P9-CKY-220

1800   1850   1900   1950

1787 ■
Society for Alleviating the Miseries of Public Prisoners established in Philadelphia

■ **1789**
Jeremy Bentham, *An Introduction to the Principles of Morals and Legislation*

■ **1790**
Pennsylvania passes legislation nearly identical to England's Penitentiary Act of 1779

1827 ■
Elizabeth Gurney Fry, *Observations in Visiting, Superintendence and Government of Female Prisons*

■ **1817**
Good Time Law passed in New York

■ **1777**
John Howard, *The State of the Prisons of England and Wales*

■ **1841**
John Augustus develops the concept of probation

1867 ■
Wines and Dwight, *Report on the Prisons and Reformatories of the United States and Canada*

1868 ■
Amendment 14 to the Constitution guarantees due process of law and equal protection of the law

■ **1870**
Declaration of Principles developed at international conference in Cincinnati, Ohio; creation of National Prison Association

1871 ■
Ruffin v. Commonwealth upholds judicial "hands off" policy

■ **1840**
Alexander Maconochie and Walter Crofton develop the concept of parole

■ **1878**
Massachusetts Probation Act

■ **1876**
Cesare Lombroso, *Criminal Man*

■
1833
Alexis de Tocqueville and Gustave de Beaumont, *On the Penitentiary System in the United States*

Folsom prison

1939
George Rushe, *Punishment and Social Structure*

■
1916
Thomas Mott Osborne, *Society and Prisons*

1924 ■
Congressional authorization of Federal Bureau of Prisons

■ **1929**
National Commission on Law Observance and Enforcement (Wickersham Commission)

■ **1899**
Illinois Juvenile Court Act

1948 ■
U.N. creates special section on prevention of crime and treatment of offenders

■ **1910**
Federal parole law enacted

■ **1925**
Federal Probation Act

■ **1930**
Federal Bureau of Prisons established

■
1780
Use of torture abolished in France

■ **1790**
Walnut Street Jail, first penitentiary, established in Philadelphia

■ **1772**
Ghent Maison de Force established in France

■ **1772**
Connecticut Newgate Prison

■ **1776**
Transportation to the American colonies from England ends

■ **1787**
Transportation of English offenders to Australia begins

1825 ■
House of Refuge established in New York

■ **1819**
Auburn State Penitentiary established in New York

1825 ■
Western State Penitentiary established in Pittsburgh

19th c. women's prison

1859 ■
State Lunatic Asylum for Insane Convicts established in Auburn, New York

■ **1829**
Eastern Penitentiary established in Cherry Hill, Pennsylvania

■ **1834**
Pennsylvania abolishes public executions

■ **1847**
Michigan first state to abolish death penalty

1873 ■ ■ **1876**
State Reformatory, first independent, female-run prison for women, established in Indiana

Elmira Reformatory established in Elmira, New York

■ **1865**
House of Shelter, a reformatory for women run by Zebulon Brockway, established in Detroit

■ **1877**
Reformatory Prison for Women established in Framingham, Massachusetts

■ **1895**
Fort Leavenworth becomes first federal prison

■ **1864**
Halfway house for women established in Boston

1880 ■
Massachusetts establishes statewide probation system

■ **1899**
First juvenile court established in Cook County (Chicago)

■ **1925**
Prison at Stateville, Illinois, based on Bentham's panopticon design

■
1927
Warden Mary Belle Harris opens federal institution for women in Alderson, West Virginia

■ **1930**
Thirty states and federal government use probation

■ **1934**
Alcatraz opens

■ **1935**
Execution of 199 offenders in United States: highest rate in 20th century

■ **1936**
Last public execution, Owensboro, Kentucky

1800   1850   1900   1950

CORRECTIONAL THOUGHT

1950 **1960** **1970** **1980** **1990** **2000**

1954
National Prison Association becomes American Correctional Association

1958
Gresham Sykes, *The Society of Captives*

1971
American Friends Service Committee, *Struggle for Justice*

1974
Robert Martinson, *What Works?*

1973
National Advisory Commission on Criminal Justice Standards and Goals

1980
John Irwin, *Prisons in Turmoil*

1977
James B. Jacobs, *Stateville*

1967
In re Gault requires counsel for juvenile offenders

1971
David Rothman, *The Discovery of the Asylum*

1987
John J. Dilulio, Jr., *Governing Prisons*

1967
President's Commission on Law Enforcement and Administration of Justice

1968
Crime and Safe Streets Act

1973
Minnesota Community Corrections Act

1970
Holt v. Sarver declares Arkansas prison system unconstitutional

1972
Furman v. Georgia declares death penalty as currently administered unconstitutional

1964
Cooper v. Pate: State prisoners may sue officials in federal courts

1965
California Probation Subsidy Act

1976
Gregg v. Georgia upholds death penalty law

1980
Ruiz v. Estelle declares Texas prison system unconstitutional

1990
David Garland, *Punishment and Modern Society*

1993
Three-strikes law passed in Washington

1991
Wilson v. Seiter: Prisoners must show official deliberate indifference to prove cruel and unusual conditions

2000
California Proposition 36: drug treament instead of jail

1998
Pennsylvania Board of Probation and Parole v. Scott: Evidence seized without a warrant may be used in a revocation hearing

2000
Illinois death penalty moratorium

1996
Prisoner Litigation Reform Act

1995
Michael Tonry, *Malign Neglect*

1995
Franklin Zimring and Gordon Hawkins, *Incapacitation*

1996
Crime Control Act promotes truth-in-sentencing

2007
Jonathan Simon, *Governing Through Crime*

2003
Prison Rape Elimination Act

2006
Bruce Western, *Punishment and Inequality*

Surveillance cameras

2007
Todd R. Clear, *Imprisoning Communities*

CORRECTIONAL PRACTICE

1983
Electronic monitoring used in Florida and New Mexico

1982
Intensive probation supervision established in Georgia

1977
California, Illinois, and Michigan first states to use determinate sentencing

1983
Boot camps originate in Georgia and Oklahoma

1987
United States sentencing guidelines in effect

2004
Sentencing guidelines under judicial scrutiny

1995
Reparative sentencing enacted in Vermont

1997
Executions reach new high

1999
Violent crime reaches lowest level in 25 years

1993–2005
Death sentences drop 60%

1995
U.S. incarceration population tops 1,000,000

1971
Prison riot in Attica, New York

1950 **1960** **1970** **1980** **1990** **2000**

CHAPTER 4

The Punishment of Offenders / 69

CHAPTER 5

The Law of Corrections / 101

CHAPTER 6

The Correctional Client / 133

PART 2
CORRECTIONAL PRACTICES

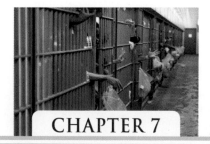

CHAPTER 7

Jails: Detention and Short-Term Incarceration / 169

CHAPTER 8

Probation / 199

CHAPTER 9

Intermediate Sanctions and Community Corrections / 233

CHAPTER 10

Incarceration / 259

CHAPTER 11

The Prison Experience / 285

CHAPTER 12

Incarceration of Women / 309

CHAPTER 13

Institutional Management / 337

CHAPTER 14

Institutional Programs / 371

CHAPTER 15

Release from Incarceration / 407

CHAPTER 16

Making It: Supervision in the Community / 431

CHAPTER 17

Corrections for Juveniles / 469

PART 3
CORRECTIONAL ISSUES AND PERSPECTIVES

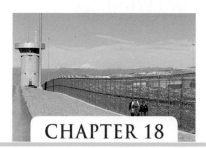

CHAPTER 18

Incarceration Trends / 505

CHAPTER 21

Surveillance and Control in the Community / 569

CHAPTER 22

Community Justice / 583

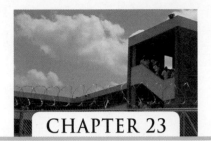

CHAPTER 23

American Corrections: Looking Forward / 603

American Corrections was inspired by our shared belief that undergraduates must be exposed to the dynamics of corrections in a manner that captures their attention and encourages them to enter the field. The Ninth Edition continues this tradition.

Corrections is so rich in history, innovative in practice, and challenged by societal problems that it deserves to be taught in a way that is both interesting and accurate. Fortunately, our teaching and research cover different areas of corrections, so each of us can focus on our strengths while challenging the others to do their best work. We hope that this book reflects our enthusiasm for our field and the satisfaction we have found in it.

The dynamic and constantly changing field of corrections has undergone major changes during the past few years. Although crime rates have fallen, the number of people under correctional supervision has climbed. Pressured by the public to "do something" about crime, political leaders have enacted policies to toughen the punishment of offenders. Laws requiring truth-in-sentencing, "three strikes and you're out," and sex offender notification resulted directly from this public concern. These policies have crowded prisons and jails, swamped probation and parole caseloads, and tripled correctional costs. Yet a shift in public policy may again be underway. In some states, rehabilitative programs have again appeared, alternatives to incarceration are being examined, and reentry to the community has again demanded attention.

The downturn in the economy has placed great fiscal burdens on public agencies. At all levels of government—federal, state, and local—budgetary deficits have greatly affected corrections. As criminal justice students know, corrections has little to no control over the inflow of offenders to community corrections, jails, and prisons; nonetheless, correctional budgets also often face cuts imposed by fiscally strapped governments. To operate with the resources mandated, some correctional systems have had to release prisoners, cut back rehabilitative programs, expand community supervision caseloads, lay off staff, and take other actions to save money.

To address these problems, the public as well as professionals are increasingly focusing their attention on research by scholars who have demonstrated the shortcomings of correctional practices and have urged alternatives. In the Ninth Edition, we thus not only examine the history of corrections and the exciting changes that have occurred to make the field what it is today, but we also look to the future of corrections by examining research-based solutions to current problems.

In *American Corrections*, Ninth Edition, we offer an accurate analysis of contemporary corrections that is based on up-to-date research. By acknowledging the problems with the system, we hope that our exposition will inspire suggestions for change. We believe that when human freedom is at stake, policies must reflect research and be formulated only after their potential effects have been considered carefully. In other words, we hope that any changes we inspire will be good ones. We also hope that a new generation of students will gain a solid understanding of all the aspects of their complex field.

■ THE APPROACH OF THIS TEXT

In learning about corrections, students gain a unique understanding of how social and political forces affect the way organizations and institutions respond to a particular segment of the community. They learn that social values come to the fore in the correctional arena because the criminal sanction reflects those values. They also learn that in a democracy, corrections must operate not only within the framework of law but also within the boundaries set by public opinion. Thus, as a public activity, corrections is accountable to elected representatives, but it must also compete politically with other agencies for resources and "turf."

Two key assumptions run throughout the book. One is about the nature of corrections as a discipline; the other concerns the best way to analyze correctional practices:

- ■ **Corrections is interdisciplinary.** The academic fields of criminal justice, sociology, psychology, history, law, and political science contribute to our understanding of corrections. This cross-fertilization is enriching, yet it requires familiarity with a vast literature. We have structured our text with a strong focus on coherence to make this interdisciplinary approach comprehensive yet accessible.

- ■ **Corrections is a system.** In our book the concept of a system serves as a framework for analyzing the relationships among the various parts of corrections and the interactions between correctional professionals and offenders. The main advantage of this perspective is that it allows for dispassionate analysis of correctional practices.

■ ORGANIZATION

Correctional officials and political leaders are continually asking, "Where is corrections headed?" In this Ninth Edition of American Corrections we explore the context, practices, and special issues of corrections in three major sections.

New to this edition are part-opening Guest Perspectives by recognized experts who discuss correctional innovations and ideas related to the topics presented in that part. Michael Thompson, Director of the Council of State Governments Justice Center, opens Part 1: The Correctional Context by discussing justice reinvestment. He emphasizes the current economic "crisis"—as correctional costs, especially those related to incarceration, eat up more and more of state and local budgets. He supports a new "justice reinvestment" strategy designed to reduce correctional costs while increasing public safety. Part 2: Correctional Practices opens with a Guest Perspective by Scott Talbott, a U.S. Probation Officer in Arizona. In it he argues for evidence-based practices in community supervision. This approach emphasizes the importance of having correctional professionals employ research-supported methods of probation and parole supervision to help reduce recidivism. To open Part 3: Correctional Issues and Perspectives, Deborah Mukamal, Director of the Prisoner Reentry Institute at John Jay College of Criminal Justice, describes the Justice Corps, a program established to assist young adult offenders as they return to their neighborhoods. Each of these Guest Perspectives lays the groundwork for the chapters that follow.

In Part 1 we describe the historical issues that frame our contemporary experience of corrections. We examine the general social context of the corrections system (Chapter 1) and the early history of correctional thought and practice (Chapter 2). We also focus on the distinctive aspects of correctional history in America

(Chapter 3), analyze current theory and evidence on methods of punishment (Chapter 4), and survey the impact of law on corrections (Chapter 5). In Chapter 6, we portray the correctional client: the offender. We consider the offender in relation to criminal legislation, criminal justice processing, and larger societal forces that are associated with crime. Part 1 thus presents the foundations of American corrections: context, history, goals, organizations, and offenders.

In Part 2 we look at the current state of the major components and practices of the system. The complexity of correctional organization results in fragmentation and ambivalence in correctional services. Jails and other short-term facilities are scrutinized in Chapter 7; probation in the community, by which most offenders are handled, in Chapter 8; and the new focus on intermediate sanctions in Chapter 9. Because imprisonment remains the core symbolic and punitive mechanism of corrections, we examine it in detail. We discuss incarceration (Chapter 10); the prison experience (Chapter 11); the incarceration of women (Chapter 12); institutional management (Chapter 13); and educational, industrial, and treatment programs in correctional institutions (Chapter 14). In being both descriptive and critical, we hope to raise questions about current incarceration policies. In Chapters 15 and 16 we examine the process of releasing prisoners from incarceration and the ways offenders adjust to supervised life in the community. In Chapter 17 we describe the separate system of corrections for juveniles. Thus, in Part 2 we focus on the development, structure, and methods of each area of the existing corrections system, portraying them in light of the continuing issues described in Part 1.

In Part 3 we analyze those current correctional issues and trends that are important enough to deserve individual attention: incarceration trends (Chapter 18); race, ethnicity, and corrections (Chapter 19); the death penalty (Chapter 20); surveillance and control in the community (Chapter 21); and community justice (Chapter 22). In Chapter 23, "American Corrections: Looking Forward," we take both a retrospective view of American corrections and a view toward its future. These chapters are designed to raise questions in the minds of readers so that they can begin to grapple with important issues.

■ SPECIAL FEATURES

Several features make this book an especially interesting introduction to corrections.

- ■ **Opening vignettes:** Each chapter opens with a description of a high-profile correctional case. Taken from today's headlines, each vignette dramatizes a real-life situation that draws the student into the chapter's topic. Instructors find these "lecture launchers" an important pedagogical tool to stimulate interest. For example, Chapter 15, "Release from Incarceration," describes the release of former NFL star quarterback Michael Vick to community supervision and contrasts his situation to that of most offenders returning to society.

- ■ **Focus boxes:** In this feature, the real-world relevance of the issues discussed in the text is made clear by vivid, in-depth accounts by correctional workers, journalists, prisoners, parolees, and the relatives of those who are in the system. In this Ninth Edition we have increased the number and variety of these Focus boxes, which are placed into three categories: People in Corrections, Correctional Policy, and Correctional Practice. We believe students will find that the material in each Focus box enhances their understanding of the chapter topic.

- ■ **Do the Right Thing boxes:** Correctional workers are often confronted with ethical dilemmas. In each of these boxes we present a scenario in which an ethical question arises. We then provide a writing assignment in which students examine the issues and consider how they would act in such a situation.

■ **Myths in Corrections:** Faculty told us that they spend much of their classroom time debunking popular myths about corrections. In this new edition most chapters contain a special boxed feature presenting research that challenges correctional myths.

■ **Careers in Corrections:** In appropriate chapters throughout the book, students will find one or more boxes in which a particular correctional occupation is described. The material includes the nature of the work, required qualifications, earnings and job outlook, plus a source of more information.

■ **Glossary:** One goal of an introductory course is to familiarize students with the terminology of the field. We have avoided jargon in the text but include terms that are commonly used in the field. Such indispensable words and phrases are set in bold type, and the term and its definition have been placed in the margin. A full glossary with definitions of all terms is located at the back of the book.

■ **Graphics:** We have created tables and figures that clarify and enliven information so that it can be perceived easily and grasped accurately. For this new Ninth Edition, tables and figures have been fully updated wherever possible.

■ **Photographs:** The Ninth Edition contains an enlarged program of dynamic photographs spread throughout the book. These reveal many aspects of corrections ordinarily concealed from the public eye. The photographs provide students with a real view of correctional policies and practices.

■ **Other student aids:** At the beginning of each chapter is an outline of the topics to be covered, followed by a set of learning objectives. These tools are designed to guide students as they progress through the chapter. Each chapter also refers students to interesting websites where they can learn more about topics discussed. Many chapters also offer brief biographies of people who have made an impact on the field of corrections. At the end of each chapter students can find a summary keyed to the learning objectives, a list of any key terms presented in the chapter, discussion questions, and suggestions for further reading.

Other Changes in the Ninth Edition

As textbook authors we have a responsibility to present current data, provide coverage of new issues, and describe innovative policies and programs. Toward this end we have completely updated and rewritten this edition, line by line. We have been assisted by the comments of an exceptionally knowledgeable team of reviewers who pointed out portions of the text their students found difficult, suggested additional topics, and noted sections that should be dropped. Among the new or expanded topics found in this Ninth Edition are the following:

■ **Death penalty:** Introduction in the 1970s of lethal injections as an execution method has resulted in a flurry of court cases challenging this approach as a violation of the cruel and unusual punishment clause of the Eight Amendment to the Constitution. In 2008 this claim was examined by the U.S. Supreme Court, which ruled in *Baze v. Rees* that attorneys for the death row inmates had not proved that lethal injection was in conflict with the amendment. However, this is likely not the last word on this issue, as botched executions continue to command headlines and new cases enter the judicial system. Other issues surrounding the death penalty such as the effectiveness of counsel, execution of the insane, and execution for child rape are examined in Chapters 4 and 18. As an ever-increasing number of death row inmates are being released because new evidence has shown that they were erroneously convicted, use of the death penalty will continue to provide a major source of debate among legislators, scholars, and correctional officials.

- **Incarceration trends:** Although rates of violent crime have dropped to 1970 levels, the incarceration rate continues to climb. This increase in the prison and jail populations conflicts with the budgetary crisis facing state and local governments. In many states the corrections system faces pressure to reduce the number of prisoners to meet budgetary limits. In other states overcrowding has led to demands by the judiciary that prison populations be reduced. This issue has a direct impact on parole supervision at a time when caseloads are high.

- **Reentry:** Each year more than 700,000 offenders are released from prison and returned to their communities. Disturbingly, the largest group of new admissions to prison in some states are recidivists. In response, assisting felons in the reentry process has become a major focus of correctional policy. The problems encountered by parolees as they adjust to the community is dealt with extensively in Chapters 15 and 16.

- **Evidence-based practice:** There has been a growing movement for "evidence-based" practice in dealing with those under community supervision—probation or parole. Public statements by Attorney General Holder and the development of programs within the U.S. Justice Department's Office of Justice Programs has spurred this thrust. Probation and parole officers are encouraged to make decisions based on methods that have been shown to be effective by well-designed research methods.

- **Correctional law:** The right of habeas corpus for alleged terrorist detainees has remained an important issue since 9/11. For example, the U.S. Supreme Court's recent decision in *Boumediene v. Bush* entitles detainees at Guantanamo Bay to challenge their confinement.

- **Incarceration of women:** As the number of female prisoners has increased, so too has research on the impact of maternal incarceration on children. Administrators in several states have devised programs to provide opportunities for women to maintain contact with their children.

- **Private prisons:** Since the advent of private prisons in the 1970s, questions have been raised as to whether they are more cost-effective than public prisons. Until recently, research on this question has been lacking. As states deal with severe budgetary problems, the future of private prisons remains uncertain.

- **The prison experience:** Prison gangs have been a major problem in some correctional systems for some time. Different strategies have been developed to deal with these gangs. Prison rape is also an issue that has brought a national spotlight on inmate safety. New evidence provides national estimates on the prevalence of sexual violence in prisons and how correctional officials handle victimization reports.

SUPPLEMENTS

An extensive package of supplemental aids accompanies this edition of *American Corrections*. Supplements are available to qualified adopters. Please consult your local sales representative for details.

For the Instructor

Instructor's Resource Manual with Test Bank Fully updated and revised by Dana Greene of New Mexico State University, the *Instructor's Resource*

Manual with Test Bank for this edition includes learning objectives, detailed chapter outlines, chapter summaries, key terms and figures, class discussion questions, media suggestions, and a complete test bank. Each chapter's test bank contains approximately 65 multiple-choice, true-false, fill-in-the-blank, matching, and essay questions, which are coded according to difficulty level, and which include a full answer key.

eBank Lesson Plans   The Lesson Plans bring accessible, masterful suggestions to every lesson. The Lesson Plans includes a sample syllabus, learning objectives, lecture notes, discussion topics, in-class activities, a detailed lecture outline, and assignments. Lesson Plans are available on the PowerLecture resource and the instructor website, or by emailing your local representative and asking for a download of the eBank files.

JoinIn™ on TurningPoint®   Spark discussion and assess your students' comprehension of chapter concepts with interactive classroom quizzes and background polls developed specifically for use with this edition of *American Corrections*. Also available are polling/quiz questions that enable you to maximize the educational benefits of the ABC® News video clips we custom-select to accompany this textbook. Cengage Wadsworth's exclusive agreement with TurningPoint software lets you run our tailor-made Microsoft® PowerPoint® slides in conjunction with the "clicker" hardware of your choice. Enhance how your students interact with you, your lecture, and each other. *For college and university adopters only. Contact your local Cengage representative to learn more.*

PowerLecture DVD   This instructor resource includes Microsoft® PowerPoint® lecture slides with graphics from the text, making it easy for you to assemble, edit, publish, and present custom lectures for your course. The PowerLecture DVD also includes video-based polling and quiz questions that can be used with the JoinIn on TurningPoint personal response system, and integrates ExamView testing software for customizing tests of up to 250 items that can be delivered in print or online. Finally, all of your media teaching resources in one place!

Criminal Justice Media Library   This engaging resource provides students with more than 300 ways to investigate current topics, career choices, and critical concepts.

WebTutor™ ToolBox on Blackboard® and WebCT®   WebTutor ToolBox presents a powerful combination: easy-to-use course management tools for WebCT or Blackboard and content from this text's rich companion website, all in one place. You can use ToolBox as is from the moment you log on or, if you prefer, customize the program with web links, images, and other resources.

WebTutor™   Jumpstart your course with customizable, rich, text-specific content within your Course Management System. Whether you want to web-enable your class or put an entire course online, WebTutor delivers. WebTutor offers a wide array of resources including media assets, test bank, practice quizzes and additional study aids. Visit webtutor.cengage.com to learn more.

Classroom Activities for Criminal Justice   This valuable booklet, available to adopters of any Wadsworth criminal justice text, offers instructors the best of the best in criminal justice classroom activities. Containing both tried-and-true favorites and exciting new projects, its activities are drawn from the full spectrum of criminal justice subjects, including introduction to criminal justice, criminology, corrections, criminal law, policing, and juvenile justice, and can be customized to fit any course. Novice and seasoned instructors alike will find it a powerful tool to stimulate classroom engagement.

Internet Activities for Criminal Justice In addition to providing a wide range of activities for any criminal justice class, this useful booklet helps familiarize students with Internet resources they will use both as students of criminal justice and in their criminal justice careers. *Internet Activities for Criminal Justice* allows instructors to integrate Internet resources and addresses important topics such as criminal and police law, policing organizations, policing challenges, corrections systems, juvenile justice, criminal trials, and current issues in criminal justice. Available to adopters of any Wadsworth criminal justice text, and prepared by Christina DeJong of Michigan State University, this booklet will bring current tools and resources to the criminal justice classroom.

The Wadsworth Criminal Justice Resource Center—www.cengage .com/criminaljustice Designed with the instructor in mind, this website features information about Cengage Wadsworth's technology and teaching solutions, as well as several features created specifically for today's criminal justice student. Supreme Court updates, timelines, and hot-topic polling can all be used to supplement in-class assignments and discussions. You'll also find a wealth of links to careers and news in criminal justice, book-specific sites, and much more.

For the Student

Companion Website—www.cengage.com/criminaljustice/clear The Companion Website provides many chapter-specific resources, including chapter outlines, learning objectives, glossary, flash cards, crossword puzzles, web links, ABC videos, and tutorial quizzing.

CL eBook CL eBook allows students to access Cengage Learning textbooks in an easy-to-use online format. Highlight, take notes, bookmark, search your text, and, in some titles, link directly into multimedia: CL eBook combines the best aspects of paper books and ebooks in one package.

Careers in Criminal Justice Website This unique website helps students investigate the criminal justice career choices that are right for them with the help of several important tools:

- Career Profiles: Video testimonials from a variety of practicing professionals in the field as well as information on many criminal justice careers, including job descriptions, requirements, training, salary and benefits, and the application process.
- Interest Assessment: Self-assessment tool to help students decide which careers suit their personalities and interests.
- Career Planner: Résumé-writing tips and worksheets, interviewing techniques, and successful job search strategies.
- Links for Reference: Direct links to federal, state, and local agencies where students can get contact information and learn more about current job opportunities.

Wadsworth's Guide to Careers in Criminal Justice, Third Edition
This handy guide, compiled by Caridad Sanchez-Leguelinel of John Jay College of Criminal Justice, gives students information on a wide variety of career paths,

including requirements, salaries, training, contact information for key agencies, and employment outlooks.

Writing and Communicating for Criminal Justice This book contains articles on writing skills, along with basic grammar review and a survey of verbal communication on the job, that will give students an introduction to academic, professional, and research writing in criminal justice. The voices of professionals who have used these techniques on the job will help students see the relevance of these skills to their future careers.

Handbook of Selected Supreme Court Cases, Third Edition This supplementary handbook covers almost 40 landmark cases, each of which includes a full case citation, an introduction, a summary from WestLaw, excerpts from the case, and the decision. The updated edition includes *Hamdi v. Rumsfeld*, *Roper v. Simmons*, *Ring v. Arizona*, *Atkins v. Virginia*, *Illinois v. Caballes*, and much more.

Current Perspectives from InfoTrac These readers, designed to give students a deeper taste of special topics in criminal justice, include free access to InfoTrac College Edition. The timely articles are selected by experts in each topic from within InfoTrac College Edition. They are available free when bundled with the text.

- Terrorism and Homeland Security
- Cybercrime
- Juvenile Justice
- Policy in Criminal Justice
- Crisis Management and National Emergency Response
- Racial Profiling
- New Technologies and Criminal Justice
- White Collar Crime

Terrorism: An Interdisciplinary Perspective This 80-page booklet discusses terrorism in general and the issues surrounding the events of September 11, 2001. This information-packed booklet examines the origins of terrorism in the Middle East, focusing on Osama bin Laden in particular, as well as issues involving bioterrorism, the specific role played by religion in Middle Eastern terrorism, globalization as it relates to terrorism, and the reactions and repercussions of terrorist attacks.

Crime Scenes 2.0: An Interactive Criminal Justice CD-ROM Recipient of several New Media Magazine Invision Awards, this interactive CD-ROM allows students to take on the roles of investigating officer, lawyer, parole officer, and judge in excitingly realistic scenarios. Available *free* when bundled with *American Corrections*. An online instructor's manual is also available.

Internet Guide for Criminal Justice, Second Edition Intended for the novice user, this guide provides students with the background and vocabulary necessary to navigate and understand the web, then provides them with a wealth of criminal justice websites and Internet project ideas.

■ ACKNOWLEDGMENTS

In writing this Ninth Edition of *American Corrections*, we were greatly assisted by people who merit special recognition. Instructors and students who used prior editions were most helpful in pointing out its strengths and weaknesses; we took their comments seriously and hope that new readers will find their educational needs met more fully. We also gratefully acknowledge the valuable contributions of the following reviewers:

MARK S. BROWN, University of South Carolina–Columbia
ASHLEY G. BLACKBURN, University of North Texas
MEGAN COLE, Brown College
JESSIE L. KRIENERT, Illinois State University
IRYNA MALENDEVYCH, University of Central Florida
PATRICK F. McMANIMON, JR., Kean University
TREVOR MILTON, State University of New York–College at Old Westbury
MICHAEL SEREDYCZ, University of Wisconsin–Parkside

We have also been assisted in writing this edition by a diverse group of associates. Chief among them is Carolyn Henderson Meier, Senior Acquisitions Editor, who supported our efforts and kept us on course. Shelley Murphy, our Development Editor, reviewed our efforts and made important suggestions in keeping with the goals of this revision. Michelle Williams, Marketing Manager for Criminal Justice at Wadsworth, has skillfully guided the presentation of *American Corrections*, Ninth Edition, to faculty and students. Erin Abney, Assistant Editor, has managed the organization and improvement of the complete set of ancillaries that accompany the text. The project has also benefited much from the attention of Christy Frame, Production Manager. The talented Marsha Cohen designed the interior of the book. Ultimately, however, the full responsibility for the book is ours alone.

Todd R. Clear
tclear@rutgers.edu

George F. Cole
georgefrasercole@gmail.com

Michael D. Reisig
reisig@asu.edu

PART 1

Michael Thompson
Director, Council of State Governments
Justice Center

JUSTICE REINVESTMENT
A New Strategy for State Corrections

State and county officials are facing a "crisis" in their criminal justice systems as correctional costs, particularly those related to incarceration, eat up more and more of state and local budgets. In the face of severe budgetary pressures and increased prison costs, important educational, training, and rehabilitative programs are being slashed. The impact of this reality is devastating, in that as community-based programs dwindle, recidivism rates rise, with the result that prison growth accelerates. To fund expansion of the prison system, dollars are siphoned from effective criminal justice policies and redirected to build more cells.

When policy makers exhaust all options for funding additional prisons, some dangerous scenarios emerge. Policy makers begin to consider releasing offenders indiscriminately and in mass numbers. This policy is especially scary considering that safeguards in the community such as treatment, supervision, and employment services have likely been greatly diminished because of the fiscal pressures described earlier.

A crime-fighting strategy based exclusively on building more prisons is not the solution. Evidence demonstrates that policy makers should not assume that simply incapacitating more people will provide a corresponding increase on public safety. For example, over the past seven years, Florida has increased its incarceration rate 16 percent, while New York's rate has gone in the opposite direction, decreasing 16 percent. Despite this difference, over the same period the drop in New York's crime rate was double that of Florida's. In short, while New York invested considerably less money in prisons than did Florida, New York delivered greater public safety to its residents.

In response to the current situation, members of the bipartisan Council of State Governments have developed a new strategy called *justice reinvestment*. This strategy is designed to cut

THE CORRECTIONAL CONTEXT

correctional spending, reduce failure rates of people released from prison, and increase public safety. Justice reinvestment has three phases:

- Analyze crime and correctional data and develop policy options to reduce spending on corrections and reinvest in strategies to increase public safety and strengthen communities.
- Implement enacted policy options effectively.
- Establish and track indicators of key correctional and public safety trends to ensure accountability.

From our work so far, we have learned that each state faces its own distinct challenge; there is no "one-size-fits-all" justice reinvestment program. Instead, justice reinvestment is a *strategy* that aims to ensure that policy makers use data to shape their correctional policy and to inform decisions about the allocation of resources in those neighborhoods where most people released from prison and jail return.

In terms of reinvestment, every state has a handful of "high-stakes" communities in which most people return when released from prison or jail. These communities are disproportionately made up of minority and poor residents. These communities are also often blighted and lack resources. Reinvesting in these geographic areas generates significant improvements to public safety and reduces overall correctional expenditures.

A justice reinvestment strategy can only be applied where there is a bipartisan commitment among the state's leaders to work together to address the criminal justice challenges. Without a bipartisan commitment from these stakeholders, these changes provide fodder for political games and otherwise serve no useful purpose.*

Part 1 of American Corrections, 9th edition—The Correctional Context—describes the corrections system, its history, the way offenders are punished, the law as it relates to prisoners and correctional officials, and the clients of corrections. As you study these chapters, consider the remarks of Director Thompson and the "justice reinvestment" that the Council of State Governments proposes. What do you think the strategies might accomplish? What are some of the difficulties that must be overcome for the strategy to work?

*Adapted from the statement given by Michael Thompson at the Hearing on Justice Reinvestment, Commerce, Justice, Science, and Related Agencies, Appropriations Subcommittee, U.S. House of Representatives, April 1, 2009.

© Suzanne DeChillo/The New York Times/Redux Pictures

LEARNING OBJECTIVES

After reading this chapter, you should be able to . . .

1 Describe the range of purposes served by the corrections system.

2 Define the systems framework and explain why it is useful.

3 Name the various components of the corrections system today and describe their functions.

4 Identify at least five key issues facing corrections today.

5 Discuss what we can learn from the "great experiment of social control."

Over the past 40 years the American corrections system has seen a sustained period of remarkable growth, with the number of people in prison, on probation, or on parole at record highs.

OVER THE PAST 35 YEARS, Americans have experienced one of the greatest policy experiments in modern history. Never before have we seen such growth of the penal system—an expansion that has lasted for a full generation. In 1973 the prison incarceration rate was 96 per 100,000 Americans. Every year since then, the number of prisoners has increased—during periods when crime went up, but also during periods when crime declined; during good economic times and bad; during times of war and times of peace.

At first, for most of the 1970s, the growth stemmed from rising rates of crime. But correctional population growth continued during the 1980s, when crime rates stabilized. They continued to grow throughout the 1990s, even though crime rates fell by more than 50 percent between 1993 and 2007.[1] Since 1990, the swelling prison population seems due entirely to tougher criminal justice policies rather than changes in crime rates.[2] See "Myths in Corrections" on page 4 for more.

By 2008—after 35 years of steady growth—the U.S. imprisonment rate reached 506 per 100,000.[3] Correctional budgets had also grown by over 600 percent during that time. There are today over 3,200 people on death row and another

THE CORRECTIONS SYSTEM

- **THE PURPOSE OF CORRECTIONS**

- **A SYSTEMS FRAMEWORK FOR STUDYING CORRECTIONS**
  - Goals
  - Interconnectedness
  - Environment
  - Feedback
  - Complexity

- **THE CORRECTIONS SYSTEM TODAY**

- **KEY ISSUES IN CORRECTIONS**
  - Managing the Correctional Organization
  - Working with Offenders
  - Upholding Social Values

140,000 serving life sentences. Counting prisons and jails, almost 2.3 million citizens are incarcerated, making the total incarceration rate over 760 per 100,000 citizens, a stunning 1 percent of all adults.[4] When all forms of corrections are taken into account—including probation, parole, and community corrections—more than 3 percent of all adults are under some form of correctional control.[5] The extensive growth of the correctional population since 1980 is shown in **Figure 1.1**.

Some say that when prison populations grow, crime rates decline, because prisons prevent crime. But between 1973 and the early 1990s, we saw both imprisonment growth and *increases* in crime. Most observers concluded that when more people commit crime, more people end up behind bars. This suggests that as crime declines, so will correctional caseloads. But studies show that, aside from the 1970s, there has been little relationship between the nation's crime rate and the size of its prison population.[6] Again, since 1990, the swelling prison population seems to be entirely due to tougher criminal justice policies rather than changes in crime rates.[7]

Nor does it seem that this 35-year pattern is changing. The prison population briefly fell in the second half of 2000—the first drop in the prison population since 1972—but quickly resumed its pattern of growth. In 2005, the total incarceration rate grew by 2.7 percent nationally, the highest rate of growth in six years. By any measure, the U.S. corrections system has seen a sustained period of remarkable, steady growth for more than a generation. As said, this has never happened before in the United States—or anywhere else. (See the Focus box "The Great Experiment in Social Control" on page 6.) If these rates continue, almost 7 percent of people born in 2001 will go to prison at some time during their lives.[8] Imagine 14 friends or relatives; then, imagine one of them incarcerated.

Yet there is a glimmer of change, as a new liberal-conservative consensus emerges. This new consensus centers on a growing idea that the penal system, especially prisons, has grown too much. Some believe that "mass incarceration" has become a problem in its own right, but concerns about burgeoning probation caseloads and high jail counts have arisen as well. Both liberals and conservatives rightfully worry that the expansion of corrections has affected some groups more than others. About one-third of all African American men in their twenties are under some form of correctional control. In inner-city areas of

Chapter

1

MYTHS IN CORRECTIONS

HIGH U.S. CRIME RATES

THE MYTH: The United States has such a large prison system, compared with the prison systems of other countries, because it has so much more crime.

THE REALITY: Compared with the burglary rates of Australia and England, America's is the lowest, and its assault and robbery rates fall in between those of the other two countries. Its incarceration rate is four times higher than that of either country.

Sources: Patrick A. Langan and David P. Farrington. *Crime and Justice in the United States and in England and Wales.* 1981–96 (Washington, DC: Bureau of Justice Statistics, November 1998); The Sentencing Project, *New Incarceration Figures: Growth in Population Continues* (Washington, DC: The Sentencing Project, December 2006).

Detroit, Baltimore, and Philadelphia, as many as half of this group are under penal supervision. Nearly 12 percent of all African American men 20–40 years old—the age of most fathers—are now locked up. One in six male African Americans have been to prison.[9]

Both liberals and conservatives also share a concern that the cost of corrections, nearly $70 billion a year, is out of line. Prison budgets—by far the most expensive portion of the penal system—grow even when monies for education and others services lag. Probation caseloads and daily jail populations have also grown, and they cost money, too. With growing public concern about the quality of schools and health care, people of all political persuasions are tempted to ask if so much money is needed for corrections. They are especially leery about continuing to invest in what many political leaders, especially conservatives, see as a system that is not as effective as it ought to be.[10]

Corrections, then, is a topic for public debate as never before. A generation ago, most people knew very little about corrections. Prisons were alien "big houses,"

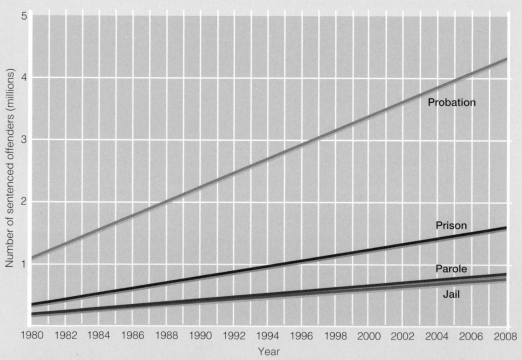

Figure 1.1

Correctional Populations in the United States, 1980–2008

Although the increase in prison populations receives the most publicity, a greater proportion of correctional growth has occurred in probation and parole.

Sources: Latest data available from the Bureau of Justice Statistics correctional surveys, http://www.ojp.usdoj.gov/bjs/: *Annual Survey of Jails, Annual Parole Survey, Annual Probation Survey, National Prisoner Statistics Population Mid-year Counts.*

infused with mystery and located in remote places. The average American had no direct knowledge of "the joint" and no way of learning what it was like. Most people did not even know what probation or parole were, much less have an opinion about their worth. More than 7.5 million Americans are now in the corrections system. Of today's men in their thirties, almost one in 28 has been to prison; if current patterns continue, 11 percent of male children born this year (a third of male African Americans born this year) and 2 percent of female children will go to prison.[11] Add to these numbers the impact on fathers and mothers, brothers and sisters, aunts and uncles, and husbands, wives, and children, and you have an idea of how pervasive corrections is today—especially for poor Americans and people of color.

Further, crime stories dominate our news media. Read any local newspaper or watch any local nightly newscast and you will encounter a crime story that raises questions about corrections: Should the offender have been released? Is the sentence severe enough? Should laws for this type of crime be tougher? In short, corrections now maintains a profound place, not only in the public eye, but also in the public experience. But are the images we form—images based on media reports and our own experiences—accurate? Do they tell us all we need to know about corrections?

The coming years will be an exciting period for people interested in corrections. A growing consensus, crossing the political divide, places us on the verge of a new era in correctional policy, characterized by a search for innovative strategies to deal with crime that are more effective and less costly—financially and socially—than the policies that have dominated the landscape for almost 40 years. This is a time when those who study corrections can help shape a new generation of policies and practices. The demand for correctional professionals will continue to grow, but openness to new ideas will be greater than ever before.

People who study corrections want to learn more about the problems that rivet attention. They want to see beyond the three-minute news story, to understand what

The **Bureau of Justice Statistics** is a major source of criminal justice data; see the corresponding link at www .cengage.com/criminaljustice/ clear.

To get a short summary of all the crime stories in the news, subscribe to the **Criminal Justice Journalists' daily summary** by going to the corresponding link at www .cengage.com/criminaljustice/ clear.

© Jim West/The Image Works

One of every 43 Americans is under some form of correctional supervision. Most offenders live among us in the community.

is happening to people caught in the system. And they suspect that what seems so simple from the viewpoint of a politician arguing for a new law, or from the perspective of a news reporter sharing the latest crime story, may in fact be far more complex for the people involved.

FOCUS ON

CORRECTIONAL POLICY

The Great Experiment in Social Control

Almost half of the current U.S. population, including most of the readers of this book, were born after 1971. For them, it is entirely "normal" to see yearly increases in the number of Americans in prison, in jail, and under correctional supervision. For their entire lives, they have seen corrections grow in good economic times and bad, during periods of rising crime and of dropping crime, while the "baby boom" generation (Americans born in the decade after World War II) hit their twenties and thirties—the peak crime-prone age—and clogged the criminal justice system.

The large and growing correctional populations that seem so normal have not always been so. From 1900 until about 1970, U.S. prison populations were quite stable, hovering between 90 and 120 inmates per 100,000 citizens. After over 35 years of steady growth, the rate of incarceration is now five times as high as it was in 1973. It has reached its highest point in U.S. history—by most accounts the highest in the world.

We might call this phenomenon the "great experiment in social control," for it has defined a generation of Americans who have witnessed the greatest expansion in government control ever undertaken by a democratic state. Researchers have tried to explain the sources of this growth. Some of it stems from increases in crime, but most of this crime growth occurred during the first half of the "experiment." Some is due to increased effectiveness at apprehending, arresting, and convicting criminals. But this aspect of the "experiment" is minor compared with changes in punishment policy. In the United States, the chances of a felon getting a prison sentence instead of probation have increased steadily for several decades, to the point where the chance of getting a probation sentence is now a fraction of what it used to be.

So, more people are going to prison, and they are serving longer terms as well. Further, the strictness of postrelease supervision has also increased, so that more probationers than before are being sent back to prison because of a failure to abide by strictly enforced rules. This triple whammy—less probation, longer prison terms, and stricter postsentencing supervision—has fueled a continuing increase in correctional populations, especially prison populations, even when crime rates are dropping.

Some scholars have tried to explain the unprecedented punitiveness of the late twentieth-century U.S. policy (see "For Further Reading"). They discuss the importance of American politics and culture, and they expressly point to the effects of two decades of the "war on drugs." Yet *why* this punitiveness occurred is far less interesting than *what* its results have been. Over the coming years, researchers, scholars, and intellectuals will begin to try to understand what we have learned from this great experiment.

The effects of this experiment in social control fall into three broad categories: its effects on crime, on society, and on the pursuit of justice. First, and most important, how has the growth of corrections affected rates of crime? Because so many factors affect crime, we cannot easily distinguish the effects of a growing corrections system from other effects, such as the economy or times of war. Researchers who have tried to do so have reached divergent conclusions, but even the most conservative scholars of the penal system now seem to agree that further growth will have little impact on crime.[12] Others note that because the crime rate today is about the same as it was in the early 1970s, when the penal system began to grow, the corrections system has not likely had a large effect on crime.[13]

Second, there is a growing worry that a large corrections system—especially a large prison system—damages families and communities, and increases racial inequality.[14] For example, more than 1.5 million children have parents in prison, and one of five African American children have a parent who has been to prison.[15] How do these experiences affect their chances in life? And what does it mean that more than one in four male African Americans will end up in prison?

Third, how does a large penal system affect the pursuit of justice? Do people feel more confidence in their justice system? Is it right to have people who break the law end up punished the way America punishes them? In this great experiment in social control, have we become a more just society?

AP Photo/Carlo Allegri, Pool

The 2005 trial of the late Michael Jackson on child molestation charges dominated the national news media for months. Americans seem to be fascinated by celebrity misdeeds. For every high-profile case, innumerable others exist that get only local attention. Yet all crime stories raise questions about corrections.

One theme in this book is that things are not as simple as they look. New laws and policies seldom achieve exactly what they were intended to do, and they often have unintended consequences. In this text we explore the most important issues in penology, from the effectiveness of rehabilitation to the impact of the death penalty, with the knowledge that each has more than one side.

We begin with a seemingly simple question: What is the purpose of corrections? In exploring the answer to this question, you will discover a pattern that recurs throughout the book. Any important correctional issue is complicated and controversial. The more you learn about a given issue, the more you will see layers of truth, so that your first findings will be bolstered by evidence and then challenged by further investigation and deeper knowledge.

In the end we think you will see that there are few easy answers, but plenty of intense questions. Near the beginning of each chapter we present questions for inquiry that each chapter will explore. We hope that these will help focus your exploration of corrections and serve as a study guide, along with the summary at the end of each chapter.

■ THE PURPOSE OF CORRECTIONS

It is 11:00 A.M. in New York City. For several hours, a five-man crew has been picking up trash in a park in the Bronx. Across town on Rikers Island, the view down a corridor of jail cells shows the prisoners' hands gesturing through the bars as they converse, play cards, share cigarettes—the hands of people doing time. About a thousand miles to the south, almost four hundred inmates sit in isolated cells on Florida's death row. In the same state, a woman on probation reports to a community control officer. On her ankle she wears an electronic monitoring device that tells the officer if she leaves her home at night. On the other side of the Gulf of Mexico, sunburned Texas inmates in stained work clothes tend crops. Almost due north in Kansas, an inmate grievance committee in a maximum-security prison reviews complaints of guard harassment. Out on the West Coast, in San Francisco, a young man on his way to work checks in with his

corrections
The variety of programs, services, facilities, and organizations responsible for the management of individuals who have been accused or convicted of criminal offenses.

social control
Actions and practices, of individuals and institutions, designed to induce conformity with the norms and rules of society.

parole officer and drops off a urine sample at the parole office. All these activities are part of **corrections**. And all the central actors are offenders.

Punishing people who break society's rules is an unfortunate but necessary part of social life. From the earliest accounts of humankind, punishment has been used as one means of **social control**, of compelling people to behave according to the norms and rules of society. Parents chastise their children when they disobey family rules, groups ostracize individuals who deviate from expected group norms, colleges and universities expel students who cheat, and governments impose sanctions on those who break the law. Of the various ways that societies and their members try to control behavior, criminal punishment is the most formal, for crime is perhaps the most serious type of behavior over which a society must gain control.

In addition to protecting society, corrections helps define the limits of behavior so that everyone in the community understands what is permissible. The nineteenth-century sociologist Emile Durkheim argued that crime is normal and that punishment performs the important function of spotlighting societal rules and values. When a law is broken, citizens express outrage. The deviant thus focuses group feeling. As people unite against the offender, they feel a sense of mutuality or community. Punishing those who violate the law makes people more alert to shared interests and values.

Three basic concepts of Western criminal law—offense, guilt, and punishment—define the purpose and procedures of criminal justice. In the United States, Congress and state legislatures define what conduct is considered criminal.

The police, prosecutors, and courts determine the guilt of a person charged with a criminal offense. The postconviction process then focuses on what should be done with the guilty person.

The central purpose of corrections is to carry out the criminal sentence. The term *corrections* usually refers to any action applied to offenders after they have been convicted and implies that the action is "corrective," or meant to change offenders according to society's needs. Corrections also includes actions applied to people who have been accused—but not yet convicted—of criminal offenses. Such people are often under supervision, waiting for action on their cases—sitting in jail, undergoing drug or alcohol treatment, or living in the community on bail.

When most Americans think of corrections, they think of prisons and jails. This belief is strengthened by legislators and the media, which focus much attention on

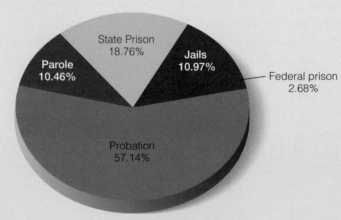

Figure 1.2
Percentage of People in Each Category of Correctional Supervision

Although most people think of corrections as prisons and jails, in fact over two-thirds of offenders are supervised within the community.

Sources: Latest data available from Bureau of Justice Statistics correctional surveys, http://www.ojp.usdoj.gov/bjs/: *Annual Survey of Jails, Annual Parole Survey, Annual Probation Survey, National Prisoner Statistics Population Midyear Counts.*

incarceration and little on community corrections. As **Figure 1.2** shows, however, over two-thirds of all people under correctional supervision are living in the community on probation or parole.

Corrections thus encompasses all the legal responses of society to some prohibited behavior: the variety of programs, services, facilities, and organizations responsible for managing people accused or convicted of criminal offenses. When criminal justice researchers, officials, and practitioners speak of corrections, they may be referring to any number of programs, processes, and agencies. Correctional activities are performed by public and private organizations; involve federal, state, and local governments; and occur in a variety of community and closed settings. We can speak of corrections as a department of the government, a subfield of the academic discipline of criminal justice, an approach to the treatment of offenders, and a part of the criminal justice system.

Corrections is all these things and more.

■ A Systems Framework for Studying Corrections

Because it reflects social values, corrections is as complex and challenging as the society in which we live today. Corrections is a legal intervention to deter, to rehabilitate, to incapacitate, or simply to punish or achieve retribution.

Having a framework will help you sort out the complex, multidimensional nature of corrections. In this book we use the concept of the corrections system as a framework for study. A **system** is a complex whole consisting of interdependent parts whose operations are directed toward common goals and influenced by the environment in which they function. Interstate highways, for example, make up a transportation system. The various components of criminal justice—police, prosecutors, courts, corrections—also function as a system.

system
A complex whole consisting of interdependent parts whose operations are directed toward common goals and influenced by the environment in which they function.

Goals

Corrections is a complicated web of disparate processes that, ideally, serve the goals of fair punishment and community protection. These twin goals—punishment and protection—not only define the purpose of corrections but also serve as criteria by which we evaluate correctional work. Correctional activities make sense when they seem to punish offenders fairly or offer some sense of protection. The thought of an unfair or unsafe correctional practice distresses most people.

When these two functions of punishment and protection do not correspond, corrections faces goal conflict. For example, people may feel it is fair to release offenders on parole once they have served their sentences, but they may also fear any possible threats the parolees pose to the community. Further, such goal conflicts can cause problems in the way the system operates.

Interconnectedness

Corrections can be viewed as a series of processes: sentencing, classification, supervision, programming, and revocation, to name but a few. Processes in one part of the corrections system affect, in both large and small ways, processes in the rest of the system.

For example, when a local jail changes its policies on eligibility for work release, this change will affect the probation caseload. When a parole agency implements new drug-screening practices, the increased number of violators uncovered by the new policy will affect jails and prisons within the system. When writers fail to check their facts for a presentence investigation report, poorly reasoned correctional assignments may result.

Corrections has links with other criminal justice agencies. The police, sheriff, prosecutor, and judiciary all play roles with regard to correctional clients. What are some of the problems that develop out of these necessary links?

AP Images/Jessica Hill, Pool

These processes all affect one another because offenders pass through corrections in a kind of assembly line with return loops. After criminals are convicted, a selection process determines which offender goes where, and why. This sifting process is itself uncertain and often hard to understand. Most, but not all, violent offenders are sent to prison. Most, but not all, violators of probation or parole rules receive a second chance. Most,

FOCUS ON

CORRECTIONAL PRACTICE

Probation's Interconnectedness with the Worlds of Law Enforcement and Social Services

For many years, communities in California have been distressed by the problems of youth gangs. In 2008, 13 cities came together to form their own local Gang Prevention Networks. The Network is comprised of elected officials, prominent citizens, the heads of law enforcement and prosecution, school officials, faith-based organizations, and social services. The main purpose of Networks is to coordinate actions of law enforcement and social services to "blend prevention, intervention, and enforcement."

Probation has become an important part of the work of the group, because it is centrally involved in many of the aspects that relate to youth who are either involved in gangs or at risk of doing so. Many gang members end up on probation, of course, when they are convicted of crimes. But probation is also deeply involved in the school system, working with school officials on a range of projects. Probation serves the courts by

providing them with information about people who are awaiting sentencing, and probation officers often serve the arrest warrants of people who commit crimes while under supervision. Finally, probation is one of the major agencies making referrals to various community-level services, as its clients and their families seek help with a range of problems. Probation officers also often find that in working with a person who is formally under supervision, they often also spend time working informally with their brothers and other family members.

This description illustrates the vital role probation plays in crime prevention—and it shows how probation is central to and closely interconnected with the host of private and public agencies that try to reduce the problem of gangs.

Source: John A Calhoun, "The Essential Role Played by Probation in California's 13-City Gang Prevention Network," *Perspectives Magazine* 33 (no. 1, Winter 2009): 47–50.

but not all, offenders caught committing crimes while supervised by correctional authorities will receive a greater punishment than offenders not under supervision. **Figure 1.3** shows examples of interconnections among correctional agencies as they deal with offenders who have been given different sentences. (See also the Focus box "Probation's Interconnectedness with the Worlds of Law Enforcement and Social Services.")

Environment

As they process offenders, correctional agencies must deal with outside forces such as public opinion, fiscal constraints, and the law. Thus, sometimes a given correctional agency will take actions that do not seem best suited to achieving fairness or public protection. At times correctional agencies may seem to work at odds with each other or with other aspects of the criminal justice process.

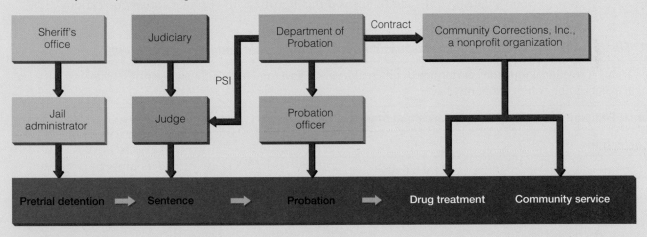

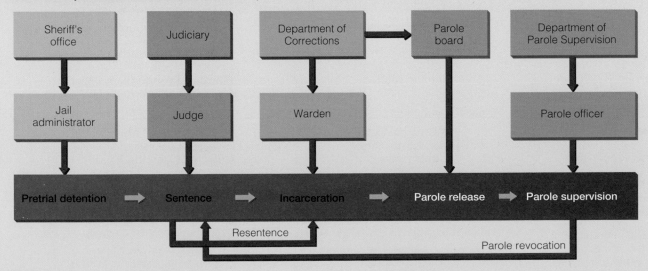

Figure 1.3
Interconnectedness of Correctional Agencies in Implementing Sentences

Note the number and variety of agencies that deal with these two offenders. Would you expect these agencies to cooperate effectively with one another? Why or why not?

Corrections has a reciprocal relationship with its environment. That is, correctional practices affect the community, and community values and expectations in turn affect corrections. For example, if the prison system provides inadequate drug treatment, offenders return to the community with the same drug problems they had when they were locked up. When citizens subsequently lose confidence in their corrections system, they tend not to spend tax dollars on its programs.

Feedback

Systems learn, grow, and improve according to the feedback they receive about their effectiveness. When a system's work is well received by its environment, the system organizes itself to continue functioning this way. When feedback is less positive, the system adapts to improve its processes.

Although feedback is crucial for corrections, this system has trouble obtaining useful feedback. When things go well, the result is the absence of something—no new crimes or no prison riots—that is, something that *might* have occurred but did not. Figuring out such things is difficult at best. In contrast, when corrections fails,

TABLE 1.1 *The Distribution of Correctional Responsibilities in Philadelphia County, Pennsylvania*

Note the various correctional functions performed at different levels of government by different agencies. What correctional agencies does your community have?

Correctional Function	Level and Branch of Government	Responsible Agency
Adult Corrections		
Pretrial detention	Municipal/executive	Department of Human Services
Probation supervision	County/courts	Court of Common Pleas
Halfway houses	Municipal/executive	Department of Human Services
Houses of corrections	Municipal/executive	Department of Human Services
County prisons	Municipal/executive	Department of Human Services
State prisons	State/executive	Department of Corrections
County parole	County/executive	Court of Common Pleas
State parole	State/executive	Board of Probation and Parole
Juvenile Corrections		
Detention	Municipal/executive	Department of Public Welfare
Probation supervision	County/courts	Court of Common Pleas
Dependent/neglect	State/executive	Department of Human Services
Training schools	State/executive	Department of Public Welfare
Private placements	Private	Many
Juvenile aftercare	State/executive	Department of Public Welfare
Federal Corrections		
Probation/parole	Federal/courts	U.S. courts
Incarceration	Federal/executive	Bureau of Prisons

Sources: Taken from the annual reports of the responsible agencies.

everybody knows: The media report new crimes or expose scandals in administration. As a result, corrections systems and their environments tend to overrespond to correctional failure but remain less aware of success.

Complexity

As systems grow and mature, they tend to become more complex. Thirty years ago, the "three P's"—probation, prisons, and parole—dominated correctional practice. Today all kinds of activities come under the heading of corrections, from pretrial drug treatment to electronically monitored home confinement; from work centers, where offenders earn money for restitution, to private, nonprofit residential treatment programs.

The complexity of the corrections system is illustrated by the variety of public and private agencies that compose the corrections system of Philadelphia County, Pennsylvania, as **Table 1.1** shows. Note that offenders are supervised by various service agencies operating at different levels of government (state, county, municipal) and in different branches of government (executive, judicial).

■ THE CORRECTIONS SYSTEM TODAY

The American corrections system today employs over seven hundred thousand administrators, psychologists, officers, counselors, social workers, and others. The federal government, the 50 states, over three thousand counties, and uncounted municipalities and public and private organizations administer corrections at an average annual cost of over $60 billion.[16]

Corrections consists of many subunits, each with its own functions and responsibilities. These subunits—probation offices, halfway houses, prisons, and others—vary in size, goals, clientele, and organizational structure. Some are administered in institutions; others, in the community. Some are government agencies; others are private organizations contracted by government to provide specific services to correctional clients. A probation office is organized differently from a halfway house or a prison, yet all three are part of the corrections system and pursue the goals of corrections.

There are, however, important differences among subunits of the same general type. The organization of a five-person probation office working closely with one judge in a rural setting, for example, differs from that of a more bureaucratized 100-person probation office in a large metropolitan system. Such organizational variety may help or hinder the system of justice.

Federalism, a system of government in which power and responsibility are divided between a national government and state governments, operates in the United States. All levels of government—national, state, county, and municipal—are involved in one or more aspects of the corrections system. The national government operates a full range of correctional organizations to deal with the people convicted of breaking federal laws; likewise, state and local governments provide corrections for people who have broken their laws. However, most criminal justice and correctional activity takes place at the state level. Only about 1 percent of individuals on probation, 10 percent of those on parole, and 11 percent of those in prison are under federal correctional supervision.

Despite the similarity, from state to state, of behaviors that are labeled criminal, important differences appear among specific definitions of offenses, types and severity of sanctions, and procedures governing the establishment of guilt and treatment of offenders. In addition, many variations in how corrections is formally organized appear at the state and local levels. For example, four state corrections systems—California, Florida, New York, and Texas—handle more than one in three state prisoners, and about two-fifths of all offenders under correctional control in the United States, but each of these four states has developed different organizational configurations to provide corrections (see the Focus box "The Big Four in Corrections").

Look at the **federal prison system** by going to the corresponding link at www .cengage.com/criminaljustice/ clear.

federalism
A system of government in which power and responsibilities are divided between a national government and state governments.

FOCUS ON
CORRECTIONAL PRACTICE

The Big Four in Corrections

Four states from four different regions in the United States dominate the correctional scene: California, Texas, New York, and Florida. They account for almost a third of all prisoners and nearly two-fifths of all offenders under correctional control (see Table 1 for a breakdown of the key numbers).

TABLE 1 *The Big Four by the Numbers*

	Prison	Probation	Parole
California	173,670	325,069	120,753
Florida	102,388	279,760	4,528
New York	60,347	119,405	52,225
Texas	172,506	427,080	102,921

Sources: Bureau of Justice Statistics, most recent reports for each state.

California

California has the largest prison population in the United States; about one in every eight state prisoners in the United States is incarcerated in the California system. The enormity of the California prison system results largely from the enormity of the state itself, as shown by the fact that California's imprisonment rate (471 inmates per 100,000 residents) is just above the national average for states (450 per 100,000).

The California adult corrections system is administered by the Adult Authority, which is a part of the state executive branch of government. Juvenile institutions are administered by the Youth Authority. Adult and juvenile probation services are provided by the executive branch at the county level and administered by a chief probation officer. A portion of the county probation costs is subsidized by the state, but these subsidies compose a smaller part of the budget than they did in the 1980s. Local taxes pay for jails and probation services, and predictably these services have been hit quite hard by funding caps placed on government services. Jails and probation compete with schools and hospitals for scarce funds. One result is that jails are filled to capacity and priority is given to sending prisoners to the state facilities, which are themselves overcrowded (but funded by a different tax base). Probation caseloads have also grown—for example, from 100 per officer a decade ago to over 300 per officer now in Los Angeles County. Californians seem to want to be tough on law violators

but not to have to pay for it. The most pressing question in California, especially given the state's huge budget deficit, is how to reconcile these two concerns.

As the new millennium got underway, there was a big surge in the state's prison population as a result of landmark three-strikes legislation in 1994 imposing long sentences on felony recidivists. Even though California's voters approved a requirement in 2000 that most drug offenders be given drug treatment rather than incarceration, California's prison system continued to grow. Eventually, the pressures on the California prison system became a national news story, as the prison health care system was declared unconstitutional, and the state was ordered by the federal courts to reduce its prison population by over 40,000 inmates.[17] With a powerful public employee union—the California Correctional Peace Officers Association—representing 55,000 correctional employees, it is not clear how the system can reduce its costs without facing strong political resistance.[18]

Florida

Florida is a bellwether state, because its current age profile reflects where the nation is headed: to be composed of a large number of retirees and a large number of young people. And if Florida is a sign of things to come, corrections in the United States as a whole will continue to grow, because its sentencing policies have sustained one of the fastest-growing prison populations in the nation, even as its crime rate has declined.

The state of Florida administers all institutional and community-based correctional services regionally, and regional directors have considerable autonomy. The five adult regional administrators report to the secretary of the Department of Corrections and manage all institutional and field services. Juvenile corrections is housed within the Department of Health and Rehabilitative Services and operates in 11 districts. Thus, Florida unifies corrections under the executive branch, with separate adult and juvenile functions. Parole supervision was all but abolished in 1984, when Florida enacted its new determinate-sentencing system, and the system now manages a handful of people who face very long parole periods under previous laws.

When Florida passed its sentencing-guideline system in order to overcome widespread sentencing disparity, institutional admissions skyrocketed. Alarmed, Florida administrators started the Community Control Project, providing close supervision (often with electronic monitoring) to divert offenders from prison. The program is the largest diversion effort in the nation, taking in about a thousand new offenders per month. Florida's prison admissions have been dropping for more than a decade, but prison populations continue to grow because sentences are longer than they were before. Since 1990, the rate of growth in Florida prisoners has almost doubled the national average, even though Florida's current incarceration rate remains just about the national average (458 per 100,000 versus 450 per 100,000).

Florida Governor Charlie Crist is a strong proponent of prison expansions, but he recently had to put a $184 million prison-expansion plan on hold when the state's revenues began to dry up during the economic downturn and the state faced a $5 billion shortfall in funds. Moreover, judges, faced with mounting pressures from jail crowding and cuts in probation, have reduced their sentences to local facilities and increased their use of prison terms.[19]

New York

The corrections system in New York was for many decades regarded as innovative. The reformatory was a New York invention, as was modern parole. Today, however, people regard New York as a large, stable, well-administered bureaucracy no longer on the cutting edge.

The Department of Corrections manages adult institutional corrections; the Division of Youth Services manages juvenile institutions and aftercare. Probation is a county function: A chief probation officer, who is accountable to the county chief executive, administers adult and juvenile services. The state's Division of Probation carries out a coordinating function for probation. The Division of Parole administers both parole release and supervision. New York operates decentralized correctional services with strong state coordination.

As in almost all states, the New York corrections system was overcrowded for many years. Moreover, it faced an added burden—New York City corrections, with its mammoth correctional facility at Rikers Island. For years, the New York City corrections system put pressure on the state operations, because many New York City prisoners were awaiting assignment to state facilities. In the last few years, however, dropping crime rates in New York City have relaxed the pressure in both city and state corrections systems, as the Rikers Island population began to fall.

In the first half of the 1990s, tightening revenues raised concern among correctional leaders in New York. As one of his first acts as governor, George Pataki proposed loosening the laws for minor repeat offenders, hoping that it would ease pressure on the corrections system. The legislature repealed the so-called Rockefeller Drug Laws (passed in the 1970s) that made New York one of the toughest states in the country on drug offenders. A boot camp program has also shortened incarceration for some of those drug offenders. Since 1990, New York has ranked fifth smallest among the 50 states in rate of growth in prisoners, and public policy makers' fears that the prison budget would come to strain the state's revenues were further alleviated by a reduction of almost 15 percent in the number of prisoners between 2000 and 2008.

Texas

In terms of corrections, Texas earns its reputation of "bigness": The rate of Texans under correctional control is higher than the equivalent rate in any other state in the Union, save Georgia. Nearly one in nine of the nation's probationers live in Texas, which has a correctional control rate two-thirds higher than the national average.

All adult corrections in Texas are housed under the Department of Criminal Justice, which is supervised by a nine-person board appointed by the governor. This department administers corrections through three separate divisions: institutions, parole supervision, and probation. In addition, the parole board reports to the Board of Criminal Justice. The Institutional Division, in addition to managing all state custodial facilities, monitors the local jails. The Texas Youth Commission handles all juvenile institutions and aftercare. Organized on a county basis, adult and juvenile probation are run separately by chief probation officers locally appointed by the county judiciary. Standards for both probation functions are established and monitored by state authority. Adult probation is monitored by the Department of Criminal Justice; juvenile probation, by the Juvenile Probation Commission. Because Texas has over two hundred counties, coordinating the work of these commissions is extremely complicated.

Through most of the 1990s, Texas corrections operated under something of a siege mentality. As a result of a series of lawsuits, Texas prisons had a tight population cap, forcing the rest of the system to be more cautious in incarcerating offenders. Obviously, decision-making fragmentation made it nearly impossible to develop a coordinated response to the prison-overcrowding problem. A federal judge eventually threatened to fine the state over $500,000 a day if it failed to

(Continued)

FOCUS ON

CORRECTIONAL PRACTICE (Continued)

comply with court-ordered standards. An emergency legislative session was called, and all parts of the system were pressured to develop responses to control prison crowding. A few years later, the state's systematic response to overcrowding—combined with the nation's most aggressive prison-building program—resulted in a relaxation of judicial scrutiny of the prison system. A major debate among policy makers between a correctional policy of punitiveness and one of rehabilitation

has been resolved in favor of the latter approach, and this, too, is reducing the pressure on the prison system.[20]

Sentencing reform in the late 1980s doubled the prison population in less than a decade, but this trend has since abated. Texas's 3.1 percent decline in prisoners since 2000 was one of the largest declines in the country, and state leaders now proclaim that the number of prisoners no longer exceeds prison capacity.

---

prison

An institution for the incarceration of people convicted of serious crimes, usually felonies.

jail

A facility authorized to hold pretrial detainees and sentenced misdemeanants for periods longer than 48 hours. Most jails are administered by county governments; sometimes they are part of the state government.

The extent to which the different levels of government are involved in corrections varies. The scope of the states' criminal laws is much broader than that of federal criminal laws. As a result, just over 300,000 adults are under federal correctional supervision. There are 102 federal **prisons** and 1,719 state prisons.[21] **Jails** are operated mainly by local governments, but in six states they are integrated with the state prison system.

As noted in **Figure 1.4**, criminal justice costs are borne by each level of government, with well over 90 percent of correctional costs falling on state and local governments. In most states, the agencies of community corrections—probation and intermediate sanctions—are run by the county government and are usually part of the judicial branch. However, in some jurisdictions the executive branch runs them, and in several states this part of corrections is run by statewide organizations.

That the United States is a representative democracy complicates corrections. Officials are elected, legislatures determine the objectives of the criminal law system and appropriate the resources to carry out those objectives, and political parties channel public opinion to officeholders on such issues as law and order. Over time the goals of correctional policies have shifted. For example, between 1940 and 1970, corrections was oriented toward liberal rehabilitative policies; since about 1970, conservative, get-tough crime control policies have influenced corrections. Questions of crime and justice are thus inescapably public questions, subject to all the pressures and vagaries of the political process.

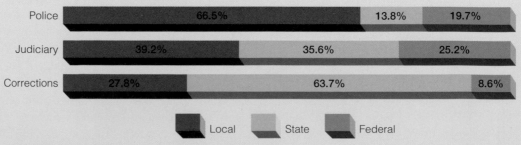

Figure 1.4

Distribution of Justice System Expenditures by Level of Government

State and local governments bear the brunt of the costs of correctional activities.

Source: BJS *Bulletin*, May 2004.

Clearly, corrections encompasses a major commitment on the part of American society to deal with people convicted of criminal law violations. The increase in the number of offenders under supervision in the past decade has caused a major expansion of correctional facilities, staff, and budgets; some might say that corrections is now a big business.

Spending for corrections has risen more dramatically than for any other state function, jumping a whopping 538 percent between 1982 and 2001. During this period, state legislatures increased operating appropriations for corrections by an average of 10.4 percent annually (excluding construction costs), compared with a 4.1 percent increase for Medicaid and a 5.1 percent increase for higher education.[22] Many states now spend more on corrections than on all public higher education.

■ KEY ISSUES IN CORRECTIONS

Like all other government services, corrections is buffeted by frequently shifting social and political forces that greatly complicate administration. These forces are also part of what make corrections so interesting to study. In this section we describe some of the controversies, issues, and themes that arise in the study of corrections. These are divided into three main areas: managing the correctional organization, working with offenders, and upholding social values.

Managing the Correctional Organization

The ways in which different correctional organizations are managed depend on various factors, including goals, funding, bureaucracy, and interagency coordination.

GOALS ■ The theory inherent in the term *corrections*, the assumption that offenders can be "corrected," faces much dispute. For example, some people believe that we cannot ever rehabilitate most offenders, that only social maturation can influence most people to abide by the law. Others argue that the penal system should not be concerned with the future behavior of criminals, that the only appropriate response to wrongdoing is punishment. Yet from the end of World War II until the 1970s, the corrective function was so widely accepted that treatment and reform of offenders were virtually the only issues in criminal justice deemed worthy of serious attention.

Corrections has constantly faced the challenge of deciding which goals to emphasize. Conflict over goals stems precisely from the shifting forces that directly influence corrections. Political ideology, for example, often colors the analysis and development of correctional policy. Liberals believe that corrections should follow one path; conservatives, another. Goals set by conflicting interests do not usually mesh.

In response to conflicting political forces, correctional leaders offer conflicting (or at least divergent) justifications for a given policy in order to maintain an appearance of consensus. A program of private-industry employment for prison inmates, for instance, can be commended to liberals as rehabilitative training, to free-enterprise advocates as expansion of the private sector, and to conservatives as a get-tough policy designed to make prisoners pay the costs of their incarceration. Although this tactic helps preserve support for the prison's industrial operations, it also creates managerial problems for correctional leaders, because when the program is implemented, the goals of treatment, profit, and punishment may well conflict.

Further, correctional leaders who state precise objectives risk alienating various important groups or constituencies. Thus, they tend to frame goals as vague generalities, such as "to protect the public" or "to rehabilitate offenders." The effects of this vagueness extend well beyond public relations; often it is difficult for correctional staff members to make goal-oriented choices, because they are unsure of what the leaders want.

To see what one criminologist is doing to try to **improve corrections**, go to the corresponding link at www .cengage.com/criminaljustice/ clear.

Corrections depends on funding from county, state, or federal legislatures. Here, the Michigan senate tries to deal with a major budgetary shortfall. Corrections must compete not only with other criminal justice agencies for funds but also agencies supporting education, transportation, social welfare, and so on. What strategies might correctional officials use to secure adequate resources?

AP Images/Al Goldis

This has led some observers to argue that corrections does not work to achieve an overriding goal, but rather seeks to balance stated and unstated goals so that no single goal is sacrificed.

FUNDING ■ At all political levels, corrections is only one of many services operated by government and paid for by tax revenues. Thus, corrections must vie for funding, not only with other criminal justice agencies but also with agencies supporting education, transportation, social welfare, and so on. Per capita spending on all criminal justice activities ranges from less than $100 in West Virginia to more than $400 in Alaska and New York.

Understandably, corrections does not always receive the funding it needs; people may want garbage collected regularly more than they want quality correctional work performed. Recall, too, that corrections is largely invisible until a problem occurs, such as when a parolee commits a heinous crime or a prison riot breaks out. An even greater difficulty stems from the perceived undesirability of those corrected; it is not easy to win larger budgets to help people who have broken the law.

Conflict among the branches and levels of government also creates problems for corrections. Local governments are often responsible for correctional programs for minor offenders; state governments handle longer-term, more-serious offenders. Often the two levels vie for operating funds, and each seeks to avoid responsibility for offenders supervised by the other. Given this fragmentation, correctional services and programs may overlap.

Officials of the executive branch often complain that legislatures enact correctional codes and prescribe operational responsibilities without providing sufficient funds to carry them out. Both branches complain that court rulings set unfair constraints on their ability to handle assigned offenders. In developing and implementing policies, correctional agents must consider not only the sociopolitical environment but also the government setting in which corrections functions.

One result of funding squabbles is dispute over organizational "turf." Most probation offices are attached to the judiciary and funded by county governments. Do they then fall within the domain of corrections, or do they belong to the judiciary? Should the sheriff be in charge of transporting offenders from jail to prison, or should the prison administrators be responsible? To what extent should social service agencies become involved with the needs of correctional clients in a halfway house? Should parole officers or the police be responsible for tracking down offenders who have violated the conditions of their release?

Struggles for resources also occur between corrections and related social service agencies. A department of corrections may vie with a department of mental health for funds to set up a drug rehabilitation program; both departments may view the new resources as a way to expand. Often, correctional departments take such empire-building actions to keep themselves strong and viable.

BUREAUCRACY ■ Michael Lipsky has provided perhaps the most vivid portrait of the problems facing correctional workers. He coined the term **street-level bureaucrats** to refer to the following:

> *Public service workers who interact directly with citizens in the course of their jobs, [including] teachers, police officers and other law enforcement personnel, social workers, judges, public lawyers and other court officers, health workers and many other public employees who grant access to government programs and provide services within them.*[23]

Lipsky's provocative generalizations about street-level bureaucrats apply to virtually all individuals who have face-to-face contact with offenders. They work with inadequate resources and face ever-increasing demands. Frequently they find themselves theoretically obligated to provide higher-quality treatment for their clients than they can afford. Thus, street-level bureaucrats soon learn that "with any single client they probably could interact flexibly and responsibly. But if they did this with too many clients, their capacity to respond flexibly would disappear."[24] Probation officers, for example, may feel obliged to find jobs for their probationers. If they took time to do so, however, they could not provide other services. An officer may genuinely desire to work hard for those probationers who show promise, but not for others. Officers facing such conflicts may become alienated from their clients because they cannot satisfy their clients' needs—maintaining a working relationship proves too frustrating.

Limited resources force administrators of service bureaucracies to monitor carefully the way workers apply their time and energies. Bureaucracies that process people develop categories for their clients, seeking to use personnel or agency resources in the best way and to succeed with some clients, even though they cannot succeed with them all.

Lipsky concludes that delivering street-level policy through bureaucracy presents an inherent contradiction. One person delivering service to another suggests human interaction, caring, and responsibility. But delivering service through a bureaucracy suggests detached, inflexible treatment based on limited resources. Conflicting, ambiguous goals, combined with difficulties in measuring work performance, may reduce effectiveness and commitment to the work. Thus, the bureaucratic model guarantees that services are delivered only up to a point and that goals are never fully achieved.

Is Lipsky's conclusion too pessimistic, or is it just realistic? Certainly correctional workers and their clients face formidable obstacles. Workers must make daily decisions under conditions of technical uncertainty and sporadic negative feedback; offenders must comply both with legal mandates and with less-explicit parameters established by the needs of the correctional organization. Yet bureaucratic worker–client relationships offer benefits as well. As their time and tasks grow more structured, workers have less discretion and thus less capacity to abuse their positions. Further, limited organizational resources force agencies to clarify their goals and to direct services toward those people who most need staff time. And, given the extensive power of correctional agencies, conditions in bureaucracies may restrain abuse of state power.

INTERAGENCY COORDINATION ■ Managing correctional agencies is further complicated by the fact that most corrections systems comprise several loosely related organizations that are themselves bureaucracies. Thus decision making is dispersed—no one person can implement the full range of correctional practices. For example, the sheriff who runs the jail and the probation officer who runs the pretrial release program are both affected by jail crowding and delays in sentencing hearings. Even so, they may resist working together, because each is busily protecting an area of managerial control.

For data on **correctional expenditure**, go to the corresponding link at www .cengage.com/criminaljustice/ clear.

street-level bureaucrats
Public-service workers who interact directly with citizens in the course of their work, granting access to government programs and providing services within them.

Furthermore, line workers in corrections, those in direct contact with offenders, seldom influence organizational policies, even though they must implement those policies daily. Corrections itself cannot determine the type and number of its clients. Others in the criminal justice system, primarily judges, do that, and correctional officials cannot halt or regulate the flow. Thus, the efforts of correctional workers are sometimes sporadic, uncoordinated, or inconsistent merely because various bureaucracies are loosely interconnected.

Within the corrections system, a great deal of policy is formally interconnected. In some states as many as half or more of all inmates go to prison because they have violated a requirement of probation or parole; in other states, these rule violators are less frequently sent to prison. In other words, the enforcement policies of the supervising agencies help determine prison intake. In most systems, however, prison authorities have little control over policies for enforcing probation rules. Similarly, a probation officer's caseload is determined by the number of people on probation and the length of their probation terms: Even though officers have a finite amount of time for supervision, they generally have little or no control over their caseloads. As offenders flow through the system—from probation to revocation to prison to work release to parole—one agency determines the workload of the next.

These informal interconnections create an uneasy tension. Agency directors understandably may take steps to protect their piece of the system from encroachment by the rest of it. Each correctional unit commonly insulates itself from the pressures faced by the other units, because the others often produce unwanted caseload increases; for example, crowded jail conditions may encourage judges to put more offenders on probation.

That very isolation makes it more likely that the other units will run into problems resulting from a lack of cooperation, and these problems will haunt all the units when the corrections system as a whole is criticized. (See the Focus box "Correctional Interconnectedness in Alabama.")

FOCUS ON

CORRECTIONAL PRACTICE

Correctional Interconnectedness in Alabama

Here is a description of the ways a crisis in one correctional agency can affect other agencies:

Alabama's prisons are full, and the county jails are so crowded that dozens of inmates have been left to sleep on tables and floors. It's a decades-old situation that reached a crisis point in 2000, when a state with one of the nation's highest incarceration rates finally had to expand its prison system to accommodate a crushing growth in prisoners. Today, with more than 27,000 people incarcerated in Alabama, or 591 per 100,000 residents (only five states have higher rates), Alabama is a case study in correctional crisis.

Under a consent arrangement in the year 2000, the state prison system agreed to accept inmates who had been in county jails more than 30 days after being sentenced to a state prison term. But backlogs soon built up and by 2001, about 2,000 state prisoners had been in county jails longer than 30 days. Soon after that, two sheriffs armed with their own court orders rounded up more than 200 state prisoners from county jails and dropped them off at state lockups.

"They're somebody else's problem now," Sheriff Jim Woodward said. In Morgan County, a federal judge last month ordered 104 state inmates moved from the jail, where he said conditions were so cramped it resembled a "slave ship." In Houston County, where the 200-bed jail had 300 prisoners, a judge had threatened to leave state inmates handcuffed to a prison fence if the state didn't take them. The crisis came when a judge ordered a halt to the mass transfer of prisoners to state prisons that were already full themselves.

"This is not a situation where counties, quite frankly, should be doing what they're doing today," then-Governor Don Siegelman said at the time. "They should look for alternatives and not simply wash their hands of the situation."

Working with Offenders

"People work" is central to corrections because the raw material of the system consists of people—staff and offenders. In working with offenders, correctional staff must deal with uncertain technologies, engage in exchange relationships with offenders, and follow uncertain correctional strategies.

PROFESSIONAL VERSUS NONPROFESSIONAL STAFF ■ The term *staff* refers to probation officers, correctional officers, counselors, and others responsible for the daily management and supervision of offenders. The correctional staff includes both professional and nonprofessional employees. For example, psychologists, counselors, and administrators usually hold at least one college degree. They view themselves as members of various professions, with all the rights that adhere to such callings. They believe they should be able to work without supervision and to make decisions without always consulting rulebooks or guidelines. These professional employees work closely with nonprofessional staff, such as jail or prison correctional officers. The nonprofessional staff frequently have only a high school education, and they function under close, often paramilitary (military-style)

© John Birdsall/The Image Works

"People work" is central to corrections. Staff must work closely with offenders, using uncertain technologies, engaging in exchange relationships, and following uncertain strategies.

His successor, Governor Robert Riley, faced the crisis head on. In 2004, a year when many Alabama state agencies had to deal with budget cuts of 10–20 percent, corrections received a whopping 6.9 percent budget increase to pay for additional staff and facilities in order to reduce the crowding problem and bring medical facilities in line with court requirements.

Alabama's current prison crisis recalls the problems in the early 1980s when a federal judge, with the approval of then-Governor Fob James, ordered the mass release of nonviolent offenders because of prison overcrowding. A decade earlier, a judge had described Alabama's prison system as "barbaric" and ruled state inmates have a constitutional right to adequate living conditions.

But the state today still relies heavily on county jails to house its inmates, paying them $1.75 per inmate for food even though officials say it costs counties about $30 a day to house each prisoner. This is especially expensive, since three-quarters of those entering the Alabama prison system are serving sentences for either drug crimes or property crimes, not violence.

"State prisons are full, county jails are full, and the probation officers are loaded up with cases," said Allen Tapley, the executive director of the Sentencing Institute, a private research group. Correctional experts and prison officials say the solution includes more community correctional programs, drug courts, and parole for inmates with convictions for nonviolent offenses. But those are a tough sell in a political environment that favors jail time even for nonviolent crimes.

Source: Adapted from Judith Green and Kevin Pranis, *Alabama Prison Crisis* (New York: Justice Strategies, October 2005); "Mass Transfer Creates Crisis for Alabama Prisons," http://www.usatoday.com/news/nation/2001-05-09-ala-prison.htm, June 19, 2001.

supervision and enforce rules with physical means when necessary. The different perspectives of these two groups and the ways they communicate with each other have caused problems—for example, conflicts over the best ways to deal with offenders and distrust of each other's motives and expertise—in some types of correctional organizations.

technology
A method of applying scientific knowledge to practical purposes in a particular field.

UNCERTAIN TECHNOLOGIES ■ The term **technology** refers to methods of applying scientific knowledge to practical purposes in a particular field. Correctional technologies are not as sophisticated as those of, say, engineering, but their subjects—human beings—are far more complex. Methods of dealing effectively with offenders are highly uncertain. Although knowledge of human behavior has developed during the past century, the validity of the various approaches for treating offenders—such as group therapy, behavior modification, and anger management—remains in doubt.

Thus, corrections is expected to implement programs of questionable value. Correctional organizations face a serious problem: Not all released prisoners adjust successfully to free society; not all mental health referrals of offenders result in emotional adjustment; not all probationers prove trustworthy. Correctional decisions are prone to error. In fact, correctional organizations may approach the technical problem of human ignorance about humans by seeking to reduce types of error rather than to eliminate error altogether.

Further, any organization develops routines just to keep it operating. Like most people, workers in correctional organizations want regular and predictable responsibilities. They do not want to venture into uncharted seas where they may make an uninformed decision and then be penalized for it. Uncertainty declines when people reduce operations to routines—patterns that repeat and thus become familiar. Recognizing these routines is essential for understanding corrections.

EXCHANGE ■ A key facet of corrections is the degree of interdependence between staff and offenders. The unarmed, outnumbered correctional officer assigned to a prison or jail has surprisingly little raw power with which to exact cooperative behavior. Similarly, a probation officer can do little with a probationer who resists the officer's influence. Meanwhile, the prisoner depends on the work of the correctional officer, and the parolee often feels powerless under supervision. Thus, staff and offenders are interdependent: To achieve personal goals, each depends on the other. The officer needs the offender's cooperation to convince superiors that the officer is performing properly; the offender needs the officer's recommendation for favorable termination of parole.

exchange
A mutual transfer of resources based on decisions regarding the costs and benefits of alternative actions.

The interdependence of people in corrections makes the concept of exchange important to understanding their daily world. **Exchange** occurs when two parties trade promises or concessions that make each person's work easier or more predictable. A probationer, for example, cooperates by reporting regularly and attending an alcohol treatment program; in return, the officer is more likely to overlook incidental, minor violations of probation. Each party's situation is made easier by the voluntary decisions of the other.

Because exchange relations between staff and offenders are quite important, they often are subject to informal enforcement. For instance, a rowdy inmate is removed from his cell and placed in solitary until he "settles down" and recognizes officials' authority. A juvenile on probation is arrested and "detained" (locked up) for the weekend while awaiting a hearing on her truancy from school, even though officials have no intention of revoking her probationary status. Conversely, a guard who is hostile or condescending to inmates finds it takes much longer to return prisoners to their cells for the morning count or to quiet down noisy prisoners. Subtle and not-so-subtle pressures unceasingly reinforce the need for keepers and the kept to stay aware of each other's needs.

In sum, correctional transactions almost uniformly involve some aspect of worker–offender contact and interaction. Because staff members and offenders

FOCUS ON CORRECTIONAL POLICY

Is the Great Experiment in Social Control Too Expensive?

Many people think that the "Great Experiment" in incarceration came about as a result of policies enacted by legislators to make sentences more punitive. This is true, but a recent analysis by the criminologist William Spelman sheds new light on this phenomenon.[25] He found good evidence that the size of a state's prison population is related to both the amount of crime it has and the policies it enacts to deal with crime. But he also found that prison expansion is also related to other kinds of expenditures a state makes. Specifically, states that have more revenues available for a variety of programs and services, including health and education, also spend more on prisons, and as their commitment to other services grows, so does their commitment to incarceration growth. Recently, good fiscal times meant growth in imprisonment, as the cost of prisons grew faster than any other public sector investment—aside from Medicaid.[26]

If investment in prison during the 1980s and 1990s was partly product of state revenues, then it should come as no surprise that the economic recession of 2009 has led to a host of new policies designed to close prisons and reduce prison expenditures. For example, when Colorado closed its women's prison and moved their female prisoners into co-correctional facilities with men, it saved $5 million. The national trend to contain prison growth extends even to states with historically high prison populations, such as Texas and Louisiana, as well as very conservative states, such as Kentucky and Nevada.[27]

But the dollar costs of corrections are only a part of the total cost of the largest prison system in the world. New research has shown how the growing prison population has tended to increase racial inequality,[28] distorted electoral politics,[29] and damaged families and communities.[30] All of these effects are costly for society, even if a state's budget does not reflect them. Overall, many leading thinkers have begun to agree that the U.S. prison system needs to be scaled back.

---

depend on each other to achieve their goals, each person can influence evaluations made by the other. This process must be managed through screening and processing routines, staff training and evaluation programs, and so forth. (See the Focus box "Is the Great Experiment in Social Control Too Expensive?")

UNCERTAINTY IN CORRECTIONAL STRATEGIES ■ Throughout the chapters to come, we explore an important theme: that correctional workers and managers cannot predict with certainty what effect their choices will have on the system. How does the correctional official organize staff, choose programs, and manage offenders when the consequences of such actions are so ambiguous? Given this uncertainty, organizational theorists say that the correctional environment is unstable and that, as a result, one of management's main concerns is avoiding negative feedback from the community—the courts, political leaders, the public, and so forth.

Because the effectiveness of correctional strategies that deal directly with offenders is so uncertain, organizations often place greater emphasis on secondary technologies in which they have more confidence—the design of a prison's security apparatus, a computer-based offender-tracking system for probation, and so on. But the core work of corrections concerns the interactions of people—staff and offenders—which will always remain hard to predict and control, no matter what the technology.

There are two points of interest here. First, offenders obviously are handled in a variety of ways. Who determines what happens to offenders, and how they make this determination, is a key issue in this book. Second, and even more central, corrections gets its "business" from not only the courts but also itself. Policies and practices determine how strictly the rules will be enforced, how dire the consequences will be when they are broken, and how much latitude staff will have in assigning offenders to programs. See "Do the Right Thing" for more.

For numerous publications about the field of corrections, visit the website of the **American Correctional Association**, listed at www.cengage.com/criminaljustice/clear.

DO THE RIGHT THING

Governor Wilma James faces a crisis. Her state's Department of Revenue just informed her that tax revenues will be down because of the struggling economy, and she must find a way to reduce the budget by $6 billion, a whopping 4 percent of the overall budget. Some costs are fixed and cannot be cut, including health care and pension payments. Other costs are dear to the hearts of her constituency, such as education and child welfare. She has decided she needs to impose cuts on several cherished programs, including the prison system. The correctional commissioner has told her that he can absorb some budget cuts by greater efficiencies in his prison programs, but if she wants to reduce costs immediately, she has to authorize the early release of prisoners. There are choices. She can let a large number of people convicted of drug-related crimes go, but the commissioner tells her that some of them pose a high risk to the community. She can give early release to people who are considered low risk, but some of them have been convicted of serious crimes.

What should she do?

WRITING ASSIGNMENT: Write an essay on reducing prison populations. Is this a wise thing to do? Why or why not? How would you approach doing this? What is the best way to reduce the costs of corrections? Is it a short-term problem or a long-term one?

Upholding Social Values

All these problems combine to make the field of corrections controversial and therefore engrossing for those who study it. Yet, as compelling as these problems may be, they are only a sidelight to the central appeal of the field of corrections. The questions that corrections raises concerning social control are fundamental to defining society and its values. Seemingly every aspect of the field brings up issues centering on deeply held values about social relations. For example, what kinds of services and treatment facilities should inmates infected with HIV/AIDS receive? Should corrections be more concerned with punishing offenders for crimes or with providing programs to help them overcome the problems in their lives that contribute to crime? Is placing surveillance devices in people's homes a good idea or an invasion of privacy? Questions of interest to researchers, students, and citizens hardly end here. Crucial public and private controversies lurk at every turn. In your own studies and throughout your life, you will find you cannot answer the questions inherent in these controversies without referring to your own values and those of society.

People who undertake careers in corrections often do so because they find the field an excellent place to express their most cherished values. Probation and parole officers frequently report that their original decision to work in these jobs stemmed from their desire to help people. Correctional officers often report that the aspect of their work they like best is working with people who are in trouble and who want to improve their lives. Administrators report that they value the challenge of building effective policies and helping staff perform their jobs better. The field of corrections, then, helps all these individuals to be fully involved with public service and social life. Corrections is interesting to them in part because it deals with a core conflict of values in our society—freedom versus social control—and it does so in ways that require people to work together.

SUMMARY

1 Describe the range of purposes served by the corrections system.

Corrections is a means of social control. It holds people accused of crimes; carries out criminal sentences imposed by courts, including both confinement and community supervision; and provides services for rehabilitation.

2 Define the systems framework and explain why it is useful.

A system is a complex whole consisting of interdependent parts whose operations are directed toward common goals and influenced by the environment in which they function. It is a useful concept because it helps us understand how the various aspects of corrections can affect the others.

3 Name the various components of the corrections system today and describe their functions.

Corrections consists of many subunits. There are both federal and state corrections systems. Institutional corrections include prisons and jails, and they confine people who have been sentenced by the courts (or, in the case of jails, who are awaiting trial). Community corrections supervises people who are either awaiting trial or have been sentenced by the court but are living in the community. There are also private organizations that provide various services to people under correctional authority. Important differences exist among subunits of the same general type.

4 Identify at least five key issues facing corrections today.

Corrections faces several issues: dealing with conflicting goals; obtaining adequate funding; making the bureaucracy of correctional services more effective; coordinating correctional activity across different agencies; and dealing with correctional uncertainty.

5 Discuss what we can learn from the "great experiment of social control."

The growth in the corrections system has resulted mostly from deliberate policies that increase the severity of sentences. Changes in crime rates have had little effect on this growth.

KEY TERMS

corrections (p. 8)	jail (p. 16)	street-level bureaucrats (p. 19)
exchange (p. 22)	prison (p. 16)	system (p. 9)
federalism (p. 13)	social control (p. 8)	technology (p. 22)

FOR DISCUSSION *2 questions and answer them.*

1. Contrast the role of crime with the role of politics in the growth of corrections. Why is this contrast important?
2. What do you see as some of the advantages and disadvantages of the systems concept of corrections?
3. Corrections is a system in which technologies of uncertain validity are used. What are some of the dangers of using these technologies? What safeguards, if any, should be applied?
4. Assume that the legislature has stipulated that rehabilitation should be the goal of corrections in your state. How might people working in the system displace this goal?
5. What does Lipsky mean by the term *street-level bureaucrat*? Give some examples of how street-level bureaucrats act.
6. Suppose you are the commissioner of corrections for your state. Which correctional activities might come within your domain? Which most likely would not?

FOR FURTHER READING

Cole, George F., and Christopher E. Smith. *The American System of Criminal Justice.* 12th ed. Belmont, CA: Wadsworth, 2010. Introduces the American system of criminal justice.

Domanick, Joe. *Cruel Justice: Three Strikes Politics and the Politics of Crime in America's Golden State.* Berkeley, CA: University of California Press, 2004. Analyzes the development of three-strikes legislation in California and discusses its impact.

Herivel, Tara, and Paul Wright, eds. *Prison Profiteers: Who Makes Money from Mass Incarceration?* New York: New Press, 2008. Papers on the economics and politics of private prisons and jails.

Rafael, Steven, and Michael Stoll, eds. *Do Prisons Make Us Safer: The Benefits and Costs of the Prison Boom.* New York: Russell Sage Foundation, 2009. Studies concerning the effects of incarceration on crime, families, and society.

Tonry, Michael. *Thinking about Crime and Sensibility in American Penal Culture.* Oxford University Press, 2004. Provides an assessment of the growth of punishment in the United States, and compares this pattern to those of other nations during the same period.

Walker, Samuel. *Sense and Nonsense about Crime: A Policy Guide.* 6th ed. Belmont, CA: Wadsworth, 2004. Examines crime control practices that do not work and those that have some potential for success.

Western, Bruce. *Punishment and Inequality in America.* New York: Russell Sage Foundation, 2006. A statistical study of the effects of incarceration on social inequality.

NOTES

[1] Shannon M. Catalano, "Criminal Victimization, 2005," BJS *Bulletin*, September 2006, p. 1.

[2] Jennifer C. Karberg and Allen J. Beck, "Trends in U.S. Correctional Populations: Findings from the Bureau of Justice Statistics" (paper presented at the National Committee on Community Corrections, Washington, DC, April 16, 2004).

[3] Heather C. West and William J. Sabol, *Prison Inmates at Midyear 2008—Statistical Tables* (Washington, DC: Bureau of Justice Statistics, March 2009), 4.

[4] Pew Charitable Trusts, One in 100: *Behind Bars in America, 2008* (Philadelphia: Author, 2008), 5.

[5] Pew Charitable Trusts, *One in 31: The Long Reach of Corrections* (Philadelphia: Author, March 2009), 1.

[6] Alfred Blumstein and Allen Beck, "Reentry as a Transient State between Liberty and Recommitment," in *Prisoner Reentry and Crime in America*, edited by Jeremy Travis and Christy Visher (New York: Cambridge University Press, 2005), 50–79.

[7] Jennifer C. Karberg and Allen J. Beck, "Trends in U.S. Correctional Populations: Findings from the Bureau of Justice Statistics" (paper presented at the National Committee on Community Corrections, Washington, DC, April 16, 2004).

[8] Thomas P. Bonczar, "Prevalence of Imprisonment in the U.S. Population, 1974–2001," BJS *Special Report*, August 2003, p. 2.

[9] Ibid.

[10] See the special issue of *Policy Today* 4 (no. 3, March 2007).

[11] Bonczar, "Prevalence of Imprisonment."

[12] Raymond V. Liedka, Anne Morrison Piehl, and Bert Useem, "The Crime Control Effects of Incarceration: Does Scale Matter?" *Criminology and Public Policy* 5 (no. 2, 2006): 245–76.

[13] Franklin E. Zimring and Gordon Hawkins, *Incapacitation* (Chicago: University of Chicago Press, 1997).

[14] Bruce Western, *Punishment and Inequality in America* (New York: Russell Sage Foundation, 2006).

[15] Rucker C. Johnson, "Ever Increasing Levels of Incarceration and the Consequences for Children," in *Do Prisons Make Us Safer? The Benefits and Costs of the Prison Boom*, edited by Steven Rafael and Michael Stoll (New York: Russell Sage Foundation, 2009), 177–206.

[16] BJS *Bulletin*, May 2004, p. 1.

[17] Solomon Moore, "Court Panel Orders California to Reduce its Prison Population by 55,000 in Three Years," *New York Times*, February 10, 2009, p. A-12.

[18] See Joan Petersilia, "California's Correctional Paradox of Excess and Deprivation," in *Crime and Justice, a Review of Research*, vol. 37 (Chicago: University of Chicago, 2008), 207–78.

[19] "Economy Bogs Down Florida Governor's Pro-Prison Position," *Orlando Sentinel*, May 13, 2009, pp. 1, 8.

[20] Mike Ward, "Drug Program Gets Credit for Halting Prisoner Increase," *American Statesman*, February 20, 2009, p. 12.

[21] James J. Stephan, *Census of State and Federal Correctional Facilities, 2005* (Washington, DC: Bureau of Justice Statistics, October 2008), 1.

[22] Stan C. Proband, "State Correctional Budgets up 5.1 Percent in 1998," *Overcrowded Times* 9 (April 1998): 1.

[23] Michael Lipsky, *Street-Level Bureaucracy* (New York: Russell Sage Foundation, 1980), 3.

[24] Ibid., pp. 37–38, 81, 99 (quote from p. 81).

[25] William Spelman, "Crime, Cash, and Limited Options: Explaining the Prison Boom," *Criminology and Public Policy* 8 (no. 1, February 2009): 29–78.

[26] Solomon Moore, "Prison Spending Outpaces All but Medicaid," *New York Times*, March 3, 2009, p. A-10.

[27] Judith Greene, "Positive Trends and Best Policies in Criminal Justice Reform: A National Overview" (testimony given to the New Jersey Legislature, May 6, 2009), http://www.justicestrategies.net.

[28] Bruce Western, *Punishment and Inequality in America* (New York: Russell Sage Foundation, 2006).

[29] John Guetzkow and Bruce Western, "The Political Consequences of Mass Imprisonment," in *Remaking Democracy and Public Policy in an Age of Inequality*, edited by Joe Soss, Jacob Hacker, and Suzanne Metler (New York: Russell Sage Foundation, 2009), 228–42.

[30] Anthony C. Thompson, *Releasing Prisoners, Redeeming Communities* (New York: New York University, 2008).

© Gianni Dagli Orti/CORBIS

LEARNING OBJECTIVES

After reading this chapter you should be able to . . .

1 Understand the major forms of punishment from the Middle Ages to the American Revolution.

2 Discuss the Age of Reason and how it affected corrections.

3 Understand the contribution of Cesare Beccaria and the classical school.

4 Explain the contribution of Jeremy Bentham and the utilitarians.

5 Discuss the work of John Howard and its influence on correctional reform.

The brutality of the execution of Robert-François Damiens, convicted of attempting to assassinate King Louis XV of France, raises questions about the purpose of this type of punishment.

A HUSH FELL OVER THE FRENCH courtroom on March 2, 1757, as the chief judge rose to read the sentence on Robert-François Damiens, convicted of trying to assassinate King Louis XV:

> He is to be taken and conveyed in a cart, wearing nothing but a shift, holding a torch of burning wax weighing two pounds; in the said cart to the Place de Greve, where on a scaffold that will be erected there, the flesh will be torn from his breasts, arms, thighs and calves with red-hot pinchers, his right hand, holding the knife with which he committed the said parricide, burnt with sulphur, and, on those places where the flesh will be torn away, poured molten lead, boiling oil, burning resin, wax and sulphur melted together and then his body drawn and quartered by four horses and his limbs and body consumed by fire, reduced to ashes and his ashes thrown to the winds.[1]

Newspapers recorded that Damiens's death was even more horrible than the sentence required. Because the horses were not able to pull him "limb from limb," the executioners resorted to hacking off Damiens's arms and legs. All this occurred while the man was still alive.

What was the point of this punishment? What did the state hope to achieve through this atrocity? Why does this execution

THE EARLY HISTORY OF CORRECTIONAL THOUGHT AND PRACTICE

- ### FROM THE MIDDLE AGES TO THE AMERICAN REVOLUTION
  Galley Slavery
  Imprisonment
  Transportation
  Corporal Punishment and Death

- ### ON THE EVE OF REFORM

- ### THE AGE OF REASON AND CORRECTIONAL REFORM
  Cesare Beccaria and the Classical School

Jeremy Bentham and the "Hedonic Calculus"
John Howard and the Birth of the Penitentiary

- ### WHAT REALLY MOTIVATED CORRECTIONAL REFORM?

seem so horrible to us today? After all, public corporal punishment was the norm for thousands of years, and people pursued it with gusto.

Until the 1800s punishments were public spectacles throughout Europe and America. Crowds taunted the condemned as the executioner or sheriff conducted whippings, burnings, pilloryings, and hangings on orders of the king or court. Punishment-as-spectacle was used to control crime and to exhibit the sovereign's power. Yet only a few decades after Damiens's 1757 execution, a major change took place in Europe and the United States. Efforts were being made to devise a rational, reformative model of criminal sanctions focused on the mind and soul, not the body. With the development of the penitentiary in the 1830s as a place where offenders could reflect on their misdeeds, repent, and prepare for life as crime-free citizens, torture as a public spectacle disappeared. By the 1900s punishments were carried out within prisons or in the community under the supervision of correctional staff who saw themselves not as instruments of suffering but as social workers, managers, and technicians of reform.

Like other social institutions, corrections reflects the vision and concerns of the larger community. For example, in their post–Revolutionary War idealism, Americans strongly believed crime could be eliminated from this rich new nation if offenders were isolated from bad influences and encouraged to repent. Similarly, in the early 1900s, inspired by a new faith in the behavioral sciences, penology veered sharply toward a psychological

Chapter

2

approach to offender rehabilitation. Later, though, as crime rose in the late 1960s, public opinion demanded another shift in correctional policy, toward greater emphasis on crime control.

In this chapter we examine the broad European antecedents to American correctional thought and practice. In Chapter 3, this historical overview continues through an examination of corrections in the United States from colonial times to the present. Later in the book, the history of such specific correctional practices as prison industry, probation, and parole is discussed in greater detail. Let us begin here by examining the correctional practices of earlier times.

FROM THE MIDDLE AGES TO THE AMERICAN REVOLUTION

The earliest-known comprehensive statements of prohibited behavior appear in the Sumerian Law of Mesopotamia (3100 B.C.E.) and the Code of Hammurabi, developed by the king of Babylon in 1750 B.C.E. These written codes were divided into sections to cover different types of offenses and contained descriptions of the punishments to be imposed on offenders. Another important ancestor of Western law is the Draconian Code, promulgated in classical Greece in the seventh century B.C.E. This code was the first to erase the distinction between citizens and slaves before the law. Attributed to Drakon, the code described legal procedures and also the forms of punishment that could be inflicted: "stoning to death; throwing the offender from a cliff; binding him to a stake so that he suffered a slow death and public abuse while dying; or the formal dedication of the offender to the gods."[2] Lesser punishments might be the forbidden burial of offenders and the destruction of their houses.

In Rome the law of the Twelve Tables (450 B.C.E.) and the code compiled by Emperor Justinian in 534 C.E. helped lay the groundwork of European law. As in Greece and

During the Middle Ages various punishments were imposed on the body of the offender. This sixteenth-century German engraving has the title *The Usual Punishments*. Can you identify them?

Die verschiedenen im Mittelalter üblichen Strafen und Hinrichtungsarten
Ulrich Tenglers Laienspiegel, Augsburg 1509

Bibliotheque Nationale, Paris, France, Archives Charmet/The Bridgeman Art Library International

other ancient societies such as Egypt and Israel, Roman lawbreakers were made into slaves, exiled, killed, imprisoned, and physically brutalized.[3] In most of Europe, forms of legal sanctions that are familiar today did not appear until the beginning of the Middle Ages, in the 1200s. Before that time, Europeans viewed responses to crime as a private affair, with vengeance a duty to be carried out by the person wronged or by a family member. Wrongs were avenged in accordance with the **lex talionis**, or law of retaliation. This principle underlays the laws of Anglo-Saxon society until the time of the Norman conquest of England in 1066. During the Middle Ages the **secular law** of England and Europe was organized according to the feudal system.[4] In the absence of a strong central government, crimes among neighbors took on the character of war, and the public peace was endangered as feudal lords sought to avenge one another's transgressions. In response, in England by the year 1200 a system of **wergild**, or payment of money as compensation for a wrong, had developed as a way of reducing the frequency of violent blood feuds. During this period the custom of treating offenses as personal matters to be settled by individuals gradually gave way to the view that the peace of society required the public to participate in determining guilt or innocence and in exacting a penalty.

Criminal law thus focused on maintaining public order among people of equal status and wealth. Given the parties involved, the main criminal punishments were penance and the payment of fines or restitution. Lower-class offenders without money received physical punishment at the hands of their masters.

During this same period the church, as the dominant social institution, maintained its own system of ecclesiastical punishments, which made a great impact on society as a whole. Especially during the Inquisition of the 1300s and 1400s, the church zealously punished those who violated its laws. At the same time, it gave refuge from secular prosecution to people who could claim **benefit of clergy**. In time, benefit of clergy was extended to all literate people.

In the later Middle Ages, especially during the 1400s and 1500s, the authority of government grew, and the criminal law system became more fully developed. With the rise of trade, the breakdown of the feudal order, and the emergence of a middle class, other forms of sanction were applied. In addition to fines, five punishments were common in Europe before the 1800s: galley slavery, imprisonment, transportation, corporal punishment, and death. As we discuss later, each of these punishments had a specific purpose, and the development of each was linked to ongoing social conditions. Realize that at the time, with neither a police force nor other centralized instruments of order, deterrence was the dominant purpose of the criminal sanction. Thus, before the 1800s people believed that one of the best ways to maintain order was to intimidate the entire population by publicly punishing offenders.

Galley Slavery

Galley slavery was the practice of forcing men to row ships. Now popularly identified with ancient Rome or Greece, galley slavery was not formally abolished throughout Europe until the mid-1700s.[5] However, by the 1500s the practice had begun to wane with the advent of heavy sailing ships. At first exclusively for slaves or men captured in battle, galley slavery came to be the lot of some convicts, often as a reprieve from the gallows. According to a 1602 proclamation by Queen Elizabeth I, the galleys were considered more merciful than ordinary civil punishments, even though the oarsmen might remain in chains for life.[6]

Imprisonment

Until the late Middle Ages, prisons were used primarily for the detention of people awaiting trial. In ancient times, offenders were incarcerated in cages, in rock quarries, or even in chambers under the Roman Forum while they awaited punishment. Short imprisonment as punishment was used in Italy, France, Germany, and England for petty crime, often for those unable to pay their fines or debts.[7] Some inmates in the medieval prison were "not cast out of urban life"; rather, they were able to roam

lex talionis
Law of retaliation; the principle that punishment should correspond in degree and kind to the offense ("an eye for an eye and a tooth for a tooth").

secular law
The law of the civil society as distinguished from church law.

wergild
"Man money"; money paid to relatives of a murdered person or to the victim of a crime to compensate them and to prevent a blood feud.

benefit of clergy
The right to be tried in an ecclesiastical court, where punishments were less severe than those meted out by civil courts, given the religious focus on penance and salvation.

You can find an excellent **criminal justice history** resource site listed at the corresponding link at www.cengage.com/criminaljustice/clear.

galley slavery
Forced rowing of large ships or galleys.

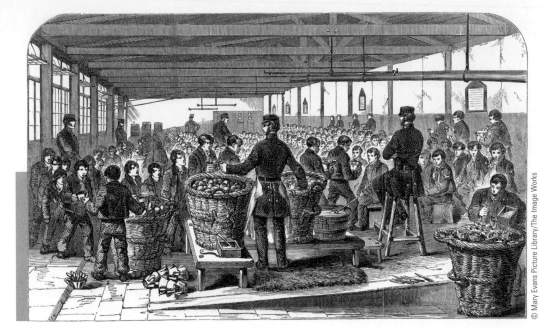

© Mary Evans Picture Library/The Image Works

Bridewell Houses were workhouses established throughout England for the employment and housing of offenders. Here, young men at the Tothill Fields Bridewell House have dinner in silence under strict supervision.

the city as licensed beggars, debtors seeking settlement of the claims against them, who could plead with their families for sustenance. But for most offenders prior to the 1800s, incarceration provided punishments far greater than mere detention.[8]

Conditions in these jails were appalling. Men, women, and children, healthy and sick, were locked up together. The strong preyed on the weak, there was no sanitation, and disease was epidemic. Furthermore, authorities made no provision for the inmates' upkeep. Often the warden viewed his job as a business proposition, selling food and accommodations to his charges. The poor thus had to rely for survival on alms brought to them by charitable people and religious groups.

Attempts to reform prisons began in the 1500s. With the disintegration of feudalism, political power became more centralized and economies began to shift from agriculture to manufacturing. As links to feudal landlords dissolved, the rural poor wandered about the countryside or drifted to the cities. The emphasis of the Protestant Reformation on the importance of hard work and on the sinfulness of sloth stirred European reformers to urge that some means be found to provide work for the idle poor. Out of these concerns the **house of correction** or "workhouse" was born.

house of correction
Detention facility that combined the major elements of a workhouse, poorhouse, and penal industry by both disciplining inmates and setting them to work.

In 1553 London's Bishop Nicholas Ridley persuaded Edward VI to donate Bridewell Palace as the first house of correction. By a law passed in 1609 each English county was required to provide "Bridewells" or houses of correction. These facilities did not serve merely as a place of detention, as did the jail; they instead combined the main elements of a workhouse, poorhouse, and penal institution. Whereas jails were thought to promote idleness among the inmates, the house of correction was expected to instill "a habit of industry more conducive to an honest livelihood."[9] The inmates—primarily prostitutes, beggars, minor criminals, and the idle poor such as orphans and the sick— were to be disciplined and set to work. The products made in the house of correction were to be sold on the market, so that the facility would be self-sufficient and not need government subsidy. The term *Bridewell House* came to be used for all versions of the English house of correction.

Information about **England's "house of corrections"** can be found at the corresponding link at www.cengage.com/criminaljustice/clear.

Institutions similar to the English house of correction appeared in Holland, France, Germany, and Italy. Visiting these places in 1775, the English penal reformer John Howard was impressed by their cleanliness, discipline, and emphasis on rehabilitation through Bible study and regularity of habits. A motto carved over the doorway to one institution succinctly defined the authority of the law with regard to the inmates: "My hand is severe but my intention benevolent." This motto influenced the later development of the penitentiary.

Of the European institutions, the Milan House of Correction, built in 1755, and a similar institution in Ghent, the Maison de Force, built in 1772, attracted particular attention. The latter did so because of its design. It was an octagonal building surrounding a central yard. Eight long pavilions radiated from the center, allowing the separation of inmates by the seriousness of the crime, by sex, or by status as a member of the noncriminal poor. The prisoners worked in common areas during the day and were segregated at night.

Conditions in England's Bridewells deteriorated as the facilities increasingly housed criminals rather than poor people. In the 1700s the labor power provided by the inmates was no longer economically profitable, and the reformative aim of the institution vanished.

The Prison Act of 1865 formally joined the jail and the house of correction. The resulting institution became known as a prison—a place of punishment for those serving terms of up to two years.[10] As we will see, elements of the houses of correction were later incorporated into the penitentiary and the industrial prison of the nineteenth century.

© Art Media/Heritage/The Image Works

In addition to England, other European countries transported offenders to their colonies. In 1852 France began sending convicts to Devil's Island, French Guiana. It was not until 1951 that the last prisoner was transported there.

Transportation

From ancient times people who have disobeyed the rules of a community have been cast out, or banished. With the breakdown of feudalism and the worsening of economic conditions in the 1600s, prisons and houses of correction in England and Europe filled to overflowing. The New World represented a convenient place to send French, Spanish, and English offenders, a place from which they would probably not return.[11] For Russians, **transportation** to Siberia often meant death.

Initially, English prisoners could choose transportation in place of the gallows or the whipping post. (See the Focus box "Shaming: An Ancient Technique of Social Control.") With passage of the Vagrancy Act of 1597, transportation became prescribed. By 1606, with the settlement of Virginia, the transportation of convicts to North America became economically important for the colonial companies for whom they labored. It also helped relieve the overcrowded prisons of England.

Transportation seemed so successful that in 1717 a statute was passed allowing convicts to be given over to private contractors, who then shipped them to the colonies and sold their services. Prisoners who returned to England before their terms expired were to be executed. The Transportation Act of 1718 made transportation the standard penalty for noncapital offenses. From 1718 to 1776 an estimated 50,000 British convicts were shipped to the American colonies. In 1772 three-fifths of male convicts were transported.[12]

With the onset of the American Revolution, transportation from England temporarily halted. By this time questions also had been raised about the appropriateness of the policy. Some critics argued that it was unjust to send convicts to live in a country where their lives would be easier than at home. But perhaps more importantly, by the beginning of the 1700s American planters had discovered that African slaves were better workers and economically more profitable than English convicts. The importation of black slaves increased dramatically, the prisons of England again became overcrowded, and large numbers of convicts were assigned to live in **hulks** (abandoned ships) along the banks of the Thames.

British transportation began again in 1787, to different locales. Over the next 80 years, 160,000 prisoners were transported from Great Britain and Ireland to New South Wales, Tasmania, and other parts of Australia. As the historian Robert Hughes explains,

> *Every convict faced the same social prospects. He or she served the Crown or, on the Crown's behalf, some private person, for a given span of years. Then came a pardon or a ticket-of-leave, either of which permitted him to sell his labor freely and choose his place of work.*[13]

transportation
The practice of transplanting offenders from the community to another region or land, often a penal colony.

hulks
Abandoned ships the English converted to hold convicts during a period of prison crowding between 1776 and 1790.

For a **Victorian's description of a hulk**, see the corresponding link at www .cengage.com/criminaljustice/clear.

For more on the **transportation of English convicts to Australia**, see the corresponding link at www .cengage.com/criminaljustice/ clear.

An ancient punishment, shaming sometimes does not work as officials expect. The public (and media-covered) shaming of these prostitutes in Shenzhen in China created an angry nationwide backlash.

© Photoshot /Landov

FOCUS ON CORRECTIONAL PRACTICE

Shaming: An Ancient Technique of Social Control

From ancient times, communities have used *shaming*—holding someone up for public humiliation—as a way to punish petty criminals and reinforce social values. The punishment of shaming can range from being forced to describe one's own crime to being displayed in a public place where one often was subjected to verbal or even physical abuse. In colonial America offenders were often placed in stocks in the public square, where citizens shamed them. In Nathaniel Hawthorne's *The Scarlet Letter,* the Puritan Hester Prynne must wear an "A" announcing her adultery. Although many believe that shaming is banned by the UN Convention on Human Rights, the terms are not precisely defined and many modern judges use this type of punishment. Examples of modern forms of shaming include requiring sex offenders to post a sign in their front yard announcing their offense, or drunk drivers to place a bumper sticker on their car revealing their DUI conviction.

In China, television viewers in 2006 saw a scene reminiscent of the Cultural Revolution, which had ended in 1976. A hundred or so prostitutes and a few pimps were paraded in front of a jeering crowd, their names revealed, and then taken to jail.

This act of public shaming was intended as the first step in a two-month campaign by the authorities in the southern city of Shenzhen to crack down on prostitution. But the event prompted an angry nationwide backlash, with many people supporting the prostitutes because of the violation of their human rights and expressing outrage in one online forum after another.

While the voices condemning the behavior of the city and its police force were the most energetic, some supported the crackdown. "Perhaps you've never been to Shenzhen, or you've been there and you don't have a thorough understanding of the place," wrote one contributor to an Internet forum. "A person who really knows Shenzhen would feel that this is not harsh enough, because the prostitution industry has become so prosperous here."

The parading of the arrested prostitutes came after a television station had broadcast a report about prostitution in the city's Futian district, where sex is openly traded by streetwalkers and pimps and in bathhouses and karaoke clubs.

Instead of jumping on the bandwagon against prostitution, which is illegal but omnipresent in China, many commentators aimed their criticism at the government for its hypocrisy in not acting against the rich underworld that operates the sex trade.

Shaming has been an element of social control in many cultures throughout history. Would this approach work in the United States today? Would some groups in U.S. society respond more readily than others? Why? Why not?

Sources: Drawn from John Braithwaite, *Crime, Shame and Reintegration* (New York: Cambridge University Press, 1989); Howard W. French, "As Vice Dragnet Recalls Bad Old Days, Chinese Cry Out," *New York Times,* December 13, 2006, p. A3.

However, in 1837 a committee of Parliament reported that, far from reforming criminals, transportation created thoroughly depraved societies. Critics argued that the Crown was forcing Englishmen to be "slaves until they were judged fit to become peasants."[14] The committee recommended a penitentiary system in which offenders were confined and set to hard labor. This recommendation was only partially adopted; not until 1868 did all transportation from England cease.[15]

Corporal Punishment and Death

Although **corporal punishment** and death have been used throughout history, the sixteenth through eighteenth centuries in Great Britain and Europe were particularly brutal. For example, the German criminal code of 1532 specified,

> *An ordinary murderer or burglar merits hanging in chains or beheading with the sword. A woman who murders her infant is buried alive and impaled, a traitor is drawn and quartered. Other grave offenders may be burned to death, or drowned, or set out to die in agony upon the wheel with their limbs smashed.*[16]

corporal punishment
Punishment inflicted on the offender's body with whips or other devices that cause pain.

Pain for punishment

Because they considered the publicity of punishment a useful deterrent, authorities carried sanctions out in the market square for all to see. The punishments themselves were harsh: Whipping, mutilation, and branding were used extensively, and death was the common penalty for a host of felonies. For example, some 72,000 people were hanged during the reign of Henry VIII (1509–1547), and in the Elizabethan period (1558–1603) vagabonds were strung up in rows of 300–400 at a time.[17] (The modern equivalent would be 15,000–23,000 Americans strung up at once.) Capital punishment could either be a "merciful" instant death (beheading, hanging, garroting, or burying alive), or a prolonged death (burning alive or breaking on the wheel). As Pieter Spierenburg notes, prolonged death was practically unknown in England, "although a famous pamphlet of 1701 argued that hanging did not effectively deter potential lawbreakers."[18]

Those criminals who were not executed faced various mutilations—removing a hand or finger, slitting the nostrils, severing an ear, or branding—so that the offenders could be publicly identified. Such mutilation usually made it impossible for the marked individual to find honest employment. In sum, almost every imaginable torture was used in the name of retribution, deterrence, the sovereignty of the authorities, and the public good.

The reasons for the rise in the severity of punishments during this period are unclear but are thought to reflect the expansion of criminal law, the enhanced power of secular authorities, an increase in crime (especially during the eighteenth century), and changes in the economic system. For example, the number of crimes for which the English authorized the death penalty swelled from 50 in 1688 to 160 in 1765 and reached 225 by 1800. Some of the new statutes made capital crimes of offenses that had previously been treated more leniently, and other laws criminalized certain activities for the first time. But the criminal law, popularly known as the Bloody Code, was less rigid than it seemed; it allowed judicial discretion, and lesser punishments were often given.[19]

London, as well as other cities, doubled in population from 1600 to 1700, although the overall population of England and Wales rose by only 25 percent. Because of the population increases and the accompanying widespread poverty, the incidence of crime in the cities ballooned. The rise in the number of prosecutions and convictions may also have represented a response by government and the elite to the threat posed to public order by the suddenly outsized working-class population. As Georg Rusche and Otto Kirchheimer argue, the rise of capitalism led to economic, rather than penal, considerations as the basis for punishment.[20]

On test Ceasar…
wrote book 1764

ON THE EVE OF REFORM

As noted previously, by the middle of the 1700s England was inflicting capital and corporal punishment extensively, transporting large numbers of convicts overseas, and facing the problem of overcrowded jails and houses of correction; yet crime continued its upward curve. England, the most advanced and powerful country in the world, was ready for correctional reform.

At this stage, economic and social factors, particularly concerning labor, began to reshape the nature of penal sanctions. Other important influences stemmed from altered political relationships and changes in the power of the church and the organization of secular authority.

Around the same time, the revolutionaries in the American colonies, with their liberal ideas about the relationship between citizen and government and their belief in human perfectibility, were setting the stage for a shift in penal policies.

In view of all these considerations, we can arbitrarily designate 1770 as the eve of a crucial period of correctional reform on both sides of the Atlantic.

■ THE AGE OF REASON AND CORRECTIONAL REFORM

During the 1700s Western scholars and social activists, particularly in England and France, engaged in a sweeping reconception of the nature of society. In this remarkable period, known as **The Enlightenment, or the Age of Reason**, new ideas based on rationalism, the importance of the individual, and the limitations of government replaced traditional assumptions. Revolutions occurred in America and France, science made great advances, and the industrial revolution came into full swing.

Until the 1700s European society had generally been static and closed; individuals had their place in a hierarchy of fixed social relationships. The Enlightenment represented a liberal reaction against this feudal and monarchical tradition. The Reformation had already ended the religious monopoly held by the Catholic Church, and the writings of such Protestant thinkers as Martin Luther and John Calvin encouraged a new emphasis on individualism and the social contract between government and the governed. The triumph of William of Orange in the Glorious Revolution of 1688 brought increased power to the English Parliament, and the institutions of representative government were strengthened. The 1690 publication of John Locke's two treatises on government further developed the ideas of a liberal society, as did the writings of the French thinkers Montesquieu and Voltaire.

Finally, advances in scientific thinking led to a questioning attitude that emphasized observation, experimentation, and technological development. Sir Isaac Newton argued that the world could be known and reduced to a set of rules. The scientific revolution had a direct impact on social and political thought because it encouraged people to question established institutions, use the power of reason to remake society, and believe that progress would ultimately bring about a just community.

What impact did these political and social thinkers of the Enlightenment have on corrections? As we have emphasized, ideas about crime and justice are part of larger philosophical and scientific movements. Because of the ideas that gained currency in the 1700s, people in America and Europe began to rethink such matters as the procedures to be used to determine guilt, the limits on a government's power to punish, the nature of criminal behavior, and the best ways to correct offenders. Specifically they began to reconsider how criminal law should be administered and to redefine the goals and practices of corrections. During this period the classical school of criminology emerged, with its insistence on a rational link between the gravity of the crime and the severity of the punishment. Proponents of the social contract and utilitarian philosophies emphasized limitations on the power of government and proposed the need to erect a system of graduated criminal penalties to deter crime. Further, political liberals and religious groups encouraged reform of the prison system.

All these factors produced a major shift in penal thought and practice. Penal codes were rewritten to emphasize adaptation of punishment to the offender. Correctional practices moved away from inflicting pain on the body of the offender, toward methods that would set the individual on a path of honesty and right living. Finally, the penitentiary developed as an institution in which criminals could be isolated from the temptations of society, reflect on their offenses, and thus be reformed.

Of the many individuals who actively promoted the reform of corrections, three stand out: Cesare Beccaria (1738–1794), the founder of what is now called the classical school of criminological thought; Jeremy Bentham (1748–1832), a leader of reform in England and the developer of a utilitarian approach to crime and punishment; and John Howard (1726–1790), the sheriff of Bedfordshire, England, who helped spur changes that resulted in the development of the penitentiary.

The Enlightenment, or the Age of Reason
The 1700s in England and France, when concepts of liberalism, rationality, equality, and individualism dominated social and political thinking.

Cesare Beccaria and the Classical School

The rationalist philosophy of the Enlightenment, with its emphasis on individual rights, was applied to the practices of criminal justice by the Italian scholar **Cesare Beccaria** in his 1764 book *On Crimes and Punishments*. He argued

CESARE BECCARIA (1738–1794)
Italian scholar who applied the rationalist philosophy of the Enlightenment to the criminal justice system.

classical criminology
A school of criminology that views behavior as stemming from free will, that demands responsibility and accountability of all perpetrators, and that stresses the need for punishments severe enough to deter others.

Learn more about **Cesare Beccaria** at the corresponding link at www .cengage.com/criminaljustice/ clear.

that the true aim and only justification for punishment is utility: the safety it affords society by preventing crime.[21] This was the first attempt to explain crime in secular, or worldly, terms instead of religious terms. The book also pointed to injustices in the administration of criminal law. In particular, Beccaria focused on the lack of a rational link between the gravity of given crimes and the severity of punishment. From this movement came **classical criminology**, whose main principles are as follows:

1. The basis of all social action must be the utilitarian concept of the greatest good for the greatest number of people.

2. Crime must be considered an injury to society, and the only rational measure of crime is the extent of the injury.

3. Prevention of crime is more important than punishment for crimes. To prevent crime, laws must be improved and codified so that citizens can understand and support them. *So they can know what to do what not to do.*

4. Secret accusations and torture must be abolished. Further, the accused have a right to speedy trials and to humane treatment before trial, as well as every right to bring forward evidence on their behalf.

5. The purpose of punishment is crime deterrence, not social revenge. Certainty and swiftness in punishment, rather than severity, best secure this goal.

6. Imprisonment should be more widely employed, and better physical quarters should be provided, with prisoners classified by age, sex, and degree of criminality.

Beccaria summarized the thinking of those who wanted to rationalize the law: "In order for punishment not to be, in every instance, an act of violence of one or many against a private citizen, it must be essentially public, prompt, necessary, the least possible in the given circumstances, proportionate to the crime, dictated by laws."[22]

Beccaria's ideas took hold especially in France; many of them were incorporated in the French Code of 1791, which ranked crimes on a scale and affixed a penalty to each. In the United States, James Wilson, the leading legal scholar of the postrevolutionary period, credited Beccaria with having influenced his thinking, notably with regard to the deterrent function of punishment. Through Wilson, Beccaria's principles had an important effect on reform of the penal laws of Pennsylvania, which laid the foundation for the penitentiary movement.[23]

Jeremy Bentham and the "Hedonic Calculus"

"The greatest good for the greatest good for people"

utilitarianism
The doctrine that the aim of all action should be the greatest possible balance of pleasure over pain, hence the belief that a punishment inflicted on an offender must achieve enough good to outweigh the pain inflicted.

Jeremy Bentham, one of the most provocative thinkers and reformers of English criminal law, is best known for his utilitarian theories, often called his "hedonic calculus." Bentham claimed that one could categorize all human actions and, either through pleasurable (hedonic) incentives or through punishment, direct individuals to desirable activities. Undergirding this idea was his concept of **utilitarianism**, the doctrine that the aim of all action should be "the greatest happiness of the greatest number." As Bentham noted, an act possesses utility "if it tends to produce benefit, advantage, pleasure, good or happiness . . . or to prevent the happening of mischief, pain, evil or unhappiness to the party whose interest is considered."[24] Thus, according to Bentham, rational people behave in ways that achieve the most pleasure while bringing the least pain; they are constantly calculating the pluses and minuses of potential actions.

In Bentham's view, criminals were somewhat childlike or unbalanced, lacking the self-discipline to control their passions by reason. Behavior was not preordained, but rather was an exercise of free will. Thus, crime was not sinful, but the result of improper calculation. Accordingly the criminal law should be organized so that the offender would derive more pain than pleasure from a wrongful act. Potential offenders, recognizing that legal sanctions were organized according to this scheme, would be deterred from committing antisocial acts.

JEREMY BENTHAM (1748–1832)

English advocate of utilitarianism in prison management and discipline. Argued for the treatment and reform of prisoners.

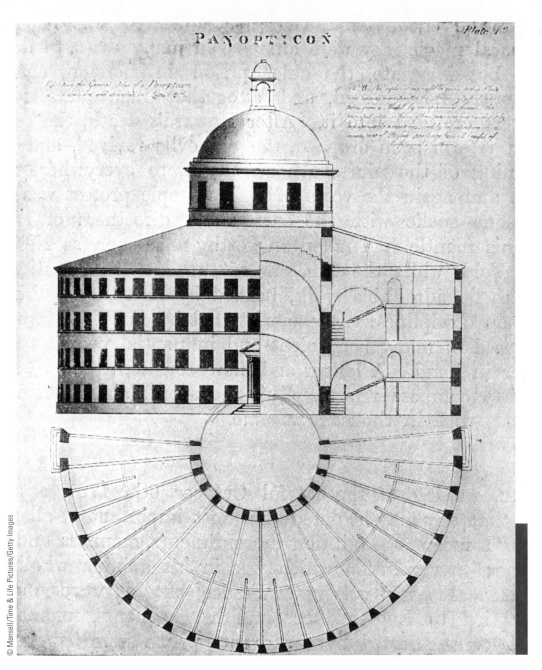

PANOPTICON

In 1796 Jeremy Bentham designed the "panopticon" so that each prisoner was kept in a cell set in such a way as to prevent him from being aware of whether or not he was under observation by the staff.

© Mansell/Time & Life Pictures/Getty Images

Bentham sought to reform the criminal laws of England so that they emphasized deterrence and prevention. The goal was not to avenge an illegal act, but to prevent the commission of such an act in the first place. Because excessive punishment was unjustified, the punishment would be no more severe than necessary to deter crime: not "an act of wrath or vengeance," but one of calculation tempered by considerations of the social good and the offender's needs.[25]

Bentham developed plans for a penitentiary based on his utilitarian principles. The design of his "panopticon," or "inspection house," called for a circular building with a glass roof and cells on each story around the circumference. This arrangement would permit a prison inspector in the center of the building to keep out of sight of the prisoners yet view their actions through a system of blinds. The panopticon was never constructed in England; one was proposed for France but never adopted, as was one for Ireland. Two panopticon-type prisons actually were constructed in the United States. Western State Penitentiary, modeled to some extent on Bentham's ideas, opened in Pittsburgh in 1825. The fullest expression of the style was the prison in Stateville, Illinois,

You can find additional information about **Jeremy Bentham** at the corresponding link at www.cengage.com/criminaljustice/clear.

See a virtual **panopticon** at the corresponding link at www.cengage.com/criminaljustice/clear.

where four circular cellhouses were built from 1916 to 1924. Described by an architect as "the most awful receptacle of gloom ever devised and put together with good stone and brick and mortar,"[26] the panopticon was quickly abandoned.

John Howard and the Birth of the Penitentiary

Probably no individual did more for penal reform in England than **John Howard**—county squire, social activist, and Sheriff of Bedfordshire. Like many members of the new merchant class, Howard had a social conscience and was concerned about conditions among the poor. On being appointed high sheriff of Bedfordshire in 1773, he exercised the traditional but usually neglected responsibility of visiting the local prisons and institutions. He was shocked by what he saw, especially when he learned that the jailers received no regular salary but made their living from the prisoners and that many people who had been discharged by the grand jury or acquitted at their trials were still detained because they could not pay their discharge fees.[27]

Howard expanded his inspections to the prisons, hulks, and houses of correction outside his jurisdiction in England, and then to those in other parts of Europe. In England the prisons were overcrowded, discipline was lacking, and sanitation was unheard of—thousands died yearly from disease. Even members of the free community feared "prison fever," for the disease often infected courthouse personnel and others in contact with offenders. At the time, seven years of imprisonment was viewed as a de facto penalty of death.

Howard thought that England should copy some of the prisons he had visited in Belgium, Holland, Germany, and Italy. In particular, he was favorably impressed by the separate confinement of inmates at night after their common daytime tasks. Of the Maison de Force in Ghent he wrote, "The convicts were properly lodged—fed—clothed—instructed—worked. The utmost regularity, order, cleanliness prevailed; there was no drunkenness; no riot; no excessive misery; no irons, no starvation."[28]

Howard's descriptions of conditions in English penal institutions, in his book *The State of Prisons in England and Wales,* horrified the public. Of particular concern was the lack of discipline. After his report to the House of Commons, Howard, along with Sir William Blackstone and William Eden, drafted the Penitentiary Act of 1779, a curious amalgam of traditional and progressive ideas that greatly affected penology.

The Penitentiary Act originally called for creating houses of hard labor where people who would otherwise have faced transportation would instead be imprisoned for up to two years. The act was based on four principles set down by Howard: (1) secure and sanitary structure, (2) systematic inspection, (3) abolition of fees, and (4) a reformatory regimen. Prisoners were to be confined in solitary cells at night but were to labor silently in common rooms during the day. The labor was to be "of the hardest and most servile kind, in which Drudgery is chiefly required and where the Work is little liable to be spoiled by Ignorance, Neglect or Obstinancy"—such work as sawing stone, polishing marble, beating hemp, and chopping rags.[29] The legislation further detailed such items as the prisoner's diet, uniforms, and conditions of hygiene.

Perhaps influenced by his Quaker friends, Howard came to believe that the new penal institution should be a place not merely of industry but also of contrition and penance. The twofold purpose of the penitentiary was to punish and to reform offenders through solitary confinement between intervals of work, the inculcation of good habits, and religious instruction so that inmates could reflect on their moral duties.

JOHN HOWARD (1726–1790)

English prison reformer whose book The State of Prisons in England and Wales *contributed greatly to the passage of the Penitentiary Act of 1779 by the House of Commons.*

The Penitentiary Act and follow-up legislation passed in 1782 and 1791 attracted political support from a variety of sources. Legalists sought to deter crime, philanthropists wanted to help humanity, conservatives thought products made by convict labor would save money, and pragmatic politicians wanted to solve the disquieting prison situation. Philanthropists and other social reformers believed solitary confinement was the best way to end the evil of inmate association and to allow reflection. Bentham agreed, because he believed the penitentiary would help deter crime by being onerous to but not destructive of the offender.

■ WHAT REALLY MOTIVATED CORRECTIONAL REFORM?

Was it just the humanistic concerns of the Quakers and individuals such as Bentham and Howard that prompted this era of criminal law reform, or were other forces at work as well? Apparently reform sprang as much from the emergence of the middle class as from humanism. The new industrialists may have been concerned about the existing criminal law because, paradoxically, its harshness helped some offenders escape punishment: Jurors would not convict people accused of petty property offenses for which death was prescribed. In petitions to Parliament, groups of businessmen complained that their property was not protected if offenders could expect to escape punishment.[30] They wanted swift and certain sanctions, and their demands coincided with the moral indignation of Bentham, Howard, and other reformers.

Traditional scholarship on corrections has emphasized the humanitarian motives of reformers seeking a system of benevolent justice. However, other scholars have focused on the underlying economic or social factors that account for shifts in correctional policies. They do not accept the standard version that such people as Beccaria, Bentham, and Howard were motivated by concern for their fellow humans when they advocated a particular perspective on the problem of criminality. The revisionists suggest, for example, that until 1700 the size of the incarcerated population in England was linked to the economic demand for workers. The penitentiary may thus represent not the product of the humanitarian instincts unleashed by the Enlightenment, but a way to discipline the working class to serve a new industrial society.

Changes took place in England's prisons, and new institutions were constructed along lines suggested by Howard and Bentham, but not until 1842, with the opening of Pentonville in North London, did the penitentiary plan come to fruition. Meanwhile, the concept of the penitentiary had traveled across the Atlantic to the new American republic, where it developed.

SUMMARY

1 Understand the major forms of punishment from the Middle Ages to the American Revolution.

From the Middle Ages to the American Revolution, corrections consisted primarily of galley slavery, imprisonment, transportation, corporal punishment, and death.

2 Discuss the Age of Reason and how it affected corrections.

In the latter part of the eighteenth century, the Enlightenment (Age of Reason) brought changes in penal policy. Rather than stressing physical punishment of the offender, influential Enlightenment thinkers such as Beccaria, Bentham, and Howard sought methods for reforming offenders. The reforms were first proposed in Europe and later fully developed in America.

3 Understand the contribution of Cesare Beccaria and the classical school.

Beccaria applied the rationalist philosophy of the Enlightenment, with its emphasis on individual rights, to the practices of the criminal justice system. Beccaria set forth six principles on which his reforms were based. These principles set the foundation for the classical school of criminology.

4 Explain the contribution of Jeremy Bentham and the utilitarians.

Best known for his utilitarian theories, often called his "hedonistic calculus," Bentham claimed that one could categorize all human actions. His idea of "utilitarianism" proposed that the aim of all actions was the "greatest happiness for the greatest number." Criminals were somewhat childlike or unbalanced, lacking the self-discipline to control their passions.

5 Discuss the work of John Howard and its influence on correctional reform.

Howard investigated conditions in European prisons and jails. He was shocked by what he found in English correctional facilities. He rallied legislative interest in reform and was a major proponent of the penitentiary. Parliament passed the Penitentiary Act of 1779 based on Howard's principles: (1) a secure and sanitary structure, (2) systematic inspections, (3) abolition of fees, and (4) a reformatory regimen.

Key Terms

Beccaria, Cesare (p. 37)
benefit of clergy (p. 31)
Bentham, Jeremy (p. 38)
classical criminology (p. 38)
corporal punishment (p. 35)
The Enlightenment, or the Age
   of Reason (p. 37)

galley slavery (p. 31)
house of correction (p. 32)
Howard, John (p. 40)
hulks (p. 34)
lex talionis (p. 31)
secular law (p. 31)
transportation (p. 34)

utilitarianism (p. 38)
wergild (p. 31)

For Discussion

1. In what ways have changes in the social, economic, and political environment of society been reflected in correctional policies?
2. How do you suppose the developments discussed in this chapter eventually brought about the separation of children from others in the prison system?
3. How have the interests of administrators and the organizations they manage distorted the ideals of penal reformers?
4. Some people believe the history of corrections shows a continuous movement toward more-humane treatment of prisoners as society in general has progressed. Do you agree? Why or why not?
5. How may specific underlying social factors have influenced the development of correctional philosophies?

FOR FURTHER READING

Foucault, Michel. *Discipline and Punish*. New York: Pantheon, 1977. Describes the transition from a focus on punishment of the body of the offender to the use of the penitentiary to reform the individual.

Geltner, G. *The Medieval Prison: A Social History*. Princeton, NJ: Princeton University Press, 2008. Argues that prisons existed in Europe in the thirteenth and fourteenth centuries.

Hughes, Robert. *The Fatal Shore*. New York: Knopf, 1987. Traces the colonization of New South Wales and the impact of transportation.

Ignatieff, Michael. *A Just Measure of Pain*. New York: Pantheon, 1978. Recounts the coming of penal institutions to England during the latter part of the eighteenth century.

Morris, Norval, and David J. Rothman, eds. *The Oxford History of the Prison*. New York: Oxford University Press, 1995. Fourteen articles by scholars examining the prison from ancient times to the present.

Spierenburg, Pieter. *The Spectacle of Suffering*. New York: Cambridge University Press, 1984. Examines the role of public punishment in preindustrial Europe and its ultimate disappearance by the middle of the nineteenth century.

NOTES

1 Michel Foucault, *Discipline and Punish* (New York: Pantheon, 1977), 4.

2 Edward M. Peters, "Prisons before the Prison: The Ancient and Medieval Worlds," in *The Oxford History of the Prison*, edited by Norval Morris and Michael Tonry (New York: Oxford University Press, 1995), 5.

3 Peters, "Prisons before the Prison," pp. 3–47.

4 Pieter Spierenburg, *The Spectacle of Suffering* (New York: Cambridge University Press, 1984), 14.

5 Pieter Spierenburg, "The Body and the State: Early Modern Europe," in *The Oxford History of the Prison*, edited by Norval Morris and David J. Rothman (New York: Oxford University Press, 1995), 75.

6 For a description of the treatment of galley slaves, see George Ives, *A History of Penal Methods* (Montclair, NJ: Patterson Smith, 1970), 104.

7 John H. Langbein, "The Historical Origins of the Sanction of Imprisonment for Serious Crime," *Journal of Legal Studies* 5 (1976): 37.

8 G. Geltner, *The Medieval Prison* (Princeton, NJ: Princeton University Press, 2008), p. 4; Peters, "Prison before the Prison." See also Roger Matthews, *Doing Time: An Introduction to the Sociology of Imprisonment* (New York: St. Martin's Press, 1999), 5–9.

9 Adam J. Hirsch, *The Rise of the Penitentiary* (New Haven, CT: Yale University Press, 1992), 14.

10 Matthews, *Doing Time*, p. 8.

11 A. Roger Ekirch, *Bound for America: The Transportation of British Convicts to the Colonies 1718–1775* (New York: Oxford University Press, 1987).

12 Spierenburg, "The Body and the State," p. 76.

13 Robert Hughes, *The Fatal Shore* (New York: Knopf, 1987), 282.

14 Ibid.

15 Ibid., p. 162.

16 Langbein, "Historical Origins," p. 40.

17 Georg Rusche and Otto Kirchheimer, *Punishment and Social Structure* (New York: Russell & Russell, [1939] 1968), 19.

18 Spierenburg, "The Body and the State," p. 54.

19 Michael Ignatieff, *A Just Measure of Pain* (New York: Pantheon, 1978), 27.

20 Rusche and Kirchheimer, *Punishment and Social Structure*, p. 96.

21 Mark M. Lanier and Stuart Henry, *Essential Criminology* (Boulder, CO: Westview Press, 1998), 67.

22 Harry E. Barnes and Negley K. Teeters, *New Horizons in Criminology* (New York: Prentice-Hall, 1944), 461.

23 Francis Edward Devine, "Cesare Beccaria and the Theoretical Foundation of Modern Penal Jurisprudence," *New England Journal of Prison Law* 7 (1981): 8.

24 Gilbert Geis, "Jeremy Bentham," in *Pioneers in Criminology*, edited by Herman Mannheim (Montclair, NJ: Patterson Smith, 1973), 54.

25 Ignatieff, *Just Measure of Pain*, p. 27.

26 Geis, "Jeremy Bentham," p. 65.

27 Anthony Babington, *The English Bastille* (New York: St. Martin's Press, 1971), 103.

28 Barnes and Teeters, *New Horizons in Criminology*, p. 481.

29 Ignatieff, *Just Measure of Pain*, p. 93.

30 Michael Russigan, "A Reinterpretation of Criminal Law Reform in Nineteenth-Century England," *Journal of Criminal Justice* 8 (1980): 205.

The Library Company of Philadelphia

LEARNING OBJECTIVES

After reading this chapter you should be able to . . .

1 Describe "The Great Law" of Pennsylvania and note its importance.

2 Distinguish the basic assumptions of the penitentiary systems of Pennsylvania and New York.

3 Discuss the elements of the Cincinnati Declaration.

4 Understand the reforms advocated by the Progressives.

5 Discuss the assumptions of the medical model, regarding the nature of criminal behavior and its correction.

6 Illustrate how the community model reflected the social and political values of the 1960s and 1970s.

7 Describe the forces and events that led to the present crime control model.

Located outside Philadelphia, Eastern State Penitentiary became the model of the Pennsylvania system of "separate confinement." The building was designed to ensure that each offender remained separated from all human contact so that he could reflect on his misdeeds.

ON OCTOBER 25, 1829, Charles Williams, an 18-year-old African American from Delaware County, Pennsylvania, began serving a two-year sentence for larceny at the Eastern State Penitentiary, located in Cherry Hill outside of Philadelphia. The newly constructed facility was described at the time as "the most imposing in the United States."[1] Williams was assigned to a cell measuring 12 by 8 by 10 feet with an attached 18-foot-long exercise yard. The cell was furnished with a fold-up metal bedstead, a simple toilet, a wooden stool, a workbench, and eating utensils. Light came from an 8-inch window in the ceiling; the window could be blocked to plunge the cell into darkness as a disciplinary measure.

Charles Williams became Prisoner Number 1 at Eastern, a model of the separate confinement penitentiary viewed at the time as a great advance in penology. For the two years of his sentence, Williams would be confined to his cell and exercise yard, his only human contact being a weekly visit by the chaplain. Every measure was taken to ensure that the prisoner would not be distracted from his moral rehabilitation. Officials could inspect the interior of the cell through a peephole without the resident knowing. Food was inserted through an opening in the wall, designed so that the inmate

THE HISTORY OF CORRECTIONS IN AMERICA

could not see the guard. Solitary labor, Bible reading, and reflection on his own behavior were viewed as the keys to providing the offender with the opportunity to repent.

Few Americans realize that their country gave the world its first penitentiary, an institution created to reform offenders within an environment designed to focus their full attention on their moral rehabilitation. This goal of reform reflected a major shift in correctional thinking. Remember that brutal public punishments such as the dismemberment of Damiens had occurred with some regularity just 60 years before Williams entered Eastern. Thought about both human nature and the purpose of punishment had changed dramatically.

English trends and practices greatly influenced American corrections, especially during its formative years. Although the work of Cesare Beccaria and the development of the Milan House of Correction affected penal policies throughout much of the Western world, corrections in colonial America followed English ideas and policies. Further, although these transatlantic ties have continued over the years, American correctional institutions and practices have developed in decidedly American ways in responding to social and political pressures within the United States.

This chapter surveys the historical changes in correctional thought and practices in the United States. We focus on seven periods: the colonial period, the arrival of the penitentiary, the reformatory movement, the progressive movement, and the rise of the medical model, the community model, and the crime control model. As each period is discussed, we emphasize the ways in which correctional goals reflected ideas current at the time.

Chapter

3

■ THE COLONIAL PERIOD

THE WHIPPING-POST AND PILLORY AT NEW CASTLE, DELAWARE.—SKETCHED BY RANU GIDEN.—[SEE PAGE 721.]

Until the early 1800s Americans followed the European practice of relying on punishment that was physically brutal, such as death, flogging, and branding.

© CORBIS

During the colonial period, most Americans lived under laws and practices transferred from England and adapted to local conditions. In New England the Puritans maintained a strict society, governed by religious principles, well into the middle of the eighteenth century, and they rigorously punished violations of religious laws. As in England, banishment, corporal punishment, the pillory, and death were the common penalties. In 1682, with the arrival of **William Penn**, Pennsylvania adopted "The Great Law," which was based on humane Quaker principles and emphasized hard labor in a house of correction as punishment for most crimes. Death was reserved for premeditated murder. The Quaker Code survived until 1718, when it was replaced by the Anglican Code, which was already in force in other colonies. The latter code listed 13 capital offenses, with larceny the only felony not punishable by death. Whipping, branding, mutilation, and other corporal punishments were prescribed for other offenses, as were fines. Enforcement of this code continued throughout the colonies until the Revolution.

Unlike the mother country, with its crowded hulks, jails, and houses of correction, the colonies seldom used institutions for confinement.[2] Instead, banishment, fines, death, and the other punishments just mentioned were the norm. As David Rothman writes, the death penalty was common:

> The New York Supreme Court in the pre-Revolutionary era regularly sentenced criminals to death, with slightly more than twenty percent of all its penalties capital ones. When magistrates believed that the fundamental security of the city was in danger, as in the case of a slave revolt in 1741, the court responded with great severity (burning to death thirteen of the rebellion's leaders and hanging nineteen others). Even in less critical times the court had frequent recourse to the scaffold for those convicted of pickpocketing, burglary, robbery, counterfeiting, horse stealing, and grand larceny as well as murder.[3]

Jails held people awaiting court action or those unable to pay their debts. Only rarely were convicted offenders jailed for their whole sentences; the stocks, whipping post, or gallows were the places for punishment. Punishments were public spectacles, because "rubbing the noses of offenders in the community context was an essential part of the process of ripping and healing, which criminal justice was supposed to embody."[4] In keeping with the Calvinist doctrine of predestination, little thought was given to reforming offenders; such people were considered naturally depraved.[5]

■ THE ARRIVAL OF THE PENITENTIARY

Until the beginning of the 1800s, America remained sparsely populated and predominantly rural. In 1790 the entire population numbered less than four million, and no city had more than 50,000 inhabitants. By 1830 the rural population had more than doubled and the urban population had more than tripled.

WILLIAM PENN (1644–1718)

English Quaker who arrived in Philadelphia in 1682. Succeeded in getting Pennsylvania to adopt "The Great Law" emphasizing hard labor in a house of correction as punishment for most crimes.

Growth was accompanied by rapid social and economic changes that affected all aspects of life. Colonial life had been oriented toward the local community; everyone knew everyone else, neighbors helped one another as needed, and the local clergy and elite maintained social control. In the nineteenth century, however, social problems could no longer be handled with the help of neighbors. In an increasingly heterogeneous urban and industrial society, responsibility for the poor, insane, and criminal became the province of the state and its institutions.

With the Revolution, the ideas of the Enlightenment gained currency (see Chapter 2), and a new concept of criminal punishment came to the fore. This correctional philosophy, based on the ideas of Beccaria, Bentham, and Howard, coincided with the ideals of the Declaration of Independence, which took an optimistic view of human nature and a belief in each person's perfectibility.[6] Social progress was thought possible through reforms to match the dictates of "pure reason." Emphasis also shifted from the assumption that deviance was part of human nature, to a view that crime was caused by forces in the environment. The punitive colonial penal system based on retribution thus was held to be incompatible with the idea of human perfectibility.

Reformers argued that if Americans were to become committed to the humane and optimistic ideal of human improvability, they had to remove barbarism and vindictiveness from penal codes and make reformation of the criminal the primary goal of punishment. Thomas Jefferson and other leaders of the new republic worked to liberalize the harsh penal codes of the colonial period. Pennsylvania led the way with new legislation that sought "'to reclaim rather than destroy,' 'to correct and reform the offenders,' rather than simply to mark or eliminate them."[7] Several states, including Connecticut (1773), Massachusetts (1785), New York (1796), and Pennsylvania (1786), added incarceration with hard labor as an alternative to such public punishments as whippings and the stocks. For example, the Massachusetts State Prison, which opened in 1805, was designed as a workhouse; inmates labored from dawn to dusk making shoes and nails as a means of "destroying [their] 'habit of idelness' [sic] and replacing it with a 'habit of industry' more conducive to an honest livelihood."[8]

Incarceration, in the tradition of the English workhouse, developed in the immediate aftermath of the Revolution. The **penitentiary**, as conceptualized by the English reformers and their American Quaker allies, first appeared in 1790, when part of Philadelphia's Walnut Street Jail was converted to allow separate confinement. The penitentiary differed markedly from the prison, house of correction, and jail. It was conceived as a place where criminal offenders could be isolated from the bad influences of society and one from another so that, while engaged in productive labor, they could reflect on their past misdeeds, repent, and be reformed. As the word *penitentiary* indicates, reformers hoped that while offenders were being punished, they would become penitent, see the error of their ways, and wish to place themselves on the right path. They could then reenter the community as useful citizens.

The American penitentiary attracted the world's attention, and the concept was incorporated at Millbank and Pentonville in England and in various other locales in Europe. By 1830 foreign observers were coming to America to see this innovation in penology; they were excited by the changes being made in the United States. For instance, France sent Alexis de Tocqueville and Gustave Auguste de Beaumont, England sent William Crawford, and Prussia sent Nicholas Julius. By the middle of the century, the U.S. penitentiary in its various forms—especially the Pennsylvania and New York systems—had indeed become world famous.

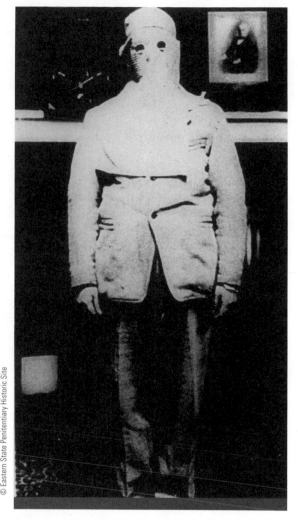

© Eastern State Penitentiary Historic Site

One aspect of separate confinement stipulated that prisoners should have no visual or verbal contact with other inmates. Prisoners were hooded when it was necessary to move them within the penitentiary.

penitentiary
An institution intended to isolate prisoners from society and from one another so that they could reflect on their past misdeeds, repent, and thus undergo reformation.

The Pennsylvania System

As in England, Quakers set about to implement their humanistic and religious ideas in the new nation; in Philadelphia their efforts came to fruition. For Quakers, penance and silent contemplation could allow one to move from the state of sin toward perfection.

BENJAMIN RUSH (1745–1813)

Physician, patriot, signer of the Declaration of Independence, and social reformer, Rush advocated the penitentiary as a replacement for capital and corporal punishment.

The penitentiary thus provided a place where individuals, on their own, could be reformed.

Quakers were among the Philadelphia elite who in 1787 formed the reformist Society for Alleviating the Miseries of Public Prisons. Under the Quaker leadership of **Benjamin Rush** and others such as Benjamin Franklin, the society urged replacement of capital and corporal punishment with incarceration. Members had been communicating with John Howard, and their ideals in many ways reflected his.

In 1790 the group was instrumental in passing legislation almost identical to England's Penitentiary Act of 1779. The 1790 law specified that an institution was to be established in which "solitary confinement to hard labour and a total abstinence from spirituous liquors will prove the most effectual means of reforming these unhappy creatures."[9]

To implement the new legislation, the existing three-story Walnut Street Jail in Philadelphia was expanded in 1790 to include a "Penitentiary House" for the solitary confinement of "hardened and atrocious offenders." The plain stone building housed eight cells on each floor and had an attached yard. Each cell was dark and small (only 6 feet long, 8 feet wide, and 9 feet high). From a small grated window high on the outside wall, inmates "could perceive neither heaven nor earth." Inmates were classified by offense: Serious offenders were placed in solitary confinement without labor; the others worked together in shops during the day under a strict rule of silence and were confined separately at night.[10]

Soon, when the Walnut Street Jail became overcrowded, the legislature approved construction of additional institutions for the state: Western Penitentiary on the outskirts of Pittsburgh and Eastern Penitentiary in Cherry Hill, near Philadelphia. The opening of Eastern in 1829 marked the full development of the penitentiary system based on separate confinement. In the years between Walnut Street and Eastern, other states had adopted aspects of the Pennsylvania system. **Separate confinement** was introduced by Maryland in 1809, by Massachusetts in 1811, by New Jersey in 1820, and by Maine in 1823, but Eastern became the fullest expression of the concept of rehabilitation through separate confinement.

Eastern Penitentiary was designed by John Haviland, an English immigrant and an acquaintance of John Howard. One of the most imposing and expensive public structures of its day, the facility apparently was modeled after the Maison de Force at Ghent. Cell blocks extended from a central hub like the spokes of a wheel. Each prisoner ate, slept, worked, and received religious instruction in his own cell. The inmates did not see peers; in fact, their only human contact was the occasional visit of a clergyman or prison official.[11]

As described by Robert Vaux, one of the original reformers, the Pennsylvania system was based on the following principles:

separate confinement
A penitentiary system developed in Pennsylvania in which each inmate was held in isolation from other inmates, with all activities, including craft work, carried on in the cells.

Eastern Penitentiary
is today a national historical landmark where visitors are welcome. Learn about current exhibits, events, and links at the corresponding website listed at www.cengage.com/criminaljustice/clear.

1 Prisoners would not be treated vengefully but should be convinced that through hard and selective forms of suffering they could change their lives.
2 Solitary confinement would prevent further corruption inside prison.
3 In isolation, offenders would reflect on their transgressions and repent.
4 Solitary confinement would be punishment because humans are by nature social beings.
5 Solitary confinement would be economical because prisoners would not need long periods of time to repent, and therefore fewer keepers would be needed and the costs of clothing would be lower.[12]

The Pennsylvania system of separate confinement soon became controversial. Within five years of its opening, Eastern endured the first of several investigations carried out over the years by a judicially appointed board of inspectors. The reports detailed the extent to which the goal of separate confinement was not fully observed, physical punishments were used to maintain discipline, and prisoners suffered mental breakdowns because of the isolation. Separate confinement had declined by the

Reprinted with permission of the American Correctional Association, Alexandria Virginia

The New York Penitentiary at Auburn, New York, emphasized a congregate system of discipline, obedience, and work. Warden Elam Lynds believed that convicts were incorrigible and that industrial efficiency was the overriding purpose of the prison.

1860s when crowding required doubling up in each cell, yet it was not abolished in Pennsylvania until 1913.[13]

The New York (Auburn) System

Faced with overcrowded facilities such as Newgate Prison, built in Greenwich Village in 1797, the New York legislature in 1816 authorized a new state prison in Auburn. Influenced by the reported success of the separate confinement of some prisoners in the Walnut Street Jail, the New York building commission decided to erect a portion of the new facility on that model and to authorize an experiment to test its effectiveness. The concept proved a failure—sickness, insanity, and suicide increased markedly among the prisoners. The practice was discontinued in 1824, and the governor pardoned those then held in solitary.

In 1821 **Elam Lynds** was installed as warden at Auburn. Instead of duplicating the complete isolation practiced in Pennsylvania, Lynds worked out a new **congregate system** of prison discipline whereby inmates were held in isolation at night but congregated in workshops during the day. The inmates were forbidden to talk or even to exchange glances while on the job or at meals. Lynds was convinced that convicts were incorrigible and that industrial efficiency should be the overriding purpose of the prison. He instituted a reign of discipline and obedience that included the lockstep and the wearing of prison stripes. Furthermore, he considered it "impossible to govern a large prison without a whip. Those who know human nature from books only may say the contrary."[14]

congregate system
A penitentiary system developed in Auburn, New York, in which inmates were held in isolation at night but worked with other prisoners during the day under a rule of silence.

ELAM LYNDS (1784–1855)

A former army officer, Lynds was appointed warden of the newly opened Auburn prison in 1821. He developed the congregate system and a regimen of strict discipline. Inmates were known only by their number, wore striped clothing, and moved in lockstep. In 1825 he was commissioned to oversee construction with inmate labor at Ossining (Sing Sing), New York.

contract labor system
A system under which
inmates' labor was sold on a
contractual basis to private
employers who provided the
machinery and raw materials
with which inmates made
salable products in the
institution.

Whereas inmates of the Pennsylvania penitentiaries worked in their cells, those in New York were employed in workshops both as therapy and as a way to finance the institution. Convict labor for profit through a **contract labor system** became an essential part of Auburn and other northeastern penitentiaries. Through this system of "free" convict labor, the state negotiated contracts with manufacturers, who then delivered raw materials to the prison for conversion into finished goods. By the 1840s Auburn was producing footwear, barrels, carpets, carpentry tools, harnesses, furniture, and clothing. During this period, inmates also built the new prison at Ossining-on-the-Hudson (Sing Sing). Wardens at Auburn and other prisons that adopted the New York (often called Auburn) system seemed to be more concerned with instilling good work habits and thus preventing recidivism (relapse into crime) than with rehabilitating prisoners' character.

Debating the Systems

Throughout this era, the preferred structure of prison systems was hotly debated. Advocates of both the Pennsylvania and the New York plans argued on public platforms and in the nation's periodicals over the best methods of punishment (see **Table 3.1**). Underlying the debates were questions about disciplining citizens in a democracy and maintaining conformity to social norms in a society that emphasized individualism. Participants included some of the leading figures of the time. As each state considered new penal construction, it joined the debate.

What divided the two camps was the way in which reformation was to be brought about. Proponents of the New York system maintained that inmates first had to be "broken" and then socialized by means of a rigid discipline of congregate but silent labor. Advocates of Pennsylvania's separate system rejected such harshness and, following Howard, renounced physical punishments and any other form of human degradation. The New Yorkers countered that their system cost less, efficiently tapped convict labor, and developed individuals who eventually would be able to return to the community with the discipline necessary for the industrial age. The Pennsylvanians responded that New York had sacrificed the principal goal of the penitentiary (reformation) to the accessory goal (cost-effectiveness) and contended that exploiting inmates through large-scale industry failed to promote the work ethic and only embittered them.

The Pennsylvania model looked back to an earlier, crafts-oriented, religious society, whereas the New York model looked forward to the emerging industrial age. John Conley argues that the Pennsylvania model lost out because it embraced an outdated

TABLE 3.1 *Comparison of Pennsylvania and New York (Auburn) Penitentiary Systems*

	Goal	Implementation	Method	Activity
Pennsylvania (Separate System)	Redemption of the offender through the well-ordered routine of the prison	Isolation, penance, contemplation, labor, silence	Inmates are kept in their cells for eating, sleeping, and working	Bible reading, work on crafts in cell
New York (Auburn) (Congregate System)	Redemption of the offender through the well-ordered routine of the prison	Strict discipline obedience, labor, silence	Inmates sleep in their cells but come together to eat and work	Work together in shops making goods to be sold by the state

labor system. In contrast, the New York system, as practiced at Auburn, was consistent with the new demands and challenges of factory production, which "would provide the state with a means of exploiting the labor of inmates to defray the expenses of the institution and possibly earn a profit for the state."[15] In this sense Auburn served as forerunner of the industrial prison that would dominate until the rise of organized labor in the twentieth century.

In addition to clarifying some hazy issues in the writings of Bentham and Howard, this debate contributed to decisions in several states and in Europe about how one should design and run penitentiaries. Most European visitors favored the Pennsylvania model, and the First International Prison Congress, held in 1846 in Germany, endorsed it by a large majority. The separate system was soon incorporated in correctional facilities in Germany, France, Belgium, and Holland.

Initially, many American states—New York in 1797, Massachusetts in 1805, and New Jersey in 1836—built penitentiaries with at least a portion devoted to separate confinement, but within a few years they shifted to the New York style. By 1840 hard labor organized under the contract system achieved dominance in northeastern penitentiaries.[16]

As prison populations increased, the Pennsylvania system proved too expensive. In addition, the public became concerned by reports that prisoners were going insane because they could not endure long-term solitary confinement. Design for construction during the nineteenth century almost entirely followed the New York model (see **Figure 3.1**). Yet not until the end of that century did Pennsylvania, the birthplace of the penitentiary, finally convert to the congregate system. In 1971, Eastern Penitentiary closed. (See the Focus box "From Eastern State to Pelican Bay: The Pendulum Swings.")

Read about the origins of **Auburn State Prison** at the website of the New York Correction History Society, listed at www.cengage.com/criminaljustice/clear.

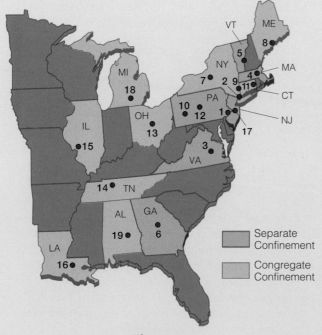

City	Prison	Year built
1. Philadelphia, PA	Walnut Street Jail	1790
2. New York City, NY	Newgate Prison	1797
3. Richmond, VA	Virginia Penitentiary	1800
4. Charlestown, MA	Massachusetts State Prison	1805
5. Windsor, VT	Vermont State Prison	1809
6. Milledgeville, GA	Georgia Penitentiary	1817
7. Auburn, NY	Auburn State Prison	1819
8. Thomaston, ME	Maine State Prison	1823
9. Ossining, NY	Sing Sing	1825
10. Pittsburgh, PA	Western Penitentiary	1826
11. Wethersfield, CT	Connecticut State Prison	1827
12. Cherry Hill, PA	Eastern Penitentiary	1829
13. Columbus, OH	Ohio Penitentiary	1830
14. Nashville, TN	State Prison	1831
15. Alton, IL	State Prison	1833
16. Baton Rouge, LA	State Prison	1835
17. Trenton, NJ	State Prison	1836
18. Jackson, MI	State Prison	1838
19. Wetumpka, AL	State Prison	1841

Figure 3.1
Early Prisons in the United States
Source: Norman Johnston, *Forms of Constraint: A History of Prison Architecture* (Urbana: University of Illinois Press, 2000).

FOCUS ON

CORRECTIONAL POLICY

From Eastern State to Pelican Bay: The Pendulum Swings

Eastern State Penitentiary, built in Cherry Hill (now the Fairmount neighborhood of Philadelphia), holds the distinction of being the first correctional institution in the world based on the system of separate confinement. When it opened in 1829, prisoners were held in their own cell for the duration of their sentence. Food was passed through a slot in the cell door, there was a small window to let in light, and prisoners could use an attached exercise yard. There was no opportunity for human contact except for occasional visits from the chaplain or prison officials. The purpose of these arrangements was to allow the offender time to reflect on his misdeeds and, through penitence, correct his life without the distractions of other inmates or the outside world. Not surprisingly, many inmates held under these conditions of solitary confinement went mad. In 1890 the U.S. Supreme Court condemned the Pennsylvania system, noting that a considerable number of prisoners became insane, others committed suicide, while still others survived the ordeal but were not reformed. Long-term solitary confinement was by the twentieth century considered cruel and outmoded.

In the 1970s, as the United States experienced a rise in crime, the punishment pendulum swung away from the rehabilitation emphasis of the 1950s toward a much more punitive approach with long sentences of incarceration. Beginning in the 1980s, solitary confinement came back into correctional practice. During the 1990s, 40 states and the Federal Bureau of Prisons built "super-max" prisons to hold the most disruptive, violent, and incorrigible offenders. Unlike Pennsylvania's Eastern State Penitentiary, the super-max prison is not designed to transform the prisoner but to contain his behavior.

California's Pelican Bay institution and the federal penitentiary at Florence, Colorado, are examples of prisons designed to hold the "toughest of the tough." As with Eastern State Penitentiary, offenders in super-max facilities spend up to 23 hours a day in their 8-by-10-foot concrete cells, in silence and with little human contact. They are shackled whenever they are taken out of their cells—during recreation, showers, and weekend visits (through security glass). Many of the super-max facilities have had to add mental health units to deal with the estimated one-third of inmates whose minds deteriorate under the conditions first developed at Eastern and now continued at Pelican Bay, Marian, Florence and up to 40 other super-max institutions.

Are there differences between Pennsylvania's separate confinement policy and today's super-max prisons? Should we expect this new approach to succeed where the similar policies of the 1830s failed?

Sources: Drawn from V. Beiser, "The Cruelest Prison," *Los Angeles Times Magazine*, October 19, 2003, pp. 12–17, 33; A. Cusac, *Cruel and Unusual: The Culture of Prisons in America* (New Haven, CT: Yale University Press, 2009).

■ DEVELOPMENT OF PRISONS IN THE SOUTH AND WEST

Historical accounts of American corrections tend to emphasize the nineteenth-century reforms that took place in the populous states of the Northeast. Scholars often neglect penal developments in the South and the West. Prisons, some following the Pennsylvania Model, were built in four southern states—Georgia, Kentucky, Maryland, and Virginia—by 1817. Later prisons such as the ones built in Jackson, Mississippi (1842), and Huntsville, Texas (1848), followed the Auburn model. But further expansion ended with the Civil War. With the exception of San Quentin (1852), the sparse population of the West did not lend itself to construction of many prisons until the latter part of the nineteenth century.

Southern Penology

With the end of the Civil War, southern legislatures passed "Black Codes" designed to control newly freed African Americans by making it "a crime to have a gun, be out after a certain hour, or utter 'offensive language' in the presence of white women."[17]

Following the Civil War, southern states leased their prisoners to private entrepreneurs as field hands, railroad builders, loggers, and miners.

Conviction resulted in harsh punishments. At the same time, southerners faced the task of rebuilding their communities and economy. Because of the devastation of the war and depression in the agriculturally based economy, funds to construct new prisons remained scarce, even the face of an increasing population of convicts. Given these challenges, a large African American inmate labor force, and the states' need for revenue, southern states saw the development of the **lease system** and penal farms.

Although originating in Massachusetts in 1798, the leasing of convicts to private entrepreneurs took hold in the South first in Kentucky (1825) and then in other southern states before the war. Businesses in need of workers could negotiate with the state for the labor and care of prisoners. This was particularly true in Alabama, Arkansas, Florida, Georgia, Louisiana, and Mississippi.[18] In 1866 Alabama turned over the state prison to a contractor who worked the inmates in building a railroad through the heart of the state's mineral region.[19] Texas leased the Huntsville Penitentiary inmates to a firm that used them as laborers on railroad construction, wood milling, and cotton picking.[20] As Edgardo Rotman notes, these entrepreneurs, "having no ownership interest in them (the prisoners), exploited them even worse than slaves."[21] The death rate of prisoners soared. See "Do the Right Thing" to consider further the problems surrounding inmate labor.

The South's agrarian economy and the great number of African American offenders also provided the basis for the penal farm, a state-run plantation that grew crops to feed the inmates and to sell on the market. Large-scale penal farms developed mainly in the latter part of the century, particularly in Louisiana, Mississippi, and Texas. Upset by the failure of authorities to collect profits from lessees of convict labor, the people of Mississippi adopted a constitutional provision to end all contracts by 1895. Prison officials then purchased the 15,000-acre Parchman Farm, which served for many at the time as a model for southern penology.[22] In many southern states, penal farms remain a major part of corrections.

lease system
A system under which inmates were leased to contractors who provided prisoners with food and clothing in exchange for their labor. In southern states, the prisoners were used as field laborers.

The **convict lease system in Texas** is described at the corresponding link at www.cengage.com/criminaljustice/clear.

DO THE RIGHT THING

It is 1887. As a legislator you must vote on a bill to extend or end the prisoner-leasing contract between the Natchez Coal and Mining Company and the state of Mississippi. You know that the contract brings money into the state treasury and relieves the prison system by housing, feeding, and guarding the more than 800 prisoners who are leased to the mining company. But you also know that the working conditions are horrendous and the death rate of the prisoners is high. Tales of

guards beating the prisoners have become a major issue in the state, and journalists have uncovered corruption in the decision to award the contract to the company.

WRITING ASSIGNMENT: Should you vote to extend the leasing contract? What facts might influence you to vote one way or the other? Write a letter to your constituents explaining your position.

Western Penology

Settlement in the West did not take off until the California gold rush of 1849; only during the latter part of the nineteenth century did most western states enter the Union. Except in California, the prison ideologies of the East did not greatly influence penology in the West. Prior to statehood, prisoners were held in territorial facilities or in federal military posts and prisons. Until Congress passed the Anti-Contract Law of 1887, restricting the employment of federal prisoners, leasing programs were used extensively in California, Montana, Oregon, and Wyoming. In their eagerness to become states, some of the last of the territories included anticontract provisions in their new state constitutions.[23]

In 1850 California became the first western state to be admitted to the Union. The old Spanish jails had become inadequate during the time of the gold rush and, "following frontier traditions," the care of convicts was placed in the hands of a lessee. In 1852 the lessee chose Point San Quentin, a spit of land surrounded by water on three sides. Using convict labor, the lessee built two prison buildings. In 1858, when San Quentin became overcrowded and reports of deaths, escapes, and the brutal discipline of the guards came to public attention, the state took over the facility.[24]

The Oregon territory had erected a log prison structure in the 1850s, but with rumors of official corruption, it was soon leased to a private company. On joining the Union in 1859, the state discontinued the lease system. In 1866 the legislature decided to build a prison in Salem on the Auburn plan. It was completed in 1877. Yet, with labor difficulties and an economic depression in the 1890s, responsibility for the prison was again turned over to a lessee in 1895.[25]

■ THE REFORMATORY MOVEMENT

Unfortunately, ways in which reforms are implemented often do not match the high ideals of social activists. Legislators and governors may be willing to support the espoused goals of change, but putting the ideals into practice requires leadership, money, public support, and innovative administrators. Thus, soon after a given innovation, correctional facilities become overcrowded, discipline wanes, programs are abandoned, and charges of official misconduct erupt. The subsequent investigation typically recommends changes that may or may not be implemented—and the cycle continues.

By the mid-1800s, reformers had become disillusioned with the penitentiary. Neither the New York nor the Pennsylvania systems nor any of their imitators had achieved rehabilitation or deterrence. This failure was seen as resulting from poor administration rather than from weakness of the basic concept. Within 40 years of being built, penitentiaries had become overcrowded, understaffed, and minimally financed. Discipline was lax, brutality was common, and administrators were viewed as corrupt. For example, at Sing Sing in 1870, investigators discovered that "dealers were publicly supplying prisoners with almost anything they could pay for" and that convicts were "playing all sorts of games, reading, scheming, trafficking."[26] This reality was a far cry from the vision of John Howard and Benjamin Rush.

In 1865 the New York Prison Association commissioned **Enoch Cobb Wines** and Theodore Dwight to undertake a nationwide survey of prisons. After visiting 18 prisons and houses of correction, they published their *Report on the Prisons and Reformatories of the United States and Canada* in 1867. None of the prisons they visited viewed reformation of its inmates as a primary goal or deployed resources to further reformation. Inadequacies in the physical plants, lack of staff training, and poor administrative practices were in evidence. However, the researchers were most upset by the extent to which corporal punishment was used for discipline. The report emphasized that prisons should prepare inmates for release by allowing them to "advance toward freedom by moving through progressively liberal stages of discipline."[27]

Across the Atlantic, a controversy that directly influenced American corrections developed. In England, Alexander Maconochie urged the **mark system** of graduated terms of confinement. Penalties would be graded according to the severity of the crime, and offenders would be released from incarceration according to their performance. A certain number of marks would be given at sentencing, and prisoners could reduce the number by voluntary labor, participating in educational and religious programs, and good behavior. Maconochie thus argued for sentences of indeterminate length and a system of rewards. Through these incentives, offenders would be reformed so that they could return to society.

Maconochie's ideas were not implemented in England. However, in Ireland in 1854 Sir Walter Crofton adopted practices similar to the mark system that came to be known as the Irish or *intermediate* system. On conviction, prisoners spent a period in solitary confinement and then were sent to public work prisons where they could earn positive marks (rather than removing initial marks against them). When they had enough marks, they were transferred to the intermediate stage, or what today might be called a *halfway house*. The final test was a *ticket-of-leave*, a conditional release that was the precursor of the modern parole system.[28] Again, theory and practice bridged the continents as Maconochie's and Crofton's ideas traveled across the Atlantic.

Cincinnati, 1870

By 1870 a new generation of American penal reformers had arisen. Among them were Gaylord Hubbell, warden of Sing Sing, who had observed the Irish system in operation; Enoch C. Wines, secretary of the New York Prison Association; Franklin Sanborn, secretary of the Massachusetts State Board of Charities; and Zebulon Brockway, head of Detroit's Michigan House of Correction. Like the Quakers, these penologists were motivated by humanitarian concerns, but they also understood how prisons operated.

The National Prison Association (predecessor of the American Correctional Association) and its 1870 meeting in Cincinnati embodied the new spirit of reform. In its famous Declaration of Principles, the association advocated a new design for penology: that prison operations should stem from a philosophy of inmate change, with reformation rewarded by release. Sentences of indeterminate length would replace fixed sentences, and proof of reformation, rather than mere lapse of time, would be a requirement for a prisoner's release. Classification of prisoners on the basis of character and improvement would encourage the reformation program. Penitentiary practices that had evolved during the first half of the nineteenth century—fixed sentences, the lockstep, rules of silence,

ENOCH COBB WINES (1806–1879)

A guiding force of American corrections from 1862, when he became the secretary of the New York Prison Association and served so until his death. Organizer of the National Prison Association in 1870 and a major contributor to the Cincinnati Declaration of Principles.

mark system
A system in which offenders are assessed a certain number of marks, based on the severity of their crime, at the time of sentencing. Prisoners could reduce their term and gain release by reducing marks through labor, good behavior, and educational achievement.

The reformatory movement emphasized education and training, such as this training course in blacksmithing at Elmira Reformatory, New York, 1898. On the basis of their achievement and conduct, offenders moved forward toward release.

Reprinted with permission of the American Correctional Association, Alexandria, Virginia

ZEBULON BROCKWAY (1827–1920)

Reformer who began his career in penology as a clerk in Connecticut's Wethersfield Prison at age 21. In 1854, while superintendent of the Monroe County Penitentiary in Rochester, New York, he began to experiment with ideas on making prisons more rehabilitative. He put his theories to work as the superintendent at Elmira State Reformatory, New York, in 1876, retiring from that institution in 1900.

and isolation—were now seen as debasing and humiliating, and as destroying inmates' initiative.

Given the leadership roles of clergy in the National Prison Association, it is not surprising that, like the activists who had promoted the penitentiary in the 1830s, those gathered at Cincinnati still saw crime as a sort of moral disease that should be treated by efforts at moral regeneration.

Like the Quakers before them, the 1870 reformers looked to institutional life as the way to effect rehabilitation. Inmates would be made into well-adjusted citizens, but the process would take place behind walls. The Cincinnati Declaration could thus in good faith insist that "reformation is a work of time; and a benevolent regard to the good of the criminal himself, as well as to the protection of society, requires that his sentence be long enough for the reformatory process to take effect."[29]

Elmira Reformatory

reformatory
An institution for young offenders that emphasized training, a mark system of classification, indeterminate sentences, and parole.

The first **reformatory** took shape in 1876 at Elmira, New York, when **Zebulon Brockway** was appointed superintendent. Brockway believed that diagnosis and treatment were the keys to reform and rehabilitation. He questioned each new inmate to explore the social, biological, psychological, and "root causes" of the offender's deviance. An individualized work-and-education treatment program was then prescribed. Inmates adhered to a rigid schedule of work during the day, followed by courses in academic, vocational, and moral subjects during the evening. Inmates who did well achieved early release.[30]

Designed for first-time felons between the ages of 16 and 30, the approach at Elmira incorporated a mark system of classification, indeterminate sentences, and parole. Once the courts had committed an offender to Elmira, the administrators could determine the release date; the only restriction was that the time served could not exceed the maximum prescribed by law for the particular offense.

The indeterminate sentence was linked to a three-grade system of classification. Each offender entered the institution at grade 2, and if the inmate earned nine marks a month for six months by working hard, completing school assignments, and causing no problems, he could be moved up to grade 1, which was necessary for release. If he failed to cooperate and violated rules of conduct, thus showing poor self-control and an indifference to progress, he would be demoted to grade 3. Only after three months of satisfactory behavior could he reembark on the path toward eventual release.[31] In sum, this system placed "the prisoner's fate, as far as possible, in his own hands."[32]

Elmira's proclaimed success at reforming young felons was widely heralded, and over the next several decades its program was emulated in 20 states. Brockway's annual reports claimed that 81 percent of inmates released from Elmira underwent "probable reformation." An article that appeared in the *Journal of the American Social Science Association*, "How Far May We Abolish Prisons?" echoed this optimism. The author's answer to the title question was "to the degree that we put men into reformatories like Elmira, for it reforms more than 80 percent of those who are sent there."[33] Brockway even weathered an 1893 state investigation into charges of brutality at Elmira, which revealed that the whip and solitary confinement were used there regularly. However, in 1900 he was forced to resign in the face of mounting criticism of his administration.

By 1900 the reformatory movement had spread throughout much of the nation, yet by the outbreak of World War I in 1914, it was already declining. In most institutions, the architecture, the attitudes of the guards, and the emphasis on discipline differed little from past orientations. Too often, the educational and rehabilitative efforts took a back seat to the traditional emphasis on punishment. Even Brockway admitted that it was difficult to distinguish between inmates whose attitudes had changed and those who merely lived by prison rules. Being a good prisoner became the way to win parole, but this did not mean that the prisoner had truly changed.

Look for a web link to the **history of Elmira Reformatory** at www.cengage.com/criminaljustice/clear.

Lasting Reforms

Although the ideals of Wines, Brockway, and the other leaders of the reformatory movement were not realized, these men made several major contributions to American corrections. The indeterminate sentence, inmate classification, rehabilitative programs, and parole were first developed at Elmira. The Cincinnati Declaration of Principles set goals that inspired prison reformers well into the twentieth century. Still more changes were to come before that, however. In the mid-nineteenth century, the United States entered a period of significant social change. The nation faced problems arising from two new demographic changes: the gradual shift of the population from the countryside to the cities and the influx of immigrants. Thus, the stage was set for progressive reforms.

■ THE RISE OF THE PROGRESSIVES

The first two decades of the 1900s, called the Age of Reform, set the dominant tone for U.S. social thought and political action until the 1960s.[34] Industrialization, urbanization, technological change, and scientific advancements had revolutionized the American landscape. A group known as the Progressives attacked the excesses of this emergent society, especially those of big business, and placed their faith in state action to deal with the social problems of slums, adulterated food, dangerous occupational conditions, vice, and crime.

The Progressives, most of whom came from upper-status backgrounds, were optimistic about the possibility of solving the problems of modern society. Focusing in particular on conditions in cities, which had large immigrant populations, they believed

The mission of probation during the Progressive era was to provide guidance, friendship, and assistance to offenders. Critics have said that the real goal was to indoctrinate offenders with middle-class values.

that civic-minded people could apply the findings of science to social problems, including penology, in ways that would benefit all. Specifically, they believed that society could rehabilitate criminals through individualized treatment.

Individualized Treatment and the Positivist School

The scholar David Rothman uses two words to epitomize the Progressive programs: *conscience* and *convenience*. The reforms were promoted by benevolent and philanthropic men and women who sought to understand and cure crime through a case-by-case approach. They believed that the reformers of the penitentiary era were wrong in assuming that all deviants were "victims of social disorder" and that the deviants "could all be rehabilitated with a single program, the well-ordered routine" of the prison.[35]

The Progressives thought it necessary to know the life history of each offender and then devise a treatment program specific to that individual. This meant that correctional administrators would need the discretion to diagnose each criminal, prescribe treatment, and schedule release to the community. From this orientation, the phrase "treatment according to the needs of the offender" came into vogue, in contrast to "punishment according to the severity of the crime," which had been the hallmark of Beccaria and the reformers of the early 1800s.

Rothman argues that because discretion was required for the day-to-day practice of the new penology, correctional administrators responded favorably to it. The new discretionary authority made it easier for administrators to carry out their daily assignments. He also notes that those Progressives committed to incarceration were instrumental in promoting probation and parole, but supporters of the penitentiary used the requirement of discretion to expand the size of the prison population.

The Progressives had faith that the state would carry out their reforms with justice. In the same way that they looked to government programs to secure social justice, they assumed that the agents of the state would help offenders. Rothman notes,

> In criminal justice, the issue was not how to protect the offender from the arbitrariness of the state, but how to bring the state more effectively to the aid of the offender. The state was not a behemoth to be chained and fettered, but an agent capable of fulfilling an ambitious program. Thus, a policy that called for the state's exercise of discretionary authority in finely tuned responses was, at its core, Progressive.[36]

positivist school
An approach to criminology and other social sciences based on the assumption that human behavior is a product of biological, economic, psychological, and social factors and that the scientific method can be applied to ascertain the causes of individual behavior.

As members of the **positivist school**, the Progressives looked to social, economic, biological, and psychological rather than religious or moral explanations for the causes of crime, and they applied modern scientific methods to determine the best treatment therapies. Recall that the classical school of Beccaria and Bentham had emphasized a legal approach to the problem, focusing on the act rather than the criminal. In contrast, the scientific positivist school shifted the focus from the criminal act to the offender. By the beginning of the twentieth century, advances in the biological and social sciences provided the framework for the reforms proposed by the Progressives.

Although the positivist school comprised several theoretical perspectives, most of its practitioners shared three basic assumptions:

1 Criminal behavior is not the result of free will but stems from factors over which the individual has no control: biological characteristics, psychological maladjustments, and sociological conditions.

Chicago Daily News/Library of Congress, Prints and Photographs Division

2 Criminals can be treated so that they can lead crime-free lives.

3 Treatment must center on the individual and the individual's problem.

Progressive Reforms

Armed with their views about the nature of criminal behavior and the need for state action to reform offenders, the Progressives fought for changes in correctional methods. They pursued two main strategies: (1) improve conditions in social environments that seemed to be breeding grounds for crime and (2) rehabilitate individual offenders. Because they saw crime as primarily an urban problem, concentrated especially among the immigrant lower class, the Progressives sought through political action to bring about changes that would improve ghetto conditions: better public health, landlord–tenant laws, public housing, playgrounds, settlement houses, education. However, because they also believed that criminal behavior varied among individuals, a case-by-case approach was required.[37]

By the 1920s the Progressives had succeeded in gaining wide acceptance of four portions of their program: probation, indeterminate sentences, parole, and juvenile courts. These elements had been proposed at the 1870 Cincinnati meeting, but the Progressives and their allies in corrections implemented them throughout the country.[38]

1 *Probation.* This alternative to incarceration fitted nicely into the Progressive scheme, for it recognized individual differences and allowed offenders to be treated in the community under supervision.

2 *Indeterminate Sentences.* Although the sentences were called "indeterminate," state legislatures nearly always set a minimum and maximum term, within which the correctional process of rehabilitation could operate. Fixed sentences were retained for lesser offenses, but during this period more than three-quarters of convicted offenders whose maximum terms exceeded five years were serving indeterminate sentences.

3 *Parole.* Although the idea of parole release had been developed in Ireland and Australia in the 1850s, and Zebulon Brockway had instituted it at Elmira in 1876, not until the mid-1920s did it really catch on in the United States. Like probation, parole expanded greatly during the Progressive period. By the mid-1920s, well over 80 percent of felons sentenced in the major industrialized states left prison via parole.[39]

Although the reforms of the Progressives were much criticized, probation, indeterminate sentences, and parole remain dominant elements of corrections to this day. Perhaps, as Rothman suggests, this is because they provide authority to criminal justice officials and affirm the vitality of the rehabilitative idea.[40] However, these three crucial reforms provided the structure for yet another change in corrections.

■ THE RISE OF THE MEDICAL MODEL

Even before psychiatry began to influence U.S. society, the idea that criminals are mentally ill was popular in correctional circles. At the 1870 Cincinnati congress, one speaker described a criminal as

> *a man who has suffered under a disease evinced by the perpetration of a crime, and who may reasonably be held to be under the dominion of such disease until his conduct has afforded very strong presumption not only that he is free from its immediate influence, but that the chances of its recurrence have become exceedingly remote.*[41]

Certainly much Progressive reform was based on the idea that criminals could be rehabilitated through treatment, but not until the 1930s were serious attempts made to

HOWARD GILL (1890–1989)

A prison reformer in the Progressive tradition, Gill designed Massachusetts's Norfolk Prison Colony to be a model prison community. Norfolk provided individual treatment programs and included inmates on an advisory council to deal with community governance.

medical model

A model of corrections based on the assumption that criminal behavior is caused by social, psychological, or biological deficiencies that require treatment.

Howard Gill: First one to come up with it and proving it.

implement what became known as the **medical model** of corrections. Under the banner of the newly prestigious social and behavioral sciences, the emphasis of corrections shifted to treating criminals as people whose social, psychological, or biological deficiencies had caused them to engage in illegal activity.

One early proponent of the medical model was **Howard Gill**, who became the superintendent of the Norfolk State Prison Colony, Massachusetts, in 1927. Gill tried to create a "community" of inmates within secured walls. He helped design Norfolk in the style of a college campus, staffed not only with guards but also with professionals who provided treatment programs: educators, psychiatrists, and social workers. Inmates wore ordinary clothing, not prison garb, and participated with staff on advisory councils dealing with matters of community governance. During the Depression, Gill's policies came under increasing fire. An escape by four inmates triggered a backlash that led to his removal in 1934. Gill continued his progressive reform work through several prison-related posts in the federal government until he entered academia in 1947.[42]

The concept of rehabilitation as the primary purpose of incarceration took on national legitimacy in 1929, when Congress authorized the new Federal Bureau of Prisons to develop institutions that would ensure the proper classification, care, and treatment of offenders. **Sanford Bates**, the first director of the bureau, had served as the president of the American Correctional Association and promoted the new medical model.

The 1950s came to be known as the Era of Treatment as many states, particularly California, Illinois, New Jersey, and New York, fell in line with programs designed to reform prisoners.

Most other states, as well as political leaders everywhere, adopted at least the rhetoric of rehabilitation, changing statutes to specify that treatment was the goal of their corrections system and that punishment was an outdated concept. Prisons were thus to become something like mental hospitals that would rehabilitate and test the inmate for readiness to reenter society. In many states, however, the medical model was adopted in name only: Departments of prisons became departments of corrections, but the budgets for treatment programs remained about the same.

Because the essential structural elements of parole, probation, and the indeterminate sentence were already in place in most states, incorporating the medical model required only adding classification systems to diagnose offenders, as well as treatment programs to cure them.

Initially the number of psychiatrists and therapeutic treatment programs was limited, but it increased sharply after World War II. Group therapy, behavior modification, shock therapy, individual counseling, psychotherapy, guided group interaction, and many other approaches all became part of the "new penology." Competing schools of psychological thought debated the usefulness of these techniques, many of which were adopted or discarded before their worth had been evaluated.[43] However, the administrative needs of the institution often superseded the treatment needs of the inmate: Prisoners tended to be assigned to the facilities, jobs, and programs that had openings rather than to those that would provide the prescribed treatment.

California adopted the medical model more thoroughly than did any other state. During the administration of Governor Earl Warren, authorization was granted for the construction of specialized prisons and the California Adult Authority. Felony offenders received indeterminate sentences, the lengths of which were determined by the nine members of the Authority; these nine had almost complete power to classify, distribute, and treat prisoners, and ultimately determine their release. California developed a full range of treatment programs, including psychotherapy and group therapy. By the 1970s many California prisons were in turmoil, the value of treatment programs had come into question, and disparities

SANFORD BATES (1884–1972)

The first director of the Federal Bureau of Prisons, Bates advocated prison reform throughout his career. After becoming the president of the American Correctional Association in 1926, he also played an important role in the development of programs in New Jersey and New York.

in the release decisions of the Adult Authority had begun to be questioned. Not surprisingly, California became one of the first states to move toward determinate sentencing and away from the medical model.[44]

Maryland's Patuxent Institution, which opened in 1955, is probably the best example of a prison built according to the principles of the medical model. Patuxent was founded to treat adults given indeterminate sentences and judged to be "defective delinquents." Its administrators had broad authority to control intake, to experiment with a treatment milieu, and to decide when to release "patients." Throughout the period of incarceration, a patient was diagnosed and treated through a variety of programs and therapies.

Critics of treatment programs in American prisons pointed out that even during the 1950s, when the medical model reached its zenith, only 5 percent of state correctional budgets were allocated for rehabilitation. Although states adopted the rhetoric of the medical model, custody remained the overriding goal of institutions. Some argued that it was impossible to develop the rapport with inmates that was needed to cure their personality difficulties; others asserted that custody always took precedence over treatment in the daily running of prisons.

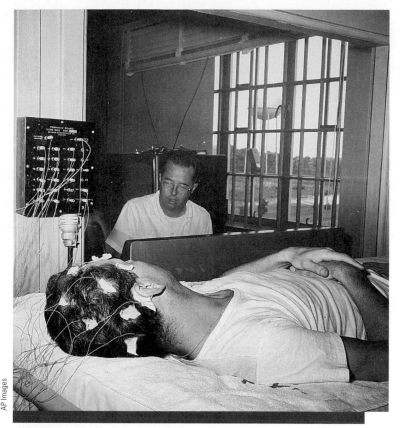

AP Images

Every inmate entering Maryland's Patuxent Institution received a brain examination to determine if any physical condition would retard or prevent rehabilitation, which was the prison's goal.

■ FROM MEDICAL MODEL TO COMMUNITY MODEL

As we have seen, social and political values greatly influence correctional thought and practices. During the 1960s and 1970s, U.S. society experienced the civil rights movement, the war on poverty, and resistance to the Vietnam War. Americans also challenged government institutions dealing with education, mental health, juvenile delinquency, and adult corrections. In 1967 the President's Commission on Law Enforcement and Administration of Justice reported,

> *Crime and delinquency are symptoms of failures and disorganization of the community. . . . The task of corrections, therefore, includes building or rebuilding social ties, obtaining employment and education, securing in the larger senses a place for the offender in the routine functioning of society.*[45]

This analysis was consistent with the views of **community corrections** advocates, who felt that the goal of the criminal justice system should be the reintegration of offenders into the community.

The inmate riot and hostage taking at New York State's Attica Correctional Facility aided the move toward community corrections. On the morning of September 13, 1971, after four days of negotiations, a helicopter began dropping CS gas (an incapacitating agent) on the inmates milling around in the prison yard. After the gas came a rain of bullets from state police guns, which hit 128 men and killed 29 inmates and 10 hostages. With the exception of the massacres of Native Americans in the late nineteenth century, it was the "bloodiest one-day encounter between Americans since the Civil War."[46] For many, the hostilities at Attica showed prisons to be counterproductive and unjust. They urged officials to make decarceration through community corrections the goal and pressed greater use of alternatives to incarceration such as probation, halfway houses, and community service.

community corrections
A model of corrections based on the assumption that reintegrating the offender into the community should be the goal of the criminal justice system.

You can find more on the **Attica riots** at the corresponding link at www.cengage.com/criminaljustice/clear.

Community corrections called for a radical departure from the medical model's emphasis on treatment in prison. Instead, prisons were to be avoided because they were artificial institutions that interfered with the offender's ability to develop a crime-free lifestyle. Proponents argued that corrections should turn away from psychological treatment in favor of programs that would increase offenders' opportunities to become successful citizens. Probation would be the sentence of choice for nonviolent offenders so that they could engage in vocational and educational programs that increased their chances of adjusting to society. For the small portion of offenders who had to be incarcerated, time in prison would be only a short interval until release on parole. To further the goal of reintegration, correctional workers would serve as advocates for offenders as they dealt with government agencies, providing employment counseling, medical treatment, and financial assistance.

The reintegration idea prevailed in corrections for about a decade until the late 1970s, when it gave way to a new punitiveness in criminal justice in conjunction with the rebirth of the determinate sentence. Advocates of reintegration claim, as did advocates of previous reforms, that the idea was never adequately tested. Nevertheless, community corrections remains a significant idea and practice in the recent history of corrections.

■ THE CRIME CONTROL MODEL: THE PENDULUM SWINGS AGAIN

Beginning in the late 1960s, the public became concerned about rising crime rates. At the same time, studies of treatment programs challenged their worth and the Progressive assumption that state officials would exercise discretion in a positive way. Critics of rehabilitation attacked the indeterminate sentence and parole, urging that treatment be available on a voluntary basis but that it not be tied to release. In addition, proponents of increased crime control called for longer sentences, especially for career criminals and violent offenders.

The Decline of Rehabilitation

According to critics of rehabilitation, its reportedly high recidivism rates prove its ineffectiveness. Probably the most thorough analysis of research data from treatment programs was undertaken by Robert Martinson for the New York State Governor's Special Committee on Criminal Offenders. Using rigorous standards, he surveyed 231 English-language studies of rehabilitation programs in corrections systems. They included such standard rehabilitative programs as educational and vocational training, individual counseling, group counseling, milieu therapy, medical treatment (plastic surgery, drugs), parole, and supervision. Martinson summarized his findings by saying, "With few and isolated exceptions, the rehabilitative efforts that have been reported so far have had no appreciable effect on recidivism."[47]

Critics of the rehabilitation model have also challenged as unwarranted the amount of discretion given to correctional decision makers to tailor the criminal sanction to the needs of each offender. In particular, they have argued that the discretion given to parole boards to release offenders is misplaced, because board decisions are more often based on the whims of individual members than on the scientific criteria espoused by the medical model.

crime control model of corrections
A model of corrections based on the assumption that criminal behavior can be controlled by more use of incarceration and other forms of strict supervision.

The Emergence of Crime Control

As the political climate changed in the 1970s and 1980s, and with the crime rate at historic levels, legislators, judges, and officials responded with a renewed emphasis on a **crime control model of corrections**. By 1980 the problem of crime and punishment had become an intense subject for ideological conflict, partisan politics, and legislative action.[48]

The critique of the rehabilitation model led to changes in the sentencing structures of more than half of the states and to the abolition of parole release in many. The new determinate sentencing laws were designed to incarcerate offenders for longer periods. In conjunction with other forms of punishment, the thrust of the 1980s centered on crime control through incarceration and risk containment.

The punitive ethos of the 1980s and 1990s appeared in the emphasis on dealing more strictly with violent offenders, drug dealers, and career criminals. It was also reflected in the trend toward intensive supervision of probationers, the detention without bail of accused people thought to present a danger to the community, reinstitution of the death penalty in 37 states, and the requirement that judges impose mandatory penalties for people convicted of certain offenses or having extensive criminal records. By the end of the century, the effect of these "get-tough" policies showed in the record numbers of prisoners, the longer sentences being served, and the size of the probation population. Some observers point to these policies as the reason why the crime rate has begun to fall. Others ask whether the crime control policies have really made a difference, given demographic and other changes in the United States. **Table 3.2**, which traces the history of correctional thought and practices in the United States, highlights the continual shifts in focus.

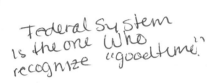
Federal System is the one who recognize "good time".

TABLE 3.2 *History of Corrections in America*

Note the extent to which correctional policies have shifted from one era to the next and how they have been influenced by various societal factors.						
Correctional Model						
Colonial (1600s–1790s)	**Penitentiary (1790s–1860s)**	**Reformatory (1870s–1890s)**	**Progressive (1890s–1930s)**	**Medical (1930s–1960s)**	**Community (1960s–1970s)**	**Crime Control (1970s–Present)**
Features Anglican Code Capital and corporal punishment, fines	Separate confinement Reform of individual Power of isolation and labor Penance Disciplined routine Punishment according to severity of crime	Indeterminate sentences Parole Classification by degree of individual reform Rehabilitative programs Separate treatment for juveniles	Individual case approach Administrative discretion Broader probation and parole Juvenile courts	Rehabilitation as primary focus of incarceration Psychological testing and classification Various types of treatment programs and institutions	Reintegration into community Avoidance of incarceration Vocational and educational programs	Determinate sentences Mandatory sentences Sentencing guidelines Risk management
Philosophical Basis Religious law Doctrine of predestination	Enlightenment Declaration of Independence Human perfectability and powers of reason Religious penitence Power of reformation Focus on the act Healing power of suffering	NPA Declaration of Principles Crime as moral disease Criminals as "victims of social disorder"	The Age of Reform Positivist school Punishment according to needs of offender Focus on the offender Crime as an urban, immigrant ghetto problem	Biomedical science Psychiatry and psychology Social work practice Crime as signal of personal "distress" or "failure"	Civil rights movement Critique of prisons Small is better	Crime control Rising crime rates Political shift to the right New punitive agenda

■ WHERE ARE WE TODAY?

During the first decades of the twenty-first century, the time may be ripe for another look at correctional policy. The language now used in correctional journals differs markedly from that found on their pages 30 years ago. The optimism that once suffused corrections has waned. For the first time in three decades, the financial and human costs of the retributive crime control policies of the 1990s are now being scrutinized. With budget deficits in the billions, states are facing the fact that incarceration is expensive. Are the costs of incarceration and surveillance justified? Has crime been reduced because of correctional policies? Are we safer today than before?

Michael Tonry and Joan Petersilia make the important point that during the past quarter century federal and state lawmakers have enacted policies based on the propositions about the crime-preventive effects of harsher and more-certain punishment. The validity of these propositions, they argue, is the fundamental question still to be answered.[49] What does the experience of contemporary crime control policies indicate about the future of corrections in the United States?

SUMMARY

1 Describe "The Great Law" of Pennsylvania and note its importance.

With the arrival in 1682 of William Penn, Pennsylvania adopted "The Great Law," which was based on Quaker principles and emphasized hard labor in a house of correction as punishment for most crimes. Death was reserved for premeditated murder.

2 Distinguish the basic assumptions of the penitentiary systems of Pennsylvania and New York.

The penitentiary ideal, first incorporated in Pennsylvania, emphasized the concept of separate confinement. Inmates were held in isolation, spending their time at craft work and considering their transgressions. In the New York (Auburn) congregate system, inmates were held in isolation but worked together during the day under a rule of silence.

3 Discuss the elements of the Cincinnati Declaration.

A Declaration of Principles was adopted at the 1870 meeting of the National Prison Association, held in Cincinnati. The declaration stated that prisons should be organized to encourage reformation, rewarding it with release. It advocated indeterminate sentences and the classification of prisoners based on character and improvement. The reformers viewed the penitentiary practices of the nineteenth century as debasing, humiliating, and destructive of inmates' initiative.

4 Understand the reforms advocated by the Progressives.

The Progressives looked to social, economic, biological, and psychological rather than religious or moral explanations for the causes of crime. The advocated the development of probation, indeterminate sentences, treatment programs, and parole.

5 **Discuss the assumptions of the medical model, regarding the nature of criminal behavior and its correction.**

Beginning in the 1930s reformers put forward the medical model of corrections, which viewed criminal behavior as caused by psychological or biological deficiencies. They held that corrections should diagnose and treat these deficiencies using a variety of programs and therapies. When "well," the offender should be released.

6 **Illustrate how the community model reflected the social and political values of the 1960s and 1970s.**

During the 1960s and 1970s, dissatisfaction with the medical model led to the development of community corrections. Influenced by the civil rights movement, protests against the Vietnam War, and the war on poverty, reformers held that prisons were to be avoided because they were artificial institutions that interfered with the offender's ability to develop a crime-free lifestyle. Offenders should instead receive opportunities for success in the community, and corrections should emphasize the rebuilding of an offender's ties to the community.

7 **Describe the forces and events that led to the present crime control model.**

The rise of crime in the late 1960s and questions about the effectiveness of rehabilitative programs brought pressure to shift to a crime control model of corrections, with greater use of incarceration and other forms of strict supervision.

KEY TERMS

Bates, Sanford (p. 60)
Brockway, Zebulon (p. 56)
community corrections (p. 61)
congregate system (p. 49)
contract labor system (p. 50)
crime control model of corrections (p. 62)

Gill, Howard (p. 60)
lease system (p. 53)
Lynds, Elam (p. 49)
mark system (p. 55)
medical model (p. 60)
penitentiary (p. 47)

Penn, William (p. 46)
positivist school (p. 58)
reformatory (p. 56)
Rush, Benjamin (p. 48)
separate confinement (p. 48)
Wines, Enoch Cobb (p. 55)

FOR DISCUSSION

1. Why do you think the idea of the penitentiary first caught on in the United States?
2. The prison has engendered a continuing fascination in U.S. culture. What other methods might the general public find acceptable as ways to punish offenders?
3. How do you think offenders will be punished in the United States in the future? What philosophical and technical developments would buttress the approaches you foresee?
4. We seem to be constantly driven by images of a "crime-free society." As a result, we adopt drastic solutions as though being crime-free were possible. Is it?

FOR FURTHER READING

Christianson, Scott. *With Liberty for Some.* Boston: North-eastern University Press, 1998. Examines the paradox of a country that prides itself as the citadel of individual liberty, yet has maintained five centuries of imprisonment.

Friedman, Lawrence M. *Crime and Punishment in American History.* New York: Basic Books, 1993. An excellent historical overview of the American criminal justice system.

Hindus, Michael S. *Prison and Plantation: Crime, Justice, and Authority in Massachusetts and South Carolina, 1767–1878.* Chapel Hill: University of North Carolina Press, 1980. Shows the differences between corrections in the emerging industrial Northeast and the plantation system of the South.

Kann, Mark E. *Punishment, Prisons and Patriarchy: Liberty and Power in the Early American Republic.* New York: New York University Press, 2005. Presents the view that in the postrevolutionary period reformers coupled their legacy of liberty with a penal philosophy that denied liberty, especially to marginal Americans.

Pisciotta, Alexander W. *Benevolent Repression: Social Control and the American Reformatory-Prison Movement.* New York: New York University Press, 1994. Argues that reformatories, although dedicated to humane, constructive, and charitable treatment, worked instead to tame and train criminal elements of the working class.

Rothman, David J. *Conscience and Convenience.* Boston: Little, Brown, 1980. Examines Progressive-era reforms to individualize treatment for deviants and therefore solve the problems of crime and mental illness.

———. *The Discovery of the Asylum.* Boston: Little, Brown, 1971. Describes changes in the ways Americans treated criminals, the mentally ill, and the poor during the eighteenth and early nineteenth centuries.

Sullivan, Larry E. *The Prison Reform Movement: Forlorn Hope.* Boston: Twayne, 1990. A concise history of American penology from the eighteenth century to the present.

NOTES

[1] Negley K. Teeters and John D. Shearer, *The Prison at Philadelphia's Cherry Hill* (New York: Columbia University Press, 1957), 63.

[2] David J. Rothman, "Perfecting the Prison: United States, 1789–1865," in *The Oxford History of the Prison,* edited by Norval Morris and David J. Rothman (New York: Oxford University Press, 1995), 112.

[3] David J. Rothman, *The Discovery of the Asylum* (Boston: Little, Brown, 1971), 51.

[4] Lawrence M. Friedman, *Crime and Punishment in American History* (New York: Basic Books, 1993), 48.

[5] Adam J. Hirsch, *The Rise of the Penitentiary* (New Haven, CT: Yale University Press, 1992), 8.

[6] Louis P. Masur, *Rights of Execution* (New York: Oxford University Press, 1989), 24.

[7] Gordon S. Wood, *The Radicalism of the American Revolution* (New York: Knopf, 1992), 193.

[8] Hirsch, *Rise of the Penitentiary,* p. 14.

[9] Blake McKelvey, *American Prisons* (Montclair, NJ: Patterson Smith, 1977), 8.

[10] Norman Johnston, *Forms of Constraint: A History of Prison Architecture* (Urbana: University of Illinois Press, 2000), 68.

[11] Norman Johnston, *Eastern State Penitentiary: Crucible of Good Intentions* (Philadelphia: Philadelphia Museum of Art, 1994). Eastern State Penitentiary is now a museum open to the public.

[12] Thorsten Sellin, "The Origin of the Pennsylvania System of Prison Discipline," *Prison Journal* 50 (Spring–Summer 1970): 15–17.

[13] Teeters and Shearer, *Prison at Philadelphia's Cherry Hill,* ch. 4.

[14] Gustave de Beaumont and Alexis de Tocqueville, *On the Penitentiary System in the United States and Its Application to France* (Carbondale: Southern Illinois University [1833] 1964), 201.

[15] John A. Conley, "Prisons, Production, and Profit: Reconsidering the Importance of Prison Industries," *Journal of Social History* 14 (Winter 1980): 55.

[16] Martha A. Myers, *Race, Labor, and Punishment in the New South* (Columbus: Ohio State University Press, 1998), 6.

[17] Mary Ellen Curtin, *Black Prisoners and Their World, Alabama, 1865–1900* (Charlottesville: University Press of Virginia, 2000), 6.

[18] Matthew Mancini, *One Dies, Get Another: Convict Leasing in the American South, 1866–1928* (Columbia: University of South Carolina Press, 1996); Myers, *Race, Labor, and Punishment,* 8.

[19] Curtin, *Black Prisoners,* p. 63.

[20] Donald R. Walker, *Penology for Profit: A History of the Texas Prison System 1867–1912* (College Station: Texas A&M University Press, 1988).

[21] Edgardo Rotman, "The Failure of Reform, United States, 1865–1965," in *The Oxford History of the Prison,* edited by Norval Morris and Michael Tonry (New York: Oxford University Press, 1995), 176.

[22] McKelvey, *American Prisons,* 213–14; William Banks Taylor, *Down on Parchman Farm* (Columbus: Ohio State University Press, 1999).

[23] McKelvey, *American Prisons,* p. 229.

[24] Shelley Bookspan, *A Germ of Goodness: The California State Prison System, 1851–1944* (Lincoln: University of Nebraska Press, 1991), 6–14.

[25] McKelvey, *American Prisons,* pp. 228–33.

[26] David J. Rothman, *Conscience and Convenience* (Boston: Little, Brown, 1980), 18.

[27] Rotman, "Failure of Reform," p. 172.

[28] Elizabeth Eileen Dooley, "Sir William Crofton and the Irish or Intermediate System of Prison Discipline," *New England Journal of Prison Law* 575 (Winter 1981): 55.

[29] Rothman, *Conscience and Convenience,* p. 70.

[30] Rotman, "Failure of Reform," p. 174.

[31] Alexander W. Pisciotta, *Benevolent Repression: Social Control and the American Reformatory-Prison Movement* (New York: New York University Press, 1994), 20.

[32] Ibid., p. 41.

[33] W. M. F. Round, "How Far May We Abolish Prisons?" *Journal of the American Social Science Association* 325 (1897): 200–201, as cited in Rothman, *Conscience and Convenience*, p. 55.

[34] Richard Hofstader, *The Age of Reform* (New York: Knopf, 1974).

[35] Rothman, *Conscience and Convenience*, p. 5.

[36] Ibid., p. 60.

[37] Ibid., p. 53.

[38] Ibid., p. 99.

[39] Rotman, "Failure of Reform," p. 183.

[40] Rothman, *Conscience and Convenience*, p. 99.

[41] Quoted in Jessica Mitford, *Kind and Usual Punishment* (New York: Knopf, 1973), 96.

[42] Thomas C. Johnsen, "Howard Belding Gill," *Harvard Magazine*, September–October 1999, p. 54.

[43] Karl Menninger, *The Crime of Punishment* (New York: Viking Press, 1969), 19.

[44] Larry E. Sullivan, *The Prison Reform Movement: Forlorn Hope* (Boston: Twayne, 1990), 71.

[45] U.S. President's Commission on Law Enforcement and Administration of Justice, *The Challenge of Crime in a Free Society* (Washington, DC: U.S. Government Printing Office, 1967), 7.

[46] New York State Special Commission on Attica, *Attica: The Official Report of the New York State Special Commission on Attica* (New York: Bantam Books, 1972), xi.

[47] Robert Martinson, "What Works? Questions and Answers about Prison Reform," *Public Interest* 35 (Spring 1974): 22.

[48] Michael Tonry, *Sentencing Matters* (New York: Oxford University Press, 1996), 3.

[49] Michael Tonry and Joan Petersilia, "American Prisons at the Beginning of the Twenty-first Century," in *Prisons*, edited by Michael Tonry and Joan Petersilia, vol. 26 of *Crime and Justice: A Review of Research*, edited by Michael Tonry (Chicago: University of Chicago Press, 1999), 3.

© REUTERS/Shepard/Landov

In 2009 former Wall Street financier Bernard Madoff was sentenced to 150 years in prison for a $65 billion fraud scheme that he operated for more than 20 years.

LEARNING OBJECTIVES

After reading this chapter you should be able to . . .

1 Understand the goals of punishment.

2 Be familiar with the different forms of the criminal sanction.

3 Explain how different factors affect the sentencing process.

4 Discuss the problem of unjust punishment.

"ALL RISE!" The people in the Manhattan federal courtroom stood as U.S. District Court Judge Denny Chin mounted the dais. On that 29th day of June 2009, the courtroom was packed with attorneys, reporters, and onlookers. Judge Chin was about to sentence a former Wall Street financier, Bernard Madoff, who pleaded guilty in March to 11 counts of securities and mail fraud, lying to the Securities and Exchange Commission, and perjury. The sentencing took place during the worst economic crisis in the United States since the 1930s.

Having operated a $65 billion fraud scheme for more than 20 years that ensnared private foundations, millionaires, and several hundred small investors, Madoff had become the poster children for Wall Street greed and fraud.

Before the sentencing, several victims stood at the lectern in the courtroom and told the court wrenching stories of how Madoff's fraud had changed their lives. One victim said, "My life will never be the same. I am financially ruined and will worry every day about how I will take care of my wife." Attempting to frame his experience, another victim stated, "The fallout from having your entire life savings robbed from right under your nose is like nothing you can

THE PUNISHMENT OF OFFENDERS

- ### THE PURPOSE OF CORRECTIONS
  Retribution (Deserved Punishment)
  Deterrence
  Incapacitation
  Rehabilitation
  New Approaches to Punishment
  Criminal Sanctions: A Mixed Bag?

- ### FORMS OF THE CRIMINAL SANCTION
  Incarceration
  Intermediate Sanctions
  Probation
  Death
  Forms and Goals of Sanctions

- ### THE SENTENCING PROCESS
  The Administrative Context
  Attitudes and Values of Judges
  The Presentence Report
  Sentencing Guidelines
  The Future of Sentencing Guidelines

- ### UNJUST PUNISHMENT
  Sentencing Disparities
  Wrongful Convictions

describe."[1] Judge Chin told those gathered in the courtroom that he received letters from more than 100 victims. One of the letter writers, a widow who invested her life savings with Madoff shortly after her husband died, wrote that Madoff told her, "Your money is safe with me."[2]

Speaking in court, Judge Chin noted that he received not one letter on Madoff's behalf. Chin said Madoff's crimes "were extraordinarily evil" and "the amount of fraud . . . was staggering."[3] Judge Chin then sentenced Madoff to 150 years in prison—the maximum allowed under federal sentencing guidelines. The federal system does not allow for parole, but Madoff can reduce his sentence by 15 percent with good behavior, which will make him eligible for release in 127 years.

Crucial to every decision in the criminal justice process is the question "Is it just?" Should Madoff have been given rehabilitative treatment, probation, community service, or imprisonment? Did justice serve Madoff's victims? Did the sentence support society's need for the maintenance of right conduct? What rationale governed the punishment?

These types of questions are central to the mission of corrections. In this chapter we examine the goals of corrections, note the various forms of the criminal sanction, and discuss the sentencing process. As we explore these topics, we will examine their links to one another and to the historical and philosophical issues developed in Chapters 2 and 3.

Chapter

■ THE PURPOSE OF CORRECTIONS

Rationales for punishment are influenced by the broad philosophical, political, and social themes of their era. Prevailing ideas about the causes of crime are closely tied to questions of responsibility and hence to the rationale for specific sanctions. As explained in Chapter 2, the ideas of the classical school of criminology, founded by Cesare Beccaria, squared nicely with the concepts of the Age of Reason, as did Jeremy Bentham's utilitarianism. In the context of the times, "making the punishment fit the crime" was more humane because it sought to do away with the brutal punishments often inflicted for trivial offenses. With the rise of science and the development of positivist criminology toward the end of the 1800s, new beliefs emerged about criminal responsibility and the desirability of designing punishment to meet the needs of the offender. The positivists considered criminal behavior to be the result of sociological, psychological, or biological factors and therefore directed correctional work toward rehabilitating the offender through treatment.

Before further examining the goals of the criminal sanction, we should consider what the term *punishment* actually means. Herbert Packer argues that punishment is marked by these three elements:

1 An offense.

2 The infliction of pain because of the commission of the offense.

3 A dominant purpose that is neither to compensate someone injured by the offense nor to better the offender's condition but to prevent further offenses or to inflict what is thought to be deserved pain on the offender.[4]

Note that Packer emphasizes two major goals of criminal punishment: inflicting deserved suffering on offenders and preventing crime.

Criminal sanctions in the United States have four goals: retribution (deserved punishment), deterrence, incapacitation, and rehabilitation. In Chapter 22 we describe the movement to make restorative and community justice a fifth goal of the criminal sanction. Here, as we discuss each of the four traditional justifications for punishment, bear in mind that although judges often state publicly that their sentencing practices accord with a particular goal, conditions in correctional institutions or the actions of probation officers may be inconsistent with that goal. Thus, sentencing and correctional policies may be carried out in such a way that no one goal dominates or, in some cases, that justice itself is not demonstrably served.

Retribution (Deserved Punishment)

retribution
Punishment inflicted on a person who has infringed on the rights of others and so deserves to be penalized. The severity of the sanction should fit the seriousness of the crime.

Retribution is punishment inflicted on a person who has violated a criminal law and so deserves to be punished. The biblical expression "an eye for an eye, a tooth for a tooth" illustrates the philosophy underlying retribution. Retribution means that those who commit a particular crime should be punished alike, in proportion to the gravity of the offense or to the extent to which others have been made to suffer. Retribution is deserved punishment; offenders must "pay their debts." This idea focuses on the offense alone, not the future acts of the criminal or some other purpose such as reform or deterrence. Offenders must be penalized for their wrongful acts, simply because fairness and justice require that they be punished.

With the Age of Reason and the development of utilitarian approaches to punishment, the idea of retribution lost much of its influence (see Chapter 2). However, some scholars claim that the desire for retribution is a basic human emotion. They maintain that if the state does not provide retributive sanctions to reflect community revulsion at offensive acts, citizens will take the law into their own hands to punish offenders. Under this view, the failure of government to satisfy the people's desire for retribution could produce social unrest. Retribution helps the community emphasize the standards it expects all members to uphold.

This argument may not be valid for all crimes, however. If a rapist is inadequately punished, then the victim's friends, family, and other members of the community may be tempted to exact their own retribution. But what about a young adult who smokes marijuana? If the government failed to impose retribution for this offense, would the community care? The same apathy may hold true with respect to offenders who commit other small, nonviolent crimes. But even in these seemingly trivial situations, retribution may be useful and necessary to remind the public of the general rules of law and the important values it protects.

Since the late 1970s, retribution as a justification for the criminal sanction has aroused new interest. This has occurred largely because of dissatisfaction with the philosophical basis and practical results of rehabilitation. Using the concept of "just deserts" (or deserved punishment) to define retribution, some theorists argue that one who infringes on the rights of others deserves to be punished. This approach is based on the philosophical view that punishment is a moral response to harm inflicted on society. In effect, these theorists believe that basic morality demands that wrongdoers be punished. Andrew von Hirsch, a leading writer on punishment, says that "the sanctioning authority is entitled to choose a response that expresses moral disapproval: namely, punishment."[5] According to von Hirsch and others, punishment should be applied only to exact retribution for the wrong inflicted and not primarily to achieve other goals such as deterrence, incapacitation, or rehabilitation.[6]

Deterrence

Many people think of criminal punishment as a way to affect the future choices and behavior of individuals. Politicians frequently talk about being "tough on crime" so as to send a message to would-be criminals. This approach goes back to the eighteenth century. Recall from Chapter 2 that Jeremy Bentham was struck by what seemed to be the pointlessness of retribution. Other reformers adopted his theory of utilitarianism, which holds that human behavior is governed by the individual's calculation of the benefits versus the costs of one's acts. Before stealing money or property, for example, potential offenders consider the punishment that others have received for similar acts and are thereby deterred.

Modern thinking distinguishes two types of deterrence.[7] **General deterrence** presumes that members of the general public will be deterred by observing the punishments of others and will conclude that the costs of crime outweigh the benefits. For general deterrence to be effective, the public must be constantly reminded about the likelihood and severity of punishment for various acts. They must believe they will be caught, prosecuted, and given a specific punishment if they commit a particular crime. Moreover, the punishment must be severe enough to impress them well enough to avoid committing crimes. For example, public hanging was once considered an effective general deterrent.

general deterrence
Punishment of criminals that is intended to be an example to the general public and to discourage the commission of offenses by others.

By contrast, **specific deterrence**, also called **special or individual deterrence**, targets the decisions and behavior of offenders who have already been convicted. Under this approach, the amount and kind of punishment are calculated to discourage the criminal from repeating the offense. The punishment must be sufficiently severe to make the criminal conclude, "The consequences of my crime were too painful. I won't commit that crime again, because I don't want to risk being punished again."

specific deterrence (special or individual deterrence)
Punishment inflicted on criminals to discourage them from committing future crimes.

The concept of deterrence poses obvious difficulties.[8] Deterrence assumes that all people act rationally and think before they act. It does not account for the many people who commit crimes under the influence of drugs or alcohol, or who suffer from psychological problems or mental illness. Deterrence also does not account for people who act impulsively in stealing or damaging property. In other cases, the low probability of being caught defeats both general and specific deterrence. To be generally deterrent, punishment must be perceived as fast, certain, and severe. But punishment does not always come about this way.

Knowledge of the effectiveness of deterrence is limited. For example, social science cannot measure the effects of general deterrence; only those who are not deterred come to the attention of researchers. A study of the deterrent effects of punishment would have to examine the impact of different forms of the criminal sanction on various potential lawbreakers. How can anyone determine how many people—or even if *any* people—stopped themselves from committing a crime because they were deterred by the prospect of prosecution and punishment? Therefore, while legislators often cite deterrence as a rationale for certain sanctions, no one really knows the extent to which sentencing policies based on deterrence achieve their objectives. Because contemporary U.S. society has shown little ability to reduce crime by imposing increasingly severe sanctions, the effectiveness of deterrence for many crimes and criminals should be questioned.[9]

Incapacitation

incapacitation
Depriving an offender of the ability to commit crimes against society, usually by detaining the offender in prison.

Incapacitation assumes that society can, by detention in a correctional facility or by execution, remove an offender's capacity to commit further crimes. Many people express such sentiments by urging, "Lock 'em up and throw away the key!" In primitive societies, banishment from the community was the usual method of incapacitation. In early America, offenders often agreed to move away or to join the army as an alternative to some other form of punishment. Today, imprisonment is the usual method of incapacitation. Offenders can be confined within secure institutions and effectively prevented from committing additional harm against society for the duration of their sentence. Capital punishment is the ultimate method of incapacitation.

Any sentence that physically restricts an offender can have an incapacitating effect, even when the underlying purpose of the sentence is retribution, deterrence, or rehabilitation. Sentences based primarily on incapacitation, however, are future oriented. Whereas retribution requires focusing on the harmful act of the offender, incapacitation looks at the offender's potential actions. If the offender will likely commit future crimes, then the judge may impose a severe sentence—even for a relatively minor crime.

Under the theory of incapacitation, for example, a woman who kills her abusive husband as an emotional reaction to his verbal insults and physical assaults could receive a light sentence. As a one-time impulse killer who felt driven to kill by unique circumstances, she is not likely to commit additional crimes. By contrast, someone who shoplifts merchandise from a store and has been convicted of the offense on 10 previous occasions may receive a severe sentence. The criminal record and type of crime indicate that he or she will commit additional crimes if released. Thus, incapacitation focuses on characteristics of the offenders instead of characteristics of the offenses.

Does it offend the American sense of justice that a person could receive a severer sentence for shoplifting than for manslaughter? This question raises one criticism of incapacitation. Questions arise also about how to determine the length of sentence. Presumably, offenders will not be released until the state is reasonably sure that they will no longer commit crimes. However, can any person's behavior be accurately predicted? Moreover, on what grounds can the state punish people for anticipated future behavior that it cannot accurately predict?

selective incapacitation
Making the best use of expensive and limited prison space by targeting for incarceration those offenders whose incapacity will do the most to reduce crime in society.

In recent years, greater attention has been paid to the concept of **selective incapacitation**, whereby offenders who repeat certain kinds of crimes are sentenced to long prison terms. Research suggests that a relatively small number of offenders commit a large number of violent and property crimes.[10] Burglars, for example, tend to commit many offenses before they are ultimately caught. Thus, these "career criminals" should be locked up for long periods.[11]

Although the idea of confining or closely supervising repeat offenders is appealing, it is also quite expensive to do so. In addition, selective incapacitation raises several moral and ethical questions. Because the theory looks at aggregates—the total harm of a certain type of crime versus the total suffering to be inflicted to reduce its incidence—policy makers may tend to focus on cost-benefit comparisons, disregarding serious issues of justice, individual freedom, and civil liberties.

Rehabilitation

rehabilitation
The goal of restoring a convicted offender to a constructive place in society through some form of vocational or educational training or therapy.

Rehabilitation refers to the goal of restoring a convicted offender to a constructive place in society through some form of vocational or educational training or therapy. Many people believe that rehabilitation is the most appealing modern justification for use of the criminal sanction. These Americans want offenders to be treated and resocialized so they will lead a crime-free, productive life. Over the last century, rehabilitation advocates have argued that techniques are available to identify and treat the causes of criminal behavior. If the offender's criminal behavior is assumed to result from some social, psychological, or biological imperfection, the treatment of the disorder becomes the primary goal of corrections.

The goal of rehabilitation is oriented solely toward the offender and does not imply any consistent relationship between the severity of the punishment and the gravity of the crime. People who commit lesser offenses may receive long prison sentences if experts believe that the offenders need a long period to become rehabilitated. By contrast, a murderer may win early release by showing signs that the psychological or emotional problems that led to the killing have been corrected.

According to the concept of rehabilitation, offenders are treated, not punished, and will return to society when they are "cured." Consequently, judges should not set a fixed sentence but ones with maximum and minimum terms so that parole boards may release inmates when they have been rehabilitated. Such sentences are known as indeterminate sentences because the judge does not set a fixed release date. The indeterminate sentence is justified by the belief that if prisoners know when they are going to be released, they will not make an effort to engage in the treatment programs prescribed for their rehabilitation. If, however, they know they will be held until cured, they will cooperate with counselors, psychologists, and other professionals seeking to treat their problems. (See more on indeterminate sentences later in this chapter.)

From the 1940s until the 1970s, the goal of rehabilitation was so widely held that treatment and reform of the offender were generally regarded as the only issues worthy of serious attention. Experts assumed that crime was caused by problems affecting individuals and that modern social sciences had the tools to address those problems. Since the 1970s, however, studies of rehabilitative programs have challenged the idea that we really know how to cure criminal offenders.[12] Moreover, scholars no longer take for granted that crime is caused by identifiable, curable problems such as poverty, lack of job skills, low self-esteem, and hostility toward authority. Instead, some argue that one cannot identify the cause of criminal behavior for individual offenders. Norval Morris argues that coerced prison treatment programs not only waste resources but also infringe on human rights.[13]

Clearly, many legislatures, prosecutors, and judges have abandoned the rehabilitation goal in favor of retribution, deterrence, or incapacitation. Yet on the basis of opinion polls, researchers have found public support for rehabilitative programs.[14] Prison wardens have also supported such programs.[15]

restorative justice
Punishment designed to repair the damage done to the victim and community by an offender's criminal act.

New Approaches to Punishment

During the past decade, many people have called for shifts away from punishment goals that focus either on the offender (rehabilitation, specific deterrence) or the crime (retribution, general deterrence, and incapacitation). Some have argued that the current goals of the criminal sanction leave out the needs of the crime victim and the community. Crime has traditionally been viewed as violating the state, but people now recognize that a criminal act also violates the victim and the community.[16] In keeping with the focus of police, courts, and corrections on community justice (see Chapter 22), advocates are calling for **restorative justice** to be added to the goals of the criminal sanction.

The restorative justice perspective views crime as more than a violation of penal law. The criminal act

© Rose Howerter/The Oregonian

Restorative justice seeks to repair the damage done to the victim and the community by an offender's criminal act. Susanna Cooper sits next to David Myers as she looks at a photo of his dead wife. Cooper pled guilty to vehicular homicide in the death of Elaine Myers, received a 34-month prison sentence, and agreed to enter into talks with the victim's family.

practically and symbolically denies community. It breaks trust among citizens and requires community members to determine how "to contradict the moral message of the crime that the offender is above the law and the victim beneath its reach."[17] Crime victims suffer losses involving damage to property and self. The primary aim of criminal justice should be to repair these losses. Crime also challenges the essence of community, to the extent that community life depends on a shared sense of trust, fairness, and interdependence.

Critics say that the retributive focus of today's criminal justice system denies the victim's need to be acknowledged and isolates community members from the conflict between offender and victim. By shifting the focus to restorative justice, sanctions can provide ways for the offender to repair harm. Others warn, however, that society should approach restorative justice with caution because many procedural safeguards are impaired.[18]

The restorative process involves the participation of the offender, the victim, and the community. The offender must take responsibility for the offense, agree to "undo" the harm through restitution, and affirm a willingness to live according to the law. The victim must specify the harm of the offense and the resources necessary to restore the losses suffered; the victim must also lay out the conditions necessary to diminish any fear or resentment toward the offender. The community facilitates the restorative process, emphasizes to the offender the norms of acceptable behavior, provides support to restore the victim, and offers opportunities for the offender to perform reparative tasks for the victim and the community. Finally, it provides ways for the offender to get the help needed to live in the community crime free.

Research suggests that restorative justice programs can be effective. For example, Nancy Rodriguez's study of juveniles in Arizona revealed that adolescents who participated in restorative justice programs were less likely to recidivate than juveniles in her comparison group. Interestingly, Rodriguez found that restorative justice programs were most effective at reducing recidivism for girls and juvenile offenders with less-extensive criminal histories.[19] Based on their extensive review of the research literature on restorative justice, Lawrence Sherman and Heather Strang conclude that restorative justice programs reduce recidivism among property and violent offenders. However, such programs seem to be more effective when crimes involve a personal victim. Sherman and Strang also found evidence that restorative justice programs benefit the victims of crime. In particular, victims who willingly meet with offenders experience fewer posttraumatic stress symptoms.[20] Additional research must be conducted before we can reach more-definitive conclusions about the effectiveness of restorative justice programs.

For information on **restorative justice** in the Minnesota Department of Corrections, visit the corresponding link at www .cengage.com/criminaljustice/ clear.

Criminal Sanctions: A Mixed Bag?

How should society justify the use of criminal sanctions? Should the purpose be deterrence or incapacitation? What about retribution and rehabilitation? Justifications for specific sanctions usually overlap. A term of imprisonment may be philosophically justified by its primary goal of retribution but also serve the secondary functions of deterrence and incapacitation. General deterrence is such a broad concept that it adapts to the other goals, except possibly rehabilitation.

However, rehabilitation clearly conflicts with the other goals. For example, the deterrent power of incarceration depends primarily on being unpleasant. If incarceration consists mainly of a pleasant rehabilitative experience, it loses its deterrent power. By the same token, the more unpleasant prison life is, the less suitable an environment it is for most rehabilitation programs.

Trial judges carry the heavy burden of fashioning a sentence that accommodates these values in each case. A judge may sentence a forger to a long prison term as an example to others, even though this person poses little threat to community safety and probably does not need correctional treatment. The same judge may impose a shorter sentence on a youthful offender who has committed a serious crime yet who may be a good candidate for rehabilitation if quickly reintegrated into society.

To see how these goals might be enacted in real life, consider again the sentencing of Bernard Madoff. **Table 4.1** shows various hypothetical sentencing statements that Judge Chin might have given, depending on prevailing correctional goals.

TABLE 4.1 *Hypothetical Punishments for Bernard Madoff*

At sentencing, the judge usually gives reasons for the punishment imposed. Here are some statements U.S. District Court Judge Denny Chin *might* have made, depending on the correctional goal he wanted to promote.	
Goal	**Judge's Statement**
Retribution	I am imposing this sentence because you deserve to be punished for the fraud and other crimes committed against the investors who trusted you with their life savings. Your criminal behavior in this case is the basis for your punishment. Justice requires me to impose a sanction that reflects the value the community places on right conduct.
Deterrence	I am imposing this sentence so that your punishment for fraud and other crimes will serve as an example and deter others who may contemplate similar actions. In addition, I hope that the sentence will deter you from ever again committing such an act.
Incapacitation	I am imposing this sentence so that you will be unable to violate the law while imprisoned. Because you have not been convicted of prior offenses, selective incapacitation is not warranted.
Rehabilitation	The trial testimony of your psychiatrists and the information contained in the presentence report make me believe that aspects of your personality led you to violate the law. I am therefore imposing this sentence so that you can be treated in ways that will rectify your behavior so you will not break the law again.

As we next consider the ways that these goals are applied through the various forms of punishment, keep in mind the underlying goal or mix of goals that justifies each form of sanction.

■ FORMS OF THE CRIMINAL SANCTION

Incarceration, intermediate sanctions, probation, and death are the ways the criminal sanction, or punishment, is applied in the United States. Most people think of incarceration as the usual punishment. As a consequence, much of the public believes that offenders receiving alternatives to incarceration, such as probation, are "getting off." However, community-based punishments such as probation and intermediate sanctions are imposed far more often than prison sentences.

Many judges and researchers believe that the sentencing structures in the United States are both too severe and too lenient. That is, many offenders who do not warrant incarceration are sent to prison, and many who should be given more-restrictive punishments receive minimal probation supervision.

Advocates for more-effective sentencing practices increasingly support a range or continuum of punishment options, with graduated levels of supervision and harshness.[21] As **Figure 4.1** shows, simple probation lies at one end of this range, and traditional incarceration lies at the other. As noted by certain researchers, "An expanded range of sentencing options gives judges greater latitude to exercise discretion in selecting punishments that more closely fit the circumstances of the crime and the offender."[22] They argue that by using this type of sentencing scheme, authorities can maintain expensive prison cells for violent offenders. At the same time, less-restrictive community-based programs can be used to punish nonviolent offenders.

Michael Tonry notes that as recently as 1975 a distinctively "American" system of sentencing and corrections had formed:

Then every state and the federal government used [an] indeterminate sentencing system in which legislatures set maximum authorized sentences; judges chose among imprisonment, probation, and fines, and set maximum sentences; correctional officials had broad powers over good time and furloughs; parole boards set release dates; and virtually all these decisions were immune from appellate review.[23]

PROBATION

Offender reports to probation officer periodically, depending on the offense, sometimes as frequently as several times a month or as infrequently as once a year.

INTENSIVE SUPERVISION PROBATION

Offender sees probation officer three to five times a week. Probation officer also makes unscheduled visits to offender's home or workplace.

RESTITUTION AND FINES

Used alone or in conjunction with probation or intensive supervision and requires regular payments to crime victims or to the courts.

COMMUNITY SERVICE

Used alone or in conjunction with probation or intensive supervision and requires completion of set number of hours of work in and for the community.

SUBSTANCE ABUSE TREATMENT

Evaluation and referral services provided by private outside agencies and used alone or in conjunction with either simple probation or intensive supervision.

Figure 4.1
Escalating Punishments to Fit the Crime

This list includes generalized descriptions of many sentencing options used in jurisdictions across the country.

Source: *Seeking Justice: Crime and Punishment in America* (New York: Edna McConnell Clark Foundation, 1997), 32–33.

There is now no standard approach. Some states have retained parole release; some have abolished it. Many states have sentencing guidelines, others have determinate sentences, and many have retained indeterminate sentences. Mandatory minimums, three-strikes laws, and truth-in-sentencing have affected all jurisdictions in diverse ways.

As we examine the various forms of criminal sanctions, bear in mind that complex problems are associated with applying these legally authorized punishments. Although the penal code defines the behaviors that are illegal and specifies the procedures for determining guilt, the legal standards for sentencing—for actually applying the punishment—have not been as well developed. In other words, the United States has no common laws of sentencing. Thus, judges have discretion in determining the appropriate sentence within the parameters of the penal code.

Incarceration

Imprisonment is the most visible penalty imposed by U.S. courts. At the end of 2006, there were nearly 2.3 million Americans in prison or jail.[24] Many people think that imprisonment significantly deters potential offenders. However, incarceration is expensive. It also creates problems of reintegrating offenders into society upon release.

In penal codes, legislatures stipulate the type of sentences and the amount of prison time that may be imposed for each crime. Three basic sentencing structures are used: (1) indeterminate sentences, (2) determinate

AP Images/Rob Carr

Of all correctional measures, incarceration represents the greatest restriction on freedom. These inmates are part of America's huge incarcerated population. Since 1980 the number of Americans in prisons and jails has quadrupled.

DAY REPORTING

Clients report to a central location every day where they file a daily schedule with their supervision officer showing how each hour will be spent — at work, in class, at support group meetings, etc.

HOUSE ARREST AND ELECTRONIC MONITORING

Used in conjunction with intensive supervision; restricts offender to home except when at work, school, or treatment.

HALFWAY HOUSE

Residential settings for selected inmates as a supplement to probation for those completing prison programs and for some probation or parole violators. Usually coupled with community service work and/or substance abuse treatment.

BOOT CAMP

Rigorous military-style regimen for younger offenders, designed to accelerate punishment while instilling discipline, often with an educational component.

PRISONS AND JAILS

More-serious offenders serve their terms at state or federal prisons, while county jails are usually designed to hold inmates for shorter periods.

sentences, and (3) mandatory sentences. Each type of sentence makes certain assumptions about the goals of the criminal sanction, and each provides judges with varying degrees of discretion.

INDETERMINATE SENTENCES ■ When the goal of rehabilitation dominated corrections, legislatures enacted **indeterminate sentences** (often termed *indefinite sentences*). In keeping with the goal of treatment, indeterminate sentencing gives correctional officials and parole boards significant control over the amount of time a prisoner serves. Penal codes with indeterminate sentencing stipulate a minimum and maximum amount of time to be served in prison (for example, 1–5 years, 3–10 years, 10–20 years, 1 year to life, and so on). At the time of sentencing, the judge informs the offender about the range of the sentence. The offender also learns that he or she will probably be eligible for parole at some point after the minimum term has been served. The parole board decides on the actual release date.

DETERMINATE SENTENCES ■ Dissatisfaction with the rehabilitation goal and support for the concept of retribution (deserved punishment) led many legislatures in the 1970s to shift to **determinate sentences**. With a determinate sentence, an offender is imprisoned for a specific period (for example, 2 years, 5 years, 10 years). At the end of the term, minus credited good time (discussed later in this chapter), the prisoner is automatically freed. The time of release is tied neither to participation in treatment programs nor to a parole board's judgment concerning the offender's likelihood of returning to criminal activities.

Some determinate sentencing states have adopted penal codes that stipulate a specific term for each crime category. Others allow the judge to choose a range of time to be served. Some states emphasize a determinate **presumptive sentence**; the legislature or a commission specifies a term based on a time range (for example, 14–20 months) into which most cases should fall. Only in special circumstances should judges deviate from the presumptive sentence. Whichever sentencing scheme is used, however, the offender theoretically knows at sentencing the amount of time to be served.

indeterminate sentence
A period of incarceration with minimum and maximum terms stipulated, so that parole eligibility depends on the time necessary for treatment; closely associated with the rehabilitation concept.

determinate sentence
A fixed period of incarceration imposed by a court; associated with the concept of retribution or deserved punishment.

presumptive sentence
A sentence for which the legislature or a commission sets a minimum and maximum range of months or years. Judges are to fix the length of the sentence within that range, allowing for special circumstances.

AP Images/Jim McKnight

Mandatory sentences can impose severe punishments on first offenders or those who commit nonviolent crimes if they are convicted of offenses, such as drug crimes, that legislatures treat as especially harmful to society. Here Denise Smith, serving a 10- to 20-year drug sentence in New York, wipes away a tear as she talks about being so far away from her children. Should judges have the power to individualize sentences depending on the prior record of each defendant and circumstances of each crime?

mandatory sentence

A sentence stipulating that some minimum period of incarceration must be served by people convicted of selected crimes, regardless of background or circumstances.

MANDATORY SENTENCES ■ Politicians and the public have continued to complain that offenders are released before serving terms that are long enough, and legislatures have responded.[25] All states and the federal government now require **mandatory sentences** (often called *mandatory minimum sentences*), stipulating some minimum period of incarceration that people convicted of selected crimes must serve. The judge may consider neither the circumstances of the offense nor the background of the offender, and he or she may not impose sentences that do not involve incarceration. Mandatory prison terms are most often specified for violent crimes, drug violations, habitual offenders, or crimes in which a firearm was used.

The "three strikes and you're out" laws, now adopted by several states and the federal government, provide one example of mandatory sentencing.[26] These laws require that judges sentence offenders who have three felony convictions (in some states two or four convictions) to long prison terms, sometimes to life without parole.[27] Research shows that California's three-strikes law has increased the size of the prison population. Many of these inmates received their third strike for nonviolent crimes. These prisoners are also disproportionately African American and Latino.[28] This law has also effected a substantial aging of the prison population that will eventually result in soaring health costs.[29] Three-strikes laws have also been linked to lower rates of plea bargaining and to causing desperate offenders to violently resist arrest.[30] Yet research shows that the laws have had little impact on reducing rates of serious crime.[31]

In March 2003 the U.S. Supreme Court in two 5–4 rulings upheld California's three-strikes law. The offenders in the two cases argued that their third felonies were minor and their long sentences were unconstitutional "cruel and unusual" punishments. Leondro Andrade's third felony was for stealing two videotapes, for which he was sentenced to 50 years without the possibility of parole. Gary Ewing's theft of golf clubs earned him a sentence of 25 years to life. Justices in the majority said that the California law reflected a legislative judgment and that the court should not second-guess this policy choice. The four justices in the minority argued that there was a "gross" disparity between the pettiness of the crime and the severity of the sentence.[32]

Although legislators may assume that mandatory sentences will be imposed and criminal behavior reduced, this intent may be thwarted by the decisions of judges

Families Against Mandatory Minimums is a national organization that seeks to reduce the use of stiff sentences; go to the corresponding link at www .cengage.com/criminaljustice/ clear.

and prosecutors. California prosecutors vary greatly as to whether they make charges under the three-strikes law. The law is used much less in San Francisco, for example, than in San Diego.[33] Regional voter support for the law may account for the disparity.

The three-strikes law in California has affected the courts and corrections, but the impact has not been as dramatic as initially predicted. Some researchers argue that the law "has been absorbed and accommodated" in the criminal justice system through plea bargaining and the continued exercise of discretion by prosecutors and judges. They believe that the law's politically symbolic effect has proved much greater than its operational impact.[34] In November 2004, voters turned down a proposal to reform California's three-strikes law. See "Myths in Corrections" for more.

Use of mandatory minimum sentences greatly expanded during the 1980s as a weapon in the war on drugs. This has caused a great increase in the number of drug offenders, most for a nonviolent offense, spending long terms in America's prisons. Research has shown that these laws hit mostly low-level street dealers, mules, and addicts rather than the "kingpins" who import and distribute drugs to the market. Across the country, mandatory prison terms are applied more often to African American drug offenders than to their white counterparts.[35]

Faced with prison overcrowding and constricted budgets, officials are apparently now having second thoughts about mandatory sentences. In many states mandatory minimum drug laws have come under attack. Given the research that has been conducted on the effects of mandatory minimums, Michael Tonry contends that "mandatory penalties are an idea whose time long ago passed."[36]

MYTHS IN CORRECTIONS

THREE STRIKES AND YOU'RE OUT

THE MYTH: Three-strikes laws that require judges to sentence offenders with three felony convictions to long prison terms, such as life without parole, deter would-be criminals and reduce the overall crime rate.

THE REALITY: Research shows that after taking into account how often three-strikes laws are used and considering other factors related to crime, three-strikes laws have virtually no deterrent effect on crime.

Sources: John L. Worrall, "The Effect of Three-Strikes Legislation on Serious Crime in California," *Journal of Criminal Justice* 32 (July–August 2004): 283–96.

THE SENTENCE VERSUS ACTUAL TIME SERVED ■ Regardless of the discretion judges have to fine-tune the sentences they give, the prison sentences that are imposed may bear little resemblance to the amount of time served. In reality, parole boards in indeterminate-sentencing states have broad discretion in release decisions once the offender has served a minimum portion of the sentence.

Most states have provisions for **good time**, by which days are subtracted from prisoners' minimum or maximum term for good behavior or for participating in various types of vocational, educational, or treatment programs. Correctional officials consider these policies necessary for maintaining institutional order and reducing crowding. The possibility of receiving good-time credit provides an incentive for prisoners to follow institutional rules. Prosecutors and defense attorneys also take good time into consideration during plea bargaining. In other words, they think about the actual amount of time a particular offender is likely to serve.

The amount of good time one can earn varies among the states, usually from 5 to 10 days a month. In some states, once 90 days of good time are earned, they are vested; that is, the credits cannot be taken away as a punishment for misbehavior. Prisoners who then violate the rules risk losing only days not vested.

Judges in the United States often prescribe long periods of incarceration for serious crimes, but good time and parole reduce the amount of time spent in prison. **Figure 4.2** compares the estimated time actually served by offenders sent to state prisons with the mean sentence they received. Note that the national average for time served is 27 months, or 51 percent of the mean sentence of 53 months. This type of national data often hides the impact of variations in sentencing and releasing laws in individual states. In many states, because of prison crowding and release policies, offenders serve less than 51 percent of their sentences. In other states, where three-strikes and truth-in-sentencing laws are employed, the average time served will be much longer than the national average.

good time
A reduction of an inmate's prison sentence, at the discretion of the prison administrator, for good behavior or for participation in vocational, educational, and treatment programs.

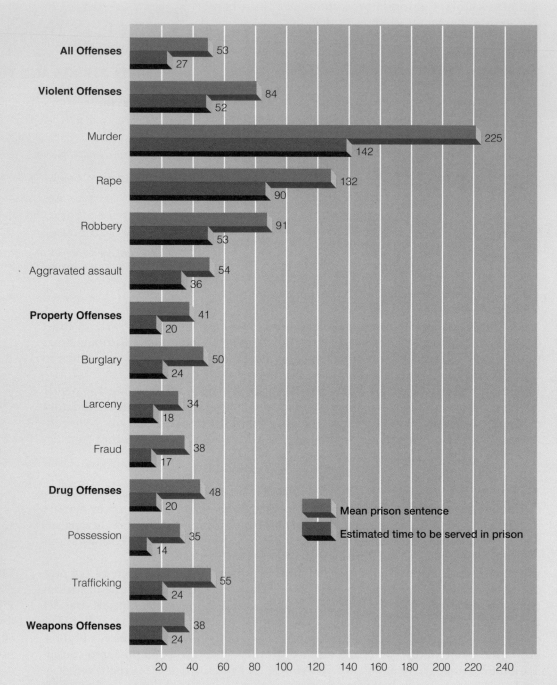

Figure 4.2

Estimated Time to be Served in State Prison, by Offense

Many offenders serve one-half or less of their mean sentence. Why is there such a difference between the sentence and the actual time served?

Source: Bureau of Justice Statistics, *Felony Sentences in State Courts, 2002* (Washington, DC: U.S. Government Printing Office, December 2004), 4.

TRUTH-IN-SENTENCING ■ *Truth-in-sentencing* refers to laws that require offenders to serve a substantial proportion (usually 85 percent for violent crimes) of their prison sentence before being released on parole. These laws have three goals: (1) providing the public with more-accurate information about the actual length of sentences, (2) reducing crime by keeping offenders in prison for longer periods, and (3) achieving a rational allocation of prison space by prioritizing the incarceration of particular classes of criminals (such as violent offenders).[37] Critics maintain that truth-in-sentencing increases prison populations at a tremendous cost.

Truth-in-sentencing has become such a politically attractive idea that the federal government allocated most of the $10 billion for prison construction, authorized under the Violent Crime Control and Law Enforcement Act of 1994, only to those states that met the 85 percent goal.[38] However, an evaluation of the federal government's incentive grant program reveals that although all states received some money from the program, few states actually enacted new truth-in-sentencing laws to qualify for federal funding. When the program ended, the federal government had awarded only $2.7 billion of the authorized $10 billion to states. The program had resulted in only 50,000 new prison beds.[39]

The sentence imposed by the judge may be viewed as the beginning of corrections. Here former Nebraska running back Thunder Collins is escorted from the courthouse following his sentence to life for the murder of Timothy Thomas during a drug deal that "got out of hand."

Intermediate Sanctions

Prison crowding and the low levels of probation supervision have spurred interest in the development of **intermediate sanctions**, punishments less severe and costly than prison, but more restrictive than traditional probation.[40] Intermediate sanctions provide a variety of restrictions on freedom, such as fines or other monetary sanctions, home confinement, intensive probation supervision, restitution to victims, community service, boot camp, and forfeiture of possessions or illegally gained assets.

In advocating intermediate punishments, Norval Morris and Michael Tonry stipulate that these sanctions should be used in combination, to reflect the severity of the offense, the characteristics of the offender, and the needs of the community.[41] In addition, intermediate punishments must be supported and enforced by mechanisms that take seriously any breach of the conditions of the sentence. Too often criminal justice agencies have devoted few resources to enforcing sentences that do not involve incarceration. If the law does not fulfill its promises, offenders may feel they have "beaten" the system, which makes the punishment meaningless. Citizens viewing the system's ineffectiveness may develop the attitude that nothing but stiffer sentences will work. (See Chapter 9 for a full discussion of intermediate sanctions.)

intermediate sanctions
A variety of punishments that are more restrictive than traditional probation but less severe and costly than incarceration.

Probation

The most frequently applied criminal sanction in the United States is **probation**, a sentence that an offender serves in the community under supervision. Nearly 60 percent of adults under correctional supervision are on probation (approximately 4.2 million adults in 2006).[42] Probation is designed to maintain supervision of offenders while they try to straighten out their lives. As a judicial act, granted by the grace of the state, probation is not extended as a right. Conditions are imposed specifying how an offender will behave throughout the length of the sentence. Probationers may be ordered to undergo regular drug tests, abide by curfews, enroll in educational programs or remain employed, stay away from certain parts of town or certain people, or meet regularly with probation officers. If the conditions of probation are not met, the supervising officer may recommend to the court that the probation be revoked and that the remainder of the sentence be served in prison. Probation may also be revoked for committing a new crime. (See Chapter 8 for a full discussion of probation.)

Although probationers serve their sentences in the community, the sanction is often tied to incarceration. In some jurisdictions, the court can modify an offender's prison sentence, after a portion is served, by changing it to probation. This is often referred to as **shock probation** (or *split probation*). An offender is released after a period of incarceration (the "shock") and resentenced to probation. An offender on probation may be required to

probation
A sentence allowing the offender to serve the sanctions imposed by the court while he or she lives in the community under supervision.

shock probation
A sentence in which the offender is released after a short incarceration and resentenced to probation.

AP Images/Nati Harnik, File

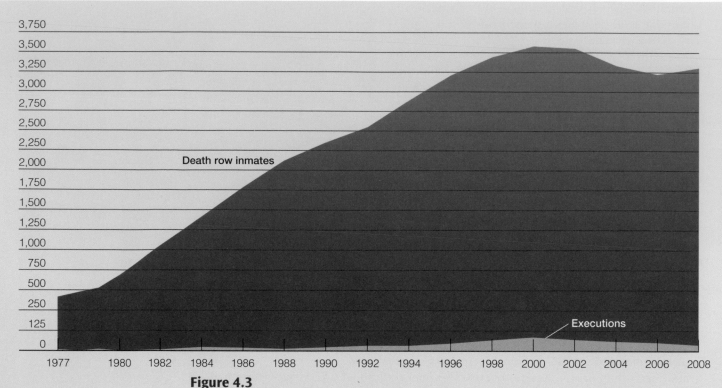

Figure 4.3

People under Sentence of Death and People Executed, 1977–2008

Since 1976 hundreds of new offenders have been added to death row each year, yet the number of executions has never been greater than 98. What explains this situation?

Source: Death Penalty Information Center, http://www.deathpenaltyinfo.org, June 3, 2009.

spend intermittent periods, such as weekends or nights, in jail. Whatever the specific terms of the probationary sentence, it emphasizes guidance and supervision in the community.

Probation is generally advocated as a way of rehabilitating offenders whose crimes are less serious or whose past records are clean. It is viewed as both less expensive and more effective than imprisonment, which may embitter youthful or first-time offenders and mix them with hardened criminals so that they learn more-sophisticated criminal techniques.

Death

Although other Western democracies abolished the death penalty years ago, the United States continues to use it. Capital punishment was imposed and carried out regularly before the late 1960s. Amid debates about the constitutionality of the death penalty and with public opinion polls showing increasing opposition to it, the U.S. Supreme Court suspended use of the death penalty from 1968 to 1976.[43] The Court eventually decided that capital punishment does not violate the Eighth Amendment's prohibition on cruel and unusual punishments. Executions resumed in 1977 as a majority of states began, once again, to sentence murderers to death.

The number of people facing the death penalty increased dramatically for over two decades, as **Figure 4.3** reveals. Only during the last several years has this increase leveled off and declined. On January 1, 2009, 3,297 people awaited execution in the United States.[44] Over one-half of those on death row are in the South, with the greatest number found in Florida, Texas, Alabama, and North Carolina. Although on average about 226 people are sent to death row each year, since 1976 the annual number of executions has never exceeded 98 (in 1999). Is this situation the result of the appeals process or of the lack of will on the part of political leaders and a society that is perhaps uncertain about the taking of human life? The death penalty may have more significance as a political symbol than as a deterrent to crime.

Articles and information in **support** of the death penalty can be found at the corresponding link at www.cengage.com/criminaljustice/clear.

Since January 2000, when Governor George Ryan of Illinois called for a moratorium on executions in his state, questions about the fairness of capital punishment have dominated public debate. Congress and state legislatures have seen bills introduced for a national moratorium on executions, for competent counsel in death row cases, and for inmates to have easier access to DNA tests needed to challenge their convictions. In 2007 only 122 people were added to death row, the smallest such number since executions resumed in 1977. Only 37 people were executed in 2008. Will the United States eventually join the other industrial democracies and stop executing criminals? This is an important question, which Chapter 20 addresses.

Forms and Goals of Sanctions

The criminal sanction takes many forms, and offenders are punished in various ways to serve various purposes. **Table 4.2** summarizes how these sanctions operate and how they reflect the underlying philosophies of punishment. Note that incarceration,

TABLE 4.2 *The Punishment of Offenders*

The goals of the criminal sanction are carried out in a variety of ways, depending on the provisions of the law, the offenders' characteristics, and the judge's discretion. To achieve punishment objectives, judges may impose sentences that combine several forms.

Form of Sanction	Description	Purpose
Incarceration	Imprisonment	
Indeterminate sentence	Specifies a maximum and minimum length of time to be served	Incapacitation, deterrence, rehabilitation
Determinate sentence	Specifies a certain length of time to be served	Retribution, incapacitation, deterrence
Mandatory sentence	Specifies a minimum amount of time that must be served for given crimes	Incapacitation, deterrence
Intermediate Sanctions	Punishment for those requiring sanctions more restrictive than probation but less restrictive than prison	
Fine	Money paid to the state by offender	Retribution, deterrence
Restitution	Money paid to victim by offender	Retribution, incapacitation, deterrence
Forfeiture	Seizure by the state of property either illegally obtained or acquired with resources illegally obtained	Retribution, incapacitation, deterrence
Community service	Requires offender to perform work for the community	Retribution, deterrence
Home confinement	Requires offender to stay in home during certain times	Retribution, incapacitation, deterrence,
Intensive probation	Requires strict and frequent reporting to probation officer	Retribution, incapacitation, deterrence
Boot camp/Shock probation	Short-term institutional sentence emphasizing physical development and discipline, followed by probation	Retribution, incapacitation, deterrence
Probation	Allows offender to serve a sentence in the community under supervision	Retribution, incapacitation, rehabilitation
Death	Execution	Retribution, incapacitation, deterrence

intermediate sanctions, probation, and death can each be used to achieve one or more punishment goals. As you examine the sentencing process, notice how judges use their discretion to set the punishment within the provisions of the law and the characteristics of the offender.

Scholars have called attention to "invisible punishments." Jeremy Travis points out that not all punishments are as visible to the public as are prisons and community corrections. Although the number of offenders in state prison and on probation and parole has dramatically increased in recent decades, laws and regulations that diminish the rights and privileges of ex-offenders and their families have also expanded. These invisible punishments include (1) denying felons the right to vote, (2) allowing termination of parental rights, (3) establishing a felony conviction as grounds for divorce, (4) restricting access to certain occupations, and (5) barring felons from public welfare programs and benefits (such as public housing, student loans, and food stamps).[45] Much of the debate has centered on felons' voting rights. Forty-eight states restrict voting rights for citizens convicted of a felony. This represents over five million Americans, or 2 percent of the voting-age population. Only 26 percent of these people are incarcerated in correctional facilities.[46]

■ THE SENTENCING PROCESS

Regardless of how and where the decision is made—misdemeanor court or felony court, plea bargain or adversarial context, bench or jury trial—judges are responsible for imposing sentences. The often difficult task of sentencing involves more than applying clear-cut principles to individual cases. In one case, a judge may decide to sentence a forger to prison as an example to others, although she poses no threat to community safety and probably does not need rehabilitative treatment. In another case, the judge may impose a light sentence on a youthful offender who, although having committed a serious crime, may be a good risk for rehabilitation if he can be moved quickly back into society.

Legislatures establish the penal codes that set forth the sentences judges may impose. These laws generally give judges discretion in sentencing. Judges may combine various forms of punishment in order to tailor the sanction to the offender. The judge may specify, for example, that the prison terms for two charges are to run either concurrently (at the same time) or consecutively (one after the other), or that all or part of the period of imprisonment may be suspended. In other situations, the offender may receive a combination of a suspended prison term, probation, and a fine. Judges may also suspend a sentence as long as the offender stays out of trouble, makes restitution, or seeks medical treatment. They may also delay imposing any sentence but retain power to set penalties at a later date if the offender misbehaves.

When a judge gazes at a defendant and pronounces sentence, what thinking has gone into his or her decision? Within the discretion allowed by the code, various elements in the sentencing process influence the decisions of judges. In the Focus box, Judge Robert Satter relates some of the difficulties of sentencing. Social scientists believe several factors influence the sentencing process: (1) the administrative context of the courts, (2) the attitudes and values of judges, (3) the presentence report, and (4) sentencing guidelines.

The Administrative Context

The administrative context within which judges impose sentences greatly influence their decisions. As a result, we can find differences, for example, between the assembly-line style of justice in the misdemeanor courts and the more-formal proceedings found in felony courts.

MISDEMEANOR COURT: ASSEMBLY-LINE JUSTICE ■ Misdemeanor or lower courts have limited jurisdiction because they normally can only impose prison sentences of less than one year. These courts hear about 90 percent of criminal cases.

FOCUS ON PEOPLE IN CORRECTIONS

A Trial Judge at Work: Judge Robert Satter

I am never more conscious of striving to balance the scales of justice than when I am sentencing the convicted. On one scale is society, violated by a crime, on the other is the defendant, fallible, but nonetheless human . . .

George Edwards was tried before me for sexual assault, first degree. The victim, Barbara Babson, was a personable woman in her late twenties and a junior executive in an insurance company. She described on the stand what had happened to her:

I was returning to my Hartford apartment with two armloads of groceries. As I entered the elevator, a man followed me. He seemed vaguely familiar but I couldn't quite place him. When I reached my floor and started to open my door, I noticed him behind me. He offered to hold my bags. God, I knew right then I was making a mistake. He pushed me into the apartment and slammed the door. He said, "Don't you know me? I work at Travelers with you." Then I remembered him in the cafeteria and I remembered him once staring at me. Now I could feel his eyes roving over my body, and I heard him say, "I want to screw you." He said it so calmly at first, I didn't believe him. I tried to talk him out of it. When he grabbed my neck, I began to cry and then to scream. His grip tightened, and that really scared me. He forced me into the bedroom, made me take off my clothes.

"Then," she sobbed, "he pushed my legs apart and entered me."

"What happened next?" the state's attorney asked.

He told me he was going to wait in the next room, and if I tried to leave he would kill me. I found some [pieces of] cardboard, wrote HELP! on them, and put them in my window. But nobody came. Eventually I got up the courage to open the door, and he had left. I immediately called the police.

Edwards's lawyer cross-examined her vigorously, dragging her through the intimate details of her sex life. Then he tried to get her to admit that she had willingly participated in sex with the defendant. . . .

Edwards took the stand in his own defense. A tall man with bushy hair, he was wearing baggy trousers and a rumpled shirt. In a low voice he testified that the woman had always smiled at him at work. He had learned her name and

address and gone to her apartment house that day. When he offered to help her with her bundles, she invited him into her apartment. She was very nice and very willing to have sex. He denied using force. I did not believe him. I could not conceive that Miss Babson would have called the police, pressed the charges, and relived the horrors of the experience on the stand if the crime had not been committed as she testified. The jury did not believe him either. They readily returned a verdict of guilty. First-degree sexual assault is a class B felony punishable by a maximum of twenty years in the state prison. If I had sentenced Edwards then, I would have sent him to prison for many years. But sentencing could take place only after a presentence report had been prepared by a probation officer. . . .

Before the rescheduled date, I had weighed the factors, made up my mind, and lived with my decision for several days. In serious criminal cases I do not like to make [a] snap judgment from the bench. I may sometimes allow myself to be persuaded by the lawyers' arguments to reduce a preconceived sentence, but never to raise it. . . .

I gaze out the courtroom window, struggling for the words to express my sentence. I am always conscious that the same sentence can be given in a way that arouses grudging acceptance or deep hostility.

Mr. Edwards, you have committed a serious crime. I am not going to punish you to set an example for others, because you should not be held responsible for the incidence of crime in our society. I am going to punish you because, as a mature person, you must pay a price for your offense. The state's attorney asks for twenty years because of the gravity of the crime. Your attorney asks for a suspended sentence because you are attempting to deal with whatever within you caused you to commit the crime. Both make valid arguments. I am partially adopting both recommendations. I herewith sentence you to state prison for six years.

Edwards wilts. His wife gasps. I continue.

However, I am suspending execution after four years. I am placing you on probation for the two-year balance of your term on the condition that you continue in psychiatric treatment until discharged by your doctor. The state is entitled to punish you for the crime that you have committed and the harm you have done. You are entitled to leniency for what I discern to be the sincere effort you are making to help yourself.

Edwards turns to his wife, who rushes up to embrace him. Miss Babson nods to me, not angrily, I think. She walks out of the courtroom and back into her life. As I rise at the bench, a sheriff is leading Edwards down the stairwell to the lockup.

Did Judge Satter strike the appropriate balance in this case? If you were judging this case, how would you sentence Edwards? What facts from the case would consider when making your decision?

Source: Robert Satter, *Doing Justice: A Trial Judge at Work* (New York: Simon & Schuster, 1990), 170–181. Copyright © 1990 by Robert Satter. Reprinted by permission of the author.

Whereas felony cases are processed in lower courts only for arraignments and preliminary hearings, misdemeanor cases are processed completely in the lower courts. Only a minority of cases adjudicated in lower courts end in jail sentences. Most cases result in fines, probation, community service, restitution, or a combination of these punishments.

Many lower courts are overloaded and allocate minimal time to each case. Judicial decisions here are mass-produced because actors in the system share three assumptions. First, any person appearing before the court is guilty, because the police and prosecution have presumably filtered out doubtful cases. Second, the vast majority of defendants will plead guilty. Third, those charged with minor offenses will be processed in volume, with dozens of cases being decided in rapid succession within a single hour. The citation will be read by the clerk, a guilty plea entered, and the sentence pronounced by the judge for one defendant after another.

Defendants whose cases are processed through the lower-court assembly line may seem to receive little or no punishment. However, people who get caught in the criminal justice system experience other punishments, whether or not they are ultimately convicted. Time spent in jail awaiting trial, the cost of a bail bond, and days of work lost make an immediate and concrete impact. Poor people may even lose their jobs or be evicted from their homes if they fail to work and pay their bills for just a few days. For most people, simply being arrested is devastating. Measuring the psychological and social price of being stigmatized, separated from family, and deprived of freedom is impossible.[47]

FELONY COURTS ■ Felony cases are processed and offenders are sentenced in courts of general jurisdiction. Because of the seriousness of the crimes, the atmosphere is more formal and generally lacks the chaotic, assembly-line environment of misdemeanor courts. Caseload burdens can affect how much time is devoted to individual cases. Exchange relationships among courtroom actors can facilitate plea bargains and shape the content of prosecutors' sentencing recommendations. That is, sentencing decisions are ultimately shaped, in part, by the relationships, negotiations, and agreements among the prosecutor, defense attorney, and judge. **Table 4.3** shows the types of felony sentences imposed for different offense classifications.

Attitudes and Values of Judges

All lawyers recognize that judges differ from one another in their sentencing decisions. The differences can be explained in part by the conflicting goals of criminal justice, by administrative pressures, and by the influence of community values. Sentencing decisions also depend on judges' attitudes about the offender's blameworthiness, the protection of the community, and the practical implications of the sentence.[48]

Blameworthiness concerns such factors as offense severity (such as violent crime or property crime), the offender's criminal history (such as recidivist or first timer),

TABLE 4.3 *Types of Felony Sentences Imposed by State Courts*

Note that although we often equate a felony conviction with a sentence to prison, well over a fourth of felony offenders receive probation.			
Most Serious Conviction Offense	**Prison**	**Jail**	**Probation**
All offenses	40%	30%	28%
Violent offenses	54	24	20
Property offenses	37	31	30
Drug offenses	37	30	30
Weapon offenses	44	28	27
Other offenses	34	35	29

Source: Bureau of Justice Statistics, *Felony Sentences in State Courts, 2004* (Washington, DC: U.S. Government Printing Office, July 2007), 4.

and role in commission of the crime (such as leader or follower). For example, a judge might impose a harsh sentence on a repeat offender who organized others to commit a serious crime.

Protection of the community is influenced by similar factors such as dangerousness, recidivism, and offense severity. However, it focuses mostly on the need to incapacitate the offender or to deter would-be offenders.

Finally, the practicality of a sentence can affect judges' decisions. For example, judges may take into account the offender's ability to "do time," as in the case of an elderly person. They may also consider the impact on the offender's family; a mother with children may call for a different sentence than a single woman would. Finally, costs to the corrections system may play a role in sentencing, as judges consider the size of probation caseloads or prison crowding.[49]

The Presentence Report

Even though sentencing remains the judge's responsibility, the **presentence report** is an important ingredient in the judicial mix. Usually a probation officer investigates the convicted person's background, criminal record, job status, and mental condition to suggest a sentence that is in the interests of both the offender and society. Although the presentence report serves primarily to help the judge select the sentence, it also helps in the classification of probationers, prisoners, and parolees for treatment planning and risk assessment. In the report, the probation officer makes judgments about what information to include and what conclusions to draw from that information. In some states, however, probation officers present only factual material to the judge and make no sentencing recommendation. Because the probation officer does not necessarily follow evidentiary rules, presentence reports include hearsay statements as well as firsthand information. (See Chapter 8 for an example of a presentence report.)

Although presentence reports are represented as diagnostic evaluations, critics point out that they are not scientific and often reflect stereotypes. John Rosecrance argues that in practice the presentence report primarily serves to maintain the myth of individualized justice. He found that the present offense and the prior criminal record determine the probation officer's final sentencing recommendation.[50] He learned that officers begin by reviewing the case and typing the defendant as one who should fit into a particular sentencing category. Investigations are then conducted mainly to gather further information to support their early decision.

The presentence report is one means by which judges ease the strain of decision making. The report lets judges shift partial responsibility to the probation department. Because a substantial number of sentencing alternatives are available to judges, they

presentence report
Report prepared by a probation officer, who investigates a convicted offender's background to help the judge select an appropriate sentence.

The history of the **presentence investigation report** is found at the corresponding link at www.cengage.com/criminaljustice/clear.

Seated in her chambers, Judge Carla Tolle read the presentence investigation report of the two young men she would sentence when court resumed. She had not heard these cases. As often happened in this overworked courthouse, the cases had been given to her only for sentencing. Judge Mark Krug had handled the arraignment, plea, and trial.

The codefendants had held up a convenience store in the early morning hours, terrorizing the young manager and taking $47.50 from the till. As she read the reports, Judge Tolle noticed that they looked pretty similar. Each offender had dropped out of high school, had held a series of low-wage jobs, and had one prior conviction for which probation had been imposed. Each had been convicted of Burglary 1, robbery at night with a gun.

Then she noticed the difference. David Breen had pleaded guilty to the charge in exchange for a promise

of leniency. Richard Lane had been convicted on the same charge after a one-week trial. Judge Tolle pondered the decisions that she would soon have to make. Should Lane receive a stiffer sentence because he had taken the court's time and resources? Did she have an obligation to impose the light sentence recommended for Breen by the prosecutor and the defender?

There was a knock on the door. The bailiff stuck his head in. "Everything's ready, Your Honor."

"Okay, Ben, let's go."

WRITING ASSIGNMENT: Put yourself in Judge Tolle's shoes and render a decision in the Breen and Lane cases. First, provide your sentencing decision. Next, discuss the factors that you considered during the decision-making process. Finally, explain which factors influenced you the most and why.

often rely on the report for guidance. But two questions often arise: (1) Should judges rely so much on the presentence report? and (2) Does the time spent preparing it represent the best use of probation officers' time? "Do the Right Thing" illustrates some of the difficulties faced by a judge who must impose a sentence with little more than the presentence report to consider.

Sentencing Guidelines

sentencing guidelines
An instrument developed for judges that indicates the usual sanctions given previously for particular offenses.

Since the 1980s, **sentencing guidelines** have been established in the federal courts and adopted or been considered in at least 20 states.[51] States that adopt guidelines do so in hopes of accomplishing various goals; these may include reducing disparity in sentencing for similar offenses, increasing and decreasing punishments for certain types of offenders and offenses, establishing truth-in-sentencing, reducing prison crowding, and making the sentencing process more rational.[52] Although statutes provide a variety of sentencing options for particular crimes, guidelines point the judge to more-specific actions that have been given previously in similar cases. The range of sentencing options provided for most offenses allows for the seriousness of the crime and the criminal history of an offender.[53] In some states guidelines are used for intermediate sanctions.[54]

Legislatures and, in some states and the federal government, commissions construct sentencing guidelines as a grid of two scores.[55] As shown in **Table 4.4**, one dimension relates to the seriousness of the offense, the other to the offender's criminal history. The offender score is obtained by totaling the points allocated to such factors as the number of juvenile, adult misdemeanor, and adult felony convictions; the number of times incarcerated; the status of the accused at the time of the last offense, whether on probation or parole or escaped from confinement; and employment status or educational achievement. Judges look at the grid to see what sentence should be imposed on a particular offender who has committed a specific offense. Judges may go outside of the guidelines if aggravating or mitigating circumstances exist; however, they must provide a written explanation of their reasons for doing so.[56]

TABLE 4.4 *Minnesota Sentencing Guidelines Grid (Presumptive Sentence Length in Months)*

The italicized numbers within the grid denote the range within which a judge may sentence without the sentence being deemed a departure. Offenders with no imprisonment felony sentences are subject to jail time according to law.

LESS SERIOUS ← → MORE SERIOUS

CRIMINAL HISTORY SCORE

	0	1	2	3	4	5	6 or more
Murder, second degree (intentional murder; drive-by shootings)	306 *261–367*	326 *278–391*	346 *295–415*	366 *312–439*	386 *329–363*	406 *346–480[a]*	426 *363–480[a]*
Murder, third degree Murder, second degree (unintentional murder)	150 *128–180*	165 *141–198*	180 *153–216*	195 *166–234*	210 *179–252*	225 *192–270*	240 *204–288*
Assault, first degree Controlled substance crime, first degree	86 *74–103*	98 *84–117*	110 *94–132*	122 *104–146*	134 *114–160*	146 *125–175*	158 *135–189*
Aggravated robbery, first degree Controlled substance crime, second degree	48 *41–57*	58 *50–69*	68 *58–81*	78 *67–93*	88 *75–105*	98 *84–117*	108 *92–129*
Felony DWI	36	42	48	54 *46–64*	60 *51–72*	66 *57–79*	72 *62–86*
Assault, second degree Felon in possession of a firearm	21	27	33	39 *34–46*	45 *39–54*	51 *44–61*	57 *49–68*
Residential burglary Simple robbery	18	23	28	33 *29–39*	38 *33–45*	43 *37–51*	48 *41–57*
Nonresidential burglary	12[b]	15	18	21	24 *21–28*	27 *23–32*	30 *26–36*
Theft crimes (over $2,500)	12[b]	13	15	17	19 *17–22*	21 *18–25*	23 *20–27*
Theft crimes ($2,500 or less) Check forgery ($200–$2,500)	12[b]	12[a]	13	15	17	19	21 *18–25*
Sale of simulated controlled substance	12[b]	12[a]	12[a]	13	15	17	19 *17–22*

Presumptive commitment to state imprisonment. First-degree murder is excluded from the guidelines by law and continues to be a mandatory life sentence.

■ Presumptive stayed sentence; at the discretion of the judge, up to a year in jail and/or other nonjail sanctions can be imposed as conditions of probation. However, certain offenses in this section of the grid always carry a presumptive commitment to state prison.

[a] M.S. § 244.09 requires the Sentencing Guidelines to provide a range of 15% downward and 20% upward from the presumptive sentence. However, because the statutory maximum sentence for these offenses is no more than 40 years, the range is capped at that number.

[b] One year and one day.

Sentencing guidelines are expected to be reviewed and modified periodically so that recent decisions will be included. Given that guidelines are constructed on the basis of past sentences, some critics argue that because the guidelines reflect only what has happened, they do not reform sentencing. Others question the choice of characteristics included in the offender scale and charge that some are used to mask racial criteria.[57] Paula Krautt found differences in drug-trafficking sentences

To see an essay by a DEA agent that weighs the **impacts of sentencing guidelines on federal drug offenders**, visit the corresponding link at www .cengage.com/criminaljustice/ clear.

The **U.S. Sentencing Commission** helps define punishments for federal offenses; visit them using the corresponding link at www .cengage.com/criminaljustice/ clear.

among federal district and circuit courts.[58] However, Lisa Stolzenberg and Stewart D'Alessio studied the Minnesota guidelines and found, compared with preguideline decisions, an 18 percent reduction in disparity for the prison/no prison outcome and a 60 percent reduction in disparity of length of prison sentences.[59] Then again, Brian Johnson found that when judges departed from the sentencing guidelines, disparities were revealed that were based not only on race and ethnicity but also on the mode of conviction.[60]

One impact of guidelines is that sentencing discretion has shifted from the judge to the prosecutor.[61] The ability of prosecutors to choose the charge and to plea bargain has affected the accused: They now realize that they must plead guilty and cooperate in order to avoid the harsh sentences specified for some crimes (such as crack cocaine possession or operating a continuing criminal enterprise). In fact, federal drug laws give prosecutors discretion to ask judges to give sentence reductions for offenders who have provided "substantial assistance in the investigation or prosecution of another person."

Sentencing guidelines have led to the development of a rich body of appellate case law.[62] Until the advent of guidelines, the right of defendants or prosecutors to appeal the terms of a sentence was limited. Challenges of judicial interpretations of the guidelines have now increased so that a common law of sentencing is developing. In most states, either party may appeal any departures from the guidelines. For example, if the guidelines call for a 36-month prison sentence and the judge imposes 60 months, the defendant can appeal.[63] Whereas in 1975 virtually all appeals challenged only the conviction, today sentencing issues may be the sole or primary basis in about half of the cases appealed.[64]

Although guidelines make sentences more uniform, many judges object to having their discretion limited in this manner. For example, many federal judges objected to legislation signed by President George Bush in April 2003 limiting the power of judges to hand down a lesser sentence than called for in the guidelines.[65] Speaking before the American Bar Association in August 2003, Supreme Court Justice Anthony Kennedy said that the sentencing guidelines specify prison terms that are too long and called for the scrapping of mandatory minimum terms for some federal crimes.[66] Many scholars and judges view the U.S. Sentencing Commission Guidelines as impossibly complex, politically motivated, and unduly harsh.[67] Michael Tonry has called the guidelines "the most disliked sentencing reform initiative in the United States" in the twentieth century.[68] However, Peter Rossi and Richard Berk found a fair amount of agreement between the sentences prescribed in the guidelines and those desired by the general public.[69]

The Future of Sentencing Guidelines

On January 12, 2005, the Supreme Court transformed criminal sentencing by returning much of the discretion that was taken from federal judges in 1984 with the institution of sentencing guidelines. The Court presented its 5–4 decision, *United States v. Booker*, in two parts.[70] In the first part the justices said that the guidelines violated a defendant's rights to trial by jury, because judges had the power to make factual findings that increased sentences beyond the maximum that would be supported by the evidence presented to the jury. Freddie J. Booker had been convicted of intending to distribute at least 50 grams of cocaine base, for which the guidelines recommend a sentence of 20 to just over 22 years. The judge, however, imposed a 30-year sentence because he learned that Booker had distributed 10 times that amount of cocaine in the weeks prior to his arrest, a fact that had not been presented to the jury. The majority of the justices said that this violated the Sixth Amendment.

In the second part of the *Booker* decision, the justices said that the guidelines should be treated as discretionary rather than mandatory. Justice Breyer, writing for the majority in this portion of the decision, said that judges should consult the guidelines and take them into account. He said that the guidelines should be understood as being advisory and that they could be appealed for reasonableness. Some observers noted that judges would still rely heavily on the guidelines, while others said that such an advisory system would give federal trial judges more sentencing power than ever.[71]

The *Booker* case is the latest in a series of recent decisions that have thrown into doubt the constitutionality of the federal sentencing guidelines and those of many states. For most observers, it was the logical outcome of a line of legal development that began with *Apprendi v. New Jersey* (2000). In that case, the Supreme Court invalidated New Jersey's hate-crime statute, which increased the sentence for an ordinary crime if the judge found that the act was motivated by bias. The court said that, other than a previous conviction, "any fact that increases the penalty for a crime beyond the prescribed statutory maximum must be submitted to a jury and proved beyond a reasonable doubt."[72] Until the *Apprendi* decision, many state and federal drug indictments did not specify a quantity of drugs in the indictment, allowing the judge to include that information in calculating the sentence. Typically, drug laws impose a series of escalating sentences, depending on drug quantity. Questions were immediately asked about the constitutionality of these laws.

In June 2004 the Supreme Court, following the rationale established in *Apprendi*, struck down Washington State's sentencing guidelines (*Blakely v. Washington*), which permitted judges to enhance a defendant's sentence by using information that had not been proved beyond a reasonable doubt to a jury.[73] In this case, the judge added 37 months to the sentence for kidnapping; as justification, the judge cited "deliberate cruelty," a finding not supported by admissions in Blakely's plea bargain and not proved before the jury. Writing for the 5–4 majority, Justice Scalia said that this provision of the guidelines violates the right to trial by jury, because "the judge's authority to sentence derives wholly from the jury's verdict."[74] Quickly following the Court's announcement of the *Blakely* decision, several federal judges declared the federal sentencing guidelines to be unconstitutional.[75]

Although the *Booker* decision might seem to end federal and state guidelines, members of the House of Representatives and the Senate indicated that there would be a renewed struggle between the congressional and judicial branches regarding sentencing policies.[76] Conservatives have been highly critical of judges who have imposed sentences lighter than those called for in the guidelines, while liberals have argued that judges must have the discretion to tailor the punishment to fit the criminal and the crime. Sentencing guidelines and efforts to restrict the discretion of judges are not yet over.

Timothy Cole, sentenced in 1986 to 25 years in prison for a rape he did not commit, was exonerated in 2009. Cole died in prison in 1999. Appearing in court, his family asked that he be pardoned. Texas law does not deal with cases where the person to be pardoned is dead. Cole's family is rightfully frustrated.

AP Images/Harry Cabluck

■ UNJUST PUNISHMENT

Unjust punishment can occur because of sentencing disparities and wrongful convictions. The prison population in most states contains a higher proportion of African American and Hispanic men than appears in the general population. Are these sentencing disparities caused by racial prejudices and discrimination, or are other factors at work? Wrongful conviction occurs when an innocent person is nonetheless found guilty by plea or verdict. It also includes those cases in which the conviction of a truly guilty person is overturned on appeal because of due process errors.

Sentencing Disparities

sentencing disparity
Divergence in the lengths and types of sentences imposed for the same crime or for crimes of comparable seriousness when no reasonable justification can be discerned.

A central question is whether gender, racial, ethnic, or class sentencing disparity is the result of discrimination. **Sentencing disparity** occurs when widely divergent penalties are imposed on offenders with similar criminal histories who have committed the same offense, but when no reasonable justification can be discerned for the disparity. As shown in **Figure 4.4**, the average prison sentence length for white offenders is 58 months, compared with 63 months for African Americans. The most pronounced difference concerns violent offenses, where African American offenders, on average, are sentenced to longer periods than are whites—108 months versus 95 months.

In contrast, discrimination occurs when criminal justice officials either directly or indirectly treat someone differently because of their race, ethnicity, gender, or class. The fact that African Americans and Hispanics receive harsher punishments than do whites may simply mean that minorities happen to commit more-serious crimes than do whites; if true, this would account for the sentencing disparity. However, if officials singled out members of these groups for harsh punishment because of their race or ethnicity, that would be discrimination.

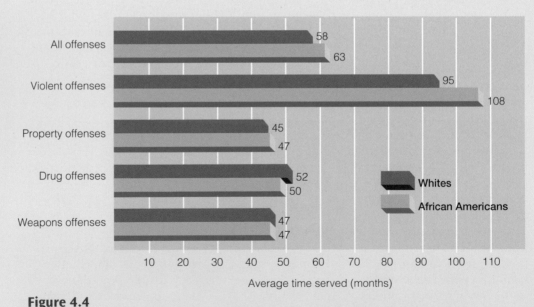

Figure 4.4

Average Length of Prison Sentence Imposed in State Court, by Offense

For many types of offenses, white and African American offenders receive prison sentences that are similar in terms of length. Why is there such a difference between racial groups in sentence length for violent offenses?

Source: Christopher Hartney and Linh Vuong, *Created Equal: Racial Disparities in the US Criminal Justice System* (Oakland, CA: National Council on Crime and Delinquency, March 2009), 14.

The research on racial disparities in sentencing has failed to produce consistent results. Studies of sentencing in Pennsylvania, for example, found that there is a "high cost of being black, young (21–29 years), and male." Sentences given these offenders resulted in a higher proportion going to prison and incurring longer terms.[77] A later analysis of Pennsylvania data, however, found that Hispanic defendants received the harshest penalties.[78] While supporting the Pennsylvania results, research in Chicago, Kansas City, Missouri, and Miami found variation among the jurisdictions as to sentence length.[79] A recent meta-analysis, conducted by Ojmarrh Mitchell, that included 71 published studies found evidence that racial disparities in sentencing are present in cases involving drug offenses and imprisonment. Mitchell concludes that the inconsistencies in sentencing disparity research are largely due to methodological factors.[80]

Do sentencing disparities stem from the prejudicial attitudes of judges, police officers, and prosecutors? Are African Americans and Hispanics viewed as a "racial threat" when they commit crimes of violence and drug selling, which are thought to be spreading from the urban ghetto to the "previously safe places of the suburbs"?[81] Are enforcement resources distributed so that certain groups are subject to closer scrutiny than are other groups?

Scholars have pointed out that the relationship between race and sentencing is complex and that judges consider many defendant and case characteristics. According to this view, judges assess not only the legally relevant factors of blameworthiness, dangerousness, and recidivism risk but also race, gender, and age characteristics. The interconnectedness of these variables, not judges' negative attitudes, is what culminates in the disproportionately severe sentences given to young African American men.[82] Laws dealing with the possession and sale of crack cocaine raise interesting questions regarding sentencing disparity and racial discrimination. (See the Focus box "Politics and Sentencing: The Case of Crack Cocaine.")

Wrongful Convictions

A serious dilemma for the criminal justice system concerns people who endure **wrongful conviction**. Whereas the public expresses much concern over those who "beat the system" and go free, people pay comparatively little attention to those who are innocent, yet convicted.

The development of DNA (deoxyribonucleic acid) technology has increased the number of people convicted by juries and later exonerated by science. This technology compares the DNA of the suspect with the DNA in biological substances found on the victim or at the crime scene. Tests conducted on 18,000 cases found that more than 25 percent of the prime suspects were excluded from prosecution prior to trial because there was no match.[83] The Innocence Project reports that, as of June 2009, there have been 238 criminal cases in which the convicted person was exonerated because of DNA evidence. Among the exonerated, 17 served time on death row. The average age at the time of the wrongful conviction was 26 years. The exonerees spent an average of 12 years in prison, which amounts to a total of 2,968 years for the group.[84]

In recent years the number of "innocence projects" has mushroomed nationally. These projects have played a key role in exonerating prisoners through DNA testing, pressing states to pass postconviction DNA statues, implementing videotaped interrogations in police departments, and reforming eyewitness identification procedures.[85]

In October 2004 Congress passed the Justice for All Act. This act includes funds to implement DNA testing on a nationwide backlog of more than 300,000 rape kits and other crime-scene evidence and ensures access to postconviction DNA testing for those serving time in prison.[86]

Why do wrongful convictions occur? Experts usually cite such factors as eyewitness error, unethical conduct by police and prosecutors, community pressure, false accusations, inadequacy of counsel, and plea-bargaining pressures. Beyond the fact that the real criminal is presumably still free in such cases, the standards of our society are damaged when an innocent person has been wrongfully convicted.

Visit the **Sentencing Project**, a major reform organization, using the corresponding link at www.cengage.com/criminaljustice/clear.

wrongful conviction
Occurs when an innocent person is found guilty by either plea or verdict.

You can learn more about the **Innocence Project** at the corresponding link at www.cengage.com/criminaljustice/clear.

FOCUS ON CORRECTIONAL POLICY

Politics and Sentencing: The Case of Crack Cocaine

In 1986 the American public first heard about crack cocaine. It was said to be extremely addictive and cheaper than the powdered form of cocaine. Citing the cocaine-induced death of Len Bias, an all-American basketball player and Boston Celtics draft choice, the media spread the fear that crack not only was the drug of choice in the ghetto but was being used by middle-class, suburban Americans.

To address this new problem, Congress passed the Anti-Drug Abuse Act in the fall of 1986. The new law specified that conviction for possession or distribution of 5 grams of crack cocaine (the weight of about two pennies) would mean a mandatory five-year sentence with no parole. Possession of greater amounts or operating a "continuing criminal enterprise" (drug trafficking) could lead to life sentences with no parole. At that time people did not notice that the crack penalty equaled a 100:1 ratio, compared with conviction for possession or distribution of the more-expensive powdered cocaine. In other words, before a powdered cocaine user or seller received a five-year sentence, he or she would have to possess 500 grams of the powdered substance.

The impact of the 1986 law was immediate. From 1988 to 1989, the number of drug offenders incarcerated shot up by more than 5,500, at the time the largest one-year increase ever recorded by the Federal Bureau of Prisons.

In 2008 nearly 20,000 federal prisoners were serving sentences for crack cocaine offenses. Approximately 82 percent of defendants sentenced in federal court for dealing crack were African American. The disparity between punishments for crack and powdered cocaine offenders soon became a major issue for African Americans.

After studying the issue of racial disparity, the U.S. Sentencing Commission recommended that the legal distinction be dropped and that the penalties be calibrated the same way, at the 100:1 ratio (100 grams of crack or powdered cocaine equals one year in prison). However, Congress and the Clinton administration rejected this recommendation.

In a recent case, *Kimbrough v. United States*, the Supreme Court ruled that federal judges could use discretion to shorten prison terms for offenders convicted of crack cocaine crimes. The ruling was intended to reduce the disparity between crimes involving crack and powdered cocaine. Federal efforts to reduce sentencing disparity were aided in March 2008 when new sentencing guidelines for crack cocaine went into effect. The new federal guidelines reduce the average sentence for crack possession from 10 years and 1 month to 8 years and 10 months. The law is retroactive, which means that it applies to all federal prisoners convicted under the old sentencing guidelines.

Does the new law adequately address the disparity between the sentences given in crack cocaine cases and those given in cases involving the powdered form of cocaine? Why did it take lawmakers so long to address this perceived injustice?

Sources: Joseph T. Hallinan, *Going Up the River* (New York: Random House, 2001), 44–45; *Kimbrough v. United States,* 522 U.S. 85 (2007); Bill Mears, "Justices: Judges Can Slash Crack Sentences," *CNN,* December 10, 2007, http://www.cnn.com/2007/US/law/12/10/scotus.crack.cocaine/index.html; Solomon Moore, "Rules Lower Prison Terms in Crack Cases," *New York Times,* November 2, 2007, http://www.nytimes.com/2007/11/02/us/02crack.html?hp; *New York Times,* October 24, 1995, p. A18; *Newsweek,* November 6, 1995, p. 81; "Thousands of Crack Sentences Being Reduced," *MSNBC.com,* March 3, 2008, http://www.msnbc.msn.com/id/23454471.

How many people are wrongfully convicted each year in the U.S.? This is a difficult question to answer. A recent study conducted by Robert Ramsey and James Frank asked criminal justice professionals (prosecutors, defense attorneys, judges, and police officers) to estimate how frequently wrongful convictions occur in felony cases. The results indicate that professionals believe such errors occur in 0.5 percent to 1 percent of felony cases in the legal jurisdiction in which they work, and in 1 percent to 3 percent of felony cases nationwide. These same people indicated that a wrongful conviction rate less than 0.5 percent was acceptable.[87]

How should the wrongfully convicted be compensated for the time they spent in prison? What is the value of a life unjustly spent behind bars? Increasingly, legislatures have had to face these questions. Several states and the federal government now have laws to provide compensation, but these laws vary widely in their definition of an appropriate payout. Virginia compensates the wrongly convicted at a rate of 90 percent of the state's annual per capita income—about $30,000 a year for up to 20 years of imprisonment. Alabama pays a minimum of $50,000 per year, while New Jersey provides up to $20,000 per year or twice the person's preprison salary, whichever is greater.

Money may provide some compensation, but as one lawyer from New York asks, "What's missing your child's first day of school worth? Not being with your parents as they lay dying? Having your parents go to their graves with you branded a convict?"[88] Compensation can be much higher when in the hands of a jury. In October 2006 a U.S. District Court jury awarded $9 million in damages to Alejandro Dominguez, who spent four years in prison after being wrongfully convicted because of the victim's false identification. After DNA evidence proved his innocence, Dominguez was pardoned, which made him eligible for $60,000 in compensation from the Illinois Court of Claims.[89]

Whether unjust punishments result from racial discrimination or wrongful conviction, they do not serve the ideals of justice. Unjust punishments raise fundamental questions about the criminal justice system and its links to the society it serves.

SUMMARY

1 Understand the goals of punishment.

In the U.S., criminal sanctions have four goals. Retribution (or deserved punishment) entails punishing an offender because they deserve to be penalized. Deterrence involves administering punishment to discourage members of the general public (general deterrence) and the criminal (specific deterrence) from committing future crimes. Incapacitation keeps the offender from committing future crimes by incarcerating them or putting them to death. Rehabilitation attempts to restore the convicted offender to a constructive place in society through the use of educational or vocational training or therapy.

2 Be familiar with the different forms of the criminal sanction.

Four forms of criminal sanction are used in the United States: incarceration, intermediate sanctions, probation, and death. Incarceration can take place in a jail or prison. A variety of sentencing structures are used (indeterminate, determinate, and mandatory). Intermediate sanctions are penalties that are severer than probation but less severe than incarceration. Judges use these sanctions in combination to reflect the severity of the crime, the characteristics of the offender, and the needs of the community. Probation is a sentence that the offender serves in the community. Conditions are imposed specifying how an offender is to behave throughout the sentence. If the conditions are not met, the supervising officer may recommend to the court that probation be revoked. Death is the least frequently used sanction. The death penalty may have more significance as a political symbol than as a deterrent to crime.

3 Explain how different factors affect the sentencing process.

Several factors influence the sentencing process. First, the administrative context of the courts play a role in sentencing. Misdemeanor courts are run like an assembly line. Because judges hear a large number of cases on a daily basis, they allocate minimal time to each case. In felony courts, the crimes are more serious and the proceedings are more formal. Second, sentencing decisions depend on judges' values and attitudes about the offender's blameworthiness, which includes such factors as the severity of the offense, the offender's criminal history, and the offender's role in commission of the crime. Third, the presentence report, which is usually prepared by a probation officer, provides background information about the offender that helps the judge select the sentence. Finally, sentencing guidelines provide judges with information on the usual sanctions given previously to particular offenses. Sentencing guidelines are intended to reduce disparity in sentencing offenders who commit similar crimes, establish truth-in-sentencing, and make the sentencing process more rational.

4 **Discuss the problem of unjust punishment.**

Unjust punishments can occur because of sentencing disparities and wrongful convictions. Sentencing disparity occurs when widely divergent penalties are imposed on offenders with similar criminal histories who have committed the same offense, but when no reasonable justification can be discerned for the disparity. Wrongful conviction occurs when an innocent person is found guilty by either plea or verdict. DNA evidence has helped exonerate innocent people who have been wrongly convicted. To create a system that is more just, reformers want to reduce sentencing disparities and wrongful convictions.

KEY TERMS

determinate sentence (p. 77)
general deterrence (p. 71)
good time (p. 79)
incapacitation (p. 72)
indeterminate sentence (p. 77)
intermediate sanctions (p. 81)
mandatory sentence (p. 78)

presentence report (p. 87)
presumptive sentence (p. 77)
probation (p. 81)
rehabilitation (p. 72)
restorative justice (p. 73)
retribution (p. 70)
selective incapacitation (p. 72)

sentencing disparity (p. 92)
sentencing guidelines (p. 88)
shock probation (p. 81)
specific deterrence (special or individual deterrence) (p. 71)
wrongful conviction (p. 93)

FOR DISCUSSION

1. Should one goal dominate how judges assign criminal sanctions? If not, how would you organize the different goals? By the amount of harm offenders cause? By offender criminal history? By some other factor?

2. Can all offenders be rehabilitated? What kinds of offenders are most likely to benefit from rehabilitation efforts? How should the corrections system deal with offenders who are difficult to rehabilitate?

3. How much discretion should judges, prosecutors, and parole board members have in administering the criminal sanction? Should one of these positions enjoy higher levels of discretion relative to the others? If yes, what justifies such a view?

4. Suppose you are a state lawmaker. What factors would influence your vote on how criminal sanctions should be used? What factors would you ignore?

5. How would you respond to the argument that individuals who are wrongfully convicted are simply casualties of the war on crime? How would you feel if your friend or relative was wrongfully convicted? If you had a friend who was exonerated of a crime he or she did not commit, what government compensation would be best?

FOR FURTHER READING

Domanick, Joe. *Cruel Justice: Three Strikes and the Politics of Crime in America's Golden State*. Berkeley, CA: University of California Press, 2004. Traces the events that led to the passage of California's three-strikes law and identifies the barriers that prevented subsequent attempts to revise the law.

Gould, Jon B. *The Innocence Commission: Preventing Wrongful Convictions and Restoring the Criminal Justice System*. New York: New York University Press, 2007. Examines 12 cases of wrongful conviction in Virginia and points to ways that similar mistakes can be avoided in the future.

Loury, Glenn C. *Race, Incarceration, and American Values*. Cambridge, MA: MIT Press, 2008. Presents the argument that the growing use of incarceration in the United States is not a result of rising crime rates, but instead a product of a generation-old decision to become more punitive as a society.

McLaughlin, Eugene, Ross Fergusson, Gordon Hughes, and Louis Westmareland, eds. *Restorative Justice: Critical Issues*. London: Sage, 2003. A collection of essays from well-known scholars that address conceptualizing, institutionalizing, and contesting restorative justice.

Spohn, Cassia C. *How Do Judges Decide? The Question for Fairness and Justice in Punishment*. 2nd ed. Thousand Oaks, CA: Sage, 2009. A comprehensive overview of punishment, the sentencing process, disparity in sentencing, and sentencing reform.

von Hirsch, Andrew. *Doing Justice*. New York: Hill & Wang, 1976. Represents the best statement of the "just deserts" model, with recommendations for implementing it.

NOTES

[1] "Victims at Madoff Sentencing Describe Agony of Losing Financial Security," http://www.chicagotribune.com, June 29, 2009.

[2] Robert Frank and Amir Efrati, "'Evil' Madoff Gets 150 Years in Epic Fraud," *Wall Street Journal*, http://online.wsj.com/article/SB124604151653862301.html, June 30, 2009.

[3] Jack Healy, "Madoff Is Sentenced to 150 Years for Ponzi Scheme," *New York Times*, http://www.nytimes.com/2009/06/30/business/30madoff.html?_r=1, June 30, 2009.

[4] Herbert L. Packer, *The Limits of the Criminal Sanction* (Stanford, CA: Stanford University Press, 1968), 33–34.

[5] Andrew von Hirsch, *Doing Justice* (New York: Hill & Wang, 1976), 49.

[6] Norval Morris, "Punishment, Desert, and Rehabilitation," in *Equal Justice under Law,* U.S. Department of Justice, Bicentennial Lecture Series (Washington, DC: U.S. Government Printing Office, 1977), 137–67.

[7] Travis C. Pratt, Francis T. Cullen, Kristie R. Blevins, Leah E. Daigle, and Tamara D. Madensen, "The Empirical Status of Deterrence Theory: A Meta-Analysis," in *Taking Stock: The Empirical Status of Criminological Theory—Advances in Criminological Theory,* vol. 15, edited by Francis T. Cullen, John Paul Wright, and Kristie R. Blevins (New Brunswick, NJ: Transaction, 2006), 367–95.

[8] Mark C. Stafford and Mark Warr, "A Reconceptualization of General and Specific Deterrence," *Journal of Research in Crime and Delinquency* 30 (May 1993): 123–35.

[9] Daniel S. Nagin, "Criminal Deterrence Research at the Outset of the Twenty-first Century," in *Crime and Justice: A Review of Research,* vol. 23, edited by Michael Tonry (Chicago: University of Chicago Press, 1998), 1–42.

[10] Todd R. Clear, *Harm in American Penology* (Albany: State University of New York Press, 1994), 103.

[11] Kathleen Auerhahn, "Selective Incapacitation and the Problem of Prediction," *Criminology* 37 (November 1999): 703–34.

[12] Robert Martinson, "What Works? Questions and Answers about Prison Reform," *Public Interest* 35 (Spring 1974): 25–54.

[13] Morris, "Punishment, Desert, and Rehabilitation."

[14] Brandon K. Applegate, Francis T. Cullen, and Bonnie S. Fisher, "Public Support for Correctional Treatment: The Continuing Appeal of the Rehabilitative Ideal," *Prison Journal* 77 (September 1997): 237–58.

[15] Francis T. Cullen, Edward J. Latessa, Velmer S. Burton, Jr., and Lucien X. Lombardo, "The Correctional Orientation of Prison Wardens: Is the Rehabilitative Ideal Supported?" *Criminology* 31 (February 1993): 69–92.

[16] John Braithwaite, *Restorative Justice and Responsive Regulation* (New York: Oxford University Press, 2002).

[17] Todd R. Clear and David R. Karp, *Community Justice Ideal: Preventing Crime and Achieving Justice* (Washington, DC: National Institute of Justice, 1999), 85.

[18] Leena Kurki, "Restorative and Community Justice in the United States," in *Crime and Justice: A Review of Research,* vol. 27, edited by Michael Tonry (Chicago: University of Chicago Press, 2000), 235–303.

[19] Nancy Rodriguez, "Restorative Justice at Work: Examining the Impact of Restorative Justice Resolutions on Juvenile Recidivism," *Crime and Delinquency* 53 (July 2007): 355–79.

[20] Lawrence W. Sherman and Heather Strang, *Restorative Justice: The Evidence* (London: Smith Institute, 2007), 8.

[21] Norval Morris and Michael Tonry, *Between Prison and Probation: Intermediate Punishments in a Rational Sentencing System* (New York: Oxford University Press, 1990).

[22] *Seeking Justice: Crime and Punishment in America* (New York: Edna McConnell Clark Foundation, 1997), 32–33.

[23] Michael Tonry, "The Fragmentation of Sentencing and Corrections in America," in *Sentencing and Corrections: Issues for the Twenty-first Century* (Washington, DC: National Institute of Justice, September 1999), 12.

[24] Bureau of Justice Statistics, *Probation and Parole in the United States, 2006* (Washington, DC: U.S. Government Printing Office, July 2008), 2.

[25] Although public opinion polls show high support for mandatory sentences in the abstract, support quickly diminishes when the questions present particular circumstances. See Brandon K. Applegate, Francis T. Cullen, Michael G. Turner, and Jody L. Sundt, "Assessing Public Support for Three-Strikes-and-You're-Out Laws: Global versus Specific Attitudes," *Crime and Delinquency* 42 (October 1996): 517–34.

[26] David Schultz, "No Joy in Mudville Tonight: The Impact of Three Strikes' Laws on State and Federal Corrections Policy, Resources, and Crime Control," *Cornell Journal of Law and Public Policy* 9 (2000): 557–83.

[27] Michael Vitiello, "Three Strikes: Can We Return to Rationality?" *Journal of Criminal Law and Criminology* 67 (Winter 1997): 395–463.

[28] Scott Ehlers, Vincent Schiraldi, and Jason Ziedenberg, *Still Striking Out: Ten Years of California's Three Strikes* (Washington, DC: Justice Policy Institute, September 2004).

[29] Kathleen Auerhahn, "Selective Incapacitation, Three Strikes, and the Problem of Aging Prison Populations: Using Simulated Modeling to See the Future," *Criminology and Public Policy* 1 (2002): 353–88; Ryan S. King and Marc Mauer, *Aging Behind Bars: "Three Strikes" Seven Years Later* (Washington, DC: The Sentencing Project, 2001), 4.

[30] Walter J. Dickey, "The Impact of 'Three Strikes and You're Out' Laws: What Have We Learned?" *Corrections Management Quarterly* 1 (Fall 1997): 55–64.

[31] John L. Worrall, "The Effect of Three-Strikes Legislation on Serious Crime in California," *Journal of Criminal Justice* 32 (July–August 2004): 283–96.

[32] *Lockyer, Attorney General of California v. Andrade,* 538 U.S. 63 (2003); *Ewing v. California,* 538 U.S. 11 (2003).

[33] Franklin E. Zimring, Gordon Hawkins, and Sam Kamin, *Punishment and Democracy: Three Strikes and You're Out in California* (New York: Oxford University Press, 2001), 219.

[34] Ibid., pp. 220–21.

[35] Charles Crawford, "Gender, Race, and Habitual Offender Sentencing in Florida," *Criminology* 38 (February 2000): 263–80; Human Rights Watch, *Punishment and Prejudice: Racial Disparities in the War on Drugs* (New York: Author, 2000).

[36] Michael Tonry, "Criminology, Mandatory Minimums, and Public Policy," *Criminology and Public Policy* 5 (February 2006): 54.

[37] Marc Mauer, "The Truth about Truth-in-Sentencing," *Corrections Today* 58 (February 1, 1996): 51–59.

[38] Steven R. Donziger, *The Real War on Crime: The Report of the National Criminal Justice Commission* (New York: Harper Perennial, 1996), 24. See also William J. Sobol, Katherine Rosich, et al., *The Influences of Truth in Sentencing on Changes in States' Sentencing Practices and Prison Populations* (Washington, DC: Urban Institute, 2002).

[39] Susan Turner, Peter W. Greenwood, Terry Fain, and James R. Chiesa, "An Evaluation of the Federal Government's Violent Offender Incarceration and Truth-in-Sentencing Incentive Grants," *Prison Journal* 86 (September 2006): 364–85.

[40] Morris and Tonry, *Between Prison and Probation*.

[41] Ibid.

[42] Bureau of Justice Statistics, *Probation and Parole*, p. 2.

[43] T. J. Keil and Gennaro F. Vito, "Fear of Crime and Attitudes toward Capital Punishment: A Structural Equations Model," *Justice Quarterly* 8 (December 1991): 447.

[44] Deborah Fins, *Death Row U.S.A.* (New York: NAACP Legal Defense and Educational Fund, Winter 2009), 1.

[45] Jeremy Travis, "Invisible Punishment: An Instrument of Social Exclusion," in *Invisible Punishment: The Collateral Consequences of Mass Imprisonment*, edited by Marc Mauer and Meda Chesney-Lind (New York: New Press, 2002), 17–18.

[46] Christopher Uggen, Angela Behrens, and Jeff Manza, "Criminal Disenfranchisement," *Annual Review of Law and Social Science* 1 (2005): 308; Christopher Uggen and Jeff Manza, *Locked Out: Felon Disenfranchisement and American Democracy* (New York: Oxford University Press, 2006).

[47] Malcolm M. Feeley, *The Process Is the Punishment* (New York: Russell Sage Foundation, 1979).

[48] Darrell Steffensmeier and Stephen Demuth, "Ethnicity and Judges' Sentencing Decisions: Hispanic-Black-White Comparisons," *Criminology* 39 (February 2001): 145–78.

[49] Darrell Steffensmeier, John Kramer, and Cathy Streifel, "Gender and Imprisonment Decisions," *Criminology* 31 (1993): 411.

[50] John Rosecrance, "Maintaining the Myth of Individualized Justice: Probation Presentence Reports," *Justice Quarterly* 5 (June 1988): 235.

[51] Kevin R. Reitz, "The Status of Sentencing Guidelines Reforms in the United States," in *Penal Reform in Overcrowded Times*, edited by Michael Tonry (New York: Oxford University Press, 2001), 31–33.

[52] U.S. Department of Justice, *Sentencing Guidelines: Reflections on the Future* (Washington, DC: U.S. Government Printing Office, June 2001), 2.

[53] Julian V. Roberts, "The Role of Criminal Record in the Sentencing Process," in *Crime and Justice: A Review of Research*, vol. 22, edited by Michael Tonry (Chicago: University of Chicago Press, 1997), 303–62.

[54] Michael Tonry, "Intermediate Sanctions in Sentencing Guidelines," in *Crime and Justice: A Review of Research*, vol. 23, edited by Michael Tonry (Chicago: University of Chicago Press, 1998), 199–253.

[55] Michael Tonry, "Sentencing Commissions and Their Guidelines," in *Crime and Justice: A Review of Research*, vol. 17, edited by Michael Tonry (Chicago: University of Chicago Press, 1993), 140–41.

[56] John H. Kramer and Jeffrey T. Ulmer, "Sentencing Disparity and Departures from Guidelines," *Justice Quarterly* 13 (March 1996): 81.

[57] Joan Petersilia and Susan Turner, "Guideline-Based Justice Prediction and Racial Minorities," in *Crime and Justice: A Review of Research*, vol. 15, edited by Norval Morris and Michael Tonry (Chicago: University of Chicago Press, 1987), 151–81.

[58] Paula Krautt, "Location, Location, Location: Interdistrict and Intercircuit Variation in Sentencing Outputs for Federal Drug-Trafficking Offenses," *Justice Quarterly* 19 (December 2002): 633–71.

[59] Lisa Stolzenberg and Stewart J. D'Alessio, "Sentencing and Unwarranted Disparity: An Empirical Assessment of the Long-Term Impact of Sentencing Guidelines in Minnesota," *Criminology* 32 (May 1994): 301–10.

[60] Brian D. Johnson, "Racial and Ethnic Disparities in Sentencing Departures across Modes of Conviction," *Criminology* 41 (May 2003): 449–90.

[61] John Wooldredge and Timothy Griffin, "Displaced Discretion under Ohio Sentencing Guidelines," *Journal of Criminal Justice* 33 (2005): 301.

[62] Richard S. Frase, "Sentencing Principles in Theory and Practice," in *Crime and Justice: A Review of Research*, vol. 22, edited by Michael Tonry (Chicago: University of Chicago Press, 1997), 398.

[63] Cassia Spohn, *How Do Judges Decide?* (Thousand Oaks, CA: Sage, 2002), 229.

[64] Joy A. Chapper and Roger A. Hanson, "Managing the Criminal Appeals Process," *State Court Journal* 12 (1988): 4; Roger A. Hanson, *Time on Appeal* (Williamsburg, VA: National Center for State Courts, 1996), 56.

[65] *New York Times*, December 8, 2003, p. A14.

[66] *Boston Globe*, August 10, 2003, p. A16.

[67] David J. Rothman, "The Crime of Punishment," *New York Review of Books*, February 17, 1994, pp. 34–38.

[68] Tonry, "Sentencing Commissions," 138.

[69] Peter H. Rossi and Richard A. Berk, *Just Punishments: Federal Guidelines and Public Views Compared* (New York: Aldine DeGruyter, 1997).

[70] *United States v. Booker*, 543 U.S. 220 (2005).

[71] Jan Crawford Greenburg, "High Court Voids Mandatory Sentencing in Federal Courts," *Chicago Tribune*, January 13, 2005, p. 1.

[72] *Apprendi v. New Jersey*, 500 U.S. 466 (2000).

[73] *Blakely v. Washington*, 124 S. Ct. 2531 (2004).

[74] Linda Greenhouse, "Justices in 5–4 Vote, Raise Doubts on Sentencing Rules," *New York Times*, June 26, 2004, p. 1.

[75] Adam Liptak, "U.S. Judge Overturns Guidelines for Sentences," *New York Times*, June 30, 2004, p. A12.

[76] Carl Hulse and Adam Liptak, "New Fight over Controlling Punishments Is Widely Seen," *New York Times*, January 13, 2005, p. A29.

[77] Darrell Steffensmeier, Jeffery Ulmer, and John Kramer, "The Interaction of Race, Gender, and Age in Criminal Sentencing: The Punishment Cost of Being Young, Black, and Male," *Criminology* 36 (November 1998): 789.

[78] Steffensmeier and Demuth, "Ethnicity and Judges' Sentencing Decisions."

79 Cassia Spohn and David Holleran, "The Imprisonment Penalty Paid by Young, Unemployed Black and Hispanic Male Offenders," *Criminology* 38 (February 2000): 281–306.

80 Ojmarrh Mitchell, "A Meta-Analysis of Race and Sentencing Research: Explaining the Inconsistencies," *Journal of Quantitative Criminology* 21 (December 2005): 439–66.

81 Charles Crawford, Ted Chiricos, and Gary Kleck, "Race, Racial Threat, and Sentencing of Habitual Offenders," *Criminology* 36 (August 1998): 502.

82 Samuel Walker, Cassia Spohn, and Miriam DeLone, *The Color of Justice* (Belmont, CA: Wadsworth, 1996), 154.

83 C. Ronald Huff, "Wrongful Conviction and Public Policy: The American Society of Criminology Presidential Address," *Criminology* 40 (2002): 1–18.

84 See http://www.innocenceproject.org, June 6, 2009.

85 Tresa Baldas, "Exoneration as a Cottage Industry," *National Law Journal*, http://www.nlada.org/DMS/Documents/1096991865.88/PubArticleNLJ.jsp%3Fid%3D1096473926982, October 4, 2004.

86 "Anti-Crime Legislation Passes Congress," http://www.CJReform.org, October 9, 2004.

87 Robert J. Ramsey and James Frank, "Wrongful Conviction: Perceptions of Criminal Justice Professionals Regarding the Frequency of Wrongful Conviction and the Extent of Systematic Errors," *Crime and Delinquency* 53 (July 2007): 436–70.

88 Christian Davenport, "Putting Price on Time of Wrongful Conviction," *Boston Sunday Globe*, October 10, 2004, p. 4.

89 Michelle Tsai, "18 Years in Prison? Priceless," http://www.Slate.com/id/2166483, May 18, 2007.

AP Images/Tomas van Houtryve

An alleged unlawful enemy combatant is escorted through Camp X-Ray, the government's detention center in Guantanamo Bay, Cuba. The legal status of these detainees and their rights under the U.S. Constitution have generated a great deal of controversy.

LEARNING OBJECTIVES

After reading this chapter you should be able to . . .

1 Discuss the foundations that support the legal rights of prisoners.

2 Explain the role of the U.S. Supreme Court in interpreting correctional law.

3 Understand the constitutional rights of prisoners.

4 Be familiar with the alternatives to litigation.

5 Explain the rights of offenders under community supervision.

6 Discuss how the law affects correctional personnel.

ON OCTOBER 17, 2006, President George Bush signed the Military Commissions Act (MCA) into law at a White House ceremony. Supporters viewed the MCA as an important tool in the war on terror that, among other things, eliminated the ability of "unlawful enemy combatants" to file a writ of habeas corpus in U.S. federal courts.[1] Within hours of the MCA becoming law, lawyers from the Justice Department notified the federal courts that they no longer had jurisdiction over the writs filed by Guantanamo Bay prisoners.

A writ of habeas corpus is a legal device that allows detained individuals to request an evidentiary hearing so that a judge can examine the legality of their confinement in a jail, prison, or mental hospital. Habeas corpus has a long tradition in common-law countries that predates American independence. According to Eric Freedman, a law professor at Hofstra University, habeas corpus was "established by the prisoners who were tossed into the Tower of London by the king, and it was preserved in the Constitution."[2] Article III, Section 9 of the U.S. Constitution reads, "The privilege of the writ of habeas corpus shall not be suspended, unless when in a case of rebellion or invasion the public safety may require it." Civil libertarians argue that 9/11 and the war on terror do not meet these criteria.

THE LAW OF CORRECTIONS

What troubled many civil libertarians was the ambiguity of the definition of an "unlawful enemy combatant." Michael Dorf, a Columbia University law professor, noted that the MCA could allow the "government to declare a permanent resident alien—including someone who has been residing lawfully in the United States for decades—to be an enemy combatant, and lock him up, potentially forever . . . never [allowing him] an opportunity to challenge his detention or treatment in a U.S. court."[3]

For many Americans, the idea that enemy combatants can challenge their imprisonment in U.S. military detention facilities seems absurd. They believe that prisoners of the war on terror do not have the same rights as American citizens. For others, however, placing limits on the use of habeas corpus is a very serious matter to be undertaken only under extraordinary circumstances, and the war on terror does not rise to this level of seriousness. Many legal experts believed the Supreme Court would eventually rule that the MCA's restriction of habeas corpus petitions was unconstitutional. On June 12, 2008, the experts proved to be correct. In *Boumediene v. Bush,* the Court ruled that the detainees at Guantanamo Bay are entitled to file writs of habeas corpus and challenge their confinement before civilian judges.[4]

It is reasonable to ask where future restrictions on habeas petitions might be targeted. These petitions can be used to address issues related to the legality of confinement, including individuals held in police custody without being charged with a crime, individuals awaiting

Chapter

5

trial who believe their bail is excessive, and prisoners who remain incarcerated past the expiration of their sentence. In 2007 more than 22,000 state and federal prisoners filed habeas petitions.[5]

Since the late 1960s federal and state courts have become increasingly involved in correctional matters other than habeas petitions. Although much of correctional law concerns claims by inmates that their rights have been violated, judges have also insisted that the due process rights of probationers and parolees be upheld. In some jurisdictions, the courts have declared entire corrections systems to be operating in ways that violate the Constitution. The courts have also ruled on claims by correctional personnel regarding employment discrimination, affirmative action, collective bargaining, and liability for job-related action.

In this chapter, we examine the legal foundations on which correctional law is based, analyze the constitutional rights of offenders, and explore the rights and liabilities of correctional personnel.

THE FOUNDATIONS OF CORRECTIONAL LAW

Four foundations support the legal rights of individuals under correctional supervision: (1) constitutions, (2) statutes, (3) case law, and (4) regulations. Most correctional litigation has involved rights claimed under the U.S. Constitution. State constitutions generally parallel the U.S. Constitution but sometimes confer other rights. Legislatures are of course free to grant additional rights to offenders and to authorize correctional departments to adopt regulations that recognize those rights.

Constitutions

constitution
Fundamental law contained in a state or federal document that provides a design of government and lists basic rights for individuals.

Constitutions contain basic principles and procedural safeguards, and they describe the institutions of government (legislature, judiciary, and executive), the powers of government, and the rights of individuals. Constitutional rights are basic protections held by individuals against improper limitations of their freedom. For example, the first 10 amendments to the United States Constitution, together known as the Bill of Rights, provide protection against government actions that would violate basic rights and liberties. Several have a direct bearing on corrections because they uphold freedom of religion, association, and speech; limit unreasonable searches and seizures; require due process; and prohibit cruel and unusual punishments.

States have their own constitutions that parallel the U.S. Constitution and contain protections against state and local governments. During the early 1960s the U.S. Supreme Court decided to require state governments to respect most of the rights listed in the Bill of Rights. Before that time the Bill of Rights protected citizens only against actions of the federal government. As a result of Supreme Court decisions, the power of all government officials is limited by the U.S. Constitution and their own state constitution.

The courts of each state are empowered to declare correctional conditions and practices in violation of either the state or the federal constitution. While most state constitutions do not give offenders any greater rights than those granted by the U.S. Constitution, some do. For example, a California court has ruled that electronic surveillance of prisoners violates the privacy guarantees of state statutes; an Oregon court has ruled that the state constitutional guarantee against "unnecessary rigor" in correctional practices provides grounds to stop certain genital searches.[6] Rulings such as these would not likely have occurred if the cases had been tried in the federal courts.

When convicted of a crime, an individual does not lose all his or her constitutional rights. However, some rights may be limited when they are outweighed by legitimate government interests and when the restriction is reasonably related to those interests. The courts have recognized three specific interests as justifying some restrictions on the constitutional rights of prisoners: (1) the maintenance of institutional order, (2) the maintenance of institutional security, and (3) the rehabilitation of inmates. Thus, on a case-by-case basis, the courts must ask the following: Are proposed restrictions reasonably related to preserve these interests? Later in this chapter, we discuss specific amendments to the U.S. Constitution and decisions of the U.S. Supreme Court as they relate to prisoners' rights.

Statutes

Statutes are laws passed by legislatures at all levels of government. Within the powers granted, the U.S. Congress is responsible for statutes dealing with problems concerning the entire country. Thus, laws passed by Congress define federal crimes and punishments, allocate funds for criminal justice agencies of the national government, and authorize programs in pursuit of criminal justice policies. Each state legislature enacts laws that govern the acts of its governments (state and local) and individuals within their borders, and that appropriate funds for state agencies such as corrections. The penal codes of the national and state governments contain statutes defining criminal behavior.

statute
Law created by the people's elected representatives in legislatures.

Statutes are written in more-specific terms than are constitutions. Courts nonetheless must often interpret the meaning of terms and rule on the legislature's original intention. For example, in 1998 the Supreme Court was asked to rule whether the Americans with Disabilities Act of 1990 applied to state prisoners. The case, brought by a Pennsylvania offender, was opposed by most states. In a unanimous decision, the Court said that "the statute's language unmistakably includes state prisons and prisoners within its coverage."[7]

State legislatures may grant specific rights to inmates beyond those conferred by the state constitutions or the U.S. Constitution. Some state laws have created "liberty interests" that cannot be denied without due process of law. Some states also have enacted "right-to-treatment" legislation and other statutes that charge correctional officials with particular duties. Prisoners may sue officials who fail to fulfill their statutory duties and obligations. If such claims are upheld, inmates may be entitled to collect monetary damages from the responsible officials and/or to receive a court ruling ordering a practice stopped.

Case Law

Court decisions, often called **case law**, are a third foundation of correctional law. The United States operates under a common-law system in which judges create law or modify existing law when they rule in specific cases. In deciding the cases presented to them, U.S. judges are guided by constitutional provisions, statutes, and decisions in other cases. These prior rulings, also known as **precedent**, establish legal principles used in making decisions on similar cases. When such a case arises, the judge looks to the principles arising from earlier rulings and applies them to the case being decided. The judges' ability to adjust legal principles when new kinds of situations arise makes the common law, or case law, flexible so as to respond to changes in society.

case law
Legal rules produced by judges' decisions.

precedent
Legal rules created in judges' decisions that serve to guide the decisions of other judges in subsequent similar cases.

As we have noted, constitutions often have phrases that lack clear, definite meanings. Consider, for example, the Eighth Amendment's phrase "cruel and unusual punishments," which judges have had to interpret in various cases. In the Florida case of *Ford v. Wainwright* (1986), the U.S. Supreme Court was asked to consider whether it was cruel and unusual punishment to execute an offender who became mentally ill while incarcerated. In his opinion for the Court, Justice Thurgood Marshall concluded that the Eighth Amendment prohibits the state from executing a prisoner who is insane.

He said that, in common law, executing an insane person has little retributive value, has no deterrence value, and simply offends humanity.[8] He also said that Florida's procedures for determining a prisoner's sanity were inadequate.

With this decision, *Ford v. Wainwright* became a precedent (and part of case law) that judges are to use when the execution of a mentally ill death row inmate is challenged. The decision also alerts states that their procedures for determining sanity should not resemble those of Florida.

Regulations

regulations
Legal rules, usually set by an agency of the executive branch, designed to implement in detail the policies of that agency.

Regulations are rules made by federal, state, and local administrative agencies. The legislature, president, or governor gives agencies the power to make detailed regulations governing specific policy in areas such as health, safety, and the environment.

A department of corrections may create regulations regarding the personal items prisoners may have in their cells, when prisoners can have visitors, how searches are to be carried out, the ways that disciplinary procedures will be conducted, and so forth. Often these regulations are challenged in court. For example, weekend visiting hours in some prisons are regulated so that half of the inmates are eligible for a visit on Saturday and the other half on Sunday. This is justified because of the great numbers who swamp the visiting area on weekends. However, a challenge to the regulation might be mounted by those who for religious reasons cannot travel on the designated day.

Regulations are a form of law that guides the behavior of correctional officials. They are often the basis of legal actions filed by prisoners and correctional employees, who may claim that the regulations violate constitutional protections or statues or that officials are not following the regulations.

■ CORRECTIONAL LAW AND THE U.S. SUPREME COURT

For most of U.S. history, the Bill of Rights was interpreted as protecting individuals only from acts of the federal government. These important constitutional rights were viewed as having no bearing on cases where citizens felt unjustly abused by state and local laws. This meant that the Bill of Rights had little influence over criminal justice, because the vast majority of cases are in state courts and corrections systems.

The Fourteenth Amendment, ratified in 1868, barred states from violating a person's right to "due process" and "equal protection" of the law. But not until the 1920s did the Court begin to name specific rights that the Fourteenth Amendment protected from infringement by states. Only during the 1960s, under the leadership of Chief Justice **Earl Warren,** did the Court begin to require that state officials abide by the specific provisions of the Bill of Rights.

hands-off policy
A judicial policy of noninterference concerning the internal administration of prisons.

Prior to the 1960s the courts maintained a **hands-off policy** with respect to corrections. Judges in some states applied their states' constitutions to correct abuses in jails and prisons. However, most judges followed the belief of the Virginia judge in *Ruffin v. Commonwealth* (1871) that prisoners did not have rights.[9] Judges also argued that the separation of powers among the three branches of government prevented them from interfering in the operations of any executive agency. Judges supposed that, because they were not penologists, their intervention in the internal administration of prisons would disrupt discipline.

EARL WARREN (1891–1974)

The 14th chief justice of the United States (1953–1969), Earl Warren began his public career in 1919 as the district attorney of Alameda County, California. He was elected California's attorney general in 1938 and governor in 1942, then twice reelected. President Dwight Eisenhower later appointed him as chief justice. Under his leadership, the Court enormously affected American law and provided support and impetus for significant social changes.

The End of the Hands-off Policy

Although prior to the 1960s individual state court judges occasionally ordered sheriffs and prison officials to change

© Dennis Brack/Landov

The Supreme Court of the United States has the final word on questions concerning interpretations of the Constitution. During the 1970s the Court ended the hands-off policy and greatly extended the rights of prisoners.

conditions and policies in specific correctional facilities, the U.S. Supreme Court decision in *Cooper v. Pate* (1964) signaled the end of the hands-off policy.[10] The court said that through the Civil Rights Act of 1871 (referred to here as Section 1983), state prisoners were *persons* whose rights are protected by the Constitution.[11] The act imposes **civil liability** on any person who deprives another of constitutional rights. It allows suits against state officials to be heard in the federal courts. Because of *Cooper v. Pate* the federal courts now recognize that prisoners may sue state officials over such things as brutality by guards, inadequate nutrition and medical care, theft of personal property, and the denial of basic rights.[12]

At the time, the federal courts were seen as being more likely to rule in the prisoner's favor than were the state courts.[13] As James Jacobs points out, "Just by opening a forum in which prisoners' grievances could be heard, the federal courts destroyed the custodian's absolute power and the prisoners' isolation from the larger society. And the litigation in itself heightened prisoners' consciousness and politicized them."[14]

Although Section 1983 is the most commonly used legal action to challenge prison and jail conditions, inmates may also seek relief filing a **habeas corpus** petition. As we saw at the beginning of the chapter, this is an ancient legal writ in which prisoners (or pretrial detainees) ask the courts to examine the legality of their imprisonment and ask for release from illegal confinement. In recent years the Supreme Court has issued several decisions limiting opportunities for prisoners to file habeas corpus petitions. In 1996 Congress passed the Anti-Terrorism Act, which imposes a one-year limit from the time of conviction to file a federal habeas petition. It also passed the Prison Litigation Reform Act, which makes filing lawsuits more difficult for prisoners, especially if they have previously had cases dismissed as frivolous. As was noted previously, the Military Commissions Act of 2006 restricts unlawful enemy combatants from filing habeas petitions. In 2008, however, the U.S. Supreme ruled that such restrictions were unconstitutional.[15] Fred Cheesman and his associates argue, however, that the number of state prisoners using the federal courts to challenge the validity of their convictions and the conditions of their confinement will continue to rise as the size of the incarcerated population also rises.[16]

The number of habeas corpus petitions filed in federal courts by federal prisoners decreased by 13 percent from 2006 to 2007. The number of habeas petitions filed by state inmates also decreased (19,195 in 2006 to 19,139 in 2007). **Figure 5.1** presents trends in prisoner habeas corpus petitions since 1966. Remember that prisoners filing habeas petitions are asking to be released from illegally imposed confinement, whereas

civil liability
Responsibility for the provision of monetary or other compensation awarded to a plaintiff in a civil action.

habeas corpus
A writ (judicial order) asking a person holding another person to produce the prisoner and to give reasons to justify continued confinement.

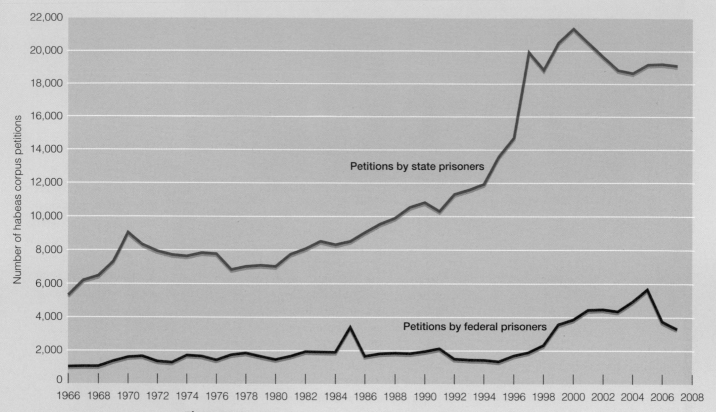

Figure 5.1

Trends in Prisoner Habeas Corpus Petitions Filed in U.S. District Courts

The higher number of habeas corpus petitions filed by state inmates is partially explained by the larger number of prisoners housed in state facilities compared with the number in federal institutions.

Sources: Bureau of Justice Statistics, *Sourcebook of Criminal Justice Statistics, 1977* (Washington, DC: U.S. Government Printing Office, 1978), Table 5.28; Ann L. Pastore and Kathleen Maguire, eds., *Sourcebook of Criminal Justice Statistics,* Table 5.65.2007, http://www.albany.edu/sourcebook/pdf/t5652007.pdf, June 15, 2009.

the Section 1983 civil rights cases seek improvements in prison conditions, return of property, or compensation for abuse by officers. But merely filing a case in court does not mean that it will be heard. A large number of Section 1983 cases are dismissed because the plaintiff did not follow the court's rules or because there was no evidence of a constitutional rights violation. Very few cases actually go to trial and are decided in favor of the prisoner.[17] The number of Section 1983 cases increased by approximately 11.6 percent from 2006 to 2007 for federal prisoners. During the same period, the number of Section 1983 cases also increased by nearly 1.2 percent for state inmates.[18]

Prisoner-inspired litigation skyrocketed after *Cooper v. Pate.* The number of suits brought by state prisoners in federal courts alone rose from 218 in 1966 to a high of 40,569 in 1995. Additional cases, of course, were filed in state courts. This onslaught of prisoner litigation drew criticism from correctional officials who said they spent time and resources responding to the suits, conservatives who opposed federal intervention in prison administration, and legislators who argued that judges should refrain from making public policy.[19]

Access to the Courts

Supreme Court decisions that eased prisoner access to the courts assisted this increase in filings. Until the 1970s many states limited communication between prisoners and their attorneys, prohibited jailhouse lawyers, and did not provide prison law libraries.

These limitations were imposed on the grounds of institutional security, but prisoners need access to the courts to ensure that officials have followed the law.

The leading case on access to courts is *Johnson v. Avery* (1969).[20] Johnson, a Tennessee inmate, was disciplined for violating a regulation prohibiting one inmate from assisting another with legal matters. The Supreme Court ruled that prisoners are entitled to receive legal assistance from other prisoners unless alternative resources are provided to help prepare necessary legal documents. However, the Court said that the prison could impose reasonable regulations on "jailhouse lawyers" in keeping with the need for order and security.

In a second case, *Bounds v. Smith* (1977), the Supreme Court extended the principle of prisoner access by addressing the question of law libraries. North Carolina had libraries in only seven of its 77 prisons. Inmates could be transported to a library for one day of legal research. The Court ruled that this was inadequate. It held that "the fundamental constitutional right of access to the courts requires prison authorities to assist inmates in the preparation and filing of meaningful legal papers by providing prisoners with adequate law libraries or adequate legal assistance from persons trained in the law."[21]

But is the mere presence of a law library enough to satisfy the constitutional needs of inmates for access to the courts? What did the Court in *Bounds* mean by "adequate legal assistance"? The Supreme Court addressed these questions in the 1996 case of *Lewis v. Casey.*[22] A lower federal court had held that the Arizona Department of Corrections was not providing adequate legal assistance to inmates. It ordered more training for library staff, updating of legal materials, photocopying services, better access to the library, and so forth. In its ruling the Court said that *Bounds* did not create an abstract, freestanding right to a law library or legal assistance but that inmates must show that the inadequacy of the library hindered efforts to pursue a legal claim.

The Prisoners' Rights Movement

As an outgrowth of the civil rights movement, organizations such as the NAACP's Legal Defense and Education Fund and the National Prison Project of the American Civil Liberties Union became concerned about prisoners' rights. In the climate of the times,

Supreme Court decisions, argument calendar, schedules, and visitor's guide are available at the corresponding link at www.cengage.com/criminaljustice/clear.

TM & Copyright © 20th Century Fox Film Corp./courtesy Everett Collection

The first prisoners' rights decisions by the U.S. Supreme Court concerned the most egregious violations of constitutional rights, such as the conditions at the Cummins Farm Unit of the Arkansas State Prison, as depicted in the film *Brubaker*.

PEOPLE IN CORRECTIONS

From a Lonely Prison Cell, an Inmate Wins an Important Victory

Somewhere in the bowels of Camp J of the Louisiana State Penitentiary at Angola, not far from where three guards kicked, punched and pummeled him, . . . prisoner No. 91888, Keith J. Hudson, may be savoring something few lawyers anywhere have known in recent years: He took a civil liberties case to the Supreme Court of the United States, and won.

By a vote of 7 to 2, the Justices agreed with Mr. Hudson that prison beatings can be unconstitutionally "cruel and unusual, even if they result only in split lips and bloody noses rather than concussions and broken bones." . . .

For the 32-year-old Mr. Hudson, the ruling was the culmination of nine years of legal work, in which he read precedents from the law books brought to his cell by prison messengers, and hunted and pecked his legal briefs on a portable typewriter. Mr. Hudson, serving a 20-year sentence for armed robbery, could not argue his case personally; that case was handled by Alvin Bronstein of the American Civil Liberties Union's national prison project.

In a handful of homemade documents, written in a patois of street talk and legalese, Mr. Hudson offered his version of events in the early morning of October 30, 1983.

The pummeling split his lip, broke his dental plate and left him "bleeding and swelling about the face and bruised about the body," Mr. Hudson wrote in a typewritten account dotted with misspellings, typos, fractured grammar and uneven margins. He said he quickly filed a complaint seeking "fifty thousand dollars" in damages and an order "to prohibit further crulity [sic] to myself and other inmates housed in Camp J."

At a hearing, Mr. Hudson produced and questioned two corroborating witnesses, cited his rights under the First, Eighth, and Fourteenth Amendments to the Constitution, recounted the guards' racist, crude, curse-ridden comments, and told the judge that he had suffered "not only mental and physical anguish but a permanent psychological scar for life." Convinced, the judge awarded Mr. Hudson $800 in damages. But, a three-judge panel of the Federal Court of Appeals for the Fifth Circuit reversed the decision. The judges concluded that the force the guards used was unreasonable, excessive, unnecessary, wanton—and constitutional. Mr. Hudson asked the Supreme Court to review the case.

In his typewritten petition, he contended that the appellate judges had misread the Constitution. "This ruling falls short, because of its negligence in also considering the *mental injury* sustained, which is more significant than physical damage," he ruled. The Court resoundingly agreed.

Source: David Margolick, "At the Bar," *New York Times*, March 6, 1992, p. B8. Copyright © 1992 by the New York Times Co. Reprinted by permission.

---

many groups placed legal protections for inmates high on their political agendas. It was no longer unheard-of for prisoners to sue wardens or commissioners of corrections. Efforts such as those of Keith Hudson often resulted in major changes in the law (see the Focus box "From a Lonely Prison Cell, an Inmate Wins an Important Victory").

The first successful prisoners' rights cases involved the most excessive prison abuses: brutality and inhuman physical conditions. In 1967, for example, the Supreme Court invalidated a Florida inmate's confession of rioting after he had been thrown naked into a "barren cage," filthy with human excrement, and kept there for 35 days.[23] The notorious Cummins Farm Unit of the Arkansas State Prison (depicted in the film *Brubaker*) was declared in violation of the Eighth Amendment by a federal district court in 1971. In that case the judge, noting that Arkansas relied on trusties (inmates who serve as "guards") for security and housed inmates in barracks, ruled that leaving them open to "frequent assaults, murder, rape, and homosexual conduct," was unconstitutional.[24]

By the end of the 1970s, federal judges had imposed changes on prisons and jails in nearly every state. In addition, important decisions were made requiring due process in probation and parole. By 1990 most of the worst abuses had been corrected, and judges stopped expanding the number and nature of prisoners' rights. As Malcolm Feeley and Edward Rubin note, "Over the course of a single decade, the federal courts fashioned a comprehensive set of judicially enforceable rules for the governance of American prisons."[25]

We have seen that over the past four decades, prisoners have pursued rights guaranteed in the U.S. Constitution by filing Section 1983 petitions (42 U.S.C. 1983) in the federal courts. They have asserted that civil rights found in the Bill of Rights have been violated. We now examine the case law that has evolved as the Supreme Court has considered inmate claims that their constitutional rights have been violated.

■ CONSTITUTIONAL RIGHTS OF PRISONERS

The rights applicable to inmates are essentially summarized in a handful of phrases in four of the amendments to the U.S. Constitution. Three of these—the First, Fourth, and Eighth Amendments—are part of the Bill of Rights. The fourth, the Fourteenth Amendment, became effective in 1868. In this section we present the text of these amendments and discuss rights under them in some detail.

Realize that constitutional rights are not absolute and may conflict with the broader needs of society. Courts must examine government rules to determine exactly which behaviors have been infringed on and which have not. The Supreme Court did not fully address these boundaries with regard to prisoners' rights until 1987. Lacking guidance from the higher courts, "lower courts developed a number of contradictory tests to resolve these cases."[26]

Some lower courts have held rules in conflict with First Amendment protections to be unconstitutional unless they were the **least restrictive method** of dealing with an institutional problem. For example, a court struck down the punishment of inmates for writing inflammatory political tracts, because officials could merely have confiscated the material.[27] Other courts have stated that a right may be limited if it interferes with a **compelling state interest** such as the goal of maintaining security. A rule prohibiting the receipt of nude photographs of wives and girlfriends was found unconstitutional. The court ruled that the right to receive such photographs was protected; however, because other inmates might be aroused by the sight of them, a rule against their display would have been proper as a security measure.[28] Limitations on the receipt of certain publications have also been upheld on the grounds that they present a **clear and present danger** "to the security of a prison, or to the rehabilitation of prisoners."[29]

With courts using different methods to distinguish constitutional from unconstitutional policies, the Supreme Court needs to set standards. Guidance for the lower courts was first enunciated in *Turner v. Safley* (1987), in which the Court upheld a Missouri ban on correspondence among inmates in different correctional institutions. Justice O'Connor, writing for a 5–4 majority, said that such a regulation was valid only if it was "reasonably related to legitimate penological interests."[30] She specified the four elements of the **rational basis test**:

1 There must be a rational connection between the regulation and the legitimate interest put forward to justify it.

2 There must be alternative means of exercising the right that remain open to prison inmates.

3 There must be a minimal impact of the regulation on correctional officers and other inmates.

4 There must be no less-restrictive alternative available.

This test is the current standard for the analysis of not only prisoners' First Amendment claims but other constitutional claims as well.[31]

The First Amendment

Amendment I: *Congress shall make no law respecting an establishment of religion, or prohibiting the free exercise thereof; or abridging the freedom of speech, or of the press; or the right of the people peaceably to assemble, and to petition the government for a redress of grievances.*

---

least restrictive methods
Means of ensuring a legitimate state interest (such as security) that impose fewer limits to prisoners' rights than do alternative means of securing that end.

compelling state interest
An interest of the state that must take precedence over rights guaranteed by the First Amendment.

clear and present danger
Any threat to security or to the safety of individuals that is so obvious and compelling that the need to counter it overrides the guarantees of the First Amendment.

rational basis test
Requires that a regulation provide a reasonable, rational method of advancing a legitimate institutional goal.

Since the 1940s, the Supreme Court has maintained that the First Amendment holds a special position in the Bill of Rights because it guarantees those freedoms essential in a democracy. Because of the preferred position of this amendment, it is not surprising that some of the early prisoners' rights cases concerned rights protected by it: access to reading materials, noncensorship of mail, and freedom of religious practice. **Table 5.1** shows some of the most significant cases decided under this amendment.

SPEECH ■ Since the 1970s, courts have extended the rights of freedom of speech and expression to prisoners, requiring correctional administrators to show why restrictions on these rights must be imposed. For example, in 1974 the Supreme Court ruled that censorship of mail was permissible only when officials could demonstrate a compelling government interest in maintaining security.[32] The result has been a marked increase in communications between inmates and the outside world. However, the decision in *Turner v. Safley* allowed Missouri to ban correspondence between inmates at different institutions as a means of combating prison gangs and communicating escape plans.[33] The Court reaffirmed this in 2001 when it said that regulations concerning mail among prisoners are valid if they meet the *Turner* test, without regard to whether the letters contain information relevant to a legal case.[34]

TABLE 5.1 *Selected Interpretations of the First Amendment as Applied to Prisoners*

The Supreme Court has made numerous decisions affecting prisoners' rights to freedom of speech and expression and freedom of religion.	
Case	**Decision**
Procunier v. Martinez (1974)	Censorship of mail is permitted only to the extent necessary to maintain prison security.
Turner v. Safley (1987)	Inmates do not have a right to receive mail from one another, and this mail can be banned if "reasonably related to legitimate penological interests."
Beard v. Banks (2006)	Prison policies that deny magazines, newspapers, and photographs to the most incorrigible inmates in the prison system in an effort to promote security and rule compliance are constitutional.
Fulwood v. Clemmer (1962)	The Muslim faith must be recognized as a religion, and officials may not restrict members from holding services.
Gittlemacker v. Prasse (1970)	The state must give inmates the opportunity to practice their religion but is not required to provide a member of the clergy.
Cruz v. Beto (1972)	Prisoners who adhere to other than conventional beliefs may not be denied the opportunity to practice their religion.
Kahane v. Carlson (1975)	An Orthodox Jewish inmate has the right to a diet consistent with his religious beliefs unless the government can show cause why it cannot be provided.
Theriault v. Carlson (1977)	The First Amendment does not protect so-called religions that are obvious shams, that tend to mock established institutions, and whose members lack religious sincerity.
O'Lone v. Estate of Shabazz (1987)	The rights of Muslim prisoners are not violated when work makes it impossible for them to attend religious services if no alternative exists.

The right of free speech also includes access to publications. Prisoners generally receive books and magazines only directly from the publisher. The Pennsylvania Department of Corrections (PDC) instituted a ban on such periodicals in their Long Term Segregation Unit, which requires inmates to remain in their cells 23 hours a day. PDC officials noted that doing so was necessary for rehabilitative and security purposes. They argued that depriving inmates of these materials provides an incentive for good behavior and helps improve security, because inmates cannot use such materials to start cell fires or use them to throw feces on unsuspecting officers. The Court said that the PDC's justifications were sufficient, and it noted the need to induce law-abiding behavior among the most difficult prisoners.[35]

RELIGION ■ The First Amendment prevents Congress from making laws respecting the establishment of religion or prohibiting its free exercise. Cases concerning the free exercise of religion have caused the judiciary some problems, especially when the practice in question may interfere with prison routine and the maintenance of order.

The growth of the Black Muslim religion in prisons set the stage for suits demanding that this group be granted the same privileges as other faiths (special diets, access to clergy and religious publications, and opportunities for group worship). In the 1960s many wardens believed the Muslims were a radical political group posing as a religion. They did not grant them the benefits extended to people who practiced conventional religions.

In an early case (*Fulwood v. Clemmer*, 1962), a federal court ruled that officials must recognize the Black Muslims as a religion and allow them to hold worship services as inmates of other faiths do. It did not accept the view that the Muslims posed a "clear and present danger."[36] In another religion case (*Cruz v. Beto*, 1972), the justices declared that a Buddhist prisoner must be given reasonable opportunities to practice his faith, like those given prisoners belonging to religions more commonly practiced in the United States.[37]

However, in *O'Lone v. Estate of Shabazz* (1987), the court ruled that a Muslim's free-exercise rights were not violated by prison officials who would not alter his work schedule so that he could attend Friday afternoon Jumu'ah services.[38] Shabazz's assignment took him outside the prison, and officials claimed that returning him for services would create a security risk. The justices ruled that the policy was related to a legitimate penological interest.

Muslim, Orthodox Jew, Native American, and other prisoners have gained some of the rights considered necessary for the practice of their religions. Court decisions have upheld prisoners' right to be served meals consistent with religious dietary laws, to correspond with religious leaders and possess religious literature, to wear a beard if one's belief requires it, and to assemble for services. In sum, members of religious minorities have broken new legal ground on First Amendment issues.

Religious freedom is a continuing issue, as seen in the Religious Freedom Restoration Act passed by Congress and signed into law by President Bill Clinton in 1993 (42 U.S.C. 2000bb). This legislation came in response to a 1990 Supreme Court decision, unrelated to corrections, upholding denial of unemployment compensation to two drug treatment counselors dismissed for using peyote during a Native American religious ceremony.[39] Religious leaders immediately became concerned that the Court had weakened First Amendment protections for believers. A broad coalition of groups pressured Congress to restore the requirement that the government must show a compelling interest before it can limit the free exercise of religion. The act seemed to have undermined the *Turner* and *Shabazz* decisions.[40] In 1997, however, the Supreme Court declared that Congress did not have the authority to enact such legislation (*City of Boerne v. Flores*).[41] To overcome the Court's objections, Congress passed the Religious Land Use and Institutionalized Persons Act in 2000. Although much of the litigation surrounding the act concerns land-use regulations and churches' use of their property (as in the *Flores* case), Section 3 prevents government from imposing "substantial burden on a person residing in or confined to an institution," such as prisoners. Cases about kosher diets, beards on Muslims, head coverings, and religious services have been heard in the lower federal courts, but the Supreme Court has yet to consider the constitutionality of the act.

Cornell Law School provides **U.S. Supreme Court opinions.** See the corresponding link at www.cengage.com/criminaljustice/clear.

You can learn more about the **Religious Land Use and Institutionalized Persons Act** at the corresponding link at www.cengage.com/criminaljustice/clear.

The Fourth Amendment

Amendment IV: *The right of the people to be secure in their persons, houses, papers, and effects, against unreasonable searches and seizures, shall not be violated, and no warrants shall issue but upon probable cause, supported by oath or affirmation, and particularly describing the place to be searched, and the persons or things to be seized.*

The Fourth Amendment was designed to protect areas of privacy from government intrusion such as searches. However, on entering a correctional institution, prisoners surrender most of their rights to privacy. The amendment prohibits only "unreasonable" searches and seizures. Thus regulations viewed as reasonable to maintain security and order in an institution may be justified.

Table 5.2 outlines some of the Supreme Court's Fourth Amendment opinions. They reveal the fine balance between the right to privacy and institutional need.

Two principal types of searches occur in prisons: searches of cells and searches of the person. In *Hudson v. Palmer* (1984), the Supreme Court made clear that the Fourth Amendment does not apply within the confines of the prison cell. However, the Court noted that this does not necessarily mean that prisoners have no protections against the harmful consequences of some searches. For example, if the inmate's property is damaged or destroyed, the prisoner may file a lawsuit against the correctional officers.[42]

Searches of the person may be conducted at different levels of intrusiveness: metal detectors, pat-down searches of clothed inmates, visual "strip" (nude) searches, and body cavity searches. Correctional administrators must craft regulations to demonstrate clearly that the level of intrusiveness is related to a legitimate institutional need and not conducted with the intent to humiliate or degrade.[43]

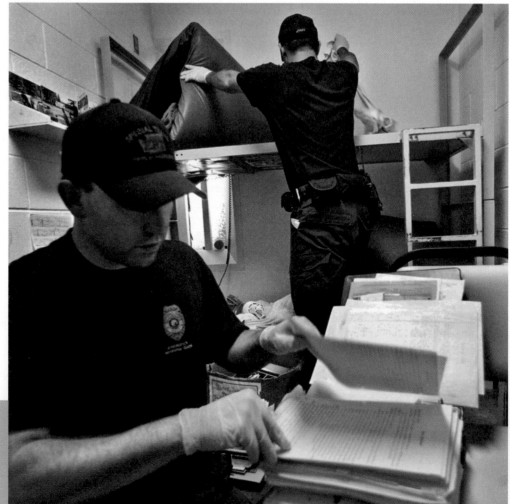

Correctional officers at McNeil Island Corrections Center in Washington conduct a search an inmate's cell for contraband. Do such searches violate the Fourth Amendment?

AP Images/The News Tribune, Drew Perine

TABLE 5.2 *Selected Interpretations of the Fourth Amendment as Applied to Prisoners*

The Supreme Court has often considered the question of unreasonable searches and seizures.	
Case	**Decision**
Lanza v. New York (1962)	Conversations recorded in a jail visitor's room are not protected by the Fourth Amendment.
U.S. v. Hitchcock (1972)	A warrantless search of a cell is not unreasonable, and documentary evidence found there is not subject to suppression in court. It is not reasonable to expect a prison cell to be accorded the same level of privacy as a home or automobile.
Bell v. Wolfish (1979)	Strip searches, including searches of body cavities after contact visits, may be carried out when the need for such searches outweighs the personal rights invaded.
Hudson v. Palmer (1984)	Officials may search cells without a warrant and seize materials found there.

The most intrusive personal searches involve body cavity examinations. This may require a visual or digital examination of the inmate's body openings, an X-ray, or the forced taking of a laxative if it is believed that contraband has been hidden in the body. For example, inmates in Bureau of Prisons facilities, including those in pretrial detention, are required to expose their body cavities for visual inspection following every contact visit with a person from outside the institution. In *Bell v. Wolfish* (1979), judges argued that this requirement did violate the Fourth Amendment. However, in a 5–4 decision, the Court said that "balancing the significant and legitimate security interests of the institution against the privacy interests of the inmates, we conclude that they can [conduct the searches]."[44] The privacy rights of the prisoners could be suspended for security purposes.

To justify a digital examination to probe the anus or vagina, however, the courts have ruled that there must be reasonable suspicion based on factual circumstances to justify such procedures. For example, if an officer observes an inmate receiving a small packet from a visitor and it is not found after pat-down and strip searches, a body cavity search may be justified.[45]

With the employment of both male and female correctional officers in all institutions, lawsuits have been brought to stop opposite-sex officers from viewing and searching inmates' bodies. Some courts have ruled that staff members of one sex may not supervise inmates of the opposite sex during bathing, use of the toilet, or strip searches.[46] Here, the inconvenience of ensuring that the officer is of the same sex as the inmate does not justify the intrusion. Yet the courts have upheld the authority of female guards to pat down male prisoners, excluding the genital area.[47] Complicating this issue is the claim that nondiscrimination laws are violated if male or female officers are not allowed to carry out the same job responsibilities, including opposite-sex searches.[48]

In general, the courts have favored the security and safety interests of prison officials when dealing with search and seizure issues. Only the most intrusive physical searches have come under scrutiny and must be justified on the grounds that officers expected to find contraband.

The Eighth Amendment

Amendment VIII: *Excessive bail shall not be required, nor excessive fines imposed, nor cruel and unusual punishments inflicted.*

The Constitution's prohibition of cruel and unusual punishments has been tied to prisoners' need for decent treatment and minimal health standards. The courts have applied three principal tests under the Eighth Amendment to determine whether conditions are unconstitutional: (1) whether the punishment shocks the general conscience of a civilized society, (2) whether the punishment is unnecessarily cruel, and (3) whether the punishment goes beyond legitimate penal aims. **Table 5.3** summarizes some of the major Eighth Amendment cases.

Federal courts have ruled that although some aspects of prison life may be acceptable, the combination of various factors—the **totality of conditions**—may be such that life in the institution constitutes cruel and unusual punishment. This concept developed from the 1976 decision in *Pugh v. Locke*. Here, Federal District Court Judge Frank M. Johnson, Jr., found that "the evidence . . . establishes that prison conditions [in Alabama] are so debilitating that they necessarily deprive inmates of any opportunity to rehabilitate themselves or even maintain skills already possessed."[49]

When brutality, unsanitary facilities, overcrowding, and inadequate food have been found, judges have used the Eighth Amendment to order sweeping changes and, in some cases, to take over the administration of entire prisons or corrections systems. In these cases, wardens have been ordered to follow specific procedures and to spend money on certain improvements.

Several dramatic cases demonstrate this point. In Georgia, for example, prison conditions were shown to be so bad that judges demanded change throughout the state.[50] In *Ruiz v. Estelle* (1980), described more fully in the Focus box, the court ordered the Texas prison system to address unconstitutional conditions. Judicial supervision of the system continued for a decade, finally ending in 1990.

totality of conditions
The aggregate of circumstances in a correctional facility that, when considered as a whole, may violate the protections guaranteed by the Eighth Amendment, even though such guarantees are not violated by any single condition in the institution.

TABLE 5.3 *Selected Interpretations of the Eighth Amendment as Applied to Prisoners*

The Supreme Court is called on to determine whether correctional actions constitute cruel and unusual punishment.	
Case	**Decision**
Ruiz v. Estelle (1975)	Conditions of confinement in the Texas prison system are unconstitutional.
Estelle v. Gamble (1976)	Deliberate indifference to serious medical needs of prisoners constitutes the unnecessary and wanton infliction of pain, and thus violates the Eighth Amendment.
Rhodes v. Chapman (1981)	Double-celling and crowding do not necessarily constitute cruel and unusual punishment. It must be shown that the conditions involve "wanton and unnecessary infliction of pain" and are "grossly disproportionate" to the severity of the crime warranting imprisonment.
Whitley v. Albers (1986)	An innocent prisoner mistakenly shot in the leg during a disturbance does not suffer cruel and unusual punishment if the action was taken in good faith to maintain discipline rather than for the mere purpose of causing harm.
Wilson v. Seiter (1991)	Prisoners must not only prove that prison conditions are objectively cruel and unusual but also show that they exist because of the deliberate indifference of officials.
Overton v. Bazetta (2003)	Regulations suspending visiting privileges for two years for those prisoners who have "flunked" two drug tests does not constitute cruel and unusual punishment. The regulations relate to legitimate penological interests.

CORRECTIONAL POLICY

The Impact of *Ruiz v. Estelle*

In December 1980, William W. Justice, a federal judge for the Eastern District of Texas, issued a sweeping decree against the Texas Department of Corrections. He ordered prison officials to address a host of unconstitutional conditions, including overcrowding, unnecessary use of force by personnel, inadequate numbers of guards, poor health care practices, and a building-tender system that allowed some inmates to control other inmates.

Eastham is a large maximum-security institution housing recidivists over the age of 25 who have been in prison three or more times. It is tightly managed and has served as the depository for troublemakers from other Texas prisons. To help with these hard-core criminals, the staff used to rely on a select group of inmates known as building tenders (BTs). By co-opting the BTs with special privileges, officials could use them and their assistants, the turnkeys, to handle the rank-and-file inmates.

In May 1982 Texas signed a consent decree, agreeing to dismantle the building-tender system by January 1983. BTs were reassigned to ordinary prison jobs; stripped of their power, status, and duties; and moved to separate cell blocks for their protection. At the same time, Eastham received 141 new officers, almost doubling the guard force, to help pick up the slack. These reforms were substantial and set off a series of shifts that fundamentally altered the guard and inmate societies.

With the removal of the BTs and turnkeys, with restrictions on the unofficial use of force by guards, and with the institution of a prisoner discipline system emphasizing due process, fairness, and rights, the traditional social structure of Eastham came under severe strain. Major changes took place within the prison community related to interpersonal relations between the guards and inmates, the organization of inmate society, and the guard subculture and work role.

Guards and Inmates

Formerly, ordinary inmates had been subject to an all-encompassing, totalitarian system in which they were "dictated to, exploited, and kept in submission." But with the new relationship between the keepers and the kept, inmates challenged the authority of correctional officers and were more confrontational and hostile. In response to the assaults on their authority, the guards cited inmates for infractions of the rules. The changes in the relationship between guards and inmates resulted from many factors. First, there were more

guards. Second, the restrictions on the guards meant that physical reprisals were not feared. Third, the guards no longer had the BTs to act as intermediaries. Finally, the social distance between guards and prisoners had diminished. The last factor is important because one result of the civil rights movement is that prisoners were no longer viewed as "nonpersons." Inmates now had rights and could invoke due process rules to challenge decisions of guards and other officials. As a result, guards had to "negotiate, compromise, or overlook many difficulties with inmates within the everyday control system."

Reorganization within the Inmate Society

The purging of the BT-turnkey system created a power vacuum characterized by uncertainty. One outcome was a rise in the amount of inmate–inmate violence. Whereas in the past the BTs had helped settle disputes among inmates, during the postreform period these conflicts more often led to violence in which weapons were used. Violent self-help became a social necessity. As personal violence escalated, so did inmate gang activities. Gang members knew that they had to have the assistance of others if they were threatened, assaulted, or robbed. For nongang prisoners, heightened levels of personal insecurity meant that they had to rely on themselves and avoid contact with inmates known for their toughness.

Guard Subculture and Work Role

The court-imposed reforms upset the foundations of the guard subculture and work role. The guards' world of work was no longer well ordered, predictable, or rewarding. Among rank-and-file guards, fear of the inmates increased. On removal of the BTs, guards were assigned to cell-block duty for the first time; this placed them in close contact with inmates. The fact that most of the guards were new to prison work meant that they were hesitant to enforce order. Many officers believed that because they could not physically punish inmates and have their supervisors back them up, it was best not to enforce the rules at all. They thought that their authority had been undermined and that the new disciplinary process was frustrating. Many preferred simply to look the other way.

The court-ordered reforms brought Eastham's operations more in line with the constitutional requirements of fairness and due process but disrupted an ongoing social system. Before the *Ruiz* decision, the prison had been run on the basis of paternalism, coercion, dominance, and fear. Guards exercised

FOCUS ON

CORRECTIONAL POLICY (*Continued*)

much discretion over inmates, and they used the BTs to help maintain order and to provide information. During the transition to a new bureaucratic-legal order, levels of violence and personal insecurity increased. Authority was eroded, combative relations between inmates and officers materialized, and inmate gangs developed to provide security and autonomy for members.

Judicial supervision of the Texas prison system as a result of this case lasted for a decade and ended on March 31, 1990.

Source: Adapted from James W. Marquart and Ben M. Crouch, "Judicial Reform and Prisoner Control: The Impact of *Ruiz v. Estelle* on a Texas Penitentiary," *Law and Society Review* 19 (1985): 557–86. See also *Ruiz v. Estelle*, 503 F.Supp. 1265 (S.D.Tex. 1980).

In *Hutto v. Finney* (1978), the Supreme Court upheld a lower court's decision that confinement in Arkansas's segregation cells for more than 30 days was cruel and unusual. In that decision the Court also summarized three principles with regard to the Eighth Amendment:

1 Courts should consider the totality of conditions of confinement.

2 Courts should specify in remedial orders each factor that contributed to the violation and that required a change in order to remove the unconstitutionality.

3 Where appropriate, courts should enunciate specific minimum standards that, if met, would remedy the total constitutional violation.[51]

The Court has indicated, however, that unless extreme conditions are found, courts must defer to correctional officials and legislators. Yet the federal courts have intervened in states where institutional conditions or specific aspects of their operation violate the Eighth Amendment.

Of particular concern to correctional officials are court orders requiring an end to prison crowding. For example, the courts have stated that cells must afford each inmate at least 60 square feet of floor space. However, in *Rhodes v. Chapman* (1981), the Supreme Court upheld double-bunking (two inmates in a cell designed for one person) in Ohio as not constituting a condition of cruel and unusual punishment. To prove violation of the Eighth Amendment, the Court noted, it must be shown that the punishment either "inflicts unnecessary or wanton pain or is grossly disproportionate to the severity of the crime warranting punishment." Unless the conditions in the Ohio prison were "deplorable" or "sordid," the Court declared, the courts should defer to correctional authorities.[52]

The Fourteenth Amendment

Amendment XIV: *All persons born or naturalized in the United States, and subject to the jurisdiction thereof, are citizens of the United States and of the state wherein they reside. No state shall make or enforce any law which shall abridge the privileges or immunities of citizens of the United States; nor shall any state deprive any person of life, liberty, or property without due process of law, nor deny to any person within its jurisdiction the equal protection of the laws.*

One word and two clauses of the Fourteenth Amendment are relevant to the question of prisoners' rights. The relevant word is *state*, which is found in several of the

Brandon McKelvey/The Daily Texan

Since the 1960s, prisoners such as Roderick Johnson have been able to sue state officials for violation of their civil rights under the Fourteenth Amendment to the U.S. Constitution. In 2004 Johnson sued Texas prison officials in the U.S. District Court, charging that they had permitted him to be raped and sold as a sexual slave over an 18-month period.

clauses of the Fourteenth Amendment. Recall that by the 1970s the Supreme Court had ruled that, through the Fourteenth Amendment, the Bill of Rights restricts state governments.

The first important clause concerns procedural due process. **Procedural due process** requires that all individuals be treated fairly and justly by government officials and that decisions be made according to procedures prescribed by law. Prisoners sometimes file claims based on the due process clause when they believe that state statutes or administrative procedures have not been followed regarding, for example, parole release, intraprison transfers, transfers to administrative segregation, and disciplinary hearings.

The second important clause is the **equal protection** clause. Claims that prisoners have been denied equal protection of the law concern issues of racial, gender, or religious discrimination.

DUE PROCESS IN PRISON DISCIPLINE ■ Administrators have the discretion to discipline inmates who break institutional rules. Until the 1960s disciplinary procedures could be exercised without challenge, because the prisoner was physically

procedural due process
The constitutional guarantee that no agent or instrumentality of government will use any procedures other than those procedures prescribed by law to arrest, prosecute, try, or punish any person.

equal protection
The constitutional guarantee that the law will be applied equally to all people, without regard for such individual characteristics as gender, race, and religion.

The 1974 case of *Wolff v. McDonnell* extended certain due process rights to prisoners in disciplinary hearings, including procedures to guarantee due process. Here, a correctional officer briefs inmates about the steps in the disciplinary process.

confined, lacked communication with the outside, and was legally in the hands of the state. In addition, formal rules of prison conduct either did not exist or were vague. For example, disrespect toward a correctional officer was an infraction, but the characteristics of "disrespect" were not defined. The word of the correctional officer was accepted, and the inmate had little opportunity to challenge the charges.

In a series of decisions in the 1970s, the Supreme Court began to insist that procedural due process be part of the most sensitive of institutional decisions: those by which inmates are sent to solitary confinement and the methods by which good-time credit can be taken away because of misconduct.

The 1974 case of *Wolff v. McDonnell* extended certain due process rights.[53] The Supreme Court specified that when a prisoner faces serious disciplinary action that may result in segregation or the withdrawal of good time, the state must follow certain minimal procedures that conform to the guarantee of due process:

1. The prisoner must be given 24-hour written notice of the charges.
2. The prisoner has the right to present witnesses and documentary evidence in defense against the charges.
3. The prisoner has the right to a hearing before an impartial body.
4. The prisoner has the right to receive a written statement from that body concerning the outcome of the hearing.

However, the Court also recognized the special conditions of incarceration. It further stated that prisoners do not have the right to cross-examine witnesses and that the evidence presented by the offender shall not be unduly hazardous to institutional safety or correctional goals.[54]

As a result of the Supreme Court's decisions, some of which are outlined in **Table 5.4**, prison officials have established rules that provide some elements of due process in disciplinary proceedings. In many institutions, a disciplinary committee receives charges, conducts hearings, and decides guilt and punishment. Such committees usually include administrative personnel, but sometimes they also include inmates or citizens from the outside. Even with these protections, prisoners are still powerless and may risk further punishment if they challenge the warden's decisions too vigorously.

TABLE 5.4 *Selected Interpretations of the Fourteenth Amendment as Applied to Prisoners*

The Supreme Court has ruled concerning procedural due process and equal protection.	
Case	**Decision**
Wolff v. McDonnell (1974)	The basic elements of procedural due process must be present when decisions are made concerning the disciplining of an inmate.
Baxter v. Palmigiano (1976)	Although due process must be accorded, an inmate has no right to counsel in a disciplinary hearing.
Vitek v. Jones (1980)	The involuntary transfer of a prisoner to a mental hospital requires a hearing and other minimal elements of due process such as notice and the availability of counsel.
Sandin v. Conner (1995)	Prison regulations do not violate due process unless they place atypical and significant hardships on a prisoner.

EQUAL PROTECTION ■ In 1968 the Supreme Court firmly established that racial discrimination may not be official policy within prison walls.[55] Segregation can be justified only as a temporary expedient during periods when violence between races is demonstrably imminent. Equal protection claims have also been upheld in relation to religious freedoms and access to reading materials of interest to racial minorities. For instance, the cases brought by members of the Black Muslim religion, discussed previously, concerned both the First Amendment right to religious freedom and the Fourteenth Amendment right to equal protection.

The most recent cases concerning equal protection deal with issues concerning female offenders. Although the U.S. Supreme Court has yet to rule, state and lower federal courts have considered several relevant cases. In *Pargo v. Elliott* (1995), Iowa female inmates argued that their equal protection rights were violated because programs and services were not at the same level as those provided male inmates. The court ruled that, because of differences and needs, identical treatment is not required for men and women. It was concluded that there was no evidence of "invidious discrimination."[56] In the next few years, the U.S. Supreme Court is likely to consider equal protection for female prisoners.

A Change of Judicial Direction

The early years of the prisoners' rights movement brought noteworthy victories. As noted previously, the Supreme Court's decision in *Cooper v. Pate* (1964) allowed prisoners to sue state officials in the federal courts when their constitutional rights had been denied. But it was not until 1974, in *Wolff v. McDonnell,* that the Court "provided the kind of clarion statement that could serve as a rallying call for prisoners' rights advocates."[57] In that case Justice Byron White, speaking for the court, wrote,

> *Lawful imprisonment necessarily makes unavailable many rights and privileges of the ordinary citizen, a retraction justified by the considerations underlying our penal system. . . . But though his rights may be diminished by the needs and exigencies of the institutional environment, a prisoner is not wholly stripped of constitutional protections when he is imprisoned for crime.*[58]

This language, and that contained in the Court's decisions in several subsequent cases, provided the movement with a symbolic lift. It gave prisoners' rights advocates the feeling that the Supreme Court was backing their efforts.

During the past 30 years, the Supreme Court has been less supportive of the expansion of prisoners' rights, and a few decisions reflect a retreat. In *Bell v. Wolfish* (1979), the Court asked if the particular restrictions under question were intended as punishment or as an "incident of some other legitimate governmental purpose." The justices also seemed to take great pains to say that "prison administrators . . . should be accorded wide-ranging deference in the adoption and executing of policies."[59] This ruling was followed by *Rhodes v. Chapman* (1981), in which the Court held that to prove an Eighth Amendment violation, the inmate must show that the punishment was unnecessary or out of proportion to the prison-rule violation. Again, the justices said that in most cases the court should defer to correctional authorities.[60]

The emergence of the doctrine that "due deference" must be given to administrators to run their prisons has struck some observers as a return to the hands-off doctrine.[61] Justices seem unwilling to intervene in problems of administration, but they have expressed a willingness to hear cases involving substantive rights issues, as in the following 1985 federal circuit court opinion:

> *In the great majority of cases it would be sheer folly for society to deny prison officials discretion to act in accordance with their professional judgment. At the same time it would be an abrogation of our responsibility as judges to assume such judgments (or, more precisely, to reassume) a "hands-off" posture, requiring categorical acquiescence in such judgments.*[62]

The concept of deliberate indifference surfaced in *Daniels v. Williams* (1986). Here the Court said that an inmate could sue for damages only if officials had inflicted injury intentionally or deliberately.[63] This reasoning was extended in the 1991 case of *Wilson v. Seiter,* where the Court ruled that a prisoner's conditions of confinement are not unconstitutional unless it can be shown that administrators had acted with "deliberate indifference" to basic human needs.[64] The opinion cites *Estelle v. Gamble* (1976) and *Whitley v. Albers* (1986) to present other Eighth Amendment cases requiring a showing of correctional officials' motives in order to prove a constitutional violation.[65]

Many scholars believe that the deliberate-indifference requirement indicates a shift from the use of objective criteria (proof that the inmate suffered conditions protected by the Eighth Amendment) to subjective criteria (the state of mind of correctional officials, namely, deliberate indifference) in determining whether prison conditions are unconstitutional. Other scholars believe that the impact of *Wilson* will not be great.[66]

Besides upholding deliberate indifference, recent rulings and laws have also limited prisoners' access to the federal courts, suggesting that the pace of prisoners' right cases will continue to decrease. For example, in *McCleskey v. Zant* (1991), the Court ruled that all habeas corpus claims must be raised in the initial petition.[67] Also, in *Colman v. Thompson* (1991), the Court stated that a habeas petition should not be considered even when attorney error resulted in violations of state procedural rules.[68] Thus, although prisoners have a right to access to the courts via law libraries and the assistance of other inmates, the reality is that access has been diminished, especially for those prisoners who lack counsel and are likely to be tripped up by the stricter procedural rules.

After years of complaining and lobbying by governors and state attorneys general, Congress acted in 1996 to make it more difficult for prisoners to file civil rights lawsuits and for judges to make decisions affecting prison operations. The Prison Litigation Reform Act limits the authority of federal judges to order remedies and maintain supervision over correctional institutions as a result of civil rights lawsuits. Judges' orders affecting prisons automatically expire after two years unless new hearings are held to demonstrate that rights violations continue to exist. The act also made it more difficult for prisoners to seek a waiver of court fees. In addition, as we have seen, prisoners are prohibited from filing additional civil rights lawsuits if they previously had three lawsuits dismissed as frivolous. The only exception to this rule is if prisoners need to file lawsuits when they are in imminent danger of serious physical harm. Thus, a prisoner who has three prior dismissals cannot file a civil rights lawsuit about a new violation of religious freedom rights, because such rights do not concern the prisoner's safety. As shown in **Figure 5.2**, the number of Section 1983 lawsuits filed in federal courts has dropped by about 43 percent since the act was passed.

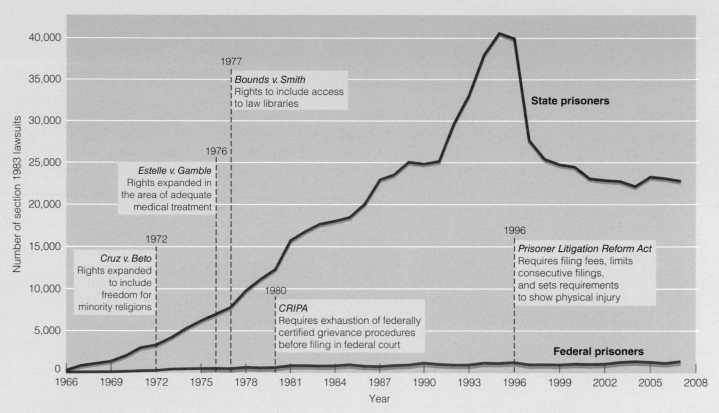

Figure 5.2

Section 1983 Lawsuits

The number of Section 1983 lawsuits among state prisoners has dropped dramatically since the passage of the Prison Litigation Reform Act of 1996.

Sources: Bureau of Justice Statistics, *Sourcebook of Criminal Justice Statistics, 1977* (Washington, DC: U.S. Government Printing Office, 1978), Table 5.28; Ann L. Pastore and Kathleen Maguire, eds., *Sourcebook of Criminal Justice Statistics,* Table 5.65.2007, http://www.albany.edu/sourcebook/pdf/t5652007.pdf, June 15, 2009.

Various aspects of the Prison Litigation Reform Act (PLRA) have been challenged in court, but the U.S. Supreme Court has endorsed the provisions of the law. For example, in *Booth v. Churner* (2001), the Court ruled that a prisoner seeking monetary damages must first complete available prison administrative processes before filing a lawsuit, even if that process does not make provisions for awarding monetary damages.[69] The Court recently ruled that various procedural rules implemented by lower courts, such as rules intended to enforce the PLRA's exhaustion requirement, are not required by the act and that imposing them exceeds proper judicial limits.[70]

Historically speaking, the Rehnquist Court era (1986 to 2005) was a period in which "the Supreme Court firmly halted the expansion of constitutional rights for offenders."[71] Although the Supreme Court and Congress may be less sympathetic toward prisoners' claims, the lower federal courts and many state courts continue to support judicial intervention to uphold civil rights. A return to a strict hands-off policy seems highly unlikely, but greater deference is being given to prison administrators. Many scholars believe the era of institutional reform has ended.[72]

The position of the American Civil Liberties Union on the **Prison Litigation Reform Act** is found through the corresponding link at www .cengage.com/criminaljustice/ clear.

Impact of the Prisoners' Rights Movement

The prisoners' rights movement can probably be credited with general changes in American corrections since the late 1970s.[73] The most obvious changes are improvements in institutional conditions and administrative practices. Law libraries and legal assistance are now generally available, communication with the outside is easier, religious practices are protected, inmate complaint procedures have been developed, and due process requirements are emphasized. Prisoners in solitary confinement undoubtedly suffer less neglect than they did before. Although overcrowding remains a major problem, many conditions have greatly improved and the most brutalizing elements of prison life have diminished.[74]

Although individual cases may have made only a dent in correctional bureaucracies, real changes have occurred over time. The prisoners' rights movement has clearly influenced correctional officials. The threat of lawsuits and public exposure has placed many in the correctional bureaucracy on guard. For example, wardens and their subordinates may now be refraining from traditional disciplinary actions that might result in judicial intervention. One can argue whether or not such changes will ultimately prove useful. On the one hand, this wariness may have merely further bureaucratized corrections, requiring staff to to protect themselves from lawsuits by preparing extensive and time-consuming documentation of their actions. On the other hand, judicial intervention has forced corrections to rethink existing procedures and organizational structures. As part of the wider changes in the "new corrections," new administrators, increased funding, reformulated policies, and improved management procedures have, at least in part, been influenced by the prisoners' rights movement. The actual impact of extending constitutional rights to prisoners has not yet been measured, but evidence suggests that court decisions have had a broad effect.

■ ALTERNATIVES TO LITIGATION

Although many prisoners do have legitimate legal claims, correctional specialists, judges, and even lawyers are questioning the suitability of lawsuits as the only means to resolve them. Annually more than 22,000 state prisoners petition the federal courts to halt certain correctional practices or to seek monetary awards for damages. The courts deem many of these suits frivolous and dismiss them for failure to state legitimate claims. Among the remainder, only a few are decided in ways that affect anyone but the litigant.

Litigation is a cumbersome, costly, and often ineffective way to handle such claims. Except for class actions and isolated individual grievances, most prisoner cases resemble disputes settled in small claims courts. As former Chief Justice Burger has said, "Federal judges should not be dealing with prisoner complaints which, although important to a prisoner, are so minor that any well-run institution should be able to resolve them fairly without resort to federal judges."[75]

Still another problem is that, although most suits that prisoners file under 42 U.S.C. 1983 are dismissed before trial, the remaining cases force correctional officials to expend time and resources in litigation, to face the possibility of being sued personally, and to risk the erosion of their leadership. Correctional administrators have charged that much prisoner litigation is designed merely to "hassle" them.[76]

From the prisoner's perspective, litigation may be neither effective nor satisfying. Most prisoners face three problems: (1) they generally lack legal representation, (2) constitutional standards are difficult to meet, and (3) even if a suit succeeds, changes in policies or financial compensation may take a long time.

Four alternatives to litigation appear in the corrections systems of various states: (1) inmate grievance procedures, (2) an ombudsman, (3) mediation, and (4) legal assistance. All are designed to solve problems before the inmate feels compelled to file suit, but mediation and legal assistance can also be invoked after a suit has been initiated.

News of the current actions of the Supreme Court are found on the website of **On the Docket**, listed at www.cengage .com/criminaljustice/clear.

Inmate Grievance Procedures

Although informal procedures for hearing inmates' complaints have existed for many years, only since the mid-1970s have formal grievance mechanisms been widely used. All states and the Federal Bureau of Prisons now have grievance procedures.

Most corrections systems use a three-step inmate grievance process. A staff member or committee in each institution usually receives complaints, investigates them, and makes decisions. If the prisoner is dissatisfied with the outcome, he or she may appeal the case to the warden and ultimately to the commissioner of corrections. Reports indicate that some grievances are more easily resolved than others. For example, many inmates complain that they are not receiving proper medical treatment, but because medical personnel can usually document the treatment provided, such complaints normally subside. The many complaints of lost personal property are another matter. Most involve items deposited at the reception center at the time of arrival but not transferred with the prisoner to another institution. Staff members often cannot account for missing property, and the process for receiving compensation for property lost or damaged can be complicated. Probably the most difficult situation to resolve is alleged brutality by a guard. Such a complaint virtually always comes down to the inmate's word against the officer's, because staff members rarely testify against other officers.

The inmate-grievance procedure can help defuse tensions in correctional facilities. It also serves as a management tool. By attentive monitoring of the complaint process, a warden can discern patterns of inmate discontent that may warrant actions to prevent the development of deeper problems.

The Ombudsman

Ombudsman programs are the second most common dispute-resolution mechanisms in corrections. Begun in Sweden, such programs have been used successfully throughout the United States for more than two decades. An **ombudsman** is a public official with full authority to investigate citizens' complaints against government officials.

Ombudsman programs succeed if inmates have quick and easy access to the office. When inmates respect their ombudsman, his advice as to the merits of grievances may help reduce the number of frivolous claims; when ombudsmen see merit in claims, they can try to convince authorities that it would be in their interest to resolve the matters out of court.

Mediation

Mediation is a consensual and voluntary process in which a neutral third party assists disputants in reconciling their differences. The informality of the process stands in contrast

AP Images/Daytona Beach News-Journal, Nigel Cook

Online materials for **alternative dispute resolution and mediation** are found through the corresponding link at www.cengage.com/criminaljustice/clear.

ombudsman
A public official who investigates complaints against government officials and recommends corrective measures.

Access the **prison ombudsman** for Northern Ireland through the corresponding link at www.cengage.com/criminaljustice/clear.

mediation
Intervention, in a dispute, by a third party to whom the parties in conflict submit their differences for resolution and whose decision (in the correctional setting) is binding on both parties.

Law libraries and legal assistance are now available in most prisons. "Jailhouse" lawyers not only assist other inmates with their legal questions, but they can also discourage frivolous suits.

to the complex, cumbersome procedures of the courtroom. Proponents point out that, in the mediation process, straightforward questions can be asked so that underlying issues can be explored. This feature offers a special advantage to prisoners, most of whom would not have counsel were they to take their cases to court. Mediation is particularly effective when the essence of a complaint is not a conflict of abstract principles but a problem requiring an administrative solution. However, it has not lived up to its potential in the correctional arena, because in many cases neither party seems willing to be bound by the decision.

Legal Assistance

Learn about the **Prison Legal Services of Michigan** by using the corresponding link at www.cengage.com/criminaljustice/clear.

As noted previously, the Supreme Court has emphasized that prisoners must have access to legal resources so that they can seek postconviction relief.[77] Since the early 1970s, several legal-assistance mechanisms have been developed in correctional institutions, including staff attorneys to assist inmates with their legal problems, inmate ("jailhouse") lawyers, and law school clinics.

Providing legal assistance may seem counterproductive if the goal of correctional administrators is to avoid litigation, but lawyers do more than simply help prisoners file suits. They also advise on the legal merits of complaints and thus can discourage frivolous suits. Further, counsel can help determine the underlying issues of a complaint and therefore frame questions in terms that people with legal training will understand.

■ LAW AND COMMUNITY CORRECTIONS

Although public attention and most correctional law concerns prisons and jails, a majority of convicted offenders are supervised in the community. However, as with prisoners, offenders in the community do have rights, and courts have addressed issues concerning due process and searches and seizures.

As discussed in Chapter 4, probation is a type of community sentence, and parolees are offenders released to community supervision after spending a portion of their sentence in prison. Probation is imposed by a judge and is administered by probation officers. Parole is usually granted by a parole board and is administered by parole officers. Eligibility for parole is stated in the law, as are the release criteria. Even in those states with determinate sentencing and mandatory release, parolees receive supervision for a specified length of time.

There is no *right* to parole. In *Greenholtz v. Inmates of the Nebraska Penal and Correction Complex* (1979), the U.S. Supreme Court made clear that the state grants release on parole and that individuals do not have a right to be conditionally released before expiration of a sentence.[78] Supporting the authority of parole and pardons boards, the Court ruled in *Connecticut Board of Pardons v. Dumschat* (1981) that an inmate did not have a right to learn why his request for commutation (reduction) of his life sentence was denied. The inmate claimed he had some expectation of commutation, because three-fourth of lifers in that state received commutation and thereby became eligible for parole.[79]

Constitutional Rights of Probationers and Parolees

While in the community as probationers and parolees, offenders must live according to conditions specified at the time of their sentencing or parole release. Should these conditions be violated, community supervision may be revoked and the offender sent to prison for the remainder of the sentence. But does this mean that probationers and parolees do not enjoy the constitutional rights of ordinary citizens? As Justice Scalia has said, "It is always true of probationers (as we have said it to be true of parolees) that

Celebrity heiress Paris Hilton and her attorneys are seen in a California courtroom. Judge Michael T. Sauer found that she had violated her probation, and he sentenced her to 45 days in jail. Hilton had been driving while her license had been suspended for a prior reckless driving conviction in which she had been sentenced to probation. Which Supreme Court decisions apply to this case?

they do not enjoy 'the absolute liberty to which every citizen is entitled, but only . . . conditional liberty properly dependent on observation of special restrictions.'"[80]

The conditions placed on probationers and parolees may interfere with their constitutional rights. Such conditions typically limit the right of free association by denying offenders contact with their crime partners or victims. But courts have struck down conditions preventing parolees from giving public speeches and receiving publications. The case of *Griffin v. Wisconsin* (1987) provides a good example of the clash between the Bill of Rights and community corrections.[81] Learning that Griffin might have a gun, probation officers searched his apartment without a warrant. The Supreme Court noted the practical problems of obtaining a search warrant while the probationer was under supervision. The Court said that the probation agency must be able to act before the offender damages himself or society. In Griffin's case, the Court felt that the agency had satisfied the Fourth Amendment's reasonableness requirement.

In a 1998 case, *Pennsylvania Board of Probation and Parole v. Scott,* a closely divided Court ruled that evidence that would be barred by the exclusionary rule from use by the prosecution in a criminal trial can be used in parole-revocation hearings.[82] Officers, without a search warrant, found guns in the home of a paroled murderer who was barred from owning weapons. The Court upheld revocation of the offender's parole. A unanimous Supreme Court later upheld a condition of probation that required the offender to submit to searches at any time, with or without a warrant.[83] More recently, the case of *Samson v. California* (2006) involved a police officer who stopped and searched a motorist he knew was on parole. The officer found methamphetamines in the parolee's car. At trial the defense argued that the drugs were inadmissible as evidence because the officer did not have a warrant. The trial court denied the defense motion. Later the Supreme Court ruled that because parolees in the legal custody of the state have reduced privacy rights and because the defendant signed a written consent to suspicionless searches by a parole or peace officer, the warrantless search was constitutional.[84]

Revocation of Probation and Parole

When probationers or parolees do not obey their conditions of release, they may be sent to prison. As fully discussed in Chapters 8 and 16, if the offender commits another crime, probation or parole will likely be revoked. For minor violations of the conditions (such as missing an Alcoholics Anonymous meeting), the supervising officer has discretion as to whether to ask for revocation.

The Supreme Court has addressed the question of due process when revocation is being considered. In *Mempa v. Rhay* (1967), the justices determined that a probationer had the right to counsel in revocation and sentencing hearings before a deferred prison sentence could be imposed.[85] In *Morrissey v. Brewer* (1972), they ruled that parolees facing revocation must be given due process through a prompt informal inquiry before an impartial hearing officer.[86] The Court required a two-step revocation hearing process. In the first stage, a hearing officer determines whether there is probable cause that a violation has occurred. Parolees have the right to be notified of the charges against them, to know the evidence against them, to be allowed to speak on their own behalf, to present witnesses, and to confront the witnesses against them. In the second stage, the revocation hearing, the parolee must receive a notice of charges and the disclosed evidence of the violation. The parolee may cross-examine witnesses. The hearing body determines if the violation is sufficiently severe to warrant revocation. It must give the parolee a written statement outlining the evidence and giving reasons for the decision.

In the following year the Supreme Court applied the *Morrissey* procedures to probation revocation proceedings in *Gagnon v. Scarpelli* (1973).[87] But in *Gagnon* the Court also looked at the right to counsel. It ruled that there was no absolute requirement but that in some cases probationers and parolees might request counsel, which should be allowed on a case-by-case basis depending on the complexity of the issues, mitigating circumstances, and the competence of the offender.

■ LAW AND CORRECTIONAL PERSONNEL

Just as law governs relationships among correctional personnel, inmates, probationers, and parolees, laws and regulations also define the relationships between administrators and their staff. With the exception of those working for private and nonprofit organizations, correctional personnel are public employees. In this section we look at two important aspects of correctional work. First, as public employees, all correctional employees are governed by civil service rules and regulations. Second, correctional clients may sue state officials under Section 1983 of the United States Code. We will examine the liability of correctional personnel with regard to these suits.

Civil Service Laws

From the time a public employee is recruited until he or she leaves public service, civil service rules and regulations govern the work environment. Civil service laws set the procedures for hiring, promoting, assigning, disciplining, and firing public employees. Such laws protect public employees from arbitrary actions by their supervisors. Workplace rules also develop through collective-bargaining agreements between unions and the government. Where correctional personnel can join unions, the bargaining process develops rules concerning assignments, working conditions, and grievance procedures. These agreements carry the force of law.

Like their counterparts in the private sector, government employees are protected from discrimination. With the Civil Rights Act of 1964, Congress prohibited employment discrimination based on race, gender, national origin, and religion. Subsequent federal legislation prohibits discrimination against people with disabilities (Americans with Disabilities Act) and age discrimination (Age Discrimination in Employment Act). States have their own antidiscrimination laws. All such laws have increased the number of minorities and women who work in corrections.

Unlike many public employees, those who work in corrections face a difficult position. Offenders have not chosen to be incarcerated nor supervised in the community. They thus do not look on correctional personnel as offering them assistance.

Correctional employees must assert authority to control the behavior of individuals who have shown that they lack self-control or have little regard for society's rules. Whether in prison, in a probationer's home, or on the street, this responsibility creates pressures and difficult—sometimes dangerous—situations.

Correctional personnel also face pressures from their supervisors. If they expect to succeed in their job and gain promotions, they must carry out their duties in a professional manner that will please their supervisors, who may not always appreciate the quick decisions that must be made on the "front line."

Liability of Correctional Personnel

As noted, in *Cooper v. Pate* (1964) the Supreme Court said that Section 1983 provides a means not only for prisoners but also probationers and parolees to bring lawsuits against correctional officials. The statute says that "any person" who deprives others of their constitutional rights while acting under the authority of law may be liable in a lawsuit.[88]

In subsequent decisions, the Court further clarified the meaning of Section 1983. In *Monell v. Department of Social Services of the City of New York* (1978), the Court said that individual officers and the agency may be sued when the agency's "customs and usages" violate a person's civil rights. If an individual can show that harm was caused by employees whose wrongful acts were the result of these "customs, practices, and policies, including poor training and supervision," then the employees can be sued.[89] This position was strengthened in *Hope v. Pelzer* (2002). The Court denied qualified immunity to Alabama correctional officials who had handcuffed an inmate to a hitching post in the prison yard and denied him adequate water and bathroom breaks. The decision emphasized that a reasonable officer would have known that using a hitching post in this manner was a violation of the Eighth Amendment prohibition on cruel and unusual punishments.[90]

With the increased use of private prisons, questions have arisen as to the liability under Section 1983 of private contractors. Correctional Services Corporation, which operates a community center under contract with the Federal Bureau of Prisons, was sued for a civil rights violation for making a prisoner with a heart condition climb five flights of stairs instead of permitting him to use an elevator; this triggered a heart attack and fall on a staircase. The Court held in a 5–4 ruling that a Section 1983–type action could not be brought against the contractor. The inmate should have filed a grievance through the Bureau of Prison's administrative process or brought a regular tort lawsuit for injunctive relief.[91]

In Section 1983 litigation, correctional employees may be sued as individuals in their personal capacity, as opposed to their official capacity as a state employee. Usually, attorneys for the state will defend the case, and most states will assume responsibility for any financial damages awarded the plaintiff. However, if the court finds the employee to have acted intentionally or maliciously or to have committed a criminal act against a client, he or she may be responsible for paying the legal defense and the damages the jury awards.

How should correctional workers protect themselves from civil rights suits? Clair Cripe, formerly the general counsel of the Federal Bureau of Prisons, suggests five rules for correctional employees:

1. Follow agency policies and the instructions of supervisors. By following policies, the staff member will be in step with the professional expectations of the agency's management. From a legal standpoint, the employee should follow the policies to ensure compliance with legal standards and avoid lawsuits.

2. Obtain good training. Staff members need to know the areas of their performance that expose them the most to liability.

3. Become familiar with the law directly affecting the job. This is true whatever the specialty—casework, security, health care, probation, parole, or institutional programs.

4 To ensure a good defense when being sued, find a good mentor. Although correctional workers receive formal training, they gain on the job much knowledge of how things "really" work.

5 Keep good records. If correctional employees are called to testify at a trial or grievance hearing, good records are invaluable.[92]

Although huge financial settlements make headlines and the number of Section 1983 filings is large, few cases come to trial and very few correctional employees must personally pay financial awards to plaintiffs. However, no correctional employee wants to be involved in such legal situations. Not only are they time-consuming and emotionally draining, but the mere fact of being sued can seriously damage a professional career.

SUMMARY

1 Discuss the foundations that support the legal rights of prisoners.

Four foundations support the legal rights of individuals under correctional supervision. The first, constitutions, not only provide the design of the government, but also list the basic rights of individuals. Individuals do not lose all of their constitutional rights after being convicted of a crime. Some of the rights of prisoners, however, are outweighed by legitimate government interests (maintaining institutional order, maintaining institutional security, and rehabilitating inmates). Statutes are laws passed by elected officials in legislatures. Statutes may provide specific rights to inmates beyond those conferred by the state constitutions or the U.S. Constitution. Case law refers to the legal rules produced by judges. Prior judicial rulings serve to guide the decisions of other judges who must rule on similar cases. Finally, regulations are rules set by agencies in the executive branch of government. For example, a department of corrections may create regulations on the type of personal items inmates are allowed to have in the cells.

2 Explain the role of the U.S. Supreme Court in interpreting correctional law.

Traditionally, the U.S. Supreme Court maintained a hands-off policy with respect to corrections. Because prisoners were viewed as not having rights, judges did not interfere with prison operations. In the 1960s, however, this policy was abandoned, and the Court issued a series of decisions that broadly outlined the rights of prisoners, including providing inmates with access to the federal courts to sue prison officials for denying them basic rights. Today's Court is comparatively less active in correctional matters, but it occasionally rules on cases to clarify constitutional issues in correctional settings.

3 Understand the constitutional rights of prisoners.

The rights of inmates can be summarized in a handful of phrases in four amendments to the U.S. Constitution—the First, Fourth, Eighth, and Fourteenth. The First Amendment addresses rights related to access to reading materials, noncensorship of mail, and freedom of religious practices. The Fourth Amendment provides protection against government intrusion (searches and seizures). However, prisoners surrender most of their privacy rights when they enter prison. In correctional facilities, the Fourth Amendment concerns searches of cells and searches of the person. The Eighth Amendment protects inmates against cruel and unusual punishments. The federal courts have intervened in states where prison conditions or specific aspects of their operation were found to violate the Eighth Amendment. Finally, the Fourteenth Amendment helps to ensure procedural due process and equal protection to prisoners. These two clauses of the Fourteenth Amendment are very important when prisoners are disciplined for violating institutional rules.

4 Be familiar with the alternatives to litigation.

Four alternatives to litigation are present in the corrections systems of various states. Inmate grievance procedures usually involve a three-step process: (1) an inmate files a complaint, (2) a prison staff member (or grievance officer) investigates the matter, and (3) the investigator issues a decision. Another alternative, the ombudsman, involves an official who receives complaints, investigates, and recommends corrective measures. The effectiveness of this approach is contingent on whether inmates respect the ombudsman. Mediation entails a third party reviewing the matter and making a decision that is binding on both prison officials and inmates. This approach is most effective when the complaint involves a problem that requires an administrative solution. Finally, legal assistance by staff attorneys, inmate lawyers, and law school clinics can advise inmates on the legal merits of their complaints and assist inmates in framing their complaints in legal terms.

5 Explain the rights of offenders under community supervision.

Like inmates in correctional facilities, convicted offenders in the community also have rights. But they do not enjoy the same rights as ordinary citizens. For example, various conditions are placed on parolees, such as limiting their right to associate with their partners in crime and with victims. In instances when parole supervision is being revoked, offenders possess various due process rights. For example, parolees have the right to be notified of the charges against them, to know the evidence against them, to be allowed to speak on their own behavior, to present witnesses, and to confront the witnesses against them. As for the right to counsel, the Supreme Court has ruled that it should be allowed on a case-by-case basis.

6 Discuss how the law affects correctional personnel.

Law and regulations define the relationships between prison administrators and their staff. All correctional employees working in public prisons are governed by civil service rules and regulations. Civil service laws set the procedures for hiring, promoting, assigning, disciplining, and firing public employees. Such laws protect public employees from arbitrary actions by their supervisors. Workplace rules also develop through collective-bargaining agreements between unions and the government. A second way that the law affects correctional personnel relates to the ability of convicted offenders to sue correctional officials under Section 1983 of the United States Code. Section 1983 provides a means not only for prisoners but also probationers and parolees to bring lawsuits against correctional officials. The statute says that "any person" who deprives others of their constitutional rights while acting under the authority of law may be liable in a lawsuit. Few of these cases come to trial, and very few correctional employees must personally pay financial awards to plaintiffs.

KEY TERMS

case law (p. 103)
civil liability (p. 105)
clear and present danger (p. 109)
compelling state interest (p. 109)
constitution (p. 102)
equal protection (p. 117)
habeas corpus (p. 105)

hands-off policy (p. 104)
least restrictive methods (p. 109)
mediation (p. 123)
ombudsman (p. 123)
precedent (p. 103)
procedural due process (p. 117)
rational basis test (p. 109)

regulations (p. 104)
statute (p. 103)
totality of conditions (p. 114)
Warren, Earl (p. 104)

FOR DISCUSSION

1. What difficulties might you, as a correctional officer, foresee in attempting to run your unit of the institution while at the same time upholding the legal rights of the prisoners?
2. Suppose that you are a prison warden. A group of prisoners calling themselves "The Sun Devils" claims that they are a religious organization. They request that the institution grant them permission to chant at the sun at noon each day as part of their First Amendment rights. How would you determine whether you must grant these requests?
3. Should convicted offenders under parole supervision enjoy the same constitutional rights as law-abiding citizens? If not, which rights should be withheld? Should these rights be granted after the offender successfully completes parole?
4. Which of the following alternatives to litigation—inmate grievance procedures, ombudsman, and mediation—do you believe is most effective in maximum-security prisons for men? What factors make these alternatives less effective at resolving inmate complaints?
5. As a correctional officer, what steps would you take to protect yourself from inmate lawsuits? How can prison officials limit the number of lawsuits filed by inmates?

FOR FURTHER READING

Anderson, Lloyd C. *Voices from a Southern Prison*. Athens: University of Georgia Press, 2000. Case study of the 10-year litigation to reform the Kentucky State Reformatory as seen through the eyes of the three inmates who brought the litigation, as well as the perspective of the judge, the reform-minded head of the Kentucky corrections system, and a journalist.

Carroll, Leo. *Lawful Order: A Case Study of Correctional Crisis and Reform*. New York: Garland, 1998. Examination of the Rhode Island prison system over a 25-year period, focusing on the impact of *Palmigiano v. Garrahy*.

Cripe, Clair A., and Michael G. Pearlman. *Legal Aspects of Corrections Management*. 2nd ed. Boston: Jones & Bartlett, 2005. An excellent text geared primarily to correctional administrators.

DiIulio, John J., Jr., ed. *Courts, Corrections, and the Constitution*. New York: Oxford University Press, 1990. Contains a collection of essays that examine the capacity of judges to intervene in ways that improve the quality of life behind bars.

Feeley, Malcolm M., and Edward L. Rubin. *Judicial Policy Making and the Modern State: How Courts Reformed America's Prisons*. New York: Cambridge University Press, 1998. Examines the prison reform movement as an example of judicial policy making.

Martin, Steve J., and Sheldon Ekland-Olson. *Texas Prisons: The Walls Came Tumbling Down*. Austin: Texas Monthly Press, 1987. Recounts the history of the Texas prison system, focusing on the rise of the writ-writers, the case of *Ruiz v. Estelle*, and the impact of Judge William Justice's decision.

Smith, Christopher E. *Law and Contemporary Corrections*. Belmont, CA: Wadsworth, 2000. A text that examines the law as applied to prisons, probation, parole, and correctional personnel.

NOTES

[1] Sheryl Gay Stolberg, "President Signs New Rules to Prosecute Terror Suspects," *New York Times*, October 18, 2006, p. 20.

[2]. David G. Savage, "Critics Say Tribunals Law Limits Key Layer of Redress," *Chicago Tribune*, October 18, 2006, p. 5.

[3] Michael C. Dorf, "Why the Military Commissions Act Is No Moderate Compromise," http://www.writ.news.findlaw.com/dorf/20061011.html, October 11, 2006.

[4] *Boumediene v. Bush*, 553 U.S. (2008); Robert Barnes, "Justices Say Detainees Can Seek Release," *Washington Post*, June 13, 2008, p. A01.

[5] Ann L. Pastore and Kathleen Maguire, eds., *Sourcebook of Criminal Justice Statistics*, Table 5.65.2007, http://www.albany.edu/sourcebook/pdf/t5652007.pdf, June 15, 2009.

[6] *Delancie v. Superior Court of San Mateo County*, 31 Cal. 3d 865 (1982); *Sterling v. Cupp*, 290 Ore. 611, 625 P.2d 123 (1981).

[7] *Pennsylvania Department of Corrections et al. v. Yeskey*, 524 U.S. 206 (1998).

[8] *Ford v. Wainwright*, 477 U.S. 399 (1986).

[9] *Ruffin v. Commonwealth*, 62 Va. 790 (1871).

[10] Donald H. Wallace, "Prisoners' Rights: Historical Views," in *Correctional Contexts*, 2nd ed., edited by Edward J. Latessa et al. (Los Angeles: Roxbury, 2001), 229–38; Christopher E. Smith, "The Prison Reform Litigation Era: Book-Length Studies and Lingering Research Issues," *Prison Journal* 83 (September 2003): 337–58.

[11] *Cooper v. Pate*, 378 U.S. 546 (1964).

[12] Note that federal prisoners cannot use Section 1983 to bring suits charging federal officials of violating their constitutional rights. But the Supreme Court in *Bivens v. Six Unknown Federal Narcotics Agents*, 403 U.S. 388 (1971) and later cases have allowed federal prisoners to sue federal officials. Thus, federal prisoners bring *"Bivens suits,"* not Section 1983 actions.

[13] Clair A. Cripe, *Legal Aspects of Corrections Management* (Gaithersburg, MD: Aspen, 1997), 53.

[14] James B. Jacobs, *New Perspectives on Prisons and Imprisonment* (Ithaca, NY: Cornell University Press, 1983), 37.

15 *Boumediene v. Bush,* 553 U.S. (2008).

16 Fred Cheesman, II, Roger A. Hanson, and Brian J. Ostrom, "A Tale of Two Laws: The U.S. Congress Confronts Habeas Corpus Petitions and Section 1983 Lawsuits," *Law and Policy* 22 (April 2000): 104.

17 Roger A. Hanson and Henry W. K. Daley, *Challenging the Conditions of Prisons and Jails: A Report on Section 1983 Litigation* (Washington, DC: Bureau of Justice Statistics, 1995).

18 Pastore and Maguire, *Sourcebook.*

19 John A. Fliter, *Prisoners' Rights: The Supreme Court and Evolving Standards of Decency* (Westport, CT: Greenwood Press, 2001), 1–4.

20 *Johnson v. Avery,* 393 U.S. 413 (1969).

21 *Bounds v. Smith,* 430 U.S. 817 (1977).

22 *Lewis v. Casey,* 64 U.S.L.W. 4587 (1996).

23 *Brooks v. Florida,* 389 U.S. 413 (1967).

24 *Holt v. Sarver,* 442 F.2d 308 (8th Cir. 1971).

25 Malcolm M. Feeley and Edward Rubin, *Judicial Policy Making and the Modern State: How the Courts Reformed America's Prisons* (New York: Cambridge University Press, 1998), 14.

26 Michael Mushlin, *Rights of Prisoners,* 2nd ed. (Colorado Springs, CO: Shepard's/McGraw-Hill, 1993), 257.

27 *Brown v. Wainwright,* 419 F.2d 1308 (5th Cir. 1969).

28 *Pepperling v. Crist,* 678 F.2d 787 (9th Cir. 1982). However, the U.S. Court of Appeals for the Seventh Circuit, in *Trapnell v. Riggsbuy,* 622 F.2d 290 (7th Cir. 1980), found absolute prohibition a "narrowly drawn and carefully limited response to a valid security problem."

29 *Sostre v. Otis,* 330 F.Supp. 941 (S.D.N.Y. 1971).

30 *Turner v. Safley,* 482 U.S. 78 (1987).

31 John McLaren, "Prisoners' Rights: The Pendulum Swings," in *Prisons: Today and Tomorrow,* edited by Joycelyn M. Pollock (Gaithersburg, MD: Aspen, 1997), 357. See also *O'Leon v. Estate of Shabazz,* 107 S. Ct. 2400 (1987).

32 *Procunier v. Martinez,* 416 U.S. 396 (1974).

33 *Turner v. Safley,* 482 U.S. 78 (1987).

34 *Shaw v. Murphy,* 532 U.S. 223 (2001).

35 *Beard v. Banks,* 548 U.S. 521 (2006).

36 *Fulwood v. Clemmer,* 206 F.Supp. 370 (D.C. Cir. 1962).

37 *Cruz v. Beto,* 450 U.S. 319 (1972).

38 *O'Lone v. Estate of Shabazz,* 482 U.S. 342 (1987).

39 *Employment Division of Oregon v. Smith,* 494 U.S. 872 (1990).

40 Jack E. Call and Charles Samarkos, "The Impact of the Religious Freedom Restoration Act on Prisoners' Rights," *Corrections Today* 58 (April 1996): 136–42.

41 *City of Boerne v. Flores,* 117 S. Ct. 2157 (1997).

42 *Hudson v. Palmer,* 468 U.S. 517 (1984).

43 *Smith v. Fairman,* 678 F.2d 52 (7th Cir. 1982).

44 *Bell v. Wolfish,* 441 U.S. 520 (1979).

45 *United States v. Oakley,* 731 F.Supp 1363 (S.D. Ind. 1990).

46 *Lee v. Downs,* 641 F.2d 1117 (4th Cir. 1981).

47 *Smith v. Fairman,* 678 F.2d 52 (7th Cir. 1982).

48 Katherine Bennett, "Constitutional Issues in Cross-Gender Searches and Visual Observation of Nude Inmates by Opposite-Sex Officers: A Battle Between and Within the Sexes," *Prison Journal* 75 (1995): 90–112.

49 *Pugh v. Locke,* 406 F.2d 318 (1976).

50 Bradley S. Chilton, *Prisons under the Gavel: The Federal Court Takeover of Georgia Prisons* (Columbus: Ohio State University Press, 1991).

51 *Hutto v. Finney,* 98 S. Ct. 2565 (1978).

52 *Rhodes v. Chapman,* 452 U.S. 337 (1981).

53 *Wolff v. McDonnell,* 418 U.S. 539 (1974).

54 Ibid.

55 *Lee v. Washington,* 390 U.S. 333 (1968).

56 *Pargo v. Elliot,* 49 F.3d 1355 (1995).

57 Jacobs, *New Perspectives,* p. 42.

58 *Wolff v. McDonnell,* 418 U.S. 539 (1974).

59 *Bell v. Wolfish,* 441 U.S. 520 (1979).

60 *Rhodes v. Chapman,* 452 U.S. 337 (1981).

61 Charles H. Jones, "Recent Trends in Corrections and Prisoners' Rights Law," in *Correctional Theory and Practice,* edited by Clayton A. Hartjen and Edward E. Rhine (Chicago: Nelson Hall, 1992), 119.

62 *Abdul Wali v. Coughlin,* 754 F.2d 1015 (2nd Cir. 1985).

63 *Daniels v. Williams,* 474 U.S. 327 (1986).

64 *Wilson v. Seiter,* 111 S. Ct. 2321 (1991).

65 *Estelle v. Gamble,* 429 U.S. 97 (1976); *Whitley v. Albers,* 475 U.S. 312 (1986).

66 Jack E. Call, "Prison Overcrowding Cases in the Aftermath of *Wilson v. Seiter,*" *Prison Journal* 75 (September 1995): 390–405.

67 *McCleskey v. Zant,* 111 S. Ct. 1454 (1991).

68 *Colman v. Thompson,* 111 S. Ct. 2546 (1991).

69 *Booth v. Churner,* 532 U.S. 731 (2001).

70 *Jones v. Bock,* 549 U.S. (2007).

71 Christopher E. Smith, "Prisoners' Rights and the Rehnquist Court Era," *Prison Journal* 87 (December 2007): 473.

72 Smith, "Prison Reform Litigation Era."

73 Feeley and Rubin, *Judicial Policy Making,* 366–75.

74 James B. Jacobs, "Judicial Impact on Prison Reform," in *Punishment and Social Control,* edited by Thomas G. Blomberg and Stanley Cohen (New York: Aldine DeGruyter, 1995), 63–76.

75 Warren E. Burger, "Chief Justice Burger Issues Year-End Report," *American Bar Association Journal* 62 (1976): 189–90.

76 Jeffrey H. Maahs and Rolando V. del Carmen, "Curtailing Frivolous Section 1983 Inmate Litigation: Laws, Practices, and Proposals," *Federal Probation* 59 (December 1995): 53–61.

77 *Johnson v. Avery,* 393 U.S. 499 (1969).

78 *Greenholtz v. Inmates of the Nebraska Penal and Correction Complex,* 442 U.S. 1 (1979).

79 *Connecticut Board of Pardons v. Dumschat,* 452 U.S. 458 (1981).

80 *Griffin v. Wisconsin,* 483 U.S. 868 (1987).

81 Ibid.

82 *Pennsylvania Board of Probation and Parole v. Scott,* 524 U.S. 357 (1998).

83 *United States v. Knights,* 534 U.S. 112 (2001).

84 *Samson v. California,* 547 U.S. 843 (2006).

85 *Mempa v. Rhay,* 389 U.S. 128 (1967).

86 *Morrissey v. Brewer,* 408 U.S. 471 (1972).

87 *Gagnon v. Scarpelli,* 411 U.S. 778 (1973).

88 *Cooper v. Pate,* 378 U.S. 546 (1964).

89 *Monell v. Department of Social Services of the City of New York,* 436 U.S. 658 (1978).

90 *Hope v. Pelzer,* 536 U.S. 730 (2002).

91 *Correctional Services Corporation v. Malesko,* 534 U.S. 61 (2001).

92 Cripe, *Legal Aspects,* pp. 75–77.

© Tom Dahlin/Getty Images

LEARNING OBJECTIVES

After reading this chapter you should be able to . . .

1 Understand how the criminal justice system operates as a large selection process to determine who ends up in the corrections system.

2 Describe some of the main similarities among and differences between the general population and people who end up under correctional authority.

3 Identify different types of offenders in the corrections system and the kinds of problems they pose for corrections.

4 Describe the classification process for people under correctional authority and know why it is important.

5 Understand important problems and limitations in classifying people under correctional authority.

Among the thousands of fans in this stadium, how many are likely to be under correctional supervision? What are the characteristics of a "typical" offender? Would you recognize one sitting next to you?

CHANCES ARE, someone in this class with you, studying corrections, has been incarcerated. In fact, it is likely that more than one of your class members has been to jail, probably just an overnight stay for some public-order infraction or another. Perhaps one of your classmates has been to prison as well and has now joined you in studying the system that once held him—or, less likely, her—captive. It may strike you as odd to think that someone you see almost every day might have been locked behind bars, but statistics say that in a typical group of 30 or so young adults, probably at least one has been locked up, usually for a minor offense. As noted in Chapter 1, more than 3 percent of all adults in the United States are currently under some form of correctional control. This large group extends into all kinds of households, neighborhoods, and social groups.

THE CORRECTIONAL CLIENT

Still, the idea that one of "us" might be under correctional authority can be unsettling. We are used to thinking of offenders as somehow different from "normal" citizens, so when we encounter someone who has been on probation or imprisoned, we wonder both about how that person received a criminal sentence, and also about our preconceptions of offenders. Who are offenders? What gets them into trouble? What should we think of them?

Actually, anyone can get into trouble. So one answer to the question "What are offenders like?" is that they can be like any of us. Yet when we look at offenders as a group, we see that while they come from every walk of life, in fact the powerful and wealthy rarely encounter the criminal justice system. The typical client of the criminal justice system is a young, male minority member from a poor neighborhood. For example, African Americans make up less than one-seventh of the U.S. population but nearly half of the accused and convicted people in the justice system. Men comprise under half of the general population but nearly nine-tenths of the justice system population. Half of those entering state prisons are between 18 and 27 years old.

In this chapter, we examine why correctional clients, as a group, seem to differ so markedly from the general population. The reasons are not clear, but they generally have to do with the selection process that determines who gets charged, prosecuted, and convicted. Exactly how this selection process produces the subjects for corrections is a matter of some controversy.

Chapter

6

■ SELECTION FOR THE CORRECTIONS SYSTEM

The process leading to conviction might suggest that becoming a correctional client is quite difficult—as if corrections had to be "broken into," like a career. There is some truth to this idea. As **Figure 6.1** shows, we can view the criminal justice system as a filtering process, because it operates as a large offender-selection bureaucracy. At each

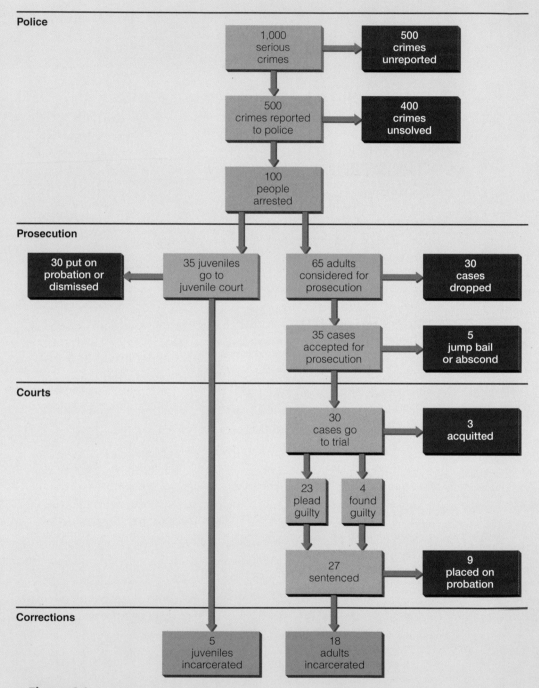

Figure 6.1
Criminal Justice as a Filtering Process

Decisions at each point in the system result in some cases being dropped while others are passed on to the next point. Are you surprised by the small portion of cases that remain?

Sources: Data in this figure have been drawn from many sources, including Bureau of Justice Statistics, *Sourcebook of Criminal Justice Statistics, 1999* (Washington, DC: U.S. Government Printing Office, 2000), and BJS *Bulletin,* February 1988.

stage, some defendants are sent on to the next stage, while others are either released or processed under changed conditions. Note that few suspects who are arrested are then prosecuted, tried, and convicted. Some go free because the police decide that a crime has not been committed or that the evidence is not sound. The prosecutor may decide that justice would be better served by sending the suspect to a substance abuse clinic. Many defendants will plead guilty, the judge may dismiss charges against others, and the jury may acquit a few defendants. Thus, the criminal justice system is often described as a filtering process or a funnel—many cases enter it, but only a few result in conviction and punishment. These few are the clients of corrections.

You can find the **Uniform Crime Reports** through the corresponding link at www .cengage.com/criminaljustice/clear.

What other factors can influence who becomes a correctional client? One factor is a policy decision that street crimes—committed disproportionately by the underprivileged—warrant more attention from police than do corporate or white-collar crimes committed by the middle and upper classes. This is especially true with regard to drug offenses, where the police focus greater attention on low-income sellers rather than suburban buyers.

The decision to grant bail and the amount required is a second factor influencing the filtering process. People with "stakes" in the community, such as homeowners and those with good jobs, are likely to be released on bail or their own recognizance pending trial. This decision may be made on the assumption that they will appear to face the charges because they have a lot to lose if they do not show up. People without jobs or property are more likely to be held in custody to make sure they will not flee. Bail for these people may be set so high they cannot pay, thus making it impossible to live in the community awaiting trial.

A defendant freed on bail has often been portrayed to the court as a solid citizen, someone for whom probation would be appropriate. The pretrial detainee, by contrast, often appears in court wearing dingy jail garb, looking for all the world like a person for whom being locked up would not much disrupt life.

Once a person is convicted, a range of punishments of escalating severity may be imposed (see Figure 4.1, pp. 76–77). The judge bases the sentence not only on the offense but also on the defendant's criminal history. Two-thirds of those convicted receive a community sentence such as a fine or probation. However, those convicted of serious crimes and those who have had previous contact with corrections are more likely than petty offenders or first timers to receive terms of incarceration (see **Figure 6.2**).

If current criminal justice policies seem defensible and reasonable—and few people advocate that we abandon them—then they must also be seen as a double-edged sword: People unfortunate enough to have few resources and to have had prior contacts with the justice system are generally treated the most harshly. The result is a correctional population that differs significantly from the general population. The distinctiveness of the correctional population is not lost on the offenders themselves. They recognize that many other people's charges were dropped or reduced but theirs were not, and that other offenders avoided the full penalties of the law by tapping resources they did not have.

Herein lies one of the most significant consequences of the filtering process in criminal justice: Despite their guilt, many offenders feel unjustly treated in comparison with others. Perhaps not surprisingly, these offenders are often not easy to manage in the probation, jail, or prison setting.

The obvious contrast between correctional populations and the general community also leads some critics to view criminal justice as a mechanism for social control of minorities and the lower classes (see **Table 6.1**). Historical studies of American corrections show that in earlier eras members of the newest immigrant groups filled the prisons out of proportion to their numbers in the general population. Since the Civil War, African Americans have consistently made up the largest group in southern prisons, but elsewhere the largest group has changed over time: first Germans, Irish, and Italians, and now African Americans and Hispanics. Further, although this idea of ethnic succession is not entirely consistent with recent research, our prisons and jails undeniably hold disproportionate numbers of poor, disadvantaged, and minority citizens.

However, even if many correctional clients share characteristics of social class, race, and sex, they also have important differences. In the sections that follow, we classify correctional clients according to some of those differences and discuss the implications of such classifications for correctional programming.

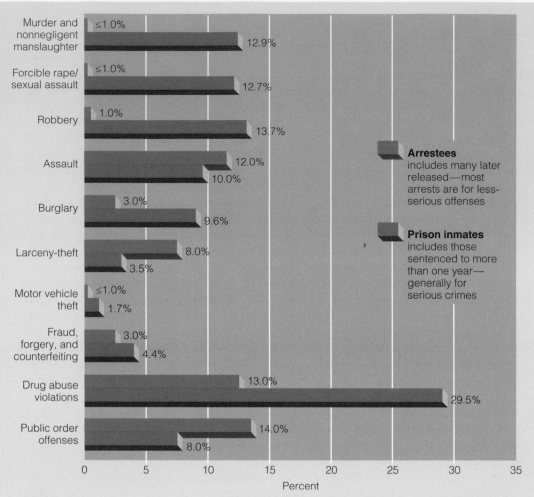

Figure 6.2

Percentages of People Arrested and Imprisoned for Offenses in 11 Categories

The justice system acts as a selection filter, increasingly bringing more-serious cases forward for severer punishments.

Sources: BJS *Bulletin,* March 2009; *Sourcebook,* http://www.albany.edu/sourcebook/.

TABLE 6.1 *Comparison of Gender and Race/Ethnicity of People under Different Types of Correctional Supervision*

These numbers show the percentage of offenders who receive probation, jail time, or prison sentences in two categories: gender and race/ethnicity. Women tend to spend far less time incarcerated than do men and are more likely to receive probation. Keep in mind that although the percentages of whites and blacks here are similar, the black percentages represent a much larger proportion of the African American community than the white percentages do of the white population.

	Probation	Jail	Parole	Prison
Male	77%	87%	88%	93%
Female	23	13	12	7
White	55	43	42	34
Black	29	39	37	40
Hispanic	13	16	19	20
Other	3	2	2	6

Note: Data are rounded. Hispanics may be of any race.
Sources: BJS *Bulletin,* December 2008; March 2009.

■ TYPES OF OFFENDERS AND THEIR PROBLEMS

In some respects, every offender assigned to corrections is unique; no two are exactly alike. Thus, in referring to "types" of offenders, individuals may be grouped because they share an important characteristic (such as type of offense) even when they differ in some other vital characteristic (such as prior record, social class, or intelligence). Any attempt to describe groups of offenders reflects a decision to generalize about people while potentially sacrificing individualism. For example, we tend to talk about "sex offenders" or "professional criminals" as though they all behaved in the past (and will behave in the future) in the same way. Although this approach simplifies policy making and correctional programming, it bears little resemblance to reality. Therein lies the peril of grouping offenders: If we forget that the grouping is done only to enable correctional officials to take action, we will inevitably distort portraits of individual offenders.

To be honest, then, our discussion of criminal categories will contain disputable statements about groups of offenders with whom corrections must work. Keep this in mind as you read about types of offenders. Whether situational offender or career criminal or elderly offender, some individuals fit into a group nicely, while others are more difficult to place; certainly, all individuals within a group will vary in some respects.

The groupings are made for our convenience, to help us understand the types of people corrections manages and the ways in which their characteristics influence the work of corrections. We also offer a series of personal stories to illustrate the types. Each is a true story; some are classics, like the story of Johnnie Baxstrom, about whom the United States Supreme Court once deliberated. Others, like Susan Smith, are people whose stories once dominated the news. There are a few old friends, like Archie and Nevin, whose stories we have used over the years because, even though they are decades old, their lives still reflect those of many of the mostly faceless people who go through the corrections system today. We also introduce our good friend, Michael Santos, a federal prisoner whose writing appears throughout this book. We tell these stories, current and historical, to give a human face to the people who go through the corrections system. Even the most troubling stories illustrate a central point about corrections—it is a system of people whose lives have depth and meaning well beyond the convenient labels we use to characterize their crimes.

situational offender
A person who in a particular set of circumstances has violated the law but who is not given to criminal behavior under normal circumstances and is unlikely to repeat the offense.

AP Images

Susan Smith confessed to murdering her sons by drowning. The situation and the circumstances leading to this crime are complicated and tragic.

The Situational Offender

Most people convicted of a felony are not arrested again. Some studies estimate that this is true for 80 percent of first-time offenders. Of course, some undoubtedly commit further crimes and are simply never caught, but most do not commit a second offense. The person entering the corrections system and having committed what appears to be a one-time offense is called a **situational offender**. In their classic study, Martin Haskell and Lewis Yablonsky described this type of offender as one who (1) confronted a problem requiring action, (2) took action that violated the criminal law, (3) was caught and given the status of criminal, and (4) until the time of the offense was committed to the normative system of our society and was indistinguishable from other people.[1] Thus, the situational offender "made a mistake" and "paid a debt to society" for that mistake (see the Focus box "Susan's Story").

FOCUS ON PEOPLE IN CORRECTIONS

Susan's Story

On October 25, 1994, Susan Smith released the brake on her maroon Mazda Protege and watched as it rolled into John D. Long Lake and took six endless minutes to sink, drowning her two sons, Michael (aged three years) and Alex (aged 14 months), who were strapped into their car seats inside. She then flagged down a passing motorist and told a panicky, concocted story claiming she had been carjacked and her children kidnapped by a young black man. In front of the television cameras, with her estranged husband David by her side, she tearfully pleaded for the return of the children unharmed.

Nine days later, Susan Smith confessed to the murders. Stunned Americans asked themselves how a mother could kill her own babies so cold-heartedly.

There is no easy answer to the question. Susan Smith is a situational offender, but her situation, and the circumstances leading to her crime, are complicated and tragic. No single fact explains her actions, of course, but when the totality of her life is presented, a picture emerges of a weak woman who had been victimized most of her life and who sought desperately to cling to a lover who rejected her because of her children.

The list of calamities befalling Susan Smith is devastating. Her father committed suicide when she was six years old, only a month after her parents' divorce. By the time she was 15, she was a victim again, repeatedly sexually molested by her stepfather, Beverly Russell, a pillar of the small town of Union, South Carolina, and a seemingly exemplary member

The situational offender presents many problems for corrections. First, the crime is usually a serious, violent crime (often murder or aggravated assault), and the offender usually knew the victim well (often a spouse or other family member). For such a crime, a severe punishment is thought appropriate. Even though only an extremely small percentage of murderers commit murder again, fear of the situational offender, together with outrage at the offense, often results in lengthy incarceration.

Yet once the situational offender begins the sentence, there is little for corrections to do. The person typically has a positive orientation toward accepted social values, a solid work history, and good basic employment skills. The prognosis for successful readjustment while on parole is extremely good. However, other than help in adjusting to the life crisis of imprisonment, few positive programming options exist for the situational offender. Correctional officers thus find managing the time served by these essentially adjusted offenders troublesome, because the officers can take few positive actions. Although situational offenders may participate in programs as a means of self-improvement, their time in prison remains mainly a matter of simply serving the sentence.

Moreover, with prison crowding, it is precisely the situational offenders who correctional officials and parole boards believe are most appropriate for early release, because these offenders pose little threat to the public. The spaces they vacate can house far more serious criminals. Granting early release to a situational offender opens the corrections system to criticism, however. Citizens inevitably react against what they may see as coddling and a failure of justice. Furthermore, the one situational offender out of 20 who murders again can destroy the careers of the officials who allowed parole. Therefore, situational offenders often remain in prison while other felons, those who actually represent more threat to society but less threat to corrections, are released.

The Career Criminal

career criminal
A person who sees crime as a way of earning a living, who has numerous contacts with the criminal justice system over time, and who may view the criminal sanction as a normal part of life.

One of the most slippery concepts in the classification of offenders is the so-called career criminal. When the criminologist Walter Reckless first developed the idea of the **career criminal**, he had in mind a specific set of attributes:

1 Crime is his way of earning a living, his main occupation.

2 He develops technical skills useful to the commission of his crimes.

of the Christian Coalition. When the abuse was discovered, Susan's mother seemed to blame Susan for the crime and chose not to prosecute. After a brief interval, the sexual assaults resumed, and they continued into Susan's early twenties, even after she was married to David Smith and bore their two children.

The marriage was no haven either, and it ended after three years under accusations of infidelity by both parties. In the time between her marital separation and the murders of her children, Susan had a series of sexual encounters, including an affair with a steady boyfriend named Tom Findlay and with Tom's father, who also happened to be Susan's boss.

When Tom broke off their affair, saying he did not want to raise another man's children, Susan's desperate need for love and fear of losing it must have erupted into an compulsion that ended in the frenzied decision to take her children's lives.

After hearing testimony about Susan's pitiful life, a jury sentenced her to life in prison without parole. But her troubles followed her into the prison system. Two correctional officers have been arrested, accused of having sexual relations with her, and when she took out an ad for a pen pal in 2003, many people reacted with exasperation. The nation was appalled by her act, but many felt pity for her after hearing the string of events that led her to kill her children. Her persistent problems, though, make the sympathy wear thin.

© Reuters/CORBIS

Career criminal, former Mafia hit man, and turncoat, Salvatore "Sammy the Bull" Gravano listens to the reading of charges against him in a Phoenix, Arizona, courtroom. In a 181-count criminal complaint, the state leveled 12 felony charges against the one-time Gambino crime family henchman for his alleged role in the syndicate and related conspiracy, drug, weapons, and money-laundering crimes.

3 He started as a delinquent child and progressed toward criminality.

4 He expects to do some time in prison as a "cost" of doing this type of work.

5 He is psychologically normal.[2]

Reckless attributed these characteristics to a small, more or less undifferentiated group of offenders who worked at crime, including organized-crime figures, white-collar criminals, and professional criminals who worked continuously at an illegal occupation (see the Focus box "Archie's Story"). However, the conception of career

FOCUS ON

PEOPLE IN CORRECTIONS

Archie's Story

Archie left home at age 13 and traveled around the country as a transient, sometimes supporting himself as a truck driver. Archie claims to have committed about five hundred burglaries, five hundred auto thefts, and five robberies before his 18th birthday. Of them, he was arrested for only one robbery. As he was not convicted, however, he has no juvenile record. Even in this early phase of his criminal career, Archie was quite sophisticated in his MO (*modus operandi*, or "method of operating"). He used theatrical makeup to disguise himself for his burglaries and robberies, including contact lenses of various colors. He recalls being fairly violent and obsessed about his small size. He injured one of his robbery victims when the man tried to resist.

Archie's first incarceration did not come until his mid-thirties. For this conviction he served several years in a California prison. Although his rap sheet shows nine arrests for drug violations and petty theft, the only serious prison time he served before his present term was for an auto theft conviction.

Before his first incarceration, Archie was employed much of the time, but his main source of income was crime. His wife was a heroin addict. Between his 18th birthday and his first incarceration, he estimates that he committed about 100 grand thefts, 100 burglaries, and 12 robberies. His average take per robbery was about $2,500. He was never arrested for any of these crimes. He used the loot mainly to support his wife's drug habit and for partying.

The main targets of Archie's robberies were savings and loan banks or payroll offices. His MO was to disguise himself in full theatrical makeup and to enter the savings and loan carrying a sawed-off shotgun, which he would point at a young female employee.

The main targets of Archie's burglaries were pawnshops or businesses. His few residential burglaries were at private homes where an informer had told him a valuable collection or large sums of money were kept. His typical MO was to make the acquaintance of the prospective victim and gain access to his home to learn where the valuables were kept. Within a month after befriending the victim, Archie would burglarize his house. He also performed insurance fraud burglaries in which the "victim" would indicate the articles he wanted stolen. Archie would burglarize the house at a prearranged time, stealing the articles that had been specified and selling them to a fence. The fence would profit, Archie would profit, and the insurance company would reimburse the victim for the items stolen.

Archie reports having shot victims when they tried to resist, in both burglaries and robberies. He also mentions having retaliated against two heroin addicts who were friends of his wife and who apparently had tried to kill him. Archie says that both were seriously injured. Archie relates that his first conviction and incarceration occurred because his wife informed on him when he was trying to stop her from using drugs.

After release from the first incarceration, in his late thirties, Archie remained on the street about five years before being incarcerated for his present term. During this period he committed only four robberies, at large stores or markets, and they yielded very large amounts of money. As in his earlier years, he engaged in elaborate planning for each crime. Archie was convicted by a jury on two counts of armed robbery with a prior felony conviction, and he is serving two concurrent sentences of five-to-life; he is also serving two consecutive five-to-life sentences for use of a firearm in these robberies.

Source: Joan Petersilia, Peter W. Greenwood, and Marvin Lavin, *Criminal Careers of Habitual Felons* (Washington, DC: U.S. Government Printing Office, 1978), 100–101.

criminals has recently changed. Given research ranging from studies of a group of men born in Philadelphia in 1958 to interviews with convicted and imprisoned adults in California, Texas, and Michigan, scholars in the 1980s concluded that a small group of active criminals commits a majority of all crimes.[3] This led to a significant shift in thinking about career criminals. Instead of applying the term to someone whose work is crime, policy makers began to use it to refer to any offender with several convictions or arrests. Thus, a person with as few as three or four convictions now is commonly labeled a career criminal. This may seem a bit odd to most of us; we would hardly call our own jobs a career if we had been seen at work only three or four times.

Of course, many individuals who are repeatedly convicted actually do admit to more crimes, sometimes many more than the handful for which they are being punished. Peter Greenwood's famous study of robbers, for example, found that as many as half of those with multiple convictions for robbery admitted to having committed a large number of robberies for which they had not been caught.[4] Undeniably, this small minority made something of a career out of that crime. Still, many repeaters—almost half of Greenwood's sample, for example—are not high-rate offenders. That is, the mere existence of multiple convictions does not imply a career in crime as Reckless defines it; the person may simply be a frequent offender (have committed several crimes in the past few years) who shifts from one type of crime to another.

Why, then, this recent trend to paint the picture of the career criminal with such a broad brush? Part of the answer has to do with political pressures. With the devaluation of rehabilitation in the 1970s came renewed confidence in incapacitation as the appropriate correctional course. But if incapacitation was the political catchword, what group would be the target? Previous studies had unearthed so few career criminals that this notion was not promising for crime control hard-liners. If the career criminal concept could be expanded to include virtually all multiple repeaters, however, then the target group for this newly popular policy would be large indeed.

Corrections has borne the cost of this conceptual shift. Much as in the case of violent situational criminals, pressure has grown to keep repeaters in prison longer to prevent them from pursuing their predatory "careers." Yet these criteria result in nonprofessional but intermittent offenders being misclassified as career criminals. One result is that they contribute to prison overcrowding. California's three-strikes legislation, discussed in Chapter 1, specifies a sentence of 25 years to life for the third felony conviction. It is meant to catch career criminals early in their careers, but critics point out that it ends up putting a large number of petty repeaters behind bars for a very long time.

Without question, our prisons hold some career criminals—professional offenders committed to lives of crime. But we must examine the accuracy of the overall label and recognize that any decision to classify offenders has social and political significance.

The Sex Offender

Although a wide array of legislation regulates sexual conduct, corrections commonly deals with three basic types of **sex offenders:** (1) rapists (sexual assaulters), (2) child molesters (pedophiles), and (3) to a lesser extent, prostitutes. Each subclass of sex offender has a variety of economic, psychological, and situational motivations, and for each the correctional response is deeply influenced by prevailing public opinion about the crimes themselves. See "Myths in Corrections" for more.

THE RAPIST ■ With the resurgence of feminism in the 1960s and 1970s, the justice system's response to rape became a major political issue. Indeed, to discuss rape under the heading of "sex offenses" risks ignoring that it is primarily an act of violence against women. In her classic study, *Against Our Will,* Susan Brownmiller persuasively argued that rape needed to be reconceptualized; it is not a sex crime but a brutal personal assault: "To a woman the definition of rape is fairly simple. . . . A deliberate violation of emotional, physical and rational integrity and . . . [a] hostile, degrading act of violence."[5] When rape is placed where it truly belongs, within the context of modern criminal violence and not within the purview of archaic masculine codes, the crime retains its unique dimensions, taking its place with armed robbery and aggravated assault. The link between lethal violence and sexual assault is illustrated by the fact that about half of all murders of women committed by acquaintances and two-thirds of those by strangers occurred in the process of sexual assaults.[6]

The widespread reconception of rape—the recognition that it is not sexually motivated but represents a physical intrusion fueled by a desire for violent coercion—

sex offender
A person who has committed a sexual act prohibited by law, such as rape, child molestation, or prostitution, for economic, psychological, or situational reasons.

MYTHS IN CORRECTIONS

SEX OFFENDERS AND VIOLENCE

THE MYTH: The offenders commit crimes of violence typically victimizing unsuspecting strangers.

THE REALITY: Most sexual offenses occur between people who are acquainted with each other and involve coercion but not violence.

Source: Karen Terry, *Sexual Offenses and Offenders; Theory, Practice and Policy* (Belmont, CA: Wadsworth. 2006).

The website of the **Rape, Abuse and Incest National Network** contains important data and support resources for rape; see the corresponding link at www.cengage.com/criminaljustice/clear.

led to two broad shifts in criminal justice. The first was a move to redefine the crime of rape as a gender-neutral "sexual assault" or even as a special case of the general crime of assault.

The second was a trend toward harsher sentences for convicted rapists. The sexual assaulter presents particular difficulties for correctional management. The truly violent sex offender may well be a security risk inside the prison, for the same irrational attitudes and unpredictable behavior patterns displayed before conviction might also occur during incarceration. More likely, however, the rapist will become a target for inmate violence. In the prisoner subculture, "crazies," including many rapists, are near the bottom of the pecking order. Such offenders commonly are subjected to humiliating physical and sexual attacks as a form of inmate domination. Thus, whether unpredictably violent or predictably vulnerable to attack, the incarcerated sexual assaulter is a security risk.

THE CHILD MOLESTER ■ Few offenses are so uniformly reviled or carry so great a stigma as child molestation does. However, only in recent years, with more-open discussion of sexual issues, have scholars focused significantly on convicted child molesters.

The picture of the child molester that emerges is more tragic than disgusting (see the Focus box "Nevin's Story"). As many as 90 percent of child molesters were themselves molested as children, and sex offenders are about twice as likely as other offenders to report being sexually victimized as a child.[7] Child molestation is a complex crime involving many factors; it ordinarily stems from deep feelings of personal inadequacy on the part of the offender. As many as 20 percent of child molesters are over 50 years old, and many cases involve ambivalent feelings of attachment between adults and children that gradually become converted into sexual contact. Many child molesters are of borderline intelligence. Some victims of molestation are confused by the crime and feel guilty about it because of their emotional attachment to their molesters. They usually are aware that the act is "wrong" or "bad." If the act arouses pleasurable feelings, the situation is further complicated.

The child molester is often the most despised offender in court and in prison. An incarcerated molester is almost certain to be the target of repeated threats, physical violence, and routine hostility from other prisoners. Moreover, because most prison systems have little treatment options for molesters, this offender's experience in prison typically is quite bleak. As a result, some states have set aside special institutions or cell blocks for molesters in order to ensure their safety.

THE PROSTITUTE ■ Prostitution is more an economic than a sexual crime; that is, it is an illegal business transaction between a service provider and a customer. Public opinion about prostitution is ambivalent; public policy seems to fluctuate between "reform" legislation designed to legalize and regulate prostitution and wholesale police roundups of "hookers and pimps" to "clean up" the streets. The AIDS epidemic has fueled renewed concern about prostitutes' transmission of the disease. In response, some courts have ordered infected prostitutes to refrain from practicing their trade. In any event, prostitution exists (even flourishes) in virtually every section of the country, and when prostitutes or their pimps are punished, the sentence generally is probation or a fine.

A study of female street prostitutes in the Los Angeles County Jail found that many began their work at age 15, and one-third got started through family or friends. Seventy per-

In 2005 John E. Couey abducted 9-year old Jessica Lunsford, raped and buried her alive. Couey's blasé demeanor at his trial galvanized the public to demand that actions be taken to prevent "sexually violent predators" from living in the community. Couey remains on Florida's death row.

AP Images/John VanBeekum, Pool

FOCUS ON

PEOPLE IN CORRECTIONS

Nevin's Story

For as long as he can remember, Nevin has relived in his dreams the experience of being forced to have oral sex with a man when he was about five years old. At the age of 49, serving a 5–10-year term for the sexual assault of a 10-year-old boy, Nevin confronted correctional authorities in Connecticut with a problem. He has filed a lawsuit to force the state to provide treatment for him after his release from the maximum-security prison in Somers. He has no money to pay for treatment, and he says flatly that he will never be able to resist the attraction he feels toward young boys.

Nevin's criminal record stretches back 35 years. He has been in and out of prisons in Connecticut, New York, and Pennsylvania for all but five of those years. He estimates that he has sexually assaulted about a thousand boys during his lifetime, and he has said that he has never had any difficulty finding willing partners. "I hang out where the prostitutes hang out, and they [boys] approach me. That solves the problem. I walk down Forty-second Street in New York City, and in 15 minutes I have five kids asking if they can go home with me, because I'm known as that type of person." Nevin prefers dark-haired, dark-skinned youngsters and says that he has paid various fees. "I'd pay 20 dollars. I'd pay 50 cents."

Pedophilia, preference for children as sexual objects, is an extremely difficult abnormality to cure. Psychologists believe pedophiles are generally sane and in all other respects are good citizens, but they cannot control this one aspect of their lives. Sexual aversion therapy has been used in some cases. At the Somers Prison it was used until 1975, when it was stopped as a result of a lawsuit filed by child molesters who said that they were being denied parole release unless they underwent the treatment. The technique involved the application of electric shocks to the genital area when photographs of nude children were flashed on a screen. Injections of Depo-Provera are also being used with some pedophiles at the Sexual Disorders Clinic at Johns Hopkins University Hospital, Baltimore. The drug blunts the male sexual drive, and success has been reported when its use is accompanied by therapy. Depo-Provera, however, is not approved for use in the prison setting.

Nevin has written to the Superior Court asking for treatment upon release. The Department of Correction says it has given him treatment, cannot hold him longer than his sentence, and cannot provide treatment after release. Should Nevin be able to prove that the state has an obligation to provide treatment, providing that treatment would be up to another state agency, such as the Department of Mental Health?

Nevin acknowledges he has a responsibility "not to engage in this type of behavior." Nevin is more concerned with the rights of the boys he fears will become his next victims than he is with the protection of his own rights. In his letter to the court he wrote, "I believe it is time we consider the rights of the people to be safe in their homes and to be secure in the knowledge that their children can go to school safely without being molested." Because he is sane, Nevin cannot be involuntarily committed to a state mental hospital. What should be done? What of the pedophiles who are not so concerned about their problem as Nevin is?

Source: Adapted from the *Hartford Courant*, October 12–14, 1984. Reprinted by permission of the Los Angeles Times reprints.

---

cent had children, but 90 percent of these did not have custody of them. The study found that street prostitutes tend to be children of dysfunctional families, brought up without parents in an atmosphere of drug use and sexual assault.[8] Child prostitution is a special version of this problem, because the sexual exploitation of these children has such a lasting impact on them. One study has estimated that as many as 300 teenagers work as prostitutes in one active New York City area, alone, many of them boys.[9]

Because prostitution is an economic crime, correctional caseworkers must find a substitute vocation for offenders. This is not easy, for many prostitutes lack education and marketable skills, and many are addicted to drugs. Further, many attempt to leave the trade but few succeed until age, illness, or disability renders them less productive. Because prostitution is more a nuisance than a threat to the public, caseworkers tend to accord such cases low priority, as do the courts and prosecutors. Therefore, prostitution often receives marginal enforcement of laws and indifferent punishment.

To learn about the **Mary Magdalene Project**, an organization providing sanctuary to prostitutes, go to the corresponding link at www .cengage.com/criminaljustice/ clear.

CONCERN ABOUT THE SEX OFFENDER   ■   In 2005, when John E. Couey abducted nine-year-old Jessica Lunsford from her bedroom in the middle of the night, raped her, and eventually murdered her, a nation watched the case with horror. Couey had a long criminal record with over 24 arrests and including a conviction for the assault of a woman during a burglary for which he was sentenced to 10 years. The sight of Couey idly scribbling on a notepad as the most gruesome facts of his crime were put in evidence—little Jessica had been repeatedly raped and was buried alive, suffocating to death in a plastic bag—galvanized a response to deal with what many referred to as "sexually violent predators," people who repeatedly victimized others sexually and seemed incapable of stopping themselves from escalating their violence. Many sex offenders are recidivists, because treatment often does not succeed. In recent years 16 states have enacted "sexually violent predator" statutes. These laws are based on the belief that society needs a way to keep potentially dangerous "perverts" off the streets after their sentences have been served. Many states are placing released sex offenders under longer terms of intense supervision, while others have imposed tougher sentencing measures. All states now have laws requiring public notification when sex offenders are paroled.

Partly in response to fears about repeat sexual violence committed by "sexually violent predators," new laws call for a range of close controls to be placed on people convicted of sex crimes, from broad community notification when they move into the neighborhood after release from prison to GPS monitoring of their whereabouts, 24 hours a day. The most drastic type of legislation, passed by 19 states, allows correctional authorities to propose indefinite "civil commitment" of people classified as "violent sexual predators," which in practice means they will be confined for life (or until cured) in a mental institution devoted to them. These new laws seem harsh, but the courts have upheld them as constitutional.[10]

Concern about sex offenders is understandable but not always completely appropriate. One of the most authoritative studies of 10,000 sex offenders released from prison found that they were four times more likely than other offenders to be rearrested for a sex offense within three years of their release.[11] Yet this figure could be misleading. Only 5.3 percent of the 10,000 sex offenders were rearrested for a sex crime (compared with a mere 1.3 percent of the others released that year). To complicate matters further, sex offenders as a group were far less likely to be rearrested for *any* kind of offense; 43 percent of sex offenders have a new arrest after three years, compared with 68 percent of all others. Another study has found that juveniles who are convicted of sex-related crimes are no more likely to be arrested for sex crimes as adults than are other types of juvenile delinquents.[12] So while it is clear that sex offenders pose a different kind of risk than do other offenders, it is equally clear that many sex offenders do quite well after release from prison.

The new laws are quite popular, but they raise important questions about the reach of the laws and fairness in dealing with people who commit sex crimes. On the one hand, research has not shown promising results for treatment programs. This suggests that civil-commitment programs are not likely to help those sent there. Indeed, there appear to be problems in the management of some civil-commitment centers, with poorly trained staff and difficulties in maintaining control.[13] On the other hand, alarm about sex offenders may be overblown. Studies have consistently shown that not only do convicted sex offenders have lower-than-average rates of new crimes after they have served their sentences, they even appear to have low rates of new *sex* offenses; the average sex offender neither specializes in certain kinds of sex crimes nor is persistent in crime, generally.[14] The John E. Coueys of this world are extremely rare, and it turns out that trying to predict who they are is nearly impossible (see the section on classification, later in this chapter).

The Substance Abuser

Substance abuse and addiction fundamentally influence the nature of the correctional population. As noted by the National Center on Addiction and Substance Abuse, crime and alcohol/drug abuse in America are joined at the hip. They found that four out of five jail and prison inmates "had been high when they committed their crimes, had stolen to support their habit or had a history of drug and alcohol abuse that led them to commit crime."[15]

Criminal law typically distinguishes between the use of illegal drugs and the illegal use of alcohol. In the case of drugs, any unauthorized possession of a controlled substance is prohibited. Laws against the mere possession of some drugs are so strict that, in the federal system as well as many states, prison terms are mandatory for such offenses. In contrast, possession of alcohol is prohibited only for minors. The criminal justice system becomes involved in alcohol offenders' lives primarily because of their conduct under the influence of alcohol. Because the difference between these two types of offenders is important for correctional policy, we discuss them here separately.

THE DRUG ABUSER ■ Our culture is a drug-using culture, from aspirin and caffeine to marijuana and cocaine. Not surprisingly, then, substance abuse figures prominently in criminal behavior (see the Focus box "Mary Lou's Story"). Nearly one-third of state prison inmates serving time for violent offenses were under the influence of an illegal drug when they committed the crime.[16] As **Figure 6.3** shows, from 55 to 76 percent of offenders arrested in 12 U.S. cities tested positive for an illegal drug at the time of their arrest. While only about 2 percent of the U.S. adult population abuse drugs, over half of those in prison admit to doing so.[17]

The **drug abuser** presents both treatment and management problems for corrections. The offender may have been convicted for possession or sale of drugs or for some other offense committed as a result of their use. Thus, correctional personnel must address the effects of drug dependency while the client is in detention, on probation, in prison, or on parole. The drug abuser also represents a potential control problem for correctional staff because of a high likelihood of rearrest.

Information on **commonly abused drugs** can be found at the website of the National Institute on Drug Abuse, listed at www.cengage.com/criminaljustice/clear.

drug abuser
A person whose use of illegal chemical substances disrupts normal living patterns to the extent that social problems develop, often leading to criminal behavior.

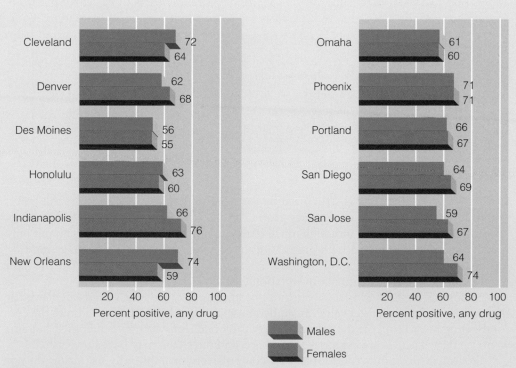

Figure 6.3
Drug Use by Booked Arrestees in 12 U.S. Cities
A large proportion of felony arrestees are under the influence of drugs at the time of their arrest.

Source: National Institute of Justice, *ADAM: 2002 Annual Report* (Washington, DC: U.S. Government Printing Office, April 2003).

PEOPLE IN CORRECTIONS

Mary Lou's Story

Mary Lou looks much older than her 25 years. She was brought up in Chicago in a family of six children, where the only income was her mother's monthly welfare check. She is now approaching the time of her release from prison after serving a sentence for driving the getaway car involved in the armed robbery of a drugstore.

A school dropout at age 16, Mary Lou met Frankie, a flashy dude who seemed to have money to spend yet was always on the street. Soon she was doing drugs with Frankie, and even though her girlfriends warned her that he was a junkie and a pimp, she moved into his apartment; by then, she had graduated to heroin. During their first weeks together, they were high much of the time—sleeping through the morning, getting a fix, then cruising the streets in Frankie's Buick, dropping in at bars and apartments to visit what seemed like an endless number of his friends.

When Frankie's money ran low, he told Mary Lou she was going to have to "hustle" if she expected to live with him. She told him she wouldn't and moved in with a girlfriend. Within a day, she was feeling so bad that she had to borrow money for a fix. Faced with her habit and an empty pocketbook, Mary Lou hustled. She turned two tricks the first night, but her second customer beat her up. Shaken by the experience and hurting for heroin, she returned to the only person she thought could help her—Frankie. He was not happy to see her, because another girl had already taken her place, but he agreed to help if she would hustle for him. During the next six months she was able to make enough money to retain Frankie's protection and to support her habit.

With the onset of winter, the streets of Chicago turned cold, and the supply of heroin on the streets suddenly tightened in response to a strong law enforcement effort. By this time both Mary Lou and Frankie were heavy users. After two frantic days of trying to find affordable heroin, Frankie decided to rob a drugstore. In a haze, Mary Lou drove him to the store, parked in an alley, and waited while Frankie, armed with a gun, entered the store. Within minutes he came dashing back, a burglar alarm blaring in his wake. Mary Lou gunned the Buick down the alley and into the street, where it struck another car. Frankie jumped out and ran off. A stunned Mary Lou just sat behind the wheel while a crowd formed and an officer arrived to investigate the accident.

It took little detective work for the police to link the collision to the robbery. They arrested Frankie back at his apartment and took him to the station house for booking. Mary Lou was already there when he was brought in. Held in the Cook County jail awaiting court action, she endured agonizing withdrawal from heroin.

At the suggestion of her public defender, Mary Lou pleaded guilty to a reduced charge of abetting an armed robbery and was sentenced to a three- to five-year term.

The street addict's life is structured by the need to get money to support the habit, and that need often leads to property crime. Studies of the relationship between drugs and crime have found that although much of the money for supporting a drug habit may be legitimately obtained, a high proportion of drug users admit to income-generating crimes. Even if an addict supports only a small fraction of the habit's cost through crime, this can translate into many violations.

Habits costing $50–$150 a day are not uncommon. Because stolen goods are fenced at much less than their market value, an addict must steal goods worth several times the cost of the drug just to support the habit. Robbery is more directly lucrative than theft but also more chancy: There is always a risk of violence, and the victim may have little cash.

Treatment programs for people who compulsively or habitually use drugs do not have high success rates, and some are controversial. As the social movement against heroin grew in the 1950s and 1960s, support for clinical treatment of addiction also grew, and special drug treatment facilities were opened to house addicts as a special population of incarcerated offenders. Civil-commitment procedures were often used to send convicted offenders to such facilities, where their incarceration term frequently exceeded what they would otherwise have received. Evaluations of these programs showed dismal results. For example, one of the early long-term follow-up studies of

100 treated prisoners found only 10 instances of five or more consecutive years of abstinence following hospitalization.[18]

Thus, substance abusers represent a serious dilemma for corrections. By definition, their behavior is compulsive and likely to be repeated. Although the mere act of drug abuse is not considered a serious offense, the collateral acts of predatory crime and violence are considered quite serious.

Since the 1980s, federal policies have sought to combat drug abuse by providing tougher criminal sanctions. Punishments for drug possession and sales were made considerably harsher, especially in the federal courts, where sentences of 10 years or longer became routine. There was also a renewed emphasis on treatment for drug addiction, and some of these prison-based programs had better results than the earlier civil-commitment programs did. Yet most experts believe the dual-track strategy of punishment and treatment has not yet appreciably lowered drug abuse among citizens and offenders.

THE ALCOHOL ABUSER ■ Unlike marijuana, heroin, and other controlled substances, alcohol is widely available and relatively inexpensive, and its consumption is an integral part of life in the United States. Only when alcohol leads to problems such as unemployment, family disorganization, and crime does society become concerned (see the Focus box "Bill's Story").

The **alcohol abuser's** problem translates into crime much less directly than that of the drug user. Where many addicts must engage in a criminal act just to get the drug of their choice, the alcoholic need only go to the corner store. However, alcoholics produce far more disastrous consequences than heroin addicts do. According to some estimates,

alcohol abuser
A person whose use of alcohol is difficult to control, disrupting normal living patterns and frequently leading to violations of the law while under the influence of alcohol or in attempting to secure it.

FOCUS ON PEOPLE IN CORRECTIONS

Bill's Story

Bill Gunderson is only 39 years old but he looks 60. His eyes are sunken; his face is bony, pockmarked, and stubbly. He is bundled up in layer on layer of clothing, topped by a grease-stained, military-green overcoat. His hair, clotted in bunches and standing out all over his head, combines with his physique to give him the appearance of a scarecrow. On this day in late December, Gunderson is stumbling among the crowd of affluent holiday shoppers on King Street in Alexandria, Virginia, looking for handouts and having little success. They can immediately tell that he is drunk.

Being drunk is Gunderson's normal state. Because he has no home, he is often drunk in public and has been arrested repeatedly on this charge since he arrived in Alexandria two months before. "The cops pick me up whenever I get too drunk, not because they want to," Gunderson says. "A couple of times they just took my bottle and poured it on the street. But usually they pick me up. It's for my own health, I reckon."

After his first arrest, Gunderson was driven directly to the city's detoxification center, a six-bed facility designed to relieve some of the burden on the Alexandria Correctional Center. "They gave me a bed, let me take a shower, and gave me some coffee," Gunderson says. But after a few hours he

began to go into withdrawal, and because the detox center is not staffed or equipped to administer sedatives to ease the pain, Gunderson left in search of the only relief he knows—another bottle of wine. "I was shaking so bad, but the only thing they told me was, 'Hey, you gotta go through it.'"

The second time Gunderson was arrested, the detox center refused to admit him and the police took him to jail. Every time after that—Gunderson guesses it has happened 16 times in a month and a half—he has gone straight to jail. He is always released after a few hours and told to appear later for trial. Gunderson says he has never appeared in court and has no intention of doing so. "They don't care," he says with a toothless grin. "Why should they?" Sheriff Michael Norris of Alexandria admits that the police do not track down drunks like Gunderson for court appearances. The offense is punishable only by a $10 fine, and no matter what the police do, they are likely to pick up the same offender on the same charge a few days later. "It's just a merry-go-round," Sheriff Norris says.

Source: D. Whitford, "Despite Decriminalization, Drunks Still Clog Our Nation's Jails," *Corrections Magazine,* April 1983, p. 31. Reprinted by permission of the Edna McConnell Clark Foundation.

alcohol use contributes to almost 100,000 deaths annually, about six times the total number of homicides reported to the police. Alcohol is more closely associated with crimes of violence than is any illegal drug, and the number of alcohol-related traffic fatalities is about the same as the number of homicides. Alcohol use impairs coordination and judgment, reduces inhibitions, and confuses understanding; criminal acts can easily follow. Thus, a drunk's drive home may become vehicular homicide, a domestic dispute may become aggravated assault, a political debate or quarrel over money may become disorderly conduct, and a night of drinking may lead to burglary or auto theft. It has been estimated that one-third of those in jail are under the influence of alcohol at the time of their offense.[19]

Although research on alcoholic offenders has focused on the incarcerated, these offenders appear in other correctional environments as well. One survey found that offenders convicted of driving while intoxicated (DWI) made up 14 percent of probationers, 7 percent of jail inmates, and 2 percent of state prisoners.[20] Like drug abusers, alcoholics present problems for probation officers, community treatment providers, and parole officers. Because some alcoholics become assaultive when they drink, dealing with them is neither pleasant nor safe.

Other problems are related to the treatment of alcohol abusers. To some extent, these problems stem from Americans' generally ambivalent attitude toward alcohol use, which is seen as recreational behavior rather than deviance. Consequently, treatment programs seem to work best when they focus on getting people to recognize the nature of their own patterns of alcohol use rather than on alcohol use per se. This is one reason why the program of Alcoholics Anonymous (AA) has consistently proved the most successful of alcohol treatment methods: It provides intensive peer support to help people face their own personal inability to manage alcohol use.

Despite its general success, AA may be of limited usefulness to criminal offenders, many of whom come from lower social classes that appear less responsive to AA's middle-class orientation. Moreover, AA views itself as a strictly voluntary treatment program; individuals must want to help themselves to subscribe to it. This characteristic often clashes with the coercive nature of treatment in corrections, which may require attendance at AA meetings as a condition of the sentence. The poor fit between AA's voluntary peer group structure and the involuntary nature of corrections may explain why studies find these programs somewhat ineffective with offenders convicted of public drunkenness.

The Mentally Ill Offender

Alex Ocasio, inmate no. 91A9788, held in New York's Stormville maximum-security prison, is a paranoid schizophrenic who not only hears voices that aren't there but must endure the taunts of other inmates who call him "bug" for the medication ("bug juice") that he and many other mentally ill prisoners must drink every night. Ocasio, serving time for robbery, is one of an estimated 15,000 mentally ill prisoners held in the New York system alone. Nationwide almost 800,000 inmates in prisons and almost 500,000 in jails suffer from some form of mental health problem.[21] People behind bars who are approaching release to the community are about five times more likely to suffer from schizophrenia or other psychotic disorders, and are twice as likely to suffer from depression and stress disorder.[22] In addition, about 550,000 probationers have a mental condition or have stayed overnight in a mental hospital at some point in their lives.[23]

Few images disturb people more than that of the "crazy," violence-prone criminal whose acts seem random, senseless, or even psychopathic. To understand such people better, correctional professionals often roughly classify them as "disturbed" or **mentally ill offenders**—people whose rational processes do not seem to operate in normal ways (see the Focus box "Johnnie's Story," p. 150). Mentally ill offenders are less able than most people to think realistically about their conduct, including criminal conduct. Not all mentally ill offenders are violent or psychopathic. Recent studies show that only 3 percent of the violent behavior in the United States is attributable to mental disorder, and people with mental illness are more likely to be victims of crime than perpetrators of violence.[24] Yet those citizens whose mental disorders translate into criminality present significant problems for corrections.

mentally ill offender
A "disturbed" person whose criminal behavior may be traced to diminished or otherwise abnormal capacity to think or reason, as a result of psychological or neurological disturbance.

Nationally, 43 percent of state prisoners report mental illness. Group therapy is one of the most used treatments in the prison context.

The classification of most violent offenders as "mentally ill" is now recognized as both an overgeneralization and a social issue. For one thing, not all violent offenders are demonstrably mentally ill. For another, the decision to apply the label "sick" (which the term *psychopath* or *sociopath* implies, *-path* meaning ill person) makes the person seem somehow less whole and makes it easier to justify extreme correctional measures.

There is some overlap between what we described as the career criminal and the so-called psychopath. Both engage in frequent criminal activity. The intended distinction between them is made clear in the original description of the psychopath: "an asocial, aggressive, highly impulsive person, who feels little or no guilt and is unable to form lasting bonds of affection with other human beings.[25] Thus, the psychopath lacks attachment to people or rules, whereas a career criminal is motivated by economic gain. However, in practice this distinction is problematic because it presumes knowledge of another person's private thoughts. Who can prove that another individual never feels love, affection, or guilt and should therefore be labeled psychopathic? Who can prove that the same individual might not also be motivated by material gain?

The central problem with the mental health model of criminality is that we cannot observe people's minds; we can only infer their inner feelings and thoughts from their behavior. When we see people behaving in outrageous or bizarre ways, we are tempted to infer that their mind or emotions work in strange ways. We call these people "sick" or "emotionally ill" even when there is no evidence of an illness, in the sense of the flu or other physical disease. In earlier times, deities, witches, and instincts were considered to cause a variety of odd or criminal behaviors. As Thomas Szasz has argued, today we use the term *mental illness* to explain behaviors we do not understand, even if the behavior is not caused by a "disease of the brain."[26]

Our need to explain some criminal behavior as mental illness can easily lead us to overgeneralize and ascribe mental illness to all criminals. In 1969 the National Commission on the Causes and Prevention of Violence recognized the problem when it concluded famously that (1) research evidence does not support the popular idea that the mentally ill are overrepresented in the population of violent criminals and (2) people identified as mentally ill generally pose no greater risk of committing violent crimes than does the population as a whole.[27]

FOCUS ON

PEOPLE IN CORRECTIONS

Johnnie's Story

Johnnie Baxstrom was a black male, born on August 12, 1918, in Greensboro, North Carolina. He quit school when he was seventeen, while he was in the eleventh grade. As described by his hospital notes, throughout his childhood "he had what he termed 'fainting headaches.'" He said it felt as though someone were beating on the side of his temple and that he would black out in school. He was hospitalized from May 29, 1956, to June 8, 1956, for head injury. Diagnosis: "Idiopathic Epilepsy and residuals from Bilateral Subdural Hematoma, following skull fracture."

Baxstrom had a very irregular job record showing that he worked only for short times at a variety of unskilled positions. He did have a good military record; he entered the armed forces in September 1943 and received an honorable discharge in March 1946. He was married three times. Baxstrom's criminal record is a lengthy list of drinking and property offenses. However, his first offense did not occur until he was thirty, which was two years after his getting out of the military service and while he was living with his second wife. He was charged with assaulting a female with a dangerous weapon, but the case was never disposed of in the courts. Again in 1950, he was arrested on two counts of assault and one of larceny in Baltimore. . . . He was found not guilty of all charges. His first conviction occurred six months later. He received a twelve-month sentence on the road gang for an "affray [offensive] assault on a female." Over the next few years, Baxstrom appears to have taken up a wandering lifestyle involving no work. Between 1951 and 1958,

when he was sentenced to Attica, Baxstrom was arrested twelve times . . . for such things as trespassing on Southern Railway property, drunkenness, vagrancy, disorderly conduct, intoxication, and one time for robbery for which he received and served a one-year sentence in the Maryland House of Corrections.

On October 21, 1958, Baxstrom was arrested in Rochester, New York, for attacking a police officer with an ice pick. According to hospital records, he stabbed the officer in the face, forehead, and collarbone. . . . Apparently Baxstrom was drinking in a bar where he got into a fight with another patron. During the fight Baxstrom pulled a knife or ice pick and stabbed the other combatant. This other combatant turned out to be a police officer in civilian clothes. For this act, he received a two-and-a-half to three-year sentence. The conviction was for assault, second-degree. He was admitted to Attica State Prison.

While in Attica, Baxstrom was reported to "often have epileptic fits during which he was aggressive, assaultive toward guards and inmates. He also used obscene language." Because of this, he was transferred administratively to Dannemora prison, on a civil commitment. In 1966, in a landmark case, the U.S. Supreme Court (383 US 107) held that an administrative civil commitment of a prisoner to mental hospital without basic due process of law was unconstitutional.

Source: H. J. Steadman and J. J. Cocozza, *Careers of the Criminally Insane* (Lexington, MA: Lexington Books, 1974), 43–45. Reprinted by permission.

This conclusion underscores the problem for corrections that mentally ill offenders represent: Their mental illness is often a separate issue from their criminality, and dealing with their criminality may not require treatment of their mental illness. In other words, the fact that a person has mental or emotional problems and is an offender does not necessarily mean that he or she will continue to offend until the mental or emotional problems are resolved. But for those who suffer from a mental illness, obtaining and maintaining treatment can be important. Of prisoners who have been diagnosed with a serious mental illness, two-thirds were not in treatment or off their prescribed medication at the time of their arrest.[28]

The general public links mental illness, crime, and the insanity defense because of a handful of highly publicized trials, such as that of John Hinckley, the would-be assassin of Ronald Reagan. But only about 8 percent of convicted or accused people in mental hospitals are there because they were found not guilty by reason of insanity. Another 6 percent are in hospitals because they have been judged to be mentally disordered sex offenders, and 32 percent have been found to be incompetent to stand trial. The largest group (54 percent), and the group of greatest concern to corrections, consists of offenders who became mentally ill after having been imprisoned.[29]

Why do some offenders become mentally ill while serving their terms? We must recognize that incarceration is stressful, even for the emotionally strong. Prisoners lose contact with families and other sources of emotional support. Often they feel humiliated by being convicted and sentenced to prison. Then they must face the strains of prison life, which are often augmented by unsafe and burdensome prison conditions. For some prisoners, the strain proves too much—they lose their emotional stability.

Institutional care for mentally ill offenders has paralleled historical shifts in corrections. There were early efforts to separate the mentally ill from other incarcerated offenders, but not until 1859 did the first institution built specially for such people, the New York State Lunatic Asylum for Insane Convicts, open near Auburn Prison. The facility held both convicted and nonconvicted patients, and it later received patients judicially transferred from civil hospitals.

Today, all states have either separate facilities for mentally ill criminals or sections of mental hospitals reserved for them. In some states the department of corrections controls these institutions, and in others the department of mental health does. In the coming decade, corrections will face an increased number of mentally ill clients. Much of the increase is related to a major policy shift in the mental health field: **deinstitutionalization**. With the availability of drugs that inhibit aberrant behavior, it became possible to release a multitude of mental patients to the community. Unfortunately, under- or even unsupervised former patients often fail to take their medication and then commit deviant or criminal acts. Because of their behavior, some are shuttled back and forth between the mental hospital and jail or prison. Mentally ill offenders have high rates of homelessness, unemployment, alcohol and drug use, and physical and sexual abuse prior to their current arrest.

Nearly 20 percent of violent offenders incarcerated or on probation are mentally ill. Unlike the mentally ill in state prisons, the majority of mentally ill offenders in jail or on probation have committed a property or public-order offense. Many of these criminal behaviors are relatively minor offenses.

Mentally ill offenders generally receive treatment from correctional personnel while awaiting disposition of their cases or from probation officers working cooperatively with mental health workers. When sentenced to probation, these offenders may be required to participate in mental health treatment programs. Counseling, medication, and group therapy are the most common treatments.

deinstitutionalization
The release of a mental patient from a mental hospital and his or her return to the community.

The Mentally Handicapped Offender

The 43-year-old man entered the Dunkin' Donuts shop, approached the counter, and demanded, "All your money and a dozen doughnuts." With his finger pointed inside his pocket, he announced that he had a gun and would use it. When the police arrived, they found the man standing outside the shop eating the doughnuts—just as they had found him after several previous holdups. The man's name is Eddie; he has an IQ of 61. He has served prison sentences for this type of offense, but almost immediately upon release he commits another such crime.

Ron, a 33-year-old man who functions at the level of a 10-year-old, was sentenced to a five-year prison term for bank robbery. He was easily identified by the police because he had signed his name on the holdup note he had given to the teller.

Charlie, who has an IQ of 85, set fire to a trash barrel in the hallway of his apartment building. A psychotic tenant, panicked by the smoke, jumped out of the window and was killed by the fall. Charlie is awaiting trial for murder.

These cases point to another problematic type of person for the corrections system: the **mentally handicapped offender**, often referred to as mentally retarded or developmentally disabled. An estimated 2 to 3 percent of the U.S. population is mentally handicapped (having IQs below 70). Among the incarcerated population, about 5 percent (50,000) are in this category, and a much higher percentage of those on probation or under juvenile care are mentally handicapped. In California alone, correctional agencies handle 22,000 adults and juveniles who are classified as mentally handicapped.[30]

mentally handicapped offender
A person whose limited mental development prevents adjustment to the rules of society.

Like other Americans, mentally handicapped people commit crimes, but there is no proved link between their disability and a propensity for criminal behavior. Their criminality may result from the fact that they do not know how to obtain what they want without breaking the law (see the Focus box "Donald's Story"). It may also result from the fact that they are easily duped by people who think deviant behavior is a joke or who use them to secure something illicitly for themselves. Mentally handicapped people also are disproportionately poor, so if they need or want something, they may commit a crime to get it. Further, because they cannot think quickly, they get caught more often than do other criminals. As a Los Angeles police officer told one researcher, "They are the last to leave the scene, the first to get arrested, and the first to confess."[31]

FOCUS ON PEOPLE IN CORRECTIONS

Donald's Story

Donald stole to survive. Often he took food from grocery stores. Sometimes he broke into diners to cook meals for himself in the middle of the night.

"I'd never break into anybody's house," Donald said. "That would be wrong. People have to work too hard for their money. I only break into stores." He doesn't understand that when he steals from businesses, he hurts the people who own them. He is mentally retarded.

Donald, whose IQ is in the 60s (100 is normal), spent most of his life in Ladd School, Rhode Island's institution for the retarded. In 1967, when he was twenty-four years old, he was released and given a job washing dishes in an East Greenwich, Rhode Island, restaurant.

"It wasn't enough money," said Donald. "It was only $30 a week. If I paid for my room, I couldn't eat. So I quit. I had to survive somehow, so I would go out and steal. I didn't know how to do no job."

Asked why he didn't go on welfare, he replied, "I didn't know about that stuff. Nobody ever told me anything about it. It's hard to get on welfare. You have to write stuff on papers."

Arrests came one after the other, Donald's court records show. One was for breaking into a diner and stealing thirty-five cents. At one point, Donald found a job at a Providence laundry and for a few months the break-ins stopped.

"All I did was fold clothes from the dryer," he recalled. "There was me and another guy. Then they decided one person could do it, and they got rid of my helper. I got scared. I couldn't do it alone. So I just quit."

So it was back to the break-ins.

Donald often got caught and was continually before the courts. But the judges never knew what to do with him; Rhode Island has no program for retarded offenders. Sometimes they put him on probation, and on several occasions they sent him to the state mental hospital for observation.

But no one helped Donald get a job. Finally, the judges lost patience and started sending Donald to prison. He has served at least three prison sentences, although court records are unclear and Donald is not sure there were not more. He is not good with numbers. When asked, he didn't know his age, which is thirty-seven.

On July 30, 1978, police records show that Donald was out of prison again. At 10:02 that night, a burglar alarm went off at a Providence factory building. Police found Donald hiding behind a door with a glass cutter in his pocket. As usual, Donald confessed. "I felt like getting some money," he told police. "I didn't know where to get it. Then I tried to get it in there."

A sympathetic judge put Donald on probation on the condition that he voluntarily live at the state mental hospital until a better arrangement could be made for him. Since then, Donald hasn't done any stealing. "Don't need to," he said. "I eat for free now."

Every weekday, after breakfast at the mental hospital, Donald takes the bus to downtown Providence and walks the streets looking for a job. He's been doing it for more than a year now, without success.

"If only I can get a job, maybe I can get out of the hospital," he said. "But I can't read and write. I can't do the forms. They ask you where you live. I live in a nuthouse. They ask about your last job." What's his future? "I don't know," he said. "I don't want to steal no more. It ain't worth it. I wish when I got in trouble a cop had shot me. So I wouldn't have to do it no more."

Source: B. DeSilva, "Donald's Story," *Corrections Magazine,* August 1980, p. 27. Reprinted by permission of the Edna McConnell Clark Foundation.

The majority of the offenses committed by mentally handicapped people are classified as property or public-order crimes. This is not to say that they do not also commit serious violent crimes; among the incarcerated, a higher proportion of mentally handicapped offenders than others have been convicted of homicide and other crimes against persons. Because of the special circumstances that are often involved when a mentally handicapped person commits a very serious crime, numerous states have prohibited their execution, regardless of the nature of the crime.[32] In 2002 the U.S. Supreme Court ruled in *Atkins v Virginia* that it violates the Eighth Amendment of the U.S. Constitution (prohibiting cruel and unusual punishment) to execute a person of who is mentally handicapped.[33]

Programs that deal with mentally handicapped individuals have recently focused on deinstitutionalization. Like the mentally ill, the mentally handicapped have been returned to the community, where they are expected to live, work, and care for themselves with minimal supervision. Because they have difficulty adjusting to the rules of the community, they often come to the attention of the criminal justice system.

What can corrections do for or with this special category of offender? Obviously, the usual routines of probation, diversion, incarceration, and community service will not work. Mentally handicapped individuals typically are not comfortable with change, are difficult to employ outside of sheltered workshops, and are not likely to improve significantly in terms of mental condition or social habits. As such, they violate probation or break prison rules and are further penalized. While incarcerated, they are often the butts of practical jokes and exploited as scapegoats or sexual objects. Recent litigation has called attention to the fact that these offenders require special programs, and the Americans with Disabilities Act (ADA) provides federal oversight to local correctional programs for those suffering from mental disabilities.

Appropriate correctional programs for mentally handicapped offenders need to be developed. In many prisons and jails, such inmates are segregated with others who have special needs. This strategy has been criticized because some mentally disabled offenders are preyed on by others in the unit. In several states, such as Massachusetts and Texas, there are programs within probation and parole to provide additional assistance and services to the mentally handicapped. Day reporting centers are used in some states, as are halfway houses. These programs aim at helping mentally disabled offenders gain the skills and discipline they need to live independent and crime-free lives.

Some observers believe that mentally handicapped offenders are less criminals than misfits who lack training in how to live in a complex society; they belong not in prison but in a treatment facility where they can learn rudimentary survival skills. Criminal justice practitioners often argue that mentally handicapped offenders constitute a mental health problem, but because they have committed crimes, mental health agencies do not want them. Thus they are shunned by both camps and get little help from either.

The Offender with HIV/AIDS

For the foreseeable future, Human Immunodeficiency Virus (HIV—and its full-blown symptomatic stage, Acquired Immune Deficiency Syndrome, or AIDS)—will have a major impact on American corrections. This is true, even though the most recent data show that rates of HIV and AIDS in prisons and jails are, for the first time in a decade, beginning to decline, even while rates of infections in the general population are increasing. In 2004 nearly 6,000 prisoners in U.S. prisons and jails had verified cases of AIDS, and more than 23,000 were HIV positive (1.7 percent of all prisoners, down from 2.3 percent six years earlier). More than 200 inmates died of AIDS in 2004, about 6 percent of all deaths in custody, but this is an 82 percent decrease from 1995.[34] Applying these ratios to probation means that perhaps 90,000 of those offenders are HIV positive. Further, these numbers underestimate the scope of the problem, because many HIV-infected offenders are undiagnosed.

The offender with HIV or AIDS confronts probation and parole officers with several problems. For jail and prison administrators, the problems stem mainly from policy issues concerning the people under their supervision. Institutional administrators must

To learn more about **HIV testing and medical policy,** go to the Centers for Disease Control by using the corresponding link at www .cengage.com/criminaljustice/ clear.

PEOPLE IN CORRECTIONS

Mike's Story

Mike Camargo lay in his hospital bed in the prison ward of Bellevue Hospital in New York City. Camargo was a pretrial detainee accused of selling drugs to an undercover police officer the previous summer. When he was conscious, he felt sharp, stabbing pains in his arms and feet. He could hardly move, much less sit up. Camargo was told that he suffered from pneumonia and toxoplasmosis.

Six weeks later he was transferred to an intensive care unit of the hospital. He had gone into shock because the bacteria growing in his brain deprived his nervous system of necessary oxygen. His inability to breathe was also caused by other bacteria clogging his heart valves. Mike Camargo's life had been spent in petty crime as a small-time drug dealer. The cops had caught him more than once, and he had served several sentences. Now he was dying of AIDS.

Later that year, Camargo's presence was required for a court appearance before Justice Sheindlin of the Supreme Court of New York in the Bronx. Dr. Jonathan Cohn, Camargo's attending physician at Bellevue Hospital, was subpoenaed by Camargo's lawyer to explain the defendant's absence. Cohn was placed under oath, and he then graphically explained to the court why he believed Camargo's deteriorating condition made producing the prisoner, much less continued prosecution, futile.

Over the prosecutor's objection, the court granted the defendant's motion to dismiss in the interest of justice. Justice Sheindlin explained to the prosecutor that although the defendant was a recidivist, it was doubtful he could be regarded as a threat to the safety or welfare of society. To impose incarceration on this minor drug dealer would be absurd given his imminent death. Further, the court noted that no sentence would compare with the many diseases now attacking the defendant.

The typical AIDS prisoner is much like Mike Camargo: He was in his early thirties. He was an intravenous drug user who had been incarcerated for a drug-related crime. And he died of AIDS-related pneumonia.

Source: Adapted from Patricia Raburn, "Prisoners with AIDS: The Use of Electronic Processing," *Criminal Law Bulletin,* May–June 1988, pp. 213–14. Reprinted by permission. Copyright © 1988 by Warren, Gorham & Lamont Inc., 210 South Street, Boston, MA 02111.

develop policies covering such matters as ways to prevent disease transmission, housing those infected, and medical care for inmates in the last stages of AIDS. In determining what actions should be taken, administrators have found that a host of legal, political, budgetary, and attitudinal factors limit their ability to make the best decisions (see the Focus box "Mike's Story").

PREVENTION ■ AIDS is a communicable disease that occurs when the HIV virus breaks down the human immune defenses so that the body becomes unable to combat infections. The virus is transmitted in contaminated blood and semen, primarily by needle sharing related to intravenous drug use and by sexual activity. HIV is difficult to transmit; scientific evidence shows that it is not passed on through casual contact. HIV transmission rates are 5 times higher in prisons than in the general population.[35]

A key way to prevent AIDS transmission is knowledge about the virus. If people do not understand how the virus is transmitted and how to prevent transmission, they run a higher risk of acquiring and transmitting the disease. We know that the "feeder population" for correctional institutions—young, poor, undereducated, minority men and boys—know very little about AIDS.

The long incubation period of the disease—the time between infection and the appearance of outward symptoms—also makes preventing the spread of AIDS difficult. Carriers may engage in unsafe drug taking and sex without knowing they are infecting others. Although most infected offenders were infected with HIV before they were incarcerated, transmission within the institution remains a problem.

In most prisons, educational programs now inform staff and inmates about the disease and how it spreads. Some observers have suggested that hypodermic needles and condoms be made available to prisoners so that if they do engage in intravenous drug taking and homosexual behavior, they will be protected. However, because these behaviors violate prison rules, administrators are reluctant to legitimize them. The policy of testing all residents and new inmates for the HIV antibody has been widely debated. **Figure 6.4** shows the testing policies of state corrections systems. Opponents of systemwide testing argue that there is no evidence of higher transmission rates in prisons than in the free community and thus no reason to screen. Further, because it is allegedly impossible to keep test results confidential, infected individuals will be stigmatized while incarcerated and discriminated against in insurance, housing, and employment upon release. Finally, policies have been developed to ensure that correctional personnel and inmates do not become infected while handling blood or body fluids in their duties. Using protective coverings, avoiding needle injuries, and taking care in handling diseased bodies have all become standard operating procedure.

HOUSING ■ If inmates are found to be HIV-positive or to have AIDS, what should be done? When they do become ill, unquestionably they should be cared for in a medical facility. But what about inmates who test positive yet may not become ill for several years? Should they be housed in a segregated facility or remain in the general population? Should they be protected from the hostility of other inmates and staff?

Correctional administrators have chosen various housing options, depending on such factors as the number of infected inmates in a given population and the availability and cost of separate facilities. Most corrections systems segregate inmates with AIDS but keep asymptomatic HIV carriers in the general population. On a case-by-case

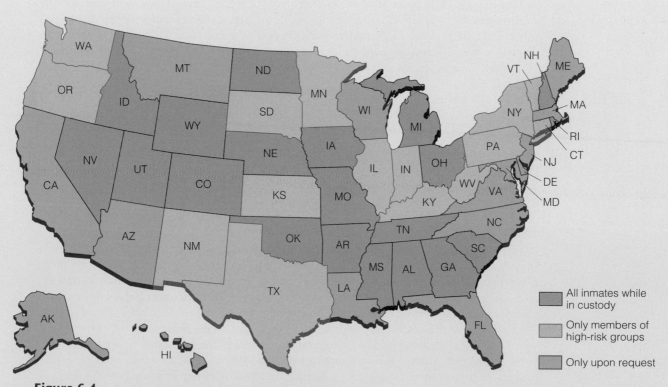

Legend:
- All inmates while in custody
- Only members of high-risk groups
- Only upon request

Figure 6.4
HIV Testing Policies in State Corrections Systems

Twenty states test all inmates for HIV while in prison. Fifteen states test only members of high-risk groups. In addition, all states test inmates on request or medical referral.

Source: BJS *Bulletin,* November 2004, p. 6.

basis, most administrators segregate prisoners who display high-risk behavior, who need protection, or whose medical condition calls for separate housing.

In some systems HIV-infected people are kept in the general population but given special treatment to reduce the possibility that they will transmit HIV to others. For example, in some states they are assigned single cells, whereas in others they are housed together in double cells. These policies have been criticized at some institutions because making particular cell arrangements for HIV-infected inmates announces their condition to staff and other inmates.

When inmates exhibit AIDS-related symptoms, they are usually confined to a hospital or infirmary. In some states (such as New Jersey) such inmates are placed in a hospital in the community; in other states (such as California) they are placed in a correctional medical facility. In states with a large number of prisoners carrying the virus, segregated housing is the policy, even when they show no symptoms of AIDS. California, for example, now houses all HIV-infected inmates in a wing of the Correctional Medical Facility at Vacaville to prevent transmission and to provide medical and counseling services to the group in the most effective way.

MEDICAL CARE ■ Corrections has a legal responsibility to furnish medical care to people under its supervision. Because AIDS patients face serious psychological as well as physical problems, they require counseling and support services for themselves and their families.

Medical services for AIDS patients are costly, ranging from $50,000 to $145,000 annually per patient; in some high-cost areas, extended acute medical care can run as high as $300,000. States with a large number of HIV-positive and AIDS-infected prisoners face costs that could easily constitute a major portion of their entire correctional budgets.

The release of inmates with AIDS after they complete their sentences also raises difficult issues. On humanitarian grounds, one could argue that executive clemency or parole should be granted so that AIDS patients do not spend their last days in prison, yet there is a moral—and probably a legal—obligation to ensure that they are not simply "dumped" on the streets.

The Elderly Offender

Crime—at least predatory street crime—is the province of young men. In visiting a prison, one is struck by the predominant numbers of young men, especially minorities. America's prison population has traditionally been young and poor, but in recent years it has been aging. In 2008, U.S. prisons and jails held more than 74,000 offenders over 55 years old, an increase of three-quarters compared with the elderly population in 1996. Nearly one in five prisoners is over the age of 44.[36]

The prison population is growing older for two reasons. First, the U.S. population in general is aging. Second, and more important, sentencing practices have changed. Consecutive lengthy sentences for heinous crimes, long mandatory minimum sentences, and life sentences without parole mean that more men who enter prison will spend most or all of the rest of their lives behind bars.

The elderly prisoners can be divided into three general groups. Most were young when they first entered prison facing very long terms for particularly serious crimes such as murder or brutal sexual assault (see the Focus box "Grant's Story"). A few first enter prison in their old age, usually convicted of either financial crimes such as embezzlement or sexual assaults such as molestation or pedophilia. Finally there are the experienced committed criminals, those who have been in prison before (usually more than once) but who are returning on yet another conviction. Obviously, then, elderly offenders vary in terms of criminal history and prison sophistication, but they also differ significantly from their younger peers, as we discuss shortly.

Although recent attention has focused on elderly prisoners, the ranks of those on probation and parole are increasingly populated by the aged. Probation has always

In the California Medical Facility, nurse Debbie Coluter assists an elderly inmate with Alzheimer's disease to his cell. Older and terminally ill inmates cost two to three times as much to incarcerate as younger prisoners, costing taxpayers billions of dollars.

had to deal with elderly offenders whose low-level public-order, property, and motor vehicle crimes have enabled them to be given community sentences. But, like their nonoffender counterparts, elderly probationers have special needs for employment, housing, and the maintenance of family ties. In many cases, probation officers must provide extra supervision to ensure that elderly probationers adhere to the conditions of their sentence.

FOCUS ON

PEOPLE IN CORRECTIONS

Grant's Story

Grant Cooper knows he lives in prison, but there are days when he cannot remember why. His crimes flit in and out of his memory like flies through a hole in a screen door, so that sometimes his mind and conscience are blank and clean.

He used to be a drinker and a drifter who had no control over his rage. In 1978, in an argument with a man in a breadline at the Forgotten Man Ministry in Birmingham, Alabama, his hand automatically slid into his pants pocket for a knife.

He cut the man so quick and deep that he died before his body slipped to the floor. Mr. Cooper had killed before, in 1936 and in 1954, so the judge gave him life. Back then, before he needed help to go to the bathroom, Mr. Cooper was a

dangerous man. Now he is 77, and since his stroke in 1993 he mostly just lies in his narrow bunk at the Hamilton Prison for the Aged and Infirm, a blue blanket hiding the tubes that run out of his bony body. Sometimes the other inmates put him in a wheelchair and park him in the sun. . . .

Mr. Cooper travels only in his mind. "I don't know if they'll ever set me free," he said, looking up from his bed, a pair of black-framed glasses sitting crooked on his face.

"I don't know. I don't reckon so."

Some days, if he forgets enough, he already is.

Source: Rick Bragg, "Where Alabama Inmates Fade into Old Age," *New York Times*, November 1, 1995, pp. A1, A18. Copyright © 1995 by The New York Times Co. Reprinted by permission.

Corrections also faces a huge increase in the number of aged parolees as those imprisoned in their youth for long terms are released to community supervision. Imagine the problems faced by, say, a 55-year-old, poorly educated, unskilled man who has spent the last 15–20 years behind bars on a drug offense. Parole faces the challenge of helping these ex-offenders make the transition to living in a society they have not confronted for more than a decade.

The most obvious difference between most offenders and the elderly has to do with health. Aging prisoners have more trouble handling the physical strains of prison life than do the younger inmates, and the aged usually need increased medical care. Elderly offenders also have different social interests. Whereas younger inmates enjoy physical sports and competitive recreation, older inmates, like older men on the outside, may prefer solitude and less-strenuous interaction. These differences between elderly prisoners and rank-and-file inmates translate into significantly greater per-inmate operating costs for the former, because of the need for special health, recreational, and housing services: One year's incarceration for an inmate over 60 years old costs more than three times the overall average cost per inmate.

Even though many elderly inmates have committed quite serious crimes, studies indicate that age reduces the chance that the prisoner will violate prison rules. Older prisoners often are more stable and dependable than their youthful counterparts, and they frequently occupy positions of trust within the prison. Upon release, these inmates typically pose little risk to the public. The adjustment problem facing most elderly offenders has to do with the way extended prison terms tend to institutionalize them. When a person spends many years in prison, the routines of the prison become debilitating. The prison regime controls all of the inmate's time and takes away most personal autonomy and decision making. After years of being told what to do almost every waking hour, a person will find it difficult to relearn how to make even the simplest decisions.

With prison space a valuable resource, some administrators believe that elderly offenders should be released to the community so that their cells can be reallocated to those young offenders still able to commit serious crimes.

The Long-Term Prisoner

long-term prisoner
A person who serves a lengthy period in prison, such as 10 years or more, before his or her first release.

More prisoners serve long sentences in the United States than do prisoners in any other Western nation (see the Focus box "Michael's Story"). The median prison sentence is now almost five years, and people convicted of violent crimes get a median sentence of almost eight years.[37] But about 24 percent of all prisoners end up serving sentences of over 25 years, and another 9 percent are serving life sentences. Most **long-term prisoners** have been convicted of violent or drug offenses. These prisoners are often the same people who will become elderly inside prison walls, with all the attendant problems just discussed. Those who are returned to the community at perhaps age 55 following 20 years of incarceration face daunting prospects in terms of adjustment, employment, and housing.

There is no one standard way that a long-term prisoner reacts to the time in prison. Studies show substantial differences in the way the long-termer responds, with some prisoners but not others experiencing severe stress, depression, and other health problems. When severe emotional stress occurs, it tends to take place earlier rather than later in the sentence.

Long-term prisoners are not generally seen as control problems—they are charged with disciplinary infractions about half as often as are short-term inmates—but they do present a management problem for prison administrators. Program managers have to find ways of making prison life livable for those who are going to be there a long time.

According to Timothy Flanagan, one of the foremost authorities on long-term inmates, this involves three main principles: (1) maximizing opportunities for the inmate to exercise choice in living circumstances, (2) creating opportunities for meaningful living, and (3) helping the inmate maintain contact with the outside world.[38]

FOCUS ON
PEOPLE IN CORRECTIONS

Michael's Story

Just after his 24th birthday, Michael Santos was sentenced to 45 years in prison on nonviolent continuing criminal enterprise charges for his participation in cocaine trafficking. Under U.S. Sentencing Commission guidelines, which are expressly designed to deal harshly with drug dealers, Santos will serve at least 85 percent of the sentence: over 38 years. He will be in his sixties when he is released.

Michael Santos's case illustrates a growing trend in American corrections—prisoners serving long terms. His sentence is an almost unimaginable length of time. For many of you reading this book, it is more than two times your current age. What must it mean to a man in his twenties to hear a judge impose such a sentence? How can a person face it?

In a recent scholarly paper on the topic, Santos mused on some of the dread and distress he felt facing his future: "Would my life be reduced to a prison registration number, being counted periodically as I waited for paint to peel off prison walls and years to pass away?"

Long-term prisoners must confront three main areas of concern. First, there is the inevitable shock, dismay, and sense of injustice on hearing the sentence pronounced. Even when lawyers have prepared the defendant for the worst, something ruinous occurs when the judge reads the sentence aloud. And even when the crime has been particularly heinous, the offender experiences disbelief and angry disheartenment on hearing the penalty, as though in some way it were disconnected from the crime itself.

Second, there is the problem of personal loss. Santos realized that the long term was "likely to rip apart my relationships." He had married only a few months before his arrest, and he had little hope that the marriage could survive the fissure of imprisonment. But even if the marriage did not end, he had to wonder about what its quality would be—its intimacy and its potential for meaningful family life with no children and restricted contact. No matter how much love was present, it seemed woefully inadequate to overcome the abyss of 45 years in prison.

Whenever Santos wondered about the future, he had countless other inmates' stories to advise him of the possibilities: mates who had long since abandoned them in painful, often acrimonious splits; children who felt that their fathers had deserted them, an accusation nearly impossible to dispute from behind the prison wall. Even the salvaged relationships seemed strained and unappealing.

Third, there is the challenge of finding meaningful ways to while away the interminable hours among society's outcasts. Like most long-term prisoners, Santos spent the first years involved in legal wrangles, trying to overturn his conviction or obtain clemency. But after these initial years, "an ocean of depression swallowed me." The biggest battle is simply how to cope, how to escape the inviting sinkhole of hopelessness.

Michael Santos has now served over 20 years of his 45-year term. He fights every day for self-respect and for his future. To give his prison time meaning, he has completed bachelor's and master's degrees. He has continued to write, publishing on topics of correctional policy and administration. And he battles the system—against desperate odds—to get his sentence reduced. But in the end he struggles with hopelessness: "The coming of the Messiah," he protests, "seems closer than my release from prison."

Source: Adapted from Michael G. Santos, "Facing Long-Term Imprisonment," in *Long-Term Confinement: Policy, Science and Correctional Practice,* edited by Timothy J. Flanagan (Thousand Oaks, CA: Sage, 1995), 36–40.

■ CLASSIFYING OFFENDERS: KEY ISSUES

Our descriptions of the categories of offenders should make clear that several factors frustrate attempts to classify correctional clients. Problems center on overlap and ambiguity in classification, the programmatic needs of corrections, behavioral probabilities, sociopolitical pressures, and individual distinctions.

Overlap and Ambiguity in Offender Classifications

Some sex offenders may also be alcoholics; some situational offenders may have emotional problems (perhaps even stemming from their new status as offender);

AP Images/Jerry Lai

What level of custody, and access to what type of programs, should be given to multimillionaire Conrad Black, sentenced to six and a half years in prison for swindling investors out of millions of dollars?

some career criminals may be addicts. A classification system that has so much overlap cannot give correctional decision makers much guidance as to appropriate treatment. Should an addicted multiple burglar be treated as a career criminal or as an addict?

To combat ambiguities in classification, correctional administrators have started using **classification systems**. These systems apply a set of objective criteria to all inmates in order to arrive at an appropriate classification. The criteria usually include such factors as current and prior offense histories, previous experiences in the justice system, and substance abuse patterns. By using objective criteria, these systems reduce the unreliability of the offender's classification, and by limiting the criteria to a few relevant facts, the systems avoid overlap.

classification systems
Specific sets of objective criteria, such as offense history, previous experience in the justice system, and substance abuse patterns, applied to all inmates to determine an appropriate classification.

Offense Classifications and Correctional Programming

Some critics argue that the most important requirement for any correctional classification system is that it should improve our ability to manage and treat offenders effectively. As such, if the categories described leave many correctional programming decisions unresolved, what good are they?

When one considers offenders, the normal response is to ask first what the person's crime is and then what the person's criminal history is. The nine classes of offenders we have described probably constitute 80 percent or more of the felony offenders managed by corrections, yet in each case the category is so broad that it does not answer the important question, How should this offender be managed? Broad categories can help portray the nature of offenders, but the programmatic needs of corrections require much narrower and more-precise classification systems. In particular, corrections must be able to identify the offender's potential risk to correctional security and to the community.

Behavioral Probabilities

Human behavior may be impossible to predict, but we can certainly make educated guesses about a person's likely future behaviors. Thus, we can say confidently that a five-time check forger is likely to commit a similar offense again, just as a first-time offender is unlikely to do so. We know, of course, that the check forger may stop offending after the fifth time, just as the first-time offender may continue. But, on average, our educated guesses will more often than not be right. This is often thought of as a probabilistic approach to classification.

Recent classification systems have included probabilistic concepts. Officials try to see which offender characteristics are associated with reinvolvement in crime. The approach resembles the one used by automobile insurance companies, whose actuaries recognize that even though many teenagers do not have accidents, teenagers as a group have much higher accident rates than do adult drivers. Therefore, teenagers pay higher premiums, because they represent a greater risk.

Similarly, offenders who have characteristics associated with higher risk can be classified as more likely to pose a threat and so can be required to pay a penological "premium": higher bail or no bail, closer supervision on probation or parole, tighter security in institutions, and so on. Even though most offenders will not commit more offenses, probabilistic classification thus serves corrections in this practical way.

Sociopolitical Pressures

One of the most frustrating aspects of offender classification is that the public response to crime frequently makes classification an emotionally charged issue. As a result, in managing offenders, corrections often must respond to changing public demands.

At one time or another, each group of offenders we described has endured intense public hostility. In the 1940s and 1950s, for instance, public outrage over narcotics use led to stiff penalties for their sale and promoted the establishment of addiction hospitals across the United States. In the 1950s and 1960s, public concern with the "psychopath" led to the establishment of long-term treatment facilities just for the "dangerous" offender, such as Maryland's famous Patuxent Institution. More recently, attention has focused on high-rate offenders, and policies have sought to incapacitate them selectively or collectively.

In each case, public alarm about crime has produced new labeling patterns in the criminal justice system, with special handling mandated for all those who match the label. Difficulties arise, however, because the labels are often broadly applied (partly because of the overlap in any classification system) and the handling is usually severer than necessary. Those who object to the frequent "reform" movements in corrections recognize that misapplying labels can do great harm. Yet in many instances the accuracy of the label and its application matter little to correctional policy makers, who face the worse problem of responding to the public demand for "action" to "crack down" on one type of crime or another. The problem is more political than penological.

Distinctions in Classification Criteria

We all classify the people around us. We think, *John is a Democrat, Nancy is a nice person, Tim is untrustworthy,* and so on. We realize that these terms do not fully describe the individuals but serve only as rough labels that help us gauge how they may behave or think in a given situation. In reality we know that sometimes John may sound like a Republican, Nancy may be grumpy, and Tim may keep his word. Certain tendencies may characterize a person's behavior, but it is seldom fixed.

Given the variability of human behavior, offender classification must be seen as a rough way of grouping people. Being precise about the criteria used for grouping is equally important. Three general kinds of criteria are used to classify offenders:

1 *Offense criteria* classify offenders as to the seriousness of the crime committed.

2 *Risk criteria* classify offenders as to the probability of future criminal conduct.

3 *Program criteria* classify offenders as to the nature of correctional treatment appropriate to the person's needs and situation.

Each type of criteria does not lead to the same correctional consequence as the others. That is, if we apply offense criteria to an offender, the suggested correctional strategy will differ from the consequence suggested by applying the risk or program criteria. For example, many offenders who committed serious crimes most likely will not do so again, many offenders who have few treatment needs still represent a risk to the community, and so on. Thus, corrections systems need to apply all three classification systems to determine the most appropriate way to manage any given offender.

SUMMARY

1 **Understand how the criminal justice system operates as a large selection process to determine who ends up in the corrections system.**

We can view the criminal justice system as a filtering process, because it operates as a large offender-selection bureaucracy. At each stage, some defendants are sent on to the next stage, while others are either released or processed under changed conditions. Note that few suspects who are arrested are then prosecuted, tried, and convicted. Some go free because the police decide that a crime has not been committed or that the evidence is not sound. The prosecutor may decide that justice would be better served by sending the suspect to a substance abuse clinic. Many defendants will plead guilty, the judge may dismiss charges against others, and the jury may acquit a few defendants. Thus, the criminal justice system is often described as a filtering process or a funnel—many cases enter it, but only a few result in conviction and punishment. These few are the clients of corrections.

2 **Describe some of the main similarities among and differences between the general population and people who end up under correctional authority.**

Historical studies of American corrections show that in earlier eras members of the newest immigrant groups filled the prisons out of proportion to their numbers in the general population. Since the Civil War, African Americans have consistently made up the largest group in southern prisons, but elsewhere the largest group has changed over time: first Germans, Irish, and Italians, and now African Americans and Hispanics. Further, although this idea of ethnic succession is not entirely consistent with recent research, our prisons and jails undeniably hold disproportionate numbers of poor, disadvantaged, and minority citizens.

3 Identify different types of offenders in the corrections system and the kinds of problems they pose for corrections.

This chapter presents nine main types of people under correctional authority: the situational offender, the career criminal, the sex offender, the substance abuser, the mentally ill offender, the mentally handicapped offender, the offender with HIV/AIDS, the elderly offender, and the long-term prisoner. Each group as its own special characteristic that creates treatment and management issues for correctional authorities. The main issues that differentiate these types of offenders are (1) the risk they represent to the community, (2) their need for special kinds of correctional programming, and (3) distinctions that need to be made among people within each group.

4 Describe the classification process for people under correctional authority and know why it is important.

Correctional authorities need to answer a question about every person under their supervision: "How should this offender be managed?" Broad categories can help portray the nature of offenders, but the programmatic needs of corrections require much narrower and more-precise classification systems. In particular, corrections must be able to identify the offender's potential risk to correctional security and to the community. This is the purpose of classification. In classifying offenders, correctional administrators put them into groups based on the seriousness of their offense, the security risks they pose to the prison, and their treatment needs.

5 Understand important problems and limitations in classifying people under correctional authority.

Five main challenges to the classification of correctional clients have been identified: overlap and ambiguity in offender classifications, programming, behavioral probabilities, sociopolitical pressures, and distinctions in classification criteria. There are no easy answers to any of these problems, but the success of correctional classification systems depends on minimizing the negative implications of each challenge.

KEY TERMS

alcohol abuser (p. 147)

career criminal (p. 138)

classification systems (p. 160)

deinstitutionalization (p. 151)

drug abuser (p. 145)

long-term prisoner (p. 158)

mentally handicapped offender (p. 151)

mentally ill offender (p. 148)

sex offender (p. 141)

situational offender (p. 137)

FOR DISCUSSION

1. Is the process by which correctional clients are selected discriminatory? What might be done to reduce actual or perceived discrimination?

2. How does the classification of correctional clients reflect the fragmentation of corrections?

3. What role should public opinion play in categorizing various offenders for the purpose of punishing them?

4. Is classifying offenders according to the probability of future criminal conduct a good idea? What are the dangers of the practice? What are its advantages?

5. What policy recommendations would you make with regard to the way career criminals are handled?

FOR FURTHER READING

Aday, Ronald. *Aging Prisoners: Crisis in American Corrections*. Westport, CT: Praeger, 2003. Summarizes studies of the needs and problems of elderly offenders.

Goulding, Dot, *Recapturing Freedom: Issues Relating to the Release of Long-Term Prisoners into the Community*. Sydney: Hawkins Press, 2007. A study of the special obstacles faced by prisoners who are released from prison after serving long sentences.

Hobbs, Richard. *Bad Business*. New York: Oxford University Press, 1995. Studies professional criminals through interviews to understand their motivations and methods of work.

Human Rights Watch. *Ill Equipped: U.S. Prisons and Offenders with Mental Illness*. New York: Author, 2003.

Describes case studies of the "crisis" in mental health treatment in U.S prisons and provides a series of recommendations for improvement of care.

McVay, Douglas A., ed. *Drug War Facts*. Washington, DC: Common Sense for Drug Policy, 2003. Presents a compendium of facts about drug crime, drug treatment, and drug policy, with a special emphasis on the need for reform.

Terry, Karen J. *Sexual Offenses and Offenders: Theory, Practice and Policy*. Belmont, CA: Wadsworth, 2006. Covers deviant sexual behavior, types of sex offenders, theories of sexual offending, treatment for sex offenders, and management and supervision policies regarding sex offenders.

NOTES

[1] Martin R. Haskell and Lewis Yablonsky, *Criminology: Crime and Criminality* (Chicago: Rand McNally, 1974), 264.

[2] Walter C. Reckless, *The Crime Problem* (New York: Appleton- Century-Crofts, 1961), 153–77.

[3] Alfred Blumstein, Jacqueline Cohen, Jeffrey Roth, and Christy Visher, *Criminal Careers and "Career Criminals"* (Washington, DC: National Academy of Sciences, 1986).

[4] Peter Greenwood, *Selective Incapacitation* (Santa Monica, CA: Rand Corporation, 1982).

[5] Susan Brownmiller, *Against Our Will* (New York: Simon & Schuster, 1975), 376–77.

[6] Lawrence A. Greenwood, *Sex Offenses and Offenders: An Analysis of Data on Rape and Sexual Assault* (Washington, DC: U.S. Government Printing Office, 1997).

[7] Ibid., p. 23.

[8] Mary Magdalene Project, *Beyond 2000: Research Report on Street Prostitution*, http://www.prostitution -recovery.org.

[9] Ric Curtis, "Commercial Sexual Exploitation of Children in New York City" (paper presented to the American Society of Criminology, November 2007).

[10] Rudolph Alexander, Jr., "The Supreme Court and the Civil Commitment of Sex Offenders," *Prison Journal* 84 (no. 3, September 2004): 361–78.

[11] Bureau of Justice Statistics, *Recidivism of Sex Offenders Released from Prison in 1994* (Washington, DC: U.S. Government Printing Office, October 2003).

[12] Franklin E. Zimring, Wesley G. Jennings, Alex R. Piquero, and Stephanie Hays, "Investigating the Continuity of Sex Offending: Evidence from the Philadelphia Birth Cohort," *Justice Quarterly* 26 (no. 1, March 2009): 58–76.

[13] Abby Goodnough and Monica Davey, "A Record of Failure at a Center for Sex Offenders," *New York Times*, March 5, 2007, pp. A-1, 16.

[14] Terrance D. Miethe, Jodi Olson, and Ojmarrh Mitchell, "Specialization and Persistence in the Arrest Histories of Sex Offenders: A Comparative Analysis of Alternative Measures and Offense Types," *Journal of Research in Crime and Delinquency* 43 (2006): 204–29.

[15] *Behind Bars: Substance Abuse and America's Prison Population* (New York: National Center for Addiction and Substance Abuse, 1997); *New York Times*, January 9, 1998, p. A1.

[16] Helene R. White and Rolf Loeber, *Substance Abuse and Criminal Offending: Policy Brief* (New Brunswick, NJ: Rutgers University Center for Behavioral Health Services and Criminal Justice Research, April, 2009).

[17] BJS *Bulletin*, October 2006, p. 7.

[18] George E. Vaillant, "A 20-Year Follow-up of New York Narcotic Addicts," *Archives of General Psychiatry* 29 (August 1973): 237–41.

[19] Doris J. James, *Profile of Jail Inmates, 2002*, BJS *Special Report*, July 2004.

[20] BJS *Special Report*, June 1999, p. 1.

[21] BJS *Bulletin*, September 2006, p. 1.

[22] National Commission on Correctional Healthcare, *The Health Status of Soon to Be Released Inmates* (Washington, DC: National Institute of Justice, May 2000).

[23] "United States: Mentally Ill Mistreated in Prison," *Human Rights News* (New York: Human Rights Watch, 2003).

[24] John Monahan, "Mental Illness and Violent Crime," in *Research in Review* (Washington, DC: National Institute of Justice, October 1996).

[25] William McCord and Joan McCord, *The Psychopath* (New York: Van Nostrand, 1964), 2.

[26] Thomas S. Szasz, *Law, Liberty, and Psychiatry* (New York: Macmillan, 1963), 12.

[27] U.S. National Commission on the Causes and Prevention of Violence, *Crimes of Violence* (Washington, DC: U.S. Government Printing Office, 1969), 444.

[28] Andrew P. Wilper, Steffie Woolhandler, J. Wesley Boyd, et al., "The Health and Health Care of U.S. Prisoners: Results of s Nationwide Survey," *American Journal of Public Health*, January 15, 2009, http://www.biomedexperts.com/Abstract.bme/19150898/The_health_and_health_care_of_US_prisoners_results_of_a_nationwide_survey.

[29] Statistics based on Bureau of Justice Statistics, *Report to the Nation on Crime and Justice* (Washington, DC: U.S. Government Printing Office, 1983), 68.

[30] Joan Petersilia, "Justice for All? Offenders with Mental Retardation and the Criminal Justice System," *Prison Journal* 77 (no. 4, December 1997): 358–80.

[31] Joan Petersilia, *Doing Justice? Criminal Offenders with Developmental Disabilities* (Berkeley: California Policy Research Center, University of California, 2000), 5.

[32] Peggy M. Tobolowsky, "Capital Punishment and the Mentally Retarded Offender," *Prison Journal* 84 (no. 3, September 2004): 340–60.

[33] *Atkins v Virginia,* 536 U.S. 304 (2002).

[34] BJS *Bulletin,* November 2006, pp. 1–3.

[35] Christopher Krebs, "High-Risk HIV Transmission Behavior in Prison and the Prison Subculture," *Prison Journal* 82 (no. 1, March 2002): 19–49.

[36] BJS *Bulletin,* December, 2009.

[37] Tracey Kyckelhahn and Thomas H. Cohen, *Felony Defendants in Large Urban Counties, 2004: Statistical Tables* (Washington, DC: Bureau of Justice Statistics, April 2008).

[38] Timothy J. Flanagan, "Adaptation and Adjustment among Long-Term Prisoners," *Federal Prisons Journal* 2 (no. 2, Spring 1991): 45–51.

PART 2

Photo by R. Scott Stipe; provided courtesy of Scott Talbott

Scott Talbott
United States Probation Officer,
United States District Court,
District of Arizona

EVIDENCE-BASED PRACTICES: THE NEW FACE OF COMMUNITY SUPERVISION

Probation, parole, community supervision, and *supervised release* are terms commonly used to describe court-ordered and/or postrelease supervision of offenders convicted of violating federal or state criminal laws. While there are subtle differences from one jurisdiction to another, the core functions of the officers responsible for supervising the offender in the community are very similar.

When a convicted offender reenters the community, either at the sentencing stage or after a term of incarceration, he or she is usually not free from correctional supervision. Instead, most offenders usually serve a term of community supervision. Based on the standard and special conditions imposed by the court or releasing authority, the supervising probation or parole officer is responsible for monitoring the offender. The officer's primary objectives are as follows:

- Enhance community safety
- Reduce the likelihood of recidivism
- Aid in the offender's reintegration into society

These three objectives are accomplished by assessing the risks and needs of the offender, making appropriate referrals for services, and responding to violations in an appropriate and professional manner.

Today there is a move toward evidence-based community supervision practices. Unlike the traditional approach, which emphasized making repeated contacts with offenders and enforcing compliance with court-ordered conditions of supervision, evidence-based supervision calls for correctional professionals to employ research-supported methods and interventions to help reduce the risk of recidivism. This change in orientation is consistent with the old saying, "Don't work harder—work smarter." While using tried-and-true correctional practices sounds good in theory, they can be difficult to implement. Like employees in other professions, correctional professionals can be resistant to change.

CORRECTIONAL PRACTICES

The United States Probation Office in the District of Arizona, for example, is actively using several evidence-based strategies to supervise offenders. Several years ago the department replaced the less-effective "minimum contact per offender" requirement with a more-purposeful quality of contact philosophy. Now, instead of simply requiring officers to make a specific number of contacts per offender to ensure compliance with release conditions, contemporary officers meet with offenders to evaluate their needs and make referrals to social service agencies if necessary. In this way officers now strike a more-balanced approach to their work. They provide law enforcement services to ensure community safety, as well as social work services to help offenders live law-abiding lives. Additionally, the use of consistent and swift graduated sanctions is strongly recommended when addressing violations of supervision. Finally, the Arizona office encourages the concentration on and allocation of resources for medium- and high-risk offenders, as well as the early release from supervision of compliant, low-risk offenders.

An important component of evidenced-based practice is the use of statistically validated risk/needs assessment tools for case planning and management. While assessing offenders' risks and needs has always been a part of the supervision process, with officers priding themselves on their ability to use their instincts to assess risks and needs, target interventions, and deliver services, the evidence-based approach employs research-validated assessment tools. A second component of evidence-based practice is the use of motivational interviewing techniques. In contrast to the traditional and often confrontational methods used in the past, motivational techniques focus on empowering the offender and eliciting behavioral change.

Evidence-based practice is an exciting development in community supervision. Officers already use many of the recommended strategies, but now such strategies are becoming more formalized and backed up by systematic research. Evidence-based practice in community corrections systems assists probation officers in reducing recidivism risk and promoting positive behavioral change.[*]

Although the public views corrections as primarily concerned with prisons and jails, almost three-quarters of offenders are supervised within the community. In Part 2 we examine correctional practices in both the community and institutions. The chapters that follow are organized to cover the ways offenders are dealt with, start to finish—from jail detention to sentences of probation, intermediate sanctions, or incarceration, to release and reentry into the community. By focusing on the day-to-day practices of corrections, Part 2 shows correctional professionals in action.

[*]Written especially for this text by Scott Talbott, who has worked in community supervision since 1993. Before becoming a U.S. probation officer in 2001, he worked as a community corrections officer for the Washington State Department of Corrections.

AP Images/Damian Dovarganes

LEARNING OBJECTIVES

After reading this chapter you should be able to . . .

1 Describe the history of the jail and its current function in the criminal justice system.

2 Describe who is in jails, and why they are there.

3 Discuss the kinds of jails in the United States.

4 List the main issues facing jails today.

5 Outline the problem of bail and list the main alternatives to bail.

6 Outline the problems of jail administration.

7 Describe new developments in jails and jail programs.

8 Critically assess the future of the jail.

The American jail has been called the ultimate ghetto because most of the more than 11 million people who pass through jail each year are poor. They are held awaiting disposition of their cases, serving sentences of under one year or awaiting transfer to state prison. The Men's Central Jail in Los Angeles is the largest in the nation.

JAILS ARE A STRANGE CORRECTIONAL HYBRID: part detention center for people awaiting trial, part penal institution for sentenced misdemeanants, part refuge for social misfits taken off the streets. Jails hold men, women, and juveniles of all colors who have been accused of violating the law. Jails are the traditional dumping ground not only for criminals but also for petty hustlers, derelicts, junkies, prostitutes, the mentally ill, and disturbers of the peace, mainly from the poorer sections of cities. Thus, jail's functions include those of the workhouse of the past.

Students interested in improving corrections during their future careers could find no area that more obviously needs reform than U.S. jails. Among the institutions and programs of the corrections system, jail is the one most neglected by scholars and officials and least known to the public. Uniformly jam-packed and frequently brutalizing, jails almost never enhance life. Many criminal justice researchers agree that of all correctional agencies, jails are the oldest, most numerous, most criticized, and most stubbornly resistant to reform.

JAILS: DETENTION AND SHORT-TERM INCARCERATION

Jails are in such a state of decline that the estimated cost to bring them up to acceptable standards far exceeds what the nation can afford, at least in the foreseeable future. Further, conditions in many jails are getting worse, because sentenced felons are held there while awaiting vacancies in overcrowded state prisons. Therefore scholars, administrators, policy makers, and elected officials agree that using jail for any offender should be avoided whenever possible. Yet jail represents nearly all Americans' initial contact with corrections. For many people, this will be their only time in a correctional institution, and the impression it leaves will greatly influence their views of the criminal justice system.

With an estimated 13 million jail admissions per year, more people directly experience jails than experience prisons, mental hospitals, and halfway houses combined.[1] Even if we consider that some portion of this total is admitted more than once, probably at least 7 to 8 million people are detained in a jail at some time during the year.

In this chapter, we examine problems of operating jails and how some individuals avoid pretrial detention. We also raise questions about the role of corrections in this type of facility, where prisoners generally sit idle without access to treatment and rehabilitative programs.

Chapter

7

■ THE CONTEMPORARY JAIL: ENTRANCE TO THE SYSTEM

Jails are the entryway to corrections. They house both accused individuals awaiting trial and sentenced offenders, usually serving one-year terms or less. People appealing sentences are often held in jail as well, as are those awaiting transfer to other jurisdictions. Nationally over 785,000 people are under jail authority any given day; more than nine-tenths of them are behind bars, with the remainder under some form of community release.[2]

Some people argue that jails lie outside corrections. For one thing, they claim that most of the nation's 2,876 jails are really a part of law enforcement, because sheriffs administer them. For another, they note that sentenced offenders make up only about half of the jail population and that pretrial detainees, who compose most of the other half, should not fall within the scope of correctional responsibility. Finally, they suggest that because most jails have neither treatment nor rehabilitative programs, they should be excluded from corrections.

We believe that jails are an important part of corrections and demonstrate many complexities of the system. Administered by locally elected officials, jails are buffeted by the local politics of taxation, party patronage, and law enforcement. Jail practices also affect probation, parole, and prison policies.

Jails are perhaps the most frustrating component of corrections for people who want to apply treatment efforts to help offenders. Of the enormous numbers of people in jail, many need a helping hand. But the unceasing human flow usually does not allow time for such help—nor are the resources available in most instances.

Origins and Evolution

Jails in the United States descend directly from feudal practices in twelfth-century England. At that time, an officer of the crown, the *reeve*, was appointed in each *shire* (what we call a county) to collect taxes, keep the peace, and operate the *gaol* (jail). The *shire reeve* (from which the word *sheriff* evolved), among other duties, caught and held in custody, until a formal court hearing determined guilt or innocence, people accused of breaking the king's law. With the development of the workhouse in the sixteenth century, the sheriff took on added responsibilities for vagrants and the unemployed who were sent there. The sheriff made a living by collecting fees from inmates and by hiring out prison labor.

English settlers brought these traditions and institutions with them to the American colonies. After the American Revolution, the local community elected law enforcement officials—particularly sheriffs and constables—but the functions of the jail remained unchanged. Jails were used to detain accused persons awaiting trial, as well as to shelter misfits who could not be taken care of by their families, churches, or other groups.

The jails often were in the sheriffs' homes and run like the sheriffs' households. Detainees were free to dress as they wished and to contribute their own food and necessities. "So long as they did not cost the town money, inmates could make living arrangements as pleasant and homelike as they wished."[3] Local revenues paid room and board for detainees who could not make independent contributions.

In the 1800s the jail began to change in response to the penitentiary movement. Jails retained their pretrial detention function but also became facilities for offenders serving short terms, as well as housing vagrants, debtors, beggars, prostitutes, and the mentally ill. Although the fee system survived, other changes took place. The juvenile reformatory movement and the creation of hospitals for the criminally insane during the latter part of the nineteenth century siphoned off some former jail inhabitants. The development of probation also removed some offenders, as did adult reformatories and state farms, and inmates now were segregated by sex. However, even with these innovations,

To learn more about jail history, see the corresponding link at www .cengage.com/criminaljustice/ clear.

the overwhelming majority of accused and convicted misdemeanants were held in jail. This pattern has continued to modern times.

Population Characteristics

Not until 1978 did the Bureau of the Census, for the Bureau of Justice Statistics, conduct a complete nationwide census of jails. Repeated every five years by local officials, this census contains information on inmates in jails that hold people beyond arraignment (that is, usually more than 48 hours). Excluded from the count are people in federal and state facilities. An annual survey of the top one-third largest jails, which hold about 75 percent of the inmate population, supplements these five-year nationwide counts.

The most recent National Jail Census shows that about 86 percent of inmates are men, nearly two-thirds are under 35 years old, just over two-fifths are white, and most have little education and a very low income.[4] The demographic characteristics of the jail population differ from those of the national population in many ways: People in jail are younger and disproportionately African American, and most are unmarried (see **Figure 7.1**).

As with prisons, jail populations vary from region to region and from state to state. The proportion of a state's population in jail, known as the *jail rate*, is high in the West and South (see **Figure 7.2**). In many states where prisons are filled to capacity, sentenced felons awaiting transfer sit in jails.

One of the most troubling trends in jails is the increasing rate of incarceration for African Americans. **Figure 7.3** shows the changes in these rates since 1990; most of the increase in jail population over the past decade has been due to a more than doubling

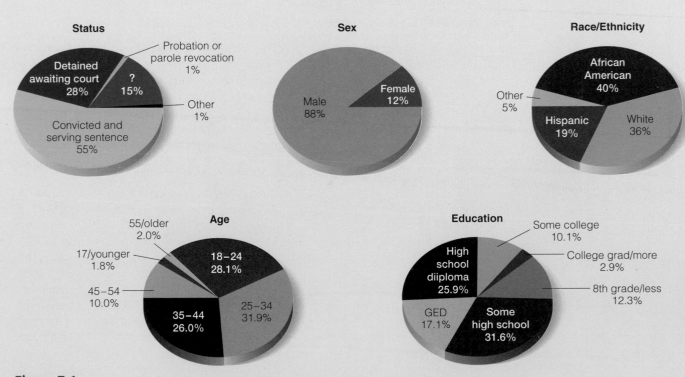

Figure 7.1
Characteristics of Adult Jail Inmates in U.S. Jails

Compared with the American population as a whole, jails are disproportionately inhabited by men, minorities, the poorly educated, and those with low incomes.

Sources: Bureau of Justice Statistics: *Bulletin,* May 2006, p. 8; *Statistical Tables,* March 2009.

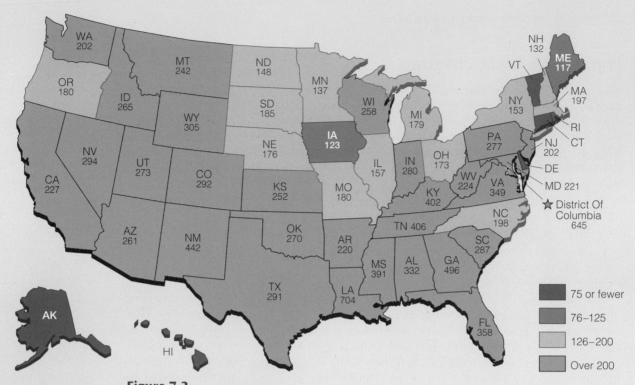

Figure 7.2

People Incarcerated in Local Jails per 100,000 Population, by State

What accounts for the fact that incarceration rates in jails differ from state to state?

Note: Six states—Alaska, Connecticut, Delaware, Hawaii, Rhode Island, and Vermont—have integrated jail-prison systems; therefore, information for these states is not given.

Source: BJS *Bulletin*, May 2006, p. 9.

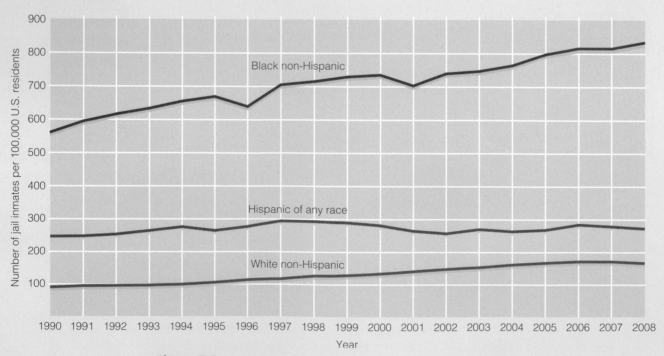

Figure 7.3

Jail Incarceration Rates by Race and Ethnicity, 1990–2008

What can explain the phenomenal increase in the incarceration rate of African Americans?

Source: Bureau of Justice Statistics, http://www.ojp.usdoj.gov/bjs/glance/tables/jailrairtab.htm, April 29, 2009.

of the number of African Americans in jails. As we discuss in Chapter 18, this trend applies to all of corrections, not just jails.

Administration

Of the 2,876 jails in the United States, 80 percent have a county-level jurisdiction, and most are administered by an elected sheriff. An additional 600 or so municipal jails are in operation. Only in six states—Alaska, Connecticut, Delaware, Hawaii, Rhode Island, and Vermont—are jails for adults administered by state government. There are also an estimated 13,500 police **lockups** (or drunk tanks) and similar holding facilities authorized to detain people for up to 48 hours. The Federal Bureau of Prisons operates 11 jails for detained prisoners only, holding 11,000 inmates. There are 47 privately operated jails, under contract to state or local governments, and they house 2.4 percent of the total jail population.[5]

The capacity of jails varies greatly. The 50 largest jurisdictions hold almost one-third of the nation's jailed inmates. The two jurisdictions with the most inmates, Los Angeles County and New York City, together hold about 33,300 inmates in multiple jails, or 4 percent of the national total. The Los Angeles County Men's Central Jail alone holds almost 20,000 people, but most jails are much smaller, with well more than half holding fewer than 50 people each.[6] However, the number of these small facilities is dwindling because of new jail construction and the creation of regional, multicounty facilities.

As facilities to detain accused people awaiting trial, jails customarily have been run by law enforcement agencies. We might reasonably expect that the agency that arrests and transports defendants to court should also administer the facility that holds them. Typically, however, neither sheriffs nor deputies have much interest in corrections. They often think of themselves as police officers and of the jail as merely an extension of their law enforcement activities. In some major cities, municipal departments of correction, rather than the police, manage the jails.

Many experts argue that jails have outgrown police administration. Jails no longer serve simply as holding places but now represent one of the primary correctional facilities in the criminal justice system. In fact, much correctional work is directed toward jail inmates. Probation officers conduct presentence investigations in jails, alcohol and drug abusers receive treatment in many facilities, and inmates perform community service or work toward reintegration out of some facilities. Therefore, the effective administration of jails requires skills in offender management and rehabilitation that are not generally included in law enforcement training. This point was well made over 40 years ago by the U.S. President's Commission on Law Enforcement and the Administration of Justice: "The basic police mission of apprehending offenders usually leaves little time, commitment, or expertise for the development of rehabilitative programs, although notable exceptions demonstrate that jails can indeed be settings for correctional treatment."[7]

Jail administrators face problems that good management practices cannot always overcome. One problem is that some jails cannot send their prisoners to state facilities after they are sentenced. Many state prisons are so crowded that they refuse to accept sentenced offenders until space becomes available. In recent years, up to 1 in 20 of those in jail had been sentenced to prison but awaited prison space to open up. In Louisiana, 45 percent of the state's prisoners are held in local jails, and the figure is one-third for Kentucky and over one-fourth for Tennessee. Indeed, in the South, 1 of every 10 state prisoners is being held in a local jail. In 2008, jails held 47,934 inmates, of whom 20,785 were being held for immigration and customs violations.[8] Such special populations have further complicated the problem of jail management.

Another problem is that many jails still receive funds through a **fee system**, whereby the costs of housing, food, and services are averaged and a standard amount (say, $10 per day per prisoner) is remitted to the sheriff's department. This creates an incentive for poor jails to skimp on food, services, and prisoner support. Often the sheriff uses money saved on housing prisoners to augment the kinds of law enforcement services that attract public support and are therefore helpful at the polls.

lockup
A facility authorized to hold people before court appearance for up to 48 hours. Most lockups (also called drunk tanks or holding tanks) are administered by local police agencies.

fee system
A system by which jail operations are funded by a set amount paid per day for each prisoner held.

CAREERS IN CORRECTIONS Correctional Officer—Local Jails

NATURE OF THE WORK

Most jails are operated by county governments, three-quarters under the jurisdiction of an elected sheriff. The approximately 150,000 correctional officers in the jail system admit and process more than 7 million people a year in either pretrial or sentenced categories. Officers must supervise individuals during the most dangerous, postarrest phase, when arrestees may be most stressed and violent. The constant turnover of the jail population is an additional problem in terms of maintaining security and stability.

REQUIRED QUALIFICATIONS

Candidates for employment must be at least 18 to 21 years of age, be a U.S. citizen, and have a high school education, no felony convictions, and some work experience. They must be in good health and meet formal physical fitness, eyesight, and hearing standards. Some local departments provide training for officers according to criteria set by the American Jail Association. In some states, regional training academies are available to local correctional agencies. On-the-job training is a major resource for officer candidates.

EARNINGS AND JOB OUTLOOK

Job opportunities for correctional officers employed in county jails depend on local budgetary constraints even in the face of increases in the jail population. Salaries for entry-level correctional officers vary greatly, with the highest being in the Northeast and the lowest in the rural South. Median annual earnings of correctional officers and jailers were $35,760 in May 2006. The middle 50 percent earned between $28,320 and $46,500. The lowest 10 percent earned less than $23,600, and the highest 10 percent earned more than $58,580.

MORE INFORMATION

For more information, see the *Occupational Outlook Handbook,* **Correctional Officers**, found at the corresponding web link at www.cengage.com/criminaljustice/clear.

The Influence of Local Politics

Because of the close links between jail administration and local politics, fiscal pressures and political conservatism greatly affect jails. Fiscally sound measures often are ignored because of political pressures. For example, pretrial release programs are cost-efficient and a proved means of reducing institutional crowding, yet the public's fear of crime often makes the programs politically infeasible. Conversely, political pressures may support expanded use of jail confinement for misdemeanant offenders or probation violators (particularly when crime is a potent electoral issue), but funds to expand or upgrade the jail's capacity to handle these additional offenders are often lacking. The jail is a crime control service but also a drain on revenues. The tension between these two public interests is often expressed in local debates over capital expenditures for jail construction. Because revenues often are insufficient, many jails are overcrowded and cannot house all the inmates assigned to their supervision, and some are released or placed in other facilities.

It is very hard to wrest control of local facilities away from a politically sensitive office such as that of sheriff or police chief. Jail employees constitute a large block of political patronage for elected officials to distribute to political supporters. Political appointees spend most of their time administering the jail, but during political campaigns they hustle votes and money for their bosses. Even when jail employees are civil servants, political considerations can affect hiring and promotion. Because few politicians willingly surrender control over such a potential political force as the jail, change is slow. See "Careers in Corrections" for more about what it means to work in a local jail.

FOCUS ON CORRECTIONAL POLICY

Private Jails

The town of Hardin, Montana (population 3,600) was like a lot of other small, rural towns—it was looking for a way to create jobs. So in 2007 the town's residents financed the building of a new, state-of-the-art private jail capable of holding 464 inmates—Two Rivers Correctional Facility—on the promise that it would provide steady employment for over 100 locals.

It is easy to understand the economic appeal of the project, as the county's unemployment rate hovers around 10 percent and Hardin's central business district has seen much better days. The town paid for the jail through sale of revenue bonds. Once it was built, the town turned the facility over to a for-profit prison-management firm to start the hiring.

But nobody came. The facility has remained empty, and the $27 million of bonds went into default a year later.

For months, correctional officers Glyn and Rae Perkins, husband and wife, were the only employees at the 96,000-square-foot facility. They were laid off on January 23, 2009. "Those of us who were involved had such high hopes," she says. "The state blocked us at every stage. It could've been such a good thing. I sit here now, watching businesses close and people wondering if they'll lose their houses. It's sad."

Soon enough, a new source of hope appeared. A campaign pledge from President Barack Obama to close the U.S. facility holding suspected terrorists at the naval base at Guantanamo Bay, Cuba, became an executive order. Quickly, the jail's backers made a new pitch. Why not house those 240 detainees at Two Rivers? Hardin's City Council last week passed a resolution to entice the detainees their way, saying they could provide "a safe and secure environment, pending trial and/or deportation."

Reaction from Montana's three-man congressional delegation was swift and unanimous, but hardly supportive.

"I understand the need to create jobs, but we're not going to bring al-Qaeda to Big Sky Country—no way, not on my watch," said Senator Max Baucus, a Democrat. Many local taxpayers are livid at Hardin officials. "It's been a complete fiasco since the beginning, and I don't see how they built it without any solid contracts," says Mike Carpata, a forester with the Bureau of Indian Affairs, as he shopped for reloading supplies at Lammer's Trading Post, where locals and members of the Crow Tribe come to buy guns and ammo or beading supplies, or to sell for quick cash their saddles, buffalo robes, and beaded-buckskin ceremonial costumes.

Others remain supportive of the jail project—and the enterprise of the town's administrators. The store's fourth-generation owner, George Lammers, noting the drastic difference between subtropical, humid Gitmo and dry, wintry Hardin, says, "This place would be torture for some of those boys." But, he allows, "I think it would be great for all the law enforcement people to be here. It would help our housing market. Our city fathers wanted the economic benefits, but I guess they didn't foresee the political controversies."

On a Saturday morning, two 30-ish sisters who had been up all night partying wobbled along the sidewalk then slouched in the sun against one of many vacant storefronts lining Center Avenue. They said they needed a ride out of town and were afraid they might be picked up by the police and jailed, but then laughed with some relief when reminded that the closest lockup, the Big Horn County Jail, was now so overcrowded that it was turning away misdemeanor offenders.

Source: Adapted from Pat Dawson-Hardin, "The Montana Town That Wanted to Be Gitmo," *Time*, May 3, 2009, http://www.time.com/time/nation/article/0,8599,1894373,00.html.

Regional Jails

Most local jails are located away from major population centers, and many hold as few as 30 people. Although the state may provide a portion of their operating funds, the smallest jails lack essential services, such as medical care, that must be provided no matter how few people may need them.

One recent trend designed to remedy these problems is regionalization: the creation of combined municipal-county or multicounty jails. This multijurisdictional or **regional jail**, fiscally sound though it may be, has been slow to catch on, because it negatively affects several interest groups. Local political and correctional leaders do not want to give up their autonomy or their control over patronage jobs, and reformers often object to moving inmates away from their communities. Citizens who oppose having regional

regional jail
Facility operated under a joint agreement between two or more government units, with a jail board drawn from representatives of the participating jurisdictions, and having varying authority over policy, budget, operations, and personnel.

jails "in their backyard" make finding locations to build regional jails difficult. Nevertheless, the number of jails in the United States actually dropped in the mid-1990s, as outmoded facilities were closed in favor of building new, always larger—and often regional—replacement facilities. In 1993, for example, only 17 percent of all jail inmates were housed in facilities holding 2,000 or more prisoners, but today that figure is over 30 percent, largely as a result of new facilities such as regional jails. A new trend is for regional jails to be privately run. (See the Focus box "Private Jails" for more.)

■ PRETRIAL DETENTION

On June 30, 2009, Federal Judge David Hittner revoked the bond of Texas financier R. Allen Stanford, a billionaire accused of masterminding a $7 billion fraud against 30,000 investors. What factors do you think the judge considered?

AP Images/David J. Phillip

Imagine that you have been arrested by the police and accused of a crime. They have handcuffed you, read you your rights, and taken you to the station for booking. Frightened, you have a hundred questions, but the police treat you as if your fears were irrelevant to their work. You may be angry with yourself for what you have done. You may be frustrated that you cannot seem to control the flow of procedure: fingerprints, mug shots, long waits while detectives and prosecutors discuss you without acknowledging your presence. Slowly you begin to understand that you have acquired a new status: accused offender.

Then you are taken to the detention section of the jail. If it is an advanced facility, you are placed in a holding room for an intake interview. There your situation is explained to you, you are asked questions about your background that will help determine how best to manage you while you are in jail, and you are told what you can expect next. If, however, you are in one of many jails with no formal intake procedure, you are simply put in the holding tank. If you are a man, several strangers likely will be in the cell with you, men whose stories you do not know and whose behavior you cannot predict. If you are a woman, you probably will be by yourself. In either case, once the guard leaves, you are on your own behind bars, and the full extent of your situation begins to sink in. This can be an especially trying period for those detainees who are thrust into a hostile and threatening environment, as discussed in "Do the Right Thing."

In such circumstances, many people panic. In fact, the hours immediately following arrest are often a time of crisis, stemming from the arrested person's sense of vulnerability and hopelessness, fear of lost freedom, and sheer terror. Over one-third of the deaths that occur in jails are suicides. Not surprisingly, most of these suicides happened within the first 6–10 hours after lockup, and most psychotic episodes occur during or just after jail intake.

Other factors can exacerbate the crisis brought on by arrest and detention. Often the arrestee is intoxicated or on drugs, a state that may have contributed to the crime for which the person is being held. Sometimes the criminal behavior stems from an emotional instability that may worsen in detention. Especially for young offenders, the oppressive reality can trigger debilitating depression. Unquestionably one of the most crucial times for arrestees is the period immediately following arrest. (See the Focus box "Jimmy's First Day in Jail.")

DO THE RIGHT THING

Ted Bliss entered the office of Dick Steele, Warden of the Montville County Jail.

"Dick, we can't put Josh Welch into the general population—he'll be eaten alive! With the Latin Kings and the CRIPS trying to impress each other, that young white kid is going to be jail meat."

"I know, Ted, but what can we do? The place is crowded; I can't separate by race or by gang. This is no hotel where someone gets his own room and special services. We've got one 30-man dorm for the detainees, and 20 beds in the other wing for those under sentence. I know he's going to have trouble, but he's just going to have to work it out himself."

"But you could put him over in the sentenced wing. There's a bed there, and those guys are less aggressive. It's these young gang members just off the street who try to impress each other by being so macho. They really put the pressure on the new boys."

"I know, but we can't make exceptions."

WRITING ASSIGNMENT: Does Warden Steele have an ethical obligation to protect Josh Welch? Should Officer Bliss continue to pressure for a policy exception? What would you do if you were Ted Bliss? Write a memo to the warden, formally explaining your position and detailing how you'll handle the situation.

FOCUS ON
PEOPLE IN CORRECTIONS

Jimmy's First Day in Jail

Jimmy James sat in the back of the Mountain View police car, his hands cuffed behind his back. He had never been arrested before, and thoughts about jail tormented his mind. When Jimmy saw news reports depicting the crowded conditions and violence, he didn't pay much attention. The trauma of confinement was the furthest thing from his mind. Yet he found trouble by downloading nude pictures from the Internet. Facts later revealed that the girls in the pictures were underage, and Jimmy now faced felony charges for child pornography.

The police officers drove in to a basement garage and parked their vehicle. After one of the officers opened the car's rear door, Jimmy stepped out, his heart pounding. The officer gripped Jimmy by the handcuff, making him feel as if he were a dog on a leash. The officer guided Jimmy into an elevator. When the door opened again, Jimmy saw the madness of the large King County Jail.

Jimmy's legs shook as he walked into the jail's administrative area. His first stop was booking. To his right were prisoners packed in a series of open holding cages. The cages resembled the dog pound, he thought, though instead of yelping and barking dogs, Jimmy heard the blustering cacophony that came from scores of young, seemingly angry men. He hoped the officers would not lock him inside with the other prisoners.

As the jail staff took Jimmy into custody, the officers lost interest in him. He was fingerprinted, positioned for his mug shot, and then led toward the bullpens.

"Can I go into that one?" Jimmy gestured toward the bullpen that held only three prisoners seated on a bench, each of whom looked contrite.

"No can do," the jailer said. "That's the misdemeanor tank. You're in with the felons, Class A."

The jailer unlocked the gate to the most crowded cage. "Step inside," the jailer ordered.

Jimmy hesitated, and the prisoners taunted him. "Step inside, bitch," he heard one prisoner yell. "Don't get scared now. What is it homey, you too good to be in here with us?"

"Get in," the jailer ordered.

Jimmy walked into the cage. Once the jailer locked the gate behind him, Jimmy passed his cuffs through the bars and the jailer freed his wrists. Then the jailer walked away, leaving the prisoners to themselves.

The crowd of strangers frightened Jimmy. He was 21, shorter than average height with a slender build. Hi sand-colored hair was thinning prematurely. He didn't have

anywhere to sit, so he walked toward the back of the cell and leaned against the wall.

A larger prisoner stepped toward Jimmy. "What up big dog?"

Jimmy didn't know how to respond. He nodded his head.

"Where you from?"

Jimmy didn't want to talk to anyone. He stood silent against the wall, with hunched shoulders and bowed his head toward the floor.

"I'm sayin'," the aggressive prisoner persisted, "you ain't tryin' to talk?"

Jimmy kept silent.

"Okay, okay," the prisoner said. "I feel ya. But check dis out. Wussup wit dat watch?"

Jimmy looked up, realizing his efforts at disappearing were not working. "What do you mean?"

"I'm sayin', wassup wit dat watch? You know some'nes gonna take it up off you once you get to the block."

"Why?"

"You's in jail fool. Straight gangstas up in here. Best let me hold it for you. I'm a take care it, make sure you get it back when your daddy post bail."

Jimmy thought for a split second. He didn't want any problems. The watch wasn't fancy, just a simple digital model with an alarm. Knowing he probably wouldn't see it again, he unfastened the Velcro band and handed it over.

"Dats wassup homey," the prisoner strapped the prize on his wrist. "I'm a take good care you up in here. What dey got you up in here for youngun?"

"Internet porn."

"Internet porn. Wus dat?"

"Internet porn, you know, downloading nude pictures from the web."

"They be lockin' mothafuckas up for dat?"

"Well the models were underage."

The prisoner smiled. "Oh you be likin' dem kids."

"I didn't know the models were underage."

"Uh-huh. Was dey little girls or little boys?"

"They were young women. I'm not gay you know."

"Ain't no one sayin' you was gay. I's just axin', dat's all. But check dis out, youngun. When we gets up on da block, don't be talkin' 'bout your case. Just stay close to me. I'm a look out for ya."

The jailer returned to the bullpen. He unlocked the gate and called names to step out. Jimmy made his way through the crowd, as did his unnamed protector. The jailer handed the men a roll of dingy sheets, a threadbare blanket, and a brown sack that held two pieces of white bread with bologna. The prisoners marched through the jail's corridor, passing through various sliding gates until they reached a housing unit. "Grab a mat," the jailer ordered, "and find yourself a home on the floor."

Jimmy couldn't believe he would have to live in such conditions. Sleeping mats were everywhere. A list on the wall posted 30 names waiting for cell space. The bathrooms were open, lacking a modicum of privacy. A stench of dried urine permeated the air. Noise from table games, aggressive voices, and a television blasting rap songs contributed to the frenetic energy in the housing unit. He would go crazy if he had to stay in jail long, Jimmy thought.

"Don't even sweat it," the larger prisoner said. "We goin' crash right here. I'm a look out for ya, youngun."

Jimmy quivered. He sat on the mat that he had dropped, held his knees, and waited, afraid for what might happen next.

Source: Written by Michael Santos.

To find out about **standards for jails** and current issues about jails, visit the American Jail Association, using the corresponding link at www.cengage.com/criminaljustice/clear.

Detainees differ in their need for help during this period. Those under the influence of a mind-altering substance need time to overcome its effects; others need to be left alone; still others need communication and advice. Jails lack the programmatic flexibility to accommodate the range of needs. However, the early confinement period also represents a mental health opportunity, because an individual in crisis is most likely to respond positively to efforts at help. Unfortunately, the jail is not ordinarily well suited to provide aid in the first hours of detention. Elaborate mental health measures are neither feasible nor necessarily required. However, even simple human contact—conversation with correctional staff, involvement in some activity, communication about what the detainee is likely to be experiencing—is frequently enough to reduce many initial anxieties.

Special Problems of Detainees

Beyond the initial crisis of being arrested and jailed, people who are detained for an extended period often face serious problems. The most significant are mental health problems, substance dependency, medical needs, and legal problems. Because so many jail inmates have these problems, jails often have been referred to as the social agency of last resort.

MENTAL HEALTH PROBLEMS ■ Growing attention is being paid to the mental health of arrestees whose behavior, while not seriously criminal, is socially bizarre—those who are only partially clothed, who speak gibberish or talk loudly to themselves, who make hostile gestures, and so on. These people, whose behavior is unpredictable and to some extent uncontrollable, formerly were transported to mental institutions where they could be treated. But with the nationwide deinstitutionalization movement, they have become outpatients of society, and they often spend time in jail instead of receiving the psychiatric treatment they once might have received. Almost two-thirds of jail prisoners have a history of mental problems; for one-fifth of people in jails, there is a very recent history of mental disorder.[9] (See **Figure 7.4**.) But many jails do not offer any form of psychological care at all, and only a minority of jail inmates receive mental health treatment.

Observers say the number of inmates considered mentally ill is increasing. However, police have few alternatives to confinement for people who behave oddly or self-destructively, even if they are more nuisances than criminals. Moreover, unstable people often respond to the stress of jail with emotional outbursts and irrational behavior. Jails not only draw from but also add to the ranks of the mentally disturbed.

Most jails lack resources to provide care for mentally ill offenders.[10] Three-fourths of all jails have no rehabilitative staff, and among the remainder the vast majority of rehabilitative personnel lack training to deal with severe cases of mental and emotional stress, particularly when threats of self-injury are involved. Consequently, mentally disturbed inmates often languish in jails, where they are abused by other inmates, misunderstood by correctional workers, and left untreated by professional personnel.

The news is not all bad, however; some positive steps have been taken to divert the mentally ill from jail. Many jails now screen new arrivals for mental health problems, with specially trained counselors interviewing and evaluating pretrial detainees. Inmates with mental health problems are usually referred to local social service agencies for treatment and may be diverted from criminal prosecution in order for treatment to proceed.

SUBSTANCE DEPENDENCY ■ Nationally, half of all people placed in jail were under the influence of alcohol or an illegal drug at the time of arrest, and over two-thirds, more than 400,000 jail inmates, have a history of substance abuse. More than half of those entering jail have a history of failed drug treatment, often during previous jail or probation terms.[11] The most dramatic problems posed by offenders' drug abuse occur during withdrawal, when the addict's body reacts to the loss of the substance on which it has grown dependent. Both alcoholics and drug addicts suffer withdrawal, but it is especially painful for the latter group and may last as long as a week. Addicts may attempt suicide to escape the pains of withdrawal, and a higher percentage of drug addicts than nonaddicts succeed in the attempt. Early identification of the

Detained alcoholics and drug addicts must undergo withdrawal in jails where there are few treatment resources for them.

© Ulrik Jantzen/Contrasto/Redux Pictures

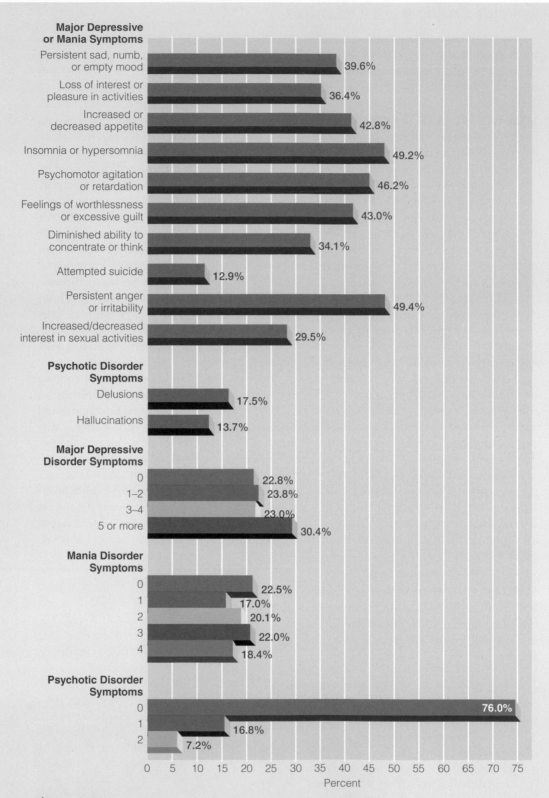

Figure 7.4

Percentage of Jail Inmates with Mental Health Symptoms in Past 12 Months or Since Admission

Source: BJS *Special Report*, September 2006, p. 2. Data are based on inmate self-report in the *Survey of Inmates in State and Federal Correctional Facilities, 2004,* and the *Survey of Inmates in Local Jails, 2002.*

drug addict is therefore a high priority in urban jails, for withdrawal symptoms can be assuaged by methadone maintenance or release to an addiction treatment facility. Despite the short stays of inmates in jails, treatment programs designed especially for jails have shown some success. Despite the great need for substance abuse treatment in jails, only 16 percent of those in jail receive it while there.[12]

Every jail regularly houses alcoholic offenders, many of whom, during the initial hours of confinement, are physically sick, hallucinating, and paranoid. These symptoms tend to be viewed as inconveniences rather than as conditions requiring treatment. Few jails provide any real form of treatment, and treatment by outside agencies is often just as rare because agencies prefer voluntary clients to offenders.

Since the first detoxification center in the United States was established in St. Louis in 1966, the national trend has been toward treating public drunkenness as more of a medical than a criminal problem. These detox centers are quasi-voluntary facilities for recidivist inebriates, many of whom have no other place to go. The centers provide shelter, medical care, food, clothing, and counseling for residents, most of whom are taken there by police.

MEDICAL NEEDS ■ Detainees have many medical needs, ranging from minor scrapes and bruises sustained during arrest and booking to major injuries sustained during the crime and its aftermath. To these injuries can be added the routine health deficiencies of any lower-class citizen: infections, poor nutrition, lack of dental care, and so forth. Taken together, more than one-third of those in jail report a physical ailment of some sort.[13] Even so, almost half of the nation's jails do not screen routinely for infectious diseases, such as tuberculosis.

For the most part, citizens who end up in jail, on either charges or sentences, lack medical insurance, and so whatever medical care they receive is provided by the jail itself. Almost 60 percent of America's jails make prisoners pay for at least some of the medical care they receive; two-thirds of those require payment for all services. Forty percent provide the health care through on-site staff or other government employees. Even in the jails that seek to address inmate health problems, services are problematic, and many inmates have complained about the quality of care being offered.

Today the most pressing medical issue in jails relates to the offender with AIDS, estimated at just over 1 percent of jailed inmates nationally.[14] About 7 percent of all jail deaths are AIDS-related.[15] As noted in Chapter 6, jail officials should be in a position to provide certain treatments for arrestees with HIV/AIDS, and all correctional workers should take standard precautions around these offenders. The main problems have to do with staff training, because many jail employees have misconceptions about how the disease is spread. This can lead to mishandling of HIV/AIDS-infected inmates. The poor response to HIV-positive inmates in jails is exacerbated by the fact that about nearly half of all jails do not routinely screen for the virus. Yet there is good news as well. Nationally, HIV rates in jails are down markedly since 1996, dropping by more than one-fourth, and AIDS as a cause of death during custody has also declined since that time.[16]

LEGAL NEEDS ■ Pretrial detainees need access to legal assistance. In the emotionally stressful postarrest period, suspects need information about what will happen prior to their trial. They also need legal help in securing release through bail or diversion. If release is not possible, they must have help in preparing their case, negotiating with the prosecutor about charges, or directing the attorney to people who may provide an alibi or exonerating evidence. Not surprisingly, research consistently shows that people locked up in jail until trial suffer a disadvantage in preparing their defense. People in jail are likely to need a public defender, an appointed counsel, or an attorney provided by contract. Unfortunately, because they must process large numbers of cases for relatively small fees, criminal defense attorneys cannot spend much time locating witnesses, conducting investigative interviews, and preparing testimony. So for many detainees these essential defense plans are only partially pursued.

Detainees can expect to spend long periods without seeing an attorney. In fact, most have only one or two hurried conversations with their attorneys before they appear in court. To add insult to injury, detainees are brought to court in shackles and jail-issue clothing, in dramatic contrast to well-groomed defendants who have been able to remain free. Detainees who were once employed have long since been fired. In short, detainees have relatively dim prospects.

PRETRIAL DETAINEES' RIGHTS ■ Unlike prisoners, pretrial detainees have not been convicted of the crimes for which they are being held. Technically, they are innocent, yet they are detained under some of the worst conditions of incarceration. In the 1970s several courts reasoned that such people should suffer no more restrictions than are necessary to ensure their presence at trial and that legal protections for detainees should exceed those of sentenced prisoners.

However, in 1979 the U.S. Supreme Court overruled the lower courts by limiting pretrial detainees' rights. As discussed in Chapter 5, the Court in *Bell v. Wolfish* ruled that conditions can be created to make certain that detainees are available for trial and that administrative practices designed to manage jails and to maintain security and order are constitutional.[17] The justices said that restrictions other than those that ensure court appearance may legitimately be imposed on detainees and that when jail security, discipline, and order are at stake, detainees may be treated like other prisoners.

Release from Detention

One of the most startling facts about U.S. jails is that more than half of their occupants are awaiting trial. For many, this pretrial detention will last a long time: The average delay between arrest and sentencing is more than six months.[18] In urban jails, the wait is often longer because of heavy court backlogs. Remarkably, despite the constitutional right to a speedy trial, in some court systems defendants can expect to languish in jail for up to a year or more before their cases come to trial.

The hardship of pretrial detention exerts pressure on defendants to waive their rights and plead guilty. Further, as we have seen, it undermines their defense (see **Figure 7.5**). And delay, often a useful defense tactic because it can weaken the prosecutor's case, imposes a further penalty on the detained defendant.

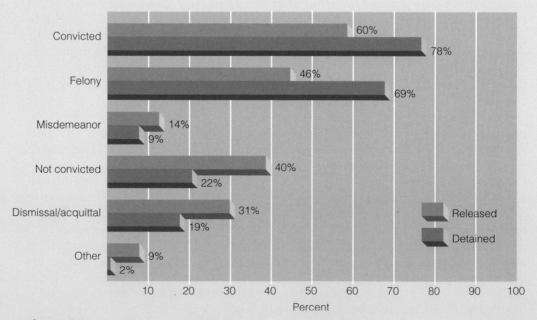

Figure 7.5
Pretrial Release and Adjudication Outcome
Most who are released pending trial do better at trial than those who are not.

Source: Bureau of Justice Statistics, *Pretrial Release of Felony Defendants in State Courts*, November 2007, Table 5.

Small wonder, then, that recent years have seen a major emphasis on programs to facilitate the release of offenders awaiting trial. Rates of pretrial release have gradually grown from less than 50 percent in the early 1960s to nearly 90 percent in some of today's largest urban areas. Nationally, 62 percent of felony defendants awaiting trial are released prior to the disposition of their case, half of them within a day.[19] Even so, the proportion of people in jail who are there because they are awaiting trial has increased from about half to nearly two-thirds in the last 10 years.[20] Today, jail overcrowding is accelerating the development of new mechanisms for pretrial release, one of the simplest ways to reduce a jail's population. Innovative alternatives to the traditional bail system have enabled police departments to sustain high volumes of arrests, even when local jails are severely overcrowded and under court order to reduce daily populations.

Paradoxically, jail crowding may have exacerbated the problem of pretrial populations. As mentioned, the 1990s saw a trend to close down old, dilapidated jails and replace them with newer, larger facilities. The proportion of jail inmates housed in large jails (over 2,000 capacity) has almost doubled since 1993. Jail capacity increased by more than one-third. But many of the new spaces were taken not by sentenced prisoners but by pretrial detainees, as the proportion of jail prisoners serving sentences remains just over half.[21]

■ THE BAIL PROBLEM AND ALTERNATIVES

When someone is arrested for a crime, the court seeks to ensure that the defendant will appear at the appointed time to face charges. Judges traditionally have responded to this need by requiring that the person post **bail**, normally ranging from $1,000 to $25,000 (although higher amounts may be required), to be forfeited if the accused fails to appear. See **Figure 7.6** to see what bail amounts judges set.

Defendants have two principal ways to make bail. They may post the full amount to the court, where it is held until the case is decided. Or they may pay a set fee to a **bondsman**, who posts the amount with the court; the fee varies, depending on the jurisdiction.

Dissatisfaction with the bail process stems from several factors. First, many defendants—in some studies over 90 percent of pretrial detainees—are practically indigent and cannot afford bail. Second, money is a weak incentive for appearance in

bail
An amount of money, specified by a judge, to be posted as a condition for pretrial release to ensure the appearance of the accused in court.

bondsman
An independent businessperson who provides bail money for a fee, usually 5–10 percent of the total.

Figure 7.6
Amount of Bail Set by the Judge

Most judges set low bail amounts for defendants, yet even these amounts are hard for some indigent people to raise.

Source: Bureau of Justice Statistics, *Felony Defendants in Large Urban Counties, 2002* (Washington, DC: U.S. Department of Justice, 2006), 16.

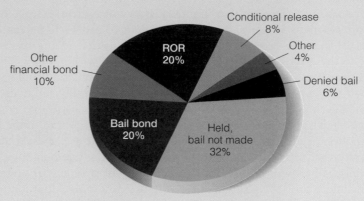

Figure 7.7
Pretrial Release Outcomes

Source: Bureau of Justice Statistics, *Pretrial Release of Felony Defendants in State Courts* (Washington, DC: U.S. Government Printing Office, November 2007), Table 1.

court in many cases, because the people who can afford bail are the ones most likely to appear at trial without the threat of its forfeiture. Perhaps the most disquieting factor is that human freedom can be had for a price. Imprisoning people merely because they are too poor to pay for their release seems antithetical to our cultural ideals and our concept of justice.

To avoid the problems of bail, some jurisdictions have increased the use of citations and summonses. For nonserious offenses, police can give the accused a "ticket" specifying a court appearance date and thus avoid having to take the accused into custody. Experiments with this approach indicate that it effectively reduces demands for short-term detention space. See **Figure 7.7** for more on pretrial release.

Release on Recognizance

release on recognizance (ROR)
Pretrial release because the judge believes the defendant's ties in the community are sufficient to guarantee the defendant's appearance in court.

By far the most successful approach allows defendants to be released solely on their promise to appear at trial, a practice known as **release on recognizance (ROR)**. ROR programs assume that ties to the community (residence, family, employment) give people an incentive to keep their promise to appear and to retain their status in the community.

ROR defendants frequently have higher appearance rates than do defendants freed through various bail programs; they also have lower rearrest rates and higher rates of sentences to probation rather than prison. ROR programs have demonstrated clearly that the vast majority of accused people can be safely released into the community on their promise to return for trial. Loss of bail is an unnecessary threat. The rate of willful failure to appear in most jurisdictions is normally less than 5 percent.

Despite the benefits of ROR, questions arise. Because ROR requires that defendants have ties to the community, only a small number of defendants can usually participate. One national analysis of ROR found that women are more likely than men to be released, and African Americans are less likely than whites. Moreover, these effects vary from one region of the country to another, with African Americans least likely to be released on recognizance in the West and South, even when controlling for other factors related to the release decision (offense, age, and previous record).[22]

day reporting center
Facility where offenders such as pretrial releasees and probation violators attend daylong intervention and treatment sessions.

Some jurisdictions have begun to experiment with pretrial release under some form of supervision. Nationally, about 73,000 jail inmates are under some form of supervised release. Forty percent of these are supervised by probation officers or other counselors or are under pretrial supervision, 8 percent attend **day reporting centers**, 25 percent perform community service (these are discussed more fully in Chapter 9), and 19 percent are under **electronic monitoring**.[23] These approaches show promise, as at least one study has shown that jail inmates who stay longer on monitoring have lower recidivism rates.[24]

Pretrial Diversion

As an alternative to adjudication, **pretrial diversion** began with the belief that formally processing people through the criminal justice system is not always beneficial. Each of the three main reasons advanced in support of pretrial diversion has provoked controversy:

1 Many offenders' crimes are caused by special problems—vagrancy, alcoholism, emotional distress—that cannot be managed effectively through the criminal justice system.

2 The stigma attached to formal criminal labeling often works against rehabilitation and promotes an unnecessarily harsh penalty for a relatively minor offense.

3 Diversion is cheaper than criminal justice processing.

For the most part, correctional leaders agree that jails can do little for inmates who have mental, emotional, or alcohol-related problems. For such people, social programs are more suitable than jails. There is less agreement about appropriate treatment for those whose problems are less clearly beyond their own control—unemployed and unskilled youths, multiple drug users, and episodic offenders, to name a few. Their marginal criminality may stem primarily from their disadvantaged status, and their status can be seen as at least partly their own fault. Diversion from the criminal justice system is controversial, because to some critics it allows some people to "get off easy." Yet the rationale for diverting them is attractive. The jail sanction does little to alter their disadvantaged status; indeed, the stigma of a conviction often decreases their chances of becoming productive citizens. A more-enlightened policy would deflect them from criminal justice processes and instead put them into reparations programs. That is, in fact, the precise aim of most pretrial diversion.

The mixed success of pretrial diversion programs highlights a persistent problem of criminal justice reform. Innovations designed to reduce the overall intrusiveness of the system, no matter how well intentioned, often backfire and instead expand its capacity for social control. The process, called "**widening the net**," occurs when a new program is applied to offenders with crimes less serious than those of the people for whom it was originally designed; rather than focusing on the more-serious offenders, it increases the scope of corrections.

If pretrial diversion programs are to meet their objectives, they must be applied to offenders who otherwise would be treated more harshly. This is not easy to accomplish, because many criminal justice system officials distrust programs that are more lenient or more oriented to community service than are their current practices.

Conduct during Pretrial Release

People who are awaiting trial would seem to have a special incentive to behave well. If they show up for court with a job and prospects for a good future, it will be harder for a judge to impose a sentence of confinement. If they show they can adjust well to the community during the period between the arrest and the trial, then the judge will likely take that into account when imposing a sentence.

It may be surprising, then, that many defendants do not behave well during their period of release before trial. While the vast majority—78 percent—of defendants on some form of pretrial release show up for every court hearing, more than one in five do not. These are called **absconders**, and unless there is some good reason they missed the court date, a warrant is sent out for their arrest. They are considered fugitives. Nationally, one-fourth of these fugitives (6 percent of all defendants) remain at large at least one year after they were supposed to have their trial.[25]

electronic monitoring
Community supervision technique, ordinarily combined with home confinement, that uses electronic devices to maintain surveillance on offenders.

pretrial diversion
An alternative to adjudication in which the defendant agrees to conditions set by the prosecutor (for example, counseling or drug rehabilitation) in exchange for withdrawal of charges.

widening the net
Increasing the scope of corrections by applying a diversion program to people charged with offenses less serious than those of the people the program was originally intended to serve.

absconders
People who fail to appear for a court date and have no legitimate reason.

The failure to appear for trial is not the only form of misbehavior that happens when people are released before trial. Almost one in five (18 percent) of all people released while awaiting trial are rearrested before their trial date arrives, two-thirds for a felony.[26] The high arrest rate of pretrial releases represents a significant concern to people interested in jail reform. They wonder if some sort of supervision or treatment program would help keep these numbers down. They also see that high rates of arrests for this population lead to questions about the effectiveness of the pretrial system.

Preventive Detention

preventive detention
Detention of an accused person in jail, to protect the community from crimes the accused is considered likely to commit if set free pending trial.

Even as ROR and other prerelease programs have moved forward, the heightened public concern about misconduct by people who are released while awaiting trial has led to a political movement to prevent pretrial release, especially release on bail. With **preventive detention**, defendants who are regarded as dangerous or likely to commit crimes while awaiting trial are kept in jail for society's protection. In 1984 the Comprehensive Crime Control Act authorized the holding of an allegedly dangerous defendant without bail if the judge finds that no conditions of release would ensure the defendant's appearance at trial and at the same time ensure the safety of the community.

The notion of the need for protection from accused criminals has been subjected to sustained analysis. Many scholars believe that holding in custody a person who has not been convicted of committing a crime but who someone thinks might commit a crime violates the due process provisions of the Constitution. Others argue that the practice is impractical and potentially nefarious. But as we have seen, less than one in five of all defendants who are released pending trial are arrested for another crime before trial, and many of those are not convicted of the new crime.

Political pressure to incorporate the public's safety concerns into release decisions has become so strong that well over half of the states have laws allowing preventive detention. The U.S. Supreme Court, in *Schall v. Martin* (1984) and *United States v. Salerno* (1987), approved preventive-detention practices.[27]

■ THE SENTENCED JAIL INMATE

MYTHS IN CORRECTIONS

JAILS ARE FOR MISDEMEANANTS

MYTH: Jail sentences are more for misdemeanants than they are for felons.

FACT: Nearly 40 percent of felony defendants are eventually sentenced to jail, a rate that is almost the same as prison sentences for felonies.

Source: Bureau of Justice Statistics, *Felony Defendants in Large Urban Counties, 2002* (Washington, DC: U.S. Department of Justice, 2006), iii.

The sentenced jail inmate presents special difficulties for the correctional administrator, mainly because of the short duration of the term and the limitations of the jail's physical plant. By definition, jail terms are shorter than prison terms—typically 30–90 days for a misdemeanor. Felons commonly serve from six months to a year, in some occasions serious felons (convicted of sexual assault or robbery, for example) will serve two years or more.[28] (See "Myths in Corrections.") In many cases the sentence ultimately imposed is "time served," because the judge believes that the time already spent in pretrial detention—when by law the person was presumed innocent—is sufficient, or more than sufficient, punishment for the offense committed. The real punishment is not the sentence, but rather the impact on the offender of the unpleasant, costly, and harmful conditions of life behind bars from arrest up to case disposition. In short, the process is the punishment.

Of those sentenced to additional jail time, misdemeanants constitute the forgotten component of local criminal justice operations. Over half were under criminal justice system supervision at the time of their arrest—probation, parole, or pretrial release—and

© MONICA ALMEIDA/The New York Times/Redux Pictures

Nicholle Brockett is serving her 21-day sentence for drunk driving in a "pay-to-stay" cell at the jail in Santa Ana, California. The special cell costs her $82 a day. At least 12 such jails are found in California for offenders whose crimes are relatively minor and who have the cash. The clients in these jails are segregated from the general population. They have access to cell phones and in some jails to laptop computers as well. Critics ask if these jails send the wrong message about equality within the justice system.

these people are well known to the justice system. Nearly three-quarters have previously been sentenced to probation or confinement. They also have a range of treatment needs. More than four-fifths have a history of illegal drug use; 29 percent were unemployed, and of the employed, 40 percent earned less that $1,000 a month. More than one-third have experienced a serious physical injury, and almost one-fifth were abused.[29] Most have not graduated from high school, and many are illiterate; yet educational programming is unlikely to yield results in such a short time, especially with adults.

Their short terms make treatment difficult. For example, offenders can rarely earn a high school equivalency diploma in one or two months, and prospects for continued education after release are dim. Similar impracticalities are inherent in job-training programs, which may require 25–30 weeks to complete. In addition, job-placement prospects are spotty for the former inmate, who may not even have the help of a parole or probation officer in looking for work. Treatment programs for the mentally ill, the emotionally disturbed, and alcoholics and drug addicts suffer from the same time constraints.

The jail facility also limits program opportunities. Jobs within the institution are few, and most inmates have no real work. Those assigned to work details find the labor menial and monotonous: janitorial, kitchen, and laundry tasks. Still, they are lucky: The vast majority of inmates simply languish in small cells. Recreational options may consist of a small library of donated books, a Ping-Pong table, and a few card tables; few jails have basketball courts, weight rooms, and the like. Whatever the resources, recreational time is carefully rationed. Contact with friends and relatives is the only thing that sustains many prisoners in jail, but visiting hours often are limited to a few minutes each week.

In sum, with isolated exceptions, jail time is the worst kind of time to serve as a correctional client. For corrections, jail is an expensive and largely ineffective proposition—a revolving door that leads nowhere.

To ameliorate these problems, reformers have begun to emphasize the importance of carefully planned and supported reentry programs. Jail administrators are to begin preparing for the sentenced jail inmate's release from the first day of confinement,[30] and partnerships with community supervision agencies are encouraged to provide more support for the person who is returning to the community from the jail.[31]

■ ISSUES IN JAIL MANAGEMENT *Maggie*

American jails are faced with numerous problems, many of them age-old: lack of programs, poor financial resources, antiquated facilities, and so on. Here we discuss five of the most important issues related to jail: legal liability, jail standards, personnel matters, jail crowding, and the jail facility itself.

Legal Liability

As discussed in Chapter 5, jail employees may be legally liable for their actions (42 U.S.C. 1983). Whenever a government official (such as a correctional officer) uses his or her authority to deprive a citizen of civil rights, the victim can sue the official to halt the violation and to collect damages (both actual and punitive) and recoup legal costs. Supervisors, including wardens, also can be liable for the actions of staff members—even if they were not aware of those actions—if it can be shown that they should have been aware. Lack of funds does not excuse an administrator from liability for failing to train staff sufficiently or to provide basic, constitutionally required custodial arrangements. Local governments that administer the jails are also liable for injurious conduct.

Many people believe that court decisions awarding civil judgments under Section 1983 are an open invitation for prisoners to sue, and sue they do. Prisoners have litigated just about every conceivable aspect of the conditions of incarceration, from hours of recreation to quality of food. The most successful suits have been those showing that an employee's action has contributed to a situation that harmed a prisoner.

The threat of litigation has forced jails to develop basic humane practices for managing offenders. Civil damages and legal fees of more than $1 million have been awarded often enough to draw the attention of sheriffs, jail managers, and local government officials. Budgets for jails have been increased to reflect the additional costs of developing training programs, classification procedures, and managerial policies to prevent actions leading to liability suits.

Jail Standards

One of the best ways to reduce litigation is to develop specific standards for the practices and procedures that routine jail operations entail. Standards are important for at least three reasons. First, they indicate proactive criteria for jail management, which help eliminate the "Monday morning quarterback" (rehashed in hindsight) aspect of much litigation. If jails are following standard procedures, they cannot be held as accountable as they otherwise would for problems inmates experience during incarceration. Second, standards provide a basis by which administrators can evaluate staff performance: They need merely determine whether staff are complying with operational standards. Third, standards facilitate the planning and evaluation of jail programs by giving program managers a target to consider in their work.

Even so, authorities are uncertain about the best way to design and implement jail standards. Some experts argue that standards should be binding. Generally this means that an oversight agency visits each jail in the state and determines whether its programs are consistent with the standards. Jails that fail to comply with standards are given a deadline by which to meet them. If they do not, they may be fined—or even closed down.

Other experts argue that because jails differ so much in size and needs and because so many of them suffer from underfunding and inadequate facilities, holding all jails accountable for meeting the same inflexible set of standards is unreasonable. These experts push for voluntary guidelines by which program goals for jail operations would be set by groups such as the American Correctional Association and monitored by teams of professionals.

The bottom line is that if jail administrators do not implement standard practices, the courts will intervene. Even new jails are not immune to this problem. In the late 1980s, jails commonly came under court orders soon after opening, and sometimes even before opening.

Personnel Matters

Local correctional workers are among the most poorly trained, least educated, and worst paid employees in the criminal justice system. Many take custodial positions on a temporary basis while awaiting an opening in the ranks of the sheriff's law enforcement officers. Of the approximately 240,000 jail employees noted in the last census, about 72 percent performed direct custody functions, 13 percent were clerical and maintenance workers, 7 percent were professionals, and 1 percent were in education.[32]

Personnel problems facing jail administrators stem from several factors, but the primary one is probably a combination of low pay and poor working conditions. Local correctional workers earn substantially less than firefighters and police officers in the same jurisdiction. And whenever these correctional workers can, they leave for better-paying jobs with less-stressful working conditions. Many correctional employees, however, have only limited education and do not fare well in competition for better positions, so they must stay where they are.

Understaffing further exacerbates these poor working conditions. Jails are 24-hour operations. Assuming that the typical jurisdiction has a 40-hour workweek with normal holidays and leave time, nearly five full-time employees are required to fill one position around the clock. The national ratio of inmates to custodial employees in jails is about 4.3 to 1, which translates to about 25 to 1 for each staff workday. In essence, each jail employee must be able to control 25 inmates or more, which helps account for the common practice of simply locking the doors and leaving inmates in their cells all day.

Not surprisingly, local correctional workers are often an unhappy bunch. Turnover is extraordinarily high, with many jails reporting complete staff turnover every two or three years. The effects are disastrous. No matter what the level of staffing, proper security must be maintained in the jail, so there is pressure to move new employees directly into the ranks, despite the fact that training at a state academy may last 30–60 days—and classes may not start for several months. The dilemma is obvious and has prompted the Jail Division of the National Institute of Corrections in Longmont, Colorado, to make the training of jail staff instructors a high national priority. This strategy seeks to increase the number of qualified trainers for jail workers so that no new employee lacks the necessary preparation for the assignment. At best, however, this is a stopgap. In the long run, society must improve pay rates and working conditions to make jail employment more attractive.

Jail Crowding

The number of people confined in jails reached nearly crisis proportions in the early 1990s. The jail population, which had remained fairly stable during the 1970s, more than doubled between 1983 and 1993, and it has increased by a third since 1993. Much of this crowding stems from the expectation that jails are to handle a wide range of people, including drug addicts, the mentally ill, and alcoholics. Further, hundreds of jails have been forced to close as a result of litigation, and over one in seven jails now operates under a court order of one type or another, typically related to crowding.[33]

In some cases, jail crowding has worsened for yet another reason: The state corrections system does not immediately accept sentenced offenders who should be

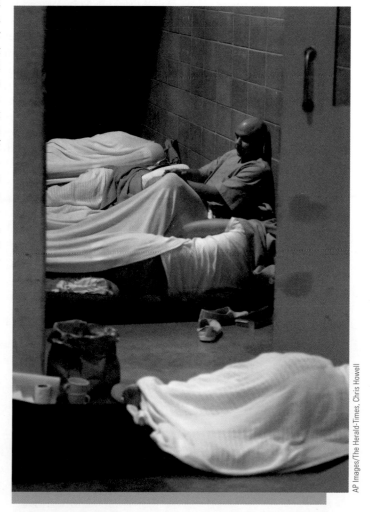

Because of crowding, some prisoners in the Monroe County Jail in Bloomington, Indiana, must sleep on the floor of the indoor recreation facility. Jail and prison crowding is a major problem.

AP Images/The Herald-Times, Chris Howell

serving time in prisons but for whom there is no space. This situation has led to problems for sheriffs and jail administrators. One sheriff in Arkansas brought inmates to the state penitentiary, chained them to the fence, and tried to leave them there; state officials armed with shotguns and a court order made him take the inmates back. Judges frustrated with prison crowding may also sentence to jail low-level offenders who would otherwise have gone to prison.

Jail administrators know that crowding can produce problems in jail management. Cells intended to hold one or two people are holding three, four, even five inmates. It is not uncommon for prisoners to sleep in hallways, with or without mattresses. Direct and immediate consequences of overcrowding are violence, rape, and a variety of health problems. In addition, some evidence indicates that prolonged exposure to seriously crowded conditions reduces the life expectancy of inmates. Certainly tempers flare in close quarters, and the vulnerable inmate becomes a likely victim. And remember: Many of the people subjected to these conditions have not yet been tried and must be presumed to be innocent.

There are many possible solutions to jail crowding. Two center on people detained before trial: (1) increasing the availability of release options, such as ROR and supervised release, and (2) speeding up trials.[34] Other ameliorative measures are directed toward people serving time and include work release sentences, which at least relieve crowding for part of the day. Yet less than half of all jails currently have some form of work release programs, and barely a third have provisions for weekend sentences. About 2 percent of the jail population—12,000 people—serve their sentences on weekends in order to reduce crowding.[35] **Table 7.1** shows the kinds of programs that enable jailed inmates to be placed in the community.

Oddly, building new jails—or increasing the capacity of existing facilities—apparently has little effect on the problem of crowding. Instead, policies regarding the use of jails, combined with crime rates in the jurisdiction served by the jails, seem to determine the amount of crowding. Wide variations exist among jurisdictions in patterns of jail usage, controlling for population served. Some jails were heavily used, others less so. The most crowded jails tended to be those housing "pass-through" populations—arrestees and detainees—and these tended to be larger facilities as well. This may explain the common phenomenon of new jails with expanded capacities opening, only to suffer renewed conditions of crowding. The solution to crowding is not as much jail capacity as it is jail policy.

TABLE 7.1 *Jail Inmates in the Community*

To reduce crowding, many jails have developed programs that enable some inmates to remain in the community instead of being confined.	
Type of Program	**Number of Inmates**
Weekender programs	12,325
Electronic monitoring (EM)	13,539
Home detention (no EM)	498
Day reporting	5,758
Community service	18,475
Other pretrial supervision	12,452
Other work programs	5,808
Treatment programs	2,259
Other outside programs	1,739
Total	72,853

Source: Bureau of Justice Statistics, *Statistical Tables*, March 2009, p. 8.

There are other reasons why jail expansion is today not as popular as it once was. Building new facilities is extremely expensive, costing on average $40,000–$50,000 per cell—meaning that a facility for 1,000 can cost $50 million to build and another $25 million annually to run. At a time when local governments are pressed to fund other priorities, such as education and health care, these costs seem extravagant. This is especially true because most people who go to jail do not return to the community as more-capable citizens, and so the jail acts more like a revolving door than a correctional service. In short, while jail growth has been a major dynamic in correctional policy for nearly 30 years, policy makers increasingly desire to stem the growth and look for other ways to deal with minor criminal activity and with people who are awaiting trial.[36]

New-generation jails, such as this one in Fort Collins, Colorado, are designed to increase the interaction of inmates with correctional officers. How might this style of jail influence your work as a correctional officer?

The Jail Facility

According to a survey of sheriffs, almost 30 percent of all jail cells are at least 50 years old, despite an unprecedented construction boom to replace old facilities. As we have just seen, jails are expensive structures; at their most expensive, they can cost as much as $100,000 per cell to build—and perhaps $200,000 per cell when financing is taken into consideration. Running a physically outmoded jail can be more expensive still.

In many jails, even such basic items as radios and television sets are lacking. With idle time, poor physical security, and little or no chance to participate in programs, prisoners are often cheek to jowl, day in and day out. Crowded cells make for threatening environments that may translate into potentially costly lawsuits. Often the only way to counteract poor security in older jails is to hire extra staff. For these reasons and others, many jurisdictions have turned toward what is called the **new-generation jail**. This jail, through its unique design and set of programs, attempts to use the physical plant to improve the staff's ability to manage and interact with the inmate population and to provide services. Three general concepts are employed: podular design, interaction space, and personal space.

The **podular unit** (derived from *pod* and *modular*) is a living area for a group of inmates that defines a post or a watch. The podular unit replaces the old cell blocks. Twelve to 25 individual cells are organized into a unit (the pod) that serves as a self-contained minijail. Typically the cell doors open into a common living area where the inmates of the pod can congregate.

The new-generation jail tends to reinforce interaction of various sorts. For example, inmates have greater freedom to interact socially and recreationally, and correctional staff are in direct physical contact with them throughout the day, an approach called **direct supervision**. In older jails, bars and doors separate correctional officers from inmates; the new-generation jail places them in the same rooms with inmates. The inmates are also given personal space and may stay in their individual cells to pursue their own interests when they wish. They may even have keys to their own quarters within the pod.

The new structure offers several advantages over older jails. First, its economics are flexible. When jail populations are low, whole pods can be temporarily shut down, saving personnel and operational costs. Second, minimum standards for recreation time and nonlockup time can be met routinely without costly construction or renovation. Third, supervising the staff is less demanding, for staff have greater autonomy to manage

new-generation jail
A facility with a podular architectural design and management policies that emphasizes interaction of inmates and staff and provision of services.

podular unit
Self-contained living areas, for 12–25 inmates, composed of individual cells for privacy and open areas for social interaction. New-generation jails are made up of two or more pods.

direct supervision
A method of correctional supervision in which staff members have direct physical interaction with inmates throughout the day.

To find out about **direct-supervision jails**, visit the website of the National Institute of Corrections, listed at www .cengage.com/criminaljustice/ clear.

their pods. Fourth, policy makers have learned that new-generation jails are as much as 20 percent cheaper to construct, and they provide more-effective inmate security and supervision. Finally, there is some evidence that the new-generation concept results in less violence and fewer inmate infractions, leaving staff feeling more secure in their work.[37]

The greatest advantages, however, are programmatic. In larger jails, pods can serve specialized offender groups who share a need, such as for remedial educational services, or who for any reason (for example, AIDS, gang affiliation, or offense type) need to be segregated from the rest of the jail population. Thus, the needs of the inmate can become a more significant factor in the nature of the confinement.

Placing correctional staff in closer contact with inmates also has benefits. Prisoners often show symptoms of depression or behave disruptively because of stress or the emotional strain of confinement; this can become more troublesome without appropriate staff response. When correctional officers are physically closer to inmates, they can more readily become aware of feelings or behavior that may require attention. Further, the physical structure can potentially moderate staff–inmate conflict. By getting to know one another better, staff and inmates can maintain better interactions. Thus, in the long run the new-generation jail is thought to be one way to help overcome the correctional officer's traditional alienation from inmates. The new-generation concept may lead to changes in staff attitudes toward inmates; however, one recent study comparing attitudes of correctional officers in new-generation jails versus traditional jails found few differences in their overall outlook about the job.[38]

More recently, the concept of the new-generation jail has evolved in recent years to embrace the idea of **therapeutic justice**, a philosophy of reorienting the jail experience from being mostly punitive to being mostly rehabilitative. (See the Focus box "Community Model for Jails" for more.)

In the 1980s administrators became enamored of the tight management approaches that the criminologist John DiIulio advocated (see Chapter 13). DiIulio's "control model" emphasizes running prisons safely and securely. The control model asserts that a manager's first priority is to exert total control over the population at all times. This control is achieved by isolating prisoners as much as possible and limiting interpersonal contact. However, research on the new-generation jail has called his ideas into question, at least as concerns the jail. Studies show that an alternative "employee investment" approach, in which staff and inmates are seen as resources to be developed rather than problems to be controlled, is more successful in achieving the results DiIulio sought with his control model. This is one reason that many experts now agree that the direct-supervision jail offers the best route toward improved staff morale, reduced staff sick leave, reduced injury to staff and inmates—and even reduced maintenance costs.

Despite its advantages, all is not well with the new-generation jail. For one thing, it is hard to sell the concept to a public who underestimates the painfulness of the jail experience and sees the new system as a means of coddling offenders. That more than half of jail inmates typically have *not* yet been convicted of a crime does not dampen the public's desire for harsh punishment of offenders. Jail administrators need to inform political decision makers about the fiscal and programmatic advantages of the new jail.

A second problem is more troubling: Many new jails become outmoded between the planning stage and completion of construction. Legal standards may change, creating new requirements for cell space, recreational space, visitation areas, and the like. Inadequate attention may have been given to possible programmatic needs. Often the very existence of a new jail leads to such an enthusiastic response by judges and other criminal justice officials that the new facility quickly becomes crowded.

Finally, the number of cells that should be built into a new jail is controversial. Planners often argue that new jails need to be more spacious than old jails to accommodate growing numbers of offenders. Architects pleading for large jails often use projections of burgeoning jail populations to support expansion. Critics respond that jail populations grow to meet available capacity, and they cite numerous new jails of doubled capacities that became overcrowded the day they opened. There is a need, they say, for policies to keep jail populations under control as well as facilities to house those populations.

therapeutic justice
A philosophy of reorienting the jail experience from being mostly punitive to being mostly rehabilitative.

FOCUS ON
CORRECTIONAL PRACTICE

Community Model for Jails

For most of history, jails have been perceived as punitive, custodial institutions. Their primary purpose has been to hold people who are accused of crimes (custody) and confine them after they are sentenced for the crime (punishment). Many experts believe that this emphasis has proved a failure, leading to violence and despair within the jail and high rates of recidivism for those who leave jail.

Recently, the Center for Therapeutic Justice, an advocacy group specializing in jail reform, has begun disseminating a new way of thinking about the way jails should be run. They call their new approach the community model.

Based on social learning theory, the **community model for jails** begins with a basic idea about what jails need: a new culture for inmates and staff that more closely mirrors the community life outside the jail, the life in which people are expected to function after they leave the jail. The idea is that the typical jail culture, which is based on power, conflict, and control, cannot teach the attitude and skills a person needs to "make it" in the community. Instead, the jail needs to teach interpersonal responsibility based on self- (and mutual) respect. The idea is that personal respect and responsibility are precisely the skills that are needed for productive community life once a person leaves the jail.

The community model is created by building a prosocial, self-governing inmate unit within the jail. In this unit the norm of mutual aid is taught and reinforced, and the people in the jail (staff and inmates alike) work together to create a culture based on positive community values, such as self-control, interpersonal competence, and abstinence from substance abuse. The community model replaces the conflict of the traditional jail with a spirit of cooperation and support, and in doing so promotes long-term behavior change.

The community model is usually not initially a jailwide phenomenon. Instead, it develops in a separate part of the jail. This demonstrates to inmates and staff alike the possibilities it offers for a better jail culture and environment. The model incorporates treatment approaches that have been proved effective, and it builds into them a democratically elected, inmate-led program based on building motivation, compliance, and a positive attitude toward the hard work of building a community and strengthening personal responsibility. After the community model is fully developed, it is less expensive to run than the traditional jail, and its proponents claim it reduces violence and increases program participation—with the promise of long-term change and lower rates of recidivism.

Source: Lance Forsythe, Aretha Hicks, Penny B. Patton, and V. Morgan Moss, "Center for Community Justice's Community Model: The Jail Administrator's Best Friend," *American Jails,* January–February 2006, pp. 35–41.

■ THE FUTURE OF THE JAIL *Chamber*

Few government functions in the United States are under assault from as many camps as is the jail. Reform groups call for more-humane jail conditions; the media expose jails as cruel, crowded, and counterproductive; inmates sue their keepers for mistreatment, often successfully; and experts describe jails as failures.

In some respects the jail's importance to the criminal justice system has seldom been greater than it is today. With many prisons more crowded than they are legally permitted to be, jails have become a backup resource for managing the many offenders for whom the state lacks space. As local governments experiment with ways to improve the credibility of the criminal justice system, solutions seem inevitably to involve the jail—for work release, for enforcing court orders for probationers, for new laws against drunkenness, and for other initiatives. Local decision makers have more control over jails and jail policy than over facilities operated by state correctional agencies.

Moreover, the jail is an expensive item in county and municipal budgets. The average cost of a day in jail varies greatly, but for a large urban jail it can be quite high. A day in New York City's Rikers Island—the nation's most expensive stay—costs $228, and the next most expensive, the Multnomah County (Portland, Oregon) jail, is no bargain at $103 per day. Even in the "cheap" jails in Houston ($27 per day) and Phoenix

community model for jails
An innovative model for jail administration that promotes a sense of community among staff and inmates alike, while using community to promote rehabilitative change.

($25 per day) the price adds up, as one bed can cost $10,000 per year.[39] Further, for many of these municipalities, the overall costs of jail place a major strain on budgets. One-fourth of the Harris County (Houston) annual budget goes to law enforcement, with more than three-quarters of a million dollars spent daily on sentenced and unsentenced detainees.[40] Over the last quarter century, jail costs have grown 50 percent faster than all other municipal criminal justice costs.

Perhaps because of the jail's budgetary costs and system centrality, two general trends—if they continue—bode well for its future. First, many jurisdictions have renovated or replaced jail facilities since the early 1970s. The overwhelming difficulties associated with decrepit physical plants are at least partially overcome by this new construction. Second, many jurisdictions are joining together to build and maintain a single jail to serve their collective needs. Although political problems abound in such an arrangement—politicians resist giving up authority over jail budgets—this movement seems to be gaining adherents.

SUMMARY

1 Describe the history of the jail and its current function in the criminal justice system.

Jails in the United States descend from feudal practices in twelfth-century England, in which the *shire reeve* (from which the word *sheriff* evolved) caught and held in custody people accused of breaking the king's law. English settlers brought these traditions and institutions with them to the American colonies. Today jails are the entryway into the criminal justice system and a place of confinement for less-serious law violators.

2 Describe who is in jails, and why they are there.

There are two kinds of people in jail: those who are awaiting trial and those who are sentenced to terms of confinement of less than a year. Jails also house mostly young men, particularly young men of color. The majority of those in jail are serving sentences for crimes, with the remainder awaiting adjudication of charges (including probation and parole revocation).

3 Discuss the kinds of jails in the United States.

The smallest jails are police lockups. Most other jails are run by county governments, although there are also municipal jails under the authority of the larger cities. In some areas, regional jails serve multiple city and county governments.

4 List the main issues facing jails today.

Jails struggle with the need to provide services to people who are awaiting trial, in part because their stay may be short and they are also not yet convicted of any crimes. Jails also face issues affecting detainees, especially mental health problems, substance abuse, medical problems, and legal needs.

5 Outline the problem of bail and list the main alternatives to bail.

Being held in bail is damaging to a defendant's life circumstances, as well as being detrimental to his/her chances at trial and sentence. Financial bail systems discriminate against the poor, who comprise the vast majority of jail detainees. Bail alternatives, such as release on recognizance and pretrial diversion apply to only a portion of those awaiting trial.

6 Outline the problems of jail administration.

Jail administrators are legally liable for their treatment of people incarcerated in their facility. They must meet certain written standards, even if their facility lacks sufficient finds to meet them. Because jails often pay their employees less than do other justice-related institutions, recruiting and retaining high-quality personnel remains difficult. Finally, jail crowding and outmoded jail facilities make maintaining good programs extremely difficult.

7 Describe new developments in jails and jail programs.

To deal with the problems of jails, there has been a recent movement to increase the use of the new-generation jail, in which jail detainees are kept in podular units instead of cells and security is maintained by direct-supervision methods. Another new idea is to implement the community model for jails.

8 Critically assess the future of the jail.

Although jails are an expensive part of local government budgets, they are widely neglected by scholars and officials, and the public knows little about them. The prospects of jails are looking up, though, owing to extensive efforts to renovate old jails and build new ones, and to design these replacements in ways that facilitate better services and improved security.

KEY TERMS

absconders (p. 185)
bail (p. 183)
bondsman (p. 183)
community model for jails (p. 193)
day reporting center (p. 184)
direct supervision (p. 191)

electronic monitoring (p. 185)
fee system (p. 173)
lockup (p. 173)
new-generation jail (p. 191)
podular unit (p. 191)
pretrial diversion (p. 185)

preventive detention (p. 186)
regional jail (p. 175)
release on recognizance (ROR) (p. 184)
therapeutic justice (p. 192)
widening the net (p. 185)

FOR DISCUSSION

1. How do local politics affect jail administration? Should political influence be as extensive as it is? Does it help or hinder good correctional practices?
2. What special problems and needs do jail detainees have? Why? What problems do these needs pose for jail administrators?
3. What are the pros and cons of preventive detention? How might it affect crime control? Due process?
4. How would you balance tensions between jail management and public safety?
5. What are some problems you would expect to encounter if you were in charge of providing rehabilitative programs in a jail?

FOR FURTHER READING

Cornelius, Gary. *The American Jails: Cornerstone of Modern Corrections.* Upper Saddle River, NJ: Prentice-Hall, 2007. A contemporary critical assessment of the state of jails in America and the new directions in jail policy and practice.

Goldfarb, Ronald. *Jails: The Ultimate Ghetto.* Garden City, NY: Doubleday, 1975. Classic and still accurate critique of the American jail.

Irwin, John. *The Jail.* Berkeley: University of California Press, 1985. Classic description of the jail experience and inmates' reaction to it.

Kerle, Kenneth E. *Exploring Jail Operations.* Hagerstown, MD: American Jail Association, 2003. Provides a contemporary analysis of problems facing jails and analyzes the potential for jail reform.

Miller, Rod. *Developing a Jail Industry.* Washington, DC: Bureau of Justice Assistance, U.S. Government Printing Office, August 2003. Covers practical and conceptual issues in the design and implementation of work programs in jails.

Schwartz, Sunny. *Dreams from the Monster Factory: A Tale of Prison, Redemption, and One Woman's Fight to Restore Justice to All.* New York: Scribner, 2009. Describes the "Resolve to Stop the Violence" project in a San Francisco jail, an approach that joins offenders and victims in a philosophy of empowerment and accountability.

Wynn, Jennifer. *Inside Rikers.* New York: St. Martin's Press, 2001. Describes the lives of inmates and staff involved in the New York City Jail at Rikers Island.

NOTES

[1] Bureau of Justice Statistics, *Jail Inmates at Midyear 2008—Statistical Tables* (Washington, DC: U.S. Government Printing Office, March 2009). Based on estimated 260, 075 admissions per week (see Table 4).

[2] BJS *Bulletin,* December 2009, p. 2.

[3] David Rothman, *Discovery of the Asylum* (Boston: Little, Brown, 1971), 56.

[4] Bureau of Justice Statistics, *Statistical Tables,* March 2009, p. 5.

[5] Ibid.

[6] Bureau of Justice Statistics, *Statistical Tables,* March 2009, p. 7.

[7] U.S. President's Commission on Law Enforcement and the Administration of Justice, *Task Force Report: Corrections* (Washington, DC: U.S. Government Printing Office, 1967), 79.

[8] Bureau of Justice Statistics, *Statistical Tables,* March 2009, p. 6.

[9] BJS *Special Report,* September 2006, p. 2.

[10] Rick Ruddell, "Jail Intervention for Inmates with Mental Illness," *Journal of Correctional Health Care* 12 (no. 2, Winter 2006): 118.

[11] BJS *Special Report,* July 2005.

[12] BJS *Special Report,* July 2004, p. 2.

[13] BJS *Special Report,* November 2006.

[14] BJS *Bulletin,* December 2004, p. 8; see also Bureau of Justice Statistics, *Deaths in Custody Reporting Program,* http://www.ojp.usdoj.gov/bjs/dcrp/tables/dcst06lj1.htm, June 29, 2009.

[15] BJS *Bulletin,* December 2004, p. 7.

[16] Ibid., p. 9.

[17] *Bell v. Wolfish,* 441 U.S. 520 (1979).

[18] BJS *Bulletin,* December 2004, p. 9; October 2001, p. 9.

[19] Bureau of Justice Statistics, *Pretrial Release of Felony Defendants in State Courts* (Washington, DC: U.S. Government Printing Office, November 2007), 7.

[20] Bureau of Justice Statistics, *Prison and Jail Inmates at Midyear 2006* (Washington, DC: U.S. Government Printing Office, 2007), 32, 37.

[21] BJS *Bulletin,* July 2004, p. 2.

[22] Sheila Royo Maxwell and Jessica Davis, "The Salience of Race and Gender in Pretrial Release Decisions: A Comparison across Multiple Jurisdictions," *Criminal Justice Policy Review* 10 (no. 4, 2000): 491–502.

[23] Bureau of Justice Statistics, *Statistical Tables,* March 2009, p. 8.

[24] Randy R. Gainey, Brain K. Payne, and Mike O'Toole, "The Relationships between Time in Jail, Time on Electronic Monitoring, and Recidivism: An Event History Analysis of a Jail-Based Program," *Justice Quarterly* 17 (no. 4, 2000): 734–52.

[25] Bureau of Justice Statistics, *Felony Defendants in Large Urban Counties, 2002* (Washington, DC: U.S. Government Printing Office, 2006), 21.

[26] Ibid., p. 21.

[27] *Schall v. Martin,* 467 U.S. 253 (1984); *United States v. Salerno,* 481 U.S. 739 (1987).

[28] BJS *Special Report,* July 2004, p. 5.

[29] Ibid, pp. 8–10.

[30] Jeff Mellow, Debbie Mukamal, Stefan LoBuglio, Amy Solomon, and Jenny W. L. Osborne, *The Jail Administrator's Toolkit for Reentry* (Washington, DC: Urban Institute, 2008).

[31] Amy Solomon, Jenny W. L. Osborne, Stefan LoBuglio, Jeff Mellow, and Debbie Mukamal, *Life after Lock-up: Improving Reentry from Jail to the Community* (Washington, DC: Urban Institute, 2008).

[32] Bureau of Justice Statistics, *Census of Jails, 1999* (Washington, DC: U.S. Government Printing Office, 2002), 25.

[33] Ibid., p. 16.

[34] Mark A. Cunniff, *Jail Crowding: Understanding Jail Population Dynamics* (Washington, DC: National Institute of Corrections, January 2002).

[35] BJS *Bulletin,* May 2004, p. 9.

[36] Amanda Petteruti and Nastassia Walsh, *Jailing Communities: The Impact of Jail Expansion and Effective Public Strategies* (Washington, DC: Justice Policy Institute, April 2008).

[37] James Williams, Daniel Rodeheaver, and Denise Huggins, "A Comparative Evaluation of a New Generation Jail," *American Journal of Criminal Justice* 23 (no. 2, 1999): 78–89.

[38] Brandon K. Applegate and Eugene Paoline, III, "Jail Officers' Perceptions of the Work Environment in Traditional versus New Generation Facilities," *American Journal of Criminal; Justice* 31 (2007): 64–80.

[39] George Camp and Camille Camp, *The Corrections Yearbook, 2000: Jails* (Middletown, CT: Criminal Justice Institute, 2001), 39.

[40] Jessie Bogan, "America's Jail Crisis," *Forbes,* July 13, 2009, http://www.forbes.com/2009/07/10/jails-houston-recession-business-beltway-jails.html.

© Modesto Bee/ZUMA Press

Stanislaus County, California, probation officer Jeff Brandon talks with David Tubera, a probationer, during a routine check. Over four million Americans are under probation supervision.

THE NEW YORK CITY Probation Department is one of the most overworked and underappreciated organizations in the nation's largest city. Probation officers in New York say they have, for years, felt their efforts are poorly understood and badly supported by the city that pays their salaries. With 274 probation officers responsible for 44,517 cases, the average caseload is an untenable 162 probationers per officer. Relief seems a financial impossibility in a city that grapples with perennial financial strains and faces growing numbers in the city's court system, most of whom end up on probation. An improvement in public perception of probation seems an even more Herculean task, given the general public indifference (or worse, antagonism) toward probation.

To combat the unwieldy caseloads, a few years ago the department undertook what the *New York Times* called "a bold experiment," setting up a two-tiered system of supervision: Violent offenders were to be seen often in individual and group counseling sessions; nonviolent offenders would not see a probation officer but would report electronically to kiosks that would use laser techniques to read their fingerprints. This new system had the desired result of easing the workload of probation officers, allowing them to focus

PROBATION

their attention on the most serious cases. But it did nothing about the poor public appraisal of the value of probation in the first place. In fact, the idea that convicted felons would be monitored by machines seemed to give further support to a general public distrust of probation in New York City.

In response the probation officials in the city have decided to create another two-tiered system: high-risk caseloads and reporting caseloads. High-risk cases are those probationers whose background and personal characteristics show that they pose a risk to the community. These probationers are supervised closely in caseloads of 65 that are organized by neighborhood in order to promote more-extensive contact between officer and probationer. A subset of the high-risk category that is termed "special offender"—sexual predators, gang members, and selected violent or high-volume offenders—receives even closer supervision. The rest of probationers are placed in a "reporting unit," where they receive services and make regular reports but are subject to limited direct supervision.[1]

The plan has two aims. First, to help improve public safety, it seeks to provide a better level of supervision to problematic probationers who live in certain neighborhoods. Second, and just as important, to improve probation's image with the public, the plan has officers beginning this work in the neighborhoods where probationers live.

Chapter

8

These two innovations speak volumes about modern probation. Instead of dealing with petty offenders, today's probation departments are increasingly called on to deal with tough, even violent, offenders. Yet they are asked to handle this more-difficult workload with decreasing levels of funding. In New York City, probation officials are trying to forge a new way out of this dilemma. If the experiment works, probation in New York and other big cities will change substantially.

Most people would say that probation needs to change. Although few citizens or political leaders give it much respect, it is by far the most extensively used form of corrections in the United States. Over half of all adults under correctional authority are serving probation sentences. In 2007 this included more than 4.2 million people, or nearly three times the number of adults in prisons.[2] Escalating prison growth has captured the public's attention, but since 1985 the U.S. probation population has actually grown at a faster rate than the incarcerated population.

Despite the wide use of probation, media critics tend to give it short shrift, often portraying it as "a slap on the wrist." This notion is so widespread that a well-known scholarly work on correctional policy once referred to probation as "a kind of standing joke."[3] These views sharply contrast with official policies. For example, during the past decade alone, the government devoted over a quarter of a billion dollars in federal funds to improve and expand probation, and supervision in the community is becoming the sanction for more and more offenders. Further, advocates of intermediate sanctions point to probation as the base on which to build greater punishments.

What is really true about probation? How effective is it? How important is it today? In this chapter, we describe the function of probation in corrections and review numerous studies of probation supervision and court services. Although in today's correctional environment probation is increasingly coupled with a variety of intermediate sanctions, in this chapter we consider traditional probation services (intermediate sanctions are covered in Chapter 9).

Visit the website of the **American Probation and Parole Association**, listed at www.cengage.com/criminaljustice/clear.

Our review will demonstrate that, as in most other areas of corrections, probation agencies work amid social and political ambivalence about punishment. This ambivalence, together with uncertainty about treatment methods, leaves probation in a quandary: We ordinarily rely heavily on it in sentencing offenders, but we show limited confidence in its corrective capacities.

■ THE HISTORY AND DEVELOPMENT OF PROBATION

Probation is basically the idea that, in lieu of imprisonment, the offender is allowed to live in the community under supervision and demonstrate a willingness to abide by its laws. In this country probation began with the innovative work of **John Augustus**, who was the first to provide bail for defendants under authority of the Boston Police Court in 1841. The roots of probation, however, lie in earlier attempts, primarily in England, to mitigate the harshness of the criminal law.

JOHN AUGUSTUS (1785–1859)

A Boston boot-maker known as the first probation officer. In helping people brought before the Boston courts, he acted as counsel, provided bail, and found housing for the accused.

Benefit of Clergy

From the 1200s until the practice was abolished in 1827, people accused of serious offenses in England could appeal to the judge for leniency by reading in court the text of Psalm 51. The original purpose of this benefit of clergy was to protect people under church authority, such as monks and nuns, from the power of the king's law. Because this benefit was gradually extended to protect ordinary citizens from capital punishment, Psalm 51 came to be known as the "neck verse." The requirement that the person be able to read favored the upper social classes. Eventually, common thugs memorized the verse so they could pretend to read it before the court and thus avail themselves of its protection; judges then became more arbitrary in granting the benefit. In the United States benefit of clergy was criticized because of its unequal application and baffling legal character—charges often directed at probation today.

Judicial Reprieve

Judges have long understood the need to grant leniency to some offenders, and they regularly seek ways to deflect the full punitive force of the law. In nineteenth-century England, **judicial reprieve** became widespread. If an offender requested it, the judge could suspend either the imposition or execution of a sentence for a specified length of time, on condition of good behavior by the offender. At the end of that time, the offender could apply to the Crown for a pardon.

In the United States, judicial reprieve took a different form and led to a series of legal controversies. Rather than limiting the duration of the reprieve, many judges suspended imposition of punishment as long as the offender's behavior remained satisfactory. The idea was that the reprieved offender who remained crime-free need not fear the power of the court; the offender who committed another crime, however, was subject to punishment for both crimes.

In 1916 the U.S. Supreme Court declared the discretionary use of such indefinite reprieves unconstitutional.[4] The Court recognized the occasional need to suspend a sentence temporarily because of appeals and other circumstances, but it found that indefinite suspension impinged on the powers of the legislative and executive branches to write and enforce laws. With this decision, the practices of probation became subject to the provisions of the states' penal codes.

Recognizance

In a search for alternative means to exercise leniency in sentencing, nineteenth-century judges began to experiment with extralegal forms of release. Much of this innovation occurred among the Massachusetts judiciary, whose influence on modern probation was enormous.

One of the trailblazers was Boston Municipal Court Judge Peter Oxenbridge Thatcher, the originator of the practice of **recognizance**. In 1830 Thatcher sentenced Jerusha Chase "upon her own recognizance for her appearance in this court whenever she was called for."[5] In 1837 Massachusetts made recognizance with monetary sureties into law. What made this important was the implied supervision of the court—the fact that the whereabouts and actions of the offender were subject to court involvement.

Both reprieve and recognizance aimed at humanizing the criminal law and mitigating its harshness. The practices foreshadowed the move toward individualized punishment that would dominate corrections a century later. The major justifications for probation—flexibility in sentencing and individualized punishment—already had strong support. Yet an institutionalized way of performing recognizance functions was still needed.

As the first probation officer, John Augustus was the first to formalize court leniency. Because his philanthropic activities made Augustus a frequent observer in the Boston Police Court, the judge deferred sentencing a man charged with being a common drunkard and released him into Augustus's custody. At the end of a three-week probationary period, the man convinced the judge that he had reformed, therefore receiving a nominal fine.

Courtesy of The Bostonian Society Old State House Museum

JOHN AUGUSTUS.

judicial reprieve
A practice under English common law whereby a judge could suspend the imposition or execution of a sentence on condition of good behavior on the part of the offender.

recognizance
A formally recorded obligation to perform some act (such as keep the peace, pay a debt, or appear in court when called) entered by a judge to permit an offender to live in the community, often on posting a sum of money as surety, which is forfeited by nonperformance.

To learn about
John Augustus, go to the
corresponding link at www
.cengage.com/criminaljustice/
clear.

Besides being the first to use the term *probation*, Augustus developed the ideas of the presentence investigation, supervision conditions, social casework, reports to the court, and revocation of probation. He screened his cases "to ascertain whether the prisoners were promising subjects for probation, and to this end it was necessary to take into consideration the previous character of the person, his age, and the influences by which he would in future be likely to be surrounded."[6] His methods were analogous to casework strategies: He gained offenders' confidence and friendship and, by helping them get a job or aiding their families in various ways, he helped them reform.

The Modernization of Probation

Probation eventually extended to every state and federal jurisdiction. As it developed, the field underwent a curious split. Augustus and his followers had contributed a humanitarian orientation that focused on reformation. In contrast, the new probation officers were drawn largely from the law enforcement community—retired sheriffs and policemen—who had their own orientation.

The strain between the so-called law enforcer role of probation, which emphasizes surveillance of the offender and close controls on behavior, and the social worker role, which emphasizes provision of supportive services to meet offenders' needs, continues today—with no resolution in sight. Advocates of the law enforcement model argue that conditions for community control must be realistic, individualized, and enforceable. Proponents of the social work model believe that supervision must include treatment to help the offender become a worthwhile citizen. Each view has dominated at one time or another in the past half-century.

In the 1940s leaders in probation and other correctional branches began to embrace ideas from psychology about personality and human development. Probation began to emphasize a medical model, with rehabilitation as its overriding goal. This new focus moved probation work—or at least its rhetoric—into the realm of the professions. Although only a very small number of probation departments fully implemented this approach, the ideas underlying it dominated the professional literature.

The medical model remained influential through the 1960s, when the reintegration model came to the fore. This model assumed that crime is a product of poverty, racism, unemployment, unequal opportunities, and other social factors. Probation was seen as central because it was the primary existing means of working with the offender in the problem's context—the offender's community. Methods of probation began to change from direct service (by psychological counseling) to service brokerage: After being assessed, clients were put in touch with appropriate community service agencies. Government studies heralded the reintegrative approach, and federal funds were shifted to community-based correctional agencies (discussed in Chapter 9), including probation agencies.

In the latter part of the 1970s, thinking about probation changed again in a way that continues to this day. The goals of rehabilitation and reintegration have given way to an orientation widely referred to as *risk management*. The goal here is to minimize the probability that an offender will commit a new offense, especially by applying tight controls over the probationer's activities and maintaining careful surveillance. Risk management combines values of the just deserts model of the criminal sanction with the idea that the community deserves protection.

Today offenders are placed on probation in one of four ways. Most commonly, judges impose a sentence of probation directly (60 percent). Sometimes the judge imposes a sentence of probation that is suspended pending good behavior (22 percent). For still other offenders who are already on probation, an additional sentence is imposed but its activation is suspended (9 percent). Finally, the court may require that some period of incarceration be served prior to probation; this is called a "split sentence" (9 percent). This last option was quite popular in the 1990s, but its use has waned in the last few years. This may be because many probationers face jail while awaiting trial or because prison space is limited.

In addition, judges may implement their sentencing arrangements, including the following:

1 *Modification of sentence:* The original sentencing court reconsiders an offender's prison sentence within a limited time frame and modifies it to probation.

2 *Shock incarceration:* An offender sentenced to incarceration is released after a period of confinement (the shock) and resentenced to probation.

3 *Intermittent incarceration:* An offender on probation spends weekends or nights in a local jail.

Who gets probation? In the past it was thought that probation should be reserved for first-time offenders who have committed lesser crimes. This has changed over time, so that today 51 percent of probationers have been convicted of a felony, and about one-fifth are convicted of a violent crime. The characteristics of probationers are shown in **Figure 8.1**. See also "Myths in Corrections."

Clearly, probation practices reflect the social forces of the time. For instance, the emphasis on psychiatric social work flowed naturally from the idea of corrections as reformative, a vision held by religious and social reformers of the day. Further, the reintegration movement represented a shift from imprisonment toward services such as job training and education. This was consistent with President Lyndon Johnson's vision of the Great Society, which would create equal opportunities for all citizens and would eliminate discrimination, poverty, and injustice. When the Great Society failed to materialize, attention turned to the responsibility of society to protect its citizens from crime. Thus, the recent emphasis on risk management sprang from widespread public demands that the justice system be streamlined and that it focus on reducing crime. Many see combining probation with periods of incarceration as a way to make it "tougher" and more-effective against crime.

Today, there has been a growing interest in probation's role as a part of **community justice**, a philosophy that emphasizes reparation to the victim and the community, problem-solving strategies instead of adversarial procedures, and increased citizen involvement in crime

community justice
A model of justice that emphasizes reparation to the victim and the community, approaching crime from a problem-solving perspective, and citizen involvement in crime prevention.

MYTHS IN CORRECTIONS

WHO IS ON PROBATION?

THE MYTH: Probation is a sanction that is reserved for low-level offenders.

THE REALITY: Compared with people in prison, twice as many probationers have been convicted of assault, and one-third more have been convicted of burglary. Further, the number of people convicted of sexual assault is 80 percent of the number in prison for that offense.

Source: BJS *Bulletin*, November 2006.

© The Plain Dealer/Landov

Probation officers work closely with judges, especially regarding sentence options. In many jurisdictions the judges want to know the progress of the offenders under supervision.

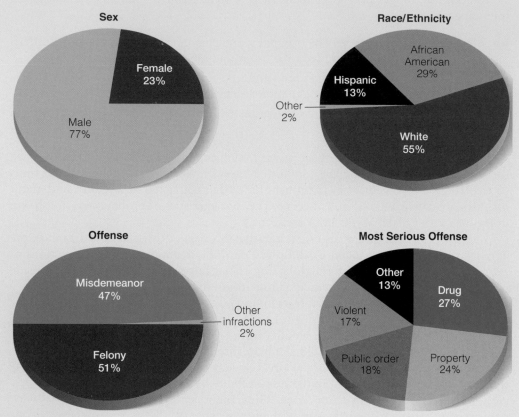

Figure 8.1
Characteristics of Adults on Probation

Although probation was originally used mainly for first-time offenders convicted of lesser crimes, many of today's probationers have been sentenced for felonies and other serious offenses.

Sources: Bureau of Justice Statistics, *Statistical Tables*, December 2006, p. 6; December 2008, p. 6.

prevention.[7] By breaking away from traditional bureaucratic practices, community justice advocates hope to develop a more flexible and responsive form of local justice initiatives—and many see probation as leading the way. (See Chapter 22 for more.)

■ THE ORGANIZATION OF PROBATION TODAY

Originating in court, the first probation agencies were units of the judicial branches of city and county governments, primarily in the eastern United States. The first full-time federal probation officer was appointed in 1927. As the idea of probation caught on and moved westward, variations in its organization were attempted. Probation has been placed in the executive branch, it has been subjected to statewide unification, and it has been consolidated with parole. **Figure 8.2** shows the seven jurisdictional patterns of probation organization nationwide. "Careers in Corrections" offers a view of work as a federal probations officer (compare this with the Careers box on state and county probation officers, later in the chapter.)

The organization of probation involves three issues concerning whether it should be (1) centralized or decentralized, (2) administered by the judiciary or the executive branch, and (3) combined with parole services or not.

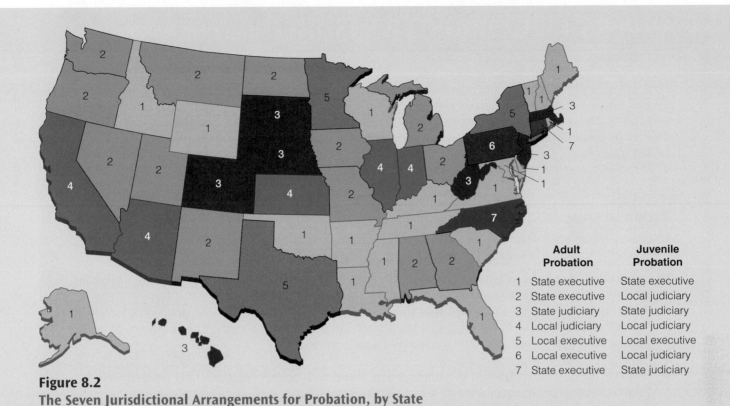

Figure 8.2

The Seven Jurisdictional Arrangements for Probation, by State

The organization of probation varies depending on the traditions and politics of state and local governments.

Source: American Correctional Association, *ACA Directory 2000* (College Park, MD: American Correctional Association, 2000).

	Adult Probation	Juvenile Probation
1	State executive	State executive
2	State executive	Local judiciary
3	State judiciary	State judiciary
4	Local judiciary	Local judiciary
5	Local executive	Local executive
6	Local executive	Local judiciary
7	State executive	State judiciary

Should Probation Be Centralized or Decentralized?

The centralization issue concerns the location of the authority that administers probation services. Proponents of decentralization argue that an agency administered by a city or county instead of a state is smaller, more flexible, and better able to respond to the unique problems of the community. Because decentralized probation draws its support from the community and local government, it can offer more-appropriate supervision for its clients and make better use of existing community resources than centralized probation can.

In contrast, centralization places authority for a state's probation activities in a single statewide administrative body. Proponents of this approach assert that local probation has tended to follow outdated practices and to lack professionalism. State agencies, they argue, are larger, can train staff to take a variety of roles, and can implement broader programs with greater equality in supervision and services.

Who Should Administer Probation?

Though the recent trend has been away from judicially administered probation, many observers (especially those who seek greater accountability in probation) believe that the probation function rightfully belongs under the judiciary. The usual claim is that, under judicial administration, probation is more responsive to the desires of the sentencing judge, who is more likely to scrutinize supervision when it is performed by

CAREERS IN CORRECTIONS   Probation Officer—Federal

NATURE OF THE WORK

Federal probation and pretrial services officers are appointed by the judiciary in each of the 94 Federal District Courts. The primary mission of these officers is to supervise and investigate offenders and defendants as ordered by the judicial officer. The work includes preparing reports, for the United States District Court, the United States Parole Commission, and the Federal Bureau of Prisons, regarding the background and activities of offenders charged with or having been found guilty of federal offenses.

REQUIRED QUALIFICATIONS

To qualify for an entry-level position as a federal probation and pretrial services officer, candidates must meet certain minimum requirements, which include

- A bachelor's degree in an academic field such as criminal justice, sociology, psychology, human relations, business, or public administration.
- Progressively responsible experience after completion of the bachelor's degree in such fields as probation, pretrial services, parole, or corrections, or work in addiction treatment. A master's degree in one of the accepted fields may be substituted for the required work experience.
- Good physical condition and health.
- Because the position is classified as hazardous duty, first-time appointees must not have reached their 37th birthday at the time of appointment.

EARNINGS AND JOB OUTLOOK

Federal probation and pretrial services officers are classified and paid under a system that combines General Schedule (GS) grades and salary. They receive hazardous duty pay and are eligible for benefits accorded other federal employees. Entry-level salaries range from $39,000 to $76,000, depending on experience. Employment with the United States Probation office is "at will." The job outlook for these officers is promising, as probation caseloads rise and the number of federal prisoners returning to the community increases.

MORE INFORMATION

You can obtain additional information about this occupation from the website for **Probation Officer Careers, Jobs, and Training Information**; see the link at www.cengage.com/criminaljustice/clear.

judicial employees. Also, the morale of probation officers who work closely with judges may be higher than that of other probation officers.

Proponents of placing probation under the executive branch argue that the judiciary is ill prepared to manage a human services operation. To coordinate and upgrade the quality of a human services operation such as probation requires the full attention of professional public administrators. It is argued that placing probation under the executive branch results in better allocation of probation services, increased interaction and administrative coordination between corrections and allied human services, increased access to the legislature and the budgeting process, and more-appropriate service priorities.

Should Probation Be Combined with Parole?

Probation and parole both supervise offenders who are serving portions of their sentences in the community. Indeed, the growth in use of split sentences and shock probation means that probation often begins after a jail or even prison term—just as with parole.

Because of these similarities, many states have placed probation and parole functions under a single agency, which promotes more-efficient hiring and training practices. Arguably, such comprehensive approaches also promote the professionalization of community supervision officers.

Some experts suggest, however, that subtle but important distinctions between probationers and parolees are hard to sustain in a unified system. Probationers are usually less deeply involved in criminal lifestyles, while parolees always face serious problems in reentering the community after longer incarceration (see Chapter 16). These differences call for different handling, which some people believe can best be done by separate agencies.

No solution to the problem of how to organize probation is at hand. Rather than searching for a single "best" way to organize probation, considering how it will work in a given state or region may be more fruitful. For example, in jurisdictions with a tradition of strong local government, decentralized probation under the executive branch may be best, whereas states with a strong central bureaucracy or strong judiciary may choose to place probation there. **Figure 8.3** shows that states vary dramatically in their use of probation. Further, no clear pattern has appeared in the relationship between the way probation is organized and how frequently it is used.

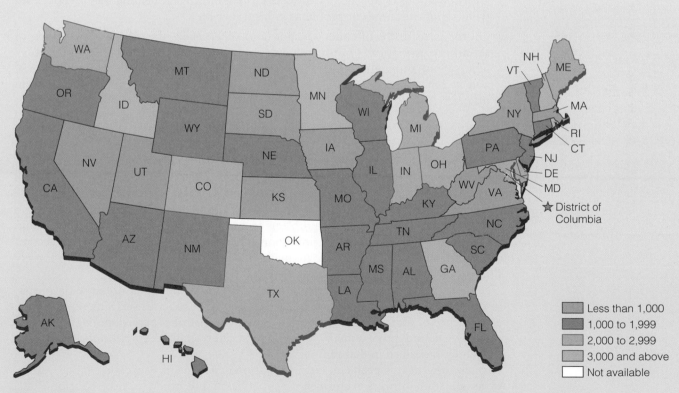

Figure 8.3
State Variations in Use of Probation

Some states make greater use of probation as a criminal sanction than others. Unlike incarceration rates, which are higher in the southern and western states, there is no regional pattern in probation use.

Source: Bureau of Justice Statistics, *Statistical Tables*, December 2008, p. 3.

■ THE DUAL FUNCTIONS OF PROBATION: INVESTIGATION AND SUPERVISION

presentence investigation (PSI)

An investigation and summary report of a convicted offender's background, which helps the judge decide on an appropriate sentence. Also known as a presentence report.

Probation officers have traditionally performed two major functions: investigation and supervision. Regardless of the specifics of a given probation agency's structure or practices, certain aspects of investigation and supervision are uniform.

Investigation involves the preparation of a **presentence investigation (PSI)**, which the judge uses in sentencing an offender. Typically the court orders the PSI after the offender's conviction (often on a guilty plea). Before the sentencing date, the probation officer conducts the investigation and prepares the PSI.

The PSI process typically begins with an interview of the offender to obtain basic background information. The probation officer then seeks to verify, clarify, and explore the information derived (or omitted) from the initial interview. The final PSI document summarizes the officer's findings, evaluates the offender, and often recommends a sentence.

Supervision begins once an offender is sentenced to probation. Supervision policies and practices vary greatly among agencies but usually involve three steps:

1 The probation officer establishes a relationship with the offender and defines the roles of officer and offender.

2 The officer and offender establish supervision goals to help the offender comply with conditions established by the court (often directed at helping the offender confront significant needs or problems in his or her life).

3 On the basis of the offender's response to supervision, the officer decides how to terminate probation. Options include early termination because of satisfactory adjustment, termination because the sentence has expired, or revocation because of a new conviction or violation of probation conditions set by the judge or probation officer.

Investigation and supervision are divergent functions. In investigating clients and preparing PSIs, probation officers work primarily with other human service professionals—teachers, officials, psychologists, and so forth. Probation officers also have a sense of partnership with the judge: Both parties seek the best sentence and therefore value useful, accurate information on which to base the disposition. These relationships may reinforce the officers' self-esteem. Supervision, by contrast, is fraught with uncertainty and error. With no standard solutions to the problems faced by most probationers, many of whom are troubled and hard to manage, probation supervisors may find little sense of accomplishment. Further, the rewards are intangible: Work consists of a series of tasks loosely connected to possible rehabilitation.

This difference between the two functions often puts informal pressure on probation officers to give investigation a higher priority than supervision. Superiors can see the excellence of an investigation more readily than that of supervision; in effect, then, producing a sound, professionally appealing PSI can seem more important than serving the offender described in that report.

To circumvent this problem, large probation departments "specialize" their staff—they assign some officers exclusively to supervision and others to investigation. This, however, produces some inefficiency. For example, the supervising officer must learn much of the information that the presentence officer already knows. Similarly, when probationers are convicted of new offenses, the supervising officer is often the best person to write a PSI, given his or her familiarity with the case. Ironically, specialization does not necessarily protect the supervision function. Frequently the best staff members are assigned to the PSI units, and top priority is given to maintaining an adequate PSI workforce, even in the face of unwieldy supervision caseloads.

In any case a probation system whose workers are specialized is much easier to manage. Such a system enhances accountability for the timeliness and accuracy of PSIs and more easily ensures the operation of supervision routines according to agency policies. Therefore, the trend is toward specialization of these functions, almost as if they were two different jobs.

The Investigative Function

As noted earlier, the presentence investigation serves mainly to help the judge select an appropriate sentence. It also helps with the eventual classification decisions that the offender may encounter regarding probation, incarceration, and parole agencies; it facilitates treatment planning and parole decisions; and it serves as a document for systematic research.

Learn more about the **history and uses of the PSI**; see the corresponding link at www .cengage.com/criminaljustice/ clear.

PURPOSE ■ Apart from its many other uses, the PSI plays its most important role in the sentencing process. This is especially true because there are no uniformly accepted guidelines or rationales for sentencing. Individual judges, even in the same court system, may weigh factors in the case differently. The PSI must therefore be comprehensive enough to provide necessary information to judges with a variety of sentencing perspectives.

The rehabilitative goal requires assessment of the offender's treatment needs. The consensus is that imprisonment has limited rehabilitative value, so in practice a commitment to rehabilitation poses two questions: (1) Does the offender have special problems, circumstances, or needs that led to the criminal behavior? and (2) Can these problems be overcome by community services combined with careful supervision to prevent further criminal involvement?

The increasingly popular goal of community protection leads to other questions. With risk management in mind, the probation officer assesses the likelihood that the offender will continue criminal behavior if allowed to remain in the community. Estimates of risk are based on degree of prior criminal involvement, stability of the offender's lifestyle, and pattern of prior adjustment to correctional treatment.

In practice two circumstances constrain the influence of the PSI in sentencing. First, because goals are unclear, judges often seek some balance between rehabilitation and risk management. Rather than pursue a single value in sentencing, judges ordinarily ask a more-complicated question: If this offender is not a risk to the community, is there some rehabilitative reason to keep him or her in the community—a reason strong enough to overcome the objection that probation tends to depreciate the seriousness of the offense?

© image100/Alamy

The presentence investigation (PSI) plays an important role in sentencing. The PSI often contains information about special problems that influenced commission of the criminal act. Probation officers must gather information about offenders from family members, educators, and employers to complete this report.

The second constraint is plea bargaining. When the sentence has already been proposed in the process of negotiation between the prosecutor and the defense attorney, the role of the PSI is altered. Instead of helping the judge decide the case, the PSI helps determine whether the negotiated agreement is appropriate. To counter this problem, some probation officials argue that PSIs should be written before the defendant's initial plea. Although support exists for this innovation, it is unclear whether in the long run PSIs written before plea bargaining would be feasible for most cases.

According to some, such continued constraints mean that the PSI's importance is vastly overestimated. Often, they say, the sentence is determined by facts about the case—the offense, the plea agreement—that are far more obvious than anything the PSI can uncover. Others argue that the traditional PSI is a relic of the medical model of corrections, when judges relied on clinical assessments of defendants awaiting sentencing.[8] Small wonder some studies have shown that rather than read it in its entirety, most judges scan a PSI for a few relevant facts so they can make sure their intended decision makes sense.[9]

CONTENTS ■ For many years the ideal PSI was thought to be a lengthy narrative description of the offense and offender, culminating in a recommendation for sentencing and a justification for that recommendation (see the Focus box "Sample Presentence Report"). Early PSI-writing manuals stressed length and breadth of coverage. Now, however, people are questioning the assumption that more is better. Information theory suggests that PSIs that are short and to the point are not necessarily less useful than long ones.

A shortened, directed, and standardized PSI format is becoming more common. This approach may seem less professional, but in practice it places even greater responsibility on the probation officer. It requires the officer to know the case and the penal code well enough to know precisely what information the judge will require to evaluate the sentencing options.

To be useful, PSIs must offer valid and reliable information. Two techniques improve validity and reliability: verification and objectivity. *Verification* occurs when PSI information is cross-checked with some other source for accuracy. If the offender states during the PSI interview he or she has no drinking problem, for example, the investigator questions the offender's family, friends, and employer before writing "No apparent problem" in the PSI.

Objectivity is aided by avoiding vague conclusions about the case. For instance, rather than describe the offender as *immature* (a term subject to various interpretations), the PSI writer might describe the offender's observed behaviors that suggest immaturity: poor work attendance, lack of understanding of the seriousness of the offense, and so forth.

The victims' rights movement of the 1970s included a drive to have the PSI reflect not just the offender's circumstances but also the impact of the crime on the victim. Called **victim impact statements**, this new section of the standard PSI required the probation officer to interview the victim and determine, in the victim's own words, the damage caused by the crime. Victims' advocates claimed that adding these statements to the PSI would let the judge better appraise the seriousness of the crime and choose a sentence that best served both offender and victim. Critics worried that the judge would be unfairly prejudiced by articulate victims and those who overestimated their true losses. However, experience has shown that the addition of victim impact statements to PSIs has not increased the willingness of judges to impose harsh sentences.

RECOMMENDATIONS ■ Sentencing recommendations in PSIs are controversial, because a person without authority to sentence is nevertheless suggesting what the sentence should be. For this reason, not all probation systems include it in the PSI. Yet there is a well-established tradition of sentence recommendations by nonjudicial court actors; normally the judge solicits recommendations from the defense and prosecution, as well as the probation officer. But what the probation officer says may carry extra weight because presumably it is an unbiased evaluation of the offender based on thorough research by someone who understands the usefulness of probation and is familiar

victim impact statements
Descriptions in PSIs of the costs of the crime for the victim, including emotional and financial losses.

FOCUS ON
CORRECTIONAL PRACTICE

Sample Presentence Report

State of New Mexico
Corrections Department
Field Service Division
Santa Fe, New Mexico 87501
Date: January 4, 2010
To: The Honorable Manuel Baca
From: Presentence Unit, Officer Brian Gaines
Re: Richard Knight

Appearing before Your Honor for sentencing is 20-year-old Richard Knight who, on November 10, 2009, pursuant to a Plea and Disposition Agreement, entered a plea of guilty to Aggravated Assault Upon a Peace Officer (Deadly Weapon) (Firearm Enhancement), as charged in Information Number 10-5736900. The terms of the agreement stipulate that the maximum period of incarceration be limited to one year, that restitution be made on all counts and charges whether dismissed or not, and that all remaining charges in the Indictment and DA Files 39780 be dismissed.

Prior Record

The defendant has no previous convictions. An arrest at age 15 for disorderly conduct was dismissed after six months of "informal probation."

Evaluation

The defendant is an only child, born and raised in Albuquerque. He attended West Mesa High School until the 11th grade, at which time he dropped out. Richard declared that he felt school was "too difficult" and that he decided that it would be more beneficial for him to obtain steady employment rather than to complete his education. The defendant further stated that he felt it was "too late for vocational training" because of the impending one-year prison sentence he faces, due to the Firearm Enhancement penalty for his offense.

The longest period of time the defendant has held a job has been for six months with Frank's Concrete Company. He has been employed with the Madrid Construction Company since August 2008 (verified). Richard lives with his parents, who provide most of his financial support. Conflicts between his mother and himself, the defendant claimed, precipitated his recent lawless actions by causing him to "not care about anything." He stressed the fact that he is now once again "getting along" with his mother. Although the defendant contended that he doesn't abuse drugs, he later contradicted himself by declaring that he "gets drunk every weekend." He noted that he was inebriated when he committed the present offense.

In regard to the present offense, the defendant recalled that other individuals at the party attempted to stab his friend and that he and his companion left and returned with a gun in order to settle the score. Richard claimed remorse for his offense and stated that his past family problems led him to spend most of his time on the streets, where he became more prone to violent conduct. The defendant admitted being a member of the 18th Street Gang.

Recommendation

It is respectfully recommended that the defendant be sentenced to three years incarceration and that the sentence be suspended. It is further recommended that the defendant be incarcerated for one year as to the mandatory Firearm Enhancement and then placed on three years probation under the following special conditions:

1. That restitution be made to Juan Lopez in the amount of $662.40
2. That the defendant either maintain full-time employment or obtain his GED [general equivalency diploma]
3. That the defendant discontinue fraternizing with the 18th Street Gang members and terminate his own membership in the gang

with community resources. These considerations may explain why judges so often follow the recommendations in the PSI.

The congruence of the PSI recommendation and the sentences range from 70 to over 90 percent. Of course, it is hard to know whether judges are following the officers or whether the officers' experience has given them the ability to come up with recommendations the judges select. If the reason for the congruence between the probation officer's recommendations and the sentences imposed is the judge's confidence in the officer's analysis, that confidence may be misplaced. One evaluation found that "in only a few instances did the offenders they recommended for probation behave significantly better than those they recommended for prison."[10] The study speculated that perhaps this prognostic inaccuracy arose because officers did not have time to verify information reported in the PSI, because of their heavy caseloads.

The recommendation may be most useful when a plea-bargaining agreement includes a sentence. In such cases the PSI is a critical check on the acceptability of the negotiated settlement, permitting the judge to determine whether any factors in the offense or in the offender's background might indicate that the agreement should be rejected.

DISCLOSURE ■ In view of the importance of the PSI to the sentencing decision, one would think the defendant would have a right to see it. After all, it may contain inadvertent irrelevancies or inaccuracies that the defense would want to dispute at the sentencing hearing.

Nevertheless, in many states the defense does not receive a copy of the report. The case most often cited in this regard is *Williams v. New York* (1949), in which the judge imposed a death sentence on the basis of evidence in the confidential PSI despite the jury's recommendation of a life sentence.[11] The Supreme Court upheld the judge's decision to deny the defense access to the report, although without such access the defense was incapable of challenging its contents at the sentencing hearing.

Cases and state law since 1949 have reduced the original restrictive impact of *Williams*. At least one circuit court has held, for example, that the PSI cannot refer to illegally seized evidence excluded from a trial.[12] And 16 states require full disclosure of the PSI. In the other states, the practice is generally to "cleanse" the report and then disclose it. Cleansing involves deleting two kinds of statements: (1) confidential comments from a private citizen that, if known to the offender, might endanger the citizen, and (2) clinical statements or evaluations that might be damaging to the offender if disclosed. Moreover, many judges allow the defense to present a written challenge of any disclosed contents of the PSI.

PRIVATE PSIs ■ Private investigative firms have recently begun to provide judges with PSIs. These firms work in one of two ways. Some contract with defendants to conduct comprehensive background checks and provide judges with creative sentencing options as alternatives to incarceration. In this approach, often called **client-specific planning**, the firm serves as an advocate for the defendant at the sentencing stage. In the second approach, the court hires a private investigator to provide a neutral PSI.

Privately conducted PSIs have sparked controversy. Because the defendant pays for client-specific planning, many people view it as an unfair advantage for upper- and middle-class offenders who can afford the special consideration the advocacy report provides. These concerns are well taken; as advocates of private PSIs point out, their reports often result in less-severe sentences for their clients.

The neutral private PSI also raises serious issues. Proponents say that private investigators do what the probation department does—only better. Yet critics question whether private firms ought to be involved in the quasi-judicial function of recommending sentences. Moreover, the liability of private investigators for the accuracy and relevance of the information they provide to courts is unclear. Also, private PSIs, when purchased by the court, probably cost taxpayers more than do the traditional alternatives.

The Supervision Function

Offenders placed on probation supervision come from a mix of backgrounds, and the charges against them represent a range of seriousness. Compared with inmates in prison and jail, probationers are more likely to be white and slightly more likely to be female (see **Table 8.1**). Of the 4.1 million offenders on probation, about one in six were convicted of a violent offense, and another two in six of a property offense. Half had at least one conviction before they were arrested on the charge leading to probation. The variety of offenders requires a range of supervision strategies.

client-specific planning
Process by which private investigative firms contract with convicted offenders to conduct comprehensive background checks and suggest to judges creative sentencing options as alternatives to incarceration.

To learn about **client-specific planning**, visit the website of the National Center on Institutions and Alternatives, listed at www.cengage.com/criminaljustice/clear.

TABLE 8.1 *Ethnicity and Sex of Probationers and Prisoners*

	Race				Sex	
Probationers are more likely to be white and female than are offenders who are confined in prison or jail.						
	White	*African American*	*Hispanic*	*Other*	*Male*	*Female*
Probation	55%	29%	13%	2%	77%	23%
Jail	43	40	17	NA	89	11
Prison	36	42	20	2	91	9

Sources: BJS *Special Report*, December 2008; March 2009.

As in the case of PSIs, probation supervision follows universally accepted standards. Indeed, both probation officers and clients generally enjoy wide latitude. To show how this latitude is exercised in practice, we describe the three major elements of supervision: the officer, the offender, and the bureaucracy.

THE OFFICER ■ The probation officer faces role conflict in virtually every aspect of the job. Most of this conflict has its genesis in the uneasy combination of two responsibilities: (1) enforcing the law and (2) helping the offender. Although the responsibilities may be compatible, they often are not.

The chief conflict between the officer's two roles arises from the use of power and authority. In human relations these terms have very specific meanings. **Power** is the ability to force a person to do something he or she does not want to do. **Authority** is the ability to influence a person's actions in a desired direction without resorting to force. Thus, a person who chooses to exercise power in a relationship can almost always be shown to lack authority.

The problem of power and authority is a thorny one for probation officers. Officers are expected to exercise the power of law in controlling offenders under their supervision. This is one reason that in many jurisdictions probation officers are legally classified as "peace officers," with the power of arrest. Yet the actual power of the role is less than it seems: Short of exercising their formal power to arrest or detain probationers, probation officers normally can do little to force compliance with the law. And the powers of arrest and revocation are themselves carefully constrained by case law and statutes.

The lack of substantive power explains why probation officers rely heavily on their authority: It is a more-efficient and ultimately more-effective tool. The techniques of authority in probation are like those in social casework, but many people question their applicability in a role permeated by the power of law. They point out that the principles of social work have long been based on self-determination, which lets clients decide the nature, goals, and duration of the intervention—a condition not always feasible in the probation setting.

Despite such skepticism, professionals have tried to understand how probation officers might use authority as a positive tool. These officers use three different types of authority in their work:

1. Irrational authority, based solely on power
2. Rational authority, derived from the officer's competence in deciding on the best approach to take
3. Psychological authority, the most influential type, reflecting acceptance by both client and officer of each other's interest in jointly determined goals and strategies of supervision

The most effective probation officers combine all three types of authority, rather than resorting to the formal power of their role. This concept is difficult to execute.

power
The ability to force a person to do something he or she does not want to do.

authority
The ability to influence a person's actions in a desired direction without resorting to force.

The officer is attempting to gain the offender's trust and confidence so that, guided by a measure of rational or (better) psychological authority, the offender will change patterns that tend to promote involvement in crime. Yet both parties know that the officer can wield raw power should the offender falter. Often the message is simply, "Let me help you—or else!" This kind of mixed message leads to manipulation by both officer and probationer and can make the supervision relationship seem inconsistent.

In response to the complicated nature of their authority, probation officers often define their role in very simplistic terms, as if choosing between two incompatible sets of values: protecting the public versus helping offenders, enforcing the law versus doing social work, and so on. But such simplistic classification does not resolve the ambiguities of the probation officer's job. The officer frequently is given only vague guidelines for supervision, resulting in wide disparities at times. Recently, probation specialists have argued that the probation officers' roles can best be melded through a new technique referred to as motivational interviewing. This is "an approach that was first developed and applied in the field of addictions but has broadened and become a favored approach for use with numerous populations . . . [of] 'involuntary clients,'" such as probationers.[13]

motivational interviewing
A method for increasing the effectiveness of correctional treatment, by having the probation officer interact with the client in ways that promote the client's stake in the change process.

Motivational interviewing involves a variety of interpersonal techniques that increase the effectiveness of correctional treatment, by having the probation officer interact with the client in ways that promote the client's stake in the change process. The strategy promises to do the following:

- Help the officer get "back into the game" of behavior change
- Identify effective tools for handling resistance and help keep difficult situations from getting worse
- Keep the probation officer from doing all the work
- Place the responsibility for behavior change on the probationer[14]

Even for the most effective probation officers, however, role conflict makes the job difficult. Probation officers are now held accountable for any abridgment of the community's safety resulting from acts of commission or omission in performing their duties. In practice this means they must make reasonable efforts to monitor the behavior of clients and to exercise caution with those whose backgrounds make them potential risks to the community. The most famous case that established this principle involved a

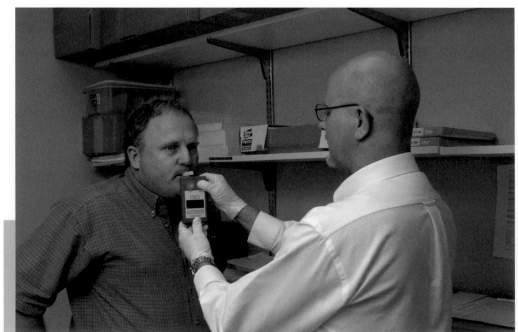

Frequent substance-abuse testing is a condition of probation for many offenders. Administering these tests has become part of the officer's supervisory role.

© Bob Daemmrich/The Image Works

probationer convicted of sexual assault. His probation officer helped him get a job as a maintenance worker in an apartment complex, giving him access to keys to various apartments. In placing the probationer, the officer withheld his client's past record from the employer. The probationer sexually assaulted several apartment residents, who later sued the probation officer for covering up the probationer's record. The court decided in favor of the victims, ruling that probation officers indeed are liable for their conduct as government employees.[15]

The liability of probation officers (and parole officers as well) is an area of law not yet well formulated. This issue has certainly made operational procedures in probation more important than ever. To defend against possible allegations of misconduct,

CAREERS IN CORRECTIONS — Probation Officer: State and County

NATURE OF THE WORK

State and county probation officers have two main functions. First, they conduct investigations and write reports about and recommendations on offenders for the courts, keeping the judge up to date on offenders compliance with the conditions of their probation terms. Second, they supervise probationers' adjustment to the community, maintaining contact with them and providing guidance based on the risk levels and specific needs of the probationers. Officers usually are required to spend more time with offenders who need more rehabilitation and counseling or with those who pose a higher risk than others. Agencies and jurisdictions also can determine the maximum number of cases an officer is allowed to manage. Officers may handle anywhere from 20 to 100 cases at any given time.

REQUIRED QUALIFICATIONS

Prospective probation officers are expected to have a four-year degree in criminal justice, social work, or some other related field, though specific requirements vary among states. A master's degree or related work experience is recommended and even required by some employers. Written, psychological, physical, and oral testing is ordinarily part of the application process, and good mental and physical health is a prerequisite to working as a probation officer. Convicted felons may be disqualified from this field of employment. Computer-related knowledge and skills are helpful, and strong interpersonal abilities are needed as well, since probation officers interact with a wide range of people in the pursuit of their duties. Because of the large number of reports a correctional treatment specialist or probation officer will produce over his or her career, candidates should possess strong writing skills. Newly hired officers and specialists receive additional on-the-job training for up to one year after being hired.

EARNINGS AND JOB OUTLOOK

Probation officers earned a median of $39,600 in 2004. The two middle quartiles earned from $30,770 to $50,550. The top 10 percent earned greater than $66,000, while the lowest 10 percent brought in less than $25,810. Local government officers and specialists earned a median $39,450 compared with the state median of $38,720 in 2002. Jobs in urban areas tended to result in higher wages. The employment growth rate for probation officers and correctional treatment specialists is expected be average through 2012. However, many officers and specialists are projected to retire between now and 2012, creating many job opportunities in addition to those generated by natural job growth.

MORE INFORMATION

Information about state and county employment opportunities can be found at various state and local official probation websites, including the website for **Probation Officer Careers, Jobs, and Training Information**; see the link at www.cengage.com/criminaljustice/clear.

probation officers need to document their actions so that they can meet any potential challenge. See "Careers in Corrections" for more on the work of state and county probation officers.

THE OFFENDER ■ The offender's response to supervision strongly influences the overall effectiveness of probation. Some offenders respond favorably to probation and get along well with their probation officers; others are resentful or resistant.

The offender's response to probation depends in part on his or her perception of the officer's power. Most probationers believe they have little effect on the supervision process. Although probation officers' real power is limited by law and bureaucracy, offenders may see the officer as occupying a commanding role. Officers decide on the style of supervision—whether supportive or controlling—and offenders have little direct influence on even this decision. Therefore, probationers often perceive themselves as relatively powerless in the face of potentially arbitrary decisions by the officers.

Probationers thus commonly resent their status, even when most people think they should be grateful for "another chance." In response many probation officers try to involve the client in determining goals and strategies and in actively solving problems, rather than simply requiring the offender to seek assistance. Such strategies are aimed at reducing the perceived discrepancy between the power of the officer and the powerlessness of the client.

THE BUREAUCRACY ■ All supervision activities take place in the context of a bureaucratic organization, which imposes both formal and informal constraints. *Formal constraints* are the legal conditions of probation, whether standard, punitive, or treatment; these are set by the court or written into law. **Standard conditions**, imposed on all probationers, include reporting to the probation office, notifying the agency of any change of address, remaining gainfully employed, and not leaving the jurisdiction without permission. **Punitive conditions**, including fines, community service, and some forms of restitution, are designed to increase the restrictiveness or painfulness of probation. A punitive condition usually reflects the seriousness of the offense. **Treatment conditions** force the probationer to deal with a significant problem or need, such as substance abuse. An offender who fails to comply with a condition is usually subject to incarceration; thus, one main purpose of the officer's supervision is to enforce compliance with the conditions.

In spite of conceptual distinctions, in practice the rationale for different conditions can become blurred. Standard conditions regarding drug treatment may be imposed because they are thought to increase the impact of drug treatment; restitution may be seen as an important part of an offender's change in attitude. In fact, there is some evidence that paying restitution results in lower rearrest rates, suggesting that it can be both a punitive and a treatment condition.[16]

Until recently most probation agencies had to enforce large numbers of conditions of all types, perhaps because the sentencing judges believed that the more conditions they imposed, the greater the control over the offender. In fact, the reverse is often true: With numerous conditions, some quite meaningful to the offender and others not, all the conditions can lose credibility. If the offender disobeys a trivial condition, the probation officer may well choose to look the other way, leading the probationer to wonder if *any* conditions will be enforced. Moreover, scattershot conditions cloud the officer's authority and overall plan to assist the client.

The formal constraints imposed by the organizational policy often pale before the *informal constraints* imposed by bureaucratic pressures. Three such pressures are (1) case control, (2) case management structure, and (3) competence.

Case control pressures emerge because judges, prosecutors, administrators, and community members all expect probation officers to "make" probationers abide by the conditions and legal requirements of probation. But the officer can do little to "make" the offender cooperate, for real power (such as the threat of revocation) is usually limited. Consequently, officers must rely on their discretion and individual supervision style, often minimizing or deliberately ignoring formal requirements in order to persuade the offender to cooperate.

standard conditions
Constraints imposed on all probationers, including reporting to the probation office, reporting any change of address, remaining employed, and not leaving the jurisdiction without permission.

punitive conditions
Constraints imposed on some probationers to increase the restrictiveness or painfulness of probation, including fines, community service, and restitution.

treatment conditions
Constraints imposed on some probationers to force them to deal with a significant problem or need, such as substance abuse.

FOCUS ON

CORRECTIONAL PRACTICE

Sample Supervision Plan

SUPERVISION PLAN

Client _____ Richard Knight

Probation Officer _____ Brian Gaines

Supervision Level _____ Hvigh

_____X____ Regular

_____ Minimum

Richard Knight will:

1. Provide check stubs showing monthly restitution payment of $50.
2. Obtain GED assessment from Nuestra Familia Educational Center.

3. Complete job-training course at New Mexico Technical High School.
4. Keep curfew of 8 P.M. on weekdays and 10 P.M. on weekends.

Signed: *Richard Knight*

Probation Officer: _____ Brian Gaines

Client: _____ Richard Knight

Date: _____ January 6, 2010

Similarly, the often large caseloads that bureaucracies generate and the unpredictability of the job produce a need for case management structure. This is achieved by documenting the officer's activities and by maintaining such routines as scheduled reporting days (when offenders come for office visits) and field days (when officers make home visits). But regular schedules do not always meet the demands of the caseload, nor do established operating procedures always lead to positive results. Such structure can limit the officer's creativity and intensity, as well as the agency's overall responsiveness.

Finally, the pressure for competence that a correctional bureaucracy exerts can demoralize a probation staff. Officers simply cannot manage all of their cases effectively—there is no surefire approach to take with offenders. Further, the officer typically receives little feedback about successes but much about failures. The result is an unintentional but systematic attack on the officer's sense of competence. Many officers react with cynical, defensive stances: Probationers cannot be changed unless they want to be, probationers are losers, and so forth. When several probation officers within an office develop this kind of cynicism, their negativism can pollute the whole working atmosphere.

In sum, the informal world of supervision is best understood as a complex interaction between officers (who vary in style, knowledge, and philosophy) and offenders (who vary in responsiveness and need for supervision) in a bureaucratic organization that imposes significant formal and informal constraints on the work. (See the Focus box "Sample Supervision Plan" for more.)

■ THE EFFECTIVENESS OF SUPERVISION

In light of such complexity, the effectiveness of probation supervision is difficult to assess. It depends on several factors: the skills of the officer, the availability of services such as employment counseling or drug treatment, and the needs and motives of the probationer. For many years, experts believed that reducing probation officers' caseloads could make supervision more effective. They reasoned that smaller caseloads would let officers devote more attention to each case, improving services. Frequently cited standards called for caseloads of 35 to 50, although such figures had never been justified by empirical study. During the 1960s and 1970s, dozens of experiments were conducted to find the optimal caseload. Yet subsequent reviews of those studies showed that caseload

recidivism
The return of a former correctional client to criminal behavior, as measured by new arrests or other problems with the law.

reduction alone did not significantly reduce **recidivism**—the return of a former correctional client to criminal behavior, as measured by new arrests or other problems with the law—among adult probationers. Even the field's most effective advocate for probation and parole supervision, the American Probation and Parole Association, has been unable to uncover a link between the size of a caseload and the effectiveness of supervision.[17]

Why don't smaller caseloads improve supervision effectiveness? Perhaps the assumption that "more supervision is better supervision" is too simplistic. Many factors—including the overall supervision experience, classification of offenders, officers' competence, treatment types, and policies of the probation agency—contribute to effectiveness more than does caseload.

Case Management Systems

Case management systems help focus the supervision effort of probation officers on client problems, which are identified using a standardized assessment of probationer risks and needs. In 1980 the National Institute of Corrections (a division of the Federal Bureau of Prisons) developed what it calls a "model system" of case management. This model has five principal components—statistical risk assessment, systematic needs assessment, contact supervision standards, case planning, and workload accounting— each designed to increase the effectiveness of probation supervision.

1. *Statistical risk assessment:* Because fully accurate predictions are impossible, there is pressure to assess risk conservatively—to consider the client a risk even when the evidence is ambiguous. This tendency toward overprediction (estimating that a person's chance of being arrested is greater than it actually is) means officers will spend time with probationers who actually need little supervision. The use of statistically developed risk assessment instruments reduces overprediction and improves the accuracy of risk classifications.

2. *Systematic needs assessment:* Subjective assessments of clients' needs often suffer from probation officers' biases and lack of information. With systematic needs assessment, officers can more consistently and comprehensively address probationers' problems by evaluating them according to a list of potential needs.

3. *Contact supervision standards:* Probation officers understandably tend to avoid "problem" clients and spend more time with cooperative ones. Ideally, however, those who pose the greatest risk and have the greatest needs require the most time. Based on the two assessments, offenders are classified into supervision levels. Each level has a minimum supervision contact requirement, with the highest-risk or highest-need offenders receiving the most supervision.

4. *Case planning:* The broad discretion given probation officers to supervise their clients can lead to idiosyncratic approaches. When a probation officer must put the supervision plan in writing, the result is likely to be a better fit between the client's problems and the officer's supervision strategy. In addition, the officer's work is more easily evaluated.

5. *Workload accounting:* Because different cases have varying supervision needs, simply counting cases can misrepresent the overall workload of an agency. A better system for staffing the agency involves time studies that estimate the number of staff needed to carry out supervision.

This five-part model has enjoyed widespread support from probation and parole administrators, and studies show that it reduces recidivism.[18] Risk assessment tools have been validated on a wide variety of probationer populations.[19] It has come to be considered standard practice in virtually every large probation agency in the United States, and several other countries have adopted it.

Structured case management systems help probation staff to decide which approach to supervision clients most need: intensive supervision, special services, or traditional probation monitoring. When clients are placed in the most appropriate supervision approach, probation effectiveness increases.

Learn about the way **case management systems** work in community supervision; see the corresponding link at www.cengage.com/criminaljustice/clear.

Evidence-Based Supervision

Researchers have begun to investigate systematically the differences between programs that work—that is, programs that reduce recidivism—and those that do not. This endeavor is called **evidence-based practice**. Studies suggest that among the most important characteristics of programs for probationers, four stand out:

■ Focus the program on high-risk probationers (risk principle).

■ Provide greater levels of supervision to higher-risk clients (supervision principle).

■ Provide treatment programs designed to meliorate the problems that produce the higher risk level (treatment principle).

■ Make referrals to treatment programs (referral principle).[20]

These "effectiveness" principles matter greatly in the design of probation-supervision programs. In one study of 66 community-based programs in Ohio, for example, meeting these principles was found to be an important determinant of each program's overall effectiveness. Just as important, failing to follow these principles often meant programs did *worse*.[21] (See **Figure 8.4**.) One of the key findings of this line of research is that surveillance-oriented supervision programs do not seem to work very well.[22] Overall, the

evidence-based practice
Using correctional methods that have been shown to be effective by well-designed research studies.

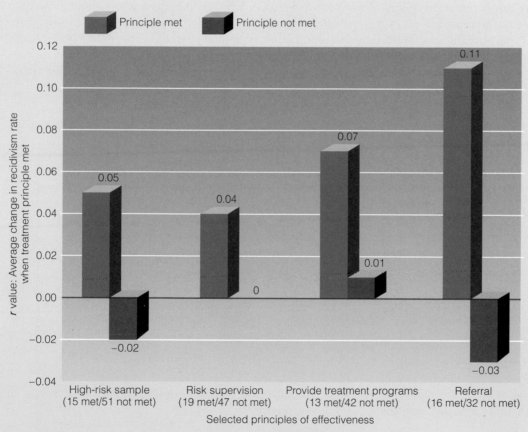

Figure 8.4

The Effectiveness of Evidence-Based Programming in Community Supervision Programs

Community-based programs that follow four principles of effective programs reduce recidivism rates, whereas programs that fail to do so often make recidivism rates increase.

Source: Christopher T. Lowenkamp, Jennifer Pealer, Edward J. Latessa, and Paula Smith, "Adhering to the Risk and Need Principles: Does It Matter for Supervision-Based Programs?" *Federal Probation* 70 (no. 3, December 2006), http://www.uscourts.gov/fedprob/December_2006/adhering.html, June 14, 2007.

evidence-based movement in community supervision has tended to support the value of programs, when they are applied to high-risk probationers and use methods that are designed to reduce the risk.[23] Some people suggest that this line of research supports a range of specialized services for probationers with special types of problems. Despite strong support for the use of case management systems, recent studies have found that most probation officers do not use case management principles in the way they supervise their probationers.[24]

Specialized Supervision Programs

The needs of probationers vary dramatically. Sex offenders require different supervision strategies than do cocaine addicts; mentally ill offenders must be handled differently than embezzlers. However, because caseloads often exceed 100 probationers per officer, officers have begun to group probationers with similar problems into a single caseload. This specialization allows the probation officer to develop more expertise in handling each problem, and it promotes a concentrated supervision effort.

Studies show that this approach has promise. For example, employment-counseling programs and support services improve employment possibilities, and specialized treatment for sex offenders on probation reduces their recidivism. Specialized services have been found to be more effective than traditional services for otherwise difficult subgroups of probationers, including domestic violence cases[25] and probationers with mental illness.[26]

Recent interest in the problem of substance abuse has increased the attention given to probationers affected by drugs and alcohol. Several specialized programs designed to combat probationers' drug use typically take advantage of new techniques for drug surveillance and treatment. **Urinalysis** determines if an offender is using drugs. **Antabuse**, a

urinalysis
Technique used to determine whether someone is using drugs.

Antabuse
A drug that, when combined with alcohol, causes violent nausea; it is used to control a person's drinking.

FOCUS ON

CORRECTIONAL POLICY

Dealing with the Drug Offender

Drug-involved offenders present problems and opportunities to probation. The main problem is that many such offenders lead disorganized lives and consequently have trouble abiding by even the simplest rules of probation, such as reporting and remaining employed. The main opportunity is that getting a drug offender to stay off drugs is one of the most effective ways to prevent crime.

There is no easy way to help drug-involved offenders stay clean. In developing a training program regarding the supervision of drug offenders, the American Probation and Parole Association identified several "principles" in supervising drug offenders:

1. *Use urine tests to confirm behavior.* Effective supervision is impossible unless the probation officer knows reliably whether the probationer is truly "clean." Drug testing—more frequent early in the sentence and gradually tailing off—is the best way to know the truth.
2. *Know the pharmacology of drugs.* Different drugs have different effects. Knowing those effects can help in the early

identification of relapse, and it can help the officer understand the sometimes erratic behavior of the probationer.

3. *Expect "slips," especially at first.* Recovery from drug addiction is a lifelong process. Almost no one who is truly addicted walks away from drugs the first time. The probation officer needs to be prepared for "slips," even in the most motivated client.
4. *Have realistic goals.* Abstinence is the right goal, but it is more reasonable to aim the supervision strategy a bit lower: reduce the duration of "slips" and increase the time between them.
5. Have a graduated program of enforcement sanctions.

When a client fails, do not start with prison as a first response. Instead, begin with a rapid response (say, a curfew) and gradually escalate the severity if the failures continue. Save prison or jail as a last resort.

Source: Todd R. Clear, Val B. Clear, and Anthony Braga, "Intermediate Sanctions for Drug Offenders," *Prison Journal*, 73 (Summer 1993): 178–98.

drug that stimulates nausea when combined with alcohol, inhibits drinking. **Methadone**, a drug that reduces craving for heroin, spares addicts from painful withdrawal symptoms. These approaches are often combined with close surveillance in order to reinforce abstinence during probation (see the Focus box "Dealing with the Drug Offender").

Another new specialized program pairs the probation officer more closely with street police officers. Officers who work in tandem with the police are often given caseloads of especially tough probationers. The police liaison allows for more-effective searches and arrests and gives probation officers access to police information about probationers.

The difficulty with specialized supervision programs is what to do with the "ordinary" offender slated for traditional services. Often probation officers regard "regular" probation as a less-attractive function, and conflict among the specialized units can become a serious management problem. As a consequence, such programs, even when successful, require extensive managerial support.

Even so, specialization of supervision will likely continue to grow in popularity. One reason why has to do with an increasing recognition of the seriousness of the problems faced by probationers and parolees. In one sample of probationers, 40 percent were under the influence of alcohol at the time of their offense and 14 percent had been using illegal drugs.[27] Statistics such as these point to the importance of providing specialized programs for probationers whose problems with drugs or alcohol lead to repeated criminality and revocation.

methadone
A drug that reduces the craving for heroin; it is used to spare addicts from painful withdrawal symptoms.

Performance-Based Supervision

Questions about the effectiveness of community supervision have spawned **performance-based supervision**, an approach that emphasizes "results" in setting priorities and selecting activities. The focus on results affects both the strategies and the agencies of client supervision.

The performance-based movement has called for a new emphasis on public safety in probation.[28] Rather than promoting an amorphous belief in offender rehabilitation, this new philosophy of probation squarely accepts responsibility for adopting approaches that help enhance the safety of the public. One of the most cogent expressions of this new philosophy is called "broken windows probation" because it adopts

performance-based supervision
An approach to probation that establishes goals for supervision and evaluates the effectiveness of meeting those goals.

© Jeff T. Green/The New York Times/Redux

Sex offenders require supervision strategies different from those for drug addicts. Officers with specialized probation caseloads are required to make frequent unannounced visits to their clients.

the view that probation should be responsible for doing everything it can—even in dealing with problems of public disorder—to improve public safety (see the Focus box "The Broken Windows Model"). By accepting public safety as a primary aim, probation leaders recognize the critical role probation can play, not just in reducing crime, but also in enriching community life by contributing to a sense of personal security and quality of life. The "broken windows" idea enables probation to embrace new problem-solving and partnership strategies that have proved successful for law enforcement. (These strategies are discussed in depth in Chapter 22.)

Probation organizations that adopt a performance-based orientation express the focus on public safety in two ways. First, they choose supervision strategies that reflect what is known about the effectiveness of supervision. In most cases, this means providing the most attention to the highest-risk cases, emphasizing the reduction of the kinds of problems that most contribute to crime, and consistently reinforcing crime-free behaviors. Second, they set goals for improved supervision outcomes with their clients. Measuring whether these goals are accomplished gives the probation administrator the ability to know if the supervision methods are "performing correctly" or need to be changed.

FOCUS ON CORRECTIONAL POLICY

The Broken Windows Model

In March 1997 a group of probation administrators formed a Reinventing Probation Council and began meeting in New York City with the idea of developing a new approach to probation supervision. The group included several of the most prominent national spokespersons in the field, and it was led by the prominent correctional critic, John DiIulio, a professor at the University of Pennsylvania. The result of their meetings, which occurred at regular intervals over three years, was a call for a new vision for probation supervision—an approach they called "broken windows" probation.

The new vision begins with a frank admission that traditional probation supervision has failed to protect the public because it has failed to hold probationers accountable for their conduct. The result is a system of probation that serves neither the public nor the victims of crime and also fails to provide what probationers need in order to comply with the law and reclaim their roles as citizens. To remedy this situation, the group called for seven new strategies to be adopted by probation supervision:

1. *Place public safety first.* Adopt an organizational mission that gives primary importance to the safety of the community.
2. *Supervise probation in the neighborhood, not in the office.* Take the work of the probation officer out of the office and into the field, where it will have more impact on probationer behavior.

3. *Rationally allocate resources.* Provide more supervision to high-risk cases; provide special supervision to cases with special problems.
4. *Provide for strong enforcement of probation conditions and a quick response to violations.* Make sure probationers comply with their conditions, and do not let probation violators languish without attention.
5. *Develop partners in the community.* Build good working relationships with the police, social services, and local community leaders such as clergy and neighborhood associations.
6. *Establish performance-based initiatives.* Set individual organizational goals and evaluate whether they have been accomplished.
7. *Cultivate strong leadership.* Build the basis for a generation of new leaders in probation who share the vision for the future.

The announcement of the broken windows model has received a great deal of fanfare in the profession—not to mention some criticism. But the ideas promoted by the model are already gaining ground in probation departments around the country, and it appears that what the model proposes is increasing in popularity around the country.

Sources: Reinventing Probation Council, *Transforming Probation through Leadership: The "Broken Windows" Model* (New York: Center for Civic Innovation at the Manhattan Institute, 2000); Faye Taxman and James Byrne, "Fixing Broken Windows Probation," *Perspectives* 25 (no. 2, Spring 2001): 22–29.

In short, the performance movement shifts the focus of supervision plans from activities to results—from what probation officers do to what they accomplish. The test of probation, in this circumstance, is how well the sentence turns out in the end.

Is Probation Effective Regardless?

Almost all studies of the effectiveness of probation supervision compare different probation strategies. They often find no difference in outcomes, and even when there is a difference, it is typically modest. The frequency of such weak results for probation studies leads some scholars to conclude that probation "doesn't work" or that its effects are minimal at best. This often makes prison seem a more-powerful option by comparison, even if it is much more expensive than probation.

Again, these studies almost always compare one kind of probation to another. They do not compare probation with "doing nothing," because doing nothing is not a reasonable option. Yet what if probation is considerably better than "doing nothing"? What if the various *methods* of probation vary little in their impact, but probation itself works?

We have no completely convincing studies of this question (what judge would want to engage in an experiment where a sentence of "nothing" was routinely given to a random sample of convicted felons?). But a recent study suggests that probation works perhaps far better than most people might suspect. Designed to find out whether the personal relationships of probationers affected their likelihood of being arrested, the study followed a sample of probationers for the first eight months of their probation term. The study found that a few case factors predicted the likelihood of new criminal behavior (carrying guns or using drugs or alcohol) but, overall, the entire sample exhibited a large and abrupt reduction in criminal activity immediately following being placed on probation, and the initial reduction lasted the duration of the study. This reduction in criminality had little to do with life circumstances but instead appeared to be a general effect of the probation sentence.[29]

This work is bolstered by a recent study reported by the New York City Criminal Justice Agency that compared traditional New York City probation, more heavily funded "alternatives to incarceration" (such as those discussed in Chapter 9), and jail. The researchers concluded that when it came to preventing new arrests, probation was as effective as lauded "alternative" sanctions and more effective than jail.[30] Another study compared probation supervision of drug offenders with imprisonment; it concluded that probationers had fewer arrests and convictions under probation, even accounting for the time the prison group spent behind bars.[31]

While a few studies are not enough to prove a point, the result is good news for probation. It may be that the fact of being on probation itself matters more than the kind of probation one experiences.

■ REVOCATION AND TERMINATION OF PROBATION

Probation status ends in one of two ways: (1) The person successfully completes the period of probation or (2) the person's probationary status is revoked because of misbehavior. Revocation can result from a new arrest or conviction or from a *rules violation,* a failure to comply with a condition of probation. Rules violations that result in revocations are referred to as **technical violations.**

Revocations for technical violations are somewhat controversial, because behaviors that are not ordinarily illegal—changing one's residence without permission, failing to attend a therapy program, neglecting to report to the probation office, and so forth—can result in incarceration. Some years ago, technical violations were common whenever probationers were uncooperative. Today probation is revoked when the rules violation persists or poses a threat to the community. Probation officers have broad discretion to investigate potential rules violations and even new crimes. The U.S. Supreme Court has ruled that people on probation may be searched when the probation officer

technical violation
The probationer's failure to abide by the rules and conditions of probation (specified by the judge), resulting in revocation of probation.

has a "reasonable suspicion" that a crime or rules violation may have occurred.[32] This means that probation officers do not need search warrants, nor do they have to have "probable cause" to believe a crime has occurred, the higher standard for searches that applies to citizens who are not under correctional supervision.

Although patterns vary across the country, the most common reason for a revocation is a new offense by the probationer. Sometimes the court waits for conviction on the new offense before revoking probation, but if the offense is serious enough, probation is immediately revoked. In such cases a technical violation is alleged, even though the real basis for revocation is the new offense. (See the Focus box "Sample Revocation Form," for a look at a technical violation.)

According to most studies of probation revocation, from one-fifth to one-third of probationers fail to abide by the terms of their probation. A widely publicized Rand Corporation study, however, found much higher rates of violation, raising the concern

FOCUS ON CORRECTIONAL PRACTICE

Sample Revocation Form

ORDER OF REVOCATION, STATE OF NEW MEXICO

In the 1st District Court of New Mexico, Santa Fe

Defendant: <u>Richard Knight</u>
Case Number: 2010-00235
Matter: *State of New Mexico v. Richard Knight*
Date: April 15, 2010

The above named defendant has been charged with the violation of probation, as follows:

1. Failure to make restitution as ordered by the court
2. Association with the 18th Street Gang in violation of the order of the court

On <u>January 4, 2010</u> the defendant was convicted of the crime of <u>Aggravated Assault Upon a Peace Officer (Deadly Weapon) (Firearm Enhancement), as charged in Information Number 10-5736900</u> and was notified of his rights, and given a copy of the probation order of the court.

On March 23, 2010, Probation Officer <u>Brian Gaines</u> informed the court of probable cause that the probationer was in violation of the following probation conditions:

1. That restitution be made to Juan Lopez in the amount of $662.40
2. That the defendant discontinue fraternizing with the 18th Street Gang members and terminate his own membership in the gang

Defendant was (1) provided with a copy of the alleged violations, (2) informed that any statement s/he made could be used against him/her, (3) informed of the right to obtain assistance of counsel and to have one provided if indigent, and (4) informed of the date of the probation revocation hearing.

Pursuant to this allegation, the defendant:

  <u>X</u> admitted the violations
  _____ asked for a hearing on the charges
  <u>X</u> waived counsel
  _____ sought the assignment of counsel due to indigency status

The court finds that

  <u>X</u> sufficient evidence exists to support the allegation of a violation of probation
  _____ the evidence of a violation of probation is insufficient

In finding that a violation of probation has occurred, the court relied on the following evidence: <u>testimony by the probation officer that restitution had not been paid; testimony by the probation officer that he observed the defendant in the company of gang members; admission under oath by the defendant that these allegations were true.</u>

Based on the courts finding of a violation of probation, the following sentence is ordered:

1. A jail term of 30 days
2. Attendance in the Gang Violence Reduction Program of the probation department
3. Intensive probation supervision following release from jail

Signed: <u>*Judge Manuel Baca*</u>

of probation administrators. For 40 months the Rand researchers followed a sample of probationers from two urban California counties, who had been placed on probation for FBI Index crimes. More than one-third were reincarcerated for technical violations or new offenses; of these, 65 percent were arrested for a felony or misdemeanor, and 51 percent were actually convicted of a crime. In other words, many of these probation "failures" remained on probation after their convictions, even though the crimes were often serious. This study found that once a person is placed on probation, serious misbehavior does not necessarily result in removal from the community.[33]

Other follow-up studies have supported the overall results of the Rand study. When we look at annual exits from probation, we see a similar picture: **Figure 8.5** shows recent statistics showing the ways in which probationers in the United States ended their terms. Note that about two-thirds completed their terms successfully.

Replications of this type of follow-up study outside of "big-corrections states" such as California and Texas have found somewhat lower levels of serious misbehavior by probationers. Perhaps probation works well in some areas but less well in others, partly depending on the nature of the person placed on probation. The kind of person placed on probation varies dramatically from place to place. One study of felony sentencing found that rates of probation sentences for robbers varied among 14 cities from a low of less than 1 percent to a high of 13 percent, and probation sentences varied from 2 to 40 percent.[34] Probation agencies that supervise more-serious offenders can be expected to have higher rates of revocation. In locations where probationers have serious criminal histories, some probation departments have begun to collaborate with police departments to improve the public-safety effectiveness of both agencies. See "Do the Right Thing" for more.

Because revocation of probation is a serious change in the offender's status, the courts have ruled that the offender has several due process rights in the revocation procedure. As discussed in Chapter 5, the U.S. Supreme Court has ruled that a probationer has the right to counsel at a revocation and sentencing hearing.[35] In a later decision, the Supreme Court further clarified revocation procedures.[36] The approved practice is to handle the revocation in three stages:

1 *Preliminary hearing (sometimes waived):* The facts of the arrest are reviewed to determine if there is probable cause that a violation has occurred.

2 *Hearing:* The facts of the allegation are heard and decided. The probation department presents the evidence to support the allegation, and the probationer has an opportunity to refute the evidence. Specifically, the probationer has the right to

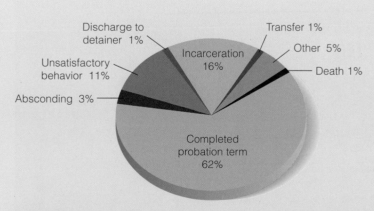

Figure 8.5

Termination of Probation in the United States

Most probationers who finish their probation terms do so satisfactorily, but about one in six end up in prison.

Source: Bureau of Justice Statistics, *Statistical Tables*, December 2008, p. 15.

DO THE RIGHT THING

As you look over the Recommendation for Revocation Report sent to you by Officer Sawyer, you are struck by the low-level technical violations used to justify sending James Ferguson, a minor drug offender, to prison. Sawyer cites Ferguson's failure to attend all the drug treatment sessions, to complete his community service, to pay a $500 fine. You call Sawyer in to discuss the report.

"Bill, I've looked over your report on Ferguson and I'm wondering what's going on here. Why isn't he fulfilling the conditions of his probation?"

"I'm really not sure, but it seems he just doesn't want to meet the conditions. I think he's got a bad attitude, and I don't like the guys he hangs around with. He's always mouthing off about the 'system' and says I'm on his case for no reason."

"Well, let's look at your report. You say that he works for Capital Services cleaning offices downtown from midnight till 8 A.M. yet has to go to the drug programs three mornings a week and put in 10 hours a week at the Salvation Army Thrift Store. Is it that he isn't trying or does he have an impossible situation?"

"I think he could do it if he tried, but also, I think he's selling cocaine again. Perhaps he needs to get a taste of prison."

"That may be true, but do you really want to revoke his probation?"

WRITING ASSIGNMENT: What's going on here? Is Sawyer recommending revocation because of Ferguson's attitude and the suspicion that he is selling drugs again? Do the technical violations warrant prison? Write a memo explaining what you would recommend, and why, if you were Ferguson's probation officer.

Probation officers often require the assistance of police officers in bringing a client to court for possible revocation of probation. In Bakersfield, California, police and probation officers cooperate in rounding up violators. As a probation officer, when might you require assistance?

© The Bakersfield Californian/Zuma Press

see written notice of the charges and the disclosure of evidence of the violation, to testify and to present witnesses and evidence to contradict the allegations, to cross-examine adversarial witnesses, to be heard by a neutral and detached officer, and to review a written statement of findings. Unless unusual grounds exist to deny counsel, the probationer also has the right to an attorney.

3 *Sentencing:* With an attorney present, the judge decides whether to impose a term of incarceration and, if so, the duration of the term. This stage is more than a technicality, because after a minor violation, probation is often reinstated with greater restrictions.

For those who successfully complete probation, the sentence is terminated. Ordinarily the probationer is then a completely free citizen again, without obligation to the court or to the probation department.

■ PROBATION IN THE COMING DECADE

With the new century, many dramatic changes are coming in probation. Caseloads of traditional probation are growing well beyond reasonable management: 200- and even 300-person caseloads are no longer unusual. In many locales, traditional probation has seen a deterioration in quality of supervision, because of loss of staff and increase in cases. Yet the importance of probation for public safety has never been greater. Studies now suggest that putting offenders on probation actually makes them *less* likely to commit new crimes than if they had been sent to prison instead.[37] As a result of the renewed emphasis on public safety, many agencies have also experienced a resurgence of intensive and structured supervision for selected offenders (see Chapter 9).

Since that first day in 1841 when John Augustus looked for a better way of working with criminals, probation has continued to grow. What was once known as an "alternative to incarceration" is now the number-one sentencing option used by judges all across the United States.

During the last 25 years, probation has gone through three major changes in emphasis, from rehabilitation to surveillance to risk management. Probation now finds itself on the brink of what could be another major directional change. More and more jurisdictions are indicating that probation must take responsibility for the desired behavioral changes in probationers.

This leaves us with two increasingly divergent types of probation in the future. One is largely a paper exercise. Whatever services are provided will be done through brokerage: The probation officer serves as a referral agent, involving the probationer in single-focus community service agencies (such as drug treatment programs) that work with a variety of community clients, not just with offenders. In the second type of probation, the remaining probationers—a minority of all offenders, to be sure—will be watched closely and will receive first-rate supervision and control from highly trained professionals working with reasonable levels of funding and programmatic support.

The use of brokerage is not necessarily a bad idea. Proponents argue that specialists can provide treatment superior to what a generalist can offer and that communities ought to provide such assistance to offenders. Yet community agencies are not always quick to offer services to offenders; they prefer to work with voluntary clients, not those who avail themselves of services only under threat of the law.

Probation administrators are also changing the way they want to be evaluated. Most of the time—and in most of the studies cited in this chapter—probation's effectiveness is determined by rearrest rates: High rates are seen as a sign of ineffective supervision. Yet administrators know that high rearrest rates can also mean that staff is watching high-risk clients vigilantly, something most citizens would applaud. From this viewpoint, recidivism rates do not offer the sole means of evaluating a probation department.

Instead, some feel probation should also be evaluated by a series of "performance indicators" that better reveal whether probation is doing its job.[38] These indicators include numbers of community service projects performed by probationers, amount of probation fees and restitution collected, employment rates, amount of taxes paid, and days free of drug use. However, detractors claim that even if these performance indicators are high, the public is interested in crime as a bottom line—and that means recidivism rates matter most.

In many respects, then, probation finds itself at a crossroads. Although its credibility is probably as low as it has ever been, its workload is growing dramatically and, in view of the crowding in prisons and jails, will probably continue to do so. Under the strain of this workload and on-again, off-again public support, probation faces a serious challenge: Can its methods of supervision and service be adapted successfully to high-risk offenders? Many innovations are being attempted, but it is unclear whether such new programs actually improve probation or detract from it. Certainly they expand the variety of probation sanctions, making them more applicable to more offenders. But do they strengthen the mainstream functions of probation—investigation and supervision? These functions must be improved for probation to succeed in its current challenge.

SUMMARY

1 Describe the history and development of probation, including how it is organized today.

Probation stems from European practices that attempted to alleviate the harshness of the criminal law. In the United States, probation goes back to the 1830s, when John Augustus volunteered to "stand bail" for people in the Boston Police Court. Today probation exists as a sentencing option in every state of the United States, operated by courts or by correctional departments.

2 Describe the two functions of probation.

Probation officers have traditionally performed two major functions: investigation and supervision. Investigation involves the preparation of a presentence investigation (PSI), which the judge uses in sentencing an offender. Supervision begins once an offender is sentenced to probation, and it involves establishing a relationship with the offender, setting supervision goals to help the offender comply with conditions established by the court, and deciding how to terminate probation on the basis of the offender's response to supervision.

3 Discuss the purpose and content of the presentence investigation report.

The PSI plays its most important role in the sentencing process. Because individual judges, even in the same court system, may weigh factors in a case differently, the PSI must be comprehensive enough to provide necessary information to judges with varying sentencing perspectives. A shortened, directed, and standardized PSI format is becoming more common. This approach places greater responsibility on the probation officer, who must discern precisely what information the judge will require to evaluate the sentencing options.

4 Describe the major issues involved in the presentence investigation.

PSIs present three major issues: (1) Whether to make sentencing recommendations. These are controversial, because a person without authority to sentence is nevertheless suggesting what the sentence should be. For this reason, not all probation systems include it in the PSI. (2) Whether to disclose the contents of the PSI to the defendant. In many states, the defense does not receive a copy of the report. In the other states, the practice is generally to "cleanse" the report of confidential comments and clinical statements, then disclose it. (3) Whether private investigative firms ought be allowed to provide judges with PSIs paid for by the defendant. In this approach, the firm serves as an advocate for the defendant at the sentencing stage.

5 **Describe the dynamics that occur among the probation officer, the probationer, and the probation bureaucracy.**

Probation officers face role conflict in that they must both enforce the law and help the offender. The responsibilities are often incompatible. The offender's response to supervision depends in part on his or her perception of the officer's power. Most probationers believe they have little effect on the supervision process. Although probation officers' real power is limited by law and bureaucracy, offenders may see the officer as occupying a commanding role. All supervision activities take place in the context of a bureaucratic organization, which imposes both formal and informal constraints. Formal constraints are the legal conditions of probation.

6 **Discuss the different kinds of probation conditions and tell why they are important.**

Standard conditions, imposed on all probationers, include reporting to the probation office, notifying the agency of any change of address, remaining gainfully employed, and not leaving the jurisdiction without permission. Punitive conditions, including fines, community service, and some forms of restitution, are designed to increase the restrictiveness or painfulness of probation. A punitive condition usually reflects the seriousness of the offense. Treatment conditions force the probationer to deal with a significant problem or need, such as substance abuse.

7 **Define** *recidivism* **and describe its importance to probation.**

Recidivism is the return of a former correctional client to criminal behavior, as measured by new arrests or other problems with the law. It is the basis on which we decide if a probation strategy is working or not.

8 **Define** *evidence-based practice* **and discuss its importance.**

Evidence-based practice centers on an understanding of the differences between programs that work—that is, programs that reduce recidivism—and those that do not. Studies suggest that, among the most important characteristics of programs for probationers, four stand out: (1) focusing the program on high-risk probationers (risk principle), (2) providing greater levels of supervision to higher-risk clients (supervision principle), (3) providing treatment programs designed to meliorate the problems that produce the higher risk level (treatment principle), and (4) making referrals to treatment programs (referral principle).

9 **Describe what is known about the effectiveness of probation supervision.**

Studies of the effectiveness of probation supervision find little or no difference in outcomes for different probation strategies. This often makes prison seem a more-powerful option by comparison, even though it costs much more than probation. But some recent studies suggest that probation works perhaps far better than most people might suspect. In preventing new arrests, probation may be as effective as lauded "alternative" sanctions and more effective than jail or prison.

10 **Discuss the revocation of probation, including "technical" revocation.**

Probation status ends in one of two ways: (1) the person completes the period of probation or (2) the person's probationary status is revoked because of misbehavior. Revocation can result from a new arrest or conviction or from a rules violation, a failure to comply with a condition of probation. Rules violations that result in revocations are called technical violations. Revocations for technical violations are somewhat controversial, because behaviors that are not ordinarily illegal can result in incarceration.

KEY TERMS

Antabuse (p. 220)
Augustus, John (p. 200)
authority (p. 213)
client-specific planning (p. 212)
community justice (p. 203)
evidence-based practice (p. 219)
judicial reprieve (p. 201)

methadone (p. 221)
motivational interviewing (p. 214)
performance-based supervision (p. 221)
power (p. 213)
presentence investigation (PSI) (p. 208)
punitive conditions (p. 216)
recidivism (p. 218)

recognizance (p. 201)
standard conditions (p. 216)
technical violation (p. 223)
treatment conditions (p. 216)
urinalysis (p. 220)
victim impact statements (p. 210)

FOR DISCUSSION

1. How does the use of probation affect the corrections system? Why is it used so extensively?
2. How does the presentence investigation report affect accountability for the sentence that is imposed?
3. How do you think the investigative and supervisory functions of probation can be most effectively organized? What would the judges in your area say about your proposal? What would the department of corrections say?
4. Given the two major tasks of probation, how should officers spend their time? How do they actually spend their time?
5. Why might some probationers be kept in the community after a technical violation, rather than having their probation revoked?

FOR FURTHER READING

Festervan, Earlene. *Women Probationers: Supervision and Success*. Lanham, MD: American Correctional Association, 2004. A description of the interviewing, assessing, counseling, and supervision strategies used with women on probation.

Jones, Justin, and Rita Hyde Jones. *Tales of the Caseload*. Lexington, KY: American Probation and Parole Association, 2004. Provides a professional probation officer's perspective on the assessment and supervision of probationers in contemporary society.

Kleiman, Mark. *When Brute Force Fails: How to Have Less Crime and Less Punishment*. Princeton, NJ: Princeton University Press, 2009. Discusses the best ways to enforce probation and parole conditions in order to make community corrections a genuine alternative to incarceration.

Meloy, Michelle. *Sex Offenses and the Men Who Commit Them: An Assessment of Sex Offenders on Probation*. Cambridge, MA: Northeastern University Press, 2006. A study of 150 male sex offenders placed on probation in a large metropolitan probation department.

Towl, Graham J. *Psychology in Probation Services*. Malden, MA: Blackwell, 2005. A description of techniques for those interested in the application of psychology to the work of probation services.

Wooton, Harold B. *Justice . . . Is Just Us*. New York: iUniverse, 2009. A novel with a realistic portrayal of a probation officer, written by a former chief probation officer.

NOTES

1 *The New Look of Adult Supervision* (New York: New York City Department of Probation), http://www.nyc.gov/html/prob/html/restructure.html#look, March 22, 2007.
2 Lauren E. Glaze and Thomas P. Bonczar, *Probation and Parole in the United States, 2007—Statistical Tables* (Washington, DC: Bureau of Justice Statistics, December 2008).
3 Robert Martinson, "California Research at the Crossroads," *Crime and Delinquency* 22 (April 1976): 191.
4 *Ex parte United States*, 242 U.S. 27 (1916); often referred to as *Killits*.
5 *John Augustus, First Probation Officer* (New York: Probation Association, 1939), 30. First published as *John Augustus, A Report of the Labors of John Augustus, for the Last Ten Years, in Aid of the Unfortunate* (Boston: Wright & Hasty, 1852).
6 Ibid., p. 34.
7 Todd R. Clear and Eric Cadora, *Community Justice*. Belmont, CA: Wadsworth, 2003.
8 Jeanne B. Stinchcombe and Darryl Hippensteel, "Presentence Investigation Reports: A Relevant Justice Model Tool or a

Medical Model Relic," *Criminal Justice Policy Review* 12 (no. 2, June 2001): 164–77.

9 Michael D. Norman and Robert C. Waldman, "Utah Presentence Investigation Reports: User Group Perceptions of Quality and Effectiveness," *Federal Probation* 64 (no. 2, 2000): 7–12.

10 Joan Petersilia, Susan Turner, James Kahan, and Joyce Peterson, *Granting Felons Probation: Public Risks and Alternatives* (Santa Monica, CA: Rand, 1985), 39, 41.

11 *Williams v. New York*, 337 U.S. 241 (1949).

12 *Verdugo v. United States*, 402 F.Supp. 599 (1968).

13 Michael D. Clark, "Motivational Interviewing for Probation Staff: Increasing the Readiness to Change," *Federal Probation* 69 (no. 2, December 2005), http://www.uscourts.gov/fedprobe/June_2006/interviewing.html, June 14, 2007.

14 List adapted from Michael D. Clark, Scott Walters, Ray Gingerich, and Melissa Meltzer, "Motivational Interviewing for Probation Officers: Tipping the Balance toward Change," *Federal Probation* 70 (no. 1, June 2006): 38–44.

15 *Rieser v. District of Columbia*, 21 Cr.L. 2503 (1977).

16 Maureen C. Outlaw and R. Barry Ruback, "Predictors and Outcomes of Victim Restitution Payments," *Justice Quarterly* 16 (no. 4, December 1999): 847–61.

17 Mario Papparozzi and Gary Hinzman, "Caseload Size in Probation and Parole," *Perspectives* 29 (no. 2, Spring 2005): 23–25.

18 Patricia M. Harris, Raymond Gingrich, and Tiffany Whitaker, "The 'Effectiveness' of Differential Supervision," *Crime and Delinquency* 50 (no. 3, Summer 2004): 235–71.

19 Christopher T. Lowenkamp, Brian Lovins, and Edward J. Latessa, "Validating the Level of Service Inventory-Revised and the Level of Service Inventory: Screening Version with a Sample of Probationers," *Prison Journal* 89 (no. 2, June 2009): 189–204.

20 P. Gendreau, S. French, and A. Taylor, "What Works (What Doesn't) Revised 2002: The Principles of Effective Correctional Treatment" (unpublished manuscript, University of New Brunswick, St. John, Canada, 2002).

21 Christopher T. Lowenkamp and Edward J. Latessa, "Increasing the Effectiveness of Correctional Programming through the Risk Principle: Identifying Offenders for Residential Placement," *Criminology and Public Policy* 4 (no 2, Spring 2005): 263–82.

22 S. Aos, M. Miller, and E. Drake, *Evidence-Based Adult Corrections Programs: What Works and What Does Not* (Olympia: Washington State Institute for Public Policy, 2006).

23 William D. Burrell, "Probation and Parole Case Management: An Evidence-Based Framework for the Future," *Community Corrections Report*, May–June 2008, pp. 51–56.

24 James Bonta, Tanya Rugge, Terri-Lynne Scott, Guy Bourgon, and Annie K. Yessine, "Exploring the Black Box of Community Supervision," *Journal of Offender Rehabilitation*, 47 (no. 3, 2008): 248–70.

25 Matthew T. DeMichele, Ann Crowe, Andrew Klein, and Doug Wilson, "'What Works' in the Supervision of Domestic Violence Offenders: Promising Results from a Study in Rhode Island," *Perspectives* 30 (no. 1, Summer 2006): 46–57.

26 Jennifer L. Skeem and Paula Emke-Francis, "Probation and Mental Health: Responding to the Challenges," *Perspectives* 28 (no. 3, Summer 2004): 22–27.

27 BJS *Special Report*, March 1998, p. 1.

28 Caliber Associates, "From Theory to Practice: The Lifecycle Document for the Results-Based Management Framework for the Federal Probation and Pretrial Services System," *Federal Probation* 70 (no. 2, September 2006): 88–98.

29 Doris Layton-MacKenzie and Spencer De Li, "The Impact of Formal and Informal Social Controls on the Criminal Activities of Probationers," *Journal of Research in Crime and Delinquency* 39 (no. 3, August 2002): 243–76.

30 Jukka Savolainen, *The Impact of Felony ATI Programs on Recidivism* (New York: New York City Criminal Justice Agency, April 2003).

31 Cassia Spohn and David Holleran, "The Effect of Imprisonment on Recidivism Rates of Felony Offenders: A Focus on Drug Offenders," *Criminology* 40 (no. 2, May 2002): 297–328.

32 *United States v Knight*, (00-1260) 534 U.S. 112 (2001).

33 Petersilia et al., *Granting Felons Probation*, p. 39.

34 Stephen Klein, Patricia Ebener, Allan Abrahamse, and Nora Fitzgerald, *Predicting Criminal Justice Outcome: Measuring What Matters* (Santa Monica, CA: Rand, 1991).

35 *Mempa v. Rhay*, 389 U.S. 128 (1967).

36 *Gagnon v. Scarpelli*, 411 U.S. 778 (1973).

37 Paul Nieuwbeerta, Daniel S. Nagin, and Arjan A. J. Blokland, "Assessing the Impact of First-Time Imprisonment on Offenders' Subsequent Criminal Career Development: A Matched Samples Comparison," *Journal of Quantitative Criminology*, in press.

38 Michael J. Elbert, "Early Termination from Probation," *Perspective* 32 (no. 2, Spring 2008): 54–58.

© AP Images/Danny Moloshok

LEARNING OBJECTIVES

After reading this chapter you should be able to . . .

1 Describe the rationale for nonincarceration penalties.

2 Describe the rationale for intermediate sanctions.

3 Illustrate the continuum-of-sanctions concept.

4 Explain some of the problems associated with intermediate sanctions.

5 List the various types of intermediate sanctions and who administers them.

6 Describe what it takes to make intermediate sanctions work.

7 Assess the role of the new correctional professional.

8 Explain how community corrections legislation works and describe its effectiveness.

9 Critically assess the future of probation, intermediate sanctions, and community corrections.

Singer Chris Brown pled guilty to one count of felony assault against his former girlfriend Rihanna. He received five years of probation, 180 days of community service, and a protective order to stay away from Rihanna.

PRISON IS EXPENSIVE, no doubt about it. Over 60 billion dollars is spent on corrections each year. More than 90 percent of that goes to pay for incarceration, even though more than two-thirds of people under correctional authority are under community supervision. A year behind bars costs 25 to 50 times as much as a year on probation. In many states the correctional budget exceeds the higher-education budget. Years of growth in prison expenditures have often been matched by an equivalent drop in education dollars.

More and more, policy makers look at the prison budget and wonder if there is a less-expensive way to carry out punishments. Especially in times when state-level revenues are tight and governors face the possibility of having to cut popular health and education programs, prison costs come under scrutiny.[1]

Undeniably, prison costs more than probation because it provides total control over a person's life in a way probation cannot. For this reason, people who want to save money by doing something less expensive than prison have been uneasy with probation as the only alternative. As Norval Morris and Michael Tonry have noted, "Prison is used excessively; probation is used even more excessively; between the two is a near vacuum of purposive and enforced punishments."[2]

Intermediate Sanctions and Community Corrections

Chapter

9

Judges know that prison is often too much and probation is, just as often, not enough. For the first-time offender whose crime is neither violent nor unusual, and who has solid links to the community such as a good job, judges generally feel comfortable with a probation term. But the truly first-time, nonviolent felon is unusual. Much more commonly, a felony conviction is not the defendant's first crime. Too often probation or some other sanction has been tried before, and the person has ended up in trouble again.

Just as often the crime is serious enough, of course, but not alarming: The person was caught once again using drugs (or was implicated in another theft, or was caught with an illegal handgun, or got drunk and got in a fight). What good would another term of probation do? What message would it send?

Yet just as clearly, a prison term makes little sense. The 24 months or so of a typical sentence[3] will require $50,000 or more from the taxpayer; this seems expensive in view of the minor costs of the crime itself. Further, people who go to prison do not have better prospects of making it than do people who remain in the community.

There are other considerations. Most defendants have dependents—a spouse and children—and what will happen to them, when the person goes to prison? Increasingly, research shows that children and families suffer many hardships, ranging from financial to psychological, when a loved one goes to prison.[4] One of those hardships costs everyone in the long run: In the United States, children of people who go to prison are more likely than others to end up in trouble with the law and eventually in prison themselves.[5]

And what about the victims? They always seem to want the toughest penalty the law provides, but sending offenders to prison will gain them little. Too many victims leave court feeling alienated from justice, whatever the sentence. Further, they all face the uphill battle of recovering from the emotional and practical costs of crime, a battle the sentence does little to help. At least probationers can be ordered to pay restitution. With probation officers' caseloads exceeding 100, though, what can one realistically expect?

Finally, many types of nonprison sentences seem to lead to lower recidivism rates.[6] Perhaps going to prison makes people less likely to obey the law, or staying in the community makes adjustment to a law-abiding life easier. But if the idea is to help people turn their lives around, in most cases the judge has far better choices than sending them to prison.

For all of these reasons, our society benefits from choices that fall between probation and prison—intermediate sanctions that are more exacting than probation but less costly and with fewer collateral consequences than prison. In this chapter we present and analyze nonprobation programs designed to keep offenders in local community corrections instead of prisons.

■ THE CASE FOR INTERMEDIATE SANCTIONS

Learn about the latest **policy research on community corrections**; go to the corresponding link at www.cengage.com/criminaljustice/clear.

The enormous cost of incarceration is a powerful practical argument for community-based alternatives. But there are other reasons why we need a range of correctional strategies between probation and imprisonment, including: (1) imprisonment is too restrictive for many offenders, (2) traditional probation does not work with most offenders, and (3) justice is well served by having options in between. In the following sections, we explore these arguments in more detail.

Unnecessary Imprisonment

Americans have traditionally tended to equate prison with punishment. When someone is sentenced to something other than prison, many people suspect that the offender "got off"; when an offender receives a short prison sentence, many think he or she "got a break." Yet to treat prison as the primary means of punishment is wrong on two grounds.

First, most sanctions in Western democracies do not involve imprisonment. In the United States, probation is the most common sanction: For every offender in prison or jail, three are on probation or parole. In Europe this is even more evident. Germany, for example, imposes fines as a sole sanction on two-thirds of its property offenders; in England, the figure approaches half. Community service is the preferred sanction for most property offenders in England. Further, Sweden, the Netherlands, France, Austria—and virtually every other European Common Market country—use such

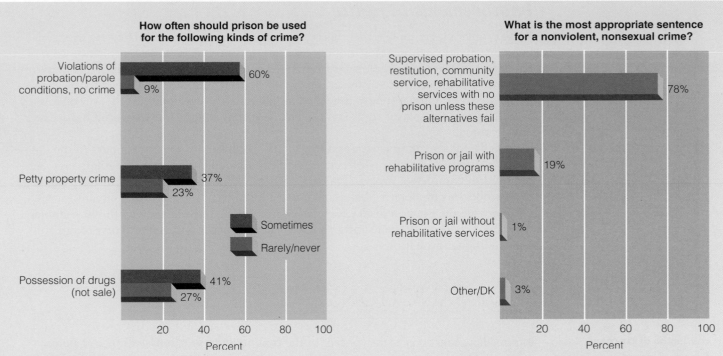

Figure 9.1
Public Opinion about Punishment

Source: Christopher Hartney and Susan Marchionna, "Attitudes of U.S. Voters toward Nonserious Offenders and Alternatives to Incarceration," NCCD *Focus*, June 2009, pp. 1–10.

sanctions far more than incarceration. Because nonprison sanctions are a worldwide phenomenon, it makes little sense to think of them as lack of punishment.

Second, prison is simply not effective in most cases. We expect prison to teach the offender something and deter him or her from a life of crime, but evidence speaks to the contrary. Studies now show that people who go to prison do worse after their release than they would have done under a sentence to a community penalty.[7] Along these lines, public sentiment about nonprison punishment appears to be changing. A recent national survey sponsored by the National Council on Crime and Delinquency found that nonprison punishments are thought to be the sanction of choice for people convicted of nonviolent, nonsexual offenses (see **Figure 9.1**).

If prison is neither the most common nor the most effective sanction, why does it dominate our thinking on punishment? Perhaps it is time to recognize that corrections can and should develop nonincarcerative sanctions that fill the gap between prison and probation.

Visit the website of the **International Community Corrections Association**, listed at www.cengage.com/criminaljustice/clear.

Limitations of Probation

As we said in Chapter 8, probation may not work with serious offenders. Because probation officers handle 100 or more offenders at a time, the average probationer gets maybe 15 minutes of contact per week—hardly meaningful supervision. Further, in many cases this supervision does not really address the offender's problems. The probation officer may check the person's pay stubs and test for drug use. But in the limited time available, little may happen to help the probationer achieve a change in lifestyle.

Intermediate sanctions can improve traditional probation supervision in two ways. First, they can intensify supervision. Second, they can provide specialized programs better suited to address the offender's needs.

Improvements in Justice

Judges sometimes complain that their sentencing choices are limited. They say they confront an offender whose crime does not warrant prison but for whom probation seems inadequate. Developing an array of sanctions between these two extremes lets judges better match the sentence to the crime. Similarly, when an offender breaks probation or parole rules, some response is needed to maintain the credibility of the rules. However, sending the violator to prison for behavior that is not otherwise criminal seems unwarranted.

Finally, intermediate sanctions allow a closer tailoring of the punishment to the offender's situation. For many offenders, a fine is adequate punishment. Others may be required to complete a drug treatment program. Still others can be confined to home for a while. In sum, intermediate sanctions, tailored to fit the offender's circumstances, may provide the greatest justice for many. This may be one reason why public opinion surveys so consistently find support for intermediate sanctions as alternatives to prison and traditional probation.

■ CONTINUUM OF SANCTIONS

continuum of sanctions
A range of correctional management strategies based on the degree of intrusiveness and control over the offender, along which an offender is moved according to his or her response to correctional programs.

Intermediate sanctions fit the concept of the **continuum of sanctions**—a range of punishments that vary in intrusiveness and control, as shown in **Figure 9.2.** Probation plus a fine or community service may be appropriate for minor offenses, whereas six weeks of boot camp followed by intensive probation supervision may be right for serious crimes.

The continuum-of-sanctions concept also incorporates a range of correctional management strategies that vary in intrusiveness and control. Offenders are initially assigned to a level of control, depending on the seriousness of their offense and their prior record. They may then move to a less- or a more-restrictive level, depending on how well they do at each level. For example, a person might start with a 7:00 P.M. curfew, a community service obligation, and mandatory treatment programs on the weekends. If those restrictions are satisfactorily met for six months, the person might have the curfew rescinded.

Many jurisdictions have developed a continuum of sanctions, and its advantages now seem plain. First, it increases the corrections system's flexibility. As jails and prisons become more crowded, selected offenders can be moved to less-restrictive options, such as work release programs. Second, it allows more-responsive management of individual offenders.

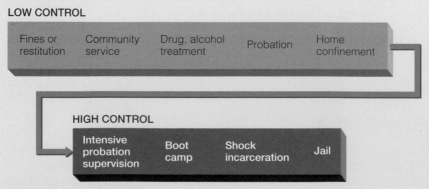

Figure 9.2
Continuum of Sanctions

Judges may use a range of intermediate sanctions, from those exerting a low level of control to those exerting a high level.

Thus, if a person on regular probation is not reporting, a brief home confinement can be followed by a return to probation. Finally, it costs less than other alternatives.

Both state and county agencies can benefit from using a continuum of sanctions. Further, it can be either codified into law or operated as a practice agreed to by the various correctional agencies. For instance, in Maricopa County, Arizona, the combined resources of multiple agencies—the jail, treatment centers, and probation—are used to develop the punishment system along a continuum of sanctions. This meets the same aims as Delaware's sentencing accountability system, but it is neither a part of penal law nor operated by a single state agency.

■ PROBLEMS WITH INTERMEDIATE SANCTIONS

Despite the growing range of available alternatives to incarceration and parole, all is not well with the intermediate sanctions movement. Problems arise in selecting which agencies will operate the process and which offenders receive the sanctions. Further, intermediate sanctions often inappropriately "widen the net."

Selecting Agencies

Administrators of such traditional correctional agencies as jails, prisons, probation, and parole often argue that they should also administer intermediate sanctions. They claim to have the staff and the experience to design new programs for special offender subgroups, and they suggest that to maintain program coherence, they ought to operate all correctional processes. Critics counter that because traditional correctional organizations must give highest priority to traditional operations, they cannot adequately support midrange alternatives. Therefore, new agencies, both public and private, should run intermediate programs. Other critics believe that intermediate sanctions programs will inevitably be controlled by the probation and prison systems—especially because these systems need intermediate sanctions to resolve swollen caseloads and overcrowded facilities.

Selecting Offenders

A second issue has to do with selecting appropriate offenders for alternative programs. One school of thought emphasizes selection by seriousness of offense; the other concentrates on the offender's problems. A focus on the offense usually eliminates some crime categories from consideration. Many argue that violent or drug-marketing offenses are so abhorrent that a nonincarcerative program is not appropriate. Yet these offenders are often best able to adjust to these programs. Moreover, to the degree that these programs are needed to reduce prison overcrowding, they must include some serious offenders.

In practice, both the crime and the criminal are considered. Certain offenses are so serious that the public would not long tolerate intermediate punishments for them (even though there are many instances of successful community-based control of murderers and other serious offenders). At the same time, judges want programs to respond to the needs of the offenders they sentence.

Underlying this issue is the thorny problem of **stakes**. Most of us would be willing to bet $1 on a 1-in-10 chance of winning $10, yet few of us would be willing to bet $1,000 on a 1-in-10 chance of winning $10,000. The odds are the same, but we stand to lose so much more in the second case. Similarly, intermediate sanctions programs often are unwilling to accept offenders convicted of serious crimes, particularly violent crimes, even though the chances of the offenders' successfully completing a program may be quite good. If those offenders commit additional serious crimes, the damage to the community and—through negative publicity—to the corrections system can be substantial. With some offenders the stakes are simply too high, regardless of the amount of risk.

stakes
The potential losses to victims and to the system if offenders fail; stakes include injury from violent crimes and public pressure resulting from negative publicity.

Widening the Net

A third major problem with selecting offenders for intermediate sanctions is *widening the net* (see Chapter 7). In some ways, this problem is potentially the most damaging, because it strikes at the very core of the intermediate sanctions concept. Critics argue that instead of reducing the control exerted over offenders' lives, the new programs actually have increased it. You can readily see how this might occur. With the existence of an alternative at each possible point in the system, the decision maker can select a more-intrusive option than ordinarily would have been imposed. Community service, for instance, can be added to probation; shock incarceration can be added to a straight probation term.

Available evidence reveals that implementing intermediate sanctions has had three consequences:

1 *Wider nets:* The reforms increase the proportion of people in society whose behavior is regulated or controlled by the state.

2 *Stronger nets:* By intensifying the state's intervention powers, the reforms augment the state's capacity to control people.

3 *Different nets:* The reforms create new jurisdictional authority or transfer it from one agency or control system to another.

Learn about the **history of community corrections and intermediate sanctions** by visiting the website of the National Criminal Justice Reference Service, listed at www.cengage.com/criminaljustice/clear.

■ VARIETIES OF INTERMEDIATE SANCTIONS

How the various sanctions programs relate to one another depends on the jurisdiction running them. For example, one county may use intensive supervision in lieu of a jail sentence; another may use it for probation violators. We have organized our description of the main types of intermediate sanctions according to which agencies administer them—the judiciary, probation departments, or correctional departments.

Sanctions Administered by the Judiciary

The demand for intermediate sanctions often comes from judges dissatisfied with their sentencing options. In courts that have managerial authority over probation, this discontent has translated into new probation programs. Other courts have sought to expand their sentencing options by relying more on programs within their control, such as pretrial diversion, forfeiture, fines, community service, and restitution. These programs aim primarily at reducing trial caseloads, especially focusing on less-serious offenders who ought not to tie up the court system. The programs also seek to impose meaningful sanctions without incarceration.

PRETRIAL DIVERSION ■ The functions of pretrial diversion, especially as a jail alternative, were examined in Chapter 7. Because courts have extremely broad discretion in the pretrial phase of adjudication, some have sought to apply this discretion to a greater range of offenders.

Pretrial-diversion programs typically target petty drug offenders. A new strategy in Wayne County (Detroit), Michigan, exemplifies this practice. First-time arrestees for drug possession are "fast-tracked" into drug treatment programs within hours of arrest. They are promised that if they successfully complete the drug treatment program, the charges against them will be dropped. This kind of treatment-based diversion program depends on cooperation between the court and prosecution. Judges indicate their willingness to delay trial if prosecutors are willing to drop charges against less-serious offenders who change their own lives. See "Myths in Corrections" for information on the effectiveness of drug testing.

MYTHS IN CORRECTIONS

DRUG TESTING

THE MYTH: Drug testing for people under community supervision deters them from drug use.

THE REALITY: The rate of drug testing has been found to have no relationship to the amount of a person's drug use.

Source: Rudy Haapanen and Lee Britton, "Drug Testing for Youthful Offenders on Parole: An Experimental Evaluation," *Criminology & Public Policy* 1 (no. 2, 2002): 217–44.

FINES ■ Over $1 billion in fines is collected annually in the United States. Yet, compared with other Western democracies, the United States makes little use of fines as the sole punishment for crimes more serious than motor vehicle violations; nationally about 1 percent of felons receive fines as the sole penalty.[8] Instead, fines typically are used with other sanctions, such as probation and incarceration. For example, it is not unusual for a judge to impose two years' probation and a $500 fine.

Many judges cite the difficulty of enforcing and collecting fines as the reason they do not make greater use of this punishment. They note that offenders tend to be poor, and many judges fear that fines would be paid from the proceeds of additional illegal acts. Other judges are concerned that relying on fines as an alternative to incarceration would let affluent offenders "buy" their way out of jail while forcing the poor to serve time.

In Europe fines are used extensively, are enforced, and are normally the sole sanction for a wide range of crimes. The amounts are geared to both the severity of the offense and the resources of the offender. To deal with the concern that fines exact a heavier toll on the poor than on the wealthy, Sweden and Germany have developed the **day fine**, which bases the penalty on the offender's income. For example, a person making $36,500 a year and sentenced to 10 units of punishment would pay $3,650; a person making $3,650 and receiving the same penalty would pay $365. In the United States the day fine has been tested in five jurisdictions, located in Arizona, Connecticut, Iowa, New York, and Washington.

day fine
A criminal penalty based on the amount of income an offender earns in a day's work.

FORFEITURE ■ With passage of the Racketeer Influenced and Corrupt Organizations Act (RICO) and the Continuing Criminal Enterprise Act (CCE) in 1970, Congress resurrected forfeiture, a criminal sanction that had lain dormant since the American Revolution. Through amendments in 1984 and 1986, Congress improved ways to implement the law, making prosecution easier. Similar laws are now found in several states, particularly with respect to controlled substances and organized crime.

Forfeiture, in which the government seizes property derived from or used in criminal activity, can take both civil and criminal forms. Under civil law, property used in criminal activity (for example, automobiles, boats, or equipment used to manufacture illegal drugs) can be seized without a finding of guilt. Under criminal law, forfeiture is imposed as a consequence of conviction and requires that the offender relinquish various assets related to the crime. These assets can be considerable. For example, in 1990, state and federal officials confiscated $1 billion worth of assets from drug dealers.

However, forfeiture is controversial. Critics argue that confiscating property without a court hearing violates citizens' constitutional rights. In 1993 the U.S. Supreme Court restricted the use of summary forfeiture. Now the use of this form of sanction has waned.[9]

forfeiture
Government seizure of property and other assets derived from or used in criminal activity.

COMMUNITY SERVICE AND RESTITUTION ■ Although for years judges have imposed community service and restitution, few judges have used them as exclusive sanctions. Recently, with prisons overcrowded and judges searching for efficient sentencing options, interest in these sanctions has increased.

Community service requires the offender to provide a specified number of hours of free labor in some public service, such as street cleaning, repair of run-down housing, or hospital volunteer work. **Restitution** is compensation for financial, physical, or emotional loss caused by an offender, in the form of either payment of money to the victim or to a public fund for crime victims.

Both alternatives rest on the assumption that the offender can atone for his or her offense with a personal or financial contribution to the victim or to society. They have been called *reparative alternatives,* because they seek to repair some of the harm done. Such approaches have become popular because they force the offender to make a positive contribution to offset the damage, thus satisfying a common public desire that offenders not "get away" with their crimes.

The effectiveness of these programs is mixed. Studies have found that, without such programs, many—perhaps most—of the offenders who were ordered to provide community service and restitution would have been punished with a traditional probation sentence. This bodes poorly for community service as a real solution for correctional crowding. Nor have community service and restitution programs proved especially

community service
Compensation for injury to society, by the performance of service in the community.

restitution
Compensation for financial, physical, or emotional loss caused by an offender, in the form of either payment of money to the victim or to a public fund for crime victims, as stipulated by the court.

Ivy Supersonic, a member of Howard Stern's "wack pack," performs community service after pleading guilty to harassment and identity theft.

© Bryan Smith/ZUMA Press

effective at reducing the criminal behavior of their participants; in fact, they seem to have somewhat higher failure rates than do the regular supervision cases.[10] Yet offenders subjected to restitution experience it as both punitive and rehabilitative. And community service cases may end up having lower rearrest rates than would be expected if they had been sentenced differently.

In sum, community service and restitution show that simply implementing a so-called alternative does not always achieve the aims of intermediate sanctions. In order not to widen the net, careful attention must be paid to selecting appropriate offenders. And judicial decision making must be controlled to ensure that people who enter the programs are those who otherwise would have been incarcerated.

Sanctions Administered by Probation Departments

One basic argument for intermediate sanctions is that probation, as traditionally practiced, is inadequate for large numbers of offenders. Probation leaders have responded to this criticism by developing new intermediate sanctions programs and expanding old ones. New programs often rely on increased surveillance and control. Old programs often are revamped to become more efficient and expanded to fit more probationers.

DAY REPORTING (TREATMENT) CENTERS ■ Fairly recently, as prisons became more and more crowded, judges grew reluctant to incarcerate probation violators except when the violation involved a new crime. As a result, probationers in some jurisdictions came to realize that they could disregard probation rules with relative impunity. Probation administrators found that the lack of credibility with clients severely hampered their effectiveness.

The solution seemed to be the development of probation-run enforcement programs. For example, Georgia has experimented with **probation centers**, where persistent probation violators reside for short periods. Massachusetts and New York City have instituted *day reporting centers*, where violators attend daylong intervention and treatment sessions (see Chapter 7). Minnesota and other states have established **restitution centers**, where those who fall behind in restitution are sent to make payments on their debt. These centers have been found to reduce the amount of jail time clients end up serving and reduce their recidivism rates.[11]

All of these types of centers are modeled after an innovation developed in Great Britain in the 1970s. In the United States, these facilities vary widely, but all provide a credible option for probation agencies to enforce conditions when prisons are overcrowded. All of them, regardless of specific type, are usually referred to as day reporting centers. Most day reporting centers use a mix of common correctional methods. For example, some provide a treatment regime comparable to that of a halfway house—but without the problems of running a residential facility. Others provide contact levels equal to or greater than intensive supervision programs, in effect creating a community equivalent to confinement.

So far there are few evaluations of these programs. Initial studies suggest that day reporting does not result in lower rearrest rates than do other intensive supervision methods.[12] One problem common to newly established intermediate sanctions programs is that stringent eligibility requirements result in small numbers of cases entering the program. But some evidence is promising: Evaluations of jail-run day reporting centers find that program participants have lower levels of drug use and absconding, but because participants were carefully screened before acceptance, applicability may be limited to low-risk cases.[13]

Day reporting centers are growing in popularity faster than evidence concerning their effectiveness is appearing, with hundreds of programs now operating in more than half of the states. The real test of these programs will involve two issues: (1) how much do they improve probation's credibility as a sanction and (2) how well do they combat jail and prison crowding? These questions remain unanswered.

INTENSIVE SUPERVISION ■ **Intensive supervision probation (ISP)** has sprung up around the country, and it seems ideally suited to the pressures facing corrections. Because ISP targets offenders who are subject to incarceration, they should help alleviate crowding; because they involve strict supervision, they respond to community pressures to control offenders.

What constitutes intensive supervision? Even the most ambitious programs require only daily meetings between officers and offenders. Such meetings, which might last 10 minutes or less, can never occupy more than a minuscule portion of the offender's waking hours. So, no matter how intensive the supervision, substantial trust must still be placed in the probationer.

Early evaluations of ISP programs in Georgia, New York, and Texas found that intensive supervision can reduce rearrest rates. Nevertheless, these programs were not received without controversy. For one thing, the low number of rearrests came at a cost. All evaluations of intensive supervision found that, probably because of the closer contact, probation officers uncovered more rules violations than they did in regular probation.

Read about **community service programs**; see the corresponding link at www.cengage.com/criminaljustice/clear.

probation center
Residential facility where persistent probation violators are sent for short periods.

restitution center
Facility where probationers who fall behind in restitution are sent to make payments on their debt.

intensive supervision probation (ISP)
Probation granted under conditions of strict reporting to a probation officer with a limited caseload.

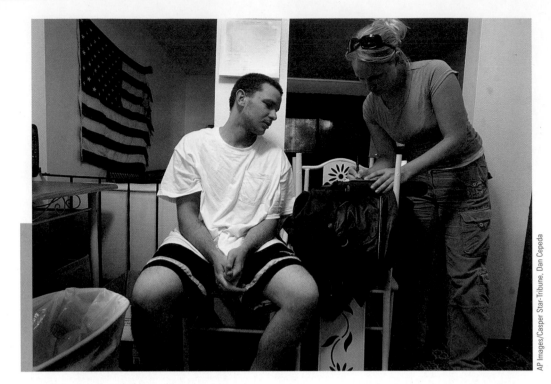

Intensive supervision probation (ISP) requires offenders to live in the community under strict conditions of reporting. Probation officer Bridget Wiggins fills out a report on Kyle Allison during a visit in Casper, Wyoming.

AP Images/Casper Star-Tribune, Dan Cepeda

Therefore, ISP programs often had higher technical failure rates than did regular probation, even though ISP clients had fewer arrests.

This was precisely what researchers found in a series of important experiments testing ISP effectiveness. Offenders in California were randomly assigned to either ISP or regular probation. Results indicated no differences in overall rearrest rates but substantial differences in probation failure rates. ISP clients did much worse under the stricter rules—possibly because ISP makes detecting rules violations easier.[14] In sum, these programs not only failed to reduce crime but actually cost the public more than if the programs had not been started in the first place.

Despite questions about the effectiveness of ISP, the approach has enjoyed wide support from correctional administrators, judges, and even prosecutors. The close supervision has revitalized the reputation of probation in the criminal justice system. It has also demonstrated probation's ability to enforce strict rules, ensure employment, support treatment programs, and so forth. Given the positive public relations, ISP is likely here to stay.

Although intensive supervision may satisfy public demands for control measures, probationers continue to need various forms of assistance. Many offenders face serious personal problems—unemployment, emotional and family crises, substance abuse—that require service or treatment. Therefore, officers still have to juggle the roles of helper and controller. On paper the conflicts between these roles in ISP programs may seem less extreme, but in practice they may well continue and perhaps be exacerbated by the mixed messages of the programs.

home confinement

Sentence whereby offenders serve terms of incarceration in their own homes.

HOME CONFINEMENT ■ Under **home confinement**, offenders are sentenced to incarceration but serve those terms in their own homes. Variations are possible. For instance, after a time some offenders might be allowed to go to work or simply leave home for restricted periods during the day; others might be allowed to maintain employment for their entire sentence. Whatever the details, the concept revolves around using the offender's residence as the place of punishment.

On the surface, the idea of home confinement is appealing. It costs the state nothing to house the offender; the offender pays for lodging, subsistence, and often even the cost of an electronic monitor. More importantly, significant community ties can be maintained—to family, friends (restricted visitation is ordinarily allowed), employers, and community groups. The punishment is more visible to the community than if the offender were sent to prison. The goals of reintegration, deterrence, and financial

AP Images/Chris O'Meara

In Tampa, Florida, Circuit Judge Wayne Timmerman presides over the sentencing of former middle school teacher Debra Lafave, who pleaded guilty to having sex with a 14-year-old student. She was sentenced to three years of home confinement and seven years of probation.

responsibility are served simultaneously. When people know a little bit about home confinement, they tend to favor it for many kind of crimes. In one study, for example, a college class learned that home confinement can be experienced as quite punitive when they experienced a daylong house restriction as a class assignment.[15]

Evaluations of home confinement provide a few impressions of how the program works. Anecdotal evidence suggests that the effectiveness of home confinement seems to wear off after a few months; it is increasingly difficult to enforce detention conditions as the sentence rounds into its second half-year. The program seems best suited to low-risk offenders who have relatively stable residences.

ELECTRONIC MONITORING ■ One of the most popular new approaches to probation supervision is surveillance by electronic monitors. Electronic monitoring is ordinarily combined with and used to enforce home confinement. The number of offenders currently being monitored is difficult to estimate, because the equipment manufacturers consider this to be privileged information. However, the best estimates are that about 20 different companies provide electronic monitoring for more then 100,000 offenders.[16] Only about 11,500 of them, however, are on these programs having been sentenced to, and then diverted from, a jail sentence.[17] For the rest, electronic monitoring is a condition of a probation sentence.

Two basic types of electronic-monitoring devices exist. Passive monitors respond only to inquiries; most commonly the offender receives an automated telephone call from the probation office and is told to place the device on a receiver attached to the phone. Active devices send continuous signals that are picked up by a receiver; a computer notes any break in the signal.

Advocates of these systems point out that they are cheaper than incarceration (especially because the offender often pays to use the system) and tougher than probation. Yet even if most of the 11,500 people under electronic monitoring as a condition of a jail sentence have been truly diverted from confinement, that is less than 2 percent of the total jail population. Nonetheless, these systems are also more humane than prison or jail, because offenders keep their jobs and stay with their families. In addition, probation officers are free to spend more time addressing the offenders' needs rather than providing surveillance. Florida's community control offenders may have somewhat lower rearrest rates than do similar offenders sentenced to jail, and this large program of electronic monitoring is believed to save the state of Florida a considerable amount of money.[18] On the other hand, a study of a Kentucky program found that 69 percent

Read a series of **studies of intensive supervision** using the corresponding link at www.cengage.com/ criminaljustice/clear.

of offenders put on electronic monitoring had a new arrest within five years,[19] and another study of electronic monitoring for violent offenders found that it had no effect on success rates of parolees.[20]

Some observers point out that only offenders who own telephones and can afford the $25–$100 per week these systems cost to rent are eligible. In addition, confinement to the home is no guarantee that crimes will not occur. Many crimes—child abuse, drug sales, and assaults, to name a few—commonly occur in offenders' residences.

Moreover, the reliability of these devices has recently become an issue. Some offenders have figured out how to remove the monitors without detection; others have been arrested at the scene of a crime—even though the monitoring system indicated they were safely at home. They can also intrude on the privacy of the family and be unduly stressful for the offender and his or her family.

Despite these drawbacks, the use of electronic monitoring likely will continue to increase, along with technological advances. Recently, Global Positioning Systems, which use satellite tracking devices to monitor offenders' whereabouts, have become more feasible. These new approaches provide 24-hour verification of an offender's exact location.[21] (See Chapter 21 for a description.)

Sanctions Administered by Correctional Departments

Correctional agencies have had to develop intermediate sanctions to manage the burgeoning load of offenders. Some correctional agencies rely on electronic monitoring to support an early-release program, but shock incarceration and boot camps are the two most common responses to overcrowding.

shock incarceration
A short period of incarceration (the "shock"), followed by a sentence reduction.

SHOCK INCARCERATION ■ The fact that the deterrent effect of incarceration wears off after a very short term of imprisonment has led to experimentation with **shock incarceration**. The offender is sentenced to a jail or prison term; then, after the offender has served 30 to 90 days, the judge reduces the sentence. The assumption is that the offender will find the jail experience so distasteful that he or she will be motivated to "stay clean."

Shock incarceration is controversial. Its critics argue that it combines the undesirable aspects of both probation and imprisonment. Offenders who are incarcerated lose their jobs, have their community relationships disrupted, acquire the label of convict, and are exposed to the brutalizing experiences of the institution. Further, the release to probation reinforces the idea that the system is arbitrary in decision making and that probation is a "break" rather than a truly individualized supervision program. It is hard to see how such treatment will not demean and embitter offenders. Many studies of shock incarceration showed no improvement in recidivism rates. Nonetheless, interest has remained high, leading to a new form of the shock technique called boot camp.

boot camp
A physically rigorous, disciplined, and demanding regimen emphasizing conditioning, education, and job training. Designed for young offenders.

BOOT CAMP ■ One variation on shock incarceration is the **boot camp**, in which offenders serve a short institutional sentence and then go through a rigorous, paramilitary regimen designed to develop discipline and respect for authority. The daily routine includes strenuous workouts, marches, drills, and hard physical labor.

Proponents of boot camp argue that many young offenders get involved in crime because they lack self-respect and cannot order their lives. Consequently, the boot camp model targets young first offenders who seem to be embarking on a path of sustained criminality. Evaluations show that young offenders given boot camp may improve in self-esteem. But critics argue that military-style physical training and the harshness of the experience do little to overcome problems that get inner-city youths in trouble with the law. In fact, follow-ups of boot camp graduates show they do no better than other offenders after release.[22] This ineffectiveness has led several authorities to close down their boot camps. Even more troubling are the recent charges of fatal physical abuse which, in Florida, have led to the closing of all boot camps in the state (see the Focus box "Teenager's Death Leads Florida to Close Boot Camp").[23]

Military-type drilling and physical workouts are part of the regimen at most boot camps, including this one in Pendleton, California. Evaluations of boot camps have reduced the initial optimism about this approach. Boot camps have been closed in many states.

FOCUS ON
CORRECTIONAL PRACTICE

Teenager's Death Leads Florida to Close Boot Camp

Seven former guards at Bay County juvenile boot camp and a nurse were charged with aggravated manslaughter in the death of 14-year-old who died on January 6, 2006, while in custody at the camp.

Martin Lee Anderson, who entered the Bay County Sheriff's Office Boot Camp January 5 because of a probation violation, complained of breathing difficulties and collapsed while doing push-ups, sit-ups and other exercises. He died after midnight the next day at a Pensacola hospital.

A staff report prepared later explained that Anderson had resisted repeated attempts to get him to complete the exercises. The Bay County Sheriff's Office said he was restrained for being "uncooperative."

In the initial autopsy, Bay County Medical Examiner Dr. Charles Siebert said Anderson suffered internal bleeding because he had the sickle cell trait that led to hemorrhaging.

"It was a natural death," he said.

However, Anderson's parents, Gina Jones and Robert Anderson, contested the autopsy, alleging that their son was beaten to death by guards at the boot camp.

After a videotape surfaced showing guards hitting and kneeing Anderson at the military-style facility while he was being restrained, they had the boy's body exhumed. On a silent, grainy, 80-minute videotape of the teen's entry process, staffers were shown hitting Anderson from behind and using various takedown methods against him. Near the end of the confrontation, guards appeared to become more concerned, and several ran in and out of the scene. A few minutes later, emergency medical personnel took him away on a gurney.

A second autopsy conducted by Dr. Vernard Adams determined that Anderson had died by suffocation at the hands of sheriff's officials who had shoved ammonia capsules up the boy's nose, blocked the boy's mouth, and forced him to inhale the ammonia that caused his vocal cords to spasm, blocking his airway.

In an incident report, the guards said they had used the capsules five times on Anderson in order to get his cooperation.

The family sued the Department of Juvenile Justice and the Bay County Sheriff's office for $40 million, and the suit was eventually settled for $4.8 million.

The camp has been closed.

Sources: Adapted from "Eight Charged with Manslaughter in Florida Boot Camp Death," *North County Gazette*, November 28, 2006, http://www.northcountrygazette.org; "Teen's Death at Florida Boot Camp Reported Not of Natural Causes; Parents Seek Justice," *Jet*, April 3, 2006.

Studies show that only boot camps that are carefully designed, target the right of-fenders, and give them rehabilitative services are likely to save money and reduce re-cidivism.[24] Too many boot camps overemphasize discipline, to the detriment of the graduates. In fact, in Maricopa County, a special group had to be set up for boot camp graduates because their failure rates were so high after leaving the program.

Do boot camps work? There is no firm answer, but results to date have not been promising. Perhaps job training and education would be more beneficial than physical training. The intentionally harsh tactics of boot camp are brutal, especially for impres-sionable young offenders, and even when they are combined with a heavy emphasis on rehabilitation programming, they appear to fail to reduce rearrest rates.[25] Neverthe-less, the approach has proved popular with a public that is searching for new ways to handle offenders.

■ MAKING INTERMEDIATE SANCTIONS WORK

Intermediate sanctions have not been used long enough to allow a complete evalua-tion of their effectiveness. Only a few of the hundreds of programs attempted since the mid-1980s have been studied. Summaries of the value of intermediate sanctions note frequent failures to achieve goals, but that certainly does not mean the idea should be abandoned.

One evaluation problem is that intermediate sanctions often profess lofty goals such as improving justice, saving money, and preventing crime. Yet the limited record on intermediate sanctions suggests that these goals are not always accomplished. If inter-mediate sanctions are to work, they must be carefully planned and implemented. Even then they must overcome obstacles and resolve such issues as sentencing philosophies and practices, offender selection criteria, and surveillance and control methods.

Sentencing Issues

The most important issue concerning the use of intermediate sanctions has to do with sentencing philosophy and practice. In recent years, greater emphasis has been placed on deserved punishment: the idea that similar offenses deserve penalties of similar se-verity. Intermediate sanctions could potentially increase the number of midrange pun-ishments and thereby improve justice.

Yet advocates of deserved punishment argue that it is not automatically evident how intermediate sanctions compare with either prison or probation in terms of severity, nor is it clear how they compare with one another. For example, placing one offender on intensive probation while ordering another to pay a heavy fine may violate the equal punishment rationale of just deserts.

When intermediate sanctions are used to reduce prison crowding, the issue becomes even murkier. For example, is it fair for some offenders to receive prison terms while others receive the intermediate sanction alternative?

principle of interchangeability
The idea that different forms of intermediate sanctions can be calibrated to make them equivalent as punishments despite their differences in approach.

For intermediate sanctions to be effective, exchange rates consistent with the **principle of interchangeability** must be developed so that one form can be substituted for or added to another form. In other words, different forms of intermediate sanctions must be cali-brated to make them equivalent as punishments despite their differences in approach. For example, two weeks of jail might be considered equal to 30 days of intermittent confine-ment or two months of home confinement or 100 hours of community service or one month's salary. (See **Table 9.1** for a reminder from Chapter 7 of how many offenders serve various intermediate sanctions as an alternative to jail.)

Advocates say that, in terms of intrusiveness, a short prison sentence can be roughly equivalent to some intensive supervision programs or residential drug treatment and that various forms of intermediate sanctions can be made roughly equivalent to one another. It is clear, both from studies and from experience, that some offenders would rather be in prison than be placed on tough intermediate sanctions. Thus, one can

TABLE 9.1 *Persons under Jail Supervision Assigned to Intermediate Sanctions*

Of the 820,000 people who are under some form of jail supervision, more than one in 12 are in an intermediate sanction program.	
Intermediate Sanction Program	**Number**
Weekender programs	12,325
Electronic monitoring	13,539
Home detention	498
Day reporting	5,758
Community service	18,475
Other pretrial supervision	12,452
Other work programs	5,808
Treatment programs	2,259
Other	1,739
Total	72,853

Source: Bureau of Justice Statistics, *Statistical Tables*, March 2009, p. 8.

Read about how Ohio has tried to reorganize **community-based correctional incentives** at the corresponding link at www.cengage.com/criminaljustice/clear.

design intermediate sanctions that equal incarceration in terms of intrusion, thereby upholding the principles of deserved punishment.

Yet these studies are troubling in that they find substantial differences across racial groups in the preference for prison over intermediate sanctions. For example, African Americans and Hispanics are more likely than whites to rate prison as preferable to the intermediate sanction. This raises a concern that widespread adoption of intermediate sanctions may further exacerbate racial disparities in prison populations.

In practice some observers have tried to structure this principle of interchangeability by describing punishment in terms of units: A month in prison might count as 30 units; a month on intensive supervision might count as 10. Thus, a year on ISP would be about the same as a four-month prison stay. To date, no one has designed a full-blown system of interchangeability, though both the federal sentencing guidelines and those in Oregon embrace the concept of punishment units. The future will likely bring attempts to create interchangeability based on equivalence of punishments.

Selection of Offenders

If intermediate sanctions are to work, they must be reserved for appropriate offenders; which offenders are chosen, in turn, depends on a program's goals. No matter the program's goals, however, intermediate sanctions must be made available regardless of race, sex, or age.

THE TARGET GROUP ■ Intermediate sanctions have two general goals: (1) to serve as a less-costly alternative to prison and (2) to provide a more-effective alternative to probation. To meet these goals, intermediate sanctions managers search for appropriate offenders to include in their program—often a difficult task. Yet there are plenty of prison-bound offenders who seem appropriate candidates for intermediate sanctions: One study of offenders entering California prisons found that as many as one-fourth would have been suitable for intermediate sanctions.[26]

Because of judges' reluctance to divert offenders from prison, many intermediate sanctions programs billed as prison alternatives actually serve as probation alternatives. As an example, consider boot camp programs, which are usually restricted to first-time

© AP Images/Dee Marvin

Which offenders should be selected for intermediate sanctions rather than prison? Some research shows that, in fact, many offenders would have received probation, rather than incarceration, if the intermediate sanction had not been available. Do intermediate sanctions mainly widen the net?

property offenders aged 16 to 25. Boot camp, then, cannot be considered an effective prison alternative, because young, first-time property offenders seldom go to prison.

Probation alternatives (often called probation enhancements) face a similar problem. Theoretically they should be restricted to the highest-risk offenders on probation—those needing the most surveillance and control. Typically, however, the conservatism inherent in new programs makes the truly high-risk cases ineligible for the program.

Clearly, when intermediate sanctions are applied to the wrong target group, they cannot achieve their goals. When prison alternatives are applied to nonprison cases, they cannot save money. When probation-enhancement programs are provided to low-risk clients, they cannot reduce much crime.

One possible solution is to use intermediate sanctions as backups for clients who fail on regular probation or parole. This practice would increase the probability that the target group was composed of high-risk, prison-bound offenders.

PROBLEMS OF BIAS ■ Race, sex, and age bias are of particular concern for intermediate sanctions. Because getting sentenced to an intermediate sanction involves official (usually judicial) discretion, the concern is that white, middle-class offenders will receive less-harsh treatment than will other groups. In fact, unless program administrators work hard to widen their program's applicability, nonwhites will be most likely to remain incarcerated rather than receive alternative sanctions, and minorities may be more likely to face tougher supervision instead of regular probation.

Alternative sanctions also tend to be designed for men, not women. One could argue that this is reasonable because men make up over 80 percent of the correctional population, but the patently unfair result may be that special programs are available *only* to men. Moreover, some experts on female offenders challenge the design of intermediate sanctions, which is often based on tough supervision. They argue that measures for many women offenders should instead emphasize social services.

Solutions to the problem of bias are neither obvious nor uncontroversial. Most observers recognize that some discretion is necessary in placing offenders in specialized programs. They believe that, without the confidence of program officials, offenders are likely to fail. This means that automatic eligibility for these programs may not be a good idea. It may be necessary to recognize the potential for bias and to control it by designing programs especially for women, for example, making certain that cultural factors are taken into account in selecting offenders for them.

Surveillance and Control

Intermediate sanctions have, for the most part, been developed during a period in which correctional policy has been enmeshed in the politics of "getting tough on crime." Not surprisingly, most of these alternatives tend to emphasize their toughness. Boot camps are described as providing no-nonsense discipline; intensive supervision expressly incorporates surveillance and control as primary strategies. Certainly this rhetoric is useful in obtaining public support for the programs. But do the programs themselves benefit from being so unabashedly tough?

Growing evidence indicates that the tough aspects of intermediate sanctions may not be totally positive. As we have seen, when both the requirements of supervision and the surveillance of offenders increase, more violations are detected and more probationers face revocation of probation. However, if "being tough"—upgrading standards and their enforcement—has no impact on crime, but instead merely costs more money (through the need to process more violators), where is the benefit? For example, in California over half of all prison admissions are probation or parole violators, many of whom have not been accused of a new crime.[27] Some people wonder whether the costs of stricter measures outweigh the benefits.

■ THE NEW CORRECTIONAL PROFESSIONAL

Without a doubt, the advent of intermediate sanctions has changed the work world of the professional in corrections. The long-standing choice between prison and probation now includes community and residential options that run the gamut from tough, surveillance-oriented operations to supportive, treatment-based programs. The kinds of professionals needed to staff these programs vary from recent college graduates to experienced and well-trained mental health clinicians. Central to this growth, however, are three major shifts in the working environment of the new correctional professional.

First, nongovernment organizations have emerged to administer community corrections programs. Hundreds of nonprofit agencies, such as CASES, now dot the correctional landscape (see the Focus box). These organizations contract with probation and parole agencies to provide services to clients in the community.

FOCUS ON

CORRECTIONAL PRACTICE

CASES: Center for Alternative Sentencing and Employment Services

CASES, or the Center for Alternative Sentencing and Employment Services, is a nonprofit "alternative to incarceration" agency operating in New York City. Its mission is "to increase the understanding and use of community sanctions that are fair, affordable, and consistent with public safety."

CASES was established in 1989 to serve as a home for the Court Employment Project (CEP) and the Community Service Sentencing Project (CSSP), both originally developed by the Vera Institute of Justice. CEP is a diversion program for prison-bound young offenders that provides them with job skills and then places them into entry-level jobs. CSSP is a work program, operating from 9:00 A.M. to 4:30 P.M., Monday through Friday, that provides a way for serious misdemeanants to perform community service instead of going to jail. From these two programs, CASES services have grown to include nine special programs for youthful offenders, four alternative programs for adult offenders, four

special programs targeting mental health, and a new program to prevent parole revocation. With a staff of 180 and an annual budget of $12 million, CASES provides services and supervision for almost 14,000 offenders a year. A new CASES budget comes mostly from contracts with the court system of the city of New York, though it also receives grants from state and federal agencies. The contracts have performance benchmarks that tie the amount of the contract to successful program outcomes.

Studies of CASES programs have confirmed that these programs work and that CASES contracts save the city of New York money. This innovative approach to alternatives to incarceration has won numerous awards, including the Significant Achievement Award from the American Psychiatric Association for the Nathaniel Project, a community-based alternative for mentally ill offenders.

For more information on **CASES and the Nathaniel Project**, see the corresponding link at www.cengage.com/criminaljustice/clear.

To see how a study of one state's **intermediate sanctions strategies** led to important changes in policy, go to the corresponding link at www.cengage.com/criminaljustice/clear.

Second, an increased emphasis on accountability has reduced individual discretion. Professionals currently work within boundaries, often defined as guidelines, that specify policy options in different case types. For instance, a staff member may be told that each offender must be seen twice a month in the office and once a month in the community and that each time a urine sample must be taken. Rules such as these not only constrain discretion but also provide a basis for holding staff accountable.

Third, the relationship between the professional and the client has become less important than the principles of criminal justice that underlie that relationship. Instead of training in psychology and counseling, for instance, the new correctional professional receives training in law and criminal justice decision making. This means that the sources of job satisfaction have shifted from helping offenders with their problems toward simply shepherding offenders through the system.

Thus, the new correctional professional is more accountable for decision making and is more oriented toward the system in carrying out agency policy. This has significant implications for the motivation and training of staff, but it also means that, in the traditional three-way balance among offender, staff, and bureaucracy, the last has grown in importance. (See "Careers in Corrections" to learn about one type of correctional professional: addiction treatment specialists.)

CAREERS IN CORRECTIONS Addiction Treatment Specialist

NATURE OF THE WORK

Drug and alcohol abuse is a major problem that is often linked to criminal behavior. Correctional addiction treatment specialists, also known as clinical social workers or addiction counselors, may work with offenders either in prisons or in community health organizations. Offenders are usually referred to treatment by the courts or by probation, prison, or parole authorities. Addiction treatment is a major component of community corrections.

Addiction treatment specialists assess and treat individuals with substance problems, including abuse of alcohol or drugs. They develop treatment plans by examining an offender's institutional files and gathering information from family members and other counselors. Treatment is through individual and group therapy in either outpatient or residential settings. Twelve-step programs are often incorporated into the treatment regimen.

REQUIRED QUALIFICATIONS

A bachelor's degree in social work plus training in addiction therapies are normally the minimal requirements for entry into this position. Some states require a master's degree, certification in addiction treatment, and supervised work experience.

EARNINGS AND JOB OUTLOOK

The Bureau of Labor Statistics expects that the demand for treatment specialists will grow rapidly over the next decade, because substance abusers are increasingly being placed into community treatment programs instead of being sent to prison. The median annual salary for an addition treatment specialist was $32,500 in 2002, with the lowest 10 percent earning less than $22,000.

MORE INFORMATION

You can obtain additional information about this occupation from the website of the U.S. Department of Labor's *Occupational Outlook Handbook* or on the website of the **National Association of Social Workers**; both are listed at www.cengage.com/criminaljustice/clear.

■ COMMUNITY CORRECTIONS LEGISLATION

Most correctional clients in the United States are under state or county authority. Corrections systems located only a few miles apart can vary dramatically in philosophy and practice because of differences in community values, interests, and politics. In most states, judges, prosecutors, and sheriffs are elected by voters in each county. These officials have extensive discretion concerning the disposition of offenders. Their decisions often reflect the political and social realities of their community. For instance, a person who crosses the border from Utah to Nevada goes from a state with one of the lowest incarceration rates in the United States to a state with one of the highest, even though their crime rates are nearly identical.

The differences in the style and philosophy of correctional programs in different localities reflect a basic truth about law and order: Beliefs about right and wrong, as well as values about how to deal with wrongdoers, differ from one locality to the next. Over the years the concept of community corrections has revolved around many themes, but one core idea has endured—that local governments know best how to deal with their own crime problems. As such, local and state laws reflect unique ways of implementing community corrections, even though they share similar goals. As we will see in the following discussions, the implementation and evaluation of community corrections must take local differences into account.

Reducing Reliance on Prison

Community corrections legislation is best understood in terms of its goal to reduce reliance on prisons. In pursuit of this goal, it embraces a wide spectrum of alternatives to incarceration among which judges and other criminal justice system officials can choose.

In the late 1960s and early 1970s, several states considered legislation that would establish financial and programmatic incentives for community corrections. For example, in 1965 California passed the Probation Subsidy Act, which sought to reimburse counties for maintaining offenders in the local corrections system instead of sending them to state facilities. Lawmakers developed a formula to determine the number of offenders who ordinarily would be sent to state institutions and to pay the counties a specified sum for each offender not sent to prison. The counties could then use the money to strengthen probation and other local correctional services in order to handle the additional offenders.

In 1973 Minnesota passed the first Comprehensive Community Corrections Act, which funded local corrections systems with money saved by state corrections when individuals were not sentenced to state facilities. Colorado in 1976 and Oregon in 1978 passed legislation patterned after Minnesota's law. The experiences of these pioneering states in community corrections was so well regarded that by 1995 more than half of U.S. states had passed community corrections legislation. By 2007 the vast majority of states had done so, as shown in **Figure 9.3**.

Community corrections legislation is based on the idea that local justice systems have little incentive to keep their own offenders in local corrections. State-administered institutions are funded by state tax revenues, and it costs communities little to send large numbers of offenders there. In contrast, it costs local citizens much more to keep offenders in jail or on local probation, because their taxes pay for those services.

Yet incarceration in a state prison costs substantially more than local incarceration or probation (see **Table 9.2**). In the long run, centralized, state-administered punishments seem to be more expensive than local corrections. If we also acknowledge that many offenders are sentenced to state prison when this extreme punishment is not necessary, we can easily see that the financial incentives that favor imprisonment run contrary to good correctional policy.

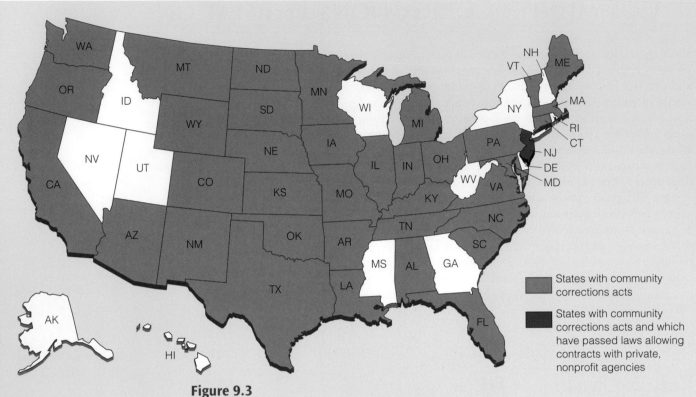

Figure 9.3
States with Community Corrections Acts

Many states provide financial incentives for local governments to keep offenders in local correctional agencies instead of sending them to state prisons.

Source: Mary Shilton, "Community Corrections Acts by State," 2007, http://centerforcommunitycorrections.org/?page_id=78, September 24, 2009.

TABLE 9.2 *Costs of Incarceration and Intermediate Sanctions in Four States*

In a study of Colorado, North Carolina, Ohio, and Virginia, intermediate sanctions proved far less expensive than imprisonment.	
Correctional Method	**Cost per Year per Offender**
Prison	$24,911
Jail	17,491
Probation	1,217
Intensive supervision	3,208
Community service	3,862
Day reporting	3,893
House arrest	563
Electronic monitoring	2,815
Halfway house	17,491
Boot camp	33,190

Source: Based on data from *Seeking Justice: Crime and Punishment in America* (New York: Edna McConnell Clark Foundation, 1997), 34. Adjusted for inflation by the authors.

The payback system must establish some formula for determining baseline prison commitment rates—that is, what number of offenders would normally be expected to be sent to prison. Sending fewer to prison would qualify for payback funds. Further, this formula must be applied to all the state's jurisdictions. This idea has problems, of course. Local corrections systems do not contribute equally to overincarceration of offenders; for example, urban and rural areas are bound to contribute differently. The funding formula, then, is likely to result in some serious inequities. For instance, California's formula did not adjust for counties that traditionally had restricted their use of incarceration; as a consequence, subsidies given to "progressive" counties were unlikely to be equal to those given to more "conservative" ones. Then California's original 1965 rate of payback ($4,000 per offender) was not adjusted for inflation, and by 1975 this amount was worth less than $2,500 per offender. In contrast, Minnesota's formula included an inflation factor and permitted adjustments for a locality's crime rate and the capacity of its corrections system. Even so, the formula was criticized for providing lesser financial incentives to cities, which had more offenders and correspondingly larger corrections systems.

Evaluation of Community Corrections Legislation

The main thrust of community corrections legislation—to limit dependence on prison—comprises three aims:

1 To reduce the rate and number of people sentenced to state correctional facilities

2 To reduce tax revenues spent on corrections by transferring both the costs and the funding to less-expensive local correctional facilities

3 To reduce prison populations

Have these aims been achieved? The answer is complicated.

Several evaluations of California's Probation Subsidy Act have been made. All agree on one point: The availability of probation subsidies resulted in several local policy shifts and local compensatory decisions. Adult and juvenile commitments to state facilities decreased immediately following the enactment of the probation subsidy. These early findings led supporters of the subsidy to conclude that it was extremely effective at reducing commitments.

Closer inspection showed that, in the local justice systems, the general intrusiveness of corrections increased for both adult and juvenile offenders. More were given jail terms, and more received tighter control through commitment to local drug treatment and mental health facilities. Thus, the overall effect of the subsidy was primarily to transfer the incarceration of offenders from state-funded prisons to state-subsidized local corrections—hardly a resounding victory for community corrections.

The community corrections movement has had limited impact on prison populations in most states that have enacted such legislation. Generally, their prisons remain crowded. Parole decisions appear to have become more conservative in California and Minnesota, thus counterbalancing the modest reduction in commitments achieved by community corrections legislation. Thus, some critics have argued that the movement toward community corrections is little but a surface shift in policies that emphasize incarceration, and the talk of community corrections reform enables the corrections field to continue its costly practices while creating an image of fiscal responsibility.

So, has community corrections legislation failed? The results are not entirely conclusive. All studies have found that some offenders were shifted to local corrections, and this is encouraging. The problem is this: How can administrators control local correctional programs to ensure that the prison commitments are actually reduced under the new policies, as the legislation intended? The community corrections acts that allow local government to contract with private, nonprofit businesses that provide services to offenders claim that they create private jobs while reducing commitments to prison, and this aspect of community corrections acts may benefit all concerned.

CORRECTIONAL POLICY

Community Corrections Today

The Pew Charitable Trusts has been trying to help states deal with their problems of burgeoning prison populations. To do this, they advocate a series of measures that create fiscal and programmatic incentives for decision makers to keep convicted offenders in local corrections systems rather than sending them to state prisons. They stress a five-point agenda:

1. *Evidence-based practices:* Develop supervision and services based on studies of "what works" to reduce recidivism.
2. *Earned-compliance credits:* Provide incentives for people under community corrections to reduce the length of their sentences when they successfully complete programs.
3. *Administrative sanctions:* When correctional clients struggle under community-based alternatives, develop administrative sanctions (such as house arrest) for dealing with them rather than returning them to prison.

4. *Performance-incentive funding:* When community programs reduce recidivism, increase their funding.
5. *Performance measurement:* Make sure you know whether programs are having their intended effects.

The key idea underlying the Pew model is "justice reinvestment." That is, the program intends to divert a large number of people from prison, thus saving money. But some of those savings are designed to be spent in communities that suffer from high rates of crime and are the homes to large numbers of people who have been involved in the criminal justice system. In this way, programs that work can be strengthened, and communities that face substantial problems related to crime can start to improve.

Source: Pew Charitable Trusts, *Pew Policy Framework to Strengthen Community Corrections* (Philadelphia: Author, December 15, 2008).

To see what the **Pew Charitable Trusts** is doing about correctional policy, go to the corresponding link at www .cengage.com/criminaljustice/ clear.

Certainly, community corrections is no panacea. The desire to reduce the number of offenders in prison must be supported by procedures to control the manner in which offenders are handled in local programs. (See the Focus box "Community Corrections Today" for one foundation's suggestions.)

■ THE FUTURE OF INTERMEDIATE SANCTIONS AND COMMUNITY CORRECTIONS

What does the future hold for intermediate sanctions and community corrections? Certainly, those who support these programs must address three recurrent problems.

First, some way must be found to overcome the seemingly immutable tendency of the criminal justice system to resist placing offenders in less-restrictive options and to keep increasing the level of corrections. As we have seen, studies of nonprison alternatives find that even the most successful programs enroll only a minority of offenders who would otherwise have been incarcerated. The usual pattern is first to place offenders in prison and then to release them to the community. New alternative programs are filled with people who formerly would have been placed on regular probation. Nonprison programs, whether intermediate sanctions or community corrections programs, must improve their ability to obtain the kinds of offenders for which they are intended.

Second, community support for these programs must increase. Too often citizens fear the offenders in their midst. Active measures must be taken to allay those fears, to help citizens become comfortable with a correctional mission that recognizes a wide array of programs rather than favoring incarceration.

Third, the purposes of these sanctions must be clarified. No program can operate successfully for long without clearly defined goals. The goals of most programs today state vague and often competing generalizations: rehabilitation, reduction of overcrowding, protection of the community, reintegration, cost-effectiveness, and so on.

While no legitimate government operation can reject any of these considerations, they must prioritize and clarify some of their objectives before these new forms of correctional functions can take their rightful place as core operations in the overall system.

SUMMARY

1 Describe the rationale for nonincarceration penalties.

Per year, incarceration costs between 25 and 50 times as much as probation. For certain crimes, prison is too harsh a punishment and probation not harsh enough. Neither probation nor prison guarantees that offenders will "make it" once their term is served. Further, children and families suffer financial, psychological, and other hardships when one of their loved ones goes to prison. Many victims leave court feeling alienated from justice, whatever the sentence. Finally, a range of nonprison sentences seem to lead to lower recidivism rates. For all of these reasons, there needs to be a choice between probation and prison—some intermediate sanction that is more exacting than probation but less costly and with fewer collateral consequences than prison.

2 Describe the rationale for intermediate sanctions.

Intermediate sanctions have arisen because many people believe that a sentence to probation is not strict enough, but prison is too extreme. To implement intermediate sanctions, many jurisdictions have developed the continuum-of-sanctions concept, which offers a range of correctional options between prison and probation. To be effective, intermediate sanctions have to target the right group of offenders and place less emphasis on surveillance and control and more emphasis on services.

3 Illustrate the continuum-of-sanctions concept.

Corrections systems have developed a range of punishments that vary in intrusiveness and control, providing choices that fall between probation and prison. Probation plus a fine or community service may be appropriate for minor offenses, whereas six weeks of boot camp followed by intensive probation supervision may be right for serious crimes.

4 Explain some of the problems associated with intermediate sanctions.

Problems with intermediate sanctions center on selecting appropriate agencies to run them, selecting the right offenders to place in them, and avoiding widening the net.

5 List the various types of intermediate sanctions and who administers them.

Courts offer pretrial diversion, fines, forfeiture, community service, and restitution; probation departments offer day reporting centers, intensive supervision, home confinement, and electronic monitoring; correctional departments offer shock incarceration and boot camps.

6 Describe what it takes to make intermediate sanctions work.

To make intermediate sanctions work, there must be interchangeability of sanctions so that penalties in the community can be compared with penalties in confinement. The right offenders need to be selected for the right programs, and problems of bias must be avoided. Surveillance and control must be carefully used so that sanctions do not backfire.

7 Assess the role of the new correctional professional.

The new correctional professional can work within a context of strong bureaucratic guidelines and high expectations of accountability. They are at ease dealing with nongovernment agencies, and they possess a range of skills at motivating offenders to use an array of correctional services.

8 Explain how community corrections legislation works and describe its effectiveness.

When communities keep offenders locally instead of sending them to prison, they save the state money. Community corrections legislation gives the money that was saved back to these communities to fund local programs that manage those offenders. These strategies work when the cost incentives are large enough to reward communities for keeping offenders locally, and when jail is not used as a replacement for prison.

9 Critically assess the future of probation, intermediate sanctions, and community corrections.

Community-based correctional approaches face challenges of getting public support for keeping offenders in community programs instead of sending them to incarceration. They must clarify their mission and become more-crucial components of the correctional array of programs. Justice reinvestment strategies offer one viable way of doing this.

KEY TERMS

boot camp (p. 244)
community service (p. 239)
continuum of sanctions (p. 236)
day fine (p. 239)
forfeiture (p. 239)

home confinement (p. 242)
intensive supervision probation (ISP) (p. 240)
principle of interchangeability (p. 246)
probation center (p. 240)
restitution (p. 239)

restitution center (p. 240)
shock incarceration (p. 244)
stakes (p. 237)

FOR DISCUSSION

1. How do intermediate sanctions work better—as a way of improving on probation, or as a way of avoiding the negatives of imprisonment? Why?
2. Should intermediate sanctions be run by traditional probation and prison systems or by new agencies seeking to serve as alternatives to them?
3. What does the California probation subsidy program tell us about the interdependence of various elements of corrections?

4. Why do states with similar crime rates sometimes have different incarceration rates?
5. Do you think that intermediate sanctions are acceptable to the general public in the current political climate?

FOR FURTHER READING

Byrne, James M., Arthur J. Lurigio, and Joan Petersilia. *Smart Sentencing: The Emergence of Intermediate Sanctions.* Newbury Park, CA: Sage, 2005. Explores various issues in the design and implementation of intermediate sanctions programs, with special reference to programs in the United States.

Caputo, Gail. *Intermediate Sanctions in Corrections.* Denton: University of North Texas, 2004. A description of the major forms of intermediate sanctions and their effectiveness in saving money and reducing costs.

Duff, Anthony. *Punishment, Communication, and Community.* New York: Oxford University Press, 2005. A well-regarded philosophical exploration of the basis for and strategies of punishment in the community.

Golash, Deirdre. *The Case against Punishment: Retribution, Crime Prevention, and the Law.* New York: NYU Press, 2005. A legal and philosophical exploration of the drawbacks of a retributive punishment system.

Morris, Norval, and Michael Tonry. *Between Prison and Probation: Intermediate Punishments in a Rational Sentencing System.* Oxford, England: Oxford University Press, 1990. Original and classic description of intermediate punishments

that can sanction offenders more severely than can nominal probation but less severely than incarceration.

Rex, Sue. *Reforming Community Penalties.* London: J.C.B. Mohr, 2005. An assessment of strategies for improving community-based correctional programs.

Worrall, Anne, and Clare Hoy. *Punishment in the Community: Managing Offenders, Making Choices.* Portland, OR: Willan, 2005. A critical assessment of the programs and policies of community-based programs, with special attention to the United Kingdom.

Notes

1 Michael Jacobson, *Downsizing Prisons: How to Reduce Crime and End Mass Incarceration* (New York: New York University Press, 2005).

2 Norval Morris and Michael Tonry, *Between Prison and Probation: Intermediate Punishments in a Rational Sentencing System* (New York: Oxford University Press, 1990), 3.

3 Median time served for felons sentenced to prison for property crimes is about 24 months: Bureau of Justice Statistics, *Statistical Tables,* July 2007, Table 1.5.

4 Joseph Murray, "The Effects of Imprisonment on the Families and Children of Prisoners," in *The Effects of Imprisonment,* edited by Allison Liebling and Shadd Maruna (Portland: Willan, 2005), 442–92.

5 Joseph Murray, Carl-Gunnar Janson, and David Farrington, "Crime in Adult Offspring of Prisoners: A Cross-National Comparison of Two Longitudinal Samples," *Criminal Justice and Behavior* 34 (2007): 133–49.

6 Paula Smith, Claire Coggin, and Paul Gendreau, *The Effects of Prison Sentences and Intermediate Sanctions on Recidivism* (Ottawa: Solicitor General of Canada, 2002).

7 Daniel S. Nagin, Francis T. Cullen, and Cheryl Lero Jonson, "Imprisonment and Reoffending," *Crime and Justice: A Review of Research* (forthcoming). See also Amy Elizabeth Lerman, "The People Prisons Make: Effects of Incarceration on Criminal Psychology," in *Do Prisons Make Us Safer? The Benefits and Costs of the Prison Boom,* edited by Steven Raphael and Michael Stoll (New York: Russell Sage Foundation, 2009), 151–76.

8 U.S. Department of Justice, *Felony Defendants in Large Urban Courts* (Washington, DC: U.S. Government Printing Office, December 2003), 32.

9 *Austin v. United States,* 61 Lw. 4811 (1993).

10 For a detailed description of these programs, see Gail Caputo, *Intermediate Sanctions in Corrections* (Denton: University of North Texas Press, 2004), chs. 7 and 8.

11 Freda Solomon, "The CASES Day Custody Program," *Research Brief* series, no. 20 (New York: New York City Criminal Justice Agency, May 2009).

12 Liz-Marie Marciniak, "The Addition of Day Reporting to Intensive Supervision Probation: A Comparison of Recidivism Rates," *Federal Probation* 64 (no. 2, June 2001): 34–39.

13 Rachel Porter, Sophia Lee, and Mary Lutz, *Balancing Punishment and Treatment: Alternatives to Incarceration in New York City* (New York: Vera Institute of Justice, 2002).

14 Joan Petersilia and Susan Turner, *Intensive Supervision for High-Risk Offenders: Three California Experiments* (Santa Monica, CA: Rand Corporation, 1990).

15 Jeanne B. Stinchcomb, "Prisons of the Mind: Lessons Learned from Home Confinement," *Journal of Criminal Justice Education* 13 (no. 3, 2002): 463–78.

16 "The 2002–2003 Electronic Monitoring Survey," *Journal of Electronic Monitoring* 15 (no. 1, Winter–Spring 2002): 5.

17 BJS *Bulletin,* October 2006.

18 William D. Bales, Laura F. Bedard, Susan T. Quinn, David T. Ensley, and Glen P. Holley, "Recidivism of Public and Private State Prison Inmates in Florida," *Criminology and Public Policy* 4 (no. 1, 2005): 57–82.

19 Robert Stanz and Richard Tewksbury, "Predictors of Success and Recidivism in a Home Incarceration Program," *Prison Journal* 80 (no. 3, 2000): 326.

20 M. Finn and S. Muirhead-Steves, "The Effectiveness of Electronic Monitoring with Violent Male Parolees," *Justice Quarterly* 19 (no. 2, 2002): 293–312.

21 Greg Frost, "Florida's Innovative Use of GPS for Community Corrections," *Journal of Offender Monitoring* 15 (no. 2, Spring 2002): 6–9.

22 Dale Parent, *Correctional Boot Camps: Lessons from a Decade of Research* (Washington, DC: U.S. Department of Justice, June 2003).

23 Associated Press, "Parents Want Charges in Boot Camp Death; Video Appears to Show Guards Restraining, Hitting Teen," February 18, 2006, http://www.msnbc.msn.com/id/11396434/. See also Jeff Lincoln, "US: Students Protest Juvenile's Death in Florida 'Boot Camp,'" World News Service, April 25, 2006, http://www.wsws.org/articles/2006/apr2006/boot-a25.shtml.

24 Megan C. Kurlychek and Cynthia A. Kempinen, "Beyond Boot Camp: The Impact of Aftercare on Offender Reentry," *Criminology and Public Policy* 5 (no. 2, 2006): 363–88.

25 Catherine A. Kempinen and Megan C. Kulychek, "An Outcome Evaluation of Pennsylvania's Boot Camp: Does Rehabilitative Programming with a Disciplinary Setting Reduce Recidivism?" *Crime and Delinquency* 49 (no. 4, 2003): 681.

26 Joan Petersilia, "California's Correctional Paradox of Excess and Deprivation," *Crime and Justice: A Review of Research* 37 (2008): 207–78.

27 Joan Petersilia, *Understanding California Corrections* (Berkeley: CA: Policy Research Center, May 2006).

© AP Images/Mark Foley

LEARNING OBJECTIVES

After reading this chapter you should be able to . . .

1 Explain how today's prisons are linked to the past.

2 Discuss the goals of incarceration.

3 Be familiar with the organization of incarceration.

4 Discuss the factors that influence the classification of prisons.

5 Explain who is in prison.

New arrivals ("fish") begin processing at the North Florida Reception Center Prison. This involves classification as to security level, housing, and program needs. It is here that inmates also begin to shed their civilian identity through medical and mental health screenings, drug testing, IQ measurement, showers, hair cuts, and the issuance of rule books and uniforms.

"STAINLESS-STEEL HANDCUFFS snugly fastened around subdued wrists. Waiting at an outer gatehouse. Watching the uniformed reception officer dispassionately size me up. Then escorted past double fences, inner fences, through steel doors, electronic steel grilles into the inner sanctum of concrete and steel.

"Fear. The kind that chews at the stomach and makes the fingers tremble. Fear of known and unknown hidden dangers.

"The atmosphere is tense and strange. Still wearing street-side clothes, I am a curiosity. After a number of rights and lefts and double-locked stairways, we come to Admitting and Processing.

"Catalogued, tagged, photographed, and deloused. Issued, not issued, acceptable, not acceptable, and then ordered into a cell slightly bigger than a walk-in closet. When that door slams shut, an ache of mental and emotional pain seizes the senses brutally and completely."

INCARCERATION

This description was written for this text by Wayne B. Alexander, who is serving a life term for murder and other crimes. It shows how depersonalizing, jarring, and terrifying entrance into prison can be. Incarceration is something no person would want to endure. (For more of this narration, see the Focus box "Realization" on the next page.)

Of the approximately 7.2 million adults under correctional supervision in the United States, only about 2.25 million are in jails and prisons.[1] Yet when the subject of the criminal sanction arises, the general public thinks first of incarceration. And it is prison that legislators and politicians have in mind when they consider changes in the penal code or annual appropriations for corrections.

In this chapter and three of the four that follow, we focus primarily on the incarceration of male adults, who make up about 93 percent of the prison population.[2] Our discussion links the modern prison with the history of American corrections so that we can understand its antecedents.

Chapter 10

FOCUS ON PEOPLE IN CORRECTIONS

Realization

Hearing the cell door slam shut the first time, there is a gripping realization, almost spiritual for some, that the consequences of crime are terribly real. Every memory, all of the past, good and bad, returns to haunt. Every single indelible moment is etched upon the mind's eye at some point, and painful memories invade conscious thought. The act, the arrest, pretrial and trial, conviction and sentencing, and most of all the last three hours flood involuntarily into mind and heart.

I look around at the cool, unforgiving gray concrete walls and feel the hopelessness. The helplessness of my predicament. The accommodations are welded and brazed and anchored into the concrete to last for years of use.

The gnawing fear that has been building steadily since hearing the door slam shut prompts me to jump up and test the door to see if it's really locked. It is.

Coming to terms with this reality begins one of the many emotional storms raging inside me. The raw fear penetrates and subsides, and the fight to control myself from crying out or pleading like a small child is a constant struggle.

This sensation of being torn apart from within by conflicting emotions vying for control is the most frightening human experience known. Nothing compares to the realization that I am being confined and controlled so totally. "Oh, God, no," I cry to myself. "Please don't let this be!"

After two hours the door slides back and a shout—"Chow!"—is heard. Steel doors slam, keys clang, and there is the shuffling of hundreds of feet. The strange, listless, angry, and embittered faces of the others offer painful insight into this subculture.

Lock in! 8:30 P.M. Until the morning meal, that door will be locked. Can I make it? The struggle rages again as I feel tears well up behind fatigued eyes. After two hours a uniformed arm pokes a flashlight into the cell for a moment and withdraws. Counted, and counted and counted again, I am among the best-monitored individuals outside an intensive care unit in the country. More than a half-dozen times a day I am counted to ensure that I still suffer. In addition, clothes, underwear, property, and every file about me bears the assigned number that was issued during the processing.

I didn't know until this day that it was possible to tag, count, and store human beings like merchandise in a warehouse. Yet in this modern maximum-security "correctional institution," the insidiously antiseptic ritual of accepting an individual and transforming him into a number is as normal as sending youngsters on their way to school every morning on a yellow bus.

The consequences, again, become sparklingly clear and real. By committing a crime, I have plunged headlong into this nightmare of living death. I am condemned and I am so sorry; God, I'm sorry. I look around and realize there is no one to tell it to. In that moment I come to the realization that I have been forsaken. I have been cast out of a free society and branded with a number, never to achieve a position of trust or a level of responsibility that I might be capable of. I have come to the place of punishment and proved that the criminal justice system is alive and well in America.

I, the convicted, the incarcerated, come face-to-face with all these truths, only to sit mute upon my bunk, isolated by a society I so desperately want to apologize to.

Source: Written especially for this text by long-term prisoner Wayne B. Alexander, convicted of murder and other crimes.

■ LINKS TO THE PAST

Reformers are frustrated by the sheer durability of prisons. For example, the oldest prison in America—New Jersey's State Prison in Trenton, which opened in 1798 and was rebuilt in 1836—still houses offenders. Structures of stone and concrete are not easily redesigned when correctional goals change. So, elements of major reform movements can be found within the walls of many older prisons. In line with the Quakers' belief that offenders could be redeemed only if removed from the distractions of the city, many correctional facilities still operate in rural areas—Stateville (Illinois), Attica (New York), Walla Walla (Washington)—far from most of the inmates' families, friends, and communities. Although many modern prisons feature "campus" settings, the stronghold remains the primary architectural style. Life on the "inside" varies with the type and locale of the institution and the characteristics of the inmates. Yet a prison is still a prison, whatever it is called and however it is constructed.

The image of the "big house," popularized in countless movies and television shows, is still imprinted on the minds of most Americans, although it has long ceased to be a realistic portrayal—if indeed it ever was. Moreover, much social science literature about prison society is based on studies conducted in big houses, or maximum-security prisons, during the 1950s. Fictional depictions of prison life are typically set in the big-house fortress where the inmates are tough and the guards are just as tough or tougher. But American correctional institutions have always been more varied than movies or novels portray them.

Although big houses predominated in much of the country during the first half of the twentieth century, many prisons, especially in the South, did not conform to this model. Racial segregation was maintained, prisoners were used as farm labor, and the massive walled structures were not as common as in the North.

The typical big house of the 1940s and 1950s was a walled prison with large, tiered cell blocks, a yard, shops, and industries. The prisoners, in an average population of about 2,500 per institution, came from both urban and rural areas, were usually poor, and, outside the South, were predominately white. The prison society was essentially isolated; access to visitors, mail, and other communication was restricted. Prisoners' days were very structured, and guards enforced the rules. There was a basic division between inmates and staff; rank was observed and discipline maintained. In the big house few treatment programs existed; custody was the primary goal.

During the 1960s and early 1970s, when the rehabilitation model was dominant, many states built new prisons and converted others into "correctional institutions." Treatment programs administered by counselors and teachers became a major part of prison life, although the institutions continued to give priority to the custody goals of security, discipline, and order.

The civil rights movement of the early 1960s profoundly affected prisoners, especially minority inmates. Prisoners demanded their constitutional rights as citizens and greater sensitivity to their needs. As discussed in Chapter 5, the courts began to take notice of the legal rights of prisoners. As inmates gained more legal services, the traditional judicial hands-off policy evaporated. Suddenly, administrators had to respond to the directives of the judiciary and run the institutions according to constitutional mandates.

During the past 40 years, as the population of the United States has changed, so has the prison population. The number of African American and Hispanic inmates has greatly increased. More inmates come from urban areas and more have been convicted of drug-related and violent offenses than before. Incarcerated members of street gangs, which are often organized along racial lines, frequently regroup inside prison and contribute to elevated levels of violence. Another major change has been

The Stateville Correctional Center, in Illinois is an example of the "big house," typical of prisons that predominated during the first half of the twentieth century. These large, multitiered cell blocks are now viewed as being not in keeping with today's penology.

the rising number of correctional officers joining public employee unions, along with their use of collective bargaining to improve working conditions, safety procedures, and training.

Further, the focus of corrections has shifted to crime control, which emphasizes the importance of incarceration. As a result, the number of people in prison has increased. Some politicians argue that offenders have it too "cushy" and that prisons should return to the strict regimes found in the early twentieth century. Many states have removed educational and recreational amenities from their institutions.

The number of people in America's prisons has increased substantially over the past decade. Tensions have built within the overcrowded institutions. Although today's correctional administrators seek to provide humane incarceration, they must struggle with limited resources. The modern prison faces many of the difficult problems that confront other parts of the criminal justice system: racial conflicts, legal issues, limited resources, and growing populations. Despite these challenges, can prisons still achieve their objectives? The answer to this question depends, in part, on how we define the goals of incarceration.

■ THE GOALS OF INCARCERATION

Citing the nature of the inmates and the need to protect the staff and the community, most people consider security the dominant purpose of a prison. High walls, razor wire, searches, checkpoints, and regular counts of inmates serve the security function: Few inmates escape. More important, such features set the tone for the daily operations. Prisons are expected to be impersonal, quasi-military organizations where strict discipline, minimal amenities, and restrictions on freedom carry out the punishment of criminals.

Three models of incarceration have predominated since the early 1940s: custodial, rehabilitation, and reintegration. Each reflects one style of institutional organization.

custodial model
A model of correctional institutions that emphasizes security, discipline, and order.

1 **The custodial model** assumes that prisoners have been incarcerated for the purpose of incapacitation, deterrence, or retribution. It emphasizes security, discipline, and order, which subordinate the prisoner to the authority of the warden. Discipline is strict, and most aspects of behavior are regulated. This model prevailed in corrections before World War II, and it continues to dominate most maximum-security institutions.

rehabilitation model
A model of correctional institutions that emphasizes the provision of treatment programs designed to reform the offender.

2 The **rehabilitation model**, developed during the 1950s, emphasizes treatment programs designed to reform the offender. According to this model, security and housekeeping activities are preconditions for rehabilitative efforts. As all aspects of the organization should be directed toward rehabilitation, professional treatment specialists enjoy a higher status than do other employees. Treatment programs exist in most contemporary institutions. But since the rethinking of the rehabilitation goal in the 1970s, very few prisons continue to conform to this model.

reintegration model
A model of correctional institutions that emphasizes maintenance of the offender's ties to family and the community as a method of reform, in recognition of the fact that the offender will be returning to the community.

3 The **reintegration model** is linked to the structures and goals of community corrections. Recognizing that prisoners will be returning to society, this model emphasizes maintaining offenders' ties to family and community as a method of reform. Prisons following this model gradually give inmates greater freedom and responsibility during their confinement, moving them to halfway houses or work release programs before releasing them under some form of community supervision.

Although one can find correctional institutions that conform to each of these models, most prisons are mainly custodial. Nevertheless, treatment programs do exist, and even some of the most custodial institutions attempt to prepare inmates for reentry into free society. Because prisons are expected to pursue many different and often

Some legislators have argued that weightlifting, basketball, and other physical actiivies in prison are frills that should be restricted. Wardens, however, believe that these activities are important ways to keep prisoneners busy and reduce tensions. Does this type of recreation serve an incarceration goal?

incompatible goals, it would seem that they are almost doomed to fail. Charles Logan believes that the mission of prisons is confinement and that the basic purpose of imprisonment is to punish offenders fairly through terms of confinement proportionate to the seriousness of the crimes. He summarizes the mission of the prison as follows: "to keep prisoners—to keep them in, keep them safe, keep them in line, keep them healthy, and keep them busy—and to do it with fairness, without undue suffering, and as efficiently as possible."[3] If the purpose of prisons is punishment through confinement under fair and just conditions, what are the implications for correctional managers? Following these criteria, what measures should we use to evaluate prisons?

■ ORGANIZATION FOR INCARCERATION

All 50 states and the federal government operate prisons. Offenders are held in 1,292 confinement facilities, nearly 92 percent of which are operated by the states, and the remainder by the federal government and private companies. The largest percentage of state confinement facilities are located in the South (47 percent), while 20 percent are located in the Midwest, 18.5 percent in the West, and 14.5 percent in the Northeast.[4] For the most part, prisons, as distinguished from jails, house convicted felons and those misdemeanants who have been sentenced to terms of more than one year. Note, however, that various state governments and the federal government differ in terms of bureaucratic organization for incarceration, number and types of institutions, staffing, and size of offender populations. We now look at the federal and state systems in turn.

Federal Bureau of Prisons

In 1930 Congress created the Federal Bureau of Prisons within the Department of Justice. The bureau was responsible for "the safekeeping, care, protection, instruction, and discipline of all persons charged or convicted of offenses against the United States." Before 1930, administrators of the seven federal prisons then in operation functioned with little control by Washington. Today the bureau is highly centralized, with a director (appointed by the president), six regional directors, and a staff of over 35,000, who supervise more than 201,000 prisoners. To carry out its tasks, the Federal Bureau of Prisons has a network of over a hundred facilities ranging from penitentiaries to correctional institutions, detention centers, prison camps, and halfway houses.[5]

The jurisdiction of federal criminal law, unlike that of the states, is restricted to crimes involving interstate commerce, certain serious felonies such as bank robbery, violations of other federal laws, and crimes committed on federal property. Historically, federal prisons have housed bank robbers, extortionists, people who commit mail fraud, and arsonists. But since the initiation of the war on drugs in the 1980s, the number of drug offenders in federal prisons has steadily increased. Drug offenders currently constitute about 53.3 percent of the federal inmate population. There are fewer violent offenders in federal prisons than in most state institutions. Federal prisoners are often a more-sophisticated type of criminal, from a higher socioeconomic class, than the typical state prisoner. Interestingly, over 53,000—about 27 percent—of federal inmates are citizens of other countries.[6] **Figure 10.1** presents some key characteristics of federal prisoners.

With the introduction of federal sentencing guidelines in 1987, the average length of imprisonment increased substantially. Further, the total number of offenders is greater now than in previous decades. In fact, the federal government does not have enough pretrial detention space to house most people accused of violating the federal criminal law, so about two-thirds of pretrial detainees are housed in state or local facilities on a contractual basis. The U.S. Marshals Service is responsible for placing these prisoners. Although all 50 states have laws requiring their correctional facilities to accept federal pretrial detainees, the marshals typically enter into intergovernmental service agreements with receptive jails. Local officials fear that sophisticated federal prisoners will bring lawsuits challenging the conditions of their confinement and believe that federal officials expect the higher federal standards to be maintained at local expense.

The Bureau of Prisons currently operates 102 confinement facilities.[7] These facilities are classified using five security levels, ranging from "minimum" to "high" security. The bureau has one maximum-security prison (or "super max"), located in Florence, Colorado. The bureau is organized so that the wardens report to one of the regional offices. Regional office staff deal with a variety of matters, including health and psychological services, financial management, inmate discipline, and food service. Technical assistance is also provided to institutional and community corrections personnel by regional office staff.[8]

Historically, the federal system has enjoyed a good reputation and has been viewed as an innovator in the field of corrections. In fact, John DiIulio went so far as to suggest that responsibility for all state prison operations be delegated to the Federal Bureau of Prisons.[9] Do you think that this would ensure the humane treatment of prisoners?

The **Federal Bureau of Prisons** website is listed at www.cengage.com/criminaljustice/clear.

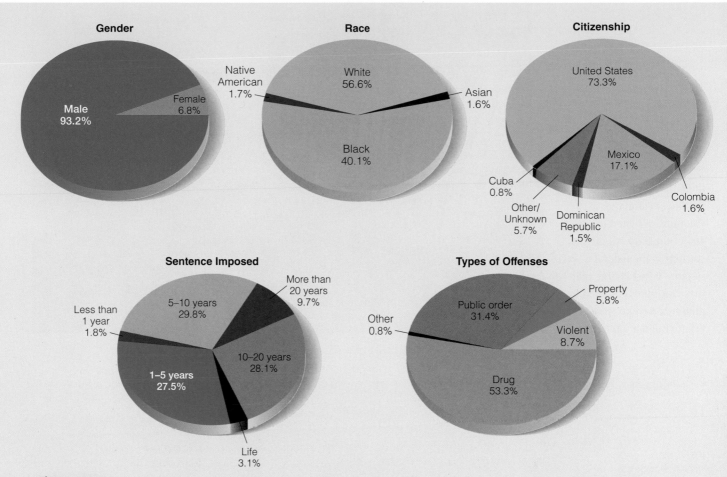

Figure 10.1

Characteristics of Federal Prison Inmates in 2007

Federal prisoners tend to be male, white, and convicted of drug offenses. A sizable portion of federal inmates are not U.S. citizens, and over half of federal inmates received sentences ranging from 5 to 20 years.

Sources: Federal Bureau of Prisons, *State of the Bureau,* 2007 (Washington, DC: U.S. Government Printing Office, 2007), 52; Bureau of Justice Statistics, *Prisoners in 2007* (Washington, DC: U.S. Government Printing Office, December 2008), 22.

State Prison Systems

Although states vary considerably in how they organize corrections, the executive branch of each state government administers its prisons. This point is important because probation is often part of the judiciary, parole may be separate from corrections, and in most states jails are run by county governments.

Commissioners of corrections, normally appointed by state governors, are responsible for the operation of prisons. As discussed in Chapter 13, each institution is administered by a *warden* (often called a *superintendent*), who reports directly to the commissioner or a deputy commissioner for institutions. The number of employees in state correctional agencies has risen dramatically during the past decade: Upwards of 390,000 people—administrators, officers, and program specialists—work in state institutions.[10]

To a great extent, the total capacity of a state's prisons reflects the size of the state's population. Yet, as discussed in Chapter 18, the number of offenders in a state's institutions reflects more than just crime rates and social factors. Sentencing practices, legislative appropriations for corrections, and politics can also affect incarceration rates.

In addition to organization, states vary considerably in the number, size, type, and location of correctional facilities. Louisiana's state prison at Angola, for example, has

About 20,000 inmates are now held in at least 57 "super-max" prisons such as the Administrative Maximum Facility in Florence, Colorado, designed to house 400 of the most "predatory" convicts in the federal system. Critics charge that these facilities, designed to minimize human contact, violate human rights.

© Stephen Ferry/Getty Images/Liaison

1. Bullock Correctional Facility
2. Draper Correctional Facility,
   Elmore Correctional Facility,
   Thomas F. Staton Correctional Facility
3. Easterling Correctional Facility
4. J. O. Davis Correctional Facility,
   G. K. Fountain Correctional Facility,
   Holman Correctional Facility
5. Hamilton Work Release Center
6. Limestone Correctional Facility
7. Childersburg Work Release Center
8. Kilby Correctional Facility
9. St. Clair Correctional Facility
10. Alex City Work Release Center
11. Elba Work Release Center
12. Julia Tutwiler Correctional Facility
13. Ventress Correctional Facility
14. Donaldson Correctional Facility
15. Bibb County Correctional Facility
16. Atmore Work Release Center
17. Decatur Work Release Center
18. Birmingham Work Release Center
19. Camden Work Release Center
20. Mobile Work Release Center
21. Loxley Work Release Center

Figure 10.2
The Alabama Prison System

The number and variety of institutions for felons in Alabama is typical of most medium-sized states. What factors might influence the location of penal institutions?

Source: Alabama Department of Corrections, http://www.doc.state.al.us/map.asp, June 23, 2009.

an inmate population of approximately 5,200, whereas institutions for inmates with special problems frequently house fewer than 100. Some states (such as New Hampshire) have centralized incarceration in a few institutions, and other states, such as California, New York, and Texas, have a wide mix of sizes and styles—secure institutions, diagnostic units, work camps, forestry centers, and prerelease centers. For example, Alabama has 29 institutions, which include maximum- and medium-security facilities, a cattle ranch, an institution for the aged and infirm, a women's prison, and an honor farm (see **Figure 10.2**).[11]

Information about **Washington's Department of Corrections** is found at the corresponding link at www.cengage.com/criminaljustice/clear.

■ THE DESIGN AND CLASSIFICATION OF PRISONS

Since the era of John Howard in England and the Quakers in Philadelphia, penologists have pondered the optimal design of prisons. In all eras, attempts were made to design correctional institutions that would advance the prevailing purpose of the criminal sanction.[12] In this section we discuss some of the changes and concepts in prison design. A cardinal principle of architecture is that form follows function: The design of a structure should serve the structure's purpose. During the early 1800s some English and American architects specialized in designing penitentiaries that would accommodate contemplation, industry, and isolation, thought to be the necessary conditions for moral reform. Efforts during the penitentiary era were directed at building institutions that would promote penance. When prison industry became the focus after the Civil War, a different design was proposed to enhance the efficiency of the workshops. When punishment through custody reigned supreme, the emphasis was on the fortress-like edifice that ensured security. And during the rehabilitation era of the 1950s and 1960s, new prisons were built in styles thought to promote treatment. At all times, however, the plans of the architects had to be "realistic" regarding cost.

The design and operational characteristics of today's prisons vary considerably from state to state. Some states and the federal government have created smaller facilities. But even with the prison-building boom of the 1990s, many institutions remain old and large. The antiquated megaprisons found in many states have all the maintenance and operational problems of old, heavily used buildings.

Today's Designs

The buildings constructed to suit the purposes of one era often cannot be easily adapted to suit those of succeeding eras or changes in the sizes and characteristics of prison populations. At the same time, prisons are built to last, which means form may not continue to serve function. Unlike the nineteenth-century prisons, which were designed as grand fortresses, today's construction is greatly influenced by cost. After a cross-country tour of many prisons, Joseph Hallinan described the modern correctional facility as a "concrete econo-box," low and bunkered and anonymous. From a distance it resembles a hospital or suburban high school. It has no guard towers, because guards are expensive. It has no walls; fences are cheaper.[13]

During the prison construction boom of the 1990s, many states chose the concrete econo-box. However, four basic models account for the designs of most U.S. prisons.

THE RADIAL DESIGN ■ Prisons of the early nineteenth century tended to follow the **radial design** of Eastern Penitentiary (see **Figure 10.3a**). A control center at the hub makes it possible to monitor movement. From this central core, one or more "spokes" can be isolated from the rest of the institution if trouble erupts. Even though Auburn Prison was administered to contrast with the separation and silence practiced at Eastern, it also had the radial design. At other present-day locations, such as Leavenworth (Kansas) and Rahway and Trenton (New Jersey), the old design persists, but few newer prisons have been built to such specifications.

radial design
An architectural plan by which a prison is constructed in the form of a wheel, with "spokes" radiating from a central core.

a. Radial design

b. Telephone-pole design

c. Courtyard style

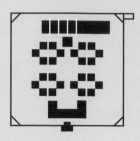

d. Campus style

Figure 10.3
Prison Designs Used in the United States
These four basic designs are used throughout the country for most prisons housing adult felons. Each style has certain features related to the goals of "keeping and serving" the prisoners. How does architecture influence the management of these institutions?

telephone-pole design
An architectural plan for a prison, calling for a long central corridor crossed at regular intervals by structures containing the prison's functional areas.

THE TELEPHONE-POLE DESIGN ■ In a prison based on the **telephone-pole design**, a long central corridor (the pole) serves as the means for prisoners to go from one part of the institution to another (see **Figure 10.3b**). Jutting out from the corridor are cross-arms, each containing the prison's functional areas: housing, shops, school, recreation area, and so on. The central pole allows continuous surveillance, as well as independently controlled access to each functional area.

The telephone pole is the design most commonly used for maximum-security prisons in the United States. For example, Graterford (Pennsylvania), Marion (Illinois), and Somers (Connecticut) are designed in this fashion. Built for custody, these prisons can house inmates according to classification levels, with certain housing areas designated for inmates with special needs, for those whose conduct merits extra privileges, and so on.

William Nagel notes that the telephone-pole design cuts off inmates from the world and that daily and seasonal variations are lost. For these reasons, he believes confinement here "prepares [the inmate] only for confinement," not for reentry to the community.[14]

courtyard style
An architectural design by which the functional units of a prison are housed in separate buildings constructed on four sides of an open square.

THE COURTYARD STYLE ■ Some of the newer correctional facilities, including some maximum-security prisons, are built in **courtyard style** (see **Figure 10.3c**). In these facilities, the functional units of a prison are housed in separate buildings constructed on four sides of an open square. Movement along the endless corridors, which is common in the telephone-pole design, is replaced by movement across the courtyard to the housing units and other functional areas. In some facilities of this type, such functional units as the dining hall, gym, and school are located in the yard area.

campus style
An architectural design by which the functional units of a prison are individually housed in a complex of buildings surrounded by a fence.

THE CAMPUS STYLE ■ A design long used for juvenile and women's correctional facilities, the **campus style** has been used for some newer institutions for men as well (see **Figure 10.3d**). Relatively small housing units are scattered among the shops, school, dining hall, and other units of the facility. This style is thought to be an important development not only because of the humane features of the design but also because individual buildings can be used more flexibly. As in courtyard-style prisons, inmates and staff must go outdoors to get from one part of the facility to another. Although the campus style might appear to provide less security than more-conventional facilities, modern prison fences keep escapes to a minimum. Most facilities of this type serve medium- and minimum-security populations.

The Location of Prisons

Most prisons for adults are located in rural areas. Originally, the rationale was that inmates would more readily repent if isolated from urban distractions and family contacts. When more prisons were built later in the nineteenth century, the country setting was retained because the institutions maintained farms contributing to their self-sufficiency. Now, even though most prison inmates come from cities and reintegration is an important correctional goal, new institutions are still being built in the countryside. Many view this as counterproductive because urban families have difficulty visiting their loved ones in rural prisons and meaningful work or educational release programs for inmates are impractical. In addition, prison administrators must rely on the local labor pool to recruit workers. This usually means that rural whites are hired to guard urban African Americans.

Although the choice of rural settings stems partly from land costs, political factors also figure in the decision. Many citizens believe that serious offenders should be incarcerated, but not in their community. This attitude is often referred to as the NIMBY syndrome (Not In My Back Yard!). Some people fear that a prison will lower property values; this concern prevents criminal justice planners from locating facilities in areas that have the resources and will to oppose prison construction. Another concern residents have with prison construction includes community problems caused by people who visit prison inmates.[15]

Alternatively, some economically depressed localities have welcomed prison construction. They believe prisons will bring jobs and revitalize the local economy. Research shows, however, that new prisons do not always improve economic conditions in depressed rural communities. Many new prison employees may live in neighboring counties and commute to work, local residents might lack the qualifications necessary for prison work, and local business may not be awarded contracts to supply newly constructed prisons with goods and services.[16] For these and other reasons, some communities have had second thoughts about the impact of prisons on their economic development.

The Classification of Prisons

State prisons for men usually are classified according to the level of security deemed necessary: maximum, medium, and minimum. Thirty-eight states and the federal government have created prisons that exceed maximum security, which are frequently called "super-max" prisons. A national survey found that 40 states currently operate super-max prisons.[17] These facilities house approximately 20,000 prisoners and are designed to hold the most disruptive, violent, and incorrigible offenders.[18] California's Pelican Bay Institution and Virginia's Red Onion Institution are examples of prisons designed to hold the "toughest of the tough" and the "worst of the worst" (see the Focus box "Maximum Takes on a New Meaning at This Prison").

With changes in the number of prisoners and their characteristics, the distinction between maximum and medium security has disappeared in some systems. Crowding has forced administrators to use medium-security facilities to house inmates requiring maximum security. Some penologists believe that many inmates now in maximum-security facilities could be housed at lower levels. Others argue that the higher security level is necessary given the tough orientation of today's inmates. They also argue that prison space is so expensive that it must be used cost-effectively.

Most states have so few female prisoners that they are all housed in one institution; those who require higher levels of security are segregated. In contrast, male inmates are assigned to a specific type of facility depending on a variety of factors, including the seriousness of the offense, the possibility of an attempt to escape, and the potential for violent behavior. Because many states do not have an institution designed for each level of security, a facility is often divided into sections for different categories of prisoners. Such facilities are referred to as "multilevel" facilities. There are no national design or classification standards, so a maximum-security facility in one state may be run as a medium-security facility in another. Nevertheless, some generalizations can be made.

Learn about **Virginia's super-max prison** at the corresponding link at www.cengage.com/criminaljustice/clear.

FOCUS ON
CORRECTIONAL PRACTICE

Maximum Takes on a New Meaning at This Prison

The state will soon begin transferring its most dangerous and disruptive inmates to the 300-cell, fortress-like Northern Correctional Institution in Somers, Connecticut's first "super maximum" security prison.

The inmates at Northern will be confined to individual 7-foot-by-12-foot concrete-encased cells 23 hours a day. When they are allowed out for a shower or fresh air, they will be handcuffed and in leg irons.

The cells are unpainted. No pictures will be allowed on the walls. Each has a small steel sink and toilet in one corner and a small steel desk with circular steel pull-out stool at the other end. The mattress on the metal bed frame has been X-rayed for possible contraband. "The word has already gotten out on this place through the inmate network," said David May, the warden, "and the word is that it's a place where you don't want to be."

The new prison is for those men among the state's 15,000 inmates who present "chronic management problems," said Mr. May. "Something like this within the prison system is a major deterrent."

The concrete, bunker-style building is further reinforced by three fences: a 12-foot outer chain link fence topped with razor wire, a middle electrified fence that sets off lights and alarms if touched, and a 14-foot steel fence that curves inward, making it virtually impossible for someone to scale it.

Inside, newly arrived inmates will be admitted to Phase One, the most restricted and claustrophobic of the cell areas, where sensory deprivation is the main tool in instigating behavioral changes. No radio or television is allowed. There is minimal contact with others. One visit is allowed each week, but it is conducted with the inmate behind thick glass; the only communication is by speaker telephone. All meals are eaten in the cell. "The opportunities for socializing are extremely limited," Mr. May said.

Compliant inmates can progress to Phase Two, where they will be allowed out of their cells for classes and therapeutic programs and may win use of a radio and restricted television viewing. "We will have classes on anger management, communication skills, problem solving, decision making, things these inmates don't know how to do," Mr. May said. "They don't know how to assert themselves without laying a hand on someone."

In Phase Three inmates would be allowed communal dining with a handful of other inmates and limited time playing basketball in a prison gymnasium. The ultimate goal would be to transfer inmates back to a less confined facility, although some may stay indefinitely if their behavior continues to be a problem, Mr. May said.

Leo Arone, regional director of the Department of Correction, said the "super max" prisons have had mixed success across the country, especially where recalcitrant inmates are transferred as a last resort and where they are forced to finish out their full sentences, even if the sentence is life without parole.

Perhaps most notorious is Pelican Bay, in northern California, which . . . was ordered by a Federal judge . . . to stop abuses. The judge, Thelton E. Henderson, noting near-total isolation and use of excessive force in the prison, said conditions there "may well hover on the edge of what is humanly tolerable."

Warning of the limitations of such prisons, Mr. Arone said, "If you lock a dog in a pen and throw food inside three times a day and never talk to him, after a year when you open the pen you're going to have a killer."

Source: Jacqueline Weaver, "Maximum Takes on a New Meaning at This New Prison," *New York Times,* February 19, 1995, p. 1. Copyright © 1995 by The New York Times Co. Reprinted by permission.

---

maximum-security prison
A prison designed and organized to minimize the possibility of escapes and violence; to that end, it imposes strict limitations on the freedom of inmates and visitors.

THE MAXIMUM-SECURITY PRISON ■ Usually an imposing edifice surrounded by high stone walls studded with guard towers, the **maximum-security prison** (sometimes called a *closed custody prison*) is designed to prevent escapes and to deter prisoners from harming one another. There are 355 such facilities in the United States that house about 38 percent of all state prisoners.[19]

Inmates live in cells, each with its own sanitary facilities. The barred doors may be operated electronically so that an officer can confine all prisoners to their cells with the flick of a switch. Because the purpose of this type of facility is custody and discipline, it embraces a military-style approach to order. Prisoners follow a strict routine.

For many prisoners the yard can be a dangerous place. It is here that assaults and stabbings may occur. How would you deal with such an environment as an inmate? As a correctional officer?

Head counts are frequent, and surveillance of behavior—often through closed-circuit television—eliminates privacy.

These structures are built to last. Many that were built at the turn of the century, when custody was the dominant model of incarceration, are still in use, even though their design makes it difficult to adapt many of them to rehabilitation and reintegration. The old prisons are not alone in their bad repute; a newer prison, Walpole State Prison in Massachusetts, built in the 1950s, has been described as the "concrete horror," one of the most dehumanizing facilities in the United States. Some of the most well-known prisons, such as Attica (New York), Stateville (Illinois), and Yuma (Arizona), are maximum-security facilities.

THE MEDIUM-SECURITY PRISON ■ There are 438 **medium-security prisons** in the United States (holding 43 percent of state inmates).[20] From the outside these facilities resemble maximum-security prisons, but these facilities are organized differently and the inmate routines are less rigid. Prisoners have more privileges and contact with the outside world through visitors, mail, and access to radio and television. The medium-security prisons usually place greater emphasis on work and rehabilitative programs. Although the inmates may have committed serious crimes, they are not perceived as intractable, hardened criminals. Some of the newer medium-security facilities have a campus or courtyard style, although the razor-wire fences, guard towers, and other security devices remain. In some states, a medium-security prison seems much closer to maximum than to minimum security.

THE MINIMUM-SECURITY PRISON ■ The **minimum-security prison** (926 facilities housing 19 percent of state inmates) houses the least violent offenders, long-term felons with clean disciplinary records, and inmates who have nearly completed their term.[21] The minimum-security prison lacks the guard towers and walls usually associated with correctional institutions. Often, chain-link fencing surrounds the buildings. Prisoners usually live in dormitories or even in small private rooms rather than cells. There is more personal freedom: Inmates may have television sets, choose their own clothes, and move about casually within and among the buildings. The system relies on rehabilitation programs and offers opportunities for education and work release. It also offers re-integration programs and support to inmates preparing for release. Some states and the Federal Bureau of Prisons operate minimum-security prison camps where inmates work

medium-security prison
A prison designed and organized to prevent escapes and violence, but in which restrictions on inmates and visitors are less rigid than in maximum-security facilities.

minimum-security prison
A prison designed and organized to permit inmates and visitors as much freedom as is consistent with the concept of incarceration.

© Justin Sullivan/Getty Images

Read about how the **North Carolina Department of Correction** classifies and assigns inmates to different custody levels; go to the corresponding link at www.cengage.com/ criminaljustice/clear.

on forest conservation and fight wildfires. To the outsider, minimum-security prisons may seem to enforce little punishment, but the inmates remain segregated from society and their freedoms are restricted. It is still a prison.

Private Prisons

U.S. taxpayers spend approximately $38.2 billion annually on prisons. About $3.3 billion is on inmate medical care, $1.2 billion on feeding prisoners, and $996 million for utilities (electricity, heating oil, water).[22] To accomplish these sorts of tasks, many jurisdictions contract with private companies to furnish food and medical services, educational and vocational training, maintenance, industrial programs, and other services. Although private enterprise has long played a role in American corrections, the scope of services purchased from profit-seeking organizations has expanded greatly in recent decades. In fact, governments now hire corporations to house prisoners in privately owned facilities.

Douglas McDonald has identified four basic forms of public and private involvement in corrections, as shown in **Figure 10.4**. His model distinguishes between ownership and operating authority. Some institutions are both owned and operated by either government or a private enterprise. Others, however, may be owned by government and operated under contract by a private entity, or owned by a private entity and operated by government on a lease or lease-purchase agreement.

Over the past 25 years, entrepreneurs have made inroads in the corrections arena by building and operating private facilities. Private entrepreneurs argue they can build and run prisons as effectively, safely, and humanely as any level of government. They propose also that they can do so more efficiently, which saves taxpayers money. Pressured by prison and jail crowding, rising staff costs, and growing public sentiment regarding inefficient government, politicians in the early 1980s found such proposals appealing. In 1986 Kentucky's Marion Adjustment Center became the first privately owned and operated facility for the incarceration of adult felons classified to at least a level of minimum security.

Although a recent development, private management of entire institutions for adult felons has already become a growth industry. By the end of 2007, privately operated facilities housed 125,975 inmates.[23] The private-prison business is dominated by the Corrections Corporation of America (CCA), which is the fifth-largest correctional system

Inmates wait for a gate to open remotely at Florence, Arizona, a facility of Corrections Corporation of America. CCA dominates the private-prison business. Questions have arisen as to whether privately owned and operated prisons really reduce costs.

Photo by Earnie Grafton/San Diego Union-Tribune/ZUMA Press. © Copyright 2006 by San Diego Union-Tribune

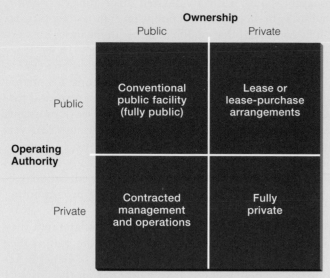

	Ownership	
	Public	Private
Public	Conventional public facility (fully public)	Lease or lease-purchase arrangements
Private	Contracted management and operations	Fully private

Operating Authority

Figure 10.4
Four Basic Forms of Public and Private Involvement in Correctional Administration

Ownership and operating authority are the key variables that help us differentiate forms of correctional administration.

Source: Douglas McDonald, "Private Penal Institutions," in *Crime and Justice: A Review of Research,* vol. 16, edited by Michael Tonry (Chicago: University of Chicago Press, 1992), 365.

in the United States. CCA currently manages over half of the beds under contract with private operators. Today, because many states now have excess capacity in their prisons, the growth of the private-prison industry is expected to level off somewhat.

PRACTICAL AND ETHICAL ISSUES ■ Private prisons remain quite controversial, giving rise to several issues. For example, advocates of privately operated prisons claim that their facilities provide the same level of care as do state-run facilities. But

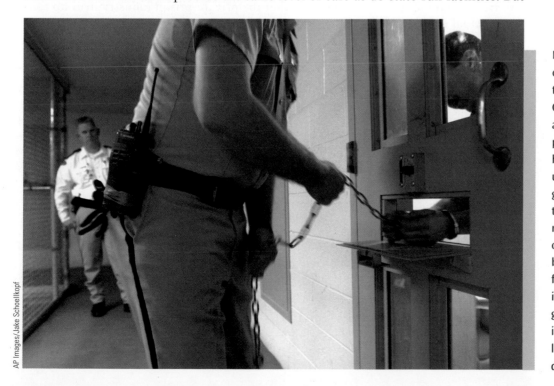

AP Images/Jake Schoellkopf

Major John Beard (rear), chief of security at the Guadalupe County Correctional Facility, watches as an inmate is handcuffed prior to being taken from his cell in the segregation unit. The murder of a guard by prisoners at this private facility and murders of inmates at other private facilities have been seen as wake-up calls for New Mexico to review its corrections system in general and private prisons in particular. What practical, legal, and ethical questions do private prisons pose?

MYTHS IN CORRECTIONS

PRIVATE VERSUS PUBLIC PRISONS

THE MYTH: Private prisons are more cost-effective than public prisons.

THE REALITY: Research shows that private prisons are no more cost-effective than public prisons. A variety of other factors, such as security level, inmate population size, and the age of the facility, influence a prison's daily per diem cost.

Source: Travis C. Pratt and Jeff Maahs, "Are Private Prisons More Cost-Effective Than Public Prisons? A Meta-analysis of Evaluation Research Studies," *Crime and Delinquency* 45 (July 1999): 358–71.

researchers have not yet validated this claim consistently. One study of 48 private and public juvenile correctional facilities concluded that public and private facilities are very similar in terms of environmental quality.[24] The evidence regarding prison programming shows that differences exist between state and private adult institutions: Compared with private prisons, a greater proportion of state and federal correctional facilities provide access to work programs (96.7 versus 55.9 percent), education programs (92.7 versus 59.5 percent), and counseling programs (97.3 versus 74.2 percent).[25] But the percentage of privately owned facilities providing prisoners with basic adult education, secondary education, and vocational training programming has increased substantially since 1995.[26]

Supporters of prison privatization also claim that they can run prisons more cheaply than do the states. (See "Myths in Corrections.") However, the U.S. General Accounting Office issued a report comparing the costs of public and private prisons. After reviewing five separate studies, it could not determine whether privatization saved money.[27] Another study concluded that private prisons were no more cost-effective than public prisons.[28] In cases where cost savings can be shown, such savings are fairly modest and result from reductions in staffing, fringe benefits, and other personnel-related costs.[29] For example, research has shown that private prisons pay new officers less and provide employees with nearly 60 hours less preservice training than do public prisons.[30] Not surprisingly, correctional officer unions continue to oppose private prisons.

Questions about accountability of service providers to public correctional officials are also raised. Critics charge that the profit incentive may result in poor services, as evidenced by a detainee uprising at a jail in Elizabeth, New Jersey, run by the Esmore Correctional Services Corporation for the Immigration and Naturalization Service. Undercutting a bid by the Wackenhut Corporation by $20 million, Esmore violated the contract through understaffing, abuse of detainees, inadequate physical conditions, and health hazards. A movement is growing for greater government regulation of private prisons. In Ohio, Texas, Tennessee, and several other states, legislatures have enacted or are considering new laws to ensure that the private-prison industry lives up to its contractual obligations.[31]

More generally, private prisons point to an important philosophical question. Should governments delegate social control functions to private, profit-seeking entities? Michael Reisig and Travis Pratt argue that prison administration is a basic government function that should not be delegated to private concerns. John DiIulio agrees and believes that doing otherwise corrodes the moral bond between citizens and the government.[32] Another concern is whether private companies will always act in ways consistent with the public interest. Unlike their public counterparts, private-prison corporations need to fill their cells to be profitable. Some fear that correctional policy may become skewed because contractors will use political influence to build more facilities and to continue programs not in the public interest.

The web link for the **Corrections Corporation of America** is found at www.cengage.com/criminaljustice/clear.

The experience of Cornell Corrections illustrates this problem. Cornell built a 300-bed facility in Rhode Island only to find that the federal prisoners slated to be housed there at $83 a day did not materialize. Rhode Island's political leaders pressed the U.S. Justice Department to fill the facility, but to no avail. Facing angry bondholders and investors, Cornell hired an attorney to scour the country for states seeking beds for their prisoners. Only after North Carolina agreed to send 232 prisoners (including 18 murderers) to Rhode Island was Cornell's fiscal crisis relieved, at least temporarily.[33]

LEGAL ISSUES ■ Recall that Section 1983 allows prisoners to sue public officials for constitutional violations. Because private companies are acting "under the color of state law," it had originally been assumed that they could be sued under Section 1983.

But are guards employed by a private-prison company provided with the "qualified immunity" of government employees who perform similar correctional work? Qualified immunity shields state employees from liability as long as their conduct does not violate "clearly established" rights. In 1997 the U.S. Supreme Court examined the question of the liability of guards in private prisons. The Court said that private prison guards did not have this legal protection and are fully liable for their actions when they violate a protected right.[34] In a later case the Court ruled that federal inmates in privately operated facilities may sue individual employees alleged to have violated their constitutional rights, but prisoners cannot sue the corporation itself.[35] A former attorney for the Massachusetts Department of Correction, Stanley Adelman, commented that the law regarding legal liability and private prisons is "complex and, to put it mildly, not always logically consistent."[36]

Are Section 1983 suits filed against private facilities qualitatively different than suits filed by inmates housed in public correctional institutions? A recent study addressed this question. After reviewing a matched sample of Section 1983 suits, the authors of the study found that suits filed by inmates in privately operated facilities more often focused on living and physical conditions, such as religious freedom, harassment, and cruel and unusual punishment. Suits against public facilities more often alleged violations relating to medical treatment and physical security. Interestingly, when evaluating the judicial statements that were issued in response to inmate suits, the authors found that those concerning private facilities "carried greater levels of admonishment" and were "much more stern and corrective in nature."[37]

The idea of privately run correctional facilities has recently stimulated much interest among the general public and within the criminal justice community. But privatization itself has a long history in criminal justice, dating as far back as the English practice of transporting convicts to North America and Australia. Jeremy Bentham, well-known for his panopticon prison design, was himself an entrepreneur who unsuccessfully pursued a contract to construct and operate a prison.[38] There may be further privatization of prison services, or privatization may become only a limited venture initiated at a time of prison crowding, fiscal constraints on governments, and revival of free-enterprise ideology. In any case, the controversy about privatization has forced correctional officials to rethink some strongly held beliefs. In this regard, the possibility of competition from the private sector may have a positive impact.

■ WHO IS IN PRISON?

The age, education, and criminal history of the inmate population influence how correctional institutions function. What are the characteristics of inmates in the nation's prisons? Do most inmates have long records of serious offenses, or are many of them first-time offenders who have committed minor crimes? Do some inmates have special needs that dictate their place in prison? These questions are crucial to understanding the work of correctional professionals.

Data on the characteristics of prisoners are limited. The Bureau of Justice Statistics reports that a majority of prisoners are men, members of minority groups, and convicted of violent crimes.[39] Approximately 40 percent of state prisoners have not completed high school or its equivalent (see **Figure 10.5**).[40]

Recidivists and those who are convicted of violent crimes make up an overwhelming portion of the prison population. Research shows that 44 percent of prisoners are rearrested within the first year after release. Within three years about 25 percent of all released inmates will return to prison.[41] Most of today's prisoners have a history of persistent criminality. Four additional factors affect correctional operations: the increased number of elderly prisoners, the many prisoners with HIV/AIDS, the thousands of prisoners who are mentally ill, and the increase in long-term prisoners.

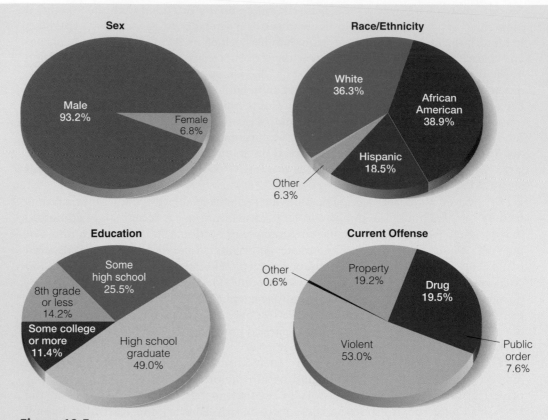

Figure 10.5

Characteristics of State Prisoner Inmates

State prisoners tend to be male and of a racial or ethnic minority, have at least a high school education, and have been convicted of violent offenses.

Sources: Bureau of Justice Statistics: *Education and Correctional Populations* (Washington, DC: U.S. Government Printing Office, January 2003), 2; *Prisoners in 2007* (Washington, DC: U.S. Government Printing Office, December 2008), 21.

Elderly Prisoners

Correctional officials have become increasingly aware of the growing number of inmates over age 55. Elderly prisoners have unique service needs regarding housing, medical care, programs, and release. Although older prisoners still make up a small proportion of the total inmate population, their numbers continue to rise and may become a major problem for corrections within the next decade.

■ *Housing:* Administrators believe that the elderly should usually remain in the general prison population, but with special accommodations. These accommodations can range from assigning older inmates to a bottom bunk to housing them in a separate wing with special architectural features, such as grab bars in cells and showers. Some states have specialized facilities for frail inmates and those with physical or mental disabilities.[42] Separate facilities and wings also prevent younger, tougher inmates from preying on the elderly.

■ *Medical care:* Elderly prisoners are those most likely to develop chronic illnesses such as heart disease, stroke, and cancer. The cost of maintaining an elderly inmate is much higher than that of maintaining a younger one. The aging prisoner population has no doubt contributed to rising health care expenditures. Spending for medical care in U.S. prison systems totals $3.3 billion annually.[43] Ironically, while in prison, the offender's life may be prolonged and medical care better than if he or

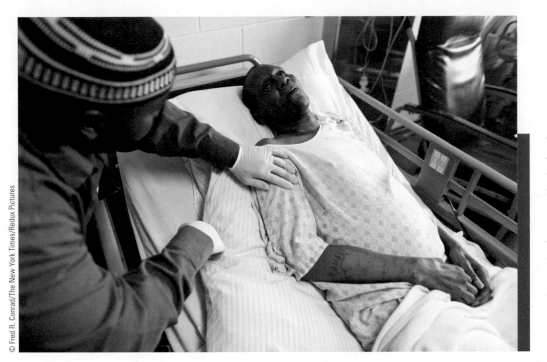

One-third of all inmates are over 50 years old. As courts have given longer sentences and parole has been tightened, more and more prisoners can expect to die while incarcerated. Seventy-five prisons now have hospice programs where palliative care is given. In many facilities, inmate volunteers tend dying comrades.

she were discharged. To care for dying prisoners, a number of states have created facilities that provide hospice care.[44]

■ *Programs:* Work assignments, recreation, and rehabilitative programs must be tailored to fit the physical and mental abilities of the elderly. For example, older inmates may work part time or engage in greenhouse or craft programs. Exercise designed to keep the elderly inmate active contributes to overall health. Work helps increase feelings of self-worth. Even life skills programs for the elderly help these prisoners think ahead toward their release date.

■ *Release:* Preparation for release of the elderly to community supervision or to hospice services requires time and special efforts by correctional staff. These include dealing with multiple government and social service agencies to ensure that social security and Medicare benefits will be available upon release and that medical care will continue. Staff must be proactive "to ensure that those who are eligible for release do not stay in prison because they have no place to go."[45]

Research indicates that as people get older, they become less dangerous. Only 1 percent of serious crime is committed by people over 60. But not all elderly prisoners are the same. Some elderly inmates are first-time offenders who committed their crime after age 50. Others are habitual criminals who have been in and out of prison most of their lives. Finally, some received long sentences and aged in prison.[46] Prisoner advocates argue that not all elderly prisoners should remain incarcerated until they die. Many states are considering community alternatives for low-security elderly prisoners. The Project for Older Prisoners (POPS) aims at culling low-risk geriatrics from overcrowded prisons. The alternative to releasing elderly prisoners seems to be to maintain an ever-larger population of them in prison geriatric wards.

Prisoners with HIV/AIDS

In the coming years AIDS is expected to be the leading cause of death among men aged 25 to 44.[47] With a significant percentage of the male inmate population under 35, correctional officials must cope with the problem of HIV—the human immunodeficiency virus that causes AIDS—as well as AIDS and related health issues. In 2005 there were 22,480 state and federal inmates with HIV or AIDS. The rate of confirmed AIDS cases

Information about prison **hospice programs for terminally ill inmates** can be found at the corresponding link at www.cengage.com/ criminaljustice/clear.

Learn more about the **Project for Older Prisoners** at the corresponding link at www .cengage.com/criminaljustice/ clear.

in state and federal prisons is 2.5 times higher than the rate in the total U.S. population. The high rate of infection among inmates can be explained by prisoners' high-risk behaviors, such as intravenous drug use, needle sharing, and unprotected sex. In 2005, 203 AIDS-related inmate deaths took place in federal and state prisons.[48] AIDS is the second-leading cause of death in prison, behind "natural causes."[49]

Homosexual activity among men is one way HIV is transmitted in prison populations. Although such behavior is forbidden, many inmates engage in homosexual behaviors at one time or another. But rates of HIV infection are higher among female prisoners (2.2 percent) than male prisoners (1.7 percent).[50] One study found that childhood sexual abuse is linked to HIV/AIDS risk-taking behavior among female prisoners.[51] Some argue that the government has a compelling interest to educate prisoners about the risky behaviors associated with HIV transmission.[52]

To deal with HIV/AIDS, prison officials have proposed a variety of policies. As they decide what actions their institution should take, however, they must face a host of legal, political, medical, budgetary, and attitudinal factors. Only 20 states test all new inmates for HIV. Other states conduct tests only if an inmate is in a high-risk group, if there is evidence to suggest the inmate is HIV-positive, or if the prisoner recently assaulted another inmate or staff member.[53] Policies concerning segregated housing for infected prisoners are especially controversial (see "Do the Right Thing").

Mentally Ill Prisoners

Mass closings of public hospitals for the mentally ill began in the 1960s. At the time new psychotropic drugs made treating patients in the community seem a more-humane alternative to hospitalization. It also promised to be less expensive. Soon, however,

DO THE RIGHT THING

The policy directive was precise: All inmates will be tested for HIV. All inmates found to be positive will be placed in Wing A, regardless of their physical condition, conviction offense, or time remaining in their sentence.

Testing for the deadly virus began at Elmwood State Prison soon after Warden True's directive was posted. All 753 inmates were tested over a three-week period, and every new prisoner, before entering the institution, had blood drawn at the medical unit for testing.

Six weeks after the directive was posted, the results were known. Most of the inmates breathed a sigh of relief in learning they were not positive. For a few, however, the call to report to the doctor was a prelude to a medical death sentence. The news that they had tested positive was traumatic. Most cursed, others burst into tears, still others sat in stunned silence.

The new policy was leaked to the press. The state chapter of the American Civil Liberties Union and the Howard Association for Prisoners' Rights called for a meeting with Warden True. In a press conference, they protested the "state's invasion of privacy" and the "discriminatory segregation of gays and drug users, most of the latter being African American and Hispanic." They emphasized that because it would be years before most of the infected would develop a "full" case of AIDS, correctional officials should respond with compassion, not stigmatization.

Warden True told reporters that he was responsible for the health of all inmates and that the policy had been developed to prevent transmission of the disease. He said that although the HIV inmates would be segregated, they would have access to all facilities available to the general inmate population but at separate times. He denied that he intended to stigmatize the 20 prisoners who had thus far tested positive.

WRITING ASSIGNMENT: Put yourself in Warden True's shoes. What factors would you consider in developing a policy for dealing with HIV in your facility? Next, discuss alternatives to testing and segregation that might be used to control the spread of HIV in correctional facilities. Finally, discuss whether it is ethical to segregate inmates with HIV/AIDS from the general prison population.

people saw that community treatment works only if patients take their medication. Widespread homelessness was the most public sign that the community treatment approach had its shortcomings. With the expansion of prisons and the greater police emphasis on public-order offenses, many mentally ill individuals are now arrested and incarcerated. These inmates tend to catch a revolving door from homelessness to incarceration and then back to the streets.

The incarceration rate of the mentally ill is considerably higher than that of the general population. Approximately 56 percent of state prison inmates have a history or symptoms of mental health problems. Homelessness prior to incarceration is more than twice as high among mentally ill prisoners than other prisoners.[54] Mental illness is more likely among offenders convicted of violent crimes and less likely among drug offenders. Mental health also varies by race, age, and gender. Inmates who are white, female, and under the age of 25 experience mental health problems more frequently than do other inmates.[55]

Mentally ill prisoners pose particular challenges for correctional professionals. For example, mentally ill inmates in state and federal prisons are more likely to be involved in fights than are other inmates, and about 58 percent of mentally ill state prisoners have been formally charged with rule violations.[56] Correctional workers are usually unprepared to deal with the mentally ill. Further, although some inmates benefit from the regular medication they receive in jail or prison, others suffer as the stress of confinement deepens their depression, intensifies delusions, or leads to mental breakdown. Some commit suicide.

The availability and type of mental health treatment programs in prison vary. The two most common types involve therapy/counseling or dispensing medications.[57] One in every eight inmates in state prisons receives counseling services, and approximately one in ten receives psychotropic medications. In some states, such as Maine, Hawaii, and Oregon, approximately 20 percent of inmates receive psychotropic medications.[58] Although dispensing medication can help keep these inmates stable and functioning, some observers fear that prisons tend to overmedicate prisoners.[59]

Long-Term Prisoners

More prisoners serve long sentences in the United States than in any other Western nation. One survey found that nearly 310,000 prisoners are currently serving at least 20-year sentences. Of these inmates, about 10 percent are serving "natural life," which means there is no possibility of parole.[60] The number of inmates serving natural life has nearly tripled since 1992. These long-term prisoners are often the same people who will become elderly offenders, with all the attendant problems. Each life sentence costs taxpayers an estimated $1 million.[61] The "get-tough" sentencing policies of the last 30 years—three-strikes, mandatory minimums, truth-in-sentencing—have altered the composition of the lifer population, which now includes more nonviolent offenders than before.[62]

Frederick Maue, Chief of Clinical Services at the Pennsylvania Department of Corrections, comments that severe depression, feelings of hopelessness, and other health problems are common among long-term prisoners. Such emotional stress tends to take place earlier in the sentence as these inmates lose contact with their families.[63] Addressing the mental health needs of this special population is critical to preventing sudden suicide attempts.

Long-term prisoners generally are not seen as control problems. They are charged with disciplinary infractions far less frequently than are short-term inmates. Rather, administrators must face the challenge of making the lives of such prisoners bearable. Experts suggest that administrators follow three main principles when managing long-term inmates: (1) maximize opportunities for the inmate to exercise choice in living circumstances, (2) create opportunities for meaningful living, and (3) help the inmate maintain contact with the outside world.[64] Many long-term inmates will eventually be released after spending the best years of their lives behind bars. Will these offenders be able to support themselves when they return to the community?

SUMMARY

1 Explain how today's prisons are linked to the past.

Contemporary prisons are shaped by the past in many ways. For example, many prisons in operation today were built over 100 years ago. These prisons were designed to reflect the correctional goals of the time, such as removing inmates from the distractions of the city. Many of these prisons are walled structures with large, tiered cell blocks that are located in rural areas. Although the primary goal today is custody, most prisons also provide inmates with programs. This feature of the modern prison can be traced back to the 1960s and 1970s when the rehabilitation model was dominant. Finally, inmates in today's correctional facilities have various constitutional rights that prison officials must respect. These rights were largely established in the 1960s.

2 Discuss the goals of incarceration.

Three models of incarceration have been used since the 1940s, each of which reflects different goals and styles of institutional organization. First, the custodial model emphasizes security, discipline, and order for the purposes of incapacitation, deterrence, or retribution. This model prevailed prior to World War II. The rehabilitation model, which developed during the 1950s, views every aspect of organization as directed toward reforming the offender. Toward this end, a variety of treatment programs are used. Finally, the reintegration model emphasizes the maintenance of the offender's ties to family and the community. Prisons that employ this model recognize that most inmates will one day return to the community. Accordingly, inmates are gradually given greater freedom and responsibility as they approach release.

3 Be familiar with the organization of incarceration.

American prisons are operated at the federal and state levels. Many of these prisons are very old and located in rural areas. State and federal facilities for men operate at different security levels, such as maximum and minimum security, which restrict inmate movement to a greater or lesser degree. Because so few women are imprisoned, most states house female offenders in a single facility. Most prison facilities are owned and operated by governments; however, many states and the federal government contract with private corporations that provide prison services, including housing inmates in privately owned facilities.

4 Discuss the factors that influence the classification of prisons.

State prisons for men are usually classified using three security classifications—maximum, medium, and minimum. A number of states also operate "supermax" prisons, where the most disruptive, violent, and incorrigible inmates are housed. Maximum-security prisons are designed to prevent escapes and to deter inmates from harming one another. Custody is emphasized in these prisons, which are usually run in a military-like fashion. Medium-security prisons are less rigid, and rehabilitation programs are more widely used. Compared with inmates in maximum-security prisons, those in medium-security facilities have more privileges and contact with the outside world. Finally, minimum-security prisons house the least violent offenders, prisoners who are nearing release, and long-term inmates with clean disciplinary records. Many of these facilities have work release programs. Prisoners in these facilities usually live in dormitories or small private rooms rather than cells.

5 Explain who is in prison.

The overwhelming majority of inmates in both federal and state prisons are male. A majority of federal inmates are drug offenders, and federal prisoners tend to come from a higher socioeconomic class than do state prisoners. The majority of federal inmates are white. In state prisons, a large number of inmates are members of racial and ethnic minority groups. A majority of prisoners are convicted of violent crimes. Correctional officials must increasingly deal with the problems of special populations, including elderly prisoners, prisoners with HIV/AIDS, mentally ill prisoners, and long-term prisoners. Elderly prisoners have unique service needs regarding housing, medical care, programs, and release. Testing inmates for HIV/AIDS and segregating infected prisoners raises civil rights issues. Mentally ill prisoners tend to get into fights and break rules more often than do other inmates, and treatment varies by institution. Finally, the number of long-term prisoners has increased greatly, presenting corrections with the task of making the lives of such prisoners bearable.

KEY TERMS

campus style (p. 268)

courtyard style (p. 268)

custodial model (p. 262)

maximum-security prison (p. 270)

medium-security prison (p. 271)

minimum-security prison (p. 271)

radial design (p. 267)

rehabilitation model (p. 262)

reintegration model (p. 262)

telephone-pole design (p. 268)

FOR DISCUSSION

1. Is the custodial model most appropriate for organizing prisons that operate at different security levels? What model should be used to organize a minimum-security facility?
2. What are some of the strengths and weaknesses of various prison designs? Are some designs better than others?
3. What questions emerge regarding the practice of contracting with private, for-profit organizations to operate correctional facilities? Should the job of operating prisons be the sole responsibility of the government?
4. Which characteristics of the prison population may present major problems for the managers of institutions?
5. If you were a warden, how would you handle long-term prisoners?

FOR FURTHER READING

Hallett, Michael A. *Private Prisons in America: A Critical Race Perspective.* Chicago: University of Illinois Press, 2006. Views the prison privatization movement as the latest attempt to oppress and legally discriminate against African American men.

Hallinan, Joseph T. *Going Up the River: Travels in a Prison Nation.* New York: Random House, 2001. From California to North Carolina and from New York to Texas, Hallinan explores one of America's growth industries: its prisons.

Keve, Paul W. *Prisons and the American Conscience.* Carbondale: Southern Illinois University Press, 1991. Recounts the history of U.S. federal corrections from 1776.

Wright, Richard A. *In Defense of Prisons.* Westport, CT: Greenwood Press, 1994. Critiques the critics of incarceration and analyzes deterrence and incapacitation in support of the prison.

NOTES

1 Bureau of Justice Statistics, *Probation and Parole in the United States, 2006* (Washington, DC: U.S. Government Printing Office, December 2007), 2.

2 Bureau of Justice Statistics, *Prisoners in 2007* (Washington, DC: U.S. Government Printing Office, December 2008), 1.

3 Charles H. Logan, "Criminal Justice Performance Measures in Prisons," in *Performance Measures for the Criminal Justice System* (Washington, DC: U.S. Government Printing Office, October 1993), 13.

4 Bureau of Justice Statistics, *Census of State and Federal Correctional Facilities, 2005* (Washington, DC: U.S. Government Printing Office, October 2008).

5 "About the Bureau of Prisons," http://www.bop.gov/about/index.jsp, December 26, 2008.

6 Federal Bureau of Prisons, *State of the Bureau, 2007* (Washington, DC: U.S. Government Printing Office, 2007), 52.

7 Bureau of Justice Statistics, *Census*, Appendix Table 2.

8 Federal Bureau of Prisons, *State of the Bureau*, 9–10.

9 John J. DiIulio, *No Escape: The Future of American Corrections* (New York: Basic Books, 1991), 203–10.

10 Bureau of Justice Statistics, *Census*, Appendix Table 12.

11 Alabama Department of Corrections, http://www.doc.state.al.us, June 23, 2009.

12 Norman Johnston, *Forms of Constraint: A History of Prison Architecture* (Urbana: University of Illinois Press, 2000).

13 Joseph T. Hallinan, *Going Up the River: Travels in a Prison Nation* (New York: Random House, 2001), xvi.

14 William G. Nagel, *The New Red Barn: A Critical Look at the American Prison* (New York: Walker, 1973), 40.

15 Randy Martin and David L. Myers, "Public Response to Prison Siting: Perceptions of Impact on Crime and Safety," *Criminal Justice and Behavior* 32 (April 2005): 143–71.

16 Ryan Scott King, Marc Mauer, and Tracy Huling, "An Analysis of the Economics of Prison Siting in Rural Communities," *Criminology and Public Policy* 3 (July 2004): 453–80.

17 Daniel P. Mears, "A Critical Look at Supermax Prisons," *Corrections Compendium* 30 (September–October 2005): 6–7, 45–49.

18 Chad S. Briggs, Jody L. Sundt, and Thomas C. Castellano, "The Effect of Supermaximum Security Prisons on Aggregate Levels of Institutional Violence," *Criminology* 41 (November 2003): 1341–76.

19 Bureau of Justice Statistics, *Census*, Appendix Tables 5 and 11.

20 Ibid., Appendix Tables 5 and 11.

21 Ibid., Appendix Tables 5 and 11.

22 Bureau of Justice Statistics, *State Prison Expenditures, 2001* (Washington, DC: U.S. Government Printing Office, June 2004), 6.

23 Bureau of Justice Statistics, *Prisoners in 2007*, Appendix Table 13.

24 Gaylene Styve Armstrong and Doris Layton MacKenzie, "Private versus Public Juvenile Facilities: Do Differences in Environmental Quality Exist?" *Crime and Delinquency* 49 (October 2003): 542–63.

25 Bureau of Justice Statistics, *Census*, Appendix Tables 16, 18, and 19.

26 Bureau of Justice Statistics, *Education and Correctional Populations* (Washington, DC: U.S. Government Printing Office, January 2003), 4.

27 U.S. General Accounting Office, *Private and Public Prisons: Studies Comparing Operational Costs and/or Quality of Service* (Washington, DC: U.S. Government Printing Office, August 1996).

28 Travis C. Pratt and Jeff Maahs, "Are Private Prisons More Cost-Effective Than Public Prisons? A Meta-Analysis of Evaluation Research Studies," *Crime and Delinquency* 45 (July 1999): 358–71.

29 James Austin and Garry Coventry, "Emerging Issues on Privatizing Prisons," *Corrections Forum* 10 (December 2001): 11.

30 Curtis Blakely, "Private and State Run U.S. Prisons Compared," *Probation Journal* 51 (2004): 254–56.

31 *New York Times*, April 15, 1999, p. 1.

32 Michael D. Reisig and Travis C. Pratt, "The Ethics of Correctional Privatization," *Prison Journal* 80 (June 2000): 210–22; DiIulio, *No Escape*, pp. 180–203.

33 *New York Times*, November 24, 1995, p. 1.

34 *Richardson v. McKnight*, 521 U.S. 399 (1997).

35 *Correctional Services Corporation v. Malesko*, 534 U.S. 61 (2001).

36 Stanley E. Adelman, "Supreme Court Rules on Potential Liabilities of Private Corrections," *Corrections Today* 64 (July 2002): 28.

37 Curtis R. Blakely and Vic W. Bumphus, "An Analysis of Civil Suits Filed against Private and Public Prisons: A Comparison of Title 42: Section 1983 Litigation," *Criminal Justice Policy Review* 16 (March 2005): 85.

38 Malcolm M. Feeley, "Entrepreneurs of Punishment: The Legacy of Privatization," *Punishment and Society* 4 (July 2002): 327–33.

39 Bureau of Justice Statistics, *Prisoners in 2007*, p. 21.

40 Bureau of Justice Statistics, *Education and Correctional Populations*, p. 2.

41 Bureau of Justice Statistics, *Recidivism of Prisoners Released in 1994* (Washington, DC: U.S. Government Printing Office, June 2002), 3.

42 Anthony A. Sterns, Greta Lax, Chad Sed, Patrick Keohane, and Ronni S. Sterns, "The Growing Wave of Older Prisoners: A National Survey of Older Prisoner Health, Mental Health and Programming," *Corrections Today* 70 (August 2008): 70–76.

43 Bureau of Justice Statistics, *State Prison Expenditures*, p. 1.

44 Sterns et al., "Growing Wave of Older Prisoners," p. 71.

45 Joann Brown Morton, "Implications for Corrections of an Aging Prison Population," *Corrections Management Quarterly* 5 (Winter 2001): 84.

46 Connie Neeley, Laura Addison, and Delores Craig-Moreland, "Addressing the Needs of Elderly Offenders," *Corrections Today* 59 (August 1997): 120–23.

47 Centers for Disease Control and Prevention, http://www.cdc.gov/men/lcod/04all.pdf, June 24, 2009.

48 Bureau of Justice Statistics, *HIV in Prisons, 2005* (Washington, DC: U.S. Government Printing Office, September 2007).

49 Bureau of Justice Statistics, *Suicide and Homicide in State Prisons and Local Jails* (Washington, DC: U.S. Government Printing Office, August 2005), 2.

50 Bureau of Justice Statistics, *HIV in Prisons, 2005*, p. 1.

[51] Janet L. Mullings, James W. Marquart, and Deborah J. Hartley, "Exploring the Effects of Childhood Sexual Abuse and Its Impact on HIV/AIDS Risk-Taking Behavior among Women Prisoners," *Prison Journal* 83 (December 2003): 442–63.

[52] Barbara H. Zaitzow, "Whose Problem Is It Anyway? Women Prisoners and HIV/AIDS," *International Journal of Offender Therapy and Comparative Criminology* 45 (December 2001): 673–90.

[53] Bureau of Justice Statistics, *HIV in Prisons, 2004* (Washington, DC: U.S. Government Printing Office, November 2006), 6.

[54] Bureau of Justice Statistics, *Mental Health Problems of Prison and Jail Inmates* (Washington DC: U.S. Government Printing Office, September 2006), 1.

[55] Ibid., p. 4.

[56] Ibid., p. 10.

[57] Kenneth Adams and Joseph Ferrandino, "Managing Mentally Ill Inmates in Prisons," *Criminal Justice and Behavior* 35 (August 2008): 913–27.

[58] Bureau of Justice Statistics, *Mental Health Treatment in State Prisons, 2000* (Washington, DC: U.S. Government Printing Office, July 2001), 1.

[59] Terry A. Kupers, *Prison Madness* (San Francisco: Jossey-Bass, 1999), 9.

[60] Camille Graham Camp, *The 2002 Corrections Yearbook: Adult Corrections* (Middletown, CT: Criminal Justice Institute, 2003).

[61] Marc Mauer, Ryan S. King, and Malcolm C. Young, *The Meaning of "Life": Long Prison Sentences in Context* (Washington, DC: The Sentencing Project, 2004), 3.

[62] Ibid., p. 13.

[63] Frederick R. Maue, "An Overview of Correctional Mental Health Issues," *Corrections Today* 63 (August 2001): 8.

[64] Timothy J. Flanagan, "Adaptation and Adjustment among Long-Term Prisoners," *Federal Prison Journal* 2 (Spring 1991): 41–51.

AP Images/SEVANS

LEARNING OBJECTIVES

After reading this chapter you should be able to . . .

1 Discuss the "inmate code" and talk about where the values of the prison subculture come from.

2 Be familiar with the prison economy.

3 Explain the different types of prison violence.

4 Discuss what can be done about prison violence.

Self-proclaimed neo-Nazi Joseph Druce strangled fellow inmate John Geoghan in the protective custody unit of the Souza-Baranowski Correctional Center in Massachusetts. The murder raised multiple questions as to why prison staff did not prevent the incident.

SHORTLY BEFORE noon on August 23, 2003, the 22 inmates housed in the protective custody unit at the Souza-Baranowski Correctional Center in Lancaster, Massachusetts, were returning to their cells. As the doors clanged shut, prison staff discovered that an inmate was out of place.

Locked in his 68-year-old neighbor's cell, the heavily tattooed, self-proclaimed neo-Nazi Joseph L. Druce jammed the door shut from the inside by placing a toothbrush, nail clippers, and a book he had cut in two into the door tracks. This would slow the guards' entry.

Druce tied his elderly victim's hands behind his back, threw him to the cell floor, and began strangling him with a pair of socks. Officers arriving on the scene had trouble getting the cell door open. Druce continued his violent assault, jumping off the frail victim's bed, landing on his chest, snapping his ribs, and puncturing his lungs.

Approximately eight minutes passed before officers were able to make their way into the cell. The elderly prisoner,

THE PRISON EXPERIENCE

John J. Geoghan, a former Catholic priest serving a 9- to 10-year sentence for molesting a 10-year-old boy, received medical attention but died two hours later at a local hospital.

Questions quickly emerged: How could something like this happen in a protective custody unit? Why was Geoghan housed in the same unit as a prisoner who was convicted of murdering a homosexual man and who openly professed his hatred for gays? Why didn't prison staff prevent the incident? Was Geoghan's claim that prison officers had previously assaulted and harassed him related to the incident?

It is no secret that prisons can be violent places. After all, prisons house violent offenders under crowded conditions. We can better understand the causes of prison violence and patterns of victimization by examining the social and personal dimensions of life behind the prison walls. Druce, for example, described the Geoghan murder as "a prize" that also showed the world "that child predators must be dealt with more stringently."[1] But is Druce the "typical" inmate one finds in American prisons? Can we assume that violence is this rampant throughout the corrections system? If you were entering prison for the first time, what should you expect?

Even the most hardened criminal must be tense on entering (or reentering) prison. For the "fish," the newcomer, the first few hours and days engender tremendous worry and anxiety. "What will it be like? How should I act? Will I be able to protect myself?" Like an immigrant starting out in a new country, new prisoners have trouble with the language, finding strange customs and unfamiliar rules. Unlike the immigrant, however, the prisoner does not have the freedom to choose where and with whom to live. (See the Focus box "Going In: The Chain.")

What does being incarcerated mean to inmates, guards, and administrators? How do prisons function? Are the officers really in charge, or do the inmates "run the joint"? As we examine the different dimensions of prison life, imagine you are visiting a foreign land and trying to learn about its culture and daily activities. Although the prison may be located in the United States, the traditions, language, and relationships appear foreign to most visitors.

Chapter

11

FOCUS ON CORRECTIONAL PRACTICE

Going In: The Chain

Michael Santos

Have you ever had a time in your life when you just wanted to die, when you thought death would be easier than facing the problems that you know are waiting for you? That was the feeling I had when I was 23 years old, just after a federal judge in Seattle sentenced me to serve 45 years in prison for a nonviolent drug crime.

I remember my thoughts and experiences clearly as I was beginning that term. I had already been detained for about a year—awaiting my trial—before the judge sentenced me. A few weeks after conviction and the imposition of sentence, I knew I'd soon be on my way to prison. It would be a new experience, and one I wasn't looking forward to beginning.

My journey began when one of the guards from the jail came by my cell door early on a Saturday morning to wake me. "Roll up!" he hollered. "Roll up" is jail vernacular ordering a prisoner to pack all belongings and prepare for movement. The moment he said it, I felt it. His words were hanging in the air, like a threat, letting me know I was on my way to a place from where some don't return. "Okay, let's go," I said to myself as I tried to pump up my heart.

I didn't have much, as the jail really limits the amount of personal property a prisoner can keep. The guard marched me to a smoke-filled room where my ankles were shackled together and my wrists were cuffed to a chain wrapped around my waist. There were several other prisoners in the room. We were all chained together, because we were to ride the bus that would deliver us to prison.

I didn't know where I was going, not for several hours anyway. Then I found out. I was off to the U.S. Penitentiary in Atlanta. "Damn," I thought, "why would they be sending me to Atlanta? I'm from Seattle."

It didn't much matter what I thought. I was beginning to realize my thoughts didn't matter to anyone but me. When I was arrested, I pretty much lost my identity and became chattel, property of the U.S. government. Prison guards regulated everything in my life: the clothes I wore, the food I ate, the time I slept, the mail I sent or received. Lawyers even spoke for me. All I did was go through the motions of being human; someone else was always directing me. That is what it means to lose freedom.

What I did begin to think about was my own mortality. What was I going to be after release? I was a young man then, but I wouldn't walk the streets again until I was well over 50 years old. I'd been an adult for only a few years before I got locked up; now prison was going to be my life. Who would I be after release? An old man with nothing: no home, no automobile, no assets. A couple of friends might buy me a doughnut and a cup of coffee, but I'd have nowhere to go. I'd have to start life from nothing—at over 50—and that was a chilling feeling.

The month-long bus ride was hell. We left Seattle, but rather than going directly to Atlanta, we worked our way across the West picking up and dropping off prisoners. I was restrained during the whole time, and the people sitting around me were, for the most part, guys who seemed like they'd been doing time forever. Most were covered with tattoos. I guess the tattoos were supposed to be frightening or something, like they were going to make the prisoner scarier and somehow meaner; they worked. I was learning everyone had their own way of dealing with time. Yet I had enough experience after my year in the county jail to know that I'd do my time alone.

When the bus finally approached the huge penitentiary in Atlanta, I was awestruck by the enormous wall that enveloped the entire prison. It stood 40 feet high, clearly separating

■ PRISON SOCIETY

The 1934 publication of Joseph Fishman's *Sex in Prison* marked the beginning of the scientific study of inmate subcultures in maximum-security institutions.[2] Since that time social scientists have studied the prison as a functioning community with its own values, roles, language, and customs. In other words, the inmates of a maximum-security prison do not serve their time in isolation. Rather, prisoners form a society with traditions,

the prisoners inside from the community. And the heavily armed guards standing outside the bus made clear there was nothing nice behind that wall.

I was scared, but I was determined to do whatever it took to make it through. I told myself repeatedly I was ready, but now, in retrospect, I realize I could never be ready. There was no room for fear, but fear was everywhere. I could smell it on the bus, on the men. We all waited, looking outside the windows in silence. I knew the only way I was going to make it was to stand up and face it, to go through it; it was with this absolute resolve that I was determined to return to the world.

Finally, the guards began calling us off by last name and prison number. It is not easy walking with a 12-inch chain connected to each ankle, and wrists bound to a chain that runs around the waist, but when my name was called, I managed to wobble through the bus's aisle, hopped down the steps, then began the long march up the stairs leading to the fortress. As I was moving to the prison's doors, I remember glancing over my shoulder, knowing it would be the last time I'd see the world from the outside of prison walls for a long time.

Once I was inside, the plain concrete walls reminded me my time was not going to be easy. As I was getting settled inside the walls, walking through the crowded halls, staring at the desperate faces, I felt the pressure. It was like I was on the road with a million drunk drivers all at once! They were angry with no apparent reason, as if they woke up in the morning and didn't even know themselves why they were mad.

Standing in line to eat breakfast is like going through a busy intersection when the traffic lights don't work; it's easy to crash, to get into a wreck without warning. Bam! That was how fast things happen in the penitentiary. I learned that killers stand 5 feet 6 to 5 feet 8. People who appear harmless are frequently the most dangerous men in the penitentiary.

And there is no such thing as a fair fight in prison. You see guys over 6 feet tall, 220 pounds, hitting 5 feet 8, 150-pound guys with a piece of pipe when the smaller guy isn't looking. Fighters get respect from the other prisoners for this kind of thing, that is, recognition for doing "the right thing." I've seen people stabbed and piped in the showers, [the] chow hall, the yard, the theater. People wore phone books taped to their bodies to protect themselves as they walked to the yard. Shanks [knives] were planted everywhere. Prison is really a gladiator school; a battle zone full of desperate men—a place where no one wants to be.

I remember reading somewhere that there are no atheists in foxholes, as every soldier placed in that situation is praying to God. Similarly, there really are no pacifists in prison, as even the most docile-seeming prisoner is capable of extreme violence, and often for no apparent reason. All prisoners feel the tension [that] no matter where a man walks behind the walls, the threat of death is ever present. Seasoned prisoners want newcomers to either run with them or run away from them. They want to mold the way a prisoner behaves, who his friends are, and what he does. I refused to let the others dictate the kind of person I would be, so I pursued my own goals and decided to keep to myself while inside.

Serving a prison term is a consuming experience. Since I didn't want to be consumed, and didn't want to become like many of the people around me, I committed myself to building a better life and focusing on the future, on life outside of prison walls. I knew my road in prison would be long. I was certain the prisoners around me could make the road longer, and none of them could make it shorter. And that's why I've always structured my time to help me avoid them.

Source: Michael Santos is now serving his time in a minimum-security prison camp; 2009 marked the 22nd year of his 45-year sentence. Reprinted by permission.

norms, and a leadership structure. Some may choose to associate with only a few close friends; others form cliques along racial or "professional" lines.[3] Still others may be the politicians of the convict society; they attempt to represent convict interests and distribute valued goods in return for support. Just as a social culture exists in the free world, a prisoner subculture exists on the "inside." Membership in a group provides mutual protection from theft and physical assault, the basis of wheeling-and-dealing activities, and a source of cultural identity.

A link to a website devoted to **communications by and with prisoners** is found at www.cengage.com/ criminaljustice/clear.

The concept of the prisoner subculture helps us understand inmate society. Like members of other groups who interact primarily among themselves and are physically separated from the larger world (groups such as soldiers, medical patients, or monks), inmates develop their own myths, slang, customs, rewards, and sanctions. However, the notion that the prisoner subculture is isolated, separate, and opposed to the dominant culture may now be misleading, because contemporary prisons are less isolated from the larger society than were big-house prisons. Although prisons do create special conditions that compel inmates to adapt to their environment, the culture of the outside world penetrates prison walls through television, magazines, newspapers, and contact with visitors and family. In short, the prison is very much a product of institutional and political relationships between the prison and the larger society.

Norms and Values

inmate code
A set of rules of conduct that reflect the values and norms of the prison social system and help define for inmates the image of the model prisoner.

As in any society, the convict world has certain distinctive norms and values. Often described as the **inmate code**, these norms and values develop within the prison social system and help define the inmate's image of the model prisoner. As Robert Johnson notes, "The public culture of the prison has norms that dictate behavior 'on the yard' and in other public areas of the prison such as mess halls, gyms, and the larger program and work sites."[4] Prison is an ultramasculine world. The culture breathes masculine toughness and insensitivity, impugns softness, and emphasizes the use of hostility and manipulation in one's relations with fellow inmates and staff. It makes caring and friendly behavior, especially with respect to the staff, look servile and silly.[5]

Charles Terry, a former inmate, says that male prisoners must project an image of "fearlessness in the way they walk, talk, and socially interact."[6] Inmates must never show emotion about pain; such feeling is seen as weakness. Terry believes that humor is one of the ways some inmates cope. It is used to bridge the gap between a normal and a convict identity.

The code also emphasizes the solidarity of all inmates against the staff. The two primary rules of the inmate code are "do your own time" and "don't inform on another convict." Following his New Jersey study, Gresham Sykes refined the rules embodied in the code as follows:

1 *Don't interfere with inmate interests.* Never rat on a con, don't be nosy, don't have a loose lip, and don't put a guy on the spot.

2 *Don't quarrel with fellow inmates.* Play it cool, don't lose your head, do your own time.

3 *Don't exploit inmates.* Don't break your word, don't steal from cons, don't sell favors, and don't welsh on bets.

4 *Maintain yourself.* Don't weaken, don't whine, don't cop out, be tough, be a man.

5 *Don't trust the guards or the things they stand for.* Don't be a sucker, guards are hacks and screws, the officials are wrong and the prisoners are right.[7]

How does the "fish," the newcomer, learn the norms and values of the prison society? In jail awaiting transfer to the prison, the fish hears from fellow inmates exaggerated descriptions of what lies ahead. The bus ride to prison and the processing through the prison reception center further initiate the novice. The actions of the staff at the reception center, the folktales passed on by experienced cons, and the derisive shouts of the inmates on the inside all serve as elements of a degradation ceremony that shocks the new prisoner into readiness to begin the **prisonization** process. But not all prisoners complete this process. In his pioneering work, Donald Clemmer suggests that such factors as a short sentence, continuation of contacts with the outside, a stable personality, and refusal to become part of the group may weaken prisonization.[8]

prisonization
The process by which a new inmate absorbs the customs of prison society and learns to adapt to the environment.

The prisoner subculture designates inmates according to the roles they play in that society and the extent to which they conform to the code. Among the roles described in

the literature are "right guy" or "real man" (an upholder of prisoner values and interests), "square John" (an inmate with a noncriminal self-concept), "punk" (a passive homosexual), "rat" (an inmate who squeals or sells out to the authorities), and "gorilla"
or "wolf" (an aggressive inmate who pursues his own self-interest at others' expense).[9]
TJ Granack, sentenced to serve 15–30 years for first-degree attempted murder, lists 15
survival tips for beginners. See some of these in the Focus box "Survival Tips for Beginners" and note how many conform to the inmate code.

A single, overriding inmate code probably does not exist in present-day institutions.
Instead, convict society is organized along racial, ethnic, and age lines.[10] Adherence to
the inmate code also differs among institutions, with greater modifications to local situations found in maximum-security prisons. Still, the core commandments as described
by Sykes 50 years or so ago remain.

Reflecting tensions in U.S. society, many prisons are today marked by racially motivated violence, organizations based on race, and voluntary segregation by inmates by
race whenever possible, such as in recreation areas and dining halls.

Do prisoners reject the views of conventional society? Research by Lucia Benaquisto
and Peter Freed found that a vast majority of inmates hold views on law and justice
similar to those held by the general public. But as individuals they also view themselves
as exceptions; it is the "other inmates" whose norms are contrary to those of society.

FOCUS ON CORRECTIONAL PRACTICE

Survival Tips for Beginners

Okay, so you just lost your case. Maybe you took a plea bargain. Whatever. The point is you've been sentenced. You've
turned yourself over to the authorities and you're in the county
jail waiting to catch the next chain to the R Units [receiving]
where you'll be stripped and shaved and photographed and
processed and sent to one of the various prisons in your state.

So what's a felon to do? Here are some survival tips that
may make your stay less hellish:

1. *Commit an Honorable Crime.* Commit a crime that's considered, among convicts, to be worthy of respect. I was
   lucky. I went down for first degree attempted murder, so
   my crime fell in the "honorable" category. Oh, goodie. So I
   just had to endure the everyday sort of danger and abuse
   that comes with prison life.

2. *Don't Gamble.* Not cards, not chess, not the Super Bowl.
   And if you do, don't bet too much. If you lose too much,
   and pay up (don't even think of doing otherwise), then
   you'll be known as [the] rich guy who'll be very popular
   with the vultures.

3. *Never Loan Anyone Anything.* Because if you do, you'll be
   expected to collect one way or another. If you don't collect
   you will be known as a mark, as someone without enough
   heart to take back his own.

4. *Make No Eye Contact.* Don't look anyone in the eye. Ever.
   Locking eyes with another man, be he a convict or a guard,

is considered a challenge, a threat, and should therefore
be avoided.

5. *Pick Your Friends Carefully.* When you choose a friend,
   you've got to be prepared to deal with anything that person may have done. Their reputation is yours, and the
   consequences can be enormous.

6. *Fight and Fight Dirty.* You have to fight, and not according
   to Marquis of Queensbury rules, either. If you do it right,
   you'll only have to do it once or twice. If you don't, expect
   regular whoopings and loss of possessions.

7. *Mind Your Own Business.* Never get in the middle of anyone else's discussion/argument/confrontation/fight. Never
   offer unsolicited knowledge or advice.

8. *Keep a Good Porn Collection.* If you *don't* have one, the
   boys will think you're funny.

9. *Don't Talk to Staff, Especially Guards.* Any prolonged discussions or associations with staff makes you susceptible
   to rumor and suspicion of being a snitch.

10. *Never Snitch.* Or even *appear* to snitch. And above all,
    avoid the real thing. And if you do, you'd better not get
    caught.

Source: From TJ Granack, "Welcome to the Steel Hotel: Survival Tips
for Beginners," in *The Funhouse Mirror*, edited by Robert Gordon Ellis
(Pullman, WA: Washington State University Press, 2000), 6–10.

Contemporary prison society is divided along racial, ethnic, and gang subgroups—there is no inmate code to which all prisoners subscribe.

© Adam Tanner/The Image Works

The researchers suggest that, while incarcerated, the inmate must live and survive in an environment "where his movements and options are constrained, his person is insecure, and personal control is highly limited."[11] Thus, many inmates conform to the subculture even though their own values run contrary to the inmate code.

Interviews with ex-convicts in California paint a picture of prison society that is in greater turmoil than it has been in the past. The presence of gangs, changes in the type of person now incarcerated, and changes in prison policy have all contributed to this turmoil. As the researchers found, "All these elements coalesced to create an increasingly unpredictable world in which prior loyalties, allegiances, and friendships were disrupted."[12]

Given a changing prison society without a single code of behavior accepted by the entire population, administrators face a much more difficult range of tasks. They must be aware of the different groups, recognize the norms and rules that members hold, and deal with the leaders of many cliques rather than with a few inmates who have risen to top positions in the inmate society.

Prison Subculture: Deprivation or Importation?

Where do the values of the prison subculture come from? How do they become integrated into a code? Sykes argues that the subculture arises within the prison in response to the pains of imprisonment.[13] These pains include the deprivation of liberty, autonomy, security, goods and services, and heterosexual relationships. Only through full integration into prison society can inmates adapt to and compensate for these deprivations.

An alternative theory holds that the values of the inmate community are primarily imported into prison from the outside world. John Irwin and Donald Cressey suggest that the prisoner subculture really combines three subcultures: convict, thief, and "straight."[14] They believe that the system of values, roles, and norms that exists in the adult prison results from the convergence of the convict and the thief subcultures. The convict subculture is found particularly among state-raised youths who have been in and out of foster homes, detention centers, reform schools, and correctional institutions since puberty. They are used to living in a single-sex society, know the ways of institutional life, and in a sense make prison their home. People who belong to the thief subculture consider crime a career and are always preparing for the "big score." Irwin and Cressey note that thieves must exude a sense of "rightness" or "solidness" to be considered a "right guy" by their peers. Finally, the "square Johns" bring the culture of

state to state and from facility to facility. For example, inmates in some prisons have televisions, civilian clothing, and hot plates. Not all prisoners enjoy these luxuries, nor do they satisfy lingering desires for a variety of other goods. Some state legislatures have decreed that amenities will be prohibited and that prisoners should return to Spartan living conditions.

Recognizing that prisoners do have some needs that are not met, prisons have a commissary or "store" from which residents may periodically purchase a limited number of items—toilet articles, tobacco, snack foods, and other items—in exchange for credits drawn on their "bank accounts." The size of a bank account depends on the amount of money deposited on the inmate's entrance, gifts sent by relatives, and amounts earned in the low-paying prison industries.

However, the peanut butter, soap, and cigarettes of the typical prison store in no way satisfy the consumer needs and desires of most prisoners. Consequently, an informal underground economy is a major element in prison society. Many items taken for granted on the outside are highly valued on the inside. For example, talcum powder and deodorant take on added importance because of the limited bathing facilities. Goods and services unique to prison can take on exaggerated importance. For example, unable to get alcohol, offenders may seek a similar effect by sniffing glue. Or, to distinguish themselves from others, offenders may pay laundry workers to iron a shirt in a particular way, a modest version of conspicuous consumption.

Mark Fleisher found an inmate running a "store" in most every cell block in the U.S. Penitentiary at Lompoc. Food stolen (from the kitchen) for late-night snacks, homemade wine, and drugs (marijuana) were available in such stores.[20]

When David Kalinich studied the State Prison of Southern Michigan in Jackson, he learned that a market economy provides the goods (contraband) and services not available or allowed by prison authorities.[21] Through interviews, Kalinich established the prices being charged (in 1980). For example, a pint of liquor smuggled in from the outside cost $15 or six cartons of cigarettes. "Spud juice," an alcoholic drink made on the grounds by the inmates, sold for $5 a quart or 15 packs of cigarettes. Kalinich found that the prison economy, like a market on the outside, responded to the forces of supply and demand and that risk of discovery replaced some of the risk associated with business in the free world. (See a description of the prison economy in the Focus box "Carnalito, the Hustler" on the following page.)

As a principal feature of prison culture, this informal economy reinforces the norms and roles of the social system and influences the nature of interpersonal relationships. The extent of the economy and its ability to produce desired goods and services—food, drugs, alcohol, sex, preferred living conditions—vary according to the extent of official surveillance, the demands of the consumers, and the opportunities for entrepreneurship. Their success as "hustlers" determines the luxuries and power inmates can enjoy.

Because real money is prohibited and a barter system is somewhat restrictive, the standard currency in the prison economy is cigarettes. They are not contraband, are easily transferable, have a stable and well-known standard of value, and come in "denominations" of singles, packs, and cartons. Furthermore, they are in demand by smokers. Even those who do not smoke keep cigarettes for prison currency. As more prisons adopt "nonsmoking" policies, cans of tuna fish have emerged as the form of currency.

Certain positions in the prison society enhance opportunities for entrepreneurs. For example, inmates assigned to work in the kitchen, warehouse, and administrative office steal food, clothing, building materials, and even information to sell or trade to other prisoners. The goods may then become part of other market transactions. Thus, exchanging a dozen eggs for two packs of cigarettes may result in reselling the eggs as egg sandwiches, made on a hot plate, for five cigarettes each. Meanwhile, the kitchen worker who stole the eggs may use the income to get a laundry worker to starch his shirts or a hospital orderly to provide drugs or a "punk" to give him sexual favors. "Sales" in the economy are one to one and are also interrelated with other underground market transactions.

Economic transactions may lead to violence when goods are stolen, debts remain unpaid, or agreements are violated. Disruptions of the economy may occur when officials conduct periodic "lockdowns" and inspections. Confiscation of contraband

FOCUS ON

PEOPLE IN CORRECTIONS

Carnalito, the Hustler

Carnalito, a prisoner from Mexico, was convicted in Texas at age 15 for a drug offense and was sentenced to five years. He arrived at Fort Dix, a low-security federal prison, when he was 18. He makes his living as a hustler within the prison economy.

At five each morning Carnalito begins his day by taking his customer's dirty clothes to the prison laundry where he washes, dries, and neatly folds them before returning them. For this service he receives three dollars' worth of commissary goods (canned tuna, postage stamps, and cigarettes) from each customer. By using Carnalito, his clients are able to avoid the frustration of waiting in line to use the machines and watching over their clothes to avoid theft.

While the clothes are washing, Carnalito performs his assigned duties as a unit orderly, cleaning the first-floor bathrooms of his housing unit. For this work the administration credits 10 dollars each month to his commissary account as "inmate performance pay." Carnalito also does the cleaning duties of three other inmate orderlies who each pay him 15 dollars a month; thus he earns another 45 dollars' worth of commissary items.

By noon each day, having finished his assigned duties, Carnalito begins to gather the ingredients to prepare dinner for a group of five inmates. This group does not want to suffer the frustrations of eating in the dining hall among hundreds of other prisoners where fights often break out. Instead, they

pay Carnalito a total of $200 per month for cooking their dinner six nights a week. For this fee, Carnalito procures vegetables from kitchen hustlers. He pays them with commissary items and assumes the risk of hiding the vegetables from the guards. The vegetables are combined with commissary items, provided by the dinner group, to complete the meal. The group sends the fee to Carnalito's mother in Mexico.

After providing for his own needs, Carnalito still has about $200 worth of commissary items each month from his earnings. He distributes these excess items by "running a store," allowing others to buy packs of cigarettes or bags of coffee at any time on credit. For every two packs, however, Carnalito requires that his customers pay three packs back.

Not counting the $200 that his clients send outside for his cooking services, Carnalito earns approximately $400 through his cleaning services and the store. Whenever he accumulates too many commissary items, he makes a deal with other prisoners who buy these goods at 80 cents on the dollar; the purchasers send the money to Carnalito's address in Mexico.

Carnalito works hard within the prison economy, but through his work, he accumulates at least $500 each month that is deposited in his Mexican bank account. If all continues to move according to plan, he expects to be released from prison in a few years. He will be twenty-one, with nearly $20,000 in U.S. currency in his bank account. He plans to open a business in Mexico upon release.

Source: Written especially for this text by Michael Santos.

---

may result in temporary shortages and price readjustments, but gradually business returns. The prison economy, like that of the outside world, allocates goods and services, provides rewards and sanctions, and is closely linked to the society it serves.

■ VIOLENCE IN PRISON

Prisons offer a perfect recipe for violence. They confine large numbers of men in cramped quarters, some of whom have histories of violent behavior. While incarcerated, these men are not allowed contact with women and live under highly restrictive conditions. Sometimes these conditions, coupled with the inability of administrators to respond to inmate needs, spark collective violence, as in the riots at Attica, New York (1971); Santa Fe, New Mexico (1980); Atlanta, Georgia, (1987); and Lucasville, Ohio (1993). In Chapter 13, we examine collective violence from a management perspective.

Although prison riots are widely reported in the news media, few people are aware of the level of everyday interpersonal violence in U.S. prisons. For example, each year

AP Images/The Advocate-Messenger, Clay Jackson

Officers race to enter the Northpoint Training Center, a medium security men's prison near Burgin, Kentucky, as inmates riot. The damage was so extensive that the facility had to be closed and the inmates transferred.

34,000 inmates are physically attacked by other inmates.[22] Even so, some evidence suggests that prisons are becoming less violent. In 2003 the homicide rate was 4 per 100,000 inmates, which is substantially lower than it was in 1980 (54 homicides per 100,000 inmates). Similarly, the suicide rate among state prisoners was 16 per 100,000 inmates in 2003, which is also lower than the rate reported in 1980 (34 suicides per 100,000 inmates).[23] However, scholars have pointed out that studies tend to focus on only the types of violence that are officially recorded, not the full range of prisoner victimization. Further, great numbers of prisoners live in a state of constant uneasiness, always looking out for people who might demand sex, steal their possessions, or otherwise harm them. In any case, some researchers have suggested that the level of violence varies by offender age, institutional security designation, and administrative effectiveness.[24]

Violence and Inmate Characteristics

For the person entering prison for the first time, anxiety and fear of violence are especially high. As one fish asked, "Will I end up fighting for my life?" Gary, an inmate at Leavenworth, told the journalist Pete Earley, "Every convict has three choices, but only three. He can fight (kill someone), he can hit the fence (escape), or he can fuck (submit)."[25] Inmates who are victimized are significantly more likely than others to be depressed and experience symptoms associated with posttraumatic stress such as nightmares.[26] Even if a prisoner is not assaulted, the potential for violence permeates the environment of many prisons, adding to the stress and pains of incarceration. Assaults in our correctional institutions raise serious questions for administrators, criminal justice specialists, and the general public. What causes prison violence, and what can be done about it? We consider these questions when we examine the three main categories of prison violence: prisoner–prisoner, prisoner–officer, and officer–prisoner. But first we discuss three characteristics that underlie these behavioral factors: age, attitudes, and race.

AGE ■ Studies have shown that young men between 16 and 24, both inside and outside prison, are more prone to violence than are older men. Not surprisingly, 93 percent of adult prisoners are men, 54 percent were convicted of a violent offense, and 16 percent are under age 25.[27] Studies also show that young prisoners face a greater risk of being victimized than do older inmates.[28]

Besides having greater physical strength than their older counterparts, young prisoners also lack the commitments to career and family that inhibit antisocial behavior. In addition, many have difficulty defining their position in society. Thus, they interpret many interactions as challenges to their status.

Machismo, the concept of male honor and the sacredness of one's reputation as a man, requires physical retaliation against those who insult one's honor. Observers have argued that many homosexual rapes are not sexual but political—attempts to impress on the victim the aggressor's male power and to define the target as passive or "feminine." Some inmates adopt a preventive strategy, trying to impress others with their bravado, which may result in counterchallenges and violence. Young inmates may seek to establish a reputation by retaliating for slurs on their honor, sexual prowess, and manliness. The potential for violence among such prisoners is obvious.

ATTITUDES ■ Some sociologists posit that a subculture of violence exists among certain socioeconomic, racial, and ethnic groups. This subculture is found in the lower class; in its value system, violence is "tolerable, expected, or required."[29] Arguments are settled and decisions are made by the fist rather than by verbal persuasion. Many inmates bring these attitudes into prison with them. Some support for this theory exists. For example, one large study of male prisoners in the federal system found much higher rates of prison violence by African American inmates than white inmates. This may reflect the higher rates of violence among African Americans in the inner city, which, like the prison, "elicit challenges to selfhood and expectations of danger that evoke predatory as well as protective violent responses."[30]

RACE ■ Race has become a major divisive factor in today's prisons. Racist attitudes have become part of the inmate code. Forced association, having to live with people one would not likely associate with on the outside, exaggerates and amplifies racial conflict. Violence against members of another race may be how some inmates deal with the frustrations of their lives. The presence of gangs organized along racial lines contributes to violence in prison.

Prisoner–Prisoner Violence

Although prison folklore may attribute violence to sadistic guards, most prison violence occurs between inmates. Hans Toch observed that inmates are "terrorized by other inmates, and spend years in fear of harm. Some inmates request segregation, others lock

Two former Mexican Mafia inmates have chosen to live out their life sentences in protective custody. Rubin Davis (top bunk), was initiated into the gang in Calipatria State Prison in California by murdering a rival gang member on his second day. After rising to the top ranks of the gang he refused to order the murder of a rival gang member's wife and children. He denounced the gang and moved into the Sensitive Housing Unit for his own protection.

© Mark Allen Johnson/Zuma Press

themselves in, and some are hermits by choice."[31] The Bureau of Justice Statistics reports that the rate of prisoner–prisoner assault in U.S. prisons is 28.0 attacks per 1,000 inmates.[32] But official statistics likely do not reflect the true amount of prisoner–prisoner violence, because many inmates who are assaulted do not make their victimization known to prison officials.

PRISON GANGS ■ Racial or ethnic gangs (also referred to as "security threat groups") are now linked to acts of violence in most prison systems. Gangs make it difficult for wardens to maintain control. By continuing their street wars inside prison, gangs make some prisons more dangerous than any American neighborhood. Gangs are organized primarily to control an institution's drug, gambling, loan-sharking, prostitution, extortion, and debt-collection rackets. In addition, gangs protect their members from other gangs and instill a sense of macho camaraderie.

A link for a website designed to help parole officers **identify and interpret prison gang tattoos** can be found at www.cengage.com/criminaljustice/clear.

Contributing to prison violence is the "blood in, blood out" basis for gang membership: A would-be member must stab a gang's enemy to be admitted; once in, he cannot drop out without endangering his own life. Given the racial and ethnic foundation of gangs, violence between them can easily spill into the general prison population. Some institutions have programs that offer members a way out of gang life. Referred to as "deganging," these programs educate members and eventually encourage them to renounce their gang membership. Critics say that for many this supposed change merely provides a "way of getting out of lock-down status; proponents counter with, 'So what? Their behavior within the prison setting has been modified.'"[33]

Prison gangs exist in the institutions of most states and the federal system. For example, a study by the American Correctional Association found that in the early 1990s there were more than 46,000 gang members in the federal system and in the prisons of 35 states.[34]

Although prison gangs are small, they are tightly organized and have even arranged the killing of opposition gang leaders housed in other institutions. Research has shown that prisons infested with gangs tend to experience the greatest number of inmate homicides.[35] Administrators say that prison gangs tend to pursue their "business" interests, yet they also contribute greatly to inmate–inmate violence as they discipline members, enforce orders, and retaliate against other gangs. Marie Griffin and John Hepburn found that gang-affiliated inmates are more likely to be involved in violent misconduct than are nongang inmates, independent of their race, age, and criminal history.[36]

AP Images

Sergeant Stephanie Howard records the body markings on an inmate as others wait their turn in the Lexington Reception and Assessment Center in Oklahoma. Records of tattoos and other markings signifying gang membership are used to identify those likely to engage in violence.

The racial and ethnic basis of gang membership has been well documented in California. Beginning in the late 1960s, a Chicano gang—the Mexican Mafia, whose members had known one another in Los Angeles—took over the rackets in San Quentin. In reaction, other gangs were formed, including a rival Mexican gang, La Nuestra Familia; CRIPS (Common Revolution in Progress); the Texas Syndicate; the Black Guerrilla Family; and the Aryan Brotherhood (see **Table 11.1**).[37] Gang conflict in California prisons became so serious in the 1970s that attempts were made to break up the gangs by dividing members among several institutions. As of 2002, however, California had the largest number of prison gang members (5,342), followed by Texas (5,262). Data from 41 different jurisdictions shows that nearly 5 percent of inmates are validated gang members.[38]

Administrators use a variety of strategies to weaken gang influence and to reduce violence.[39] These strategies include identifying members, segregating housing and work assignments, restricting possession or display of gang symbols, conducting strip searches, monitoring mail and telephone communications, and providing only no-contact visits.[40] Some correctional departments transfer key gang members to other states in the hope of slowing or stopping a prison gang's activity.

Many facilities segregate rival gangs by housing them in separate units of the prison or moving members to other facilities. However, prison officials tend to believe that segregation policies are ineffective and expensive.[41]

Administrators have also set up intelligence units to gather information on gangs. The Florida Department of Corrections Security Threat Intelligence Unit monitors the thousands of gang members incarcerated in Florida prisons. The information that the unit collects is regularly provided to federal, state, and local law enforcement agencies upon request. Thirty days prior to the release of a gang member, the unit provides a report to law enforcement officials in the county in which the inmate was convicted. These reports provide law enforcement officials with valuable information, such as the address where the former inmate will be residing, gang affiliation, a list of nicknames and aliases, criminal history, description of tattoos, and a photograph of the individual.[42]

TABLE 11.1 *Characteristics of Major Prison Gangs*

These gangs were founded in the California prison system during the late 1960s and 1970s. They have now spread across the nation and are viewed as the major security threat groups in most corrections systems.

Name	Makeup	Origin	Characteristics	Enemies
Aryan Brotherhood	White	San Quentin, 1967	Apolitical. Most in custody for crimes such as robbery.	CRIPS, Bloods, BGF
Black Guerrilla Family (BGF)	African American	San Quentin, 1966	Most politically oriented. Anti-government.	Aryan Brotherhood, EME
Mexican Mafia (EME)	Mexican American/ Hispanic	Deuel Vocational Center, Los Angeles, late 1950	Ethnic solidarity, control of drug trafficking.	BGF, NF
La Nuestra Familia (NF)	Mexican American/ Hispanic	Soledad, 1965	Protect young, rural Mexican Americans.	EME
Texas Syndicate	Mexican American/ Hispanic	Folsom, early 1970s	Protect Texan inmates in California.	Aryan Brotherhood, EME, NF

Source: Major Prison Gangs, http://www.dc.state.fl.us/pub/gangs/prison.html, March 30, 2007.

PROTECTIVE CUSTODY ■ For many victims of prison violence, protective custody is the only way to escape further abuse. Most prison systems have such a unit, along with units for disciplinary and administrative segregation. Nearly six thousand state prisoners are in protective custody.[43] Inmates who seek protective custody may have been physically abused, have received sexual threats, have reputations as snitches, or fear assault by someone they crossed on the outside who is now a fellow inmate. Referred to as the "special management inmates," they pose particular problems for prison administrators, who must provide them with programs and services.[44]

Life is not pleasant for these inmates. Often their physical condition, programs, and recreational opportunities are little better than those for inmates who are in segregation because of misbehavior. Usually they are let out of their cells only briefly to exercise and shower. Their only stimulation is from books, radio, and television. Inmates who ask to "lock up" have little chance of returning to the general prison population without being viewed as a weakling—a snitch or a punk—to be preyed on. Even when administrators transfer such inmates to another institution, their reputations follow them through the grapevine.

PRISON RAPE ■ Given how regularly violent sexual assaults are portrayed in the media, the public's belief that sexual assault is common in most American prisons is not too surprising. Until recently, there were no reliable national data on prison sexual violence. On September 4, 2003, the Prison Rape Elimination Act was signed into law. The law calls for the gathering of national statistics on prison rape, the development of guidelines, and the establishment of grants to help states address the problem. In 2007 the Bureau of Justice Statistics released nationwide statistics on the prevalence of prison sexual violence (see "Myths in Corrections"). According to the report, perpetrators of inmate–inmate sexual violence tend to be male (85 percent) and either black (49 percent) or white (39 percent). Victims are more likely to be male (82 percent), under the age of 40 (84 percent), and white (72 percent).[45] Other studies have found that victims tend to be the following:

- First-time, nonviolent offenders
- Those convicted of a crime against a minor
- Inmates who are physically weak
- Prisoners who are viewed as effeminate
- Offenders who are not affiliated with a gang
- Those who are believed to have "snitched" on other prisoners[46]

The Bureau of Justice Statistics report also shows that most acts of prisoner–prisoner sexual violence involve a single victim (92 percent) and one assailant (90 percent). Incidents involving two or more perpetrators make up only 10 percent of known incidents of inmate–inmate sexual violence.[47]

Prison administrators confront various challenges in their attempts to combat sexual violence. For example, officials report that inmates have reservations about reporting sexual victimization. Some victims of sexual violence fear that prison officials will not protect them from retaliation if they report the incident. Other inmates believe that officials will not take their allegation seriously.[48] Another problem is that many sexual assaults are not reported in a timely manner. One study conducted in the Texas prison system found that only 30 percent of allegations of sexual assault were reported on the day in which the event reportedly occurred. Time lapse is one of the primary

MYTHS IN CORRECTIONS

SEXUAL VIOLENCE IN STATE PRISONS

THE MYTH: Because state prisons are filled with predatory, violent offenders who are deprived of heterosexual relationships, sexual violence happens with great regularity.

THE REALITY: In 2006 there were an estimated 4,516 allegations of sexual violence in state prisons. Taking into account the size of the inmate population, the rate of sexual violence against state prisoners is approximately 3.75 attacks per 1,000 inmates.

Source: Bureau of Justice Statistics: *Sexual Violence Reported by Correctional Authorities, 2006* (Washington, DC: U.S. Government Printing Office, August 2007), 3.

Just Detention International is an organization that is working to end sexual violence in prison; see the link at www.cengage.com/criminaljustice/clear.

of allegations of sexual assault were reported on the day in which the event reportedly occurred. Time lapse is one of the primary reasons why prison officials only used rape kits and forensic exams in 20 percent of all alleged sexual assaults.[49]

Prisoner–Officer Violence

The mass media have focused on riots in which guards are taken hostage, injured, and killed. Violence against officers typically occurs in specific situations and against certain individuals. Yearly, inmates assault approximately 18,000 prison staff members.[50] Correctional officers do not carry weapons within the institution, because a prisoner could seize them. However, prisoners do manage to get lethal weapons and can use the element of surprise to injure an officer. In the course of a workday, an officer may encounter situations that require the use of physical force against an inmate—for instance, breaking up a fight or moving a prisoner to segregation. Because such situations are especially dangerous, officers may enlist others to help minimize the risk of violence. The officer's greatest fear is unexpected attacks. These may take the form of a missile thrown from an upper tier, verbal threats and taunts, or an officer's "accidental" fall down a flight of stairs. The need to remain constantly watchful against personal attacks adds stress and keeps many officers at a distance from the inmates.

Besides physical injury, an attack can compromise an officer's authority. After such an incident, administrators often have no alternative but to transfer the officer to tower duty.

Officer–Prisoner Violence

A fact of life in many institutions is unauthorized physical violence by officers against inmates. Stories abound of guards giving individual prisoners "the treatment" when supervisors are not looking. Many guards view physical force as an everyday, legitimate procedure. In some institutions, authorized "goon squads" comprising physically powerful officers use their muscle to maintain order.

From time to time, the media present incidents of the excessive and illegal use of force by prison officials. Such an incident at the Forest Hays, Jr., State Prison occurred in northwestern Georgia when A. G. Thomas, an aide to the state prison commissioner, touched off a bloody attack on prisoners when he grabbed an unresisting inmate by the hair during a shakedown raid and dragged him across the floor. Seeing Thomas assault an inmate, some correctional officers assumed that "it was o.k. to do it. If Mr. Thomas can slam one, then we can slam one, too." The commissioner "watched in another cell

When officers must remove an uncooperative or violent prisoner from a cell, trained cell extraction teams must ovewhelm the prisoner through the use of force while also limiting the risk of injury to themselves. Such events are often filmed to prevent false claims that officers used excessive force. Are there precautions that these officers should take to avoid injury to themselves or to the prisoners?

© Joel Gordon 2008—Model Released—All Rights Reserved

block while inmates, some handcuffed and lying on the floor, were punched, kicked, and stomped by guards." The incidents led to a lawsuit in federal court. Georgia agreed to pay $283,000 to settle suits brought by 14 inmates beaten at Hays.[51]

Probably the worst cases of officer–prisoner violence in recent years have occurred at the California State Prison at Corcoran. Between 1989 and 1995, 43 inmates were wounded and 7 killed by officers firing assault weapons—the most killings in any prison. Guards even instigated fights between rival gang members. During these "gladiator days," tower guards often shot the gang members after they had been ordered to stop fighting. Each shooting was justified by state-appointed reviewers.[52]

How do we tell when prison officers are using force legitimately and when they are using it to punish individual prisoners? Correctional officers are expected to follow departmental rules in their dealings with prisoners, but supervisors rarely observe staff–prisoner confrontations. Further, prisoner complaints about officer brutality are often not believed until the officer involved gains a reputation for harshness. Still, wardens may feel they must support their officers to retain, in turn, their officers' support. Levels of violence by officers against inmates are undoubtedly lower today than in years past. Nevertheless, officers are expected to enforce prison rules and may use force to uphold discipline and prevent escapes. Further, definitions of appropriate force for the handling of particular situations typically are vague (see Chapter 13).

Americans were shocked when pictures of U.S. military personnel mistreating Iraqi prisoners surfaced in April 2004. The pictures showed soldiers humiliating detainees by hooding them, parading them around naked, and placing them in sexually humiliating positions. Allegations of other abuses also surfaced, including pouring cold water over naked prisoners' bodies, beatings, and threats of rape. Others argued that conditions at U.S. prisons are not much better. For example, unknown numbers of inmates in U.S. prisons are ill-treated, whether by officer brutality, neglect of medical needs, or administrative failure to prevent violent victimization, such as forcible rape.[53] Some criminologists were not surprised by the guards' actions. They noted that the tactics were similar in intensity to those of the college students acting as "guards" in the famous Stanford prison experiment conducted by Philip Zimbardo in 1971. Highly publicized events, such as the Abu Ghraib incident, serve as a reminder: Prisons should not be run in the shadows but must be subjected to the bright lights of public scrutiny.

Decreasing Prison Violence

Lee Bowker points to five factors that contribute to prison violence: inadequate supervision by staff members, architectural design that promotes rather than inhibits victimization, the easy availability of deadly weapons, the housing of violence-prone prisoners near relatively defenseless people, and an overall high level of tension produced by close quarters.[54] The physical size and condition of the prison and the relations between inmates and staff also affect violence.

THE EFFECT OF ARCHITECTURE AND SIZE ■ Prison architectural design is thought to influence the amount of violence in an institution. Many prisons are not only large but also contain areas where inmates can avoid supervision. The new-generation prisons—with their small housing units, clear sight lines, and security corridors linking housing units—are largely designed to limit these opportunities and thus prevent violence.

The fortress-like prison certainly does not create an atmosphere for normal interpersonal relationships, and size of the largest institutions can create management problems. The massive scale of the megaprison, which may hold up to 3,000 inmates, provides opportunities for aggressive inmates to hide weapons, dispense private "justice," and engage more or less freely in other illicit activities. Size may also result in some inmates "falling through the cracks," being misclassified and forced to live among more-violent offenders.[55]

The relationship between prison crowding and violence is unclear.[56] Some studies have shown that as personal space shrinks, the number of violent incidents rises. The inconsistent research findings may be partially explained by the fact that crowding is measured in several different ways (for example, number of people per area, amount

For more on the **Zimbardo experiment**, which simulated guard–prisoner violence, as well as **connections between Zimbardo's research and Abu Ghraib**, go to the two corresponding websites listed at www.cengage.com/criminaljustice/clear.

of space per person, amount of unshared space per person).[57] Further, inmate perceptions of crowding seem to depend on several factors, such as institutional experiences during incarceration. For example, one study revealed that prisoners who received few visits from friends and family, as well as those who were recently victimized, were more apt than other prisoners to say that the facilities housing them were crowded.[58] Clearly, increasing the size of an institution's population strains the limits of dining halls, athletic areas, educational and treatment programs, medical care, and so forth. To maintain quality of life, prisons need increased resources to offset such strains. In some institutions the population has more than doubled without increases in violence. Good management seems to be a major factor in keeping conditions from deteriorating.

THE ROLE OF MANAGEMENT ■ The degree to which inmate leaders are allowed to take matters into their own hands can affect the level of violence among inmates. When administrators run a tight ship, security measures prevent sexual attacks in dark corners, the making of "shivs" and "shanks" (knives) in the metal shop, and open conflict among inmate groups. A prison must afford each inmate defensible space, and administrators need to ensure that every inmate remains secure, free from physical attack.

Effective prison management may decrease the level of violence by limiting opportunities for attacks. Wardens and correctional officers must therefore recognize the types of people under guard, the role of prison gangs, and the structure of institutions. John DiIulio argues that no group of inmates is "unmanageable [and] no combination of political, social, budgetary, architectural, or other factors makes good management impossible."[59] He points to such varied institutions as the California Men's Colony, New York City's Tombs and Rikers Island, the Federal Bureau of Prisons, and the Texas Department of Corrections. At these institutions, good management practices have resulted in prisons and jails where inmates can "do time" without fearing for their personal safety. Wardens exert leadership and manage their prisons effectively, so that problems do not fester and erupt into violent confrontations.

Measures suggested to reduce violence are not always clear-cut nor applicable to all situations. The following steps have been proposed:

1 Improve classification so that violence-prone inmates are separated from the general population.

2 For inmates fearful of being victimized, create opportunities to seek assistance from staff.

3 Increase the size, racial diversity, and training of the custody force.

4 Redesign facilities so that all areas can be put under surveillance; there should be no "blind spots." Use smaller institutions.

5 Install grievance mechanisms or an ombudsperson to help resolve interpersonal or institutional problems.

6 Augment the reward system to reduce the pains of imprisonment.

unit management
Tactic for reducing prison violence by dividing facilities into small, self-contained, semiautonomous "institutions."

One administrative strategy that has helped bring order to violence-marked institutions is **unit management**.[60] This approach divides a prison into many small, self-contained "institutions" operating in semiautonomous fashion within the confines of a larger facility. Each of the units houses between 50 and 100 inmates, who remain together as long as release dates allow and who are supervised by a team of correctional officers, counselors, and treatment specialists. The assumption is that, by keeping the units small, staff will get to know the inmates better and recognize problems early on, and group cohesion will emerge. Further, because the unit manager has both authority and accountability, policies presumably will be enforced consistently and fairly. The unit-management approach to violence reduction has proved successful in several state and federal institutions.[61]

In sum, prisons must be made safe. Because the state puts offenders there, it has a responsibility to prevent violence and maintain order. To eliminate violence from prisons, officials may have to limit movement within the institution, contacts with the outside, and the right to choose one's associates. Yet these measures may run counter to the goal of producing men and women who will be responsible citizens when they return to society.

SUMMARY

1 Discuss the "inmate code" and talk about where the values of the prison subculture come from.

The inmate code is a set of norms and values that develops in the prison social system. It defines the model prisoner in the eyes of inmates and provides a code of conduct for living in prison. An inmate who projects toughness, keeps his distance from the staff, and does his "own time" is held in high regard. A prisoner who is emotionally weak, snitches on fellow inmates to the staff, and gets involved in other people's business does not enjoy high status. Some scholars argue that the inmate code develops as a response to the prison environment; adaptive roles reflect ways to relieve the pains of imprisonment. Others argue that the prison subculture is primarily imported from the world outside the prison walls.

2 Be familiar with the prison economy.

Prisons feed, clothe, and house inmates. In some states prisoners are allowed comforts, such as televisions sets, that are provided by friends and family members. Inmates can also purchase certain goods from the prison commissary (or store). However, an informal economy exists in most prisons to satisfy inmates' consumer demands. Some inmates take advantage of their job assignments to steal goods and provide services in the prison economy. Because real money is prohibited, the standard currency in the prison economy is cigarettes. This form of currency is often used because they are not contraband, they are easily transferable, they have a well-known standard of value, and they can be used in denominations (singles, packs, and cartons). In states that have adopted nonsmoking policies, cans of tuna fish are used as a form of currency.

3 Explain the different types of prison violence.

The most common type of prison violence involves one inmate attacking another inmate. However, the true extent of this type of violence is unknown because many incidents do not come to the attention of prison officials. In comparison, prisoner–officer violence is less common. Examples of this type of violence include physical assaults, thrown objects, and verbal threats. Officer–prisoner violence is tightly regulated. However, officers are allowed to use physical force in certain situations, such as attempting to break up a fight between inmates. Instances of inmate abuse by officers sometimes comes to the attention of the general public, but such occurrences are undoubtedly less frequent today than in years past.

4 Discuss what can be done about prison violence.

The architectural design and size of prison facilities is thought to contribute to prison violence. Many older prisons contain areas where inmates can avoid supervision. New-generation prisons are designed to provide staff with clear sight lines and security corridors linking housing units. These features limit opportunities for violence. Older prisons are frequently much larger than newly constructed facilities. Managing large numbers of inmates increases the chances that some inmates will be misclassified and forced to live among violent inmates. Thus, reducing the size of the inmate population is thought to be another way of preventing violence. Finally, effective prison management can reduce prison violence. When administrators run a tight ship, security measures prevent attacks, the making of weapons, and conflict among inmate groups. To succeed, prison managers must recognize the types of people under their guard, the role of prison gangs, and the structure of their institutions.

KEY TERMS

inmate code (p. 288)
prisonization (p. 288)
unit management (p. 304)

FOR DISCUSSION

1. Imagine that you are a new prisoner. What are your immediate concerns? How will you deal with them? What problems do you expect to face?
2. Do the values of the prison culture result from the deprivations of prison, or do inmates bring them from the outside? What was the case 50 years ago?
3. If you were the warden of a maximum-security prison for men, what policies would you adopt to prevent violence in the institution?

FOR FURTHER READING

Byrne, James, Don Hummer, and Faye Taxman. *The Culture of Prison Violence*. Boston: Allyn and Bacon, 2008. A comprehensive review of the causes, prevention, and control of violence in prisons.

Carroll, Leo. *Lawful Order: A Case Study of Correctional Crisis and Reform*. New York: Garland, 1998. History of Rhode Island's adult correctional institutions over the past 40 years. Examines the transformation of these institutions in response to changes in the external environment.

Johnson, Robert. *Hard Time: Understanding and Reforming the Prison*. 3rd ed. Belmont, CA: Wadsworth, 2002. The author uses historical information and prisoners'

personal accounts to paint a realistic portrait of life inside the prison walls.

Santos, Michael G. *Inside: Life Behind Bars in America*. New York: St. Martin's Press, 2006. Capturing the voices of his fellow prisoners, Santos makes the tragic and inspiring stories of men—from the toughest gang leaders to the richest Wall Street criminals—come alive.

Useem, Bert, and Peter Kimball. *States of Siege: U.S. Prison Riots, 1971–1986*. New York: Oxford University Press, 1989. A contemporary classic that surveys prison riots with case studies of the upheavals at Attica, Joliet, Santa Fe, Jackson, and Moundsville and considers the nature and causes of prison riots.

NOTES

1 William T. Crew, "Letter from Alleged Killer Tells of His Motivation," *Catholic Free Press* (Worcester, MA), September 12, 2003, http://www.poynter.org/dg.lts/id.46/Aid.47906/column.htm.

2 Joseph Fulling Fishman, *Sex in Prison* (New York: National Liberty Press, 1934).

3 Leo Carroll, *Hacks, Blacks, and Cons: Race Relations in a Maximum Security Prison* (Lexington, MA: Lexington Books, 1974).

4 Robert Johnson, *Hard Time*, 3rd ed. (Belmont, CA: Wadsworth, 2002), 100.

5 Don Sabo, Terry A. Kupers, and Willie London, "Gender and the Politics of Punishment," in *Prison Masculinities*, edited by Don Sabo, Terry A. Kupers, and Willie London (Philadelphia: Temple University Press, 2001), 3, 7.

6 Charles M. Terry, "The Function of Humor for Prison Inmates," *Journal of Contemporary Criminal Justice* 13 (February 1997): 26.

7 Gresham M. Sykes, *The Society of Captives* (Princeton, NJ: Princeton University Press, 1958), 63–108.

8 Donald Clemmer, *The Prison Community* (New York: Holt, Rinehart & Winston, 1940), 299–304.

9 Sykes, *Society of Captives*, pp. 84–108.

10 Carroll, *Hacks, Blacks, and Cons;* John Irwin, *Prisons in Turmoil* (Boston: Little, Brown, 1980); Sabo, Kupers, and London, "Gender and the Politics of Punishment."

11 Lucia Benaquisto and Peter J. Freed, "The Myth of Inmate Lawlessness: The Perceived Contradiction between Self and Other in Inmates' Support for Criminal Justice Sanctioning Norms," *Law and Society Review* 30 (1996): 508.

12 Geoffrey Hunt, Stephanie Riegal, Tomas Morales, and Dan Waldorf, "Changes in Prison Culture: Prison Gangs and the Case of the Pepsi Generation," in *Criminal Justice: Politics and Policies*, 7th ed., edited by George F. Cole and Marc G. Gertz (Belmont, CA: Wadsworth, 1998), 435–47.

13 Sykes, *Society of Captives*, p. 107.

14 John Irwin and Donald R. Cressey, "Thieves, Convicts, and the Inmate Culture," *Social Problems* 10 (1962): 142–55.

15 Edward Zamble and Frank J. Porporino, *Coping, Behavior, and Adaptation in Prison Inmates* (New York: Springer-Verlag, 1988).

16 Ibid., p. 13.

17 Irwin, *Prisons in Turmoil*, p. 67.

[18] Pete Earley, *The Hot House: Life inside Leavenworth* (New York: Bantham Books, 1992), 44.

[19] Virgil L. Williams and Mary Fish, *Convicts, Codes, and Contraband* (Cambridge, MA: Ballinger, 1974), 40.

[20] Mark S. Fleisher, *Warehousing Violence* (Newbury Park, CA: Sage, 1989), 151–52.

[21] David B. Kalinich, *Power, Stability, and Contraband* (Prospect Heights, IL: Waveland Press, 1980).

[22] Bureau of Justice Statistics, *Census of State and Federal Correctional Facilities, 2000* (Washington, DC: U.S. Government Printing Office, October 2003), 8–10.

[23] Bureau of Justice Statistics, *Suicide and Homicide in State Prisons and Local Jails* (Washington, DC: U.S. Government Printing Office, August 2005).

[24] Angela S. Maitland and Richard D. Sluder, "Victimization and Youthful Prison Inmates: An Empirical Analysis," *Prison Journal* 78 (no. 1, March 1998): 55.

[25] Earley, *Hot House*, pp. 55–56.

[26] Andy Hochstetler, Daniel S. Murphy, and Ronald L. Simons, "Damaged Goods: Exploring Predictors of Distress in Prison Inmates," *Crime and Delinquency* 50 (July 2004): 436–57.

[27] Bureau of Justice Statistics, *Prisoners in 2007* (Washington, DC: U.S. Government Printing Office, December 2008).

[28] John D. Wooldredge, "Inmate Lifestyles and Opportunities for Victimization," *Journal of Research in Crime and Delinquency* 35 (November 1998): 489.

[29] Marvin E. Wolfgang and Franco Ferracuti, *The Subculture of Violence* (London: Tavistock, 1967), 263.

[30] Miles D. Harer and Darrell J. Steffensmeier, "Race and Prison Violence," *Criminology* 34 (August 1996): 342.

[31] Hans Toch, *Peacekeeping: Police, Prisons, and Violence* (Lexington, MA: Lexington Books, 1976), 47–48.

[32] Bureau of Justice Statistics, *Census of State and Federal Correctional Facilities, 2000*, p. 10.

[33] Peter M. Carlson, "Prison Interventions: Evolving Strategies to Control Security Threat Groups," *Corrections Management Quarterly* 5 (Winter 2001): 14.

[34] American Correctional Association, *Gangs in Correctional Facilities: A National Assessment* (Washington, DC: National Institute of Justice, 1994), 21.

[35] Michael D. Reisig, "Administrative Control and Inmate Homicide," *Homicide Studies* 6 (February 2002): 84–103.

[36] Marie L. Griffin and John R. Hepburn, "The Effect of Gang Affiliation on Violent Misconduct among Inmates during the Early Years of Confinement," *Criminal Justice and Behavior* 33 (August 2006): 419–48.

[37] Alfonso J. Valdez, "Prison Gangs 101," *Corrections Today* 71 (February 2009): 40–43.

[38] Camille Graham Camp, *The 2002 Corrections Yearbook: Adult Corrections* (Middletown, CT: Criminal Justice Institute, 2003), 37.

[39] C. Ronald Huff and Matthew Meyer, "Managing Prison Gangs and Other Security Threat Groups," *Corrections Management Quarterly* 1 (Fall 1997): 10–18.

[40] Gary Hill, "Gangs inside Prison Walls around the World," *Corrections Compendium* 29 (January–February 2004): 26; Chad Trulson, James W. Marquart, and Soraya K. Kawucha, "Gang Suppression and Institutional Control," *Corrections Today* 68 (April 2006): 26–31.

[41] G. W. Knox, "A National Assessment of Gangs and Security Threat Groups in Adult Correctional Institutions: Results of the 1999 Adult Corrections Survey," *Journal of Gang Research* 7 (2000): 1–45.

[42] Michelle Jordan, "Florida STG Intelligence Unit Aims to Keep Communities Safe," *Corrections Today* 71 (February 2009): 28–31.

[43] Camp, *2002 Corrections Yearbook*, p. 46.

[44] Richard A. McGee, George Warner, and Nora Harlow, "The Special Management Inmate," in *Incarcerating Criminals*, edited by Timothy J. Flanagan, James W. Marquart, and Kenneth G. Adams (New York: Oxford University Press, 1998), 99–106.

[45] Bureau of Justice Statistics, *Sexual Violence Reported by Correctional Authorities, 2006* (Washington, DC: U.S. Government Printing Office, August 2007), 4.

[46] Kim English and Peggy Heil, "Prison Rape: What We Know Today," *Corrections Compendium* 30 (September–October 2005): 2.

[47] Bureau of Justice Statistics, *Sexual Violence, 2006*, p. 4.

[48] Janine M. Zweig and John Blackmore, *Strategies to Prevent Prison Rape by Changing the Correctional Culture* (Washington, DC: U.S. Department of Justice, October 2008).

[49] James Austin, Tony Fabelo, Angela Gunter, and Ken McGinnis, *Sexual Violence in the Texas Prison System* (Washington, DC: JFA Institute, March 2006).

[50] Bureau of Justice Statistics, *Census of State and Federal Correctional Facilities, 2000*, p. 10.

[51] Joseph T. Hallinan, *Going Up the River: Travels in a Prison Nation* (New York: Random House, 2001), 110–111.

[52] Mark Arax and Mark Gladstone, "State Thwarted Brutality Probe in Corcoran Prison, Investigators Say," *Los Angeles Times*, July 5, 1998, p. 1.

[53] "The Dark Side of America," *New York Times*, May 17, 2004, p. 24A.

[54] Lee H. Bowker, "Victimizers and Victims in American Correctional Institutions," in *Pains of Imprisonment*, edited by Robert Johnson and Hans Toch (Beverly Hills, CA: Sage, 1982), 64.

[55] Anthony E. Bottoms, "Interpersonal Violence and Social Order in Prisons," in *Crime and Justice: An Annual Review of Research*, vol. 26, edited by Michael Tonry and Joan Petersilia (Chicago: University of Chicago Press, 1999), 205–81.

[56] Travis W. Franklin, Cortney A. Franklin, and Travis C. Pratt, "Examining the Empirical Relationship between Prison Crowding and Inmate Misconduct: A Meta-Analysis of Conflicting Research Results," *Journal of Criminal Justice* 34 (July–August 2006): 401–12.

[57] Benjamin Steiner and John Wooldredge, "Rethinking the Link between Institutional Crowding and Inmate Misconduct," *Prison Journal* 89 (no. 2, June 2009): 205–33.

[58] John Wooldredge, "Explaining Variation in Perceptions of Inmate Crowding," *Prison Journal* 77 (no. 1, March 1997): 35.

[59] John J. DiIulio, *No Escape: The Future of American Prisons* (New York: Basic Books, 1990), 12.

[60] Christopher A. Innes and Vicki D. Verdeyen, "Conceptualizing the Management of Violent Inmates," *Corrections Management Quarterly* 1 (Fall 1997): 9.

[61] J. Forbes Farmer, "A Case Study in Regaining Control of a Violent State Prison," *Federal Probation* 55 (1988): 41–47.

© Tim Rue/Corbis

LEARNING OBJECTIVES

After reading this chapter you should be able to . . .

1 Explain why women prisoners are called the "forgotten offenders."

2 Be familiar with the history of the incarceration of women.

3 Explain how interpersonal relationships in women's prisons differ from those in men's prisons.

4 Be familiar with the special issues that incarcerated women face.

5 Discuss the problems women face when they are released to the community.

Arriving at the California Institute for Women in Corona, Joseph Calder of Yucaipa is first off the bus in anticipation of a Mother's Day visit. In California's "Get on the Bus" program, children from throughout the state are reunited with their incarcerated mothers on this special day.

A LARGE GROUP of children and adults gather around a bus waiting for the doors to open so they can board. It is Mother's Day, and the children are bustling with excitement about the bus ride that will take them to see their mothers. Where are the children going? To a restaurant for a fancy dinner? To a public park for a picnic? To a family cookout to feast on hot dogs and hamburgers? Not today. These children are participants of the Get on the Bus program. Operated by the Center for Restorative Justice, the program transports children from urban areas to visit their mothers who are serving time in California prisons.

At midyear 2007, an estimated 809,800 prisoners in state and federal facilities were parents of children under age 18, an increase of 79 percent since 1991. Most of these prisoners

INCARCERATION OF WOMEN

are fathers, but around 8 percent are mothers. Nationwide the number of mothers incarcerated in federal and state prisons has increased 131 percent since 1991. These women are more likely than male prisoners to have lived with their children prior to incarceration.[1] They experience difficulty staying in touch with their children, because most states only have one or two prisons for women. Transportation is difficult, visits are short and (at best) infrequent, and phone calls are expensive and irregular.

The Get on the Bus program is an annual event coinciding with Mother's Day. Since the program began in 1991, it has transported thousands of children to visit their incarcerated mothers. To qualify for the program, inmates must have good conduct for one year. Although the trip can be long, Wendy Hill, the Associate Director for Female Offender Programs and Services, believes it is worth it: "Every child wants to see, hug and talk with their mother, whether they are incarcerated or not." Hill believes that the program helps kids stay connected with their mothers, and it even reduces the chance that mothers will return to prison.[2]

Because women make up such a small proportion of the prison population, a far larger portion of correctional budgets goes to institutions for men. Yet female offenders usually have greater health, program, and security needs than do their male counterparts. In this chapter we review the history of women's incarceration and examine the life of women behind bars.

Chapter

12

■ WOMEN: THE FORGOTTEN OFFENDERS

Often referred to as the "forgotten offenders," women traditionally have received discriminatory treatment from judges, few program resources from prison administrators, and little attention from criminal justice scholars. This neglect may stem from several facts: They make up a small proportion of the correctional population, their criminality is generally not serious, and their place in the criminal justice system merely reflects the common societal attitude that puts all women in a subservient position.

Compared with prisons for men, those for women are fewer and smaller. Joanne Belknap argues that this has resulted in a three-pronged form of institutionalized sexism:

1 Women's prisons generally are located farther from friends and families, making visits from children, other family members, and friends more difficult, particularly for the poor.

2 The relatively small number of women in prison and jail is used to "justify" the lack of diverse educational, vocational, and other programs available to incarcerated women.

3 The relatively small number of women in prison and jail is used to "justify" low levels of specialization in treatment and failure to segregate the more-serious and mentally ill offenders from the less-serious offenders (as is done in male prisons and jails).[3]

AP Images/Matt Rourke

Although they make up about just seven percent of the incarcerated population, the number of women prisoners is increasing faster than that of men. Becky Pemberton is serving a 35-year sentence at the Mabel Bennett Women's Prison in McLoud, Oklahoma, for stealing money out of cash registers in six states over three days.

Since the women's movement, scholars have more actively sought to understand women's criminality, the nature of the subculture of women's institutions, and the special problems of this offender population. In a period when equal opportunity has become public policy, paternalistic and discriminatory decisions by judges, probation officers, wardens, and parole boards concerning female offenders have been both criticized and litigated in court. Although women prisoners have brought fewer legal cases contesting the conditions of confinement than have men, the right to equal protection under law has prompted state and federal judges to intervene in several disputes.[4]

Female offenders are incarcerated in 98 confinement facilities for women and 93 facilities that house men and women separately.[5] Women make up only 6.8 percent of the federal prison population and 6.8 percent of inmates incarcerated in state correctional facilities.[6] However, the growth rate in number of incarcerated women has exceeded that of men since 1995. From 1995 to 2005 the male population in state and federal correctional facilities increased by 34 percent, whereas that of women increased by 57 percent.[7] This growth has been particularly acute in the federal system, which because of the war on drugs has had to absorb an additional 6,000 female inmates in the past 20 years.[8] The number of women now incarcerated in prisons is more than 114,000.[9] Barbara Owen and Barbara Bloom argue that the increased number of women in prison has significantly affected program delivery, housing conditions, medical care, staffing, and security.[10] **Figure 12.1** shows the incarceration rate for women in each state.

Some researchers have postulated that as women advance toward a position of equality with men in society, their behavior will become increasingly similar to men's, and so criminality among women will increase. As one observer noted, "Women wearing judges' robes or corporate

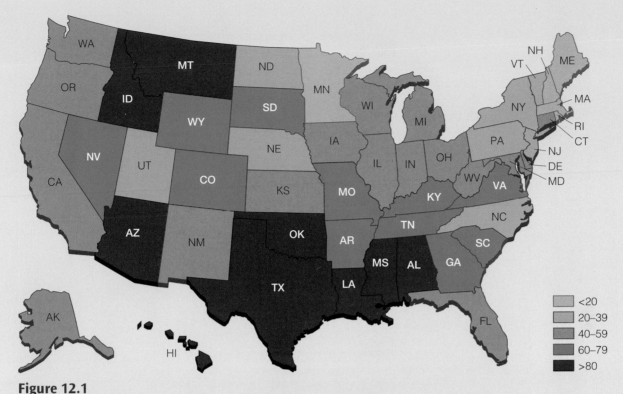

Figure 12.1

Rate of Female Imprisonment per 100,000 Female Residents

What accounts for the varying rates of female incarceration in different regions of the country?

Source: Natasha A. Frost, Judith Greene, and Kevin Pranis, *Hard Hit: The Growth in the Imprisonment of Women, 1977–2004* (New York: Women's Prison Association, 2006), 33.

pinstripes have become everyday images of society's changing gender roles. But what about women attired in Day-Glo prison jumpsuits?"[11] Others argue that differences in socializing women and men make it unlikely that the criminality of women will approach that of men, especially in terms of violent crimes.

Women account for 24.2 percent of all arrests for the serious crimes tabulated by the Uniform Crime Reports (see **Figure 12.2**), but women represent about 68 percent of people arrested for prostitution and commercialized vice, 44.1 percent of those arrested for fraud, and about 38 percent of those arrested for forgery.[12] Women are more likely than men to be serving sentences for drug offenses and other nonviolent property crimes.[13] Given that there are far fewer female offenders and that their crimes generally are far less serious than men's, many observers argue that it is rational for correctional public policy to focus on men.

Still, like the incarceration rate, the rate of arrests for women have increased more than that for men over the past decade, particularly for drug and certain Index offenses—robbery and burglary.[14] Showing direct links between women's status and their criminality is impossible, but as they have moved into jobs from which they were formerly excluded, they may have gained the opportunities and skills to commit criminal acts. As Freda Adler remarked many years ago, "When we did not permit women to swim at the beaches, the female drowning rate was quite low. When women were not permitted to work as bank tellers or presidents, the female embezzlement rate was low."[15] Others challenge this view, pointing out that most property offenses committed by women consist of petty fraud and shoplifting, crimes unrelated to occupation. Owen and Bloom found that the increased incarceration of women is a product of the war on drugs.[16] However, as Nichole Rafter suggests, the feminization of poverty since 1960 has meant that women and children now comprise 80 percent of the poor in the United States. She and other scholars believe that the poverty of young, female, single heads of

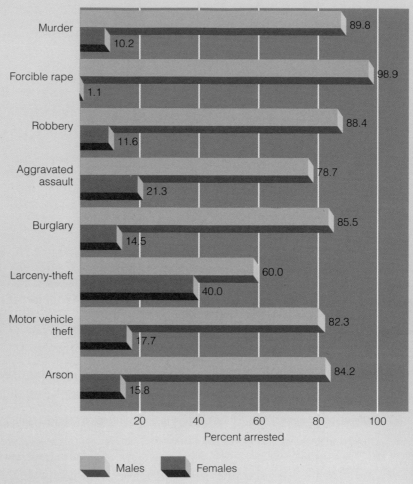

Figure 12.2

Percentage of Men and Women Arrested for Index Crimes

Although many more men than women are arrested, the proportion of arrests of women is highest for larceny-theft. What might account for these data?

Source: Federal Bureau of Investigation, *Crime in the United States, 2007*, Table 42, http://www.fbi.gov/ucr/cius2007/data/table_42.html, August 17, 2009.

Learn about **Hollywood's depiction of women prisoners** by reading reviews of the many films about them; find the web link at www.cengage.com/criminaljustice/clear.

households, and the way society treats them, has contributed to the increase in women's crime, particularly property offenses.[17]

Women convicts traditionally have received lighter sentences than men for similar offenses. Judges have stated that when they sentence women, they feel compelled to treat them differently from men, and not only because children often are involved. Researchers believe this differential treatment arises from the fact that most jurists are men and hold typically male attitudes: Women are the weaker sex and require gentle treatment. Other scholars believe women are now being sentenced harshly whether they are first-time drug offenders or have been convicted of assaults against their intimate partners.

■ HISTORICAL PERSPECTIVE

In the early 1800s reformers began to press for separate correctional facilities and programs for female offenders. Prior to that time, all prisoners—men, women, children—in Europe and in the United States were housed together in jails and prisons. Historical records indicate that women were punished the same as men: lashed, transported,

Reprinted with permission of the American Correctional Association, Alexandria, Virginia

Well into the twentieth century, female inmates were trained for stereotypically "feminine" occupations—ironing, laundry work, and cooking.

imprisoned, and hanged. After John Howard's exposé of prison conditions in England in 1777 and the development of the penitentiary in Philadelphia, people began to address the issue of corrections for women. Although the sexes were segregated, the conditions under which women prisoners lived were atrocious.

Elizabeth Gurney Fry, a middle-class English Quaker, was the first person to press for changes in the treatment of sentenced women and children. When Fry and several other Quakers visited London's Newgate Prison in 1813, they were shocked by the conditions in which the female prisoners and their children lived. Describing that first visit, Fry wrote, "The railing was crowded with half-naked women, struggling for the front situations with the most boisterous violence, and begging with the utmost vociferation." Fry felt she was venturing into a den of wild beasts, "shuddering when the door was closed upon her and she was locked in with such a herd of novel and desperate companions."[18] She advocated for separate facilities for women, with a domestic atmosphere, to be staffed by women. As a result, a parliamentary committee in 1818 heard evidence about conditions in the prisons, and reforms were ordered. Her 1827 book, *Observations in Visiting, Superintendence and Government of Female Prisons*, influenced the movement to reform American prisons for women.

The Incarceration of Women in the United States

News of Fry's efforts quickly reached the United States.[19] Although reformers were excited about the development of the penitentiary, the issue of corrections for women had not yet been broached. In 1844 Sarah Doremus and Abby Hopper Gibbons formed the Women's Prison Association in New York, with the goal of improving the treatment of female prisoners and separating them from male prisoners. Elizabeth Farnham, the head matron of the women's wing at Sing Sing from 1844 to 1848, sought to implement Fry's ideas but was thwarted by the male overseers and legislators and was forced to resign.

ELIZABETH GURNEY FRY (1780–1845)

Born in Norwich, England, Elizabeth Fry was second only to John Howard as a nineteenth-century advocate of prison reform in Europe. In 1817 she helped organize the Association for the Improvement of Female Prisoners in Newgate, then the main prison in London. This group, made up of wives of Quaker businessmen, worked to establish prison discipline, separation of the sexes, classification of criminals, female supervision for women inmates, adequate religious and secular instruction, and the useful employment of prisoners. Largely through her efforts, such reforms rapidly moved to other prisons in England and abroad.

Few women were incarcerated in the United States in the nineteenth century. Unlike their European counterparts, American judges were unwilling to pronounce women guilty of crime unless they were habitual offenders.[20] The women who were convicted, as inspectors at Sing Sing noted in 1844, were "the most abandoned representatives of their sex." At this time, prison was "the end of the road for women too far lost to virtue to offer much hope for redemption." Because only men were believed to have the ability to reason, and women supposedly were motivated solely by emotions, women who committed crimes posed a much more-serious threat to order: As they had gone against their "nature" and were not amenable to reason, how could they be reformed? "It seems to have been regarded as a sufficient performance of the object of punishment, to turn them loose within the pen of the prison and there leave them to feed upon and destroy each other."[21]

Until 1870 most women inmates were housed in the same prisons and treated essentially the same as men.[22] Separate quarters were gradually established for female convicts in prisons intended primarily for men. Most incarcerated women were convicted for crimes against public order, especially prostitution, alcoholism, and vagrancy. The few women sentenced for more-serious offenses were in out-of-the-way quarters without exercise yards, visitors' rooms, or even fresh air and sunlight. At Auburn in 1820, for example, "together, unattended, in a one-room attic, the windows sealed to prevent communication with men, the female prisoners were overcrowded, immobilized, and neglected."[23] Conditions of women imprisoned in other eastern and midwestern states before the Civil War have been similarly documented. All such reports indicate that the offenders were disregarded, sexually exploited, forced to do chores to maintain the prison, and kept in unsanitary facilities.

The **Prison Activist Resource Center** has a section on imprisoned women; see the web link at www.cengage.com/criminaljustice/clear.

The Reformatory Movement

As we noted in Chapter 3, the 1870 meeting of the National Prison Association in Cincinnati marked a turning point in American corrections. Although the Declaration of Principles did not address the problems of female offenders in any detail, it endorsed separate, treatment-oriented prisons. Right after the Civil War, the House of Shelter, a reformatory for women, opened in Detroit. Run by Zebulon Brockway, it became the model for reformatory treatment. The first independent female-run prison was established in Indiana in 1873, followed by the Massachusetts Reformatory-Prison for Women in 1877 and the Western House of Refuge at Albion (Michigan) in 1893.[24]

The Quakers continued to pursue prison reform. In 1869 Sarah Smith and Rhoda M. Coffin were appointed to inspect correctional facilities for women. They found "the state of morals in our southern prisons in such a deplorable condition that they felt constrained to seek some relief for the unfortunate women confined there."[25] Women volunteers in corrections, following the example of Elizabeth Fry, became quite active in serving others, acting out their religious convictions. Maud Booth, a leader of the Salvation Army, expressed this zeal: "We must work for regeneration, the cleansing of the evil mind, the quickening of the dead heart, the building up of fine ideals. In short, we must bring the poor sin-stained soul to feel the touch of the Divine hand."[26]

Three principles guided female prison reform during this period: (1) separation of women prisoners from men, (2) provision of differential care, and (3) management of women's prisons by female staff. Rafter summarizes these principles: "Operated by and for women, female reformatories were decidedly 'feminine' institutions, different from both custodial institutions for women and state prisons and reformatories for men."[27]

Like the penitentiary movement, advocates of women's reformatories favored rural correctional institutions, in areas away from the unwholesome conditions of the city. However, the reformatory for women did not emulate the fortress-like penitentiary but instead resembled cottages around an administration building. Many states adopted this plan, expecting that such housing for 20 to 50 women at a time would create a homelike atmosphere. For example, at the Massachusetts Reformatory Prison for Women in Framingham, which opened in 1877, the inmates lived in private rooms rather than cells, had iron bedsteads and bed linens, and, if they behaved well, "could decorate their quarters, enjoy unbarred windows, and have wood slats instead of grating on their doors."[28] Inmates had opportunities to learn domestic skills suitable to their "true" female nature. The expectation was that upon release they would apply these skills in domestic service or in their own homes.

The women in these reformatories were primarily convicted of petty larceny, prostitution, or "being in danger of falling into vice." They tended to be viewed as errant or misguided women who needed help and protection within a female environment, rather than being seen as dangerous criminals who had to be isolated to safeguard society. The upper-middle-class Protestant women active in prison reform may have removed from the offenders the stigma of "fallen women," but they developed programs that treated the offenders as children. As Rafter points out, the women who lobbied state administrations for reformatories believed they were being helpful, "but in the course of doing good . . . [they] perpetuated the double standard that required women to conform to more difficult moral rules than men and punished them if they failed to do so."[29]

Strongest in the East and Midwest, the reformatory movement gradually spread to parts of the South and West. In the South, corrections was tied to the lease system of farm labor. When African American women and children began to appear in large numbers before the criminal courts after the Civil War, officials had difficulty persuading farm leaseholders to accept these "dead hands," so the states created separate asylum farms for them.[30]

As time passed, the original ideals of the reformers faltered, overcome by societal change, administrative orthodoxy, and legislative objections. In 1927 the first federal prison for women opened in Alderson, West Virginia, with **Mary Belle Harris** as warden. She believed that much criminality among women resulted from dependency on men. She wanted her inmates to acquire skills to break this bondage and give them self-respect. These aims were incorporated into the programs at Alderson, which soon became a national model.

By the 1930s, as the country moved away from rural and domestic values, increases in the offender population and greater emphasis on custodial care made reformatories seem out of touch with reality. Thus, by 1935 the women's reformatory movement had "run its course, having largely achieved its objective [establishment of separate prisons run by women] in those regions of the country most involved with Progressive reforms in general."[31]

MARY BELLE HARRIS (1874–1957)

Born in Pennsylvania, Mary Belle Harris is chiefly known as the first warden of the Federal Institution for Women. She began her work in corrections in 1914 when she became the superintendent of the Women's Workhouse on Blackwell Island, New York City. She worked to create classification systems, developed educational programs, and pushed for intermediate sentences and parole. These aims were incorporated into the programs at Alderson, which soon became a national model.

The Post–World War II Years

No distinctive correctional model for women has arisen since the 1940s, perhaps because recent theories about the causes and treatment of criminal behavior do not discriminate between the sexes. As women increasingly have been arrested for more-serious crimes, and more drug law violators incarcerated, custody has become a larger goal than reformation. Rehabilitative programs, many based on psychological or sociological premises, were implemented in women's institutions in the 1940s and 1950s, as they had been in men's facilities. However, some scholars have argued that attention and resources were devoted mainly to men's institutions and that the less-serious offenders found in women's prisons received lower priority than did the serious ones. Further, educational and vocational programs for women have been geared toward traditionally "feminine" occupations—hairdressing, food preparation, secretarial skills—that perpetuate gender stereotypes. With less emphasis on rehabilitation, along with the rise in prison populations during the 1970s and 1980s, corrections for women was forced to defer to the rising concern about male offenders.

Today people's demands that women be treated the same as men have increased. However, as Rafter points out, "Equal treatment usually means less adequate treatment."[32] She argues that inferior care is the rule today and that gender differences are not taken into account.

Katja Heinemann/Aurora Photos

Best-selling author Wally Lamb is the volunteer facilitator of a writing workshop at York Correctional Institution in Connecticut. In their book, *Couldn't Keep It to Myself: Testimonies from Our Imprisoned Sisters*, eleven members of the workshop describe how they were "imprisoned by abuse, rejection, and their own self-destructive impulses long before they entered the criminal justice system."

■ WOMEN IN PRISON

Learn about **contemporary efforts to reform the lives of women in prison** by visiting the website of the California Coalition for Women Prisoners; see the link at www .cengage.com/criminaljustice/ clear.

Life in women's prisons both resembles and differs from that in institutions for men. Women's facilities are smaller, with looser security and less-structured inmate–staff relationships; the underground economy is not as well developed; and female prisoners seem less committed to the inmate code. Women also serve shorter sentences than do men, so women's prison society is more fluid as new members join and others leave.

Most women's prisons have the outward appearance of a college campus, often seen as a cluster of "cottages" around a central administration/dining/program building. Generally, those facilities lack the high walls, guard towers, and cyclone fences found at most prisons for men. Recent years, however, have seen a trend to upgrade security for women's prisons by adding razor wire, higher fences, and other devices to prevent escapes.

These characteristics of correctional facilities for women are offset by geographic remoteness and inmate heterogeneity. Few states operate more than one institution for women, so inmates generally live far from children, families, friends, and attorneys (see the Focus box "Excerpts from a Prison Journal").

There is less pressure to design effective treatment programs for women than for men. Kristy Holtfreter and Merry Morash maintain that correctional programming for women offenders has traditionally been based on assumptions about male criminality.[33] Barbara Bloom and other scholars argue that programs need to be developed that are gender sensitive, recognizing that female offenders are often victimized by family

FOCUS ON

PEOPLE IN CORRECTIONS

Excerpts from a Prison Journal

"The Rose"

This is an interview with myself. I've decided to write a book on things happening to me. . . . Maybe someone else will read it and learn. I'm sitting in jail.

"Jail?" you say.

Sure. Haven't you ever seen one? That's the place you always believed, and were told, the bad people go. It's not true. They send good people there too. Look at me. I'm in a 12-by-20-foot cell with two other "criminally oriented" females. They're OK. One is here for not returning a car to the dealer she borrowed it from—known by some as grand theft auto. The other is in here for writing too many checks on an account with no money.

The bunks are always too high, the mattresses are flimsy, and the pillows are falling apart. The window's got no glass in it; the cold north breeze blows in and freezes your ass off. So, if you ever plan on going to jail, hope it's in the summer.

The wind blows in, sending shivering chills up your spine. Oh! what you'd give to stand outside, with the sunshine beaming down, the birds singing, a tree to touch, a decent glass to drink out of, a proper plate to have your food on, a fork to eat with, a room without names all over the walls. . . . Hanging your towels over the heater to dry so you'll have a dry towel the next time you take a shower. The heater is a little portable thing that looks like someone took their frustration out on it. And you have to put everything up so it doesn't get wet, because the shower leaks and splatters all over everywhere. . . . Days of dripping shower, which is the worst sound in the world.

It's a sixty-eight-year-old building with steam heaters that whistle, jailers walking around with keys jingling, the elevator up and down all the time. They never come to get you. The phone rings from sunup to sundown. No calls for you. Calls only yours to be made when it's your turn. Knowing down inside no call will help you out of this mess.

The guys still flirt, no matter where—even through a little window in the door. . . . One of the girls is sitting under the sink having an obscene pipe conversation with Gary next door. He says it'll make him feel good, going down in history as an obscene pipe caller.

You'll never believe this. They're not trying to break out, just "escape to rape"—each other. I can hear the spoons digging now. Maybe they'll make it—by next year! The "escape to rape" fell through. We all knew it would, but it gave us

something to do last night. We must've laughed for four hours straight. We got to do something. You can't just sit around and cry and find someone else to blame things on. A year is a long time when you live it in a box.

I made the news. Not like most of the people I went to school with. I'm going to write what it says so I'll never forget what Clovis, New Mexico, is really like.

[They spelled my name right!], convicted of issuing a worthless check and distribution of a controlled substance, is charged with being an habitual offender. District Judge gave Ms. a two-year state penitentiary sentence with one year suspended and to be served on parole probation.

Ms. was originally given a suspended one-year sentence for issuing a worthless check. She was also previously given a five-year deferred penitentiary sentence for distribution of a controlled substance and was placed on probation.

Maybe someday I'll understand all this.

The worst feeling in the world was walking away and hearing my son scream for his mom. Knowing that I had to come back upstairs and be locked up. That's the hell in this hole—knowing people are close at hand and you can't touch or feel them.

I think what makes this so hard is that it's Christmastime. I'm almost crazy thinking I'm going to miss Santa Claus, Christmas carols, and my boys' smiling faces Christmas morning.

It's getting close to the time of my departure from a town I grew up in, learned to love. I feel a great loss as I'm going away knowing that returning may be a long ways away. Every passing moment brings thoughts I never conceived of having. I've never felt so alone. I've never felt so lost. I've never had so much taken from me in such a short time.

The strain of waiting for tomorrow has made me nervous, nauseous, and nuts. The three N's. Sounds like a bad disease. I go to a fate that I have no concept of, praying and hoping that I can handle it.

(Later, from the State Penitentiary)

I came through the gate knowing very well that it will be many months before I will be able to leave. The Annex (for women) is a building separate from the Big House (for men). I've only been here thirty minutes and I'm already talking like a convict. They gave me a number and issued me two blankets, dark green; two sheets, white; two towels, white; soap; toothbrush and toothpaste. They gave me some books, paper, pen, and envelopes, brought me to this square box half the

(Continued)

size of the county jail cell. It has one of the hardest beds I've ever seen, a toilet, a sink, a footlocker, two small bookcases, and a window. You can look out and see desert.

So far the women and matrons here seem very adaptable and willing to help. I've already had cookies, two glasses of milk, and two cups of hot chocolate brought to me before I sleep in my new box, sweet box. Don't get me wrong. I'll take all my days of working, bill collectors, children crying—and headaches, worries, and woes. I'll take my problems just not to hear that steel door slam shut and the key turn in the lock,

a matron walk down the hall leaving me with an empty feeling, and a sound of clanking, jangling keys falling off in the distance.

Source: The 24-year-old author of this journal chose the pen name "The Rose." Her identity has been disguised to protect her and her family, including two sons, aged two and six. These excerpts were written in the first five days following her conviction, while she was awaiting transfer from county jail to state prison. She served nine months in both maximum- and minimum-security facilities. Edited by Sue Mahan, from her interview notes.

members and intimate partners.[34] Bloom further notes that studies of female offenders highlight the importance of relationships. Criminal involvement often comes through relationships with family members, significant others, or friends. Successful programs relate to the social realities from which the women come and to which they will return.

Effective programming begins with effective classification in terms of housing assignments, therapeutic approaches, and educational and vocational opportunities. In many institutions, the small number of clients limits the extent to which the needs of individual offenders can be recognized and treated. Housing classifications are often so broad that dangerous or mentally ill inmates are mixed with women who have committed minor offenses and have no psychological problems. Similarly, available rehabilitative approaches may be limited, especially if correctional departments fail to recognize women's problems and needs, because of the relatively small population of female inmates.

Belknap points out that the regime of women's prisons has been described as "discipline, infantilize, feminize, medicalize, and domesticize."[35] The tendency to treat women like children and the emphasis on "domesticating" them has been well documented. Belknap also notes, however, that discipline for incarcerated women is generally overly harsh compared with that for men. For example, Texas female prisoners are far more likely to be cited for rule infractions, especially minor ones, and to receive severer punishments.[36] Drugs are extensively used to "calm" inmates, and vaginal searches are frequently used to discover contraband. Coramae Mann notes, "What is ironic about this procedure is that these vagina examinations are frequent, yet the preventive Pap test for cervical cancer is not often given."[37]

Characteristics of Women in Prison

What are the characteristics of women in America's prisons? The Bureau of Justice Statistics reports that almost 70 percent of them are 25–45 years old, about half are racial or ethnic minorities, and about 40 percent have not completed high school or its equivalent (see **Figure 12.3**).[38] The main factors distinguishing incarcerated women from men are the nature of offenses, sentence lengths, patterns of drug use, and correctional history.

OFFENSE ■ Although the public commonly believes most female prisoners are incarcerated for minor offenses such as prostitution, sentences for such crimes are usually served in jails; prisons hold the more-serious offenders, both male and female. According to the Bureau of Justice Statistics, at the end of 2005 approximately 35 percent of female state prisoners were serving sentences for violent offenses (compared with

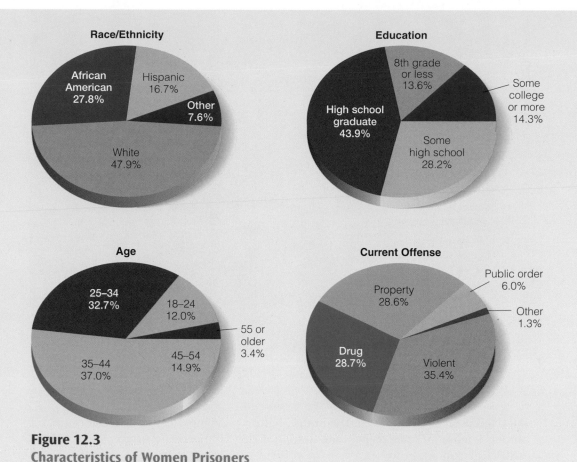

Figure 12.3
Characteristics of Women Prisoners

Sources: Bureau of Justice Statistics: *Education and Correctional Populations* (Washington, DC: U.S. Government Printing Office, January 2003), 5; *Prisoners in 2007* (Washington, DC: U.S. Government Printing Office, December 2008), 19, 21.

54 percent of male prisoners), 28.6 percent were serving for property offenses (versus 18.5 percent of men), 28.7 percent for drug-related offenses (versus 18.9 percent of men), and 6 percent for public-order offenses (versus 7.7 percent of men).[39] The most significant difference between the sexes concerns violent offenses.

SENTENCE ■ For all types of crimes, women prisoners receive shorter maximum sentences than do men. For example, the average prison sentence for murder is 192 months for women and 245 months for men. Differences between men and women are also present for property offenses (47 months for men, 34 months for women), drug offenses (52 months for men, 41 months for women), and weapons offenses (47 months for men, 41 months for women).[40] Shorter sentences are quite frequently a result of women's less-serious criminal background, especially regarding the use of violence, when compared with their male counterparts. Nevertheless, women offenders also serve long sentences in prison.

In their study of adjustment patterns among women prisoners in Virginia who have long-term (more than 10 years), medium-term (2 to 10 years), and short-term (less than 2 years) sentences, Caitlin Thompson and Ann Loper found that long- and medium-term inmates reported higher levels of conflict, such as feeling anger, when compared with their short-term counterparts. The study also revealed that short-term inmates committed significantly fewer nonviolent and institutional infractions, such as theft and failure to obey smoking rules. The study recommends that correctional interventions target women prisoners in specific sentence groups. More specifically, women who are serving longer sentences should be given priority for receiving specialized programming that addresses conflict resolution and stress related to prison life.[41]

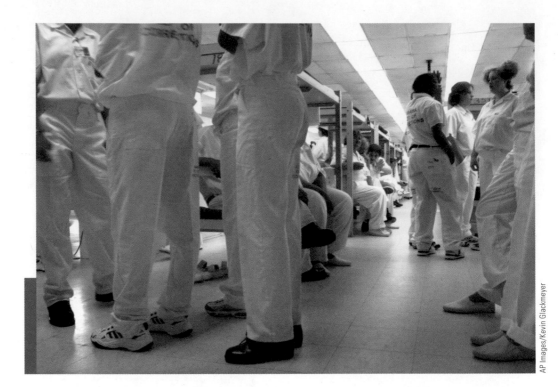

AP Images/Kevin Glackmeyer

In this crowded prison, inmates stand around or sit on bunks in a dorm that holds 250 women. What is the impact of this environment?

DRUG USE ■ Drug use in the month before their most recent offense is greater among female (59.3 percent) than among male (55.7 percent) state prisoners. For federal prisoners, however, this type of drug involvement is higher for men (50.4 percent) than women (47.6 percent), but this gender gap was even wider in the mid-1990s. Methamphetamine use prior to incarceration is higher among female than among male state and federal prisoners. A higher percentage of female state prisoners (60.2 percent) had symptoms consistent with drug dependence or abuse during the 12 months prior to entering prison than did male state prisoners (53.0 percent). Among federal inmates, gender differences for drug dependence and abuse are modest (45.7 percent for men, 42.8 percent for women).[42] The extent of drug use has policy implications, because it indicates that a large percentage of female offenders need medical assistance while going through withdrawal in jails, and they need treatment programs while incarcerated. (See "Myths in Corrections.")

MYTHS IN CORRECTIONS

PROFILES OF WOMEN OFFENDERS

THE MYTH: The life experiences of all women under correctional supervision are characterized by prior emotional, physical, and sexual abuse; substance abuse; turbulent family and intimate relationships; and economic marginalization.

THE REALITY: A recent study found that a sizable portion of women offenders (nearly 20 percent of the sample) reported relatively little prior domestic abuse, few drug-related problems, and little reliance on public assistance. Among this group, greed appeared to be the primary motivation for committing crime.

Source: Michael D. Reisig, Kristy Holtfreter, and Merry Morash, "Assessing Recidivism Risk across Female Pathways to Crime," *Justice Quarterly* 23 (September 2006): 384–405.

CORRECTIONAL HISTORY ■ About 65 percent of the female prisoners (compared with 77 percent of male prisoners) had a history of prior convictions before their current sentence. Differences between men and women on this variable seem related primarily to experiences as juveniles: More men than women reported having been on probation and incarcerated as youths. About 33 percent of women prisoners were on probation at the time of their incarcerating arrest, compared with 20 percent of male inmates.[43]

Drug offenses seem to account for the great increase of women in prison. Survey data collected by the National Council on Crime and Delinquency found that drug dependence was the main factor women offenders cited for committing their crime.[44] The upsurge in drug offenders and gang members has changed

was the main factor women offenders cited for committing their crime.[44] The upsurge in drug offenders and gang members has changed the character of the inmate society in many prisons for women. Delia Robinson, a veteran Connecticut inmate, told Andi Rierden that she especially disdains the young troublemakers who

> come in off the streets looking like zombies, bone thin and strung out on crack cocaine. "You can tell them by the abscesses on their bodies from shooting liquid dope cut with meat tenderizer. Before long these inmates fatten up on the prison's starchy food and the junk they order from commissary, smuggle in their drugs, and sleep around with women, even though they likely have a boyfriend or husband on the outside. Once released, they'll return to the streets, get arrested and then return to the Farm [prison]. Once settled in they'll unite with old flames and 'just chill.'"[45]

The Subculture of Women's Prisons

Much of the early research on women's prisons focused on types of relationships between female offenders. As in all types of prisons, same-sex relationships were observed, but unlike those in male prisons where such relationships are often coerced, sexual relationships between women prisoners appeared more voluntary. Interestingly, researchers reported that female inmates tended to form pseudofamilies in which they adopted various roles—father, mother, daughter, sister—and interacted as a unit, rather than identifying with the larger prison subculture.[46] Such cooperative relationships help relieve the tensions of prison life, assist the socialization of new inmates, and permit individuals to act according to clearly defined roles and rules.

When David Ward and Gene Kassebaum studied sexual and family bonding at the California Institute for Women in Frontera in the early 1960s, they found homosexual roles but not familial roles. The women at Frontera seemed to adapt less well to prison, and they did not develop the solidarity with one another that Donald Clemmer and Gresham Sykes found in male institutions. Yet societal expectations for gender and social roles of women were important in the prisoner subculture.[47]

We need to consider recent shifts in prison life when considering the existing research on women in prison. Just as the subculture of male prisons has changed since the pioneering research of Clemmer and Sykes, the climate of prisons for women has undoubtedly changed. Through interviews with a small group of women prisoners, Kimberly Greer found support for the idea that prisons for women are less violent, involve less gang activity, and do not have the racial tensions found in men's prisons. However, Greer also observed that women's interpersonal relationships were less stable and less familial than in the past. The inmates reported higher levels of mistrust and greater economic manipulation.[48] Thus, we must approach past research with caution.

Researchers do not agree on the extent and nature of same-sex relationships in women's prisons. Imogene Moyer, for example, points out that the evidence must be analyzed within a framework that recognizes factors in each institutional setting. Before generalizations about social relationships can be made with any confidence, researchers must assess policies designed to keep prisoners separate, average length of time served, distance from relatives, and level of regimentation.[49] Robert Leger found that the lesbians he surveyed had longer sentences, were arrested younger, were more likely to have been previously confined, and had served more time, compared with the heterosexual women with whom they were imprisoned.[50]

A more-explicit attempt to compare the subculture of women's prisons with that of men's was made by Rose Giallombardo. Like John Irwin and Donald Cressey, Giallombardo hypothesized that many subcultural features of the institution are imported from the larger society. For example, she found that female inmates express and fulfill social needs through prison homosexual marriage and kinship. Giallombardo suggests that, in many ways, the prison subcultures of men and women are similar, with one major exception: The informal social structure of the female prison is somewhat collectivist. It is characterized by warmth and mutual aid extended to family and kinship members; male prisoners adapt by self-sufficiency, a convict code, and solidarity with other inmates.[51]

The debate over whether the subculture of prisoners is due to deprivation or is imported has led some interesting findings in women's institutions. When Esther Heffernan began her study in a women's institution, she expected to find a unitary inmate social structure arising from within the institution, as Clemmer and Sykes had. But Heffernan found no "clear-cut pattern of acceptance or rejection of the inmate social system, nor any relatively uniform perception of deprivations." Unlike male maximum-security prisons, the prison Heffernan studied—like most other women's prisons—had a diverse population with the whole spectrum of offenses. Heffernan shows what Irwin and Cressey only suggest: Prisoners with similar orientations developed "distinctive norms and values, a pattern of interrelationships and certain roles that served their own prison needs."[52] The typical offender brings these orientations with them to the prison.

In a more-recent study of prison culture, Barbara Owen found that the inmates in the Central California Women's Facility have developed various styles of doing time.[53] Based on the in-prison experience, these styles correspond to the day-to-day business of developing a program of activities and settling into a routine. Owen discovered that one's style of doing time stems from one's commitment to a deviant identity and the stage of one's criminal and prison career. These elements influence the extent to which an inmate is committed to the "convict code" and participating in "the mix."

The vast majority of inmates, according to Owen, want to avoid "the mix"—"behavior that can bring trouble and conflict with staff and other prisoners." A primary feature of "the mix" is anything for which one can lose good time or be sent to administrative segregation. Being in "the mix" is involves "homo-secting," fighting, using drugs, and being involved in conflict and trouble. Owen found that most women want to do their time and go home, but some "are more at home in prison and do not seem to care if they 'lose time.'"[54] The culture of being "in the mix" is not imported from the outside but is internal to the prison, as some inmates prefer the pursuit of drugs, girlfriends, and fighting.

Male versus Female Subcultures

Comparisons of male and female prisons are difficult because most studies have been conducted in either male or female institutions, and most follow theories and concepts

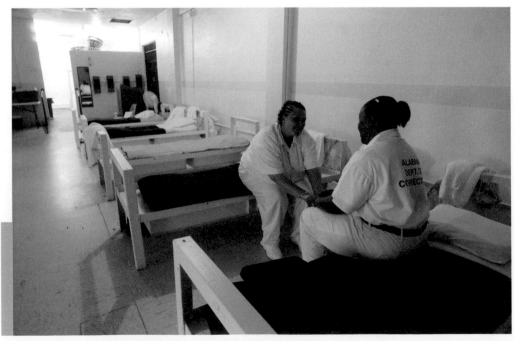

Compared with the convict society of prisons for men, many women prisoners, such as these in Tutwiler Women's Prison in Alabama, develop strong bonds of support and friendship.

AP Images/Dave Martin

first developed in male prisons. The following, however, helps clarify subcultural differences:

- Over half of male inmates, but only a third of female prisoners, are serving time for violent offenses.
- Women's prisons are less violent than prisons for men.
- Women are more responsive than men to prison programs.
- Men's prison populations are divided by security levels, but most women serve time in facilities where the entire population is mixed.
- Men tend to segregate themselves by race; this is less true for women.
- Men rarely form intimate relationships with prison staff, but many women share personal information with their keepers.

Some critics say that, despite these differences, the current practice of imprisoning women is based on assumptions about violent men.

A major difference between male and female prisons relates to interpersonal relationships. In male prisons, individuals act for themselves and are evaluated by others according to how they adhere to the inmate code. As James Fox notes in his comparative study of one women's prison and four men's correctional facilities, men believe they must demonstrate physical strength and avoid mannerisms that may imply homosexuality. To gain recognition and status within the convict community, the male prisoner must strictly adhere to these values. Men form cliques, but not the family networks found in prisons for women. Male norms emphasize autonomy, self-sufficiency, and the ability to cope with one's own problems, and men are expected to "do their own time." Fox also found little sharing in the men's prisons.[55]

Women place less emphasis on achieving status or recognition within the prisoner community. Fox also observed that women place fewer restrictions on sexual and emotional conduct. As noted previously, in women's prisons, close ties seem to exist among small groups that are similar to families. These groups provide emotional support and share resources.[56]

While it is true that female prisons are less violent than male facilities, violence still takes place in female institutions. A recent study of more than 7,000 male and female state prisoners found that certain types of violence, such as slapping, hitting, kicking, and biting were more common among the women than the men. However, the types of violence used by male inmates were typically more serious. For example, male prisoners were much more likely to threaten or harm another inmate with a shank (knife).[57]

The differences between male and female prison subcultures have been attributed to the nurturing, maternal qualities of women. Some critics argue that such a conclusion stereotypes female behavior and assigns a biological basis to personality where no basis exists. Of importance as well is the issue of inmate–inmate violence in male and female prisons. The little research that has been conducted indicates that women are less likely than men to engage in violent acts against other inmates.[58]

■ ISSUES IN THE INCARCERATION OF WOMEN

As noted, the number of incarcerated women has increased immensely over the past 15 years. Many states seem to believe that they should run women's prisons as they do prisons for men, with the same policies and procedures. Joycelyn Pollock believes that when prisons emphasize parity and use a male standard, women ultimately lose. She says that "equality of sentencing has led to staggering increases of women in prison, equality in prison programming has led to more vocational programs, but [equality] has also led to more security measures [and] more formalist approaches to supervision."[59]

Although departments of corrections have been playing "catch up" to meet the challenge of crowded facilities, problems persist. These include sexual misconduct by officers, lack of educational and training programs, demands for medical services, and the needs of mothers and their children. We examine each of these issues and the policy implications they pose for the future.

Sexual Misconduct

As the number of women prisoners has increased, cases of sexual misconduct by male correctional officers have escalated. Sexual misconduct includes any behavior that is sexual in nature (either consensual or nonconsensual) that is directed toward an inmate by an employee, official visitor, or agency representative. Such acts include (1) touching genitalia, breast, or buttocks in a way that is intended to arouse, abuse, or gratify sexual desire, (2) using threats or making requests for sexual acts, and (3) indecent exposure and staff voyeurism for sexual gratification.[60] Sexual misconduct is harmful in that it jeopardizes facility security, creates stress and trauma for those involved, exposes the agency and staff to potential lawsuits, creates a hostile work environment, and victimizes the vulnerable.[61]

Monetary civil judgments awarded to women for mistreatment while in prison can be costly. For example, officials in Virginia reportedly reached a $10 million out-of-court settlement in class-action suits brought by nine women who said they were sexually abused by a half-dozen correctional officers and an instructor. One of the inmates, a convicted murderer, was impregnated by a correctional officer.[62]

To deal with the problem of sexual abuse in prison, states have enacted statutes prohibiting sexual relations with correctional clients. Despite these laws, corrections still greatly needs better sexual harassment policies, training of officers, and screening of recruits. Some correctional administrators say that part of the problem is the large number of men guarding women.

Educational and Vocational Programs

A major criticism of women's prisons is that they lack the variety of vocational and educational programs usually available in male institutions and that existing programs tend to conform to stereotypes of "feminine" occupations—cosmetology, food service, housekeeping, and sewing.[63] Such training does not correspond to the wider opportunities available to women in today's world. The programs also are less ambitious

As the number of women prisoners has increased, cases of sexual misconduct by male correctional officers have escalated. At a public hearing before the National Prison Rape Elimination Commission, Hope Hernandez testifies how she was raped by an officer while she was confined. The commission was formed to help prevent prison sexual assaults.

AP Images/Eric Risberg

than those in men's prisons, which offer training for "real-world" jobs. Both men's and women's facilities usually offer educational programs so inmates can become literate and earn general equivalency diplomas (GEDs). Such programs seem quite important, considering that upon release most women must support themselves and many are financially responsible for children.

Research conducted in the 1970s confirmed that fewer programs were offered in women's than in men's institutions and that the existing programs lacked variety.[64] In 1979, in the case of *Glover v. Johnson*, a federal court ruled that programs in women's prisons must be substantially equal to those offered to men and that the programs must be based on the interests and needs of women.[65] Merry Morash and her colleagues noted changes during the 1980s, but they, too, found that gender stereotypes shaped

AP Images/The Dickinson Press, Thomas E. Hammel

Evette Seewalker joins two pieces of metal together using the gas-welding process she has learned through a program at North Dakota's Women's Correctional Rehabilitation Center. Critics charge that, unlike this program, many training programs in women's prisons are for "feminine" jobs.

vocational programs.[66] The American Correctional Association reported in 1990 that the few work assignments for incarcerated women do teach marketable skills.[67]

To get a good job, workers must have the education necessary to meet the needs of a complex workplace. However, most female offenders are undereducated and unskilled, which limits future occupational opportunities. In some institutions, less than half of the inmates have completed high school. Some corrections systems assign these women to classes so they can earn a GED, and other inmates can do college work through correspondence study or courses offered in the institution.

Critics of corrections have pointed out that, although the female workforce in the broader community has greatly expanded since the 1970s and women now occupy positions formerly reserved for men, female prisoners are not being prepared for such jobs. Upon release, however, most women prisoners have no one to depend on but themselves. They must find a job that will provide income and advancement. Without means of support, the released offender faces a life dependent on welfare or engaged in illegal activity to fulfill her children's needs and her own. Programs to train offenders for postrelease vocations that can improve their socioeconomic condition are essential if offenders are to succeed in the community.[68]

Medical Services

Women's prisons also lack proper medical services. Yet, compared with men, women usually have more-serious health problems, because of their socioeconomic status and limited access to preventive medical care. They also have a higher incidence of mental health problems.[69] Many women have gynecological problems as well. Government statistics show that a higher percentage of female than male prison inmates (2.2 percent versus 1.7 percent) tested positive for HIV.[70] A higher percentage of female than male state prison inmates reported a medical problem since admission, such as arthritis, asthma, cancer, heart problems, liver problems, hepatitis, and sexually transmitted disease.[71]

Pregnant women also need special medical and nutritional resources. In 2004, 4.1 percent of female state prisoners were pregnant when they entered prison. Nearly 95 percent of these women received an obstetric exam, and about 54 percent received pregnancy care.[72] Pregnancies raise numerous issues for correctional policy, including special diets, abortion rights, access to delivery room and medical personnel, and length of time that newborns can remain with incarcerated mothers. Most pregnant inmates are older than 35, have histories of drug abuse, have had prior multiple abortions, and carry sexually transmitted diseases. All of these factors indicate the potential for a high-risk pregnancy requiring special medical care.

Further, pregnant inmates must not only cope with the physical aspects of incarceration but also endure psychological stress over whether to have an abortion, who should care for the child after birth, and separation from the child. Many prison systems are allowing nursing infants to stay with their mothers, creating in-prison nurseries, developing special living quarters for pregnant women and new mothers, instituting counseling programs, and improving standards of medical care.

Saying that corrections must "defuse the time bomb," Leslie Acoca argues that the failure to provide women inmates with basic preventive and medical treatments, such as immunizations, breast cancer screening, and management of chronic diseases, is resulting in more-serious health problems that are more-expensive to treat. She says that poor medical care for the incarcerated merely shifts costs to overburdened community health care systems after release.[73]

Mothers and Their Children

Of great concern to many incarcerated women is the fate of their children. Over 60 percent of female inmates in state prisons are mothers of minor children. On any given day, the mothers of an estimated 131,000 minor children are incarcerated in state prisons. Nearly 58 percent of imprisoned mothers do not see their children during their prison sentence. About 61 percent of incarcerated mothers lived with their children prior to being sent to prison. Many of these women were single caretakers. Because of this, many children of incarcerated mothers are cared for by friends and relatives, while 10.9 percent are in state-funded foster care.[74]

Anxiety about children bothers all imprisoned mothers, especially if strangers are caring for their children. One study of prison mothers found that 13 percent had at least one child requiring special education, 15 percent said one or more had become a ward of the court, and 10 percent said one or more of their children had been arrested as a juvenile.[75] Beth Huebner and Regan Gustafson's research shows that maternal incarceration adversely affects the life chances of imprisoned women's children. Specifically, they found that children of incarcerated women are nearly three times more likely to be convicted of crime as an adult as are individuals whose mother has not been incarcerated.[76] Enforced separation of children from their mothers can be devastating for both. Many women fear that neither they nor the children will be able to adjust to each other when they are reunited after their long separation.

In most states, babies born in prison must be placed with a family member or a social agency within three weeks of birth. Critics have expressed great concern about such early termination of mother–infant bonding, so some innovative programs now let them stay together longer. For example, at the Ohio Reformatory for Women, prisoners may live with their babies in dorm rooms. These mothers take classes on parenting, learn how to administer CPR, and learn the proper way to use a car seat. Terry Collins, the director of the Department of Rehabilitation and Correction, says the program gives women a chance "while clean and sober and free from violence on the outside, to bond with their babies." Ohio officials believe that strengthening the bond between mother and baby will reduce the likelihood of the mother returning to prison. Only 3 percent of mothers who have participated in the program have returned to prison.[77] Other prisons have developed prison nurseries. Advocates argue that these programs prevent placing the children of incarcerated women in foster care and also allow mothers and children to bond during an important stage in child development.[78] Although prison nursery programs are now more common than they were a decade ago, over 80 percent of state departments of corrections do not have such programs in place. Lorie Goshin and Mary Byrne note that the number of infants involved in prison nursery programs is only a small fraction of the number of children whose mothers are incarcerated. The researchers also point out that nursery programs do not address the large number of older children who are left behind when their mothers are sent to prison.[79] See the Focus box for the story of Maria, who gave birth while incarcerated.

The **Chicago Legal Advocacy for Incarcerated Mothers** assists families of women prisoners; see the web link at www.cengage.com/criminaljustice/clear.

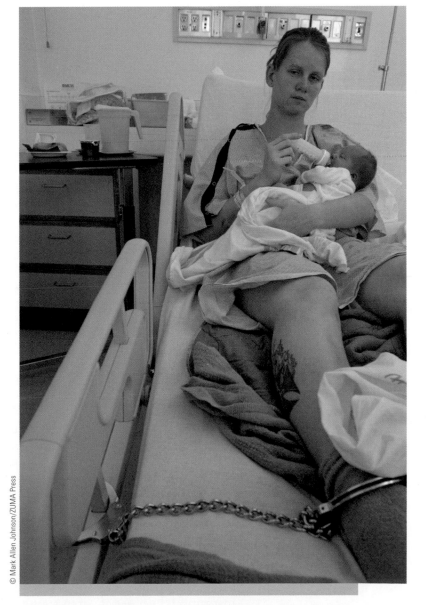

© Mark Allen Johnson/ZUMA Press

Laura Strange, a California inmate, was shackled to her bed during labor, delivery, and recovery. California has since banned this policy, but it is still found in some other states.

PEOPLE IN CORRECTIONS

Maria's Story

Maria is a soft-spoken woman in her mid-30s, of mixed African-American and Hispanic descent. Her slimness belies the fact that she delivered her second child less than three months ago in a nearby hospital.

Maria believes that she is extremely fortunate compared to most of the other pregnant and postpartum inmates who live in her housing unit. She is one of a handful of prison mothers participating in a small local program that provides foster mothers from the surrounding community to care for newborns. The foster mothers bring the children to the prison regularly for visits and help prepare both mother and child to live together successfully after the mother's release.

Without this program, Maria would have lost contact with her baby during the first months of his life because the child would have been sent immediately to a child welfare agency in Maria's county of commitment, hundreds of miles away from the prison. Maria describes the intense depression of the pregnant women she lives with who cannot participate in the program because of its limited size. She says that not knowing what will happen to their infants after delivery is the "worst thing" for these women.

For Maria, the most difficult aspect of childbearing while incarcerated was returning from the hospital to the prison 10 hours after delivery without her baby and without medication to dry up her milk. She reports that in the days following the birth, her breasts became painfully engorged with milk and that she consequently developed an infection and high fever. She observes that other postpartum inmates in her unit have experienced the same problem.

Maria recalls that on the day of her last arrest she went to a local store to put some baby clothes on layaway because she had recently discovered that she was pregnant. She entered the store with her boyfriend who proceeded to steal a stack of Levi 501 jeans, which he hoped to sell for money to buy drugs. Maria claims that she had stopped using drugs due to her pregnancy and fear of HIV infection and that she had begged her boyfriend before they went shopping not to jeopardize their freedom by shoplifting. When the boyfriend was caught in the act of stealing, she was arrested also.

Because of her extensive history of past arrests and her status as a parolee and because she would not inform on her boyfriend, Maria was convicted for shoplifting and violation of parole and was sentenced to two years in state prison. Her boyfriend was not convicted and served no time for his offense. . . . Once she entered prison, her boyfriend [the father of her second child] severed all contact with her and has made no inquiries regarding their baby.

Source: Leslie Acoca, "Hearts on the Ground: Violent Victimization and Other Themes in the Lives of Women Prisoners," *Corrections Management Quarterly* 1 (Spring 1997): 50.

Imprisoned mothers have difficulty maintaining contact with their children. Because most states have only one or two prisons for women, mothers may be incarcerated 150 or more miles away. Transportation is difficult, visits are short and infrequent, and phone calls are uncertain and irregular. When the children do visit the prison, the surroundings are strange and intimidating. In some institutions children must conform to the rules governing adult visitation: strict limits and no physical contact. Other correctional facilities, however, seek ways to help mothers maintain links to their children and nurture their relationships. For example, the Dwight Correctional Center in Illinois schedules weekend retreats similar to camping trips for women and their children.

Programs to address the needs of imprisoned mothers and their children are being designed and implemented. In some states children may meet with their mothers at almost any time, for extended periods, and in playrooms or nurseries where physical contact is possible. Some states transport children to visit their mothers; some institutions even let children stay overnight with their mothers. But few programs, according to Merry Morash and Pamela Schram, "get beyond the assumption that all that is needed is retraining in parenting skills, or that women's needs are limited to the parenting area."[80] One national survey shows that 90 percent of states

Patty Prewitt plays with her granddaughters at the Women's Eastern Reception, Diagnostic and Correctional Center at Vandalia, Missouri. Prewitt is part of the 4-H LIFE program, which tries to create a healthy envionment for offenders and members of their family.

make "parenting classes" available to women prisoners and nearly 75 percent provide "special visiting areas." Far fewer, however, allow overnight visits (28 percent) or have nurseries (7 percent), both of which many believe can help nurture the bond between mother and child.[81]

The emphasis on community corrections as it developed in the 1970s gave rise to programs in which youngsters could live with their mothers in halfway houses. These programs have not expanded as much as expected, however, in part because children upset prison routine. Many states have furlough programs that let inmates visit relatives and children in their homes during holiday periods and some weekends.

■ RELEASE TO THE COMMUNITY

Women face a variety of problems and challenges upon release from prison: Many of these women are poor, have lost custody of their children and would like it back, have serious health care needs, and have extensive substance abuse histories. Additionally, 60 to 70 percent of women released from incarceration have nowhere to go and must find a place to live.[82] Stable housing is essential for women to regain custody of their children, and it also provides a base from which to hunt for a job, get health care, and receive substance abuse treatment. But obtaining housing is complicated by several factors, including skeptical landlords, who may view women parolees as either financial or security risks, and federal restrictions on subsidized housing.[83]

Despite cutbacks in funding for offender services, some programs do help women make the transition from prison to the community. The Sarah Powell Huntington House (SPHH) in New York City helps women parolees reunite with their children, by providing stable housing and helping women develop living and parenting skills. Over the last 10 years, SPHH has helped 328 women who, on average, stay in the program for 10 months.[84] Are programs that address the needs of women parolees effective? Kristy Holtfreter and her associates found that impoverished women parolees are 83 percent less likely to reoffend if given access to housing and life skills training.[85] Overall, the research indicates that a significant majority of women offenders need some assistance to reenter society successfully. Those who do not have friends and family to lean on will need state-funded resources to become self-sufficient, overcome the stigma of having been convicted of a felony, and stay out of prison.[86]

It is a joyous day when a prisoner is released and can return to her family.

© Myrleen Ferguson Cate/PhotoEdit

SUMMARY

1 Explain why women prisoners are called the "forgotten offenders."

Female prisoners make up a small portion of the correctional population. The offenses women commit are usually less serious than those committed by men. Some observers claim that women's place in the criminal justice system reflects broader societal attitudes that place all women in a subservient position. Unfortunately, the status of "forgotten offender" has several negative consequences, including discriminatory treatment from judges, few prison programs, and little attention from criminal justice scholars.

2 Be familiar with the history of the incarceration of women.

Until 1870 women were incarcerated in the same prisons as men. Elizabeth Fry helped reform prisons in England by advocating for the separation of the sexes, female supervision for women inmates, and the useful employment of prisoners. In the United States, separate quarters were gradually established for female convicts in prisons intended mainly for men. The conditions under which women prisoners lived were atrocious. Women offenders were mostly convicted of public order crimes, like prostitution, alcoholism, and vagrancy. In the 1870s the reformatory movement was underway, advocating (1) separation of women prisoners from men, (2) provision of differential care, and (3) management of women's prisons by female staff. In 1927 the first federal prison for women opened in Alderson, West Virginia, with Mary Belle Harris as warden. She believed that much criminality among women resulted from dependence on men. She wanted her inmates to acquire skills and develop self-respect. No distinctive correctional model for women has arisen since the 1940s. Rehabilitative programs were implemented in women's institutions in the 1940s and 1950s, as they had been in men's facilities. Educational and vocational programs for women have been geared toward traditionally "feminine" occupations—hairdressing, food preparation, secretarial skills—that perpetuate gender stereotypes. With less emphasis on rehabilitation, along with the rise in prison populations during the 1970s and 1980s, corrections for women was forced to defer to the rising concern about male offenders.

3 Explain how interpersonal relationships in women's prisons differ from those in men's prisons.

Men form cliques, and norms in male prisons emphasize autonomy, self-sufficiency, and the ability to cope with one's own problems. Men are expected to "do their own time," and they share very little with one another. In contrast, women develop close ties and form small groups that are similar to families that provide emotional support and share resources. Women also place fewer restrictions on sexual and emotional conduct.

4 Be familiar with the special issues that incarcerated women face.

Four important issues in women's prisons are sexual misconduct, educational and vocational programs, medical services, and mothers and their children. (1) Sexual misconduct, or instances where prison officials sexually exploit female inmates, threatens facility security, creates stress and trauma for those involved, exposes the agency and staff to potential lawsuits, creates a hostile work environment, and victimizes people who are vulnerable. To deal with this problem, states have enacted statutes prohibiting sexual relations with correctional clients. (2) Women's prisons lack the variety of vocational and educational programs usually available in male institutions, and existing programs tend to conform to stereotypes of "feminine" occupations. (3) Women's prisons lack proper medical services, even though women usually have more-serious health problems than do men, as well as gynecological needs. (4) A majority of women prisoners were the primary caretakers of children before entering prison, and over half of these women do not see their children while serving their sentence. Some states have implemented visitation programs to address this issue.

5 Discuss the problems women face when they are released to the community.

Many female ex-prisoners have serious health care needs and have extensive histories of substance abuse. What is more, many women who are released from prison are poor and would like to regain custody of their children. Many of these women have no place to go and must find a place to live, but federal laws restricting subsidized housing and landlords who are reluctant to rent to a former prison inmate can make doing so difficult. Research has demonstrated that women offenders benefit from assistance when reentering society, such as help from friends and family and state-funded resources, to become self-sufficient and stay out of prison.

KEY TERMS

Fry, Elizabeth Gurney (p. 313)
Harris, Mary Belle (p. 315)

QUESTIONS FOR DISCUSSION

1. How has fragmentation of corrections among federal, state, and local governments affected the quality of services for female offenders?
2. If they commit similar crimes, should women receive the same sentences as do men? How might the unequal treatment of male and female offenders be rationalized?
3. Imagine you are the administrator of a women's correctional center. What problems would you expect to encounter? How would you handle these problems?
4. What parental rights should prisoners have? Should children be allowed to live in correctional facilities with their mothers? What problems would this practice create?
5. How do the social structures of male and female correctional institutions differ? Why do you think they differ in these ways?

FOR FURTHER READING

Freedman, Estelle B. *Their Sisters' Keepers*. Ann Arbor: University of Michigan Press, 1981. Traces the history of the development of prisons for women in the United States.

Kruttschnitt, Candace, and Rosemary Gartner. *Marking Time in the Golden State: Women's Imprisonment in California*. New York: Cambridge University Press, 2005. Using a variety of data sources, the authors explore women inmates' responses to the prison regime and social relations between one another.

Lamb, Wally, and Carolyn Adams Goodwin. *Couldn't Keep It to Myself: Testimonies from Our Imprisoned Sisters*. New York: HarperCollins, 2003. A collection of vivid life portraits written by inmates housed at Connecticut's maximum-security prison for women.

Morash, Merry, and Pamela J. Schram. *The Prison Experience: Special Issues of Women in Prison*. Prospect Heights, IL: Waveland, 2002. The authors explain the realities of prison life for women, paying special attention to such topics as motherhood, staff sexual misconduct, mental illness, and gender-responsive programming.

Rierden, Andi. *The Farm: Life inside a Women's Prison*. Amherst: University of Massachusetts Press, 1997. A case study of changes in the inmate population and administration during the late 1980s to early 1990s at Connecticut's Niantic Correctional Institution.

NOTES

1 Bureau of Justice Statistics, *Parents in Prison and Their Minor Children* (Washington, DC: U.S. Government Printing Office, August 2008).

2 "Sister Suzanne Jabro: The Fuel That Has Fired up 'Get on the Bus' for Nearly a Decade," *CDRC News*, June 2008, http://www.cdcr.ca.gov/News/CDCR_News/page_7.html, September 28, 2009.

3 Joanne Belknap, *The Invisible Woman: Gender, Crime, and Justice* (Belmont, CA: Wadsworth, 1996), 97.

4 Nichole Hahn Rafter, "Gender and Justice: The Equal Protection Issue," in *The American Prison*, edited by Lynne Goodstein and Doris MacKenzie (New York: Plenum Press, 1989), 89.

5 Bureau of Justice Statistics, *Census of State and Federal Correctional Facilities, 2000* (Washington, DC: U.S. Government Printing Office, October 2003), 6.

6 Federal Bureau of Prisons, *State of the Bureau 2007* (Washington, DC: U.S. Government Printing Office, 2007), 52; Bureau of Justice Statistics, *Prisoners in 2007* (Washington, DC: U.S. Government Printing Office, December 2008), Appendix Table 10.

7 Bureau of Justice Statistics, *Prisoners in 2005* (Washington, DC: U.S. Government Printing Office, November 2006), 4.

8 Mark S. Fleisher, Richard H. Rison, and David W. Helman, "Female Inmates: A Growing Constituency in the Federal Bureau of Prisons," *Corrections Management Quarterly* 1 (Fall 1997): 28–35.

9 Bureau of Justice Statistics, *Prisoners in 2007*, p. 1.

10 Barbara Owen and Barbara Bloom, "Profiling Women Prisoners: Findings from National Surveys and a California Sample," *Prison Journal* 75 (no. 2, June 1995): 166.

11 Clifford Krauss, "Women Doing Crime, Women Doing Time," *New York Times*, July 3, 1994, p. 3.

12 Federal Bureau of Investigation, *Crime in the United States, 2007*, http://www.fbi.gov/ucr /cius2007/data/table_42.html, Table 42, August 17, 2009.

13 Owen and Bloom, "Profiling Women Prisoners," p. 167.

14 Federal Bureau of Investigation, *Crime in the United States, 2007*, Table 33.

15 Freda Adler, "Crime, an Equal Opportunity Employer," *Trial Magazine*, January 1977, p. 31.

16 Owen and Bloom, "Profiling Women Prisoners," p. 182.

17 Nichole Rafter, *Partial Justice: Women, Prisons and Social Control* (New Brunswick, NJ: Transaction, 1990), 178.

18 E. R. Pitman, *Elizabeth Fry* (New York: Greenwood, [1884] 1969), 55.

19 Lucia Zedner, "Wayward Sisters: The Prison for Women," in *The Oxford History of the Prison*, edited by Norval Morris and David J. Rothman (New York: Oxford University Press, 1995), 333.

20 Feeley and Little point out that for much of the eighteenth century almost half of those indicted for felony offenses in London were women. The proportion dropped in the nineteenth century as the roles of women changed in the economy, the family, and society. See Malcolm M. Feeley and Deborah L. Little, "The Vanishing Female: The Decline of Women in the Criminal Process, 1687–1912," *Law and Society Review* 25 (1991): 720–57.

21 W. Davis Lewis, *From Newgate to Dannemora: The Rise of the Penitentiary in New York, 1796–1888* (Ithaca, NY: Cornell University Press, 1965), 158–59.

22 Nichole Hahn Rafter, "Equality or Difference?" *Federal Prisons Journal* 3 (Spring 1992): 17.

23 Estelle B. Freedman, *Their Sisters' Keepers* (Ann Arbor: University of Michigan Press, 1981), 15.

24 Zedner, "Wayward Sisters," p. 353.

25 Sara F. Keely, "The Organization and Discipline of the Indiana Women's Prison" (proceedings of the 58th Annual Congress of the National Prison Association, 1898), 275, quoted in Rose Giallombardo, *Society of Women: A Study of a Women's Prison* (New York: Wiley, 1966), 7.

26 Maud Ballington Booth, "The Shadow of Prison" (proceedings of the 58th Annual Congress of the National Prison Association, 1898), 275, quoted in Giallombardo, *Society of Women*, p. 46.

27 Nichole Hahn Rafter, "Prisons for Women, 1790–1980," in *Crime and Justice*, vol. 5, edited by Michael Tonry and Norval Morris (Chicago: University of Chicago Press, 1983), 147.

28 Freedman, *Their Sisters' Keepers*, p. 69.

29 Rafter, "Prisons for Women," p. 165.

30 Lewis, *From Newgate to Dannemora*, p. 213.

31 Rafter, "Prisons for Women," p. 165.

32 Rafter, "Equality or Difference?" p. 19.

33 Kristy Holtfreter and Merry Morash, "The Needs of Women Offenders: Implications for Correctional Programming," *Women and Criminal Justice* 14 (2003): 137–60.

34 Barbara Bloom, "Gender-Responsive Programming for Women Offenders: Guiding Principles and Practices," *Forum of Correctional Research* 11 (September 1999): 22–28.

35 Belknap, *Invisible Woman*, p. 98.

36 Dorothy S. McClellan, "Disparity and Discipline of Male and Female Inmates in Texas Prisons," *Women and Criminal Justice* 5 (1994): 71–97.

37 Coramae Richey Mann, *Female Crime and Delinquency* (Tuscaloosa: University of Alabama Press, 1984).

38 Bureau of Justice Statistics, *Prisoners in 2007*, 19, 21; *Education and Correctional Populations* (Washington, DC: U.S. Government Printing Office, January 2003), 5.

39 Bureau of Justice Statistics, *Prisoners in 2007*, Appendix Table 10.

40 Bureau of Justice Statistics, *State Court Sentencing of Convicted Felons, 2004—Statistical Tables*, Table 2.6. Revised July 25, 2007, http://www.ojp.usdoj.gov/bjs/pub/html/scscf04/tables/scs04206tab.htm.

41 Caitlin Thompson and Ann B. Loper, "Adjustment Patterns in Incarcerated Women: An Analysis of Differences Based on Sentence Length," *Criminal Justice and Behavior* 32 (December 2005): 714–32.

42 Bureau of Justice Statistics, *Drug Use and Dependence, State and Federal Prisoners, 2004* (Washington, DC: U.S. Government Printing Office, October 2006).

43 Bureau of Justice Statistics, *Women Offenders* (Washington, DC: U.S. Government Printing Office, December 1999), 9.

44 Leslie Acoca, "Hearts on the Ground: Violent Victimization and Other Themes in the Lives of Women Prisoners," *Correctional Management Quarterly* 1 (Spring 1997): 44–55.

45 Andi Rierden, *The Farm: Life Inside a Women's Prison* (Amherst: University of Massachusetts Press, 1997), 18.

46 Esther Heffernan, *Making It in Prison* (New York: Wiley, 1972).

47 David Ward and Gene G. Kassebaum, *Women's Prisons: Sex and Social Structure* (Hawthorne, NY: Aldine, 1965), 140.

48 Kimberly R. Greer, "The Changing Nature of Interpersonal Relationships in a Women's Prison," *Prison Journal* 80 (no. 4, December 2000): 442–68.

49 Imogene L. Moyer, "Differential Social Structures and Homosexuality among Women in Prisons," *Virginia Social Science Journal* (April 1978): 13–14, 17–19.

50 Robert G. Leger, "Lesbianism among Women Prisoners: Participants and Nonparticipants," *Criminal Justice and Behavior* 14 (December 1987): 463.

51 Rose Giallombardo, *Society of Women*.

52 Heffernan, *Making It in Prison*, pp. 16–17.

53 Barbara Owen, *"In the Mix": Struggle and Survival in a Women's Prison* (Albany: State University of New York Press, 1998).

54 Ibid., p. 179.

55 James G. Fox, *Organizational and Racial Conflict in Maximum-Security Prisons* (Lexington, MA: Lexington Books, 1982), 100–102.

56 Ibid., pp. 100–101.

57 Nancy Wolff and Jing Shi, "Type, Source, and Patterns of Physical Victimization: A Comparison of Male and Female Inmates," *Prison Journal* 89 (no. 2, June 2009): 172–91.

58 Candace Kruttschnitt and Sharon Krmopotich, "Aggressive Behavior among Female Inmates: An Exploratory Study," *Justice Quarterly* 7 (June 1990): 370.

59 Joycelyn M. Pollock, *Counseling Women in Prison* (Thousand Oaks, CA: Sage, 1998), 42.

60 Bureau of Justice Statistics, *Sexual Violence Reported by Correctional Authorities, 2006* (Washington, DC: U.S. Government Printing Office, August 2007), 9.

61 Susan W. McCampbell and Elizabeth P. Laymen, *Training Curriculum for Investigating Allegations of Staff Sexual Misconduct with Inmates* (Tamarac, FL: Center for Innovative Public Policies, 2000), 3.

62 "$10M Settlement in Prison Sex Abuse Case," *CBSNews.com*, April 19, 2008, http://www.cbsnews.com/stories/2008/04/19/national/main4029273.shtml, September 28, 2009.

63 Clarice Feinman, "An Historical Overview of the Treatment of Incarcerated Women: Myths and Realities of Rehabilitation," *Prison Journal* 63 (no. 2, 1983): 12–26.

64 Ruth M. Glick and Virginia V. Neto, *National Study of Women's Programs* (Washington, DC: National Institute of Law Enforcement and Criminal Justice, 1977); Ralph R. Arditi, Frederick Goldbert, Jr., M. Martin Hartle, John H. Peters, and William Phelps, "The Sexual Segregation of American Prisons," *Yale Law Journal* 82 (1973): 1229.

65 *Glover v. Johnson*, 478 F.Supp. 1075 (1979).

66 Merry Morash, Robin N. Haarr, and Lila Rucker, "A Comparison of Programming for Women and Men in U.S. Prisons in the 1980s," *Crime and Delinquency* 40 (April 1994): 197–221.

67 American Correctional Association, *The Female Offender: What Does the Future Hold?* (Alexandria, VA: Kirby Lithographic Company, 1990).

68 Barbara Bloom, Barbara Owen, and Stephanie Covington, *Gender-Responsive Strategies for Women Offenders* (Washington, DC: U.S. Government Printing Office, May 2005), 9.

69 Bureau of Justice Statistics, *Mental Health Problems of Prison and Jail Inmates* (Washington, DC: U.S. Government Printing Office, September 2006), 4.

70 Bureau of Justice Statistics, *HIV in Prisons, 2005* (Washington, DC: U.S. Government Printing Office, September 2007), 1.

71 Bureau of Justice Statistics, *Medical Problems of Prisoners—Statistical Tables*, Table 2. Revised April 22, 2008, http://www.ojp.usdoj.gov/bjs/pub/html/mpp/tables/mppt02.htm.

72 Ibid., Table 10.

73 Leslie Acoca, "Defusing the Time Bomb: Understanding and Meeting the Growing Health Care Needs of Incarcerated Women in America," *Crime and Delinquency* 44 (January 1998): 49–69.

74 Bureau of Justice Statistics, *Parents in Prison*.

75 Acoca, "Defusing the Time Bomb."

76 Beth M. Huebner and Regan Gustafson, "The Effect of Maternal Incarceration on Adult Offspring Involvement in the Criminal Justice System," *Journal of Criminal Justice* 35 (May–June 2007): 283–96.

77 "Babies Are Pampered in Prison," *Corrections Today* 68 (December 2006): 12.

78 Women's Prison Association, *Mothers, Infants and Imprisonment: A National Look at Prison Nurseries and Community-Based Alternatives* (New York: Author, May 2009), 5.

79 Lorie Smith Goshin and Mary Woods Byrne, "Converging Streams of Opportunity for Prison Nursery Programs in the United States," *Journal of Offender Rehabilitation* 48 (May 2009): 271–95.

80 Merry Morash and Pamela J. Schram, *The Prison Experience: Special Issues of Women in Prison* (Prospect Heights, IL: Waveland, 2002), 99.

81 Joycelyn M. Pollock, "Parenting Programs in Women's Prisons," *Women and Criminal Justice* 14 (2002): 131–54.

82 Women's Prison Association, *A Report on the First Ten Years of the Sarah Powell Huntington House* (New York: Author, 2004).

83 Women's Prison Association, *WPA Focus on Women and Justice: Barriers to Reentry* (New York: Author, October 2003).

84 Women's Prison Association, *Report on the First Ten Years.*

85 Kristy Holtfreter, Michael D. Reisig, and Merry Morash, "Poverty, State Capital, and Recidivism among Women Offenders," *Criminology and Public Policy* 3 (March 2004): 201.

86 Beth E. Richie, "Challenges Incarcerated Women Face as They Return to Their Communities: Findings from Life History Interviews," *Crime and Delinquency* 47 (July 2001): 368–89.

AP Images/Phil Coale

LEARNING OBJECTIVES

After reading this chapter you should be able to . . .

1 Be familiar with the principles used to organize the functioning of prisons.

2 Discuss the importance of prison governance.

3 Discuss the different job assignments that correctional officers are given.

4 Understand the negative consequences of boundary violations and job stress among prison staff.

Police investigators mark the location of evidence outside the Federal Correctional Institution in Tallahassee, Florida. Two people were killed when a gunfight broke out between federal agents and prison guards as the agents tried to arrest six guards on charges that they traded alcohol and drugs for sex with female inmates.

SHORTLY BEFORE 8:00 A.M. on June 21, 2006, two federal officers died during a gunfight at the Federal Correctional Institution (FCI) in Tallahassee, Florida. One of the fallen officers was 17-year veteran William "Buddy" Sentner, 44, a special agent from the U.S. Department of Justice's Office of the Inspector General.[1] Agent Sentner had just arrived at the FCI, a low-security federal women's facility, to serve an arrest warrant stemming from a federal indictment accusing several correctional officers with committing various crimes. The other fatally wounded officer, Ralph Hill, was one of the prison guards named in the arrest warrant.[2]

The indictment in the Tallahassee case alleged that five FCI officers had engaged in sexual relationships with various female inmates at the facility in exchange for contraband, including cosmetics, jewelry, chewing gum, cigars, and cigarettes over a four-year period.[3] The sixth officer was accused of telling inmates involved in the scandal not to participate with law enforcement officials who were investigating the allegations. After federal agents arrived on the scene, FCI officer

INSTITUTIONAL MANAGEMENT

Ralph Hill emerged from a secured area in the lobby and began firing a handgun in the direction of the agents, killing agent Sentner. Agents returned fire, killing Hill.[4]

The remaining FCI officers faced several charges. Three of the guards pleaded guilty to mail fraud and received sentences ranging from probation to one year in prison.[5] The two remaining cases went to trial, resulting in guilty verdicts involving witness tampering and accepting illegal gratuities.[6] These two officers were sentenced to one year in prison.[7]

Boundary violations occur when the social distance between prison officers and inmates breaks down, and inappropriate relationships develop. Behavior that blurs, minimizes, or disrupts the social distance between captors and captives can take many forms, including instances where prison officials abuse their power to obtain sexual favors.[8] Such behavior violates departmental policies because it jeopardizes prison order, constitutes an abuse of legal authority, and violates public trust. Such relationships can result in employees being fired from their jobs, sued by the inmates involved, and prosecuted for violating criminal statutes.

The prison differs from almost every other institution or organization in modern society. It has unique physical features, and it is the only place where a group of employees manage a group of captives. Prisoners must live according to the rules of their keepers and with restricted movements. When reading this chapter, keep in mind that prison managers

Chapter

13

1. Cannot select their clients
2. Have little or no control over the release of their clients
3. Must deal with clients who are there against their will
4. Must rely on clients to do most of the work in the daily operation of the institution—work they are forced to do and for which they are not paid
5. Must depend on the maintenance of satisfactory relationships between clients and staff

Given these unique characteristics, how should prisons be run? Further, wardens and other key personnel are asked to perform a difficult job, one that requires skilled and dedicated managers. What rules should guide them?

Remember that a wide range of institutions fall under the heading of "prison." Some are treatment centers serving a relatively small number of clients; others are sprawling agricultural complexes; still others are ranches or forest camps. Although new facilities have opened in recent years, many prisons remain as large, fortress-like institutions with comparable management structures and offender populations.

In this chapter, we look at how institutional resources are organized to achieve certain goals. At a minimum, prisoners must be clothed, fed, kept healthy, provided with recreation, protected from one another, and maintained in custody. In addition, administrators may face the tasks of offering vocational and educational programs and using inmate labor in agriculture or industry. To accomplish all this in a community of free individuals would be taxing. To do so when the population consists of some of the most antisocial people in the society is surely a Herculean undertaking, one that depends on organization.

■ Formal Organization

formal organization
A structure established for influencing behavior to achieve particular ends.

The University of Texas, the General Motors Corporation, and the California State Prison at Folsom are very different organizations, each created to achieve certain goals. Differing organizational structures let managers coordinate the various parts of the university, auto manufacturer, and prison in the interests of scholarship, production, and corrections.

A **formal organization** is deliberately established for particular ends. If accomplishing an objective requires collective effort, people set up an organization to help coordinate activities and to provide incentives for others to join. Thus, in a university, a business, and a correctional institution, the goals, rules, and roles that define the relations among the organization's members (the organization chart) have been formally established.

compliance
Obedience to an order or request.

Amitai Etzioni, an organization theorist, uses the concept of compliance as the basis for comparing types of organizations. **Compliance** is obedience to an order or directive given by another person. In compliance relationships, an order is backed up by one's ability to induce or influence another person to carry out one's directives.[9] People do what others ask, because those others have the means—remunerative, normative, or coercive—to get the subjects to comply. **Remunerative power** is based on material resources, such as wages, fringe benefits, or goods, which people exchange for compliance. **Normative power** rests on symbolic rewards that leaders manipulate through ritual, allocation of honors, and social esteem. **Coercive power** depends on applying or threatening physical force to inflict pain, restrict movement, or control other aspects of a person's life.

remunerative power
The ability to obtain compliance in exchange for material resources.

normative power
The ability to obtain compliance by manipulating symbolic rewards.

coercive power
The ability to obtain compliance by the application or threat of physical force.

Etzioni argues that all formal organizations employ all three types of power, but the degree to which they rely on any one of them varies with the desired goal. Thus, although the University of Texas probably relies mainly on normative power in its relationships with students and the public, it relies on remunerative power in relationships with faculty and staff. Although General Motors is organized primarily for manufacturing, it may appeal to "team spirit" or "safety employee of the month" campaigns to meet its goals. And although the warden at Folsom may rely on remunerative and normative powers to manage staff to make it the best correctional facility in the United States, in working with prisoners he relies primarily on coercive power. The presence in high-custody institutions of "highly alienated lower participants" (prisoners), Etzioni says, makes the application or threat of force necessary to ensure compliance.[10]

Coercive power undergirds all prison relationships, but correctional institutions vary in their use of physical force and in the degree to which the inmates are alienated. Correctional institutions can be placed on a continuum of custody or treatment goals. At one extreme is the highly authoritarian prison, where the movement of inmates is greatly restricted, staff–inmate relationships are formally structured, and the prime emphasis is on custody. In such an institution, treatment goals take a back seat. At the other extreme is the institution that emphasizes the therapeutic aspect of the physical and social environment. Here the staff collaborates with inmates to overcome the inmates' problems. Between these ideal types lie the great majority of correctional institutions.

However, this custody–treatment continuum may neglect other aspects of imprisonment. As noted in Chapter 10, Charles Logan points out that we expect a lot of prisons "to correct the incorrigible, rehabilitate the wretched, deter the determined, restrain the dangerous, and punish the wicked." He proposes that we analyze prisons according to the goals of the "confinement model." In this model, the purpose of imprisonment is to "punish offenders—fairly and justly—through lengths of confinement proportionate to the gravity of the offense."[11] Thus, the mission with respect to prisoners has five features:

1 *Keep them in:* The facility must be secure, such that inmates cannot escape and contraband cannot be smuggled in.

2 *Keep them safe:* Inmates and staff need to be kept safe, not only from each other but from various environmental hazards as well.

3 *Keep them in line:* Prisons run on rules, and the ability of prison administrators to enforce compliance is central to the quality of confinement.

4 *Keep them healthy:* Inmates are entitled to have care for their medical needs.

5 *Keep them busy:* Constructive activities, such as work, recreation, education, and treatment programs, are antidotes to idleness.[12]

Prison work entails accomplishing this mission in a fair and efficient manner, without causing undue suffering. The state may run correctional institutions with other goals as well, but these are the main objectives.

The Organizational Structure

For any organization to be effective, its leaders and staff must know the rules and procedures, the lines of authority, and the channels of communication. Organizations vary in their organizational hierarchy, in their allocation of discretion, in the effort expended on administrative problems, and in the nature of the top leadership.

AP images/J. D. Cavrich

Warden Brian Clark talks with inmate William Carroll in a cell-block area. "Management by walking around" is a style that some successful wardens have adopted to achieve the goals of their prisons. This means that they must take a hands-on and proactive role, paying close attention to details rather than waiting for problems to arise.

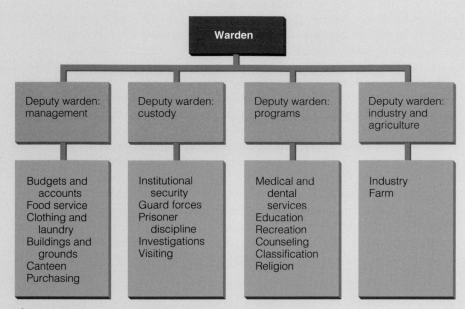

Figure 13.1

Formal Organization of a Prison for Adult Felons

The formal organization of an institution may say little about those political and informal relationships among staff members that really govern how the prison operates.

unity of command
A management principle holding that a subordinate should report to only one supervisor.

chain of command
A series of organizational positions in order of authority, with each person receiving orders from the one immediately above and issuing orders to the one(s) immediately below.

span of control
A management principle holding that a supervisor can effectively oversee only a limited number of subordinates.

line personnel
Employees who are directly concerned with furthering the institution's goals and who are in direct contact with clients.

staff personnel
Employees who provide services in support of line personnel; examples of staff personnel include training officers and accountants.

CONCEPTS OF ORGANIZATION ■ The formal administrative structure of a prison is a hierarchy of staff positions, each with its own duties and responsibilities, each linked to the others in a logical chain of command. As **Figure 13.1** shows, the warden is ultimately responsible for the operation of the institution. Deputy wardens oversee the functional divisions of the prison: management, custody, programs, and industry and agriculture. Under each deputy are middle managers and line staff who operate the departments. Functions are subdivided according to prison size and population.

Three principles are commonly used to organize the functioning of hierarchically structured organizations: unity of command, chain of command, and span of control. **Unity of command** is the idea that it is most efficient for a subordinate to report to only one superior. If a worker must respond to orders from two or more superiors, chaos ensues. Unity of command is tied to the second concept, **chain of command**. Because the person at the top of the organization cannot oversee everything, he or she must rely on lower-ranking staff to pass directives down. For example, the warden asks the deputy warden to have custody conduct a shakedown; the deputy warden passes the directive to the captain of the guard, who then has the lieutenant in charge of a particular shift carry out the search. The term **span of control** refers to the extent of supervision by one person. If, for example, a correctional institution offers many educational and treatment programs, the deputy warden for programs may not be able to oversee them all effectively. This deputy warden's span of control is stretched so far that a reorganization and further division of responsibilities may be required.

Two other concepts clarify the organization of correctional institutions: line and staff. **Line personnel** are directly concerned with furthering the institution's goals. They have direct contact with the prisoners; such personnel include the custody force, industry and agricultural supervisors, counselors, and medical technicians. **Staff personnel** support line personnel. They usually work under the deputy warden for management, handling accounting, training, purchasing, and so on.

The custodial employees make up a majority of an institution's personnel. They normally are organized along military lines, from deputy warden to captain to correctional officer. The professional staff (about 25 percent of the personnel), such as clinicians, teachers, and industry supervisors, are separate from the custodial staff and have little in common with them. All employees answer to the warden, but the treatment personnel and the civilian supervisors of the workshops have their own titles and salary scales. Their responsibilities do not extend to providing special services to the custodial employees. The top medical and educational personnel may formally report to the warden but in fact look to the central office of the department of corrections for leadership.

The multiple goals and separate employee lines of command often cause ambiguity and conflict in the administration of prisons. For example, the goals imposed on prisons are often contradictory or unclear. Conflicts between different groups of personnel (custodial versus treatment staff) and between staff and inmates present significant challenges to prison administrators.

THE WARDEN ■ The warden is the chief executive of the institution. The attitude that he or she brings to the job affects the organization. Not long ago the prison warden was an autocrat who ran the institution without direction from departments of corrections or the intrusion of courts, labor unions, or prisoner support groups.[13] Things are quite different today. Contemporary prison wardens need a broad set of skills to manage large groups of employees and to operate facilities in a way that keeps inmates, staff, and society safe. The primary duties and tasks of prison wardens are summarized in **Table 13.1**.

The prison warden is the institution's main contact with the outside world. Responsible for operating the prison, he or she normally reports to the deputy commissioner for institutions in the central office of the department of corrections. When the warden directs attention and energy outward (to the central office, parole board, or legislature), he or she delegates the daily operation of the prison to a deputy, usually the person in charge of custody. In recent years wardens in most states have lost much of their autonomy to managers in the central office who handle such matters as budgets, research and program development, public information, and legislative relations. The warden's job security, however, still rests on the ability to run the institution effectively and efficiently. At the first sign of trouble, the warden may be forced to look for a new job, and in some states the top management of corrections seems to be in constant flux. In short, today's prison warden must function effectively despite decreased autonomy and increased accountability.

Copyright © Joel Gordon 2008 - Model Released - All Rights Reserved

In some prisons, correctional officers work according to military-style rules. Here the oncoming shift of correctional officers is briefed on operational issues that may arise during their next eight hours.

MANAGEMENT ■ Bureaucracies tend to increase the personnel and resources used to maintain and manage the organization. This tendency can especially prevail in public bureaucracies, which strongly emphasize financial accountability and reporting to higher government agencies. Correctional institutions are no exception. Bureaucratic functions often fall to a deputy warden for management, who is responsible for

TABLE 13.1 *Primary Duties and Tasks of Prison Wardens*

Contemporary prison wardens place great emphasis on maintaining safety and security. They are also responsible for mundane but important duties such as managing the budget and presiding over the physical plant.

Duties		Tasks		
Administer safety and security operations	Approve security and safety policies and procedures	Ensure facility compliance	Assess safety and security systems	Manage intelligence operations
Manage human resources	Promote equal employment opportunities	Manage staff recruitment process	Authorize/ recommend hiring staff	Ensure staff development
Manage critical incidents	Review and approve emergency plans	Monitor emergency scenarios	Ensure readiness of emergency response team	Command intelligence team
Manage the budget	Compile budget requests	Establish budget priorities	Submit and justify budget requests	Monitor and control overtime
Foster a healthy institutional environment	Maintain frequent and direct contact with inmates	Provide meaningful inmate programs	Provide quality inmate-support services	Provide fair inmate-grievance system
Preside over the physical plant	Administer physical plant maintenance plan	Ensure facility safety, security, and sanitation inspections	Monitor allocation of space	Monitor and allocate resources

Source: Rick Ruddell and Tommy Norris, "The Changing Role of Wardens: A Focus on Safety and Security," *Corrections Today* 70 (October 2008): 39.

housekeeping tasks: buying supplies, keeping up the buildings and grounds, providing food, maintaining financial records, and the like. Some states, however, centralize many of these tasks in the office of the commissioner, to promote accountability and coordination among constituent institutions. For example, buying supplies from one warehouse that serves all state agencies has decreased the discretion of prison management to contract locally for provisions.

Most personnel assigned to manage services for correctional institutions have little contact with the prisoners; in some facilities they work in buildings separate from the main plant. Only personnel who provide services directly, such as the head of food services, have direct contact with the prisoners.

CUSTODIAL PERSONNEL ■ Later in this chapter we examine in detail the role of the correctional officer. Here, simply note that in most institutions the custodial force has graded ranks (captain, lieutenant, officer), with pay differentials and job titles following the chain of command, as in the military. Unlike the factory or the military,

CAREERS IN CORRECTIONS   Correctional Officer: State

NATURE OF THE WORK

There are 300,000 state correctional officers who work in the great array of reformatories, prisons, prison camps, and penitentiaries that comprise American corrections. Regardless of the setting, they maintain order within the institution and enforce rules and regulations. To keep the facility secure, officers must often search inmates and their living quarters for contraband, settle disputes, enforce discipline, and communicate prisoner requests to higher levels. Officers may be assigned to housing units, perimeter patrols, or inmate work assignments. Correctional officers usually work an eight-hour day, five days a week, on rotating shifts.

REQUIRED QUALIFICATIONS

Correctional officers must be at least 18 to 21 years of age, be a U.S. citizen with no felony convictions, and have at least a high school education and some work experience. Most states require qualifying examinations, including personality screenings. Candidates must be in good health and meet fitness, eyesight, and hearing standards. The American Correctional Association sets training guidelines for recruits. Most states have training academies with instruction on legal restrictions, custody procedures, interpersonal relationships, use of firearms, and self-defense. After graduation from the academy, trainees typically receive several weeks or months of training in the job setting under the supervision of an experienced officer.

EARNINGS AND JOB OUTLOOK

As states have had to deal with the explosion of the prison population, the number of correctional officers has markedly increased during the past three decades. Although such expansion has slowed in recent years, in part because of budgetary constraints, turnover in the officer corps should provide future openings. With regional variation, the median annual earnings for state correctional officers is $34,000, with entry-level salaries of about $22,000.

MORE INFORMATION

See the **American Correctional Association** website, through the link found at www.cengage.com/criminaljustice/clear.

which have separate groups of supervisors and workers or officers and enlisted personnel, the prison requires its lowest-status employee, the correctional officer, to be both a supervisor (of inmates) and a worker (for the warden). This causes role conflict and makes officers vulnerable to corruption by the inmates. Officers know the warden is judging their performance by the way they manage the prisoners, and they can seldom manage without at least some cooperation from the prisoners. Officers ease up on some rules so prisoners will more willingly comply with other rules and requests. "Careers in Corrections" offers a view of work as a state correctional officer.

PROGRAM PERSONNEL ■ The contemporary correctional institution is concerned not only with punishing but also with encouraging prisoners' participation in educational, vocational, and treatment programs. Such programs have been a part of corrections since the late 1800s, but the enthusiasm for rehabilitation that swept corrections after World War II created a wider variety of programs, as discussed in Chapter 14. Here we need only mention that rehabilitative and educational personnel find it difficult to achieve their goals in institutions whose primary mission is custody.

Copyright © Joel Gordon - Model Released - All rights reserved

Line personnel have direct contact with prisoners and make up over 60 percent of an institution's personnel. The visitor's room is one place where officers must enforce rules that apply to both inmates and civilians.

INDUSTRY AND AGRICULTURE PERSONNEL ■ Since the invention of the penitentiary, inmate labor has been used for industry and agriculture. As we show in Chapter 14, the importance of these functions has varied over time and among regions. In some southern prisons, most of the inmates' time is spent tending crops. In the Northeast, prison farms have disappeared because they are uneconomical and ill matched to the urban backgrounds of most inmates.

Like other programs, industrial and agricultural production is usually administered outside of the strict custodial hierarchy. But unlike educational or treatment programs, work in a factory or farm requires supervisors. Administrators must often mediate disputes over the need for officers in guard towers or housing units, for example, and the need for officers in fields or factories.

The Impact of the Structure

The organizational structure of correctional institutions has changed over time. The traditional custodial prison was run as an autocracy, with the warden dominating the guard force and often disciplining employees as strictly as inmates. When rehabilitation became a goal, and treatment and educational programs were incorporated, a separate structure for programs, often headed by a deputy warden, was added. Its employees were professionals in the social and behavioral sciences, who frequently clashed with autocratic wardens who emphasized custody.

As some institutions began to focus on rehabilitation, correctional planners and scholars frequently contrasted the traditional prison organization with a collaborative model. For example, a 1967 U.S. presidential commission report referred optimistically to the future correctional institution in which a dedicated and professionally trained staff would work with other administrators and with prisoners to identify inmates' problems and to strive for rehabilitation.[14] Such an institution would require structural changes to deemphasize the traditionally rigid control function, enlarge the decision-making role of treatment personnel, and allow input from the prisoners about the operation of the facility. However, by the 1980s it was hard to find either prisons being run this way or correctional leaders advocating that they be so run. Some observers say that no more than a few institutions really followed the collaborative organizational style.

Correctional institutions are more humanely administered today than they were in the past. This change is in part a response to the presence of rehabilitative personnel and programs, the increased training and professionalism of correctional personnel, the intrusion of the courts, and the growth of citizen observer groups that monitor operations. Society will no longer tolerate the harsh conditions once prevalent in prisons. For example, the deplorable situation at the Cummins Farm Unit at Arkansas State Prison (described in Chapter 5) probably could not now exist for long, because the media would expose it.

A formal organizational chart does not convey the whole story of a prison's organization; no chart can show how the people who occupy the positions actually perform. As theorists explain, an informal organization, with its own rules and procedures, chain of command, and channels of communication, exists alongside the formal structure. Every organization has individuals who ignore directives, bypass the chain of command in communicating to the top, and negotiate with others who perform parallel or associated functions.

How, then, do prisons function? How do prisoners and staff try to meet their own goals? Although the U.S. prison may not conform to the ideal goals of corrections, and the formal organization may little resemble the ongoing reality of the informal relations, order is kept and a routine is followed.

■ GOVERNING PRISONS

Traditionally, prison sociologists have looked at prisons as social systems rather than institutions to be governed. Until fairly recently, our understanding of life inside prison was based on **inmate balance theory**. This perspective was developed in the pioneering works of Donald Clemmer and Gresham Sykes. This theory provides insights on the maintenance of order and prevention of collective violence.[15] According to this view, for the prison system to operate effectively, officials must tolerate minor infractions, relax security measures, and allow inmate leaders to keep order. When officials go too far in asserting their authority by cracking down on inmate privileges, the delicate balance of shared authority is upset, which in turn unleashes collective disorder.[16]

inmate balance theory
A governance theory that posits that, for a prison system to operate effectively, officials must tolerate minor infractions, relax security measures, and allow inmate leaders to keep order.

Criminologists have written about the effects of prison conditions on inmates, racial and ethnic cleavages, inmate argot and roles, and the informal distribution of authority in prisons. However, as John DiIulio notes, sociological research on prison society does little to help correctional officials manage inmates and staff. In fact, most criminological research about prisons implies that administrators can do little to govern, because—despite formal rules and regulations—institutions are run mainly through the informal social networks of the keepers and the kept (see **Table 13.2** for one set of formal rules of conduct). DiIulio finds shocking the extent to which correctional officials seem to have accepted sociological explanations for institutional conditions, rather than correcting faulty management practices.[17]

DiIulio and others have developed an alternative explanation of prison disorder, which has been dubbed **administrative control theory**.[18] This perspective posits that disorder results from "unstable, divided, or otherwise weak management."[19] Thus, when officials lose control over their institutions, collective disorder and other unruly inmate behaviors become more likely. This administrative breakdown has several effects:

administrative control theory
A governance theory that posits that prison disorder results from unstable, divided, or otherwise weak management.

1. Inmates come to believe their conditions of confinement are not only bad, but unjust.
2. Officials become indifferent to routine security measures and the day-to-day tasks of prison management.
3. Weak management permits gangs and other illicit groups to flourish. These groups, in turn, may help mobilize disturbances.[20]

What distinguishes a well-run prison from a substandard prison? DiIulio argues that the crucial variable is not the ethnic or racial distribution of the population, the criminal records of the inmates, the size of the institution, the degree of crowding, or the level of funding. What is important is *governance*: the sound and firm management of inmates and staff.

TABLE 13.2 *Rules of General Conduct, Michigan Department of Corrections*

1. All residents are expected to obey directions and instructions of members of the staff. If a resident feels he/she has been dealt with unfairly, or that he/she has received improper instructions, he/she should first comply with the order and then follow the established grievance procedures outlined later in this booklet.

2. Any behavior considered a felony or a misdemeanor in this state also is a violation of institutional rules. Such acts may result in disciplinary action and/or loss of earned good time in addition to possible criminal prosecution.

3. Any escape, attempt to escape, walk away, or failure to return from a furlough may result in loss of good time and/or a new sentence through prosecution under the escape statute. At one time or another, most persons in medium or minimum custody have felt restless and uneasy. When this happens, we urge you to see your counselor or the official in charge for guidance and advice. Occasionally, the department has asked that those who have walked away impulsively not be prosecuted when they have turned themselves in immediately after the act, realizing their mistake.

4. Any resident may, if they feel they have no further recourse in the institution, appeal to the Director of Corrections, Deputy Director, the Attorney General, state and federal courts, Michigan Civil Rights Commission or the Governor in the form of sealed and uncensored mail.

5. Reasonable courtesy, orderly conduct, and good personal hygiene are expected of all residents. Standards for haircuts, beards, and general appearance are listed later in this rule book.

6. Residents cannot hold any group meetings in the yard. Meetings for all legitimate purposes require staff approval; facilities, if available, will be scheduled for this purpose and necessary supervision provided.

7. While residents are permitted to play cards and other games, gambling is not allowed. In card-playing areas there shall be no more than four persons at a table. Visible tokens or other items of value will be sufficient evidence of gambling. Games are prohibited during working hours on institutional assignments.

8. All typewriters, calculators, radios, TVs, electric razors, and other appliances, including musical instruments, must be registered with the institutional officials by make, model, and serial number.

9. Items under Paragraph 8 cannot be traded, sold, or given away without written approval of the Deputy Warden or Superintendent.

10. Residents cannot operate concessions, sell services, rent goods, or act as loan sharks or pawnbrokers.

11. All items of contraband are subject to confiscation.

12. When a resident desires to go from one place to another for a specific and legitimate reason, he/she should obtain a pass from the official to whom [he/she is] responsible, such as the housing unit supervisor, work foreman, teacher, etc.

13. No resident is allowed to go into another resident's cell or room unless specifically authorized.

Source: Michigan Department of Corrections, *Resident Guide Book* (Lansing: Michigan Department of Corrections, n.d.).

What quality of life should be maintained in a prison? DiIulio states that a good prison "provides as much order, amenity, and service as possible given the human and financial resources."[21] *Order* is defined as the absence of individual or group misconduct threatening the safety of others—for example, assaults, rapes, and other forms of violence or insult. A basic assumption should be that, because the state sends offenders to prison, it is responsible for ensuring their safety there. *Amenity* is anything that enhances the inmates' creature comforts, such as good food, clean bedding, and recreational opportunities. This does not mean that prisons are to function as luxury hotels, but contemporary standards stipulate that correctional facilities should not be deleterious to inmates' mental and physical health. Finally, *service* includes programs designed to improve the life prospects of inmates: vocational training, remedial education, and work opportunities. Here, too, we expect inmates to be engaged in activities during incarceration that will make them better people and enhance their ability to lead crime-free lives upon release.

If we accept the premise that well-run prisons are important for inmates, staff, and society, what are some of the problems that correctional administrators must address? The correctional literature points to four factors that make governing prisons different from administering other public institutions: (1) the defects of total power, (2) the limited rewards and punishments, (3) the co-optation of correctional officers, and (4) the strength of inmate leadership. After we review each of these factors, we will consider the administrative systems and leadership styles that can help make prisons safe and humane and serve inmates' needs.

The Defects of Total Power

In his classic study of the New Jersey State Prison, Sykes emphasized that, although in formal terms correctional officials have power to induce compliance from the prisoners, in fact that power is limited and in many ways depends on inmate cooperation.[22] It is from this perspective that the inmate balance theory of management evolved.

Much of the public believes that prisons are run in an authoritarian manner; correctional officers give orders and inmates follow them. Strictly enforced rules specify what the captives may and may not do. Staff members have the right to grant rewards and to inflict punishment. In theory any inmate who does not follow the rules can be placed in solitary confinement. Because the officers have a monopoly on the legal means of enforcing rules

Governing a society of captives is more complicated than the simplistic belief that officers give orders and inmates follow them. In the Maryland Correctional Institute at Hagerstown, officer D. L. Stephens escorts inmates back to their housing area following recreation. Stephens is often outnumbered 75 to 1 as he attempts to keep order. What tactics might he use to gain the cooperation of inmates?

MYTHS IN CORRECTIONS

PRISON DISORDER AND MASS INCARCERATION

THE MYTH: The massive increase in the number of prisoners has resulted in American prisons becoming more disorderly.

THE REALITY: A study of prison disorder found that riots, correctional staff murders, inmate homicides, and escapes are rarer today after adjusting for the size of the inmate population than in the 1970s and 1980s.

Source: Burt Useem and Anne M. Piehl, "Prison Buildup and Disorder," *Punishment and Society* 8 (2006): 87–115.

and can be backed up by the state police and the National Guard if necessary, many people believe that no question should arise as to how the prison is run.

Certainly, we can imagine a prison society made up of hostile and uncooperative inmates ruled by force. Prisoners can be legally isolated from one another, physically coerced until they cooperate, and put under continuous surveillance. Although all these things are possible, the public would probably not tolerate such practices for long, because people expect correctional institutions to be run humanely.

Also, prisoners, unlike members of other authoritarian organizations such as the military, do not recognize the legitimacy of their keepers and therefore are not always moved to cooperate. No sense of duty propels prisoners to compliance. This is an important distinction, because duty is the backbone of most social organizations. With it, rules are followed—and need not be explained first.[23]

The notion that correctional officers have total power over inmates has many other flaws. As Sykes points out, "The ability of the officials to physically coerce their captives into the paths of compliance is something of an illusion as far as the day-to-day activities of the prison are concerned and may be of doubtful value in moments of crisis."[24] Forcing people to follow commands is an inefficient way of making them carry out complex tasks; efficiency is further diminished by the ratio of inmates to custody staff (10.3 to 1 in federal prisons and 4.9 to 1 in state facilities) and by the potential danger.[25] (See "Myths in Corrections.")

Of course, physical coercion is used to control prisoners. Such tactics may violate criminal statutes and administrative procedures, but they have long occurred in prisons throughout the United States—and cannot be considered idiosyncratic or sporadic. A study of a Texas prison, for example, found that a small but significant percentage of the officers used physical punishment. Force both controlled the prison population and induced cohesion among officers, maintaining a status differential between officers and inmates and helping officers win promotions.[26]

Rewards and Punishments

Correctional officers often rely on rewards and punishments to gain cooperation. To maintain security and order among a large population in a confined space, they impose extensive rules of conduct. Instead of using force to ensure obedience, however, they reward compliance and punish rule violations by granting and denying privileges.

Several policies may be followed to promote control. One is to offer cooperative prisoners rewards such as choice job assignments, residence in the honor unit, and favorable parole reports. Inmates who follow the rules receive good time. Informers may also be rewarded, and administrators may ignore conflict among inmates on the assumption that it keeps prisoners from uniting against authorities.

The system of rewards and punishments has some deficiencies. One is that the punishments for rule breaking do not represent a great departure from the prisoners' usual circumstances. Because inmates are already deprived of many freedoms and valued goods—heterosexual relations, money, choice of clothing, and so on—not being allowed to attend, say, a recreational period does not carry much weight. In addition, according to the inmate code in a particular prison, the defiant convict may gain standing among the other prisoners. Finally, authorized privileges are given to the inmate at the start of the sentence and are taken away only if rules are broken, but few further rewards are authorized for progress or exceptional behavior. However, as an inmate approaches release, opportunities for furloughs, work release, or transfer to a halfway house can serve as incentives to obey rules.

Gaining Cooperation: Exchange Relationships

One way that correctional officers obtain inmate cooperation is by tolerating minor rule infractions in exchange for compliance with major aspects of the custodial regime. The correctional officer plays the key role in the interpersonal relationships among the prisoners and serves as the link to the custodial bureaucracy. The correctional officer

> *must supervise and control the inmate population in concrete and detailed terms . . . [and] must see to the translation of the custodial regime from blueprint to reality and engage in the specific battles for conformity. Counting prisoners, periodically reporting to the center of communications, signing passes, checking groups of inmates as they come and go, searching for contraband or signs of attempts to escape—these make up the minutiae of [the officer's] eight hour shift.*[27]

Officers and prisoners are in close association both day and night—in the cell block, workshop, dining hall, recreation area, and so on. Although the formal rules require a social distance between the officers and inmates, their close physical proximity makes them aware that each depends on the other. To look good to their superiors, the officers need the cooperation of the prisoners, and the inmates count on the officers to relax the rules or occasionally look the other way. For example, officers in a midwestern prison told the researcher Stan Stojkovic that flexibility in rule enforcement was especially important as it related to the ability of prisoners to cope with their environment. As one officer explained, "Phone calls are really important for guys in this place. . . . You cut off their calls and they get pissed. So what I do is give them a little extra and they are good to me."[28]

Even though officers are backed by the state and have the formal authority to punish any prisoner who does not follow orders, they often discover that the best course of action is to make "deals" with the inmates. As a result, officers buy compliance or obedience in some areas by tolerating rule breaking elsewhere.

Officers are expected to maintain "surface order." They must ensure that the inmates conform voluntarily to the most important rules, things run smoothly, and no visible trouble and no cause for alarm emerge. Because officers' job performance is judged on the ability to maintain surface order, both officers and prisoners have a tacit understanding and bargain accordingly. Stojkovic summarizes the assumptions underlying the accommodative relationships between officers and inmates as follows:

1. Negotiations are central to prisoner control, because correctional officers cannot have total control over the inmates.

2. Once an officer defines a set of informal rules with prisoners, the rules must be respected by all parties.

3. Some rule violations are "normal" and consequently do not merit officers' attention or sanctioning.[29]

Correctional officers must be careful not to pay too high a price for the cooperation of their charges. Under pressure to work effectively with prisoners, officers may be blackmailed into doing illegitimate favors in return for cooperation. When leadership is thus abdicated, authority passes to the inmates.

Inmate Leadership

In the traditional prison of the big-house era, administrators enlisted the inmate leaders to help maintain order. As Richard Korn and Lloyd McCorkle wrote in 1954,

> *Far from systematically attempting to undermine the inmate hierarchy, the institution generally gives it covert support and recognition by assigning better jobs and quarters to its high-status members provided they are "good inmates." In this and other ways the institution buys peace with the system by avoiding battle with it.*[30]

Descriptions of the contemporary maximum-security prison, however, raise questions about administrators' ability to run institutions in this way. When the racial, offense, and political characteristics of inmate populations of many prisons began to change in the mid-1960s, the centralized convict leadership structure was replaced by multiple centers of power. As official authority broke down, some institutions became violent, dangerous places.

Prisons seem to function more effectively now than they have in the recent past. Although prisons are more crowded, riots and reports of violence and escapes have declined.[31] In many prisons the inmate social system may have reorganized, so that correctional officers again can work through prisoners respected by fellow inmates. Yet some observers contend that when wardens maintain order in this way, they enhance the positions of some prisoners at the expense of others. The leaders profit by receiving illicit privileges and favors, and they increase their influence among inmates by distributing benefits.

Disciplining Prisoners

Maintaining order can be burdensome to prison administrators, given the factors just discussed. In an earlier era, prisoners were kept in line with corporal punishment. Today, withholding privileges, erasing good-time credits, and placing inmates in "the hole" (the adjustment center, or administrative segregation) constitute the range of punishments available to discipline the unruly. The Supreme Court has curbed administrators' discretion in applying these punishments: Procedural fairness must accompany the process by which inmates are sent to solitary confinement and in the method by which good-time credit can be lost because of misconduct.

On entering the prison, the newcomer receives a manual, often running up to a hundred pages, specifying the rules that govern almost all aspects of prison life, from permitted clothing to dining-room conduct and standards of personal hygiene. Prominently listed are types of behavior that can result in disciplinary action: rioting, gambling, sexual activity, possession of currency, failure to obey an order, and so on. Prisoners are warned that some rule infractions also violate the state's criminal law and may be handled by the criminal justice system. An institutional committee, however, handles most inmate rule violations. This disciplinary committee may commit an inmate to punitive segregation for the number of days specified for each class of offense or hand down other sanctions. The manuals vary from state to state; some merely list violations and

Keeping cell phones out of the hands of inmates has become a major correctional problem. At the Brockbridge Correctional Facility in Jessup, Maryland, all officers are searched before going on duty. What does this practice say about administrators' confidence in their officers?

Kevin Clark/The Washington Post

allow disciplinary committees to exercise their discretion when determining the appropriate punishment.

THE DISCIPLINARY PROCESS ■ Custodial officers act like police officers with regard to most prison rules. Minor violations may warrant merely a verbal reprimand or warning, but more-serious violations can earn the prisoner a "ticket": a report forwarded to higher authority for action. Some corrections systems distinguish between major and minor violations. Major tickets go to the disciplinary committee; minor ones receive summary judgment by a hearing officer, whose decision may be appealed to a supervising captain, whose decision may, in turn, be appealed to the committee. In some systems, all disciplinary reports go to a hearing officer, who investigates the charges, conducts the hearing, and determines the punishment. The commissioner of corrections can review hearing officers' decisions and reduce punishments but not increase them.

Such procedures are relatively new. Less than 40 years ago, formal codes of institutional conduct either did not exist or were ignored; the warden had full discretion in punishment, and inmates had no opportunity to challenge the charges. In a series of decisions beginning in 1970, the U.S. Supreme Court granted inmates certain limited procedural rights: to receive notice of a complaint, to have a fair hearing, to confront witnesses, to have help in preparing for the hearing, and to be given a written statement of the decision (see Chapter 5).[32] However, the Court has also emphasized the need to balance prisoner rights with state interests. Thus, two years after it guaranteed prisoners fundamental due process rights, the Court ruled that counsel was not included.[33]

As a result most prisons developed rules that specify some elements of due process in disciplinary proceedings. In many institutions a disciplinary committee receives charges, conducts hearings, and determines guilt and punishment. Normally, disciplinary committees comprise three to five members of the correctional staff, including representatives of custody, treatment, and classification, with a senior officer acting as chairperson. Sometimes the committees also include inmates or outside citizens.

As part of the procedure, the inmate is read the charge and is allowed to present his or her version of the incident and to present witnesses. In some institutions, an inmate advocate may help the prisoner. If the inmate is found guilty, a sanction is imposed. The inmate can usually appeal the decision to the warden and ultimately to the commissioner. Even with these protections, prisoners may still feel powerless and fear further punishment if they challenge the disciplinary decisions of the warden too aggressively.

SANCTIONS ■ Administrative segregation and loss of privileges and good time are the sanctions most often imposed for violating institutional rules. The privileges lost may include visits, mail, access to the commissary, and recreational periods.

The most severe sanction by a disciplinary committee is confinement in administrative segregation. Most institutions limit the amount of time that an inmate can spend in segregation and regulate conditions with respect to food, medical attention, and personal safety. Twenty days of continuous administrative segregation is the maximum in many prisons, but inmates can be returned to "the hole" after a token period outside.

Maintaining order among offenders who live in close proximity under conditions of deprivation is a challenge. Officers recognize they must walk a narrow line between being too restrictive and overly permissive. They must recognize, too, that their objective is to encourage cooperation and conformity to the rules. But they must also understand that rewards and punishments are limited and that courts now insist that due process be observed in disciplining and proceeding against violators. This presents a tall order, but with good management practices the objective can be reached. One index of a poorly run institution is a large number of disciplinary violations, showing that staff and prisoners cannot prevent disruptive behavior or function with mutual tolerance, let alone respect.

Leadership: The Crucial Element of Governance

As Edwin Sutherland and Donald Cressey have observed, any prison is made up of the synchronized actions of hundreds of people, some of whom hate and distrust each other, love each other, fight each other physically and psychologically, think of each other as stupid or mentally disturbed, "manage" and "control" each other, and vie with each other for favors, prestige, power, and money.[34] Still, most prisons do not fall into disarray, although at times certain institutions have approached chaos. Examples include Soledad in California, during a period of racial and political unrest in the 1960s; Walla Walla in Washington in the 1970s, when an experiment with inmate self-government was attempted; and the Eastham Unit and some other Texas prisons prior to court-ordered reforms in the 1980s. But these are exceptions, and many correctional facilities are well governed. How, then, does management effect a reasonable quality of life in U.S. prisons?

FOCUS ON CORRECTIONAL POLICY

A Model Prison

Set in the woods outside of Bradford, Pennsylvania, is the Federal Correctional Institution, McKean. Opened in 1989 as a medium-security facility, it houses more than 1,000 male inmates. Until he retired in July 1995, McKean's warden was Dennis Luther, an administrator who, during his 16 years in prison work, gained a reputation for unorthodox policies.

At a time when politicians were railing against "country club" prisons and the need to "make 'em bust rocks," Luther ran an institution that earned a 99.3 accreditation rating from the American Correctional Association, the highest in the Bureau of Prisons. Badly overcrowded and with an increasing number of violent offenders, McKean cost taxpayers $15,370 a year for each inmate, well below the federal average of $21,350. Amazingly, in six years there were no escapes, no murders, no suicides, and only three serious assaults against staff and six recorded against inmates.

How did he do it? According to Luther, each prison has its own culture, which is often violent and abusive, based on gangs. The staff in such institutions feel they are unable to change it. At McKean, Luther set out to build a different type of culture, based on unconditional respect for the inmates as people. As he says, "If you want people to behave responsibly, and treat you with respect, then you treat other people that way." This credo has been translated into 28 beliefs, the product of Luther's years of experience. These "Beliefs about the Treatment of Inmates" are posted all over the institution to remind both staff and inmates alike of their responsibilities. They include the following:

1. Inmates are sent to prison *as* punishment and not *for* punishment.

2. Correctional workers have a *responsibility* to ensure that inmates are returned to the community no more angry or hostile than when they were committed.

3. Inmates are *entitled* to a safe and humane environment while in prison.

4. You must believe in man's *capacity* to change his behavior. . . .

10. Be *responsive* to inmate requests for action or information. Respond in a timely manner and respond the first time an inmate makes a request. . . .

12. It is important for staff to *model* the kind of behavior they expect to see duplicated by inmates. . . .

14. There is an *inherent value* in self-improvement programs such as education, whether or not these programs are related to recidivism. . . .

18. Staff *cannot*, because of their own insecurities, lack of self-esteem, or concerns about their masculinity, condescend or degrade inmates. . . .

26. Inmate discipline must be *consistent* and *fair*.

Merely posting the "Beliefs" in prominent places will not create a superior prison culture. The credo must be put into practice. Here are some examples:

1. *Frontline staff:* If you want to get frontline staffers to treat inmates with respect, top managers must treat staffers with respect. Luther has said, "Line-level people have good ideas, not only about how to do their job, but about how to do your job better." With this in mind, he created the Line Staff Advisory Board, a rotating group of frontline

Management styles vary, even in bureaucracies. In his study of prison management in California, Michigan, and Texas correctional facilities, John DiIulio argues that prisons should be run in a paramilitary fashion with strict adherence to official rules, regulations, and policies.[35] Others note the value of alternative approaches. For example, Hans Toch argues that prison administrators should involve staff in problem-solving activities.[36] In his study of higher-custody state prisons, Michael Reisig found that flexible and adaptive managerial approaches are most effective at maintaining low levels of prison disorder.[37] Despite the controversy regarding which management style works best, the consensus among practitioners and researchers is that the quality of prison life is mainly a function of management. The Focus box "A Model Prison" describes the unique management practices of Warden Dennis Luther.

workers who meet with him to talk through complaints, suggestions, and rumors.

2. *"Management by walking around":* Through contact with staff and inmates in the dining hall, on the yard, and in the cell blocks, a warden becomes a visible presence who can hear suggestions and complaints. Often he or she can nip problems before they fester and explode. This presence sets an example of the extent to which the warden is concerned about the problems of inmates and staff.

3. *Inmate involvement:* Regular "town hall" meetings with inmates provide opportunities for two-way communication. Proposed changes in regulations or procedures are first brought to the inmates for comment (for example, items to be offered in the commissary).

4. *Inmate Benefit Fund:* The Inmate Benefit Fund (IBF) was created to generate money inmates could use to purchase items for which taxpayer dollars were not available. Using their own funds, inmates could order from Bradford stores and restaurants items that would ease their stay in McKean. Orders were placed with the IBF and delivered to the institution for a modest handling charge. With 2,000 inmates, substantial sums were generated by these surcharges. The inmates could use these funds to purchase additional educational and recreational programs for the population. Besides helping inmates gain access to these programs, the IBF spending contributed to the local economy.

5. *Education:* McKean has a higher percentage of inmates enrolled in classes than does almost any other federal prison. Luther believes prison time should be spent preparing

offenders for their return to the community. Courses are taught by staff members of the prison's education department, professors from neighboring colleges, and inmates. The inmates teach adult continuing education courses and act as mentors and tutors.

Luther expects inmates to be responsible, and he holds them to a higher standard than found in most prisons. For example, after a few minor incidents, the warden ordered "closed movement" during evening hours. This restricted inmate activity and was meant to be permanent. A group of inmates asked if he would restore "open movement" if the prison was incident-free for 90 days. Luther agreed, and the prison has remained "open."

Inmates who meet the standards are rewarded. Weekly inspections are held in each cell block, and inmates who score high receive additional privileges. Those whose disciplinary record is clean and excel in the programs can earn their way to the "honor unit." And those who show consistently good behavior are allowed to attend supervised picnics on Family Day.

Dennis Luther is convinced his methods will work in any prison, even those plagued by violence, overcrowding, and gangs. Many staff members feel the same way. They believe McKean is a shining example of the difference good management can make.

Sources: Adapted from Tom Peters, *Liberation Management* (New York: Knopf, 1992), 247–55; Robert Worth, "A Model Prison," *Atlantic Monthly*, November 1995, pp. 38–44. Dennis Luther has retired from the Federal Bureau of Prisons.

Prison systems perform well if leaders can cope with the political and other pressures that contribute to administrative uncertainty and instability. In particular, management is successful when prison directors

1 Are in office long enough to learn the job, make plans, and implement them.

2 Project an appealing image to a wide range of people, both inside and outside of the organization.

3 Are dedicated and loyal to the department, seeing themselves as engaged in a noble and challenging profession.

4 Are highly hands-on and proactive, paying close attention to details and not waiting for problems to arise. They must know what is going on inside, yet also recognize the need for outside support. In short, they are strangers neither in the cell blocks nor in the aisles of the state legislature.[38]

From this perspective, making prisons work is a function of administrative leadership and the application of sound management principles. DiIulio's research challenges the traditional assumption of many correctional administrators that "the cons run the joint." Rather, as the success of such legendary administrators as George Beto of Texas, William Fauver of New Jersey, Anna Kross of New York's Rikers Island, and William Leeke of North Carolina demonstrate, prisons can be managed so that inmates can serve their time in a safe, healthy, and productive environment.[39]

CORRECTIONAL OFFICERS: THE LINCHPIN OF MANAGEMENT

Over the past 25 years, the correctional officer's role has changed greatly. No longer responsible merely for "guarding," the correctional officer is now considered a crucial professional who has the closest contact with the prisoners and performs a variety of tasks. Officers are expected to counsel, supervise, protect, and process the inmates under their care (see the Focus box "A Day on the Job—in Prison"). In many jurisdictions, hours are long, pay is low, entry requirements are minimal, and turnover is high. Given these conditions, why would someone want to enter this field?

Who Becomes a Correctional Officer?

The early criminal justice literature either ignored the prison officer or painted a picture of an individual with a "lock psychosis" resulting from the routine of numbering, counting, checking, and locking. Some prison studies gave the impression that officers were incompetent and psychologically inferior, performing the only job they could get. They were viewed as the primary opponents of rehabilitation, at loggerheads with both inmates and administrators. Some observers have referred to guards in general as "frightened, hostile people,"[40] and the report of the commission that investigated the 1971 Attica riots labeled the guards there as racists. Who are the correctional officers? Have they been accurately depicted? What kind of person accepts a job that offers low pay and little hope of advancement?

Studies have shown that a primary incentive for becoming a correctional officer is the security of a civil service job. In addition, because most correctional facilities are located in rural areas, prison work often is better than other available jobs, and overtime or part-time work often can supplement the salary. Until the push of the last 30 years for greater professionalism among correctional workers, many guards joined the ranks because they had few employment opportunities.

Today, because of the demand for well-qualified correctional officers, most states have given priority to recruiting quality personnel. Salaries differ from state to state.

Read an interview with an experienced correctional officer; see the web link at www.cengage.com/criminaljustice/clear.

FOCUS ON

PEOPLE IN CORRECTIONS

A Day on the Job—in Prison

Phil Carvalho holds the rank of senior correctional officer. He has covered virtually every custody assignment in the eight years he has been in a prison that has been jarred by inmate riots and strikes by its personnel. Since last January, his post has been Ten Block, the segregation unit where Massachusetts houses up to sixty of its toughest and most incorrigible inmates. . . .

Ten Block is a steel, barred island within the walled continent of the prison . . . insulated and isolated for those who live there and those who work there. It is an island cut off from the institutional mainland by more than the click, bang of steel. Because it confines or segregates those who have assaulted guards and inmates, it is often territory that is ostracized by other guards and inmates.

When Carvalho arrives, nine young officers already are beginning to fill cardboard trays with muffins, cereal, and paper cups of coffee from the kitchen wagon. Like Carvalho, all are volunteers for Ten Block.

"Yeah, you gotta be crazy to work here," one of them says, "but it's got good days off." Most of the officers have been spit at by some of their charges. Some have been hit by urine and excrement.

Before Carvalho has a chance to move through the door of the cubicle that serves as an office, one of the three phones inside rings.

"Ten. Carvalho."

The phone is sandwiched between the cheek and the shoulder of the 220-pound, six-foot two-inch Carvalho. For the next eight hours, it will ring incessantly, with rare moments of silence. For Carvalho, the telephone is something more than an electronic instrument.

He growls at it, purrs into it, persuades, cajoles, allowing the cadence of his voice to vary with the purpose of his message. "Yeah, right. Hey, sweetheart, do me a favor." . . .

An officer comes into the cubicle with a handful of small brown envelopes. Carvalho counts them, records the total and the time in the dog-eared logbook in front of him.

"Medication," he says. "O.K., give 'em out."

Ten Block distributes medication more frequently than meals. Four times a day, inmates may receive prescriptions that include sedatives, tranquilizers, and sleeping pills. During the morning distribution, fourteen of twenty-eight inmates on the first floor receive pills. Five milligrams of Valium four times a day plus a sleeping pill at night is not unusual.

"I can't understand it," says Carvalho. "These guys when they're on the street can't be gettin' that medication. Impossible. Some of 'em need it for their nerves. Being in this situation they need something to calm them down. But the pain pills they put out, the depressants . . . it's unbelievable." . . .

"Yeah, Charlie?"

"Listen, Phil, you gotta get that son-of-a-bitch out of here." . . . The voice in the dimly lighted cell details a complaint against an officer on the three-to-eleven shift.

Other inmates shout their own litany of complaints. Hands holding mirrors protrude from the other fourteen cells in the section, giving their owners a glass reflected picture of the officer and the visitor.

"The only thing I can tell you," Carvalho responds, "is that I've got to get McLaughlin down here."

Thomas McLaughlin is deputy superintendent at Walpole. He is one of the key reasons why Phil Carvalho volunteered for Ten Block. "He backs you up. And he's there when you need him. All these guys," Carvalho says, pointing to the young officers, "they're there when you need 'em." . . .

When McLaughlin arrives, Carvalho takes him through the corridor where the inmates are complaining about the officer. They move from cell to cell like army medics making rounds in a crowded hospital. The deputy superintendent is a listener. Occasionally, he asks a question, sometimes he nods, but his face shows neither a flicker of sympathetic agreement nor cynical disbelief. Later, he tells Carvalho there will be a meeting with the night officer at the end of the shift.

"Hey, Phil . . . Phil . . ." Another voice from the cell in the corridor. Carvalho again moves into the narrow hallway.

"Hey, Phil, I need a legal visit. My case comes up on the fourteenth."

"O.K. I'll take care of it."

From a hall phone, Carvalho dials an extension, "Yeah, Phil Carvalho. I need a legal visit for . . . " . . .

The demands made on Carvalho are not phrased in convoluted euphemisms. They are direct. They deal with basic wants in the limited, cramped world of the segregation unit . . . an appointment for a visitor, a phone call to a relative . . . some writing paper. Sometimes the demands attempt to stretch the narrow boundaries of Ten Block. Either way, the answers are equally direct. Carvalho's booming voice, intoning, "I'll try," or "Yes," or "No," leaves little room for doubt.

(Continued)

FOCUS ON PEOPLE IN CORRECTIONS (*Continued*)

The noon food wagon arrives, and the officers dish out the meal into the paper trays. After the inmates are served, the officers grab a tray and bring it into the office, a few at a time. Some have brought their lunch and eat it piecemeal between running upstairs or into the cell corridors. Elsewhere in the prison, most corrections officers eat in the staff mess hall. In Ten Block, there is no formal sit down dining.

Carvalho, between bites, dials the phone again. "Yeah, Russ. He's back in Block Three. Yeah, he's back. My count is fifty-eight." The count of inmates is reported to control at the beginning of the shift, at noon, or whenever any inmate leaves or returns to Ten Block. . . .

The clock on the office wall ticks the shift slowly to an end.

Fifty minutes and twenty-seven traffic-congested miles later, Carvalho is back in his private world on the outer fringes of suburbia. He is greeted by his wife and his 14-year-old daughter, Cheryl. . . . Supper is on the table a half hour later. The small talk is about an afternoon shopping trip in search of parochial school uniforms for Cheryl. There is no small talk about Ten Block.

Source: Edgar May, "A Day on the Job—in Prison," *Corrections Magazine*, December 1976, 6–11. Reprinted by permission of the Edna McConnell Clark Foundation.

In Louisiana, for example, entry-level pay for correctional officers is $15,953 a year. In other states, such as Massachusetts, New Jersey, Nevada, and Rhode Island, new officers make over $30,000 a year.[41] In addition to their salaries, most officers can earn overtime pay to supplement their base salary.

Over the past 40 years, federal courts, the 1964 Civil Rights Act, and affirmative action programs have dramatically changed the racial and gender composition of the correctional officer force. Today, approximately 30 percent of correctional officers belong to minority groups, and 23 percent are women.[42] How do these increases in the number of minority and female officers shape the work environment among correctional officers? Scott Camp and Neal Langan found in their study of over 4,000 staff

With the great expansion of corrections during the last 40 years, recruits must pass stringent physical and academic requirements. The length of preservice training programs varies from state to state from a few weeks to several months.

© Melanie Stetson Freeman/The Christian Science Monitor/Getty Images

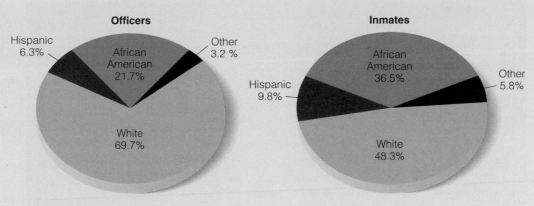

Figure 13.2

Racial/Ethnic Composition of Correctional Officers and Inmates, Adult Systems Nationwide

Although the racial/ethnic composition of correctional officers does not match that of the inmate population, great strides toward such a match have been made during the past 40 years.

Source: Camille Graham Camp, *The 2002 Corrections Yearbook: Adult Corrections* (Middletown, CT: Criminal Justice Institute, 2003), 30, 158.

members employed in 98 prisons that white and male employees believe that women and racial/ethnic minorities have better opportunities regarding career advancement. Their analysis suggests, however, that such opportunities do not differ between men and women, nor between whites and members of racial and ethnic minority groups.[43] **Figure 13.2** shows the racial/ethnic composition of correctional officers and inmates in adult systems.

Women officers are no longer limited to work with women prisoners. In state prisons, an estimated 67,480 correctional officers (or 25.5 percent) are women. Many of these women work in adult male correctional facilities. In the Federal Bureau of Prisons, women make up only 13 percent of the correctional officer force.[44]

Just as female police officers often have found themselves excluded from certain assignments and from full integration into the force, women who work in corrections also must deal with discrimination.[45] In a study of women officers in two prisons for men, Lynn Zimmer found that their male counterparts were opposed to sexual integration of the guard force.[46] Male officers argued that women could not handle the violence and confrontations with inmates that occur in prisons. A study by Richard Tewksbury and Sue Carter Collins, however, found that female correctional officers reportedly respond as aggressively to inmate aggression and misbehavior as do their male coworkers.[47] In some states male prisoners raised the issue of privacy when female officers were assigned to cell-block duty; courts have upheld inmate objections regarding women supervising shower and toilet facilities.[48]

What do male inmates think of the female officers who supervise them? A Texas study examined inmate perceptions of whether female officers performed as well as men. Surprisingly, minimum-custody inmates had a relatively low opinion of the ability of women to perform correctional officers' tasks. However, maximum-custody inmates had high opinion of their competency and "felt that such officers would be calm and cool in problem situations."[49] Female officers are thought to exert a "softening" influence on the environment, making it more livable and less violent.

To prepare officers for prison work, most states require cadets to complete a preservice training program. In some states, preservice programs for officers resemble the military's basic training, with a similar emphasis on physical training, discipline, and classroom work. During the typical program, recruits receive training in a variety of

The presence of female correctional officers in a men's maximum-security prison shocks some people. Here officer Kim Hill checks an inmate for contraband inside a wing of the Texas Department of Criminal Justice's Beto Unit.

topics, including report writing, communicable diseases, inmate manipulation, self-defense, inmate classification, and use of force. In states with large Latino populations, preservice training also includes basic Spanish.[50] The length of preservice training varies from state to state. For example, cadets in California and Michigan receive 640 hours of training. In contrast, training for new recruits in Kentucky lasts 40 hours.[51]

The classroom work, however, often bears little resemblance to problems confronted in the cell block or on the yard. Therefore, on completing the course, the new officer is placed under the supervision of an experienced officer. On the job, the new officer experiences real-life situations and learns the necessary techniques and procedures. Through encounters with inmates and officers, the recruit becomes socialized to life behind walls and gradually becomes part of that subculture.[52]

For most correctional workers, being a custodial officer is a dead-end job. Although officers who perform well may be promoted to higher ranks such as correctional counselor, few ever move into administration. However, in some states and in the Federal Bureau of Prisons, people with college degrees can move up the career ladder to management positions without having to advance through the ranks of the custodial force.

Role Characteristics

The public has traditionally characterized the correctional officer as a mindless and brutal custodian. This stereotype may be true for some guards who seek order at any price and use violence to achieve it. The image of toughness "is exalted in the guard subculture, and is the public image (though not the private reality) adopted by most officers."[53] However, officers also have their own, private view of their work, which Robert Johnson defines in terms of human service. That is, officers help prisoners adapt and cope with prison life in a mature way. Johnson believes that the human service role makes the officer's job more meaningful, rewarding, and ultimately less stressful.[54]

Correctional officers, then, are human service providers expected to engage in "people work" within an organizational setting. Human service activities undertaken by officers include (1) providing goods and services, (2) acting as referral agents or advocates, and (3) helping with institutional adjustment problems.[55]

Officers are expected to help inmates deal with their personal problems. However, because they work in a bureaucracy, they are also expected to treat clients impersonally and to follow formally prescribed procedures. Fulfilling these contradictory role expectations is difficult, and the long-term physical proximity of officers and inmates heightens this difficulty. "Careers in Corrections" offers a closer view of the work of a federal correctional officer.

Although most prison work is thought to be routine, guarding is not an undifferentiated occupation. Officers supervise the cell blocks, dining areas, and shops; transport prisoners to hospitals and courts; take turns serving on the disciplinary board; perch with rifles in guard towers; and protect the prison gates. Unscheduled activities range from offering informal counseling to breaking up fights to escorting prisoners on family visits in the community.

In most states the custodial staff is organized into ranks of officer, sergeant, lieutenant, and captain. Each sergeant supervises a complement of officers in one area of the prison—housing unit, hospital, and so on. The lieutenants are the main disciplinarians of the institution, conducting shakedowns, breaking up fights, and supervising the removal

CAREERS IN CORRECTIONS — Correctional Officer: Federal Bureau of Prisons

NATURE OF THE WORK

Making up the largest part of the Federal Bureau of Prisons workforce, correctional officers maintain security and inmate accountability in order to prevent disturbances, assaults, and escapes. They monitor and supervise the work assignments of inmates. They also report orally and in writing on inmate conduct and usually maintain a daily log of their activities. Officers are expected to respond to inmate needs by directing them to appropriate educational, health, and release planning resources within the institution. About 14,000 officers work in federal correctional institutions.

REQUIRED QUALIFICATIONS

To qualify for an entry-level position as a correctional officer, candidates must meet one of the following criteria required by the Federal Bureau of Prisons:

■ A bachelor's degree in any field of study
■ At least three years of qualifying work experience such as being a supervisor, teacher, counselor, probation/parole officer, or security guard
■ A combination of undergraduate education and qualifying work experience that equals three years

As a condition of employment, new federal correctional officers must undergo 200 hours of formal training within the first year of employment. They also must complete 120 hours of specialized training at the Federal Bureau of Prisons residential training center at Glynco, Georgia, within 60 days after appointment.

EARNINGS AND JOB OUTLOOK

The U.S. Department of Labor says that opportunities for correctional officers are expected to be excellent. Layoffs are rare because of the increasing inmate population. The starting salary for federal correctional officers is about $25,000, but it is slightly higher in areas where prevailing local pay levels are higher.

MORE INFORMATION

See the **Bureau of Prisons** website, found at www.cengage.com/criminaljustice/clear.

of inmates to segregation. The few captains on a staff have primarily administrative responsibilities and serve as the link between custodial personnel and the warden and other top management officials.

The military nomenclature and organization extend to the relationships among staff members. Officers are subject to inspections; in some institutions their superiors may give them "tickets" (disciplinary reports). When they are housed in quarters attached to the facility, rules govern their off-duty behavior. To guard against officers' smuggling contraband into the institution, the staff is subject to rigorous discipline. That the rules for and organization of the officers parallel those that govern the inmates is not lost on the correctional staff. "We're all doing time here," they say, "except that we're doing it in eight-hour shifts."

Job Assignments

Officers may be assigned to one of seven job assignments. These vary according to their location within the institution, the duties required, and the nature of the contact with the inmate population. Assignments include (1) block officer, (2) work detail supervisor, (3) industrial shop and school officer, (4) yard officer, (5) administration building assignment, (6) wall post, and (7) relief officer.[56]

BLOCK OFFICERS ■ Compared with other correctional staff, officers in the cell blocks have the closest contact with prisoners and the greatest potential for inducing behavior change in them. Work in the housing units of some prisons is dangerous because the officers do not carry weapons, are greatly outnumbered, and can be easily overwhelmed by the prisoners.

In units housing 300–400 inmates, the five to eight block officers are responsible for moving their charges to the dining hall, work sites, infirmaries, and the like. They must oversee unit maintenance, watch for potential breaches of security, handle inmates' personal problems and answer their questions, enforce rules, ensure inmate safety, and carry out the warden's orders. As such, the cell block officer must have both management and leadership skills.

WORK DETAIL SUPERVISORS ■ Inmates provide labor for feeding, cleaning, and maintaining the institution. A portion of the custodial staff must supervise various work details connected with these tasks. The work area is more relaxed than the cell block. The work groups are small, the officer and prisoners may engage in conversation, and esprit may develop as they work. This is especially true when people work a particular job and shift for an extended time. In the kitchen, laundry, welding shop, or hospital, for example, the inmate–officer relationship is analogous to worker and foreman in a factory.

Studying field operations at a plantation-style southern prison, Ben Crouch found officers to be focused on two goals: "completing the agriculture task at hand and returning to the building the same number of inmates 'turned out' at the beginning of the day."[57] Officers showed little interest in the rules of dress and demeanor that concerned building personnel. Although most fights between inmates were stopped immediately, on some occasions the two antagonists were allowed to "duke it out," which was unheard-of in the cell blocks. Crouch found that officers in the field adopted a paternalistic style, evoking the unequal relationship of parent to child. Social distance between inmate and supervisor in the field was not as great as inside, so informality arose between them.

INDUSTRIAL SHOP AND SCHOOL OFFICERS ■ Officers assigned to the industrial shops and prison school primarily have maintenance and security responsibilities. They work alongside civilians, such as shop supervisors, teachers, and counselors. Here the correctional officers act principally to ensure that the inmates who are supposed to be in the shops or school are there at the appointed time. The officers keep attendance, ascertain the whereabouts of absentees, attempt to prevent pilfering, and handle inmate problems and complaints.

YARD OFFICERS ■ As Lucien Lombardo observes, "In the blocks inmates are at home; in the school, shops, and on work details they are at work; but in the yard inmates are 'on the street.'" The yard is probably the most unstructured environment in the prison. Officers maintain a presence in the area, but they have no specific duties other than "supervising" the inmates. They are expected to preserve order and to be concerned about security. According to one guard, "In the yard it's mainly the observation of key individuals—the supposed troublemakers. You keep an eye on them so they're not causing any trouble that the prison doesn't need."[58]

ADMINISTRATION BUILDING ASSIGNMENTS ■ Officers in the administration building have very little contact with the inmates and interact mainly with administrators, officials from the commissioner's office, and civilians. They provide security at the gates, supervise the visitors' room, and escort outsiders to offices. Because the appearance and behavior of these officers may color the general public's impression of the institution, they are selected carefully.

WALL POSTS ■ Officers assigned to the towers or along the walls have almost no contact with inmates. With nothing but telephone and weapon, the tower guard is solitary and bored. Traditionally, these assignments have been reserved for new recruits and partially incapacitated veterans or for officers who do not get along with inmates. In more-violent prisons some correctional officers have sought to flee frustration and trouble by transferring from the cell blocks, dormitories, and yard to the safety of the towers.

RELIEF OFFICERS ■ Relief officers are assigned to a variety of tasks, depending on vacancies in the staff due to vacations and sick days. Because they work for only short periods in any particular area of the institution, they do not develop close contacts with the inmates. Relief officers are experienced workers who can step into any assignment as needed.

Problems with the Officer's Role

Prison officers must deal with conflicting custodial and treatment goals. They are held responsible for preventing escapes, maintaining order, and ensuring the smooth functioning of the institution; yet they are also expected to counsel inmates and demonstrate an understanding attitude. Beyond the incompatibility of those roles lies the impossible rehabilitative ideal of treating each inmate as an individual in a large people-processing institution. Officers must use discretion yet somehow be both custodial and therapeutic. Thus, if they enforce the rules, they may be considered too rigid, but if their failure to enforce rules threatens security, orderliness, or maintenance, they are not doing their job. They must do all of this in a tense environment where, on average, the ratio is one officer to four and a half inmates.

The correctional officer is the key figure in the penal equation, the one on whom the whole system depends. Given the current emphasis on humane custody, the officer must be able to influence inmates positively.

Job Stress and Burnout

Recruiting and training qualified correctional officers is only half of the equation. Retention is also important. In some states, such as Arkansas (42.3 percent turnover rate), Tennessee (39.0 percent), and South Carolina (36.7 percent), turnover among correctional officers exceeds more than a third of the entire officer force. In comparison, the national average is about 17 percent.[59] High turnover requires correctional departments to allocate scarce resources to recruitment and training. An important part of the correctional administrator's job is to identify and deal with the problems that lead to turnover among prison staff.

Prison work can be stressful. After all, officers are responsible for supervising clients who are there against their will. Research shows that several factors contribute to job

© Jack Kurtz/The Image Works

Correctional officers are the linchpin of mangement because they are in constant contact with the inmates. They must enforce the rules and yet gain the cooperation of the prisoners—a difficult job!

stress among correctional officers, including relationships with co-workers, departmental policies, and the length of time on the job.[60]

High stress levels can make managing the prison more difficult and can harm prison staff. For example, one study found that federal correctional officers with higher levels of job stress took more days of sick leave.[61] Stressed-out correctional officers experience more problems at home because they displace their frustration onto their spouse or children. Heart disease, eating disorders, and other health problems associated with substance abuse are also linked to officers' stress levels. High stress levels can also lead to frustration, negative work-related attitudes, and emotional exhaustion. In short, job stress can lead to burnout.[62]

The research on job burnout shows that prison work affects male and female correctional officers differently. For example, research shows that female officers are more likely than their male counterparts to develop a concern for inmates' well-being,[63] and they more often express a sense of accomplishment and personal achievement in their work.[64] In the past, female officers experienced higher levels of job stress and burnout, compared with men. These new findings suggest that women are learning to cope better with the stressors associated with prison work. This is not to say, however, that women no longer experience problems on the job. In their study of correctional staff in the Pacific Northwest, Victor Savicki and his associates found that female correctional officers frequently faced gender-based harassment. Further, harassment contributed to job stress, burnout, and lack of organizational commitment among female officers.[65]

A correctional administrator's ability to reduce job stress and burnout can lead to many positive outcomes. For example, reducing officers' stress levels can result in significant financial savings. Fewer resources are expended recruiting, hiring, training, and orienting new officers, as well as covering overtime costs to fill the shifts of officers taking stress-related sick time. Retaining experienced officers can also have a positive impact on safety levels; seasoned officers are the ones best equipped to deal with potentially explosive situations involving inmates. Effectively reducing job stress is good for staff morale, and it demonstrates management's concern for employees. Stress and burnout are among the issues that correctional employees' unions address. Initiatives to address these factors can help foster positive relations between the prison administration and unions.[66] Correctional work is stressful, but prison administrators can reduce the negative effects of stress and burnout by addressing the issue head-on.

Boundary Violations

When social distance breaks down, officers are more prone to commit **boundary violations**. In their study of a southern state prison system, James Marquart and his colleagues identified three types of violations: "general boundary violations," such as staff–inmate exchanges of material goods or written correspondence; "dual relationships," such as disclosing personal information to inmates or excessive flirting; and "staff–inmate sexual contact," which includes intercourse and other sexual acts.[67]

Marquart and his associates found that 80 percent of violations involved dual relationships. These interactions always appeared consensual and were initiated primarily by inmates. Often these relationships involved the exchange of deeply personal letters with romantic overtones. In more than half of these cases, the employee was fired. The least common were general boundary violations (8 percent). Many of these cases probably go undetected by prison officials. These violations usually took place in newer prisons, which were staffed with inexperienced employees.

Incidents involving staff–inmate sexual contact (12 percent) are the most serious. Ninety-five percent of these cases resulted in the employee either being terminated or handing in his or her resignation. The following vignette is a typical example:

> In a written statement, Officer Adams admitted that she loved inmate D and was involved in a personal relationship with D going on two years. Adams stated that she got to know D through casual conversations, which eventually grew into the present relationship. Adams also stated that she was in love with D and had discussed marriage and life together after he was released. Adams admitted that the two had engaged in acts of sexual intercourse in the chapel. She also admitted that she placed $350 in D's trust fund.[68]

The situations surrounding prison employees' boundary violations varied. Some violations were characterized as "rescue situations" where prison staff members felt sorry for inmates and violated departmental policy in an attempt to help them. Employees

boundary violations
Behavior that blurs, minimizes, or disrupts the social distance between prison staff and inmates, resulting in violations of departmental policy.

DO THE RIGHT THING

Shortly after beginning his career as an officer at Pinewood Correctional Complex, Vincent Fernandez was unexpectedly reunited with an old acquaintance, Larry Simpson, who was serving a five- to ten-year sentence. The two hadn't seen each other in years, but they shared many childhood memories from the time when Fernandez's sister babysat both of them. Early on, lessons from the academy stuck with Fernandez, and he tried to keep an appropriate level of social distance between himself and inmate Simpson.

Both men were assigned to the kitchen. As months passed, the personal bond between Fernandez and Simpson strengthened. They frequently reminisced about the "good ol' days," talked sports, and discussed the trials and tribulations of mutual friends. Over time Fernandez became increasingly puzzled about how Simpson could have ended up behind bars.

Eventually, Fernandez was transferred to another prison approximately 180 miles away from Pinewood, which meant he would no longer have regular contact with Simpson. A few weeks later, while working at his new facility, an inmate approached Fernandez and passed him an envelope. It was a letter from Simpson. Simpson explained that his wife had recently filed for divorce and that he was deeply troubled by the situation. He asked Fernandez to write back and advise him on what he should do. Officer Fernandez felt conflicted. On the one hand he wanted to comfort and support his old friend. On the other, he knew that departmental regulations strictly prohibited written correspondence between staff and inmates.

WRITING ASSIGNMENT: First, explain what you think Fernandez should do in this situation. Next, describe the potential harm of Fernandez corresponding with his childhood friend. Describe what you think would happen if Fernandez's sergeant found out he was communicating with Simpson. Finally, do you think that Fernandez should report Simpson for contacting him?

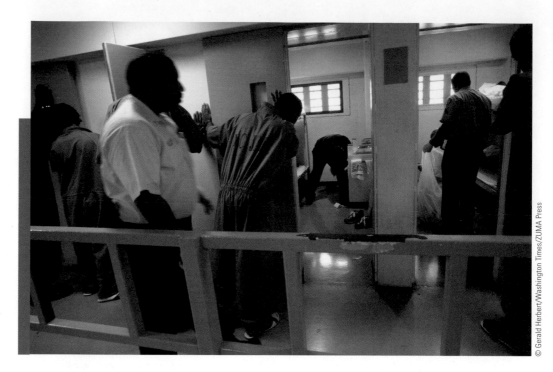

Corporal punishment and excessive use of force are not permitted, yet officers at times must confront inmates who challenge their authority and do not obey the rules. During this surprise search for contraband, two inmates are handcuffed and lined against the wall as officers search their cell. What other tactics might be used to control the situation?

© Gerald Herbert/Washington Times/ZUMA Press

involved in these situations seldom expressed remorse for their actions. "Lovesickness situations" frequently involved dual relationship violations where staff members were romantically involved with inmates. Three-quarters of these situations involved female prison employees who viewed the inmate as a friend or intimate partner. Although rare, some situations were "predatory," which usually involved male staff members abusing their power to obtain sexual favors from female inmates.[69]

Boundary violations among correctional staff are serious issues that prison managers must confront, because such violations contribute to disorder, potentially jeopardize officers' safety, and can result in costly lawsuits. For example, a federal lawsuit filed against the Michigan Department of Corrections, *Nunn v. MDOC* (1996), alleging sexual misconduct and harassment by staff members against female inmates, resulted in a $3,787,000 settlement agreement.[70] To prevent boundary violations, prison officials seek to recruit well-qualified cadets; they also design preservice training programs that emphasize the need for social distance and that prepare employees to defend themselves against inmate manipulation (see "Do the Right Thing" on page 363). The many tasks prison staff are asked to carry out may seem like an almost impossible mandate.

Use of Force

Although neither corporal punishment nor excessive force is permitted, correctional officers are allowed to use force in many situations. They often confront inmates who challenge their authority or are attacking other inmates. Though unarmed and outnumbered, officers must maintain order and uphold institutional rules. Under these conditions, they feel justified in using force.

When and how much force may be used? All correctional agencies now have formal policies and procedures with regard to the legitimate use of force. In general, these policies allow only levels of force necessary to achieve legitimate goals. Officers violating these policies may face an inmate lawsuit and dismissal. Christopher Smith lists five situations in which it is legally acceptable for officers to use force.[71]

1 *Self-defense:* If officers are threatened with physical attack, they may use a level of force that is reasonable to protect themselves from harm.

2 *Defense of third persons:* As in self-defense, an officer may use force to protect an inmate or another officer. Again, only reasonably necessary force may be used.

3 *Upholding prison rules:* If prisoners refuse to obey prison rules, officers may need to use force to maintain safety and security. For example, if an inmate refuses to return to his or her cell, using handcuffs and forcefully transferring the prisoner may be necessary.

4 *Prevention of a crime:* Force may be used to stop a crime, such as theft or destruction of property.

5 *Prevention of escapes:* Officers may use force to prevent escapes, because they threaten the well-being of society and order within correctional institutions. Although escape from a prison is a felony, officials may not shoot the fleeing inmate at will, as in the past. Today agencies differ as to their policies toward escapees: Some limit the use of deadly force to prisoners thought to be dangerous, while others require warning shots. However, officers in Nebraska and Texas may face disciplinary action if they fail to use necessary deadly force. Although the U.S. Supreme Court has limited the ability of police officers to shoot fleeing felons, the rule has not been applied to correctional officers.

Correctional departments have detailed sets of policies on the use of force. However, correctional officers face many challenges to their self-control and professional decision making. Inmates often "push" officers in subtle ways such as moving slowly, or they use verbal abuse to provoke officers. Correctional officers are expected to run a "tight ship" and maintain order, often in situations where they are outnumbered and dealing with troubled people. In confrontational situations, they must defuse hostility yet uphold the rules—a difficult task at best.

Collective Bargaining

Collective bargaining for prison workers is a fairly recent phenomenon. The first prison employee unions with collective-bargaining rights were established in 1956 in Washington, D.C., and New York City. However, the movement did not register major gains until the 1970s, when many states passed laws permitting unionization by public employees. By 1981, correctional employees were unionized in 29 of 52 jurisdictions (state, federal, and District of Columbia).[72]

The unions representing correctional staff include national public employee associations, such as the American Federation of State, County, and Municipal Employees (AFSCME), whose membership includes 85,000 correctional employees, and locally based state organizations, such as the California Correctional Peace Officers Association (CCPOA), with over 30,000 members. These unions seek to increase wages and benefits, improve working conditions, combat efforts to privatize corrections, and lobby for legislation. Such lobbying efforts have not gone unnoticed among commissioners and other correctional administrators, who often solicit the help of organized labor at budget time.

The **Pennsylvania State Corrections Officers Association** maintains a website; see the link at www.cengage.com/criminaljustice/clear.

Because members are public employees, the law prohibits them from striking. But work stoppages and "sickouts" have occurred, and several commissioners have lost their jobs under union pressure. For example, in 1979 the 7,000 officers of the New York State system went on strike for 17 days, forcing the governor to call up more than 12,000 National Guard troops to maintain order.[73] In Connecticut 800 officers went on strike for three days, and 100 officers called in sick at the New Jersey State Prison. Although these work stoppages were settled within a short time, they made an impact beyond the specific issues in dispute.

The great expansion of the incarcerated population over the past decade has brought more than a 400 percent increase in the number of correctional officers nationwide. In some states this growth has greatly increased union power and resulted in more-formal relationships between employees and administrations: A labor contract stipulates the rights and obligations of each side, and wardens can no longer dictate working conditions. Thus, unionization has brought officers not only better work compensation and job security but also greater control over their work. Seniority now determines work assignments, and officers play a greater role in setting institutional policies. Nonetheless, many people fear that unions and pro-inmate groups may form alliances on certain issues to oppose the administration.

SUMMARY

1 Be familiar with the principles used to organize the functioning of prisons.

Prisons are bureaucracies. Accordingly, three organizational principles help explain how they function. Supervision of subordinates follows the principle of unity of command—the idea that each employee reports to only one superior. Following the chain of command principle, each person receives orders from the superior immediately above and issues orders to those immediately below him or her. Finally, the span of control principle refers to staff members' ability to supervise only a limited number of subordinates.

2 Discuss the importance of prison governance.

Prison governance refers to the sound and firm management of inmates and staff. Effective governance is challenging for correctional administrators because the power that officers possess to control inmates is limited, officers have few legitimate rewards to provide inmates for good behavior, and available punishments do not represent much of a departure from the inmates' daily routines. Correctional administrators who successfully govern their institutions do not rely on inmate leadership to control the population, but rather apply sound management principles to prison operations.

3 Discuss the different job assignments that correctional officers are given.

Officers are assigned different jobs. Block officers, for example, work in housing units. They do not carry weapons and are greatly outnumbered by inmates. They answer inmates' questions, enforce rules, and watch for potential security breaches, among other things. Work detail supervisors are officers who oversee small groups of inmates who feed their fellow prisoners, clean the cell blocks, and maintain the facility. Yard officers are not only expected to maintain a visible presence but also to preserve order and address security threats. The wall post officer has little contact with inmates. These officers are assigned to the tower or are responsible for patrolling the wall (or fence). This job assignment can be very lonely and boring. Finally, relief officers do not form close ties with inmates but can fill in wherever needed.

4 Understand the negative consequences of boundary violations and job stress among prison staff.

Boundary violations occur when the social distance between prison staff and inmates breaks down and interpersonal relationships form in violation of departmental policy. These relationships can result in higher levels of prison disorder, can jeopardize officer safety, and can result in costly lawsuits. The negative consequences of job stress among prison staff are twofold. First, job stress contributes to turnover. When staff members resign their positions, new employees have to be recruited and trained, which drains resources from correctional budgets. Second, the physical effects of job stress on prison employees are quite serious and include heart disease, eating disorders, and substance abuse. Correctional officers who experience job stress also possess more-negative attitudes toward their work and report higher levels of emotional exhaustion.

KEY TERMS

administrative control theory (p. 345)
boundary violations (p. 363)
chain of command (p. 340)
coercive power (p. 338)
compliance (p. 338)

formal organization (p. 338)
inmate balance theory (p. 345)
line personnel (p. 340)
normative power (p. 338)
remunerative power (p. 338)

span of control (p. 340)
staff personnel (p. 340)
unity of command (p. 340)

FOR DISCUSSION

1. How have American prisons changed since the big-house era? What do these changes mean for management?
2. As the superintendent of a prison, what sort of management problems do you face? What people can help you solve them?
3. How is the idea of total power in the institutional setting defective?

4. As a correctional officer assigned to manage a 40-man housing unit in a maximum-security prison, what problems might you face? How would you handle them?
5. Would you like to be a correctional officer? What aspects of the job make it attractive? What aspects make it unattractive?

FOR FURTHER READING

Bright, Charles. *The Powers That Punish*. Ann Arbor: University of Michigan Press, 1996. An in-depth analysis of the powerful social and political forces that shaped the emergence and operations of one of the world's largest walled prisons—Michigan's Jackson State Prison—in the mid-twentieth century.

Conover, Ted. *New Jack: Guarding Sing Sing*. New York: Random House, 2000. Denied permission to write about the lives of correctional officers, Conover became one himself and served a year at Sing Sing. The book provides an officer's view of a maximum-security institution.

DiIulio, John J., Jr. *Governing Prisons*. New York: Free Press, 1987. Represents a major critique of the sociological view

of prisons, and argues that governance by correctional officials is the key to maintaining good prisons and jails.

Jacobs, James B. *Stateville*. Chicago: University of Chicago Press, 1977. A classic study of a maximum-security prison. Discusses the transformation process of Stateville Penitentiary from a prebureaucratic to a bureaucratic organization over a half century.

Useem, Bert, Camille Graham Camp, and George M. Camp. *Resolution of Prison Riots*. New York: Oxford University Press, 1996. Drawing from the events of eight prison riots, the authors discuss effective strategies and procedures for dealing with collective inmate protests.

NOTES

[1] Officer Down Memorial Page, http://www.odmp.org/officer.php?oid=18337, April 7, 2007.

[2] "Timeline of Events," *Tallahassee Democrat,* June 22, 2006, p. A3.

[3] Ibid.

[4] Daniela Velazquez, "Correctional Officer Gives His Account of Shootout," *Tallahassee Democrat,* June 24, 2006, p. A1.

[5] Chitra Subramanyam: "Federal Prison Guard Pleads Guilty," *Tallahassee Democrat,* September 7, 2006, p. A1; "Second FCI Guard Pleads Guilty," *Tallahassee Democrat,* September 15, 2006, p. A1; "Third FCI Guard Says He's Guilty," *Tallahassee Democrat,* October 4, 2006, A1; "Prison, Probation for 2 FCI Guards," *Tallahassee Democrat,* December 15, 2006, p. A1.

[6] Chitra Subramanyam, "Verdict Is Mixed for FCI Officers," *Tallahassee Democrat,* November 4, 2006, p. A1.

[7] "Prison for Guards over Sex with Inmates," *USA Today,* http://www.usatoday.com/news/nation/2007-01-10-guards-jailed_x.htm, April 5, 2007.

[8] James W. Marquart, Maldine B. Barnhill, and Kathy Balshaw-Biddle, "Fatal Attraction: An Analysis of Employee Boundary Violations in a Southern Prison System, 1995–1998," *Justice Quarterly* 18 (December 2001): 877–910.

[9] Amitai Etzioni, *A Comparative Analysis of Complex Organizations* (New York: Free Press, 1961), 3.

[10] Ibid., pp. 5–7, 27.

[11] Charles Logan, "Criminal Justice Performance Measures for Prisons," in *Performance Measures for the Criminal Justice System* (Washington, DC: U.S. Government Printing Office, October 1993), 23.

[12] Ibid., pp. 27–28.

[13] James B. Jacobs, *Stateville* (Chicago: University of Chicago Press, 1977).

[14] U.S. President's Commission on Law Enforcement and Administration of Justice, *Task Force Report: Corrections* (Washington, DC: U.S. Government Printing Office, 1967), 19–57.

[15] Donald Clemmer, *The Prison Community* (Boston: Christopher, 1940); Gresham M. Sykes, *The Society of Captives* (Princeton, NJ: Princeton University Press, 1958).

[16] Bert Useem and Michael D. Reisig, "Collective Action in Prisons: Protests, Disturbances, and Riots," *Criminology* 37 (November 1999): 735.

[17] John J. DiIulio, *Governing Prisons* (New York: Free Press, 1987), 13.

[18] Ibid.; Bert Useem and Peter A. Kimball, *States of Siege: U.S. Prison Riots, 1971–1986* (New York: Oxford University Press, 1989).

[19] Useem and Reisig, "Collective Action in Prisons," p. 735.

[20] Ibid., p. 737.

[21] DiIulio, *Governing Prisons*, p. 12.

[22] Sykes, *Society of Captives*, p. 41.

[23] John R. Hepburn, "The Exercise of Power in Coercive Organizations: A Study of Prison Guards," *Criminology* 23 (1985): 145–64.

[24] Sykes, *Society of Captives*, p. 49.

[25] Bureau of Justice Statistics, *Census of State and Federal Correctional Facilities, 2005* (Washington, DC: U.S. Government Printing Office, October 2008), 5.

[26] James Marquart, "Prison Guards and the Use of Physical Coercion as a Mechanism of Prisoner Control," *Criminology* 24 (1986): 347–66.

[27] Sykes, *Society of Captives*, 53.

[28] Stan Stojkovic, "Accounts of Prison Work: Corrections Officers' Portrayals of Their Work Worlds," *Perspectives on Social Problems* 2 (1990): 211–30.

[29] Ibid., p. 223.

[30] Richard Korn and Lloyd W. McCorkle, "Resocialization within Walls," *Annals* 293 (1954): 191.

[31] Burt Useem and Ann M. Piehl, "Prison Buildup and Disorder," *Punishment and Society* 8 (2006): 87–115.

[32] *Wolff v. McDonnell,* 94 S. Ct. 2963 (1974).

[33] *Baxter v. Palmigiano,* 425 U.S. 308 (1976).

[34] Edwin H. Sutherland and Donald R. Cressey, *Criminology* (Philadelphia: Lippincott, 1970), 536.

[35] DiIulio, *Governing Prisons*, p. 237.

[36] Hans Toch, "Trends in Correctional Leadership," *Corrections Compendium* 27 (November 2002): 8–9, 23–25.

[37] Michael D. Reisig, "Rates of Disorder in Higher-Custody State Prisons: A Comparative Analysis of Managerial Practices," *Crime and Delinquency* 44 (April 1998): 229–44.

[38] DiIulio, *Governing Prisons*, p. 242.

[39] John J. DiIulio, *No Escape: The Future of American Corrections* (New York: Basic Books, 1991), ch. 1.

[40] James B. Jacobs and Norma Crotty, *Guard Unions and the Future of Prisons* (Ithaca: New York State School of Industrial and Labor Relations, 1978), 2.

[41] Editor, "Wages and Benefits Paid to Correctional Employees," *Corrections Compendium* 28 (January 2003): 8–26.

[42] Camille Graham Camp, *The 2002 Corrections Yearbook: Adult Corrections* (Middleton, CT: Criminal Justice Institute, 2003), 158.

[43] Scott D. Camp and Neal P. Langan, "Perceptions about Minority and Female Opportunities for Job Advancement: Are Beliefs about Equal Opportunities Fixed?" *Prison Journal* 85 (no. 4, December 2005): 399–419.

[44] Bureau of Justice Statistics, *Census of State and Federal Correctional Facilities, 2005*, Appendix Table 12.

[45] Nancy C. Jurik, "Organizational Barriers to Women Working as Corrections Officers in Men's Prisons," in *Incarcerating Criminals,* edited by Timothy J. Flanagan, James W. Marquart, and Kenneth G. Adams (New York: Oxford University Press, 1998), 136–48.

[46] Lynn E. Zimmer, *Women Guarding Men* (Chicago: University of Chicago Press, 1986).

[47] Richard Tewksbury and Sue Carter Collins, "Aggression Levels among Correctional Officers: Reassessing Sex Differences," *Prison Journal* 86 (no. 3, September 2006): 327–43.

[48] Mark R. Pogrebin and Eric D. Poole, "The Sexualized Work Environment: A Look at Women Jail Officers," *Prison Journal* 77 (no. 1, March 1997): 41–57.

[49] Kelly A. Cheeseman, Janet L. Mullings, and James W. Marquart, "Inmate Perceptions of Security Staff across Various Custody Levels," *Corrections Management Quarterly* 5 (Spring 2001): 44.

[50] Editor, "Correctional Officer Education and Training," *Corrections Compendium* 28 (February 2003): 11–22.

[51] Ibid., p. 11.

[52] Ben M. Crouch and James W. Marquart, "On Becoming a Prison Guard," in *The Administration and Management of Criminal Justice Organizations,* 2nd ed., edited by Stan Stojkovic, John Klofas, and David Kalinich (Prospect Heights, IL: Waveland Press, 1994), 301.

[53] Robert Johnson, *Hard Times: Understanding and Reforming the Prison* (Belmont, CA: Wadsworth, 2002), 201.

[54] Ibid.

[55] Lucien X. Lombardo, "Alleviating Inmate Stress: Contributions from Correctional Officers," in *The Pains of Imprisonment,* edited by Robert Johnson and Hans Toch (Prospect Heights, IL: Waveland Press, 1988), 285–97.

[56] Lucien X. Lombardo, *Guards Imprisoned* (New York: Elsevier, 1981), 3.

[57] Ben M. Crouch, "The Book vs. the Boot: Two Styles of Guarding a Southern Prison," in *The Keepers,* edited by Ben M. Crouch (Springfield, IL: Thomas, 1980), 207–24.

[58] Lombardo, *Guards Imprisoned*, p. 42.

[59] Camp, *2002 Corrections Yearbook*, p. 170.

[60] Eugene A. Paoline, Eric G. Lambert, and Nancy Lynne Hogan, "A Calm and Happy Keeper of the Keys: The Impact of ACA Views, Relations with Coworkers, and Policy Views on the Job Stress and Job Satisfaction of Correctional Staff," *Prison Journal* 86 (no. 2, June 2006): 182–205; see also Stephen S. Owen, "Occupational Stress among Correctional Supervisors," *Prison Journal* 86 (no. 2, June 2006): 164–81; Gaylene S. Armstrong and Marie L. Griffin, "Does the Job Matter? Comparing Correlates of Stress among Treatment and Correctional Staff in Prisons," *Journal of Criminal Justice* 32 (2004): 577–92.

[61] Eric G. Lambert, Calvin Edwards, Scott D. Camp, and William G. Saylor, "Here Today, Gone Tomorrow, Back Again the Next Day: Antecedents of Correctional Officer Absenteeism," *Journal of Criminal Justice* 33 (2005): 165–75.

[62] Peter Finn, *Addressing Correctional Officer Stress: Programs and Strategies* (Washington, DC: U.S. Government Printing Office, 2000), 11–17.

[63] Robert D. Morgan, Richard A. Van Haveren, and Christy A. Pearson, "Correctional Officer Burnout: Further Analyses," *Criminal Justice and Behavior* 29 (April 2002): 144–60.

[64] Joseph R. Carlson, Richard H. Anson, and George Thomas, "Correctional Officer Burnout and Stress: Does Gender Matter?" *Prison Journal* 83 (no. 3, September 2003): 277–88.

[65] Victor Savicki, Eric Cooley, and Jennifer Giesvold, "Harassment as a Predictor of Job Burnout in Correctional Officers," *Criminal Justice and Behavior* 30 (October 2003): 602–19.

[66] Finn, *Addressing Correctional Officer Stress*, p. 7.

[67] Marquart, Barnhill, and Balshaw-Biddle, "Fatal Attraction," p. 906.

[68] Ibid., p. 899.

[69] Ibid., pp. 900–905.

[70] Senate Fiscal Agency, *Status of Lawsuits against the State of Michigan, FY 1999–2000 Update* (Lansing, MI: Senate Fiscal Agency, 2001), 6.

[71] Christopher R. Smith, *Law and Contemporary Corrections* (Belmont, CA: Wadsworth, 1999), ch. 6.

[72] David Duffee, "Careers in Criminal Justice: Corrections," in *Encyclopedia of Crime and Justice,* edited by Sanford H. Kadish (New York: Free Press, 1983), 1232.

[73] Jacobs and Crotty, *Guard Unions,* p. 3.

© Karl Rabe

These prisoners at Eastern Correctional Facility in New York are among the graduates of a unique program sponsored by Bard College, in which inmates can complete work for a degree while incarcerated.

LEARNING OBJECTIVES

After reading this chapter you should be able to . . .

1 Describe how correctional programs help address the challenge of managing time in the correctional setting.

2 Describe the ways that security acts as a constraint on correctional programs offered in institutional settings.

3 Know the meaning of the "principle of least eligibility" and illustrate its importance.

4 Understand the importance of the classification process and how "objective classification" works.

5 Describe the major kinds of institutional programs that are offered in correctional institutions.

6 Analyze recent developments in the field of correctional rehabilitation.

7 Describe the main types of correctional industries and define how each works.

8 Understand the current pressures facing correctional programming policies.

TRAVIS DARSHAN dropped out of school when he was 14. When he was 17, he was arrested with two friends for robbing and killing a taxi driver. Today he and eight other New York State prisoners are taking college classes as students at Bard College, an elite private college in upstate New York. They attend classes in one of the prison classrooms, usually used for GED purposes. Sitting in a circle, they refer to their books and talk with energy about what they have been studying. Travis's fellow students include Wes Caines, who has served 17 years for a shootout in which one man died and another was seriously injured; Salih Israel, serving 20 to 40 years for shooting a woman in the course of a robbery; and Reshawn Hughes, who before prison had never read a book.

Their European history professor, Tabetha Ewing, speaks about the class in glowing terms. "It was the most amazing experience," Ewing says. "We had an immediate rapport. And they took themselves and the work so seriously that I didn't have a moment to consider the absence of a guard." Was the class dumbed down for people behind bars? Not at all, she says.

INSTITUTIONAL PROGRAMS

"Once I was there three weeks, I just made it harder," she says. Ewing had to make the course harder because the inmates studied harder.

The student-inmates have a room where they can study if they have free time during the day. Computers there do not have Internet access. However, they do much of their studying at night in their cells, surrounded by a constant din.

Travis Darshan acknowledges that his cell does not provide an ideal study situation, but he says he manages to block the noise out. "When I begin to read, I try to focus in on my studies. And you kind of go into another world," he says. "You know, instead of hearing that noise, you just block it out. The distractions aren't available when your mind is centered on what you're reading."[1]

The Bard College program is a rarity in the U.S. prison system. Yet in many ways it functions as all prison programs do: occupying time, developing skills, helping the prison run well, and—perhaps most importantly—giving hope. In this chapter we examine the wide variety of prison programs in today's prisons. We investigate the role these programs play in prison life, and we evaluate their effectiveness from the viewpoint of both inmates and management.

Chapter

14

■ MANAGING TIME

The median time served in U.S. prisons is about 27 months.[2] Imagine where you were that many months ago and what you were doing. Now imagine you had spent every day, every hour, since then living behind bars. Think of what you would have missed. Think, too, of how long the prison term would have seemed to have lasted—decades, an eternity.

The theme in prison, the one thread that links all prisoners, is time: "time in the joint," "doing time," "good time," "time left," "straight time." "How much time did you get?" "When do you come up for parole?" "What's your maximum release date?" Many cells prominently display calendars, and some inmates carefully mark the passing of each day.

Institutional programs mitigate the oppressiveness of time. They also provide opportunities for prisoners to improve their lives, whether the programs involve counseling, education, or merely recreation. When rehabilitation is a dominant correctional goal, the parole board sees participation in a treatment program as an indication of readiness for supervision in the community. Perhaps the main merit of programs is that they keep prison time from becoming dead time. When minutes crawl, the soul grows bitter.

Prison administrators use institutional programs to help manage time. Work assignments occupy the middle hours of the day, treatment and recreational periods are held before and after work assignments, and special programs (Junior Chamber of Commerce meetings, Bible study, Alcoholics Anonymous sessions) take up the remaining hours. Experienced administrators know that the more programs they offer, the less likely inmates' boredom will translate into hostility toward the staff. The less cell time,

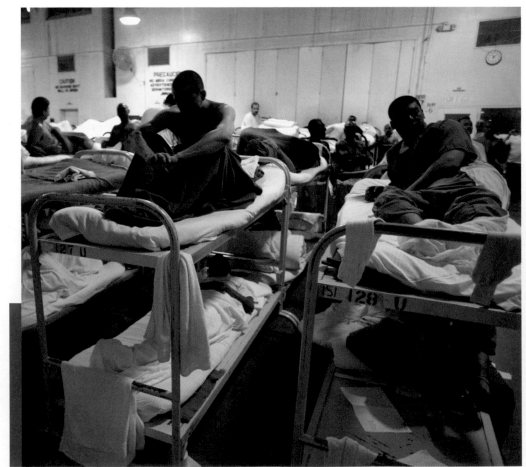

As the saying goes, "Idle hands are the devil's playground." Experienced administrators know that the more programs they offer, the less likely inmates' boredom will translate into "trouble-making." Prison overcrowding has exacerbated this problem.

© Monica Almeida/The New York Times/Redux Pictures

the fewer tensions. J. Michael Quinlan, a former director of the Federal Bureau of Prisons, has said, "It is absolutely the most important ingredient in managing a safe and secure institution to keep the inmates productively occupied, in either work or education or drug treatment or structured recreation."[3]

Administrators use prison programs as incentives for good behavior. Inmates know that when they break the rules, they will be denied access to programs, and this will make time go more slowly.

In this chapter, we use the broadest possible definition of **prison program**: any formal, structured activity that takes prisoners out of their cells and lets them do something. Programs range from group therapy sessions to chair-making factories, from baseball teams to reading groups. Some programs are designed to rehabilitate; others use inmate labor; others deal with spiritual and medical needs. All prison programs serve the fundamental need to manage time.

There are five types of programs. The most controversial is the rehabilitative program. Many such programs attempt to improve job skills or education; others use psychological, behavioral, or social treatment to try to alter the propensity for criminal behavior. A second type provides medical services to inmates. A third type is industrial. Here, prisoners make various products. The fourth type involves daily maintenance of the facility. The fifth comprises recreational programs designed to keep inmates physically fit and involved in positive activities.

prison program
Any formal, structured activity that takes prisoners out of their cells and sets them to instrumental tasks.

Constraints of Security

No matter how beneficial a program, it must not conflict with security. As the criminologist Donald J. Newman once remarked, even if a thousand evaluations showed that pole-vaulting was a valuable skill, it still would never be taught in prison.

Security requirements impinge on programs in a variety of ways. Whenever a program requires sharp tools or materials that could be fashioned into tools, heavy security prevails. This is a particular problem for maintenance, but it also affects many industrial programs. Plumbing and electrical operations use knives, pipes, hammers, and wrenches—in other words, weapons. Common prison industries such as woodworking, welding, and auto repair likewise use potentially lethal objects and materials.

Security requires tool counts, searches, and detailed accounting of materials. Often, guards search inmates twice a shift and take inventories three or more times a day. The heavy emphasis on security has two important consequences. First, unceasing surveillance further demoralizes the inmates and sharpens their sense of captivity. Prisoners are lined up and checked out so often that their consciousness of themselves as security risks is constantly reinforced. The most rudimentary tasks call for a level of control that exacerbates an already dehumanizing environment.

Second, security requirements make maintenance and industrial programs inefficient. Each time a tool is used, it must be signed out and signed in; each time material is obtained, paperwork must be done. Even coffee breaks are circumscribed by security measures. Captives are seldom the most industrious workers, and prison security measures do not improve efficiency.

Despite these negative effects, most authorities strenuously support tight control of potentially dangerous items. Even one handcrafted knife or bludgeon is a serious physical risk to inmates and staff. Yet this may not do much good; even in the most closely monitored prisons, shakedowns uncover hundreds of contrived weapons and other contraband. Prisoners are ingenious at creating weapons, even out of such items as spoons and ballpoint pens. The only remedy—however weak—is unremitting vigilance. Some programs are simply impractical, because the equipment and materials are too easily misused.

Institutional security affects rehabilitative programs in a different way. In classroom work or counseling, inmates know their interactions with other prisoners are observed closely for security violations. Even in therapy, a prisoner knows any remark made to a staff member touching on a possible violation may well generate unpleasant consequences. Here, too, security makes bridging the gap between the keepers and the kept difficult.

The effect of that gap on rehabilitative programs can be quite serious. Treatment success depends on the relationship between the therapist and the client. Many writers have analyzed this matter in some detail; a vivid description by Thomas Harris appears in his groundbreaking book *I'm OK You're OK*.[4] Harris points out that patients in therapy find it difficult to solve their problems as long as they feel what he calls "not OK": dependent, untrustworthy, incompetent. Yet these are precisely the feelings security practices arouse in prisoners. Prison therapists must therefore fight the environment in which they work: It's not easy to make a prisoner feel OK.

In short, the prison environment negatively affects every program that operates in that setting. Prisoners are often coerced into programs or treated as immature or dangerous by staff. Further, whatever prisoners learn inside, no matter how sensible, it is inevitably distorted by the fact that life inside has little resemblance to life outside, where those lessons are applied and their effectiveness judged. That is why innovators such as Dora Schriro, Commissioner of the New York City Department of Corrections, has argued for concepts such as the "parallel universe." Following this idea, administrators try to make the prison resemble, as much as possible, the outside world into which released prisoners must eventually go. Instead of being treated as docile subjects, inmates are enabled to make many decisions about their daily lives and are held accountable for those decisions.[5] Similarly, the Oregon Department of Corrections promotes an "accountability model" in which people in prison are expected to work, get training, and take responsibility for planning their lives after release.[6] Even in Texas, that bastion of "tough on crime" politics, there is active support for replacing the policies of the past with a new emphasis on education and training.[7] This kind of change is new in contemporary corrections, and it is too soon to know how well it will work and how much it will change the basic dynamic between the keepers and the kept.

Still, although the objectives of a prison program—to improve the prisoners' sense of themselves or to make them more vocationally competitive—may be laudable, achieving such objectives in a prison is difficult. The need for tight security dilutes the effectiveness of prison programs, except as a means to fill time.

The Principle of Least Eligibility

principle of least eligibility
The doctrine that prisoners ought to receive no goods or services in excess of those available to people who have lived within the law.

Institutional programs also are affected by society's expectation that prisoners will not receive for free any extra services for which law-abiding citizens must pay. According to this **principle of least eligibility**, prisoners, having been convicted of wrongful behavior, should be the least eligible of all citizens for social benefits beyond the bare minimum required by law. Taken to its extreme, the principle would prohibit many institutional benefits for offenders, such as educational courses and cosmetic surgery.

A good example is provided by what happened to the Pell Grant program in 1994. This program, which provides college loans with beneficial repayment rules, came under attack by Senator Kay Bailey Hutchison, a Texas Republican, who argued that paying tuition for college courses for inmates used $2 million and displaced 100,000 law-abiding students. Even though her facts seemed patently wrong—any student who met Pell eligibility requirements, in prison or in the community, was given funds, and of the four million grants awarded that year only 23,000 went to prisoners—the uproar led Congress to deny eligibility for prisoners. To some it simply was unfair to allow prisoners access to free-world financial benefits. The principle of least eligibility thus outweighed the fact that inmates who take educational programs while incarcerated prove the least likely to return to prison. Yet policy makers continue to recognize the value of education for prisoner rehabilitation: While Pell Grants are no longer available for prisoners, $17 million has since been made available through the Higher Education Act's "Grants for Youthful Offenders Program" for prisoner education grants for inmates under age 25 with less than five years to serve. (For one college program that survived, see the Focus box "Education in Prison.")

Offering prisoners any services of better quality than those available to law-abiding citizens is difficult for administrators to justify. The general public often is quite hostile to creative programming for inmates, and this sentiment affects virtually all programs. The story is told of a miniature golf course, built on the grounds of a Connecticut prison by inmates in their off-hours and with their own funds, that was left unused after a newspaper reporter "exposed" it in a series of stories on the "country-club prison." The principle of least eligibility reflects a strong public ambivalence about correctional programming. Surveys consistently find that citizens support rehabilitation as part of correctional policy. Yet the public also does not want programs that seem to reward criminal conduct, and they resist paying for programs that seem extravagant.[8] Therefore, prison programs frequently represent only weak versions of free-society programs. If the prison offers job-training programs, they do not prepare inmates for positions in the most prestigious or high-paying occupations. If the prison offers psychological services, they frequently take the form of group or individual counseling sessions rather than intensive therapy. Educational classes tend to be basic and barely remedial.

Consider the public reaction to a suit brought by an Oregon prisoner, who forced the state to pay $17,000 for a sex-change operation. The surgery is considered a legitimate

FOCUS ON CORRECTIONAL PRACTICE

Education in Prison

Most prisoners ended up at Eastern Correctional Facility by committing violent crimes. It's not the type of place you'd expect to walk into and find the inmates studying eighteenth-century European history. Bard College, an elite private college, is offering true liberal arts degrees to some inmates in New York State.

The program, which is privately funded, has been in this prison for six years, and the academics are tough. One inmate says he and other inmates study five or six hours a day, outside of class, to make the grade. The classes they take change each semester but what they have in common is that they're not practical courses—they're true liberal arts courses, like English, sociology, philosophy, and German.

Not every prisoner gets the opportunity; only about 10 percent of the inmates who apply to the college program are accepted. Prison life can be so routine and depressing that these men jump at the chance to escape with their minds, if not with their bodies.

Listening to them talk, one could easily have been in a college quad rather than a prison yard. They spend their free time like so many undergraduates, exercising their intellectual muscles, debating centuries-old notions of ethics, morality, and philosophy. Wes Caines, like most of these men, has children. He says his daughters were his inspiration to go to college. "I really wanted them to have a father figure who, when they looked at their father, he's more than prison,

he's more than a prisoner. So everything I've done has been in an effort to be someone that they can be proud of," he explains.

The Bard prison program isn't just at Eastern Correctional Facility—it is in four prisons in New York State and has about 120 students overall. Higher education in penitentiaries used to be common, but in 1994 Congress eliminated federal funding for prisoners to go to college, and many programs folded. The issue was this: Why give free college educations to convicts when so many students who haven't committed crimes can't afford it?

"It's a fair argument, but we treat inmates for medical reasons, we treat inmates for drug addiction—why aren't we treating inmates for educational needs?" says Commissioner Brian Fisher, the head of corrections for New York State.

Fisher says every study he's read shows that inmates given a college education are less likely to commit crimes once they are released. "Education changes people. And I think that's what prisons should do. Change somebody from one way of thinking to a different way of thinking," he says. Is this a liberal penology? Not according to Fisher, who says, "Going to prison is the punishment. Once in prison, it's our obligation to make them better than they were."

Source: Adapted from CBS News, "Maximum Security Education: How Some Inmates Are Getting a Top-Notch Education Behind Bars," *60 Minutes*, April 15, 2007.

(if unusual) procedure in free society, but many observers interpreted its free provision to a member of the least eligible class as unwarranted exploitation of the public by the offender. Yet such an operation is often justified in terms of the psychological or social well-being of the prisoner and its positive effects on future behavior.

The principle of least eligibility and the constraints of security, together, can have a devastating impact on the quality of correctional programming for mental health. These are two of the primary reasons a recent summary of the state of mental health services for people in prison concluded that "prison mental heath services are woefully deficient, crippled by under-staffing, insufficient facilities, and limited programs."[9]

■ CLASSIFICATION

classification
A process by which prisoners are assigned to types of custody and treatment.

Inmates who wish to participate in programs face still another constraint: the procedures used to classify them with respect to security and programs. At Elmira Reformatory in the 1800s, Zebulon Brockway initiated a process of **classification** so that inmates could be grouped according to custody requirements and program needs. During the rehabilitation era, classification was important because treatment was based on a clinical assessment of the inmate's needs. Although rehabilitation is less emphasized today, prison management still relies on continuing classification, which now focuses on the offender's potential for escape, violence, or victimization by other inmates.

During incarceration, prisoners may be reclassified as they encounter problems or finish treatment programs. Classification also changes if inmates transfer to another institution or if they are approaching release to the community.

The Classification Process

In most corrections systems, all prison-bound offenders pass through a reception and orientation center where, over the next three to six weeks, they are evaluated and classified. In some states, the center is a separate facility, but generally each institution has

Classification is the process of evaluating an offender's needs and developing custody and treatment programs that fit those needs.

Betsy Stein

CAREERS IN CORRECTIONS

Correctional Treatment Specialist

NATURE OF THE WORK

Correctional treatment specialists, also known as case managers or correctional counselors, work in both jails and prisons. They may also be found in probation and parole offices, as well as in community correctional centers. In jails and prisons, they develop, evaluate, and analyze the program needs and progress of inmates. In addition, they plan education and training programs to improve offenders' job skills and provide them with coping, anger management, and drug or sexual abuse counseling. As an inmate nears the end of his or her sentence, the specialists work with parole agencies to develop release plans. Correctional treatment specialists working in parole and probation agencies perform many of the same duties as their counterparts in institutions.

REQUIRED QUALIFICATIONS

In the Federal Bureau of Prisons and most state correctional agencies, entry qualifications for correctional treatment specialists require an undergraduate degree that includes 24 semester hours of social science, plus one year of professional casework experience or two years of graduate education in a social science or two years of a combination of graduate education and professional casework experience. Candidates must be 21 years old, have had no felony convictions, and possess strong writing skills. In some states, correctional treatment specialists are required to complete training sponsored by the department of corrections.

EARNINGS AND JOB OUTLOOK

Employment of correctional treatment specialists is projected to grow as fast as the average for all occupations, according to the U.S. Department of Labor. The median annual earnings for correctional treatment specialists employed by state government is about $43,000, with entry-level salaries in the low $30,000 range. Higher wages tend to be found in urban areas.

MORE INFORMATION

See the *Occupational Outlook Handbook:* **Probation Officers and Correctional Treatment Specialists**, at the corresponding website found at www.cengage.com/criminaljustice/clear.

its own reception center. Social scientists have likened reception and classification to a process of mortification. Much as the army recruit is socialized to military life by basic training, or the college student to a fraternity by pledge week, the sentenced felon is introduced to the new status of prison inmate by the reception process. This is a deliberately exaggerated degradation ceremony that seeks to depersonalize the inductee. Newcomers are stripped of personal effects and given a uniform, rule book, medical examination, and shower—in part to underscore that they are no longer free citizens.

In some systems, classification consists merely of sorting prisoners on the basis of age, severity of offense, record of prior incarceration, and institutional conduct. Such approaches serve mainly as a management tool to ensure that inmates are assigned to housing units appropriate to their custody level (low, medium, high, segregation), separated from those who are likely to victimize them (for example, separating the young, slight, and timid from the tougher men), and grouped with members of their work assignment (for example, kitchen duty).

At rehabilitative institutions, batteries of tests, psychiatric evaluations, and counseling are administered so that each prisoner can be assessed for treatment as well as custody. Because treatment resources in most prisons are limited, they must be allocated to benefit the inmates who most need them. The diagnostic process serves this purpose.

Different facilities make their classification decisions in different ways. A common arrangement is to use a committee consisting of the deputy warden and the heads of departments for custody, treatment, education, industry, and the like. This classification committee makes decisions about an inmate's program and custody status. At the hearing, caseworkers or counselors present information from presentence reports, police records, and the reception process. The inmate appears before the committee, personal needs and assignments are discussed, and decisions are made. However, because assembling so many top administrators for classification hearings is difficult, some institutions delegate the task to two or three staff members on the reception team. They make assignments according to procedures prescribed by the department of corrections and the institution's needs. "Careers in Corrections" on the previous page offers a closer view of the work of a correctional treatment specialist.

In practice, classification committees often revert to stereotypes rather than diagnostic criteria in assigning inmates. Common stereotypes include members of racial or ethnic gangs, predators who demand everything from sex to cigarettes, weak victim types, and informers seeking protection. Inmates often contribute to stereotyping by behaving in certain ways with staff. By fitting each inmate to a stereotype, the staff routinize classification, thereby serving the staff and organizational needs. Research suggests that classification results reflect these stereotypes in ways that may, in the end, have little to do with the prisoner's eventual adjustment to prison.[10]

Other classification decisions are also often made on the basis of the institution's needs rather than those of the inmate. For example, enrollment in some treatment and training programs is limited but demand is great. Thus, inmates may find that the few places in, for example, the electrician's course are filled and there is a long waiting list. On the other hand, large numbers of inmates are assigned to housekeeping tasks. See "Do the Right Thing" for more on the issues surrounding such institutional decisions.

Objective Classification Systems

As prison space becomes scarcer and more valuable, administrators feel pressured to ensure that it is used as efficiently as possible and that levels of custody are appropriate. The courts require systems of classification to "be clearly understandable, consistently

DO THE RIGHT THING

Members of the classification committee examined the case folders of the inmates who would appear before them. This morning, 10 newly admitted prisoners were to be classified as to housing and program. Each folder contained basic information about the inmate's education, prior employment, offense, sentence, and counselor's evaluation. In the small talk before the first inmate arrived, Ralph MacKinnon, the chief of the classification unit, warned the other members that the computer-programming class was filled and the waiting list was long. However, there was a great need for workers to make mattresses for state institutions.

"But Ralph, some of the guys trying to learn computer programming just can't hack it," said counselor

Michael Harris. "I've got a man coming before us who was a math major in college and has already had some computer experience. He would greatly benefit from the extra training." "That's fine, Mike, but we can't let someone jump ahead, especially when the mattress factory needs workers. I promised Jim Fox we would get him some help." "But shouldn't we put people into programs that would help them when they get out?" responded Mike.

WRITING ASSIGNMENT: If you were on the classification, committee, what would you do? Write a memo to the warden explaining your position.

applied and conceptually complete." Methods of validation must be implemented and means of redress for irregularity must be provided.[11]

New predictive and equity-based systems seek to classify inmates more objectively. *Predictive models* are designed to distinguish inmates with respect to risk of escape, potential misconduct in the institution, and future criminal behavior. Clinical, socio-economic, and criminal factors (such as previous prison escapes) are given point values, and the total point score determines the security level. *Equity-based models* use only a few explicitly defined legal variables reflecting current and previous criminal characteristics. Such variables as race, employment, and education are not used, because they are seen as unfair. However, in reality the two models frequently use similar variables to classify inmates, the main difference being that predictive models use statistical techniques. Further, careful evaluations of these models question how effective they are in locating potentially violent prisoners.[12]

Objective systems are more efficient and cheaper than other systems because line staff can be trained to administer and score the instrument without help from clinicians and senior administrators. A staff member can determine an appropriate custody level by entering relevant data, adding up total points for factor scores, and applying numerical criteria to indicate classification. Inmates who score 25 or above, for example, might be sent to maximum security, those who score 15 or below to minimum security, and the remainder to medium security. Although classification serves the program and custody goals of the institution, the process places a label on each prisoner. When prisoners become aware of the labels given them by evaluators, they interpret those labels as the viewpoint of the officials who have almost unlimited power over their lives. Inmates may even take on a new identity as a result.

Most states overclassify inmates, placing them in higher custody levels than appears necessary, simply because more high-security space is available. As a result, treatment assignments for which prisoners in maximum security are not eligible (such as work release) are simply unavailable to the vast majority of inmates. This classification policy can have further negative consequences for prisoners, because many privileges are linked to classification level. For example, in Colorado early release from prison is restricted to inmates classified as minimum security. In many states the amount of good time that can be earned is tied to security classification. Further, release on parole often depends on a record of successful participation in treatment or educational programs. Prisoners often have difficulty explaining to the parole board that they really did want to learn a skill but were given no opportunity to do so.

For the latest research on prison classification, visit the **National Institute of Corrections** by using the corresponding link at www .cengage.com/criminaljustice/ clear.

■ REHABILITATIVE PROGRAMS

Rehabilitative programs aim at reforming the offenders' behavior. Some people argue that imprisonment is so painful that it is itself reformative: Offenders change their ways to avoid repeating the experience. The reformative power of prison itself is often called its "special deterrence effect." But many scholars contend that imprisonment by itself is not reformative enough, that the inmate's prison activities must also be reformative. There is much dispute about which rehabilitative programs should be offered and emphasized, whether psychological, behavioral, social, educational and vocational, substance abuse, sex offender, or religious programs.

Psychological Programs

In prison, psychological programs seek to treat the underlying emotional or mental problems that led to criminality. Of course, this assumes that such problems are indeed the primary cause of most offenders' criminality—or even that the concept of mental illness makes sense. These assumptions underlie the medical model, discussed in Chapter 3. However, critics have challenged this model repeatedly and vigorously.

In his famous critique, the psychiatrist Thomas Szasz questioned the applicability of the medical model used for physical ailments to the human "problems in living" commonly called mental illness.[13] The notions of diagnosis, prognosis, and treatment are irrelevant to these problems and also mislead people who try to deal with them. Other critics of mental health treatment in prisons take a much less radical stance: They say mental illness is an inadequate explanation of criminal behavior. Many additional factors enter an offender's decision to behave criminally: opportunity, rational motivation, skill, acquaintances, anger. No one can demonstrate convincingly that some mental problem underlies all or even most of such decisions. Yet recent studies of prison and jail populations find very high rates of mental health problems (see **Figure 14.1**). These rates are much higher than the general population's rate but still represent only a minority of the correctional population.

The lack of consensus on diagnoses of mental illness indicates some of the drawbacks in the general concept that mental illness underlies much criminal behavior. Trained psychiatrists, for example, disagree on the diagnosis of patients' mental problems as often as half of the time. If the experts cannot agree on the nature of an "illness," then perhaps the idea of the "illness" itself has no merit.

PSYCHOTHERAPEUTIC APPROACHES   ■   The unreliability of mental illness diagnosis may be one reason why treatments have been so ineffective. Robert Martinson's groundbreaking review of treatment programs, discussed in Chapter 3, provides perhaps the starkest conclusion: With few exceptions, rehabilitative efforts had no appreciable effect on recidivism.[14] Martinson was referring to a wide variety of programs, but his conclusion applied particularly to programs designed to improve offenders' emotional or psychological functioning.

psychotherapy
In generic terms, all forms of "treatment of the mind"; in the prison setting, this treatment is coercive in nature.

The psychological approach is problematic in prison. Most experts would agree that **psychotherapy**, or "treatment of the mind," has narrow prospects for success even with motivated, voluntary, free patients. Free patients voluntarily enter a financial contract with the therapist for help; either party is free to terminate the agreement at any time. Because the client is the purchaser, it is easy to see why the therapist keeps the client's interest foremost during the treatment process.

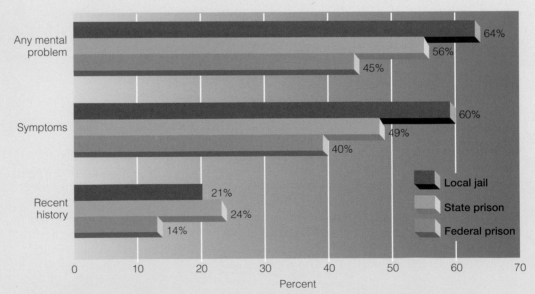

Figure 14.1
Percentage of Inmates with Mental Health Problems

A majority of people under correctional authority have a history of mental health problems; for these, problems include visible symptoms occurring recently.

Source: BJS *Special Report*, September 2006, p. 1.

In prison it is not the inmate but society who purchases the therapist's services. The interests of the purchaser assume more importance to the therapist than do those of the offender. This turns the accepted practices of most therapy upside down. The centerpiece is not the offender; instead, it is society's desire that the offender develop a crime-free lifestyle. (See "Myths in Corrections" and **Figure 14.2**.)

Because of the many problems with prison psychotherapy, programs that address inmates' emotional health have become less common in recent years. Today most prison counselors do not practice psychotherapy with inmates. While 13 percent of prisoners receive some sort of counseling, most of this prison treatment tends to focus on concrete problems that prisoners face in adjusting to the prison environment or in dealing with family crises that occur during incarceration. An additional 10 percent of prisoners receive prescription **psychotropic medications**, and only 2 percent receive 24-hour psychiatric care.[15]

MYTHS IN CORRECTIONS

PRISON AND REHABILITATION

THE MYTH: Judges should send people to prison to get rehabilitation programs.

THE REALITY: Rehabilitation programs offered in the community are twice as effective at reducing recidivism as are those same programs offered in prison.

Source: P. Gendreau, S. A. French, and A. Taylor, *What Works (What Doesn't Work)*, rev. ed., Monograph Series Project (Ottawa, Canada: International Community Corrections Association, 2002).

psychotropic medications
Drug treatments designed to ameliorate the severity of symptoms of psychological illness.

GROUP TREATMENT APPROACHES ■ Unlike psychotherapy, programs that address prisoners' emotions and thoughts tend to use group therapy, in which offenders come together to discuss mutual problems. Group treatment is considered important because humans are social animals. Most of our behavior occurs in groups, and we learn to define ourselves and to interpret our experiences in groups. This fact is particularly appropriate to criminology, because a large proportion of crime is committed by groups or in groups, and much criminal behavior is reinforced by group norms, by manipulation, and by elaborate rationalizations. Therefore, prison treatment groups are often highly confrontational. Group members are asked to "call" the manipulations and rationalizations others are using to justify their deviant behavior, and they are encouraged to participate wholeheartedly in the process. Theoretically, inmates can then come to understand their own versions of those manipulations and rationalizations.

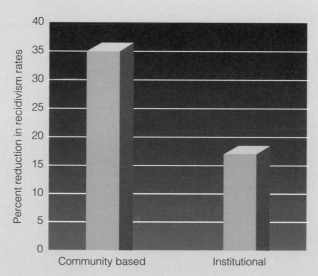

Figure 14.2
Programs in Prison versus in the Community

Rehabilitation programs offered in the community are twice as effective at reducing recidivism as are those same programs offered in prison.

Source: P. Gendreau, S. A. French, and A. Taylor, *What Works (What Doesn't Work)*, rev. ed., Monograph Series Project (Ottawa, Canada: International Community Corrections Association, 2002).

Most groups in prison use structured approaches in which the group undertakes a series of patterned discussion topics or activities that are targeted not at the offender's emotions but at thought processes. Four of the most common group approaches are reality therapy, confrontation therapy, transactional analysis, and cognitive skill building.

Reality therapy has a simple core tenet: People's problems decline when they behave more responsibly. Things get difficult when people fail to behave in ways consistent with life's realities. The therapist's role is to return the client consistently and firmly to the real consequences of his or her behavior, with particular attention to the troubles that follow inappropriate actions. Reality therapy is popular in corrections for three reasons. First, it assumes that the rules society sets for its members are inescapable. Second, its techniques are easy for staff to learn. Third, the method is short-term and thus highly adaptable to prison.

In **confrontation therapy**, a professional group leader encourages group members to confront each other's rationalizations and manipulations, which are common to criminal thoughts and actions. These sessions can become quite vocal, and inmates trying to defend themselves can get quite angry in reaction to aggressive accusations by peers. The therapy aims at pressuring inmates to give up their manipulative rationalizations and accept responsibility for the harms their crimes have caused.

Transactional analysis focuses on the roles (ego states) that people play with others. Here the aim is to help people realize that their problems commonly result from approaching the world as an angry Parent or weak Child rather than as a responsible Adult. The therapist's role is largely that of teacher; he or she spends much time explaining the concepts of transactional analysis and showing the client how to use them in analyzing his or her own life. Like reality therapy, transactional analysis is considered well suited to corrections because it is simple, straightforward, and short-term.

Cognitive skill building focuses on changing the thought patterns that accompany criminal behavior. Advocates argue that offenders develop antisocial patterns of reasoning that make them believe criminal behavior makes sense. To replace these thought patterns, offenders need to learn new skills and techniques for day-to-day living. The group leader uses a variety of procedures to teach these new skills, including role-playing and "psychodramas," that re-create emotionally stressful past occurrences. The aim of the cognitive approach is to teach offenders new ways to think about themselves and their actions.

Behavior Therapy

Correctional **behavior therapy** postulates that the differences between people labeled *deviant* and *nondeviant* lie not within the individual but in that person's responses to problems in the environment. According to this idea, what needs reformation is not the offender's mind or emotions but his or her behavior. The method seeks to change behavior directly by identifying and altering the environmental conditions that promote problem behavior. The assumption is that behavior is learned and has some positive payoff. It can be unlearned if that payoff is eliminated and a more-rewarding payoff is found for different behavior.

The target of behavior therapy in this case is not criminality per se but the variety of problem behaviors that surround a criminal lifestyle: verbal manipulation and rationalization; deficiency in social skills, such as conversation; inability to control anger and frustration; and so on. Obviously, such behavior can make it difficult to keep jobs, avoid conflict, and handle disappointment. The underlying belief is that criminal behavior typically is related to such crucial personal experiences.

Social Therapy

The broad term **social therapy** is applied to certain programs (often referred to as milieu therapy or positive peer culture) because they seek to develop a prosocial environment within the prison to help the offender develop noncriminal ways of coping outside. They are based on the idea that people learn lawbreaking values and behaviors in social

reality therapy
Treatment that emphasizes personal responsibility for actions and their consequences.

confrontation therapy
A treatment technique, usually done in a group, that vividly brings the offender face-to-face with the crime's consequences for the victim and society.

transactional analysis
Treatment that focuses on patterns of interaction with others, especially patterns that indicate personal problems.

cognitive skill building
A form of behavior therapy that focuses on changing the thinking and reasoning patterns that accompany criminal behavior.

behavior therapy
Treatment that induces new behaviors through reinforcements (rewards and punishments), role modeling, and other active forms of teaching.

social therapy
Treatment that attempts to create an institutional environment that supports prosocial attitudes and behaviors.

settings from peers to whom they attach importance. To permanently alter these values and behaviors, the peer relationships and interaction patterns must be changed.

The approach assumes that true change occurs when offenders begin to take responsibility for the social climate within which they must live. All actions are directed toward developing an inmate culture that promotes a law-abiding lifestyle with appropriate social attitudes. Such a program requires significant shifts in institutional policy to support a prosocial institutional climate. Thus (1) institutional practices must be democratic rather than bureaucratic, (2) programs must focus on treatment rather than custody, (3) humanitarian concerns have priority over institutional routines, and (4) flexibility is valued over rigidity. The creation of such a **therapeutic community** has found some success in evaluation studies, and the most recent work suggests that longer stays in therapeutic prison environments and supportive postrelease programs will lead to reductions in recidivism.[16]

Clearly, it is exceedingly difficult to turn a prison into a therapeutic community. The approach has been criticized as both inherently impractical and ineffective in reducing crime. How can a prison, intentionally established as a degrading, painful, intrusive setting, be transformed into a caring, supportive environment? How can the keepers, trained to control the kept but vulnerable to their threats, ever give up meaningful institutional authority to groups of inmates without risking their own security and that of the institution?

therapeutic community
A prison environment where every aspect of the prison is designed to promote prosocial attitudes and behavior.

Educational and Vocational Programs

One of the oldest ideas in prison programming is to teach prisoners a skill that can help them get a job upon release. Educational and vocational programs provide much to recommend their importance in prison. Offenders constitute one of the most undereducated and underemployed groups in the U.S. population. Ex-offenders have limited capability to succeed as wage earners in modern society. Many people believe that criminal behavior stems from this kind of economic incapacity, and they urge the wide use of educational and vocational programs to counter it.

EDUCATIONAL PROGRAMS ■ Nearly two-thirds of prisoners have failed to graduate from high school; two-fifths do not even have a general equivalency diploma (GED).[17] Thus, it is not surprising that programs offering academic courses are among the most popular in today's corrections system. Waiting lists for inmates who want classes are increasing.

In many systems all inmates who have not completed eighth grade—one in seven prisoners—are assigned full-time to the prison school. Many programs provide remedial help with basic reading, English, and math skills. They also permit prisoners to earn a GED. As we have seen, some institutions offer courses in cooperation with a college or university, although funding for such programs has come under attack. Recall that the Comprehensive Crime Control Act of 1994 bans federal funding to prisoners for postsecondary education. Some state legislatures have passed similar laws under pressure from people who argue that tax dollars should not be spent on the college tuition of prisoners when law-abiding students must pay for their own education. (See the Focus box "Educational Programs in Federal Prisons").

Visit the **Bard Prison Initiative college program**; see the corresponding link at www .cengage.com/criminaljustice/ clear.

Prison educational programs face several practical problems. The ability of prisoners to learn is often hampered by a lack of basic reading and computational skills. Moreover, research has increasingly shown a link between learning disabilities and delinquency; many offenders have experienced disciplinary as well as academic failure in school. Thus, prison education must cope with inmates who have neither academic skills nor attitudes conducive to learning.

Other factors exacerbate the problems of prison education. Inmates are usually well beyond the age associated with their current educational attainment, such as a 29-year-old prisoner performing at a sixth-grade level. Few available texts are appropriate for such adults. Imagine a 32-year-old two-time robber with self-inflicted tattoos struggling through a passage in a second-grade reader about Johnnie and Susie learning how to bake cookies. The sheer inappropriateness of the material to the age and interests of inmates drives many of them away from remedial schooling.

FOCUS ON

CORRECTIONAL PRACTICE

Educational Programs in Federal Prisons

Michael Santos

Educational programs are among the few activities individuals in federal prisons can pursue in order to bring meaning and hope to their lives. Such opportunities enable prisoners to escape the monotony of institutional life and to work on their personal goals and plans for their futures. Whether an individual spends time in formal classes or studies independently by using available library services, education departments are areas in the prison where the walls seem more permeable.

Prison libraries vary in size. Some of the older and larger ones hold upward of 20,000 books; those in newer institutions usually contain only a few thousand. All federal prisons participate in the interlibrary loan system, which enables an inmate to order nearly any title he or she needs from a nearby library. So although gates, walls, and gun towers isolate federal prisoners from the wider community, they still are able to learn languages and travel the world learning about different cultures through their access to literature and other educational materials.

Unfortunately, many of the men and women in prison have poor reading skills; some cannot read at all. This has always been a problem, yet the situation became even more severe after Congress passed the 1994 Comprehensive Crime Control Bill, as it tied federal prisoners' eligibility to earn good time with verification of high school equivalency. In other words, inmates who cannot pass the high school equivalency examination are ineligible to receive time off their sentences for good behavior. Furthermore, individuals who do not have a high school diploma or certificate verifying high school equivalency are limited to the amount of money they can earn from prison jobs.

Prisoners who need help developing their reading skills or preparing for the high school equivalency exam can find it in the education department of each prison. Every facility conducts adult basic education (ABE) classes and general equivalency diploma (GED) classes. In fact, Congress mandates all prisoners who lack high school equivalency to participate in GED classes for at least 120 days. Staff members usually teach these classes, though many institutions use inmate tutors to work with some inmates on an individual basis.

Inmates who complete the GED or those who already have high school diplomas can advance to the vocational technology (VT) programs. These give prisoners opportunities

Learning a marketable job skill is crucial for success upon release. At Tennessee's Turney Center Prison and Farm, inmates Max Deberry and Terry Christian have learned to make office desks. What are some of the impediments to being able to use these skills?

AP Images/John Russell

to learn trades that might translate into jobs on their release from prison. Each prison offers its own selection of VT courses, many of which culminate with actual state licenses that let successful participants ply their trades in communities outside of prison walls once their sentences are completed. Some of the more popular VT programs in federal prisons include barbering, building trades, culinary arts, horticulture, and the operation of basic computer programs.

Besides the ABE, GED, and VT classes, people in prison can also pursue collegiate studies. In fact, until the 1994 Crime Bill passed, most federal prisons had agreements with local colleges and universities.

Those agreements let nearby institutions send professors into the prison to teach classes. Many citizens complained about this practice and the 1994 Crime Bill eliminated funding for the prison college program. Still, a small minority of federal prisoners continue to prepare themselves for release by studying independently through correspondence courses at cooperating universities. Financial assistance for tuition through Pell Grants, however, is no longer available for prisoners.

Inmates in some institutions work together in order to create their own communities of learning. For example, at Federal Correctional Institution McKean, in Bradford, Pennsylvania, inmates asked the administration to designate one of the housing units as an education unit. Individuals in serious pursuit of self-improvement programs apply through the supervisor of education for assignment to that unit. Those who live in the education unit work to strengthen it in various ways. They correspond with libraries in an effort to solicit donations of books and other learning materials, they offer classes in some of the common living areas, and they work as tutors to help each other grasp concepts that might be more difficult to understand independently.

Educational programs help prisoners prepare for release. Besides that, they help prisoners move through their sentences. For the prisoner who allows his or her mind to lie dormant, time creeps at a snail's pace. Those who keep focused and work to enhance their skills in prison can document their accomplishments as time passes; in other words, educational programs empower people in prison by letting them make use of their time instead of letting the time use them.

Reprinted by permission of the author.

How successful is prison education as a rehabilitative program? Not many studies have been done on this subject. However, a recent survey of 3,000 prisoners in Maryland, Minnesota, and Ohio found that three years after release, 22 percent of the prisoners who had taken classes returned to prison, compared with 31 percent of the released prisoners who had not attended school while behind bars.[18] Recent studies show that some prisoners who obtain GEDs while incarcerated see an increase in wages upon release, but this improvement dissipates after three years.[19] Even so, the recidivism rate for these GED recipients is lower than for those who do not obtain the GED in prison.[20] Critics point out that the higher success rate may result not from the GED itself but from the better-risk prisoners being the ones who take the courses and obtain it.

VOCATIONAL PROGRAMS ■ **Vocational rehabilitation** programs attempt to teach offenders a marketable job skill. However, these programs also suffer from the principle of least eligibility: Training often centers on less-desirable jobs in industries that already have large labor pools—barbering, printing, welding, and the like. Other problems also plague prison vocational programs. Often participants are trained on obsolete or inadequate equipment, because prisons generally lack the resources to upgrade. A story is told about a popular print shop apprenticeship program at one large state reformatory, in which inmates were trained on presses donated by the local newspaper. On parole the inmates discovered that their acquired skill was unmarketable because the machinery

vocational rehabilitation
Prison programming designed to teach inmates cognitive and vocational skills to help them find employment upon release.

they had learned to operate was so inefficient that the newspaper had junked it (which was why it had been donated). Vocational programs rarely teach up-to-date skills.

Offenders also often lack the attitudes necessary to obtain and keep a job—punctuality, accountability, deference to supervisors, cordiality to co-workers. Further, they may lack the ability to locate a job opening and survive an interview. Therefore, most prisoners need to learn not only a skill but also how to act in the work world. The prison regimen, which tells prisoners what to do and where to be each moment from morning to night, can do little to develop attitudes needed outside the walls.

Yet another problem is perhaps the most resistant of all. The **civil disabilities** that attach to the former offender, discussed in more detail in Chapter 16, severely limit job mobility and flexibility. Occupational restrictions force offenders into low-paying, menial jobs, which may lead them back to crime. In one state or another, barred occupations include nurse, beautician, barber, real estate salesperson, chauffeur, worker where alcoholic beverages are sold, cashier, stenographer, and insurance salesperson. Unfortunately, some prison vocational programs actually train inmates for jobs they can never have. Further, ex-convicts may find the stigma of being a convicted offender either difficult or impossible to overcome.

Despite their detractors, prison vocational programs receive considerable support from many experts because poor job skills seem so closely tied to the problems inmates face upon release into the community. The additional income and taxes produced by vocationally trained inmates may actually offset the cost of their training programs and may also reduce recidivism among participants.

Substance Abuse Programs

The link between crime and substance abuse is strong.[21] Over half of defendants test positive for drugs at the time of arrest, and most of these arrestees need some form of drug treatment. To serve this large clientele, substance abuse treatment programs have grown rapidly in all parts of the criminal justice system, working with millions of offenders on any given day.

For years people have questioned the effectiveness of drug treatment programs for habituated offenders. Follow-up studies routinely found high rates of rearrest for those leaving these programs, and most offenders had instances of relapse as well. The failure of these programs to eradicate drug use among participants led many to believe that drug treatment did not work. Yet, more recent research has demonstrated that even though failure rates are high, drug treatment can be a valuable, cost-effective crime-reduction strategy. For example, CREST, a work release and therapeutic community program, found that the drug treatment component of this postrelease program resulted in up to a 43 percent reduction in jail recidivism.[22]

One reason for this reinterpretation of drug treatment programs is that different researchers frame the question differently. Instead of asking simply whether the offender relapses to drug use, some researchers ask a more-complex evaluation question: Do program participants return to drugs and crime at lower rates than do similar offenders who were not in the program? The usual answer is yes.

This more-complex question stems from a recognition of how difficult it is to overcome drug addiction. Even a small rate of abstinence among program participants may represent a big difference in drug use and crime compared with nonparticipants. And participants who eventually fail often spend more time drug-free on the streets before relapse, and their new crimes are less serious.[23] These effects can result in significant savings in criminal justice costs and losses of victims—as much

civil disabilities
Legal restrictions that prevent released felons from voting and holding elective office, engaging in certain professions and occupations, and associating with known offenders.

Visit the **Mental Health in Corrections Consortium** at the corresponding link at www.cengage.com/criminaljustice/clear.

Learn about the Correctional Education Association's **efforts with prisoner education** at the corresponding link at www.cengage.com/criminaljustice/clear.

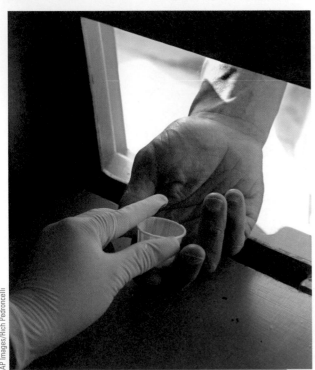

AP Images/Rich Pedroncelli

An inmate receives his medication at the California Substance Abuse Treatment Facility. Medications such as methadone are often prescribed to help addicts through the withdrawal period.

as $7 saved in costs of crime for every $1 spent on treatment[24]—and long-term reductions in recidivism.[25] Today the most effective substance abuse treatment programs share several components:

1 The program occurs in phases, with a residential treatment phase lasting between 6 and 12 months.

2 During residential treatment, participants gradually earn privileges in a therapeutic treatment setting.

3 Multiple treatment modalities are used, including individual psychotherapy, group therapy, and vocational rehabilitation.

4 Residential staff and community officials closely coordinate plans for release.

5 Treatment continues after release in the form of therapy groups augmented by drug testing.[26]

Sex Offender Programs

Many correctional officials believe that sex offenders represent the most difficult group for correctional treatment. There are several reasons for this. First, there are different types of sex offenders: Crimes vary from exhibitionism to rape to child molesting to incest. The treatment needs of one group may not correspond to the needs of another. Yet treatment programs often group all sex offenders together, perhaps because the public and prison officials tend to do so as well.

Second, some sex offenders are far more committed than others, emotionally and personally, to the kind of sexual deviance they practice. Those who are deeply devoted to a version of sexual abnormalcy may find it harder to turn away from their desires and thus may resist treatment more. Perhaps this is why some types of sex offenders have high recidivism rates.

Third, providing treatment for sex offenders in prison settings is sometimes problematic. Often sex offenders are targets of harassment, and so they are inclined to maintain a low profile. Attending treatment programs can call attention to one's status, leading to trouble with other prisoners. The incentives to deny problems with sexual deviance while incarcerated are quite high.

Various kinds of treatments have been tried, with varying degrees of success. Relapse-prevention approaches attempt to teach the offender ways to foresee inappropriate arousal before it occurs and how to prevent acting on those feelings. Interpersonal strategies work on social skills, victim awareness, and sexual identity. Other approaches try to break through patterns of denial and rationalization or to build skills in anger control and impulse control. Many treatment programs employ all of these strategies, in the hopes that they will reinforce each other and one will eventually work. Treatment programs for sexual offenders focus on helping the person to overcome the following:

- Deviant sexual arousal, interests, or preferences
- Sexual preoccupation
- Pervasive anger or hostility
- Emotional management difficulties
- Self-regulation difficulties, or impulsivity
- An antisocial orientation
- Pro-offending attitudes, or cognitive distortions
- Intimacy deficits and conflicts in intimate relationships[27]

A growing body of literature suggests that some treatments for sex offenders reduce recidivism rates. One survey of treatment programs found that sex offenders had a recidivism rate about half that of other offenders, and offering sex offenders treatment programs reduced their recidivism rate by about one-fourth, boding well for the prospects of rehabilitation for this group. Nonetheless, the researchers pointed out that "the potential impact of failed interventions [includes] potential adverse effects on the

See how programs for the treatment of sex offenders operate at the **Association for the Treatment of Sexual Abusers** and the **Center for Sex Offender Management**; see the links at www.cengage .com/criminaljustice/clear.

client and his family, when adults or juveniles [suffer] additional sexual victimization and the associated impact on the victim, victim's family, and the community."[28] Because of the important stake we have in providing effective treatment for sex offenders, experimentation with new strategies for this group will almost certainly continue.

Religious Programs

Religious programs seem substantially different from the categories discussed thus far. For most of prison history, such programs were a mainstay of prison services but were thought to be an offshoot of prison life rather than a mainstream treatment program. Recently, interest in religious strategies for social problems has grown, spawned in part by President George W. Bush's creation of a White House Office on Faith Based and Community Initiatives. People who study crime have noted an emerging literature suggesting that people who are more oriented toward religion are less likely to engage in crime.[29] For some scholars and many activists, religion is seen as an exciting new way to help prisoners change their lives. At least five states—Texas, Kansas, Minnesota, Florida, and Iowa—have opened new prison treatment facilities whose central philosophy involves religious teaching.[30] These initiatives have received a lot of attention: Advocates hope that religious programs will reduce recidivism, whereas critics worry about using tax dollars to promote religion.[31] While the courts have ruled that compulsory involvement in religious programs violates the First Amendment,[32] voluntary religious programming stands on solid constitutional ground.[33]

Because the First Amendment guarantees the right to belief and practice, religious programs are available to all prisoners, not just those in special programs. The two main religions in prison are Christianity and Islam, but U.S. prisons host the same array of faiths that the free society does. For instance, in the West and Southwest, Native Americans may fast and sit in sweat lodges, where the devotee may spend up to a day in quiet contemplation. In the Northeast and Southwest, daily Catholic masses are common. In prisons in the southern "Bible Belt," religious programs tend to be evangelical Christian.

Interviews with religious inmates indicate several reasons why religion is helpful in prison. For example, it often provides a psychological and physical "safe haven" from harsh realities and enables inmates to maintain ties with their families and with religious volunteers from the outside. Many administrators believe that inmates' strong religious groups—even those following nontraditional religions—make a prison easier to run, because these inmates help stabilize the prison culture.

Only a few studies of religion in prison have been conducted. The results of these studies are mixed. It appears that religious activity helps inmates adjust to prison psychologically, avoiding infractions.[34] A key issue is whether religious participation helps offenders stay out of trouble after release. Evidence on this is inconclusive. An early study of the Prison Fellowship's (PF) programs—a multifaceted religious training approach that works with prisoners in intensive sessions and provides follow-up support after release—found that program graduates did slightly better after release than a comparison group of non-PF inmates. The differences were most pronounced for low-risk offenders. A follow-up study, however, found that any differences in success rates for PF graduates disappeared a few months after they were released from prison.[35] A long-term study of religious programs in England had similar findings of little difference in recidivism rates for participants in religious programs, compared with the control group, although those who were most successful in the religious program had the lowest recidivism rates.[36] Why there is limited staying power for religious programs in prison remains an open question.

See the **Center for Faith-Based and Neighborhood Partnerships** at the corresponding link at www .cengage.com/criminaljustice/ clear.

The Rediscovery of Correctional Rehabilitation

After Martinson's 1974 study indicated that prison rehabilitation programs were ineffective, the number of treatment programs began to decrease. According to the new vision, prison was a place that should provide safe and secure custody while punishing offenders. Yet, even though some correctional officials willingly abandoned the rehabilitation ideal, many others believed that eradicating rehabilitation from prisons was unwise. In recent years these penologists have become a strong minority voice calling for a renewed emphasis on rehabilitative programs in corrections. In a book titled *Reaffirming Rehabilitation*, Francis Cullen and Karen Gilbert argue that correctional treatment is more humane than mere custody and punishment and that these programs can be effective when appropriately designed and implemented.[37]

Following their lead, a team of Canadian researchers analyzed a large number of recent evaluations of correctional treatment and identified six conditions under which treatment programs will be effective:

1 The programs are directed toward high-risk clients.

2 The programs respond to offenders' problems that caused the criminal behavior.

3 The treatments take into account offenders' psychological maturity.

4 The treatment providers are allowed professional discretion on how to manage offenders' progress in treatment.

5 The programs are fully implemented as intended.

6 Offenders receive follow-up support after completing the treatment programs.

Recent research that looks at a wide array of treatment programs continues to support these ideas.[38]

One of the most important elements of this research on effective treatment programs is the distinction made between "criminogenic" needs and other kinds of needs. **Criminogenic needs** are those that, when successfully addressed by treatment programs, result in lower rates of recidivism. The identification of criminogenic needs is an important advance in correctional treatment, because it enables program managers to focus their efforts on objectives that are likely to pay off in lower recidivism rates.

Although interest in rehabilitation waned when the philosophy of corrections swung toward crime control, advocates of correctional rehabilitation now point to an increase in consistent evidence that programs meeting the six criteria of success can result in considerable reductions of new criminal activity by former offenders. They argue that the time has come for a reformulation of the ethics of correctional rehabilitation: from "nothing works" to "what works, for whom, and why."[39]

criminogenic needs
Needs that, when successfully addressed by treatment programs, result in lower rates of recidivism.

Here, 2008 presidential candidate, Senator Sam Brownback, a Republican from Kansas, visited the Louisiana State Penitentiary where he spent the night in a cell and addressed inmates at a Christian service. After decades of supporting "lock 'em up" policies, many conservative legislators are now supporting rehabilitation, especially if it "saves souls and saves money."

© Thomas Dworzak/Magnum Photos

To bolster this point of view, several researchers have undertaken systematic reviews of correctional rehabilitation studies, in which a broad and careful search for all the studies ever conducted is made, then the results of those studies are statistically assessed to find patterns of results. Systematic studies are thought to be superior in giving policy makers an understanding of correctional rehabilitation, because the use of a large number of studies with a single yardstick for "success" leads to a more-reliable conclusion than do other methods.[40]

cost-benefit ratio
A summary measure of the value of a correctional program in saving money through preventing new crime.

The most powerful new studies of correctional rehabilitation programs try to express their effectiveness in **cost-benefit ratios**. A cost-benefit study begins with the recognition that crime costs money—victims suffer losses and the criminal justice system has to use its resources to combat crime. Correctional programs also cost money. Any program that can reduce crime can thus be seen as a potential money saver, at least in the long term, if the savings incurred through the crimes that have been averted outweigh the costs of the program itself. Cost benefits are expressed as ratios: When they are larger than 1, the program saves money; when they are less than 1, the program loses money. Thus, a program with a cost-benefit ratio of 2.25 saves $2.25 for every dollar it costs, while a program with a cost-benefit ratio of 0.50 loses 50 cents per dollar spent on the program.

Recent systematic cost-benefit studies have encouraged advocates for more rehabilitation programs in corrections. One summary of nine correctional intervention studies found cost-benefit ratios ranging from 1.13 to 7.14; the only programs that lost money were those operating in prisons and jails and designed primarily to incapacitate offenders.[41] Another study of 21 programs for adult offenders found that only four failed to save money; the rest saved between $237 and $9,822 per offender.[42]

Such studies have sparked a new interest in rehabilitation. The National Institute of Corrections has funded a series of demonstration programs designed to show how treatment programs can be effectively implemented in corrections. Though some scholars have doubts, many policy makers have gained a new enthusiasm for the idea of rehabilitation. After Californians passed Proposition 36, mandating treatment programs instead of prison for drug offenders, many political leaders took note. Advocates believe that the proposition, despite problems, has been an overall success.[43] This issue has ceased to be seen as primarily liberal, as conservatives such as President George W. Bush and Kansas Senator Sam Brownback have championed rehabilitation programs for people who have gone to prison.

Inmates in some states receive medical diagnosis and treatment via telecommunications. The prison medical staff follows the treatment recommendations of the specialist. If the treatment is complicated, the prisoner is transferred to a hospital.

© J. Carter Smith/CORBIS Sygma

Prison Medical Services

Inmates have a well-established right to medical treatment while incarcerated, most effectively defined by the Supreme Court in *Estelle v. Gamble*.[44] The argument for a right to medical treatment is straightforward and persuasive: Citizens who are confined do not have the capacity to obtain health insurance or sufficient funds to pay for their own health care costs, and to deny necessary treatments would be cruel. Thus, it is only fair to provide basic health care for those who are incarcerated.

This is potentially a very expensive right, because inmates as a group bring significant health problems with them to prison. Some of these problems stem from the high-risk behavior many inmates engage in prior to their incarceration. Needle use during drug abuse, for example, is the single most frequent cause of HIV transmission and is also the leading cause of **hepatitis C**, an incurable disease of the liver that kills 5 percent of those infected. Unprotected sex also accounts for high rates of sexually transmitted diseases (STDs) among prisoners. Treatment for most forms of these "lifestyle" diseases (so called because they are typically acquired as a consequence of a high-risk lifestyle) can be complicated and expensive.

The number of people who require help for these diseases is not small. Much attention has been given to HIV-positive inmates, who number over 30,000 (see Chapter 6). But less attention has been given to inmates suffering from hepatitis C, whose numbers may exceed 360,000, a stunning 18 percent of the prison population.[45] In 1995 the mortality rate in prison from AIDS was two-thirds the rate of all other causes; by 2004 the medical care for HIV and AIDS had reduced that figure to one-tenth.[46] Today the chances of dying from an infection are much greater than the chances of dying from HIV-related illnesses (see **Figure 14.3**).

The treatment regimen for these diseases involves drugs that reduce the negative effects of the diseases and slow bodily deterioration from the infection. But the most important treatment is prevention through a change in lifestyle. Prison programs that seek to halt the spread of disease within the population are educational, showing prisoners how the diseases are spread and stressing the value of abstinence from drugs

hepatitis C
A disease of the liver that reduces the effectiveness of the body's system of removing toxins.

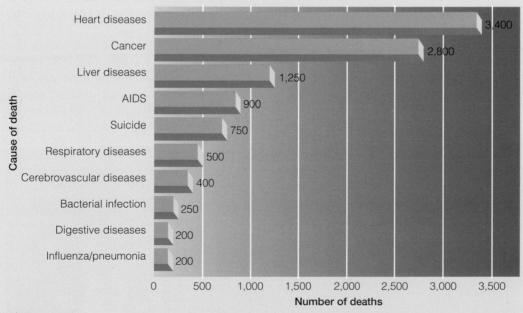

Figure 14.3
Leading Causes of State Prisoner Deaths, 2001–2004

Despite the concern about AIDS in prisons, other health factors are a more-common cause of death among people who are incarcerated.

Source: Bureau of Justice Statistics, *Data Brief*, January 2007.

and unsafe sexual contact. To date, needle-exchange programs, which have successfully reduced transmission rates on the streets, have not been tried in U.S. prisons, because critics say they indirectly support illicit drug use inside the walls.

In addition to the lifestyle diseases, prisoners suffer other maladies found in the general population. A recent study found that almost one-third of the state prison population (nearly one-fourth of the federal population) reported some debility requiring health care (see **Table 14.1**). One in five inmates reported suffering a new medical problem subsequent to arriving at the prison, and half of those serving five years or longer reported the onset of a medical problem during incarceration.[47] For these prisoners, the need for availability of "sick call" and regular medical help is no different than that of the population at large, but a prisoner's choice is restricted to whatever options the prison provides.

Most prisons offer medical services through a full-time staff of nurses, augmented by part-time physicians under contract to the correctional system. Nurses can take care of routine health care needs and dispense medicines from a secure, in-prison pharmacy; regularly scheduled visits to the prison by doctors can enable prisoners to obtain checkups and diagnoses. For cases needing a specialist, surgery, or emergency medical care, prisoners must be transported to local hospitals under close security by correctional staff. The aim is for the prison system to be able to provide a range of medical assistance to meet the various needs of the population as a whole. However, because medical care is so expensive, many prison administrators resist providing help until it is absolutely necessary. Complaints among prisoners and observers that prison medical care is "second class" are common, and one study has accused the prison authorities of purposefully abusive health care practices.[48]

While inmates' needs for health care echo those of the general population, prisoners pose two special needs, one due to poverty and the other to aging. Because prisoners as a group are very poor, they often bring to the prison years of neglect of their general health. It is surprising, for example, how many prisoners have neglected their teeth so severely that the resulting unsightly smile makes it hard to get any job requiring contact with businesses customers. A round of dental repairs can do wonders to alleviate this practical and personal problem, but outsiders might look at such free dental care as a luxury. Other consequences of being poor, such as an inadequate diet and poor hygiene, also affect the general health of the prison population.

By far, the most extraordinary health problem in contemporary corrections is the burgeoning number of elderly prisoners. Penal policies of the 1980s and 1990s have resulted in a dramatic increase in the number of offenders serving long sentences, and many of these are now beginning to grow old in prison. The number of inmates aged 50 and older doubled in the mid-1990s, and this group will likely approach 10 percent of all prisoners in coming years. The growing number of geriatric prisoners poses multiple

Follow the latest regarding infectious diseases in corrections in the **Infectious Diseases in Corrections Report** provided by the Brown University Medical School; see the corresponding link at www .cengage.com/criminaljustice/ clear.

TABLE 14.1 *Health Care Needs of Prisoners*

Many prisoners say they need medical attention for significant health impairments.		
Type of Impairment	**Percent (State)**	**Percent (Federal)**
Learning	9.9	5.1
Speech	3.7	2.2
Hearing	5.7	5.6
Vision	8.3	7.6
Mental	10.0	4.8
Physical	11.9	11.1
Total	31.0	23.4

Source: BJS *Bulletin,* January 2001, p. 1.

problems for prison authorities. Elderly inmates have more-complicated and more-numerous health problems, over all, and they eventually reach an age where they cannot work productively in prison assignments. As the length of time away from free society increases, the ability for an inmate to adjust to release decreases to the point that setting some elderly prisoners free, without family or friends, seems a difficult choice. But staying inside has its costs, too. Prisons are difficult places in which to grow old and, finally, die. Mortality rates for prisoners aged 55 or older are 50 times higher than the rates for prisoners aged 25–44.[49] The large number of geriatric inmates on the path to dying has led some prison systems to form hospice facilities where younger inmates can care for the elderly as they spend their last days on earth behind bars.[50]

The rapidly expanding cost of prison health care has led prison officials to look for ways to provide adequate health care less expensively. The managed-care strategies that are used to contain health care costs in the free world are now being used in prisons, as corrections systems seek to purchase health care on the open market rather than provide it themselves. Many prison officials are beginning to impose restrictions on health care procedures and to find ways of reducing demand among prisoners for health services. Today imprisoned offenders are the only people living in the United States who enjoy a constitutional right to adequate health care. Nevertheless, numerous state and local facilities have been found to violate basic requirements of mental health care. In fact, California's entire state prison system has been declared unconstitutional because of its poor health care.[51] Some believe that the principle of least eligibility may come into play here, making the right to medical treatment precarious, as increasing numbers of free citizens go without health care services provided to prisoners by right.

Learn about the **prison hospice movement** at the corresponding link at www .cengage.com/criminaljustice/ clear.

■ PRISON INDUSTRY

American prisoners have always worked, and making them work has been seen as a way to accomplish many correctional objectives. Historically, hard labor has served as a central part of punishment. In recent years this idea has gained new popularity with the reemergence of chain gangs in a few southern states. It was even a popular belief at one time that prisoners' labor was legally forfeited as a result of their criminality and that the state could expect to profit from their incarceration.

AP Images/Herald-Leader, Dariush Shafa

Besides mattresses and the widely known license plates, Kentucky Correctional Industries inmates also produce refurbished computers, Braille books, and wood products.

Labor was also a way to manage the restlessness and idleness of prison time. Meaningful and productive work came to be seen more recently as one of the best ways to make the long days of prison go faster, and paying inmates for their labor could help them make their hard lives less harsh through buying daily amenities and goods. Most important, labor also has been viewed as part of the reformative process. In 2002 about 3.5 percent of the 2.1 million prisoners in the United States produced goods and services worth $1.5 billion.[52]

Some scholars have declared that historians have focused too heavily on the humanitarian and reformist basis for the rise of the penitentiary and reformatory. They argue that this view does not adequately reflect economic motives for the emergence of the prison. In fact, prisons provide a captive labor pool, and restriction on inmate wages makes possible the production of goods at very low cost.

The theme of labor for profit is accompanied by a concern about idleness. Much of the history of prison industry revolves around the search for suitable ways to occupy inmates' time while also serving the financial interests of forces outside the walls. Four approaches have resulted: (1) the contract labor, piece price, and lease systems; (2) the public account system; (3) the state-use system; and (4) the public works and ways system.

The Contract Labor, Piece Price, and Lease Systems

From the first days of U.S. prisons, inmates' labor was sold to private employers, who provided the machinery and raw materials for the work they would do. The products made by this contract labor system were then sold on the open market. Alternatively, in the **piece price system**, the contractor established a purchase price for goods that inmates produced with raw materials provided by the contractor. These arrangements were extremely exploitative. Inmates worked in sweatshops, and the fees for their labor were paid to the prisons; "free" during the day, they returned to the prison at night. In the *lease system*, a variation of the piece price system, the contractor maintained the prisoners, working them for 12–16 hours at a stretch. These systems enabled many prisons in the later 1800s—even the vaunted Auburn—to operate in the black. The low wages increased the contractors' profit margins. The prisoners, of course, worked for nothing and gained nothing.

Not surprisingly, these arrangements led to extreme corruption as well as exploitation. With sizable contracts at stake, kickbacks and bribes became common practices. Further, wardens took advantage of easy opportunities to line their pockets—and caused predictable public scandals when they were caught.

Soon, organized labor began to attack the prison labor arrangements. In fact, late in the nineteenth century a coalition of humanitarian reformers and labor leaders lobbied successfully for laws prohibiting contract inmate labor. States then began to experiment with alternative forms of free-market inmate labor.

The Public Account System

When contract labor was outlawed, Oklahoma led the way in instituting the **public account system**. Instead of selling inmate labor to private entrepreneurs, the state prison itself in 1909 began to make twine, buying raw materials and using inmate labor. Similar twine-making factories existed in Minnesota and Wisconsin prisons. At first, the reform was enormously successful, reducing the costs of twine for Oklahoma farmers and generating profits that defrayed two-thirds of the costs of prison operations, but ultimately the experiment failed. The financial pressure that wardens had felt earlier did not die with the contract labor system, and they often succumbed to it by padding budgets and altering records. In any case, an industry that had such a narrow market could not sustain full employment of inmates. And when prisons began to turn a profit on goods that the private sector also produced, private industry and labor stopped cooperating.

piece price system
A labor system under which a contractor provided raw materials and agreed to purchase goods made by prison inmates at a set price.

public account system
A labor system under which a prison bought machinery and raw materials with which inmates manufactured a salable product.

Study one state's **prison industry policy** at the corresponding link at www .cengage.com/criminaljustice/ clear.

The State-Use System

In response to the problems associated with using inmate labor to produce goods for the competitive market, many states turned to a **state-use system**, in which prisoners are employed to produce goods and services used only in state institutions and agencies. Many experts consider this arrangement reasonable and beneficial, and many states mandate that their agencies must purchase goods produced by inmate labor when they are available. This requirement creates something of a state monopoly on certain products. Today the state-use system is the most common form of prison industry.

The state-use system has several advantages. Prison labor, which by many accounts is cheaper than free labor, is not allowed to compete with other labor pools in the open market. At the same time, the state can purchase some goods more cheaply. Under this system, state agencies often buy a great variety of prison-produced items—school chairs and desks, soap and paper towels, milk and eggs, and so on.

This system also has drawbacks. Even when prison products are used only by the government, the system preempts the free-labor market. Moreover, many of the goods produced within the system—license plates, for example—have no close equivalents outside, so skills the inmates acquire in prison often do not transfer to outside industries. Even when an analogous outside industry exists, prison industry is so inefficient and its methods so outmoded that prisoners often must shed what they learned there before they can succeed in private industry. Farming, for example, is a common prison industry, but the enterprise typically teaches few advanced agricultural methods; prisoners usually do manual chores, even though farmhand positions are drying up across the country. The prison farm may be good economics, but it is poor schooling.

state-use system
A labor system under which goods produced by prison industries are purchased by state institutions and agencies exclusively and never enter the free market.

The Public Works and Ways System

In a version of the state-use system called the **public works and ways system**, inmates work on public construction and maintenance projects: filling potholes, constructing or repairing buildings and bridges, and so on. This approach was introduced in the 1920s, when surfaced roads were needed.

Advocates praise the tremendous economic benefits of this system and point out that prisoners learn new skills while producing goods and services useful to society. However, prisoners do the more-arduous jobs on a project, and then outside craftspeople are hired for the skilled work. Some detractors say it is exploitation; the state receives a benefit but does not fairly compensate prisoners.

public works and ways system
A labor system under which prison inmates work on public construction and maintenance projects.

Prison Industry Today

Until very recently, the trend has been away from free-market use of prison labor and toward state monopolies. After 1940, the private use of inmate labor, once the most popular form of prison industry, vanished. One reason was that the public had become increasingly aware of the exploitative character of prison industry. Southern prison systems expanded dramatically after the Civil War, and former slaves accounted for much of this growth. The labor of most of these prisoners was contracted out in one way or another, leading some critics to argue that industrial capitalists had replaced plantation owners as exploiters of the former slaves.

With the rise of the labor movement, state legislatures passed laws restricting the sale of prisoner-made goods so as not to compete with free workers. As early as 1819, New York had required boots and shoes produced at Auburn to be labeled "State Prison." In another application of the principle of least eligibility, whenever unemployment began to soar, political pressures mounted to prevent prisons from engaging in enterprises that might otherwise be conducted by private business and free labor.

In 1900 the U.S. Industrial Commission endorsed the state-use plan, and in 1929 Congress passed the Hawes-Cooper Act, followed by additional legislation in 1935 and 1940, which banned prison-made goods from interstate commerce. In an excess of zeal, by 1940 every state had passed laws banning imports of prison-made goods from other states. These restrictions crippled production and ended the open-market system of employing prisoners. With the outbreak of World War II, however, President Franklin Roosevelt ordered the government to procure goods, for the military effort, from state and federal prisons. Later, under pressure from organized labor, President Harry Truman revoked the wartime order, and prisoners returned to idleness. By 1973 President Nixon's National Advisory Commission on Criminal Justice Standards and Goals found that few inmates throughout the corrections system had productive work.

The past decade has seen a renewed interest in channeling prison labor into industrial programs that would relieve idleness, allow inmates to earn wages that they could save until release, and reduce the costs of incarceration. In 1979 Congress lifted restrictions on the interstate sale of products made in state prisons and urged correctional administrators to explore private-sector ways to improve prison industry (see the Focus box "Prison Blues" below). In the same year, the Free Venture program of the Law Enforcement Assistance Administration made funds available to seven states to

FOCUS ON
CORRECTIONAL PRACTICE

Prison Blues

The website for one of Oregon's most competitive new retail businesses is http://www.prisonblues.com/. If you place an order, you will be buying from a government-run business operating out of Oregon's maximum-security prison, Eastern Oregon Correctional Institution, employing inmates who manufacture stylish denim jeans, shirts, and jackets.

You will also be participating in one of the most innovative semiprivate-sector programs in prison industry today: Unigroup Correctional Industries of Oregon. Made possible by Oregon Senate Bill 780 in 1984, the Prison Blues® brand was established by Inside Oregon Enterprises, a division of the Oregon Department of Corrections. It was started with a federal government grant funded by drug money seizures, and as a plan to defray incarceration costs in the state of Oregon. The inmates who make the products are paid minimum wage plus incentives. Eighty-five percent of the wage goes to victim restitution, prison maintenance, family support, and taxes. The rest they get to use personally—most of it going into a savings account available to them upon release. And, yes, inmates in Oregon's prison industries pay taxes.

Prison Blues is managed by a private-sector staff of professionals working in conjunction with correctional officers and employing an average of 50 inmates. The factory is run as closely as possible to one on the outside, though with higher security issues. The environment is bright and energetic, designed to maximize productivity, and most of the workers appreciate the time they can spend at work.

Prison Blues is certainly a winner from a business standpoint. But is it good correctional practice?

Oregon Department of Corrections officials point out that the recidivism rate of Oregon parolees is about two-thirds the national average, and they attribute some of this difference to "progressive Inmate Work Programs (IWP) with the goal of instilling inmates with important work skills and a positive work ethic."

In 1996 the factory experienced a brief shutdown due to a conflict between state and federal wage laws. Oregon voters passed Ballot Measure 49 in 1997 to resolve it, requiring prison businesses to develop partnerships with the private sector. In October 1997 the Array Corporation (d.b.a. Prison Blues) was awarded the exclusive contract to sell, market, and operate the Prison Blues brand. They now manufacture over 200,000 garments per year with the capacity to produce 500,000 for both institutions and the private sector.

To be eligible for hire, an inmate must have demonstrated good conduct and go through an interview hiring process. To keep his Prison Blues job, he has to be just as productive on the inside as people are required to be on the outside, as well as maintain good behavior within the institution. Inmates who stay in the program throughout their incarceration reenter the outside world with newfound job skills and a work ethic.

Source: Adapted from Brad Haga, "Prison Blues: Jeans Change Public Perceptions, Offer Innovative Solutions," *Corrections Compendium* 19 (October 1994): 1–4. Used with permission. Updates from the Prison Blues website: http://www.prisonblues.com.

develop industries. These programs would operate according to six principles: (1) a full workweek for inmate employees, (2) wages based on productivity, (3) private-sector productivity standards, (4) responsibility for hiring or firing inmate workers vested in industry staff, (5) self-sufficient or profitable shop operations, and (6) a postrelease job-placement mechanism. Once again, inmate labor would compete with free labor. By 1994, 16 states were engaged in Free Venture prison industry, and five states—Nevada, New Hampshire, South Carolina, Tennessee, and Washington—allowed inmates to earn wages approaching federal minimum wage.

The change in attitude toward prison industries may be related to the fact that many large U.S. firms, in search of cheap labor, have moved operations to Third World countries. The outsourcing of American jobs overseas has become a hot political issue. Because of increased shipping costs and problems of administering plants overseas, some manufacturers may view prison labor as an attractive alternative (see the Focus box "Telemarketing from Prison" below). Union opposition may weaken if it can be shown that prisoners are not taking jobs away from taxpaying free workers. Indeed, when analysts investigate prison industry, they typically find that goods made in prison are a minuscule portion of the gross domestic product, a small fraction of 1 percent of the total.

FOCUS ON CORRECTIONAL PRACTICE

Telemarketing from Prison

David Day has a bounce in his step and a glint in his eye unexpected in someone who makes nearly 400 telemarketing calls a day for less than $200 a month. That's because he has a coveted job where few exist: behind bars.

Tucked away in a corner of Oregon's largest prison, the call center looks like any other, except for the nearby guard stations, razor-wire fences, and prison yard. A guard watches over a prison call center at Snake River Correctional Institution in Ontario, Oregon.

No more than a football-field length away, employees commute from their "homes," or cells. The 40-hour workweek is Monday through Friday. A typical workday starts at 7:30 A.M. and ends at 4:00 P.M. Stellar work earns a half-day on Friday. The pay isn't great—$120 to $185 a month—but for 80 Snake River inmates, it's their first job and a diversion from life in this medium-security prison of 2,900.

Convicts work for two companies in the Oregon facility. Day and about 60 others pitch Perry Johnson consulting services to American businesses. A group of 20 inmates work for Timlin Industries, an Oregon company that sells promotional items to small businesses.

The center opened last year after a year-long push by the Oregon Department of Corrections to recruit businesses that would otherwise move offshore. The program reduces recidivism by 24 percent and teaches prisoners to work together.

"Guys are sharing business tips rather than talking about their next fix or who to knock off next," says Rob Killgore,

administrator of Oregon Corrections Enterprises, a semi-independent state agency that recruits for-profit business to prisons.

Day, 43, is one of 85 inmates who arrange business meetings from a call center at the Snake River Correctional Institution, a state penitentiary in this onion- and potato-producing town not far from the Idaho line. "I'm grateful for the opportunity. Many of us end up here because we didn't have jobs and lacked communications skills," he says on a recent morning, ponytail cascading down his state-issued denims.

About a dozen states—Oregon, Arizona, California, and Iowa, among others—have call centers in state and federal prisons, underscoring a push to employ inmates in telemarketing jobs that might otherwise go to low-wage countries such as India and the Philippines. Arizona prisoners make business calls, as do inmates in Oklahoma. A call center for the DMV is run out of an all-female prison in Oregon. Other companies are keeping manufacturing jobs in the United States. More than 150 inmates in a Virginia federal prison build car parts for Delco Remy International. Previously, some of those jobs were overseas.

At least 2,000 inmates nationwide work in call centers, and that number is rising as companies seek cheap labor without incurring the wrath of politicians and unions. At the same time, prison populations are ballooning, offering U.S. companies another way to slash costs.

(continued)

CORRECTIONAL PRACTICE (Continued)

"Prisons are prime candidates for low-skill jobs," says Sasha Costanza-Chock, a University of Pennsylvania graduate who last year completed a thesis on call centers at U.S. prisons.

Market conditions seem to favor prisons. After declining for years, call-center jobs in the United States increased by several hundred, to about 360,000, last year. At the same time, more white-collar jobs are going offshore than researchers originally thought. About 830,000 U.S. service-sector jobs, from telemarketers to software engineers, will move abroad by the end of 2005, up 41 percent from previous predictions, says Forrester Research.

About 3.5 percent of the 2.1 million prisoners in the United States produced goods and services worth an estimated $1.5 billion in 2002.

But the convicted workforce elicits as much dread as interest. Companies flinch at the prospect of a public-relations backlash should news leak out that they employ hardened criminals. Union representatives, meanwhile, call the hiring of prisoners a flagrant violation of minimum-wage laws and unfair competition to free workers.

"Quite literally, they're taking advantage of a captive audience," says Tony Daley, research economist for the Communications Workers of America, which represents 700,000 people nationwide.

Yet advances in technology and common sense have resolved those concerns today, advocates say. At Snake River prison, phone numbers are generated by computer and calls are recorded. Inmates talk to businesses, not consumers. And prisoners convicted of identification theft aren't eligible for jobs.

Katey Grabenhorst, 42, is eternally grateful one particular call-center job was available at an Oregon prison. She started working for the DMV while imprisoned and remains an employee out of jail.

The job "brought self-esteem, order, skills, and a stable income to my life," says Grabenhorst, who served nearly five years for attempted murder. "If this program wasn't available, I would have probably ended up back in prison."

"People can debate the value of prison labor, but I'm living proof it works," she says.

Source: Adapted from Jon Swartz, "Inmates vs. Outsourcing" *USA Today*, July 6, 2004, http://usatoday.com.

At this early date, the supposed efficiencies of private industry in corrections are less dramatic than expected. Inmate labor is cheaper than free labor, but recent reforms include higher wages for prisoners than those formerly paid by private contractors, and security requirements drive up costs. However, even if a renewed prison industry is neither efficient nor damaging to free-market labor, it makes sense to have inmates work. A Federal Bureau of Prisons study shows that employed inmates have fewer disciplinary infractions in prison, get better jobs when released, and stay out of trouble with the law longer than do unemployed prisoners.[53]

■ PRISON MAINTENANCE PROGRAMS

Running a prison is like running a town. The typical prison must provide every major service available in a community and more: fire department, electrical and plumbing services, janitorial maintenance, mail delivery, restaurant, drugstore, administrative record keeping, and so on. These operations must be coordinated. If only to keep the costs of these services manageable, prisoners do the bulk of the work. The one thing abundant in a prison is human resources, and perhaps the most frequent types of jobs in any given prison have to do with its day-to-day maintenance.

In most prisons, maintenance jobs constitute an elaborate pecking order of assignments and reveal something about prestige and influence within the facility. The choice jobs involve access to power. For example, a clerical job in the records room (which contains inmates' files) gives the inmate a corner on one of the most sought-after

© Michael Stravato/The New York Times/Redux Pictures

Inmates at the Cleveland Correctional Center in Texas have access to both a library and computers to assist their educational courses. In most prisons access to computers is extremely limited.

commodities in prison: information. The records room inmate can learn who is doing time for what, who is eligible for privileges (such as reclassification, reassignment, and parole), and what decisions are being made about whom. The contents of inmates' files are confidential, but it is hard to prevent the records room clerk from sneaking a look— or from trading the information for goods or favors.

Clerical support jobs are similarly prestigious. Desk assignments permit access to authority figures (and very likely to such favors as flexibility in scheduling, better food, and sometimes information) and make inmates who get them the first contributors to the institutional rumor mill. Often inmates must qualify as trusties before they are given clerical assignments.

Among the most desirable jobs are those that allow access to goods or services that can be sold within the prison economy. For example, an inmate who works in the laundry can charge two packs of cigarettes as insurance that another inmate's clothing will be returned neatly folded and without rips or tears.

Also desirable are jobs that provide access to contraband goods. For example, inmates on kitchen detail can filch extra food to trade or sell. Library assignments let prisoners make liberal use of law books and other popular reading materials. Assignments to the stockroom or to the dispensary, even with tight security on drugs and other medical items, can pay off in various ways.

Other assignments offer different kinds of benefits. The electrician's aide and the message runner, for instance, usually have flexible schedules and relatively varied tasks that make the time go more quickly.

The least desirable jobs are the most plentiful: janitorial services. New inmates must often prove themselves for later reassignment by facing mop detail and the like; such assignments are also given as disciplinary measures. Mopping halls and cleaning latrines is not particularly interesting work; repeated three or more times a day in the same areas, the tasks become painfully monotonous.

Even so, prison maintenance jobs are essential to managing the prison in two ways. First, they lower the cost of operations by eliminating the need to hire outside labor. Second, the job hierarchy provides rewards and punishments to enforce prison discipline. Prisoners who cooperate receive choice assignments; others get the dirty work.

■ PRISON RECREATIONAL PROGRAMS

When prisoners are not at work, in treatment, or in their cells, they are probably engaged in recreation. Organized recreation is a favorite pastime—and often central to the prison experience. Most men's prisons have sports teams—baseball, basketball, even football—and many regularly compete with outside teams. Many prisons also provide such activities as table tennis, weight training, music, drama, and journalism clubs.

Recreational programs have two primary functions in addition to filling time. First, they are integral to prison social life. Prisoners vary in intellect and physical capacities; variety in programs enables inmates to form positive social contacts with others who share their interests and abilities. Second, prison recreational and leisure pursuits can be rehabilitative in several ways. They can teach such social skills as cooperation and teamwork, they provide a means for prisoners to grow in experience and enhance their self-image, and they serve as a productive counterpoint to the general alienation of prison.

Recreational programs also present security risks. Whenever prisoners congregate, they can plan disruptions. Tempers can especially flare in recreation, where prisoners compete. Although prisons without leisure activities would be torture, recreation requires careful management.

Recently the public has reacted against recreational programming, feeling that free-time programs make prison too easy and even enjoyable. Politicians have thus pressed to shut down recreational programs, especially weight lifting. Administrators point out that inmates in these programs are often the best behaved; they also argue that trying to run a prison without such activities will cause prisoner unrest. Still, the popular sentiment that prison should be unbearable tends to eradicate any programming not directly related to rehabilitation.

■ PRISON PROGRAMMING RECONSIDERED

Our discussion of prison programs has focused on the types of activities used to occupy prisoners. Underlying this discussion is the question, "Is this use of prison time truly useful?" The answer is equivocal.

Offenders are often sent to prison under the assumption that educational and rehabilitative programs will prepare them to adjust to society when they are released. But most rehabilitative programs have serious shortcomings and limited effectiveness. Further, a large number of inmates are not even considered to need education, vocational training, or drug/alcohol rehabilitation. Of those who need help in these areas, often less than half actually participate in available programs. Study after study shows that even for programs that are effective, services provided in prison settings are substantially less effective than those same programs offered in the community.[54]

Nonrehabilitative programs—prison industry and maintenance—pose their own problems for administrators. The need for security severely constrains all prison practices, for example.

Yet a programless prison is unthinkable. Prisoners need structured activities so they can fill time with positive pursuits. Moreover, outside workers would not likely perform daily chores, for low wages and at some personal risk, to keep a prison operating.

Some experts have said prison programs ought to be voluntary. Their philosophical arguments in favor of free choice and against coercion and exploitation certainly sound reasonable. But given the realities of prison life—the need to run the prison, occupy time, and give both staff and prisoners hope that life will be better for inmates after they leave—it is unlikely prison programs will change in any dramatic way.

Summary

1 Describe how correctional programs help address the challenge of managing time in the correctional setting.

Institutional programs mitigate the oppressiveness of time. They also provide opportunities for prisoners to improve their lives, whether the programs involve counseling, education, or merely recreation. Prison administrators use institutional programs to help manage time. Work assignments occupy the middle hours of the day, treatment and recreational periods are held before and after work assignments, and special programs take up the remaining hours. Experienced administrators know that the more programs they offer, the less likely inmates' boredom will translate into hostility toward the staff.

2 Describe the ways that security acts as a constraint on correctional programs offered in institutional settings.

The heavy emphasis on security has two important consequences. First, unceasing surveillance further demoralizes the inmates and sharpens their sense of captivity. Second, security requirements make maintenance and industrial programs inefficient. Treatment success negatively affects the relationship between correctional counselors and clients. In short, the prison environment negatively affects every program that operates in that setting. The need for tight security dilutes the effectiveness of prison programs, except as a means to fill time.

3 Know the meaning of the "principle of least eligibility" and illustrate its importance.

According to this principle, prisoners, having been convicted of wrongful behavior, should be the least eligible of all citizens for social benefits beyond the bare minimum required by law. Taken to its extreme, the principle would prohibit many institutional benefits for offenders, such as educational courses and cosmetic surgery.

4 Understand the importance of the classification process and how "objective classification" works.

In most corrections systems, prison-bound offenders pass through a reception and orientation center where they are evaluated and classified. Such approaches serve mainly as a management tool to ensure that inmates are assigned to housing units appropriate to their custody level. At rehabilitative institutions, batteries of tests, psychiatric evaluations, and counseling are administered so that each prisoner can be assessed for treatment as well as custody. New predictive and equity-based systems seek to classify inmates more objectively. Predictive models distinguish inmates with respect to risk of escape, potential misconduct in the institution, and future criminal behavior. Equity-based models use only a few explicitly defined legal variables reflecting current and previous criminal characteristics. Objective systems are more efficient and cheaper than other systems.

5 Describe the major kinds of institutional programs that are offered in correctional institutions.

Rehabilitative programs aim at reforming behavior and help prisoners develop skills so that they can avoid a return to crime. Prison medical services help people behind bars maintain their physical health. Prison industry enables inmates to work, usually earning a wage for their efforts. Prison maintenance programs are used to keep the prison's physical plant in good running order. Prison recreational programs provide inmates with things to do in their spare time.

6 Analyze recent developments in the field of correctional rehabilitation.

After Martinson's 1974 study indicated that prison rehabilitation programs were ineffective, the number of treatment programs began to decrease. According to the new vision, prison was a place that should provide safe and secure custody while punishing offenders. Although interest in rehabilitation waned when the philosophy of corrections swung toward crime control, advocates of correctional rehabilitation now point to an increase in consistent evidence that programs can result in considerable reductions of new criminal activity by former offenders. They argue that the time has come for a reformulation of the ethics of correctional rehabilitation: from "nothing works" to "what works, for whom, and why." Recent systematic cost-benefit studies have encouraged advocates for more rehabilitation programs in corrections.

7 Describe the main types of correctional industries and define how each works.

Four approaches have been used for prison industry: (1) the contract labor system, in which inmate labor is sold to private employers who provide the machinery and raw materials for the work and sell the products; (2) the public account system, in which a prison provides machinery and raw materials with which inmates manufactured a salable products; (3) the state-use system, under which goods produced by prison industries are purchased by state institutions and agencies exclusively and never enter the free market; and (4) the public works and ways system, in which inmates work on public construction and maintenance projects such as filling potholes and repairing buildings.

8 Understand the current pressures facing correctional programming policies.

Most rehabilitative programs have serious shortcomings and limited effectiveness. Study after study shows that even for programs that are effective, services provided in prison settings are substantially less effective than those same programs offered in the community. Yet a programless prison is unthinkable. Prisoners need structured activities so they can fill their time with positive pursuits. Moreover, outside workers would not likely perform daily chores, for low wages and at some personal risk, to keep a prison operating.

KEY TERMS

behavior therapy (p. 382)
civil disabilities (p. 386)
classification (p. 376)
cognitive skill building (p. 382)
confrontation therapy (p. 382)
cost-benefit ratio (p. 390)
criminogenic needs (p. 389)

hepatitis C (p. 391)
piece price system (p. 394)
principle of least eligibility (p. 374)
prison program (p. 373)
psychotherapy (p. 380)
psychotropic medications (p. 381)
public account system (p. 394)

public works and ways system (p. 395)
reality therapy (p. 382)
social therapy (p. 382)
state-use system (p. 395)
therapeutic community (p. 383)
transactional analysis (p. 382)
vocational rehabilitation (p. 385)

FOR DISCUSSION

1. How strictly should the principle of least eligibility be applied? Support your viewpoint.
2. Are some rehabilitative programs more effective or valuable than others? Why or why not?
3. What factors limit the possibility of running prison industries as profit-making ventures? What could be done to improve the profitability of prison industries?
4. Should prisoners be forced to participate in programs? As a correctional officer, what would you do if an inmate did not want to leave his or her cell?
5. Is a programless prison a possibility?

FOR FURTHER READING

Burnside, Jonathan. *My Brother's Keeper: Faith-based Units in Prisons.* Portland, OR: Willan, 2005. A study of religious training and activity in prison walls in the United Kingdom, with a review of the recent history of prison-based religions and an assessment of the successes and failures of religious programming.

Crow, Iain. *The Treatment and Rehabilitation of Offenders.* Thousand Oaks, CA: Sage, 2001. A thorough summary of what we know about rehabilitation programs, and a series of prescriptions for designing rehabilitation programs.

Farabee, David. *Rethinking Rehabilitation: Why Can't We Reform Our Criminals?* Washington, DC: American Enterprise Institute, 2005. A call for a strategy of rehabilitation that is not based on "treatment" but rather on closer monitoring of probationers and parolees, swift application of sanctions, and indeterminate periods of community supervision.

Glaser, Daniel. *Profitable Penalties: How to Cut Both Crime Rates and Costs.* Thousand Oaks, CA: Pine Forge Press, 1997. Summarizes effective correctional practices and how those practices can be used to prevent crime, at lower correctional costs.

Greifinger, Robert, ed. *Improving Public Health through Correctional Health Care.* New York: Springer, 2007. Essays on the state of health care in the American prison system, including rehabilitation programming, drug treatment, and medical care.

Human Rights Watch. *Ill Equipped: U.S. Prisons and Offenders with Mental Illness.* New York: Author, 2003. A critical evaluation of the services provided for mentally ill prisoners in the United States, with a series of proposals for reform.

Lin, Ann Chih. *Reform in the Making: The Implementation of Social Policy in Prison.* Princeton, NJ: Princeton University Press, 2002. Describes strategies for implementing effective rehabilitation programs in the daily reality of prison life.

Myers, Martha. *Race, Labor, and Punishment in the New South.* Columbus: Ohio State University Press, 1998. Analyzes the relationship among the economy, the need for labor, business interests, and inmate labor in the South, 1870–1940.

NOTES

[1] The opening paragraphs describing the Bard College program are adapted from CBS News, "Maximum Security Education: How Some Inmates Are Getting a Top-Notch Education Behind Bars," *60 Minutes,* April 15, 2007.

[2] BJS *Bulletin,* December 2004, p. 5.

[3] *New York Times,* July 16, 1995, p. 3.

[4] Thomas Harris, *I'm OK, You're OK* (New York: Harper & Row, 1960).

[5] Dora Schriro, "Parallel Universe," http://www.afscme.org/publications/4264.cfm, November 2, 2009.

[6] Oregon Accountability Model, http://egov.oregon.gov/DOC/PUBAFF/oam_community.shtml, November 2, 2009.

[7] "Texas Prison Rehab Plans Pushed," http://www.4therapy.com/consumer/life_topics/article/8960/533/Texas+Prison+Rehab+Plans+Pushed, May 3, 2007.

[8] Nygel Lenz, "'Luxuries' in Prison: The Relationship between Amenity Funding and Public Support," *Crime and Delinquency* 48 (no. 4, October 2002): 499–525.

[9] Human Rights Watch, *Ill Equipped: U.S. Prisons and Offenders with Mental Illness* (New York: Author, 2003).

[10] Lawrence Bench and Terry D. Allen, "Investigating the Stigma of Prison Classification: An Experimental Design," *Prison Journal* 83 (no. 4, December 2003): 367–82.

[11] *Ramos v. Lamm,* 458 F.Supp. 128 (1979).

[12] James Byrne and Don Hummer, "In Search of the 'Tossed Salad Man' (and Others Involved in Prison Violence): New Strategies for Predicting and Controlling Violence in Prison," *Aggression and Violent Behavior* 12 (no. 5, 2007): 531–41.

[13] Thomas S. Szasz, *The Myth of Mental Illness* (New York: Harper & Row, 1969), 30.

[14] Robert Martinson, "What Works? Questions and Answers about Prison Reform," *Public Interest,* Spring 1974, p. 25.

[15] BJS *Special Report,* July 2001.

[16] Michael L. Prendergast, Elizabeth A. Hall, Harry K. Wexler, Gerald Melnick, and Yan Cao, "Amity Prison-Based Therapeutic Community: Five Year Outcomes," *Prison Journal* 84 (no. 1, March 2004): 36–60; William M. Burdon, Nena P. Messina, and Michael L. Prendergast, "The California Treatment Expansion Initiative: Aftercare Participation, Recidivism, and Predictors of Outcome," *Prison Journal* 84 (no. 1, March 2004): 61–80.

[17] BJS *Special Report,* January 2003.

[18] *New York Times,* November 16, 2001, p. A18.

[19] John Tyler and Jeffrey Kling, "Prison Education and Re-entry into the Mainstream Labor Market," in *Barriers to Reentry? The Labor Market for Released Prisoners in Post-industrial America,* edited by Shawn Bushway, Michael A. Stoll, and David Wieman (New York: Russell Sage Foundation, 2007), 227–56.

[20] John Tyler and Jeffrey Kling, "What Is the Value of a 'Prison GED'?" (paper presented to the Russell Sage Working Group on Incarceration and Labor, New York, March 5, 2004).

[21] Helene R. White and Rolf Loeber, *Substance Abuse and Criminal Offending: Policy Brief* (New Brunswick, NJ: Center for Behavioral Health Services and Criminal Justice Research, Rutgers University, April 2009).

[22] Kathryn E. McCollister, Michael T. French, James A. Inciardi, Clifford A. Butzin, Steven S. Martin, and Robert M. Hooper, "Postrelease Substance Abuse Treatment for Criminal Offenders: A Cost-Benefit Analysis," *Journal of Quantitative Criminology* 19 (no. 4, December 2003): 389–407.

[23] Harry K. Wexler, Gerald Melnick, and Yan Cao, "Risk and Prison Substance Abuse Treatment Outcomes: A Replication and Challenge," *Prison Journal* 84 (no. 1, March 2004): 106–20.

[24] Katherine E. McCollister, Michael T. French, Michael L. Prendergast, Elizabeth Hall and Stan Sacks, "Long-term Cost Effectiveness of Addiction Treatment for Criminal Offenders," *Justice Quarterly* 21 (no. 3, 2004): 659–82.

[25] James A. Inciardi, Stephen S. Martin, and Clifford A. Butzin, "Five-Year Outcomes of Therapeutic Community Treatment of Drug-Involved Offenders after Release from Prison," *Crime and Delinquency* 50 (no. 1, January 2004): 88–107.

[26] For a recent summary of evidence on drug abuse treatment, see *Principles of Drug Abuse Treatment for Criminal Justice Populations,* NIH Publication No. 07-5316 (Washington, DC: U.S. Government Printing Office, September 2007).

[27] Center for Sex Offender Management, *Understanding Treatment for Adults and Juveniles Who Have Committed Sex Offenses,* (Washington, DC: U.S. Department of Justice, Office of Justice Programs, November 2006).

[28] R. K. Hanson and K. Morton-Bourgon, *Predictors of Sexual Recidivism: An Updated Meta-analysis,* User Report 2004-02 (Ottawa: Public Works and Government Services Canada, 2004).

[29] Colin Baier and Bradley Wright, "'If You Love Me Keep My Commandments': A Meta-analysis of the Effect of Religion on Crime," *Journal of Research on Crime and Delinquency* 38 (January 2001): 3–21.

[30] Jacqui Goddard, "Florida's New Approach to Inmate Reform: A Faith-Based Prison," *Christian Science Monitor,* December 24, 2003.

[31] Diana B. Henriques and Andrew W. Lehren, "Religion for Captive Audiences, with Taxpayers Footing the Bill," *New York Times,* December 10, 2006, pp. 1, 42.

[32] *Americans United for Separation of Church and State v. Prison Fellowship Ministries* 509 F.3d 406 (8th Cir. 2007).

[33] See *Cutter v. Wilkinson,* 544 U.S. 709 (2005), discussed in Lynn S. Branham, "'The Devil Is in the Details': A Continued Dissection of the Constitutionality of Faith-Based Prison Units," *Ave Maria Law Review* 6 (no. 2, Spring 2008): 409.

[34] Todd R. Clear, "Does 'Getting Religion' Rehabilitate Offenders?" (National Institute of Justice Perspectives Lecture Series, Washington, DC, March 21, 2002).

[35] Byron R. Johnson, "Religious Programming, Institutional Adjustment and Recidivism among Former Inmates in Prison Fellowship Programs," *Justice Quarterly* 21 (no. 2, 2004): 329–54.

[36] Jonathon Burnside, *My Brother's Keeper: Faith-Based Unites in Prisons* (Portland, OR: Willan, 2005).

[37] Francis Cullen and Karen Gilbert, *Reaffirming Rehabilitation* (Cincinnati, OH: Anderson, 1982).

[38] Frank S. Pearson, Douglas S. Lipton, Charles M. Cleland, and Dorine S. Yee, "The Effects of Behavioral/Cognitive Programs on Recidivism," *Crime and Delinquency* 48 (no. 3, July 2002): 476–96.

[39] Francis Cullen and Paul Gendreau, "From Nothing Works to What Works: Changing Professional Ideology in the 21st Century," *Prison Journal* 81 (no. 3, September 2001): 313–38.

[40] David P. Farrington, Anthony Petrosino, and Brandon C. Welsh, "Systematic Reviews and Cost-Benefit Analyses of Correctional Interventions," *Prison Journal* 81 (no. 3, September 2001): 339–59.

[41] Brandon C. Welsh and David P. Farrington, "Monetary Costs and Benefits of Crime Prevention Programs," *Crime and Justice: A Review of Research* 27 (2000): 305–61.

[42] Steve Aos, Polly Phipps, Robert Barnowski, and Roxanne Lieb, *The Comparative Costs and Benefits of Programs to Reduce Crime* (Olympia: Washington State Institute for Public Policy, May 2001), 8.

[43] Drug Policy Alliance, *Proposition 36: Improving Lives, Delivering Results* (New York: Author, March 2006).

[44] *Estelle v. Gamble,* 95 S. Ct. 285 (1976).

[45] David Rhode, "A Health Danger from a Needle Becomes a Scourge Behind Bars," *New York Times,* August 6, 2001, pp. A1, B3.

[46] Bureau of Justice Statistics, *Data Brief,* January 2007, p. 3.

[47] BJS *Bulletin,* January 2001.

[48] John Kleinig and Margaret Leland Smith, *Discretion, Community, and Correctional Ethics* (Lanham, MD: Rowman and Littlefield, 2001).

[49] Bureau of Justice Statistics, *Data Brief*, January 2007, p. 3.

[50] Cheryl Gay Stolberg, "Behind Bars, New Effort to Care for the Dying," *New York Times,* April 1, 2001, pp. 1, 24.

[51] Robert Greifinger, ed. *Improving Public Health through Correctional Health Care* (New York: Springer, 2007).

[52] Jon Swartz, "Inmates vs. Outsourcing," *USA Today,* July 6, 2004.

[53] William G. Saylor and Gerald G. Gaes, *PREP Study Links UNICOR Work Experience with Successful Post-release Outcome* (Washington, DC: U.S. Bureau of Prisons, Office of Research and Evaluation, n.d.).

[54] Mark W. Lipsky and Francis T. Cullen, "The Effectiveness of Correctional Rehabilitation: A Review of Systematic Reviews," *Annual Review of Law and Social Science* 3 (December 2007): 297–320.

AP Images/Jason Hirschfeld

NFL quarterback Michael Vick was released from the federal penitentiary, Leavenworth, Kansas, in May 2009, after serving 18 months for operating a dog-fighting ring. Here, Vick steps out onto his deck with a federal parole agent while testing the electronic monitor worn on his ankle.

LEARNING OBJECTIVES

After reading this chapter you should be able to . . .

1 Discuss parole and explain how it operates today.

2 Be familiar with the origins and evolution of parole in the United States.

3 Discuss the different mechanisms that are used to release offenders from correctional facilities.

4 Explain how releasing authorities are organized.

5 Be familiar with the steps that are taken to ease the offender's reentry into the community.

MICHAEL VICK, NFL quarterback, was released from a federal prison in Leavenworth, Kansas, in May 2009 after serving 18 months for his part in financing and running a dog-fighting ring. His release from prison went undetected by a large group of reporters outside the Leavenworth facility. After his release, Vick returned to his home in Hampton, Virginia, to serve two additional months in home confinement. During this time, Vick worked a construction job where he made $10 an hour. He also worked at the Boys and Girls Clubs helping to run children's health and fitness programs.[1]

Michael Vick's reentry is certainly not typical of the more than 725,000 adult felons who leave state and federal prisons each year (about 2,000 daily).[2] Very few released felons attract public attention, and fewer yet serve their home detention at a suburban estate equipped with a swimming pool. Ex-prisoners are mostly men with few or no job skills. About one-third of released state inmates have a physical or mental impairment. About two-thirds of all state releasees

RELEASE FROM INCARCERATION

will return to a few metropolitan areas in their states, where they will live in poor, inner-city neighborhoods. As they leave prison, most offenders receive a new set of clothes, up to $100 in "gate money" (only in some states), instructions as to when and where to report to a parole officer, and a bus ticket home. With the great expansion of incarceration during the past three decades, the number of offenders now returning to the community has increased dramatically.

Reentry has been described as a "transient state between liberty and recommitment. It is a period of limited duration of supervision whereby an inmate moves to either full liberty in the community or is returned to prison for a new crime or for violating the conditions of release."[3] During the entry period, prisoners are on parole. For most of the twentieth century, the term *parole* referred to both a release mechanism and a method of community supervision. It is still used in this general sense, but with recent changes in sentencing and release policies, the dual usage no longer applies in many states. Now we must distinguish between a releasing mechanism and supervision. Although releasing mechanisms have changed, most former prisoners must still serve a period under supervision.

In this chapter we examine the mechanisms for prison release. Supervision of ex-inmates on parole and their adjustment to the community is discussed in Chapter 16.

Chapter

15

■ RELEASE FROM ONE PART OF THE SYSTEM TO ANOTHER

Except for the 7 percent of incarcerated felons who die in prison, all inmates will eventually be released to live in the community. Currently about 77 percent of felons are released on parole and remain under correctional supervision for a specific period. About 19 percent are released at the expiration of their sentence, having "maxed out," and are free to live in the community without supervision. There are, however, about 2,700 sex offenders in 16 states who remain in custody long after their sentence has been completed. They are being held in civil commitment programs to treat what has been judged to be a mental abnormality.[4]

parole
The conditional release of an inmate from incarceration, under supervision, after part of the prison sentence has been served.

Parole is the conditional release of an offender from incarceration but not from the legal custody of the state. Thus, offenders who comply with parole conditions and do not further violate the law receive an absolute discharge from supervision at the end of their sentences. If a parolee breaks a rule, parole may be revoked and the person returned to a correctional facility. Parole, then, rests on three concepts:

1 *Grace or privilege:* The prisoner could be kept incarcerated, but the government extends the privilege of release.

2 *Contract of consent:* The government enters into an agreement with the prisoner whereby the prisoner promises to abide by certain conditions in exchange for being released.

3 *Custody:* Even though the offender is released from prison, he or she is still a responsibility of the government. Parole is an extension of correctional programs into the community.

The Oklahoma Pardon and Parole Board provides information to the public about its responsibilities; see the corresponding website listed at www.cengage.com/criminaljustice/clear.

Only felons are released on parole; adult misdemeanants are usually released directly from local institutions on expiration of their sentences. With the incarcerated population more than quadrupling during the past 30 years, it is not surprising that the number of parolees has also grown, as shown in **Figure 15.1**. In 2006, 798,202 individuals were under parole supervision, a 262 percent increase since 1980.[5] With the massive incarcerations of the past decades, the number on parole is likely to reach one million within the next five years.

Only state and federal (not local) governments effect parole, through a variety of organizational structures. In many states, the parole board (the releasing authority) is part of the department of corrections; in others, it is an autonomous body whose members the governor appoints.

FOCUS ON CORRECTIONAL POLICY

Kansas v. Hendricks

Over a 30-year period, Leroy Hendricks was convicted of six sexual offenses against children and spent much of his adult life in prison. Every time he finished serving a prison sentence or gained parole release, he eventually victimized more children and returned to prison. After serving nearly 10 years in prison for his most recent crime—molesting two teenage boys—he was scheduled to move to a halfway house in the community as the first step toward release.

As Hendricks neared the end of his latest prison sentence, the Kansas legislature passed a new law permitting the

state to hold sex offenders in mental hospitals *after* they have served their prison sentences. As a result of Kansas's new Sexually Violent Predator Act, Hendricks was transferred from a prison to a mental hospital under a civil commitment process at the end of his sentence. Hendricks had served the prison sentence imposed for his crime. Yet, after serving his full sentence, he did not gain his freedom. The new law permitted Kansas to keep him locked up indefinitely.

Hendricks believed that detaining him after his prison sentence had been served was unfair. He took his case to

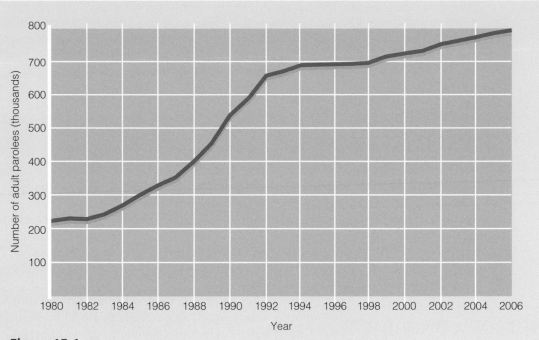

Figure 15.1

Numbers of Adults under Parole Supervision, 1980–2006

As with the incarcerated population, since 1980 the number of offenders on parole has more than tripled.

Sources: Ann L. Pastore and Kathleen Maguire, eds., *Sourcebook of Criminal Justice Statistics,* Table 6.1.2006, http://www.albany.edu/sourcebook/pdf/t612006.pdf, July 24, 2009; Bureau of Justice Statistics, *Probation and Parole in the United States, 2007 Statistical Tables* (Washington, DC: U.S. Government Printing Office, December 2008), 4.

As you read this chapter, keep in mind that, like so many other correctional activities, the decision to release is made in the context of complex and competing goals. Traditionally, parole has been justified in terms of rehabilitation. In theory, parole boards evaluate the offender's progress toward rehabilitation and readiness to abide by laws. In practice, they consider other factors as well. Even where determinate sentencing or parole guidelines are in effect, correctional officials can influence release; the decision is not as cut-and-dried as proponents have claimed.

court, claiming that the law was punishing him a second time for his crime. If that was true, the Kansas law could be violating the constitutional right not to be placed in "double jeopardy"—to be tried or punished twice for the same offense. Hendricks also argued that the law improperly imposed a new punishment on him *after* he committed his crime and served his sentence. Thus, he claimed that the Sexually Violent Predator Act was an "ex post facto law," prohibited by the U.S. Constitution because it applies new rules and punishments that did not exist at the time an offender violated previously existing laws.

In 1997 the Supreme Court tackled the issues raised by Hendricks. Hendricks remained locked up. Four of the nine justices believed Kansas had unfairly created new rules after the fact when it kept Hendricks in custody. The majority of the Supreme Court—only five justices—decided that this was not a second or after-the-fact punishment, because Kansas sought to use the law to provide "treatment" rather than to impose "punishment." Nineteen states now have laws similar to the one upheld in the Hendricks case. An estimated 2,700 sexual offenders are being held beyond the term of their sentence.

Source: *Kansas v. Hendricks,* 521 U.S. 346 (1997).

Many questions bear on the release decision no matter what procedures are followed. How will the public react? Who will be blamed if the offender commits another crime? Is the prison so crowded that an early release is necessary to open up space? How will the offender's release affect judges and prosecutors? The Focus box "*Kansas v. Hendricks*" on pages 408–409 considers the U.S. Supreme Court decision that a state can deny release to an offender who has completed his sentence.

■ ORIGINS OF PAROLE

Parole in the United States evolved during the nineteenth century following the English, Australian, and Irish practices of conditional pardon, apprenticeship by indenture, transportation of criminals from one country to another, and the issuance of tickets-of-leave. These were all methods of moving criminals out of prison. Such practices generally did not develop as part of any coherent theory of punishment or to promote any particular goal of the criminal sanction. Instead they were responses to problems of overcrowding, labor shortages, and the cost of incarceration.

As noted in Chapter 2, England relied on transportation as a major sanction until the mid-1800s. When the United States gained independence, Australia and other Pacific colonies became outlets for England's overcrowded prisons; offenders were given conditional pardons known as tickets-of-leave and sent to those outposts of the empire.

A key figure in developing parole in the 1800s was **Captain Alexander Maconochie**, who administered British penal colonies in Tasmania and elsewhere in the South Pacific and later in England. Maconochie criticized definite prison terms and devised a system of rewards for good conduct, labor, and study. He developed a classification system by which prisoners could pass through stages of increasing responsibility and freedom: (1) strict imprisonment, (2) labor on chain gangs, (3) freedom within an area, (4) a ticket-of-leave or parole with conditional pardon, and (5) full liberty. Like modern correctional practices, this procedure assumed that prisoners should be prepared gradually for release. The roots of the American system of parole can be seen in the transition from imprisonment to conditional release to full freedom.

Maconochie's idea of requiring prisoners to earn their early release caught on first in Ireland. There, **Sir Walter Crofton** built on Maconochie's idea that an offender's progress in prison and a ticket-of-leave were linked. After a period of strict imprisonment, offenders transferred to an intermediate prison where they could earn marks of commendation based on work, behavior, and education. Prisoners who graduated through Crofton's three successive levels were released on parole, with conditions. Most significant was the requirement that parolees submit monthly reports to the police. In Dublin a special civilian inspector helped releasees find jobs, visited them periodically, and supervised their activities. Crofton contributed the concepts of the intermediate prison, assistance, and supervision to the modern system of parole.

The English and Irish developments soon traveled across the Atlantic. Conditional pardons and term reductions for good time had been a part of American corrections since the early 1800s, but such offenders were released without supervision. Gaylord Hubbell,

CAPTAIN ALEXANDER MACONOCHIE (1787–1860)

Born in Scotland, Maconochie was a naval officer, geographer, and penal reformer. In 1836 he was appointed to a position in the administration of Van Diemen's Land (now Tasmania). Later, he was made superintendent of the Norfolk Island penal colony in the South Pacific. Under his direction, negative marks were given to prisoners initially but removed from the records of those who performed their tasks well, and they were released when they demonstrated their willingness to accept society's rules.

SIR WALTER CROFTON (1815–1897)

Appointed director of the Irish Convict Prisons in 1854, Crofton developed a system for offenders to work toward rehabilitation and early release by moving through three stages of increasing levels of vocational training and privileges. Prisoners were able to earn "marks" or points for good behavior. This "Irish System" significantly influenced the development of parole in the United States.

As administrator of British penal colonies in the South Pacific, Captain Alexander Maconochie devised a system of rewards for good conduct, labor, and study. Prisoners meeting his criteria were granted a ticket-of-leave, releasing them to the community.

the warden of Sing Sing, and Franklin Sanborn, the secretary of the State Board of Charities for Massachusetts, championed the Irish system. In 1870 the National Prison Association incorporated references to the Irish system into the Declaration of Principles, along with such other reforms as the indeterminate sentence and classification based on a mark system.[6]

With New York's passage of an indeterminate sentence law in 1876, Zebulon Brockway, the superintendent of Elmira Reformatory, began to release prisoners on parole when he believed they were ready to return to society. Initially, the New York system did not require police supervision, as in Ireland, because parolees were placed in the care of private reform groups. As the number of parolees increased, however, the state replaced the volunteer supervisors with correctional employees.

In the United States, as states adopted indeterminate sentencing, parole followed. By 1900, 20 states had parole systems and, by 1925, 46 states did; Mississippi and Virginia finally followed suit in 1942.[7] Beginning in 1910 each federal prison had its own parole board made up of the warden, the medical officer, and the superintendent of prisons of the Department of Justice. The boards made release suggestions to the attorney general. In 1930 Congress created the U.S. Board of Parole, which replaced the separate boards.[8]

Although used in the United States for over a century, parole remains controversial. When an offender who has committed a particularly heinous crime, such as Charles Manson, becomes eligible for parole or when someone on parole has again raped, robbed, or murdered, the public is outraged. During the 1970s both parole and the indeterminate sentence were criticized on several grounds: release was tied to treatment success, parole boards were abusing their discretion, and inmates were being held in "suspended animation." Remember, however, that although parole may be justified in terms of rehabilitation, deterrence, or protection of society, it has other effects as well. Insofar as it reduces time spent in prison, it affects plea bargaining, the size of prison populations, and the level of discipline in correctional facilities.

Crime victims can access **resources for opposing release of an inmate** at the corresponding website listed at www.cengage.com/criminaljustice/clear.

■ RELEASE MECHANISMS

From 1920 to 1973 the United States had a nationwide sentencing and release procedure. All states and the federal government used indeterminate sentencing, authorized discretionary release by parole boards, and supervised prisoners after release, and they did all of this to rehabilitate offenders.

With the 1970s came critiques of rehabilitation, a move to determinate sentencing, and the public's view that the system was "soft" on criminals. By 2002, 16 states and the federal government had abolished discretionary release by parole boards. Another five states had abolished discretionary release for certain offenses.[9] Further, in some of the states that kept discretionary release, parole boards have been reluctant

The **United States Parole Commission** still handles parole for those federal prisoners whose offense was committed prior to November 1, 1987; see the corresponding website listed at www.cengage.com/criminaljustice/clear.

to grant it. In Texas, for example, 57 percent of all cases considered for parole release in 1988 were approved; by 1998 that figure had dropped to just 20 percent.[10] Similarly, the Pennsylvania Board of Probation and Parole reduced its grant rate from the 75–80 percent range to less than 50 percent. Using a different approach, the Georgia Board of Pardons and Paroles has instituted a 90 percent rule for offenders convicted of 20 crimes. This means that these inmates, "regardless of risk or disparity in the sentence," must serve 90 percent of their time before the board will grant release.[11] Critics charge that eliminating discretionary parole has had little effect on the crime rate but has contributed greatly toward increases in prison populations.[12]

There are now five basic mechanisms for release from prison: (1) discretionary release, (2) mandatory release, (3) probation release, (4) other conditional release, and (5) expiration release. **Figure 15.2** shows the percentage of felons released by the various mechanisms.

Discretionary Release

discretionary release
The release of an inmate from prison to conditional supervision at the discretion of the parole board within the boundaries set by the sentence and the penal law.

States retaining indeterminate sentences allow **discretionary release** by the parole board within the boundaries set by the sentence and the penal law. As a conditional release to parole supervision, this approach lets the parole board assess the prisoner's readiness for release within the minimum and maximum terms of the sentence. In reviewing the prisoner's file and asking questions about the prisoner, the parole board focuses on the nature of the offense, the inmate's behavior, and participation in rehabilitative programs. This process places great faith in the ability of parole board members to predict accurately the future behavior of offenders (see the Focus box "A Roomful of Strangers").

Mandatory Release

mandatory release
The required release of an inmate from incarceration to community supervision on the expiration of a certain period, as stipulated by a determinate-sentencing law or parole guidelines.

Mandatory release occurs after an inmate has served time equal to the total sentence minus "good time," if any, or to a certain percentage of the total sentence as specified by law. Mandatory release is found in federal jurisdictions and states with determinate sentences and good-time provisions (see Chapter 4). Without a parole board to decide if the offender is ready for release and has ties to the community, such as family or a

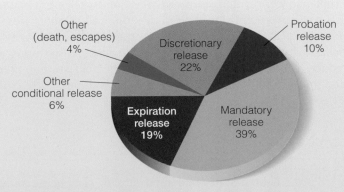

Figure 15.2
Methods of Release from State Prison

Felons are released from prison to the community, usually under supervision through various means, depending on the law.

Source: Bureau of Justice Statistics, *Probation and Parole in the United States, 2005* (Washington, DC: U.S. Government Printing Office, November 2006), 8.

FOCUS ON PEOPLE IN CORRECTIONS

A Roomful of Strangers

After four years and three months in Stanhope Correctional Facility, Ben Brooks was ready to go before the Board of Parole. He woke with butterflies in his stomach, realizing that at nine o'clock he was to walk into the hearing room to confront a roomful of strangers. As he lay on his bunk he rehearsed the answers to the questions he thought the board members might ask: "How do you feel about the person you assaulted? What have you done with your time while incarcerated? Do you think you have learned anything here that will convince the board that you will follow a crime-free life in the community? What are your plans for employment and housing?" According to prison scuttlebutt, these were the types of questions asked, and you had to be prepared to answer that you were sorry for your past mistakes, had taken advantage of the prison programs, had a job waiting for you, and planned to live with your family. You had to "ring bells" with the board.

At breakfast, friends dropped by Ben's table to reassure him that he had it made. As one said, "Ben, you've done everything they've said to do. What else can they expect?" That was the problem, *What did they expect*?

At eight-thirty, Officer Kearney came by the cell. "Time to go, Ben." They walked out of the housing unit and down the long prison corridors to a group of chairs outside the hearing room. Other prisoners were already seated there. "Sit here, Ben. They'll call when they're ready. Good luck."

At ten minutes past nine the door opened and an officer called, "First case, Brooks." Ben got up, walked into the room. "Please take a seat, Mr. Brooks," said the African American seated in the center at the table. Ben knew he was Reverend Perry, a man known as being tough but fair. To his left was a white man, Mr. MacDonald, and to his right a Hispanic woman, Ms. Lopez. The white man led the questioning.

"Mr. Brooks. You were convicted of armed robbery and sentenced to a term of five to ten years. Please tell the board what you have learned during your incarceration."

Ben paused and then answered hesitantly, "Well, I learned that to commit such a stupid act was a mistake. I was under a lot of pressure when I pulled the robbery and now am sorry for what I did."

"You severely injured the woman you held up. What might you tell her if she were sitting in this room today?"

"I would just have to say, I'm sorry. It will never happen again."

"But this is not the first time you have been convicted. What makes you think it will never happen again?"

"Well this is the first time I was sent to prison. You see things a lot differently from here."

Ms. Lopez spoke up. "You have a good prison record—member of the Toastmaster's Club, gotten your high school equivalency diploma, kept your nose clean. Tell the board about your future plans should you be released."

"My brother says I can live with him until I get on my feet, and there is a letter in my file telling you that I have a job waiting at a meat-processing plant. I will be living in my hometown but I don't intend to see my old buddies again. You can be sure that I am now on the straight and narrow."

"But you committed a heinous crime. That woman suffered a lot. Why should the board believe that you won't do it again?"

"All I can say is that I'm different now."

"Thank you Mr. Brooks," said Reverend Perry. "You will hear from us by this evening." Ben got up and walked out of the room. It had only taken eight minutes, yet it seemed like hours. Eight minutes during which his future was being decided. Would it be back to the cell or out on the street? It would be about ten hours before he would receive word from the board as to his fate.

job, mandatory release is a matter of bookkeeping to check the correct amount of good time and to make sure the sentence has been accurately interpreted. The prisoner is released conditionally to parole supervision for the rest of the sentence.

Probation Release

Probation release occurs when the sentencing judge requires a period of postcustody supervision in the community. Probation release is often tied to shock incarceration, a practice in which first-time offenders are sentenced to a short period in jail ("the

probation release
The release of an inmate from incarceration to probation supervision, as required by the sentencing judge.

shock") and then allowed to reenter the community under supervision. Since 2000, releases to probation have increased from 6 to 10 percent.[13]

Other Conditional Release

other conditional release
A probationary sentence used in some states to get around the rigidity of mandatory release by placing convicts in various community settings under supervision.

Because of the growth of prison populations, many states have devised ways to get around the rigidity of mandatory release. They place inmates in the community through furlough, home supervision, halfway houses, emergency release, and other programs.[14] These **other conditional releases** also avoid the appearance of the politically sensitive label *discretionary parole*.

Expiration Release

expiration release
The release of an inmate from incarceration without any further correctional supervision; the inmate cannot be returned to prison for any remaining portion of the sentence for the current offense.

An increasing percentage of prisoners are given an **expiration release**. These are inmates who are released from any further correctional supervision and cannot be returned to prison for their current offense. Such offenders have served the maximum court sentence, minus good time—they have "maxed out."

In the wake of the "tough on crime" policies of the last three decades, the percentage of inmates released to parole supervision, among all releasees, has dropped. Even when eligible for parole, many prisoners have bypassed the board and the controlled, supervised release it provides; instead, they have decided to "stick it out" to the expiration of their sentence and be released to the community without supervision. Nationally, up to 19 percent of prison releases are now the result of an expired term. Such prisoners are released unconditionally.[15] Critics are concerned that many offenders who "max out" have spent long terms in prison for serious, violent offenses or have spent extended periods in administrative segregation. They are often hardened, embittered, and likely to return to crime.[16]

Changes in sentencing policies during the 1970s have resulted in shifts in the percentage of prisoners released by each of the five mechanisms just described. As shown in **Figure 15.3**, recent years have seen a major decline in the percentage of prisoners released through the discretionary actions of parole boards, as well as an increase in mandatory, probation, and expiration release.

An increasing number of offenders are leaving prison at the expiration of their sentences. They have "maxed out" and leave without the requirement of parole supervision. Releasee Ronald Williams picks up his gate money at San Quentin. What is his future?

© Sacramento Bee/ZUMA Press

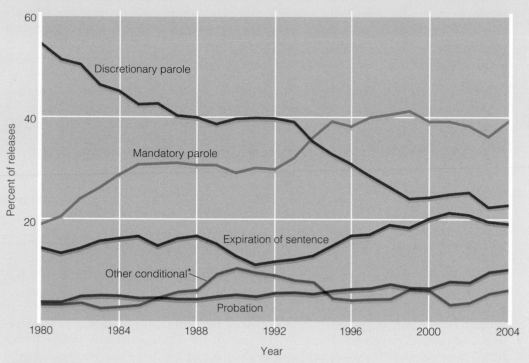

Figure 15.3

Releases from State Prison, by Method of Release

Changes in sentencing structures have resulted in a major drop in the percentage of discretionary releases, with increases in mandatory, probation, and expiration releases.

*Other conditional releases include provisional releases, supervised work furloughs, releases to home arrest or boot camp programs, conditional pardons, conditional medical releases, and unspecified releases.

Source: Bureau of Justice Statistics, *Probation and Parole in the United States, 2005* (Washington, DC: U.S. Department of Justice, November 2006), 8.

■ THE ORGANIZATION OF RELEASING AUTHORITIES

The structuring of a releasing authority raises certain questions. For example, should it be consolidated with the correctional authority or operate autonomously? How should field services be administered? Should the parole board sit full or part time? How should board members be appointed? Over the past decade, states have tended to create strong links between the paroling authority and the department of corrections, emphasizing parole board professionalism.

Consolidated versus Autonomous

Parole boards tend to be organized either inside a department of corrections (consolidated) or as an independent agency of government (autonomous). Some argue that a parole board must be independent to insulate members from the activities and influence of correctional staff. An independent parole board may be less influenced by staff considerations such as reducing the prison population and punishing inmates who do not follow rules. Critics counter that an independent parole board can become unresponsive to correctional needs and programs and is too far removed from prison activities to understand individual cases.

Whether a parole board is independent or a part of a correctional department, it cannot exist in a vacuum. Board members cannot ignore the public's attitudes and fears about crime. If a parolee commits a crime that arouses public indignation, the board members must make decisions more cautiously in order to avoid public condemnation. Parole boards may also be influenced by departments of corrections and must maintain good relations with them. For example, if an autonomous board conflicts with the department, the department might not provide the board with the information they need. Information about particular offenders might become "unavailable," or the state might provide biased information about particular offenders whom officials wish to see punished. By contrast, a board closely tied to correctional officials would more likely receive information and cooperation. However, such a board runs the risk of being viewed by prisoners and the general public as merely the rubber stamp of the department.

Field Services

Questions similar to those concerning the organization of the releasing authority surround the organization of field services. For example, should community supervision be administered by an independent paroling authority or by the department of corrections? When the parole board administers field services, proponents say, consistent policies can be developed. The need for programs that address the transition from prison to the community is increasing. Many departments have instituted such preparole programs as work release and educational release. Therefore, it is argued, the institutional staff and the parole board must be coordinated—which is easier to do if they are in the same department.

Full Time versus Part Time

A third set of questions concerns full-time versus part-time boards. Because of the increased complexity of corrections, many people, in both discretionary- and mandatory-release states, hold that administration of parole should be a full-time enterprise. The type of person who serves full time on a parole board differs considerably from the one who serves part time. Membership on a board that meets full time attracts criminal justice professionals, who usually are well paid. However, members of part-time boards, paid by the day, are thought to represent the community better, because they have other careers and are independent of the criminal justice system.

Appointment

Members of the paroling authority may be appointed by the governor or by the head of the correctional department. Some people believe that gubernatorial selection insulates the members from the department, provides "better" members, and permits greater responsiveness to public concerns. Others believe the parole mechanism should be apolitical and operated by people who really know something about corrections.

Selection of members for discretionary parole boards is often based on the assumption that people with training in behavioral sciences can tell which candidates are rehabilitated and ready to return to society. However, in many states, political considerations dictate that members should include representatives of specific racial groups or geographic areas.

■ THE DECISION TO RELEASE

An inmate's eligibility for release to community supervision depends on requirements set by law and the sentence imposed by the court. In states with determinate sentences or parole guidelines, release is mandatory once the offender has served the required amount of time. In nearly half of the states, however, the release decision is discretionary, and the

Until the 1970s, discretionary release was the primary way that offenders left prison. Diane Downes, shown on the screen, appears before the parole board via video conferencing to plead for her release after serving 25 years for shooting her children. Parole was denied.

parole board has authority to establish a release date. The date is based on the individual's rehabilitation, behavior while an inmate, and plan for reentry into the community.

Discretionary Release

Based on the assumptions of indeterminate sentences and rehabilitative programs, discretionary release is designed to allow the parole board to release inmates to conditional supervision in the community when they are deemed "ready" to live as law-abiding citizens.[17]

PROCEDURE ■ Eligibility for a release hearing in discretionary states varies greatly. Appearance before the parole board is a function of the individual sentence, statutory criteria, and the inmate's conduct before incarceration. Often the offender is eligible for release at the end of the minimum term of the sentence minus good time. In other states eligibility is at the discretion of the parole board or is calculated at one-third or one-half of the maximum sentence. However, many states provide a variety of mechanisms for release, as shown in **Table 15.1**.

As an example of the computation of parole eligibility, look again at the case of Ben Brooks (see **Figure 15.4**). At the time of sentencing, Brooks had been held in jail for six months awaiting trial and disposition of his case. He was given a sentence of a minimum of 5 years and a maximum of 10 years for robbery with violence. Brooks did well at the maximum-security prison to which he was sent. He did not get into trouble and was thus able to amass good-time credit at the rate of one day for every four that he spent on good behavior. In addition he was given meritorious credit of 30 days when he passed his high school diploma equivalency test. After serving three years and four months of his sentence, he appeared before the board of parole and was granted release into the community.

RELEASE CRITERIA ■ What factors guide the parole board decision? A parole board gives each inmate up for release a formal statement of the criteria for making the decision. These standards normally include at least eight factors concerning the inmate:

1 Nature and circumstances of offense and current attitude toward it
2 Prior criminal record
3 Attitudes toward family members, victim, and authority in general

TABLE 15.1 *Ten Release Mechanisms in South Carolina*

Until a task force on overcrowding consolidated some of the provisions, South Carolina recognized more than 10 ways to leave a prison (besides escape or death). All the following types of release have been specified in the state statutes or administrative procedures.

Type of Release	Eligibility	Calculation
Discretionary parole	All felons	"Life," eligible at 20 years. Less than 10 years, eligible at 1/4 of sentence. 10 years or more, eligible at 1/3 of sentence.
Good time	All felons	Lifers earn 15 days off maximum term for every 30 days in prison; others can earn 20 days for every 30 days in prison.
Earned work credits	All felons on special work assignments	1 day off maximum term for every 2 days in work assignment up to 180 days per year.
Extended work release	All felons with no more than 1 prior conviction	Placed on work release status 2 months before parole eligibility.
Supervised furlough I	All felons with clean disciplinary record less than 5-year sentence less than 2 prior convictions	Released 6 months before parole eligibility.
Supervised furlough II	All felons with 6 months clean record	Released 6 months before parole eligibility.
First-day-of-month rule	All felons	Released on first day of month in which eligibility is reached (after other reductions).
Emergency release provision	Felons within 90 days of eligibility for parole	When prison reaches state of crisis because of crowding, governor may roll back sentences to reduce numbers.
Provisional parole	All felons	Released 90 days before eligibility at discretion of parole board.
Christmas parole	All felons	If parole eligibility is reached between December 18 and January 30, released on December 18 at discretion of parole board.

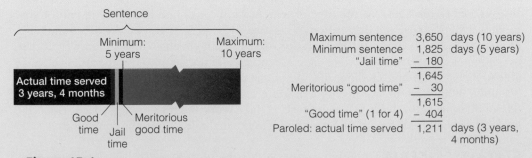

Figure 15.4
Computing Parole Eligibility for Ben Brooks

Various good-time reductions to the minimum sentence are allowed in most corrections systems to determine eligibility for parole. Note how a 5- to 10-year sentence can be reduced to a stay of three years, four months.

4 Institutional adjustment, and participation and progress in programs for self-improvement

5 History of community adjustment

6 Physical, mental, and emotional health

7 Insight into causes of past criminal conduct

8 Adequacy of parole plan

Although the published criteria may help familiarize inmates with the board's expectations, the actual decision is discretionary and is typically based on various other kinds of information as well as fundamental moral judgments about the severity of the crime, the prisoner's culpability, and the adequacy of the term served as punishment for the crime. It is frequently said that parole boards release only good risks, but as one parole board member has said, "There are no good-risk men in prison. Parole is really a decision of when to release bad-risk persons."

Other considerations weigh heavily on the parole board members. If parole is not regularly awarded to most prisoners who gain eligibility, morale among all inmates may suffer as they fear that they will not gain release when anticipated. The seeming arbitrariness of parole boards was a major cause of prison riots during the 1970s. The prospect of gaining parole is a major incentive for many prisoners to follow rules and cooperate with correctional officials.

Parole board members are also concerned about the public and the adequacy of the parole plan. They do not want public criticism for making controversial decisions. Thus, notorious offenders, such as Sirhan Sirhan, the man convicted of assassinating presidential candidate Robert Kennedy in 1968, and multiple murderer Charles Manson, are unlikely ever to gain parole release even if they behave well in prison.

THE PRISONERS' PERSPECTIVE: HOW TO WIN PAROLE ■ "If you want to get paroled, you've got to be in a program." This statement reflects one of the most controversial aspects of discretionary release: its link to treatment. Although correctional authorities emphasize the voluntary nature of most treatment services, and clinicians argue that coercive therapy cannot succeed, inmates still believe they must "play the game." Most parole boards cite an inmate's progress in self-improvement programs as one criterion for release. A Connecticut inmate noted, "The last time I went before the board they wanted to know why I hadn't taken advantage of the programs. Now I go to AA and group therapy. I hope they will be satisfied."

Although prisoners' participation in programs is technically voluntary, the link between participation and release poses many legal and ethical problems, as illustrated by the case of Jim Allen in "Do the Right Thing." In some states inmates convicted of drug or sex offenses may be expected to participate in treatment programs. However, the corrections system may not have enough places in these programs to serve all of them. Offenders may wait long periods before gaining admission, or they may be in an institution that does not have the treatment they need. Because they cannot force the prison system to transfer them to the appropriate institution, inmates may become frustrated hearing about other people gaining parole while they are not given an opportunity to prove themselves to the board. Moreover, some kinds of treatment programs, especially for sex offenders, may involve intrusive counseling therapies or medications that have lingering physical effects and a limited likelihood of success. Yet, threatened with denial of parole if they refuse to participate, prisoners may not feel able to decline such treatments.

Criteria for release on parole in Arizona are found at the corresponding website listed at www.cengage.com/criminaljustice/clear.

CONSEQUENCES OF DISCRETIONARY PAROLE ■ During a riot at New Jersey's Rahway Prison, inmates held aloft a banner that boldly proclaimed, "Abolish parole!" Why? Inmates criticize the somewhat capricious actions of some parole boards. They also point out that indeterminate sentences and discretionary release leave them in limbo. The uncertainty is demoralizing.

Attorneys in some states are available to **help prisoners gain release**; see, for example, the corresponding website listed at www.cengage.com/criminaljustice/clear.

DO THE RIGHT THING

The five members of the parole board questioned Jim Allen, an offender with a long history of sex offenses involving teenage boys. Now approaching age 45 and having met the eligibility requirement for a hearing, Allen respectfully answered the board members.

Toward the end of the hearing, Richard Edwards, a dentist who had recently been appointed to the board, spoke up: "Your institutional record is good, you have a parole plan, a job has been promised, and your sister says she will help you. All of that looks good, but I just can't vote for your parole. You haven't attended the behavior modification program for sex offenders. I think you're going to repeat your crime. I have a 13-year-old son, and I don't want him or other boys to run the risk of meeting your kind." Allen looked shocked. The other members had seemed ready to grant his release.

"But I'm ready for parole. I won't do that stuff again. I didn't go to that program because electroshock to my private area is not going to help me. I've been here five years of the seven-year max and have stayed out of trouble. The judge didn't say I was to be further punished in prison by therapy."

After Jim Allen left the room, the board discussed his case. "You know, Rich, he has a point. He has been a model prisoner and has served a good portion of his sentence," said Brian Lynch, a long-term board member. "Besides we don't know if Dr. Hankin's program works."

"I know, but can we really let someone like that out on the streets?"

WRITING ASSIGNMENT: Assume that you are a member of the parole board considering whether to release Jim Allen. Write a short essay discussing the following questions. Would you consider the results of the behavior modification program for sex offenders relevant when making your decision? Do you think the purpose of the sentence is to punish Allen for what he did, or is it for what he might do in the future? How would you vote on Allen's parole request?

When release is discretionary, the parole board's power is much like that of the sentencing judge. Detractors emphasize that, unlike the judge, the board makes its decisions outside the spotlight of public attention. In addition, they contend that, whereas sentencing is done with due process of law, a parole hearing offers few such rights.

Supporters of discretionary release maintain that parole boards can make their decisions without community pressure and can rectify sentencing errors. Arguably, legislatures often respond to public pressure by prescribing unreasonably harsh maximum sentences—30, 50, even 100 years. But most penal codes also prescribe minimum sentences that are closer to the actual times served; thus, the parole board can grant release after a "reasonable" period of incarceration.

Structuring Parole Decisions

In response to the criticism that the release decisions of parole boards are somewhat arbitrary, many states have adopted parole guidelines. Release is usually granted to prisoners who have served the amount of time stipulated by the guidelines and who meet the following three criteria:

1. They have substantially observed the rules of the institution in which they have been confined.
2. Their release will not depreciate the seriousness of the offense nor promote disrespect for the law.
3. Their release will not jeopardize the public welfare.

As with sentencing guidelines, a severity scale ranks crimes according to their seriousness, and a salient factor score measures both the offender's criminal history (drug

TABLE 15.2 *Criminal History/Risk Assessment under the Oregon Guidelines for Adult Offenders*

The amount of time to be served is related to the severity of the offense and to the criminal history/risk assessment of the inmate. The criminal history score is determined by adding the points assigned to each factor in this table.

	Factor	Points	Score
A.	No prior felony convictions as an adult or juvenile:	3	
	One prior felony conviction:	2	
	Two or three prior felony convictions:	1	
	Four or more prior felony convictions:	0	_____
B.	No prior felony or misdemeanor incarcerations (that is, executed sentences of 90 days or more) as an adult or juvenile:	2	
	One or two prior incarcerations:	1	
	Three or more prior incarcerations:	0	_____
C.	Verified period of three years conviction-free in the community prior to the present commitment:	1	
	Otherwise:	0	_____
D.	Age at commencement of behavior leading to this incarceration was _____; D.O.B. was _____		
	26 or older and at least one point received in Items A, B, or C:	2	
	26 or older and no points received in A, B, or C:	1	
	21 to under 26 and at least one point received in A, B, or C:	1	
	21 to under 26 and no points received in A, B, or C:	0	
	Under 21:	0	_____
E.	Present commitment does not include parole, probation, failure to appear, release agreement, escape, or custody violation:	2	
	Present commitment involves probation, release agreement, or failure to appear violation:	1	
	Present commitment involves parole, escape, or custody violation:	0	_____
F.	Has no admitted or documented substance abuse problem within a three-year period in the community immediately preceding the commission of the crime conviction:	1	
	Otherwise:	0	
	Total History/Risk Assessment		_____

Source: Adapted from State of Oregon, Board of Parole, *ORS* Chapter 144, Rule 255-35-015.

arrests, prior record, age at first conviction, and so on) and risk factors regarded as relevant to successful completion of parole (see **Tables 15.2** and **15.3**).

By placing the offender's salient factor score next to his or her particular offense on the severity scale, the board, the inmate, and correctional officials can calculate the **presumptive parole date** soon after the offender enters prison. This is the date by which the inmate can expect to be released if there are no disciplinary or other problems during incarceration. The presumptive parole date may be modified on a scheduled basis. The date of release may be advanced because of good conduct and superior achievement

presumptive parole date
The presumed release date stipulated by parole guidelines if the offender serves time without disciplinary or other incidents.

TABLE 15.3 *Number of Months to Be Served before Release under the Oregon Guidelines*

The presumptive release date is determined by finding the intersection of the criminal history score (Table 15.2) and the category of the offense. Thus, an offender with an assessment score between 8 and 6, convicted of a category 3 offense, could expect to serve between 10 and 14 months.

Offense Severity	Criminal History/Risk Assessment Score			
	11–9 Excellent	8–6 Good	5–3 Fair	2–0 Poor
Category 1: bigamy, criminal mischief I, dogfighting, incest, possession of stolen vehicle	6	6	6–10	12–18
Category 2: abandonment of a child, bribing a witness, criminal homicide, perjury, possession of controlled substance	6	6–10	10–14	16–24
Category 3: assault III, forgery I, sexual abuse, trafficking in stolen vehicles	6–10	10–14	14–20	22–32
Category 4: aggravated theft, assault II, coercion, criminally negligent homicide, robbery II	10–16	16–22	22–30	32–44
Category 5: burglary I, escape I, manslaughter II, racketeering, rape I	16–24	24–36	40–52	56–72
Category 6: arson I, kidnapping I, rape II, sodomy I	30–40	44–56	60–80	90–130
Category 7: aggravated murder, treason	96–120	120–156	156–192	192–240
Category 8: aggravated murder (stranger-stranger, cruelty to victim, prior murder conviction)	120–168	168–228	228–288	288–life

Source: Adapted from State of Oregon, Board of Parole, *ORS* Chapter 144, Rule 255-75-026 and Rule 255-75-035.

or postponed if there are disciplinary infractions or if a suitable community supervision plan is not developed.

The Impact of Release Mechanisms

Parole release mechanisms do more than determine the date at which a particular prisoner will be sent back into the community. Parole release also has an enormous impact on other parts of the system, including sentencing, plea bargaining, and the size of prison populations.[18]

One important effect of discretionary release is that an administrative body—the parole board—can shorten a sentence imposed by a judge. Even in states that have mandatory release, various potential reductions built into the sentence mean the full sentence is rarely served. Good time, for example, can reduce punishment even if there is no parole eligibility.

To understand the impact of release mechanisms on criminal punishment, we need to compare the amount of time actually served in prison with the sentence specified by the judge. In some jurisdictions up to 60 percent of felons sentenced to prison are released to the community after their first appearance before a parole board. Eligibility for discretionary release is ordinarily determined by the minimum term of the sentence minus good time and jail time.

Although states vary considerably, on a national basis felony inmates serve an average of two years and three months before release. In Chapter 4 (Figure 4.2, p. 80) the average time served and the percentage of the sentence served for selected offenses is shown. Note that some offenders who receive long sentences actually serve a smaller proportion of

A report by the Florida Department of Corrections about **how actual time served has changed** is found at the corresponding website listed at www.cengage.com/criminaljustice/clear.

such sentences than do offenders given shorter sentences. For example, the average robbery offender is sentenced to 91 months and serves 58 percent of the term. By contrast the average offender convicted of aggravated assault is sentenced to 54 months but serves 67 percent of the term.

The probability of release well before the end of the formal sentence encourages plea bargaining by both prosecutors and defendants. Prosecutors can reap the benefits of quick, cooperative plea bargains that look tough in the eyes of the public. Meanwhile, the defendant agrees to plead guilty and accept the sentence because of the high likelihood of early release through parole.

Beyond the benefits to prosecutors, parole discretion may benefit the overall system. Discretionary release mitigates the harshness of the penal code. If the legislature must establish exceptionally strict punishments as a means of conveying a "tough on crime" image to frustrated and angry voters, parole can effectively permit sentence adjustments that make the punishment fit the crime. Everyone convicted of larceny may not have done equivalent harm, yet some legislatively mandated sentencing schemes impose equally strict sentences. Early release on parole can be granted to an offender who is less deserving of strict punishment, such as someone who voluntarily makes restitution, cooperates with the police, or shows genuine regret.

Discretionary release is also an important tool for reducing prison populations in states with overcrowded prisons and budget deficits. Even states that abolished parole boards, instituted mandatory sentences, and adopted truth-in-sentencing laws in the 1980s are now finding loopholes that allow them to release convicts early. In December 2002 Kentucky released 567 inmates to reduce a $500 million budget deficit. Oklahoma's conservative Governor Frank Keating, who added 1,000 inmates a year to the system, asked the Pardon and Parole Board to find 1,000 nonviolent inmates to

AP Images/Tim Hacker, Pool

Parole has an impact beyond determining the date an offender is to return to the community. The probability of release well before the end of a formal sentence encourages plea bargaining. Recognizing the availability of parole, attorney Melvin McDonald listens to his client, Jennifer Mally, who was charged with 17 counts of sexual misconduct with a minor. By pleading guilty to three of the counts, the remainder was dismissed. She was sentenced to six months incarceration and required to register as a sex offender.

release early as a result of the state's budget crisis. Governors in other states, including Arkansas, California, Kansas, Michigan, Montana, Wisconsin, and Texas, have released or plan to release inmates because of prison crowding and costs.[19]

A major criticism of discretionary release is that it has shifted responsibility for many primary criminal justice decisions from a judge, who holds legal procedures uppermost, to an administrative board, where discretion rules. Judges know a great deal about constitutional rights and basic legal protections, but parole board members may not have such knowledge. In most states with discretionary release, parole hearings are secret, with only board members, the inmate, and correctional officers present. Often, no published criteria guide decisions, and prisoners are given no reason for denial or granting of parole. However, an increasing number of states permit oral or written testimony by victims as well as members of the offender's family.

Should society place such power in the hands of parole boards? Because there is so little oversight regarding their decision making and so few constraints on their decisions, some parole board members will make arbitrary or discriminatory decisions inconsistent with the constitutional system and civil rights. Generally, the U.S. legal system seeks to avoid determining people's fates through such methods.

■ RELEASE TO THE COMMUNITY

One impact of the explosive growth of the nation's prison population is the huge increase in the number of inmates who are being released to the community after serving their terms. In 2007 more than 725,000 individuals—nearly 2,000 per day—returned home from federal and state prisons.[20] Compared with those released in 1990, these "new parolees" were older, had served longer times in prison, and had higher levels of substance abuse and mental illness; more had been sentenced for drug law violations as well.[21] The problem of "making it" in the community is discussed in Chapter 16; here we describe the ways inmates are prepared for release.

The great increase in the number of ex-offenders returning to the community has stimulated action by Congress and the states to provide assistance to parolees and to reduce the staggering amount of recidivism among them. The Second Chance Act is federal reentry legislation that was first considered by Congress in 2005 and signed into law in 2008. It was designed to ensure the safe and successful return of prisoners through grants to states and communities to support reentry initiatives focused on employment, housing, substance abuse and mental health treatment, and children and family services.[22]

From the philosophy of community corrections has come the reintegration model of prison life. Here the goal is to prepare offenders for reentry into society through the gradual allocation of freedoms and responsibilities during incarceration. Where this model has been adopted, prisoners are placed at a high level of custody when they enter the institution and are periodically evaluated. As they progress, the level of custody is lowered so they can reestablish family ties and begin to heal the damage done by their crime and incarceration. Often furloughs and increased visitation are arranged. Toward the latter part of the sentence, the offender may be placed on work release, transferred to a halfway house, or given other opportunities to live in the community.

All states have some form of prison program designed to prepare the offender for release to community supervision. The offender receives prerelease counseling about the conditions of supervision, as well as help in searching for employment and a place to live. In some systems these activities begin as far as two years in advance of the targeted release date; in others they begin only after that date is confirmed (see **Table 15.4**). (See also the Focus box "Michigan Prisoner ReEntry Initiative.")

Nebraska crime victims can go online to learn about the parole system; see the corresponding website listed at www.cengage.com/criminaljustice/clear.

All states have some form of prerelease program designed to prepare inmates for reentry. The best programs assist the inmate in finding employment, finding a place to live, and reconnecting with family members.

AP Images/Damian Dovarganes

TABLE 15.4 *Eight-State Comparison of Department of Corrections Prerelease Programs*

All states provide some form of prerelease program, yet in most states they are voluntary and vary greatly in content.

Release Program	California	Georgia	Missouri	Nevada	Ohio	Pennsylvania	Texas	Washington
Required Program	No	Yes	Yes	No	Yes	No	No	No
Time before Release	45 days	Not reported	Not reported	90 days	60 days	Up to 1 year	Within 2 years	Within 2 years
Type of Programs								
Education	Yes	Yes	Yes	Yes	Yes	Yes	Yes	Yes
Job readiness	Yes	Yes	Yes	Yes	Yes	Yes	Yes	Yes
Community resources	Yes	Yes	No	Yes	Yes	Yes	Yes	Yes
Substance abuse	Yes	Yes	Yes	No	Yes	Yes	Yes	Yes
Housing	No	No	Yes	No	No	No	No	No
Furlough Options								
Available	Yes	NA	No	Yes	Yes	Yes	Yes	No
Education	Yes	NA	NA	No	Yes	No	No	NA
Family	Yes	NA	NA	Yes	No	No	Yes	NA
Other	Yes, employment, vocational	NA	NA	Yes, medical	Yes, transit control	Yes, job seeking	Yes, funeral	NA
Time limits	Less than 120 days	NA	NA	NA	NA	144 hours	2 days	NA
Special Release Facility and Assistance								
Within prison	No	No	No	No	No	Yes	Yes	No
Halfway house	Yes, reentry units	NA	Yes	No	Yes	Yes	Yes	No
Funds	Up to $200	NA	Clothing and bus	$25 plus clothing	$25–$75	NA	$100 plus bus	$40 plus bus
Follow-up	None	None	None	None	Yes	None	None	None

Source: James Austin, "Prisoner Reentry: Current Trends, Practices, and Issues," *Crime and Delinquency* 47 (July 2001): 314. Copyright 2001 by Sage Publication, Inc. Reprinted by permission of Sage Publications, Inc.

CORRECTIONAL PRACTICE

Michigan Prisoner ReEntry Initiative

It's a Thursday morning and 24-year-old Jeffery Lauderdale is planning his future—one where, he hopes, there are no prison bars. Lauderdale, of Kentwood, Michigan, has been in and out of lockups for drug convictions since age 18. Now, up for his third release from prison, he's enrolled in the four-month Intensive ReEntry Unit, a program at the Cooper Street Correctional Facility in Jackson. The unit is part of the Michigan Prisoner ReEntry Initiative which hopes to reduce the state's high recidivism rate.

With nearly half of Michigan's parolees wanted by authorities or back in prison within two years, the state is trying to better prepare inmates for release to the community. At Cooper Street inmates learn how to budget their money, interview for jobs, and put together a résumé. They also make plans to get help from community agencies once they've left prison. In the past, that help has been missing, disorganized, or late, correctional officials say.

On this morning, a four-member "transition team"—a parole officer and three people from social service agencies—is quizzing Lauderdale. The prisoner, who hopes to be released next month, sits on an upholstered chair at a conference table in a prison administrative office. He politely answers questions from the panel talking to him on a large television screen via a video conference call. He tells them he has restaurant experience and took carpentry classes in prison. "I want to be successful in staying out of prison," Lauderdale, the soon-to-be parolee, said. "I want to do what I need to do." When he was released from prison before, there was little preparation, he said. "I just went home, and that was it."

Source: Adapted from Judy Putnam, "Inmates Get New Help as They Prepare for Freedom," http://www.mlive.com, October 20, 2005.

The best of these programs provides a multiweek, full-time training program for inmates who are within 60 days of release. Inmates are given training in the attitudes needed to get and keep a job, communicational skills, family roles, money management, and community and parole resources. The prisoners and their needs are evaluated. Each prisoner is then given a list of five objectives to achieve within 30 days of being paroled, as well as the names and addresses of five public or private agencies that can be contacted for assistance. During the training program, each prisoner participates in at least one mock job interview and acquires a driver's license.

With a set of clothes, a check for $100, and a voucher good for one bus ticket, about one hundred inmates are released every weekday from Huntsville Prison in Texas. This scenario is repeated across the country, with more than 700,000 inmates being released to the community each year.

Philippe Diederich

Other programs include transfer of the participating inmates to a housing unit reserved for prereleases. One week of the four-week period is devoted to family readjustment training. With the emphasis on reintegration and community supervision, offenders are no longer confined to one cell in one institution for the duration of their terms. Instead, they move about a great deal from one security level to another and from one institution to another as they prepare for release. However, critics argue that only a small percentage of prisoners receive prerelease planning. (See "Myths in Corrections.")

Unfortunately, in most states, participating in these programs is voluntary and is available to only a small proportion of inmates. For example, in Pennsylvania certain restrictions apply and only about 1,000 are served each year; Georgia has "transitional centers," but they have a capacity of only 700. As we will see in the next chapter, the problem of prisoner reentry is serious but is only now getting national attention.

MYTHS IN CORRECTIONS

REVOLVING DOORS?

THE MYTH: "Two-thirds of these guys will be back in prison within three years."

THE REALITY: It depends on the state. More than two-thirds of parolees are returned to prison in California, yet in other states the percentage of returnees is as low as 7 percent.

Source: Fox Butterfield, "Study Calls California Parole System a $1 Billion Failure," *New York Times*, November 14, 2003, p. A14.

SUMMARY

1 Discuss parole and explain how it operates today.

Parole is the conditional release of an offender from incarceration but not from the legal custody of the state. Parolees must comply with a specified set of conditions and must not violate the law to receive an absolute discharge from supervision. If the offender breaks a rule, then parole may be revoked and the person returned to a correctional facility. Only felons are released on parole. Adult misdemeanants are usually released directly from local institutions on expiration of their sentence.

2 Be familiar with the origins and evolution of parole in the United States.

Parole in the United States evolved during the nineteenth century, following the English, Australian, and Irish practices of conditional pardon, apprenticeship by indenture, transportation of criminals, and the issuance of tickets-of-leave. After the passage of an indeterminate sentencing law in 1876, the Elmira Reformatory in New York began to release prisoners on parole. By 1900, 20 states had parole systems, and by 1946, 48 states operated parole systems. At the federal level, individual federal prisons had their own parole boards beginning in 1910. In 1930 Congress created the U.S. Board of Parole to replace separate boards.

3 Discuss the different mechanisms that are used to release offenders from correctional facilities.

In states that use indeterminate sentences, parole boards are used to grant discretionary release. When making their decision whether to release an offender, the parole board considers the nature of the offense, the inmate's behavior, and participation in rehabilitation programs. In contrast, mandatory release occurs after an inmate has served time equal to the total sentence minus good time, or to a certain percentage of the total sentence as specified by law. This form of release does not rely on the judgment of a parole board. A third release mechanism, probation release, occurs when the sentencing judge requires a period of post-custody supervision in the community. This type of release is often tied to shock incarcerations and is more common among first-time offenders. Many states also have other conditional-release mechanisms, such as placing inmates in the community through furlough, home supervision, halfway houses, or emergency release. Finally, expiration release is used when inmates have "maxed out" their sentence and are released from correctional supervision. These offenders cannot be returned to prison for their current offense.

4 Explain how releasing authorities are organized.

Parole boards tend to be organized either inside a department of corrections (consolidated) or as an independent agency of government (autonomous). Some argue that a parole board must be independent to insulate members from the activities and influence of correctional staff. Others believe that an independent parole board can become unresponsive to correctional needs and programs. Some parole boards are full time, while others are part time. Membership on a board that meets full time attracts criminal justice professionals. Members of part-time boards are thought to represent the community better, because they have other careers and are independent of the criminal justice system. Members of the paroling authority may be appointed by the governor or by the head of the correctional department. In many states political considerations dictate such appointments, and training in the behavioral sciences is not always given highest priority.

5 Be familiar with the steps that are taken to ease the offender's reentry into the community.

All states have some form of prison program designed to prepare the offender for release to community supervision. The offender receives prerelease counseling about the conditions of supervision, as well as help in searching for employment and a place to live. The best of these programs provides a multiweek, full-time training program for inmates who are within 60 days of release. Inmates are given training in the attitudes needed to get and keep a job, communicational skills, family roles, money management, and community and parole resources. Prisoners then receive a list of objectives to achieve after being paroled, as well as the names and addresses of public or private agencies that can be contacted for assistance. Other programs include transfer of the participating inmates to a housing unit reserved for prereleases. With the emphasis on reintegration and community supervision, offenders are no longer confined to one cell in one institution for the duration of their terms. Instead they move about a great deal from one security level to another and from one institution to another as they prepare for release.

KEY TERMS

Crofton, Sir Walter (p. 410)

discretionary release (p. 412)

expiration release (p. 414)

Maconochie, Captain Alexander (p. 410)

mandatory release (p. 412)

other conditional release (p. 414)

parole (p. 408)

presumptive parole date (p. 421)

probation release (p. 413)

FOR DISCUSSION

1. How does mandatory release affect the corrections system? How will corrections adjust to this harnessing of the discretion of parole boards and judges?
2. What factors should a parole board consider when it evaluates a prisoner for release?
3. Suppose, as a parole board member, you are confronted by a man who has served 6 years of a 10- to 20-year sentence for murder. He has a good institutional record, and you do not believe him to be a threat to community safety. Would you release him to parole supervision at this time? Why or why not?
4. Suppose you have been asked to decide whether the department of corrections or an independent agency should have authority over release decisions. Where would you place that authority? Why?
5. Given the current public attitude toward criminals, what do you see as the likely future of parole release?

FOR FURTHER READING

Morris, Norval. *Maconochie's Gentlemen: The Story of Norfolk Island and the Roots of Modern Prison Reform.* New York: Oxford University Press, 2001. Morris shows how Maconochie's life and efforts on Norfolk Island provide a model for the running of correctional institutions today.

Petersilia, Joan. *When Prisoners Come Home: Parole and Prisoner Reentry.* New York: Oxford University Press, 2003. A major analysis of the reentry problem, with implications for community safety.

Rhine, Edward E., William R. Smith, and Ronald W. Jackson. *Paroling Authorities: Recent History and Current Practice.* Laurel, MD: American Correctional Association, 1991. Reports the results of a national survey conducted by the ACA Task Force on Parole.

Simon, Jonathan. *Poor Discipline: Parole and the Social Control of the Underclass, 1890–1990.* Chicago: University of Chicago Press, 1993. Examines parole as dealing with the underclass and discusses the relationship among criminal threat, penal technologies, and public safety.

Travis, Jeremy, and Christy Visher, eds. *Prisoner Reentry and Crime in America.* New York: Cambridge University Press, 2005. A collection of essays by leading correctional scholars who have examined issues surrounding reentry.

NOTES

1. Larry O'Dell, "Former Quarterback Michael Vick Ends Federal Dogfighting Term, Free to Lobby for NFL Return," *Los Angeles Times,* July 20, 2009, http://www.latimes.com/sports/football/nfl/wire/sns-ap-fbn-vick-federal-sentence,0,1546813.story.

2. Bureau of Justice Statistics, *Prisoners in 2007* (Washington, DC: U.S. Government Printing Office, December 2008), 3.

3. Alfred Blumstein and Allen J. Beck, "Reentry as a Transient State between Liberty and Recommitment," in *Prisoner Reentry and Crime in America,* edited by Jeremy Travis and Christy Visher (New York: Cambridge University Press, 2005), 3.

4. *New York Times,* March 13, 2007, p. A18.

5. Ann L. Pastore and Kathleen Maguire, eds., *Sourcebook of Criminal Justice Statistics,* Table 6.1.2006, http://www.albany.edu/sourcebook/pdf/t612006.pdf, July 24, 2009.

6. Harry Elmer Barnes and Nedgley K. Teeters, *New Horizons in Criminology* (Englewood Cliffs, NJ: Prentice-Hall, 1944), 550, 553.

7. Lawrence M. Friedman, *Crime and Punishment in American History* (New York: Basic Books, 1993), 304.

8. Peter B. Hoffman, "History of the Federal Parole System: Part I (1910–1972)," *Federal Probation* 61 (September 1997): 23.

9. Joan Petersilia, *When Prisoners Come Home: Parole and Prisoner Reentry* (New York: Oxford University Press, 2003), 65.

10. Tony Fabelo, *Biennial Report to the 76th Texas Legislature* (Austin, TX: Criminal Justice Policy Council, 1999).

11. James Austin, "Prisoner Reentry: Current Trends, Practices, and Issues," *Crime and Delinquency* 47 (July 2001): 327.

12. Fox Butterfield, "Eliminating Parole Boards Isn't a Cure All, Experts Say," *New York Times,* January 10, 1999, p. 12.

13. Bureau of Justice Statistics, *Probation and Parole in the United States, 2005* (Washington, DC: U.S. Government Printing Office, November 2006), 8.

14. Pamela L. Griset, "The Politics and Economics of Increased Correctional Discretion over Time Served: A New York Case Study," *Justice Quarterly* 12 (June 1995): 307; Bureau of Justice Statistics, *Correctional Populations in the United States, 1997* (Washington, DC: U.S. Government Printing Office, November 2000), 95–104.

15. Bureau of Justice Statistics, *Probation and Parole in the United States, 2005,* p. 8.

16. Katharine Bradley and R. B. Michael Oliver, "The Role of Parole," in *Policy Brief* (Boston: Community Resources for Justice, July 2001); Petersilia, *When Prisoners Come Home,* p. 60.

17. Susette Talarico, "The Dilemmas of Parole Decision Making," in *Criminal Justice: Law and Politics,* 5th ed., edited by George F. Cole (Pacific Grove, CA: Brooks/Cole, 1988), 442–51.

18. Samuel Walker, *Taming the System: The Control of Discretion in Criminal Justice, 1950–1990* (New York: Oxford University Press, 1993), 141.

19. Fox Butterfield, "Inmates Go Free to Reduce Deficits," *New York Times,* December 1, 2002, p. A1; Charlie Cain and Norman Sinclair, "Prisons Full by Fall; Now What?" http://www.detnews.com, February 19, 2007; Andy Furillo, "Prison Pressure Welcomed," http://www.sacbee.com, March 7, 2007.

20. Bureau of Justice Statistics, *Prisoners in 2007,* 3.

21. Austin, "Prisoner Reentry," pp. 322–23.

22. Reentry Policy Council, "Second Chance Act," http://reentrypolicy.org/government_affairs/second_chance_act, October 18, 2009.

© Jose M. Osorio/The Sacramento Bee/ZUMA Press

LEARNING OBJECTIVES

After reading this chapter you should be able to . . .

1 Know the major characteristics of the postrelease function of the corrections system.

2 Define community supervision and revocation of community supervision.

3 Understand how community supervision is structured.

4 Know the constraints on community supervision.

5 Describe residential programs and how they help parolees.

6 Identify the major problems parolees confront.

7 Understand why some parolees are viewed as dangerous and how society handles this problem.

8 Describe the effectiveness of postrelease supervision.

Glenn Martin of the Fortune Society, one of New York's most successful agencies providing services to ex-prisoners, asks new parolees to raise their hands if they have a plan on how to get a job. On the first day of their release, parolees must attend this orientation, where they receive information and counseling on how to survive in the community

THIRTY-EIGHT YEAR OLD Glenn Martin is the Associate Vice President of Policy and Advocacy at the Fortune Society in New York City. The Fortune Society is one of New York City's largest and most successful nonprofit agencies providing services to people returning from prison. As VP for advocacy, Martin is the public face and voice for Fortune's work in improving the corrections system and reforming the laws that affect people who come back from prison. In this role Martin has been a tireless advocate for people who face long odds when their term of incarceration ends. He is concerned about a lot of things that affect the formerly incarcerated: health care, civil rights, family reunification—and maybe most of all, jobs.

A while back, he was speaking in a storefront church in Brooklyn, New York, to a handful of people with criminal records, about their rights and employers' hiring practices. One of the participants asked if pursuing a civil service job was a waste of time.

"Does anybody here know somebody who works with city sanitation with a conviction record?" Martin asked the

Making It: Supervision in the Community

crowd. Several of those present quickly raised their hands. "Does anybody here know somebody who works for probation with a conviction record?" More raised hands. "Does anybody here know an attorney with a criminal record?" Same thing. "You can get into these fields," Martin said. "I'm telling you, I've seen it. I've seen it. It's difficult but it's not impossible."[1]

The truth, though, is that the 720,000 people who are released from prison rarely get hired for these kinds of jobs. Glenn Martin knows this as well as anyone. He served five years in prison and two-and-a-half on parole, for robbery.

Martin's personal story is inspiring. As a youngster growing up in a tough neighborhood, he—like many of his peers—got involved in a crime that landed him in prison. But unlike so many of those he grew up with, while he was in prison he got a college education, something he says "changed everything" for him. Not only did it give him a credential he could use once he was released from prison, it also gave him a purpose in life: to help people who, like him, needed a chance to make a fresh start.

Now he runs one of the nation's most visible advocacy programs for people who are getting out of prison. It is a three-way balancing act. First, he wants to boost those who are reentering society after serving time in a prison, people who need all the encouragement and tangible support they can get. Second, he wants to be an advocate for change, trying to eliminate the many barriers people face as they try to "make it" after prison. He has to be realistic about the laws that are hard on former prisoners;

Chapter

16

until these laws are changed, ex-offenders will continue to face tough odds. Finally, he must serve as a living example of the many obstacles the formerly incarcerated people face, as well as the success that results if they are overcome.

Glenn Martin's personal story does not reflect the way things usually work out for ex-offenders. However, he provides an example of how much we all stand to benefit when people who have been to prison succeed in their second chance.

In this chapter we focus on "making it"—the struggles of former inmates to stay out of prison. Because the experience of reentry is so intensely personal, in this chapter we listen to people involved in the postrelease business—former prisoners and the parole officers who supervise them—talk about their experiences. Many ex-prisoners fail; about half of all released offenders return to prison within six years. Most are under the scrutiny of agents of the state; all face significant legal, familial, and social strains. How many of us would not be vulnerable to misconduct under such pressures? Released offenders play against a stacked deck, and the fact that so many succeed is testimony to their perseverance.

■ OVERVIEW OF THE POSTRELEASE FUNCTION

The popular notion is that once offenders have completed their prison sentences, they have paid their "debt" and are ready to start life anew. The reality is that the vast majority of offenders released from prison remain subject to correctional authority for some time. For many offenders, the parole officer represents this authority; for others, the staff of a halfway house or work release center does. The "freedom" of release is constrained: The whereabouts of offenders are monitored, and their associations and daily activities are checked.

Parolees are released from prison on condition that they abide by laws and follow rules designed both to aid their readjustment to society and to control their movement. The parolee may be required to abstain from alcohol, keep away from undesirable associates, maintain good work habits, and not leave the community without permission. These requirements, called **conditions of release**, regulate conduct that is not criminal but that is thought to be linked to the possibility of future criminality. **Figure 16.1** shows specific conditions of release in a New Jersey parole contract.

conditions of release
Restrictions on conduct that parolees must obey as a legally binding requirement of being released.

An Urban Institute report notes changes that have occurred in the parole system during the past several decades. The classic model gave parole boards the discretionary power to release inmates to community supervision. Today parole boards release only about a quarter of inmates, down from 65 percent in 1976. At the same time, reliance on parole supervision has increased significantly. Eighty percent of those released are now under parole supervision, up from 60 percent in 1960. The authors of the study make the point that under the traditional model one function of parole boards was to ensure that the offender was prepared for release with a place to stay, a job, and support from family or friends. Today most exiting prisoners are not prepared for their entrance into the community.[2]

The freedom of offenders who are released outright—either because they have completed their maximum term (the maximum sentence minus good time) or, as in the state of Maine, because there is no parole supervision—is also less complete than it may seem. The former inmate still has many serious obstacles to overcome: long absence from family and friends, legal and practical limitations on employment possibilities, the suspicion and uneasiness of the community, even the strangeness of everyday living. The outside world can seem alien and unpredictable after even a short time in the artificial environment of prison.

State of New Jersey
STATE PAROLE BOARD

Certificate of Parole

Page 1 of 4

The State Parole Board, by virtue of the authority conferred upon it by the provisions of P.L. 1979, c.441 (C.30:4-123.45, et seq.) and under the rules and regulations promulgated pursuant thereto, does hereby grant a parole to **XXXX XXXXXX, SP#XXXXXX**, who was convicted of the crime(s) and sentenced as indicated below:

Date of Sentence and Offense	County and Term	Relation and Assessment(s)
XXX XX, XXXX	XXXXXX	XX.XX
XXXXXX XXXXXXXX	XXX	

TOTAL TERM: XXX

Said inmate is now confined in the **XXXXXX XXXXXXX XXXX** by virtue of the sentence(s) imposed for the said conviction of the crime(s) aforesaid. This parole is applicable solely to said aforesaid sentence(s) and to no other, limited by and subject to the conditions annexed hereto and made a part hereof, and is effective on **XXXXXXX XXXXXX** or as soon thereafter as a suitable parole plan has been approved by the State Parole Board, and upon the further condition that the said inmate accepts the conditions contained herein and annexed hereto, as evidenced by his/her signature affixed hereto and to a copy hereof retained as a part of the record of the parolee.

This parole is subject to revocation for violation of the conditions annexed hereto and forming a part hereof.

IN TESTIMONY WHEREOF, I have hereunto set my hand, and caused our Seal to be affixed this **XXXXXX** day of **XXX** in the year of our Lord one thousand nine hundred and NINETY-THREE.

STATE PAROLE BOARD

Certifying Member(s): **XXXXXXXXXX XXXXXXX   XXXXXX XXXXXX**

GENERAL CONDITIONS OF PAROLE:

From the date of your release on parole until the expiration of your maximum sentence(s) or until you are discharged from parole, you shall continue to be under the supervision of the Bureau of Parole. A warrant for your arrest may be filed and this parole may be revoked for serious or persistent violations of the conditions of parole. You shall not be credited for time served on parole from the date a parole warrant is issued for your arrest if you are in violation of parole to the date that you are arrested and placed in confinement for violation of parole.

1. You are required to obey all laws and ordinances.
2. You are not to act as an informer for any agency which requires you to violate any conditions of your parole.
3. You are to report in person to your District Parole Supervisor or his/her designated representative immediately after you are released on parole from the institution, unless you have been given other written instructions by the institutional parole office, and you are to report thereafter as instructed by the District Parole Supervisor or his or her designated representative.
4. You are to notify your Parole Officer immediately after any arrest and after accepting any pre-trial release, including bail.
5. You are to obtain approval of your Parole Officer:
   a.   For any change in your residence or employment location.

Witness _____   Dated _____ 19 ____

_____   _____
                                              Signature

SPB-130

State of New Jersey
STATE PAROLE BOARD

XXXXX XXXXXXX, SP#XXXXXX

Certificate of Parole

Page 2 of 4

    b.   Before leaving the state of your approved residence for longer than 24 hours, except as otherwise directed for good cause by the Parole Officer.
6. You are required not to own or possess any firearm, as defined in N.J.S.2C:39-1f, for any purpose.
7. You are required not to own or possess any weapon enumerated in N.J.S.2C:39-1r.
8. You are required to refrain from the use, possession or distribution of a controlled dangerous substance, controlled substance analog or imitation controlled dangerous substance as defined In N.J.S.2C:35-2 and N.J.S.2C:35-11.
9. You are required to make payment to the Bureau of Parole of any assessment, fine, restitution, D.E.D.R. penalty and Lab Fee imposed by the sentencing court and/or the New Jersey State Parole Board.

Total Fine(s)/Penalty(s):
Total VCCB Assessment(s):
Total Restitution:

SPECIAL CONDITION(S):

You will be paroled to any outstanding detainer(s) only initially; thence upon resolution of said detainer(s), you will be released to a parole plan acceptable to the New Jersey Bureau of Parole with the following Special Conditions:

You are to participate in random urine monitoring acceptable to the District Parole Office until discharge is approved by the District Parole Supervisor. You are to refrain from the use of any controlled dangerous substance.

You are to participate in and comply with the regulations of an out-patient drug counseling program acceptable to the District Parole Office until discharge is approved by the District Parole Supervisor. You are to refrain from the use of any controlled dangerous substance.

You are to participate in a Narcotics Anonymous Program with a community sponsor acceptable to the District Parole Office until discharge is approved by the District Parole Supervisor. You are to refrain from the use of any controlled dangerous substance.

You are to participate in and comply with the regulations of an out-patient alcohol counseling program acceptable to the District Parole Office until discharge from such is approved by the District Parole Supervisor. You are to refrain from alcohol usage.

You are to participate In an Alcoholics Anonymous Program with a community sponsor acceptable to the District Parole Office until discharge is approved by the District Parole Supervisor. You are to refrain from alcohol usage.

You are to participate in mental health counseling acceptable to the District Parole Office.

I HEREBY ACKNOWLEDGE THE IMPOSITION OF THE SPECIAL CONDITION OF PAROLE THAT I ENROLL AND PARTICIPATE IN A MENTAL HEALTH COUNSELING PROGRAM. I ACKNOWLEDGE MY NEED TO PARTICIPATE IN A MENTAL HEALTH COUNSELING PROGRAM AND ACKNOWLEDGE THAT I MUST FULLY COOPERATE WITH THE TREATMENT STAFF OF THE DESIGNATED PROGRAM. I HEREBY AUTHORIZE THE DESIGNATED REPRESENTATIVES OF THE DEPARTMENT OF CORRECTIONS AND THE STATE PAROLE BOARD TO RELEASE EITHER VERBALLY OR IN WRITING ALL DIAGNOSTIC PROGNOSTIC AND TREATMENT RECORDS PERTAINING TO MY MEDICAL AND MENTAL HEALTH TO THE STAFF OF ANY MENTAL HEALTH AGENCY REQUESTED TO PROVIDE OR PROVIDING SERVICES TO ME. I ACKNOWLEDGE THAT I UNDERSTAND THAT THIS AUTHORIZATION TO RELEASE INFORMATION MAY NOT BE

Witness _____   Dated _____ 19 ____

_____   _____
                                              Signature

SPB-130

Figure 16.1
Conditions of Release, New Jersey
Newly released offenders must comply with specific conditions in order to remain in good standing on parole.

No truly "clean" start is possible. The status of former convict is nearly as stigmatizing as that of convict, and in many ways more frustrating. Most people look at the parolee askance—an embittering experience for many trying to start over.

Community Supervision

Restrictions on parolees are rationalized on the grounds that people who have been incarcerated must readjust to the community gradually so they will not simply fall back into preconviction habits and associations. Some people hold that trying to impose on parolees standards of conduct not imposed on others is both wrong and likely to fail. Moreover, new parolees find themselves in such daunting circumstances that they may have great difficulty living according to the rules.

When releasees first come out of prison, their personal and material problems are staggering. In most states they are given only clothes, a token amount of money, a copy of the rules governing their release, and the name and address of the parole officer to whom they must report within 24 hours. Although a promised job is often a condition of release, an actual job may be another matter. Most former convicts are unskilled or semiskilled, and parole stipulations may prevent them from moving to areas where they could find work. If they are African American and under age 30, they join the largest group of unemployed in the country, with the added handicap of former convict status.

Reentry problems help explain why most parole failures occur relatively soon after release—nearly one-quarter during the first six months. With little preparation, offenders move from the highly structured, authoritarian prison life into the complex, temptation-filled free world. They are expected to summon up extraordinary coping abilities; not surprisingly, the social, psychological, and material overload sends many parolees back. **Figure 16.2** summarizes some key characteristics of people released from prison.

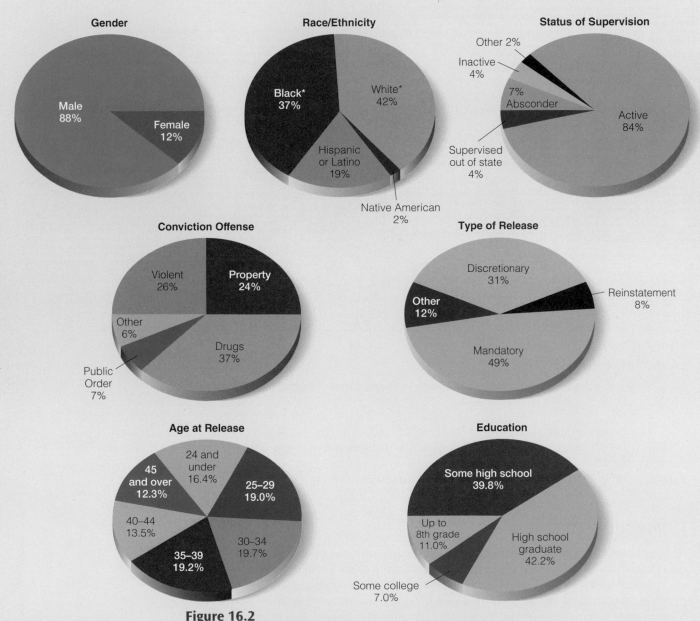

Figure 16.2

Personal Characteristics of People Released from Prison

Prison releasees tend to be men in their thirties who have an inadequate education and were incarcerated for nonviolent offenses.

*Non-Hispanic

Sources: Bureau of Justice Statistics: *Special Report,* October 2001; *Statistical Tables,* December 2008), p. 6.

Revocation

When people fail on parole, their parole is revoked and they are returned to prison to continue serving their sentences. Parole can be revoked for two reasons: (1) committing a new crime or (2) violating conditions of parole (a "technical violation"). Technical violations are controversial because they involve noncriminal conduct, such as failure to report an address change to the parole officer.

Critics of parole argue that it is improper to reimprison a parolee for minor infractions. In practice, revocations seldom result from a single rules violation—prisons are far too crowded. To be returned to prison on a technical violation, a parolee usually must show persistent noncompliance or else give the parole officer reason to believe he or she has returned to crime. Most revocations occur only when the parolee is arrested on a serious charge or cannot be located by the officer.

One of the conditions of release is that the parolee is to immediately report to his/her parole supervisor. Here a Texas couple meets with the man's officer to learn the specific elements of his parole plan.

CAREERS IN CORRECTIONS   Parole Hearing Officer

NATURE OF THE WORK

Parole hearing officers are responsible for conducting parole revocation hearings. These hearings are held to determine whether offenders have violated the conditions of their parole. Officers are responsible for determining the issues of each case, scheduling and conducting hearings, reaching impartial decisions, determining the admissibility of evidence, ensuring due process, maintaining records of evidence and testimony, and writing reports on the findings and actions taken after hearings are conducted. Reincarceration for a substantial period may result if the offender's parole is revoked.

REQUIRED QUALIFICATIONS

Background qualifications vary by state, but generally candidates must meet the following criteria:

- A bachelor's degree in criminal justice, sociology, or psychology
- Knowledge of laws regarding due process and the constitutional rights of offenders
- Knowledge of the criminal justice system, especially the parole system
- Experience as a parole officer
- Experience conducting interviews, verifying documented verbal and written information, report writing, and researching, analyzing, and interpreting laws, regulations, and policies

EARNINGS AND JOB OUTLOOK

Given the rise in the number of offenders on parole, the outlook for parole hearing officer is good. Parole hearing officers earn about $70,000 a year, but salaries vary from state to state.

MORE INFORMATION

Visit the website of the **American Probation and Parole Association**, listed at www.cengage.com/criminaljustice/clear.

Perspectives on the parolee's status in the community have changed over the years. Early reformers saw parole decisions as grace dispensed by the correctional authority. Such parole could be revoked at any time and for any reason. Later reformers viewed parole as a privilege, earned by good behavior in prison and retained by adherence to parole conditions. More recently, some commentators have begun to describe parole as a right of prisoners who have served enough time in prison, and they urge that technical violations be eliminated as a basis for return to prison. The "rights" view does not now prevail officially in any parole system, although the state of Washington strictly limits the penalties that may be imposed on technical violators.

If parole is a privilege, then its revocation is not subject to due process or rules of evidence. In some states liberal release policies have been justified on the grounds that parole can be swiftly revoked whenever the offender violates the parole rules. Under the New York statute, for example, if a parole officer has reason to believe a parolee has lapsed or is about to lapse into criminal conduct or into the company of criminals, or has violated any important condition of parole, the officer may rearrest the parolee. The officer's power to recommend revocation because the parolee is "slipping" hangs over the parolee like the proverbial sword of Damocles, suspended by a hair.

When the parole officer alleges a technical violation of parole, the U.S. Supreme Court requires a two-stage revocation proceeding. Although the Court exempted revocation proceedings from the normal requirements of a criminal trial, many due process rights must be accorded the parolee.[3] In the first stage, the parole board determines whether there is probable cause that a violation has occurred. (Probable cause is the criterion for deciding whether evidence is strong enough to uphold an arrest or to suggest issuing an arrest or warrant.) The parolee then has the right to be notified of charges, be informed of evidence, be heard, present witnesses, and confront the parole board's witnesses (providing no witness would be endangered by such a confrontation). In the second stage, the parole board decides if the violation is severe enough to warrant return to prison. See "Careers in Corrections" on the previous page for information on the career of a parole hearing officer.

The total number of parole revocations is difficult to determine. A combined revocation and recommitment rate of approximately 25 percent within three years of release has been reported for years, but newer results show a more-complicated picture of parole failure. Within three years, 68 percent are arrested for a new felony, 47 percent are convicted, and 25 percent are returned to prison for the new crime. Taking revocations for new convictions and "technical violations" together, 52 percent of released prisoners are back in prison within three years.[4] In addition, as shown in **Figure 16.3**, the percentage of successful completions as well as the percentage returned to prison shifts over time.

Technical rules violation rates vary dramatically by state (see **Figure 16.4**, p. 438). These vast differences have little to do with the way clients behave and a great deal to do with the way the system enforces its rules. (See the Focus box on California revocation practices.) When a parolee is determined to have violated a condition of parole, the parole agency has several options: (1) return the parolee to prison, (2) note the violation but strengthen supervision rather than revoke parole, (3) note the violation but take no action at that time.[5] Differences in failure rates among the states may reflect agency supervision policies, prison crowding, or political pressures to remove parolees from the community.

Nationally, 35 percent of all new prison admissions are violators of conditional release; of this group, nearly two-thirds are returned to prison for technical violations. In California, the greatest number of new prison admissions are parole violators. Most parole violations occur in the initial months following release—the highest rate of failure is in the first year of release—but parolees can fail even after years of successful adjustment.

The typical length of reconfinement for a technical parole violation varies by original charge. Specifically, those whose original charges are the most serious can expect to serve the most time for their violation, usually 13 additional months in prison, before being released a second time.[6] The guidelines of the Federal Parole Commission

The organization and mission of the of the **Texas Board of Pardons and Paroles** can be viewed at their website, listed at www.cengage.com/criminaljustice/clear.

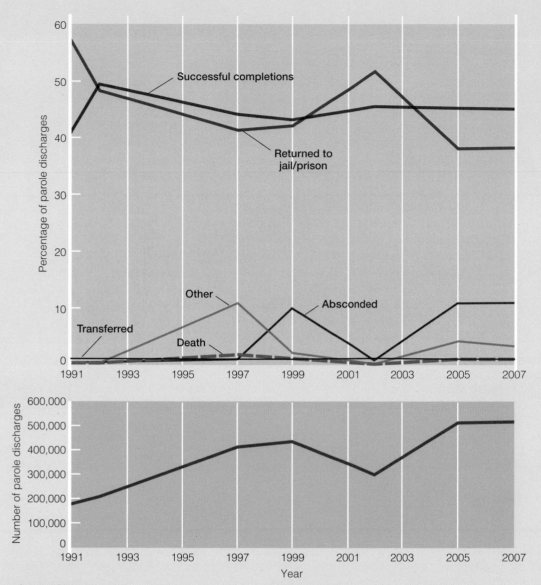

Figure 16.3

Trends in State Parole Discharges, 1991–2007

The percentage of parolees who successfully complete their term and are discharged from supervision varies over the years. What factors might account for these shifts?

*Includes those returned to prison with a new sentence or for technical parole violations and those returned pending parole revocation on new charges.

Sources: Bureau of Justice Statistics: *National Corrections Reporting Program, 1992* (Washington, DC: U.S. Department of Justice, 1995); *News Release,* August 16, 1998; *Bulletin,* October 2001, p. 6; *News Release,* October 3, 2001; *News Release,* April 6, 2004. *Statistical Tables,* December 2008.

recommend up to 8 months for revoked parolees who do not have a history of violations and 8–16 months for persistent violators, for those whose violations occur less than 8 months after release, and for those found to have a negative employment or school record during supervision. Most states do not have such guidelines. The offender whose parole is revoked may be required to serve the remainder of the unexpired sentence. **Figure 16.5** on page 439 shows the different rates of success of prisoners under parole supervision.

The **rights of victims and witnesses subpoenaed to appear before a U.S. Parole Commission revocation hearing** are found at the corresponding link at www.cengage.com/criminaljustice/clear.

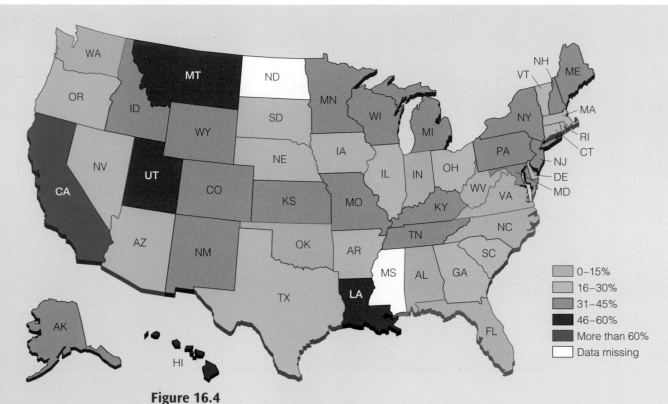

Figure 16.4
Percentage of Prison Admissions Who Are Parole Violators

States vary significantly in the percentage of prison admissions who are parole violators. What causes these differences?

Source: Jeremy Travis and Sarah Lawrence, *Beyond the Prison Gates: The State of Parole in America* (Washington, DC: Urban Institute, 2002), 23.

FOCUS ON

CORRECTIONAL PRACTICE

California: Leading the Nation in the Revocation of Ex-prisoners

When it comes to supervising parolees, California's numbers are stunning. Two-thirds of California's prison releases are back in prison within three years, compared with a 40 percent rate for the rest of the country. And over two-thirds of those who enter the California prison system are going to prison because they failed on community supervision—even though the California prison system is vastly overcrowded and one of the most expensive in the nation. Why is it so difficult to "make it" on parole in California?

The most important difference between California and the rest of the United States is that those who supervise offenders in the community—especially parole officers—are known for their strict enforcement of the rules. Parolees in California are relentlessly tested for drug use, closely moni-

tored for curfews and associations, and strictly required to work and pay their fines, restitution, and other justice fees. The toughness shows in the statistics: Compared with other parolees around the country, California parolees are nearly 50 percent more likely to be revoked for a failed drug test, and nearly one-third are more likely to be revoked for other rules violations.

Some Californians think this is good news. They say that proved risks to the community are being watched much more closely in California than anywhere else in the country. The minute a problem arises they are dealt with quickly and strictly. Others say that the high technical failure rate is misleading: California parole officers revoke their parolees on technical

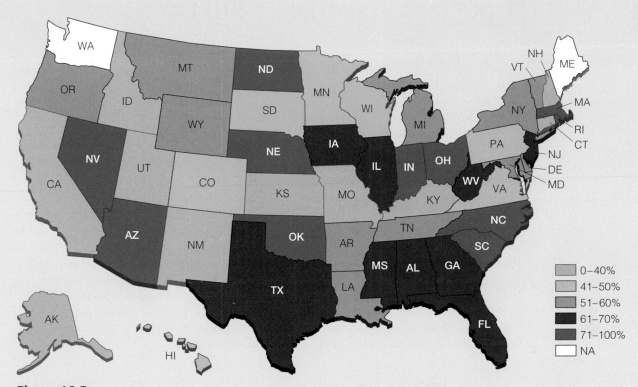

Figure 16.5
Percent Success after Release from State Prison to Parole Supervision

Why do some states seem to do a better job at helping offenders make it after prison?

Note: The most recent data available for AK, IL, NM, and OK is from 2001.

Sources: Bureau of Justice Statistics, *Special Report,* October 2001, p. 11; *Statistical Tables,* December 2008, p. 7.

grounds when there is a new felony arrest, in order to avoid the delays and due process of a trial.

Critics of California's approach point out that growing prison populations are expensive, especially in California, where a year in prison costs over $43,000 per offender. Money tends to be shifted from public education and welfare to pay for the punishments of these offenders, and when so many of them are rules violators rather than repeat felons, critics wonder if this is a wise investment. The real cynics point out that the prison guards union, which has consistently pressed for tough sentencing laws and close enforcement policies with parolees, benefits from the growth in the prison population and has increased its influence on public policy makers and pressure for more officers with higher salaries.

The truth probably lies somewhere in the middle. While a large number of prison admissions are parole violators who have not been convicted of new crimes, this group does not stay long in prison—about four months on average. Moreover, most of the people being returned for technical reasons also had a new arrest that was not prosecuted, because of the parole violation. This makes it seem that California's parole violation policy is important for public safety, but that argument may be misleading. By far most of these arrests are for misdemeanors or nonserious crimes; only 10 percent are for crimes involving violence.

Sources: BJS *Bulletin,* October 2001, p. 11; Ryken Grattet, Joan Petersilia, Jeffrey Lin, and Marlene Beckman, "Parole Violations and Revocations in California: Analysis and Suggestions for Action," *Federal Probation* 73 (no. 1, June 2009): 1–11.

■ THE STRUCTURE OF COMMUNITY SUPERVISION

Three forces influence the newly released offender's adjustment to free society: the parole officer, the parole bureaucracy, and the experiences of the offender. Carl Klockars notes that the structure of these relationships can determine the results of supervision. Klockars describes supervision as a series of stages in which attachments develop, as shown in **Figure 16.6**. In the initial stages of supervision, the strongest attachment is between the officer and the bureaucracy, with a minor attachment between the parolee and the officer and a negative attachment between the parolee and the bureaucracy. The parolee's suspicion of the bureaucracy's rules and his or her fear of its policies never change. As the parolee and officer get to know each other better, however, the officer's strongest attachment gradually shifts from the bureaucracy to the parolee. Finally, the two develop rapport, the ability to communicate positively and with mutual trust.[7]

This model explains why parolees' rule violations are often overlooked: The parole officer identifies more closely with the offender than with the bureaucracy. But the process does not always follow that pattern. Often rapport never develops, and the attachment between the parolee and the officer sours. When strain develops between the parolee and both the officer and the bureaucracy, it is very difficult for the offender to succeed.

What determines the outcome of the supervision process? The answer lies in a complex web of attitudes, situations, policies, and random events. First, consider in detail two major forces: the parole officer and the bureaucracy.

Agents of Community Supervision

Parole officers are usually asked to play two roles: cop and social worker. As cops, they can restrict many aspects of the parolee's life, enforce conditions of release, and initiate revocation for violations. In states that subscribe to the concept of parole as grace, officers may search the parolee's living quarters without warning, arrest him or her for suspected violations without bail, and suspend parole pending a hearing. One common practice is to "hold" misbehaving parolees in jail for a day or two to warn them not to challenge the officer's authority. Like other street-level bureaucrats in the criminal justice system, officers have extensive discretionary power. The officer's relationship with the offender thus has an authoritative component that can hinder the development of rapport and mutual trust.

Besides policing their charges, parole officers must act as social workers by helping parolees find jobs and restore family ties. They must mediate between parolees and

Figure 16.6
Positive and Negative Attachments at Three Stages of the Supervision Process

Parolees and their parole officers tend to develop a positive attachment as supervision proceeds.

Source: Carl B. Klockars, "A Theory of Probation Supervision," *Journal of Criminal Law, Criminology, and Police Science* 63 (1972): 550–57.

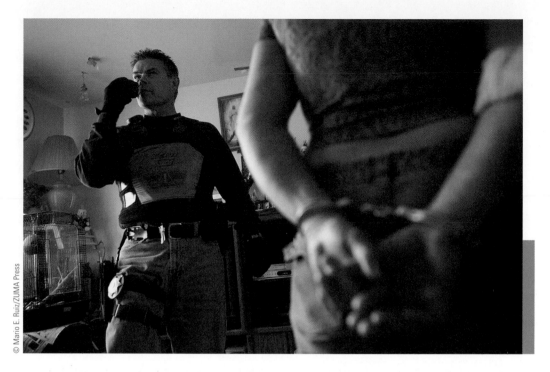

© Mario E. Ruiz/ZUMA Press

Officer Randy Hall of the Utah State Adult Probation and Parole department radios information to headquarters to report the arrest of a parolee during a home visit.

organizations and channel parolees to such human service agencies as psychiatric clinics. As caseworkers, officers must develop a relationship that fosters trust and confidence, which is not likely to develop if parolees are made constantly aware of the officers' ability to send them back to prison.

How can parole officers reconcile these conflicting role demands? One suggestion is to divide the responsibilities, so that the officer carries out the supervision and other people perform casework functions. Alternatively, the officer can be charged solely with casework, and local police can check for violations. Georgia experimented with having a team of two supervisors handle a caseload jointly. One person (often a former police officer) was the surveillance officer, and the other was the probation officer, providing assistance. However, the distinction often became vague: Parolees often looked to surveillance officers for help and saw probation officers as enforcing the conditions of supervision. Despite the conflict, it seems that any person having supervisory contact with the offender must perform both roles.

The parole officer's style has been referred to as one of two "hidden conditions" of supervision. Officers have certain expectations about how clients will behave and therefore how to treat them. Some officers take a parental approach; welfare workers approach the job as professional caseworkers; punitive officers see themselves as community protection agents; passive agents are bureaucrats. Each approach leads to a style of interaction with parolees—gruff, distant, or friendly—that informally determines the supervision process. In fact, style can overwhelm other aspects of the work. For instance, Elliot Studt's famous study of parole officers in California revealed that their individual styles were so varied that each could almost be thought of as a separate agency.[8]

The second hidden condition of supervision is the supervision plan. In most agencies, the officer and parolee develop a supervision (or treatment) plan that states what the parolee is going to do about the problems (unemployment, drug abuse, marital conflict, and so on) that hinder adjustment to the community. The officer has a great deal of discretion in developing this plan and may put a lot of energy into it or very little. This latitude may explain why officers who are oriented toward providing assistance tend to write significantly more supervision objectives for their clients and to get involved in more areas of parolees' lives than do other officers.

As street-level bureaucrats, officers are also affected by organizational demands unrelated to either assistance or control. Richard McCleary's classic study of parole officers in Cook County (Chicago) disclosed that decisions about individual parolees are influenced by the organization's definition of the situation, the officer's own perception of the parolee, and the officer's professional reputation.[9] Members of the parole bureaucracy strive to maintain desirable professional conditions: a good working atmosphere, independence from supervisory oversight, and the use of discretion. Certain parolees are viewed as threatening to the status quo because they make trouble for their officers and for the officers' superiors; they therefore elicit special responses from their officers.

McCleary believes that by typing each parolee from the start, the officer neutralizes potential trouble. On the basis of parolees' files, initial interviews, and home visits, the officer categorizes clients as sincere, criminally inclined, or dangerous. "Dangerous" refers not to parolees who are potentially violent, but rather to those few who may act irrationally or unpredictably, who do not respond to warnings, and who go out of their way to make trouble. The "dangerous" parolees are the most worrisome, for an officer has the most difficulty maintaining control over them. McCleary found that, surprisingly, one way to control them is to bargain with them:

> *All right, Johnny, this is how it is. I've got you on paper for the next seven years, but I'll make a deal with you. You give me two years of good behavior and I'll recommend you for early discharge. When I say "good behavior," though, I mean cooperation. When I tell you to do something, you do it. You don't argue with me about whether I'm right or wrong or whether it's fair or not, or even whether I have the right to tell you to do it. You just do it. If you give me two years of cooperation like that, I'll give you an early discharge.*[10]

CAREERS IN CORRECTIONS   Parole Officer

NATURE OF THE WORK

Like their probation counterparts, parole officers supervise offenders in the community through personal contact with offenders and their families. Unlike probation officers, who are generally employed by the county, parole officers are employed by the state.

In most jurisdictions they are armed peace officers with the power of arrest. As an essential ingredient in the reentry process, parole officers help offenders readjust to the community and find housing and employment. They monitor offenders' behavior to ensure that parole requirements are met. If the conditions are not met or the offender commits another crime, the officer may recommend revocation of the parole. Fieldwork may take the officer to high-crime areas where there is a risk of violence.

REQUIRED QUALIFICATIONS

Background qualifications for parole officers vary by state, but a bachelor's degree in social work, criminal justice, or a related field is usually required. Some agencies require previous experience or graduate work. Candidates must be 21 years of age, have no felony convictions, and have no restrictions on their carrying a firearm. Most parole officers receive formal training and typically work as a trainee for up to one year.

EARNINGS AND JOB OUTLOOK

The number of parole officers is expected to grow as the number of inmates leaving prison increases during the next decade. Starting salaries for parole officers vary by region, but the national median salary is $49,500.

MORE INFORMATION

Visit the website of the **American Probation and Parole Association**. See also the website for **Salary Wizard**. The web links are available at www.cengage.com/criminaljustice/clear. You can also obtain career information from your state's parole office.

Thus, parole officers represent one set of forces that affect a parolee's chance of making it. Officers can support parolees or hinder their adjustment. They "read" parolees and then decide how they will treat them. Apart from their formal power to revoke parole on the basis of violations, they have even greater informal power—to make life for parolees difficult or easy, depending on the way they approach their jobs. "Careers in Corrections" offers a closer view of the work of a parole officer.

The Community Supervision Bureaucracy

Parole officers do not work in a vacuum. Although the job often attracts people who like flexible schedules and substantial latitude, every officer works in an organizational context, usually in close contact with other officers. Parole officers therefore face limits in their approaches to cases. The limits derive from both the specific need to manage a heavier workload than is feasible in the available time and the general need to respond to organizational philosophies and policies.

WORKLOAD ■ In his award-winning essay on human services, Michael Lipsky points out that the difficulties faced by many clients of human services are so complex that "the job . . . is in a sense impossible to do in ideal terms."[11] One tool that parole organizations find useful in the face of this reality is a classification system that structures the relationship between the officer and the parolee. The system lets the parole bureaucracy prescribe rules for allocating officers' time, with priority given to the parolees most in need. The system in New York is typical (see **Table 16.1**). In general, officers spend more time with the new releasees than with those who have been out for some time. The level of supervision is later adjusted to "active" or "reduced" surveillance, depending on how the releasee functions in the community. As the officer gains confidence in the parolee, only periodic check-ins may be required. Finally, at the end of the maximum length of the sentence or at the time specified by the parole board, the former convict is discharged from supervision.

TABLE 16.1 *An Example of the Varying Levels of Supervision Provided to Releasees*

	Supervision Level		
Type of Contact	**Intensive**	**Active**	**Reduced**
Most parole systems vary amount of supervision according to the risk posed by the offender, the length of time on parole, and the response to the supervision.			
Reporting to parole office	Weekly or semimonthly	Monthly or up to but not exceeding every 2 months	Quarterly or less frequently up to and including annually
Employment check	Monthly	Every 2 months	Same as reporting
Employment visit	Every 3 months	Every 3 months	At least as frequently as reporting
Home visit	Every 3 months	Monthly	Not mentioned
Other and collateral visits	More frequently than active or reduced	Not mentioned	Not mentioned

Source: Adapted from David T. Stanley, *Prisoners among Us* (Washington, DC: Brookings Institution, 1976), 96.

Parole officers Jerry Ramirez and Guillermo Vicro Rosa talk with a parolee. Besides policing their charges, officers must act as social workers by helping parolees find jobs and restore family ties. This often leads to role conflict.

AP Images/Jeff Chiu

Reformers have long held that parole caseloads should include no more than 36 cases per officer. In reality, caseloads vary dramatically but average about 80 parolees per officer. This is smaller than the average probation caseload, but the services required by parolees are greater. There is no solid empirical evidence that smaller caseloads are more likely to lead to successful outcomes for probationers and parolees.[12]

The caseload affects how often an officer can contact each parolee and how much help can be given. Some states structure low, specialized caseloads for officers who supervise certain types of parolees, but even with specialized caseloads, time available for parolees can be minimal, often less than an hour a month. One reason for the small contact time is that officers must spend time on bureaucratic duties such as paperwork and in the field helping parolees deal with other service agencies—medical, employment, educational. Parole officers spend as much as 80 percent of their time at nonsupervisory work.

PHILOSOPHY AND POLICY ■ Originally parole officers worked directly for parole boards, and some boards still favor this arrangement because it means that the parole officer's strategies more closely follow their philosophy. In recent decades, however, parole field staffs have increasingly become part of correctional departments. With the growing emphasis on parole's links to other aspects of community corrections and on the use of prerelease programs, halfway houses, and other community-based services, the rationale is that institutional and field activities need to be coordinated months before an inmate's release on parole.

Many states combine probation and parole staffs because they perform similar functions. As pointed out, however, probation officers have ties to judges, whereas parole is seen as part of corrections. Parole has a greater law enforcement orientation: Parole agents in some states carry guns, and all are sworn officers. Agents with social work orientations thus seem more likely to gravitate toward probation.

Field service operations vary in their overall philosophy of supervision. Traditionally, parolees are assigned to their officers on the basis of where they live, so that reporting and field supervision are easier for both parties. (If an area has an unusually large number of parolees to be supervised, agencies can adjust boundaries in order to keep parole officers' caseloads roughly equal in size.) In theory, this geographic assignment helps parole officers work more closely with community service agencies in providing services to parolees. In practice, however, officers in such agencies can become isolated from their peers, their supervisors, and social services. Such officers ordinarily draw little attention to their efforts unless a client creates a problem (perhaps by a new arrest), so there is an incentive to monitor cases closely to avoid unpleasant surprises. The traditional field services agency gives its officers much latitude, and it is understood that they will be left alone until a client's behavior draws a superior's attention. They are often merely told, "Cover your bases." In recent years this traditional model of parole field services has come under criticism.

There has never been much evidence that the isolated caseload under complete discretion of a parole officer is a particularly effective way to organize the work. Moreover, a renewed emphasis on rehabilitation has led some administrators to conclude that specialization can improve services by allowing parole officers to concentrate on particular problems. Thus, one officer may handle drug users, another may supervise unemployed offenders, and so on. The argument for specialization is that homogeneous workloads make better use of staff expertise, and officers can better understand and respond to clients who have similar characteristics. Yet this strategy breeds discontent among officers because the specialties often conflict. For one thing, it is difficult to equalize workloads. Who can tell, for instance, whether it takes more or less effort to supervise 30 drug addicts than to supervise 40 sex offenders? Moreover, because officers want to think their jobs are important, they often clash over whose work (and special clientele) is the most central to the agency's mission.

Because of these problems, a premium is sometimes placed on brokering services from other agencies—referring parolees to social services that specialize in certain areas, such as employment training or drug treatment. The officer's main role then is to determine the client's most serious problems, locate agencies that handle such problems, and help the client make use of the agencies' services. Although brokering helps involve offenders with established community services, the small amount of direct contact between officers and offenders may lead to a lack of accountability and control over offenders.

In the end, this emphasis on control is what matters most in the philosophy of an agency. A parole officer can handle cases in whatever way he or she sees fit as long as the caseload is "under control." But no matter what a parole officer might believe—and no matter how skilled he or she may be—the parole officer must know where the clients are and how well they are doing. Those who are recently released from prison will always be plagued with recurring difficulties; however, without a sense that the officer is "in charge," problems can quickly arise that cause the public to question the capacity of parole to serve the community's need for safety.

CONSTRAINTS ON OFFICERS' AUTHORITY ■ Parole officers often are portrayed as having absolute authority over their clients, as being able to manage offenders in any way they see fit. It is more accurate to say that in using discretion, officers balance many constraints.

The bureaucratic context pressures parole officers to "go along with the system," just as police officers are pressured to cover for their partners. In this respect, parole resembles other correctional functions: Line workers are isolated from administration and depend on one another for support. They feel constrained to behave supportively and to let well enough alone. As one parole supervisor said,

> I won't stand for one of my parole officers (POs) second-guessing another. If I tolerated that, I'd have grudges going on here. Pretty soon I'd have an office full of snitches. A few years ago, I had a PO who couldn't keep his nose out of the other caseloads. I spoke to him about it but that didn't do any good. He thought he was the conscience of the Department of Corrections. I finally got fed up with his meddling and I gave him a taste of his own medicine. I went over to his files and found unfinished work for him to do.[13]

Parole officers perform their jobs in ways that maintain office norms without threatening their co-workers. Office norms reduce their discretion, however, because the unwritten rules often force them to take actions in regard to problems that they might otherwise have handled differently. In recent times, for example, jails and prisons have become so overcrowded that officers feel informal (but very clear) pressures not to crowd the institutions further with revocations for "nonserious" violations.

The parole bureaucracy, then, affects the offender's postrelease experience in several ways. First, it provides rules and policies for managing workloads that would otherwise be unbearable. Second, it structures the activities of parole officers according to traditional philosophical orientations. Finally, it provides a context of unwritten and informal norms that define appropriate and inappropriate officer conduct.

■ RESIDENTIAL PROGRAMS

community correctional center

A small-group living facility for offenders, especially those who have been recently released from prison.

Residential programs serve offenders when they are first released from prison. Most house between 10 and 25 offenders at any one time in medium- or minimum-security facilities. Placing heavy emphasis on involving the offenders in regular community functions, treatment staff help offenders work out plans to address their problems.

Residential programs are often referred to as **community correctional centers**. Most require that offenders live on the premises while working in the community. They usually provide counseling and drug treatment and impose strict curfews on residents when they are not working. Many of these facilities are renovated private homes or small hotels. Individual rooms, coupled with group dining and recreation areas, help these facilities achieve a homelike character. By obeying the rules and maintaining good behavior in the facility, residents gradually earn a reduction in restrictions—for instance, the ability to spend some free time in the community. The idea is to provide treatment support to the offender while promoting the step-by-step adjustment to community life.

Residential centers face problems, however. With high staff–resident ratios, they are relatively expensive to operate; they represent a real savings in costs only when they enable a jurisdiction to avoid construction of a new prison. Some centers have high failure rates—one-third or more of the residents may be rearrested in a year—but the main problems with these centers are political. Misbehavior by residents makes them unpopular with the local community. Just one serious offense can result in a strong public backlash. Citizens typically do not want groups of ex-convicts living in their midst (as noted earlier, NIMBY stands for "Not In My Back Yard"). See "Myths in Corrections" for more.

Parolees Teresa Partlow and Sandi Havel talk in their dorm-style bedroom on the campus of L.I.F.E. Tech, a center in Wetumpka, Alabama, that helps parolees with mental health or substance abuse problems make a transition back into society.

The most common type of community correctional center is the halfway house, or **work release center**. This idea originated in Wisconsin in 1913 with the passage of the Huber law, which let prisoners work in gainful occupations outside the prison as long as they returned to their cells at night.

Two kinds of work release programs are available today. In the more secure of the two, prisoners work during the day (often in groups) and then return at night to a group housing unit. In the other version, sometimes called *work furlough,* offenders work and live at home during the week and return to the prison for the weekend.

The idea underlying the halfway house is straightforward: Returning to the community after institutionalization requires an adjustment, and a relatively controlled environment improves adjustment. Because studies indicate that the highest failure rates of parolees occur in the early months of parole, this idea seems plausible. Recently halfway houses have become more than mere stopping points for prisoners released from custody; they now employ direct treatment methods (such as therapeutic community techniques) to help offenders. By these standards, how have the release programs fared?

The earliest studies of residential release programs tended to find that these offenders performed slightly worse on parole and had higher rates of return to prison than did those given regular parole supervision. Later studies have uncovered more-positive results, and today most experts agree that work release can play a role in the successful adjustment of those released from the state's prisons. Although there is still no incontestable scientific evidence that these centers "work," the research certainly indicates that remaining in prison is not preferable to work release.

One basic problem is the schizophrenic environment within which the programs operate. On the one hand, without these programs many corrections systems would be unable to manage their ballooning populations. On the other, relying on release programs makes leaders of corrections systems vulnerable to highly publicized failures, especially when a parolee commits a heinous crime.

Certainly release programs do not inevitably lead to reintegration of offenders. Perhaps the timing is faulty: Prisoners do not necessarily benefit from such assistance at the release stage. Or, more likely, the simple mechanism of graduated release may just not be up to the task of eradicating the negative impact of prison on offenders. In any case, the only thing we know for sure is that the effectiveness of programs designed to handle offenders who are being released from incarceration has been disappointing.

MYTHS IN CORRECTIONS

HALFWAY HOUSES AND PROPERTY VALUES

THE MYTH: When halfway houses or work release centers open in a neighborhood, property values go down and crime goes up.

THE REALITY: Studies find that opening a new halfway house or work release center has no effect on local crime rates or property values, and there is even some evidence that both of these aspects of neighborhoods improve.

Sources: Mary Shilton and Margot Lindsay, *Siting Half-Way House—Some Suggestions for Correctional Professionals* (Washington, DC: Center for Community Corrections, September, 2003); Washington Lawyer's Committee for Civil Rights and Urban Affairs, *Policy Brief: Studies on Halfway Houses,* http://www.washlaw.org/projects/dcprisoners_rights/studies_on_halfway_houses.htm, May 8, 2007.

work release center
A facility that allows offenders to work in the community during the day while residing in the center during nonworking hours.

■ THE OFFENDER'S EXPERIENCE OF POSTRELEASE LIFE

The new releasee faces three harsh realities: the strangeness of reentry, unmet personal needs, and barriers to success. Each must be dealt with separately; each poses a challenge to the newly released offender (see the Focus box "It's Time I Shed My Ex-convict Status").

The Strangeness of Reentry

Although release from prison can be euphoric, it can also be a letdown, particularly for parolees who return after two, three, or more years away. The images in their minds of friends and loved ones represent snapshots frozen in time, but in reality everyone has changed (as has the parolee): moved away, taken a new job, grown up, or, perhaps most disturbing, become almost a stranger. Initial attempts to restore old ties thus

FOCUS ON
PEOPLE IN CORRECTIONS

It's Time I Shed My Ex-convict Status

Twenty years ago I decided to drastically turn my life around. With a state-issued olive suit on my back, a high school equivalency diploma and $40 travel money in my pocket, I became an ex-convict. I had done my time—almost five years in all—and now had the opportunity to redeem myself. I felt almost optimistic. As the huge outer gate of New York State's Clinton prison slammed behind me, the discharge officer bid me farewell: "Get your act together," he bellowed with a mix of sincerity and humor. "I don't want to see you back here any time soon." A Department of Corrections van sat rumbling at the prison's checkpoint—my ride to the Greyhound bus depot.

Alcohol and other drugs had been my failing. Realizing I would need help, I sought an organization of other recovering addicts. Within a few days I landed a job in a metal plating factory and rented a tiny furnished apartment. On the urging of a new friend who had a similar past, I soon took my first college course. My first grade was a C, but before long I was scoring A's and B's. I also got better jobs, eventually landing a counseling job in a substance abuse treatment program. On job applications, I left questions about past arrests and convictions blank. I'd read that this would probably go unnoticed and, if it didn't it would be better to discuss such matters in person. Time passed and, in a few short years, I completed college. I went on to get my master's degree and using my graduate thesis as its foundation, I wrote a book on drugs in the workplace.

All these qualities notwithstanding, I remain, irrevocably an ex-convict. Although the years have removed all but hazy memories of addiction, hospitalization, street living and prison, I secretly carry the baggage of a former offender. As my qualifications for higher-level positions grew, so, too, did the potential for a more detailed scrutiny of my past.

On virtually every job application, the question continued to haunt me, "Have you ever been convicted of a felony or misdemeanor or denied bond in any state?" Staring blankly at the application, I would often wonder, will this nightmare ever end? For minorities, who have a higher rate of incarceration, the nightmare is even more likely to occur.

To the average person, the ex-convict is an individual of questionable character. And without the experience of meeting a rehabilitated offender, there is little chance that this image will change. It is reinforced by the fact that the only thing usually newsworthy about an ex-convict is bad news—another arrest.

Yet the real news is that many former offenders are, like me, rehabilitated members of society. No one would guess at our pasts. We don't deserve kudos for not committing crimes, but our failings should not supersede decades of personal growth and responsible citizenship. Unfortunately that's often what happens.

Under employment discrimination laws, hiring decisions cannot be made on the basis of age, sex or the color a person's skin. A job applicant does not have to reveal disability or medical condition, including former drug dependence. Employability is based on the ability to perform the essential function of the job.

No one is born an ex-convict; the title is earned and the individual must accept responsibility. Yet wouldn't it be nice if there were an ex-ex-con status? . . . To those of us who have paid our debt to society, it's a form of discrimination that undermines our efforts to continue to rebuild our lives.

Source: Walter Scanlon, "It's Time I Shed My Ex-convict Status," *Newsweek*, February 21, 2000, p. 10. All rights reserved. Reprinted by permission.

can be threatening and deeply disappointing. How many relationships—with spouses, children, and old friends—can survive unscarred the strain of long separation?

Moreover, freedom is now an unfamiliar environment. In prison, every decision about daily life is made by others, so routine decision-making skills atrophy. There are plenty of sad-funny stories about parolees looking at a menu for the first time in years and panicking at the prospect of choosing a meal and ordering it. Compare this simple task with the more-important tasks of getting a job, finding housing, and so on. Returning to the streets after years behind bars is a shock; the most normal, unremarkable events take on overwhelming significance. Max described his postrelease experience to a team of researchers:

Basically, everything had been changed. You can go in for six months and come back out and see a great change in society itself. But the main thing was trying to adjust to, say stuff like the phone system, try to adjust to the ways people are acting and what is going on in your community . . . and um, they put you out with no money and they say go make it. And that is kind of hard, it is real hard, if you are not strong you usually fall back into the things you used to do in order to get you right back into, caught back up in the same old circle. If you had a strong family support, a strong background, someone who would look out for you as far as giving you a job, giving you some money, then you might be able to survive a while. But, if not, more than likely you will go back.[14]

In time the strangeness of the free world can become a source of discomfort and pressure. To deal with this strangeness, ex-offenders are tempted to reach out to the familiar—old friends and old pastimes—and this can lead to trouble. Said one young parolee,

I wasn't tempted when I first got out because I wanted to do right, I didn't want to go back. I didn't want to be—I didn't want to have someone else controlling any life anymore. I wanted to be, you know, my own decision-maker, so therefore it was—I know not to hang out with them, you know, but it's still like pressure, you know, still pressure, do you want to come around? It's like the devil, you know, really. You know you're trying to do right, he's still going to do whatever he can to bring you back out there with him. Peer pressure is a major thing in dealing with this.[15]

Supervision and Surveillance

Most offenders released from prison are far from free. Parolees must report to a parole officer and undergo community supervision until their full sentence has been completed. The people who provide the supervision tend to define their work as "support" for the offender during this period of adjustment, but the person released might not agree.

One underlying message of supervision, no matter how supportive, is that the ex-offender is not really free. There are rules to be obeyed and authorities to heed. The promise of release, with its aura of freedom, soon dissipates into a hard reality: ex-prisoners may think they have paid their debt to society, but they cannot yet rejoin their fellow citizens. There is always the chance of running afoul of the authorities and being faced with return.

Stay out two years, wipe the slate clean, flunk a piss test, they put me back in prison again. I ain't done nothing wrong. And that is what my parole officer saying, "Wow, you ain't committed no crime." I didn't commit one then but they say I did. I couldn't afford a lawyer at the time. I work for the city of Tallahassee, I couldn't afford a lawyer. And that is another thing about we being in the project, we can't afford a good attorney to represent us in the right proper way to get us off. A lot of those cases that go on down there, they would throw them out. Because you don't have an attorney, you don't know the law, they get you. . . . It's bad on us. It is really bad.[16]

Supervision is not a uniformly adverse experience. For many parolees, the officer will serve as an important source of tangible help with problems that might otherwise never be overcome. And it seems that supervision may help, overall. In both Canada and the United States, offenders released under supervision experience fewer returns to prison for new crimes than do those who leave without supervision.[17]

The **Howard League for Penal Reform** was founded in England and has branches throughout North America. It provides assistance to ex-prisoners. See the corresponding link at www.cengage.com/criminaljustice/clear.

The Problem of Unmet Personal Needs

Parolees are aware they must meet critical needs to make it on the streets. Education, money, and a job tend to top the list. Yet they are not always realistic about how to meet their needs. Participation in vocational and educational programs in prisons has been declining over the past decade, and only a minority of prisoners in need of drug treatment receive it while incarcerated.[18] Many parolees cannot identify the specific things they must avoid doing in order to stay out of trouble.

Some parolees face even more-serious needs as they reenter the community. Three-quarters report a history of drug or alcohol abuse, almost 40,000 are HIV positive (16 percent of all HIV-positive Americans are prison releases), up to 100,000 have at least one serious mental disorder requiring psychiatric services, and many—perhaps

After 13 years in prison, Adam Gaines, right, is trying to be the father he never was to his sons, Shane and Adam, Jr. "I didn't have a role model," said Adam, Jr., who dropped out of high school. Many parolees must not only live by the rules of their release, but also deal with the problems of their families.

10 percent or more—are homeless.[19] In many cases, community supervision addresses these needs, but far too often it does not, with severe results:

> *I really tried to stay out of trouble, but it's very difficult, you know. Like once you're into a routine and the people you're hanging about with and everything, and plus you're always getting hassled by the police. . . . It was about this time that I left home . . . and I was on the streets for a very long time . . . because I was homeless, I couldn't get a . . . job . . . but I still had . . . fines that I had to pay. . . . So I am stuck in this rut. I've got to pay these fines or go to jail, and I've got to live as well. So I was committing more crimes, going back to court and getting more fines, and it was just a vicious circle. So the next thing I ended up back in prison again.[20]*

Going to prison also has a negative impact on the former prisoner's intimate relationships. Women face the problem of trying to reestablish relationships with their children, who have been raised by someone else while they were behind bars. Men find it harder to establish strong marital relationships: Going to prison reduces the chances of later being married by over 40 percent, and this effect is twice as strong for African Americans than it is for whites.[21]

In many ways, the most intractable needs have to do with treatment for mental health problems. A recent report to Congress concluded that at least 8 percent of those in jail and 13 percent of those in prison will experience "an acute episode of serious mental illness" during their incarceration.[22] The rates for community corrections fall between those of prison and jail.

Barriers to Success

Soon after release, offenders learn that they have achieved an in-between status: They are back in society but not totally free. They face restrictions beyond the close monitoring of the parole officer. (See the Focus box "In the Clutches of the System: The Story of Elaine Bartlett.") Many restrictions are statutory, stemming from a common-law tradition that people who are incarcerated are "civilly dead" and have lost all civil rights. Compounding their adjustment problems are myriad impediments to employment.

CIVIL DISABILITIES ■ The right to vote and to hold public office are two civil rights that are generally limited on conviction of a felony. Eighty percent of the states return the right to vote after some period; seven states return it after offenders have

FOCUS ON
PEOPLE IN CORRECTIONS

In the Clutches of the System: The Story of Elaine Bartlett

The award-winning book, *Life on the Outside*, tells the story of Elaine Bartlett, an African American woman from Harlem, New York City. At age 26 she was convicted of a drug crime and sentenced to serve 20 years to life under the Rockefeller Drug Laws, the toughest drug laws in the country. It was her first offense, a crime for which she served 16 years in prison. Written by Jennifer Gonnerman, the book tells Bartlett's re-entry story—how she learned to deal with her four children, now grown, and worked through the deflating web of barriers that women returning from prison must face. On her first day out, "it felt strange to ride in the backseat of the . . . van without steel cuffs around my wrists." The book recounts how Bartlett hunted for a job, dealt with the parole bureaucracy, faced distrust and racist hostility, confronted strained personal and family relationships, and tried to navigate other aspects of a range of hardships after prison. Both heartbreaking and uplifting, the book closes with Bartlett saying, "Remember when you used to look down your nose at me? Well look at me now."

Prison reformers and drug law activists have found the book compelling. They champion Bartlett's story as a case study in what is wrong with the system. It plays that function well. Bartlett deals with one crisis after another, one mind-boggling restriction after another—as well as a host of personal challenges as she tries to get her life together. Nobody who reads this story can deny the impediments that are put in peoples' paths after they have been to prison. And nobody can deny the resilience that people must display as they face the challenges of reentry.

Since the book's publication, the story has continued. In 2006 Elaine was arrested for "hindering prosecution" for helping her boyfriend try to evade the police after he allegedly killed somebody. He was later caught, convicted, and sentenced to 25 to life. She went to trial on her charges, and the jury deadlocked. She later pleaded guilty to a lesser charge (a misdemeanor) and got probation.

Sources: Jennifer Gonnerman, *Life on the Outside: The Prison Odyssey of Elaine Bartlett* (New York: Farrar, Straus & Giroux, 2004); personal communication.

---

served their full sentence, and seven disenfranchise for life anyone convicted of a felony[23] (see **Figure 16.7**, p. 452). Only through a pardon is full citizenship restored. Twenty-one states return the right to hold public office to felony offenders following discharge from probation, parole, or prison; 19 states permanently restrict that right

except for pardoned felons. Many states deny felons other civil rights, such as serving on juries, holding public office, and holding positions of public trust (which include most government jobs).

An estimated 3.9 million Americans, including 1.4 million African American men (13 percent of all black men) cannot vote because of their felony convictions. Thus, in Alabama and Florida, one-third of African American men are permanently ineligible to vote, and in Iowa, Mississippi, New Mexico, Virginia, Washington, and Wyoming, the ratio is one to four. Researchers have shown that Al Gore would have won the presidency in 2000 if felons had been allowed to vote.[24]

Voting may be the most notable civil disability of ex-prisoners, but other legal barriers also directly affect those trying to make it after a term in prison. Many of the more-recent obstructions to reentry have come about

Missy Shea of the Vermont Secretary of State's office helps inmates at the Marble Valley Regional Correctional Facility through the voter registration process. Only Maine and Vermont allow incarcerated individuals to vote.

The number of states that prohibit felons from voting . . .

. . . while in prison   48

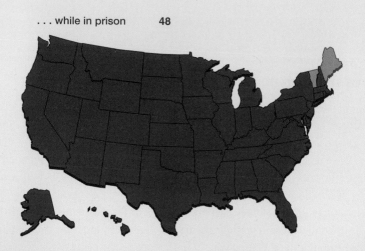

. . . while on parole   33

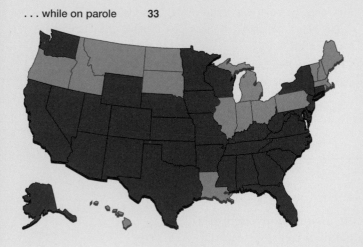

. . . while on probation   29

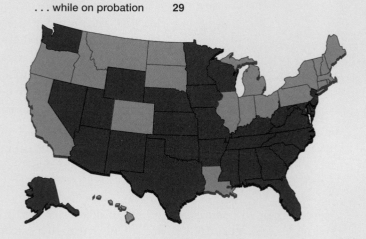

. . . after sentence is completed, for some types of felons   14

. . . after sentence is completed, for all felons   7

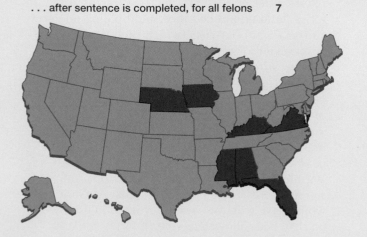

Figure 16.7
Voting Rights for Felons

Florida is the largest of seven states that can permanently strip all felons of their right to vote. States have clemency processes to restore voting rights in some cases.

Source: *New York Times,* March 28, 2004, p. 19.

through federal legislation. The Legal Action Center recently published a state-by-state analysis of legal barriers in reentry.[25] These include the following:

1 *Public assistance and food stamps:* Changes in federal welfare law that were enacted in 1996 put in place a lifetime eligibility ban for food stamps and Temporary Assistance to Needy Families (TANF—child welfare) for anyone convicted of a drug-related felony. States had the option of dropping out of some aspects of the federal ban. Only 12 states did so, leaving 38 states refusing food stamps, TANF, or both.

2 *Public housing:* Federal regulations allow any public housing authority (subsidized housing providers) to evict any person (or the person's family) when the person is arrested for a drug-related crime, and any returning felon may also be refused housing.

3 *Driver's licenses:* A 1992 federal law withheld some highway funds unless the states suspended the licenses of people convicted of a drug crime. Twenty-seven states now suspend licenses automatically.

4 *Adoptions and foster care:* Fifteen states bar those with criminal records from adopting children or serving as foster parents.

5 *Student loans:* The Higher Education Act of 1998 makes students convicted of drug-related crimes ineligible for grants, loans, or work assistance to support college.

EMPLOYMENT ■ Barriers to employment are both formal and informal. Employers hesitate to hire parolees, because they view a conviction as evidence of untrustworthiness. Thus, to the cumulative effect of statutory and informal discrimination we must add many offenders' unrealistic expectations for employment. As one parolee explains,

> *Contrary to my prison expectations, finding employment was not an easy task. In fact, it took me over six weeks to find my first job, even though, at least for the first month, I made a conscientious and continuing effort to find employment. I quickly found that I had no marketable skills. My three years' experience working for a railroad before I was imprisoned provided me with no work skills transferable to other forms of employment. Nor did my prison assignments in the tag shop (making license plates and street signs), in the soap shop (making soap), or as a cellhouse worker prove to be of any assistance. The only job openings available to me were nonskilled factory work and employment in service-oriented businesses. Finally, after six weeks, I found employment mixing chemicals in vats for placement later in spray cans. After two weeks the personnel manager told me that he had to discharge me because I had lied about my criminal history (I had). Even though my foreman spoke up for me, supposedly company policy had to be followed.[26]*

The legal barriers to employment are perhaps the most frustrating, because they constitute an insurmountable wall between the offender and job opportunities. In many states several occupations require licenses that are denied to any ex-convict. The courts have upheld these bans when the work has a connection to the criminal conduct of the offender. For example, it is constitutional for a state to forbid employment of convicted child molesters in day care centers. Other statutes bar from specified jobs any person who "gave evidence of moral turpitude or a lack of good moral character"— characteristics that many people attribute to convicts. Over the last 20 years, some employment prohibitions have been eliminated, but others have been imposed. Some of the changes are dramatic, so that in many states ex-offenders have now entered professions closed to them for centuries; yet public reaction to specific cases has resulted in new prohibitions in some locations.

Making matters worse, such statutes bar some of the jobs that former offenders have been trained to do. All states, for instance, restrict former offenders from employment as barbers (even though many prisons provide training programs in barbering), beauticians, and nurses. Further, well-paying jobs tend to be reserved for people with no criminal record. Indeed, newly released offenders may find themselves legally barred from jobs they held before they were incarcerated. In most states civil service regulations or special statutes bar or restrict the employment of former offenders. Even a prior arrest for a felony without a conviction can lead to rejection. Cities and counties

FOCUS ON CORRECTIONAL PRACTICE

Services for Parolees Reduce Their Recidivism

When Brooklyn, New York, District Attorney Charles Hynes realized that much of the work of his office had to do with prosecuting mostly minor crimes committed by people who had been previously prosecuted for crimes, he was confronting the age-old frustration of the revolving door of justice. Most people, when they think of this problem, immediately wonder if the system needs to be "tougher" in order to deter crime better. D.A. Hynes was no stranger to this perspective—he had been D.A. for 16 years and had helped the courts impose some of the toughest sentences in New York. He knew something only long-term insiders know: Many people recidivate, not because the system is too lenient, but because "making it" for former prisoners is not easy, even under the best of circumstances.

Hynes decided he wanted to try a different strategy, so in 1999 he started a new program: ComALERT (Community and Law Enforcement Resources Together). The core idea of ComALERT was simple—to provide a comprehensive array of services to people shortly after their release from prison. What made it different was locating the program in the prosecutor's office, so that the full weight of law enforcement served them—not as a threat, but as a support. The program promised help in getting jobs, finding housing, reintegrating into the community, and staying sober. When Harvard Professor Bruce Western recently completed an evaluation of ComALERT, the results were impressive. People who enter ComALERT are 15 percent less likely to be arrested or end up in prison, and those who stay in the program for the long run, availing themselves of its services over a longer period, are about 30 percent less like to do so. The program saves money, prevents crime, and reduces the hardships of reentry.

That a program of services should be so important for reentry success should not be surprising, however. For a decade, the Urban Institute has been studying reentry in dozens of locations. It has found consistently that well-designed and well-supported services lead to less recidivism.

Sources: Erin Jacobs and Bruce Western, *Report on the Evaluation of the ComALERT Prisoner Reentry Program* (New York: Kings County District Attorney's Office; October 2007); Urban Institute, http://www.urban.org/justice/corrections.cfm, October 8, 2009.

---

have more restrictions than do states. Even a prior arrest as a juvenile is an absolute bar to employment in a criminal justice occupation in many states, despite the fact that criminal justice agencies that have hired former convicts rate their job performance equal to or better than that of the average employee. (See the Focus box "Services for Parolees Reduce Their Recidivism.")

The options for most offenders remain severely limited. The quandary is real: Should offenders tell prospective employers about their criminal records and risk being denied a chance to prove themselves? Or should they lie and risk being fired if their criminal records come to light? These questions are highlighted when employers are reluctant to hire ex-convicts, especially when their crimes involved violence. One ex-offender said,

> *It took me a month to get a job. I filled out applications and did all the things that he said. I tried to practice honesty and I didn't get no contact back, nobody called me. So I kept waiting and kept praying, and I didn't even fill out an application for the job that I have now. A friend I knew before I went in, he told me to wait, you know, one day before I go to this place and sign up, he was going to talk to the man for me, and he talked to him and I got the job.*[27]

Studies have shown that prison terms damage offenders' job prospects and detach offenders from the support systems that might help them find jobs, reducing the possibility of meaningful employment from a group already facing poor job possibilities.[28] People who go to prison did not have good job prospects to begin with, and poor employment histories continue after incarceration. A one-year follow-up study of 300 men released from prison to live in Cleveland confirmed the difficult prospects faced by ex-offenders. Both employment and earning levels were quite low for this group. Only 37 percent had full-time jobs and more then half were unemployed.[29]

A similar study of Chicago parolees found that only 30 percent were employed about six months after release from prison, and less than a quarter were employed full time.[30] There is evidence that going to prison leads to a short-term increase in the likelihood of holding a job because of parole supervision, an effect that quickly erodes after time. But it also has a long-term and permanent effect on wages, reducing what a person will earn over the course of his or her work life.[31] Yet even with all these problems, getting a job really matters—studies confirm that people released from prison who are able to find work have lower recidivism rates.[32]

One important study shows how much impact the stigma of a criminal conviction has on employment prospects. The sociologist Devah Pager sent out student actors who posed as job applicants to respond to want ads. The applicants were matched in four ways. Two said they had criminal convictions; two said they did not. Two were African American; two were white. The actors who said they had a criminal conviction were less than half as likely as the others to be invited back for a second interview. The African American actors, regardless of what they said about their criminal records, were the least likely to be invited back for a second interview. That means that the noncriminal African American actor was less likely to get called back than the *criminal* white actor. This research suggests that young male African Americans who have been to prison suffer a double stigma of race *and* criminal record.[33]

Clearly, people returning from prison face bleak employment prospects. Overcoming the barriers is not easy, but one recent effort has shown promise. The Ready4Work Reentry Initiative uses a multifaceted approach by combining several social services—drug/alcohol abuse counseling, family services, job training and job placement—and having clients follow the guidance of a trained community mentor. The initiative has resulted in higher rates of employment and lower rates of recidivism.[34] Moreover, studies of the Center for Employment Opportunities (CEO), a New York City nonprofit organization, also show that poor employment prospects can be overcome. CEO initially places recently released prisoners in transitional employment work teams for minimum-wage service jobs. This starts the paychecks coming. CEO then provides job readiness and placement training during this initial phase of employment. Eventually the former prisoners are moved into long-term, permanent jobs. CEO's clients have higher rates of employment and lower rates of recidivism than do released prisoners not in the program—and only about one in 20 of their clients ends up back in prison during the first year of employment.[35]

One long-term solution for offenders is expungement of their criminal records. In theory, **expungement** means the removal of a conviction from state records. In practice, although offenders whose records have been expunged may legally say they have never been convicted, the records are kept and can be made available on inquiry. Moreover, the legal procedures for expungement are generally both cumbersome and inadequate. Expungement provides little true relief.

The same is true of a **pardon**, an executive act of clemency that effectively excuses the offender from suffering all the consequences of conviction for a criminal act. Contemporary pardons serve three main purposes: (1) to remedy a miscarriage of justice, (2) to remove the stigma of a conviction, and (3) to mitigate a penalty. Full pardons for miscarriages of justice are rare but do occur. For example, you may have read of individuals released from prison and pardoned after the discovery that the crime had been committed by someone else. Pardons are most commonly given to expunge the criminal records of first-time offenders, but overall they are given infrequently.

There is good reason to increase the use of expungements and pardons for people who have been able to keep their records clean for a certain amount of time. Recent research has revealed a "redemption" point that occurs after a period of maintaining a clean record. At this point, people who have been to prison no longer represent a greater risk of new criminality than do others of a similar age, even those who have never been arrested.[36] Further, the criminologist Joan Petersila has argued that, to speed along the postrelease return to normal life, parolees who show good adjustment in parole should be able to earn an earlier discharge from parole.[37] These proposals all recognize that being a former prisoner is a difficult status, and the sooner we can ameliorate it, the better things will be for the former prisoner and society alike.

To see one state's **innovative approach to prisoner reentry**, go to the corresponding link at www.cengage.com/criminaljustice/clear.

expungement
A legal process that results in the removal of a conviction from official records.

pardon
An action of the executive branch of the state or federal government excusing an offense and absolving the offender of the consequences of the crime.

Offenders realistically face certain misgivings about reentry: adjustment to a strange environment; the unavoidable need for job training, employment, money, and support; and limitations on opportunities. The stigma of conviction stays with the former felon. The general social condemnation of ex-convicts adds to the pressures of being monitored by a parole officer or work release counselor.

■ THE PAROLEE AS "DANGEROUS"

Few images are more disturbing than that of a recent parolee arrested for committing a new violent or sexual crime, especially when that crime is against a stranger. The most heinous of these incidents make national news and captivate the nation's attention. Examples include the arrest and conviction of the California parolee Richard Allen Davis for the brutal murder of 12-year-old Polly Klaas, which spurred a national movement toward life sentences for third-time felons, and the rape and murder of four-year-old Megan Kanka in New Jersey by a paroled sex offender, which led to a series of sex offender notification laws, called "Megan's Law" after the victim. By 1997, 32 states and the federal government had passed sex offender notification laws, and many other states were considering such laws. **Figure 16.8** shows an example of a sex offender notification bulletin from Washington State.

The fact of repeat violence fuels a public perception that parolees represent an ongoing threat to the public welfare. It also contributes to a belief that the criminal justice system is too lenient and therefore allows communities to be unsafe. For many parole officers, notification laws or their lack present an ethical dilemma (see "Do the Right Thing").

But how accurate are the public perceptions, and how necessary are the laws? Notification laws are thought to make the public feel more "in control" by letting residents know if a person with a violent criminal past is going to live nearby. However, research finds that notification laws seem to have heightened public discomfort about all ex-prisoners by calling more attention to the problem. Further, ex-prisoners report numerous problems as a consequence of public notification: three-quarters experience either threats or ostracism from a neighbor, and a similar fraction say they were evicted from a residence. Half report losing a job or being pressured by authorities.[38] Pressures that result from notification lead large numbers of sex offenders simply to ignore the requirement.

Certainly ex-offenders represent a greater risk to community safety than do other citizens. But isolated tragedies can exaggerate the actual danger to the public, especially

Parole officer Corey Burke drops by unannounced to visit a paroled sex offender in the man's apartment. Public opinion has increased the pressure on parole to intensively supervise "dangerous" offenders. Because of repeat violence by some, there is a perception that all parolees are a threat to public safety.

© Chang W. Lee/NYT Pictures/Redux

SEX OFFENDER INFORMATION BULLETIN
LEVEL 3 NOTIFICATION OF RELEASE

BULLETIN # :

SPD CASE NUMBER:	PREPARED BY DET. JAMES T.	DATE:

The Seattle Police Department is releasing the following information pursuant to RCW 4.24.550 and the Washington State Supreme Court decision in State v. Ward, which authorizes law enforcement agencies to inform the public of a sex offender's release when, at the discretion of the agency, the release of information will enhance public safety and protection.

The individual who appears on this notification has been convicted of a sex offense that requires registration with the sheriff's office in the county of their residence. Further, their previous criminal history places them in a classification level which reflects the potential to reoffend.

This sex offender has served the sentence imposed on him by the courts and has advised the King County Department of Public Safety that he will be living in the location below. HE IS NOT WANTED BY THE POLICE AT THIS TIME. THIS NOTIFICATION IS NOT INTENDED TO INCREASE FEAR; RATHER, IT IS OUR BELIEF THAT AN INFORMED PUBLIC IS A SAFER PUBLIC.

The Seattle Police Department has no legal authority to direct where a sex offender may or may not live. Unless court ordered restrictions exist, this offender is constitutionally free to live wherever he chooses.

Sex offenders have always lived in our communities; but it wasn't until passage of the Community Protection Act of 1990 (which mandates sex offender registration) that law enforcement even knew where they were living. In many cases, law enforcement is now able to share that information with you. Citizen abuse of this information to threaten, intimidate or harass registered sex offenders will not be tolerated. Further, such abuse could potentially end law enforcement's ability to do community notifications. We believe the only person who wins if community notification ends is the sex offender, since sex offenders derive their power through secrecy.

The Seattle Police Department Crime Prevention Division is available to help you set up block watches and to provide you with useful information on personal safety. Crime Prevention may be reached at 684-7555. If you have information regarding current criminal activity of this or any other offender, please call 9-1-1.

Ogden, Willard W M   3/30/68
Age 27

5'7" 155 lbs., Brown hair, Blue eyes,

Scars on right hand and right forearm.

Willard Ogden was released from the Washington State Penitentiary at Walla Walla after serving 5 years and 8 months for a conviction of Statutory Rape in the first degree and Indecent Liberties. These crimes were committed in Richmond, Washington during June and July of 1988. The victim was a 3-year-old female who resided in the same apartment complex as Ogden. The crimes were accomplished by leading the child into some woods near the apartment complex and behind a nearby school gymnasium. Ogden was often seen at the complex only in the company of small children. He sometimes offered them cookies. Ogden is an untreated sex offender who has refused deviancy treatment. He is at a high risk to reoffend. Odgen is on Post Release Supervision with the Department of Corrections. He has registered as a sex offender as required by law and has recently moved to the 800 block of Casparus St. in downtown Seattle.

Additional sex offender information:
As of the date of this bulletin, there are 8,703 sex offenders who have registered as required (since 2/28/90) and are living in Washington State. 1,900 of these are registered to King County addresses. 863 are registered to addresses within the city limits of Seattle. State-wide there are an additional 2,132 sex offenders who are required to register and have not and are actively being pursued by law enforcement.

Figure 16.8
Sex Offender Notification Bulletin, State of Washington

Is it fair to tell a person's neighbors that he has been in prison for a sex offense? How should it be done?

Source: Carl Poole and Roxanne Leib, *Community Notification in Washington State: Decision-Making and Costs* (Olympia: Washington State Institute for Public Policy, July 1995), 24.

DO THE RIGHT THING

The state had not adopted its own version of Megan's Law requiring police and neighborhood notification of the presence of a sex offender parolee in the community.

As parole officer Todd Whetzel sat in his office looking over the record of his newest client, John Paterson, the word pedophile *leaped from the paper.*

Paterson had been convicted of molesting an 11-year-old boy and had served seven years of a 10-year term before his release on parole. The 37-year-old Paterson was to live with his mother in Mansfield, the community of 50,000 where he grew up.

Examining the record, Whetzel noted that the molestation had occurred in the capital city, some two hundred miles from Mansfield. He didn't remember a

news story in the Mansfield Chronicle *about the crime or the sentence imposed. For all he knew, only Paterson, his mother, and he knew of the conviction.*

Whetzel thought about the alternatives. On the one hand, the law did not require notification, and releasing the information would violate Paterson's privacy. Certainly it would be almost impossible to help Paterson find a job if his secret were known. On the other hand, what if Paterson ended up molesting a child in Mansfield?

WRITING ASSIGNMENT: What would you do in Whetzel's place? Write two editorials, one in favor of disclosure and one against it, for the local paper.

---

considering that parolees are such a tiny proportion of the citizens on the streets. A recent study in Louisiana found that slightly over one-third of parolees were rearrested for a violent crime, but this represented less than 2 percent of all the arrests for violence statewide.[39] A national study did estimate that parolees were a much greater portion of arrests overall, between 10 and 16 percent.[40] Nonetheless, the consistent increase in ex-prisoners released from incarceration—from 180,000 in 1980 to over 700,000 today—has not been accompanied by an increase in crime nationally (see **Figure 16.9**).[41]

FOCUS ON CORRECTIONAL POLICY

Sex Offender Housing Restrictions Backfire

They used to be invisible, the four or five convicted sex offenders camping out on the Julia Tuttle Causeway connecting Miami to Miami Beach. But for three years now—pushed by local laws that bar them from living within 2,500 feet of where children gather—more and more criminals have moved in.

"At first, I thought 'Tuttle' was a halfway house," said Ricky Dorzena, 23, sitting in the encampment his probation officers recommended five months ago. "Then they said, 'No, you're staying under a bridge.'"

At least 70 convicted sex offenders live here now, in a shantytown on Biscayne Bay with trash piles clawed by crabs. It has become what even law enforcement officials call a public-safety hazard, produced by laws intended to keep the public safe. . . .

The American Civil Liberties Union filed a lawsuit in state court to strike them down. The complaint argues that Miami-Dade County's 2,500-foot restriction illegally pre-empts the

state's restriction of 1,000 feet, creating a situation in which sex offenders are more likely to flee supervision and commit new crimes. . . .

The camp is a community no one wants to exist. The first sex offenders here, like Patrick Wiese, 48, who said he served time in prison after having his stepdaughter touch him inappropriately, arrived nearly three years ago and would like to leave. Smoking a cigarette under the bridge on Thursday, Mr. Wiese said he wants to move to Homestead. He has money. He has a job at a sandwich shop, but cannot find an apartment that complies with the law.

"I've checked out 17 places," he said, after displaying his Florida license, which lists his address as "Julia Tuttle Bridge." "The probation officer says no."

In the beginning, he said, the camp was small, without many problems. But lately, it has become more tense as the

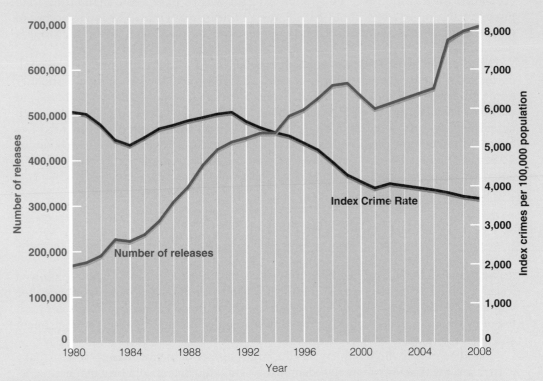

Figure 16.9

Crime Rate and Releases from State and Federal Prisons, 1980–2008

Even though the number of prisoners released into the community has increased steadily for almost three decades, crime has not increased during that time.

Sources: James P. Lynch and William J. Sabol, *Prisoner Reentry in Perspective, Crime Policy Report,* Vol. 3 (Washington, DC: Urban Institute, September 2001), p. 7, reprinted by permission; U.S. Bureau of Justice Statistics, *Bulletin,* August 2003, p. 1.

recession and the steady flow of former prisoners added residents. . . .

"Sometimes we have harmony, sometimes chaos," Mr. Wiese said. Mr. Dorzena, who said he served 17 months in jail for having sex with a 14-year-old when he was 18, smoked a cigarette beside him. "Right now," Mr. Wiese said, "we have so many people here, it's chaos."

The police agree.

John Timoney, the Miami police chief, said . . . . he had told city, state and county officials that the men (only one or two women live there) needed to be moved to more permanent homes, even if it meant changing one or more laws. He has gotten mostly studies in return, along with politicians accusing one another of shirking responsibility.

"It's like a hot potato," Chief Timoney said. "Everyone is just passing it on." . . .

Only the courts may force a change. The A.C.L.U. lawsuit argues that extreme residency restrictions contribute to homelessness, and lead sex offenders to commit more crimes because they are "living in filth and squalor, remote from family life."

For proof, it cites the state's online list of registered sex offenders and predators, which shows that 236 offenders in Miami-Dade County have skipped out on their probation, including some who used to live under the bridge on the causeway.

[Correctional officials share the A.C.L.U.'s concerns. Noting that living under an interstate was a last resort, Gretl Plessinger, a spokeswoman for the State Department of Corrections,] said: "It's not a good situation. It's not a good situation for probation officers. It's not a good situation for the offenders under the bridge, but it's also not a good situation for public safety in Miami-Dade."

Source: Gary Fineout, "Roadside Camp for Miami Sex Offenders Leads to Lawsuit," *New York Times,* July 10, 2009, p. A14. Reprinted by permission.

California's response to Polly Klaas's death was to pass a law mandating long prison terms, up to life without parole, for all third-time felons. The law is so broad it even applies to a man who recently strong-armed a pizza from a vendor along a boardwalk.

Some people worry that the public preoccupation with potential parolee criminality makes it harder for parolees to succeed. Certainly, new laws such as sex offender notification open up the possibility that some citizens will want to harass parolees and refuse to let them live in their neighborhoods. Most of the laws expressly forbid such harassment by private citizens, and a New Jersey man was arrested after he fired five bullets into the home of a paroled rapist who had lived quietly in the neighborhood for 16 years. (The Focus box "Sex Offender Housing Restrictions Backfire" on page 458 describes the problems faced by a paroled child molester.)

THE ELEMENTS OF SUCCESSFUL REENTRY

To see a documentary video about one person's experience with reentry, watch "Tracey's Story" at the corresponding link at www .cengage.com/criminaljustice/ clear.

Prison is such a harsh experience that it would seem unlikely that most who are allowed to leave would eventually return. But the problems just discussed make it easier to see why so many ex-offenders fail. Adjustment to the community is neither simple nor easy. It can be thought of as comprising two different paths: finding supports for adjustment and avoiding relapse.

Shadd Maruna, who has interviewed a large number of men who are trying to make it after serving time in prison, has identified several adjustment supports that are necessary for successful reentry.[42] Four of the most important are these:

1. *Getting substance abuse under control:* No long-term adjustment is possible unless drug and alcohol abuse are curtailed. For many newly released prisoners, this means drug treatment reinforced by drug testing. It also means cutting ties to drug-using friends.

2. *Getting a job:* For most people fresh from prison, success starts with a job good enough to provide the money to pay the bills and settle debts. The job is important, not just for the money, but for the way it redirects a person's time and energy from the negative to the positive.

3. *Getting a community support system:* Family and friends are quite important for supporting adjustment, but so are community institutions such as churches and organized athletics. Establishing good, strong contacts with these sources of support is a key to staying out of trouble, partly because the ex-offender cannot keep those supports when returning to the old way of life.

4. *Getting a new sense of "who I am":* Without a change in identity, offenders stay offenders, especially in their own minds, but also in the eyes of others. One of the keys to successful reentry is for the offender to accept that the "old me" is gone and a new person has taken over. Ex-offenders can build a new sense of self in various ways, such as thinking about the new, law-abiding version as the "real me," replacing an earlier, flawed version of the self.

relapse process
What occurs when an ex-offender's poor decision making makes adjustment problems worse, leading eventually to recidivism.

Even when offenders get jobs, find support systems, and start to develop new self-images, they can face problems that interfere with successful adjustment. Edward Zamble and Vernon Quinsey argue that failure is best understood as a **relapse process** in which offenders are faced with problem situations, lack the skills to cope with the problems, and select responses that exacerbate the problem rather than solve it.[43] An example of this occurs when an ex-offender disagrees with his or her boss. Rather than "go with the flow," the ex-offender may feel that the only way to save face is to refuse to follow the boss's instructions. When this happens a few times, the ex-offender is fired, and the poor job history that results makes getting and keeping a job even harder than before. Until the ex-offender learns how to deal effectively with the kinds of problems that set up failure, recidivism remains the likely result. Postrelease supervision is thought to be one of the main ways to teach offenders better coping skills. But does it?

■ POSTRELEASE SUPERVISION

As we have seen, postrelease supervision can be viewed as a game of three "players"—the officer, the parolee, and the administration. But how effective is that game? How do we determine its effectiveness? Further, what might the game be like in the future? Will its rules change?

How Effective Is It?

The effectiveness of corrections is usually measured by rates of recidivism, the percentage of former offenders who return to criminal behavior after release. However, because the concept of recidivism means different things to different people, the measures of recidivism also represent different things. The rates reported vary from 5 to 50 percent, depending on how one counts three things: (1) the event (arrest, conviction, parole revocation), (2) the duration of the period over which the measurement is made, and (3) the seriousness of the behavior. Typically, an analysis of recidivism is based on rearrest or reimprisonment for either another felony conviction or a parole violation for up to three years after release.

Recent figures show that less than half of those who are released from prison nationally remain arrest-free for three years. Because many of these arrests are minor, almost half of the arrested parolees successfully complete their supervision terms. Further, of 400,000 parolees who terminated supervision in 1995, 60 percent were not returned to prison.[44] But it is hard to know how much of this success results from parole work and how much reflects the sheer determination of the parolee. A recent report by the Urban Institute found almost no differences in arrest rates between people who were supervised on parole after release from prison and those who were not. This study shows that parole boards are able to select good-risk cases for early release, and when the differences in risk were taken into account, even these parolees did not do much better than people released outright from prison. They concluded that "the public safety impact of supervision is minimal and . . . does not appear to improve recidivism outcomes for violent offenders or property offender[s] released to mandatory parole [supervision]."[45] While some studies have found that mandatory-release cases do better than parolees, a recent report from the U.S. Department of

© Joel Gordon 2005—Model Released—All rights reserved

Grace Bernstein, an administrative law judge at the Harlem Parole Reentry Court in New York City, conducts a hearing to discuss and resolve issues related to parolees under supervision in the community. Should parolees be given a second chance if they violate conditions of their release, such as rules about curfews and consumption of alcohol?

Justice indicates that only 33 percent of the mandatory releases succeed, compared with 54 percent of parolees.[46] Mandatory release only seems to work for property offenders granted early parole.

People who look at results such as these argue that an important strategy for improving supervision effectiveness is case management. One element of case management is to impose on the supervision effort a structure of established approaches that will likely succeed, rather than leaving the supervision style to the officer's discretion. It is hoped that parolees will fare better, both in their criminal behavior and social adjustment, under these approaches. This kind of case management is based on tangible services such as job training and money for transportation to work, with close monitoring of progress. But the evidence regarding these strategies is mixed: A solid body of research shows that job-related services reduce recidivism and increase earnings,[47] while a handful of studies show weaker results.[48]

In short the effectiveness of parole supervision has earned, at best, mixed reviews. Yet because parolees who remain crime-free for two years often succeed thereafter, correctional administrators continue to revise parole practices in ways that will help offenders make it. A recent review of the literature on parole supervision offers this list of priorities for policy changes:

- Develop and use valid risk-assessment instruments.
- Target supervision strategies to deal with the critical needs of high-risk cases.
- Create incentives for people in reentry to succeed.
- Support those in reentry with problem-solving approaches that help them comply with parole conditions.
- Be sensible about revoking parole.[49]

reentry courts
Courts that supervise the ex-prisoner's return to the community and adjustment to his or her new life.

The limited impact of supervision has led scholars to search for new methods to deal with people who are returning to the community from prison. Some now argue that reentry needs to be bolstered by the authority of the court system, through **reentry courts**. These courts specialize in handling the problems faced by recently released prisoners. They also oversee their adjustment by adding "active judicial authority to provide graduated sanctions, positive reinforcement, and to marshal resources for offender support."[50] To date there have been no studies of the effectiveness of reentry courts. Some scholars argue that if all these courts do is increase the amount of pressure on people returning from prison, they will fail as most similar programs have failed. But if they focus on getting them involved in their communities and contributing to the welfare of their environments, they will transform the way the formerly incarcerated are seen by other citizens—and they will ultimately succeed where traditional methods have not.[51] Others have suggested that the key will be to increase the monitoring of parolees so that those who are not staying crime free will be quickly arrested and punished.[52]

What Are Its Prospects?

Although many changes have been made in the way offenders are released from prison, as noted in Chapter 15, supervision practices do not reflect these changes. Even states that have altered their release laws or policies seem to recognize that offenders need some help or control in the months after release, and research suggests that parole does help them stay crime free, at least during the early months on the outside. Therefore, most incarcerated offenders will continue to experience postrelease supervision, whether in the form of parole, work release, or some other program.

Nonetheless, the nature of supervision will likely change significantly over the next few years. Evidence increasingly suggests that supervision is not appropriate for all offenders but should be oriented toward those who are most likely to fail and who require close supervision. The broad discretionary power of the parole officer is disappearing. In its place, a much more restrictive effort is becoming popular, one in which limited special conditions are imposed and stringently enforced. The helping role of the officer—as counselor, referral agent, and so forth—is being freed from the coercive role, and the help offered is increasingly seen as an opportunity that offenders may choose not to take. Postrelease supervision is likely to be streamlined in years to come as the courts continue to review officers' decisions and their agencies' policies.

Interest in the problem of reentry has also reawakened. A broad coalition of senators recently joined with the White House to support the Second Chance Act, which provides funding for states to develop programs that will improve reentry. The Council of State Governments, after a two-year study, published a report that advocated for a long list of legal and programmatic developments to improve reentry.[53] Under Mayor Richard M. Daley, the City of Chicago has undertaken an ambitious program working with poor communities to improve the reentry of people coming to Chicago from Illinois prisons.[54]

What is not likely to change is the situation of the released offender. Poor training and poor education lead to poor job prospects; public distrust of offenders leads to discrimination. Offenders will need to hone their strategies if they are to succeed in the community.

SUMMARY

1 Know the major characteristics of the postrelease function of the corrections system.

The vast majority of offenders released from prison remain subject to correctional authority for some time. For many offenders, the parole officer represents this authority; for others, the staff of a halfway house or work release center does so. The "freedom" of release is constrained: The whereabouts of offenders are monitored, and their associations and daily activities are checked. The former inmate has many serious obstacles to overcome: long absence from family and friends, legal and practical limitations on employment possibilities, the suspicion and uneasiness of the community, even the strangeness of everyday living. The outside world can seem alien and unpredictable after even a short time in the artificial environment of prison. No truly "clean" start is possible. The status of former convict is nearly as stigmatizing as that of convict, and in many ways it is more frustrating. Most people look at the parolee askance—an embittering experience for many trying to start over.

2 Define community supervision and revocation of community supervision.

Parolees are released from prison on condition that they abide by laws and follow rules designed both to aid their readjustment to society and to control their movement. The parolee may be required to abstain from alcohol, keep away from undesirable associates, maintain good work habits, and not leave the community without permission. These requirements, called conditions of release, regulate conduct that is not criminal but that is thought to be linked to the possibility of future criminality. When people fail on parole, their parole is revoked and they are returned to prison to continue serving their sentences. Parole can be revoked for two reasons: (1) committing a new crime or (2) violating conditions of parole (a "technical violation"). Technical violations are controversial because they involve noncriminal conduct, such as failure to report an address change to the parole officer.

3 | Understand how community supervision is structured.

Three forces influence the newly released offender's adjustment to free society: the parole officer, the parole bureaucracy, and the experiences of the offender. The structure of these relationships can determine the results of supervision. The attachments among the three change over time. Initially, the officer is most attached to the bureaucracy but over time the officer's strongest attachment gradually shifts from the bureaucracy to the parolee until rapport is established. The parolee never loses suspicion of the bureaucracy. Parole officers are usually asked to play two roles: cop and social worker. But these are conflicting role demands. As street-level bureaucrats, officers are influenced by the organization's definition of the situation, the officer's own perception of the parolee, and the officer's professional reputation. Moreover, parole officers do not work in a vacuum. They face limits that derive from both the specific need to manage a heavier workload than is feasible in the available time and the general need to respond to organizational philosophies and policies. The bureaucratic context pressures parole officers to "go along with the system," just as police officers are pressured to cover for their partners.

4 | Describe residential programs and how they help parolees.

Residential programs serve offenders when they are first released from prison. Most house between 10 and 25 offenders at any one time in medium- or minimum-security facilities. Placing heavy emphasis on involving the offenders in regular community functions, treatment staff help offenders work out plans to address their problems. Residential programs usually provide counseling and drug treatment and impose strict curfews on residents when they are not working. By obeying the rules and maintaining good behavior in the facility, residents gradually earn a reduction in restrictions—for instance, the ability to spend some free time in the community. The idea is to provide treatment support to the offender while promoting the step-by-step adjustment to community life.

5 | Identify the major problems parolees confront.

Although release from prison can be euphoric, it can also be a letdown, particularly for parolees who return after two, three, or more years away. The images in their minds of friends and loved ones represent snapshots frozen in time, but in reality everyone has changed. Moreover, returning to the streets after years behind bars is a shock; the most normal, unremarkable events take on overwhelming significance. But the most significant fact is that most offenders released from prison are far from free. Parolees must report to a parole officer and undergo community supervision until their full sentence has been completed. Parolees are also aware they must meet critical needs to make it on the streets. Education, money, and a job tend to top the list, but health care is also a high priority. Offenders also learn that they have achieved an in-between status: They are back in society but not totally free. They face restrictions on opportunities including many impediments to employment.

6 | Understand why some parolees are viewed as dangerous and how society handles this problem.

Few images are more disturbing than that of a recent parolee arrested for committing a new violent or sexual crime, especially when that crime is against a stranger. Certainly ex-offenders represent a greater risk to community safety than do other citizens. But isolated tragedies can exaggerate the actual danger to the public, especially considering that parolees are such a tiny proportion of the citizens on the streets. Moreover, the consistent increase in ex-prisoners released from incarceration—from 180,000 in 1980 to over 700,000 today—has not been accompanied by an increase in crime nationally.

7 Describe the effectiveness of postrelease supervision.

The effectiveness of corrections is usually measured by rates of recidivism, the percentage of former offenders who return to criminal behavior after release. Less than half of those who are released from prison nationally remain arrest-free for three years. Because many of these arrests are minor, almost half of the arrested parolees successfully complete their supervision terms. Further, 60 percent of paroles complete their parole terms without being returned to prison. But the effectiveness of parole supervision has earned, at best, mixed reviews. The nature of supervision will likely change significantly over the next few years. Interest in the problem of reentry has reawakened, and a broad coalition supported the Second Chance Act, which provides funding for states to develop programs that will improve reentry.

KEY TERMS

community correctional center (p. 446)
conditions of release (p. 432)
expungement (p. 455)

pardon (p. 455)
reentry courts (p. 462)

relapse process (p. 460)
work release center (p. 447)

FOR DISCUSSION

1. Imagine that you have just been released from prison after a five-year term. What are the first things you will do? What problems do you expect to face?
2. It is said that probation officers tend to take a social work approach and parole officers tend to take a law enforcement approach. How might these differences in approach be explained?
3. Why are some parole officers reluctant to ask that a client's parole be revoked for technical violations? What organizational pressures may be involved?
4. Why are so many occupations closed to convicted felons?
5. Do you think neighborhood notification laws for released sex offenders increase public safety? Do these laws merely make it harder for sex offenders to succeed? Why?

FOR FURTHER READING

Bushway, Shawn, Michael A. Stoll, and David F. Weiman, eds. *Barriers to Reentry? The Labor Market for Released Prisoners in Postindustrial America.* New York: Russell Sage Foundation, 2007. A series of studies of employment-related issues facing people who are returning from prison.

Gonnerman, Jennifer. *Life on the Outside: The Prison Odyssey of Elaine Bartlett.* New York: Farrar, Straus & Giroux, 2004. The story of Elaine Bartlett, who spent 16 years in prison, and her struggle to adjust to "life on the outside": conforming to parole rules, finding a job and apartment, and reclaiming her role as head of the household.

Maruna, Shadd. *Making Good: How Ex-convicts Reform and Rebuild Their Lives.* Washington, DC: American Psychological Association, 2001. Award-winning analysis of how ex-convicts develop new personal identities and stay away from crime.

Petersilia, Joan. *When Prisoners Come Home.* New York: Oxford University Press, 2003. A comprehensive review of the research and policy about parole supervision and prison release, with recommendations for reform.

Ross, Jeffrey Ian, and Stephen C. Richards. *Beyond Bars: Rejoining Society after Prison.* New York: Penguin, 2009. Two criminologists give advice to people who are leaving prison on "how to make it."

Thompson, Anthony C. *Releasing Prisoners, Redeeming Communities.* New York: NYU Press, 2008. A survey of the problems faced by people who are reentering their communities from prison, and a guide to the kinds of policies we must enact to overcome those problems.

Travis, Jeremy. *But They All Come Back: Facing the Challenges of Prisoner Reentry.* Washington, DC: Urban Institute, 2004. A critical assessment of contemporary reentry policy, with a series of proposals for new initiatives in reentry programs.

NOTES

1 Adapted from Herbert Lowe, "Helping Ex-prisoners for Hire: Job Counselors Educate Former Inmates on How to Deal With Legal, Racial Barriers That May Prevent Them from Finding Job Opportunities," *Newsday*, January 28, 2007, p. 1.

2 Jeremy Travis and Sarah Lawrence, *Beyond the Prison Gates: The State of Parole in America* (Washington, DC: Urban Institute, 2002), 24.

3 *Morrissey v. Brewer*, 408 U.S. 471 (1972).

4 BJS *Special Report*, June 2002, p. 1.

5 Travis and Lawrence, *Beyond the Prison Gates*, p. 21.

6 BJS *Bulletin*, October 2001, p. 7.

7 Carl B. Klockars, "A Theory of Probation Supervision," *Journal of Criminal Law, Criminology, and Police Science* 63 (1972): 550–57.

8 Elliot Studt, *Surveillance and Service in Parole* (Washington, DC: U.S. Government Printing Office, 1973).

9 Richard McCleary, *Dangerous Men: The Sociology of Parole*, 2nd ed. (Albany, NY: Harrow & Heston, 1992).

10 Ibid., p. 113.

11 Michael Lipsky, *Street-Level Bureaucracy* (New York: Russell Sage Foundation, 1980), 82.

12 William D. Burrell, "Issue Paper on Caseload Standards for Probation and Parole," *Perspectives* 31 (no. 2, Spring 2007): 37–41.

13 McCleary, *Dangerous Men*, p. 63.

14 Dina R. Rose, Todd R. Clear, and Judith A. Ryder, *Drugs, Incarceration, and Neighborhood Life: The Impact of Reintegrating Offenders into the Community*, final report to the National Institute of Justice (New York: John Jay College of Criminal Justice, October 2001), 88.

15 Ibid., p. 80

16 Ibid., p. 92.

17 Amy L. Solomon, Vera Kachnowski, and Avinash Bhati, *Does Parole Work? Analyzing the Impact of Postprison Supervision on Rearrest Outcomes* (Washington, DC: Urban Institute, March 2005), 15.

18 Joan Petersilia, "Prisoner Reentry: Public Safety and Reintegration Challenges," *Prison Journal* 81 (no. 3, September 2001): 360–75.

19 Statistics taken from Jeremy Travis, Amy L. Solomon, and Michelle Waul, *From Prison to Home: The Dimensions and Consequences of Prisoner Reentry* (Washington, DC: Urban Institute, June 2001).

20 Shadd Maruna, *Making Good: How Ex-Convicts Reform and Rebuild Their Lives* (Washington, DC: American Psychological Association, 2001), 96.

21 Beth M. Heubner, "Racial and Ethnic Differences in the Likelihood of Marriage: The Effect of Incarceration," *Justice Quarterly* 24 (no. 1, March 2007): 156–83.

22 Bonita Veysey and Gislea Bichler-Robertson, "Prevalence Estimates of Psychiatric Disorders in Correctional Settings," in National Commission on Correctional Healthcare, *The Health Status of Soon-to-Be Released Inmates*, vol. 2 (Washington, DC: U.S. Government Printing Office, April 2002), 57–80.

23 *New York Times*, March 28, 2004, p. 19.

24 Christoper Uggen and Jeff Manza, "The Political Consequences of Felon Disfranchisement Law in the United States" (paper presented at the annual meeting of the American Sociological Association, Washington, DC, August 12–14, 2001).

25 Legal Action Center, *After Prison: Roadblocks to Reentry* (New York: Legal Action Center, 2004).

26 Robert M. Grooms, "Recidivist," *Crime and Delinquency* 28 (October 1982): 542–3.

27 Rose, Clear, and Ryder, *Drugs, Incarceration, and Neighborhood Life*, p. 104.

28 John C. Laub and Leanna C. Allen, "Life Course Criminology: Implications for Community Corrections," *Perspectives Magazine* 24 (no. 2, Spring 2000): 20–29.

29 Christy A. Visher and Shannon M. E. Courtney, *One Year Out: Experiences of Prisoners Returning to Cleveland* (Washington, DC: Urban Institute, April 2007). [Returning Home research brief]

30 Christy A. Visher and Vera Kachnowski, "Finding Work on the Outside: Results of the 'Returning Home' Project in Chicago," in *Barriers to Reentry? The Labor Market for Released Prisoners in Postindustrial America*, edited by Shawn Bushway, Michael A. Stoll, and David F. Weiman (New York: Russell Sage Foundation, 2007), 80–114.

31 Becky Pettit and Christopher J. Lyons, "Status and Stigma of Incarceration: The Labor Market Effects of Incarceration by Race, Class, and Criminal Involvement," in *Barriers to Reentry?* pp. 203–26.

32 Stephen Rafael and David F. Weiman, "Impact of Local Labor-Market Conditions on the Likelihood that Parolees Are Returned to Custody," in *Barriers to Reentry?* pp. 304–32.

33 Devah Pager, "Two Strikes and You're Out: The Intensification of Racial and Criminal Stigma," in *Barriers to Reentry?* pp. 151–73.

34 Shawn Bauldry, Danijela Korom-Djakovic, Wendy S. McClanahan, Jennifer McMaken, and Lauren J. Kotloff, *Mentoring Formerly Incarcerated Adults: Insights for the Ready4Work Reentry Initiative* (Philadelphia: Public/Private Ventures, 2009).

35 Center for Employment Opportunities, *A Summary of the Preliminary Findings of the Ongoing MDRC Evaluation* (New York: Author, December 2007).

36 Alfred Blumstein and Kiminori Nakamura, "Redemption in the Presence of Widespread Criminal Background Checks," *Criminology* 47 (no. 2, 2009): 327–59.

37 Joan Petersilia, "Employ Behavioral Contracting for 'Earned Discharge' Parole," *Criminology and Public Policy* 6 (no. 4, 2007): 1501–9.

38 Richard G. Zevitz and Mary Ann Farkas, "Sex Offender Community Notification: Assessing the Impact in Wisconsin," in *Research in Brief* (Washington, DC: National Institute of Justice, December 2000), 10.

39 Michael R. Geerken and Hennessey D. Hayes, "Probation and Parole: Public Risks and the Future of Incarceration Alternatives," *Criminology* 31 (no. 4, November 1993): 549–64.

40 Richard Rosenfeld, Joel Wallman, and Robert Fornango, "The Contribution of Ex-Prisoners to Crime Rates," in *Prisoner Reentry and Crime in America*, edited by Jeremy Travis and Christy Visher (New York: Cambridge University Press, 2005), 80–104.

41 James P. Lynch and William J. Sabol, *Prisoner Reentry in Perspective* [*Crime Policy Report,* vol. 3] (Washington, DC: Urban Institute, September 2001), 7.

42 Maruna, *Making Good,* p. 83.

43 Edward Zamble and Vernon Quinsey, *The Criminal Recidivism Process* (Cambridge, England: Cambridge University Press, 1997).

44 Bureau of Justice Statistics, *Correctional Populations in the United States, 1995* (Washington, DC: U.S. Government Printing Office, 1997), 130.

45 Solomon, Kachnowski, and Bhati, *Does Parole Work?* p. 15.

46 Timothy A. Hughes, Doris J. Wilson, and Allen J. Beck, "Trends in State Parole, 1990–2000," BJS *Bulletin,* October 2001, p. 1.

47 Bruce Western, *From Prison to Work: A Proposal for a National Reentry Program* (Washington, DC: Brookings Institute [The Hamilton Project], December 2008).

48 James A. Wilson, and Robert C. Davis, "Good Intentions Meet Hard Realities: An Evaluation of the Project Greenlight Reentry Program," *Criminology and Public Policy* 5 (no. 2, 2006): 303–38.

49 Peggy Burke and Michael Tonry, *Successful Transition and Reentry for Safer Communities* (Silver Spring, MD: Center for Effective Public Policy, 2006).

50 Reginald A. Wilkinson, "Prison Reform through Offender Reentry: A Partnership between Courts and Corrections" (paper presented to Pace Law School, Symposium on Prison Reform Law, October 2003), 4.

51 Shadd Maruna and Thomas LeBel, "Welcome Home? Examining the 'Reentry Court' Concept from a Strengths-Based Perspective," *Western Criminology Review* 4 (no. 2, 2003): http://wcr.sonoma.edu/v4n2/marunalebel.html.

52 David Farabee, "Reinventing Criminal Justice," *Washington Post,* February 11, 2006, p. A18.

53 Council of State Governments, *Report of the Re-entry Policy Council* (Lexington, KY: Author, 2006).

54 *Rebuilding Lives. Restoring Hope. Strengthening Communities.: Breaking the Cycle of Incarceration and Building Brighter Futures in Chicago,* final report of the Mayoral Caucus on Prisoner Reentry (Chicago: Office of the Mayor, 2006).

AP Images/Lou Toman, Pool

LEARNING OBJECTIVES

After reading this chapter you should be able to . . .

1 Understand the nature and extent of youth crime today.

2 Know the history of the development of juvenile corrections in the United States.

3 Understand the rationale for dealing differently with juvenile offenders and adult offenders.

4 Know how serious juvenile delinquency differs from most delinquency and what this implies for the juvenile justice system.

5 Know the ways juvenile offenders are sanctioned.

6 Understand the special problems youth gangs pose.

7 Envision the future of juvenile corrections.

Lionel Tate is escorted from court after a sentencing hearing. The boy, who was 12 when he killed a little girl while he was supposedly imitating professional wrestlers, was originally sentenced to life in prison without parole. Upon appeal, his life sentence was vacated and Tate was given one year of house arrest and ten years probation.

LIONEL TATE was 12 years old when he was left alone with six-year-old Eunick, a child Lionel's mother was babysitting. He killed her. He said he was playing professional wrestling with her, the way he had seen on television, but the autopsy showed he had stomped on her so forcefully that it lacerated her liver, causing her death. The judge, Joel T. Lazarus, said at sentencing that "The acts of Lionel Tate were not the playful acts of a child. . . . The acts of Lionel Tate were cold, callous and indescribably cruel." He was tried as an adult and sentenced to life imprisonment.

The case became a cause célèbre for juvenile court reform. People wondered how a 12-year-old, no matter how troubling (or troubled), could be sentenced to live the rest of his life behind bars. The case was all the more disturbing because Lionel's mother, a Florida state trooper, had turned down a plea bargain that would have resulted in a manslaughter charge and a three-year sentence.

There was no shortage of people who were appalled at this sentence, including newspaper editorial writers, citizen

CORRECTIONS FOR JUVENILES

- ■ THE PROBLEM OF YOUTH CRIME

- ■ HISTORY OF JUVENILE CORRECTIONS

  Juvenile Corrections: English Antecedents

  Juvenile Corrections in the United States

- ■ WHY TREAT JUVENILES AND ADULTS DIFFERENTLY?

  Differences between Adults and Juveniles, in Perspective

- ■ THE PROBLEM OF SERIOUS DELINQUENCY

- ■ SANCTIONING JUVENILE OFFENDERS

  Overview of the Juvenile Justice System

  Disposition of Juvenile Offenders

- ■ THE SPECIAL PROBLEM OF GANGS

- ■ THE FUTURE OF JUVENILE JUSTICE

activists, scholars, and political leaders. Even the prosecutor of the case, Ken Padowitz of Broward County, Florida, said that the penalty was too extreme, a comment the judge found infuriating. Eventually an appeals court agreed with the critics and vacated the life sentence, enabling Lionel to be freed on one year of house arrest and 10 years of probation.

But the case did not end there. Lionel was a difficult probationer, violating house arrest and being found with a knife. His probation term was extended and the supervision intensified. But in 2005, a scant 16 months after he had been released from prison, Lionel was arrested for armed robbery, after taking four pizzas at gunpoint. Lionel was now 18, representing a much less appealing case for court reform. He eventually pleaded guilty to illegal possession of a firearm and on May 18, 2006, was sentenced to 30 years in prison.

In a few short years, Lionel Tate had managed to outrage everyone. His original sentence, so extreme for a child so young, galvanized juvenile court reformers around the country and provided a case study for critics of the practice of trying juveniles in adult court. His later misconduct united people again, but this time in a kind of horror about the man-child they were confronted with. Lionel had become everyone's worst-case scenario. For those who fear juvenile violence, he embodied the basis of their fear. For those who sought to liberalize the juvenile court, he was the counterfactual case in favor of the opposite approach. Further, because Lionel is African American, his conduct fed the kind of racist fears that many hold about young black men (see Chapter 19).

Thankfully, Lionel Tate presents an extremely rare case. But when such cases come along, no matter how infrequently, they call into question the entire rationality of the juvenile justice system. On the one hand, the shocking nature of his first crime shakes the foundation of a juvenile court that treats young people as children. On the other hand, his second crimes, senseless and dismaying, occurred *after* he had been incarcerated (awaiting appeal) for longer than the three-year deal the adult system had offered in a plea bargain. It is hard to see how either system made much sense in

Chapter

17

the Lionel Tate case—but that is almost always true for extreme cases. Systems are sensibly built to handle the "usual" cases. What happens, though, with the unusual cases?

In this chapter we explore the juvenile corrections system, constructed to handle the half-million juveniles whose conduct is serious enough for corrections to be involved. This is but a fraction of the 2.2 million juveniles who are arrested and the 1.7 million who end up going to court—the vast majority of the "usual" cases involving juvenile misconduct and crime.[1]

Although separate from adult corrections, the juvenile system is linked to it at many points. What sets the juvenile correctional system apart are differences in philosophy, procedures, and programmatic emphasis. The philosophy of juvenile corrections places a higher premium on rehabilitation and prevention, as opposed to punishment, than does its adult counterpart. Less dominated by firm due process rules, the procedures of juvenile corrections support a degree of informality and discretionary decision making. This informality is in part intended to enable program administrators to develop innovative strategies that promise to keep juvenile offenders from returning to crime as adults.

■ THE PROBLEM OF YOUTH CRIME

It disturbs us to think of a child as "dangerous" or "sinister," but the daily news forces us to consider the unpleasant truth that some young people commit serious crimes. In the most recent year for which data are available, about 1,350 youths under age 18 are arrested for homicide, 3,580 for forcible rape, and a troubling 57,650 for aggravated

Fifteen-year-old Trevor Reizenstein apologizes to the court and to the victim's family for his sexual assault and attempted murder of a 5-year-old girl when he was 12. Canyon County, Idaho, Judge Thomas Ryan sentenced Reizenstein to 20 years of incarceration. When he turns 21, he will leave the juvenile facility and be transferred to prison.

AP Images/The Idaho Press-Tribune, Mike Vogt

assault.[2] Some of these cases become local or national news stories. The incidents remind us that some juveniles are capable of deeply distressing behavior. Because these cases alarm and frighten us, the need for greater confidence in the juvenile justice system has become a major issue for correctional professionals and policy makers.

Even so, extremely serious juvenile crime incidents are rare. In a nation with 75 million people 18 years of age or younger, 2.2 million arrests of juveniles took place in 2001, only 97,100 of which (just over 4 percent) were for violent crimes. After rising between 1988 and 1994, the juvenile violent crime rate has dropped by almost 50 percent; it is now the lowest it has been since at least 1980. Property crime has decreased by about half since the peak in 1991.[3] Recent research also shows that fewer juveniles are carrying guns than before.[4] Yet when Americans are asked to identify the two or three most serious problems facing children, they cite drugs and crime.

Most of us are particularly unsettled by juvenile crime for reasons beyond the numbers. Young people represent the future. We expect them to be busy growing up—learning how to become productive citizens and developing skills for a satisfying life. We do not expect them to be committing crimes that damage the quality of community life.

Because they are starting criminal behavior so young, we worry about the future—how long before a young person's criminal career fades? How much damage will be left in its wake?

Read about the **Lionel Tate case**; see the corresponding link at www.cengage.com/criminaljustice/clear.

HISTORY OF JUVENILE CORRECTIONS

Throughout history, children who have gotten in trouble have faced dire circumstances. During the Middle Ages, children were seen as property of the male head of the household, and the patriarch could deal with his possessions however he wished. Brutality was not uncommon. When a parent lacked resources, the children went without food. When parents ran afoul of the law, children lost their protectors and were left to fend for themselves. When children themselves broke the law, they faced the same kinds of punishments faced by adults. The plight of children was a factor in the reform of laws dealing with children in England during the 1600s and 1700s.

Juvenile Corrections: English Antecedents

During the early 1600s, in England, governments began to consider the plight of the child. In much the same way that the crown claimed property rights throughout the realm, children were seen as falling under the protection of the king or queen. Under the doctrine of **parens patriae**—literally, "parent of the nation"—the crown could act as guardian of any child, especially one with rights to inherited property.

The Elizabethan Poor Laws (1601) established the basis for officials to take charge of vagrant and delinquent children, placing them under the authority of church wardens and other overseers. Most ended up in poorhouses or workhouses, working under oppressive conditions akin to slavery. The same fate befell the children of widows who lacked means of support. When children broke the law, the same authorities who handled adult criminals processed them, exposing the children to adult punishments.

In the 1800s, when reformers such as John Howard visited the *gaols* and poorhouses in England, the decrepit conditions and the treatment of women and children in these dark, disease-filled facilities appalled them. As we saw in Chapter 2, reformers called for a new approach to imprisonment. The plight of children in the system helped galvanize public sentiment for change.

parens patriae
The "parent of the country"; the role of the state as guardian and protector of all people (particularly juveniles) who are unable to protect themselves.

Juvenile Corrections in the United States

Table 17.1 outlines five periods of American juvenile justice. Each period was characterized by changes that reflected the social, intellectual, and political currents of the time. During the past two hundred years, population shifts from rural to urban areas,

TABLE 17.1 *Juvenile Justice Developments in the United States*

Note : A *status offender* is a juvenile who has committed an act that is considered unacceptable for a child, such as truancy or running away from home, but that would not be a crime if committed by an adult.			
Period	**Major Developments**	**Causes and Influences**	**Juvenile Justice System**
Puritan 1646–1824	Massachusetts Stubborn Child Law (1646)	• Puritan view of child as evil • Economically margin-al agrarian society	Law provides • Symbolic standard of maturity • Support for family as economic unit
Refuge 1824–1899	Institutionalization of deviants, House of Refuge in New York established (1825) for delinquent and dependent children	• Enlightenment • Immigration and industrialization	Child seen as helpless, in need of state intervention
Juvenile Court 1899–1960	Establishment of separate legal system for juveniles; Illinois Juvenile Court Act (1899)	• Reformism and rehabilitative ideology • Increased immigration urbanization, large-scale industrialization	Juvenile court institutionalized legal irresponsibility of child
Juvenile Rights 1960–1980	Increased "legalization" of juvenile law; *Gault* decision (1967); Juvenile Justice and Delinquency Prevention Act (1974) calls for deinstitutionalization of status offenders	• Criticism of juvenile justice system on humane grounds • Civil rights movement by disadvantaged groups	Movement to define and protect rights as well as to provide services to children
Crime Control 1980-Present	Concern for victims, punishment for serious offenders, transfer to adult court of serious offenders, protection of children from physical and sexual abuse	• More-conservative public attitudes and policies • Focus on serious crimes by repeat offenders	System more formal restrictive, punitive; increased percentage of police referrals to court; incarcerated youths stay longer periods

Sources: Adapted from Barry Krisberg, Ira M. Schwartz, Paul Litsky, and James Austin, "The Watershed of Juvenile Justice Reform," *Crime and Delinquency* 32 (January 1986): 5–38; U.S. Department of Justice, *A Preliminary National Assessment of Status Offender and the Juvenile Justice System* (Washington, DC: U.S. Government Printing Office, 1980), 29.

immigration, developments in the social sciences, political reform movements, and the continuing problem of youth crime have all influenced the treatment of juveniles in the United States.

THE PURITAN PERIOD (1646–1824) ■ The English procedures were maintained in the American colonies and continued into the 1800s. The earliest attempt by a colony to deal with problem children was the passage of the Massachusetts Stubborn Child Law in 1646. With this law, the Puritans of the Massachusetts Bay Colony conveyed their view that the child was evil and that family needed to discipline youth. Those who would not obey their parents were to be dealt with by the law.

THE REFUGE PERIOD (1824–1899) ■ During the early 1800s, reformers urged the creation of institutions where delinquent, abused, and neglected children could learn good work and study habits, live in a disciplined and healthy environment, and develop "character." The first such institution was the House of Refuge in New York, which

During the nineteenth century, reformers were alarmed by the living conditions of inner-city youth, such as these homeless newsboys in New York City. As a result, reformers in Chicago ushered in the juvenile justice system.

© Bettmann/CORBIS

opened in 1825. By 1850 almost every large city had such an institution operated by private charities.

According to the reformers, residents were to be trained in job skills, provided with religious instruction, and held accountable with strict but sympathetic discipline. In practice, these ideals were difficult to attain. Most refuge houses came to resemble the adult prisons of the day, with cruelty by staff, hostilities among the inmates, and an overriding sense of harshness and alienation in daily life. Although reformers felt they were bringing a kind of "social love" into the lives of wayward youth, what in fact occurred was at best an indifferent institutionalization and at worst a kind of social oppression. Historians have pointed out that the reformers were well intentioned, but the actual impact of these reforms differed greatly from their aims.

Some have described the refuge-house movement as an aspect of the conflict between the native-born upper classes and the burgeoning inner-city immigrant poor, commonly referred to in those days as "the dangerous classes." The teeming cities alarmed the elite, who saw them as cauldrons of social problems that threatened the core of contemporary civic life.

In the mid-1800s, when frontier settlements were crying out for labor, delinquent and neglected urban children were often removed from their homes and "placed out" to these faraway places to work on farms or in small businesses. These arrangements resembled those made for the indentured servants of the previous century.

Eventually, critics began to complain about the growing abuses of the refuge house strategy. It had become apparent that the adult court system was not a satisfactory way to deal with juveniles. These courts often treated juveniles more harshly than adults who had committed the same crimes. It had also become obvious that the problems of urban youth had not been solved.

During the Progressive era at the end of the 1800s, reformers called "the child savers" worked for new ways to deal with children in trouble. A reform group in Chicago ushered in the modern juvenile justice system.

THE JUVENILE COURT PERIOD (1899–1960) ■ The first juvenile court was established by a legislative act in Cook County (Chicago) Illinois in 1899. The impetus for the reforms came from the Chicago Women's Club, which had asked the Chicago Bar Association to conduct a study of the problems of handling juvenile offenders and to recommend a model code for a new system. The thrust of the resulting legislation was to give judges broad discretion in handling juvenile cases. Judge **Julian W. Mack** presided over Chicago's juvenile court and made it a model for the nation.

Based on *parens patriae,* the new juvenile court took the role of guardian, the substitute parent to the child. Decisions about a juvenile's fate were linked less to guilt or innocence and more to "the best interests" of the child. The main tenets of the juvenile court can be summarized as informality, individualization, and intervention.

Informality was intended to move juvenile corrections away from the formality and due process requirements of the adult courtroom. Instead of rules of evidence and cross-examination, judges would run the sessions as conversations in which interested people such as parents, teachers, and social workers could comment on the case. The court was encouraged to establish a relaxed, informal atmosphere so that the needs of the child could be understood. Formal rules were thought to hinder the exploratory conversation and unnecessarily limit the potential solutions.

Individualization was based on the idea that each child ought to be treated as a unique person with unique circumstances. It was considered mistaken to handle a case solely on the basis of misbehavior type. Two children, each of whom had broken into a home, might have different needs that led each to the misconduct. Criminality was thus seen as a "symptom" of trouble, only one of the problems facing the child. By treating each child as different, better solutions to children's problems could be crafted.

Intervention was the method of the juvenile court. The final aim of all juvenile processing was "adjustment"—to help the child develop a law-abiding lifestyle. Thus, the court was not to punish children but to identify and solve the problems that led them astray and to provide treatment that would avert a life of crime.

To implement this approach, the juvenile court developed its own language, procedures, and rules. In place of standard adult processing practices, the juvenile system established a new version to achieve its new aims. **Table 17.2** compares the terminology of the adult and juvenile systems.

JULIAN W. MACK (1866–1943)

One of the foremost innovators in juvenile justice, Mack presided over Chicago's juvenile court from 1904 to 1907. He believed that the proper work of the court depended on the judge, supported by probation officers, caseworkers, and psychologists. He sought as much as possible to avoid using reformatories and tried to bring the expertise of social service professionals to the courts.

Passage of the Juvenile Court Act by Illinois in 1899 established the first separate court for delinquent, dependent, and neglected children. Judge Julian Mack presided over Chicago's juvenile court, which became a model for the nation.

© Corbis

TABLE 17.2 *Comparison of Terminology in the Adult and Juvenile Justice Systems*

Function	Adult System	Juvenile System
Taking into custody	Arrested	Detained (police contact)
Legal basis for holding	Charged	Referred to court
Formal charges	Indicted	Held on petition
Person charged	Defendant	Respondent
Determination of guilt	Trial	Hearing
Outcome of court case	Verdict	Finding
Term for "guilty"	Convicted	Adjudicated (as responsible)
Sanction	Sentence	Disposition
Custodial sentence	Incarcerated	Placed or committed
Incarceration facility	Prison	Training school
Release supervision	Parole	Aftercare

There was widespread enthusiasm for the new juvenile court model. Following the Chicago example, every state revised its penal code and established a separate juvenile court within a few years. The age of jurisdiction often varied—some states took juveniles as old as 18 or 19, whereas others allowed anyone over age 16 to be handled as an adult. The courts were given jurisdiction over delinquent, neglected, and dependent children. A **delinquent** child is one who has committed an act that if committed by an adult would be criminal. A **neglected** child is one who is not receiving proper care, because of some action or inaction of his or her parents. This includes not being sent to school, not receiving medical care, being abandoned, or not receiving some other care necessary for the child's well-being. A **dependent** child either has no parent or guardian or, because of the physical or mental disability of a parent or guardian, is not receiving proper care.

Despite the enthusiasm, problems arose with the informal approach. Sometimes, judges and attorneys ran roughshod over rights, imposing the law in ways that seemed opposed to the youngsters' true interests. Judges were allowed to tailor dispositions, but many people suspected that lower-class children and ethnic minorities received harsher, less-sympathetic treatment. Finally, the failure of intervention to stem recidivism led the community to distrust the effectiveness of juvenile court.

THE JUVENILE RIGHTS PERIOD (1960–1980) ■ By the 1960s, liberal reform groups, such as the American Civil Liberties Union, rallied to protect the rights of juveniles. In a series of decisions (see **Table 17.3**), the U.S. Supreme Court extended to juveniles many of the due process rights accorded adults.

THE CRIME CONTROL PERIOD (1980–PRESENT) ■ As Barry Feld points out, the juvenile justice system has changed dramatically in recent decades. He argues that these changes have transformed the system "from a nominally rehabilitative social welfare agency into a scaled-down second-class criminal court for young people."[5] He believes that this shift has occurred because of racial demographic and economic changes that have spurred Americans to fear "other people's children, especially minority youths charged with crimes."[6]

Conservative critics have argued that juvenile authorities treat young people far too leniently. Stories are told about crimes that would have landed an adult in jail but

delinquent
A child who has committed an act that if committed by an adult would be criminal.

neglected
Describing a child who is not receiving proper care, because of some action or inaction of his or her parents.

dependent
A child who has no parent or guardian or whose parents are unable to give proper care.

TABLE 17.3 *Major Decisions by the U.S. Supreme Court Regarding the Rights of Juveniles*

Since the mid-1960s, the Supreme Court has gradually expanded the rights of juveniles but has continued to recognize that the logic of a separate system for juvenile offenders justifies differences from some adult rights.	

Case	Significance for Juvenile Offenders
Kent v. United States (1966)	"Essentials of due process" are required by juvenile offenders.
In Re Gault (1967)	The "essentials" of due process required by *Kent*—notice, hearing, counsel, cross-examination—are specified.
In Re Winship (1970)	A standard of "beyond a doubt" is required for delinquency matters.
McKeiver v. Pennsylvania (1971)	Jury trials are not required for juvenile court hearings.
Breed v. Jones (1975)	Waiver to adult court following adjudication in juvenile court violates the constitutional guarantee against double jeopardy.
Smith v. Daily Mail Publishing Co. (1979)	The press may report certain aspects of juvenile court cases and matters.
Eddings v. Oklahoma (1982)	The age of a defendant must be considered as a mitigating factor in capital crimes.
Schall v. Martin (1984)	Preventive pretrial definition is allowed for juvenile defendants who are found "dangerous."
Stanford v. Kentucky (1989)	Minimum age for capital punishment is 16.
Roper v. Simmons (2005)	To impose the death penalty on someone for a crime committed before the age of 18 violates the Eighth Amendment prohibition of "cruel and unusual punishments."

for which a juvenile received nothing more than probation. Alarm over serious and violent juvenile offenses, particularly those committed by urban youth, has resulted in a broad public movement for increasing the use of waiver to adult court (before adjudication in juvenile court), increasing the sanctions for those remaining in juvenile court, or both. This pressure to treat juveniles as adults and to mete out stern punishment for serious crimes has eroded much of the enthusiasm for the juvenile court reforms of a century ago.

Even though the reforms of recent decades have changed the procedures and, to a lesser extent, the practices of the juvenile justice system, in many respects the underlying philosophy of the juvenile court remains very much as the original reformers intended. The justice system treats juveniles differently from adults by placing less emphasis on punishment and more on individualized treatment. The rationale for this difference is that juveniles differ in important ways from adults, ways that ought to be considered in the way the law works.

■ WHY TREAT JUVENILES AND ADULTS DIFFERENTLY?

Differences between juveniles and adults are used to justify separate justice systems. Five such differences are identified as follows.

JUVENILES ARE YOUNG AND MAY EASILY CHANGE ■ Most correctional professionals believe that juveniles are more susceptible than adults to the influence of treatment programs. Younger offenders are not as entrenched in negative peer associations, nor do they penetrate as deeply into criminal activity. Because the habits of the young are less well formed, they may be more easily altered.

But the youthfulness of juveniles is a double-edged sword. Age is a predictor of recidivism: the younger the juvenile offender—and the more serious the misconduct—the more likely that offender will be arrested again. As a consequence, correctional workers must deal with the fact that although younger offenders are more malleable, many of the young will find it hard to stay out of trouble.

JUVENILES HAVE A HIGH RATE OF "DESIST-ENCE"
■ All else being equal, age is the best predictor of recidivism: the younger the offender, the more likely that offender will fail under community supervision. But that statistic can be misleading, because juvenile offenders, as a group, have lower failure rates than do adults. Most juveniles who get in trouble with the law once never get arrested again. Despite the high success rate of juveniles, even the very young, a look at those who do fail will turn up large numbers whose criminality began at a very early age, simply because so many youths are arrested in the first place. Even studies of the most serious juvenile delinquents, though, find evidence of high rates of success: Less than one-fourth of youth who end up in custodial placements are returned to incarceration because of new offenses,[7] and even the most serious juvenile delinquents who have been labeled "chronic" by the courts are, for the most part, free of crime by the time the reach their mid-twenties.[8]

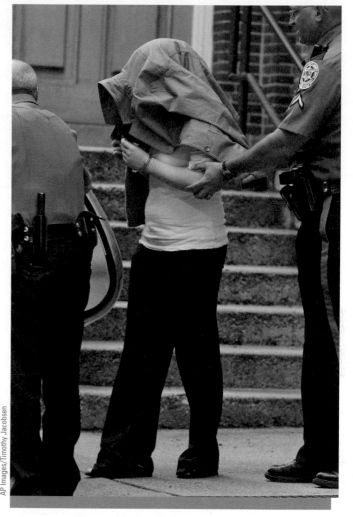

AP Images/Timothy Jacobsen

Fifteen-year-old Danielle Black is led out of the Washington County, Maryland, courthouse after a hearing on having her case of hiring a hitman to murder her father transferred to juvenile court. She was convicted in adult court and sentenced in October 2009 to 10 years of imprisonment.

JUVENILES' FAMILIES ARE AN IMPORTANT PART OF THEIR LIVES
■ For juvenile offenders, the role of family is critical to the success of correctional efforts. The juvenile is, by virtue of age, deeply connected to his or her immediate family (parents, siblings, and extended family) in ways that do not characterize adult relationships. Under the laws of most states, for example, the juvenile actually becomes a ward of the state, and the court (usually through probation officers) accepts joint responsibility for the young offender. Under the law, then, the court system is a partner with the family in the supervision effort. Many think this approach is reasonable because the child's delinquency is taken as evidence that the parents are not capable of effective supervision without support from the court.

JUVENILES ARE EASILY INFLUENCED BY THEIR PEERS
■ With isolated exceptions, juvenile crime is a group phenomenon. Young people gather to socialize, and a common part of their behavior is testing boundaries and challenging each other to try new things. We often associate "gangs" with the criminal behavior of young people, but all studies find that group criminality can arise without gangs. Especially during the preadolescence and teen years, peer relationships are the most important influences on most youths. It is not easy for youths to resist the pressure to engage in group delinquent acts.

JUVENILES HAVE LITTLE RESPONSIBILITY FOR OTHERS
■ For an adult, successful adjustment to the community involves taking on productive adult roles: parent, worker, citizen. By contrast, juveniles are typically only responsible for their own behavior.

Juvenile self-responsibility typically concerns school performance and behavior, compliance with a curfew, and developing interpersonal skills, among other things.

Differences between Adults and Juveniles in Perspective

The differences just listed underscore some of the reasons why a separate juvenile justice system makes sense to most correctional professionals: Young offenders differ from older offenders in sufficiently important ways to justify different strategies carried out by separate correctional authorities.

However, these differences do not always work out as juvenile correctional workers might intend. For example, family dynamics often contribute to delinquent behavior. Inadequate parental supervision may leave the child free enough to get into trouble. Conflicts between the child and adults may promote delinquency as the child's way of "getting back" or even unintentionally calling attention to the conflict. Abuse by parents, as well as alcoholism, drug addiction, or mental illness in parents, may contribute to problems that end in delinquency. Such adults often resist taking a positive role in the supervision effort. They may be hostile to the efforts of the correctional worker or may excuse or condone the child's misbehavior.

Peer groups can also cause problems. Minor delinquents can drift from the everyday rule-breaking of truancy, fighting, and drinking into far more serious crime. This can happen especially when the group encourages ever-greater risk taking. Although we might all remember instances of violating curfews, drinking alcohol, and other delinquent acts that seemed merely "fun," many of the most serious forms of delinquency begin with just this sort of misbehavior.

Finally, keeping a juvenile offender in the ordinary environment of most young people—schools and neighborhoods—may not be easy. When a child disrupts the school setting through aggressive or threatening behavior, the school authorities usually want that youngster removed. When neighbors fear the open violence of a gang member, the judge will face strong pressure to send that person to a juvenile institution. When a juvenile fails in the school and on the streets, few options are available to keep him or her from sinking more deeply into the corrections system.

■ THE PROBLEM OF SERIOUS DELINQUENCY

The juvenile justice system is predicated on what we might call "normal" delinquency. This idea may seem contradictory but emphasizes that delinquent behavior is common in teenage years; certainly, for young men in difficult living situations, it is almost expected. There is no legal or textbook definition of *normal*; rather, the term represents a set of assumptions about kinds of misbehaviors associated with growing up. Because some level of delinquency is, in this sense, normal, people may react to it with less alarm than to similar misbehavior by adults. People may believe that juveniles require not a punitive correctional response but a developmental one, because their behavior is a part of a common adolescent pattern.

It would be naive to think that the juvenile justice paradigm applies equally to every young person who breaks the law. As noted, for each difference between adults and juveniles, there are well-known cases where the distinction did not apply. Some juveniles are already hardened and are unlikely to change; some will continue criminal behavior well into adulthood; some lack families who will provide meaningful supervision; some are loners, unaffected by peer influences; some are already in adult roles, with jobs, spouses, and children. What should we do when a youthful offender does not act as we would expect a juvenile to act?

Status offenses are misbehaviors that are not against the law but are troubling for juveniles because the person is so young: running away, being truant, and being ungov-

status offenses
Misbehaviors that are not against the law but are troubling when done by juveniles because they are so young.

TABLE 17.4 *Percentage of Petitioned Status Offense Cases Involving Female Offenders, 1985–2002*

When girls misbehave, the juvenile justice system often treats them as status offenders rather than delinquents.	
Status Offense	**Percent of All Cases**
Runaway	61%
Truancy	46
Ungovernability	46
Liquor	30

Source: Howard N. Snyder and Melissa Sickmund, *Juvenile Offenders and Victims: 2006 National Report* (Pittsburgh: National Center for Juvenile Justice, March 2006), 191.

ernable. Society does not expect children to act this way; when they do, the juvenile court may get involved and provide a bit of structure that the parent has not given. Further, as matters of judgment, status offenses depend on social expectations. That girls are so much more likely to be involved in this kind of case than in other forms of delinquency (see **Table 17.4**) suggests that status offenses depend on ideas about what "the proper child" acts like.

One of the most important considerations is whether the behavior of the juvenile is age appropriate. What people find "normal" for different ages can vary greatly. For example, when a 14-year-old becomes angry and engages in hostile, irrational behavior, most people would think of him or her as merely "troubled." However, the same behavior by a 17-year old would be seen as immature. In the same way, when a very young juvenile—for example, a preteen—engages in an extremely violent act, we are alarmed by the antisocial behavior of a young person who should be learning to live by society's norms. Clearly, assumptions about the "normalcy" of delinquency depend on how the misbehavior fits the juvenile's age and level of development.

Similarly, people expect misbehavior to take place in a social context. It does not surprise or unduly alarm people when youths occasionally resort to delinquency as a way of becoming a member of their group. Gangs are, of course, an extreme example, but most people find even gangs understandable to a point. The lone child who commits crime for personal pleasure rather than social acceptance is comparatively rare, and people do not perceive such behavior as "normal" in a young person's development. The public also finds it hard to understand when a youngster engages in gratuitous violence. Some kids commit petty property offenses, stealing things they want or vandalizing places they resent. A few get into schoolyard fights. But children who kill each other or plot to hurt someone are deeply unsettling. The label "delinquent" seems far too weak for these acts.

Unusual juvenile criminality has been one reason why some question the wisdom of having a separate juvenile justice system. They say society ought to treat all criminal acts with the seriousness they deserve, regardless of age. To the extent that age contributed to the gravity of the act, it could be taken as an aggravating or mitigating factor in sentencing. Certainly, age would also be a consideration in designing and managing correctional programs. Offenders could be assigned to programs based partly on age and maturity. But critics of juvenile justice argue for ending the separate system of justice, because there are so many exceptions to the "norms" on which the juvenile justice system is based.

In spite of the many proposals to reform juvenile justice, so far no nationwide movement has sought to abolish juvenile court. Thus, today's most common approaches are applied within the separate system of justice for juveniles, described in the next sections.

■ SANCTIONING JUVENILE OFFENDERS

The website of the **leading government agency dealing with youth crime** is found at the corresponding link at www.cengage.com/criminaljustice/clear.

A **timeline of school shootings** is found at the corresponding link at www.cengage.com/criminaljustice/clear.

Originally, separating juvenile justice from adult justice was intended to enable justice workers to give the highest priority to preventing crime by rehabilitating delinquents. Juvenile correctional agencies provide a range of services from diversion to probation, detention, and aftercare. Although rehabilitation does indeed figure prominently in their practices, that ethic is quite fragile in reality.

Overview of the Juvenile Justice System

Juvenile corrections suffers from the same type of fragmentation as its adult counterpart does, with agencies sometimes operated under the courts, sometimes under the executive branch; sometimes housed with the institutional function, sometimes separated from it; sometimes run by counties, sometimes run by the state. Such fragmentation makes generalizing about juvenile corrections policies difficult. Nearly any policy arrangement a person can imagine exists somewhere, and what is true of one jurisdiction may not be true in the next.

In 2007, the most recent year for which we have data, almost 2.2 million juveniles (persons under age 18) were arrested, representing 15 percent of all arrests made by the police.[9] As **Figure 17.1** on the next page shows, juveniles were involved in a much smaller proportion of violent crime arrests than property crime arrests.

Less than a third of juveniles were arrested for UCR Index crimes: murder, sexual assault, aggravated assault, robbery, burglary, larceny-theft, motor vehicle theft. Of juvenile arrestees, 70 percent were male and 68 percent age 16 or older. Juvenile arrests disproportionately involved minorities. People of color comprised 17 percent of the juvenile population but were arrested out of proportion to their numbers. Especially troubling is the fact that, of those arrested for murder, 48 percent were African American; for rape, 33 percent; for robbery, 63 percent. A juvenile arrest clears proportionately fewer crimes than does an adult arrest. This is true because juveniles tend to commit crimes in groups and are more likely to be arrested for their crimes, thus clearing fewer crimes with more arrests.[10]

Such numbers are alarming: 57,650 juveniles were arrested for aggravated assault, a serious, violent personal crime. Further, arrest rates are increasing faster for girls than for boys. Yet we must take these numbers in their proper context. In all, about 0.03 percent of all Americans aged 10–17 were arrested for a violent offense in 2007. Violent crime among young people is alarming but it is not common. And the juvenile portion of all crime is dropping, as well.[11]

In fact, serious juvenile offenders (those who commit felonies) are not all violent, nor are they chronic. Violent offenders commit felonies that threaten physical harm. Chronic offenders offend in repetitive patterns. **Figure 17.2** on page 482 shows the overlap of these types of juvenile offenders—some juveniles engage in all three patterns, but most are one type of offender only. Violent offenders commit the fewest crimes.

These differences mean that the offense alone is not enough to predict whether or not the offender is someone whom society should fear. Among juveniles, the rate of false positives (incorrect predictions of dangerousness) is quite high. Studies show that instead of relying on the offense alone to identify the highest-risk juvenile offenders, we should be concerned about other factors in the juvenile's history. Among them are the following:

■ Persistent behavioral problems during the elementary school years

■ Onset of delinquency, aggression, or drug use between the ages of 6 and 11

■ Antisocial parents

■ Antisocial peers, poor school performance, impulsivity, and weak social ties between the ages of 12 and 14

■ Membership in delinquent gangs

■ Drug dealing[12]

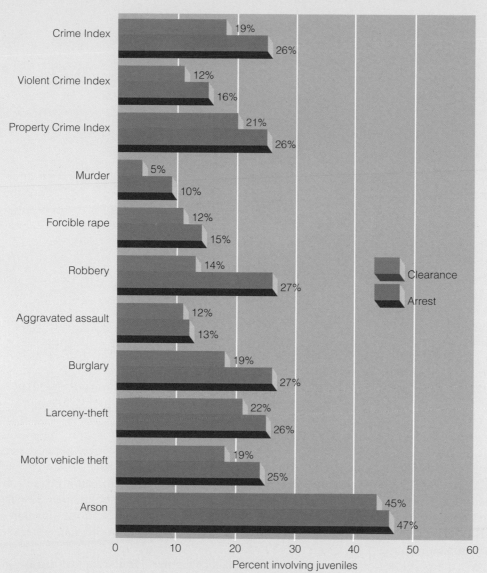

Figure 17.1

Of All Arrests, Percentage Who Are Juveniles and Percentage of Crimes Cleared by Arrests of Juveniles

Juveniles were involved in a much smaller proportion of violent crime arrests than property arrests.

*A crime that is reported to the police and is considered "solved" by virtue of at least one arrest. One arrest can clear many crimes if the offender has committed many; alternatively, if a group commits a crime, which is common for juveniles, only one crime is cleared through several arrests.

Sources: Office of Juvenile Justice and Delinquency Prevention, *Juvenile Justice Bulletin:* December 2003, p. 4; June 2009, p. 4.

Disposition of Juvenile Offenders

About 1.6 million juvenile offenders are referred to juvenile court each year. The first decision made in a juvenile court is whether or not to file a petition of juvenile jurisdiction. If the petition is granted, there is a hearing on the merits of the charges, with the intention of making the juvenile a ward of the court if the charges are sustained. Cases that are not petitioned involve informal dispositions in which the juvenile consents to whichever outcome is determined by the court.

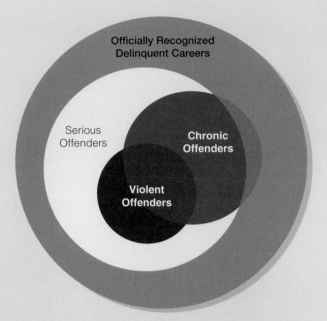

Figure 17.2
The Overlap of Violent, Serious, and Chronic Juvenile Offenders
Juvenile offenders who most concern us have important differences in their patterns of offense.

Source: Office of Juvenile Justice and Delinquency Prevention, *Juvenile Offenders and Victims: 1997 Update on Violence* (Washington, DC: U.S. Government Printing Office, 1997), 25.

As **Figure 17.3** shows, nearly half of the referrals to juvenile court do not result in a petition. Of these cases, 40 percent have their charges dismissed, and another 22 percent are assigned to an informal probation. On rare occasions, nonpetitioned juveniles receive placements, typically in mental health facilities; more commonly, some alternative sanction results.

When a petition is filed, the court must consider whether it will take jurisdiction in the case. In about 1 percent of cases, jurisdiction is waived to adult court. In the usual case, the juvenile must decide whether or not to contest the charges—if so, an adjudication hearing follows, in which the accuracy of the charges are considered. Almost half of the time, the charges are sufficiently minor, the facts are in so little dispute, or the likely disposition is sufficiently acceptable that the juvenile waives this hearing and the court proceeds directly to disposition of the charges. Without an adjudication hearing, charges are usually dismissed. It is also common for the juvenile to accept a probation term or some other moderate penalty. See "Myths in Corrections" for more.

The juvenile usually contests the charges in the petition if they are serious or the disposition is potentially severe. However, this strategy succeeds in getting the charges dismissed only 5 percent of the time. Further, even though the usual disposition is a term of probation, almost one-third of adjudicated offenders get placed in a reform school, training school, or some other institution for juveniles.

This review of the juvenile justice process shows some reasons why the process has faced criticism in recent years.

MYTHS IN CORRECTIONS

JUVENILE GANGS

THE MYTH: Gangs are a growing urban phenomenon, and youth gang numbers are rapidly increasing.

THE REALITY: Law enforcement agencies reported *declining* levels of gang activity through the 1990s, and since then the amount of gang activity as reported in national surveys has been roughly stable.

Source: Arlene Egley, Jr., and Arline K. Major, "Highlights of the 2002 Youth Gang Survey," *OJJDP Fact Sheet*, April 2004, 4.

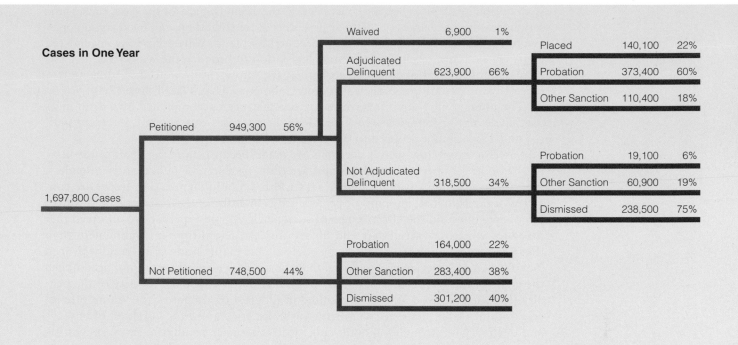

Cases in One Year

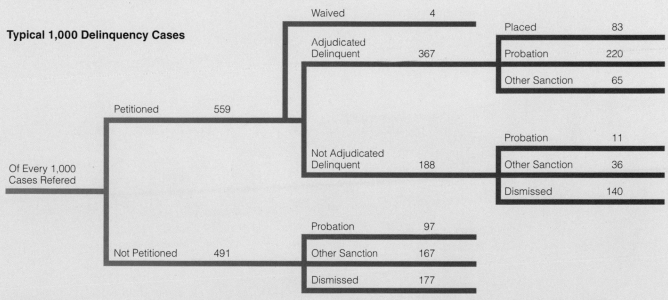

Typical 1,000 Delinquency Cases

Figure 17.3
Juvenile Court Processing of Delinquency Cases

Note: Details may not add to 100% because of rounding.

Source: Melissa Sickmund, *Delinquent Cases in Juvenile Court 2005: OJJDP Factsheet* (Washington, DC: Office of Juvenile Justice and Delinquency Prevention, June 2009), 6.

Among adult felons, for example, 77 percent of those convicted of violent crimes, as well as 66 percent of those convicted of property offenses, receive sentences involving terms of confinement.[13] This compares with confinement for only 25 percent of juveniles adjudicated for offenses against persons, and 21 percent for property offenses.[14]

WAIVER ■ Those who are uneasy with the juvenile justice system often favor an increased use of waiver to adult court. *Waiver* (also referred to as *transfer to adult court*) is an option available when the court believes the circumstances of the case, such as the seriousness of the charges or the poor prospects of rehabilitation, call for the young person to be handled under adult court procedures and laws. Waiver has long engendered controversy, but a recent surge in state legislation to broaden the waiver statutes has increased the number of crime categories that are automatically waived to adult court—especially for serious crimes such as murder and sexual assault (see **Figure 17.4**).

The public outcry about waiver has, ironically, been accompanied by a drop in its use. The overall proportion of waived delinquency cases was about 1.5 percent until the mid-1990s, but it dropped to 0.7 percent by 2005.[15]

Some question how waiver decisions are made, because more than half of the juveniles who are transferred to adult court are drug, property, or public order offenders, not violent offenders. Among juveniles transferred to adult court, 63 percent are convicted of their offense, but only 27 percent are eventually sentenced to prison.[16] Waiver opponents question the effectiveness of such results. Some experts have observed that juveniles who are waived may end up serving less actual time in confinement than those not waived on the same type of offense. One major study of juvenile waiver in New York and New Jersey concluded that the use of waiver there did not accomplish the goals of the waiver system—it did not materially increase the severity of the penalty juveniles received and often resulted in illogical treatment of the young offenders.[17] Studies have suggested that many juveniles are waived for low-level offenses,[18] and dealing with juveniles in adult court leads to higher recidivism rates, suggesting that adult punishments may actually exacerbate crimes rather than deterring them.[19] Finally, African Americans are vastly overrepresented among those cases waived to criminal court.[20]

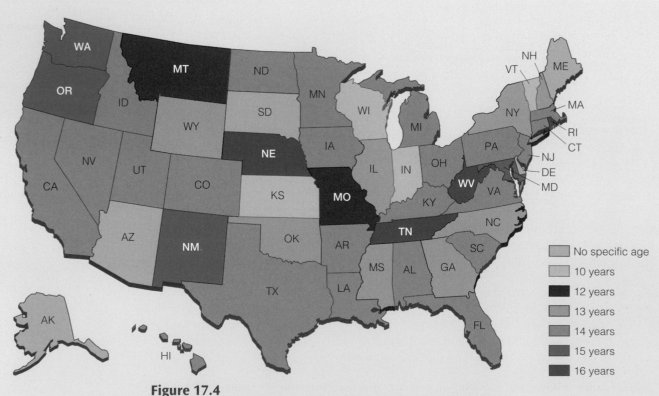

Figure 17.4
The Youngest Ages at Which Juveniles May Be Transferred to Adult Criminal Court

Source: Office of Juvenile Justice and Delinquency Prevention, *Trying Juveniles as Adults in Criminal Court* (Washington, DC: U.S. Government Printing Office, 1998), 14–15.

When 12-year-olds Jake Eakin and Evan Savoie were charged with the slaying of 13-year-old Craig Sorger, they were among the youngest youths to have their case decided in adult court. Eakin, shown in the Grant County Superior Court in Ephrata, Washington, pleaded guilty to second-degree murder, testified against Savoie and was sentenced to 14 years in prison. Savoie was found guilty of first-degree murder and received the maximum sentence of 26 years. Critics contend that juveniles should never be treated as adults.

Because the number of juveniles waived to adult court is so small, the number of juveniles serving time in adult facilities is also small. Recent data suggest that less than 2 percent of the adult prison population is under the age of 20,[21] and fewer than 7,000 juveniles were held in local jails—less that 0.01 percent of the jail population.[22] The young offender in adult facilities is a management problem because of special needs, not because of large numbers.

DIVERSION ■ The conceptual opposite of waiver is diversion. Although waiver attempts to avoid the lenient treatment of the juvenile justice system, diversion seeks to avoid burdensome consequences of formal processing. This informal adjustment to a case can occur at any stage of the juvenile justice process, but it is most often chosen prior to filing formal charges in a petition to the court.

Diversion can take two forms. The most direct form is simply to stop processing the case, in the expectation that the main objectives of the justice process have been achieved—the juvenile has realized the wrongness of the conduct and has shown a convincing willingness to refrain from it in the future. This form of diversion is seldom final—if the young person returns to court on a new referral, the old charges may be considered again with the new one.

In the second form, juveniles are diverted to specific programs. This option may be selected when the court determines that the young person's delinquency is a result of certain problems in the child's life that may best be addressed by a program designed to help the juvenile. These diversion programs often deal with developmental issues such as the child's social skills or response to frustration in school performance. Diversion to mental health treatment for emotionally disturbed youth is also commonly preferred to formal processing.

The logic of diversion is based on the developmental pattern of delinquency. It is thought that most juveniles drift into delinquent behavior gradually, as a part of growing up. As their misconduct becomes more serious, they "signal" a need for help to get off the pathway to delinquency. The diversion strategy tries to provide that help as early as possible. For example, recent studies show that misbehaviors such as stubbornness, resistance to authority, and interpersonal aggressiveness, when exhibited in preadolescence, indicate a risk of later delinquency.[23] Other studies find that truancy is

Visit the website of the **Campaign for Youth Justice,** a juvenile court waiver reform organization, listed at www.cengage.com/criminaljustice/clear.

The **National Center for Juvenile Justice** can be accessed using the corresponding link at www.cengage.com/criminaljustice/clear.

a predictor of later delinquency.[24] That is why diversion programs that help disruptive children learn to cope and those that retain children in school are considered important aspects of delinquency prevention that do not require formal juvenile processing. Whatever the logic and wisdom of diversion, it used to be the most frequent strategy for addressing complaints against juveniles. However, its popularity has diminished over the years, so that precourt diversion is now used in only one-fifth of the cases brought to the attention of the police.[25]

CORRECTIONAL PROGRAMS FOR JUVENILE OFFENDERS ■ The impact of juvenile treatment programs differs from programs for adults in two ways. First, juvenile programs show somewhat greater success than do adult programs. Second, the benefits of juvenile correctional programming considerably surpass those of their adult counterparts.

The research on the effectiveness of juvenile correctional programs identifies a handful of particularly promising strategies. Most of these programs are early intervention programs, designed to identify children at high risk of delinquency and provide a concentration of services to help them change their destinies. For youngsters aged 11–18, for example, limited basic social skills and poor school performance are two important predictors of delinquency. Programs that increase social interpersonal competence—usually through cognitively oriented skill-development strategies—and that decrease school failure tend to reduce delinquency. For girls, programs that improve family discipline and problem solving also prevent delinquency. In short, evidence increasingly suggests that the systematic support of all aspects of family life for families in which at-risk youths are being raised reduces delinquency and antisocial behavior over the long run and saves money as well, and the earlier such programs are used in the child's life, the better.[26]

For example, a study by Rand Corporation researchers found that early intervention programs prevented so much delinquency and other social problems that they saved enormous amounts of money. One program they studied, for example, was a "graduation incentives" program that established monetary and other incentives for participants who did not drop out of high school, and then provided tutoring and related assistance intensively to help them succeed. This program cost about $12,500 per participant, but it prevented more than four crimes per participant, with each crime costing well more than the program. Using cost-per-crime estimates, these researchers found that expanding available and proved early intervention programs in California would reduce crime twice as much as expanded use of incarceration would, at one-fifth the cost.[27]

Although evidence for the value of early intervention for at-risk youth is very strong, political support remains weak. A public that is willing to invest billions in bricks and mortar for more prison cells seems to see intervention programs as "soft" social welfare. Until political energy develops for expanding intervention programs, the promised benefit will remain only a promise.

DETENTION ■ Approximately 20 percent of juvenile arrestees are detained—almost 330,000 per year. Most juvenile detention is brief—the median stay is just over two weeks—until an initial appearance before a juvenile court judge (or judicial referee, who represents the court in detention hearings).[28] After a petition decision is made, most juveniles are released to their families. But about one out of five, found to endanger others or be at risk of flight, is kept in detention for days or weeks until an adjudication hearing can be scheduled.

Federal law requires that juveniles housed in adult jails be segregated from adult prisoners and be taken before a magistrate for an initial appearance within 24 hours of arrival in the facility. As minors under special protection of the court, these juveniles also have legal rights to education and basic services, yet most juveniles receive little special programming.

Such programming clearly should be a priority. Many juveniles in detention have special needs that make treatment appropriate. Juvenile delinquents disproportionately suffer from learning disabilities that make them lag in school performance—time in detention only makes matters worse after release. Still other juveniles are members of gangs, which places them at risk of assault by other members detained in the same facilities. Studies show that detention experiences significantly worsen later child behavior and increase the chance of continued delinquency.[29] In general, detention centers for juveniles are places where great strides could be made in preventing delinquency by dealing with youths in crisis, but far too little is being done.[30]

JUVENILE PROBATION ■ In 60 percent of cases, the juvenile delinquent is placed on probation and released to the custody of a parent or guardian. Further, the number of juveniles placed on probation has increased by 46 percent since 1985.[31] Often the judge orders the delinquent to undergo some form of education or counseling. The delinquent may also have to pay a fine or make restitution while on probation.

The differences between adult and juvenile probation are subtle and stem from the differences between adult and juvenile offenders, described earlier. Juvenile probation officers often try to develop personal relationships with their clients, a move discouraged for adult probation officers. To achieve this bond, juvenile probation officers often engage in recreation with their clients or accompany them to social activities. Through this bond, officers seek the youngster's trust, which they hope will form the basis for long-lasting behavioral change. Sometimes officers will mix the child on probation with other young people who are not under court supervision, to further his or her reintegration into more socially acceptable peer relationships. Often adult mentors are called in to give children effective role models; mentoring programs reduce antisocial activities and school misbehavior by as much as one-third.

In carrying out supervision, the probation officer must work closely with community social service agencies that are involved with the juvenile and the family.

Juvenile offenders newly arrived at the Texas Youth Commission Evaluation Center wait to begin psychological testing and evaluation. These youths were charged with crimes in their hometowns and ordered to this facility by the juvenile courts. After they are evaluated, they are transferred to other TYC facilities throughout the state.

Probation officers spend time in the schools, talk to teachers and guidance counselors, and learn about programs for troubled youths, such as recreational programs and youth counseling programs. Probation officers also establish close contact with family service agencies, welfare providers, and programs that support young mothers and provide substitutes for missing fathers. In some respects the probation officer serves as a linchpin for the array of community services that might help a young person stay out of trouble. "Careers in Corrections" offers a closer view of the work of a juvenile probation officer.

Although the ideals of rehabilitation and reintegration matter in all community supervision, they receive special emphasis among juvenile probation workers. It is important to recognize, however, that juvenile probation is changing. A sense of unease about how juvenile probation handles serious offending among youths has led to a new interest in the techniques and practices of adult supervision: surveillance and control.

WORKING IN THE SCHOOLS ■ Most juveniles spend a significant portion of their day in school; up to age 16, they are required by law to be in school. Juvenile justice agencies—probation in particular—typically develop school-based programs to increase overall effectiveness with youths under supervision of the juvenile court. School-based programs typically have three objectives: keep potential truants in school, reduce school violence, and improve the academic performance of at-risk youths.

CAREERS IN CORRECTIONS Probation Officer—Juveniles

NATURE OF THE WORK

Juvenile probation officers are responsible for the supervision and guidance of youths under age 18 who have been referred to them by the court, police, or social service agencies. Through the development of close ties with offenders' families, school authorities, and health agencies, probation officers help juvenile offenders meet their educational and treatment needs. They also monitor their behavior to ensure that court-ordered requirements are met. Caseload size varies by agency, by the needs of the offenders, and by the risks they pose. Caseloads for juveniles tend to be lower than those for adult probationers. Officers may be on call 24 hours a day to supervise and assist offenders.

REQUIRED QUALIFICATIONS

Background qualifications for juvenile probation officers vary by state, but a bachelor's degree in social work, criminal justice, or a related field from a four-year college or university is usually required. Some agencies require previous experience with youths or graduate work. Candidates must be 21 years of age and have no felony convictions. Most juvenile probation officers receive formal and on-the-job training.

EARNINGS AND JOB OUTLOOK

The number of probation officers for juveniles is expected to grow about as fast as other occupations during the next decade. Probation officers handling a juvenile caseload report a high level of personal satisfaction in their work. Juvenile probation officers earn about $40,000 a year.

MORE INFORMATION

Visit the website of the **American Probation and Parole Association** using the corresponding link at www.cengage.com/criminaljustice/clear. Career information can also be obtained from your state, juvenile court, or probation office.

Effective programs have been developed for each of these objectives. Successful school-safety programs focus on reducing bullying behavior and eliminating weapons and drugs on school grounds.[32] School dropout programs create networks of services within the community; this concentration of efforts seeks to increase an at-risk youth's academic self-confidence and personal commitment to staying in school. With so many juveniles processed by the juvenile justice system later returning to public schools, there is a need to find effective programs for these identified, at-risk youth.

Unfortunately, school programs do not always work as expected. Studies have found, for example, that juveniles who work while in school are more likely to engage in delinquency, and their likelihood of delinquency increases with the number of hours worked.[33] Thus, work programs that appear to offer youths transitions into adult wage-earner roles may also hasten delinquency.

INTERMEDIATE SANCTIONS FOR JUVENILES ■ The complaint that few sanctioning options exist between traditional probation and custodial dispositions is perhaps even more true in juvenile justice than in criminal justice. Only about 15 percent of delinquents receive an intermediate sanction. One reason for slowness in developing juvenile intermediate sanctions is that traditional juvenile corrections already resembles intermediate sanctions. Adult probation is interested in intensive supervision as an intermediate sanction, but adult intensive supervision probation (ISP) caseloads are often about the same size as many traditional juvenile caseloads—in the twenties or thirties.

The adult system develops electronic monitored home detention; the juvenile system has routinely used curfews that restrict youths to home except during school hours. Community service and restitution have been standard juvenile court dispositions for many years.

Some juvenile probation agencies have begun to develop intensive supervision approaches that are far more intensive than adult ISPs. A juvenile ISP officer may carry 15 cases or fewer and may well see each client almost every day—more than once a day if necessary. Police-probation partnerships intensify juvenile intensive supervision even further, because the police add surveillance to the probation services. Juvenile corrections systems have also developed work-based community service, restitution centers where young people work to pay victims back, and after-school assignments that minimize free time. Under intermediate sanctioning approaches, juveniles may be required to complete programs to increase their awareness of the impact of crimes on victims, and they may be sent to summer camps that require community service in the form of cleaning parks and other public places.

One of the most widespread new intermediate sanctions for juvenile offenders is the boot camp, described in Chapter 9. As noted there, the results have not been promising, with most studies showing that boot camp graduates do no better than do youths placed in other programs; in fact, some boot camp graduates actually do worse than those placed in other alternatives.[34] This has led to the development of specialized aftercare caseloads of boot camp graduates, to try to reduce their failure rate. See "Myths in Corrections" for more.

JUVENILE COMMUNITY CORRECTIONS ■ Despite the lukewarm evaluations of juvenile community corrections (see Chapter 22), interest has continued in this approach, for two main reasons. First, most people realize that removing a young person from the community is an extreme solution, reserved for extreme cases. Disrupting community and family relationships can interfere with long-term prospects for successful adjustment, by damaging these already fragile supports. Second, and just as compelling, for most youths the institutional stay will be short—six months to a year in custody is common. Eventually, the youth returns to the community, and the real work of successfully adjusting to community life occurs there. Advocates of community corrections ask, "Why wait?"

Community corrections offers additional advantages for juveniles. The cost of custody in a juvenile training school is usually at least double that for an adult in prison, which means there is more money to work with in creating incentives to keep offenders out of trouble and in designing and implementing effective alternatives in the community. Moreover, public opinion toward youthful offenders is not as harsh as that toward adult offenders, so it is easier to obtain public support for juvenile community corrections.[35] Finally, because youth incarceration numbers are smaller than the adult numbers, it is easier to show success in saving money by diverting offenders to local programs.

Copyright © Joel Gordon 2007 - Model Released - All rights reserved

Juvenile probation officers seek to develop personal relationships with their clients. Regular visits helps officers supervise and guide their probationers.

MYTHS IN CORRECTIONS

BOOT CAMPS AND DELINQUENCY

THE MYTH: Boot camps are effective ways of instilling discipline and preventing delinquency.

THE REALITY: Many studies of boot camps have been conducted. While some studies suggest that boot camps alter a youth's attitudes toward authority, results uniformly show that boot camps do not reduce rates of delinquency for those who attend them—and they may even make recidivism worse.

Source: Doris L. MacKenzie and Gaylene S. Armstrong, *Correctional Boot Camps: Military Basic Training or a Model for Corrections?* (Thousand Oaks, CA: Sage, 2004).

Studies of **boot camps** are reported at the corresponding link at www.cengage.com/criminaljustice/clear.

A program in Ohio, gaining national acclaim, seeks to return funds to communities that retain juvenile offenders rather than sending them to state-run schools. RECLAIM Ohio—Reasoned and Equitable Community and Local Alternatives to Incarceration of Minors—provides a significant payback to county leaders who can show that juveniles who might have been sent to training schools paid by state taxes are instead being kept in local, innovative programs designed especially for local needs. The program has proved popular because it appeals to conservative ideals of cost-effective public policy and local control, while appealing to liberal beliefs in rehabilitation of juvenile offenders.[36]

JUVENILE INCARCERATION ■ Of those juveniles declared delinquent, 22 percent are placed in public and private facilities. The national incarceration rate (including detention) per 100,000 juveniles aged 10–18 is 307. Like the adult incarceration rate, there is a wide range among the states, with the highest rate in Wyoming (606) and the lowest in Vermont (72). Nationally, 61 percent of incarcerated juveniles are held in public facilities, with the remainder in private facilities, and 94,875 offenders under age 21 are held in 2,809 facilities.[37] But juvenile placements have been dropping nationally, with an overall drop of 14 percent since 1997.[38] See **Figure 17.5** to see types of juvenile custodial facilities.

Policy makers are concerned about the overrepresentation of incarcerated African American juveniles. The Juvenile Justice and Delinquency Prevention Act of 1988 requires states to determine whether the proportion of minorities in confinement exceeds their proportion in the population. If such overrepresentation is found, states must demonstrate efforts to reduce it. *Disparity* means that the probability of receiving a particular outcome (for example, being detained in a short-term facility rather than not being detained) differs among different groups. If more African Americans are detained than others, this, in turn, may lead to more of them being adjudicated in juvenile court and may lead to a larger proportion being placed in residential facilities. **Table 17.5** shows the rate of African American overrepresentation (as a proportion of the population) at each major decision point of the juvenile corrections system. The disproportionate confinement of minority juveniles often stems from disparity at the early stages of case processing.

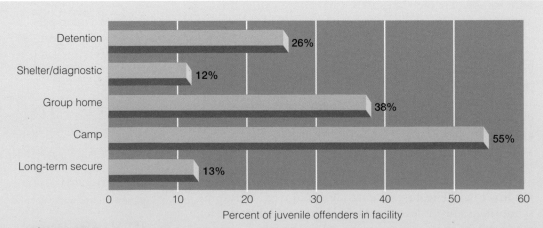

Figure 17.5

Type of Juvenile Custodial Facility

Most juvenile facilities are low security, but almost two of five juvenile facilities are for detention or long-term placement.

Source: Howard N. Snyder and Melissa Sickmund, *Juvenile Offenders and Victims: 2006 National Report* (Pittsburgh: National Center for Juvenile Justice, March 2006), 218.

Bobbie Stillman reads in her room at the Beloit Juvenile Correctional Facility in Beloit, Kansas. Nationally, more than 130,000 juveniles aged 10 to 18 are incarcerated in juvenile or adult prisons.

AP Images/Charlie Riedel

TABLE 17.5 *Overrepresentation of African Americans in the Juvenile Corrections System*

African Americans are almost twice as likely to be arrested than are whites. At subsequent stages the overrepresentation, while still a problem, is less pronounced.

	Rates per 100 Youths		
Type of Ratio[a]	White	African American	Overrepresentation of African Americans
Juvenile arrests to population[b]	6.1	11.5	1.9
Cases referred to juvenile arrests	68.9	75.6	1.1
Cases detained to cases referred	18.4	25.1	1.4
Cases petitioned to cases referred	54.9	64.7	1.2
Cases waived to cases petitioned	0.7	0.8	1.1
Cases adjudicated to cases petitioned	70.6	58.5	0.8
Placements to cases adjudicated	21.5	26.5	1.2

[a]For example, 6.1 white youths were arrested per 100 youths in the general population, 68.9 white youths out of 100 white youths who were arrested were also referred, and so forth.
[b]Population aged 10–17 equals 25,994,400 (white) and 5,431,300 (African American).

Source: Howard N. Snyder and Melissa Sickmund, *Juvenile Offenders and Victims: 2006 National Report* (Pittsburgh: National Center for Juvenile Justice, March 2006), 189.

Institutions for juvenile offenders include foster homes, residential centers, reform schools, and training schools. In recent years more juveniles are also being sent to adult prisons. These institutions vary in the degree of security and the amount of programming available. We now describe them in order of least to greatest amount of custody supervision.

Foster homes and residential centers typically take small numbers of delinquents. These locations are not considered punitive—judges use foster homes and residential centers when the juvenile's family cannot provide an adequate setting for the child's development. Foster homes are often run by a married couple, and the juveniles live in them, sometimes as cohabitants with the adults' biological children. The court pays the couple a per diem for each foster child, usually not enough to cover all the expenses involved, and the adults in the home provide supervision in cooperation with probation officers. Foster children attend the local school system and operate under whatever restrictions the foster parents and probation officer deem suitable—curfews, associations, leisure activities, and the like. Residential centers operate much like foster homes, with residents attending locals schools and living under certain restrictions. The main difference is that residential centers are run by professional staff, not adult volunteers. It may also be the case that a small amount of residential treatment programming occurs in residential centers, usually as group counseling sessions. See "Careers in Corrections" for more on being a juvenile group home counselor.

Compared with group homes, reform schools and training schools offer far less freedom to the child placed within them. They do not hesitate to impose a strict regime, and they regard one of their functions as punishment. As seen in **Figure 17.6**, the delinquents assigned to these facilities have committed serious offenses.

CAREERS IN CORRECTIONS

Juvenile Group Home Counselor

NATURE OF THE WORK

Juvenile group home counselors are responsible for supervising and guiding youths under age 18 who have been placed in a group home by a juvenile court. They spend their days with youths who reside in the home, provide one-on-one counseling, and implement treatment programs dealing with the special problems of youths. Typically they work with 8–12 youths at a time in a residential setting.

REQUIRED QUALIFICATIONS

Background qualifications for juvenile group home counselors vary by state, but a bachelor's degree in social work, criminal justice, or a related field from a four-year college or university is usually required. Some agencies require previous experience with youths or graduate work. Candidates must be at least 21 years old and have no felony convictions. Most juvenile group home counselors receive formal and on-the-job training.

EARNINGS AND JOB OUTLOOK

The number of juvenile group home counselors is expected to be stable during the next decade. Juvenile group home counselors report a high level of personal satisfaction for their work. They earn about $40,000 a year, with entry-level salaries under $25,000 in many regions.

MORE INFORMATION

Visit the website of the **American Probation and Parole Association** using the corresponding link at www.cengage.com/criminaljustice/clear. Career information can also be obtained from your state, juvenile court, or probation office.

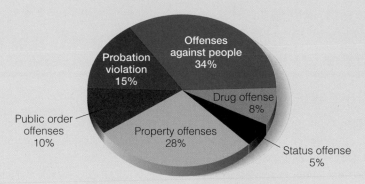

Figure 17.6

Juvenile Delinquents in Public Custodial Facilities: Types of Offenses

Some youths in confinement are there for violent crimes, but a substantial majority are confined for other, less-serious, offenses.

Source: Howard N. Snyder and Melissa Sickmund, *Juvenile Offenders and Victims: 2006 National Report* (Pittsburgh: National Center for Juvenile Justice, March 2006), 36.

These 24-hour facilities severely limit residents' freedom. School is on campus, and the residents work to maintain the facilities. In almost every way, reform schools and training schools are the equivalent of adult prisons, developed for adolescents under custody. As such, they have some of the same problems that plague adult prisons and jails: violence, sexual assault, staff–resident conflict, and disciplinary control problems. (See "Do the Right Thing.") Because the residents are younger and somewhat more volatile than adults, behavioral control is often an everyday issue, and fights and aggression are common situations. By contrast, see the Focus box "Missouri System Treats Juvenile Offenders with a Lighter Hand" for more on the Missouri Model, a promising reform movement.

DO THE RIGHT THING

Residents of the Lovelock Home had been committed by the juvenile court because they were either delinquent or neglected. All 25 boys, aged 7–15, were streetwise, tough, and interested only in getting out. The institution had a staff of social services professionals who tried to deal with the educational and psychological needs of the residents. Because state funding was short, these services looked better in the annual report than to an observer visiting Lovelock. Most of the time, the residents watched television, played basketball in the backyard, or just hung out in one another's rooms.

Joe Klegg, the night supervisor, was tired from the eight-hour shift that he had just completed on his "second job" as a daytime convenience-store manager. The boys were watching television when he arrived at seven. Everything seemed calm. It should have been, because

Joe had placed a tough 15-year-old, Randy Marshall, in charge. Joe had told Randy to keep the younger boys in line. Randy used his muscle and physical presence to intimidate the other residents. He knew that if the home was quiet and there was no trouble, he would be rewarded with special privileges such as a "pass" to see his girlfriend. Joe wanted no hassles and a quiet house so that he could doze off when the boys went to sleep.

WRITING ASSIGNMENT: Does the situation at Lovelock Home raise ethical questions, or does it merely raise questions of poor management practices? What are the potential consequences for the residents? For Joe Klegg? What is the state's responsibility? Write an essay that addresses each of these questions.

FOCUS ON CORRECTIONAL POLICY

Missouri System Treats Juvenile Offenders with a Lighter Hand

VonErrick celebrated his 14th birthday last year by committing a daylight carjacking, beating the driver to the ground. With a long record of truancy, assault, and breaking and entering, he was sent to a state group home—the same home that his two older brothers passed through after their own scrapes with the law.

Both of those brothers are out now. Tory, 16, has A grades and plans to attend college. Terry, 20, has a job and has had a clean record for four years. VonErrick was recently released and immediately started high school.

The brothers say they benefited from confinement in the Missouri juvenile system, which emphasizes rehabilitation in small groups, constant therapeutic interventions and minimal force.

Juvenile justice experts across the nation say that the approach, known as the Missouri Model, is one of several promising reform movements that strapped states are trying to reduce the costly confinement of youths. California, which spends more than $200,000 a year on each incarcerated juvenile, reallocated $93 million in prison expenses by reducing state confinement.

There is no barbed wire around facilities like Missouri Hills, on the outskirts of St. Louis. No more than 10 youths and 2 adults called facilitators live in cottage-style dormitories in a wooded setting, a far cry from the quasi penitentiaries in other states. When someone becomes unruly, the other youths are trained to talk him down. Perhaps most impressive, Missouri has one of the lowest recidivism rates in the country.

Tim Decker, director of the Missouri Division of Youth Services, said judges preferred to send youths to state facilities—Missouri Hills or the Hogan Street Regional Youth Center, with dorms that have wooden beds, male health and wellness classes, group counseling and game rooms—rather than dismal county lockups or to backlogged community programs.

"Judges have more faith in us," Mr. Decker said. "So far we're O.K., but you can't do what we do with 25 kids in a group."

Missouri Hills is clean and homey, with plush couches, stuffed animals on the bunks, and a dog rescued from the pound. The violence that plagues many juvenile prisons is also absent.

In a typical juvenile corrections environment, Mr. Decker said, if a youth becomes aggressive "you would have guards drag him into isolation" for three days.

"But," he added, "the problem is that a young person doesn't learn how to avoid that aggressive behavior and it will get worse."

In Missouri Hills, isolation rooms were used only about a dozen times last year, Mr. Decker said, and never for more than a few hours. Pepper spray is banned, and youths are taught to de-escalate fights or apply grappling holds, a form of restraint.

Mr. Decker said that upgrading facilities and training new staff cost more initially, but that the reforms would reduce recidivism, which would result in long-term savings.

VonErrick has been home for a few weeks, and his 18-year-old sister said he seemed calmer and less interested in running with the wrong crowd. Their mother, Rosie Williams, said all three of her sons seemed more focused, and she attributed the changes to the counselors at the state group home.

Source: Solomon Moore, "Missouri System Treats Juvenile Offenders with a Lighter Hand," *New York Times*, March 27, 2009, p. A13.

---

aftercare
Juvenile justice equivalent of parole, in which a delinquent is released from a custodial sentence and supervised in the community.

JUVENILE AFTERCARE ■ The term **aftercare** refers to services provided to juveniles after they have been *placed*, that is, removed from their home and put under some form of custodial care. Aftercare operates in a way similar to adult parole. It receives juveniles who have been under some form of custody—typically the state's training school, but sometimes a foster home or residential placement—and provides supervision and support during the period of readjustment to community life. The importance of aftercare rests on the fact that youths face significant obstacles of adjustment after they have been away from their homes, which makes their chances of failure quite high.

Aftercare workers know that youths who have been returned from confinement face significant adjustment problems and require substantial attention and support. First of all, a youth who has been placed in a custodial setting by the court has either engaged in some form of serious criminal behavior or has shown a pattern of persistent disobedience of less-serious laws and of court-ordered rules of behavior. In either case,

Community Gang Intervention Officer George Tejeda, right, monitors students as they depart Thomas Jefferson High School in Los Angeles, following a racially and gang-motivated brawl among more than 100 black and Hispanic students.

there is a potential for trouble. The serious offender has committed a frightening crime and faces a fearful community, a family who may not welcome his or her return, and a school system that doubts the juvenile's readiness to behave. The persistent delinquent has been a source of trouble to family, neighbors, school officials, and others and will not be received with open arms. The aftercare worker negotiates the return to the community by helping the juvenile understand the community's apprehension, while showing the community evidence that the juvenile deserves a second chance.

The aftercare worker must also closely follow the juvenile's adjustment, even while serving as advocate. The risk of recidivism is high enough that the community feels a stake in the aftercare scrutiny. All involved in the aftercare system recognize that a careful balance is needed between support and control, because these juveniles include the most serious cases in the juvenile justice system. Much is to be gained. When an aftercare worker can successfully negotiate a juvenile through the first months of return to the community, a lifetime of crime can be avoided.

■ THE SPECIAL PROBLEM OF GANGS

No discussion of juvenile justice would be complete without a comment on the special problem of gangs. The United States has 788,000 gang members, with 27,000 gangs operating in 3,350 local jurisdictions.[39] These youths are involved in perhaps a half million serious crimes.[40] Gang involvement decreased in the 1990s, but since 2000 we have seen a 40 percent increase in gang members nationally.[41]

Studies show that gangs vary widely in makeup. We worry about violent juvenile gangs, but the most common forms of gangs are far less threatening to public safety than are the notorious "Crips" or "Bloods." Indeed, joining a gang is fairly common for some groups, as **Figure 17.7** shows. Further, while most gangs are not violent, many gang members engage in positive as well as negative social behaviors. Thus, an important distinction must be made between traditional street gangs, which provide social connections and engage in many types of criminal conduct, and drug gangs, which are organized into cohesive business structures and often use violence as a method of business.

Gangs permeate the work of correctional officials. In custodial facilities, they create a profound challenge in terms of controlling the population and managing the potential for intergang conflict. In community settings, gangs provide hostile competition to the

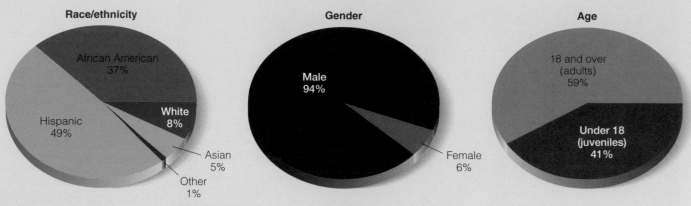

Figure 17.7
Characteristics of Youths Who Belong to a Gang

Source: Arlen Egley, Jr., and Christina E. Ritz, "Highlights of the 2004 National Youth Gang Survey," *OJJDP Fact Sheet* (Washington, DC: U.S. Office of Juvenile Justice and Delinquency Prevention, April 2006).

prosocial programs developed by correctional leaders. For the community, gangs are a primary source of fear and peril. Especially where gang members are armed, the presence of the gang can destabilize neighborhood life.

Recent initiatives have shown some success with gangs. One of the most impressive has been Operation Ceasefire, described in the Focus box.[42] This project involved a coordinated effort of prosecutors, probation officers, street-gang workers, and police to target gun use by gang members. They focused on "getting the message out" that gun violence would not be tolerated, and they backed it up by prosecuting fully any gang member involved in a gun crime. Homicides went down from weekly events to nearly zero within the first year.

CORRECTIONAL PRACTICE

Operation Ceasefire and Operation Nite Lite

One night, Boston probation officers Bill Stewart and Rick Skinner accepted an offer from their friends, police officers Bob Merner and Bob Fratalia, to spend Saturday evening in the back seat of a squad car touring the streets of Dorchester, a troubled inner-city area. Merner and Fratalia were members of the police department's gang unit who had been collaborating with probation officers in efforts to deal with a growing problem of gang violence in another troubled neighborhood, Roxbury.

A few hours into the evening, the cruising police car got an emergency call reporting a gunshot victim in a nearby street. Arriving at the scene, the four saw a crowd of about 25 residents—mostly young men—milling around a face-down body, dead from a bullet to the head. This was a familiar scene to the police, but the presence of the probation officers gave it a new twist. Stewart and Skinner recognized many of the bystanders as young men on probation and under curfew orders, who

were out on the town. The victim also turned out to be one of Stewart's probationers. In all, perhaps a dozen curfew-violating probationers were at the scene. As Stewart recalls, "They were amazed to see me out there at night with the cops. They tried to cover their faces. They knew that, unlike the cops, I could recognize them." Officer Fratalia was also amazed. Bystanders at a crime scene normally claim to have seen nothing, but Stewart was able to elicit information from the young people who faced having their probation revoked for curfew breaking.

Out of this experience, Operation Nite Lite, the simple idea of enforcing juvenile probation curfews, was born. Operation Nite Lite brings probation into the field and aims probation services at juvenile gang members with guns. Where gang violence is a serious problem, there can be no higher priority than reducing gang street violence.

Operation Nite Lite is a part of a broader effort in Boston known as Operation Ceasefire, a coordinated attempt to end

■ THE FUTURE OF JUVENILE JUSTICE

High-profile gang criminality and the recent spate of school shootings have ended the anonymity of juvenile correctional work. Public policy makers are turning their attention to the juvenile justice system, and there is reason to think that the decades of reform in adult corrections since the 1970s will be replayed in the juvenile justice arena. What will this mean?

The public today calls for get-tough measures, and we are already beginning to see the influence of this thinking on juvenile justice. There is more pressure to increase waiver of serious juveniles to the adult court, where their sentences may be longer and their punishments harsher. Local political leaders call for tougher probation, and the populations of training schools are growing. Few are surprised to see these familiar echoes of changes in the adult system arising in respect to juveniles, now that the public spotlight has landed there.

It is unlikely, however, that reform for juveniles will exactly reproduce the adult process. No matter how the papers portray extreme cases, the everyday juvenile offender remains unsophisticated and susceptible to change under appropriate programs. Most juvenile crime is still minor misbehavior, not at all like the highly charged cases of serious violence that dominate the news. To paint all juvenile offenders with a broad, adult criminal brush would not only be unwise but also inaccurate.

So, some middle ground will be found. Again, the relative anonymity of the juvenile justice system is past. Juvenile justice policy and practice will be scrutinized and pressured to conform to the stricter adult system. Few observers will note the irony that even as the pressure mounts to toughen juvenile justice, dissatisfaction remains high with the adult model toward which they are moving.

The **Urban Institute's Report on Child Welfare** is found at the corresponding link at www.cengage.com/criminaljustice/clear.

gang gun violence. Ceasefire is based on the knowledge that a few offenders account for a substantial proportion of all crime and that these offenders are often concentrated in particular city neighborhoods.

Operation Ceasefire uses two strategies. First, interagency collaboration identifies individuals and gangs at risk for committing violence. A task force of federal, state, and municipal criminal justice and social service agencies regularly meet to share information, identify gang members to be targeted, discuss tactics to increase investigation effectiveness, and develop a repertoire of interventions and strategies.

A second strategy is aimed at increasing deterrence through swift and certain sanctioning. When a violent act is committed, the various agencies can at their discretion not only arrest suspects, but also shut down drug markets, strictly enforce probation restrictions, make disorder arrests,

deal more strictly with cases in adjudication, deploy federal enforcement power, and so on.

Operation Ceasefire develops in gang members a new set of expectations regarding violent behavior. When gang members seek rehabilitative services, the program assists them. But when they persist in violent activity, the coordinated agencies hit them with undesirable sanctions until the violence stops.

The Boston program has been going strong since late 1992 and has had unexpected success. Firearm homicides have dropped from 65 per year to 21. Firearm homicides by juveniles have dropped from 10 to an astounding 0 for two years running. National attention has been focused on Boston's success story.

Source: Todd R. Clear and David R. Karp, *Community Justice: Preventing Crime and Achieving Justice, Report to the National Institute of Justice* (Tallahassee: Florida State University, 1999), 7–8.

SUMMARY

1 Understand the nature and extent of youth crime today.

Extremely serious juvenile crime incidents are rare. In a nation with 75 million people 18 years of age or younger, 2.2 million arrests of juveniles took place in 2001, only 91,100 of which (just over 4 percent) were for violent crimes. After rising between 1988 and 1994, the juvenile violent crime rate has dropped by almost 50 percent; it is now the lowest it has been since at least 1980. Property crime by juveniles has decreased by about half since its peak in 1991. Recent research also shows that fewer juveniles are carrying guns than before. Yet when Americans are asked to identify the two or three most serious problems facing children, they cite drugs and crime.

2 Know the history of the development of juvenile corrections in the United States.

American juvenile justice has gone through several historical periods. During the Puritan period (1646–1824) the Puritans of the Massachusetts Bay Colony viewed the child as evil and believed that the family needed to discipline youth. In the refuge period (1824–1899) reformers urged the creation of institutions where delinquent, abused, and neglected children could learn good work and study habits, live in a disciplined and healthy environment, and develop "character." The juvenile court period (1899–1960) focused on the idea of *parens patriae,* in that the new juvenile court took the role of guardian, the substitute parent to the child. By the 1960s liberal reform groups rallied to protect the rights of juveniles during the juvenile rights period (1960–1980). In a series of decisions, the U.S. Supreme Court extended to juveniles many of the due process rights accorded adults. Finally, in the crime control period (1980–present), the system was transformed "from a nominally rehabilitative social welfare agency into a scaled-down second-class criminal court for young people."[43]

3 Understand the rationale for dealing differently with juvenile offenders and adult offenders.

Five differences between juveniles and adults are used to justify separate justice systems: (1) Juveniles are young and may easily change. (2) Juveniles have a high rate of "desistence." (3) Juveniles' families are an important part of their lives. (4) Juveniles are easily influenced by their peers. (5) Juveniles have little responsibility for others.

4 Know how serious juvenile delinquency differs from most delinquency and what this implies for the juvenile justice system.

The juvenile justice system is predicated on what we might call "normal" delinquency, or misbehaviors that people expect juveniles to do, given their age. Serious delinquency involves status offenses, which are misbehaviors that are not against the law but are troubling for juveniles because the person is so young: running away, being truant, and being ungovernable. It would be naive to think that the juvenile justice paradigm applies equally to every young person who breaks the law. Some juveniles are already hardened; some will continue criminal behavior into adulthood; some lack families; some are loners; some are already in adult roles. Unusual juvenile criminality has been one reason why some question the wisdom of having a separate juvenile justice system. They say society ought to treat all criminal acts with the seriousness they deserve, regardless of age, because there are so many exceptions to the "norms" on which the juvenile justice system is based.

5 Know the ways juvenile offenders are sanctioned.

Juvenile offenders are sanctioned by detention, probation, intermediate sanctions, community corrections, incarceration, and aftercare. Approximately 20 percent of juvenile arrestees are briefly detained until an initial appearance before a juvenile court judge or judicial referee. About one out of five is found to endanger others or be at risk of flight, so they are kept in detention for days or weeks until an adjudication hearing can be scheduled. In 62 percent of cases, the juvenile delinquent is placed on probation and released to the custody of a parent or guardian. Often the delinquent must undergo some form of education or counseling; he or she may also have to pay a fine or make restitution while on probation. Only about 15 percent of delinquents receive an intermediate sanction: ISP and boot camps are the most common. Despite the lukewarm evaluations of juvenile community corrections, interest has continued in this approach. For most youths the institutional stay will be short—usually six months to a year. Because youths must eventually return to the community for successful adjustment to community life, advocates of community corrections ask, "Why wait?" Of those juveniles declared delinquent, 23 percent are placed in public and private facilities. Aftercare refers to services provided to juveniles after they have been placed—removed from their home and put under some form of custodial care. Aftercare operates in a way similar to adult parole.

6 Understand the special problems youth gangs pose.

The United States has 788,000 gang members, with 27,000 gangs operating in 3,350 local jurisdictions, involved in perhaps a half million serious crimes. Studies show that gangs vary widely in makeup. Most gangs are not violent, and many gang members engage in positive as well as negative social behaviors. Traditional street gangs provide social connections and engage in many types of criminal conduct, whereas drug gangs are organized into cohesive business structures and often use violence as a method of business. Gangs permeate the work of correctional officials. In custodial facilities, they create a profound challenge in terms of controlling the population and managing the potential for intergang conflict. In community settings, gangs provide hostile competition to the prosocial programs developed by correctional leaders. For the community, gangs are a primary source of fear and peril. Especially where gang members are armed, the presence of the gang can destabilize neighborhood life.

7 Envision the future of juvenile corrections.

The public today calls for get-tough measures. There is more pressure to increase waiver of serious juveniles to the adult court, where their sentences may be longer and their punishments harsher. Local political leaders call for tougher probation, and training schools are growing. Few are surprised to see these familiar echoes of changes in the adult system arising in respect to juveniles, now that the public spotlight has landed there. It is unlikely, however, that reform for juveniles will exactly reproduce the adult process. No matter how the papers portray extreme cases, the everyday juvenile offender remains unsophisticated and susceptible to change under appropriate programs. Most juvenile crime is still minor misbehavior, not at all like the highly charged cases of serious violence that dominate the news. So, some middle ground will be found.

KEY TERMS

FOR DISCUSSION

1. How has the experience of growing up changed over the last few centuries? Why are these changes important for juvenile justice?
2. How do the differences between adults and juveniles affect policies in juvenile justice? How are adults and juveniles similar under the law?
3. Are the many differences in terminology between the adult and juvenile systems important? Why or why not?
4. In what ways do juvenile institutions differ from adult institutions? How does this affect institutional management? What does this difference mean for juveniles who are housed in adult facilities?
5. Should we have a separate juvenile justice system? Why or why not?

FOR FURTHER READING

Ezell, Michel E., and Lawrence E. Cohen. *Outgrowing Serious Crime: Continuity and Change in the Criminal Offending Patterns of Chronic Offenders.* New York: Oxford University Press, 2005. Uses sophisticated statistical methods to show that many so-called "chronic" juvenile offenders give up crime by the time they reach their twenties.

Farrington, David P., and Jeremy W. Cold. *Early Prevention of Adult Anti-social Behaviour.* New York: Cambridge University Press, 2003. A series of essays and studies, by some of the most renowned scholars in criminology, reviewing the effectiveness of programs for preventing antisocial behavior.

Farrington, David P., and Brandon C. Welsh. *Saving Children from a Life of Crime.* New York: Oxford University Press, 2007. A systematic review of the studies of crime prevention for children, with a description of which kinds of programs work and which do not.

Feld, Barry C. *Bad Kids: Race and the Transformation of the Juvenile Court.* New York: Oxford University Press, 1999. Examination of the recent shift in policies regarding youth crime and the juvenile justice system in the context of race issues in U.S. society.

Klein, Malcolm W., and Cheryl L. Maxson. *Street Gang Patterns and Policies.* New York: Oxford University Press. A critical examination of knowledge about gangs and major gang-control programs across the nation.

Kupchik, Aaron. *Judging Juveniles: Prosecuting Adolescents in Adult and Juvenile Courts.* New York: NYU Press, 2006. A study of juvenile waiver that provides a critical comparison of the results of prosecuting juveniles in adult and juvenile courts.

McNamara, Robert Hartmann. *The Lost Population: Status Offenders in America.* Durham, NC: Carolina Academic Press, 2008. A comprehensive review of the current evidence about status offending and status offenders.

National Juvenile Justice Network. *Advances in Juvenile Justice Reform, 2007–2008.* Washington, DC: Author, December 2008. A listing of new programs for juvenile justice, with reviews of their effectiveness.

Tanenhaus, David S. *Juvenile Justice in the Making.* New York: Oxford University Press, 2004. A history of the juvenile court movement, with conclusions about how changes over time in the perception of youth have affected the court.

NOTES

[1] Charles Puzzanchera, "Juvenile Arrests 2007," *Juvenile Justice Bulletin,* April 2009.

[2] Ibid., p. 3.

[3] Ibid., p. 5.

[4] Rick Ruddell and G. Larry Mays, "Examining the Arsenal of Juvenile Gunslingers: Trends and Policy Implications," *Crime and Delinquency* 49 (no. 2, 2003): 231–52.

[5] Barry C. Feld, *Bad Kids: Race and the Transformation of the Juvenile Court* (New York: Oxford University Press, 1999), 3.

[6] Ibid, p. 5.

[7] Howard N. Snyder and Melissa Sickmund, *Juvenile Offenders and Victims: 2006 National Report* (Pittsburgh: National Center for Juvenile Justice, March 2006), 234.

[8] Michel E. Ezell and Lawrence E. Cohen, *Outgrowing Serious Crime: Continuity and Change in the Criminal Offending Patterns of Chronic Offenders* (New York: Oxford University Press, 2005).

[9] Puzzanchera, "Juvenile Arrests 2007," p. 1.

[10] All data taken from Snyder and Sickmund, *Juvenile Offenders and Victims: 2006.*

[11] Howard N. Snyder, "Juvenile Arrests 2004," *Juvenile Justice Bulletin,* December 2006, p. 4

[12] Howard N. Snyder, *Serious and Violent Juvenile Offenders* (Pittsburgh: National Center for Juvenile Justice, 1997).

[13] Bureau of Justice Statistics, *State Court Sentencing of Convicted Felons: Statistical Tables,* (Washington, DC: U.S. Government Printing Office, May 2005), 7.

[14] Melissa Sickmund, *Delinquency Cases in Juvenile Court* (Washington, DC: Office of Juvenile Justice and Delinquency Prevention, June 2009).

[15] Benjamin Adams and Sean Addie, *Delinquency Cases Waived to Criminal Court 2005* (Washington, DC: Office of Juvenile Justice and Delinquency Prevention, June 2009).

[16] Howard K. Snyder, "Juvenile Arrests, 2001," *Juvenile Justice Bulletin*, December 2003, p. 1.

[17] Aaron Kupchik, *Judging Juveniles: Prosecuting Adolescents in Adult and Juvenile Courts* (New York: NYU Press, 2006).

[18] Campaign for Youth Justice, *The Consequences Aren't Minor: The Impact of Trying Youth as Adults and Strategies for Reform* (Washington, DC: Campaign for Youth Justice, March 2007).

[19] Task Force on Community Preventive Services, "Effects on Violence of Laws and Policies Facilitating the Transfer of Juveniles from the Juvenile Justice System to the Adult Justice System: A Systematic Review," *American Journal of Preventive Medicine* 32 (no. 4, April 2007): 7–28)

[20] Adams and Addie, *Delinquency Cases Waived.*

[21] BJS *Bulletin*, November 2006, Table 10.

[22] BJS *Bulletin*, May 2006, Table 9.

[23] Barbara Tatem Kelley, Rolph Loeber, Kate Keenan, and Mary DeLamatre, *Developmental Pathways in Boys' Disruptive and Delinquent Behavior* (Washington, DC: Office of Juvenile Justice and Delinquency Prevention, December 1997).

[24] Eileen M. Gary, *Truancy: First Step to a Lifetime of Problems* (Washington, DC: Office of Juvenile Justice and Delinquency Prevention, October 1996).

[25] Snyder and Sickmund, *Juvenile Offenders and Victims: 2006,* p. 152.

[26] David P. Farrington and Brandon C. Welsh, *Saving Children from a Life of Crime* (New York: Oxford University Press, 2007).

[27] Peter W. Greenwood, Karyn E. Model, C. Peter Rydell, and James Chiesa, *Diverting Children from a Life of Crime: Measuring Costs and Benefits* (Santa Monica, CA: Rand, April 1996).

[28] Snyder and Sickmund, *Juvenile Offenders and Victims: 2006,* p. 215.

[29] Uberto Gatti, Richard E. Tremblay, and Frank Vitaro, "Iatrogenic Effect of Juvenile Justice," *Journal of Child Psychology and Psychiatry* 50 (no. 8, August 2009): 991–98.

[30] Kenneth E. Kerle, "Juveniles," in *American Jails: Looking to the Future* (Boston: Butterworth-Heinmann, 1998).

[31] Sarah Livsey, *Probation in Juvenile Court 2005* (Washington, DC: Office of Juvenile Justice and Delinquency Prevention, June 2009).

[32] Sandra Jo Wilson and Mark W. Lipsey, *The Effectiveness of School-based Violence Prevention Programs for Reducing Disruptive and Aggressive Behavior,* report to the National Institute of Justice (Washington, DC: Center for Evaluation Research and Methodology, Institute for Public Policy Studies, Vanderbilt University, May 2005).

[33] John Paul Wright, Francis T. Cullen, and Nicolas Williams, "Working While in School and Delinquent Involvement: Implications for Social Policy," *Crime and Delinquency* 43 (no. 2, April 1997), 203–21.

[34] David B. Wilson and Doris Layton MacKenzie, "Boot Camps," in *Preventing Crime: What Works for Children, Offenders, Victims, and Places,* edited by Brandon C. Welsh and David P. Farrington (New York: Springer, 2005), 1–36.

[35] Daniel S. Nagin, Alex R. Piquero, Elizabeth S. Scott, and Laurence Steinberg, "Public Preference for Rehabilitation versus Incarceration for Juvenile Offenders: Evidence from a Contingent Valuation Survey," *Criminology and Public Policy* 5 (no. 4, November 2006): 627–52.

[36] Christopher T. Lowenkamp and Edward J. Latessa, *Evaluation of Ohio's RECLAIM-funded Programs, Community Corrections Facilities, and DYS Facilities,* report to the Ohio Department of Youth Services (Cincinnati, OH: University of Cincinnati, August 2005).

[37] Sarah Livsey, Melissa Sickmund, and Anthony Sladky, *Juvenile Residential Facility Census, 2004: Selected Findings* (Washington, DC: Office of Juvenile Justice and Delinquency Prevention, January 2009).

[38] Antoinette Davis, Chris Tsukida, Susan Marchionna, and Barry Krisberg, *The Declining Number of Youth in Custody in the Juvenile Justice System,* NCCD Focus (San Francisco: National Council on Crime and Delinquency, August 2008).

[39] Arlen Egley and Christina O'Donnell, *The 2007 National Gang Survey* (Washington, DC: Office of Juvenile Justice and Delinquency Prevention, April 2009).

[40] G. David Curry, Richard A. Ball, and Scott H. Decker, *Estimating the National Scope of Gang Crime from Law Enforcement Data* (Washington, DC: National Institute of Justice, August 1996).

[41] Egley and O'Donnell, *2007 National Gang Survey.*

[42] David M. Kennedy, Anne M. Piehl, and Anthony A. Braga, "Youth Violence in Boston: Gun Markets, Serious Youth Offenders, and a Use-Reduction Strategy," *Law and Contemporary Problems* 59 (no. 1, 1996): 147–84.

[43] Feld, *Bad Kids,* p. 3.

PART 3

Deborah Mukamal
Director, Prisoner Reentry Institute,
John Jay College of Criminal Justice

JUSTICE CORPS

The Justice Corps is a national program that uses community service, internships, jobs, and educational opportunities as tools to reintegrate young adult offenders returning to their homes from prisons and jails. It seeks to intervene with young adult offenders before crime becomes a way of life. The Justice Corps has been described as a hybrid of the national youth corps movement, the Depression-era Job Corps program that put young people to work on community projects, and more-traditional reentry programs that help former prisoners find work, shelter, and education.

Although national in scope, programs are tailored to local needs, in particular for those neighborhoods where large numbers of people are sent to and from prison. The long-term goals of the program are to (1) help young adults stay out of the criminal justice system, (2) increase their ability to find and keep jobs and/or enroll in school, and (3) support community development in the targeted urban neighborhoods. It is hoped that the Justice Corps program will help break the recidivism cycle by providing youthful offenders with practical skills, social support, and leadership training.

The New York City Justice Corps consists of a three-phased sequence of services incorporating principles of youth, community, and workforce development into a prisoner reentry

CORRECTIONAL ISSUES AND PERSPECTIVES

program model. Beginning when they first enroll, Justice Corps members receive basic skills training and exposure to service learning for four weeks, before transitioning into service in community benefit projects for a 10–14-week period. Then, in an effort to simulate the world of work and build professional networks, Justice Corps members are placed in internships for six to eight weeks. Those who complete the three phases and graduate from the program are placed in permanent, mainstream employment and/or postsecondary educational opportunities to further their career goals. Justice Corps members are paid a stipend of $7.40 per hour for 35 hours per week during the six months of the program.

Justice Corps seeks to change the dynamics of the justice system. It seeks to interrupt the pattern of young people getting caught up in crime, cycling through the prison system, becoming evermore serious in their criminal conduct. More than that, it is an attempt to build something—citizens who contribute to their communities and their society.

Does the Justice Corps approach "work"? The New York City program is the first to be rigorously evaluated through an experimental design with random assignment of members and tracking over a two-year period. Findings from this research will have implications for the role that civic engagement can play in placing at-risk youths onto paths of self-sufficiency.

© Bob Daemmrich/AFP/Getty Images

LEARNING OBJECTIVES

After reading this chapter you should be able to . . .

1 Discuss the explanations for the dramatic increase in the incarceration rate.

2 Explain what can be done to deal with the prison population crisis.

3 Be familiar with the impact of prison crowding.

4 Discuss whether incarceration pays.

The crime control policies of the past 30 years have forced governments to build more prisons such as the super-max security federal prison in Florence, Colorado. The prison has 12-foot fences topped with razor wire and six towers with armed guards. Often a new prison is filled within a year, resulting in calls for more facilities.

THE PRISON POPULATION in the United States is large and expanding. Extensive media coverage of the increased number of Americans in prison makes the issue difficult to ignore. In 2008 the Bureau of Justice Statistics reported that 756 people per 100,000 U.S. residents were held in state or federal prisons and local jails.[1] Compared with the incarceration rate of other developed countries, America's rate is extremely high. In fact, if incarceration was an Olympic sport, the United States would win the gold medal. The silver medalist would be Russia, where the incarceration rate is 611 per 100,000 population. By comparison, the incarceration rate (per 100,000 population) of England and Wales is 148; Netherlands, 128; Australia, 126; Germany, 95; France, 85; and Ireland, 72.[2] The United States has over nine times the population of Canada but about 45 times the prison population.[3]

INCARCERATION TRENDS

A study by the Pew Charitable Trusts notes that "after a 700 percent increase in the U.S. prison population between 1970 and 2005, you'd think the nation would finally have run out of lawbreakers to put behind bars."[4] Why does the incarceration rate continue to increase in the United States? Some observers believe that, since the mid-1970s, the United States has experimented whether the crime rate can be reduced if greater numbers of offenders are imprisoned.[5] Over the past 35 years, the incarceration rate has more than quadrupled, even though the crime rate in the United States has been declining for well over two decades. Along with the steady growth in American's prison population, the amount of taxpayers' dollars spent on building and operating prisons has also substantially increased. Between 1986 and 2001, state correctional spending increased 145 percent. Running state prisons costs each resident of the United States approximately $104 each year.[6] The expansion of the prison population is difficult to understand in light of lower crime rates, state budgetary problems, and the easing of tough sentencing policies in some states. See the Focus box "State Highlights, 2011" for more.

Although nearly 2.3 million people are incarcerated in American prisons and jails, this population makes up less than one-third of people under correctional supervision. Approximately 5 million individuals are under correctional supervision in the community (probation and parole).[7] Yet when the subject of criminal sanction arises, the general public usually thinks first of incarceration. Further, it is prison that politicians have in mind when they consider changes in the penal code or annual appropriations for corrections.

In this chapter we explore explanations for the rise in incarceration. We also consider ways of dealing with prison crowding and examine its impact on the system. Finally, we evaluate the argument that incarceration is cost-effective for society.

Chapter

18

FOCUS ON

CORRECTIONAL POLICY

State Highlights, 2011

■ By 2011, without changes in sentencing and release policies, Alaska, Arizona, Idaho, Montana, and Vermont can expect to see one new prisoner for every three currently in the system.

■ Similarly, barring reforms, there will be one new prisoner for every four now in prison in Colorado, Washington, Wyoming, Nevada, Utah, and South Dakota.

■ Incarceration rates are expected to spike in Arizona and Nevada from 590 and 540 prisoners per 100,000 residents, respectively, to 747 and 640. Particularly worrisome is the growth in imprisonment of young men, the group at highest risk of criminal activity.

■ Louisiana, which has the highest incarceration rate among states, with 835 prisoners per 100,000 residents, expects that figure to hit 859 by 2011.

■ Florida is anticipated to cross the 100,000-prisoner threshold within the next five years, becoming the only state other than Texas and California to do so.

■ The report projects no growth in Connecticut, Delaware, and New York.

■ Though the Northeast boasts the lowest incarceration rates, it maintains the highest costs per prisoner, led by Rhode Island ($44,860), Massachusetts ($43,026), and New York ($42,202). The lowest costs are generally in the South, led by Louisiana ($13,009), Alabama ($13,019), and South Carolina ($13,170).

Sources: *Public Safety, Public Spending: Forecasting America's Prison Population 2007–2011* (New York: Pew Charitable Trusts, 2007), iii. Incarceration and cost data have been supplied by the individual states.

■ EXPLAINING PRISON POPULATION TRENDS

From 1930 through 1980, the incarceration rate in the United States remained fairly stable. During this period the rate of sentenced prisoners in federal and state facilities fluctuated from a low of 93 per 100,000 population in 1972 to a high of 139 in 1980. The average rate of incarceration, however, increased dramatically in the 1980s (200 per 100,000) and 1990s (389 per 100,000) (see **Figure 18.1**). This growth trend

Mass incarceration has changed the demographic and offense composition of the prison population. There are now more African Americans, Hispanics, women, and middle-aged prisoners than there were in the 1970s.

© Andrew Lichtenstein/The Image Works

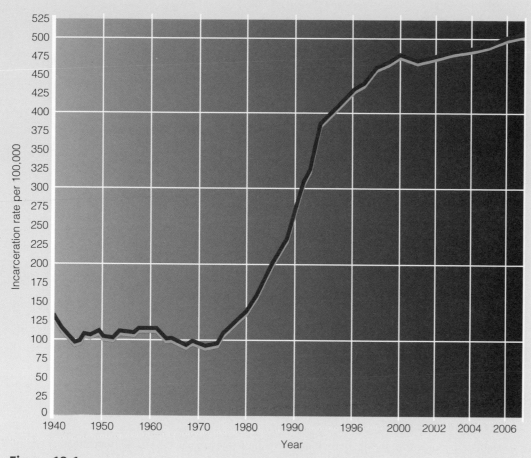

Figure 18.1

Incarceration Rate per 100,000 Population

Between 1940 and 1974, the incarceration rate of sentenced offenders held steady. Only since 1975 has a continuing increase occurred. The rate today is more than double what it was in 1988.

Sources: Ann L. Pastore and Kathleen Maguire, eds., *Sourcebook of Criminal Justice Statistics*, Table 6.28.2006, http://www.albany.edu/sourcebook, March 18, 2009; Bureau of Justice Statistics, *Prisoners in 2007* (Washington, DC: U.S. Government Printing Office, December 2008), 1.

continued into the twenty-first century. The average incarceration rate from 2000 to 2007 was 486 per 100,000.[8]

This tremendous growth has dramatically changed the demographic and offense composition of the prison population. African Americans and Hispanics now make up a large percentage of inmates in American correctional facilities. Prisoners are more likely to be middle-aged, and more women are being incarcerated. Since 1980 the percentage of inmates serving time for violent offenses has declined, and the number incarcerated for drug violations has increased.[9]

The size and growth of the prison population differs between states. As **Figure 18.2** shows, the five states with the highest incarceration rates (Louisiana, Mississippi, Oklahoma, and Alabama) are in the South. In December 2007 the South incarcerated 556 people for every 100,000 residents. Many argue that southern attitudes toward crime and punishment account for that region's high prison population. The penal codes in many southern states provide for long sentences, and inmates there spend extended periods in institutions. It is also the region with the highest African American population, which is incarcerated in numbers far greater than its proportion to the overall population.

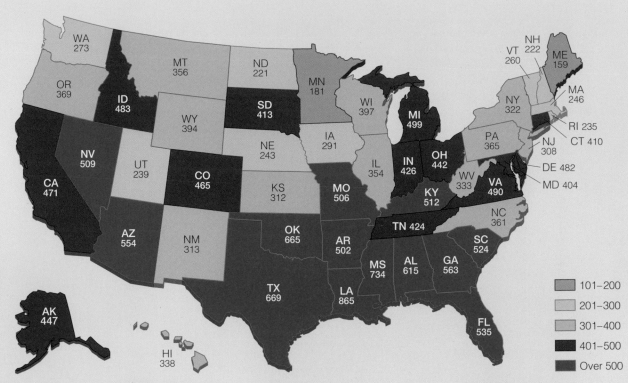

Figure 18.2

Sentenced Prisoners in State Institutions per 100,000 Population, December 31, 2007

What can be said about the differences in incarceration rates among the states? There are not only regional differences but also differences between neighboring states that seem to have similar demographics and crime characteristics.

Source: Bureau of Justice Statistics, *Prisoners in 2007* (Washington, DC: U.S. Government Printing Office, December 2008), Appendix Table 9.

Access the latest data from the Bureau of Justice Statistics on **incarceration trends** at the corresponding website at www.cengage.com/criminaljustice/clear.

The skyrocketing prison population has resulted in prison crowding. At the end of 2007 the Bureau of Justice Statistics found that 19 states and the federal government operated at or above capacity.[10] In many states new inmates have been crowded into already bulging institutions, with some making do in corridors and basements. The Bureau of Justice Statistics also found that 80,371 state and federal prisoners were being held in county jails until prison space became available.[11] The percentage of state prisoners held in jail in the South is more than double the average for the country as a whole (10.5 percent versus 5.0 percent). Specific southern states have a disproportionately large percentage of state inmates in local jails (45.5 percent in Louisiana, 35.2 percent in Kentucky, and 26.7 percent in Tennessee).[12] Judges in several states have ordered prisoners removed from jails in which crowding violates the Constitution.

Why this increase in prisoners? As we have noted, there seems to be little relationship between the crime rate and the incarceration rate. If this is the case, what factors explain the growth? Here we explore five reasons often cited for the increase: (1) increased arrests and more likely incarceration, (2) tougher sentencing, (3) prison construction, (4) the war on drugs, and (5) state and local politics. None of these reasons should be viewed as a single explanation. Rather, each contributes to the equation, with some having a greater impact than others.

Increased Arrests and More Likely Incarceration

Some analysts argue that the billions spent by federal, state, and local governments on the crime problem may be paying off. When the crime rate began to rise dramatically in the mid-1960s, the incarceration rate was proportionally low. Crime rates for serious offenses have now declined, but the estimated number of arrests for some offenses has increased dramatically. For example, in 1970 an estimated 322,300 adults were arrested for drug violations. The number of arrests in this category increased to nearly 1.7 million in 2006.[13] Only in recent years have arrest rates for violent and property crimes fallen.[14]

A large portion of the prison population is made up of offenders who are being returned to prison for new crimes or parole violations (see Chapter 16). In 2007, 62.4 percent of those entering state prisons did so directly as a result of a new court commitment, and 35.7 percent of admissions were inmates who returned to prison for violating the conditions of their parole. Prison admissions due to parole violations are a bigger problem in some states than in others. For example, parole violators made up a large percentage of admitted prisoners in California (66.3 percent) and Vermont (65.8 percent), but a relatively small percentage in North Carolina (3.1 percent) and Tennessee (5.4 percent).[15] Overall, as Alfred Blumstein and Allen Beck show, the percentage of new court commitments has flattened in recent years while the number of parolees returned to prison has increased greatly.[16]

Tougher Sentencing

Some observers think that a hardening of public attitudes toward criminals is reflected in longer sentences, in a smaller proportion of those convicted being granted probation, and in fewer inmates being released at the time of their first parole hearing.

As discussed in Chapter 4, in the past three decades the states and the federal government have passed laws that increase sentences for most crimes. In 2004 the average time served in prison was almost 5 years. Violent offenders served the longest sentences (about 7½ years). In comparison, individuals convicted of property (3 years and 9 months) and drug offenses (4 years and 3 months) served less time.[17]

New mandatory sentencing laws greatly limit the discretion of judges with regard to the length of sentences for certain offenders. The shift to determinate sentences, truth-in-sentencing laws, and a drop in release rates have contributed to the higher prison

AP Images/Devin Bruce

Not only has the number of arrests increased, but so has the likelihood of going to prison upon conviction, as well as for a longer sentence.

population. Recall, however, the difference between the sentence given by the judge and the actual time served in prison. In the past, with indeterminate sentences, most inmates went before the parole board when they had served the minimum sentence minus jail time and good time. Most were released at their first appearance before the parole board.

Prison Construction

The increased rate of incarceration may be related to the creation of additional space in the nation's prisons and the economic impact of the construction boom. Public attitudes in favor of more-punitive sentencing policies have influenced legislators to approve building more prisons. Between 1990 and 2005, over 500 prisons were built across the country, increasing the number of facilities nationwide by 42 percent.[18] A study by the Urban Institute found that Texas, the state with the greatest number of prisons (137), increased the number of its facilities by more than 700 percent between 1979 and 2000.[19] Even with the decline in the crime rate during the past decade and tougher economic times in many states, new prison construction continues.

According to organizational theorists, available public resources such as hospitals and schools are used to their fullest capacity. Prisons are no exception. When prison space is limited, judges reserve incarceration for only the most violent offenders. However, additional prisons may present a variation of the "Field of Dreams" scenario—build them and they will come. As Joseph Davey notes, "The presence of empty state-of-the-art prison facilities can encourage a criminal court judge to incarcerate a defendant who may otherwise get probation."[20] Creation of additional prison space may thus increase the incarceration rate.

For health and safety reasons, crowded conditions in existing facilities cannot be tolerated. Many states attempted to build their way out of this problem, because the public seemed to favor harsher sentencing policies, which would require more prison space. With many states holding large budget surpluses during the booming economy of the 1990s, legislatures were willing to advance the huge sums required for prison expansion. Pressures from contractors, building material providers, and correctional officer unions spurred expansion in many states. Yet many states that tried to build their way out of their crowded facilities found that as soon as a new prison came on line it was quickly filled.

The war on drugs is one of the main factors accounting for the quadrupling of the incarceration rate since 1990. Pennsylvania Attorney General Tom Corbett points to alleged members of a multimillion dollar tristate drug ring. As a result of "Operation 777" all but one member of the ring is in state custody.

The War on Drugs

Crusades against the use of drugs have recurred in American politics since the late 1800s. The latest manifestation began in 1982, when President Ronald Reagan declared another "war on drugs" and asked Congress to set aside more money for drug enforcement personnel and for prison space. This came at a time when the country was scared by the advent of crack cocaine, which ravaged many communities and resulted in an increased murder rate. In 1987 Congress imposed stiff mandatory minimum sentences for federal drug law violations, laws that many states copied. The war continued during succeeding administrations, with each president urging Congress to appropriate billions for an all-out law enforcement campaign against drugs.

The war on drugs has succeeded on one front by packing the nation's prisons with drug law offenders, but many scholars believe that this is about all it has achieved. With additional resources and pressures for enforcement, the number of people sentenced to prison for drug crimes has increased steadily. In 1980 only 19,000 or 6 percent of state prisoners had been convicted of a drug offense; by 2007 this had risen to 253,300 or 19.5 percent of inmates in state prisons.[21] The percentage in federal prisons is even higher, at 53.5 percent.[22]

State and Local Politics

Incarceration rates vary among the regions and states, but why do states with similar characteristics differ in their use of prisons? Can it be that local political factors influence correctional policies?

One might think that there would be an association among the states between crime rates and incarceration rates—the more crime, the more prisoners. Yet, as discussed earlier, some states with high crime rates do not have correspondingly high incarceration rates.[23] Even when states have similar socioeconomic and demographic characteristics—poverty, unemployment, racial composition, drug arrests—variations in incarceration rates often exist and remain difficult to explain. For example, North Dakota and South Dakota have similar social characteristics and crime rates, yet the incarceration rate in South Dakota (413 per 100,000 population) was nearly double the rate found in North Dakota (221 per 100,000).[24] One can even find similar and contiguous states such as Connecticut and Massachusetts, Arizona and New Mexico, or Minnesota and Wisconsin, where the state with the *higher* violent crime rate has the *lower* incarceration rate (see **Table 18.1**).

In recent years scholars have shown that the location of prisons makes a significant economic and political impact in some states. A good example of this relationship is found in the state of New York, which in the 1970s enacted tough sentencing laws such as 15 years to life for some nonviolent, first-time drug offenders. Over the next 20 years, the state's prison population increased dramatically. Most of the offenders ended up in new prisons located in the northern, rural, economically impoverished region of the state. One study notes that two-thirds of prisoners are from New York City, while 91 percent of prisoners are incarcerated in upstate counties.[25] The influx of inmates brought jobs to the region and legislative districts whose economy was tied to "prison payrolls and whose politics was dominated by the union that represents corrections officers."[26] Across the nation, 21 counties were found in which at least 21 percent of the residents were inmates. In Concho County, Texas, with a population of under 4,000, 33 percent of the residents were in prison.[27]

The Bureau of the Census counts prisoners as "residents" of the community where the facility is located. Since state and federal aid, such as Medicaid, foster care, and social service block grants, is distributed on the basis of population, this has meant

TABLE 18.1 *Incarceration Rates and Violent Crime Rates in Selected Neighboring States, 2007*

Politics and community values seem to vary in the amount of emphasis they place on imprisonment as a solution to crime.		
	Incarceration Rate	**Violent Crime Rate**
Arizona	554	483
New Mexico	313	664
Connecticut	410	256
Massachusetts	246	432
Minnesota	181	289
Wisconsin	397	291

Sources: Bureau of Justice Statistics, *Prisoners in 2007* (Washington, DC: U.S. Government Printing Office, December 2008), Appendix Table 6; Federal Bureau of Investigation, *Crime in the United States, 2007*, http://www.fbi.gov/ucr/cius2007/data/table_05.html, March 18, 2009.

A California political organization's website has information on the expanding **prison-industrial complex**; see the link at www.cengage.com/ criminaljustice/clear.

that aid for the distressed inner cities from which the prisoners come is diverted to the sparsely populated counties where their former residents are incarcerated. Cook County, Illinois, will lose nearly $88 million in federal benefits over the next decade because residents were counted in the 2000 Census in their county of incarceration rather than their county of origin.[28]

The addition of incarcerated residents can also influence the allocation of political representation. One study found that seven New York Senate districts meet population requirements for seats only because prison inmates are included in the count. In Wisconsin people expressed concern about the number of offenders transferred to the prisons of other states, fearing that the decennial census would not credit them to their home state, thus endangering Congressional representation.

Probably the most extensive research on the link between politics and incarceration has been done by David Greenberg and Valerie West. They analyzed variations in the levels of incarceration among the 50 states between 1971 and 1991. A basic assumption of the research is that incarceration is a response to the volume of crime, but only in part. They expected that a state's responses to crime would also be influenced by its ability to finance incarceration, by its political culture, and by levels of public anxiety and fear. Here are the main findings of this research:

1 States with high violent crime rates have higher levels of imprisonment.

2 States with higher revenues have higher prison populations.

3 States with higher unemployment and where there is a higher percentage of African Americans in the population have higher prison populations.

4 States with more-generous welfare benefits have lower prison populations.

5 States with more conservatives have not only higher incarceration rates, but their rates grew more rapidly than did the rates of states with fewer conservatives.

6 Political incentives for an expansive prison policy transcended Democratic and Republican affiliations.[29]

Examining states' criminal justice policies makes us aware of the role politics plays in the incarceration formula. As we have seen, many factors, not just the crime rate, have influenced the incarceration experiment.

Public Policy Trends

It is difficult to point to one factor as the main cause of the rapid increase in the incarceration rate during the past several decades. As we have seen, several plausible hypotheses exist. But researchers now recognize that the size of the prison population is not driven by the amount of crime; it is driven by public policy. Public policies are forged in the political arena. Politicians are aware that the public is concerned about crime; they also have little sympathy for offenders and therefore support increased punishments. In this political environment, correctional policies have emerged in Congress and in state legislatures based on the assumption that crime can be controlled through greater use of incarceration. Alfred Blumstein notes that, in a democracy, political leaders respond to public demands to deal with a problem such as crime. However, as he also notes, demands for increased punishments do not solve the problem but merely alleviate the political pressure to "do something."[30]

To "do something" about crime, government leaders have enacted policies designed to incarcerate a greater number of offenders for longer periods. This objective has been implemented through increased law enforcement and prosecution spending, mandatory-sentencing laws, truth-in-sentencing requirements, enhanced drug law enforcement, and tough parole policies. But it is not clear that these policies have succeeded.[31] Proponents of the policies argue that the decline in crime has come about because large numbers of criminals are in prison. However, some critics argue that incarcerating vast numbers of offenders has had little impact on the crime rate, is extremely expensive, and has harmed society, especially in poor minority communities.

After 35 years of policies to incarcerate more offenders for longer periods, several states have quietly started to ease their sentencing and parole laws. Four states—Connecticut, Indiana, Louisiana, and North Dakota—have dropped some laws requiring offenders to serve long times without the possibility of parole. Other states have granted judges and parole boards wider latitude in sentencing and release decisions. Greater use of intermediate sanctions and nonprison alternatives has helped lower the prison population in several states as well. A report by the Vera Institute of Justice found that, in 2003, 25 states took steps to lessen sentences and otherwise modify sentencing and correctional policy. Thirteen states made significant changes, ranging from repeal or reduction of mandatory minimum sentences for drug offenses to the expansion of treatment-centered alternatives to incarceration. Eleven states expanded emergency and early-release mechanisms. These appear to be more than fiscal belt-tightening efforts, instead reflecting shifts in correctional policies that could reduce the ever-spiraling rise of the incarceration rate.[32] See the Focus box for information on how the economic crisis has forced some states to reform their correctional policies.

Although the falling crime rate, state budget deficits, and a weakened economy may result in fewer incarcerated Americans, the U.S. prison population continues to be the highest in the developed world. Further, not all state corrections systems are taking measures to lower incarceration, so growth still continues in many states. Most state and federal correctional administrators and policy makers still face the problem of crowded prisons.

FOCUS ON CORRECTIONAL POLICY

Economic Crisis and Correctional Reform

For nearly 20 years now politicians, both Republicans and Democrats have beaten the "get-tough-on-crime" drum during their campaigns and after taking office. The results of the movement to get tougher on crime include increasingly punitive correctional policies, such as three-strikes laws and mandatory sentences, and an exploding correctional population. Although scholars and policy makers debate whether this shift in correctional philosophy has impacted the crime rate, one thing is certain: The amount of taxpayer money allocated to correctional budgets has increased substantially. The Pew Center on the States reported that state correctional budgets have quadrupled in the past two decades. In 2008 it cost $78.95 a day to keep someone in prison. Overall, state governments spend a combined $47 billion on corrections.

As the United States faces a huge economic crisis, many politicians are now considering less-punitive alternatives to the costly practice of incarcerating more offenders and building more prisons. In Kentucky, state officials now allow nonviolent offenders to be released six months early. These offenders are required to serve the remainder of their sentence at home. In California, a panel of federal judges recommended that the state release 57,000 nonviolent inmates, which would translate into $800 million in savings and also relieve problems with crowding. California's governor, Arnold Schwarzenegger, is attempting to remove low-level drug offenders from parole supervision, providing them with treatment options instead.

Such a shift in policy would have been considered political suicide just a few years ago. What is surprising to many onlookers is that many of the supporters touting correctional reform formerly advocated get-tough policies. For example, Governor Bill Richardson, who supports capital punishment, recently signed legislation repealing New Mexico's death penalty. Richardson cited cost savings as one justification for the change in law. Kansas state representative Mike O'Neal, a Republican, had previously pushed for longer sentences for sex offenders and tougher sentences for drug dealers. Recently, however, he helped develop a measure to save the state money by reducing, by 20 percent, the number of former inmates sent to prison for violating the conditions of their release, such as failing drug tests and not reporting to their parole officer. The budgetary crisis facing many states has brought about a serious discussion about whether states can continue to fund their get-tough-on-crime policies.

Sources: Kevin Johnson, "To Save Money on Prisons, Take a Softer Stance," http://www.usatoday.com, March 17, 2009; Pew Center on the States, *One in 31: The Long Reach of American Corrections* (Washington, DC: Pew Charitable Trusts, March 2009); Jennifer Steinhauer, "To Cut Costs, States Relax Prison Policies," http://www.nytimes.com, March 25, 2009.

■ DEALING WITH OVERCROWDED PRISONS

At the end of 2007, 19 state prison systems operated at or above capacity. The federal system operated at 36 percent above capacity.[33] Crowded prisons may violate constitutional standards, increase violence, decrease access to programs and services, and create major administrative problems.

Departments of corrections are usually unable to control the flow of offenders sent to them by the courts. When the number of prisoners exceeds prison capacity, administrators face an immediate need for space. The normal seven-year lag from legislative authorization to the fully operational institution is unacceptable. To deal with their overcrowded prisons, states are adopting a variety of strategies. A mixture of these strategies may best suit the needs of a particular corrections system.

Alfred Blumstein suggests four possible approaches that states may take to address overcrowding.[34] Each approach has economic, social, and political costs, and each entails a different amount of time for implementation and impact. For example, the null strategy could be implemented immediately, whereas intermediate sanctions would require several years of development to begin to reduce prison crowding. New construction would take the longest, often seven or eight years.

The Null Strategy

null strategy
The strategy of doing nothing to relieve crowding in prisons, under the assumption that the problem is temporary and will disappear in time.

Proponents of the **null strategy** say that nothing should be done, that prisons should be allowed to become increasingly congested. This, of course, may be the most politically acceptable approach in the short run; taxpayers need not pay for new construction. In the long run, however, the resulting crowding may turn prisons into powder kegs as staff members become demoralized and prisoners take control. Ultimately, the courts may declare conditions in the facilities unconstitutional and take over their administration.

Opponents of incarceration may support this approach on philosophical grounds because they fear that other strategies will only result in greater numbers being imprisoned. They may reason as well that with the prisons filled, nonviolent offenders will be placed on probation or diverted from the system.

The Construction Strategy

construction strategy
A strategy of building new facilities to meet the demand for prison space.

The approach that usually comes to mind when legislators or correctional officials confront prison crowding is to expand the size and number of facilities. But, given contemporary state budgets and the recent unwillingness of voters in some states to authorize bond issues for new prisons, the **construction strategy** may not be as feasible as it seems.

Legislatures typically estimate new prison construction costs at about $75,000 per cell. For a hypothetical 500-bed medium-security facility, this would total around $31 million. However, the true cost of constructing and operating a comparable prison only begins with that base construction cost. Additional costs such as architects' fees, furnishings, and site preparation raise the figure. For example, in Connecticut the Legislative Office of Fiscal Analysis projected the cost to construct and operate a 1,600-bed facility for 30 years as almost $2 billion.

In 2007 California Governor Arnold Schwarzenegger signed legislation to build facilities for 53,000 new prison and jail beds at a planned cost of $7.7 billion.[35] With interest on the bonds and other expenditures, the construction program could reach $15 billion. Officials said this expansion was designed to relieve the overcrowding that the federal courts have increasingly criticized. Critics argued that the plan did not include changes to the state's sentencing structure or parole system, which many experts have cited as key causes of overcrowding in California prisons and the state's recidivism rate, the highest in the nation. Nearly 70 percent of the state's convicts return to prison within three years on parole violations or new crimes.

AP Images/Rich Pedroncelli

Legislation signed by California Governor Arnold Schwarzenegger in 2007 authorized the spending of $7.7 billion for new prisons. This was before a budgetary crunch hit the state in 2009.

As noted previously, opponents of new construction believe that, given the nature of bureaucratic organizations, prison cells will always be filled. Many states that have adopted the construction strategy have found this to be true.

Intermediate Sanctions

Prisons are a costly and scarce resource. Some observers argue that, rather than merely building more institutions, corrections should reserve prison space for those violent offenders who have not been deterred by prior punishments. As discussed in Chapter 9, intermediate sanctions have been advocated as one way to punish in the community those individuals who require some kind of punishment and supervision short of incarceration. Recall that intermediate sanctions include community service, restitution, fines, boot camp, home confinement, and intensive probation supervision. Judges can fashion sentences using combinations of these punishments to fit the needs of the offender and the severity of the offense. When applied to nonserious offenders, intermediate sanctions enjoy a high level of public support (see **Figure 18.3**).

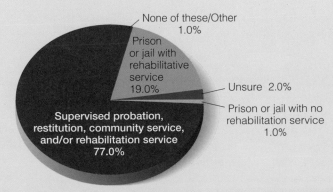

None of these/Other
1.0%

Prison or jail with rehabilitative service
19.0%

Unsure 2.0%

Prison or jail with no rehabilitation service
1.0%

Supervised probation, restitution, community service, and/or rehabilitation service
77.0%

Figure 18.3

Public Opinion on the Most Appropriate Sentence for Nonserious Offenders

When asked what they believed was the most appropriate sentence for a nonviolent, nonsexual offender, an overwhelming majority of Americans said probation, restitution, community services, and/or rehabilitation services.

Source: Christopher Hartney and Susan Marchionna, *Attitudes of U.S. Voters toward Nonserious Offenders and Alternatives to Incarceration* (Oakland, CA: National Council on Crime and Delinquency, June 2009), 6.

Some critics contend that, even if such alternatives were fully incorporated, they would affect only first-time, marginal offenders; they are not appropriate for serious criminals if crime control is a goal. They also assert that the availability of intermediate sanctions merely widens the net of social control, with the result that more citizens come under correctional supervision.

Prison Population Reduction

Corrections normally has little or no control over the intake of its raw material—offenders. Only in nine states have legislatures required that sentencing-guideline framers consider prison capacity when stipulating incarceration lengths. The main ways that correctional officials can reduce prison populations include various "backdoor strategies," such as parole, work release, and good time, to get offenders out of prison before the end of their term so as to free up space for newcomers. In recent years, however, many legislatures have mandated that higher portions of sentences be served and have reduced good-time allocations.

■ THE IMPACT OF PRISON CROWDING

Prison crowding directly affects the ability of correctional officials to do their work, because it decreases the proportion of offenders in programs, increases the potential for violence, and greatly strains staff morale. The makeup of the inmate community in terms of age, race, and criminal record also affects how institutions are operated. Because prison space is an expensive resource, we can expect—in the absence of expansion—that corrections will be working increasingly with the most serious offenders, as first-time and less-violent criminals are placed on probation for lack of cells.

As discussed both here and in Chapter 10, the overwhelming number of inmates are recidivists or have been convicted of a violent crime. A growing percentage of the admissions to prison each year are parole violators—offenders released from prison who have violated the conditions of their parole.

From 1995 through 2001, Blumstein and Beck studied court recommitment to prison for new offenses among offenders released in four states: California, New York,

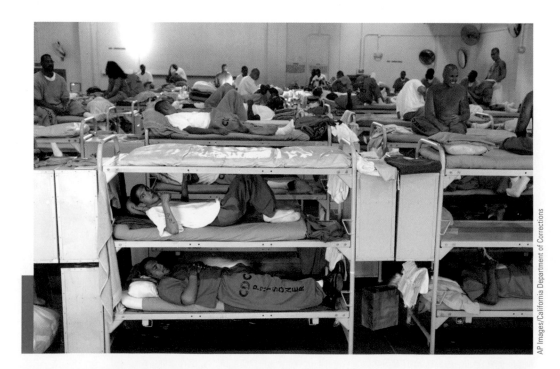

In many states prison crowding has forced the conversion of gymnasiums and dayrooms into dormitories.

AP Images/California Department of Corrections

Illinois, and Florida. The percentage returned to prison for new offenses varied greatly. California had a recommitment rate of 67 percent, New York and Illinois each had a rate of 52 percent, and Florida had 47 percent. The researchers found that 80 percent of California's recommitments stemmed from technical violations, compared with 56 percent in New York, 21 percent in Florida, and 18 percent in Illinois. The four states had similar percentages of parolees recommitted for new crimes. Some would argue that California's extensive use of technical violations is justified as a crime-prevention measure. However, the researchers argue that, compared with the other states, nothing clearly indicates that this strategy makes a meaningful difference in the criminal activity of released prisoners.[36]

A Bureau of Justice Statistics study shows that almost 60 percent of inmates have been either incarcerated or on probation at least twice; 43 percent of them, three or more times; and nearly 18 percent, six or more times. Forty-seven percent of the inmates were serving a sentence for a violent crime or had previously been convicted of a violent crime.[37] Correctional officials now face a different type of inmate, one who is more prone to violence, who has been incarcerated before, and who inhabits a prison society where racial tensions run high.

As a direct consequence of the higher incarceration rate, courts have cited several states for maintaining prisons so crowded that they violate the Eighth Amendment's prohibition against cruel and unusual punishments.[38] Courts have imposed population ceilings, specified the number of offenders per cell, set the minimum floor space per person, and ordered the removal of prisoners from overcrowded prisons and jails.

Does crowding cause inmates' ill health, misconduct, violent behavior, and postrelease recidivism? In measuring the influence of crowding, we must look further than the number of inmates housed in a prison designed for a certain capacity. The architecture of the building, the use of either cells or dormitories, inmate characteristics, management practices, and the past experiences of prisoners with regard to social density all impinge on the problem. At the least, most researchers would agree on the following points. First, prisoners housed in large, open-bay dormitories are more likely to visit clinics and to have high blood pressure than are prisoners in other housing arrangements (single-bunked cells, double-bunked cells, small dormitories, or large partitioned dormitories). Second, prisons that contain dormitories have somewhat higher assault rates than do other prisons. Finally, prisons with populations that allow less than 60 square feet per inmate tend to have high assault rates.[39]

■ DOES INCARCERATION PAY?

Opponents of current penal policies note that the United States now ranks first in the developed world for incarcerating offenders.[40] Many of these critics argue that offenders whose crimes do not warrant the severe deprivation of prison nonetheless are being sent to prison. They also argue that the policy debate does not consider many of the unintended consequences of imprisonment such as disrupted families and disintegrated communities.[41]

Supporters of incarceration believe that current policies have succeeded in lowering the crime rate. They say that most inmates have committed serious crimes, often with violence, and that they are repeat offenders. Not to incarcerate repeat offenders, they claim, is costly to society.

Is incarceration misused in the United States? One explanation of why we incarcerate more people is simply that we have more crime, compared with other countries such as England, Germany, and Japan. For example, more than 150 countries at various stages of development have lower murder rates than the United States. This point is buttressed by research comparing the likelihood of imprisonment for robbery, burglary, or theft in the United States, Canada, England, and the former West Germany.[42] Little difference among the probabilities for these crimes was found among these countries.

The propensity to incarcerate, however, is only one dimension of penal policy. As James Lynch notes, sentence length is a second important dimension. He compared the length of sentences in five industrialized democracies: Australia, Canada, England, the Federal Republic of Germany, and the United States.[43] He found that, except for homicide, the time served in confinement in the United States was generally longer than that in Australia and England for similar offenses. For Canada and the United States, the differences were minimal for violent offenses; however, sentences handed down for crimes of violence were longer in the former West Germany than in common-law countries. And whereas prisoners were kept in custody for substantially longer periods in the United States than in Australia, Canada, and England, prisoners in West Germany served longer periods than did those in the United States.

Despite a long reform tradition critical of incarceration, proponents of the current penal policies argue that prisons have value.[44] A major debate among researchers and policy makers concerns the cost-effectiveness of imprisonment, a debate sparked by a 1987 report by Edwin Zedlewski, an economist at the National Institute of Justice.[45] Zedlewski said that the annual per-prisoner cost of incarceration was $25,000. Using national crime data, he estimated that the typical offender commits 187 crimes a year when on the street, at a "social cost" of $430,000. Thus, he argued, incarceration has a benefit-cost ratio of just over 17:1. In other words, putting a thousand felons behind bars costs $25 million a year, but allowing these same felons to remain at large costs society about $430 million a year in additional crimes.

Critics immediately retorted that Zedlewski's report overstated the number of crimes committed per offender and the social costs per crime.[46] These critics pointed out that if Zedlewski's statistics were accurate, the huge increase in the prison population since 1973 should have saved almost enough money to cancel out the national debt and should have reduced crime to a negative number by 1992.[47] Obviously, this didn't happen.

However, John DiIulio and Anne Piehl used a similar approach to estimate the cost-effectiveness of imprisonment in Wisconsin. They concluded that imprisoning a typical felon costs Wisconsin $14,000 per year, but letting him roam the streets harming victims costs society $28,000 per year.[48] Still, crime in Wisconsin has increased, despite the growth in its prison population. Also employing a cost-benefit analysis, Thomas Marvell concluded that locking up each additional state prisoner prevented about 21 crimes a year. Comparing national costs of incarceration to benefits of crimes prevented, he concluded that the current size of the prison population was about right from an economic viewpoint.[49]

In light of the reduction in crime over the past decade, are current incarceration policies effective? In 1995 James Q. Wilson suggested that the United States had reached a tipping point of "diminishing returns" from its investment in prisons.[50] He argued that as states expanded incarceration, they dipped "deeper into the bucket of persons eligible for prison, dredging up offenders with shorter and shorter criminal records."[51] Other researchers support this contention, arguing that while the increase in imprisonment in the 1980s and 1990s may have prevented crime, a further increase over today's levels is unlikely to do so.[52] As the Pew Trusts study notes, "Increasing the proportion of convicted criminals sent to prison, like lengthening time served beyond some point, has produced diminishing marginal returns in crime reduction." This does not mean that incarceration will have no impact—"just that the benefits to public safety of each additional prisoner consistently decreases."[53]

Is the incarceration of *all* offenders cost effective? Studies in New Jersey, New York, Arizona, and New Mexico raise questions about the social costs of incarcerating "drug-only offenders." These are prisoners whose only adult crimes have been drug crimes. Each of these states imprisons a substantial portion of drug-only offenders. Studies have shown that, for each drug offender incarcerated, a replacement enters the market. Piehl and DiIulio believe that the incarceration of large numbers of drug offenders is not an efficient use of valuable prison space. Some of the cells could be better reserved for high-risk property and violent offenders.[54]

Again, many people point to the decline in the crime rate since the mid-1990s as an indication that mass incarceration has worked. Is this true? As with other social policy questions, we have no clear-cut answer. Researchers point to many social and economic factors as contributing to the drop in crime, such as shifts in law enforcement, economic expansion, decline in the use of crack cocaine, and demographic changes, in addition to expanded use of incarceration.[55] Bruce Western's analysis of the effects of imprisonment on crime rates from 1971 to 2001 shows that incarceration helped reduce crime and violence, but the contribution was not large. He estimates that the increase in state prison populations from 725,000 to 1.2 million inmates reduced the rate of serious crime 2 to 5 percent—one-tenth of the decline in crime between 1993 and 2001. This decline was purchased for $53 billion in incarceration costs.[56] William Spelman asks, "Whether the key to further reduction [of crime] lies in further prison expansions, or (more likely) in further improvements in these other factors, remains an open question."[57] (See "Careers in Corrections" for more on the job of a research analyst.)

Another question comes out of this debate: Should incarceration policies be judged solely by comparing prison costs with crime reduction? Critics point to the hidden costs to society that incarceration brings. These include the offenders' families being left without a wage earner and caretaker, the loss of young men to their communities, the redirection of government resources from societal needs such as health care and education, and the damage done to children by the absence of a parent.[58]

CAREERS IN CORRECTIONS — Research Analyst, State Department of Corrections

NATURE OF THE WORK

Research analysts conduct research and manage offender management databases. They also design and maintain department reporting systems, distribute monthly and quarterly reports, and provide data support to management teams. Analysts also provide data support when partnering with universities and other state agencies on research projects.

REQUIRED QUALIFICATIONS

Background qualifications vary by state, but generally candidates must meet the following criteria:

- A master's degree or higher, including multiple college-level classes in statistics
- Ability to operate statistical software programs
- Familiarity with the research methods and statistical techniques commonly used in correctional and evaluation research
- Ability to analyze and interpret data, write clearly, and prepare research reports

EARNINGS AND JOB OUTLOOK

In general, government employment related to the social sciences is projected to grow. Applicants for such positions, including those in state department of corrections, may face competition. Individuals with higher educational attainment will prove more competitive. The median annual salary for research analysts was $64,650 in 2006.

MORE INFORMATION

See the **Justice Research and Statistics Association** website, found at www.cengage.com/criminaljustice/clear.

One of the consequences of "mass incarceration" is the invisible punishment imposed on families. One in every six children in Hartford, Connecticut, has a parent in prison. Here, Marcus Maldonado hugs his daughter Elizabeth during a family visit at the Enfield Correctional Institution.

Some have also argued that removing young men from their families and friends weakens the networks of informal social control in their communities. Dina Rose and Todd Clear note that

> high-crime neighborhoods are also high-incarceration neighborhoods. In these places, children are more likely to experience family disruption, lack of parental supervision, property devoid of effective guardians, and all other manner of deteriorated informal social controls that otherwise deflect the young from criminal behavior.[59]

In summary, they argue that the "prison can never be a substitute for absent adults, family members, and neighbors in making places safe."[60]

Does incarceration pay? Until a host of crucial methodological problems are solved, no definitive answer will emerge. In particular, we need a more-accurate estimate of the number of crimes each felon commits, a better method of calculating the social costs of crime and incarceration, and a way of determining costs that includes correctional capital, operating costs, and indirect costs. Even if we were to refine the method and obtain a more-accurate view of the cost-benefit differential, certain political and moral issues would have to be addressed before a rational incarceration policy could be designed.

SUMMARY

1 Discuss the explanations for the dramatic increase in the incarceration rate.

Five factors have been put forward to explain the growing incarceration rate. First, there has been a nationwide trend for the police to make more arrests and for the courts to impose incarceration on those convicted of committing crimes. This has led not only to higher numbers of new prison admissions but also to a high number of former inmates returning to prison. Second, tougher sentencing laws have resulted in inmates spending more time, on average, in prison. Third, a large number of new prisons have been built in recent decades, greatly expanding society's ability to incarcerate offenders. Fourth, the war on drugs has resulted in the imprisonment of large numbers of drug offenders. Fifth, state and local political factors, such as the proportion of the population who are political conservatives, are also related to higher state incarceration rates.

2 Explain what can be done to deal with the prison population crisis.

Several strategies have been identified for dealing with prison crowding. The null strategy is to "do nothing." Another approach is simply to build more prisons. However, many people oppose this strategy because of the financial cost involved. Another strategy is to use intermediate sanctions for less-serious, nonviolent offenders and to reserve prison space for violent offenders. Intermediate sanctions are an attractive approach because they allow the offender to maintain ties to the community, and the sentencing judge can combine them to address the needs of the offender and the severity of the offense. Critics of the intermediate sanctions approach argue that increasing the availability of such sanctions also serves to widen the net of social control, thus increasing the number of citizens under correctional supervision. Finally, some advocate the reduction of the prison population through various "backdoor strategies," such as parole, work release, and good time.

3 Be familiar with the impact of prison crowding.

The problem of prison crowding has become more pressing as greater numbers of offenders are sentenced to prison. Correctional officials are responsible for providing humane treatment and living conditions for the offenders in their facilities. The federal courts sometimes intervene when correctional officials fail to meet their responsibilities. Measuring the effects of crowding involves more than looking at capacity; researchers also need to consider the architecture of the building, the use of either cells or dormitories, inmate characteristics, management practices, and the past experiences of prisoners.

4 Discuss whether incarceration pays.

Supporters of incarceration believe that incarceration lowers the crime rate. They argue that most prison inmates have committed serious crimes, and many of them are repeat offenders. If we do not incarcerate these offenders, society pays the price. Opponents of current penal policies note that the United States now incarcerates more of its citizens than does any other developed country in the world. These individuals also believe that many convicted offenders in correctional facilities do not require imprisonment, and that there are many unintended consequences associated with incarceration, such as disrupted families and disintegrated communities. Unfortunately, a host of crucial methodological problems in social science research make it difficult to answer whether incarceration pays.

KEY TERMS

construction strategy (p. 514)
null strategy (p. 514)

FOR DISCUSSION

1. Which of the many hypotheses advanced to explain the rise in the incarceration rate seems most plausible to you? What other reasons might be added?
2. Which of the strategies for dealing with crowded prisons seems most viable to you? What other strategy might be considered?
3. Imagine that you are incarcerated in a prison that is over capacity. What are some of the factors that will influence the way you serve your time?
4. How would you respond to the argument that the American prison is becoming a place where the urban poor receive better housing, health care, education, and job training than they do on the outside?
5. The incarceration rate has become a political issue. How would you summarize the two sides?

FOR FURTHER READING

Austin, James, and John Irwin. *It's About Time: America's Imprisonment Binge.* 3rd ed. Belmont, CA: Wadsworth, 2001. The authors argue that the "grand imprisonment experiment" that has dominated recent American crime-reduction policy has failed miserably and should be abandoned.

Jacobson, Michael. *Downsizing Prisons.* New York: NYU Press, 2005. Examines specific ways that states have begun to transform their prison systems. Offers policy solutions and strategies that can increase public safety as well as save money.

Mauer, Marc. *Race to Incarcerate.* New York: New Press, 1999. Explores the intersection of race and class that underpins the policies that have expanded incarceration. Argues that the rise in incarceration has not had a substantial impact on crime.

Mauer, Marc, and Meda Chesney-Lind, eds. *Invisible Punishment: The Collateral Consequences of Mass Imprisonment.* New York: New Press, 2002. A collection of articles examining the consequences of 30 years of get-tough policies on prisoners, ex-felons, and families and communities.

Western, Bruce. *Punishment and Inequality in America.* New York: Russell Sage Foundation, 2006. Argues that mass incarceration contributed a little to the decline in the crime rate, but the gain in public safety was purchased at a cost to the economic well-being and family life of poor minority communities.

Whitman, James Q. *Harsh Justice: Criminal Punishments and the Widening Divide between America and Europe.* New Haven: Yale University Press, 2003. Persuasive and detailed investigation of differences between U.S. and Europe in penal policy.

Zimring, Franklin E., and Gordon Hawkins. *The Scale of Imprisonment.* Chicago: University of Chicago Press, 1991. Questions the scale of society's prison enterprise compared with other criminal sanctions and with the size of the general population; calls for a political economy of imprisonment.

NOTES

[1] Bureau of Justice Statistics, *Prisoners in 2007* (Washington, DC: U.S. Government Printing Office, December 2008), 6.

[2] Roy Walmsley, *World Prison Population List,* 7th ed. (London: King's College, International Centre for Prison Studies, 2006).

[3] "Canada's Prison Population Grew in 2006: StatsCan," *CBC News,* November 21, 2007, http://www.cbc.ca/canada/story/2007/11/21/stats-prisons.html?ref=rss.

[4] *Public Safety, Public Spending: Forecasting America's Prison Population 2007–2011* (Washington, DC: Pew Charitable Trusts, February 2007), ii.

[5] Todd R. Clear, *Harm in American Penology* (Albany: State University of New York Press, 1994), 38; John Irwin and James Austin, *It's about Time: America's Imprisonment Binge* (Belmont, CA: Wadsworth, 2001).

[6] Bureau of Justice Statistics, *State Prison Expenditures, 2001* (Washington, DC: U.S. Government Printing Office, June 2004), 1.

[7] Bureau of Justice Statistics, *Probation and Parole in the United States, 2006* (Washington, DC: U.S. Government Printing Office, December 2007), 2.

[8] Ann L. Pastore and Kathleen Maguire, eds., *Sourcebook of Criminal Justice Statistics,* Table 6.28.2007, http://www.albany.edu/sourcebook/pdf/t6282007.pdf, December 31, 2008; Bureau of Justice Statistics, *Prisoners in 2007,* p. 1.

[9] Allen J. Beck, "Growth, Change, and Stability in the U.S. Prison Population, 1980–1995," *Corrections Management Quarterly* 1 (Spring 1997): 1–14.

[10] Bureau of Justice Statistics, *Prisoners in 2007,* Appendix Table 15.

[11] Ibid., Appendix Table 14.

[12] Ibid.

[13] Bureau of Justice Statistics, *Key Facts at a Glance: Estimated Arrests for Drug Abuse Violations by Age Group, 1970–2006,* http://www.ojp.usdoj.gov/bjs/glance/tables/drugtab.htm.

[14] *Sourcebook of Criminal Justice Statistics,* Table 4.2.2007, http://www.albany.edu/sourcebook/pdf/t422007.pdf, July 23, 2009.

[15] Bureau of Justice Statistics, *Prisoners in 2007,* Appendix Table 5.

[16] Alfred Blumstein and Allen J. Beck, "Reentry as a Transient State between Liberty and Recommitment," in *Prisoner Reentry and Crime in America,* edited by Jeremy Travis and Christy Visher (New York: Cambridge University Press, 2005), 61.

[17] Bureau of Justice Statistics, *Felony Sentences in State Courts, 2004* (Washington, DC: U.S. Government Printing Office, July 2007), 3.

[18] Bureau of Justice Statistics: *Census of State and Federal Correctional Facilities, 1995* (Washington, DC: U.S. Government Printing Office, August 1997), iv; *Census of State and Federal Correctional Facilities, 2005* (Washington, DC: U.S. Government Printing Office, October 2008), 1.

[19] Sarah Lawrence and Jeremy Travis, *The New Landscape of Imprisonment: Mapping America's Prison Expansion* (Washington, DC: Urban Institute, 2004), 10.

[20] Joseph Dillion Davey, *The Politics of Prison Expansion* (Westport, CT: Praeger, 1998), 84.

[21] Bureau of Justice Statistics, *Prisoners in 2007,* Appendix Table 10.

[22] Federal Bureau of Prisons, *State of the Bureau 2007* (Washington, DC: U.S. Government Printing Office, 2007), 52.

[23] David F. Greenberg and Valerie West, "State Prison Populations and Their Growth, 1971–1991," *Criminology* 39 (August 2001): 615–54

[24] Bureau of Justice Statistics, *Prisoners in 2007,* Appendix Table 6.

[25] Peter Wagner, "Detaining for Dollars: Federal Aid Follows Inner-City Prisoners to Rural Town Coffers" [pamphlet] (Springfield, MA: Prison Policy Initiative, 2002), 4.

[26] Brent Staples, "Why Some Politicians Need Their Prisons to Stay Full," *New York Times,* December 27, 2005, http://query.nytimes.com/mem/tnt.html?oref=login&tntget=2—0/1.

[27] Fox Butterfield, "Study Tracks Boom in Prisons and Notes Impact on Counties," *New York Times,* April 30, 2004, p. A15.

[28] Lawrence and Travis, *New Landscape,* p. 3.

[29] Greenberg and West, "State Prison Populations."

[30] Alfred Blumstein, "Prisons," in *Crime,* edited by James Q. Wilson and Joan Petersilia (San Francisco: Institute for Contemporary Studies, 1995), 399.

[31] Todd R. Clear, "Ten Unintended Consequences of the Growth in Imprisonment," *Corrections Management Quarterly* 1 (Spring 1997): 25–31.

[32] Jon Wool and Don Stemen, "Changing Fortunes or Changing Attitudes? Sentencing and Corrections Reforms in 2003," in *Issues in Brief* (New York: Vera Institute of Justice, 2004), 1.

[33] Bureau of Justice Statistics, *Prisoners 2007,* Appendix Table 15.

[34] Blumstein, "Prisons," p. 402.

[35] "Governor Schwarzenegger Signs Legislation to Create First Secure Community Re-entry Facility," press release, Office of the Governor, September 26, 2007, http://gov.ca.gov/index .php?/press-release/7561.

[36] Blumstein and Beck, "Reentry as a Transient State," p. 76.

[37] Bureau of Justice Statistics, *Correctional Populations in the United States, 1997* (Washington, DC: U.S. Government Printing Office, November 2000), 57.

[38] Richard B. Cole and Jack E. Call, "When Courts Find Jail and Prison Overcrowding Unconstitutional," *Federal Probation,* March 1992, pp. 29–39.

[39] Gerald G. Gaes, "The Effects of Overcrowding in Prison," in *Crime and Justice: A Review of Research,* vol. 6, edited by Michael Tonry and Norval Morris (Chicago: University of Chicago Press, 1985), 95.

[40] The Sentencing Project, "U.S. Continues to Be World Leader in Rate of Incarceration," press release, November 30, 2006.

[41] Clear, "Ten Unintended Consequences."

[42] Bureau of Justice Statistics, *Imprisonment in Four Countries* (Washington, DC: U.S. Government Printing Office, February 1987), 2. See also Warren Young and Mark Brown, "Cross-National Comparisons of Imprisonment," in *Crime and Justice: A Review of Research,* vol. 17, edited by Michael Tonry (Chicago: University of Chicago Press, 1993), 1–50.

[43] James P. Lynch, "A Cross-National Comparison of the Length of Custodial Sentences for Serious Crimes," *Justice Quarterly* 10 (December 1993): 639–60.

[44] See, for example, John J. DiIulio, Jr., "The Value of Prisons," *Wall Street Journal,* May 13, 1992; Edwin W. Zedlewski, "Why Prisons Matter: A Utilitarian Review," *Corrections Management Quarterly* 1 (Spring 1997): 15–24.

[45] Edwin W. Zedlewski, "Making Confinement Decisions," in *Research in Brief* (Washington, DC: National Institute of Justice, 1987).

[46] Franklin E. Zimring and Gordon Hawkins, "The New Mathematics of Imprisonment," *Crime and Delinquency* 34 (October 1988): 425–36.

[47] Ibid. See also Zimring and Hawkins, *Incapacitation: Penal Confinement and the Restraint of Crime* (New York: Oxford University Press, 1995), ch. 7.

[48] John J. DiIulio, Jr., "Crime and Punishment in Wisconsin," *Wisconsin Policy Research Institute Report* 3 (December 1990): 53. See also John J. DiIulio, Jr., and Anne Morrison Piehl, "Does Prison Pay?" *Brookings Review,* Fall 1991, pp. 28–35.

[49] Thomas B. Marvell, "Is Future Prison Expansion Worth the Cost?" *Federal Probation* 58 (1994): 59–62. See also Michael K. Block, "Supply Side Imprisonment Policy," in *Research Report* (Washington, DC: National Institute of Justice, 1997).

[50] James Q. Wilson, "Crime and Public Policy," in *Crime,* edited by James Q. Wilson and Joan Petersilia (Oakland, CA: ICS Press, 1995), 429–507.

[51] Ibid., p. 501.

[52] Raymond V. Liedka, Anne Morrison Piehl, and Bert Useem, "The Crime Control Effects of Incarceration: Does Scale Matter?" *Criminology and Public Policy* 5 (2006): 245–76.

[53] *Public Safety,* p. 24.

[54] Anne Morrison Piehl and John J. DiIulio, Jr., "'Does Prison Pay?' Revisited," *Brookings Review,* Winter 1995, pp. 21–25; Anne M. Piehl, Bert Useem, and John J. DiIulio, Jr., *Right-Sizing Justice: A Cost-Benefit Analysis of Imprisonment in Three States* (New York: Center for Civic Innovation at the Manhattan Institute, September 1999).

[55] Jenni Gainsborough and Marc Mauer, *Diminishing Returns: Crime and Incarceration in the 1990s* (Washington, DC: The Sentencing Project, 2000).

[56] Bruce Western, *Punishment and Inequality in America* (New York: Russell Sage Foundation, 2006), 187.

[57] William Spelman, "The Limited Importance of Prison Expansion," in *The Crime Drop in America,* edited by Alfred Blumstein and Joel Wallman (New York: Cambridge University Press, 2000), 125.

[58] Edna McConnell Clark Foundation, *Seeking Justice: Crime and Punishment in America* (New York: Author, 1997), 9–10; Clear: *Harm in American Penology,* "Ten Unintended Consequences."

[59] Dina R. Rose and Todd R. Clear, "Incarceration, Social Capital, and Crime: Implications for Social Disorganization Theory," *Criminology* 36 (August 1998): 441–80.

[60] Ibid.

© Tony Avelar/The Christian Science Monitor/Getty Images

LEARNING OBJECTIVES

After reading this chapter you should be able to . . .

1 Understand the meaning of race and ethnicity.

2 Recognize how varying visions of race and punishment influence our thinking on this issue.

3 Describe the significance of race and punishment.

The U.S. rate of imprisonment for African American men is over three times higher than the rate for white men, in proportion to their percentage of the population. How much of this difference is due to inequality and injustice?

THERE ARE MORE AFRICAN AMERICAN

MEN in prison than in college. In fact, there are four African American men in prison for every three in college (for white men, the ratio is about two in college for every prisoner). Indeed, African American men born in the 1960s are more likely to go to prison than to finish a four-year degree or serve in the military.[1] But it was not always this way. In 1980 there were *three times* more African American men in college than in prison.[2] Since then the U.S. prison system has quadrupled in size; at the same time it has surpassed college as a place for young African American men. Some have argued that the growth of the prison system was intended to be a way to imprison more African American men,[3] but not everyone agrees. Nobody, however, can dispute the disparate impact the prison system's growth has had on young men of color. The social consequences of this disparity must trouble us all.

Race and ethnicity are pervasive themes in contemporary American culture. In no area are these concepts more significant than in punishment. For one thing, people of color are far more likely than whites to be caught up in the criminal justice system. Today, almost 5,000 per 100,000 African American men and about 2,000 Hispanic men—compared

RACE, ETHNICITY, AND CORRECTIONS

- ■ THE CONCEPTS OF RACE AND ETHNICITY

- ■ VISIONS OF RACE AND PUNISHMENT
  Differential Criminality
  The Criminal Justice System Is Racist
  Society Is Racist

- ■ WHICH IS IT: RACE OR RACISM?

- ■ THE SIGNIFICANCE OF RACE AND PUNISHMENT

with about 800 white American men—were incarcerated in U.S. prisons and jails.[4] Today African Americans make up almost 40 percent of the prison population but only about 13 percent of all U.S. residents. African Americans are seven times more likely than whites to have been incarcerated at some time in a state or federal prison. If current rates continue, nearly one-third of African American children born today will go to prison during their lifetimes.[5] When all punishments—probation, intermediate sanctions, incarceration, parole—are taken into account, more than one in three African American men in their twenties are currently under correctional supervision.

These patterns begin early. Among African Americans below age 18, referrals to juvenile court occur at more than twice the rate for whites. People under 18 who are sentenced to confinement are 20 percent more likely to be African American than not.[6] In America's inner cities, the figures that emerge are astounding. In cities such as Washington, D.C., and Baltimore, Maryland, more than half of all African American adults under 40 are under some form of correctional control.

Figures such as these have alarming implications. For many Americans—especially young men of color and their families—the penal system is not an abstraction, but a reality of everyday life (this issue is discussed at greater length on Chapter 22). Those who do not report to correctional authorities probably have a brother, an uncle, or a father who does. Under these circumstances, the law represents a continuum of state presence, from the police presence on the streets to the courthouse and jail downtown to the prison out in the countryside.

This pervasiveness of corrections in the lives of people of color has evolved gradually, fueled by the 1980s war on drugs and the enormous growth of our penal system. Since 1973, the correctional population overall has increased by over 500 percent and has disproportionately affected Americans of color and their families. But sheer numbers do not tell the full story. In the everyday thinking of many Americans, crime—particularly violent street crime—is a racial phenomenon. When white Americans imagine burglars, robbers, or rapists, they often think of African American men, and they think fearfully of African American men in general. When the Lionel Tate case made headlines (see Chapter 17), part of its salience was that the case fit a paradigm of the "dangerous young black man," and media coverage fueled some of those worries. This kind of thing has crucial consequences for relations among the races in the United States.

Chapter

19

As we will see, people have differing views about where these images come from and how accurate they are. Certainly, that so many white Americans feel this way is itself an important social fact. It means that ordinary African American or Hispanic men walking down the street, minding their own business, will frequently find themselves confronted with suspicious looks or fearful, even hostile, glares from fellow citizens. How many whites have ever crossed the street in order to avoid walking near a group of young men of color who seemed, somehow, menacing? Where did the notion to fear young men of color come from?

In this chapter we explore how issues about race and ethnicity affect the corrections system. The implications are often complex. Further, strong feelings abound concerning race, class, crime, and punishment; often the debate produces more heat than light. We begin by discussing the concepts of race and ethnicity. We then focus on the indisputable fact that African Americans and Hispanics are subjected to the criminal justice system at considerably higher rates than are other ethnic and racial groups. Two questions arise: What are the causes of this disparity? What are its main effects?

■ THE CONCEPTS OF RACE AND ETHNICITY

The United States is a multiracial, multiethnic society. From colonial times, through the period of slave trade, and then through the mass migrations from all over the world, ours has been one of the most diverse societies ever to exist. By culture and by law, we are all Americans, but we are not a melting pot. Rather, we are a mosaic, with each new immigrant group seeking its place in the broader community. Where once immigrants felt great pressure to become assimilated to the dominant Euro-American society and to sacrifice their own cultural identity, the trend since the end of World War II has been to honor the many cultures the nation comprises.

Although we can point to many immigrant groups who have successfully moved up the socioeconomic ladder and into the middle class, we know that many members of both old and new groups have not. Native Americans, who lived here long before the arrival of Europeans, were decimated by disease and war, finally to be herded to reservations, where most have lived precariously. African Americans, most of whose ancestors were brought to this country as slaves, have been held back by racial discrimination and economic exploitation. Newer groups such as Hispanics and Asians also have faced discrimination, have had to work at low-wage jobs, and have been otherwise restricted in their efforts to achieve.

race
Traditionally, a biological concept used to distinguish groups of people by their skin color and other physical features.

Race and ethnicity are complex concepts. **Race** is usually assumed to be a biological concept that divides humankind into categories related to skin color and other physical features. Social scientists, however, also look at the ways in which groups define themselves and are defined by others. Today the concept of race is controversial: That so many Americans have interracial backgrounds makes accepting a purely biological approach difficult. Race is also controversial to the extent that it has political and social implications. For example, many transfers of funds from the federal government to the states for social programs are calculated according to race-based formulas.

ethnicity
Concept used to distinguish people according to their cultural characteristics—language, religion, and group traditions.

Ethnicity is a concept used to divide people according to their cultural characteristics—language, religion, and group traditions. Ethnicity is usually reported by subjects themselves, rather than stemming from an outside observer making a visual identification, as in the case of race. Although we tend to think of ethnic groups as existing among white Americans—for example Irish, Italians, Poles—the concept can also be used to distinguish ethnic groups within the black, Asian, and Hispanic communities.

Thus, in the Northeast, sizable black communities are made up of immigrants from Africa and the West Indies whose culture differs from that of the larger group of African Americans who migrated to the northern cities from the agricultural South. Asians have immigrated from many countries and are multiethnic, multilingual, and multiracial. Hispanics are also multiethnic and multiracial. We use the category "Hispanic" to distinguish Spanish-speaking Americans, yet this group is made up of people, some of whom are black and some white, from Mexico, Cuba, Puerto Rico, and other countries.

In this chapter we focus primarily on correctional issues that relate to African Americans and Hispanics. Members of these two groups are under correctional supervision out of proportion to their numbers in the general population, so issues of racial (and ethnic) disparities are most apparent with regard to these Americans.

■ VISIONS OF RACE AND PUNISHMENT

African Americans and Hispanics are subjected to the criminal justice system at much higher rates than is the white majority. A central question is whether these racial and ethnic disparities result from discrimination. A **disparity** is a difference between groups that can be explained by legitimate factors. For example, the fact that 18–24-year-old men are arrested out of proportion to their numbers in the general population is a disparity explained by the legal factor that they commit more crime. It is not thought to be the result of a public policy of singling out young men for arrest. **Discrimination** occurs when groups are differentially treated without regard to their behavior or qualifications. For example, discrimination occurs if people of color are routinely sentenced to prison regardless of their criminal history.

Explanations for the cause of racial disparities in the criminal justice system can be roughly grouped according to three themes. Some observers argue that these disparities result from the system operating as a giant sieve to differentiate offenders, so that more men of color end up under correctional authority because they commit more crimes. Others claim that the sieve is racist and that the system treats men of color more harshly than it does white men. And still others argue that the criminal justice system operates within the broader context of our society's racism and merely represents a vehicle for its expression. We consider each of these views in turn.

disparity
The unequal treatment of one group by the criminal justice system, compared with the treatment accorded other groups.

discrimination
Differential treatment of an individual or group without reference to the behavior or qualifications of the same.

Differential Criminality

Nobody denies the disparity concerning people of color in the criminal justice system. There is, however, controversy over whether the disparity results from discrimination. In their book *The Color of Justice*, Samuel Walker, Cassia Spohn, and Miriam DeLone point out that the criminal justice system is supposed to take into account differences between serious offenders and petty offenders, and such considerations might result in disparity.[7] Logically, then, more people of color will end up in corrections if they commit worse crimes and have more-serious prior records than do whites.

This general view covers a range of perspectives. The most extreme versions contend that some people are, by nature, more predisposed to commit crimes.[8] This position implies the existence of something akin to a "criminal class" of people who constitute an ongoing danger to society. When this view incorporates a conclusion that one of the predisposing factors toward criminality is having dark skin, we can see why the view is vulnerable to charges of racism. Nonetheless, some people believe that sociobiological factors result in large numbers of Hispanics and African Americans being processed by the criminal justice system.

In fact, the evidence to support a view that people of color are inherently more likely to be involved in crime is paltry at best and nonexistent at worst. **Self-report studies**, in which individuals are asked to report on their own criminal behavior, have shown that nearly everyone admits to having committed a crime during his or her lifetime, although most people are never caught. **Table 19.1** shows the results of the first self-report study, conducted with a cross-section of citizens in 1947, in which an astonishing 99 percent of

For a venue describing collaborative and comparative projects on **ethnicity and race**, go to the corresponding link at www.cengage.com/criminaljustice/clear.

self-report study
An investigation of behavior (such as criminal activity) based on subjects' responses to questions concerning activities in which they have engaged.

TABLE 19.1 *Percentage of Men and Women Who Admitted Committing Offenses, by Type of Crime, 1947*

Most adults have committed a serious offense in their lifetime.		
Type of Crime	**Men**	**Women**
Petty theft	89%	83%
Disorderly conduct	85	76
Malicious mischief	84	81
Assault	49	5
Tax evasion	57	40
Robbery	11	1
Falsification and fraud	46	34
Criminal libel	36	29
Concealed weapons	35	3
Auto theft	26	8
Other grand theft	13	11
Burglary	17	4

Source: Adapted from James Wallerstein and Clement J. Wyle, "Our Law-Abiding Law-Breakers," *Probation 35* (April 1947): 112.

respondents admitted to at least one criminal offense since turning 16.[9] A more-recent study of 4,000 public school students—now considered a classic and one of the most heavily cited studies in criminology—found that 49 percent of African American youths and 44 percent of white youths reported having committed a delinquent act during the preceding year.[10] Some self-report studies of illicit drug use have found that whites are

Are some racial and ethnic groups naturally predisposed to criminality, or do social problems of the poor contribute to higher crime rates among minority group members? What does the future hold for these two boys?

© Bob Sacha/Corbis

slightly more likely than African Americans to admit to using illegal substances, and it has been estimated that there are five times more white drug users than African American ones. Yet, African American men are admitted to prison on drug charges 13.4 times more often than are whites.[11] The argument that African Americans are more criminal than whites by nature is not sustained by the evidence.

Less-stringent versions of this argument rest on the fact that criminality is related to socioeconomic disadvantage and that many people of color suffer that to a great degree. **Figure 19.1** shows the percentage of children of whites, African Americans, and Hispanics who live in poverty; **Figure 19.2** compares the incomes of various types of families. These figures show the vast racial disparity in wealth in the United States— and studies show that this disparity is increasing.[12] Young people who live in poverty and disadvantage may develop what has been called the "code of the street," which includes a greater willingness to use violence.[13]

Social problems such as poverty, single-parent families, and unemployment contribute to higher crime rates. It is logical, then, to expect Hispanic and African American men to engage in more crimes than do whites. Not only do these higher criminality rates result from disadvantage, they also reproduce it—the victims of African American offenders are most often other people of color who live in the communities where the crimes are committed. As John DiIulio once put it, "No group of Americans suffers more when violent and repeat criminals are permitted to prey upon decent, struggling, law-abiding inner-city citizens and their children than . . . black America's silent majority."[14]

Proponents of this view point out that African American and Hispanic men are arrested more frequently and for more-serious offenses than are white men. The FBI reports that African Americans—about 12 percent of the population—account for almost two-fifths of all arrests for violent crime, and more than one-fourth of arrests for property crime.[15] But differential arrest rates are not the entire explanation. Almost three decades ago, Alfred Blumstein showed that arrest rates of African Americans explained their higher imprisonment rates for serious offenses such as homicide and robbery, but not for other crimes, notably property and drug offenses.[16]

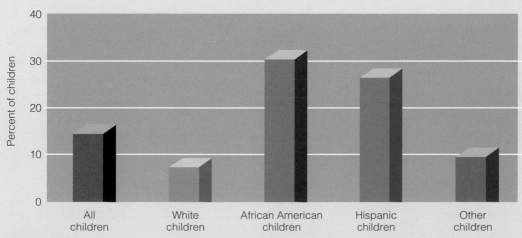

Figure 19.1

Children in Poverty, by Race and Ethnicity

One of the most disturbing aspects of contemporary American society is the increasing proportion of children who live in poverty.

Source: Sarah Fass and Nancy K. Cauthen, *Who Are America's Poor Children? The Official Story* (New York: National Center for Children in Poverty, Columbia University, November 2007), 6.

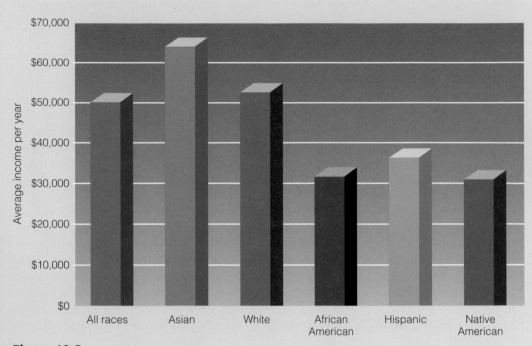

Figure 19.2
Average Family Income of Asian, White, African American, Hispanic, and Native American Families, 2007

Disparity of income continues to be a basic characteristic of U.S. society.

Source: Carmen DeNavas-Walt, Bernadette D. Proctor, and Jessica C. Smith, *Income, Poverty, and Health Insurance Coverage in the United States: 2007* (Washington, DC: U.S. Bureau of the Census, August 2008).

Those who see African Americans as more criminal because of social factors differ in their solution to the problem. Some, such as DiIulio, think we can do little other than impose long prison sentences, especially for repeat offenders, and "let 'em rot."[17] They say we need to focus our resources on today's youth in order to prevent their getting into serious crime in the first place. Others argue that we need new crime control policies that work to reduce the social problems contributing to the higher crime rates of African Americans and Hispanics. Still others contend that the social disadvantage under which these people have to live should be taken into account when they are sentenced.

The Criminal Justice System Is Racist

Racial disparities become racial discrimination if people who are otherwise similar in their criminality are treated differently by the criminal justice system because of their race. African Americans account for 30 percent of all arrests while comprising only 12 percent of the population, but just because people of color are arrested more often than whites does not mean they are more prone to crime. For example, African Americans are arrested for drug offenses at more than twice the rate of whites.[18] Yet studies show that African American youths "have substantially lower rates of use of most licit and illicit drugs"[19] and one out of 11 poor white youths say they sold illegal drugs in the previous years, compared to only one in 20 poor African American youths.[20] Sentencing for drug crimes also contributes to high rates of incarceration of African Americans. The most flagrant example has been the federal sentencing differential that punishes the possession of crack cocaine 100 times more severely than

CHAPTER 19 ■ RACE, ETHNICITY, AND CORRECTIONS 531

© Mark Peterson/Redux Pictures

Some argue that the war on drugs has targeted police resources on the urban poor. Who would be incarcerated if these same resources were targeted against the suburban consumers of drugs?

the powder version, when the only difference is that whites tend to use cocaine in its powder form, whereas inner-city people of color tend to use crack cocaine (see the Focus box "Penalties for Crack and Powder Cocaine: Are They Racist?"). State systems mirror the federal system to a lesser degree. Human Rights Watch has concluded that much of the nation's racial disparity in rates of incarceration results from drug policies that differentially select and punish African Americans at far higher rates than whites.[21]

These discrepancies do not center on drugs alone. Poor male whites, aged 15 to 18, are one-third more likely to report they have attacked someone or stolen something and almost half again as likely to damage someone's property as their African American counterparts. Nonetheless, African American youths are more likely to be arrested for *all* these crimes.[22]

Such facts raise questions about bias in the criminal justice system. Do police, prosecutors, and judges treat whites and people of color equally? A great deal of research has been conducted on race and criminal justice processing, but no simple conclusions can be drawn. Some believe that evidence of overt discrimination is weak, at best showing only small amounts of bias in decisions of police officers and judges. In 1983 the National Research Council of the National Academy of Sciences (NAS) commissioned a major review of more than 70 reports on race and criminal justice. Overall, the NAS scholars asserted that "factors other than racial discrimination in sentencing account for most of the disproportionate representation of blacks in U.S. prisons."[23] A recent summary of research on criminal justice processing shows how at each stage of the justice system, small racial disparities in case processing add up into a much larger total effect in punishments.[24]

The disparity between crime rates and punishment patterns is key to the claim by some scholars that the criminal justice system is biased against minority groups. The rate of incarceration of lower-class and minority citizens is indeed greater than even their higher rates of offending would justify.[25] (See **Figure 19.3**.) In every U.S. state, African American incarceration rates are at least twice as high as those for whites, and in some states African American rates are 10 times as high.

Figure 19.4 compares the race of offenders, as identified by victims, to the race of arrestees and shows that the odds of African American offenders being arrested are slightly higher than those of white offenders. It seems reasonable to conclude that small,

CORRECTIONAL POLICY

Penalties for Crack and Powder Cocaine: Are They Racist?

In 1987, the U.S. Congress approved a series of guidelines for sentencing people convicted of federal drug crimes. This legislation, stemming from the Sentencing Reform Act of 1984, was put into law during the height of public alarm about crack cocaine and crack-related crime. The mandatory minimum sentence for possession of 500 grams of powder cocaine was set at five years. For crack cocaine, a mere 5 grams triggered the mandatory minimum. The result was an extraordinary difference in the treatment of crack and powder cocaine—critics said that the former was punished 100 times more severely.

The difference was more than academic. About nine-tenths of federal offenders convicted of trafficking in crack cocaine are African American, and the heavy sentences they receive go a long way in explaining the larger number of African Americans serving time for drug crimes in the federal system, since those convicted of crack possession get sentences much longer than those convicted of powder cocaine possession.

Ever since the laws were enacted, people have been trying to get them changed. It has not been easy. In 1993 a federal judge tried to ignore the guidelines for four African American crack cocaine dealers, on the grounds of being unfair, but his sentences were overturned on appeal. More than once, an appeals court has said that the differential may be unfair, but it is far from unconstitutional. Twice the U.S. Sentencing Commission recommended to Congress that the penalties be revised. In 1995 they recommended that the penalties for crack

and powder be equalized. In 2002 they "unanimously and firmly" recommended that the 100–1 penalty differential be reduced "substantially." On both occasions, Congress left the guidelines intact, when various complaints were heard that a reduction in the penalty for crack would ignore how terrible the drug has been for minority communities. There is dispute about whether the pharmacological effects of crack and powder differ, but nobody claims that the problems created by one are 100 times more severe than the other. The political consequences of changing the law have perhaps been more troubling to legislators than the social consequences of leaving it as is.

It may fall to the judiciary to bring closure to this issue. When the U.S. Supreme Court ruled that sentencing guidelines must be treated as advisory rather than mandatory, some federal court judges began to sentence defendants more leniently. The 3rd Circuit Appeals Court (Philadelphia) has held that judges must weigh the seriousness of the charges in determining the sentence for crack cocaine, and may not simply impose the guidelines.

Yet another bill to reduce the disparity was recently passed in committee and moved toward a vote in the House of Representatives. Time will tell if the measure will pass.

Sources: Bill Bartel, "Bill on Cocaine vs. Crack Sentencing Passes House Panel," *Virginian-Pilot,* July 30, 2009; Gary Fields, "Judges Show More Leniency on Crack Cocaine," *Wall Street Journal,* January 12, 2006; Samuel Walker, Cassia Spohn, and Miriam DeLone, *The Color of Justice: Race, Ethnicity, and Crime in America.* 3rd ed. Belmont, CA: Wadsworth, 2004.

seemingly insignificant disparities at each stage of the criminal justice process may add up to significant overall disparities.

Criminal justice officials need not act in overtly racist ways in order to produce this kind of gap between arrest rates and punishment rates. At each stage of the process, the criminal justice system operates according to principles that, although not overtly discriminatory to men of color, may tend to disadvantage them. For example, one study found that African Americans constituted 13 percent of monthly drug users, 35 percent of arrests for drug possession, 55 percent of convictions, and 74 percent of prison sentences.[26] The number of minority arrests may be greater because police patrols are more heavily concentrated in residential areas where nonwhites live, areas where drug use may be more open and more likely to be observed by police.[27] Because pretrial-release practices take into account factors such as employment status,

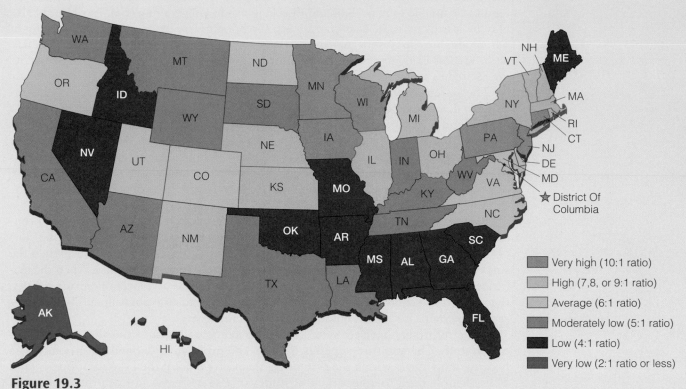

Figure 19.3

Racial Disparity in State Prison Systems: The Ratio of African American Incarceration Rates to White Rates

While southern states tend to have the highest incarceration rates of African Americans, northern states show a larger ratio of African American to white incarceration rates, meaning that the difference between the two rates is greater.

Source: The Sentencing Project, *State Rates of Incarceration by Race* (Washington, DC: Author, 2004).

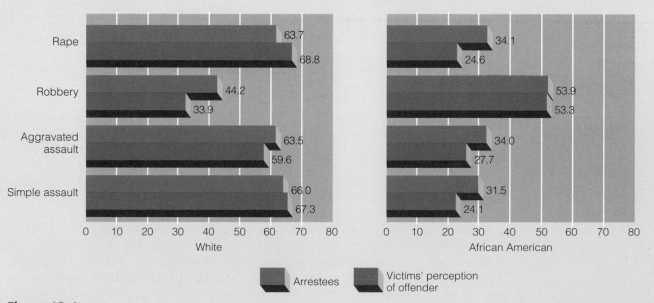

Figure 19.4

Comparison of Uniform Crime Reports and National Crime Victimization Survey Data on Offender Race

The victim's perception of the race of the offender differs from the race of those arrested.

Source: Samuel Walker, Cassia Spohn, and Miriam DeLone, *The Color of Justice: Race, Ethnicity, and Crime in America*, 3rd ed. (Belmont, CA: Wadsworth, 2004), 42, 45.

living arrangements, and prior criminal record, the underemployed and unemployed tend to be unable to make bail and thus languish in jail awaiting trial. Prosecutors also may be less likely to dismiss charges against poor, unemployed, single men—many of whom are African American—especially if they have a prior record. And poor defendants are less likely to have a private attorney. Research has shown that all these factors are related to sentence severity.

These step-by-step decisions of the system mean that African Americans, the unemployed, and the poor often appear at sentencing hearings with more-extensive prior records and fewer prospects for reform. Thus, what appears discriminatory may simply represent the functioning of an impersonal bureaucratic system. After all, evidence of discrimination in sentencing is disputable and ambiguous. One recent survey of studies of sentencing concluded that "although a number of studies have uncovered evidence of racial discrimination in sentencing, others have found no significant differences, . . . [leading to] conflicting conclusions."[28]

Perhaps criminal justice system officials, acting under the daily pressures and routines of bureaucratic decision making, use filtering criteria to move cases along. The criteria they use would be difficult to dispute: When a crime is not serious, when the suspect or defendant appears contrite and unlikely to repeat the offense, when the evidence is weak or contradictory, or when the accused has a respectable prior history, then the system chooses to dismiss the case or downgrade the punishment. Is this truly racism? Perhaps it depends on how one defines the term.

Some reformers have considered ways to eliminate racism from the criminal justice system. The solution depends on how the problem is defined. If racism exists because individuals within the system are themselves racist, then the solution is plain: These people need to adjust their attitudes or else be removed from their jobs. The problem is a bit more complicated if the problem is not racist people but disadvantageous rules and practices, such as treating the unemployed less leniently than those who have jobs. Here the solution would lie in revamping the decision-making criteria to exclude biased factors and in finding ways to control the discretion of officials to use the new criteria.

Society Is Racist

Some people claim that eliminating racism from the criminal justice system is not likely to occur, because the system is embedded in a larger racist society. In fact, the strongest voices claim that the system operates as an instrument of such racism.[29]

There is indeed evidence of broader racism in the way society asks the criminal justice system to operate. For example, some have claimed that prison is used as a place to confine people who cannot find jobs when the economy falters—and many of these unemployed are African American men.[30] Michael Tonry comments that the 1990s war on drugs was "foreordained to affect disadvantaged black youths disproportionately [and was based on] the willingness of the drug war's planners to sacrifice young black Americans."[31]

Many observers further believe that the relationship between racism and the criminal justice system is reciprocal. Devah Pager's study of employment discrimination makes the point that young African American men who have *no* criminal record are less likely to get entry-level jobs than are young white men *with* prison records. In this way, incarceration and racism mutually reinforce each other. The presence of a criminal record further damages the job prospects of young African American men, but the social stigma of being a young African American man is already a barrier to employment.[32] Whatever negative attitudes there are toward the employability of African American men, especially those who are undereducated, the large number of them who go to prison reinforces the stereotype. (See the Focus box "Incarceration and Inequality.") Thus, employers who hire young African American men tend to do so only after completing a criminal history background check, something that is not usually done at the entry level.[33]

Many believe that the criminal justice system is embedded in a larger racist society. They note that the overrepresentation of African Americans in the felony justice system means that 13 percent of African American men are permanently banned from voting. Some believe the 2000 and 2004 presidential elections won by George W. Bush would have had different outcomes if ex-felons had been allowed to vote in all states.

FOCUS ON CORRECTIONAL POLICY

Incarceration and Inequality

The sociologist Bruce Western argues that "mass incarceration"—a "penal system that is without precedent in American history, and unlike any other in the advanced democracies"—has been a cause of large, and growing, racial disparities in the United States. He uses sophisticated statistical methods and new types of data to assess the impact of mass incarceration on African American men.

For example, he shows how going to prison leads to substantial differences in life experiences. Almost one-third of all African American college dropouts are in prison, a rate almost *five times* that of whites. White men are almost 10 times more likely to graduate from college than to go to prison, while African American men are two times more likely to go to prison than to finish college.

The implications of these facts ripple their way through the lives of people who are affected by these men who cycle through the prison system. When the large numbers of men who are behind bars are included in the unemployment rate, the gap between unemployment rates for African American men and every other group in society grows. Going to prison reduces expected hourly wages and dramatically reduces the chance of employment after release—for African Americans, but not for whites. Likewise, going to prison reduces the likelihood of ever getting married for African American men, but not for whites or Hispanics, even after a child is born, and even though incarcerated men are just as likely to have children as are nonincarcerated men. Marriages of all those who have been to prison are more likely to end in divorce.

In short, the growth in the use of incarceration has had devastating effects on the African American men, the labor markets of their communities, and their families and children. These undesirable social effects of incarceration ought to be a matter of significant discussion regarding incarceration policy. For the most part, however, when new legislation about prison sentences is proposed, these matters never arise. Is that a sign of a racist society?

Source: Bruce Western, *Punishment and Inequality in America* (New York: Russell Sage Foundation, 2006); quote from p. 11.

Thus, confronted with the reality of crime committed by people of color, the criminal justice system reacts in a way that reflects public horror and revulsion by removing large numbers of people of color from their communities. Racist institutions, it is argued, help produce the higher crime rate among minorities, and then racist fears of people of color help justify treating them more harshly when they are caught.

racial threat hypothesis
The belief that white fear of African Americans is least when whites are the majority but greatest when African Americans are a substantial minority.

A significant idea underlying this point of view is the **racial threat hypothesis**, which holds that white fear of and antagonism of African Americans will be greatest in areas where the proportion of African Americans approaches that of whites, because in these areas African Americans constitute a greater perceived threat to whites. In areas that are mostly white or mostly African American, whites will feel less threatened. Studies of racial disparities in imprisonment support the racial threat hypothesis, because the rates of incarceration disparity are lowest in places where African Americans are either a very small minority or a very large minority.[34] Studies of policing also find that patterns of drug arrests of African Americans are consistent with the racial threat hypothesis.[35]

Visit the **National Association of Blacks in Criminal Justice** at the corresponding link at www.cengage.com/criminaljustice/clear.

Admittedly, the image of the "black criminal" has been useful to white people for various purposes. In the South, fear of African American rapists of white women was an excuse to lynch some young men and keep the rest in perpetual fear of summary execution. In 1988, the image of Willie Horton, an African American convicted felon released under Massachusetts Governor Michael Dukakis's administration, was purposefully used to fuel white fears of crime and help portray George Bush as "tough on crime." Bush eventually was elected president, with strong support from voters fearful of street crime. The dirty taste of the race-baiting nature of that aspect of the campaign stays with us, even 30 some years later. And in the 1990s, when Susan Smith wanted to cover up her murder of her two young sons, she invented an African American assailant—the general public believed her without batting an eye.

The overrepresentation of African Americans in the felony justice system has also led to an ominous consequence—disenfranchisement. All but four states (Vermont, Utah, Massachusetts, and Maine) forbid voting by felons who are incarcerated, but over half the states deny the right to vote to anyone under correctional supervision (whether in custody or in the community), and seven states deny the vote to all ex-felons. An estimated 13 percent of African American men—1.4 million—are *permanently* banned from voting in the states where they live.[36]

The loss of the vote has, for these Americans, denied access to political participation in a way that has racially disparate effects. Critics of this policy point out that a high percentage of African American men are, as a consequence, prevented from influencing political policies that affect their lives. The problem is not small. In Florida, for example, where nearly a half million men are denied the vote as a consequence of their felony record, if *two-tenths of a percent* of that group had voted in the 2001 election, Al Gore would almost certainly have been elected president, because he was overwhelmingly supported by African Americans who did vote. The policy is seen as so indefensible in some circles that proposals have been developed to enable some felons to vote, even if they are still under sentence.[37]

If people of color are overrepresented in the justice system because the larger society is racist, the solution may seem a bit daunting. Nobody knows a way to rapidly rid our society of policies, practices, and, perhaps most importantly, attitudes of racism. Even an optimist would think that a generation or more of vigilance to eradicate racism might be necessary.

■ WHICH IS IT: RACE OR RACISM?

We can illustrate how complicated this issue is with a hypothetical case. Suppose that Wilson, who is white, and Edwards, who is African American, were each convicted of burglary. If Wilson received probation with a $5,000 fine and 200 hours of community service while Edwards received six months in jail, would you think that the verdict was racist?

Young African American and Hispanic men contend that they are always being hassled by police. Is this racism, or effective police work?

Would it change your opinion to learn that, at sentencing, Wilson's attorney argued that a jail term would cost Wilson his job as a construction worker and would leave his unemployed wife and two children without a source of financial support? Or to learn that Edwards had no job and that his two children had already been living without his income as he sat in jail, awaiting trial? When the law tries to take into account these sorts of concerns, however reasonable they seem, it runs the risk of inadvertently penalizing those who have fewer resources.

The situation becomes even more complicated if we learn that this is Wilson's first offense but Edwards's second. The jail term makes a bit more sense for a repeat offender. But we have to keep in mind that young African American men often experience arrests that result in charges being dropped, for whatever reason. To consider such arrests at sentencing may be unfair and indirectly biased.

What if the reason Wilson received a fine is that he had a job in the first place and could afford to pay? Edwards might claim that he went to jail because he was unemployed, but that if the system would help him get a job he could pay a fine.

All these scenarios raise the question of whether the system is reasonable, biased, or simply part of a larger set of social inequities. There is no obvious answer.

Visit a website that discusses **racism and corrections**; see the corresponding link at www.cengage.com/criminaljustice/clear.

■ THE SIGNIFICANCE OF RACE AND PUNISHMENT

In some respects, it does not matter which of the competing views is most accurate. The real repercussions of racial disparities in the criminal justice system have already become a force that criminal justice policy makers must face.

The fact that such a high percentage of young African American men are behind bars must be understood in terms of what these young men cannot be doing. They cannot be earning a living, attending school, parenting their children, or supporting their partners; they cannot be voting or otherwise partaking of "free" society. We can only speculate about the implications of the fact that so many of this generation's young men of

MYTHS IN CORRECTIONS

INCARCERATION OF YOUNG FATHERS

THE MYTH: The way families are affected by incarceration of young fathers is felt equally by all racial groups.

THE REALITY: Almost one in ten (9.3 percent) of all African American children had a father in prison or jail, compared with 3.5 percent of Hispanic children and 1.2 percent of white children.

Source: Bruce Western, *Punishment and Inequality in America* (New York: Russell Sage Foundation, 2006).

color have passed through the criminal justice system. But we also must wonder whether this experience might not further alienate this group and prevent them from identifying with the society that sent them there. Does growing up with fathers, uncles, and brothers absent from home because of the system breed respect for the law, or revulsion and enmity, in the many children affected this way? Does the prison stand as a fearful symbol of deterrence or as a contemptible symbol of the inevitable power of the state to disrupt a person's life? In the effort to establish and preserve order, does the disproportionate impact of corrections on people of color instead produce suspicion and even social disruption? In short, does the heavy-handed use of the criminal justice system in minority communities exacerbate the very problems of social disorder it is trying to restore? See "Myths in Corrections" for more.

Whatever the real reason behind the disparities in the criminal justice system, many citizens believe such disparities exist because of racism, and at least as many citizens do not. The result is a polarization of attitudes about race that discolors the capacity of our society to remember its traditional values of fairness, equity, and equal opportunity.

How do we interpret the problems of race that we see in our corrections system? And what can we do to overcome them?

Most people believe there are three solutions. First, we must open the corrections system to greater participation by people who come from the groups historically disadvantaged by the disparate treatment. Special efforts to employ young men and women from minority groups will in the long run reduce the predominance of white policy makers in this area. Studies of African American police officers, judges, and correctional officers find that their decisions about cases are remarkably similar to those of their white co-workers, but their greater presence in criminal justice roles of authority benefits everyone.

Second, we must ferret out and refuse to tolerate incidents of blatant racism in justice practices or policy. This is easier said than done, of course, because there is so much disagreement about what exactly a racist policy is. For example, should people who do not have jobs be as eligible for bail as those who have stakes in the community? Should

Public pressure brought about the release after a year in prison of 14-year-old Shaquanda Cotton of Paris, Texas. She was given a seven-year sentence for shoving a teacher's aide at her high school. A 14-year-old white girl, convicted of arson for burning down her family's house, was sentenced by the same judge to probation.

© ANTONIO PEREZ/MCT/Landov

police spend as much time aggressively combating white-collar crime as they do street crime? Ensuring that criminal justice policies are free of racial and ethnic bias is nonetheless a high priority for tomorrow's correctional leaders.

Finally, we must recognize that as long as racism is a force in the larger society, any attempts to eradicate it from the criminal justice system will have only marginal prospects for success. As long as some groups are unfairly excluded from society's opportunities, they will feel less stake in obeying its laws. And the corrections system will be their adversary.

SUMMARY

1 Understand the meaning of race and ethnicity.

Race and ethnicity are complex concepts. Race is usually assumed to be a biological concept that divides humankind into categories related to skin color and other physical features. Social scientists, however, also look at the ways in which groups define themselves and are defined by others. Today the concept of race is controversial: That so many Americans have interracial backgrounds makes accepting a purely biological approach difficult. Race is also controversial to the extent that it has political and social implications. For example, many transfers of funds from the federal government to the states for social programs are calculated according to race-based formulas. Ethnicity is a concept used to divide people according to their cultural characteristics—language, religion, and group traditions. Ethnicity is usually reported by subjects themselves, rather than stemming from an outside observer making a visual identification, as in the case of race. Although we tend to think of ethnic groups as existing among white Americans—for example Irish, Italians, Poles—the concept can also be used to distinguish ethnic groups within the black, Asian, and Hispanic communities.

2 Recognize how varying visions of race and punishment influence our thinking on this issue.

There are three main viewpoints about the disproportionate involvement of people of color in the criminal justice system. (1) People argue that the proportions stem from differential criminality. More people of color end up in corrections because they commit worse crimes and have more-serious prior records than do whites. Some people believe that sociobiological factors result in large numbers of Hispanics and African Americans being processed by the criminal justice system, but there is little evidence to support this view. A less-extreme version of this argument rests on the fact that criminality is related to socioeconomic disadvantage, which many people of color suffer. (2) Some argue that the criminal justice system is racist. Racial disparities become racial discrimination if people who are otherwise similar in their criminality are treated differently by the criminal justice system because of their race. For example, African Americans are arrested for drug offenses at more than twice the rate of whites, even though African American youths have substantially lower rates of use of most legal and illegal drugs. Reforming the system depends on how we define the problem—in terms of racist attitudes or in terms of social disparities related to race. (3) Finally, some claim that society itself is racist. They argue that eliminating racism from the criminal justice system is not likely to occur, because the system is embedded in a larger racist society. Many observers further believe that the relationship between racism and the criminal justice system is reciprocal. Racist institutions, it is argued, help produce the higher crime rate among minorities, and then racist fears of people of color help justify treating them more harshly when they are caught.

3 Describe the significance of race and punishment.

The repercussions of racial disparities in the criminal justice system remain a problem that criminal justice policy makers must face. Most people believe there are three solutions. First, we must open up the corrections system to greater participation by people who come from the groups historically disadvantaged by the disparate treatment. Second, we must ferret out and refuse to tolerate incidents of blatant racism in justice practices or policy. Finally, we must recognize that as long as racism is a force in the larger society, any attempts to eradicate it from the criminal justice system will have only marginal prospects for success. As long as some groups are unfairly excluded from society's opportunities, they will feel less stake in obeying its laws.

KEY TERMS

discrimination (p. 527)
disparity (p. 527)

ethnicity (p. 526)
race (p. 526)

racial threat hypothesis (p. 536)
self-report study (p. 527)

FOR DISCUSSION

1. What are the five main reasons that people of color are overrepresented in the criminal justice system? Does overrepresentation represent a problem? What, if anything, can be done to change the pattern?
2. What impact does a high incarceration rate have on minority communities? What implications does this impact have for the effectiveness of the criminal justice system?
3. How does the close relationship between politics and criminal justice policy reflect issues of race and punishment?
4. If you were writing a sentencing code, would you give people lighter sentences if they came from disadvantaged backgrounds? Why or why not?
5. What are the most important steps to take to reduce racial differences in punishments? Why?

FOR FURTHER READING

Gabbidon, Shaun L., Helen Taylor Greene, and Vernetta D. Young, eds. *African-American Classics in Criminology and Criminal Justice.* Thousand Oaks, CA: Sage, 2002. A collection of essays by African American intellectuals, past and present, regarding race, crime, and justice.

Mincy, Robert B., ed. *Black Males Left Behind.* Washington, DC: Urban Institute Press, 2006. A series of essays on the labor market and lifetime workforce participation of black men.

Pager, Devah. *Marked: Race, Crime, and Finding Work in an Era of Mass Incarceration.* Chicago: University of Chicago Press, 2007. A series of studies that demonstrate how the growth of incarceration is the foundation for the way African American men are discriminated against in the job market.

Peterson, Ruth, Lauren Krivo, and John Hagan, eds. *The Many Colors of Crime: Inequalities of Race, Ethnicity, and Crime in America.* New York: NYU Press, 2006. An anthology of empirical and theoretical studies of the racial politics and racial outcomes of the crime and the criminal justice system.

Russell-Brown, Katherine. *The Color of Crime.* New York: NYU Press, 2009. A study of the social and political basis for racial disparity in crime and justice.

The Sentencing Project. *Reducing Racial Disparity in the Criminal Justice System: A Manual for Practitioners and Policymakers.* Washington, DC: The Sentencing Project, 2008. Explores the causes of racial disparities in the justice system and provides a series of recommendations for laws and programs to reduce disparity.

Walker, Samuel, Cassia Spohn, and Miriam DeLone. *The Color of Justice: Race, Ethnicity, and Crime in America.* 4th ed. Belmont, CA: Wadsworth, 2007. Gives an up-to-date review of studies of race, crime, and justice at all stages of the criminal justice system, from arrest to punishment.

Western, Bruce. *Punishment and Inequality in America.* New York: Russell Sage Foundation, 2006. Exhaustive empirical analysis of the way prison growth has affected young African American men and contributed to racial inequality.

NOTES

1 Bruce Western, *Punishment and Inequality in America* (New York: Russell Sage Foundation, 2006).

2 Justice Policy Institute, *Cellblocks or Classrooms? The Funding of Higher Education and Corrections and Its Impact on African American Men* (Washington, DC: Author, September 2002).

3 See Manning Marable, "Racism, Prisons, and the Future of Black America," *Peacework Magazine*, December 2001–January 2001, http://www.peaceworkmagazine.org/pwork/1200/122k05.htm.

4 Calculated from BJS *Bulletin:* May 2006, p. 8; November 2006, Table 11.

5 BJS *Special Report,* August 2003, p. 1.

6 Howard N. Snyder and Melissa Sickmund, *Juvenile Offenders and Victims: 2006 National Report* (Pittsburgh: National Center for Juvenile Justice, March 2006), 189.

7 Samuel Walker, Cassia Spohn, and Miriam DeLone, *The Color of Justice: Race, Ethnicity, and Crime in America*, 4th ed. (Belmont, CA: Wadsworth, 2007), 15–16.

8 Two classic examples are offered by James Q. Wilson and Richard J. Herrnstein, *Crime and Human Nature* (New York: Simon & Schuster, 1985) and Richard J. Herrnstein and Charles Murray, *The Bell Curve: Intelligence and Class Structure in American Life* (New York: Free Press, 1994).

9 James F. Wallerstein and Clement J. Wyle, "Our Law-Abiding Law-Breakers," *Probation* 35 (April 1947): 107–19.

10 Travis Hirschi, *Causes of Delinquency* (Berkeley: University of California Press, 1969).

11 U.S. Census Bureau, "Income Stable, Poverty Rate Increases, Percentage of Americans without Health Insurance Unchanged," *News Release*, August 30, 2005.

12 Walker, Spohn, and DeLone, *Color of Justice*, ch. 3.

13 Eric A. Stewart and Ronald L. Simmons, *The Code of the Street and African-American Adolescent Violence* (Washington, DC: U.S. Department of Justice, February 2009).

14 John J. DiIulio, Jr., "The Question of Black Crime," *Public Interest*, Fall 1994, p. 3.

15 Federal Bureau of Investigation, *Crime in the United States, 2005* (Washington, DC: Author, 2006), Table 43.

16 Alfred Blumstein, "On the Racial Disproportionality of the United States' Prison Population," *Journal of Criminal Law and Criminology* 73 (1982): 1259–81.

17 John DiIulio, "Let 'em Rot," *Wall Street Journal,* January 26, 1995, ed. page.

18 FBI, *Crime in the United States, 2005,* Table 43.

19 Lloyd D. Johnston, Patrick M. O'Malley, Jerald G. Bachman, and John E. Schulenberg, *Monitoring the Future, National Results on Adolescent Drug Use, Overview of Key Findings, 2005* (Washington, DC: National Institute on Drug Abuse, April 2006).

20 Bruce Western, *Punishment and Inequality in America* (New York: Russell Sage Foundation, 2006), 41.

21 Human Rights Watch, "Punishment and Prejudice: Racial Disparities in the War on Drugs," *Human Rights Watch Report* 12 (no. 2[G], May 2000): 20.

22 Howard N. Snyder and Melissa Sickmund, *Juvenile Offenders and Victims: 2006 National Report* (Pittsburgh: National Center for Juvenile Justice, March 2006), 125.

23 Alfred Blumstein, Jacqueline Cohen, Susan Martin, and Michael Tory, eds., *Research on Sentencing: The Search for Reform* (Washington, DC: National Academy Press, 1983), 9.

24 Christopher Hartney and Linh Vuong, *Created Equal: Racial and Ethnic Disparities in the Criminal Justice System* (San Francisco: National Council on Crime and Delinquency, March 2009).

25 Roy L. Austin and Mark D. Allen, "Racial Disparity in Arrest Rates as an Explanation of Racial Disparity in Commitment to Pennsylvania's Prisons," *Journal of Research in Crime and Delinquency* 27 (no. 2, May 2000): 200–220.

26 Fox Butterfield, "More Blacks in their 20's Have Trouble with the Law," *New York Times,* October 5, 1995, p. A18.

27 Andrew Golub, Bruce D. Johnson, and Eloise Dunlap, "The Race/Ethnicity Disparity in Misdemeanor Marijuana Arrests in New York City," *Criminology and Public Policy* 6 (no. 1, February 2007): 131–64.

28 Samuel Walker, Cassia Spohn, and Miriam DeLone, *The Color of Justice: Race, Ethnicity, and Crime in America,* 3rd ed. (Belmont, CA: Wadsworth, 2004), 243.

29 Andrew Grant-Thomas and john a. powell, "Toward a Structural Racism Framework," *Poverty and Race* 15 (no. 6, November–December 2006): 3–6.

30 Katherine Beckett and Theodore Sasson, *The Politics of Injustice: Crime and Punishment in America* (Thousand Oaks, CA: Pine Forge Press, 2000).

31 Michael Tonry, *Malign Neglect: Race, Crime, and Punishment in America* (New York: Oxford University Press, 1995), 123.

32 Devah Pager, *Marked: Race, Crime, and Finding Work in an Era of Mass Incarceration* (Chicago: University of Chicago Press, 2007).

33 Harry J. Holzer, Stephan Raphael, and Michael A. Stoll, "Perceived Criminality, Criminal Background Checks and the Racial Hiring Practices of Employers" (paper presented to the Russell Sage Working Group on Mass Incarceration and Labor, New York, March 4, 2004).

34 Bradley Keen and David Jenkins, "Racial Threat, Partisan Politics and Racial Disparities in Prison Admissions: A Panel Analysis," *Criminology* 47 (no. 1, February 2009): 209–38.

35 David Eitle and Susanne Monahan, "Revisiting the Racial Threat Thesis: The Role of Police Organizational Characteristics in Predicting Race-Specific Drug Arrest Rates," *Justice Quarterly* 26 (no. 3, September 2009): 528–61.

36 Jeff Manza and Christopher Uggen, *Locked Out: Felon Disenfranchisement and American Democracy* (New York: Oxford University Press, 2007).

37 Paul Zielbauer, "Felon Voting Law Revised in Light of 2000 Election," *New York Times,* May 15, 2001, p. A24.

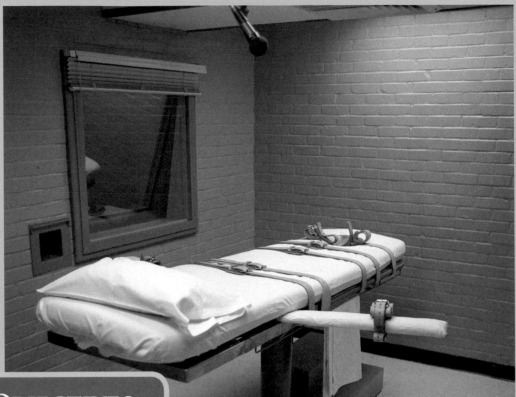

© Andrew Lichtenstein/Aurora Photos

Lethal injection is thought to be the most humane way of carrying out the death penalty. Although the U.S. Supreme Court upheld the procedure, questions remain regarding the drugs used, their administration, and the role of medical personnel in the process.

LEARNING OBJECTIVES

After reading this chapter you should be able to . . .

1 Contrast the issues in the debate over capital punishment.

2 Understand the history of the death penalty in America.

3 Discuss the legal issues that surround the death penalty.

4 Characterize the inmates on death row.

5 Speculate about the future of capital punishment.

IT TOOK MORE THAN a half hour for Angel Diaz to die by lethal injection in Florida on December 14, 2006, and then only after he had received a second dose of the chemicals. Witnesses said he appeared to be moving after the first injection, his eyes open, and at times he seemed to mouth words. He suffered 11-inch and 12-inch chemical burns on his arms in the process. Diaz's execution was the latest of several executions that were botched, including one in Ohio where the inmate raised his head in the middle of his own execution to say, "It's not working."[1] Following the Diaz execution, then-Governor Jeb Bush ordered a suspension of executions until changes in the lethal injection procedures and other reforms could be initiated.

A three-drug protocol had been developed in the late 1970s as a fail-safe execution method. Three poisonous chemicals are injected, in succession, into the bloodstream of the condemned. The first, a barbiturate, is designed to sedate the offender and suppress respiration. The second, a neuromuscular paralytic, halts breathing and body convulsions. The third, a

THE DEATH PENALTY

potassium electrolyte, stops the heart. Usually a medical examiner can confirm the death within minutes—but not always.

Over the past decade virtually every state with an active death penalty has seen legal challenges to the use of lethal injection. Courts in some states have ruled that a doctor must be present during the execution to monitor the condemned for signs of pain. The American Medical Association states that physicians who take part in executions violate medical ethics. In other cases the type of drugs, their amount, and their combination have also been attacked as inducing suffering, thus violating the cruel and unusual punishments clause of the Eighth Amendment.

In 2008 the Supreme Court addressed this issue. By a 7–2 vote in *Baze v. Rees* (2008), justices ruled that it had not been shown that the use of the three-drug lethal injection protocol violates the "cruel and unusual punishments" clause. In a separate concurring opinion, Justice John Paul Stevens wrote that *Baze* will generate debate "not only about the constitutionality of the three-drug protocol, and specifically about the justification for the use of the paralytic agent, ... but also about the justification for the death penalty itself." He said that after 30 years on the Court he had concluded that the death penalty represents "the pointless and needless extinction of life . . . that is in clear violation of the Eight Amendment."[2]

Lethal injection is the latest attempt to impose capital punishment in a way that is legal and fair and will not offend modern cultural sensibilities. Over the past hundred years capital punishment has changed from the noose to the firing squad to the gas chamber to the electric chair. Each change in technique stemmed from the idea that the new method would be more civilized and less gruesome. However, each method has had its drawbacks, resulting in bodies twitching, burning, and gagging—often for extended periods. Lethal injection was supposed to avoid at least the appearance of cruel and unusual punishment. The assumption was that the offender would merely lie down on a gurney, receive an injection, fall asleep, and die.

There seems to be a new uncertainty about capital punishment. The challenges to the use of lethal injection represent only one of several trends, including fewer executions, fewer offenders being sent to death row, increased numbers of death row inhabitants

Chapter

20

cleared by DNA, and the abolition of capital punishment in New Jersey (2007) and New Mexico (2009). Yet, as a Gallup public opinion poll in November 2008 found, more than two-thirds of people in this country still support capital punishment for murderers. Why is there such ambivalence toward the death penalty?[3]

In this chapter we focus on the moral, political, and legal issues of the death penalty debate. In addition, we examine the factors associated with death row, including the death row population, which contains a disproportionate number of poor, undereducated, minority men.

■ THE DEBATE OVER CAPITAL PUNISHMENT

AP Images/Marcio Jose Sanchez

Many opponents of capital punishment argue on humanitarian grounds that it is wrong for the state to kill people. Supporters of capital punishment argue that justice demands that offenders pay for their crimes. What other arguments do people on both sides of the issue make?

Retribution, deterrence, and incapacitation are usually cited as the reasons for keeping the death penalty. Retribution reflects the belief that one who takes another's life deserves a punishment equal to the victim's fate, deterrence reflects the hope that the execution will deter others from crime, and incapacitation reflects the desire to keep the offender from committing further crimes.

Ernest van den Haag, a supporter of capital punishment, notes that arguments about the death penalty are either moral or utilitarian. He has summarized his moral argument supporting retribution as follows: "Anyone who takes another's life should not be encouraged to expect that he will outlive his victim at public expense. Murder must forfeit the murderer's life, if there is to be justice."[4] Opponents of the death penalty argue that only God has the right to take a life; the state does not. Opponents also emphasize that mistakes can and have been made, resulting in innocent people being executed. Further, they claim that the death penalty discriminates against poor people and racial minorities, because they disproportionately receive this sentence. Van den Haag counters by claiming that abolitionists would continue to oppose capital punishment even if they could be certain that "none but the guilty are executed, and without discrimination or capriciousness."[5]

The utilitarian argument for capital punishment is based on the belief that executions of wrongdoers deter others from committing the crime. The general deterrence position sounds reasonable to most people, yet there is no effective means to prove it scientifically. Some argue that it is impossible to show if someone was actually deterred from an action because they recognized the consequences.[6]

However, over 200 studies have looked closely at murder rates, comparing states that have the death penalty with those that do not.[7] Most of these studies have found no deterrent effect of the penalty. For example, Ruth Peterson and William Bailey examined homicide rates in adjacent states over a 12-year period. They found that the murder rate in states *with* the death penalty was higher than in those without it.[8] A 2000 study found that the 12 states with no death penalty shared lower homicide rates, and four states with differing capital punishment policies—California, Michigan, New York, and Texas—did not differ in their rates (see **Figure 20.1**).[9] Richard Lempert has echoed the findings of most researchers by concluding, "The death penalty in general and executions in particular do not deter homicide."[10]

Challenging much of the deterrence research, the economist Isaac Ehrlich argued in 1975 that each execution in the United States from 1933 to 1969 prevented seven or eight murders because of the deterrent effect.[11] His findings were greeted eagerly by death penalty supporters. However, his methodology was almost immediately questioned.[12]

A panel of the National Academy of Sciences reanalyzed Ehrlich's data and found no deterrent effect.[13]

The public argument runs along the same lines as the academic debate. According to supporters, the death penalty indeed deters criminals from committing violent acts—individuals will be less likely to kill if they know that they face execution for doing so. In addition, the death penalty serves justice by paying killers back for their horrible crimes. Society exacts an appropriate measure of revenge ("an eye for an eye"), and victims' families can be reassured that the murderer received a just punishment and

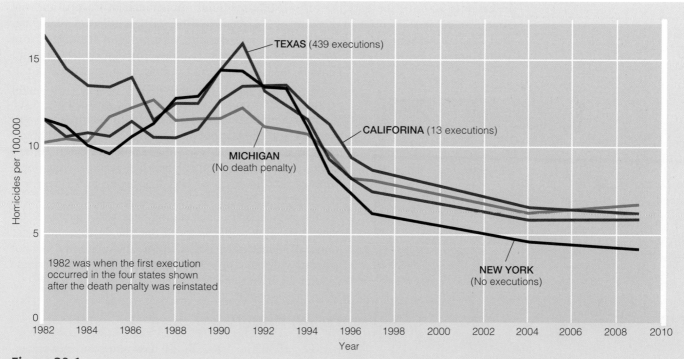

Figure 20.1

Comparing Homicide Rates and Executions in Four States

The homicide rates in four states with different approaches to the death penalty follow a similar trend. Texas has the highest number of executions. California has the largest death row population but few executions, New York abolished the death penalty in 2004 and has had no executions, and Michigan has no death penalty.

Sources: Death Penalty Information Center, http://www.deathpenaltyinfo.org, June 2009; *New York Times*, September 22, 2000, p. A19; U.S. Department of Justice, *Crime in the United States, 2008* (U.S. Government Printing Office, 2009).

Articles and information
supporting the death penalty
can be found at the corresponding
link at www.cengage.com/
criminaljustice/clear.

You can find resources considering
**ethical issues of the death
penalty** at the corresponding
link at www.cengage.com/
criminaljustice/clear.

The **Death Penalty Information
Center** is a major organization
that opposes capital punishment.
The center's website is
listed at www.cengage.com/
criminaljustice/clear.

will not kill others. By executing murderers, society emphasizes the high value placed on life. The death penalty also prevents murderers from doing further harm. Finally, the death penalty is less expensive than holding violent criminals in prison for decades or for life. By executing these serious offenders, the state can save up to $1 million in incarceration costs over the lifetime of each murderer.

According to opponents of capital punishment, there is no evidence that the death penalty deters violent crime. Many people who kill are under the influence of alcohol or drugs, psychologically disturbed, in an emotional rage, or otherwise unable to control themselves. Thus, the threat of capital punishment never enters their minds when they commit violent crimes. In addition, it is wrong for a government to participate in the intentional killing of its citizens. State-sponsored executions convey the harmful message that life is cheap and that violence is an appropriate response to violence. Further, the death penalty is applied in a discriminatory fashion. Historically, members of racial/ethnic minority groups convicted of murder have been significantly more likely to receive the death penalty than have members of the majority group. Also, poor defendants who cannot obtain pretrial release on bail and who are represented by public defenders are more likely to receive the death penalty than are other convicted murderers. Finally, innocent people have been executed.

THE DEATH PENALTY IN AMERICA

The death penalty has generated controversy ever since colonial times. As discussed in Chapter 2, until the middle of the 1700s, criminal punishment in Europe and the American colonies focused on the body of the offender. Along with mutilation, whipping, and dismemberment, death was a common punishment for a range of felonies—from premeditated murder, to striking one's mother or father (New York), to witchcraft and adultery (Massachusetts). Executions were carried out in public until the 1830s, when most were withdrawn behind prison walls.[14] In some regions, however, particularly in the West and South, public executions continued into the twentieth century. The last public execution in the United States took place on August 14, 1936, when an estimated 20,000 spectators converged on the small town of Owensboro, Kentucky.[15] The death penalty has strong historical roots in American culture.

Captain Green and Sergeant Etlinger are members of the tie-down team at Huntsville Prison in Texas. The team is responsible for all procedures from the time the inmate is escorted into the chamber until he is declared dead by medical personnel. Would you want to be a member of this team?

Yet, even though capital punishment was common, as far back as the 1600s critics argued that the death penalty was immoral, an ineffective deterrent, "a violation of the ideal of proportionality in sentencing, and a breach of the increasingly widespread belief that the criminal could be reformed."[16]

Death Row Population

Between 1930 and 1967, 3,859 men and women were executed by state and federal authorities (see **Figure 20.2**). In 1935, 199 people were put to death; after that the number of executions began to fall steadily. An average of 128 individuals per year were executed during the 1940s, 72 during the 1950s, and 19 during the 1960s until 1967, when the Supreme Court ordered a stay of executions pending a hearing on the issue. This decline led many observers to believe that the United States, like the countries of Europe, ultimately would cease applying the death penalty either by law or de facto through lack of use.[17] But this was not the case. After the Supreme Court reaffirmed

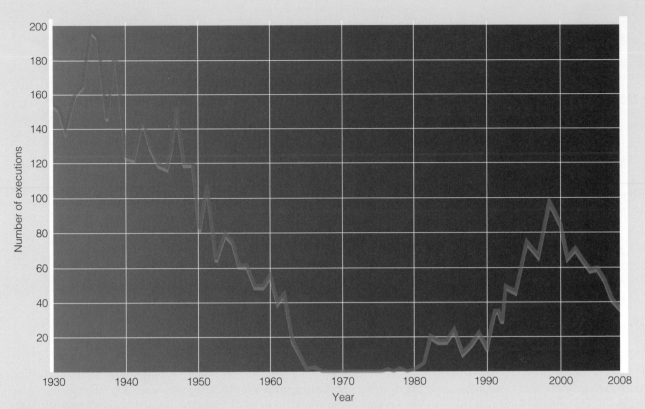

Figure 20.2
People Executed in the United States

The steady decline in executions after 1940 gave abolitionists the impression that, as in Europe, the death penalty would eventually become a thing of the past. That belief was shattered when states resumed executions in 1977.

Source: NAACP Legal Defense and Education Fund, *Death Row USA* (New York, NAACP, Winter 2009), 9.

the constitutionality of the death penalty in 1976, state legislatures quickly enacted new laws providing for the execution of convicted murderers under some circumstances, and executions resumed. From 1977 to June 2009, 1,125 men and 11 women have been executed.

The numbers of people facing the death penalty has increased dramatically since 1976. (See the Focus box "The Deathman.") As of January 1, 2009, 3,239 men and 58 women were awaiting execution. Only during the past several years has the number of people on death row begun to fall.[18] The number of people sentenced to death reached a 30-year low in 2008, when 111 inmates were sent to death row.[19] This is less than half the average of 297 who were given the death penalty each year from 1994 to 2000. Death penalty opponents argue that the decrease in sentence of death reflects a public wary of executions, "heightened by concerns about whether the punishment is administered fairly and publicity about those wrongly convicted."[20]

Public Opinion

In a democracy, public opinion usually has an important impact on public policy. Since 1936, the Gallup Organization has been asking the public, "Do you favor or oppose the death penalty for persons convicted of murder?" Responses to this question have shifted greatly over the past 80 years. Although the majority of Americans favored

FOCUS ON

PEOPLE IN CORRECTIONS

The Deathman

When Louisiana reinstated the death penalty in 1976 it needed a public executioner. Those who had held the position prior to *Furman v. Georgia* had died, grown old, or retired from the killing business. Louisiana's problem was soon solved when a Baton Rouge electrician volunteered his services. He was appointed to the post and given the alias "Sam Jones."

Why become an executioner? "I believe in it," Jones explained. He emphasized that the money he's paid has little to do with his being an executioner. On the contrary, he said that it actually costs him money. "I go in the hole on these executions," he said, "Sometimes it costs me $800 to fly and I only get $400. I usually hand that to the kids and they use it in their church, or whatever." . . .

Sam had no professional expertise as an executioner when he was hired, but it didn't matter. Louisiana was willing to allow him to learn the art of execution (using the electric chair) through on-the-job training, trial and error. He recalled his first execution, that of Robert Wayne Williams in 1983. "Everybody has their doubts when they do something for the first time and, sure, I had mine. The first time I was nervous because it was the first time. I didn't doubt I could do it, but I didn't know what to expect. I had no previous experience, and I'd never seen one [an execution] before."

Sam was shown color post-execution photographs of Robert Wayne Williams, and asked if he had seen the burns on Williams's body before. There was a long pause while he studied the pictures. "No, I've never seen that," he said, shaking his head. "That's the first time I've seen that. I didn't see that on him when they had him in the chair. It may have come

up later. I don't know what happens to 'em, what procedure the body goes through after they're electrocuted."

Asked if he had seen similar burns on any of the other eighteen men he has executed, he answered: "No, I don't remember seeing it on 'em. As soon as they take 'em out of the chair, they put 'em a body bag and they're gone."

Sam discreetly arrives at the death house shortly before the execution and waits behind the wall adjacent to the electric chair while the shackled prisoner enters the death chamber and is strapped into the chair by prison security officers. Through a small rectangular window in the wall, he observes the ritual and waits for the warden's nod—the signal for him to push the button that sends thousands of volts of electricity burning through the condemned. He departs just as secretly as he arrived. Unlike most executioners throughout history, Sam is not asked to do very much. His sole duty has been reduced to pushing a button, . . . though Louisiana's requirement that the executioner be a certified electrician implies a larger responsibility.

Sam Jones performed his last execution in Louisiana on July 22, 1991. Corrections authorities said that regardless of how executions are conducted in the future, the services of "Sam Jones" would no longer be needed, bringing his tenure as official state executioner to an end.

Source: This interview with Sam Jones was conducted by the editors of *The Angolite*, the newspaper of the Louisiana State Penitentiary. Excerpted from Wilbert Rideau and Ron Wikberg, *Life Sentences: Rage and Survival Behind Bars* (New York: Times Books, 1992), 311–18.

---

capital punishment until 1960, public support gradually declined, reaching a low of 40 percent in 1965. However, with the rise in crime in the late 1960s, opinion shifted to a tougher stance.[21] Legislators, always ready to respond to public concerns, began to press for changes in sentencing laws and urged that the death penalty be reinstituted. By 1994 a major reversal of public opinion had taken place, with 80 percent of Americans supporting the death penalty. Since that high point, the percentage has gradually dropped; by October 2008 it was 64 percent. When given an explicit alternative to the death penalty—life imprisonment with no chance for parole—the percentage of Americans favoring the death penalty drops to 48 percent. **Figure 20.3** traces these shifts in public support for the death penalty.[22]

However, some analysts argue that opinion on the death penalty is somewhat confusing. They say it is difficult to determine whether the public is supporting capital punishment in general, or whether people are merely supporting the right of the

The story of Sister Helen Prejean, "**Angel on Death Row**," is found at the corresponding website at www.cengage.com/criminaljustice/clear.

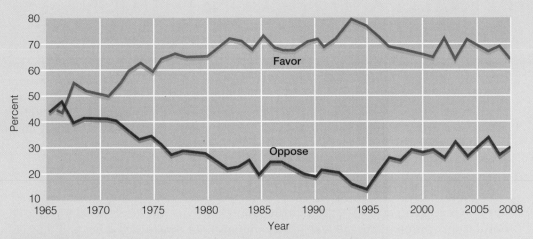

Figure 20.3
Attitudes toward the Death Penalty for People Convicted of Murder

After 1965 public opinion in favor of the death penalty increased greatly for decades. However, after climbing to a high of 80 percent in 1994, support for capital punishment for convicted murderers has generally declined. What factors may have brought about this change?

Note: Respondents were asked, "Are you in favor of the death penalty for a person convicted of murder?" Percentages do not add up to 100 because 5–7 percent of the respondents each year were undecided.

Sources: Bureau of Justice Statistics, *Sourcebook of Criminal Justice Statistics* (Washington, DC: U.S. Government Printing Office, 2000), 134; Death Penalty Information Center, http://deathpenaltyinfo.org/, June 23, 2009.

government to take a life under specific circumstances. Much depends on the wording of the question.[23]

Others point to the fact that support for capital punishment plunges when alternatives, such as life imprisonment without the possibility of parole (LWOP), are presented, as we have seen. Mark Costanzo says that the public is about evenly split when respondents are asked to choose between LWOP and death.[24] More than 20 percent of those who support capital punishment switch to LWOP when given the option. A survey of Tennessee prosecutors, public defenders, and state legislators found that support for the death penalty declines when LWOP is an option.[25] Even in such strong death penalty states as Arkansas, Georgia, Indiana, and Oklahoma, the split is about even.[26] Costanzo believes that if the public could be assured that the murderers would never be released on parole, they would be less supportive of capital punishment.[27] In their analysis of the LWOP option, Robert Lifton and Greg Mitchell found that one-third of those who support the death penalty prefer LWOP as an alternative.[28]

However, in a survey of several hundred respondents in a large U.S. city, other researchers found continued high support for the death penalty.[29] Given 17 homicide scenarios and asked the appropriate sentence—death, LWOP, or a prison term—60.8 percent called for death. This may seem low compared with the Gallup Poll results, but it is still quite high when compared with the actual percentage of murder convicts who are sentenced to death—only about 2 percent.

With 35 states and the federal government now authorizing capital punishment, 111 death sentences were pronounced in 2008.[30] Again, today almost 3,300 people wait on death row. However, as of this writing, the number of executions since 1976 has never exceeded 98 (in 1999) in any one year. Capital punishment remains a controversial issue, one that the courts, correctional professionals, scholars, and the public seem unable to resolve.

■ THE DEATH PENALTY AND THE CONSTITUTION

Death obviously differs from other punishments in that it is final and irreversible. As a result, the Supreme Court has examined the decision-making process in capital cases to ensure that the Constitution's requirements regarding due process, equal protection, and cruel and unusual punishments are fulfilled. Because life is in the balance, capital cases must be conducted according to higher standards of fairness and more-careful procedures than are other kinds of cases. Several important Supreme Court cases illustrate this imperative.

Key U.S. Supreme Court Decisions

In *Furman v. Georgia* (1972), the Supreme Court ruled that the death penalty was itself not unconstitutional, but the way it was administered constituted cruel and unusual punishment. The justices pointed to the ambiguity of the wording in the statutes of some states and the lack of systematic administration of the sentence. Although a majority of justices objected to the way in which the death penalty was applied, they could not agree on reasons why it was unconstitutional. Two justices argued that the death penalty always violates the Eighth Amendment's prohibition on cruel and unusual punishments, but other members emphasized that the procedures used to impose death sentences were arbitrary and unfair. The decision invalidated the death penalty laws of 39 states and the District of Columbia.[31]

Over the next several years, 35 states enacted new capital punishment statutes that provided for more-careful decision making and more-modern methods of execution, such as lethal injection. The new laws were tested before the Supreme Court in 1976 in the case of *Gregg v. Georgia*.[32] The Court upheld those laws that required the sentencing judge or jury to take into account specific aggravating and mitigating factors in deciding which convicted murderers should be sentenced to death. Instead of deciding the defendant's guilt and imposing the death sentence in the same proceeding, states created "bifurcated" proceedings in which a trial determines guilt or innocence, and then a separate hearing focuses exclusively on the issues of punishment. Under the *Gregg* decision, the prosecution uses the punishment-phase hearing to focus attention on the existence of "aggravating factors," such as excessive cruelty or a defendant's prior record of violent crimes. The decision makers must also focus on "mitigating factors," such as the offender's youthfulness, mental retardation, or lack of a criminal record. The aggravating and mitigating factors must be weighed together before the judge or jury can make a decision about whether to impose a death sentence. The purpose of the two-stage decision-making process is to ensure thorough deliberation before someone is given the ultimate punishment. The Court also endorsed "proportionality review," in which a higher appellate court reviews each death sentence to see if the death penalty was also imposed in similar cases.[33]

In *McCleskey v. Kemp* (1987), opponents of the death penalty felt that the U.S. Supreme Court severely limited their movement. In this case the Court rejected a challenge, on the grounds of racial discrimination, to Georgia's death penalty law.[34] Warren McCleskey, an African American, was sentenced to death for killing a white police officer during a furniture store robbery. Before the Supreme Court, McCleskey's attorney cited research showing a disparity in the imposition of the death penalty in Georgia, based on the race of the victim and, to a lesser extent, the race of the defendant. Researchers had examined over two thousand Georgia murder cases and found that defendants charged with killing whites had received the death penalty 11 times more often than had those convicted of killing African Americans. Even after compensating for 230 factors, such as the viciousness of the crime and the quality of the evidence, the study showed that the death sentence was four times more likely to be imposed when the victim was white. Although 60 percent of Georgia homicide victims are African Americans, all seven people put to death in that state since 1976 had been convicted of killing white people, and six of the seven murderers were African Americans.[35]

By a 5–4 vote, the justices rejected McCleskey's assertion that Georgia's capital-sentencing practices violated the equal protection clause of the Constitution by producing racial discrimination. The slim majority of justices declared that McCleskey would have to prove that the decision makers acted with a discriminatory purpose in deciding his case. The Court also concluded that statistical evidence showing discrimination throughout the Georgia courts did not provide adequate proof. McCleskey was executed in 1991.

In June 2002 the Supreme Court broke new ground, heartening opponents of the death penalty. First, in *Atkins v. Virginia* it ruled that execution of the mentally retarded was unconstitutional.[36] Daryl Atkins, who has an IQ of 59, was sentenced to death for killing Eric Nesbitt in a 7-Eleven store's parking lot. Justice John Paul Stevens, writing for the *Atkins* majority, noted that since 1989 a national consensus had emerged rejecting execution of the retarded. He pointed out that the number of states prohibiting such executions had gone from 2 to 18. The decision also noted that the characteristics of the mentally retarded "undermine the strength of procedural protections" guaranteed in the Constitution. This point is in keeping with the argument of experts who say retarded people's suggestibility and willingness to please lead them to confess. At trial they have problems remembering details, locating witnesses, and testifying credibly on their own behalf. However, the Court did not define *retardation* and gave little guidance to the states as to what criteria should be used.

Second, in *Ring v. Arizona* (2002) the Supreme Court ruled that juries, rather than judges, must make the crucial factual decisions as to whether a convicted murderer should receive the death penalty.[37] *Ring v. Arizona* overturned the law of that state and four others—Colorado, Idaho, Montana, and Nebraska—where judges alone decided whether there were aggravating factors that warrant capital punishment. The decision also raised questions about the procedure in four other states—Alabama, Delaware, Florida, and Indiana—where the judge decided life imprisonment or death after hearing a jury's recommendation. The *Ring* opinion also says that any aggravating factors must be stated in the indictment, thus also requiring a change in federal death penalty laws.

In 2005 the Supreme Court reduced the scope of capital punishment even further. In *Roper v. Simmons* a majority of the justices decided that offenders cannot be sentenced to death for crimes they committed before they reached the age of 18.[38] Prior to that decision, the United States was among only a half-dozen countries in the entire world with laws that permitted death sentences for juveniles. Because the Court was divided on the issue, some observers wonder if further changes in the Court's composition could lead to a reversal of this decision.

For current **death penalty issues before the U.S. Supreme Court**, go to the corresponding website listed at www.cengage.com/criminaljustice/clear.

Continuing Legal Issues

The case law since *Furman* indicates that capital punishment is legal as long as it is imposed fairly. However, opponents continue to raise several issues in litigation. Now that the mentally retarded and juvenile offenders have been excluded from eligibility for the death penalty, some people argue that offenders who are mentally ill should also be excluded. Issues have arisen about the effectiveness of representation provided for capital defendants by defense attorneys. Many critics are concerned about the impact of using death-qualified juries. Questions have also been raised about the use of capital punishment for crimes other than murder. Other cases continue to raise concerns about the lengthy periods that condemned offenders spend on death row because of appeals. Finally, issues have arisen concerning the requirements of international law on the administration of capital punishment in the United States.

EXECUTION OF THE MENTALLY ILL ■ Insanity is a recognized defense for commission of a crime because mens rea (criminal intent) is not present. But should people who become mentally disabled after they are sentenced to death be executed? The Supreme Court responded to this question in 1985 in *Ford v. Wainwright*.[39] In 1974 Alvin Ford was convicted of murder and sentenced to death. There was no suggestion at his trial or sentencing that he was mentally incompetent. Only after he was incarcerated did he begin to exhibit delusional behavior, claiming that the Ku Klux Klan was part of

Scott Panetti, a death row inmate in Texas, understands that the state intends to kill him for the murder of his wife's parents. However, he says that the state, in league with Satan, wants to kill him to keep him from preaching the Gospel. That delusion has been documented by doctors and acknowledged by judges and prosecutors. In June 2007 the U.S. Supreme Court ordered that his case be sent back to federal district court to determine whether Panetti has no "rational understanding" of the connection between the act and the execution. In March 2008 the lower court ruled that Panetti, although suffering from schizophrenia, was competent to be executed. As of December 3, 2009, no date has been set.

an elaborate conspiracy to force him to commit suicide and that his female relatives were being tortured and sexually abused somewhere in the prison.

With evidence of these delusions, Ford's counsel invoked the procedures of the Florida law governing the determination of competency of a condemned inmate. Three psychiatrists examined Ford for 30 minutes in the presence of witnesses, including counsel and correctional officials. Each psychiatrist filed a separate and conflicting report with the governor, who subsequently signed a death warrant. Ford then appealed to the Supreme Court.

Justice Thurgood Marshall, writing for the majority, concluded that the Eighth Amendment prohibited the state from executing the insane—the accused must comprehend both the fact that he had been sentenced to death and the reason for it. Marshall cited the common-law precedent that questioned the retributive and deterrent value of executing a mentally disabled person. In addition, he argued, the idea is offensive to humanity. The justices also found the Florida procedures defective because they did not provide for a full and fair hearing on the competence of the offender.

Although the Supreme Court has ruled that the insane should not be executed, the issue arose again in Arkansas in 1991.[40] Rickey Ray Rector killed two men, one of whom was a police officer. He then shot himself in the temple, lifting three inches off the front of his brain, leaving him with the mental capabilities of a small child. He was convicted at trial and given the death sentence. In prison he howled day and night, jumped around, exhibited other aspects of abnormal behavior, and seemed to have no idea that he was to be executed.

The U.S. Supreme Court rejected his appeal. The Arkansas Parole and Community Rehabilitation Board unanimously turned down a recommendation that Governor Bill Clinton commute the death sentence to life imprisonment without parole. Clinton declined to halt the execution, and Rector was given a lethal injection on January 24, 1991.

Although the Supreme Court has ruled that the insane should not be executed, how competence should be determined remains an issue. A second issue concerns the morality of treating an offender's mental illness so that he or she *can* be executed, a policy opposed by the American Medical Association. In 2003 the U.S. 8th Circuit Court of Appeals held that Arkansas could force death row inmate Charles Singleton to take antipsychotic drugs to make him sane enough to execute. Singleton was executed on January 6, 2004.[41]

EFFECTIVE COUNSEL   ■   In *Strickland v. Washington* (1984) the Supreme Court ruled that defendants in capital cases have the right to representation that meets an "objective standard of reasonableness."[42] As noted by Justice Sandra Day O'Connor, the appellant must show "that there is a reasonable probability that, but for counsel's unprofessional errors, the result of the proceeding would have been different."[43]

David Washington was charged with three counts of capital murder, robbery, kidnapping, and other felonies, and an experienced criminal lawyer was appointed as counsel. Against his attorney's advice, Washington confessed to two murders, waived a jury trial,

Further information about the **execution of the mentally ill** is found at the corresponding website listed at www.cengage.com/criminaljustice/clear.

pleaded guilty to all charges, and chose to be sentenced by the trial judge. Believing the situation was hopeless, his counsel did not adequately prepare for the sentencing hearing. On being sentenced to death, Washington appealed. The Supreme Court rejected Washington's claim that his attorney was ineffective because he did not call witnesses, seek a presentence investigation report, or cross-examine medical experts on the defendant's behalf.

In recent years, the public has learned of cases where the defense attorney's competency has been put in doubt. In 1999 the *Chicago Tribune* conducted an extensive investigation of capital punishment in Illinois. Reporters found that 33 defendants sentenced to death since 1977 were represented by an attorney who had been, or was later, disbarred or suspended for conduct that was "incompetent, unethical or even criminal." These attorneys included David Landau, who was disbarred one year after representing a Will County defendant sentenced to death, and Robert McDonnell, a convicted felon and the only lawyer in Illinois to be disbarred twice. McDonnell represented four men who landed on death row.[44]

In March 2000 a federal judge in Texas ordered the release of Calvin Jerold Burdine after 16 years on death row. At his 1984 trial, Burdine's counsel slept through long portions of the proceedings. As the judge said, "Sleeping counsel is equivalent to no counsel at all."[45]

Most death penalty defendants are indigent and are provided counsel by the state. Critics argue that defense in capital cases is a highly specialized area of the law and that inexperienced attorneys should not be assigned to indigent cases. In most jurisdictions, especially in the South, counsel appointed to represent capital defendants receive very small fees, often limited by statute to $2,500 per case. Few attorneys are willing to put in the hundreds of hours required in a capital case for these amounts. Stephen Bright estimates that he was paid less than $2 per hour for representing a capital defendant in Mississippi.[46] The defense in these cases also has limited resources to investigate the case and to call expert witnesses. One Texas lawyer delivered a 26-word statement at sentencing: "You are an extremely intelligent jury. You've got that man's life in your hands. You can take it or not. That's all I have to say." This client was executed in 1992.[47]

The right to effective counsel was reaffirmed by the Supreme Court in June 2003, when it overturned the death sentence of Kevin Wiggins. The seven-member majority declared that Wiggins's inexperienced lawyer had failed to provide adequate representation. During the sentencing phase, lawyers had failed to present mitigating evidence to the jury of the horrendous abuse Wiggins had endured throughout his childhood. In a similar situation an inexperienced attorney was appointed by an Alabama judge to assist two more-seasoned lawyers defend Holly Wood, a man charged with murdering his girlfriend. At the sentencing hearing the young attorney failed to present evidence to the jury that his client was mentally retarded and that his life should be spared. The jury, by a vote of 10–2, the minimum allowed under Alabama law, recommended death.[48] Whether the justices of the U.S. Supreme Court will create clearer or stricter standards for defense attorneys remains to be seen.

DEATH-QUALIFIED JURIES ■ Should people who are opposed to the death penalty be excluded from juries in capital cases? In *Witherspoon v. Illinois* (1968), the Supreme Court held that potential jurors who have general objections to the death penalty or whose religious convictions oppose its use cannot be automatically excluded from jury service in capital cases. However, it upheld the practice of removing, during voir dire (preliminary examination), those people whose opposition is so strong as to "prevent or substantially impair the performance of their duties." Such jurors have become known as "Witherspoon excludables." The decision was later reaffirmed in *Lockhart v. McCree* (1986).[49]

In *Uttecht v. Brown* (2007) the Supreme Court appears to have enhanced the state's ability to remove potential jurors with doubts about the death penalty. In a 5–4 decision the Court upheld the trial court judge who excused from the jury a person who had merely expressed doubts, not uniform opposition, to the death penalty.[50]

Because society is divided on capital punishment, opponents argue that death-qualified juries do not represent a cross-section of the community. Researchers have

Support for capital defense lawyers is found at the corresponding website listed at www.cengage.com/criminaljustice/clear.

also found that "juries are likely to be nudged toward believing the defendant is guilty and toward an imposition of the death sentence by the very process of undergoing death qualification."[51] Another impact is "a major bleaching of juries," according to Samuel Gross, a professor at the University of Michigan Law School: "Many more African Americans are excluded than whites." The biggest demographic predictor of attitudes toward the death penalty is race.[52]

Costanzo points to research indicating that death qualification has several impacts. First, those who are selected for jury duty are more conviction prone and more receptive to aggravating factors presented during the penalty phase. A second, subtler impact is that jurors answering the questions about their willingness to vote for a death sentence often conclude that both defenders and prosecutors anticipate a conviction and a death sentence.[53]

EXECUTION FOR CHILD RAPE   ■   Because of the heinous nature of the crime, several states have sought to enact laws permitting use of the death penalty for adults who rape children, even when the children have not been murdered. Patrick Kennedy was convicted and sentenced to death in 2004 by Louisiana for the rape of his eight-year-old stepdaughter. The sentence was upheld by the Louisiana Supreme Court. In *Kennedy v. Louisiana* (2008) the U.S. Supreme Court, in a 5–4 decision, held that a capital sentence where the crime did not involve murder was in violation of the Eighth and Fourteenth amendments.[54] The justices cited their decision in *Coker v. Georgia* (1977), which ruled that the use of the death penalty for rape of an adult was unconstitutional. Since that decision it had generally been assumed that the death penalty could only be imposed for murder.[55] The narrow division of the Court in the *Kennedy* decision has led observers to believe that a shift in the composition of the court could reverse the decision.

APPEALS   ■   Many argue that the appellate process for death sentences takes too long, traumatizes victims' families, and burdens states with millions in extra costs for defense attorneys and for housing convicted killers. Others point out that an appellate process that thoroughly examines each case is necessary, because during the 1990s, 26 percent of state death sentences were overturned during the first level of the appeals process.

A study of 1,676 cases resolved between 1992 and 2002 in 14 states found that the time from the date of the death sentence to the completion of a direct appeal was a median 966 days. Petitioning the U.S. Supreme Court added 188 days if certiorari was denied, and a median 250 days where certiorari was granted and the issues decided on the merits.[56] The 60 prisoners executed in 2005 had been under sentence of death an average of 12 years and 3 months, 15 months longer than those executed in 2004.[57] During this time, sentences were reviewed by the state courts and, through the writ of habeas corpus, by the federal courts.

The writ of habeas corpus (see Chapter 5) is the only means by which the federal courts can hear challenges by state inmates to their convictions and sentences. A long time is required to exhaust state appeals before filing a habeas corpus petition in the federal courts. Intervening court decisions have frequently reinterpreted the law to help the offender's case. Yet in two 1990 decisions the Court limited the ability of death row inmates to base appeals on new favorable rulings issued after their convictions.[58]

In a major ruling affecting death penalty appeals, the Court sharply curtailed the ability of offenders to file multiple challenges to the constitutionality of their sentences. In *McCleskey v. Zant* (1991) the Court ruled that, except in exceptional circumstances, the lower federal courts must dismiss a prisoner's second and subsequent habeas corpus petitions. Observers believe that this ruling will result in states' carrying out death sentences more quickly.[59]

In 1993 the Supreme Court further restricted appeals to the federal courts when it ruled that an offender who presents belated evidence of innocence is not ordinarily entitled to a new hearing in a federal court before execution. This ruling centered on the case of Leonel Herrera, who was convicted in Texas and sentenced to death for the

1982 murder of two police officers. Ten years later, Herrera's nephew asserted in an affidavit that, before he died in 1984, his father had confessed to the crime, asserting that Leonel had not shot the officers. Statements from three other people who previously had named Raul Herrera as the murderer were presented to the court. Texas law provides only 30 days for filing a motion for a new trial based on newly discovered evidence. The Supreme Court rejected Herrera's argument that his case should be reopened because of the new evidence. The Chief Justice, writing for the majority, observed that only in "truly persuasive" cases should a hearing be held.[60] Herrera was executed on May 12, 1993. His last words were "I am innocent; I am innocent. God bless you all."

The late Chief Justice William Rehnquist, who served as chief justice from 1986 to 2005, actively sought to reduce the opportunities for capital punishment defendants to have their appeals heard by multiple courts.[61] In 1996 President Clinton signed the Anti-Terrorism and Effective Death Penalty Act, which requires death row inmates to file habeas appeals within one year and requires that federal judges issue their decisions within strict time limits.[62]

Appellate review is a time-consuming and expensive process, but it also makes an impact. A major study of death penalty appeals found that two out of three convictions were overturned on appeal, mostly because of serious errors by incompetent defense lawyers or overzealous police officers and prosecutors. In three states—Kentucky, Maryland, and Tennessee—100 percent of appealed death sentences were overturned.[63] From 1977 through 2005, a total of 6,940 people entered prison under sentence of death. During those 29 years, 1,004 (14 percent) prisoners were executed and 3,062 (41 percent) had their death sentence removed by appellate court decisions and reviews or by commutations, or else died while awaiting execution.[64]

Michael Radelet and his colleagues examined the case of 68 death row inmates later released because of doubts about their guilt.[65] These cases account for one of every five inmates executed during the period 1970–1996. Correction of the miscarriage of about one-third of the defendants took four years or less, but it took nine years or longer for another third of the defendants. Had the expedited appeals process and limitations on habeas corpus been in effect, would these death sentences have been overturned?

INTERNATIONAL LAW ■ The last decade has seen a huge increase in the number of foreign nationals entering the United States, legally or illegally. Not surprisingly, many of these foreigners are convicted of crimes unrelated to their immigration status. As of May 2009, 126 foreign nationals from 32 countries were on death row.[66] Interestingly, four of five are in the United States legally. The rights of foreign nationals in the criminal justice system has added a new dimension to legal issues surrounding the death penalty.

The United States is a signatory of the Vienna Convention on Consular Relations, which requires notification of consular officials when a foreign national is arrested. This aspect of international law benefits Americans who face criminal punishment in foreign countries. However, individual prosecutors and police throughout the United States are apparently unaware of the law, because several dozen foreign nationals have been convicted and sentenced to death in the United States without their consular officials being informed.

Mexico, Germany, and Paraguay have filed complaints against the United States for violating the Vienna Convention in death penalty cases. In April 2004 the International Court of Justice in The Hague, Netherlands, ruled that international law had been violated and ordered the United States to review the death sentences of Mexicans held on U.S. death rows. The International Court has no power to force the United States to take action, but President George W. Bush announced in February 2005 that the United States would comply with the Vienna Convention. In light of this announcement, the Supreme Court decided not to rule on a pending case brought by a Mexican citizen on death row in Texas (*Medellin v. Dretke*).[67] Instead, the majority of justices decided to wait and see how the Texas courts would handle the cases of 12 Mexican nationals on death row. In November 2006 the Texas Court of Criminal Appeals, in a long and complex ruling, said that the president did not have the power to direct such a review.[68] Writing for the nine-member court, Judge Michael Keasler said, "We hold that the president has exceeded his constitutional authority by intruding into the independent powers of the judiciary."[69]

The issue returned to the U.S. Supreme Court in May 2007, when the justices accepted an appeal from Jose E. Medellin. In a brief filed on behalf of Medellin, U.S. Solicitor General Paul Clement urged that the Supreme Court overturn the Texas court's decision, arguing that to let that court's ruling stand would place the United States at odds with international law and the World Court. The justices, however felt differently and held in *Medellin v. Texas* (2008) that the president did not have the power to order the states to follow the Vienna Convention.[70]

Whether international law will spur additional issues and arguments concerning the death penalty remains to be seen. For example, in 2002 the Supreme Court declined to rule in a death row case that asserted a violation of the cruel and unusual punishments clause because the petitioner had spent 27 years in solitary confinement on death row under exceptionally restrictive conditions.[71] The condemned man cited judicial decisions by foreign courts, such as the Privy Council of Great Britain and the European Court of Human Rights, that stated a delay of 15 years between trial and execution can render a capital punishment conviction "degrading, shocking or cruel." Several justices of the Supreme Court have made it clear that they do not believe international law has any application to the American criminal justice system, but other justices have cited foreign cases to support specific decisions.

■ DEATH ROW INMATES

Of the 22,000 arrests each year for murder and nonnegligent manslaughter, fewer than 150 offenders receive the death penalty. The Supreme Court has ruled that juries must weigh aggravating and mitigating factors before recommending the sentence in capital cases. What other factors might contribute to the selection of only a few for execution? Does who they are, where the crime was committed, or who the prosecutor was make any difference? Is race a factor? In sum, is the process capricious, akin to a lottery, as some scholars have said?[72]

MYTHS IN CORRECTIONS

THEY MAY KILL AGAIN

THE MYTH: Public safety is often a reason given in support of the death penalty. There is concern among many that a murderer will kill again.

THE REALITY: A study of the 589 death row inmates whose sentences were converted to life imprisonment because of *Furman v. Georgia* (1972) found that of the 322 eventually paroled, 75 were returned to prison for a technical parole violation or a nonviolent crime, 32 returned to prison because of a violent crime, and only 5 killed again.

Sources: Joan M. Cheever, *Back from the Dead* (West Sussex, England: Wiley, 2006), 56.

Who Is on Death Row?

Death row inmates tend to be poorly educated men from low-income backgrounds. Further, the number of minority group members on death row is far out of proportion to their numbers in the general population (see **Figure 20.4**). The most recent data (2006) show that 65 percent of death row inmates have a prior felony conviction, 8.4 percent have a prior homicide conviction, and 27 percent were on probation or parole or in prison at the time of the capital offense.[73] (See "Myths in Corrections" for more.)

Only 58 women currently are on death row. Since 1976 only 11 women have been executed. Although one of seven arrestees for murder is a woman, judges and jurors seem reluctant to sentence women to death, as evidenced by the life-in-prison sentence given Susan Smith, convicted for murdering her two young sons. However, what some view as a double standard may end, as public attitudes toward women change.

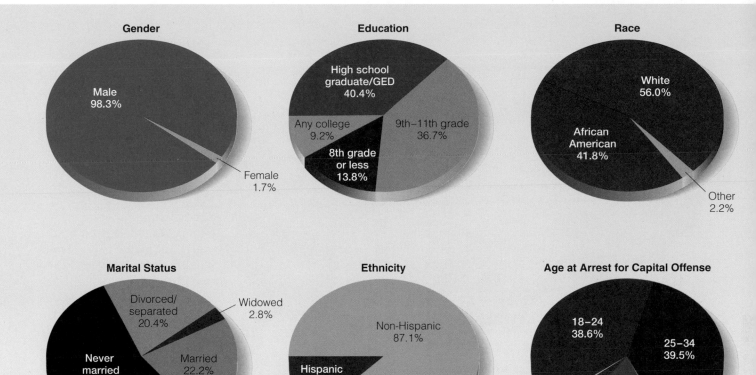

Figure 20.4
Characteristics of Death Row Inmates

Like other prisoners, death row inmates tend to be younger, less-educated men. Minority group members on death row also are disproportionately represented.

Source: Bureau of Justice Statistics, *Capital Punishment 2007—Statistical Tables,* http://www.ojp.usdoj.gov/BJS/pub/htm/cp/2007/cp07sc.htm.

Where Was the Crime Committed?

Of particular interest is the distribution of death row inmates among the states, as shown in **Figure 20.5**. About 54 percent of those under sentence of death are in the South, 25 percent in the West, and 14 percent in the Midwest. Seven percent are in the northeastern states. Also revealing is the fact that, of the 1,168 executions from 1977 to 2009, 65 percent have been carried out in five states: Texas (439), Virginia (103), Oklahoma (90), Missouri (67), and Florida (67). See also **Figure 20.6** on page 559.

Although Texas is known as the "death penalty capital of the country," the overall percentage of murderers sentenced to death there is actually lower than it is in surrounding states. For every 1,000 murders, Texas sentences 20 people to death, compared with 51 in Oklahoma, 43 in Arizona, 38 in Alabama, and 35 in Mississippi.[74]

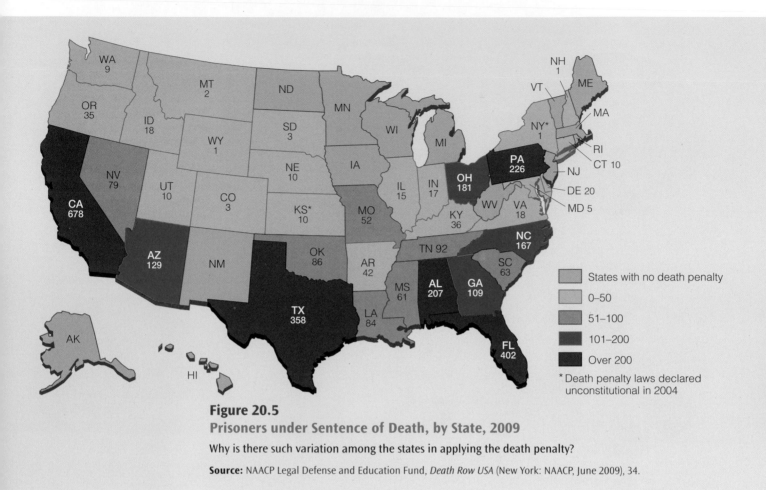

Figure 20.5
Prisoners under Sentence of Death, by State, 2009

Why is there such variation among the states in applying the death penalty?

Source: NAACP Legal Defense and Education Fund, *Death Row USA* (New York: NAACP, June 2009), 34.

Who Was the Prosecutor?

Although Harris County (Houston) has been known as the "death penalty capital" among critics of capital punishment, that "honor" has been recently eclipsed by Maricopa County (Phoenix), where in 2006 County Attorney Andrew Thomas sought the death penalty in nearly half of the first-degree murder cases. There are now 135 capital cases in trial or heading for trial in Phoenix. The huge increase has overwhelmed the public defender system and left a dozen murder defendants without representation.[75]

Even within states, the probability that a prosecutor will ask for the death penalty differs. For example, of the 289 people executed in Texas from 1977 to 2002, 67 were from the Houston area (5.3 executions per 1,000 murders), where the district attorney was a vocal advocate of the death penalty. In contrast, the district attorney in the Dallas area was more circumspect; only 26 people from that area have been executed (3.1 executions per 1,000 murders). But the real surprise is the Corpus Christi area, where 10 were executed—a whopping 13 executions per 1,000 murders.[76] The discretionary power of prosecutors and the local political environment explain many of these differences. As James Liebman, an expert on the death penalty, says, "Lots of states have death belts. In southern Georgia, there are lots of death sentences; in northern Georgia, there aren't. In Tennessee, there are tons of death sentences in Memphis and East Knoxville, but not in Nashville."[77] In New York, 83 percent of murder arrests are in New York City, yet before abolition of the death penalty, two-thirds of cases were filed in the remaining 17 percent of the state.[78] Political factors may be at work in these states to the extent that prosecuting attorneys and judges expect to be reelected if they campaign on their death penalty record.[79]

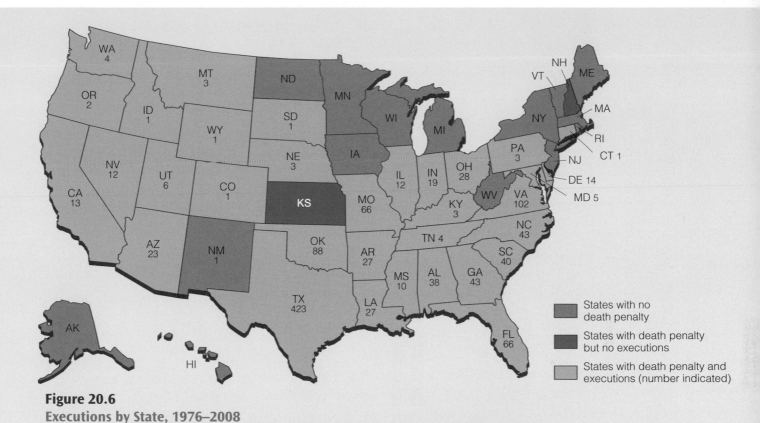

Figure 20.6
Executions by State, 1976–2008

Just over 65 percent of executions have been carried out in five southern states—Texas, Virginia, Oklahoma, Florida, and Missouri—yet the highest homicide rates are found in Louisiana, Mississippi, New Mexico, Maryland, and Nevada. What might explain the lack of correspondence between homicides and executions?

Source: NAACP Legal Defense and Education Fund, *Death Row USA* (New York: NAACP, June 2009), 10.

During his two years in office, Andrew Thomas, county attorney for maricopa county, Arizona, has nearly doubled the number of times that the office has sought the death penalty, even though the number of first-degree murder case has remained more or less the same for a decade.

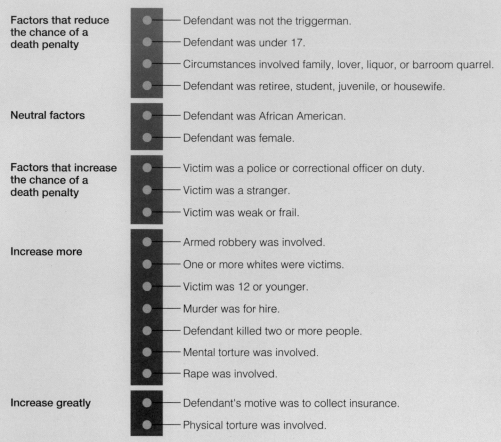

Factors that reduce the chance of a death penalty
- Defendant was not the triggerman.
- Defendant was under 17.
- Circumstances involved family, lover, liquor, or barroom quarrel.
- Defendant was retiree, student, juvenile, or housewife.

Neutral factors
- Defendant was African American.
- Defendant was female.

Factors that increase the chance of a death penalty
- Victim was a police or correctional officer on duty.
- Victim was a stranger.
- Victim was weak or frail.

Increase more
- Armed robbery was involved.
- One or more whites were victims.
- Victim was 12 or younger.
- Murder was for hire.
- Defendant killed two or more people.
- Mental torture was involved.
- Rape was involved.

Increase greatly
- Defendant's motive was to collect insurance.
- Physical torture was involved.

Figure 20.7
Imposing the Death Penalty in Georgia
Researchers have identified the various aspects of a murder that increase or decrease the chance of a death penalty in Georgia.

Source: *New York Times,* February 24, 1995, p. B4. Figure based on David Baldus, George Woodworth, and Charles Pulaski, *Equal Justice and the Death Penalty: A Legal and Empirical Analysis* (Boston: Northeastern University Press, 1990).

Was Race a Factor?

Many assume that there is an overrepresentation of African American men on death row, because they make up about 42 percent of the death row inmates yet compose only 7 percent of the U.S. population. However, recent research makes the point that African Americans commit about 50 percent of all murders nationally in states with the death penalty and those without it. The authors point out that juries are least likely to impose a death sentence in black-on-black murders (which make up the majority of murder cases involving African Americans). A death sentence is more likely in white-on-white cases and most likely when the perpetrator is African American and the victim is white.[80]

Research by David Baldus and others found that imposition of the death penalty in Georgia was influenced by the race of the murder victim and, to a lesser extent, the race of the offender.[81] Recall our earlier discussion of the Supreme Court's ruling that this did not constitute a breach of equal protection. **Figure 20.7** shows the factors influencing imposition of the death penalty in Georgia.

Is Georgia unique, or is the victim's race a determinative factor in other states? Samuel Gross and Robert Mauro examined the death penalty in Arkansas, Florida, Georgia, Illinois, Mississippi, North Carolina, Oklahoma, and Virginia. In each state, they found that the death sentence was more likely to be imposed if the victim was white rather than African American. The ratios varied from 10:1 in Georgia and Mississippi to 5:1 in Virginia.[82] A study of the death penalty in North Carolina found that, from 1993 to 1997, defendants whose victims were white were 3.5 times more likely to be sentenced to death than were defendants whose victims were people of color.[83]

Does the evidence from these states indicate racism, or do other factors play a role? Robert Bohm examined racial disparity and discrimination in two Georgia judicial circuits and suggested that institutional racism, such as the few African American prosecutors, defense attorneys, and judges in the system, is what influences capital punishment decisions. He believes that one result of the Supreme Court's decision in *McCleskey v. Kemp* is that it will be almost impossible to show racism in individual cases. Bohm quotes Georgia State Senator Gary Parker as saying, "The Supreme Court's decision in *McCleskey v. Kemp* has been interpreted by prosecutors and judges in the South as a clear message that they are not to be held accountable in the courts for racial discrimination that occurs in capital trials."[84]

A study on racial disparities in death penalty cases found that African American defendants in Philadelphia are nearly four times more likely than other defendants to be sentenced to death, even when controlling for levels of crime severity and the defendant's criminal history. The researchers also found that, unlike the South, where the victim's race is a factor, northern states show more disparity regarding the defendants' race, with African Americans more likely to be charged than whites.[85]

Whatever factors influence who receives the death penalty, the drama plays out similarly for those facing imminent death. See the Focus box "Death-Watch Logs" for a look at the circumstances surrounding a triple execution.

FOCUS ON
CORRECTIONAL PRACTICE

Death-Watch Logs

During one week in January 1997, the state of Arkansas executed Earl Van Denton, 47, and Paul Ruiz, 49, both convicted of the 1977 murders of a town marshal and park ranger after the offenders broke out of the Oklahoma prison; the state also executed Kirt Wainwright, 30, convicted in the 1988 slaying of a convenience-store worker.

Arkansas is notable for the detailed records kept by death-house guards. These "death-watch" logs provide a glimpse of the execution process. Three days before their scheduled execution, the condemned are moved from death row at the maximum-security prison near Tucker to the "death house" at the Cummins State Prison near Varner. Here are entries by the death-house guards for execution day, January 8, 1997. On the last day, the inmates are allowed no visitors besides lawyers and spiritual advisors.

1:14 A.M   Inmate Denton vomiting in commode—says he will be O.K.

1:20   Infirmary notified—says due to medication on empty stomach—O.K. to give Maalox, per Nurse Ackles. . . .

2:05   Nurse Ackles says Denton's vital signs are good. Vitals taken through trap door of cell. . . .

3:20   Inmate was asked by Sgt. McDaniel if he wanted a shot from the infirmary to stop him from vomiting. . . . Inmate Denton states that he was O.K. and did not want the shot.

4:24   Ms. Ackles entered quiet cell area with inmate Ruiz's medication. Inmate received Tylenol. Ms. Ackles advised inmate Ruiz that she would return with his Actifed. . . .

7:29   Inmate Ruiz asked for and received a banana cream roll to eat with his coffee.

8:55   Inmate Ruiz's spiritual adviser in front of cell— Ms. Pat Bane.

9:08   Inmate Ruiz sitting on bunk talking and holding the hand of his adviser through the cell's mail slot. . . .

10:17   Inmate Denton got off bunk and started to vomit in toilet. . . .

11:30   Inmate Ruiz standing in cell drinking coffee and watching TV . . . Maury Povich talk show.

FOCUS ON

CORRECTIONAL PRACTICE (*Continued*)

12:12 P.M	Inmate Wainwright asked me to give inmates Ruiz and Denton a box of cakes out of his property. This was done.
1:55	Inmate Ruiz asked if I would give inmate Wainwright a 1–2 bag of coffee out of his property.
2:08	Mr. Frank King (a prison priest) in cell area to visit with inmate Denton.
3:00	Inmate Ruiz . . . receive[s] his last meal . . . consisted of seedless grapes, salad, breadstick, crackers, salad dressing, (3) cups of coffee. Ms. Pat Bane escorted out at this time.
3:01	Inmate Wainwright received 3 cups of milk, two rolls, gravy, greens, pinto beans, rice, and four pieces of fried chicken. He refused to eat. Mr. Denton made no meal request. . . .
3:54	Inmate Ruiz . . . completed his last shower.
3:55	Inmate Ruiz handcuffed by Lieut. Moncrief and escorted back to cell. . . .
4:38	Mr. Frank King . . . and Lawyer Roy Hartestein in to visit inmate Denton.
5:35	Mr. Al Schay (a lawyer) entered cell lobby to visit with inmate Denton.
6:45	Mr. G. David Guntharp (a corrections official) entered cell lobby and told the visitor they had five minutes left to visit.
6:51	Tie-down team enter quiet cell lobby after visitors depart.

6:53	Inmate Denton exit[s] quiet cell. Mr. Denton is escorted by some half-dozen burly "tie-down" guards in riot helmets to the death chamber, roughly 20 paces away down a short hallway. They strap him to the gurney within two minutes; catheters are placed in his arms within five. He has no last words for the assembled witnesses peering in through one-way glass, . . . [Sodium thiopental, which causes unconsciousness, administered at 7:00. Second drug, the muscle relaxant pancuronium bromide, administered to collapse his diaphragm and lungs. The final drug, heart-stopping potassium chloride, is administered.] and is pronounced dead at 7:09 P.M. Mr. Ruiz follows in similar fashion less than an hour later. Mr. Wainwright, whose execution would be delayed in the chamber by a late appeal, was left. . . .
8:10	Wainwright pacing in cell, snapping his fingers and occasionally singing.
8:27	Mr. Guntharp advises the attorneys to leave. . . .
8:28	Mr. Reed approached inmate Wainwright's cell and advised it was time. Wainwright replied let's do it. . . .

Source: Tom Kuntz, "Banality, Nausea, Triple Execution: Guards on Inmates' Final Hours," *New York Times,* January 12, 1997, p. WR7. Copyright © 1997 by the New York Times Company. Reprinted by permission.

■ A CONTINUING DEBATE

Various developments in the first decade of the twenty-first century appear to indicate a weakening of support for capital punishment. In January 2000 Illinois Governor George Ryan, a longtime supporter of capital punishment, called for a moratorium on executions in his state. Ryan said that he was convinced that the system was "fraught with error," noting that since 1976, Illinois had executed 12 people yet freed 13 from death row as innocent. Since then, courts, governors, and legislatures in many of the death penalty states have acted to abolish or limit executions. The exoneration, since 1973, of 133 death row offenders, an average of five exonerations per year since 2000, has added to the concern that innocent people may be executed.[86] New Jersey abolished the death penalty in 2007, as did New Mexico in 2009. The Connecticut General Assembly passed abolition legislation in 2009 but Governor Jodi Rell vetoed it. In these states the cost of the capital punishment system has played a major role in the legislative debate. In New Jersey it was estimated that the death penalty had cost $168 million since its reinstatement in 1983—and even with this amount invested, not a single execution had taken place.

Other states' taxpayers have borne similar costs. California, with the largest death row, spends an estimated $137 million per year to maintain the system. In Maryland the death penalty has cost at least $185 million more in prosecuting and defending capital cases over the past two decades than would have been spent without the threat of execution.

Use of the death penalty has dropped in recent years. The number of death sentences have declined by more than half since the 1990s to a low of 111 in 2008, and the number of executions dropped to a 10-year low of 32 in 2009.[87]

Do these actions portend a shift in American policy and opinion regarding the death penalty? Although debate on this important public policy issue has gone on for more than two hundred years, no consensus has formed.

Opponents of the death penalty argue that poor people and members of minority groups receive a disproportionate number of death sentences. Yet some have challenged this view, claiming that there is no research to support it.[88] Opponents also cite the finality of death, in light of the number of acknowledged mistakes that have been made in the past, as sufficient reason to oppose capital punishment.[89] Nationally, as many as eight defendants have been released each year because of such factors as perjured testimony, withheld evidence, or mistakes of identification.[90]

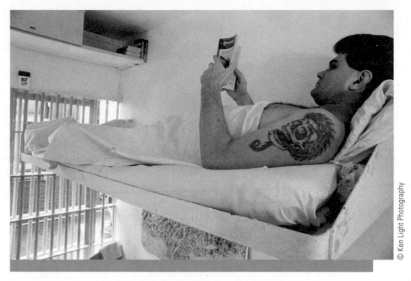

Opponents of the death penalty point to the possibility of executing an innocent person. Such appears to be the case of Cameron Todd Willingham, executed by Texas in 2004 for murdering his children by arson. Forensic experts have now concluded that the evidence of arson could not support the conclusion that he started the fire.

Opponents further note that to try, convict, and execute a murderer costs much more than trying that individual in a noncapital case and keeping him or her in prison for 20 years. A study of death penalty cases in North Carolina showed that prosecuting a capital case rather than noncapital one costs the public an extra $216,000. And if the case ultimately results in an execution, the extra cost reaches more than $2.16 million.[91] A report adopted by the Judicial Conference of the United States found the cost of defending a person who was charged with a capital offense, but for which the U.S. Attorney General did not authorize seeking the death penalty, to be $55,772. If the death penalty was sought, the defense costs were $218,112. Prosecution costs were $192,333 and $269,139, respectively.[92] Data from other parts of the nation support this view.[93]

Proponents of the death penalty claim that it deters criminals from committing violent acts and that justice demands that murderers suffer retribution, regardless of cost. They further argue that, given the high levels of violent crimes in the United States, we must retain the severest penalties. To give someone a life sentence of incarceration for murder diminishes the worth of the victim, is costly to society, and does not lessen the possibility that the offender will do further harm either while incarcerated or on parole. In answer to the charge that the death penalty is administered in an arbitrary and capricious manner, scholars such as Walter Berns and Joseph Bessette say that, in the post-*Furman* era, "the system now in place serves as a filter, reserving the death penalty for the worst offenders."[94]

Will the United States increase the pace of executions, allow the number of capital offenders in prison to grow, or provide some alternatives such as life imprisonment without parole for convicted murderers? Might the United States follow the European pattern of de facto abolition before de jure abolition? These questions remain unanswered.

SUMMARY

1 Contrast the issues in the debate over capital punishment.

Arguments for the death penalty include the following: The death penalty deters criminals from committing violent acts; it achieves justice by paying killers back for their horrible crimes; it prevents criminals from committing future acts while on parole; it is less expensive than holding offenders in prison for life. Arguments against the death penalty include the following: No hard evidence proves that the death penalty is a deterrence; it is wrong for the government to participate in the intentional killing of its citizens; the death penalty is applied in a discriminatory fashion; innocent people have been sentenced to death.

2 Understand the history of the death penalty in America.

The death penalty was common for a range of offenses during the early settlement of America. Public executions were held until the 1830s, when most of them were moved inside the prison walls. The number of states without the death penalty has increased in recent years. In some states the law is on the books yet there have been few or no executions in the last quarter century.

3 Discuss the legal issues that surround the death penalty.

The Eighth and Fourteenth amendments to the Constitution prohibit cruel and unusual punishments and require equal protection under the law, respectively. The U.S. Supreme Court has held that the death penalty is not unconstitutional unless it is administered in a cruel and unusual fashion (*Furman v. Georgia,* 1972). This position was upheld in *Gregg v. Georgia* (1976), as long as the penalty is administered fairly and the judge and jury consider mitigating and aggravating circumstances. This position has been extended to prohibit execution of the retarded or juveniles and to prohibit it in cases where the offense is not murder. Legal issues concerning execution of the mentally ill, effective counsel, death-qualified juries, the appeals process, and the impact of international law continue to appear before the Court.

4 Characterize the inmates on death row.

Death row inmates tend to be poorly educated men from low-income backgrounds. The number of minority group members is far out of proportion to their numbers in the general population. Other factors influencing who is on death row include the location of the crime, the prosecutor, and the race of the defendant and victim.

5 Speculate about the future of capital punishment.

Although the public supports the death penalty, some argue that this support is shallow. The increased number of death row inmates shown to be innocent seems to have caused a decrease in the number who receive capital punishment and the number who are executed. Several states have recently abolished capital punishment, despite public support for it.

FOR DISCUSSION

1. What are the main arguments supporting and opposing capital punishment? Which one seems to you the most important?
2. Which of the continuing legal issues should the Supreme Court scrutinize as being in violation of the Eighth Amendment?
3. Given that the death penalty has been abolished in other Western democracies, why do people in the United States support it?
4. What alternatives to death might achieve the retributive, deterrent, and incapacitative goals of capital punishment?
5. What does the future hold for the death penalty?

FOR FURTHER READING

Banner, Stuart. *The Death Penalty.* Cambridge, MA: Harvard University Press, 2002. A history of the death penalty in America from the early colonial period to the execution of Timothy McVeigh in 2001.

Beck, Elizabeth, Sarah Britto and Arlene Andrews. *In the Shadow of Death: Restorative Justice and Death Row Families.* New York: Oxford University Press, 2006. The personal stories of families victimized by murder who seek restorative justice with the person who killed their loved one.

Bedau, Hugo Adam. *Death Is Different.* Boston: Northeastern University Press, 1987. Argues that the death penalty differs from other punishments in its morality, politics, and symbolism; written by a major opponent of the death penalty.

Cheever, Joan M. *Back from the Dead.* West Sussex, England: Wiley, 2006. Follows those 589 inmates released from death row as a result of *Furman v. Georgia.* Of the "Class of '72," 322 have been paroled, 32 have been reincarcerated for a violent crime, and 5 have killed again.

Costanzo, Mark. *Just Revenge.* New York: St. Martin's Press, 1997. An excellent overview of capital punishment, exploring its symbolism, costs, expected benefits, politics, and consequences.

Galliher, John F., Larry W. Koch, David Patrick Keys, and Teresa J. Guess. *America without the Death Penalty.* Boston: Northeastern University Press, 2002. Case studies of nine states without the death penalty. Examines the relationship between death penalty abolition and such factors as economic conditions, public opinion, murder rates, and population diversity.

Prejean, Helen. *Dead Man Walking.* New York: Random House, 1993. Recounts the story of a Roman Catholic nun, the spiritual adviser to two Louisiana death row inmates, who confronts both the viciousness of these murderers and the pain of the families of their victims; written by a death penalty opponent who is also a victims' advocate.

Sarat, Austin. *When the State Kills: Capital Punishment and the American Condition.* Princeton, NJ: Princeton University Press, 2001. Argues that state killing diminishes Americans by damaging our democracy. It promises simple solutions to complex problems and offers up moral simplicity in a morally ambiguous world.

Turow, Scott. *Ultimate Punishment: A Lawyer's Reflections on Dealing with the Death Penalty.* New York: Farrar, Straus, and Giroux, 2003. A thoughtful examination of capital punishment by the novelist Turow, a member of the Illinois Governor's Commission on Capital Punishment.

Zimring, Franklin E. *The Contradictions of American Capital Punishment.* New York: Oxford University Press, 2003. Wonders why the United States has not followed other developed countries in abolishing the death penalty.

NOTES

[1] Elizabeth Weil, "The Needle and the Damage Done," *The New York Times Magazine*, February 11, 2007, p. 48.

[2] *Baez v. Rees*, 128 S. Ct. 1520 (2008).

[3] http://www.Gallup.com, November 8, 2008.

[4] Ernest van den Haag, "For the Death Penalty," *New York Times,* October 17, 1983. See also van den Haag, "Justice, Deterrence and the Death Penalty," in *America's Experiment with Capital Punishment,* edited by James R. Acker, Robert M. Bohm, and Charles S. Lanier (Durham, NC: Carolina Academic Press, 1998), 139–56.

[5] Ibid.

[6] Michael L. Radelet and Ronald L. Akers, "Deterrence and the Death Penalty: The Views of the Experts," *Journal of Criminal Law and Criminology* 87 (Fall 1996): l–16. In a survey of "top criminologists," the authors found agreement that capital punishment fails to deter.

[7] Mark Costanzo, *Just Revenge* (New York: St. Martin's Press, 1997), 96.

[8] Ruth D. Peterson and William C. Bailey, "Murder and Capital Punishment in the Evolving Context of the Post-Furman Era," *Social Forces* 66 (1988): 774–807. See also Peterson and Bailey, "Is Capital Punishment an Effective Deterrent for Murder?"

in *America's Experiment with Capital Punishment*, edited by James R. Acker, Robert M. Bohm, and Charles S. Lanier (Durham, NC: Carolina Academic Press, 1998), 157–82.

[9] Raymond Bonner and Ford Fessenden, "States with No Death Penalty Share Lower Homicide Rates," *New York Times*, September 22, 2000, p. A1.

[10] Richard O. Lempert, "The Effect of Executions on Homicides: A New Look in an Old Light," *Crime and Delinquency* 29 (1983): 88–115.

[11] Isaac Ehrlich, "The Deterrent Effect of Capital Punishment: A Question of Life and Death," *American Economic Review* 65 (1975): 397–417.

[12] William J. Bowers and Glenn L. Pierce, "The Illusion of Deterrence in Isaac Ehrlich's Research on Capital Punishment," *Yale Law Journal* 85 (1975): 187–208.

[13] L. R. Klein, B. E. Forst, and V. Filatov, "The Deterrent Effect of Capital Punishment: An Assessment of the Estimates," in *Deterrence and Incapacitation*, edited by A. Blumstein, J. Cohen, and D. Nagin (Washington, DC: National Academy of Sciences, 1978).

[14] Louis P. Masur, *Rites of Execution: Capital Punishment and the Transformation of American Culture, 1776–1865* (New York: Oxford University Press, 1989).

[15] Harry Elmer Barnes and Nedgley K. Teeters, *New Horizons in Criminology*, 3rd ed. (Englewood Cliffs, NJ: Prentice-Hall, 1959), 308.

[16] Ibid., p. 4.

[17] Franklin Zimring and Gordon Hawkins, *Capital Punishment and the American Agenda* (New York: Cambridge University Press, 1986).

[18] NAACP Legal Defense and Education Fund, *Death Row USA* (New York: NAACP, June 2009).

[19] Death Penalty Information Center, "Facts about the Death Penalty, June 12, 2009," http://www.deathpenaltyinfo.org, June 24, 2009.

[20] *New York Times*, November 15, 2004, p. A12.

[21] Thomas J. Keil and Gennaro F. Vito, "Fear of Crime and Attitudes toward Capital Punishment: A Structural Equations Model," *Justice Quarterly* 8 (December 1991): 447. The authors find a link between fear of crime in the neighborhood and a greater willingness to endorse the death penalty.

[22] http://www.deathpenaltyinfo.org, June 24, 2009.

[23] Frank P. Williams, III, Dennis R. Longmire, and David B. Gulick, "The Public and the Death Penalty: Opinion as an Artifact of Question Type," *Criminal Justice Research Bulletin* 3 (1988): 3.

[24] Costanzo, *Just Revenge*, pp. 123–28.

[25] John T. Whitehead, "'Good Ol' Boys' and the Chair: Death Penalty Attitudes of Policy Makers in Tennessee," *Crime and Delinquency* 44 (April 1998): 245–56.

[26] W. J. Bowers, M. Vandiver, and P. H. Dugan, "A New Look at Public Opinion on Capital Punishment: What Citizens and Legislators Prefer," *American Journal of Criminal Law* 22 (1994): 77–150.

[27] Costanzo, *Just Revenge*, p. 124.

[28] Robert Jay Lifton and Greg Mitchell, *Who Owns Death?* (New York: Morrow, 2000), 227.

[29] Alexis M. Durham, H. Present Elrod, and Patrick T. Kinkade, "Public Support for the Death Penalty: Beyond Gallup," *Justice Quarterly* 13 (December 1996): 705–30.

[30] http://www.deathpenaltyinfo.org, June 24, 2009.

[31] *Furman v. Georgia*, 408 U.S. 238 (1972).

[32] *Gregg v. Georgia*, 428 U.S. 153 (1976).

[33] Leigh B. Bienen, "The Proportionality Review of Capital Cases by State High Courts after *Gregg*: Only 'The Appearance of Justice'?" *Journal of Criminal Law and Criminology* 87 (Fall 1996): 130–285.

[34] *McCleskey v. Kemp*, 478 U.S. 1019 (1987).

[35] David C. Baldus, George F. Woodworth, and Charles A. Pulaski, Jr., *Equal Justice and the Death Penalty: A Legal and Empirical Analysis* (Boston: Northeastern University Press, 1990).

[36] *Atkins v. Virginia*, 122 S. Ct. 2242 (2002).

[37] *Ring v. Arizona*, 122 S. Ct. 2428 (2002).

[38] *Roper v. Simmons*, 125 S. Ct. 1183 (2005).

[39] *Ford v. Wainwright*, 477 U.S. 399 (1985).

[40] Marshall Frady, "Death in Arkansas," *New York Times*, February 23, 1993, p. 105.

[41] http://deathpenaltyinfo.org, February 18, 2007.

[42] Welsh S. White, "Effective Assistance of Counsel in Capital Cases: The Evolving Standard of Care," *University of Illinois Law Review* 1993:323.

[43] *Strickland v. Washington*, 466 U.S. 668 (1984).

[44] Ken Armstrong and Steve Mills, "'82 Death Sentence Tossed Out," *Chicago Tribune*, November 14, 1999, p. 1, and November 15, 1999, p. 1.

[45] *New York Times*, March 2, 2000, p. A19.

[46] Stephen B. Bright, "Race, Poverty and Disadvantage in the Infliction of the Death Penalty in the Death Belt," in *The Machinery of Death* (Washington, DC: Amnesty International USA, 1995).

[47] *Newsweek*, November 9, 1998, p. 64.

[48] *Wiggins v. Smith*, 000 U.S. 02-311 (2003); Adam Liptak, "Death Penalty Case Reveals Failing," *New York Times*, June 9, 2009, p. A14.

[49] *Witherspoon v. Illinois*, 391 U.S. 510 (1968); *Lockhart v. McCree*, 4776 U.S. 162 (1986).

[50] *Uttecht v. Brown*, No. 06-413 (June 4, 2007).

[51] J. Luginbuhl and M. Burkhead, "Sources of Bias and Arbitrariness in the Capital Trial," *Journal of Social Issues* 7 (1994): 103–12.

[52] Adam Liptak, "Facing a Jury of (Some of) One's Peers," *New York Times*, July 20, 2003, http://www.nytimes.com.

[53] Costanzo, *Just Revenge*, 24–25.

[54] *Kennedy v. Louisiana*, No. 07-343 (2008).

[55] *Coker v. Georgia*, 453 U.S. 584 (1977).

[56] Barry Latzer and James N. G. Cauthen, *Justice Delayed? Time Consumption in Capital Appeals: A Multi-State Study* (Washington, DC: National Institute of Justice, 2007).

[57] BJS *Bulletin*, December 2006, p. 1.

[58] *New York Times*, March 1, 1990, p. A20.

[59] *McCleskey v. Zant*, 111 S. Ct. 1454 (1991).

[60] *New York Times*, January 26, 1993, p. 1.

[61] Robert D. Pursley, "The Federal Habeas Corpus Process: Unraveling the Issues," *Criminal Justice Policy Review* 7 (June 1995): 115.

[62] *Newsweek,* May 6, 1996, p. 72.

[63] James S. Liebman, Jeffrey Fagan, and Valerie West, *A Broken System: Error Rates in Capital Cases, 1973–1995* (New York: Columbia University School of Law, 2000).

[64] BJS *Bulletin,* December 2006, p. 8.

[65] Michael L. Radelet, William S. Lofquist, and Hugo Adam Bedau, "Prisoners Released from Death Rows Since 1970 Because of Doubts about Their Guilt," *Thomas M. Cooley Law Review* 13 (1996): 907.

[66] http//www.deathpenaltyinfo.org, June 24, 2009.

[67] *Medellin v. Dretke*, 125 S. Ct. 2088 (2005).

[68] *New York Times,* November 16, 2006; http://deathpenaltyinfo .org, February 17, 2007.

[69] Marco Robbins, "Court in Texas Says Bush Wrong on Mexican Cases," *San Antonio Express News,* November 15, 2006.

[70] *Medellin v. Texas*, 552 U.S. ____ (2008).

[71] *Foster v. Florida*, 527 U.S. 990 (2002).

[72] Richard A. Berk, Robert F. Weiss, and Jack Boger, "Chance and the Death Penalty," *Law and Society Review* 27 (1993): 80; Robert E. Weiss, Richard A. Berk, and Catharine Y. Lee, "Assessing the Capriciousness of Death Charging," *Law and Society Review* 30 (1996): 607.

[73] Bureau of Justice Statistics, *Capital Punishment 2007—Statistical Tables,* http://www.ojp.usdoj.gov/bjs/pub/html/cp/2007/ cp07st.htm, October 12, 2009.

[74] John Blume, Theodore Eisenberg, and Martin T. Wells, "Explaining Death Row Population and Racial Composition," *Journal of Empirical Legal Studies* 1 (March 2004): 165–207.

[75] Jahna Berry, "Death-Penalty Backlog Strains Justice System," *Arizona Republic,* February 22, 2007, http://www.azcentral.com.

[76] "The Nation in Numbers: Mortal Justice," *Atlantic Monthly,* March 2003, pp. 40, 41.

[77] *New York Times,* February 23, 1995, p. B6.

[78] *New York Times,* January 21, 1999, p. A23.

[79] Kenneth Bresler, "Seeking Justice, Seeking Election, and Seeking the Death Penalty: The Ethics of Prosecutorial Candidates' Campaigning on Capital Convictions," *Georgetown Journal of Legal Ethics* 7 (1994): 941.

[80] Blume, Eisenberg, and Wells, "Explaining Death Row."

[81] David Baldus, Charles Pulaski, and George Woodworth, "Comparative Review of Death Sentences: An Empirical Study of the Georgia Experience," *Journal of Criminal Law and Criminology* 74 (1983): 661–85. Victim-based discrimination has been found in several southern states. See, for example, Alan Widmayer and James Marquart, "Capital Punishment and Structured Discretion: Arbitrariness and Discrimination after Furman," in *Correctional Theory and Practice,* edited by Clayton A. Hartjen and Edward E. Rhine (Chicago: Nelson-Hall, 1992), 178–96.

[82] Samuel R. Gross and Robert Mauro, *Death and Discrimination: Racial Disparities in Capital Sentencing* (Boston: Northeastern University Press, 1990), 109–10.

[83] Common Sense Foundation, "Landmark North Carolina Death Penalty Study Finds Dramatic Racial Bias" [pamphlet], Raleigh, NC, April 2001.

[84] Robert M. Bohm, "Capital Punishment in Two Judicial Circuits in Georgia," *Law and Human Behavior* 18 (1994): 335.

[85] *New York Times,* June 7, 1998, p. A22.

[86] http://www.deathpenaltyinfo.org, June 23, 2009.

[87] Ibid.

[88] Stanley Rothman and Stephen Powers, "Execution by Quota?" *Public Interest,* Summer 1994, pp. 3–17.

[89] Hugo Adam Bedau, William S. Lofquist, and Michael L. Radelet, "Miscarriages of Justice in Potentially Capital Cases," *Stanford Law Review* 40 (November 1987): 21–179.

[90] Radelet, Lofquist, and Bedau, "Prisoners Released from Death Rows," pp. 907–66.

[91] Philip J. Cook and Donna B. Slawson, with Lori A. Gries, *The Cost of Processing Murder Cases in North Carolina* (Durham, NC: Terry Sanford Institute of Public Policy, 1993).

[92] U.S. Judicial Conference of the United States, *Federal Death Penalty Cases: Recommendations Concerning the Cost and Quality of Defense Representation* (Washington, DC: U.S. Government Printing Office, 1998), 2–3.

[93] Robert M. Bohm, "The Economic Costs of Capital Punishment," in *America's Experiment with Capital Punishment,* edited by James R. Acker, Robert M. Bohm, and Charles S. Lanier (Durham, NC: Carolina Academic Press, 1998), 437–58.

[94] Walter Berns and Joseph Bessette, "Why the Death Penalty Is Fair," *Wall Street Journal,* January 1, 1998, p. A16.

© Kenneth Dickerman/The New York Times/Redux Pictures

© Kenneth Dickerman/The New York Times/Redux Pictures

LEARNING OBJECTIVES

After reading this chapter you should be able to . . .

1 Understand the goals of surveillance.

2 Know the techniques of surveillance and control now in use.

3 Describe how control is a double-edged sword.

4 Recognize the limits of control.

5 Explore how to develop an acceptable system of community control.

The technology now exists for the surveillance of probationers and parolees to be funneled to a central office. Electronic monitors worn by offenders and footage from video cameras located throughout a metropolitan area provide officials real-time data on the whereabouts of those under community supervision. What issues does this type of surveillance raise?

YOU AWAKEN in the early morning to the sound of your phone ringing. The alarm clock next to your bed tells you it is 3:45 A.M. The loud phone startles you awake, but oddly it does not surprise you. This happens every second or third day, at irregular intervals during the night.

Putting the receiver to your ear, you mutter a slight obscenity.

The voice on the other end of the line is not a human voice; it is one of those robot-voiced machines. It says, "This is the Madison County Community Control Department. Please enter your offender code." You type into the phone the last five digits of your social security number.

"Thank you," says the mechanical voice. "Please verify your identity by placing your index finger on the Veri-Pad." Next to the phone is a heat-sensing pad. You put your right index finger on it and wait for three seconds while it registers the information it is receiving from your skin.

The voice intones: "Mr. Juan Agostino, have you committed any crimes since your last observation?" You are not

SURVEILLANCE AND CONTROL IN THE COMMUNITY

unnerved by the question—it is a part of the routine for these nighttime calls. And you know the Veri-Pad is also a lie detector.

You answer, "No."

There is a slight pause. Then the voice continues: "Thank you, Mr. Agostino. You have tested negative for drugs, for alcohol, and for new crimes, and you are in residence as required. You are approved to remain in the community until the next contact." The voice clicks off.

You hang up the phone with a curious sense of annoyance but also relief. Nine months ago, you were convicted of burglary—your second conviction. If you can put up with the intrusion for another year, you will not have to go to prison.

You glance at the alarm clock, which reads, March 15, 2010 . . . 3:50 A.M. At 6:30 the alarm will go off, and you will have to get up and go to work. . . .

This scenario may sound far-fetched, but it is not. The technologies it describes either exist now and are being used or are nearly perfected.[1] They are the technologies of social control, especially designed for monitoring offenders in the community.

Perhaps you do not find the scenario particularly dismaying; if so, it is a sign of how far our society has come in the normalization of community surveillance. Thirty years ago, the description would have provoked outrage from liberals and conservatives alike. Today the techniques of community control surround us to the point where they no longer amaze or alarm us.

Chapter

21

In this chapter we explore community surveillance, an aspect of corrections that has grown more rapidly than perhaps any other in the past 20 years.[2] The steady increase since the 1980s in the percentage of new prison admissions who are probation or parole violators shows that surveillance in the community has been increasingly responsible for sending or returning offenders to prison. In fact, more than one-third of all prison admissions are probationers or parolees who failed under correctional supervision, and half of them were not convicted of a new crime but instead were sent to prison for violating the rules of probation or parole.[3]

Although this chapter argues neither for nor against this trend, it does begin with an assumption: Personal liberty—the ability to live freely with our families, in our homes and communities without being subjected to inordinate controls—is precious. Any correctional trend that touches on this supposedly inviolate aspect of American life raises profound questions.

■ THE GOALS OF SURVEILLANCE

Community surveillance of offenders has multiple goals. You might think the main goal is community protection: We keep offenders under surveillance in order to keep ourselves safe from them. Certainly the rationale for most surveillance programs and the way they are described to the public fit this goal. The rhetoric of "tough" supervision is designed to instill confidence in a doubting public that offenders living in the community pose no threat.

However, most offenders are not "dangerous," for two reasons. First, many offenders, once caught and processed by the system, do not return to crime. Second, even when offenders continue their criminal behavior, most of their crimes are petty acts that do not really endanger their victims. For most offenders, then, the aim of "protection" is not necessarily the most important reason for surveillance.

A more-basic motivation for surveillance programs is the insidious, politically driven problem of institutional overcrowding. The electoral climate of the 1980s and 1990s required politicians to promise zero tolerance for crime. Yet the cost of incarceration is such that increasing prison capacity requires increases in public spending and taxation—certainly a difficult political choice. Therefore, even as the get-tough movement has caused conditions in which a majority of offenders must reside in the community, it has also created an atmosphere in which tolerance for offenders in the community is quite limited.

Policy makers have tried to escape this bind by building correctional programs in the community around themes of surveillance, claiming that such programs are as "safe as prison." This is a debatable claim. In any case, the "tough surveillance" aspect of these new community programs serves the latent goal of allowing the corrections system to retain numerous offenders in the community without having to address the problem of public fear of crime. Thus, surveillance serves as program assurance—the public can accept having so many offenders on the streets, because the corrections system is watching them so closely.

Surveillance has other goals as well. Without some degree of surveillance, treatment providers cannot know for sure if a given treatment is working. The providers argue that some form of drug use surveillance, for instance, is essential to any drug treatment program. Deterrence-minded people argue that tough surveillance deters crime in two ways: (1) it makes offenders less willing to decide to commit a crime, because they are being watched so closely, and (2) it catches active criminals earlier in their recidivism.

The intermediate sanctions movement, discussed in Chapter 9, is an expression of this concern. It is based on the argument that, for many offenders, probation is not stringent enough, but prisons are too expensive and destructive. This has led to the creation of a range of community sanctions whose severity falls between incarceration and probation. Each of these sanctions calls for some degree of surveillance and control.

As we will see, along with surveillance technologies, systems of control also have grown. These are technical ways to limit behavior, either physically or by other means. The advent of technical surveillance has thus changed the orientation of corrections. Instead of merely applying punishment or promoting rehabilitation, the corrections system is called on to establish control over the offender's behavior in ways that prevent misconduct.

■ THE TECHNIQUES OF SURVEILLANCE AND CONTROL

Technologies of correctional surveillance and control have multiplied in recent years. Corrections uses four general types of control strategies: drugs, electronics, human surveillance, and control programs. They may be used either separately or in combination.

Drug Controls

It is perhaps ironic that a society so concerned about drug abuse uses chemicals as one of the main strategies for controlling human behavior. A long tradition of prescribing drugs for precisely this purpose exists in the United States. Although we describe here only a few such drugs, the extent of their use underscores the importance of chemical controls.

Antabuse is frequently given to alcohol abusers. As we saw in Chapter 8, when combined with alcohol, Antabuse violently nauseates a person and therefore suppresses the desire for alcohol. But it also has the side effect of seriously reducing sexual response. The drug is controversial because it is seldom taken voluntarily and its side effects are so undesirable. For example, imagine the predicament of a prisoner who wants to visit his spouse on a furlough but is required to take Antabuse as a condition of the furlough.

See the latest information about **technology in criminal justice** at the corresponding link at www .cengage.com/criminaljustice/ clear.

AP Images/Bebeto Matthews

Control of criminal behavior through the use of drugs has a long history in American corrections. In many cases the drugs must be dispensed by a nurse and consumed under supervision. Drug controls are controversial— they often have adverse side effects and are not 100 percent effective.

Depo-Provera

A "chemical castration" drug that eliminates sexual response in men.

Thorazine

A drug used to control violent or aggressive behavior caused by psychiatric problems.

Prozac

A drug used to decrease the negative emotions associated with depression.

Sometimes called "chemical castration," the drug **Depo-Provera** constrains the male sexual response. It is used to reduce or eliminate the sex drive of men convicted of certain sex offenses. The drug is fairly effective in eliminating the capacity to sustain an erection, but critics do not find this a persuasive argument in behalf of its use. They argue that the aggression inherent in sex offenses, which involves fondling children or assaulting women, is not inhibited by reduced sexual performance. Moreover, the drug does not affect the causes of sexual deviance.

The drug **Thorazine** has long been prescribed for people suffering from certain psychiatric problems that lead to violent behavior. Thorazine is a strong drug that creates a lethargic mood in its users and, by diminishing the capacity for excitement and expressive emotions, reduces the likelihood of violence. It is precisely this lowering of a person's affect that leads many to criticize its use. Chlorpromazine is used for similar problems of psychotic behavior, and it has similar side effects.

For offenders who suffer from depression, the drug **Prozac** is often prescribed. Widely used among nonoffenders, this drug decreases the low, sad feelings that accompany depression. (Zoloft and Paxil are also used, though less frequently.) Although few offenders commit crimes as the direct result of depression, it can be a contributing factor to some criminality, in that people who are unmotivated to get a job or improve their life may be undeterred by the threat of punishment for crime.

While certainly not an exhaustive list, these are some of the drugs most commonly used to control criminal behavior. These examples illustrate the range of problems addressed through drugs and the variety of physical, biological, and emotional responses these drugs produce. They also show the controversial nature of chemical controls—they often have adverse side effects, and they are never 100 percent effective.

Electronic Controls

Perhaps the most important penal innovation of the 1980s was electronic monitoring. As we saw in Chapter 9, the idea of electronic monitoring has much to recommend it: It represents "high-tech" corrections, and it costs less than prison. Since its initial application in the early 1980s, electronic monitoring has become a major industry. Today thousands of offenders are monitored each day. By 2002 at least 20 companies provided electronic monitoring products in the United States, and the market for these products is growing.[4] The technology is becoming particularly popular with sex offenders on community supervision.

The electronic age has made possible a quantum leap in surveillance technology. For example, the technology now exists for visual monitoring via telephone lines. Therefore, video screens could be used to ensure that the offender is actually at home during the phone call. The probation officer could simply call the offender on the phone and then conduct a face-to-face interview without ever leaving the office.

Routine, random video surveillance without the telephone hookup is also possible. Under this system, the probation officer could activate a video camera in the offender's home at any time and obtain direct, unbiased information about the offender's behavior and compliance with the law.

Consider also the technology of the "electric fence" that is now used to confine some dogs. It establishes a perimeter (usually the yard) outside of which the dog may not venture without getting an electric shock. This kind of technology might be easily adapted to keep certain offenders away from schools, bars, or other areas. In theory, at least, it could allow extensive freedom within the necessary restrictions. The Focus box describes efforts at electronic monitoring in England and the United States.

The ability to control a person's actions is one of the ideas behind two kinds of electronic restrictions placed on people convicted of sex crimes. The state of New Jersey requires people released from prison who have criminal histories for sex crimes to receive some form of parole supervision for life. For the highest-risk parolees with sex crime histories, GPS is used to monitor their whereabouts (as described in the Focus box). Parolees carry a cell-phone-sized monitoring device at all times while outside their homes, and this device enables the parole office to know if the person has left the state without

The **national sex offender registry** is found at the corresponding link at www.cengage.com/criminaljustice/clear.

Global Positioning System (GPS)

A type of tracking system used in corrections. The offender must carry a "bag" that transmits a signal to a satellite, allowing correctional officials to identify the person's location at all times.

FOCUS ON

CORRECTIONAL PRACTICE

Update on Electronic Monitoring: "The Bag" Beats "The Tag"

The English are not wild about "tagging offenders"—the way they refer to electronic monitoring. But their prison population has risen so drastically, by 30,000 in five years to a total of about 80,000, that some are beginning to consider the idea.

Of course, by American standards, their alarm seems misplaced. We house almost 20 times as many people in our prison systems and incarcerate our citizens at five times the rate they do. But still, when it comes to the discipline of the world of incarceration, it is all what you are used to. Americans may not understand the English unease at their present prison circumstances, but a host of electronic monitoring executives from this country have made it their business to visit England and with "aggressive marketing" convince them it is time to get into the business of tagging offenders to deal with prison growth.

In 1989 the British Home Office, the policy arm of the government, conducted an experiment with tagging as a condition of bail. The results were widely seen as a "fiasco"—more than half the tagged offenders violated their conditions or were re-arrested while under monitoring, and the program cost the equivalent of about $20,000 per offender. But that did not deter the government from undertaking a plan to use tagging on a field-test basis with curfew orders on probationers—typically unemployed men in their twenties and thirties convicted of a repeat drunkenness-related offense, such as brawling. The Home Office also funded an evaluation study.

Shortly, the program ran into problems. Magistrates (English lower-court judges) were loathe to assign the tag as a condition, and offenders were resistant to its use—only 83 offenders were sentenced to tagging in the first 12 months, and while the majority of cases did well, and the scheme cost less than $1,500 per person overall, the results still seemed meager. The Chief Probation Officers Association published an official policy statement that tagging "does not add anything that cannot already be achieved through existing community penalties."

The Home Office study had problems, as well. A proper control group was never devised, but even more important, full-scale implementation of the field experiment never occurred. There were various problems with the devices themselves, and probation staff never proved enthusiastic about using them. Eventually the Home Office suppressed the

publication of the evaluation, forcing a team of researchers to write a book on their own. Undeterred by problematic research results, the National Probation Service of England and Wales announced widespread implementation of electronic "tagging."

Disaffected with the limitations of telephone-based systems, correctional administrators have begun experimenting with **Global Positioning Systems (GPSs)**. The weakness of the traditional system was the fact that once the offender has left the property, his or her whereabouts are undetermined—all that is known is that the offender is not home. This means that the offender is monitored when under curfew but at other times is free to be anywhere—even places that are prohibited.

GPS solves that. It requires the offender to carry a "bag" (or a box) at all times. The bag transmits a signal to the satellite system developed by the U.S. military for surveillance purposes, which routes the information back to central control. What is actually being tracked is the device in the bag, but the bag has the capacity to inform central control if the offender's bracelet (and presumably the offender) has ceased to be within a short distance—say, 20 feet—of the bag. It means that the central control officer is able to know at all times where the bag is and whether the offender is nearby: 24-hour, worldwide electronic surveillance.

The companies who produce the technology charge $18 per day—about half the cost of jail. The marketers also indicate that their accuracy is far superior to that of the traditional systems and that with additional gadgetry the accuracy can be enhanced even more. The prospect of being able to monitor any offender all the time is no longer mere science fiction.

The angst about "tagging" in Europe appears to be waning, despite lukewarm findings. After less than a decade of use, there are now an estimated 40,000 offenders under electronic surveillance in Sweden, England, the Netherlands, and Belgium.

Sources: J. Robert Lilly, "Review of Electronic Monitoring Research and Policy Analysis," *Journal of Offender Monitoring* 18 (no. 1, 2005): 19, 21; J. Robert Lilly, Dick Whitfield, and Rene Leve, "Electronic Monitoring in Europe: Momentum and Caution," *Journal of Offender Monitoring* 16 (no. 2, Summer–Fall 2003): 10–13.

permission, was at or near the scene of a crime, or is in any other way in violation of legal restrictions (such as being within a school zone). Combined with polygraph testing and treatment, the program is considered a successful way to justify release of people with criminal convictions for sex crimes.[5] Another application of technology allows correctional officials to monitor the computer and Internet usage of people convicted of sex crimes and to restrict access to sexually explicit websites, under the theory that such websites stimulate the desire for repeat sexual offending.[6]

Human Surveillance

The technological advances of electronics and drugs are more systematic than mere human interaction has been. However, unlike these other techniques, personal contact allows the correctional worker to process an array of subtle information—body language, attitudes, odors, and so forth. When it comes to surveillance, no approach can fully supplant the basic strategy of increasing the offender's contact with the experienced correctional worker.

Intensive supervision systems have been used to increase both the frequency and the diversity of this surveillance contact. Reduced caseloads and minimum contact requirements for every offender under supervision increase the frequency of contact. Typically these offenders are seen at least weekly and sometimes more often than that. However, what makes the surveillance effective is not just how much contact there is, but how diverse it is. Offenders are seen at the office, in their homes, and at work; they are seen at regular intervals and in "surprise" visits. The dominant effect is an aura of surveillance in which no aspect of the offender's life is totally free of potential observation.

In short, through routine, random contacts, the correctional officer can observe a wide range of the offender's behavior in a broad array of situations. Increasing this capacity yields a deeper understanding of the offender's compliance with the law.

One of the most recent trends is to empower everyday citizens to perform their own surveillance. All 50 states now have sex offender registries, and both law enforcement and the general public have access to much of the data on these registries.[7] Sex offender notification laws enable neighbors to keep an eye on any people living near them who have been convicted of a sex crime. Similar measures being considered include sex offender license plates[8] and public access to GPS monitoring.[9] These programs have proved very popular, even though their results have sometimes been disappointing.[10] Their effect is to make the general public a source of control over people who have been convicted of certain kinds of crimes. But restrictions on sex offenders have drastically reduced the places they may live. One study estimated that only 5 percent of all housing locations would be legally available for people under sex offender registration, forcing them into "sex offender ghettos" or rural locations.[11] In Chicago, for example, housing restrictions placed on sex offenders exclude vast sections of the poor neighborhoods where most sex offenders can afford to live, and as a consequence many live in places that violate the restrictions because of proximity to a school or day care center.[12]

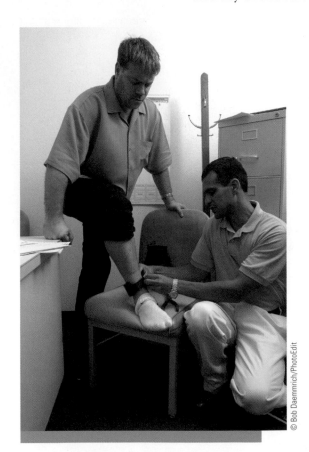

Electronic devices are increasingly being used to check on the whereabouts of probationers and parolees. Offenders can be tethered to the device and tracked using the global positioning system.

© Bob Daemmrich/PhotoEdit

Programmatic Controls

The most widely used techniques of surveillance and control are established elements of treatment programs. Drug testing is a good example. In these programs, urine samples are routinely taken to test for drug use. Normally the offender is required to submit a urine sample (with a correctional worker watching as it is "produced" to ensure that it is truly the offender's urine and not a substitute), which is then sent to a lab for testing.

Not only is this procedure awkward and invasive, it is untimely, involving substantial delay between the time of surveillance (the actual urine evaluation) and subsequent arrest and revocation if the urine proves "dirty." Recently, on-the-spot tests have been developed, usually involving a drug-sensitive strip of paper. Some are used with urine samples; others with saliva samples. In addition, because certain drugs leave no traces of their presence in the urine or saliva within hours of their use, some programs have adopted the expensive alternative of hair testing. Traces of some illegal drugs can be detected in human hair for a year or more after the drug's ingestion.

Programs also sometimes provide for systems of surveillance and control. The most famous example is Vermont's Relapse Prevention Program for sex offenders. This program trains the offender to be aware of potential signs indicating a reversion to deviant sexual behavior. These signals include sudden changes in mood, renewed drinking, loss of a job, and depression. What makes this program unusual, however, is that selected individuals living in the offender's community—family, friends, therapists, and co-workers—also are taught to look for the same signs. In effect, these people become additional eyes and ears for the correctional worker, who regularly contacts them to see if the offender is exhibiting behavioral changes that should concern the authorities. The community thus augments the system by providing additional surveillance.

The use of surveillance systems to augment treatment programs is becoming increasingly popular. One result is an expansion of surveillance to populations of offenders who would not be considered dangerous or serious. For example, electronic monitoring is now being tested to support programs for school truants and for people who have been ordered to pay child support.[13] The expansion of surveillance methods to marginally criminal populations is one of the problems critics fear in the use of this technology.

■ CONTROL: A DOUBLE-EDGED SWORD

Many of us might initially regard the idea of tighter surveillance of offenders as a good thing. Increasing the public's confidence in corrections, developing improved treatments for offenders, and improving deterrence of crime are all desirable goals. However, surveillance raises issues concerning personal freedom and politics that must be addressed.

Social Control and Personal Liberty

Various forms of surveillance are common in modern society. Parents put listening devices in infants' rooms so they can hear when the baby wakes up; banks put video monitors in their ATMs to photograph people who withdraw money; airports X-ray all bags to check for weapons; businesses and stores run checks on credit cards before each purchase. With the advent of the information age, surveillance has become a more likely option for preventing problems than ever before. (See "Myths in Corrections.")

Yet Americans also have a tradition of respect for individual privacy. We are especially suspicious of any invasion of the home, no matter what its benefits might be; thus, the increase in community surveillance comes at a price. The main cost is civil liberty. Just as studies have shown that families suffer from a member's incarceration, they also show that house arrest, electronic monitoring, and intensive supervision place stress on the family. Sometimes

MYTHS IN CORRECTIONS

SURVEILLANCE AND CRIME RATES

THE MYTH: When people are watched more closely by correctional authorities, they are less likely to engage in crimes.

THE REALITY: A host of studies in a variety of settings finds that increased surveillance is associated with higher rates of being returned to prison for misbehavior, but not lower rates of arrest for criminal conduct.

Source: Francis T. Cullen, Andrew J. Myer, and Edward J. Latessa, "Eight Lessons Learned from Moneyball: The High Cost of Ignoring Evidence-Based Corrections," *Victims and Offenders* 4 (no. 2, 2009): 197–213.

Baltimore's surveillance system includes more than 300 cameras, both portable and fixed. Here, Lucy McKeldin, a retired police officer, monitors a possible drug deal. Police claim that crime is down 15 percent in neighborhoods where cameras are installed. Critics ask if less crime is worth the resulting limits on personal liberty.

these measures infringe directly on the privacy of innocent people. For instance, think about the scenario described at the beginning of the chapter. Can you imagine the annoyance of Juan Agostino's wife whenever the phone rings in the middle of the night? Or the sense of personal violation provoked by the surreptitious video monitoring?

Critics of the new community surveillance argue that whenever the government is allowed to intervene into citizens' lives without restraint, tyranny results, as shown throughout history. Unless we jealously protect our civil liberties from intrusion by the state, freedom will inevitably and continually erode. To support their case, these critics point out that airport metal detectors were supposed to be a temporary measure when they were first developed and that the social security number was supposed to have no official use other than keeping track of social security benefits.

The advocates of control concede these points. But they also note that airplane hijackings have decreased in frequency and that life is more convenient now that we have social security numbers. Moreover, surveillance is almost always less restrictive than prison (suggesting that convicted criminals' rights to privacy are not strong), and the right to privacy might be deemed less important than the need to prevent crime. Studies of people under electronic surveillance find, for example, that they feel very strongly their loss of liberty under the device, but they equally are grateful that they did not have to go to jail.[14]

People who question technocorrections worry that when new technologies are developed for corrections, it is difficult to stop them from spreading, for they quickly become popular. Who can argue against electronic fences for criminals if it can be shown that they work? Already some city streets are blocked off to prevent drug sales. The image of a future society in which whole sections of town are cordoned off from certain people for legal reasons may not be far-fetched.

Thus, the new emphasis on correctional surveillance and control represents a major change for the community at large, as well as for corrections. We must recognize that the advocacy of technological surveillance and control changes our communities, perhaps in some ways we would not choose. And we must also acknowledge that the debate about freedom and control is a very old one that cannot be resolved in a few pages.

The Politics of Surveillance and Community Protection

Community surveillance and control are highly controversial issues in modern American politics. To better understand this controversy, we can compare traditional conservative

You can access position papers on correctional technology by reading *Tech Beat*, the award-winning magazine of the National Law Enforcement and Corrections Technology Center, through the corresponding link at www.cengage.com/criminaljustice/clear.

and liberal views about the appropriate role of government in the community and then assess how the problem of crime influences those views.

Traditionally, conservatives have opposed government intrusion into personal affairs. They seek as much autonomy as possible for individual citizens and want the government to be conservative (reluctant) in taking action. Interpersonal relations should remain unencumbered by government oversight. Yet when it comes to the problem of crime, this position is reversed: Conservatives call for broad and extensive government action and control, and the government is seen as a protector of individual and property rights. Ironically, the primary conservative spokespeople turn out to be advocates for all sorts of electronic, chemical, and human control over other citizens.

At the other end of the spectrum, the traditional liberal view calls for the use of government power to promote equal access of all citizens to the benefits of society. Thus, liberals seek programs that alleviate social inequalities; this agenda, in turn, often requires a fairly extensive level of government involvement in communities, especially in the form of ameliorative social programs. Yet when it comes to crime, liberals are suspicious of the expansion of government surveillance and control, and they seek to place firm limits on the development of these approaches. Instead of being concerned about the way crime reduces victims' access to social benefits, liberals often express their concern about potential overinvolvement by government in offenders' lives.

Why this shift? Much of it has to do with the ways in which the traditional political positions contrast the values of social order and personal liberty. Conservatives strongly emphasize social order. They view crime as a serious threat to normal social relations, as throwing the ordinary processes of human commerce out of kilter. To prevent such crime-fueled distortions of society, conservatives are willing to sacrifice offenders' interest in being free of undue government control. Although conservatives ordinarily want individuals to look out for their own interests, where crime is concerned they want government to intervene to manage the interests of private citizens.

In contrast, because they value liberty, liberals tend to be alarmed by the intrusion of government into the lives of individuals—both offenders and nonoffenders. They view any government control of citizens as inherently dangerous and believe that the cost of extending government power into the home far outweighs any potential benefits in controlling crime. While liberals want government to guarantee equal access of all citizens to the social arena, they feel that government action against crime reduces rather than advances human liberty.

There is another, more practical, issue in the politics of community surveillance and control: Which communities will be controlled? In the United States street crime is the most pervasive in the inner cities, where minorities and the poor are concentrated. Therefore, these communities are targeted for control, so that poor and minority citizens must face expanded government intrusion into their lives. This is probably another reason that the traditional viewpoints of conservatives and liberals are altered by the problem of crime. Liberals, more than conservatives, are troubled by the image of massive, government-run surveillance programs applied to minority, inner-city residents.

■ THE LIMITS OF CONTROL

A few years ago, when the first rumblings of the get-tough movement were felt, Nils Christie wrote an essay against punishment, entitled *Limits to Pain*.[15] His argument, which has become a classic criticism of penal reform, was that the focus of liberals on how reforming punishment might backfire and result in an expansion of the penal system and the number of people under government control.

His predictions turned out to be correct—though not everyone would argue this has been bad for society. Imprisonment has grown in scope and cost. At the same time, community correctional programs have become tougher, more oriented toward control and surveillance, and quicker to reincarcerate offenders who fail to comply with the strict requirements of the system. We might well ask, What are the limits of this trend?

Technology

The most direct limit on this trend is technical. All technologies have the capacity to fail, and determined offenders often can figure out a way to defeat even the most ingenious technical apparatus. The growing number of crimes committed by people who are being monitored electronically attests to this fact, as do studies that question whether people under electronic monitoring commit fewer crimes.[16]

Technologies also are limited in terms of capacity. Even though marvelous things are done with computers these days, anyone who works with them will have experienced the "bugs" that can develop in these systems. Big companies like IBM or AT&T can afford to spend large sums of money to upgrade information capability, but corrections systems need reliable computers that do not require extensive management. Thus, the correctional version of an information system is usually not state of the art. Advances in surveillance and control technologies require sophisticated technical support, which corrections often lacks.

Human Responses

A second limitation affecting control centers on people's responses to it. Those who work in corrections often choose the field because they like working with people. Many correctional workers resent the intrusion of technical surveillance into their work; others take exception to the shift in goals from helping to controlling. In either case, they may undermine the change in policy through active or passive resistance.

Offenders also resent the surveillance and control. Although they can do little about these components of their sentence directly, they can resist in indirect ways. For instance, the unenthusiastic offender may come to the probation office late, sulk during interviews, act sullenly when the officer visits the home, and generally let it be known that the tight control is unwanted.

In addition, offenders, like all of us, are relatively unpredictable. Any system of control is based partly on prediction—how the offender will respond to the system and what the offender will and will not be able to do about it. By acknowledging that offenders are not completely predictable, we also admit that there is no foolproof way to control them. One study found that an increased frequency of drug testing had no impact on the probability of failure or success for young parolees.[17] There are no guarantees.

Moral and Ethical Limits

technocorrections
The use of technological mechanisms, by corrections systems, to control offenders.

Tony Fabelo, the director of the Texas Criminal Justice Policy Council, has expressed grave concerns about the growth of **technocorrections**—the growing use of technology for control of offenders by corrections systems. He characterizes the increased reliance of correctional officials on pharmacological and electronic controls of offender behavior as a troubling new development in the field. He especially deplores "the incentives it offers to expand the net of state control in order to deal with social and behavioral problems in the name of public safety."[18]

At the same time, there is some evidence that the consequences of using technology in correctional settings have not been entirely negative. A recent study of Florida's very large program of electronic monitoring, its Community Controls System, found evidence that *both* crime and the costs of prison were averted.[19] New York City's use of ATM machines for probation reporting reduces the intrusion into the lives of thousands of probationers, while enabling probation officers to concentrate their efforts on more-serious cases.

Nonetheless, some of the scenarios about community control are downright disturbing, bringing to mind images of totalitarian regimes in which the powerful use mind control to squelch all dissent. There is, of course, a difference between dissent and crime. But when we recognize that the correctional population of the United States is disproportionately composed of young, urban, African American and Hispanic men, we should be cautious in developing whole systems of control and surveillance to surround them. After a while, it begins to appear almost as though the homes, streets, schools, and families of an entire social subgroup are being subjected to official control and invaded by surveillance technologies. The image is not attractive.

At some point, the trade-off between safety and freedom becomes a concern. In terms of street crime, some of the safest societies in history have been the totalitarian regimes of Nazi Germany and Stalinist Russia. There are worse things to live with than crime in the streets.

■ TOWARD ACCEPTABLE COMMUNITY CONTROL

How do we resolve this dilemma? Stanley Cohen has written eloquently about this problem, arguing that there is nothing inherently wrong with control.[20] The issue is who benefits from it. If the sole purpose of correctional control is to strengthen the capacity of government to rule citizens' lives and to reduce individual and community autonomy, then the control is a negative force that works to destroy communities. But if the surveillance and control are designed to maintain communities by allowing offenders to find ways to continue to live there despite their offense, then the approach is inclusive and helps build communities.

The distinction is often not obvious in practice. We can classify few of the modern correctional forms of surveillance and control as either truly inclusive or ultimately anticommunity. We can, however, begin to understand their value by asking certain questions. First, is the surveillance/control truly being used in lieu of imprisonment? That is, without this control would the offender actually be in jail or prison? Second, is the offender's risk to the community such that without this control the offender would be highly likely to engage in crime? In other words, is the surveillance/control really necessary, or is it being used to mollify public sentiment that is basically erroneous? Third, could some less-intrusive method achieve the same basic result? That is, is the technology being used only because it is high-tech, not because it succeeds better than traditional alternatives? Fourth, are steps being taken to eliminate the indirect intrusions of the surveillance into the lives of innocent individuals who live or work with the offender?

Finally, is the offender allowed opportunities to demonstrate self-control, so that the surveillance/control system can be gradually reduced? To the degree that there are positive answers to these questions, we might think of the corrections system as being necessary, limited, and focused on offenders.

SUMMARY

1 Understand the goals of surveillance.

Community surveillance of offenders has multiple goals. A main goal is community protection: We keep offenders under surveillance in order to keep ourselves safe from them. However, most offenders are not "dangerous." A more-basic motivation for surveillance programs is the problem of institutional overcrowding. Policy makers have tried to build correctional programs in the community around themes of surveillance, claiming that such programs are as "safe as prison." Surveillance has other goals as well. Without some degree of surveillance, treatment providers cannot know for sure if a given treatment is having an effect. Deterrence-minded people argue that tough surveillance deters crime because it makes offenders less willing to commit a crime, because they are being watched so closely, and it catches active criminals earlier in their recidivism.

2 Know the techniques of surveillance and control now in use.

Corrections uses four general types of control strategies: (1) Drug controls respond to a range of problems, often with adverse side effects and never 100 percent effective. (2) Electronic controls result in thousands of offenders being monitored electronically each day, through telephone systems, video systems, and GPS. (3) Human surveillance provides personal contact that allows the correctional worker to process an array of subtle information—body language, attitudes, odors, and so forth. (4) Programmatic controls use established elements of treatment programs, such as drug testing, to monitor behavior.

3 Describe how control is a double-edged sword.

Increasing the public's confidence in corrections, developing improved treatments for offenders, and improving deterrence of crime are all desirable goals. However, surveillance raises issues concerning personal freedom and politics that must be addressed. Americans have a tradition of respect for individual privacy. We are suspicious of any invasion of the home, no matter what its benefits might be; thus, the increase in community surveillance comes at a price. The main cost is civil liberty.

4 Recognize the limits of control.

The most direct limit on the trend toward surveillance is that all technologies have the capacity to fail, and determined offenders often can figure out a way to defeat even the most ingenious technical apparatus. Technologies also are limited in terms of capacity, and every technical system has its own "bugs." A second limitation affecting control centers on the resistance of both staff and clients to succumb to it; neither group is entirely predictable. Finally, the trade-off between safety and freedom becomes a concern at some point. There are worse things to live with than crime in the streets.

5 Explore how to develop an acceptable system of community control.

If the sole purpose of correctional control is to strengthen the capacity of government to rule citizens' lives and to reduce individual and community autonomy, then the control is a negative force that works to destroy communities. But if the surveillance and control are designed to maintain communities by allowing offenders to find ways to continue to live there despite their offense, then the approach is inclusive and helps build communities. If the offender is allowed opportunities to demonstrate self-control, so that the surveillance/control system can be gradually reduced, then the controls are reasonable.

KEY TERMS

Depo-Provera (p. 572)
Global Positioning System (GPS) (p. 572)

Prozac (p. 572)
technocorrections (p. 578)

Thorazine (p. 572)

FOR DISCUSSION

1. Would electronic fences be a good thing for some offenders? If so, which offenders? How would you use the fences?

2. In mandating that some offenders submit to control via drugs such as Antabuse or Depo-Provera, what trade-offs between civil liberties and community safety might be necessary?

3. What might be the value of electronically monitored house arrest for pretrial detainees?

4. Do offenders' family members have a right to privacy that protects them from correctional surveillance? Why or why not?

5. Should high school students be tested regularly for illegal drug use? Why or why not?

FOR FURTHER READING

Byrne, James M., and Donald J. Rebovich, eds. *The New Technology of Crime, Law, and Social Control.* Monsey, NY: Criminal Justice Press, 2007. Essays on the "hard" and "soft" technologies of corrections.

Cohen, Stanley. *Against Criminology.* New Brunswick, NJ: Transaction, 1988. Describes the recent history of thinking about crime control strategies, with a special emphasis on penology.

———. *Visions of Social Control.* Cambridge, MA: Polity, 1985. Assesses community-based correctional surveillance and control.

Lyon, David, ed. *Theorizing Surveillance: The Panopticon and Beyond.* Portland: Willan, 2006. A series of essays about the way surveillance has become an everyday aspect of contemporary life, and how it affects us.

Roberts, Julian. *The Virtual Prison.* New York: University of Cambridge Press, 2004. Describes the evolution of community-based penalties from systems of support and change into systems of punishment and surveillance.

Sherman, Lawrence. *Ethics in Criminal Justice Education.* Hastingson-Hudson, NY: Institute for Social Ethics, 1982. Reviews problems in criminal justice education and suggests standards.

NOTES

[1] For example, see Christopher Crucella and Douglas Stallato Kabat, "Sleep Monitoring as a Method for Detecting Alcohol and Other Drug Abuse," *Journal of Offender Monitoring* 18 (no. 1, 2005): 4, 21; Ward Vanlaar, Robyn Robertson, and Herb Simpson, "Monitoring Alcohol Use through Transdermal Alcohol Testing," *Journal of Offender Monitoring* 19 (no. 2, 2007): 26–28.

[2] Julian Roberts, *The Virtual Prison* (New York: University of Cambridge Press, 2004).

[3] BJS *Bulletin*, August 2003.

[4] "The 2002–2003 Electronic Monitoring Survey," *Journal of Electronic Monitoring* 15 (no. 1, Winter–Spring 2002): 5.

[5] New Jersey State Parole Board, "GPS Monitoring of Sex Offenders," *Corrections Forum* 17 (no. 3, May–June 2008): 55–59.

[6] Richard C. LaMagna and Marc Berejka, "Remote Computer Monitoring: Managing Sex Offenders' Access to the Internet," *Journal of Offender Monitoring* 21 (no. 1, January 2009): 11–24.

[7] Monica Davey, "Plenty of Data on Sex Offenders, but Registries Are Just a Start," *New York Times*, September 2, 2009, pp. A1, A3.

[8] Bob Driehaus, "Green License Plates Proposed to Identify Ohio Sex Offenders," *New York Times*, March 7, 2007, p. A12.

[9] Jason Peckenpaugh, "Controlling Sex Offender Reentry: Jessica's Law Measures in California," *Journal of Offender Monitoring* 19 (no. 1, 2006): 13–29.

[10] Richard G. Zevitz, "Community Notification: Its Role in Recidivism and Offender Reintegration," *Criminal Justice Studies* 10 (no. 2, 2006): 193–211.

[11] Paul A. Zanbergen and Timothy C. Hart, "Reducing Housing Options for Convicted Sex Offenders: Investigating the Impact of Residency Restriction Law Using GIS," *Justice Research and Policy* 8 (no. 2, 2006): 1–24.

[12] Lorine A. Hughes and Keri B. Burchfield, "Sex Offender Residence Restrictions in Chicago: An Environmental Injustice?" *Justice Quarterly* 25 (no. 4, December 2008): 647–73.

[13] See Rhonda Zingraff, Sheenagh Lopez, and Jennifer McCoy, "Evidence Favors Electronic Monitoring for Improvements in Child Support Collections," *Journal of Electronic Monitoring* 21 (no. 1, January 2009): 5–9; Peter A. Michel, "Truancy Reduction: An Emerging Application for Electronic Monitoring," *Journal of Electronic Monitoring* 21 (no. 2, March 2009): 12–15.

[14] Brian K. Payne and Randy R. Gainey, "The Electronic Monitoring of Offenders Released from Jail or Prison: Safety, Control, and Comparisons to the Incarceration Experience," *Prison Journal* 84 (no. 4, December 2004): 413–45.

[15] Nils Christie, *Limits to Pain* (Oxford, England: Martin Robinson, 1981).

[16] Michael P. O'Toole, "Study of Factors Affecting Recidivism of Offenders on Electronic Monitoring," *Journal of Electronic Monitoring* 17 (no. 1, Winter–Spring 2004): 5–6. See also Mary A. Finn and Suzanne Muirhead-Steves, "The Effectiveness of Electronic Monitoring with Violent Male Parolees," *Justice Quarterly* 18 (no. 2, June 2002): 293–312.

[17] Rudy Haapanen and Lee Briton, "Drug Testing for Youthful Offenders on Parole: An Experimental Evaluation," *Criminology and Public Policy* 1 (no. 2, 2002): 217.

[18] Tony Fabelo, "Technocorrections: The Promises, the Uncertain Threats," *Sentencing and Corrections: Issues for the 21st Century*, No. 5, May 2000, p. 4. [NIJ Research in Brief]

[19] Kathy G. Padgett, William D. Bales, and Thomas G. Blomberg, "Under Surveillance: An Empirical Test of the Effectiveness and Consequences of Electronic Monitoring," *Criminology and Public Policy* 5 (no. 1, 2005): 61–92.

[20] Stanley Cohen, *Against Criminology* (New Brunswick, NJ: Transaction, 1988), 104–24.

AP Images/Dan Loh

LEARNING OBJECTIVES

After reading this chapter you should be able to . . .

1 Define community justice and show how it differs from criminal justice.

2 Identify the arguments in favor of community justice.

3 Describe the problems that community justice faces.

4 Explore the future prospects of community justice.

This is Kensington, a particularly troubled section of North Philadelphia. Police officers, street crews, and inspection workers recently swept through this area, making arrests and boarding up drug houses as part of Operation Sunrise, an offensive aimed at the most crime-ridden square mile of the city. Is this one aspect of community justice?

ONE THEME throughout this book is the growth of the corrections system since the mid-1970s. It is impossible to understand the U.S. penal system without also recognizing that it is the largest in the world. As shown in Chapter 1, it incarcerates more people per capita than does any other nation, which represents several times more people than other democracies incarcerate. When we factor in the people under community supervision, the U.S. system is currently punishing one out of every 32 adults—7 percent of all male adults.[1] Nowhere in the world, and no time in history, has seen an equivalent of this massive system of punishment.

The growth of the penal system is not random. It has been concentrated among four groups, according to the following characteristics:

- *Age:* Most people in the penal system are aged 20–45.
- *Race/ethnicity:* Two-third of those under correctional control are minority group members.

COMMUNITY JUSTICE

■ *Gender:* Nearly nine-tenths of correction's clients are men.

■ *Socioeconomic status:* The penal population is dominated by poor people, the frequently unemployed, those who have little education and few skills.

These four characteristics of the penal population result in an important spatial dynamic in the correctional system: Most of the people who cycle through probation, prisons, and parole come from a limited number of impoverished communities. Not every correctional client hails from our nation's poorest places, of course; prisoners and probationers come from every neighborhood. In some places, however, the concentration of residents who have experienced the corrections system is astoundingly high. Some studies estimate that in the poorest sections of Cleveland and Baltimore, for example, almost one in five male adults is behind bars on any given day.[2] In one study, almost every family in two poor neighborhoods in Tallahassee, Florida, had a member who had gone to prison.[3]

This neighborhood effect is referred to as the **spatial concentration** of criminal justice. In these neighborhoods, arrests are common, especially for drugs, and going to prison is a common problem, alongside others such as poverty, broken families, joblessness—and crime.

Why does this happen? We have spatial concentration because American neighborhoods are segregated along racial/ethnic and income lines, and these are two of the ways corrections is concentrated. Our prisons and probation offices work with poor people of color, and the neighborhoods where they live become places where the business of corrections is a dominant theme.

Chapter

22

spatial concentration
A phenomenon of criminal justice in which certain neighborhoods have very high numbers of arrests and of people going to prison.

In these places the criminal justice system traditionally works, one case at a time, to help clean things up. People who have committed crimes are arrested, prosecuted, and punished. Increasingly, they are removed from the streets for a term of incarceration. Almost all return after a time behind bars. At times it seems the police, courts, and corrections systems work at odds with each other and with these troubled places. Police arrest "bad guys"; courts put them in prison, where they get no better and often get worse; and corrections watches them closely once they are back on the streets, waiting to start the cycle all over again. For these communities, many people are "missing" on any given day, behind bars somewhere, but because they cycle through the justice system, the actual ones who are missing change from one day to the next, and almost every young man gets his turn.

The cycling of so many residents through the justice system is now understood to produce its own list of problems for such places. There are almost 1.5 million minority children (2 million, overall) whose fathers are in prison or jail.[4] Having a father go to prison contributes to a range of developmental problems, including poor school performance, emotional problems, and even delinquency.[5] Places where many men cycle through prison are places where marriages and families are disrupted.[6] The range of social problems includes sexually transmitted diseases and teen births,[7] as well as serious juvenile delinquency.[8] Some evidence even suggests that high rates of arrests[9] and incarceration[10] *cause* crime rather than prevent it.

What is to be done? The people being processed through the justice system have committed crimes and cannot be ignored. But more of the same kind of action seems to be counterproductive. In the face of this conundrum, a growing group of reformers have argued that in these communities, community justice is a better approach. Community justice seeks not just to apprehend lawbreakers and punish them; it also seeks to improve and strengthen the communities from which they come.

In this chapter we explore the developing idea of community justice. We discuss it as a philosophy of justice and a strategy of corrections. We ultimately investigate its strengths and weaknesses as an emerging strategy for troubled communities that are hit hard not just by crime, but also by criminal justice.

■ DEFINITION OF COMMUNITY JUSTICE

Community justice is a new idea that has gathered considerable support among practitioners and policy makers across the country. A large number of municipalities have recently undertaken community justice initiatives of one sort or another. The particulars of these initiatives vary, because different places tailor strategies to the particulars of their own crime problems. However, all pursue similar goals.

The rapid growth in new and innovative community justice projects is remarkable for two reasons. First, they have arisen as a result of local desires to develop more-proactive responses to crime. Second, they receive funding not from large federal grants but rather from local resources that are redirected from traditional approaches to community justice strategies.

As you may have gathered, community justice is not a simple idea that can be explained in a single sentence. It can be thought of as at once a *philosophy* of justice, a *strategy* of justice, and a series of justice *programs*.

AP Images/Paul Vernon, File

Richard Vickers, left, talks with his block watch commander and fellow resident Bill Sieloff as they patrol their Old Oaks Neighborhood in Columbus, Ohio. Across the country neighbors are using Twitter, blogs, email, and street patrols to help ward off crime.

A Philosophy of Justice

As a philosophy, community justice is based on a pursuit of justice that goes beyond the traditional three tasks of criminal justice—the apprehension, conviction, and punishment of offenders. Community justice recognizes that crime and the problems that result from it greatly impede the quality of community life. Thus, the community justice approach not only seeks to respond to criminal events through traditional means—it also sets as a goal the improvement of quality of community life, especially for communities afflicted by high levels of crime. Robert Sampson and his colleagues have coined the term **collective efficacy** to denote the type of life that communities need to reduce crime.[11]

collective efficacy
Mutual trust among neighbors, combined with willingness to intervene on behalf of the common good, especially to supervise children and maintain public order.

A Strategy of Justice

The strategy of the community justice approach combines three contemporary justice innovations: community policing, environmental crime prevention, and restorative justice. Each of these innovations holds promise as a way of preventing crime and reviving community safety.

COMMUNITY POLICING ■ The community policing approach to law enforcement employs problem-solving strategies to identify ways to prevent crimes by getting to root causes instead of relying on arrests as a way to respond to criminal events. Rather than reacting to 911 calls for service, community policing attempts to identify crime "hot spots" and change the dynamics of those places that seem to make crime possible. Rather than keeping citizens at arm's length, police officers actively seek partnerships with residents and citizen groups in pursuit of safer streets. Rather than a hierarchical paramilitary structure, community policing seeks to decentralize decision making to officers at the local areas; it also seeks to design area-specific strategies for overcoming crime.

By the end of the 1990s, the community policing movement had become enormously successful. Over 80 percent of police departments said they practiced some form of community policing, and most observers credited the approach as being partly responsible for the drop in crime in the latter half of the decade.

A community court in San Francisco composed of a police officer, attorney, business owner, and caseworker hear the prostitution charges brought against an unidentified woman. Community courts were established in San Francisco in 1998 to redirect quality-of-life misdemeanors out of the court system and into the neighborhoods for resolution.

AP Images/Marcio Jose Sanchez

ENVIRONMENTAL CRIME PREVENTION ■ In some cities, 70 percent of crimes occur in 20 percent of the city's locations. What produces such high concentrations of crime? And what can be done about those places?

The environmental crime-prevention approach begins with an analysis of why crime tends to concentrate in certain locations and certain times. Then, environmental crime-prevention specialists try to change the places crimes tend to occur—to change them in ways that reduce crime. They bring light to darkened street corners that otherwise attract gangs as hangouts, establish procedures to keep elevators in repair so that people need not use isolated stairways to get to their apartments, change the traffic flow in streets that used to serve as drug markets, and restore open areas so that they serve as playgrounds rather than vacant lots.

RESTORATIVE JUSTICE ■ The restorative justice approach to sanctioning offenders seeks to restore the victim, the offender, and the community to a level of functioning that existed prior to the criminal event. The restorative justice approach calls for offenders to admit what they have done and take steps to make restitution. There are four basic types of restorative justice strategies: victim–offender mediation, community reparative boards, family group conferencing, and circle sentencing. In all of these strategies, victims and offenders are often brought together to identify the steps that offenders may take to help victims recover from the crime. Then the offender gets involved in programs designed to help reduce the chances of reoffending.[12]

With growing support from studies, restorative justice programs are becoming increasingly popular. (See the Focus box "Common Justice.") Research has shown that, when compared with traditional criminal justice, restorative justice programs result in greater satisfaction for both victims and offenders. Some studies also suggest that recidivism rates may be lower for some restorative justice strategies,[13] though research results are mixed.[14] Critics point out that the rhetoric of restorative justice is not always matched by the activities of corresponding programs.[15]

Programs

Programs of community justice include a varied package of methods. Listing just a few of them illustrates the range and innovative nature of community justice:

■ Crime mapping identifies where the problem of crime is most concentrated.

■ Citizen advisory groups help identify and prioritize local crime problems.

CORRECTIONAL PRACTICE

Common Justice

Danielle Sered

On the subway in New York, a group made up mostly of Christian youths attacked a group of youths who were wishing fellow passengers "Happy Hannukah." There were a number of participants in the attack and a number of people harmed. The primary male assailant already had an open hate-crime case and so was not eligible for diversion, and the least culpable of the group were given sentences of probation, a day of diversity training, and community service. Remaining was one young female defendant, who attacked and beat one of the Hannukah celebrants, pulling out her hair and causing her injury.

The case was referred to Common Justice by the District Attorney, the victim (whom Common Justice calls "the harmed party") was engaged and chose to participate, the defense counsel was contacted, and the defendant (whom Common Justice calls "the responsible party") was screened. The defendant then entered a plea of guilty to assault in the third degree as a hate crime and sentencing was suspended so she could participate in the program.

The program, Common Justice, provides an important opportunity for healing to those harmed by a range of crimes, including assault, burglary, and robbery. The project involves those harmed by younger adults (aged 16 to 24) facing felony charges. If—and only if—the harmed parties welcome the opportunity, these cases are diverted into a conferencing process designed to recognize the harm done, identify the needs and interests of those harmed, and determine a range of appropriate actions to hold the responsible party accountable. Common Justice's staff closely monitors responsible parties' compliance with the resultant agreements—which may include extensive community service, rehabilitative and educational programming, violence intervention classes, and restitution, among other sanctions—and connects those harmed by crime with appropriate services. The project serves as an alternative to incarceration for those responsible and an avenue to healing for those harmed.

Common Justice cases proceed through four stages: *engagement*, in which parties are enrolled in the program; *preparation*, in which parties and their support people (who may be family, friends, neighbors, and so forth) are prepared for the conferencing and those harmed are connected with urgently needed services; *conferencing, or dialogue*, in which the parties and their support people come together to address the harm and reach agreements that the responsible party can fulfill to make things as right as possible; and *supervision/follow-up*, in which harmed parties are supported and referred to uniquely tailored services and responsible parties are rigorously supervised as they complete their agreements.

After the conclusion of the preparatory period, Common Justice staff facilitated a dialogue between two people who had only had a terrible connection before: the program convened first one, then a second and final conference in the case. Together, the parties reached a robust and powerful set of agreements. Once they had done so, in the final go-round, the facilitator asked each person to say just a couple of words about how they were feeling. The responsible party's mother said to the harmed party,

If someone did to me what my daughter did to you, I don't know if I would have anything but hate in my heart for them. You have to be the most generous, kind, compassionate person I have ever met. Your family must be very proud of you, and they must be beautiful people to have raised someone like you. My family is indebted to you forever for what you've given us, and while I know I'll never know how you suffered, and I can't imagine what you've been through, I pray that what my daughter does in this program brings you a little bit of the peace you deserve. Thank you.

The harmed party was next to speak. She had suffered from posttraumatic stress since the incident and her life had been profoundly changed by what happened. Since becoming involved in Common Justice, those symptoms had begun to relent. She paused before speaking, and smiled, and said, "I feel relieved. I feel excited and grateful about what happened here. This is an amazing experience. I don't know what to say. . . . I feel joyful. Just joyful."

The responsible party, who had agreed to everything asked of her and was therefore faced with a demanding set of agreements to complete, when it was her turn, said (through tears) to the harmed party in a solemn and unwavering voice, "I know you've said apologies don't mean a lot to you, so instead let me just say: thank you. From the bottom of my heart, thank you. I owe you everything I have, and I won't let you down." When the participants finished going around the circle, they all broke bread together, and after requesting the harmed party's permission, the harmed and

CORRECTIONAL PRACTICE (*Continued*)

responsible party hugged. They'd only touched once before in their lives—during the violent incident that initiated this process.

This case when it occurred was cited as an example of monstrosity and hate. When the case came to Common Justice, the harmed party was understandably furious. Because of the nature of the crime, Common Justice screened the case with extraordinary care and a degree of skepticism. There was a point in the conference where it seemed uncertain whether the group would reach agreements, or to what

extent the agreements they could reach would satisfy the harmed party's needs. With the hard work of everyone in the circle, they moved to a better place than any of the participants, including the program staff, had dared to anticipate. The result stands as a testimony to what is possible between people when a process makes space for their full humanity and the best parts of themselves to emerge.

Source: Danielle Sered is Executive Director of Common Justice, a demonstration project of the Vera Institute of Justice. This essay was written specially for this book.

■ Citizen partnerships between justice agencies and citizen groups improve the legitimacy of justice programs and help justice officials tailor the programs to address community needs.

■ Local organizations of police, prosecutors, judges, and correctional officials enable them to develop local strategies of crime prevention.

■ Citizens and victims are involved in sentencing decisions to increase their confidence in the wisdom of the sanctions.

■ Offender community service gives sanctions to offenders and restores victims and their communities.

Most of all, community justice is concerned with taking seriously the problems faced by people who live with high levels of crime, some of whom are themselves involved in crime. When Walter Harrison goes to work (see the Focus box "Community Justice in Action"), he practices community justice in a way that reflects all of these particular programs, not just one or two in isolation. He is not out to arrest kids but is there to help keep them safe. He is not saying, "I am a probation officer, not a policeman"; rather, he is trying to practice probation in a way that is relevant to the particular needs of the offenders, their families, and their neighbors, each of whom is concerned about being safe.

Investigate a series of **community crime-prevention strategies** in practice; see the corresponding link at www .cengage.com/criminaljustice/ clear.

■ HOW COMMUNITY JUSTICE DIFFERS FROM CRIMINAL JUSTICE

Community justice differs from traditional criminal justice in four important ways: It is based on the neighborhood rather than on the legal jurisdiction, it uses problem-solving rather than adversarial strategies, it is restorative rather than retributive, and it strives to improve the community through a strategy called "justice reinvestment."

Neighborhoods

Neighborhoods are typically quite different from legal jurisdictions. For most important crimes, the state or federal government has legal jurisdiction within politically determined boundaries. But crime problems vary greatly within those jurisdictions. We

CORRECTIONAL PRACTICE

Community Justice in Action

Walter Harrison is a probation officer, on his way to work. But you wouldn't know it from the look of things: It is 7:00 P.M., and his destination is the local police precinct in Roxbury—a tough, inner-city neighborhood in Boston. There he will partner up with another probation officer and two police officers, members of the Gang Unit of the Boston Police Department assigned to police the gangs of Roxbury.

Their workday begins with a strategy session, in which the police-probation team reviews the files of 12 gang members they expect to see during the evening. They know the names and faces well, but the review serves as a reminder. Each gang member has a criminal record, many of which include multiple arrests for violent crimes involving guns. And each gang member is on probation for a recent conviction, with an evening curfew as a condition of probation. The team's job is to make sure that the probationers are obeying the curfew. They also want to make sure that, above all else, the young men they see are not carrying guns. This probation team wants the violence to stop.

The officers start their shift by setting priorities—who needs to be seen most, where they can expect to find problems, what new information has come to light about one of the probationers, what they have learned from recent forays into the field. After talking through their cases and setting objectives for the night's tour, they drive into the streets of Roxbury in an unmarked car. It is 8:00 P.M., the time by which every gang member on probation must be at home.

The first stop is a local park where youths congregate at night. The officers pull up near a small group of young people and look for the familiar faces of the gang members on probation. Although they recognize many of the youths—and the adolescents signal that they recognize the unmarked car—there are no probationers there. One youth approaches the car, and for a brief time he and the officers engage in an almost friendly banter. The youth's older brother is on probation and is doing well, and Harrison asks about how things are with the family. After a few minutes, the team drives off. The interaction has been calm and even cordial—everybody seems to know what is going on.

The team pulls up to a three-story run-down apartment building and makes the first curfew check. James Sampson, a 16-year-old on probation for illegal possession of a gun, lives here. The police officers do a safety check, noting the area surrounding the home and any exits from the house. The probation officers approach the front door. Sampson's mother meets them at the door and seems almost glad to see them. What proceeds is a fairly typical home visit, with routine questions about Sampson's activities, especially his new job. The officers make an effort to keep things cordial and relaxed, because they want to show respect for the probationer and his family. The visit goes well. As they leave, Sampson's mother thanks them and says with emotion that curfew means she no longer has to wonder if "my Jamie" will die on the streets in the middle of the night. It is a sentiment the team has heard before, even from the former gang members. The team heads on to its next stop. They are engaged in a new kind of correctional work in the community: "community justice."

Source: Todd R. Clear and David R. Karp, *The Community Justice Ideal: Preventing Crime and Achieving Justice* (Boulder, CO: Westview Press, 1999).

see this when we compare cities such as Miami with towns such as Lake City; both lie within Florida, but each has unique crime and justice problems. Even within a city, crime problems vary with the income levels, racial composition, and economic status of each neighborhood. The Miami neighborhoods of Liberty City and Coconut Grove show stark contrasts in their socioeconomic and crime characteristics. Would we want to apply standardized criminal justice policies to both neighborhoods? A 10-year research project in Chicago defined 343 coherent neighborhoods. Each had a different social profile and crime problem, as well as different justice concerns.[16] It follows that these local areas have different needs for justice services and priorities.

Traditional justice attempts to develop standardized approaches to crime problems that are applied uniformly across the entire legal jurisdiction. By contrast, community justice attempts to tailor strategies to fit important differences across neighborhoods within the same legal jurisdiction.

Problem Solving

Problem solving in the context of community justice differs from that of adversarial justice in its fundamental aims. The adversarial process is thought to have succeeded when the innocent citizen is found not guilty and the guilty citizen is fairly punished. In contrast, the problem-solving approach succeeds when the problem behind a crime is resolved. That is why the traditional criminal justice system is concerned almost exclusively with offenders and ends this concern once the offender's punishment has been concluded. Community justice extends its sights to solving the underlying problems faced by offenders, victims, and others in the neighborhood.

Problem solving as a core aspect of criminal justice is gaining support through a variety of means—from police decisions to correctional policy. A recent report by the National Institute of Justice found that crime fighting has evolved away from isolated arrest and prosecution strategies toward coordinated efforts that cut across agencies and levels of government. The idea is to continue to fight crime in the traditional way, by arresting and prosecuting offenders, but to try as well to identify the problems that produce the crime and address them systematically.[17]

Restoration

Follow a movement to build **community partnership against violence**; see the corresponding link at www.cengage.com/criminaljustice/clear.

Restoration is the solution sought under the problem-solving philosophy of community justice. This means that the losses suffered by the victim as a result of the crime are restored, the threat to local safety is removed, and eventually the offender returns to being a fully participating member of the community. When the crime is so serious that full restoration is not possible, community justice seeks as much restoration as can be provided.

Justice Reinvestment

justice reinvestment
A strategy to redirect funds currently spent on prisons to community public safety projects.

The most elaborate vision of community justice is expressed as **justice reinvestment**. The idea of justice reinvestment begins with the recognition that "more than $54 billion is spent annually on prisons in the United States, much of it directed toward incarcerating people for non-violent drug offenses with little or no hope of access to rehabilitation services."[18] The vast majority of these drug offenders come from disadvantaged communities where schools are poor, family life is pummeled by poverty and disruption, and chances for good jobs are minimal. These drug offenders spend up to a couple of years in prison, but they eventually return to the same disadvantages as before, with no improvement in their life prospects. In the long run the $54 billion accomplishes little more than interrupting the lives of community residents and adding to disruption in the lives of families and children.

The community justice ideal is to improve the quality of community life. Justice reinvestment is a strategy that seeks to funnel the vast resources of the criminal justice system into activities and projects that improve community life. In place of prison sentences, justice reinvestment advocates envision (1) work programs in which offenders help renovate neighborhood spaces, both public and private; (2) family programs that increase support to improve children's school performance; (3) housing strategies that provide low-cost places to live; and (4) health care support for people without health insurance. Through reallocating criminal justice funding toward education, housing, health care, and jobs, the long-term aim is to improve community life in ways that can specifically decrease crime rates and promote further improvement of the community's quality of life.

Justice reinvestment strategies rest on the idea that improving communities will not only reduce crime, it will also strengthen those communities. The evidence on this is mixed. Most programs of economic development in the community, including "weed-and-seed" programs, have had disappointing records in preventing crime,[19] and many experts believe that new strategies of this kind of work need to be developed.

TABLE 22.1 *Community Justice and Criminal Justice—Some Comparisons*

Community justice differs from criminal in the key strategies employed by each.	
Community Justice	**Criminal Justice**
Based in neighborhood.	Based in a state or local jurisdiction.
Focused on solving crime problems.	Focused on processing cases.
Uses partnerships with citizens and social service agencies.	Uses professionals who operate in isolation from citizens and other agencies.
Goal is improved community safety.	Goal is apprehension, conviction, and punishment of offenders.

Overview of Differences

These four differences—concerning neighborhoods, problem solving, restorative justice, and justice reinvestment—show how the community justice approach strikes a different path from that of traditional criminal justice. Community justice does not replace the need for criminal justice, but it fills in where the justice system fails to meet community needs.

Table 22.1 compares some of the ways that community justice differs from traditional criminal justice. The latter operates as a centralized bureaucracy staffed by professional workers whose job is to process criminal cases. Community justice strives to be a localized, community presence of specialists who develop partnerships with various agencies and citizen groups in order to deal with the problems that result from crime. Of course, community justice is not the opposite of criminal justice. All agents of justice operate under the same penal code, use the same legal authority, and face the same constitutional constraints.

Community justice is not as concerned with the individual offender as much as it is with the general issue of community safety. Because of this variation, community justice work tends to use the tools of justice in different ways and sets different priorities for taking action. For example, community-policing officers make arrests, just as traditional law enforcement officials do. But criminal justice often sees the arrest as "closing" a case, especially when it is followed by a conviction. Community justice workers see the arrest as a first part of the problem-solving process involving the impact of the crime and the future of the person who has been arrested. In cases where crimes do not result in arrest, community justice workers see just as much a need for problem solving and restoration of community safety as in those cases with arrests. Community justice concerns itself with the life of the community, and the community includes victims, offenders, and others alike.

See a **justice reinvestment project** in action; go to the corresponding link at www.cengage.com/criminaljustice/clear.

■ ARGUMENTS FOR COMMUNITY JUSTICE

Community justice has gained public support because crime damages community life, but traditional criminal justice does not address that damage. Citizens' groups and justice system leaders are coming together to develop ways to use criminal justice resources to address the damage that results from crime and crime fighting in high-crime localities. The arguments for community justice can be illustrated by three common assertions of the community justice movement.

Crime and Crime Problems Are Local

Community justice concerns itself with the quality of life in a community. Two deficits prevent a reasonable quality of life: lack of resources and lack of safety. In communities that have high concentrations of crime, these impediments to quality of life go hand in hand.

Ever since the landmark work of Clifford Shaw and Henry McKay,[20] criminologists have known that crimes tend to concentrate in certain areas. These high-crime areas are also the areas with other social problems: poverty, broken families, unemployment, and other social maladies criminologists refer to as "social disorganization." The concentration of social problems, the most troublesome of which is crime, makes these areas the least desirable places to live. People who live there tend to do so because they have few other choices. For people stuck in socially disorganized areas, life is dominated by problems of safety. Troublemakers rule the public spaces, making the streets unsafe.

Lacking financial and personal resources to create safety, residents of high-crime areas live under a permanent risk of harm. Research has shown that problems of violence stem directly from problems of social disorganization.[21] These neighborhoods also tend to become the places where offenders live after release from prison or jail or while under community supervision. **Figure 22.1** is a map of Brooklyn, New York, showing the number of prison and jail admissions in 2004. This extraordinary concentration in some neighborhoods of residents involved in the criminal justice system represents but one year's involvement. Stretched across the three to five years a typical offender is under correctional control, a picture emerges of a neighborhood of residents who are quite frequently under supervision. Part of what makes high-crime residential areas different from other places is the high concentration of justice system clients who live there.

Community justice is particularly concerned with these locations. Taking into account the families and associates, employers and neighbors of these many offenders, the distinction begins to fade between those formally under control of the state and those with whom their lives are directly intertwined. By focusing on quality of life in neighborhoods, community justice accepts responsibility for services to those who are not targets of state coercive penal control. The rationale is that as so much of community life is affected by the large number of offenders living in these locations, corrections must focus not only on the actual offenders under sentence but also on the many people whose lives they affect. Indeed, recent research suggests that place-based strategies are most effective when they are focused on quite small unit targets, such as individual blocks.[22]

Crime Fighting Too Often Damages the Quality of Life

What can be done in high-crime communities? The "trail-'em and nail-'em" approach of many criminal justice agencies seems to work poorly for offenders and their families in these areas.[23] The criminal justice system is designed as an adversarial attack on crime, implemented by identifying and accusing criminals, then removing them from the community on conviction. Nationally about 700,000 offenders are released back into the community, having served an average of just over two years in prison. The usual correctional thinking about these offenders is "individualized case management": assessing each offender's risk and needs, then developing a supervision plan for reentry.

Recently, some researchers have begun to consider the impact of high incarceration rates on community life.[24] They point out that removing offenders from the community often disrupts families and, when it becomes pervasive in a neighborhood, leads to a sense of alienation from the law. Imagine, they say, living in a neighborhood where just about everyone has been arrested and almost every man has been to prison or jail. Under those conditions the legitimacy of the legal system itself comes into question and the impact of the threat of punishment erodes. See "Myths in Corrections."

MYTHS IN CORRECTIONS

WHAT DO THEY WANT?

THE MYTH: People in poor communities want "bad guys" to be taken off their streets and sent to prison.

THE REALITY: People in poor communities tell researchers that they want to be "safe," but they also want their family members, even the ones involved in crime, not to have to go to prison.

Source: Dine R. Rose, Todd R. Clear, and Judith Ryder, "Drugs, Incarceration, and Neighborhood Life: The Impact of Reintegrating Offenders into the Community" (final report to the National Institute of Justice, October 2001).

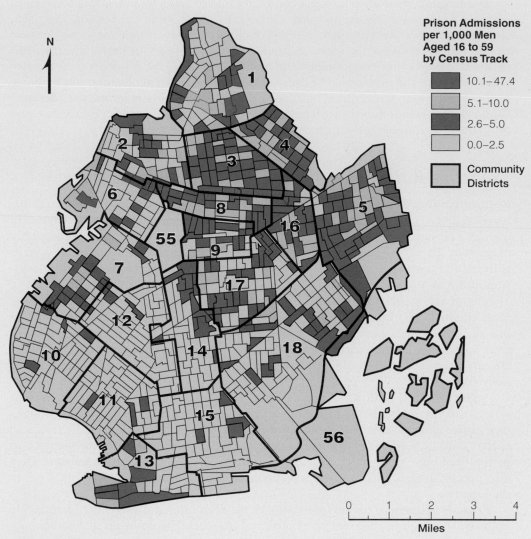

Figure 22.1

Male Residents of Brooklyn, New York, Council Districts, Admitted to Prison or Jail, 2004

The data show the residence of men admitted to prison or jail in one year. What is the impact of such a high concentration of ex-offenders living in a neighborhood?

Source: Eric Cadora and Charles Swartz, *Justice Mapping Project* (New York: Columbia University, 2007).

Problem communities in our cities may have reached critical levels of justice system involvement in residents' lives. Rather than coming from a response to violent crime, this involvement has stemmed from drug policy, one of the main reasons some neighborhoods have high rates of arrest and incarceration.[25] In several of our major cities, as noted earlier, one-fourth or more of all African American men are under some form of justice system control. In particularly hard-hit sections of some cities, as many as one-fourth of that group is behind bars.[26] This problem does not belong just to the ghettos of large cities. A study of a medium-sized southern city found one neighborhood in which 2 percent of all residents had been removed and placed in prison in one year alone, and one of the results may have been increases in crime.[27] If the community justice advocates are correct, such neighborhoods suffer repeated challenges—absorbing the losses incurred as these residents are removed, while at the same time dealing with those who have returned from prison or jail.[28]

By pursuing restorative justice, community justice seeks to ameliorate some costs of crime for these residents. By using a problem-solving, crime-prevention approach, community justice seeks to break the cycle of criminal behavior that has a grip on these communities. Studies of the federally funded "weed-and-seed" projects, which sought to work in high-crime communities and build the capacity for residents to deal more effectively with the problems that cause crime, find that where communities mobilize well in partnership with criminal justice and other social services, crime goes down.[29] While most weed-and-seed projects failed to mobilize communities effectively—and thus failed to reduce crime—the few that did had good results.

Proactive Rather Than Reactive Strategies Are Needed

Restorative justice and problem-solving strategies illustrate one of the essential differences between the philosophies of traditional criminal justice and community justice: The latter is reactive, whereas the former is proactive. Reactive approaches begin only after a crime has occurred—and only after victims and communities have suffered the costs of crime. Proactive approaches seek to prevent crimes from occurring in the first place.

The proactive approach is based on the assumption that preventing crimes is the most efficient aim of justice. Crime prevention not only saves money, because of fewer offenders processed, but also avoids costs to the victim and the community. Some fifteen years ago, the total costs to victims of felony crimes were $450 billion annually and are no doubt much higher now; the savings for each crime prevented can be considerable indeed.[30]

Advocates of traditional criminal justice often point out that one way to prevent crimes is to incapacitate the active offender by incarceration. Proponents of community justice respond that because most of those who go to prison eventually return to society, and because many of these are less capable of making it after having been to prison than before, the effects of incapacitation on the crime rate are overstated. They also present evidence that strategies based on arrest and incarceration do not work in the long run.[31]

Proactive strategies for environmental crime prevention are becoming increasingly popular. These approaches seek to identify and overcome the problems in a community

Visit the **Victim Offender Mediation Association** at the corresponding link at www.cengage.com/criminaljustice/clear.

Proactive strategies for environmental crime prevention are becoming increasingly popular. These approaches seek to identify and overcome the problems in a community that lead to crime. Here, young volunteers work together to clean trash and debris from an alley in Detroit's Corktown neighborhood.

© Jim West / The Image Works

that lead to crimes: Vacant lots that attract idle youth groups are turned into appealing playgrounds that attract children and their parents; corner liquor stores are turned into corner grocery stores; dark alleyways are cordoned off and made available to residents as backyards; drug thoroughfares have their traffic patterns rerouted to enable residents to feel safer.

Individual problem-solving strategies can also be proactive. Ex-offenders who have trouble finding a job may work on community reclamation projects for pay, and children who have limited adult supervision are encouraged to attend fun after-school programs that strengthen skills and provide adult contact outside of school settings.

David Kennedy is developing a new form of proactive strategy. In this effort he works with community leaders to present the community's norms to gangs and others involved in crime. The crime-prone members often feel connections to their families and neighbors; the work aims at using this sense of connection as a force for change. Examples of this work have yielded remarkable results in cities as diverse as Washington, D.C.; High Point, North Carolina; and Indianapolis, Indiana.[32]

The common thread in all this is to move away from an offender-based, reactive, retributive criminal justice system toward a community-based, proactive, restorative justice strategy. Community justice seeks to build a greater experience of justice by those communities hardest hit by crime.

■ PROBLEMS OF COMMUNITY JUSTICE

The image of community justice presented by its advocates is attractive. This is one reason why the concept of community justice has become more popular in recent years. Yet community justice is a new idea, and observers have raised several important questions about its prospects. In particular, three central questions have been raised, concerning individual rights, social inequality, and increased costs. Any attempt to embrace community justice will inevitably raise these issues.

Impingement on Individual Rights

In a community justice model, different communities vary in the ways they pursue public safety and improved quality of life. For example, if localities determine justice (and crime) priorities, then services such as policing and prosecution may differ in the ways they allocate resources or even take practical actions, even though they operate under identical criminal codes. How far can these differences go before they violate our belief in equality under the law? To what extent can a locality exert its unique vision of social control without infringing on freedoms of "deviant" members who are in the minority? Will a neighborhood justice movement take on characteristics of vigilantism? If so, what will stop that trend?

As citizens become more active in various aspects of the justice process, they undercut the state's role in presiding over that process. The adversarial ideal assumes that the state accuses a citizen and brings to bear evidence that supports the accusation. The dispute is between the state and the accused. Inserting neighbors and residents into that arrangement muddies the water by creating a third party to the dispute. It is unclear what the precise role of the third party ought to be—observational, participatory, advisory, or even advocative? Whichever, the presence of that party means that the state and its adversary can no longer be concerned only about each other. The concern for rights' protections extends beyond those of the accused to the rights of victims and, indirectly, to affected community members. The question is, What does the growth of interest in the community mean for the rights of criminal suspects? Because some research has shown that individual characteristics promote serious delinquency more than do community characteristics, some people wonder if a focus on communities will lead us to ignore individuals' problems that need to be addressed.[33]

We must be uneasy about the implications of any developments that undermine the protection of rights. Perhaps the finest contribution of Western civilization to modern life is the idea of the sanctity and dignity of the individual. This idea is given life in the form of legal rights, in which citizens stand equal to one another as well as to the state. Any movement toward community justice taken at the expense of this priceless heritage would impose a cultural cost of profound dimensions. Community justice ideals *will* alter established practices of substantive and procedural criminal law. The test will be to devise changes that protect precious civil liberties.

Social Inequality

Neighborhoods differ not only in their crime control priorities but also in their capacities, resources, and resilience in meeting crime problems. The same inequalities that individuals face in the United States play out as a community dynamic. The justice system really operates as two different systems, one for people with financial resources and another for the poor. Is there any assurance that the same kind of inequality will not come to characterize community justice?

This is not a small concern. The higher victimization rates of African Americans and Latinos is due, almost completely, to the fact that they live in disadvantaged places where violence persists.[34] Further, poor communities, particularly those hit hard by crime, also tend to lack resources to regulate neighborhood problems and pursue social control.[35] These communities do not come together to solve problems, and they have low rates of citizen participation in civic life. One lesson of community policing has been that, in troubled neighborhoods, getting citizens to take responsible action in regard to their crime problems is often difficult.

The more-prosperous localities will also have disproportionate political influence in many city and county governments. They will be better at organizing to influence the crime priorities, directing the funding decisions, and protecting their residents from

Neighborhoods differ not only in their crime control priorities, but also in their capacities, resources, and resilience in meeting crime problems. Poor communities lack the resources to deal with their crime problems. Prosperous communities are better at organizing to protect neighborhood members. Will community justice perpetuate these social inequalities?

© John Lei/Stock Boston, LLC

© Robert Holmes/Corbis

negative impacts of change. A community justice model that enables localities to pursue interests and preferences will inevitably raise the potential for these more-successful communities to strengthen their position in relation to other localities. Community justice cannot treat all communities as having equal importance or as being independent from one another. The most effective community organizations tend to be "neighborhood associations" that advance the needs of identifiable sections of a city, but the poorest communities tend to lack them. Therefore, we must recognize that communities exist within larger social and political systems and that local problems and the public policies created to address them must be understood within this broader context.

Inequality breeds crime. It would be a dismal irony if community justice, advanced to help places deal more effectively with their crime problems, instead contributed to the very dynamics that make those problems worse. If the problem of inequality is to be avoided, some local areas will likely require more help than others to take advantage of the promise of community justice.

Increasing Criminal Justice Costs

We spend nearly $100 billion on the criminal justice system every year. The cost of justice is increasing, and the burden it places on local areas through taxes interferes with the capacity to fund schools, provide health care, and maintain basic services. A community justice model calls for criminal justice organizations to augment current services. How will these be paid for?

The disparity between community resources and crime rates means that local revenues cannot provide the basis for funding community justice. As indicated, the very communities that most suffer from crime are least able to pay to combat it. Some mechanism for shifting financial resources from affluent communities to impoverished ones will be needed. This will obviously raise sensitive political issues, because taxpayers are leery of spending for services that do not directly benefit them.

In addition, some way of shifting costs *within* the existing justice budget will be needed. New money for new programs is scarce, and a proposal to greatly increase funding of justice work will be met with skepticism. Community justice programs that shift the onus for crime fighting to the community without providing resources to do it are doomed to fail.[36] Community justice therefore depends on a shifting of resources within existing justice functions. The overall dollar costs of justice cannot be expected to rise too much; what can occur is a change in the allocation of justice dollars to provide support for new activities in place of previous functions. Community justice calls for collaboration between criminal justice agencies and other government and community social welfare agencies and services. Coordinated efforts will enhance effectiveness by combining the resources of different agencies using similar strategies to obtain different ends. For example, while one agency's objective may be increasing employment within a neighborhood, doing so may also reduce criminal activity.

■ THE FUTURE OF COMMUNITY JUSTICE

Community justice is a new idea. It has proved very popular, but the important question of any new idea in correctional work is whether it has staying power. We might wonder whether the community justice movement will be a brief aspect of today's justice politics or, as its advocates intend, a long-term force in the reform of the justice system.

The popularity of community justice derives in part from deep dissatisfactions with contemporary justice politics. Many have become alarmed by the trends described in earlier chapters, such as the increased use of surveillance and the ever-growing size of correctional populations. Because it embraces community safety without the emphasis on "toughness" or surveillance, community justice provides an attractive alternative for many who are disillusioned with existing strategies.

For a **bibliography on restorative justice**, go to the corresponding link at www.cengage.com/criminaljustice/clear.

In some ways community justice is a throwback. Those who promote local, informal, and citizen-supported responses to crime seem to have an image of the way communities traditionally dealt with misbehavior in the past—by collective effort to overcome it. If community justice is desirable because it calls us to a nostalgic past, it is likely to be short-lived. Modern problems call for modern solutions, not fuzzy history.

Ironically, the past has also been marked by a harsh and dehumanizing approach to dealing with deviance. If the community justice movement successfully develops and demonstrates a true alternative to traditional criminal justice—with local, problem-solving, restorative, and proactive solutions to crime problems—then traditional bureaucratic justice is what will someday be a thing of the past.

SUMMARY

1 Define community justice and show how it differs from criminal justice.

As a philosophy, community justice is based on a pursuit of justice that goes beyond the traditional three tasks of criminal justice—the apprehension, conviction, and punishment of offenders. As a strategy, community justice combines three contemporary justice innovations: community policing, environmental crime prevention, and restorative justice. As a series of programs, community justice includes a varied package of methods. Most of all, community justice is concerned with taking seriously the problems faced by people who live with high levels of crime, some of whom are themselves involved in crime. Community justice differs from traditional criminal justice in four important ways: It is based on the neighborhood rather than on the legal jurisdiction, it uses problem-solving rather than adversarial strategies, it is restorative rather than retributive, and it strives to improve the community through a strategy called "justice reinvestment."

2 Identify the arguments in favor of community justice.

Community justice has gained public support because crime damages community life, but traditional criminal justice does not address that damage. Citizens' groups and justice system leaders are together developing ways to use criminal justice resources to address the damage that results from crime and crime fighting in high-crime localities. The arguments for community justice can be illustrated by three common assertions of the community justice movement: (1) Crime and crime problems are local; thus, local strategies and solutions are needed. (2) Crime fighting too often damages the quality of life, so strategies directed toward improving the quality of life are needed. (3) Proactive rather than reactive strategies are needed, because reaction never solves the original problems that lead to crime.

3 Describe the problems that community justice faces.

Three central concerns have been raised about the prospects of community justice: (1) Impingement on human rights may occur if a focus on community well-being undermines the rights of individuals accused of a crime. (2) Social inequality may result, because impoverished neighborhoods lack the human and capital resources to tackle their own problems. (3) Criminal justice costs may increase to cover the new programs and augmented services demanded by the community justice model.

4 Explore the future prospects of community justice.

We might wonder whether the community justice movement will be a brief aspect of today's justice politics or, as its advocates intend, a long-term force in the reform of the justice system. The popularity of community justice derives in part from deep dissatisfactions with contemporary justice politics. Those who promote local, informal, and citizen-supported responses to crime seem to have an image of the way communities traditionally dealt with misbehavior in the past—by collective effort to overcome it. If the call for community justice is not much more than a call for a return to the past, it will not last long. But if the community justice movement successfully develops and demonstrates a true alternative to traditional criminal justice—with local, problem-solving, restorative, and proactive solutions to crime problems—then traditional bureaucratic justice will someday be a thing of the past.

KEY TERMS

collective efficacy (p. 585)   justice reinvestment (p. 590)   spatial concentration (p. 584)

FOR DISCUSSION

1. Would you rather live in a place that practiced traditional criminal justice or in one that practiced community justice?
2. Why do you think the community justice movement is so popular? Will it last or will it be over soon? Why?
3. What impediments block greater cooperation among correctional agencies, such as probation, and other government services, such as the police or social welfare? How can these impediments be overcome?
4. Do you think citizens want to get involved in their own crime-prevention problems? Why or why not?

FOR FURTHER READING

Allen, Harry E., ed. *Repairing Communities through Restorative Justice*. Lanham, MD: American Correctional Association, 2002. Various perspectives and illustrations of the ways restorative justice can benefit victims, offenders, and communities.

Clear, Todd R. *Imprisoning Communities: How Mass Incarceration Makes Disadvantaged Places Worse*. New York: Oxford University Press, 2007. An empirical assessment of the impact of high levels of incarceration on impoverished communities.

Harcourt, Bernard E. *Illusion of Order: The False Promise of Broken Windows Policing*. Cambridge, MA: Harvard University Press, 2001. A critique of the "broken windows" theory of policing.

Hughes, Gordon, and Adam Edwards, eds. *Crime Control and Community*. Portland, OR: Willan, 2002. Presents a series of case studies of community-based crime-prevention programs.

Karp, David R., and Todd R. Clear. *What Is Community Justice?* Thousand Oaks, CA: Pine Forge Press, 2002. Provides case studies in community and restorative justice.

Weisburd, David, Wim Bernasco, and Gerben J. N. Bruinsma, eds. *Putting Crime in Its Place*. New York: Springer, 2009. A series of papers assessing crime-prevention strategies based on street-level projects.

NOTES

[1] Bureau of Justice Statistics, http://www.ojp.usdoj.gov/bjs/correct.htm, May 15, 2007.

[2] Avi Bhati, James Lynch, and William Sabol, "Baltimore and Cleveland: Incarceration and Crime at the Neighborhood Level" (paper presented at the meetings of the American Society of Criminology, Toronto, November 18, 2005).

[3] Todd R. Clear, *Imprisoning Communities: How Mass Incarceration Makes Disadvantaged Places Worse* (New York: Oxford University Press, 2007).

[4] Bruce Western, *Punishment and Inequality in America* (New York: Russell Sage Foundation, 2006), 138.

[5] Joseph Murray and David P. Farrington, "Effects of Parental Imprisonment on Children," in *Crime and Justice: A Review of Research*, vol. 3, edited by Michael Tonry (Chicago: University of Chicago, in press.)

[6] Beth M. Heubner, "The Effect of Incarceration on Marriage and Work over the Life Course," *Justice Quarterly* 22 (no. 3, 2005): 281–306.

[7] James C. Thomas and Elizabeth Torrone, "Incarceration as Forced Migration: Effects on Selected Community Health Outcomes," *American Journal of Public Health* 96 (no. 10, October 2006): 1762–65.

[8] Ralph Taylor, John Goldkamp, Phil Harris, Peter Jones, Maria Garcia, and Eric McCord, "Community Justice Impacts over Time: Adult Arrest Rates, Male Serious Delinquency Prevalence Rates within and between Philadelphia Communities" (presentation to the Eastern Sociological Society meetings, Boston, February 2006).

[9] Robert J. Kane, "On the Limits of Social Control: Structural Deterrence and the Policing of 'Suppressible' Crimes," *Justice Quarterly* 23 (no. 2, 2006): 186–213.

[10] Todd R. Clear, Dina R. Rose, Elin Waring, and Kristen Scully, "Coercive Mobility and Crime: A Preliminary Examination of Concentrated Incarceration and Social Disorganization," *Justice Quarterly* 20 (no. 1, 2003): 33–64.

[11] Robert J. Sampson, Stephen W. Raudenbush, and Felton Earls, "Neighborhoods and Violent Crime: A Multilevel Study of Collective Efficacy," *Science* 277 (August 15, 1997): 1–7.

[12] Gordon Bazemore and Mark Umbreit, "A Comparison of Four Restorative Conferencing Models," *OJJDP Bulletin*, February 2001.

[13] Joanna Shapland, Anne Atkinson, et al., *Does Restorative Justice Affect Reconviction? The Fourth Report from the Evaluation of Three Schemes* (Canberra, Australia: Ministry of Justice Research Series 10/08, June 2008).

[14] Hennessey Hayes, "Assessing Re-offending in Restorative Justice Conferences," *Australian and New Zealand Journal of Criminology* 38 (no. 1, April 2005): 77–102. See also Jeff Latimer, Craig Dowden, and Danielle Muise, "The Effectiveness of Restorative Justice Practice: A Meta-analysis," *Prison Journal* 85 (no. 2, June 2005): 127–44.

[15] Kathleen Daly, "Restorative Justice: The Real Story," *Punishment and Society* 4 (no. 1, January 2002): 55–79.

[16] Lisa L. Miller and Eric Silver, "Sources of Informal Social Control in Chicago Neighborhoods," *Criminology* 42 (no. 3, August 2004): 551–83.

[17] Malcolm L. Russell-Einhorn, "Fighting Urban Crime: The Evolution of Federal-Local Collaboration," *NIJ Research in Brief* (Washington, DC: National Institute of Justice, December 2003).

[18] Susan Tucker and Eric Cadora, *Ideas for an Open Society: Justice Reinvestment* (New York: Open Society Institute, November 2003), 1.

[19] John L. Worrall, *Crime Control in America: An Assessment of the Evidence* (Boston: Allyn and Bacon, 2005).

[20] Clifford R. Shaw and Henry D. McKay, *Juvenile Delinquency and Urban Areas* (Chicago: University of Chicago, 1942).

[21] Jeffrey D. Morenoff, Robert J. Sampson, and Stephen W. Raudenbush, "Neighborhood Inequality, Collective Efficacy, and the Spatial Dynamics of Urban Violence," *Criminology* 39 (no. 3, August 2001): 517–60.

[22] David Weisburd, Shawn Bushway, Cynthia Lum, and Sue-Ming Yang, "Trajectories of Crime at Places: A Longitudinal Study of Street Segments in the City of Seattle," *Criminology* 24 (no. 2, May 2004): 283–321.

[23] Robert J. Sampson and Stephen W. Raudenbush, "Disorder in Urban Neighborhoods—Does It Lead to Crime?" *NIJ Research in Brief* (Washington, DC: National Institute of Justice, February 2001).

[24] For a review, see Clear, *Imprisoning Communities*, ch. 5.

[25] Ryan S. King, *Disparity by Geography: The War on Drugs in American Cities* (Washington, DC: The Sentencing Project, May 2008); see also Scott Duffield Levy, "The Collateral Consequences of Seeking Order through Disorder: New York's Narcotics Eviction Program," *Harvard Civil Rights-Civil Liberties Law Review* 43 (no. 2, Summer 2008): 539–80.

[26] James P. Lynch and William J. Sabol, "Assessing the Effects of Mass Incarceration on Informal Social Control in Communities," *Criminology and Public Policy* 3 (no. 2, 2004): 267–94.

[27] Clear et al., "Coercive Mobility and Crime."

[28] Robert DeFina and Lance Hannon, "The Impact of Mass Incarceration on Poverty," *Crime and Delinquency* (forthcoming), published online February 12, 2009: http://papers.ssrn.com/sol3/papers.cfm?abstract_id=1348049.

[29] Terence Dunworth and Gregory Mills, "A National Evaluation of Weed and Seed," *NIJ Research in Brief* (Washington, DC: National Institute of Justice, June 1999).

[30] Ted R. Miller, Mark A. Cohen, and Brian Wiersema, *Victim Costs and Consequences: A New Look* (Washington, DC: National Institute of Justice, February 1996).

[31] Bernard E. Harcourt, *Illusion of Order: The False Promise of Broken Windows Policing* (Cambridge, MA: Harvard University Press, 2001); see also Ralph B. Taylor, Philip W. Harris, Peter R. Jones, and Doris Weiland, "Short-Term Changes in Arrest Rates Influence Later Short-Term Changes in Serious Male Delinquency Prevalence: A Time-Dependent Relationship," *Criminology* (in press).

[32] David Kennedy, "Making Communities Safer: Youth Violence and Gang Interventions That Work" (testimony before the House Judiciary Subcommittee on Crime, Terrorism, and Homeland Security, February 15, 2007).

[33] Per-Olaf Wikstrom and Rolf Loeber, "Do Disadvantaged Neighborhoods Cause Well-Adjusted Children to Become Adolescent Delinquents? A Study of Male Juvenile Serious Offending, Individual Risk and Protective Factors, and Neighborhood Context," *Criminology* 38 (no. 4, November 2000): 1109–43.

[34] Janet L. Lauritsen and Norman A. White, "Putting Violence in Its Place: The Influence of Race, Ethnicity, Gender, and Place on the Risk of Violence," *Criminology and Public Policy* 1 (no. 1, November 2001): 37–60.

[35] Robert J. Sampson, Jeffrey D. Morenoff, and Stephen Raudenbush, "Social Anatomy of Racial and Ethnic Disparities in Violence," *American Journal of Public Health* 95 (no. 2, February 2005): 224–32.

[36] Nancy Jurik, Joel Blumenthal, Brian Smith, and Edwardo Portillos, "Organizational Cooptation or Social Change? A Critical Perspective on Community–Criminal Justice Partnerships," *Journal of Contemporary Criminal Justice* 16 (no. 3, August 2000): 292–320.

© Greg Smith/Corbis

© Greg Smith/Corbis

LEARNING OBJECTIVES

After reading this chapter you should be able to . . .

1 Understand how the philosophy of the U.S. corrections system has changed over the years and what effects such changes have had.

2 Know the major dilemmas facing the corrections system and how they might be resolved.

3 Describe the three main challenges for the future of the U.S. corrections system and how those challenges might be faced.

Skyrocketing incarceration rates have forced state and federal governments to greatly expand their prison facilities. Inmates line up at a prison in Beeville, Texas, that was converted from the Chase Field Naval Air Station after it ceased to be used as a pilot-training facility.

AS WE PAUSE to think about the future of corrections, we might begin by asking what the American corrections system is best known for, today, across the world.

There was a time when the U.S. corrections system was the most progressive in the world. When the modern prison was invented after the American Revolution, it was envied internationally, as described in Chapter 3. When the nation's penologists met in Cincinnati in 1870, they affirmed a mission of rehabilitation that became a model for corrections systems around the globe. At the start of the twentieth century, modern probation was invented here—another innovation to be copied worldwide. For most of the nineteenth and twentieth centuries, the U.S. corrections system remained at the forefront of thinking about the best ways to deal with people who break the law, and U.S. methods were widely celebrated and emulated.

Today the U.S. corrections system no longer serves as a progressive beacon for the world's systems of punishment. If a panel of experts were asked to characterize the U.S. system, they would likely say little about forward-thinking programs or leading innovations of thought. Instead they would say that what sets the U.S. corrections system apart from all others is that it is so *big*.

AMERICAN CORRECTIONS: LOOKING FORWARD

- **FIVE CORRECTIONAL DILEMMAS**
  - Mission
  - Methods
  - Structure
  - Personnel
  - Costs

- **THREE CHALLENGES FOR THE FUTURE OF CORRECTIONS**
  - Reinvigorate a New Correctional Leadership
  - Refocus Our Investments in What Works
  - Reclaim the Moral and Ethical High Road

- **CHANGING CORRECTIONS: A FINAL VIEW**

Since the mid-1970s, by every measure, the American corrections system has grown by unprecedented amounts (see Chapters 1 and 18). Since 1973 the U.S. imprisonment rate has increased from under 100 people per 100,000 to almost 500 per 100,000. Including probation, parole, and jails, the number of people under correctional control also has more than quadrupled in that time, from under a million to over 7 million.

This growth has disproportionately affected minority group members (see Chapters 4 and 19). For example, recall that over one in three African American men in their twenties is currently under correctional control—more African American men are behind bars than attend colleges and universities. Some observers estimate that in Los Angeles about one in three African American youths will be arrested each year, though far fewer will be prosecuted. It is not hard to see why many residents in these communities believe that the criminal justice system is designed to oppress them and that the corrections system is intended to remove men from their neighborhoods.

It is also hard to believe that over the past 35 years we have deliberately created the corrections system we most want. To the contrary, most of those in charge of today's corrections system would argue that what we are doing is self-destructive and that an overhaul of the corrections system is long overdue. But there is little agreement about the best aims of reform (see Chapter 4).

This lack of agreement is one reason why it is not really accurate to refer to the unprecedented growth in corrections since the early 1970s as an "experiment." Experiments must be planned, and some hypotheses about how and why they might work must be advanced. The surge in correctional populations has resulted from disjointed, incremental policy shifts in sentencing and law enforcement practices. For example, the population of drug offenders in U.S. prisons has increased by over 700 percent since 1980, more than five times the rate of increase of other offenders; this was largely the result of the war on drugs of the 1980s and 1990s. Two decades later, almost nobody would say we have "won" that war. Now what?

In this closing chapter, we step back to look at the big picture of corrections. What can we make of the corrections system we have described in this book?

Chapter

23

Where is it headed, and what issues does it face? We explore these questions with a critical eye, because even though nobody can truly foresee the future, the way we ask ourselves about the future tells us a great deal about how we feel about the present. We begin with a discussion of five dilemmas corrections faces—indeed, has always faced throughout history. We then consider three key pressing challenges that anyone interested in corrections must undertake.

■ FIVE CORRECTIONAL DILEMMAS

A *dilemma* is a situation that forces one to choose between two unsatisfactory alternatives. Corrections faces many dilemmas—any worker in the field will attest to this. We have selected five dilemmas as particularly important, because they are what we consider "orienting" dilemmas for corrections. That is, not only must each corrections system confront them as it moves further into the twenty-first century, but the way it confronts them will profoundly affect the resolution of most other issues—from daily problems in offender management to larger considerations.

Indeed, today's difficulties and tomorrow's potential solutions are quite bound up in how these five dilemmas were faced in the past. Unlike much of the material in this book, our description of the dilemmas is not an objective restatement of facts and studies; rather, it is a subjective interpretation of many facts, studies, and observations. We return to the systems perspective as we identify five core concerns: mission, methods, structure, personnel, and costs.

Mission

Corrections lacks a clear mission. One reason for this is that it has so many different clients—offenders, the general public, other government agencies—each of which has its own expectations of corrections. In simple terms, we recognize that offenders want fairness, leniency, and assistance; the public wants protection from and punishment of criminals; government agencies want cooperation and coordination. Obviously these expectations often come into conflict. Thus, one goal of corrections ultimately must be to disentangle the expectations and establish a set of priorities for handling them.

At the same time, none of these competing expectations can be ignored. How do courts respond when corrections fails to provide rehabilitative services to offenders? How does the public respond to instances of brutal recidivism? How do government agencies manage balky correctional officials?

One common solution in corrections is to attempt to meet all expectations: provide the services that are requested, take actions to protect citizens when public safety becomes an issue, cooperate with agencies when asked to do so. The advantage of this approach is that corrections can avoid the strains that accompany goal conflict, such as making hard choices about priorities. Of course, this supposed advantage can never be fully realized. The conflicts between serving clients and protecting the community, or between coordinating government practices and providing assistance or protection, are real. When corrections tries to meet all these competing expectations equally, correctional workers must resolve the conflicts informally. Corrections must confront the problems created by ambiguity of mission. Doing so requires that choices be made. In the early 1960s most people agreed that the primary mission of corrections was the rehabilitation of offenders, but the devaluation of treatment and the movement toward harsh, mandatory sentences left a void in this area. Some observers have suggested that

To get regular updates on criminal justice, join **JUSTINFO** through the corresponding link at www.cengage.com/criminaljustice/clear.

corrections must take on the role of offender management; others have argued that the role of corrections is risk control; still others have suggested punishment as its mission. Today, community justice has worked its way into many correctional mission statements.

Whatever the choice, correctional leaders must articulate their philosophy of corrections and establish a clearer policy to guide its implementation. Both staff members and people outside the system must be aware of what corrections does and what they can expect from its efforts.

For a list of prison reform groups, go to the corresponding link at www .cengage.com/criminaljustice/ clear.

Methods

Obviously, if the correctional mission is unclear, the best correctional strategies and techniques will be ambiguous as well. When goals are in conflict, staff members have difficulty choosing among competing methods to perform their work: surveillance or service, custody or treatment. But this is not the only problem with correctional methods; much more significantly, correctional techniques often do not seem to work.

A debilitating lack of confidence results when apparently promising strategies, upon evaluation, turn out to lack merit. The list of failed correctional methods includes reduced caseloads, offender counseling, family counseling, group treatment, boot camps, and being "scared straight." These and many other methods have been promoted as the answers to various pressing problems. Each time another correctional strategy proves ineffective, the failure feeds an already pervasive feeling among workers that corrections is incapable of performing its basic functions well.

This is one reason why the short-term history of corrections seems dominated by fads. As each "innovative" technique or program is implemented, corrections is confronted by the method's limited ability to solve immediately the technical problems it was intended to solve. Consequently, it is replaced by something newer still.

The effects of these frequent changes in approach are largely negative. No firm, central technical process is allowed to develop and mature. Because corrections works with people, its central technologies should involve interpersonal communication and influence; however, the parade of new programs subtly shifts the emphasis from process to procedures. The dynamic work of corrections is stalled by the static and routinized activities that ebb and flow with each new program. Bureaucratic approaches to

© Joel Gordon Photography

The short history of corrections seems dominated by fads. One example is boot camps. People strongly expected this sanction to deter offenders, but its implementation has been fraught with problems. What is the current "innovative" fad?

offender management, such as warehousing, come to dominate the technical approach to the job. Workers become cynical about changes and about the potential of the work itself. Who can blame them? The most experienced correctional workers have seen many highly praised programs come and go, having failed to produce the expected results.

Another issue associated with correctional methods is fairness. In recent years, the concept of just deserts has become popular, and much effort has been devoted to ways to achieve it. Although the just deserts model of criminal justice is quite elaborate, it boils down to a single generalization: Offenders should be punished equally in accordance with the severity of their offenses. This seems to be a straightforward assignment.

Yet something is wanting in the doctrine of just deserts. The fact is that the most stringent correctional methods are applied in practice almost exclusively to the poor and predominantly to minorities. One is left with the feeling that merely to be "equal" in our application of state power under these circumstances is not really to be fair in the broadest sense of the term. Genuine fairness must enhance the lives and the potential of those we bring under correctional control. But if the history of corrections has taught us anything, it is that we often injure the people we try to help. We know little about how to assist offenders effectively, but it is certainly not enough just to punish them equally. The dilemma of methods is complex. Can we overcome the tradition of faddism in corrections without becoming stodgily bureaucratic in method? Can we improve the life chances of correctional clients without injuring them further despite good intentions?

Structure

Corrections is simply not in a position to influence its own fate significantly. Much of this inability has to do with its structure—internal and external. Internally, corrections is a process divided against itself. Jails, prisons, probation, and parole all struggle with one another; the practices of each become contingencies for the others. Externally, corrections represents the culmination of the criminal justice process, and it has little formal capacity to control the demand for its services. Thus, correctional leaders face two structural dilemmas.

First, their colleagues are often the ones who put the most immediate obstacles in the way of their attempts to manage their operations effectively. Second, the corrections system depends on significant factors outside of its control. The practical consequences of the structural dilemmas are sometimes quite startling.

In many jurisdictions, for example, large amounts of money have been spent renovating old jails or building new ones because the existing facilities are substandard, overcrowded, or both. Too often the new version is soon just as overcrowded as the old one was, or else it is deemed legally substandard. The fault rests with the inability of corrections to coordinate architectural planning with the programmatic needs of such nonjail agencies as the courts and probation. What initially seemed to be a problem of how much space is available really reflects a problem of how available space is used, which, in turn, is influenced by people other than jail administrators. The courts (through sentencing and pretrial release), law enforcement (through arrest), and probation/parole (through revocation) all use jail space for their own purposes. The lack of agencies to ameliorate the effects of population growth on corrections can eliminate the benefits of opening a new prison. This is only one of the deficiencies that repeatedly occur in correctional planning.

Formally, the problem of structure in corrections is one of interdependence and coordination. The ability of corrections to function effectively in some ways depends on external processes that it must respond to, influence, or at least understand. To do so, its own processes must be better coordinated with those of the external agencies that produce the dependence—and the dissension.

The problem is that there is really no easy way to coordinate these processes. Separation of powers is both a constitutional and a traditional bulwark of our government. Each agency is jealous of its own power and reluctant to reduce it by coordination or planning. Thus, when a new jail is being designed, the approval of the municipal engineering bureau is seen as a hurdle to be cleared rather than a potential resource to be tapped. Each time an interagency control is put into place, it becomes an obstacle rather than a coordinating mechanism.

Most correctional administrators find that their greatest frustrations lie in getting other agencies to avoid actions that severely constrain their ability to function. A recent trend has been the formation of "partnerships" meant to improve coordination, whether high-level commissions composed of heads of correctional, justice system, judicial, and executive-branch agencies or task forces of line-level personnel. This is a promising step, but a small one.

Get **correctional news** online at the corresponding link at www.cengage.com/ criminaljustice/clear.

Personnel

Because corrections is a people-processing operation, its personnel are its main resource. The two essential goals in regard to staff are (1) attracting the right kinds of people to work in corrections and (2) motivating them to remain once they are employed. Corrections traditionally has not done well in either area.

The initial recruitment problem frequently stems from the low starting salaries. Although salaries vary widely from place to place, correctional employees often earn less than workers in comparable positions elsewhere. For example, correctional officers frequently begin at wages lower than those of local law enforcement officers. Likewise, the starting salaries of probation and parole officers, who normally are required to have a college degree, often are not competitive with those offered to social workers and teachers.

For this reason correctional positions may be regarded as a good entry to the work world. A person new to the job market can obtain stable employment for a year or two while seeking alternative employment. The most qualified individuals find it relatively easy to move on to other occupations; less-qualified people often stay longer, some for their entire careers.

Further, as a result of collective bargaining, most correctional employees receive equal pay raises regardless of performance. Inevitably, a system of equality becomes a disincentive to employees whose work efforts surpass those of others. Too frequently, significant personnel decisions such as promotions, raises, and increased responsibilities are completely out of the hands of correctional administrators.

Courtesy of California Department of Corrections and Rehabilitation

Attracting, motivating, and retaining outstanding personnel is key to an effective corrections system. What is the future for these new officers?

In times of fiscal abundance, salary is not as great a problem, but decades of salary crunches in government employment, combined with a constricted job market, can embitter many correctional employees. The organizational culture of many correctional operations is dominated by animosity toward management and cynicism toward the job. Too often correctional employees feel unappreciated, manipulated, and alienated. Under these conditions, it is exceedingly difficult for a corrections system to perform its "peoplework" function effectively, because its most valuable resource—the staff—is demoralized.

On the surface, the solution to the personnel problem seems simple: Measure the performance of staff, reward those who are productive, and get rid of those who are not. Unfortunately this approach does not work in government employment (and may not work well in the private sector, either). For one thing, correctional performance is exceedingly difficult to assess. Although the general yardsticks of recidivism, institutional security, and so forth provide useful measures of correctional performance, they are inadequate indicators of an individual's performance. Who can say that a parolee's failure was the parole officer's fault? Indeed, it might represent an officer's successful surveillance.

Secondary performance measures, such as contacts with clients, paperwork, and training, are therefore often substituted for primary measures of job success. These secondary measures tend to be fairer because they fall within the staff's control. But for a secondary measure of performance to be useful, it must be clearly related to organizational success. In this respect, most secondary measures in corrections are inadequate. In another vein, government employment is often sought because of its purported job security; altering the personnel picture to overcome lethargy is likely to cause extreme strain among the staff.

The correctional leader's choices regarding personnel issues, unhappily, involve no short-term solutions. The answer, if there is one, lies in long-term staff development. A sound staff is built by innovative methods of selection and promotion; professional growth on the job is encouraged by incentives for education and training. "Human resource" management approaches are taken to involve staff in the operations of the organization. However, turnover at the top of the correctional hierarchy may be so great that the administrator who tries to address personnel issues may not be around to reap the rewards of his or her efforts.

Costs

One of the most notable aspects of corrections is that it is expensive. The cost of building a prison exceeds $100,000 per cell, excluding financing. Each personnel position represents expenditures equal to twice his or her annual salary when fringe benefits, retirement costs, and office supplies are included. The processing of an offender through the corrections system usually reaches at least $25,000 in direct costs and nearly half that much again in indirect costs (such as defaulted debts, welfare to families, and lost wages and taxes). The decision to punish an offender is a decision to allocate precious public resources, often irretrievably. Correctional administrators understand all this now more than ever. Allocating correctional resources wisely poses a huge challenge.

Institutional crowding, combined with fiscal restraint, has produced an unprecedented concern about correctional costs. The public is beginning to question the advisability of correctional growth. One might say that the public is exhibiting a form of political schizophrenia: The desire to punish criminals is not backed up by a willingness to pay for the punishment.

The ambivalence about punishment and funding has left correctional leaders in a bind. The arguments for expansion of large, secure facilities must be weighed against equally strong arguments for increased emphasis on community-based corrections. These arguments are in some ways easy to understand. The public continues to care deeply about controlling crime, but many prisons remain critically overcrowded.

Most correctional officials recognize that focusing on prisons is a regressive rather than a progressive approach. Many of our existing secure facilities are decrepit and need to be replaced, but the evidence is quite strong that (1) prison construction does not alleviate crowding and (2) the incapacitation strategy for crime control is both imperfect and highly prone to error. Officials also know that once a prison is built, it represents a continuing management focus for as long as it is used—in contrast to field services, which are much more responsive to change and innovation.

As we have seen, however, the nation may be on the verge of a change. One of America's worst economic recessions started in 2008, forcing virtually every state to reduce spending. One area receiving great scrutiny is corrections—especially budgets for prisons. After a generation of ever-growing correctional costs, state legislators are looking for equally effective but less-expensive ways to deal with people convicted of serious crimes. This is one of the reasons the Council of State Government's Justice Reinvestment initiative has been so popular—it reduces correctional costs in ways that promote public safety.[1]

To this puzzle must be added the recent trend toward privatization of corrections. Only time will tell if this trend will become a lasting force; meanwhile, privatization is a potential threat to administrators' ability to manage the system. Most privatization plans call for skimming off the best of the worst—the nonserious offenders who can be efficiently processed. Thus, the government-run part of the corrections system faces the possibility of having to manage only the most costly, most intractable offenders on a reduced budget.

■ THREE CHALLENGES FOR THE FUTURE OF CORRECTIONS

After nearly 35 years of correctional growth, we have not seen compelling results. If this had been a deliberate experiment, we would have a much clearer picture by now. The crime rate today is about what it was in 1973, the year prison populations first began to grow. Indeed, during most of those years, we saw crime rates much higher than those of today. Some claim that the crime rates would have been even higher had we not expanded the corrections system. However, to have the same crime rates but *seven times* the number of people under correctional supervision suggests that correctional expansion has not been an efficient crime-prevention method, to say the least.

Further, state correctional budgets have more than doubled in the past decade. At the same time, allocations for education, transportation, and the like have declined. Some argue that the fiscal consequences of a bigger corrections system have taken a toll that should be considered in evaluating this trend.

If we could go back to the early 1970s and begin again to build a corrections system with an eye toward the year 2010, would we aim for the costly, cumbersome behemoth we have today? Most people would say no.

But what are we to do? Of course, we cannot re-create history. We can, however, examine today's corrections system in light of what we want it to become. Here are three challenges for recreating corrections with an eye to the future.

Reinvigorate a New Correctional Leadership

The field of corrections will get nowhere without effective leadership. It is from its leaders that corrections will receive the vision for a new future; it is from its leaders that corrections will find the capacity to embark on the difficult road of change.

Great leaders are not so easy to come by. Many studies of leadership suggest an important idea about "fit"—how the skills of a leader need to "fit" the problems being confronted. In other words, different situations call for different kinds of leaders, because the skills needed for solving one kind of problem are not the same as those needed for a different kind. Historians tell us, for example, that Winston Churchill's tenacity and tirelessness were perfect for England during wartime, but his disinterest in give-and-take did not work well after peace was restored. When a leader's skills fit the situation, effective leadership follows.

So, what are the characteristics of the situation corrections now faces? The key consideration that the new generation of correctional leaders will face is how to redirect an enormous enterprise in need of a new vision. Numerous pressures—political, economic, and social—have created the corrections system in its current form. Leaders will have to balance these pressures effectively while promoting a new correctional agenda.

At the same time, correctional leadership will never be *solely* about a vision for the future. When Martin Horn was Commissioner of the Department of Probation and Corrections in New York City, he was one of the most successful correctional leaders in the country. He ran a complex system that includes one of the world's largest jails, Rikers Island, and one of the nation's most overstretched probation departments. Asked recently to comment on the role of a correctional leader, he emphasized three tangible results for which leaders must be responsible:

■ Acting in ways that correctional clients see as "legitimate"—that is, fair and reasonable

■ Maintaining safe, drug-free environments in prisons and jails where staff and those confined inside can stay "clean"

■ Making management "transparent" so the general public has knows how corrections is being run and has confidence in it[2]

The problem of leadership is subtle. Good leaders have strong vision for their work, but they also have an on-the-ground ability to motivate people working in the system to do their best. While education and experience are known to be important qualities in effective leadership, history also tells us that good leaders come from all walks of life and from every kind of background. The challenge facing corrections is how to attract the best leaders to the field.

Refocus Our Investments in What Works

Studies of program effectiveness have grown dramatically in recent years. Where once we would have been lucky to have a study or two to decide a course of action, we now have literally hundreds of high-quality studies to inform our work in corrections. Such studies are now common enough in corrections that a new academic society devoted to promoting them and understanding them has sprung up: The Campbell Collaboration on Criminology, which publishes the *Journal of Experimental Criminology.*

The new research has enabled researchers to go from studying correctional programs to studying *studies* of programs, looking for patterns and consistencies in findings. Called "systematic reviews," such research helps to show what kinds of programs are powerful and what kinds are not promising. For example, systematic reviews have shown that boot camps do not work but therapeutic communities often do.

So while we know a great deal about "what works," we know much less about how to get good programs into practice. Programs that have been proved ineffective have surprising staying power, while programs with a solid track record are sometimes difficult to mount. Programs that work often involve providing the kind of offender support that the general public tends to reject. Programs that fail often present appealing goals, such as "scaring kids straight," and therefore engender unwarranted support.

The criminologists David Farrington and Brandon Welsh argue for a national crime-fighting strategy that focuses not just on people who have been convicted of crimes, but also on children. They say we need the following:

■ *Early prevention measures* implemented in the early years of a child's life from (or sometimes prior to) birth through early adolescence, with a focus on reaching children and youths before they engage in delinquency in the first place

■ *Risk-focused, evidence-based programs* that identify the key risk factors for offending and implement prevention methods designed to counteract them, methods that systematic research has proved to be successful

Visit the **Campbell Collaboration on Criminology** at the corresponding link at www .cengage.com/criminaljustice/ clear.

Bobby Fox, Greene County Messenger

The Communities That Care programs sponsored the Pennsylvania Commission on Crime and Delinquency focus on crime prevention, victim assistance, and community development. Among their programs is a soccer camp for youths from six to sixteen years old designed to promote healthy development.

■ *A National Council on Early Prevention*, modeled after successful nationwide approaches used in Europe, that seeks to support the early crime-prevention strategy

■ *Local-level prevention* that collaborates with other government departments, develops local problem-solving partnerships, and involves citizens

■ *Communities That Care*,[3] a strategy of comprehensive, locally driven approaches that use promising individual, family, school, and community programs[4]

There is no dearth of crime prevention or control strategies that work. In a recent issue of *Criminology and Public Policy*,[5] 30 leading criminologists provide short essays describing policies that, in their opinion, are candidates for widespread adoption or at least wider acceptance, given the extent of research supporting them. These are not "new" ideas but well-documented ones that range from the elimination of past felony screening for employment to earned release from parole supervision. The fact that 30 such essays could be written testifies to our ample knowledge base for effective crime policy. The fact that they *needed* to be written is testimony to how far our policies now stray from what we already know makes sense. The challenge we face is bringing our practice more into line with our knowledge. This is not just a challenge of knowledge. It is also a challenge of leadership.

Reclaim the Moral and Ethical High Road

There is something disturbing about the new American punitiveness. All of us would agree that people who break the law should be punished, so the mere fact of punishment is not disturbing. Plainly, the U.S. corrections system is far more punitive today than it has been for a long time, maybe ever. Comparing the 1970s with today, people who are convicted of crimes are twice as likely to go to prison, and those who go to prison serve sentences that are nearly twice as long as before. Further, people on probation or parole face a larger set of requirements, which means they are more likely to fail and be sent to prison. But even *that* is not the heart of the matter, because people can reasonably disagree about whether U.S. prison sentences are too likely or too long, or whether supervision methods are too stringent.

What is disturbing about the U.S. corrections system is the way it has become so much *harsher* than the other systems of free societies. Here are some of the practices you can find in the U.S. system:

■ Chain gangs cleaning roads and wearing black-striped shirts

■ Men in jail made to wear pink underwear

■ Signs in yards and on cars saying the owner has been convicted of a crime

■ Children serving time in adult prisons

■ Eviction of people from their homes because of convictions of drug crimes

■ Refusals of college loans because of convictions of drug crimes

Other worrisome practices plague the U.S. corrections system. Health care in some prison systems is appallingly bad, especially for the mentally ill. In California, for example, the shockingly deficient health care for prisoners ended in a recent Federal Appellate Court ruling that ordered the state to reduce institutional crowding by releasing at least 40,000 people from the prison.[6] Routinely, correctional programs emphasize being tough and providing close surveillance over providing support and promoting change. A nationwide spate of laws demonizes sex offenders irrationally and contributes to fear and retributive actions that are counterproductive to correctional aims and democratic values. The growth of surveillance alone is cause for concern (see Chapter 21).

The social costs of the growth of the penal system have been borne most substantially by minority communities that already struggle with poverty and other forms of disadvantage. Among them are broken families, deteriorated health, teenage births, weakened labor markets, juvenile delinquency, and even more crime. As a nation committed to basic ideas of social justice, these consequences of a burgeoning corrections system must concern us (see Chapters 19 and 22).

The corrections system we have built does not highlight what is best about the American heritage: optimism, entrepreneurial spirit, and a belief in the possibilities that arise when people are allowed to pursue their dreams. There are good reasons why so many of the Western democracies around the world look elsewhere for new horizons in correctional practice.

The next generation of correctional leaders can aim the sights of the American corrections system toward higher aspirations. Part of this can be accomplished by molding a smarter corrections system, emphasizing the kinds of strategies that good studies tell us will bear fruit, and turning away from approaches that do not. But part of this will just as surely be about basic values. The challenge facing us all is how to articulate those values in a compelling way—how to clarify what corrections is all about in language and imagery that makes us, once again, a beacon of freedom and justice for the world to see.

■ CHANGING CORRECTIONS: A FINAL VIEW

MYTHS IN CORRECTIONS

CAN CORRECTIONS CHANGE?

THE MYTH: The corrections system is too buffeted by political and social forces to be able to change.

THE REALITY: The corrections system changes when people with new vision devote themselves to improving it.

Sources: Three hundred years of history and the present realities described in this book.

Throughout this book, we have portrayed corrections as a system buffeted by its environment, changing yet unchanging. External pressures arise to move correctional leadership in one direction, only to be replaced by counterpressures. One state abolishes parole release; another reinstates early-release mechanisms. One prison reduces its treatment programs; another adds professional counseling staff. The image is one of an unplanned, reactive management style rather than a planned, proactive attempt to lead corrections down a path of gradual improvement. (See "Myths in Corrections.")

Although this image is largely accurate, it, too, is changing, partly because corrections continues to develop. Several forces contribute to this change—predominantly, professional associations and government agencies.

Perhaps the greatest influence is exercised by the National Institute of Corrections (NIC), a division of the Federal Bureau of Prisons in the Department of Justice. The NIC has served as (1) a national clearinghouse of information about correctional practices, (2) a source of technical assistance to local and state correctional agencies that wish to upgrade their practices, and (3) a training operation, both basic and advanced, open to any correctional employee. The NIC has become to corrections what the FBI is to law enforcement: a strong force for professional standards, policy and procedural improvement, and general development of the field.

Similarly, the American Correctional Association (ACA) has become an active lobbyist for the field. A quarter century ago, it promulgated a set of national standards for correctional practices in jails, prisons, and field services. Correctional agencies that meet these standards may be accredited, much as universities are accredited by outside agencies. Although the ACA has faced its share of criticism, its work indicates the kind of ground-level upgrading going on in corrections today.

The American Probation and Parole Association (APPA) serves a function similar to that of the ACA but is focused on field services. It has only recently begun a highly visible national campaign to organize the profession and to develop an improved professional consciousness of the importance of field services in probation and parole.

As important as these forces for change are, a new force for steady correctional growth and development is likely to outstrip them all. That force is represented by the person who is reading this book: you, the student of corrections. For most of its history, the field has been the domain of amateurs—part-time reformers who were moved by zeal to help prisoners—and local workers who took the jobs because nothing else was available. In recent years corrections has become a field of study for people interested in long-term professional careers, perhaps people like you. This is a dramatic change, because it represents a group of potential correctional employees who can sustain the field's growth and development. This, more than any other influence, may be a stabilizing force for corrections in the years to come.

SUMMARY

1 **Understand how the philosophy of the U.S. corrections system has changed over the years and what effects such changes have had.**

There was a time when the U.S. corrections system was the most progressive in the world. For most of the nineteenth and twentieth centuries, the U.S. corrections system was at the forefront of thinking about the best ways to deal with people who break the law, and U.S. methods were widely celebrated and emulated. Instead, what sets the U.S. corrections system apart from those elsewhere in the world is that it is so *big*. Since the mid-1970s, by every measure, the American corrections system has grown by unprecedented amounts. Including probation, parole, and jails, the number of people under correctional control also has more than quadrupled in that same time, from under a million to over 7 million. It is hard to believe that over the past 35 years we have deliberately created the corrections system we most want. To the contrary, most of those in charge of today's corrections system would argue that what we are doing is self-destructive and that an overhaul of the corrections system is long overdue.

2 Know the major dilemmas facing the corrections system and how they might be resolved.

Corrections faces five core dilemmas: (1) Mission: Corrections lacks a clear mission, and it operates in an environment of competing expectations that cannot be ignored. Correctional leaders must articulate their philosophy of corrections and establish a clearer policy to guide its implementation. (2) Methods: When goals are in conflict, staff members have difficulty choosing among competing methods to perform their work: surveillance or service, custody or treatment. We must overcome the tradition of faddism in corrections and embrace the methods that improve the life chances of correctional clients. (3) Structure: Correctional leaders' colleagues are often the ones who put the most immediate obstacles in their way,

and the corrections system depends on significant factors outside of its control. Through the formation of "partnerships," the impact of structural problems can be reduced. (4) Personnel: Two essential goals are attracting the right kinds of people to work in corrections and motivating them to remain once they are employed. A sound staff is built by innovative methods of selection and promotion; professional growth on the job is encouraged by incentives for education and training. (5) Costs: Corrections is expensive. The public desire to punish criminals is not backed up by a willingness to pay for the punishment. Making the costs of correctional policies clear is an essential step in making such policies effective.

3 Describe the three main challenges for the future of the U.S. corrections system and how those challenges might be faced.

There are three challenges for re-creating corrections. (1) Reinvigorate a new correctional leadership. It is from its leaders that corrections will get the vision for a new future; it is from its leaders that corrections will find the capacity to embark on the difficult road of change. The skills of a leader need to be the right ones for the problems being confronted. Further, good leaders have a strong vision and the ability to motivate people in the system to do their best. The challenge facing corrections is how to attract the best leaders to the field. (2) Refocus our investments in what works. Studies of program effectiveness have grown dramatically in recent years. While we know a great deal about "what works," we know much less about how to get effective programs into

practice. Some argue for a national crime-fighting strategy that focuses not just on people who have been convicted of crimes, but also on children. Whatever strategies we employ, we need to focus on bringing our practice more into line with our knowledge. (3) Reclaim the moral and ethical high road. The corrections system we have built does not highlight what is best about the American heritage: optimism, entrepreneurial spirit, and a belief in the possibilities that arise when people are allowed to pursue their dreams. The challenge facing us all is how to articulate those values in a compelling way—how to clarify what corrections is all about in language and imagery that makes us, once again, a beacon of freedom and justice for the world to see.

FOR DISCUSSION

1. Why has the corrections system in the U.S. grown so much? What are the pros and cons of this growth?
2. Recall the list of objectives for correctional leadership, provided by former New York City Corrections Commissioner Martin Horn. Are these the most important goals for correctional leadership? Why or why not?
3. What philosophies might serve as alternatives to the punitive philosophy currently promoted in the U.S. corrections system? Are such alternatives feasible? Preferable? Why or why not?
4. Do you see yourself in a correctional career? What might you do to improve the correction system?

FOR FURTHER READING

Duff, Anthony. *Punishment, Communication, and Community*. New York: Oxford University Press, 2005. A philosophy of corrections that is based not on retributive punishment but on community values.

Garland, David. *The Culture of Control*: *Crime and Social Order in Contemporary Society*. Chicago: University of Chicago, 2002. An analysis of how the U.S. corrections system has changed in size and in philosophy.

Simon, Jonathon. *Governing through Crime*. New York: Oxford University Press, 2007. An examination of the politics of correctional reform.

Whitman, James Q. *Harsh Justice: Criminal Punishment and the Widening Divide between America and Europe*. New York: Oxford University Press, March 2003. Compares the history of the development of penology in the United States with that of Europe.

NOTES

[1] http://justicereinvestment.org/, October 12, 2009.

[2] Martin Horn, "Its All About Leadership" (unpublished essay).

[3] David Hawkins and Richard F. Catalano, *Communities That Care: Action for Drug Abuse Prevention* (San Francisco, CA: Jossey-Bass, 2003).

[4] David P. Farrington and Brandon C. Welsh, *Saving Children from a Life of Crime: Early Risk Factors and Effective Interventions* (New York: Oxford University Press, 2007).

[5] *Criminology and Public Policy* 6 (no. 4, 2007).

[6] *Plata, et al., v. Schwarzenegger, et al.,* U.S. District Court for California, NO. C01-1351 TEH, http://www.ca9.uscourts.gov/datastore/general/2009/08/04/Opinion%20&%20Order%20FINAL.pdf, October 12, 2009.

absconders People who fail to appear for a court date and have no legitimate reason.

administrative control theory A governance theory that posits that prison disorder results from unstable, divided, or otherwise weak management.

aftercare Juvenile justice equivalent of parole, in which a delinquent is released from a custodial sentence and supervised in the community.

alcohol abuser A person whose use of alcohol is difficult to control, disrupting normal living patterns and frequently leading to violations of the law while under the influence of alcohol or in attempting to secure it.

Antabuse A drug that, when combined with alcohol, causes violent nausea; it is used to control a person's drinking.

Augustus, John (1785–1859) A Boston boot-maker known as the first probation officer. In helping people brought before the Boston courts, he acted as counsel, provided bail, and found housing for the accused.

authority The ability to influence a person's actions in a desired direction without resorting to force.

bail An amount of money, specified by a judge, to be posted as a condition for pretrial release to ensure the appearance of the accused in court.

Bates, Sanford (1884–1972) The first director of the Federal Bureau of Prisons, Bates advocated prison reform throughout his career. After becoming the president of the American Correctional Association in 1926, he also played an important role in the development of programs in New Jersey and New York.

Beccaria, Cesare (1738–1794) Italian scholar who applied the rationalist philosophy of the Enlightenment to the criminal justice system.

behavior therapy Treatment that induces new behaviors through reinforcements (rewards and punishments), role modeling, and other active forms of teaching.

benefit of clergy The right to be tried in an ecclesiastical court, where punishments were less severe than those meted out by civil courts, given the religious focus on penance and salvation.

Bentham, Jeremy (1748–1832) English advocate of utilitarianism in prison management and discipline. Argued for the treatment and reform of prisoners.

bondsman An independent businessperson who provides bail money for a fee, usually 5–10 percent of the total.

boot camp A physically rigorous, disciplined, and demanding regimen emphasizing conditioning, education, and job training. Designed for young offenders.

boundary violations Behavior that blurs, minimizes, or disrupts the social distance between prison staff and inmates, resulting in violations of departmental policy.

Brockway, Zebulon (1827–1920) Reformer who began his career in penology as a clerk in Connecticut's Wethersfield Prison at age 21. In 1854, while superintendent of the Monroe County Penitentiary in Rochester, New York, he began to experiment with ideas on making prisons more rehabilitative. He put his theories to work as the superintendent at Elmira State Reformatory, New York, in 1876, retiring from that institution in 1900.

campus style An architectural design by which the functional units of a prison are individually housed in a complex of buildings surrounded by a fence.

career criminal A person who sees crime as a way of earning a living, who has numerous contacts with the criminal justice system over time, and who may view the criminal sanction as a normal part of life.

case law Legal rules produced by judges' decisions.

chain of command A series of organizational positions in order of authority, with each person receiving orders from the one immediately above and issuing orders to the one(s) immediately below.

civil disabilities Legal restrictions that prevent released felons from voting and holding elective office, engaging in certain professions and occupations, and associating with known offenders.

civil liability Responsibility for the provision of monetary or other compensation awarded to a plaintiff in a civil action.

classical criminology A school of criminology that views behavior as stemming from free will, that demands responsibility and accountability of all perpetrators, and that stresses the need for punishments severe enough to deter others.

classification A process by which prisoners are assigned to types of custody and treatment.

classification systems Specific sets of objective criteria, such as offense history, previous experience in the justice system, and substance abuse patterns, applied to all inmates to determine an appropriate classification.

clear and present danger Any threat to security or to the safety of individuals that is so obvious and compelling that the need to counter it overrides the guarantees of the First Amendment.

client-specific planning Process by which private investigative firms contract with convicted offenders to conduct comprehensive background checks and suggest to judges creative sentencing options as alternatives to incarceration.

coercive power The ability to obtain compliance by the application or threat of physical force.

cognitive skill building A form of behavior therapy that focuses on changing the thinking and reasoning patterns that accompany criminal behavior.

collective efficacy Mutual trust among neighbors, combined with willingness to intervene on behalf of the common good, especially to supervise children and maintain public order.

community correctional center A small-group living facility for offenders, especially those who have been recently released from prison.

community corrections A model of corrections based on the assumption that reintegrating the offender into the community should be the goal of the criminal justice system.

community justice A model of justice that emphasizes reparation to the victim and the community, approaching crime from a problem-solving perspective, and citizen involvement in crime prevention.

community model for jails A model for jail administration that promotes a sense of community among staff and inmates alike, while using community to promote rehabilitative change.

community service Compensation for injury to society, by the performance of service in the community.

compelling state interest An interest of the state that must take precedence over rights guaranteed by the First Amendment.

compliance Obedience to an order or request.

conditions of release Restrictions on conduct that parolees must obey as a legally binding requirement of being released.

confrontation therapy A treatment technique, usually done in a group, that vividly brings the offender face-to-face with the crime's consequences for the victim and society.

congregate system A penitentiary system developed in Auburn, New York, in which inmates were held in isolation at night but worked with other prisoners during the day under a rule of silence.

constitution Fundamental law contained in a state or federal document that provides a design of government and lists basic rights for individuals.

construction strategy A strategy of building new facilities to meet the demand for prison space.

continuum of sanctions A range of correctional management strategies based on the degree of intrusiveness and control over the offender, along which an offender is moved according to his or her response to correctional programs.

contract labor system A system under which inmates' labor was sold on a contractual basis to private employers who provided the machinery and raw materials with which inmates made salable products in the institution.

corporal punishment Punishment inflicted on the offender's body with whips or other devices that cause pain.

corrections The variety of programs, services, facilities, and organizations responsible for the management of individuals who have been accused or convicted of criminal offenses.

cost-benefit ratio A summary measure of the value of a correctional program in saving money through preventing new crime.

courtyard style An architectural design by which the functional units of a prison are housed in separate buildings constructed on four sides of an open square.

crime control model of corrections A model of corrections based on the assumption that criminal behavior can be controlled by more use of incarceration and other forms of strict supervision.

criminogenic needs Needs that, when successfully addressed by treatment programs, result in lower rates of recidivism.

Crofton, Sir Walter (1815–1897) Appointed director of the Irish Convict Prisons in 1854, Crofton developed a system for offenders to work toward rehabilitation and early release by moving through three stages of increasing levels of vocational training and privileges. Prisoners were able to earn "marks" or points for good behavior. This "Irish System" significantly influenced the development of parole in the United States.

custodial model A model of correctional institutions that emphasizes security, discipline, and order.

day fine A criminal penalty based on the amount of income an offender earns in a day's work.

day reporting center Facility where offenders such as pretrial releasees and probation violators attend daylong intervention and treatment sessions.

deinstitutionalization The release of a mental patient from a mental hospital and his or her return to the community.

delinquent A child who has committed an act that if committed by an adult would be criminal.

dependent A child who has no parent or guardian or whose parents are unable to give proper care.

Depo-Provera A "chemical castration" drug that eliminates sexual response in men.

determinate sentence A fixed period of incarceration imposed by a court; associated with the concept of retribution or deserved punishment.

direct supervision A method of correctional supervision in which staff members have direct physical interaction with inmates throughout the day.

discretionary release The release of an inmate from prison to conditional supervision at the discretion of the parole board within the boundaries set by the sentence and the penal law.

discrimination Differential treatment of an individual or group without reference to the behavior or qualifications of the same.

disparity The unequal treatment of one group by the criminal justice system, compared with the treatment accorded other groups.

drug abuser A person whose use of illegal chemical substances disrupts normal living patterns to the extent that social problems develop, often leading to criminal behavior.

electronic monitoring Community supervision technique, ordinarily combined with home confinement, that uses electronic devices to maintain surveillance on offenders.

The Enlightenment, or the Age of Reason The 1700s in England and France, when concepts of liberalism, rationality, equality, and individualism dominated social and political thinking.

equal protection The constitutional guarantee that the law will be applied equally to all people, without regard for such individual characteristics as gender, race, and religion.

ethnicity Concept used to distinguish people according to their cultural characteristics—language, religion, and group traditions.

evidence-based practice Using correctional methods that have been shown to be effective by well-designed research studies.

exchange A mutual transfer of resources based on decisions regarding the costs and benefits of alternative actions.

expiration release The release of an inmate from incarceration without any further correctional supervision; the inmate cannot be returned to prison for any remaining portion of the sentence for the current offense.

expungement A legal process that results in the removal of a conviction from official records.

federalism A system of government in which power and responsibilities are divided between a national government and state governments.

fee system A system by which jail operations are funded by a set amount paid per day for each prisoner held.

forfeiture Government seizure of property and other assets derived from or used in criminal activity.

formal organization A structure established for influencing behavior to achieve particular ends.

Fry, Elizabeth Gurney (1780–1845) Born in Norwich, England, Elizabeth Fry was second only to John Howard as a nineteenth-century advocate of prison reform in Europe. In 1817 she helped organize the Association for the Improvement of Female Prisoners in Newgate, then the main prison in London. This group, made up of wives of Quaker businessmen, worked to establish prison discipline, separation of the sexes, classification of criminals, female supervision for women inmates, adequate religious and secular instruction, and the useful employment of prisoners. Largely through her efforts, such reforms rapidly moved to other prisons in England and abroad.

galley slavery Forced rowing of large ships or galleys.

general deterrence Punishment of criminals that is intended to be an example to the general public and to discourage the commission of offenses by others.

Gill, Howard (1890–1989) A prison reformer in the Progressive tradition, Gill designed Massachusetts's Norfolk Prison Colony to be a model prison community. Norfolk provided individual treatment programs and included inmates on an advisory council to deal with community governance.

Global Positioning System (GPS) A type of tracking system used in corrections. The offender must carry a "bag" that transmits a signal to a satellite, allowing correctional officials to identify the person's location at all times.

good time A reduction of an inmate's prison sentence, at the discretion of the prison administrator, for good behavior or for participation in vocational, educational, and treatment programs.

habeas corpus A writ (judicial order) asking a person holding another person to produce the prisoner and to give reasons to justify continued confinement.

hands-off policy A judicial policy of noninterference concerning the internal administration of prisons.

Harris, Mary Belle (1874–1957) Born in Pennsylvania, Mary Belle Harris is chiefly known as the first warden of the Federal Institution for Women. She began her work in corrections in 1914 when she became the superintendent of the Women's Workhouse on Blackwell Island, New York City. She worked to create classification systems, developed educational programs, and pushed for intermediate sentences and parole. These aims were incorporated into the programs at Alderson, which soon became a national model.

hepatitis C A disease of the liver that reduces the effectiveness of the body's system of removing toxins.

home confinement Sentence whereby offenders serve terms of incarceration in their own homes.

house of correction Detention facility that combined the major elements of a workhouse, poorhouse, and penal industry by both disciplining inmates and setting them to work.

Howard, John (1726–1790) English prison reformer whose book *The State of Prisons in England and Wales* contributed greatly to the passage of the Penitentiary Act of 1779 by the House of Commons.

hulks Abandoned ships the English converted to hold convicts during a period of prison crowding between 1776 and 1790.

incapacitation Depriving an offender of the ability to commit crimes against society, usually by detaining the offender in prison.

indeterminate sentence A period of incarceration with minimum and maximum terms stipulated, so that parole eligibility depends on the time necessary for treatment; closely associated with the rehabilitation concept.

inmate balance theory A governance theory that posits that, for a prison system to operate effectively, officials must tolerate minor infractions, relax security measures, and allow inmate leaders to keep order.

inmate code A set of rules of conduct that reflect the values and norms of the prison social system and help define for inmates the image of the model prisoner.

intensive supervision probation (ISP) Probation granted under conditions of strict reporting to a probation officer with a limited caseload.

intermediate sanctions A variety of punishments that are more restrictive than traditional probation but less severe and costly than incarceration.

jail A facility authorized to hold pretrial detainees and sentenced misdemeanants for periods longer than 48 hours. Most jails are administered by county governments; sometimes they are part of the state government.

judicial reprieve A practice under English common law whereby a judge could suspend the imposition or execution of a sentence on condition of good behavior on the part of the offender.

justice reinvestment A strategy to redirect funds currently spent on prisons to community public safety projects.

lease system A system under which inmates were leased to contractors who provided prisoners with food and clothing in exchange for their labor. In southern states, the prisoners were used as field laborers.

least restrictive methods Means of ensuring a legitimate state interest (such as security) that impose fewer limits to prisoners' rights than do alternative means of securing that end.

lex talionis Law of retaliation; the principle that punishment should correspond in degree and kind to the offense ("an eye for an eye and a tooth for a tooth").

line personnel Employees who are directly concerned with furthering the institution's goals and who are in direct contact with clients.

lockup A facility authorized to hold people before court appearance for up to 48 hours. Most lockups (also called drunk tanks or holding tanks) are administered by local police agencies.

long-term prisoner A person who serves a lengthy period in prison, such as 10 years or more, before his or her first release.

Lynds, Elam (1784–1855) A former army officer, Lynds was appointed warden of the newly opened Auburn prison in 1821. He developed the congregate system and a regimen of strict discipline. Inmates were known only by their number, wore striped clothing, and moved in lockstep. In 1825 he was commissioned to oversee construction with inmate labor at Ossining (Sing Sing), New York.

Mack, Julian W. (1866–1943) One of the foremost innovators in juvenile justice, Mack presided over Chicago's juvenile court from 1904 to 1907. He believed that the proper work of the court depended on the judge, supported by probation officers, caseworkers, and psychologists. He sought as much as possible to avoid using reformatories and tried to bring the expertise of social service professionals to the courts.

Maconochie, Captain Alexander (1787–1860) Born in Scotland, Maconochie was a naval officer, geographer, and penal reformer. In 1836 he was appointed to a position in the administration of Van Diemen's Land (now Tasmania). Later, he was made superintendent of the Norfolk Island penal colony in the South Pacific. Under his direction, negative marks were given to prisoners initially but removed from the records of those who performed their tasks well, and they were released when they demonstrated their willingness to accept society's rules.

mandatory release The required release of an inmate from incarceration to community supervision on the expiration of a certain period, as stipulated by a determinate-sentencing law or parole guidelines.

mandatory sentence A sentence stipulating that some minimum period of incarceration must be served by people convicted of selected crimes, regardless of background or circumstances.

mark system A system in which offenders are assessed a certain number of marks, based on the severity of their crime, at the time of sentencing. Prisoners could reduce their term and gain release by reducing marks through labor, good behavior, and educational achievement.

maximum-security prison A prison designed and organized to minimize the possibility of escapes and violence; to that end, it imposes strict limitations on the freedom of inmates and visitors.

mediation Intervention, in a dispute, by a third party to whom the parties in conflict submit their differences for resolution and whose decision (in the correctional setting) is binding on both parties.

medical model A model of corrections based on the assumption that criminal behavior is caused by social, psychological, or biological deficiencies that require treatment.

medium-security prison A prison designed and organized to prevent escapes and violence, but in which restrictions on inmates and visitors are less rigid than in maximum-security facilities.

mentally handicapped offender A person whose limited mental development prevents adjustment to the rules of society.

mentally ill offender A "disturbed" person whose criminal behavior may be traced to diminished or otherwise abnormal capacity to think or reason, as a result of psychological or neurological disturbance.

methadone A drug that reduces the craving for heroin; it is used to spare addicts from painful withdrawal symptoms.

minimum-security prison A prison designed and organized to permit inmates and visitors as much freedom as is consistent with the concept of incarceration.

motivational interviewing A method for increasing the effectiveness of correctional treatment, by having the probation officer interact with the client in ways that promote the client's stake in the change process.

neglected Describing a child who is not receiving proper care, because of some action or inaction of his or her parents.

new-generation jail A facility with a podular architectural design and management policies that emphasizes interaction of inmates and staff and provision of services.

normative power The ability to obtain compliance by manipulating symbolic rewards.

null strategy The strategy of doing nothing to relieve crowding in prisons, under the assumption that the problem is temporary and will disappear in time.

ombudsman A public official who investigates complaints against government officials and recommends corrective measures.

other conditional release A probationary sentence used in some states to get around the rigidity of mandatory release by placing convicts in various community settings under supervision.

pardon An action of the executive branch of the state or federal government excusing an offense and absolving the offender of the consequences of the crime.

parens patriae The "parent of the country"; the role of the state as guardian and protector of all people (particularly juveniles) who are unable to protect themselves.

parole The conditional release of an inmate from incarceration, under supervision, after part of the prison sentence has been served.

penitentiary An institution intended to isolate prisoners from society and from one another so that they could reflect on their past misdeeds, repent, and thus undergo reformation.

Penn, William (1644–1718) English Quaker who arrived in Philadelphia in 1682. Succeeded in getting Pennsylvania to adopt "The Great Law" emphasizing hard labor in a house of correction as punishment for most crimes.

performance-based supervision An approach to probation that establishes goals for supervision and evaluates the effectiveness of meeting those goals.

piece price system A labor system under which a contractor provided raw materials and agreed to purchase goods made by prison inmates at a set price.

podular unit Self-contained living areas, for 12–25 inmates, composed of individual cells for privacy and open areas for social interaction. New-generation jails are made up of two or more pods.

positivist school An approach to criminology and other social sciences based on the assumption that human behavior is a product of biological, economic, psychological, and social factors and that the scientific method can be applied to ascertain the causes of individual behavior.

power The ability to force a person to do something he or she does not want to do.

precedent Legal rules created in judges' decisions that serve to guide the decisions of other judges in subsequent similar cases.

presentence investigation (PSI) An investigation and summary report of a convicted offender's background, which helps the judge decide on an appropriate sentence. Also known as a presentence report.

presentence report Report prepared by a probation officer, who investigates a convicted offender's background to help the judge select an appropriate sentence.

presumptive parole date The presumed release date stipulated by parole guidelines if the offender serves time without disciplinary or other incidents.

presumptive sentence A sentence for which the legislature or a commission sets a minimum and maximum range of months or years. Judges are to fix the length of the sentence within that range, allowing for special circumstances.

pretrial diversion An alternative to adjudication in which the defendant agrees to conditions set by the prosecutor (for example, counseling or drug rehabilitation) in exchange for withdrawal of charges.

preventive detention Detention of an accused person in jail, to protect the community from crimes the accused is considered likely to commit if set free pending trial.

principle of interchangeability The idea that different forms of intermediate sanctions can be calibrated to make them equivalent as punishments despite their differences in approach.

principle of least eligibility The doctrine that prisoners ought to receive no goods or services in excess of those available to people who have lived within the law.

prison An institution for the incarceration of people convicted of serious crimes, usually felonies.

prison program Any formal, structured activity that takes prisoners out of their cells and sets them to instrumental tasks.

prisonization The process by which a new inmate absorbs the customs of prison society and learns to adapt to the environment.

probation A sentence allowing the offender to serve the sanctions imposed by the court while he or she lives in the community under supervision.

probation center Residential facility where persistent probation violators are sent for short periods.

probation release The release of an inmate from incarceration to probation supervision, as required by the sentencing judge.

procedural due process The constitutional guarantee that no agent or instrumentality of government will use any procedures other than those procedures prescribed by law to arrest, prosecute, try, or punish any person.

Prozac A drug used to decrease the negative emotions associated with depression.

psychotherapy In generic terms, all forms of "treatment of the mind"; in the prison setting, this treatment is coercive in nature.

psychotropic medications Drug treatments designed to ameliorate the severity of symptoms of psychological illness.

public account system A labor system under which a prison bought machinery and raw materials with which inmates manufactured a salable product.

public works and ways system A labor system under which prison inmates work on public construction and maintenance projects.

punitive conditions Constraints imposed on some probationers to increase the restrictiveness or painfulness of probation, including fines, community service, and restitution.

race Traditionally, a biological concept used to distinguish groups of people by their skin color and other physical features.

racial threat hypothesis The belief that white fear of African Americans is least when whites are the majority but greatest when African Americans are a substantial minority.

radial design An architectural plan by which a prison is constructed in the form of a wheel, with "spokes" radiating from a central core.

rational basis test Requires that a regulation provide a reasonable, rational method of advancing a legitimate institutional goal.

reality therapy Treatment that emphasizes personal responsibility for actions and their consequences.

recidivism The return of a former correctional client to criminal behavior, as measured by new arrests or other problems with the law.

recognizance A formally recorded obligation to perform some act (such as keep the peace, pay a debt, or appear in court when called) entered by a judge to permit an offender to live in the community, often on posting a sum of money as surety, which is forfeited by nonperformance.

reentry courts Courts that supervise the ex-prisoner's return to the community and adjustment to his or her new life.

reformatory An institution for young offenders that emphasized training, a mark system of classification, indeterminate sentences, and parole.

regional jail Facility operated under a joint agreement between two or more government units, with a jail board drawn from representatives of the participating jurisdictions, and having varying authority over policy, budget, operations, and personnel.

regulations Legal rules, usually set by an agency of the executive branch, designed to implement in detail the policies of that agency.

rehabilitation The goal of restoring a convicted offender to a constructive place in society through some form of vocational or educational training or therapy.

rehabilitation model A model of correctional institutions that emphasizes the provision of treatment programs designed to reform the offender.

reintegration model A model of correctional institutions that emphasizes maintenance of the offender's ties to family and the community as a method of reform, in recognition of the fact that the offender will be returning to the community.

relapse process What occurs when an ex-offender's poor decision making makes adjustment problems worse, leading eventually to recidivism.

release on recognizance (ROR) Pretrial release because the judge believes the defendant's ties in the community are sufficient to guarantee the defendant's appearance in court.

remunerative power The ability to obtain compliance in exchange for material resources.

restitution Compensation for financial, physical, or emotional loss caused by an offender, in the form of either payment of money to the victim or to a public fund for crime victims, as stipulated by the court.

restitution center Facility where probationers who fall behind in restitution are sent to make payments on their debt.

restorative justice Punishment designed to repair the damage done to the victim and community by an offender's criminal act.

retribution Punishment inflicted on a person who has infringed on the rights of others and so deserves to be penalized. The severity of the sanction should fit the seriousness of the crime.

Rush, Benjamin (1745–1813) Physician, patriot, signer of the Declaration of Independence, and social reformer, Rush advocated the penitentiary as a replacement for capital and corporal punishment.

secular law The law of the civil society as distinguished from church law.

selective incapacitation Making the best use of expensive and limited prison space by targeting for incarceration those offenders whose incapacity will do the most to reduce crime in society.

self-report study An investigation of behavior (such as criminal activity) based on subjects' responses to questions concerning activities in which they have engaged.

sentencing disparity Divergence in the lengths and types of sentences imposed for the same crime or for crimes of comparable seriousness when no reasonable justification can be discerned.

sentencing guidelines An instrument developed for judges that indicates the usual sanctions given previously for particular offenses.

separate confinement A penitentiary system developed in Pennsylvania in which each inmate was held in isolation from other inmates, with all activities, including craft work, carried on in the cells.

sex offender A person who has committed a sexual act prohibited by law, such as rape, child molestation, or prostitution, for economic, psychological, or situational reasons.

shock incarceration A short period of incarceration (the "shock"), followed by a sentence reduction.

shock probation A sentence in which the offender is released after a short incarceration and resentenced to probation.

situational offender A person who in a particular set of circumstances has violated the law but who is not given to criminal behavior under normal circumstances and is unlikely to repeat the offense.

social control Actions and practices, of individuals and institutions, designed to induce conformity with the norms and rules of society.

social therapy Treatment that attempts to create an institutional environment that supports prosocial attitudes and behaviors.

span of control A management principle holding that a supervisor can effectively oversee only a limited number of subordinates.

spatial concentration A phenomenon of criminal justice in which certain neighborhoods have very high numbers of arrests and of people going to prison.

specific deterrence (special or individual deterrence) Punishment inflicted on criminals to discourage them from committing future crimes.

staff personnel Employees who provide services in support of line personnel; examples of staff personnel include training officers and accountants.

stakes The potential losses to victims and to the system if offenders fail; stakes include injury from violent crimes and public pressure resulting from negative publicity.

standard conditions Constraints imposed on all probationers, including reporting to the probation office, reporting any change of address, remaining employed, and not leaving the jurisdiction without permission.

state-use system A labor system under which goods produced by prison industries are purchased by state institutions and agencies exclusively and never enter the free market.

status offenses Misbehaviors that are not against the law but are troubling when done by juveniles because they are so young.

statute Law created by the people's elected representatives in legislatures.

street-level bureaucrats Public-service workers who interact directly with citizens in the course of their work, granting access to government programs and providing services within them.

system A complex whole consisting of interdependent parts whose operations are directed toward common goals and influenced by the environment in which they function.

technical violation The probationer's failure to abide by the rules and conditions of probation (specified by the judge), resulting in revocation of probation.

technocorrections The use of technological mechanisms, by corrections systems, to control offenders.

technology A method of applying scientific knowledge to practical purposes in a particular field.

telephone-pole design An architectural plan for a prison, calling for a long central corridor crossed at regular intervals by structures containing the prison's functional areas.

therapeutic community A prison environment where every aspect of the prison is designed to promote prosocial attitudes and behavior.

therapeutic justice A philosophy of reorienting the jail experience from being mostly punitive to being mostly rehabilitative.

Thorazine A drug used to control violent or aggressive behavior caused by psychiatric problems.

totality of conditions The aggregate of circumstances in a correctional facility that, when considered as a whole, may violate the protections guaranteed by the Eighth Amendment, even though such guarantees are not violated by any single condition in the institution.

transactional analysis Treatment that focuses on patterns of interaction with others, especially patterns that indicate personal problems.

transportation The practice of transplanting offenders from the community to another region or land, often a penal colony.

treatment conditions Constraints imposed on some probationers to force them to deal with a significant problem or need, such as substance abuse.

unit management Tactic for reducing prison violence by dividing facilities into small, self-contained, semi-autonomous "institutions."

unity of command A management principle holding that a subordinate should report to only one supervisor.

urinalysis Technique used to determine whether someone is using drugs.

utilitarianism The doctrine that the aim of all action should be the greatest possible balance of pleasure over pain, hence the belief that a punishment inflicted on an offender must achieve enough good to outweigh the pain inflicted.

victim impact statements Descriptions in PSIs of the costs of the crime for the victim, including emotional and financial losses.

vocational rehabilitation Prison programming designed to teach inmates cognitive and vocational skills to help them find employment upon release.

Warren, Earl (1891–1974) The 14th chief justice of the United States (1953–1969), Earl Warren began his public career in 1919 as the district attorney of Alameda County, California. He was elected California's attorney general in 1938 and governor in 1942, then twice reelected. President Dwight Eisenhower later appointed him as chief justice. Under his leadership, the Court enormously affected American law and provided support and impetus for significant social changes.

wergild "Man money"; money paid to relatives of a murdered person or to the victim of a crime to compensate them and to prevent a blood feud.

widening the net Increasing the scope of corrections by applying a diversion program to people charged with offenses less serious than those of the people the program was originally intended to serve.

Wines, Enoch Cobb (1806–1879) A guiding force of American corrections from 1862, when he became the secretary of the New York Prison Association and served so until his death. Organizer of the National Prison Association in 1870 and a major contributor to the Cincinnati Declaration of Principles.

work release center A facility that allows offenders to work in the community during the day while residing in the center during nonworking hours.

wrongful conviction Occurs when an innocent person is found guilty by either plea or verdict.

INDEX

Boldface numbers in this index refer to the page on which the term is defined.

PHOTO CREDITS

Chapter 1: 2 ©Suzanne DeChillo/The New York Times/Redux Pictures; 6 ©Jim West/The Image Works; 7 AP Images/Carlo Allegri,Pool; 10 AP Images/Jessica Hill, Pool; 18 AP Images/Al Goldis; 21 ©John Birdsall/The Image Works.

Chapter 2: 28 ©Gianni Dagli Orti/Corbis; 30 Bibliotheque Nationale, Paris, France, Archives Charmet/The Bridgeman Art Library International; 32 ©Mary Evans Picture Library/The Image Works; 33 ©Art Media/Heritage/The Image Works; 34 ©Photoshot/Landov; 39 ©Mansell/Time & Life Pictures/Getty Images.

Chapter 3: 44 The Library Company of Philadelphia; 46 ©Corbis; 47 ©Eastern State Penitentiary Historic Site; 49 Reprinted with permission of the American Correctional Association, Alexandria, Virginia; 53 ©Buyenlarge/Getty Images; 56 Reprinted with permission of the American Correctional Association, Alexandria, Virginia; 58 Chicago Daily News/Library of Congress, Prints and Photographs Division; 61 AP Images.

Chapter 4: 68 ©Reuters/Shepard/Landov; 73 ©Rose Howerter/The Oregonian; 76 AP Images/Rob Carr; 78 AP Images/Jim McKnight; 81 AP Images/Nati Harnik, File; 91 AP Images/Harry Cabluck.

Chapter 5: 100 AP Images/Tomas van Houtryve; 105 ©Dennis Brack/Landov; 107 TM & Copyright © 20th Century Fox Film Corp./courtesy Everett Collection; 112 AP Images/The News Tribune, Drew Perine; 117 Brandon McKelvey/The Daily Texan; 118 ©Creatas/photolibrary; 123 AP Images/Daytona Beach News-Journal, Nigel Cook; 125 AP Images/Mona Shafeer Edwards.

Chapter 6: 132 ©Tom Dahlin/Getty Images; 137 AP Images; 139 ©Reuters/Corbis; 142 AP Images/John VanBeekum, Pool; 149 AP Images/Mike Groll; 157 AP Images/Rich Pedroncelli; 160 AP Images/Jerry Lai.

Chapter 7: 168 AP Images/Damian Dovarganes; 176 AP Images/David J. Phillip; 179 ©Ulrik Jantzen/Contrasto/Redux Pictures; 187 ©Monica Almeida/The New York Times/Redux Pictures; 189 AP Images/The Herald-Times, Chris Howell; 191 ©Kevin Moloney/The New York Times/Redux Pictures.

Chapter 8: 198 ©Modesto Bee/ZUMA Press; 201 Courtesy of The Bostonian Society/Old State House Museum; 203 ©The Plain Dealer/Landov; 209 ©image100/Alamy; 214 ©Bob Daemmrich/The Image Works; 221 ©Jeff T. Green/The New York Times/Redux Pictures; 226 ©The Bakersfield Californian/Zuma Press.

Chapter 9: 232 AP Images/Danny Moloshok; 240 ©Bryan Smith/ZUMA Press; 242 AP Images/Casper Star-Tribune, Dan Cepeda; 243 AP Images/Chris O'Meara 245 ©Andy Kropa 2008/Redux Pictures; 248 AP Images/Dee Marvin.

Chapter 10: 258 AP Images/Mark Foley; 261 AP Images/Chicago Sun-Times, Richard A. Chapman; 263 ©Contra Costa Times/Bob Pepping/ZUMA Press; 266 ©Stephen Ferry/Getty Images/Liaison; 271 ©Justin Sullivan/Getty Images; 272 Photo by Earnie Grafton/San Diego Union-Tribune/ZUMA Press. ©Copyright 2006 by San Diego Union-Tribune; 273 AP Images/Jake Schoellkopf; 277 ©Fred R. Conrad/The New York Times/Redux Pictures.

Chapter 11: 284 AP Images/SEVANS; 290 ©Adam Tanner/The Image Works; 291 ©Kim Kulish/Corbis; 294 ©Visions of America, LLC/Alamy; 297 AP Images/The Advocate-Messenger, Clay Jackson; 298 ©Mark Allen Johnson/ZUMA Press; 299 AP Images; 302 ©Joel Gordon.

Chapter 12: 308 ©Tim Rue/Corbis; 310 AP Images/Matt Rourke; 313 Reprinted with permission of the American Correctional Associa-tion, Alexandria, Virginia; 316 Katja Heinemann/Aurora Photos; 320 AP Images/Kevin Glackmeyer; 322 AP Images/Dave Martin; 324 AP Images/Eric Risberg; 325 AP Images/The Dickinson Press, Thomas E. Hammel; 327 ©Mark Allen Johnson/ZUMA Press; 329 AP Images/Whitney Curtis; 330 ©Myrleen Ferguson Cate/PhotoEdit.

Chapter 13: 336 AP Images/Phil Coale; 339 AP images/J.D. Cavrich; 341 ©Joel Gordon; 344 ©Joel Gordon; 347 AP Images/The Herald-Mail, Ric Dugan; 350 ©Kevin Clark/The Washington Post; 356 ©Melanie Stetson Freeman/The Christian Science Monitor/Getty Images; 358 AP Images/LM Otero; 362 ©Jack Kurtz/The Image Works; 364 ©Gerald Herbert/Washington Times/ZUMA Press.

Chapter 14: 370 ©Karl Rabe; 372 ©Monica Almeida/The New York Times/Redux Pictures; 376 Betsy Stein; 384 AP Images/John Russell; 386 AP Images/Rich Pedroncelli; 389 ©Thomas Dworzak/Magnum Photos; 390 ©J. Carter Smith/Corbis Sygma; 393 AP Images/Herald-Leader, Dariush Shafa; 399 ©Michael Stravato/The New York Times/Redux Pictures.

Chapter 15: 406 AP Images/Jason Hirschfeld; 411 ©Mary Evans Picture Library/The Image Works; 414 ©Sacramento Bee/ZUMA Press; 417 AP Images/Rick Bowmer; 423 AP Images/Tim Hacker, Pool; 424 AP Images/Damian Dovarganes; 426 Phillippe Diederich.

Chapter 16: 430 ©Jose M. Osorio/The Sacramento Bee/ZUMA Press; 435 ©Bob Daemmrich/The Image Works; 441 ©Mario E. Ruiz/ZUMA Press; 444 AP Images/Jeff Chiu; 446 AP Images/Haraz Ghanbari; 450T ©Fred R. Conrad/The New York Times/Redux Pictures; 450B AP Images/Toby Talbot; 456 ©Chang W. Lee/NYT Pictures/Redux Pictures; 461 ©Joel Gordon.

Chapter 17: 468 AP Images/Lou Toman, Pool; 470 AP Images/The Idaho Press-Tribune, Mike Vogt; 473 ©Bettmann/Corbis; 474 ©Corbis; 477 AP Images/Timothy Jacobsen; 485 AP Images/The Wenatchee World/Kelly Gilli; 487 ©Larry Kolvoord/The Image Works; 489 ©Joel Gordon; 491 AP Images/Charlie Riedel; 495 AP Images/Ric Francis.

Chapter 18: 504 ©Bob Daemmrich/AFP/Getty Images; 506 ©Andrew Lichtenstein/The Image Works; 509 AP Images/Devin Bruce; 510 AP Images/The Express-Times, Joe Gill; 515 AP Images/Rich Pedroncelli; 516 AP Images/California Department of Corrections; 520 Rick Hartford/The Hartford Courant.

Chapter 19: 524 ©Tony Avelar/The Christian Science Monitor/Getty Images; 528 ©Bob Sacha/Corbis; 531 ©Mark Peterson/Redux Pictures; 535 ©Ed Kashi/Corbis; 537 AP Images/Mel Evans; 538 ©Antonio Perez/MCT/Landov.

Chapter 20: 542 ©Andrew Lichtenstein/Aurora Photos; 544 AP Images/Marcio Jose Sanchez; 546 ©Andrew Lichtenstiein/Aurora Photos; 552 ©Michael Stravato/The New York Times/Redux Pictures; 559 ©Laura Segall/The New York Times/Redux Pictures; 563 ©Ken Light Photography.

Chapter 21: 568 ©Kenneth Dickerman/The New York Times/Redux Pictures; 571 AP Images/Bebeto Matthews; 574 ©Bob Daemmrich/PhotoEdit; 576 AP Images/Matt Houston.

Chapter 22: 582 AP Images/Dan Loh; 585 AP Images/Paul Vernon, File; 586 AP Images/Marcio Jose Sanchez; 594 ©Jim West/The Image Works; 596 L ©John Lei/Stock Boston, LLC; 596 R ©Robert Holmes/Corbis.

Chapter 23: 602 ©Greg Smith/Corbis; 605 ©Joel Gordon; 607 Courtesy of California Department of Corrections and Rehabilitation; 611 Bobby Fox, Greene County Messenger.